# The HUTCHINSON
# GUIDE TO
# BRITAIN

Helicon

## STAFF AND CONTRIBUTORS

**Editorial director**
Hilary McGlynn

**Managing editor**
Elena Softley

**Project manager**
Barbara Fraser

**Contributors**
Anne Baker
Ian Chilvers
Ian Derbyshire
Clarissa Hyman
Antony Kamm
Richard Martin
David Milsted

**Contributors—*cont.***
Anna Papadoupolos
Ben Ramos
Adrian Room
Julian Rowe
Joseph Spooner
Jill Turton

**Text editors and
proofreaders**
Clare Collinson
Susan Cuthbert
Denise Dresner
Mike McGeorge
Sue Purkis
Edith Summerhayes

**Picture research**
Elizabeth Loving

**Cartography**
Olive Pearson

**Production**
John Normansell

**Design manager**
Lenn Darroux

**Page design**
Paul Saunders

# Contents

The United Kingdom of Great Britain and Northern Ireland

# Preface

FROM INVASION by the Romans to the opening of the Scottish Parliament and the National Assembly for Wales, *The Hutchinson Guide to Britain* aims to provide, through easily accessible A–Z entries, a broad grasp of the history, people, and places of Britain, and is intended to complement the more site-based information customarily found in travel guides. The book gives concise explanations of why a person, place, or event mattered, and aims to enable readers to understand the most important historical movements. The main A–Z entries are supplemented by a selection of tables, chronologies, and full-page feature essays. The essays range from the development of the English language to the impact on Britain of the two World Wars, and how the pub has been a national institution since medieval times. At the end of the book is a detailed chronology of British history since the Act of Union of 1707 to the present day, as well as a selection of useful Web sites.

The entries that can be included in a reference book of this size are highly selective, and difficult decisions have had to be made about what to include and what to exclude. For reasons of space, living people have generally been excluded from the book. For places, the policy has been to include all towns and cities with a population of over 50,000, all counties and unitary authorities, as well as small towns, villages, and natural and artificial features that have a special historical or cultural significance. These include the birthplace and chosen homes of famous figures and some of the main country houses and estates that can be visited.

Also highlighted are the building and renovation projects that Britain has undertaken to celebrate the new millennium: the London Eye, the Millennium Dome, new bridges, museums, and landmark projects in cities throughout the country.

April 2000

# List of features

## abdication crisis

The constitutional upheaval of the period 16 November 1936 to 10 December 1936, brought about by the British king ◊Edward VIII's decision to marry Wallis Simpson, a US divorcee. The marriage of the 'Supreme Governor' of the Church of England to a divorced person was considered unsuitable and the king abdicated on 10 December and left for voluntary exile in France. He was created Duke of Windsor and married Mrs Simpson on 3 June 1937.

## Aberdeen

City in northeast Scotland, situated in a low-lying coastal area on estuaries of the rivers Dee and Don; population: (1996) 219,100. Formerly part of Aberdeenshire, since 1996, as **Aberdeen City**, it has been a unitary authority with an area of 185 sq km/71 sq mi. The third largest city in Scotland, it is the main centre in Europe for offshore oil exploration, as well as an important fishing port, cultural centre, and university city. With its imposing grey architecture, it is known as the 'granite city', and it is also renowned for its year-round floral displays.

### Features

Dominating Old Aberdeen are the 15th-century cathedral of St Machar, the oldest granite building in the city, and King's College, Aberdeen's first university dating from 1495. In the newer part of the city is Marischal College, one of the largest granite buildings in the world, which united with King's College in the 19th century to form Aberdeen University. One of the city's finest architectural attractions is Provost Skene's House, built in 1545. Among its features are a painted gallery with early 17th-century panels and a 17th-century great hall. Aberdeen has a busy harbour and the redeveloped Aberdeen Maritime Museum, housed in Old Provost Ross's House,

the oldest building in Aberdeen, focuses on the history of the city's fishing, shipbuilding, and oil industries. Other attractions include the Art Gallery, St Andrew's Cathedral, and Duthie Park which includes the Winter Garden, Europe's largest indoor garden. The city has a sandy beach and its redeveloped seaside attractions include Aberdeen Fun Beach, one of Scotland's principal leisure complexes. The city hosts a variety of festivals including a folk music festival in October and the International Youth Festival.

## Aberdeenshire

Unitary authority in northeast Scotland, created in 1996 from three districts within the former

**Abdication crisis** The Duke and Duchess of Windsor on their wedding day, in France, in June 1937, six months after the Duke abdicated from the British throne. In a speech broadcast on radio on the eve of his departure for France, he said, 'I have found it impossible to discharge my duties as King as I would wish to do without the help and support of the woman I love.' Rex

Grampian region; population (1996) 226,500; area 6,308 sq km/2,436 sq mi. It is known for its mountainous western area and association with royalty (Balmoral Castle is here). The principal towns are Banff, Fraserburgh, Huntly, Peterhead, Stonehaven, and Inverurie; it is the only Scottish unitary authority with its administrative headquarters, ◊Aberdeen, outside its administrative area.

*Physical*
The southern ◊Cairngorm Mountains are in the west, while the central area is intensively farmed; in the east a coastal plain stretches towards the North Sea. The principal rivers are the Deveron, Ythan, Don, and Dee.

*Features*
The area has many examples of historic buildings and is particularly rich in castles, including that at Huntly (16th century) and, in the Dee valley, Crathes (16th century), Drum, Aboyne, and Braemar (all 17th century), and Dunnottar Castle (about 1392). Balmoral Castle, the Queen's Highland residence, is 15 km/9 mi west of Ballater in the Dee valley. The Braemar Games, the most celebrated of the ◊Highland Games, are held in September. There are 80 Sites of Special Scientific Interest, eight National Nature Reserves, three Ramsars (wetland sites), five Special Protection Areas, two Biogenetic Reserves, two National Scenic Areas, and four country parks.

*Economy*
The area is well known for cereal production, livestock, such as pedigree Angus and Beef Shorthorn cattle, and fishing, at Peterhead, Fraserburgh, and MacDuff, in particular. The eastern seaboard also serves the oil and gas industry of the North Sea and the western area has an important tourist industry; there are two skiing centres.

## Aberfan
Former coalmining village in Merthyr Tydfil unitary authority, south Wales. Coal waste from a slag heap overwhelmed a school and houses in 1966; of the 144 dead, 116 were children.

## Aberystwyth
Commercial, tourist, and educational centre in Ceredigion, mid-Wales, situated at the mouths of the rivers Ystwyth and Rheidol in Cardigan Bay; population (1991) 11,150. It is the site of the University College of Wales (1872), the National Library of Wales (1911), the College of Librarianship (Wales), the Welsh Plant Breeding Station, and the office of the Royal Commission on Ancient Monuments in Wales. It is the unofficial capital of the Welsh-speaking area of Wales. The Welsh Language Society was founded here in 1963.

The town is overlooked by Pen Dinas, an Iron Age hillfort. The remains of Edward I's castle dominate the sea front. Built by his brother, Edmund of Lancaster, it was finally completed in 1307 but was destroyed by Cromwellian forces during the Civil War. A mint was opened here by Charles I; it used silver from a local mine. Some of the coins produced can be seen in the university museum.

## Abingdon
Market town in Oxfordshire, south-central England, at the confluence of the River Ock with the Thames, 10 km/6 mi south of Oxford; population (1991) 35,200. The remains of a Benedictine abbey, founded in 675, include the 14th-century Checker Hall, now restored as an Elizabethan-type theatre, the 16th-century Long Gallery, and the 15th-century gateway. The abbey was largely destroyed in 1538 during the Dissolution of the Monasteries.

The County Hall (1677–82) houses a local museum. Other historic buildings include the Long Alley almshouses (1446). Abingdon was the county town of Berkshire until 1870. Late 20th-century excavations suggest Abingdon may be the oldest continually inhabited town in England.

## acre
Traditional English land measure equal to 4,840 square yards (4,047 sq m/0.405 ha). Originally meaning a field, it was the size that a yoke of oxen could plough in a day.

## Acton, Eliza (1799–1859)
English cookery writer and poet, whose *Modern Cookery for Private Families* (1845) influenced Mrs ◊Beeton.

*Modern Cookery* was an immediate success and there were five editions in two years. It continued in print until 1914. Acton also wrote *The English Bread Book*. Some of her poetry was published in the 1820s and 1830s.

## Adam
Family of Scottish architects and designers. **William Adam** (1689–1748) was the leading Scottish architect of his day, and his son **Robert Adam** (1728–1792) is considered one of the greatest British architects of the late 18th century, responsible for transforming the prevailing Palladian fashion in architecture to a Neo-Classical style.

William Adam trained his three sons Robert,

John, and James in his Edinburgh office. Robert travelled in Italy and Dalmatia, and was appointed architect to King George III in 1762. His commissions included the remodelling of Kenwood House (1764) and Osterley Park, London (1760s); Culzean Castle, South Ayrshire (1775); and Nostell Priory, West Yorkshire. At Kedleston Hall (1759–70) he exquisitely balanced Antiquarian and Neo-Classical influences. In his interiors, such as those at Saltram, Harewood House, Luton Hoo, and Syon House, he employed delicate stucco decoration with Neo-Classical motifs. He also earned a considerable reputation as a furniture designer.

Robert, John, and James designed and speculatively developed the district of London between Charing Cross and the Thames, which was named the Adelphi after them (Greek for 'brothers'). The area was largely rebuilt in 1936.

### Adrian IV, Nicholas Breakspear (c. 1100–1159)
Pope 1154–59; the only English pope. He secured the execution of Arnold of Brescia (1100–55), who attacked the holding of property by the Catholic Church, and crowned Frederick I Barbarossa (c. 1123–90) as German emperor. When he died, Adrian IV was at the height of a quarrel with Barbarossa over papal supremacy. He allegedly issued the controversial bull giving Ireland to Henry II of England in 1154. He was attacked for false representation, and the bull was subsequently refuted.

### Aesthetic Movement
English artistic movement of the late 19th century, dedicated to the doctrine of 'art for art's sake' – that is, art as a self-sufficient entity concerned solely with beauty and not with any moral or social purpose. Associated with the movement were the artists Aubrey Beardsley and James McNeill Whistler and writers Walter Pater and Oscar Wilde, while John Ruskin and William Morris were staunch critics of the movement.

---

*My voice as a writer has its source very much in the Caribbean region, which means that psychically you're at once connected to the Americas, Africa, Asia, and Europe.*

**Grace Nichols** British writer.
*A Virago Keepsake* (1993)

---

### Afro-Caribbean
West Indian person of African descent. Afro-Caribbeans are the descendants of West Africans captured or obtained in trade from African procurers and shipped by European slave traders to colonies in the West Indies from the 16th century. Since World War II many Afro-Caribbeans have migrated to Europe, including the UK. According to the 1991 census, there are some 500,000 Afro-Caribbeans, or black Caribbeans, living in the UK.

### agricultural revolution
Sweeping changes that took place in British agriculture over the period 1750–1850. The changes were a response to the increased demand for food from a rapidly expanding population. Major events included the ◊enclosure of open fields; the development of improved breeds of livestock; the introduction of four-course crop rotation; and the use of new crops such as turnips as animal fodder.

Recent research has shown that these changes were only part of a much larger, ongoing process of development: many were in fact underway before 1750, and other breakthroughs, such as farm mechanization, did not occur until after 1859.

The introduction of new crops – such as potatoes, red clover, and turnips – into Britain in the 17th century led to a considerable advance in farming practices, since farmers could use them to feed their livestock throughout the winter. Their use did away with the practice of slaughtering animals in the autumn and salting the meat for storage through the winter, which had been particularly detrimental to the health of the community. In the latter part of the 18th century, moreover, Jethro ◊Tull demonstrated the advantage of thorough soil cultivation, and, with the invention of the first practical mechanized seed drill in about 1701, initiated the practice of drilling rather than broadcasting seed.

*Four-course rotation*
Tull's invention allowed crops to be planted in regular rows, while the intervals between rows could be stirred and cleaned by horse-hoeing. It also afforded a place for turnips and other root crops, and eventually led to the replacement of the 'three-field' system of the village community by the four-course rotation system, which was designed to ensure that no land would need to lie fallow between periods of cultivation and, to this end, rotated crops which absorb different kinds and quantities of nutrients from the soil. The four-course rotation system was subsequently developed by enlightened landowners such as Viscount 'Turnip' Townshend (1674–1738) and

# Agriculture: Some key dates

*c.* **4400 BC** As knowledge spreads from continental Europe, communities in the British Isles begin to develop agricultural practices to replace the hunter-gatherer lifestyle.

**80 BC** The second wave of Celtic Belgae arrives in Britain from Gaul during this period. They settle mostly in the southeast and tackle the less well drained and still forested land, farming with a plough that can turn the sod.

**1128** Norman monks of the Cistercian order arrive in England and begin to farm. The order lives entirely off the land and is to introduce many improvements in agricultural practice.

**1236** The Statute of Merton (followed in 1285 by the Statute of Westminster) attempts to ensure that sufficient common land is left for the tenants of a lord who is appropriating open fields for private use, often for grazing sheep. The process is known as enclosure, and becomes widespread in the 15th and 16th centuries. It causes poverty, homelessness, and rural depopulation, leading to revolts.

**June 1381** Riots known as the Peasants' Revolt start in southeast England in reaction to a new poll tax.

**February 1607–May 1607** Resistance by English peasants to enclosures and the consequent deprivation of common land, rights, and subsistence, leads to the Midlands Rising (large-scale fence-breaking and rioting throughout the heavily enclosed counties), culminating in a peasant assembly and insurrection in Northamptonshire.

**1663** The Royal Society calls for the widespread cultivation of potatoes as a precaution against famine in Britain.

**1700–1800** The weight of cattle reaching market in England doubles over the century, thanks to the introduction of selective breeding, pedigrees, and new animal husbandry techniques.

*c.* **1701** English farmer Jethro Tull invents the first practical mechanized seed drill.

**1714** English farmer and inventor Jethro Tull introduces the horse-hoe to England from France, advocating its use for releasing nutrients from the soil.

**1788** Scottish millwright Andrew Meikle patents a threshing machine for separating the grain from the straw.

**1801, 1836, and 1845** General Enclosure Acts complete the enclosure of open fields for private use.

**1817** Irish farmer James Murray invents superphosphate, a fertilizer made from bones and sulphuric acid.

**1843** English agronomist John Bennet Lawes and English chemist Joseph Henry Gilbert establish the Rothamsted Experimental Station, Hertfordshire, England, the world's first agricultural research station.

**1845** The potato blight fungus *Phytophthora infestans* causes potato crops to fail throughout Europe. In Ireland, where the potato is a staple, over half the crop is lost causing devastating famine. Over 1 million die and 1.5 million emigrate over the next two years.

**26 June 1846** The British prime minister, Robert Peel, repeals the Corn Laws to allow the unhindered importation of grain into Ireland in an effort to alleviate the famine caused there by the failure of the potato crop.

**1873** In the first example of biological pest control, British-born US entomologist Charles Riley exports the acarid *Rhizoglyphus phylloxerae* to France to destroy aphids.

**23 July 1889** The British Board of Agriculture is founded.

**1917** The Women's Land Army is set up in Britain.

**1953** Infectious myxomatosis is introduced from continental Europe to Britain, killing millions of rabbits.

**25 October 1967** An epidemic of the cattle disease foot-and-mouth begins in Shropshire, England, ending in March 1968.

**14 October 1979** France imposes a prohibitive tariff on British lamb exports in defiance of the European Court.

**1984** The pesticide DDT is banned in Britain.

**1985** An epidemic of bovine spongiform encephalopathy (BSE), or 'mad cow disease', is reported in beef cattle in Britain; it is later traced to cattle feed containing sheep carcasses infected with scrapie; in following years the consumption of infected beef is linked to CJD (Creutzfeld Jakob disease) in humans.

**16 December 1988** The junior British health minister Edwina Currie resigns after her claim that most British eggs are infected with salmonella leads to a slump in egg sales.

**January 1996** The first genetically engineered salmon are hatched, at Loch Fyne in Scotland. The salmon contain genes from white fish as well as a salmon growth hormone gene that causes them to grow five times as fast as other salmon.

**25 March 1996** The European Union bans the export of British beef abroad following anxiety over the potential for transmission of the BSE infection to humans as CJD (Creuzfeld Jakob disease).

**27 February 1997** Scottish researcher Ian Wilmut of the Roslin Institute in Edinburgh, Scotland, announces that British geneticists have cloned an adult sheep. A cell was taken from the udder of the mother sheep and its DNA (deoxyribonucleic acid) combined with an unfertilized egg that had had its DNA removed. The fused cells were grown in the laboratory and then implanted into the uterus of a surrogate mother sheep. The resulting lamb, Dolly, came from an animal that was six years old. The news is met with international calls to prevent the cloning of humans.

**4 March 1998** The Countryside March, a demonstration in London of around 250,000 people, aims to promote understanding of the issues facing rural Britain. Issues that had caused controversy and led to the march included the 1997 bill to ban hunting with dogs, and government policies on farming.

**November 1998** The government announces a £120 million emergency aid package for Britain's farmers, especially hill farmers, partly funded by the European Union.

**November 1999** Companies developing genetically modified (GM) crops in Britain agree to enter into a voluntary ban on the growing of GM crops until 2002.

**December 1999** The EU lifts the ban on the export of British beef.

Thomas Coke (1752–1842), who used it to produce greatly increased crop yields on his farmland in Norfolk, and encouraged other farmers and landowners to use the same method. Because both Coke and Townshend lived in Norfolk, the system also became known as the 'Norfolk System'.

### Livestock farming

Other pioneers of the new farming methods developed in Britain in the latter part of the 18th century included Arthur Young (1741–1820), the first secretary of the British Board of Agriculture and the author of numerous works on agriculture; and the livestock farmer Robert Bakewell (1725–1795), who improved the quality of horned stock and sheep, largely by means of inbreeding. His work resulted in a great reduction in the age at which bullocks and sheep were ready for the butcher.

## agriculture

In 1996 74% of land in Britain was in use for agriculture, of which the majority is grassland used for grazing animals, with just under 30% used for crops. There were approximately 230,000 farm holdings (excluding very small operations) in the same year. Overall, British agriculture employs some 2% of the country's workforce. Britain's main agricultural exports are livestock (reduced from 1995 because of the BSE crisis, see ◊bovine spongiform encephalopathy), food products, agrochemicals, and agricultural machinery. See chronology on page 00 for some key dates in the history of British agriculture.

## Aintree

Racecourse situated on the outskirts of Liverpool, northwest England. The ◊Grand National steeplechase (established 1839) is held at Aintree every spring.

There is also a car-racing circuit, used only for club racing. The British Grand Prix was held here in 1955, 1957, 1959, and 1961–62.

## Albert, Prince Consort (1819–1861)

Husband of Queen ◊Victoria from 1840. A patron of the arts, science, and industry, Albert was the second son of the Duke of Saxe Coburg-Gotha and first cousin to Queen Victoria, whose chief adviser he became. He planned the Great Exhibition of 1851, the profits from which were used to buy the sites in London of all the South Kensington museums and colleges and the Royal Albert Hall, built in 1871. Albert also popularized the Christmas tree in England. He was regarded

**Albert, Prince Consort** Albert photographed with Queen Victoria in 1854; he received the title 'Prince Consort' in 1857. Victoria adored him, but government ministers resented his involvement in politics, and the British public mistrusted him because of his German origins. After his death the Queen was inconsolable and spent the next 40 years as a virtual recluse. Corbis

by the British people with groundless suspicion because of his German connections. He died of typhoid. The Queen never fully recovered from his premature death, and remained in mourning for him for the rest of her life. In his memory, she commissioned the Albert Memorial, an imposing Gothic Revival monument in Kensington Gardens, London, erected 1863–72. The monument was designed by George Gilbert Scott, who earned a knighthood from Queen Victoria for his work on it.

Resoration work on the Albert Memorial was completed in 1998.

## Albion

Name for Britain used by the ancient Greeks and Romans. It was mentioned by Pytheas of Massilia (4th century BC), and is probably of Celtic origin, but the Romans, having in mind the white cliffs of Dover, assumed it to be derived from the word *albus* (white).

## Alcock, John William (1892–1919)

English aviator. On 14 June 1919, he and Arthur Whitten Brown (1886–1948) made the first non-stop transatlantic flight, from Newfoundland to Ireland.

## Aldeburgh

Small town and coastal resort in Suffolk, eastern England, 33 km/20 mi from Ipswich; population (1991) 2,700. It maintains a small fishing fleet, serving the local market. The **Aldeburgh Festival**, founded in 1948 by the English composer Benjamin ◊Britten, is held annually at the Snape Maltings, 8 km/5 mi west of the town. It is the home of the Britten–Pears School for Advanced Musical Studies.

## Aldermaston

Village in West Berkshire, England, and site of an atomic and biological weapons research establishment, which employs some 5,000 people working on the production of nuclear warheads. During 1958–63 the Campaign for Nuclear Disarmament (CND) made it the focus of an annual Easter protest march.

## Aldershot

Town in Hampshire, southern England, 56 km/35 mi southwest of London; population (1991) 51,400. Aldershot contains the largest permanent military and training camp in the UK, dating from 1854. Cambridge Hospital (1854–1996), founded along with the camp, became the birthplace of plastic surgery in Britain. The town has many military museums, including the Aldershot Military Museum, the Airborne Forces Museum, and the Royal Corps of Transport Museum.

## Aldgate

Area and street in the City of London, connecting Fenchurch Street with Whitechapel. The old gate, which was called Eastgate in the Saxon period and, later, Alegate, was the most easterly gate of the City. Excavations have established that it was formerly the site of a Roman gate; it was rebuilt in 1608 and finally demolished in 1761. The remains of the Aldgate Pump, a water pump, can still be seen. The medieval author Geoffrey Chaucer lived in the old gatehouse.

## Aldwych

Thoroughfare in London. It was constructed between 1900 and 1905, and forms a loop on the northern side of the Strand. The name Aldwych was revived to commemorate an ancient Danish settlement in the area.

## Alexander

Three kings of Scotland:

## Alexander I (c. 1078–1124)

King of Scotland from 1107, known as **the Fierce**. He ruled over the area to the north of the rivers Forth and Clyde, while his brother and successor David ruled over the area to the south. He assisted Henry I of England in his campaign against Wales in 1114, but defended the independence of the church in Scotland. Several monasteries, including the abbeys of Inchcolm and Scone, were established by him.

## Alexander II (1198–1249)

King of Scotland from 1214, when he succeeded his father, William the Lion. Alexander supported the English barons in their struggle with King John after ◊Magna Carta. The accession of Henry III of England allowed a rapprochement between the two countries, and the boundaries between England and Scotland were agreed by the Treaty of York in 1237. By the treaty of Newcastle in 1244 he pledged allegiance to Henry III. Alexander consolidated royal authority in Scotland and was a generous patron of the church.

In 1221 he married Joanna, the sister of Henry III. In 1239, after her death, he married Marie de Coucy, with whom he had a son, Alexander III.

## Alexander III (1241–1286)

King of Scotland from 1249, son of Alexander II. After defeating the Norwegian forces in 1263, he was able to extend his authority over the Western Isles, which had been dependent on Norway. The later period of his reign was devoted to administrative reforms, which limited the power of the barons and brought a period of peace and prosperity to Scotland.

He died as the result of a fall from his horse, leaving his granddaughter ◊Margaret, the Maid of Norway, to become queen of Scotland.

## Alfred, the Great (c. 849–c. 901)

King of Wessex from 871. He defended England against Danish invasion and founded the first English navy. A new legal code came into force during his reign. He encouraged the translation of scholarly works from Latin (some he translated himself), and promoted the development of the ◊Anglo-Saxon Chronicle.

Alfred was born at Wantage, Oxfordshire, the youngest son of Ethelwulf (died 858), king of the West Saxons. In 870 Alfred and his brother Ethelred fought many battles against the Danes. Alfred gained a victory over the Danes at Ashdown in 871, and succeeded Ethelred as king in April 871 after a series of battles in which the Danes had been defeated. Five years of uneasy peace followed while the Danes were occupied in other parts of England. In 876 the Danes attacked again, and in 878 Alfred was forced to retire to the stronghold of Athelney, from where he finally emerged to win the victory of Edington, Wiltshire. By the Peace of Wedmore in 878 the Danish leader Guthrum (died 890) agreed to withdraw from Wessex and from Mercia west of Watling Street. A new landing in Kent encouraged a revolt of the East Anglian Danes, which was suppressed 884–86, and after the final foreign invasion was defeated 892–96, Alfred strengthened the navy to prevent fresh incursions.

## Alloway

Former village in South Ayrshire unitary authority, Scotland, on the River Doon, now a suburb of Ayr, lying 6 km/4 mi south of its centre. Alloway is the birthplace of Robert Burns, and is the site of several tourist attractions associated with the Scottish poet, including Burns Cottage, a museum converted from his family home; the kirk, scene of the witches' dance in *Tam o' Shanter*; the Auld Brig o' Doon over which Tam o' Shanter escaped; and the Burns Monument and gardens.

## almshouse, also known as *poor house*

House built and endowed for the support of those disabled from work by age or poverty.

Almshouses were founded by private charities and privately funded. In the Middle Ages, an almshouse was the house belonging to a monastery or a section of a monastery, where alms and hospitality were dispensed. The most ancient example in England is the hospital of St Cross, Winchester (1136). The name 'hospital' is also used for almshouses in Scotland.

## Alnwick

Town in Northumberland, England; population (1991) 7,200. It is situated 53 km/33 mi north of Newcastle, on the River Aln. **Alnwick Castle**, originally dating from the 12th century, was the home of the Percy family. It was the site of battles in 1092 and 1174 following Scottish invasions of Northumberland. The castle was much restored in the 19th century. The 15th-century Hotspur Tower was the original gateway to the town.

## Althorp

Village in Northamptonshire, England, 11km/ 7m north of Northampton, site of the **Althorp Park** estate owned by the Spencer family since 1508. ◊Diana, Princess of Wales, whose family home this was, is buried on an island in the park.

**Almshouse** A 16th-century half-timbered almshouse in Thame, Oxfordshire. Almshouses, charitable foundations to house old and needy people, are found in many ancient towns in England. This one was built by Lord Williams of Thame in the 1550s. Corbis

Earl Spencer, Diana's brother, opened a museum to her memory at Althorp in 1998.

## Alton Towers

Theme park in Alton, Staffordshire, England, 24 km/15 mi east of Stoke-on-Trent; it opened in 1979. It was once the home of the earls of Shrewsbury. The gardens of Alton Towers lie above the gorge of the River Churnet, and are decorated with statues, grottoes, ornamental fountains, and temples. They were landscaped in the early 19th century by Charles, 15th Earl of Shrewsbury. The house – originally called Alveton Lodge – was enlarged in Gothic style in the 1830s by John, the 16th Earl, who renamed it Alton Towers. It contains a picture gallery and armoury. In 1924 the estate was sold to a private company who opened it to the public.

## Ambleside

Town in the Cumbrian Lake District, England; population (1981) 3,200. It is situated 20 km/12 mi northwest of Kendal, and extends to the head of Lake Windermere in the Vale of Rothay. Ambleside is a busy tourist centre for much of the year, with many hotels and guest houses.

Ambleside's literary associations include William and Dorothy Wordsworth, who lived at nearby Grasmere and later at Rydal Mount. Harriet Martineau, who died at Ambleside in 1876, lived at The Knoll, just outside the town.

A sports festival is held here every summer which includes traditional events, such as Cumberland and Westmorland wrestling, and fell running.

## Amesbury

Town in Wiltshire, England; population (1991) 6,400. It is situated 13 km/8 mi north of Salisbury, by the River Avon, on Salisbury Plain; Stonehenge, Woodhenge, and a Roman rampart are all nearby.

**Amesbury Abbey**, the former residence of the dukes of Queensberry, was built by Inigo Jones; John Gay wrote *The Beggar's Opera* while staying as a guest here in 1727.

## Amis, Kingsley (1922–1995)

English novelist and poet. He was associated early on with the ◊Angry Young Men group of writers. His sharply ironic works include the bestselling *Lucky Jim* (1954; his first novel), a comic portrayal of life at a provincial university. His later novels include the satiric comedy *The Old Devils* (1986), for which he won the Booker Prize.

His other novels, written in a variety of genres, include the spy story *The Anti-Death League* (1966), the ghost story *The Green Man* (1969), *The Riverside Villas Murder* (1973), which imitates a classic detective story, and *The Alteration* (1976), which imagines a 20th-century society dominated by the Catholic Church. His last novel *The Biographer's Moustache* was published in 1995. He was the father of writer Martin Amis. Kingsley Amis was knighted in 1990.

## Ancient Britain

Period in Britain extending through prehistory to the Roman occupation (1st century AD).

Settled agricultural life evolved in Britain during the 3rd millennium BC. A peak was reached in Neolithic society in southern England early in the 2nd millennium BC, with the construction of the great stone circles of ◊Avebury and ◊Stonehenge. It was succeeded in central southern Britain by the Early Bronze Age Wessex culture, an aristocratic society which had strong trade links across Europe. The Iron Age culture of the ◊Celts, a warrior aristocracy that introduced horse-drawn chariots and their own distinctive art forms (see ◊Celtic art), was predominant in the last few centuries BC.

The Belgae (of mixed Germanic and Celtic stock) were responsible for the earliest British sites large and complex enough to be called towns. They settled in southern Britain, and resisted the Romans from centres such as ◊Maiden Castle, Dorset. However, they were partially Romanized in the century between the first Roman expedition to Britain under Julius Caesar (54 BC) and the Roman conquest (AD 43). For later history, see ◊Roman Britain; ◊United Kingdom.

## Anderson, Elizabeth Garrett (1836–1917)

English physician, the first English woman to qualify in medicine. Unable to attend medical school, Anderson studied privately and was licensed by the Society of Apothecaries in London in 1865. She was physician to the Marylebone Dispensary for Women and Children (later renamed the Elizabeth Garrett Anderson Hospital). She became the first woman member of the British Medical Association in 1873 and in 1908 was elected mayor of Aldeburgh, becoming the first woman mayor in Britain.

## Aneirin

Welsh poet. He wrote the core of the epic poem *Y Gododdin* (c. 600), one of the earliest known poems in Welsh. It describes a battle at Catraeth

(Catterick) where the tribe from Dun Edin (Edinburgh) were heavily defeated by the Northumbrians.

## Angevin

Term used to describe the English kings Henry II and Richard I (also known, with the later English kings up to Richard III, as the **Plantagenets**). Angevin derives from Anjou, a region in northwestern France. The **Angevin Empire** comprised the territories (including England) that belonged to the Anjou dynasty.

King John is sometimes known as the last of the Angevin dynasty because he was the last English king to reign over Anjou, which he lost in 1204.

## Anglesey, Welsh Ynys Môn (island), Sir Ynys Môn (authority)

Island and unitary authority off the northwest coast of Wales; population (1996) 71,100; area 720 sq km/278 sq mi (34 km/21 mi long and 31 km/19 mi broad). The principal towns are Llangefni (administrative headquarters), Holyhead, Beaumaris, and Amlwch.

*Physical*

Anglesey is separated from the mainland by the Menai Strait. The island has an attractive coastline and rich fauna, notably bird life, and flora.

*Features*

There is a Roman-British village at Din Lligwy. The uncompleted Beaumaris Castle was founded by Edward I in 1295. The Menai Strait is crossed by Thomas Telford's suspension bridge (1819–26; subsequently rebuilt) and the Britannia tubular railway bridge (1846–50). The village of Llanfairpwllgwyngyllgogerychwyrndrobwllllantysiliogogogoch has the longest place name in Britain. The Beaumaris festival takes place in May and June.

*Economy*

There is sheep farming and various agriculture; Anglesey was once called the granary of Wales, providing food for the mainland. Food processing and high-technology industries are now important. The Wylfa nuclear power station is located 10 km/6 mi west of Amlwch. The port of Holyhead, on the adjoining Holy Island, has a ferry service to Ireland.

## Anglesey Abbey

House in Cambridgeshire, England, 10 km/6 mi northeast of Cambridge, dating from 1600 and built on the site of an Augustinian abbey.

The landscaped garden and arboretum here were created by Lord Fairhaven who left the house and 202 ha/499 acre estate to the National Trust in 1966, along with his vast collection of furnishings and European works of art. The house has a 13th-century crypt.

## Anglo-Saxon

One of several groups of Germanic invaders (including Angles, Saxons, and Jutes) that conquered much of Britain between the 5th and 7th centuries. Initially they established conquest kingdoms, commonly referred to as the Heptarchy; these were united in the early 9th century under the overlordship of Wessex. The Norman invasion in 1066 brought Anglo-Saxon rule to an end.

The Jutes probably came from the Rhineland and not, as was formerly believed, from Jutland. The Angles and Saxons came from Schleswig-Holstein, and may have united before invading. The Angles settled largely in East Anglia, Mercia, and Northumbria; the Saxons in Essex, Sussex, and Wessex; and the Jutes in Kent and southern Hampshire.

## Anglo-Saxon art

The art of the Anglo-Saxon period of English history, from the 5th to the 11th century. Sculpted crosses and ivories, manuscript painting, and gold and enamel jewellery demonstrate a love of intricate, interwoven designs in the Anglo-Saxon period. Influences include the late Celtic arts of the native Britons, Roman styles deriving from the introduction of Christianity, and Norse art following the Viking invasions of the 8th century.

Much metalwork has survived, including simple bronze brooches, remarkable circular silver brooches with tracery and niello (infilled engraving) decoration, and gold and silver jewels with cloisonné inlays of garnet and lapis lazuli, and decoration of interlaced gold filigree. The relics of the ◊Sutton Hoo ship burial (7th century; British Museum, London) have typical Celtic ornamental patterns and include the finest examples of the Saxon goldsmiths' art yet known.

Church books of a high standard were produced by the early illuminators. In Northumbria the ◊*Lindisfarne Gospels* were embellished in the early 8th century with illuminated capital letters and elaborate paintings of the evangelists deriving unmistakably from the Celtic applied arts. In the manuscripts of southern England, in particular those produced at Winchester and Canterbury, a different style emerged in the 9th century, with delicate, lively pen-and-ink figures and heavily decorative foliage borders.

Saxon sculpture incorporated Roman, Norse, Scottish, and Irish elements, as seen in the inscriptions carved on standing stones and crosses. Great development occurred in Northumbria in the 7th century, marked in particular by Acca's cross, Hexham; and standing crosses at Ruthwell, Dumfriesshire and Bewcastle, Cumbria. In 9th-century Mercia sculpture was used to decorate churches, notably at Breedon-on-the-Hill, Derbyshire.

## Anglo-Saxon Chronicle
A history of England from the Roman invasion to the 11th century, consisting of a series of chronicles written in Old English by monks, begun in the 9th century (during the reign of King Alfred), and continuing until 1154.

The Chronicle, comprising seven different manuscripts, forms a unique record of early English history and also of the development of Old English prose up to its final stages. By 1154 Old English had been superseded by Middle English.

## Anglo-Saxon language
Group of dialects, also known as Old English, spoken between the 5th and 12th centuries by peoples of Saxon origin who invaded and settled in central and southern England in the 5th–7th centuries; thus the term properly does not include the language of the Angles who settled in the areas to the north. See ◊Old English; ◊Old English literature.

## Angry Young Men
Journalistic term applied to a loose group of British writers who emerged in the 1950s after the creative hiatus that followed World War II. They revolted against the prevailing social mores, class distinction, and 'good taste'. Their dissatisfaction was expressed in works such as Kingsley Amis's *Lucky Jim* (1954), John ◊Osborne's *Look Back in Anger* (1956), Colin Wilson's *The Outsider* (1956), John Braine's *Room at the Top* (1957), and John Wain's *Hurry on Down* (1953).

## Angus
Unitary authority on the east coast of Scotland; population (1996) 111,300; area 2,187 sq km/844 sq mi. A former county, it was part of Tayside region 1975–96. It is mountainous in the north with low hills in the south. The principal towns are Arbroath, Brechin, Carnoustie, ◊Forfar (administrative headquarters), Kirriemuir, and Montrose.

*Physical*
The Grampian Mountains in the north are dissected by the fertile valleys of the rivers Isla, Clova, Prosen, Water of Saughs, and North Esk; the wide Vale of Strathmore separates the Grampian Mountains from the low-lying Sidlaw Hills in the south.

*Features*
The area has Pictish and Iron Age remains. There are several large Iron Age hill forts, such as the two Caterthuns, and impressive souterrains (earth houses) at Ardestie and Carlungie. Other remains include brochs, sculptured stones, and hut circles. Many of these remains are situated on the fringes of the Vale of Strathmore. Glamis Castle, near Glamis village, is the 17th-century family home of the Queen Mother; she was born here. Angus has 34 Sites of Special Scientific Interest, two National Nature Reserves, three Ramsars (wetland sites), three Special Protection Areas, one National Scenic Area, and three country parks. Arbroath smokies (smoked haddock) are a local speciality.

*Economy*
Angus is essentially a rich and important agricultural area, with cereal production and some fishing (mainly in Arbroath), although the towns have a manufacturing tradition and, increasingly, a service sector base.

## Anne (1665–1714)
Queen of Great Britain and Ireland 1702–14. She was the second daughter of James, Duke of York, who became James II, and his first wife, Anne Hyde, daughter of Edward Hyde, Earl of Clarendon. She succeeded William III in 1702. Events of her reign include the War of the Spanish Succession, Marlborough's victories at Blenheim, Ramillies, Oudenarde, and Malplaquet, and the union of the English and Scottish parliaments in 1707.

## Anne of Cleves (1515–1557)
Fourth wife of ◊Henry VIII of England, whom she married in 1540. She was the daughter of the Duke of Cleves, and was recommended to Henry as a wife by Thomas Cromwell, who wanted an alliance with German Protestantism against the Holy Roman Empire. Henry did not like her looks, had the marriage declared void after six months, pensioned her, and had Cromwell beheaded for treason.

## Anne of Denmark (1574–1619)
Queen consort of James VI of Scotland (from 1603 ◊James I of Great Britain). She was the

daughter of Frederick II of Denmark and Norway, and married James in 1589. She bore him five children, two of whom survived: Charles I and Elizabeth of Bohemia. Anne was suspected of Catholic leanings and was notably extravagant but seems to have had little influence on state affairs.

## Antrim

Town in County Antrim, Northern Ireland; population (1991) 23,500. It is situated on the Six Mile Water where it enters the northeast corner of Lough Neagh, 28 km/17 mi northwest of Belfast. Antrim is a manufacturing and market town with engineering, electronics, and construction industries as well as computer-software development. The Round Tower (28 m/92 ft high) is all that remains of the 10th-century Aentrebh monastery after which the town is named.

Antrim was burnt by Scottish Covenanters in 1643; in 1798 it was the site of the **Battle of Antrim**, at which the United Irishmen were defeated by English troops.

On the outskirts of the town, in Antrim Castle Demesne, are the remains of formal gardens laid out by André Le Nôtre (also responsible for the gardens at Versailles, France). Clotworthy House, an arts centre and theatre, is located here, as is a golf course.

Castle Upton, designed in the late 18th century by Robert ◊Adam, is 9 km/5.5 mi east of Antrim at Templepatrick. Shane's Castle Park and deer park are 8 km/5 mi west of Antrim, and Randalstown Forest wildlife reserve is nearby.

A number of archaeological sites are located near Antrim: 3 km/2 mi east are the ring forts of Rathmore and Rathbeg (the possible seat of the kings of Dál nAraide during the 6th and 7th centuries); 5 km/3 mi east on Donegore Hill is a Neolithic enclosed settlement; and at nearby Ballywee ring fort excavations show evidence of house foundations and souterrains (underground dwellings).

## Antrim

County of Northern Ireland; population (1981) 642,000; area 2,830 sq km/1,092 sq mi. It occupies the northeastern corner of Northern Ireland, with a coastal eastern boundary. The principal towns and cities are ◊Belfast (county town), ◊Larne (port), Antrim, ◊Ballymena, ◊Lisburn, and ◊Carrickfergus.

### Physical

Antrim borders Lough ◊Neagh, and is separated from Scotland by the North Channel, which is only 21 km/13 mi wide at Torr Head, the narrowest point. The Antrim Mountains (highest point Trostan 554 m/1,817 ft) run parallel to the coastline. The main rivers are the Bann and the Lagan, and there are peat bogs.

### Features

The ◊Giant's Causeway, a World Heritage Site, consists of natural hexagonal and pentagonal basalt columns on the coast; other notable natural features include the Glen of Antrim and Kebble National Nature Reserve, on Rathlin Island, off the coast near Ballycastle. Bushmills Distillery, in the village of Bushmills, has the oldest known licence for distilling whiskey. There are a number of early fortifications, castles (including the 12th-century Carrickfergus Castle and romantic ruins of the 16th-century Dunluce Castle), and medieval ecclesiastical remains in the county. The village of Cushendun was built by Clough Williams-Ellis. Gobbins Cliff Path (19th century) is being restored as a millennium project. The traditional Ould Lammas Fair at Ballycastle takes place in August.

### Economy

Agriculture is important in the county (the Bann Valley is particularly fertile). There is also shipbuilding and whiskey distilling. Traditional linen production has largely been replaced by the manufacture of artificial fibres.

## Appleby, or Appleby-in-Westmorland

Market town in Cumbria, England, formerly the county town of Westmorland; population (1991) 1,300. It is situated on the River Eden, 21 km/13 mi southeast of Penrith and is known for its annual horse fair in June, attended by travellers from Ireland and elsewhere. The castle, built on the site of a Norman keep, was restored by Lady Anne Clifford in the 17th century.

The church of St Lawrence has a monument to Lady Anne, and a church organ – one of the oldest in England – which was brought here from Carlisle Cathedral in 1684.

## April Fools' Day

The first day of April, when it is customary in western Europe and the USA to expose people to ridicule by a practical joke, causing them to believe some falsehood or to go on a fruitless errand.

The victim is known in England as an April Fool and in Scotland as a gowk (cuckoo or fool).

## Apsley House

Mansion at the southeast corner of ◊Hyde Park, London. Home of the dukes of Wellington from 1820; now the Wellington Museum. It was originally built in 1771–8 for Baron Apsley, 2nd Earl Bathurst (1774–94), from designs by Robert ◊Adam.

The house was bought in 1820 by the Duke of ◊Wellington from his brother the Marquess Wellesley. The house was enlarged in 1828 by Benjamin Dean Wyatt (1775–1850), and has a palatial interior. The house and its contents were presented to the nation by the 7th Duke of Wellington in 1947. Now the Wellington Museum, it contains many Wellington relics and a famous collection of pictures captured during the Peninsular War, including Velázquez's *Water Carrier*.

It used to be known as 'No. 1, London' (being the first house that travellers reached on entering London). The Duke of Wellington held the commemorative Waterloo dinner there annually until his death.

## Archers, the

Longest-running drama serial in the world. It began on BBC radio in 1951 and continues to be broadcast in six episodes per week, with an omnibus edition on Sundays. Originally designed as a means of disseminating farming news and information, it still retains a farming advisor and refers to contemporary farming issues. The serial is set in the fictional village of Ambridge.

The programme prompted acute controversy when, in 1955, on the opening night of commercial television, it killed off a leading character in a fire. Programme-makers later admitted that this was deliberate sabotage. At its peak, also in 1955, the serial attracted 20 million listeners.

---

*In my own case I 'find' G major by singing the signature tune of 'The Archers'.*

**Antony Hopkins** English educator, conductor, writer on music, and composer.
On pitch, in *Downbeat Music Guide* (1977)

---

## architecture

### Norman

(11th–12th century) William the Conqueror inaugurated an enormous building programme. He introduced the **Romanesque style** of round arches, massive cylindrical columns, and thick walls. At Durham Cathedral (1093–*c.* 1130), the rib vaults were an invention of European importance in the development of the Gothic style.

### Gothic

The three main styles, ◊Early English, ◊Decorated, and ◊Perpendicular, are distinguishable by the design of their windows, and in particular by the development of vaulting and buttressing, whereby the thick walls and heavy barrel-vaults, the flat buttresses and the narrow windows of the 12th century came to be replaced by bolder buttresses with thinner walls between them, thinner vaults supported on stone ribs, and much larger windows filled with tracery.

---

*Ghastly Good Taste, or a depressing story of the rise and fall of English architecture.*

**John Betjeman** English poet and essayist.
Book title

---

### Tudor and Elizabethan

(1485–1603) This period saw the Perpendicular style interwoven with growing Renaissance influence. Buildings developed a conscious symmetry elaborated with continental Patternbrook details. Hybrid and exotic works result such as Burghley House, Cambridgeshire (1552–87), and Hardwick Hall, Derbyshire (1590–97).

### Jacobean

(1603–25) A transition period, with the Renaissance influence becoming more pronounced, as in Hatfield House, Hertfordshire (1607–12), and Blicking Hall, Norfolk (completed 1628).

### English Renaissance

(17th–early 18th century) The Jacobean scene of half-timbered and turreted buildings was revolutionized by Inigo ◊Jones, who introduced Palladianism with his Queen's House, Greenwich (1616–35) and Banqueting House, Whitehall (1619–22). With Christopher ◊Wren a restrained Baroque evolved showing French Renaissance influence, for example St Paul's Cathedral (1675–1710). Nicholas ◊Hawksmoor and John Vanbrugh developed a theatrical Baroque style in their design for Blenheim Palace, Oxfordshire (1705–20).

### Georgian

(18th–early 19th century) Richard Boyle Burlington, reacting against the Baroque, inspired a revival of the pure Palladian style of Inigo Jones, as in his Chiswick House, London (1725–29). William ◊Kent, also a Palladian, invented the picturesque garden, as at Rousham, Oxfordshire. Alongside the great country houses, an urban architecture evolved of plain, well-proportioned houses, defining elegant streets and squares; John Wood the Younger's Royal Crescent, Bath, was built from 1767 to 1775. The second half of the century mingled Antiquarian and Neo-Classical influences, exquisitely balanced in the work of Robert ◊Adam at Kedleston Hall (1759–70). John ◊Nash carried Neo-Classicism into the new century, his designs including Regent Street, London (begun 1811), and the Royal Pavilion, Brighton (1815–21).

### 19th century

Throughout the Victorian period Classic and Gothic engaged in the 'Battle of the Styles': Gothic for the Houses of Parliament (1840–60; designed by Charles Barry and August ◊Pugin), Renaissance for the Foreign Office (1860–75). Meanwhile advances in engineering and the needs of new types of buildings, such as railway stations, transformed the debate. Joseph Paxton's prefabricated Crystal Palace (1850–51) was the most remarkable building of the era. The Arts and Crafts architects Philip Webb and Norman Shaw brought renewal and simplicity inspired by William Morris.

### 20th century

The early work of Edwin Landseer ◊Lutyens and the white rendered houses of Charles Voysey maintained the Arts and Crafts spirit of natural materials and simplicity. Norman Shaw, however, developed an Imperial Baroque style. After World War I Classicism again dominated, grandly in Lutyens' New Delhi government buildings (1912–31). There was often a clean Scandinavian influence, as in the RIBA building, London (1932–34), which shows growing Modernist tendencies. The Modern movement arrived fully with continental refugees such as Bertholdt Lubetkin, the founder of the Tecton architectural team that designed London Zoo (1934–38).

The strong social dimension of British 20th-century architecture is best seen in the garden city andnew town movement. Welwyn Garden City was begun in 1919 and developed after World War II. The latest of the new towns, Milton Keynes, was designated in 1967. British architects have also achieved international recognition, for example, Norman Foster and Richard Rogers for their High-Tech innovative Lloyds Building, London (1979–84). Post-Modernist architecture includes the Sainsbury Wing of the National Gallery, London, designed by Robert Venturi in 1991.

---

*The British love permanence more than they love beauty.*

**Hugh Casson** English architect.
*Observer* 1964

---

In the 20th century Nikolaus ◊Pevsner did much to encourage interest in architecture, compiling a unique account of the buildings of England from stately homes to domestic architecture, in 46 volumes.

## Ardress House

17th-century manor house in County Armagh, Northern Ireland, 14 km/9 mi north of Armagh. It has two 18th-century wings added by the Dublin architect George Ensor, who married the heiress to Ardress in 1760. The Ulster Land Fund gave Ardress to the National Trust in 1960.

The decorative plasterwork in the main rooms is by Michael Stapleton, a talented stuccoist.

## Argyll and Bute

Unitary authority in western Scotland, created in 1996 from the district of the same name and part

**Architecture** Uppark, an imposing country house high on the South Downs near Chichester in West Sussex, is a good example of English Renaissance architecture. This square, red-brick building of around 1690 shows a fine sense of proportion. It was severely damaged by fire in 1989, but was painstakingly restored by its owners, the National Trust. Matthew Antrobus/National Trust Photographic Library

of Dumbarton district, which were both parts of Strathclyde region; population (1996) 89,300; area 7,016 sq km/2,709 sq mi. The area is known for its mountains, lochs, and island scenery and is a popular tourist destination. It includes the islands of Gigha, Bute, ◊Mull, Islay, ◊Jura, Tiree, Coll, Colonsay, ◊Iona, and Staffa. The principal towns are ◊Oban, Campbeltown, ◊Dunoon, ◊Helensburgh, ◊Inveraray, ◊Lochgilphead (administrative headquarters), and Rothesay.

*Physical*
Argyll and Bute is a rural area consisting of mainland and islands; the coast is heavily indented. Inland the area is mountainous; the highest peak is Ben Cruachan (1,126 m/3,693 ft). Ben Arthur (The Cobbler) is another well-known peak (884 m/2,900 ft). It has the longest peninsula in Scotland, Kintyre, extending down between the Firth of Clyde and the Atlantic; the southernmost tip is the Mull of Kintyre. Lochs Fyne and Long are the largest sea lochs; freshwater lochs include Loch Awe and Loch ◊Lomond. ◊Fingal's Cave is on the island of Staffa and Corryvrekan Whirlpool is between Jura and Scarba.

*Features*
The area is rich in Bronze, Stone, and Iron Age remains: there are standing stones, stone circles, vitrified forts, inscribed stones, and Neolithic chambered cairns. The capital of Dalriada, the ancient Scottish kingdom founded in about 503, was at Dunadd, near Crinan until shortly after the union of the Picts and Scots, whereafter it moved to Forteviut in Strathearn. Iona has the site of a monastery founded in 563 by St Columba, who made the island his base for his mission to Scotland. Inveraray Castle is a striking 18th-century neo-Gothic/Scottish baronial building. There are 112 Sites of Special Scientific Interest, seven Special Protection Areas, eight Ramsars (wetland sites), nine Special Protection Areas, one Biosphere Reserve, eight National Scenic Areas, and one regional park.

*Economy*
With land of marginal agricultural capability, and located far from the urban core, the area has a typical rural economy. Tourism, fishing, forestry, and less intensive agriculture, mainly sheep farming, are important. There is whisky distilling; whisky produced on the island of Jura is particularly noted.

## Arkwright, Richard (1732–1792)
English inventor and manufacturing pioneer who in 1768 developed a machine for spinning cotton (he called it a 'water frame'). In 1771 he set up a water-powered spinning factory and in 1790 he installed steam power in a Nottingham factory.

Arkwright was born in Preston, Lancashire, and experimented in machine designing with a watchmaker, John Kay (1704–c.1780), until, with Kay and John Smalley (died 1782), he set up the water frame, the first machine capable of producing sufficiently strong cotton thread to be used as warp. In 1771 he went into partnership with Jebediah Strutt (1726–1797), a Derby man who had improved the stocking frame, and Samuel Need (died 1781), and built a water-powered cotton mill at Cromford in Derbyshire, where he also built the first mill village for his workers. The original mill can still be visited.

In 1773 Arkwright produced the yarn ('water twist') for the first cloth made entirely from cotton; previously, the warp had been of linen and only the weft was cotton. A special act of Parliament was passed in 1774 to exempt Arkwright's fabric from the double duty imposed on cottons by an act of 1736. By 1782 Arkwright employed 5,000 workers, mainly women and children.

## Arlington Court
19th-century Neo-Grecian house in Devon, England, 11 km/7 mi northeast of Barnstaple. It was built for John Chichester, whose family owned the estate from the 14th century. The house was bequeathed to the National Trust in 1949 by Rosalie Chichester, together with over 1200 ha/2964 acres of land, including three hamlets, thirteen farms, an animal sanctuary, and a nature reserve.

The bequest also included interesting collections of costumes, pewter, 19th-century furniture, horse-drawn carriages (now displayed in the stables), model ships, and shells.

## Armagh
City and county town of County Armagh, Northern Ireland; population (1991) 14,300. The city became the religious centre of Ireland in the 5th century when St Patrick was made archbishop. Armagh was also a noted seat of learning; St Patrick founded a monastic school here, and in 1169 Rory O'Connor, the last Irish high-king, founded a 'professorship'. The city was the seat of the kings of Ulster for 700 years, and is now the seat of both the Roman Catholic and Protestant archbishops of Ireland, each of whom bears the title 'Archbishop of Armagh and Primate of All Ireland'.

The Church of Ireland cathedral occupies the traditional site of the church built by St Patrick. It houses several fine monuments, including pre-Christian stone statues (one of which is reputed to be of Queen Mhacha), and a statue of Thomas Molyneaux by Roubiliac; in the library is an annotated handwritten copy of Jonathan Swift's *Gulliver's Travels*.

Eamhain Macha, 3 km/2 mi to the west of Armagh, is a large earthwork and tumulus reputed to be the burial site of Queen Mhacha; it was also the seat of the Ulster kings until AD 332.

## Armagh (Irish *Ard Mhacha* 'the height of Mhacha' (a legendary queen))

County of Northern Ireland; population (1981) 119,000; area 1,250 sq km/483 sq mi. It borders Lough Neagh to the north and the Republic of Ireland to the south. Its principal towns and cities are ◊Armagh (county town), Lurgan and Portadown (merged to form ◊Craigavon), and Keady.

### History

Eamhain Macha was the seat of the kings of Ulster until AD 332, and the county of Armagh has been significant in many conflicts over territory, including battles over Ulster between the British and Irish during the 17th–19th centuries.

### Physical

Armagh is the smallest county of Northern Ireland. It is flat in the north, with many bogs and mounds formed from glacial deposits, and has low hills in the south, the highest of which is Slieve Gullion (577 m/1,893 ft). The principal rivers are the Bann, the Blackwater, and its tributary, the Callan.

### Features

Armagh is noted for its rich archaeological remains, including those at Eamhain Macha, a large earthwork 3 km/2 mi west of the city of Armagh, reputed to have been built by Queen Mhacha in 300 BC. Other features include Blackwater River Park, the 17th-century manor ◊Ardress House, and Camagh Forest.

### Economy

The county has good farmland, apart from the marshy areas by Lough Neagh. The north of the county is a fruit-growing and market gardening area, while to the south livestock rearing is important. Linen is manufactured (Portadown and Lurgan were the principal centres of the linen industry).

## Arnold, Matthew (1822–1888)

English poet and critic. His poem 'Dover Beach' (1867) was widely regarded as one of the most eloquent expressions of the spiritual anxieties of Victorian England. In his highly influential critical essays collected in *Culture and Anarchy* (1869), he attacked the smugness and philistinism of the Victorian middle classes, and argued for a new culture based on the pursuit of artistic and intellectual values. He was the son of Thomas Arnold, headmaster of Rugby school.

## Arnold, Thomas (1795–1842)

English schoolmaster, father of the poet and critic Matthew ◊Arnold. He was headmaster of Rugby School 1828–42. His regime has been graphically described in Thomas Hughes's *Tom Brown's Schooldays* (1857). He emphasized training of character, and had a profound influence on public school education.

---

*My object will be, if possible, to form Christian men, for Christian boys I can scarcely hope to make.*

**Thomas Arnold** English schoolmaster. Letter, on appointment to headmastership of Rugby 1828

---

## Arran

Largest island in the Firth of Clyde, lying between the Kintyre peninsula and the mainland of North Ayrshire, Scotland; area 427 sq km/165 sq mi; population (1991) 4,500. The economy is largely service based, with tourism and craft industries, such as knitwear. Other industries include whisky distilling and food processing. The island, which is mountainous to the north and undulating to the south, is a popular holiday resort. The chief town is Brodick. Machrie Moor dates from the Bronze Age (3000–4000 years ago) and has stone circles, single stones, hut circles, and burial cists. Drumadoon Point is the site of an Iron Age fort.

## art

For British art before the 10th century, see ◊Celtic art and ◊Anglo-Saxon art.

### Medieval: 10th–15th centuries

The strong traditions of Celtic art and Anglo-Saxon art continued in manuscript illumination. One of the few named figures of the period was the 13th-century illuminator and chronicler Matthew Paris. Few examples of medieval British painting survived the Reformation. The late 14th-century *Wilton Diptych* (National Gallery, London), showing Richard II presented to the Virgin and Child, is a rare example of medieval panel painting.

**Arran** The Machrie standing stones on the island of Arran, in Strathclyde region, Scotland, date from around 2000 BC. The variety of landscapes on Arran, from rocky fells in the north to gentler hills in the south, has led to it being dubbed 'Scotland in miniature'. Corel

### Tudor and Elizabethan: 15th–16th centuries

The reign of Henry VIII virtually put an end to church art. Painting survived largely through the influence and example of the German Hans ◊Holbein, who painted portraits of Henry's court. In Elizabeth's reign miniature portrait painting developed, most notably by Nicholas ◊Hilliard and his pupil Isaac Oliver.

### 17th century

British art was once again revitalized by foreign artists, in particular the Flemish painter Anthony van ◊Dyck, who settled in England to become court painter to Charles I. His Baroque elegance dominated 17th-century portraiture. Among his successors were William Dobson (1610–1646), the cavalier court painter to Charles I. During the Commonwealth and after the Restoration, the influence of foreign artists working in Britain continued, in particular Peter ◊Lely, Godfrey Kneller, and the sculptors, John Michael Rysbrack and Grinling ◊Gibbons.

### 18th century

British art at last became robustly independent, with great achievements in portraiture and landscape.

Portraiture was transformed by two outstanding figures, Thomas ◊Gainsborough and Joshua ◊Reynolds, who brought a new subtlety and refinement to portraits, their images expressing the wealth and confidence of British society. The ◊Royal Academy was founded in 1768, and as its first president Reynolds was able to promote a Classicism based on Italian High Renaissance art. Other important portraitists were Thomas Lawrence, George Romney, and John Hoppner. The fashionable portraiture of the 18th century was challenged by William ◊Hogarth, who painted contemporary life with a vigorous and unapologetic frankness. He was the first English artist to gain an international reputation. Other leading caricaturists, earthy and bitingly satirical, were James ◊Gillray and Thomas ◊Rowlandson. Their favourite targets were the Georgian court, the follies and evils of society, and, during the Napoleonic Wars, Napoleon.

Landscape painting was established in England by the work of foreign artists such as Canaletto. The first British artist to excel at landscape was Richard ◊Wilson, who painted landscape in the 'Italian manner', based on the works of Claude Lorrain. Gainsborough brought to his landscapes a more personal and romantic feeling, his influences being Dutch 17th-century landscapists.

The poet and etcher William ◊Blake was a unique figure, fashioning his own highly individual style to express a complex personal mythology. His visionary creations, among the first powerful expressions of Romanticism, briefly inspired Samuel ◊Palmer, who brought a strong note of mysticism to landscape painting.

At the very end of the century John Flaxman became the leading exponent of Neo-Classical sculpture.

### 19th century

John ◊Constable and JMW ◊Turner gave a depth and range to landscape painting which made it not only one of the most popular expressions of British art, but also one of its most important. Their achievements were complemented by a host of other landscape painters, including Richard Bonington, John Crome, John Sell ◊Cotman, Robert Cozens, Thomas ◊Girtin, and David Cox.

The ◊Pre-Raphaelite movement, which was established in the 1840s, dominated British art for the rest of the century. Its members – such as Holman ◊Hunt, Dante Gabriel ◊Rossetti, and John Everett ◊Millais – concentrated on religious, literary, and genre subjects, their style being colourful and also minutely detailed. In the late 19th century the ◊Arts and Crafts movement, led by William ◊Morris, promoted a revival of crafts and good design. Book illustration flourished under the inspiration of both the Pre-Raphaelites and the Arts and Crafts movement, its leading practitioners being Walter Crane, Kate ◊Greenaway, Arthur ◊Rackham, and Aubrey ◊Beardsley.

Among the most popular artists of the day were Edward ◊Landseer, who specialized in animal pictures; and Lord Leighton and Lawrence Alma-Tadema, both of whom made their reputations with lavish recreations of ancient Greek and Roman life.

By the end of the century British art was being influenced by French artists, in particular Edgar Degas and the Impressionists. The US-born artist James McNeill Whistler was typical, rejecting the story pictures that characterized so much Victorian art in favour of the aesthetics of form, colour, and tone. English Impressionists founded the New English Arts Club in 1886, and French influence, which continued well into the 20th century, can be seen in the work of Wilson Steer, John Singer Sargent (another American working in England), Walter ◊Sickert, and Augustus ◊John.

## 20th century

In 1910 an exhibition arranged by the critic Roger ◊Fry introduced British artists to Post-Impressionism and Fauvism. The ◊Camden Town Group was formed in 1911 to encourage artists who were bringing a new sense of form and colour to the depiction of scenes of everyday London life. Walter Sickert, Charles Ginner, and Harold Gilman were its leading figures. Artists of the ◊Bloomsbury Group, such as Duncan ◊Grant, Dora ◊Carrington, and Vanessa ◊Bell, were more adventurous in their development of the same influences.

Just before World War I Vorticism, the one specifically English art movement, was created by Wyndham ◊Lewis, one of the few artists to be directly influenced by Cubism and Futurism. Paintings by David Bomberg and sculptures by Henri Gaudier-Brzeska and Jacob ◊Epstein are among the movement's main achievements.

Between the world wars, artists soon began to reflect a wide range of styles and intentions. Matthew Smith worked in a Fauvist style and L S ◊Lowry developed a childlike naivety. Using a finely detailed realism, Stanley ◊Spencer sought to express a visionary apprehension of everyday life. Ben ◊Nicholson evolved an entirely abstract art; Paul ◊Nash, Ceri Richards, and Graham

◊Sutherland responded to Surrealism. Surrealism was also an influence on the sculptor Henry ◊Moore. Other important sculptors to emerge at this time were Barbara ◊Hepworth and Ben Nicholson (both abstract), and Jacob ◊Epstein (who soon outgrew Vorticism), Eric Gill, and Frank Dobson (all figurative).

## Post-World War II

After World War II British art became increasingly pluralistic. A strong figurative tradition was continued, in very different styles, by Francis Bacon, Lucian Freud, and others. Associated with the introduction of Pop art in the 1950s were Richard Hamilton, Peter Blake, David Hockney, and R B Kitaj. Abstract painting, which has never had a strong following in Britain, was practised by Victor Pasmore, Patrick Heron, William Turnbull, Terry Frost, and Bridget Riley, the leading figure in Op art. Outstanding among sculptors – who also have explored a range of creative possibilities – are Reg Butler, Lynn Chadwick, Kenneth Armitage, Anthony Caro, Elizabeth Frink, Eduardo Paolozzi, Richard Long, and Antony Gormley. In the late 20th century mixed and sometimes unusual media have been utilized, such as dead sheep (Damien Hirst), chocolate (Helen Chadwick, 1953–1996), and elephant dung (Chris Offili). Performance artists include Gilbert and George (who styled themselves 'living sculptures') and Bruce McLean (1944– ).

## Art Deco

Originally called 'Jazz Modern', Art Deco emerged in Europe in the 1920s and continued to influence art, architecture, and product design through the 1930s. A self-consciously modern style, it was characterized by angular, geometrical patterns and bright colours, and by the use of materials such as enamel, chrome, glass, and plastic. Art Deco style in Britain was epitomized by the innovative work of pottery designers Clarice ◊Cliff and Susie ◊Cooper. Other exponents included Betty Joel, creator of curved, easy-care, functional furniture; the cabinetmaker Ambrose Heal; the sculptor Eric Gill; industrial designer Douglas ◊Scott; and Giles Gilbert ◊Scott, who designed Battersea Power Station (1932–34) with an Art Deco interior.

Long-established pottery and glass manufacturers such as Doulton, Coulton, Crown Devon, Pilkington, and Wedgwood created Art Deco ranges, and the Carter, Stabler & Adams company, established at Poole in 1921, produced painted earthenware in the style.

## Arthur (lived 6th century AD)

Legendary British king and hero in stories of ◊Camelot and the quest for the ◊Holy Grail. Arthur is said to have been born in Tintagel, Cornwall, and been buried in Glastonbury (see ◊Avalon), Somerset. He may have been a Romano-Celtic leader against pagan Saxon invaders.

The legends of Arthur and the knights of the Round Table were developed in the 12th century by Geoffrey of Monmouth, Chrétien de Troyes, and the Norman writer Wace. Later writers on the theme include the anonymous author of *Sir Gawayne and the Greene Knight* (1346), Thomas Malory, Tennyson, T H White, and Mark Twain.

## Arthur's Seat

Hill of volcanic origin to the east of the centre of Edinburgh, Scotland; height 251 m/823 ft. It forms the core of Holyrood Park and is a dominant landmark.

The easiest ascent is from Dunsappie Loch to the south.

## Art Nouveau

Decorative style of the visual arts, interior design, and architecture flourishing from 1890 to 1910. Characterized by organic, sinuous patterns and ornamentations based on plant forms, its style was notable in the sophisticated decadence of Aubrey ◊Beardsley's illustrations, and in the fluent interior and exterior designs of Charles Rennie ◊Mackintosh.

Art Nouveau may, in part, be traced back to late Pre-Raphaelite floral patterns, as in the designs of William ◊Morris, founder of the Arts and Crafts movement. The influence of Morris and Beardsley was strongly felt in Austria, Belgium, and Germany, propagated by early numbers of the *Studio* (1893), the first issue of which contained Beardsley's work. In Italy Art Nouveau was known as *stile Liberty* after the London department store, which was celebrated for its Arts and Crafts and Art Nouveau houseware.

## Arts and Crafts movement

English social and aesthetic movement of the late 19th century which stressed the importance of manual skills and the dignity of labour. It expressed a rejection of Victorian industrialization and mass production, and a nostalgic desire to return to a medieval way of life. The movement influenced Art Nouveau and, less directly, the Bauhaus school of design.

Its roots lay in the ideas of the architect A W N Pugin and the art critic John Ruskin, both of whom believed that a country's art reflected its spiritual state and was damaged by the loss of traditional skills. The most important practitioner of their ideals was William ◊Morris, who in 1861 founded the firm of Morris, Faulkner and Co, producing a wide range of high-quality goods, including fabrics, furniture, stained glass, and wallpaper. Artists who worked for the firm included Edward ◊Burne-Jones, Dante Gabriel ◊Rossetti, and Philip Webb.

## Arts Councils

Four organizations that aid music, drama, opera, and visual arts with government funds. They came into being in April 1994 when the Arts Council of Great Britain was divided into the separate and independent Arts Councils of England, Scotland, Wales, and Northern Ireland.

## Arundel

Market town in West Sussex, southern England, on the River Arun; population (1991) 3,300. Tourism is an important summer industry.

**Arundel Castle**, the seat of the Fitzalan-Howard family, Dukes of Norfolk, was built in 1067 by the cousin of William (I) the Conqueror, Roger Montgomery, to defend the Arun valley; its large stone keep dates from the 12th century. During the English Civil War the castle was besieged from 1643 to 1644 and almost ruined by Oliver Cromwell's Parliamentary troops. It was rebuilt in the 18th century and much restoration work was carried out in 1890.

The church of St Nicholas, dating from 1380, has a pre-Reformation pulpit and 14th-century wall paintings.

## Ascot

Small town in Windsor and Maidenhead unitary authority, southern England, about 10 km/6 mi southwest of Windsor; population (1991) 6,200. The Royal Ascot race meeting, established by Queen Anne in 1711, is held annually in June. It is a social as well as a sporting event.

The June meeting is a showcase for fashion and extravagant hats, particularly on Ladies Day. Principal races include the Gold Cup, Ascot Stakes, Coventry Stakes, and the King George VI and Queen Elizabeth Stakes.

## Ashdown House

17th-century house in Oxfordshire, England, 12 km/7 mi east of Swindon. It was given to the National Trust in 1956 by Cornelia, Countess of

Craven, whose ancestor, the 1st Lord Craven, built the house for Elizabeth of Bohemia in 1665.

The house is of unusual design, and is constructed of chalk blocks with stone quoins (dressed corner-stones). It is four storeys high, and crowned by a cupola (dome) with a golden ball.

## Ashes, the

Cricket trophy theoretically held by the winning team in the England–Australia Test series.

The trophy is permanently held at ◊Lord's cricket ground no matter who wins the series. It is an urn containing the ashes of stumps and bails used in a match when England toured Australia 1882–83. The urn was given to the England captain Ivo Bligh by a group of Melbourne women. The action followed the appearance of an obituary notice in the *Sporting Times* the previous summer announcing the 'death' of English cricket after defeat by the Australians in the Oval test match.

## Ashford

Town in Kent, southeast England, 22 km/14 mi southwest of Canterbury; population (1991) 52,000. Situated close to the ◊Channel Tunnel and to the ferry ports of Folkstone and Dover, Ashford is an important commercial and industrial centre for the southeast and the site of an international passenger station which opened in 1996, offering a direct passenger rail service between Britain and Continental Europe. The French writer Simone Weil died in a sanatorium in Ashford in 1943.

## Ashmolean Museum

Museum of art and antiquities in Oxford, England, founded in 1683 to house the collections given to Oxford University by the historian and antiquary Elias Ashmole (1617–1692). Its collections include European, Near Eastern, and Oriental art and archaeology; paintings and drawings by Raphael, Michelangelo, and other Renaissance artists; watercolours by J M W Turner; and works by Pre-Raphaelite and major British and European artists of the 18th, 19th, and 20th centuries. It was the first museum in Britain to open to the public.

## Ashton, Frederick (1904–1988)

English choreographer and dancer. He was director of the Royal Ballet, London, 1963–70. He studied with Marie Rambert before joining the Sadler's Wells (now Royal) Ballet in 1935 as chief choreographer. His choreography is marked by a soft, pliant, classical lyricism. His many works and long association with Margot ◊Fonteyn, for whom he created her most famous roles, contributed to the worldwide reputation of British ballet and to the popularity of ballet in the mid-20th century.

## Ashton-under-Lyne

Industrial town and administrative headquarters of Tameside, a metropolitan district of ◊Greater Manchester, northwest England; population (1994 est) 177,000. Historically important as a cotton-milling town at the heart of the Tame Valley, Ashton-under-Lyne is the largest of Tameside's market towns. The Church of St Michael and All Angels includes magnificent stained glass dating from about 1500 and the Portland Basin Industrial Heritage Centre illustrates the industrial and social history of Tameside.

## Astor

Prominent British and US family. **Waldorf Astor**, 2nd Viscount Astor (1879–1952), was a British politician, and served as Conservative member of Parliament for Plymouth from 1910 to 1919, when he succeeded to the peerage. His US-born wife Nancy Witcher Langhorne (1879–1964), **Lady Astor**, was the first woman member of Parliament to take a seat in the House of Commons, when she succeeded her husband in the constituency of Plymouth in November 1919. She remained in parliament until 1945, as an active champion of women's rights, educational issues, and temperance.

## Astronomer Royal

Honorary post in British astronomy. Originally it was held by the director of the Royal Greenwich Observatory, the first being Joseph ◊Flamsteed. Since 1972 the title of Astronomer Royal has been awarded separately as an honorary title to an outstanding British astronomer. The Astronomer Royal from 1995 is Martin Rees. There is a separate post of Astronomer Royal for Scotland.

## Attingham Park

Late 18th-century house near Shrewsbury, Shropshire, England. It stands in a 1620 ha/4000 acre estate acquired in 1953 by the National Trust under the will of the 8th Lord Berwick. The house has a John ◊Nash picture gallery and staircase, and the park was landscaped by Humphry ◊Repton.

## Attlee, Clement, 1st Earl Attlee (1883–1967)

British Labour politician. As prime minister 1945–51 he introduced a sweeping programme of nationalization of industry and a whole new system of social services.

## Aubrey, John (1626–1697)

English biographer and antiquary. He was the first to claim ◊Stonehenge as a Druid temple. His *Lives*, begun in 1667, contains gossip, anecdotes, and valuable insights into the celebrities of his time. It was published as *Brief Lives* in 1898. *Miscellanies* (1696), a work on folklore and ghost stories, was the only work to be published during his lifetime.

## Auden, W(ystan) H(ugh) (1907–1973)

English-born US poet. He wrote some of his most original poetry, such as *Look, Stranger!* (1936), in the 1930s when he led the influential left-wing literary group that included Louis MacNeice, Stephen Spender, and C Day-Lewis. He moved to the USA in 1939, became a US citizen in 1946, and adopted a more conservative and Christian viewpoint, for example in *The Age of Anxiety* (1947).

He also wrote verse dramas with Christopher ◊Isherwood, such as *The Dog Beneath the Skin* (1935) and *The Ascent of F6* (1936), and opera librettos, notably for Igor Stravinsky's *The Rake's Progress* (1951). Auden was professor of poetry at Oxford from 1956 to 1961. He returned to live in England a year before his death.

## Augustine, St (died 605)

First archbishop of Canterbury, England. Originally prior of the Benedictine monastery of St Andrew, Rome, he was sent from Rome to convert England to Christianity by Pope Gregory I. He landed at Ebbsfleet in Kent in 597 and soon after baptized Ethelbert, king of Kent, along with many of his subjects. He was consecrated bishop of the English at Arles in the same year, and appointed archbishop in 601, establishing his see at Canterbury.

In 603 he attempted unsuccessfully to unite the Roman and native Celtic churches at a conference on the Severn. He founded Christ Church, Canterbury, in 603, and the abbey of Saints Peter and Paul, now the site of Saint Augustine's Missionary College. His Feast day is 26 May.

## 'Auld Lang Syne'

Song written by the Scottish poet Robert Burns in about 1789, which is often sung at New Year's Eve gatherings. The title means 'old long since' or 'long ago'.

## Austen, Jane (1775–1817)

English novelist. She described her raw material as 'three or four families in a Country Village'. *Sense and Sensibility* was published in 1811, *Pride and Prejudice* in 1813, *Mansfield Park* in 1814, *Emma* in 1816, and *Northanger Abbey* and *Persuasion* together in 1818, all anonymously. Many of her works have been successfully adapted for film and television.

Austen was born in Steventon, Hampshire, where her father was rector. She was sent to school in Reading with her elder sister Cassandra, who was her lifelong friend and confidante, but she was mostly taught by her father. In 1801 the family moved to Bath and after the death of her father in 1805, to Southampton, settling in 1809 with her mother and sisters in a house in Chawton, Hampshire, provided by her brother Edward (1768–1852). She died in Winchester, and is buried in the cathedral.

Jane Austen's novels deal mainly with middle-class families, set usually in rural communities, though occasionally in a town, such as Bath. Her plots hinge mostly on the development of a love affair leading to the heroine's marriage.

Her novels reveal Jane Austen as a scrupulous and conscious artist; absolute accuracy of information is allied to absolute precision of language. Describing individuals coping with ordinary life and social pressures, she probes the centres of

**Jane Austen** English novelist Jane Austen, whose uneventful life belied her ability to produce insightful novels concerning relationships and the nuances of social interaction amongst the landed gentry. Although she had several suitors, Austen never married. She died in 1817 of Addison's disease. Corbis

human experience, using a sharp, satiric wit to expose the follies, hypocrisies, and false truths of the world. She observed speech and manners with wit and precision, and her penetrating observation of human behaviour results in insights that transcend period. Her genius and place among the great English novelists was at once recognized by such critics as S T Coleridge, Robert Southey, Thomas Macaulay, and Walter Scott.

---

*For what do we live, but to make sport for our neighbours, and laugh at them in our turn?*

**Jane Austen** English novelist.
*Pride and Prejudice* (1813) ch 57

---

## Avalon
In Celtic mythology, the island of the blessed, or paradise; in the legend of King ◊Arthur, the land of heroes, ruled over by Morgan le Fay, to which King Arthur is conveyed after his final battle with Mordred. It has been identified since the Middle Ages with Glastonbury in Somerset, southwest England.

## Avebury
Europe's largest stone circle (diameter 412 m/1,350 ft), in Wiltshire, England. This megalithic henge monument is thought to be part of a ritual complex, and contains 650 massive blocks of stone arranged in circles and avenues. It was probably constructed around 3,500 years ago, and is linked with nearby ◊Silbury Hill.

The henge, an earthen bank and interior ditch with entrances on opposite sides, originally rose 15 m/49 ft above the bottom of the ditch. This earthwork and an outer ring of stones surround the inner circles. The stones vary in size from 1.5 m/5 ft to 5.5 m/18 ft high and 1 m/3 ft to 3.65 m/12 ft broad. They were erected by a late Neolithic or early Bronze Age culture. The remains that can be seen today may cover an earlier site – as may be the case at a number of prehistoric sites.

When the village of Avebury developed within the circle, many of the blocks were used for building material. In the Middle Ages many of the stones were buried.

The site was acquired by the National Trust in 1943, and the area now protected includes the majority of the stone circles; Windmill Hill, a Neolithic defensive earthwork; and a manor farm.

## Aviemore
All-year sports and tourist centre, in the Highland unitary authority, Scotland, 45 km/28 mi southeast of Inverness and adjacent to the Cairngorm Mountains. The centre specializes in winter sporting activities. It was extensively developed in the 1960s as Britain's first complete holiday and sports centre.

## Aylesbury
Market town and administrative headquarters of ◊Buckinghamshire, England, 60 km/37 mi northwest of London; population (1991) 50,000. Lying to the north of the Chiltern Hills, it has for centuries been the market centre of the Vale of Aylesbury. While modern development in the town centre has to some extent diminished its character, the King's Head Inn survives from the 15th century, and other features include the cobbled market square, the 18th-century County Hall, and some fine 17th–18th century houses. The town gives its name to a breed of large white domestic duck.

## Ayot St Lawrence
Village in Hertfordshire, southern England, 13 km/8 mi north of St Albans. The playwright George Bernard Shaw lived in the village from 1906 until his death in 1950, and his former home, Shaw's Corner, is preserved as it was in his lifetime.

## Ayr
Administrative headquarters of ◊South Ayrshire, southwest Scotland, at the mouth of the River Ayr; population (1991) 48,000. Ayr has strong associations with the poet Robert ◊Burns, who was was born at Alloway, 4 km/2.5 mi south of the town centre.

Ayr is a popular holiday resort, with a long sandy beach. It has a racecourse, which hosts the Scottish Grand National, and several golf courses. Glasgow Prestwick International Airport is 6 km/4 mi to the north of the town centre.

## Babbage, Charles
(1792–1871)
English mathematician who devised a precursor of the computer. He designed an analytical engine, a general-purpose mechanical computing device for performing different calculations according to a program input on punched cards (an idea borrowed from the Jacquard loom). This device was never built, but it embodied many of the principles on which digital computers are based.

In 1991 the British Science Museum completed Babbage's second difference engine (to demonstrate that it would have been possible with the materials then available). It evaluates polynomials up to the seventh power, with 30-figure accuracy.

## Bacon, Francis, 1st Baron Verulam and Viscount St Albans (1561–1626)
English philosopher, politician, and writer; a founder of modern scientific research. His works include *Essays* (1597; revised and augmented 1612 and 1625), characterized by pith and brevity; *The Advancement of Learning* (1605), a seminal work discussing scientific method; *Novum organum/ The New Instrument* (1620), in which he redefined the task of natural science, seeing it as a means of empirical discovery and a method of increasing human power over nature; and *The New Atlantis* (1627), describing a utopian state in which scientific knowledge is systematically sought and exploited.

## Bacon, Roger (c. 1214–1294)
English philosopher and scientist. He was interested in alchemy, the biological and physical sciences, and magic. Many discoveries have been credited to him, including the magnifying lens. He foresaw the extensive use of gunpowder and mechanical cars, boats, and planes. Bacon was known as *Doctor Mirabilis* (Wonderful Teacher).

In 1266, at the invitation of his friend Pope Clement IV, he began his *Opus majus/Great Work*, a compendium of all branches of knowledge. In 1268 he sent this with his *Opus minus/Lesser Work* and other writings to the pope. In 1277 Bacon was condemned and imprisoned by the Christian church for 'certain novelties' (heresy) and not released until 1292.

Bacon wrote in Latin and his works include *On Mirrors*, *Metaphysical*, and *On the Multiplication of Species*. He followed the maxim 'Cease to be ruled by dogmas and authorities; look at the world!'

## Baden-Powell, Robert, 1st Baron Baden-Powell (1857–1941)
British general, founder of the Scout Association. He was commander of the garrison during the 217-day siege of Mafeking (now Mafikeng) in the Second South African War (1899–1900). After 1907 he devoted his time to developing the Scout movement, which rapidly spread throughout the world.

Baden-Powell began the Scout movement in 1907 with a camp for 20 boys on Brownsea Island, Poole Harbour, Dorset. He published *Scouting for Boys* (1908) and about 30 other books. He was World Chief Scout from 1920. With his sister Agnes (1858–1945) he founded the Girl Guides in 1910.

## Bader, Douglas (1910–1982)
British fighter pilot. He lost both legs in a flying accident in 1931, but had a distinguished flying career in World War II. He was credited with 22 ½ planes shot down (20 on his own and some jointly) before being shot down and captured himself in August 1941. The film *Reach for the Sky* (1956) was based on his experiences.

## Badminton

Village in Gloucestershire, England. **Badminton House**, the seat of the Duke of Beaufort, is a mansion in the Palladian style; it has given its name to the game of badminton, and to the Badminton Library. An annual three-day equestrian event is held at Badminton, which is often attended by members of the British royal family.

## bagpipes

Any of an ancient family of double-reed folk woodwind instruments employing a bladder, filled by the player through a mouthpiece, or bellows as an air reservoir to a 'chanter' or fingered melody pipe, and two or three optional drone pipes providing a continuous accompanying harmony.

The Highland bagpipes are the national instrument of Scotland.

## Baird, John Logie (1888–1946)

Scottish electrical engineer who pioneered television. In 1925 he gave the first public demonstration of television, transmitting an image of a recognizable human face. The following year, he gave the world's first demonstration of true television before an audience of about 50 scientists at the Royal Institution, London. By 1928 Baird had succeeded in demonstrating colour television.

## Bakewell

Town in Derbyshire, England, on the River Wye, 40 km/25 mi from Derby; population (1991) 3,600. Bakewell is in the scenic surroundings of the ◊Peak District; nearby are the historic stately homes Haddon Hall and Chatsworth House.

There are Saxon remains on Castle Hill near Bakewell; the church of All Saints is mentioned in the ◊Domesday Book; on its southern side stands an 8th-century carved stone cross. Bakewell Bridge is one of the oldest bridges in England.

**Bakewell pudding**, an open almond-flavoured tart, originated here.

## Bala Lake, Welsh Llyn Tegid

Lake in Gwynedd, north Wales, about 6.4 km/4 mi long and 1.6 km/1 mi wide. It has a unique primitive species of fish, the gwyniad (a form of whitefish), a protected species from 1988. It has facilities for water sports.

## Balcon, Michael (1896–1977)

English film producer. He entered film production in the early 1920s and was instrumental in developing the career of the young Alfred

**Bagpipes** Although played in a number of regions in Britain, bagpipes are most commonly associated with Scotland. Characteristic types of tunes for the pipes are stirring marches performed by massed regimental pipers (for example at the annual Edinburgh Military Tattoo) or *pibrochs*, haunting laments for the dead played by a lone piper. Corel

◊Hitchcock. Subsequently, he was responsible for the influential Ealing comedies of the 1940s and early 1950s (see ◊Ealing Studios), such as *Kind Hearts and Coronets* (1949), *Whisky Galore!* (1949), and *The Lavender Hill Mob* (1951).

## Baldwin, Stanley, 1st Earl Baldwin of Bewdley (1867–1947)

British Conservative politician, prime minister 1923–24, 1924–29, and 1935–37. He weathered the general strike of 1926, secured complete adult suffrage in 1928, and handled the ◊abdication crisis of Edward VIII in 1936, but failed to prepare Britain for World War II.

## ballet (Italian *balletto* 'a little dance')

Western ballet as we know it today first appeared in Renaissance Italy, where it was a court entertainment. In England, the masque, a composite art form similar to the court ballet, originated in the late 16th century but was given its definitive form by the architect Inigo Jones and playwright

Ben Jonson. Masques used visual images to express moral and philosophical truths, and represented a belief in human ability to control nature; in the reign of Charles I, the 'antimasques' evolved as a mimed or danced episode preceding the main spectacle, often portraying 'grotesque' characters (a relationship may be drawn with the Italian commedia dell'arte tradition, which in turn influenced the pantomimes of English fairgrounds). The masque entertainment came to an abrupt end with the monarchy in 1649.

### 18th–19th centuries
The English choreographer John Weaver emerged in the 1700s, with his theories and 'dramatick entertainments' going back to ancient Greek traditions. In 1734 the French dramatic ballerina Marie Salle, a student with the French dancer Marie-Anne Camargo, came to London to premiere her most famous ballet, *Pygmalian*. The choreographer Jules Perrot presented his work in London in the 19th century. He was ballet master for Her Majesty's Theatre 1842–48, during which time he presented some 20 ballets, including *Ondine* (which later influenced Frederick ◊Ashton) and *Giselle* (which formed the basis of the interpretation performed today). His work in London contributed to the international expansion of Romantic ballet, which first appeared about 1830 but survives only in the ballets *Giselle* (1841) and *La Sylphide* (1832). Perrot specialized in dramatic ballets, using dance to advance the action.

### 20th century
The next major development was initiated by the Russian entrepreneur Sergei Diaghilev with his Ballets Russes, founded in 1909, which first visited London in 1911 and mounted several triumphant seasons there until the company folded with the death of Diaghilev in 1929; there were also visits to Manchester in 1919 and regional tours of England in 1927 and 1929.

In 1926 Marie ◊Rambert founded the company that developed into the Ballet Rambert, and launched the careers of choreographers such as Frederick Ashton and Anthony Tudor (1908–1987). The national company, the ◊Royal Ballet (so named in 1956), grew from foundations laid by Ninette de Valois and Frederick Ashton in 1928. The London Festival Ballet, formed in 1950, was renamed the English National Ballet in 1989. The Northern Ballet Theatre was founded in 1987.

Leading British dancers include Alicia Markova, Anton Dolin, Margot ◊Fonteyn, Antoinette Sibley, Beryl Grey, Anthony Dowell, Merle Park, and Lesley Collier; choreographers include Kenneth MacMillan, Derek Deane, artistic director of the English National Ballet, and Christopher Gable, director of the Northern Ballet Theatre from 1987.

## Ballycastle
Market town and seaside resort in the north of County Antrim, Northern Ireland; population (1991) 3,300. It is the port from which Rathlin Island is reached. Ballycastle's large Lammas Fair has been held on the last Tuesday in August since 1606.

There are a number of medieval ruins around Ballycastle, including Bonamargy friary (1 km east), an 11-m/35-ft round tower (8 km/5 mi south near Armoy), and Dunaneanie Castle (1 km west). Knocklayd Mountain (517 m/1,695 ft) is to the south, as is Ballycastle Forest. The sheer columnar basalt cliffs of Fairhead (190 m/626 ft) are 10 km/6 mi to the east, and impressive basaltic columns are also found at Grace Staples Cave to the west of Ballycastle.

## Ballymena
Town in County Antrim, Northern Ireland, on the River Braid, 45 km/28 mi northwest of Belfast; population (1991) 28,300. It was created as a Lowland Scots plantation in the 17th century.

Harryville Motte and Bailey, a 12th-century earthwork, is located on the southern outskirts of the town. Some 2 km/1 mi to the southwest is Galgorm Castle, built at the time of the plantation (1618–19), and Gracehill, a settlement established in 1746 by the Moravian Brethren sect of Protestants. Linen manufacture was introduced in Ballymena in 1733.

## Balmoral Castle
Residence of the British royal family in Scotland on the River Dee, 10 km/6 mi northeast of Braemar, Aberdeenshire. The castle, built of granite in the Scottish baronial style, is dominated by a square tower and circular turret rising 30 m/100 ft. It was rebuilt between 1853 and 1855 by Prince Albert, who bought the estate in 1852 from Robert Gordon, and gave it to Queen Victoria.

## Bamburgh Castle
Castle in the village of Bamburgh on the coast of Northumberland, England. An imposing structure of red sandstone, it is situated 26 km/16 mi southeast of Berwick, and is built on a rock rising

46 m/151 ft above the North Sea. Founded in 547 by Ida, the first king of Northumbria, it was rebuilt in Norman times, and underwent extensive restoration in the 18th and 19th centuries. It was the scene of many battles in the Border wars of the 14th century, and changed hands several times during the Wars of the Roses. Henry VI ruled briefly from Bamburgh, but after the Battle of Hexham in 1464 it became the first English castle to fall to artillery. The castle is now open to the public.

## Banbury

Market town in Oxfordshire, central England, on the River Cherwell, 40 km/25 mi north of Oxford; population (1991) 39,900. The **Banbury Cross** of the nursery rhyme 'Ride a Cock Horse to Banbury Cross' was destroyed by the Puritans in 1602, but replaced in 1859. **Banbury cakes** are made from flaky or puff pastry with a filling of dried, spiced fruit.

## Bangor

Resort and Belfast commuter town in County Down, Northern Ireland, on the shore of Belfast Lough, 20 km/12 mi northeast of Belfast; population (1991) 52,400. Bangor has the largest marina in Ireland, and the Royal Ulster Yacht Club is based here. Bangor is the site of a missionary abbey of the Celtic church founded in the 6th century, and it was here that the 7th-century prayer book, *The Antiphonary of Bangor*, one of the oldest ecclesiastical manuscripts in the world, was created; the original manuscript is now housed in Milan, but a facsimile is housed in the museum of the Bangor Heritage Centre.

## bank holiday

A public holiday when banks are closed by law. Bank holidays were instituted by the Bank Holiday Acts 1871 and 1875.

In addition to Good Friday and Christmas Day, bank holidays in England and Wales are: New Year's Day, Easter Monday, 1 May, the last Monday in May, the last Monday in August, and the first weekday after Christmas (Boxing Day). In Scotland, although there is some local variation, there are bank holidays on: New Year's Day, 2 January (and 3 January if either 1 or 2 January falls on a Sunday), the first Monday in May, the first Monday in August, and Christmas Day. Northern Ireland has all the English holidays, with the addition of St Patrick's Day (17 March) and 12 July. The Channel Islands have all the English holidays, plus Liberation Day (9 May).

## Bank of England

UK central bank founded by Act of Parliament in 1694. It was entrusted with issuing bank notes in 1844 and nationalized in 1946. It is banker to the clearing banks and the UK government.

As the government's bank, it manages and arranges the financing of the public sector borrowing requirement and the national debt, implements monetary policy and exchange-rate policy by intervening in foreign-exchange markets, sets interest rates (from 1997), and supervises the UK banking system. It is known, from its London site, as the *Old Lady of Threadneedle Street*.

## Bannockburn, Battle of

Battle on 23–24 June 1314 in which ◊Robert (I) the Bruce of Scotland defeated the English under Edward II, who had come to relieve the besieged Stirling Castle. The battle is named after the town of Bannockburn, south of Stirling, central Scotland. English losses are reckoned at about 10,000 troops against about 4,000 Scots.

## Barbican, the

Arts and residential complex in the City of London. The Barbican Arts Centre (1982) contains theatres, cinemas, and exhibition and concert halls. The architects were Powell, Chamberlin, and Bon.

## Barbirolli, John (1899–1970)

English conductor. Barbirolli excelled in the Romantic repertory, especially the symphonies of Elgar, Sibelius, Mahler, and Vaughan Williams. Trained as a cellist, he succeeded Toscanini as conductor of the New York Philharmonic Orchestra 1937–43 and was conductor of the Hallé Orchestra, Manchester, 1943–70.

## Barnsley

Industrial town and administrative headquarters of Barnsley metropolitan borough, ◊South Yorkshire, England, 26 km/16 north of Sheffield; population (1991) 75,100. Now a manufacturing and market centre, Barnsley was formerly important as a centre of the coal industry and is the site of the headquarters of the National Union of Mineworkers. Situated at the edge of the ◊Peak District National Park, Barnsley lies in an area known for its striking landscape and rich industrial history. The Cooper Art Gallery includes a collection of English drawings and 19th-and 20th-century watercolours.

## Barnstaple

Town and port in Devon, England, 96 km/60 mi northwest of Exeter; population (1981) 24,900. It is situated 10 km/6 mi from the mouth of the River Taw, and has a tidal harbour; the Taw is crossed by a 12th-century bridge with 16 arches. Barnstaple is the centre for tourism in north Devon.

## Barrett Browning, Elizabeth

English poet; see ◊Browning, Elizabeth Barrett.

## Barrie, J(ames) M(atthew) (1860–1937)

Scottish dramatist and novelist. His work includes *The Admirable Crichton* (1902) and the children's fantasy *Peter Pan* (1904).

After early studies of Scottish rural life in plays such as *A Window in Thrums* (1889), his reputation as a dramatist was established with *The Professor's Love Story* (1894) and *The Little Minister* (1897). Later plays include *Quality Street* (1901) and *What Every Woman Knows* (1908).

---

*You've forgotten the grandest moral attribute of a Scotsman, Maggie, that he'll do nothing which might damage his career.*

**James Matthew Barrie** Scottish dramatist and novelist.
*What Every Woman Knows* II

---

## Barrington Court

Tudor mansion in Somerset, England, 5 km/3 mi northeast of Ilminster. Although purchased by the National Trust in 1907, the derelict mansion and adjoining 17th-century stable block were not restored and refurnished until after World War I. The mansion has a garden designed by Gertrude ◊Jekyll.

## barrow

Burial mound, usually composed of earth but sometimes also of stones. The two main types are **long**, dating from the Neolithic period (New Stone Age), and **round**, dating from the Mesolithic period (early Bronze Age). Barrows made entirely of stones are known as cairns.

Some **long** barrows may be mere mounds, typically higher and wider at one end. The body or bodies of the deceased were usually placed in a turf-lined cavity, or a chamber of wood or stone slabs with a single entrance. This type is common in southern England from Sussex to Dorset. The remains of these stone chambers, once their earth covering has disappeared, are known as **dolmens**, and in Wales as **cromlechs**.

**Round** barrows belong mainly to the Bronze Age. In Britain they are commonly associated with the Wessex culture (2000–1500 BC). There are also some barrows from the Roman era; these have a distinctive steep and conical outline, and often contain the graves of wealthy merchant traders; similar mounds are also found in Belgic Gaul, where the traders had commercial links. The Saxons buried the remains of important chieftains in large barrows (see ◊Sutton Hoo), but clusters of small burial mounds are more commonly found.

## Barrow-in-Furness

Industrial port at the south end of the ◊Furness peninsula in Cumbria, northwest England; population (1991) 48,900. Barrow expanded in the 19th century to become a major centre of the iron and shipbuilding industries and one of Britain's busiest ports. Its steel works closed in 1983, but Barrow is still important for the manufacture of chemicals and the British Gas pipeline from Morecambe Field in the Irish Sea comes ashore here. The Dock Museum traces the history of Barrow's shipbuilding industry. Barrow is connected by bridge to Walney Island which has important nature reserves and nearby to the northeast are the ruins of Furness Abbey (1127).

## Barry, Welsh Y Barri

Port and administrative centre of the ◊Vale of Glamorgan, south Wales, 12 km/7 mi southwest of Cardiff; population (1991) 49,900. Barry includes the traditional seaside resort of **Barry Island** and within the area are the remains of Barry Castle (13th–15th century).

## Bart's

Shortened form of St Bartholomew's Hospital in Smithfield, London, one of the great teaching hospitals of England. It was founded by Henry VIII at the Reformation.

## Basildon

Industrial town in Essex, eastern England, 19 km/12 mi southwest of Chelmsford; population (1994 est) 101,000. Incorporating the old village of Basildon and several other previously independent villages, Basildon was designated a new town in 1949 – one of eight new towns developed to accommodate overspill population from London after the end of World War II.

## Basingstoke

Town in Hampshire, England, 72 km/45 mi southwest of London; population (1991) 77,800.

Formerly a small market town, Basingstoke expanded rapidly when it began to take overspill population from London in the 1960s and many of the older buildings were demolished as the town developed as a business, service, and industrial centre. The Milestones Museum, a millennium project, is a new living history museum which explores developments in transport and technology, and their effects on people's lives.

*Features*

In the nearby village of **Basing** are the ruins of Basing House, a Tudor mansion built on the site of a Norman castle, and the scene of a two-year siege during the English Civil War. Remains of the house include a 15th-century gatehouse, a dovecote, and a tithe barn. The ◊Vyne, a Tudor house now owned by the National Trust, lies north of the town.

## Bateman's

Jacobean farmhouse, 1 km/0.6 mi south of Burwash, East Sussex, England. It is built in local stone and was Rudyard ◊Kipling's home from 1902 to 1936. The house and 120 ha/296 acres, including the gardens, were left to the National Trust in 1939 by Mrs Kipling.

The stories 'Rewards and Fairies' and 'Puck of Pook's Hill' were written here; Pook's Hill can be seen from the lawn.

## Bates, H(erbert) E(rnest) (1905–1974)

English writer. He was most successful in capturing the feeling of life in the changing English countryside, and his stories are written in a simple, direct, and deeply compassionate manner. Of his many novels and short stories, *The Jacaranda Tree* (1949) and *The Darling Buds of May* (1958) particularly demonstrate the fineness of his natural observation and sensitive portrayal of character. *Fair Stood the Wind for France* (1944) was based on his experience as a squadron leader in World War II, during which he also wrote stories under the pseudonym Flying Officer X.

The five chronicles of the Larkin family began with *The Darling Buds of May*, and also included *A Breath of French Air* (1959), *When the Green Woods Laugh* (1960), *Oh! To be in England* (1963), and *A Little of What You Fancy* (1970). The novels were filmed as a television series in the 1990s.

## Bath

Historic city and administrative headquarters of ◊Bath and North East Somerset, southwest England, 171 km/106 mi west of London; population (1991) 78,700. Once the Roman town of **Aquae Sulis**, Bath flourished in the 18th century as a fashionable spa, with the only naturally occurring hot mineral springs in Britain. With its fine Roman remains and a wealth of honey-coloured 18th-century architecture, the city of Bath is a World Heritage Site and a major tourist destination. The city is also internationally known for its festivals, including the Bath International Music Festival, held in May–June.

*History*

Recognizing the medicinal and therapeutic properties of the spring water that rises here at a constant 46.5°C/116°F, the Romans established a large baths complex and a temple, dedicated to Sulis Minerva, a goddess of healing. These were built over during the medieval period and not excavated until the late 19th century. Bath was transformed in the 18th century as many members of wealthy society moved to the spa and the leading architects of the time built the elegant crescents, terraces, and squares for which it is still famous today.

*Features*

The open-air Great Bath lies at the heart of the Roman bathing complex, surrounded by pillars dating from the 19th century. The complex also includes the remains of smaller baths as well as the Roman heating system. The Roman Baths Museum, adjoining the complex, displays many Roman relics, including a bronze head of Sulis Minerva. Mineral water can be drunk from a fountain in The Pump Room, once the centre of the spa's social scene. 'Reviving Spa Culture' is a millennium project designed to create a new spa complex in the centre of Bath. The most impressive of Bath's Palladian-style architecture, much of it the work of the architects John Wood the Elder and Younger, can be seen in Queen Square, the Circus, the Assembly Rooms (1771), and the outstanding Royal Crescent. The University of Bath was established in 1966.

*Bath Abbey*

The present Abbey church, dating from 1499, is a fine example of Perpendicular Gothic architecture. Its west front includes unique carved decoration depicting angels ascending and descending ladders.

## Bath and North East Somerset

Unitary authority in southwest England, created in 1996 from part of the former county of Avon; population (1996) 158,700; area 351 sq km/136 sq mi. The principal towns and cities are ◊Bath (administrative headquarters), Keynsham, Chew Magna, Paulton, Radstock, Peasedown St John, and Midsomer Norton. The city of Bath is a World Heritage site and a magnet for tourists.

*Physical*
Part of the ◊Mendip Hills are in the south and part of the ◊Cotswold Hills in the east. The River Avon and tributaries run through the area. Chew Valley Lake is an important reservoir.

*Features*
Bath is renowned for its Roman baths with hot springs, its late Perpendicular abbey church, and its fine Regency architecture including the Royal Crescent, the Circus, and the Assembly Rooms designed by John Wood (1700–1854) and his son John Wood. Pulteney Bridge, an 18th-century shop-lined Italianate bridge designed by Robert Adam, and Beckford's Tower, built in 1827 for William Beckford, are also architectural landmarks. Elsewhere, Stanton Drew has Bronze Age stone circles, including the second largest in Britain.

*Economy*
Tourism is important to the area; the other main areas of employment are central government administration and clothing manufacture.

## Battersea
District of the Inner London borough of Wandsworth on the south bank of the Thames. It has a park and Battersea Dogs' Home (opened in 1860 for strays). Battersea Power Station (1937, designed by Giles Gilbert Scott, with an Art Deco interior), closed in 1983. Plans were approved in 1996 for its conversion into a leisure complex. Work was scheduled for completion in 2000.

## Battle
Town in East Sussex, southeast England, named after the Battle of ◊Hastings, which took place here in 1066. The remains of the Benedictine abbey of St Martin's, founded by William (I) the Conqueror to commemorate his victory over Harold II, lie nearby.

The abbey was built on the ridge above the hamlet of Senlac. It is said that the high altar was erected on the spot where Harold was killed, and the site is now marked by a memorial stone. The foundation was dissolved in 1537, but remnants of the turreted abbey gatehouse (1338) and the refectory survive.

## Battle of Britain
World War II air battle between German and British air forces over Britain 10 July–31 October 1940.

At the outset the Germans had the advantage because they had seized airfields in the Netherlands, Belgium, and France, which were basically safe from attack and from which southeast England was within easy range. The Battle of Britain had been intended as a preliminary to the German invasion plan, which Hitler postponed indefinitely on 17 September and abandoned on 10 October, choosing instead to invade the USSR. The battle has been divided into five phases: a preliminary phase; an attack on coastal targets; an attack on Fighter Command airfields; and two daylight attacks on London.

## Bayeux Tapestry
Linen hanging made about 1067–70 which gives a vivid pictorial record of the invasion of England by William (I) the Conqueror in 1066. It is an embroidery rather than a true tapestry, sewn with woollen threads in blue, green, red, and yellow. Measuring 70 m/231 ft long and 50 cm/20 in wide, it contains 72 separate scenes with descriptive wording in Latin. It is exhibited at the museum of Bayeux in Normandy, France.

## BBC, British Broadcasting Corporation
The state-owned broadcasting network. It operates television and national and local radio stations, and is financed by the sale of television licences. It is not permitted to carry advertisements but has an additional source of income through its publishing interests and the sales of its programmes. The BBC is controlled by a board of governors, each appointed by the government for five years. The BBC was converted from a private company (established in 1922) to a public corporation under royal charter in 1927. Under the charter, news programmes were required to be politically impartial. A new charter in 1996 safeguarded the BBC's role and status as a public corporation until 2006, with the licence fee guaranteed as the chief source of revenue until 2002. The first director general was John Reith (1922–38). Greg Dyke was appointed director general in 1999.

*Television*
Television services began in 1936, although they were suspended 1939–46 during World War II. A second channel, BBC2, was launched on 20 April 1964, aimed at minority interests, and in 1991 BBC World Service Television began broadcasting English-language transmissions round the world.

Under the terms of the 1989 Broadcasting Act, 25% of programmes must be supplied by external contractors. Producers are entitled to buy services

**Bayeux Tapestry** Harold II of England and William of Normandy meet in this scene from the Bayeux Tapestry. Harold had been sent to Normandy by Edward the Confessor to offer the throne of England to William. The tapestry shows Harold taken prisoner by a French count and rescued by William who subsequently knighted Harold before his return to England. The tapestry shows Harold's death at the subsequent Battle of Hastings in 1066. Corbis

for their productions inside the BBC or elsewhere. The BBC's key production centre is in London, with regional centres in Glasgow, Cardiff, Belfast, Birmingham, Manchester, and Bristol. In 1998 the BBC launched a digital channel, BBC Choice.

*Radio*

The BBC has five national radio channels, as well as a number of local regional stations. Overseas radio broadcasts (World Service) have a government subsidy. The World Service broadcasts in 47 languages, including English. Listeners have increased from 130 million a week in 1990 to over 140 million in 1998. Countries that have attempted to ban the World Service include the USSR, which jammed the airwaves for 24 years during the Cold War, and finally allowed the BBC to creep through in January 1988. Libya, Iran, and China have all attempted to stifle BBC transmissions.

*Programme library*

In March 1997 the BBC signed a 30-year agreement to open its television-programme library for commercial use in the UK for the first time. The 50–50 venture with Flextech plc will lead to new pay-TV channels that use the library.

See also ◊television and ◊broadcasting.

**Beardsley, Aubrey (1872–1898)**

English illustrator and leading member of the ◊Aesthetic Movement. His meticulously executed black-and-white drawings show the influence of Japanese prints and French Rococo, and also display the sinuous line, asymmetry, and decorative mannerisms of Art Nouveau. His work was often charged with being grotesque and decadent.

He became known through *The Yellow Book* magazine, for which he was the art editor, and through his drawings for Oscar Wilde's *Salome* (1893).

**Beatles, the**

English pop group 1960–70. The members, all born in Liverpool, were John ◊Lennon (1940– 1980, rhythm guitar, vocals), Paul McCartney (1942– , bass, vocals), George Harrison

**Beatles** From left to right Paul McCartney, George Harrison, Ringo Starr, and John Lennon, the Beatles remain the most successful British pop group ever. They topped the charts with a succession of hits, and were the first British band to gain widespread recognition in America. Their appearances often unleashed 'Beatlemania', mass adulation by hysterical teenage girls. Rex

(1943– , lead guitar, vocals), and Ringo Starr (formerly Richard Starkey, 1940– , drums). Using songs written largely by Lennon and McCartney, the Beatles dominated rock music and pop culture in the 1960s.

The Beatles gained early experience in Liverpool and Hamburg, West Germany. They had a top-30 hit with their first record, 'Love Me Do' (1962).

At the peak of Beatlemania they starred in two films, *A Hard Day's Night* (1964) and *Help!* (1965), and provided songs for the animated film *Yellow Submarine* (1968). Their ballad 'Yesterday' (1965) was covered by 1,186 different performers in the first ten years. The album *Sgt Pepper's Lonely Hearts Club Band* (1967), recorded on two four-track machines, anticipated subsequent technological developments.

The Beatles were the first British group to challenge the US dominance of rock and roll, and continued to influence popular music beyond their break-up in 1970.

## Beaton, Cecil (1904–1980)

English photographer. His elegant and sophisticated fashion pictures and society portraits often employed exotic props and settings. He adopted a more simple style for his wartime photographs of bomb-damaged London. He also worked as a stage and film designer, notably for the musicals *Gigi* (1959) and *My Fair Lady* (1965). He was knighted in 1972.

## Beaufort, Francis (1774–1857)

British admiral, hydrographer to the Royal Navy from 1829; the Beaufort scale and the Beaufort Sea in the Arctic Ocean are named after him.

Drawing up the Beaufort scale he specified the amount of sail that a full-rigged ship should carry under the various wind conditions. The scale was officially adopted by the Admiralty in 1838. Modifications were made to the scale when sail gave way to steam.

## Beaulieu

Village in Hampshire, southern England, on the estuary of the River Beaulieu and the edge of the New Forest, 9 km/6 mi southwest of Southampton. The National Motor Museum (1952) and the remains of a Cistercian abbey, established by King John in about 1204, are in the grounds of the home of Lord Montagu of Beaulieu; parts of Palace House, the family residence, were opened to the public in 1952.

Another part of the Montagu estate, the 18th-century shipyard of Buckler's Hard, is situated 3 km/2mi southwest of Beaulieu on the river estuary. Admiral Nelson's HMS *Agamemnon* was built and launched here. The yard and cottages have been restored, and the site contains a Maritime Museum.

## Beaumaris

Town and tourist resort on the Isle of Anglesey, northwest Wales; population (1991) 1,600. It is situated on Beaumaris Bay, to the north of the Menai Strait, and has a large harbour. There is an annual regatta, and a music festival is held in early summer. **Beaumaris Castle**, one of the finest European examples of the concentric type, was founded by Edward I in 1295; with Edward I's other castles in North Wales, it is classified by the United Nations as a World Heritage site.

## Bebington

Industrial town in Wirral, Merseyside, England, on the Wirral peninsula south of Birkenhead; population (1991) 60,100. Nearby is ◊Port Sunlight, originally built in 1888 as a model housing estate for workers at the Lever Brothers (now Unilever) soap and margarine factory.

## Becket, St Thomas à (1118–1170)

English priest and politician. He was chancellor to ◊Henry II 1155–62, when he was appointed archbishop of Canterbury. The interests of the church soon conflicted with those of the crown and Becket was assassinated; he was canonized in 1172.

**St Thomas à Becket** The murder of Thomas à Becket, Archbishop of Canterbury, depicted by the artist and chronicler Matthew Paris. After his death, Becket's tomb in Canterbury became one of the most important English pilgrimage sites of the Middle Ages. Philip Sauvain Picture Collection

A friend of Henry II, Becket was a loyal chancellor, but on becoming archbishop of Canterbury transferred his allegiance to the church. In 1164 he opposed Henry's attempt to regulate the relations between church and state, and had to flee the country; he returned in 1170, but the reconciliation soon broke down. Encouraged by a hasty outburst from the king, four knights murdered Becket before the altar of Canterbury cathedral. He was declared a saint, and his shrine became the busiest centre of pilgrimage in England until the Reformation.

*... they fell upon him and killed him (I say it with sorrow). I fear the anger I had recently shown against him may have been the cause of this misdeed. I call God to witness that I am extremely disturbed, but more with anxiety about my reputation than qualms of conscience.*

**Henry II** King of England.
Referring to the killing of Thomas à Becket, in a letter to Pope Alexander III, 1171

## Beddgelert

Village in Gwynedd, northwest Wales, 20 km/12 mi southeast of Caernarfon. Lying at the foot of Snowdon (1,085 m/3,560 ft), the village is close to the pass of Aberglaslyn. Its name means 'grave of Gelert'. Gelert was the hound of Llewelyn (Prince of Wales in the 13th century) and his grave is marked by a stone recalling the legend that he saved his master's child from a wolf and was then killed by Llewelyn in error.

The nearby Sygun copper mine is open to tourists. The pass of Aberglaslyn contains the rock known as the 'chair of Rhys Goch' (the 15th-century bard).

## Bede (c. 673–735)

English theologian and historian, known as **the Venerable Bede**. Active in Durham and Northumbria, he wrote many scientific, theological, and historical works. His *Historia Ecclesiastica Gentis Anglorum/Ecclesiastical History of the English People* of 731 is a primary source for early English history, and was translated into the vernacular by King Alfred.

## Bedford

Town and administrative headquarters of ◊Bedfordshire, southern England, on the River Ouse, about 80 km/50 mi north of London; population (1991) 73,900. The writer John ◊Bunyan is said to have written part of *The Pilgrim's Progress* (1678) and other works while imprisoned in Bedford gaol.

**Features**
The Bunyan Museum adjoining the Bunyan Meeting House displays artefacts associated with the life of John Bunyan and copies of *The Pilgrim's Progress* in many languages. The Cecil Higgins Art Gallery includes a collection of English watercolours, 20th-century prints, porcelain, glass, and Bedfordshire lace. Bedford has attractive riverside scenery and a pedestrian suspension bridge, built in the 1880s. Bedford is also a cosmopolitan town, with over 50 ethnic groups being represented.

## Bedfordshire
County of south central England; population (1996) 548,800; area 1,192 sq km/460 sq mi. It is associated John Bunyan, the 17th-century nonconformist preacher and author of *The Pilgrim's Progress* (1678, 1684), who lived and worked here. The principal towns are ◊ Bedford (administrative headquarters) and Dunstable. Since April 1997 ◊ Luton has been a separate unitary authority.
**Physical**
The county is low lying with part of the Chiltern Hills in the southwest; they are described as the 'Delectable Mountains' in *The Pilgrim's Progress*. The Great Ouse River and its tributary, the Ivel, run through Bedfordshire.
**Features**
Maiden Bower is an Iron Age hill fort at Houghton Regis. ◊ Whipsnade Wild Animal Park, near Dunstable (200 ha/494 acres), attracts many visitors, as does ◊ Woburn Abbey, seat of the Duke of Bedford, which also has a safari park. The Cranfield Institute of Technology is in Bedfordshire.
**Economy**
There is a diverse local economy, consisting of agriculture, manufacturing, and service industries. Agricultural production is focused on cereals (especially wheat and barley) and vegetables. Manufacturing includes agricultural machinery and motor vehicles. Minerals are extracted and local resources are used to manufacture cement and bricks. There are also research establishments.

## Bedlam, abbreviation of Bethlehem
The earliest mental hospital in Europe. It was opened in the 14th century in London and is now sited in Surrey. It is now used as a slang word meaning chaos.

## Beecham, Thomas (1879–1961)
English conductor and impresario. He established the Royal Philharmonic Orchestra in 1946 and fostered the works of composers such as Delius,

Sibelius, and Richard Strauss. He was knighted and succeeded to the baronetcy in 1916.

## Beeching Report
1963 official report on the railway network of Britain, which recommended the closure of loss-making lines and the improvement of money-making routes. Hundreds of lines and several thousand stations were closed as a result.

These closures were not evenly spread throughout the country. Networks in East Anglia, south Wales, and the West Country fared worst, whereas the densely populated southeast retained more of its routes. Richard Beeching was chair of the British Railways Board 1963–65.

## Beefeaters
see ◊ Yeomen of the Guard.

## beer
Alcoholic drink made from water and malt (fermented barley or other grain), flavoured with hops. Beer contains between 1% and 6% alcohol and is one of the oldest alcoholic drinks. See ◊ public house for a feature on the development of brewing and pubs.

---

*Good ale, the true and proper drink of Englishmen.*

**George Henry Borrow** English author and traveller.
*Lavengro* ch 48

---

## Beeton, Mrs, Isabella (1836–1865)
British writer on cookery and domestic management. She produced *Mrs Beeton's Book of Household Management* (1861), the first comprehensive work on domestic science.

*Mrs Beeton's Book of Household Management* appeared originally in monthly instalments of *The Englishwoman's Domestic Magazine* (1859–60), and was published in book form in 1861, becoming an immediate bestseller. Mrs Beeton was assistant editor of the magazine, which was published by her husband, Samuel Beeton.

## Belfast (Gaelic Beal Feirste 'the mouth of the Farset')
Capital city of ◊ Northern Ireland and industrial port in County Antrim and County Down, at the mouth of the River Lagan on Belfast Lough; population (1994 est) 290,000. A major centre of linen manufacture and shipbuilding in the 19th century, Belfast saw a decline in its traditional

industries in the 20th century and was at the centre of the sectarian conflicts known as the Troubles from 1968. In recent years, however, the city has undergone an extensive programme of urban renewal, with major investment in new industrial, business, and leisure opportunities which are contributing to the economic revival and the regeneration of the city. Stormont, seat of the Northern Ireland Assembly from 1998, is nearby and Belfast is the site of Queen's University, founded in 1849.

### History

Belfast grew up around a Norman castle built in 1177 but throughout medieval times it was a small settlement, much less important than the neighbouring port of ◊Carrickfergus, the main Anglo-Norman stronghold in the north of Ireland. For about 300 years the Lagan valley was controlled by the O'Neill family and the castle and surrounding settlement were subject to frequent dispute between the O'Neills and English forces, changing hands several times until 1574 when the lands were captured by the Earl of Essex.

With the settlement of English and Scots, Belfast became a centre of Irish Protestantism in the 17th century. An influx of Huguenots after 1685 extended the linen industry, and the 1800

Act of Union with England resulted in the promotion of Belfast as an industrial centre. Between 1831 and 1901 Belfast's population grew from 30,000 to 350,000, and it was created a city in 1888. Belfast became the capital of Northern Ireland at the time of the partition in 1920 and the first Northern Ireland parliament sat in Belfast's City Hall. After the beginning of the Troubles in 1968, sectarian violence between republicans and loyalists became part of everyday life in the city, and from 1969 British army units were present on the city's streets. The multi-party peace talks of 1997–98, leading up to the agreement of 10 April 1998, were held at Stormont, which since summer 1998 has been the seat of the Northern Ireland Assembly.

### Features

At the heart of the city is Donegall Square, the site of the grand City Hall, one of the city's principal landmarks. This imposing building, built in Portland stone, opened in 1906 and includes an impressive main dome, a lavish Italian marble staircase, and a whispering gallery. Belfast Castle, on Cave Hill, includes a Heritage Centre illustrating all aspects of the area's history. Waterfront Hall, a concert and conference venue, opened on the redeveloped waterfront in 1997 and the

**Belfast** The Parliament building at Stormont was built in 1932 to house Northern Ireland's government, and became a byword for the Unionist (Protestant) domination of political life in the province. In 1972, Stormont became redundant after the British government imposed direct rule from Westminster but in 1998 it became the seat of the Northern Ireland National Assembly. Alain Le Garsmeur/ Image Ireland/Collections

Odyssey landmark millennium project, scheduled for November 2000, is a major development project for the east side of the Lagan, including a science centre, an IMAX cinema, an indoor arena, pavilion, and public open spaces.

South of the city centre is the area known as the Golden Mile which includes the refurbished Grand Opera House, a major venue for plays and concerts, as well some old 'gin palaces', among them the restored Crown Liquor Saloon, now owned by the National Trust. Other attractions include the Ulster Museum, St Anne's Cathedral (1899), the Botanic Gardens, Belfast Zoo, and the Linenhall Library (1788) which contains a large collection of publications on Irish political events since 1968. In west Belfast the partisan murals that may be seen in the Protestant Shankill Road and Catholic Falls Road are striking evidence of the political and religious factionalism that has divided the city.

### Belgravia
Residential district of west central London, laid out in squares by Thomas Cubitt (1788–1855) between 1825 and 1830, and bounded to the north by Knightsbridge.

### Bell, Alexander Graham (1847–1922)
Scottish-born US scientist and inventor. He was the first person ever to transmit speech from one point to another by electrical means. This invention – the telephone – was made in 1876. Later Bell experimented with a type of phonograph and, in aeronautics, invented the tricycle undercarriage.

Bell also invented a photophone, which used selenium crystals to apply the telephone principle to transmitting words in a beam of light. He thus achieved the first wireless transmission of speech.

### Bell, Vanessa (1879–1961)
English painter and designer. She was one of the first English artists to paint abstracts, but most of her work was in a Post-Impressionist style. She was the sister of Virginia ◊Woolf and wife of the art critic Clive Bell, and like them she was a leading figure of the ◊Bloomsbury Group.

From 1916 she lived with Scottish painter Duncan ◊Grant, and their home at Charleston, Sussex practically became a Bloomsbury memorial.

### Belloc, Hilaire (1870–1953)
French-born British writer. He is remembered primarily for his nonsense verse for children *The*

*Bad Child's Book of Beasts* (1896) and *Cautionary Tales for Children* (1907). Belloc also wrote historical, biographical, travel, and religious books (he was a devout Catholic).

### bell ringing, or campanology
The art of ringing church bells individually or in sequence by rhythmically drawing on a rope fastened to a wheel rotating the bell, so that it falls back and strikes in time. **Change ringing** is an English art, dating from the 17th century, of ringing a patterned sequence of permutations of 5–12 church bells, using one player to each bell.

### Belvoir Castle
Neo-Gothic castle near Bottesford, Leicestershire, England; the seat of the Duke of Rutland. The original fortress of 11th to 13th centuries was rebuilt in 1528, and again in 1654–58 as a mansion. Around 1800 the 5th duke employed James Wyatt to reconvert it to a castle, altering the apartments at the same time. Further rebuilding and redecoration after a fire in 1816 included the construction of a Romanesque-style mausoleum (1820–30). The castle has an important art collection which includes works by Holbein, Poussin, Reynolds, and Gainsborough.

### Bennett, Arnold (1867–1931)
English novelist, playwright, and journalist. His major works are set in the industrial 'five towns' of the Potteries in Staffordshire (now Stoke-on-Trent) and are concerned with the manner in which the environment dictates the pattern of his characters' lives. They include *Anna of the Five Towns* (1902), *The Old Wives' Tale* (1908), and the trilogy *Clayhanger*, *Hilda Lessways*, and *These Twain* (1910–15).

### Ben Nevis
Highest mountain in the British Isles (1,344 m/4,409 ft), 7 km/4 mi southeast of Fort William, Scotland.

The northeast side of Ben Nevis has a precipice of 450 m/1,480 ft. From the summit, which consists of a large plateau, there is an extensive view of the Scottish Highlands and islands, as far as the Hebrides. There is a well-marked and easily negotiated path to the summit, but also more difficult rock-climbing routes.

### Bentham, Jeremy (1748–1832)
English philosopher, legal and social reformer, and founder of utilitarianism. The essence of his moral philosophy is found in the pronouncement

of his *Principles of Morals and Legislation* (written in 1780, published in 1789): that the object of all legislation should be 'the greatest happiness for the greatest number'.

Bentham declared that the 'utility' of any law is to be measured by the extent to which it promotes the pleasure, good, and happiness of the people concerned. In 1776 he published *Fragments on Government*. He made suggestions for the reform of the poor law in 1798, which formed the basis of the reforms enacted in 1834, and in his *Catechism of Parliamentary Reform*, published in 1817, he proposed annual elections, the secret ballot, and universal male suffrage. He was also a pioneer of prison reform.

Bentham left his body for dissection. His clothed skeleton, with a wax head, is on view at University College, London.

---

*All punishment is mischief: all punishment in itself is evil.*

**Jeremy Bentham** English philosopher, and legal
and social reformer.
*Principles of Morals and Legislation* (1789)

---

### Beowulf
Old English poem of 3,182 lines, thought to have been composed in the first half of the 8th century. It is the only complete surviving example of Germanic folk epic and exists in a single manuscript copied in England about 1000 and now housed in the Cottonian collection of the British Museum, London.

### Berkeley
Town in southern Gloucestershire, England, between Bristol and Gloucester; population (1991) 2,200. **Berkeley Castle**, in which Edward II was murdered in 1327, is regarded as one of the finest castles in England. The castle was completed in 1153 by Lord Maurice Berkeley. The Norman keep can still be seen within the great courtyard of the castle. It is still occupied, after 850 years, by the Berkeley family.

### Betjeman, John (1906–1984)
English poet and essayist, poet laureate from 1972. He was the originator of a peculiarly English light verse, nostalgic, and delighting in Victorian and Edwardian architecture. He also wrote prose works on architecture and social history which reflect his interest in the ◊Gothic

**John Betjeman** English poet John Betjeman, photographed in 1955. He was poet laureate from 1972. As well as several volumes of poetry, Betjeman wrote a blank-verse autobiography, *Summoned by Bells* (1960), and various works on architecture. Corbis

Revival. His *Collected Poems* appeared in 1958 and a verse autobiography, *Summoned by Bells*, in 1960.

Betjeman's verse, seen by some as facile, has been much enjoyed for its compassion and wit, and its evocation of places and situations. His verse is traditional in form – favouring iambic lines and a conversational clarity – and subject matter. He recalls with great precision and affection details of his childhood in north London and holidays in Cornwall.

### Betws-y-coed
Village in Conwy, north Wales, situated 25 km/15 mi south of Llandudno. It is a tourist centre for ◊Snowdonia and there are waterfalls nearby. The best known are Swallow Falls, Conwy Falls, and Fairy Glen.

The Conwy Valley Railway Museum is here, as is a motor museum. Artists are also attracted to the area, and trout and salmon are fished.

### Bevan, Aneurin (Nye) (1897–1960)
British Labour politician. Son of a Welsh miner, and himself a miner at 13, he was member of

Parliament for Ebbw Vale 1929–60. As minister of health 1945–51, he inaugurated the National Health Service (NHS). He was an outstanding speaker.

## Beveridge Report, the

Popular name of *Social Insurance and Allied Services*, a report written by William Beveridge in 1942 that formed the basis for the social-reform legislation of the Labour government of 1945–50.

Also known as the *Report on Social Security*, it identified five 'giants': illness, ignorance, disease, squalor, and want. It proposed a scheme of social insurance from 'the cradle to the grave', and recommended a national health service, social insurance and assistance, family allowances, and full-employment policies.

## Beverley

Town and administrative headquarters of the East Riding of Yorkshire, England, 13 km/8 mi northwest of Hull, and connected with the River Hull by canal; population (1991) 12,300. **Beverley Minster** (13th century) is an outstanding example of Gothic church architecture. The town hosts annual folk and early music festivals.

## Bevin, Ernest (1881–1951)

British Labour politician. Chief creator of the Transport and General Workers' Union, he was its general secretary 1921–40. He served as minister of labour and national service 1940–45 in Winston Churchill's wartime coalition government, and organized the 'Bevin boys', chosen by ballot to work in the coalmines as war service. As foreign secretary in the Labour government 1945–51, he played a leading part in the creation of NATO.

## Bewick, Thomas (1753–1828)

English wood engraver. He excelled in animal subjects, some of his finest works appearing in his illustrated *A General History of Quadrupeds* (1790) and *A History of British Birds* (1797–1804). His birthplace, Cherryburn, Mickley, Northamptonshire, is a museum of wood engraving, with many of his original blocks. Bewick's swan (*Cygnus bewicki*) is named after him.

## Bexhill-on-Sea

Seaside resort in East Sussex, England, 10 km/6 mi southwest of Hastings; population (1991) 38,900. Manufactured products include industrial machinery and scientific instruments. The centre of the seafront development is the de la Warr pavilion (1935–36), designed by the German architects Erich Mendelsohn and Serge Chermayeff.

## Bibury

Village in Gloucestershire, England. It is situated in the ◊Cotswold Hills, 11 km/7 mi north of Cirencester, on the River Coln. Bibury's riverside setting and honey-coloured old stone houses make it one of the Cotswold's most popular tourist destinations.

Arlington Row, a group of early 17th-century cottages in the village, is now the property of the National Trust; Arlington Mill, which was built in the 17th century, is now a museum.

## Big Ben

Popular name for the bell in the clock tower of the Houses of Parliament in London, cast at the Whitechapel Bell Foundry in 1858, and known as 'Big Ben' after Benjamin Hall, First Commissioner of Works at the time. It weighs 13.7 tonnes. The name is often used to mean the tower as well.

## Biggin Hill

Airport in the southeast London borough of Bromley. It was the most famous of the Royal Air Force stations in the ◊Battle of Britain in World War II.

## Billingsgate

Chief London wholesale fish market, formerly (from the 9th century) near London Bridge. It re-opened in 1982 at the new Billingsgate market, West India Dock, Isle of Dogs.

## Birdcage Walk

Area in St James's Park, London, connecting Buckingham Gate with Storey's Gate. It is named after the aviary established here during the reign of James I.

## Birkenhead

Seaport and industrial town in Wirral, Merseyside, England, opposite ◊Liverpool on the Wirral peninsula, on the west bank of the ◊Mersey estuary; population (1994 est) 93,100; Birkenhead urban area 270,200. Now linked with the east side of the Mersey by road tunnel and by rail, Birkenhead has been linked with Liverpool by ferry since the 12th century and expanded in the 19th century as a major shipbuilding town with important dock facilities. It was here that the first iron vessel in the UK was built in 1829. The last shipyard closed in 1993 and the former warehouses and industrial buildings on the Birkenhead waterfront have been redeveloped as a heritage centre. The Scout Movement was inaugurated in Birkenhead by Robert Baden-Powell in 1908.

### Features

The Williamson Art Gallery and Museum includes a collection of English watercolours and Liverpool porcelain, and a separate gallery has exhibits illustrating the history of the town's shipbuilding industry. Woodside Ferry Terminal displays the history of Mersey Ferries, and the warships HMS *Plymouth* and HMS *Onyx* are preserved here. Birkenhead Park, opened in 1847, was the first public park in the England.

## Birmingham

Second-largest city in the UK, administrative headquarters of ◊West Midlands metropolitan county, 177 km/110 mi northwest of London; population (1994 est) 1,220,000, metropolitan area 2,632,000. Birmingham, known as 'Brum' to its inhabitants, has a long-established reputation as Britain's largest manufacturing city. Lying in the heart of England, at the centre its rail and road network with an international airport nearby, it is also the site of the UK's principal conference and exhibition venues, and with its concert halls, theatres, galleries, museums, and three universities, it is now established as a major centre of culture and education. The city is highly cosmopolitan and hosts a varied programme of festivals, including the annual three-day ArtsFest and an international jazz festival.

### History

An important centre for the manufacture of swords and firearms from early times, Birmingham supplied large quantities of weapons to the Parliamentary forces of Oliver Cromwell during the English Civil War. Its location on the edge of the south Staffordshire coalfields and its skilled workforce allowed it to develop rapidly during the 18th and 19th centuries with the growth of its metal and jewellery trades. It was home to many pioneers of industry and science during the Industrial Revolution, including Matthew Bolton and James ◊Watt, who established the Soho Manufactory in the city to produce steam engines, and William Murdock, the first person to develop gas lighting on a commercial scale. During the

**Birmingham** Once known chiefly for its manufacturing industry, Britain's second city has a growing reputation for its cultural life. Created in the early 1990s, the Birmingham Royal Ballet company is seen here in its production of *Nutcracker Sweeties,* a jazz adaptation of Tchaikovsky's ballet by Duke Ellington and Billy Strayhorn. Bill Cooper/Birmingham Royal Ballet

19th century Birmingham was also a centre of religious Nonconformity, supporting the movements of Unitarianism, Wesleyan Methodism, and Baptism. In 1832 the city played an important part in the agitation leading to the ◊Reform Acts and in 1839 it was the scene of disturbances in support of ◊Chartism.

*Features*

Much redevelopment of the city has taken place in recent years with the clearing of many factories and areas of 19th-century housing. The industrial heritage of the city is now reflected in its museums, in the imposing 19th-century civic buildings in Victoria Square, and in the extensive system of canals that run through the city. Work has begun on major redevelopment of the Bull Ring shopping centre and Rotunda office complex, built during the 1960s at a time when many of the city's historic buildings were knocked down. Birmingham is the site of the National Exhibition Centre (NEC), International Convention Centre (ICC), and National Indoor Arena (NIA), and boasts a number of major tourist attractions including the National Sea Life Centre and Cadbury World, a visitor centre dedicated to chocolate in the suburb of Bournville. The Jewellery Quarter Discovery Centre illustrates the growth and decline of Birmingham's jewellery trade. Millennium Point is a landmark millennium project, scheduled for 2001, designed to create a major new science, technology, and entertainment complex, including the University of the First Age. The suburb of Edgbaston is the site of Edgbaston Cricket Ground, the University of Birmingham (1900), and of the Botanical Gardens. Just to the northeast of the city centre is one of Europe's largest motorway junctions, known as Spaghetti Junction.

*Galleries and Museums*

Birmingham has a number of excellent galleries and museums, including the Birmingham Museum and Art Gallery which houses one of the world's finest collections of Pre-Raphaelite paintings; and the refurbished Edwardian Gas Hall, a venue for touring exhibitions. The Barber Institute of Fine Arts in Edgbaston is home to an impressive collection of Renaissance and Impressionist art. The Museum of Science and Industry illustrates the industrial heritage of the city, and includes the oldest working steam engine in the world, made by Boulton and Watt in about 1779.

*Music and theatre*

Birmingham has been home to the City of Birmingham Symphony Orchestra since it was founded in 1920. Under the musical directorship of Simon Rattle from 1980 to 1998, it is now led by the Finnish conductor, Sakari Oramo, and is based in the outstanding purpose-built Symphony Hall which opened in 1991 within the ICC. Since 1990 the Birmingham Hippodrome has been home to one of Britain's principal ballet companies, the Birmingham Royal Ballet (formerly Saddlers Wells Royal Ballet).

## Birmingham Royal Ballet

Formerly the **Sadler's Wells Royal Ballet**, based in London. The company relocated to new purpose-built facilities at the Birmingham Hippodrome in 1990, when it was renamed the Birmingham Royal Ballet. David Bintley became artistic director in 1995.

The company was originally founded in 1946 as a touring company for the ◊Royal Ballet, when it was known as the Sadler's Wells Opera Ballet (later Theatre Ballet).

## Blackburn

Industrial city in northwest England, 32 km/20 mi northwest of Manchester; population (1991) 106,000. Part of the county of Lancashire until April 1998, it is now the administrative headquarters of ◊Blackburn with Darwen unitary authority. Situated on the Leeds–Liverpool canal, Blackburn was historically one of the world's most important cotton-weaving towns. Blackened by smoke from factories and chimneys, the town has benefited from anti-pollution laws and the development of smokeless zones, and with an extensive programme of redevelopment the town is forging a new profile.

*History*

Flemish weavers settled here in the 14th century, and the town grew rapidly after the completion of the Leeds–Liverpool Canal in 1816. The town prospered as the centre of Lancashire's cotton-weaving industry until the industry's decline in the 1930s and 1940s.

*Features*

A working model of the spinning jenny, invented in 1764 by James ◊Hargreaves (born near Blackburn in about 1720), can be seen at the Lewis Textile Museum. Some of Blackburn's spinning-mills, weaving sheds, and chimneys survive. The cathedral is the only Anglican cathedral in Lancashire.

## Blackburn with Darwen

Unitary authority (borough status) in northwest England, created in 1998 from part of the former county of Lancashire; population (1995)

140,300; area 136 sq km/53 sq mi. Its principal towns are ◊Blackburn (administrative headquarters) and Darwen.

*Physical*
The Leeds–Liverpool canal and River Darwen flow through the area, which lies in the western foothills of the Rossendale uplands. Darwen Hill and Tower rise to 372 m/1,220 ft.

*Features*
The Lewis Textile Museum at Blackburn, formerly Lancashire's cotton-weaving centre, presents a history of the industry. The Blackburn Museum and Art Gallery has the largest display of European icons in Britain.

*Economy*
Diverse industries include engineering, brewing, high tech (electronics, compact discs), and the manufacture of chemicals, paint, paper, textiles, leather, and carpets.

## Black Country
Central area of England, to the west and north of Birmingham, incorporating the towns of ◊Dudley, ◊Walsall, ◊Wolverhampton, and Sandwell. Heavily industrialized, it gained its name in the 19th century from its belching chimneys and mining spoil. Anti-pollution laws and the decline of heavy industry have changed the region's landscape. Coalmining in the area ceased in 1968.

The Black Country Museum was opened in 1975 at Dudley to preserve the region's industrial heritage. The area evolved with a dialect and culture distinct from that of nearby Birmingham.

## Black Death
Great epidemic of bubonic plague that ravaged Europe in the mid-14th century, killing between one-third and half of the population (about 75 million people). The cause of the plague was the bacterium *Yersinia pestis*, transmitted by fleas borne by migrating Asian black rats. The name Black Death was first used in England in the early 19th century.

It was recognized at Weymouth in August 1348, and before waning in the winter of 1349 had reduced the population of England by a third. The dramatic impact on localities is perpetuated in accounts that have entered folklore, such as the Reverend Mompesson's handling of the outbreak in the village of Eyam, Derbyshire, where he persuaded the people of the village not to flee, and so prevented the disease from spreading further.

## Blackheath
Suburb of London, lying south of Greenwich Park on the London–Dover road. It falls within the Greater London boroughs of ◊Greenwich and ◊Lewisham and takes its name from the common, where Wat Tyler encamped during the 1381 Peasants' Revolt. It developed as a residential suburb from the late 18th century.

For centuries the common was used as a place of assembly: Henry V was welcomed here after the Battle of Agincourt 1415; Henry VIII met Anne of Cleves at a Blackheath pageant; Charles II was welcomed here 1660; and the Methodist John Wesley held religious meetings on the heath in the 18th century. The common is crossed by Shooters Hill, a former haunt of highwaymen.

## Blackmore, R(ichard) D(oddridge) (1825–1900)
English novelist. His romance *Lorna Doone* (1869), set on Exmoor, southwest England, in the late 17th century, won him lasting popularity.

He published 13 other novels, including *Cradock Nowell* (1866), *The Maid of Sker* (1872), *Alice Lorraine* (1875), and *Springhaven* (1887).

## Black Mountain, Welsh Mynydd Du
Ridge of hills in the ◊Brecon Beacons National Park in Carmarthenshire and Powys, south Wales, stretching 19 km/12 mi north from Swansea. The hills are composed of limestone and red sandstone. They are estimated to be 280–295 million years old and contain a coal seam. The highest peak is Carmarthen Van (Fan Foel) at 802 m/2,630 ft.

## Black Mountains
Upland massif with cliffs and steep-sided valleys in ◊Powys and ◊Monmouthshire, southeast Wales, lying to the west of ◊Offa's Dyke largely within the ◊Brecon Beacons National Park. The highest peak is Waun Fach (811 m/2,660 ft).

## Blackpool
Seaside resort in northwest England, 45 km/28 mi north of Liverpool; population: (1997) 151,200; Blackpool urban area (1991) 261,400. Part of the county of Lancashire until April 1998, it is now a unitary authority with an area of 35 sq km/14 sq mi. In addition to being the largest and one of the most popular seaside resorts in the UK, Blackpool also provides important conference and business facilities.

*History*
Blackpool developed as a resort in the 18th century and, following the opening of the railway in 1846, workers travelled to the town from all over industrial Lancashire and Yorkshire for

'Wakes Weeks', when factories and mills closed for the annual holiday. Growth was rapid after 1879, when the borough was the first in England permitted to spend money on advertising, and large hotels, boarding houses, and lodgings were built to cater for the visitors. In spite of the changes in holiday habits resulting from the increase in car ownership and the growth in the popularity of overseas destinations, the resort still attracts many millions of visitors each year.

*Features*
Blackpool Pleasure Beach, an amusement park that includes Europe's tallest and fastest roller coaster, is one of the most visited tourist attractions in the UK, and the 157 m/518 ft-high Blackpool Tower (1894), modelled on the Eiffel Tower in Paris, attracts over one million visitors each year. Blackpool is also known for its 11 km/7 mi of promenade, and especially for their autumn 'illuminations' of coloured lights. The brash seafront, known as the Golden Mile, offers traditional seaside entertainment and there are three 19th-century piers. Other attractions include the Wintergardens, the Sandcastle Leisure Complex, the Louis Tussaud's Waxworks, the Grand Theatre, and the Sealife Centre with its large display of sharks. A tram, which first operated in 1885, transports visitors along the promenade.

## Black Prince
Nickname of ◊Edward, Prince of Wales, eldest son of Edward III of England.

## Blaenau Ffestiniog
Town in Gwynedd, northwest Wales, 15 km/9 mi northeast of Porthmadog; population with Ffestiniog (1991) 4,500. The slate quarries are no longer operating but are open to tourists. A pumped storage scheme is also open to visitors. The Ffestiniog Railway, the oldest independent railway company in the world, runs steam trains on a narrow-gauge track from Blaenau to Porthmadog.

## Blaenau Gwent
Unitary authority in south Wales, created in 1996 from part of the former county of Gwent; population (1996) 73,000; area 109 sq km/42 sq mi. Its principal towns are Ebbw Vale (administrative headquarters), Tredegar, and Abertillery.
*Physical*
The rivers Sirhowy and Ebbw flow through the area, and Mynydd Carn-y-Cefn rises to 550 m/1,800 ft.

*Features*
Part of the ◊Brecon Beacons National Park is in Blaenau Gwent. Big Pit at Ebbw Vale is a tourist attraction.
*Economy*
The area no longer depends on coal, iron, and steel industries, and former industrial land is being redeveloped.

## Blake, William (1757–1827)
English poet, artist, engraver, and visionary, and one of the most important figures of English ◊Romanticism. His lyrics, often written with a childlike simplicity, as in *Songs of Innocence* (1789) and *Songs of Experience* (1794), express a unique spiritual vision. In his 'prophetic books', including *The Marriage of Heaven and Hell* (1790), he created a vast personal mythology. He illustrated his own works with hand-coloured engravings.

*Songs of Innocence* was the first of his own poetic works that he illustrated and engraved, his highly individual style ultimately based on Michelangelo and Raphael. The complementary volume, *Songs of Experience*, which contains the poems 'Tyger! Tyger! burning bright' and 'London', expresses Blake's keen awareness of cruelty and injustice. Blake's poem 'Jerusalem' (1820) was set to music by Charles Parry.

Central themes in his work are the importance of passion and imagination, his visionary spirituality – he often claimed that he saw angels – and a political radicalism that made him a keen supporter of the French Revolution and of Mary Wollstonecraft's views on the rights of women.

## Blakeney
Village on the north coast of Norfolk, England, 10 km/6 mi east of Wells-next-the-Sea; population (1991) 1,500. A lagoon-like stretch of sea is used for sailing, and at **Blakeney Point** there is a bird sanctuary covering an area of over 4 sq km/1.5 sq mi. There is also a colony of seals.

## Blenheim Palace
House near Woodstock, Oxfordshire, England. Blenheim is the seat of the Duke of ◊Marlborough. Conceived as a national monument and virtually as a royal palace, it was the gift of Queen Anne and Parliament to the 1st Duke in gratitude for his victory over the army of Louis XIV at the Battle of Blenheim in 1704. It was built from 1705 to 1725, and designed by John ◊Vanbrugh, assisted by Nicholas ◊Hawksmoor. Grinling ◊Gibbons supervised the carving. Blenheim

Palace exemplifies Vanbrugh's style of 'heroic architecture'.

Vanbrugh's formal gardens disappeared between 1764 and 1774 when the whole park was landscaped by Capability ◊Brown, who made a lake and planted trees, reputedly arranged according to the battle plan at Blenheim. Blenheim Palace was designated a World Heritage Site in 1987.

## Bletchley

Town in Buckinghamshire, England, 72 km/45 mi northwest of London, situated just south of Milton Keynes. It was originally a railway town and has developed through the expansion of Milton Keynes.

**Bletchley Park** was the home of Britain's World War II code-breaking activities, and is now a privately run museum. German codes generated by the Enigma enciphering machine were cracked here.

## Blickling Hall

Large Jacobean house near Aylsham, Norfolk, England. It was built in rose-red brick by Henry Hobart, Lord Chief Justice of England, who pulled down the 14th-century manor house in which Anne Boleyn spent much of her childhood. Blickling Hall, its contents, and 1933 ha/4774 acres, including the village of Blickling, were left to the National Trust by the 11th Marquess of Lothian in 1940.

A family of Norwich architects called Ivory made alterations to the interior of the Hall and also built the Orangery and Temple. The 19th-century formal garden was redesigned in 1930; the park is in the style of Capability Brown and contains a lake.

## Bligh, William (1754–1817)

English sailor. He accompanied Captain James ◊Cook on his second voyage around the world (1772–74), and in 1787 commanded HMS *Bounty* on an expedition to the Pacific. On the return voyage, in protest against harsh treatment, the crew mutinied. Bligh was sent to Australia as governor of New South Wales in 1805, where his discipline again provoked a mutiny in 1808 (the Rum Rebellion).

In the *Bounty* mutiny, he and those of the crew who supported him were cast adrift in a boat with no map and few provisions. They survived, after many weeks reaching Timor, near Java, having drifted 5,822 km/3,618 mi. Many of the crew settled in the Pitcairn Islands.

## Blighty (Hindi *bilayati*, 'foreign')

Popular name for England among British troops in World War I. The term was also used to describe serious but non-fatal wounds requiring hospitalization in Britain; for example, 'He caught a Blighty one'.

## blimp

Airship; any self-propelled, lighter-than-air craft that can be steered. A blimp with a soft frame is also called a **dirigible**; a **zeppelin** is rigid-framed.

During World War I British lighter-than-air aircraft were divided into A-rigid and B-limp (that is, without rigid internal framework), a barrage balloon therefore becoming known as a blimp. The cartoonist David Low adopted the name for his stuffy character **Colonel Blimp**.

## Blitz, the

Abbreviation for Blitzkrieg (German for lightning war), applied to the attempted saturation bombing of London by the German air force between September 1940 and May 1941. It has been estimated that about 40,000 civilians were killed, 46,000 injured, and more than a million homes destroyed and damaged in the Blitz, together with an immense amount of damage caused to industrial installations.

The first raid was against London on 7–8 September 1940, and raids continued on all but 10 nights until 12 November. The raids then targeted industrial cities such as Coventry (14 November), Southampton, Birmingham, Bristol, Cardiff, Portsmouth, and Liverpool, with occasional raids on London. In spring 1941 the air defences began to take a larger toll of the attackers, due to improvements in radar for night fighters and for artillery control. The raids fell away during the early summer as Luftwaffe forces were withdrawn from the west in preparation for the invasion of the USSR.

## Bloody Assizes

Courts held by judges of the High Court in the west of England under the Lord Chief Justice, Judge ◊Jeffreys, after the Duke of Monmouth's rebellion in 1685. Over 300 rebels were executed and many more flogged or imprisoned.

## Bloomsbury

Area in the borough of Camden, London, a series of squares between Gower Street and High Holborn. It contains London University, the British Museum (1759), and the Royal Academy of Dramatic Arts. Between the world wars it was

**Blitz** Holborn Circus in London burns at the height of the Blitz. London was bombed as part of the Battle of Britain campaign by the German airforce during 1940. Corbis

the home of the ◊Bloomsbury Group of writers and artists.

## Bloomsbury Group

Intellectual circle of writers and artists based in Bloomsbury, London, which flourished in the 1920s. It centred on the house of publisher Leonard Woolf (1880–1969) and his wife, the novelist Virginia ◊Woolf. Typically Modernist, their innovative artistic contributions represented an important section of the English avant-garde.

The circle included the artists Duncan ◊Grant and Vanessa ◊Bell, the biographer Lytton ◊Strachey, and the economist John Maynard ◊Keynes. From their emphasis on close interpersonal relationships and their fastidious attitude towards contemporary culture arose many accusations of elitism.

## Blue John Cavern

Cave in Derbyshire, England. It is situated in Treak Cliff in the north of the county, 3 km/2 mi from Castleton. Blue John is the name of a distinctive local variety of fluorspar. Blue John Cavern and Treak Cliff Cavern are both open to the public.

## Blunt, Anthony (1907–1983)

English art historian and double agent. As a Cambridge lecturer, he recruited for the Soviet

secret service and, as a member of the British Secret Service 1940–45, passed information to the USSR. In 1951 he assisted the defection to the USSR of the British agents Guy ◊Burgess and Donald ◊Maclean. He was the author of many respected works on French and Italian art. Unmasked in 1964, he was given immunity after his confession.

He was director of the Courtauld Institute of Art 1947–74 and Surveyor of the Queen's Pictures 1945–1972. He was stripped of his knighthood in 1979 when the affair became public.

## Blyth

Town in Northumberland, England, on the mouth of the River Blyth where it enters the North Sea; population (1991) 77,200 (Blyth Valley district). A coal-shipping and shipbuilding port in the 19th century, Blyth is now the site of two power stations.

## Blyton, Enid (1897–1968)

English writer of children's books. She used her abilities as a trained teacher of young children and a journalist, coupled with her ability to think like a child, to produce books at all levels which, though criticized for their predictability and lack of characterization, and more recently for social, racial, and sexual stereotyping, satisfy the reader's need for security. Her bestselling series were the *Famous Five* series, the *Secret Seven*, and *Noddy*.

In 1951 she had 31 different titles published, and ten years after her death she was the fourth most translated author in the world. In 1996 Trocadero plc, a British property and leisure company, paid £14.25m for the residual copyrights in over 700 of her books.

## Boadicea
Alternative (Latin) spelling of British queen ◊Boudicca.

## Boat Race, the
Annual rowing race between the crews of Oxford and Cambridge universities. It is held during the Easter vacation over a 6.8 km/4.25 mi course on the River Thames between Putney and Mortlake, southwest London.

The Boat Race was first held in 1829 from Hambledon Lock to Henley Bridge. Up to and including the 2000 race it had been staged 148 times; Cambridge had 76 wins, Oxford 69 and there had been one dead heat in 1877. The reserve crews also have their own races. The Cambridge reserve crew is called Goldie, Oxford's is called Isis.

## Bodiam
Village in East Sussex, England. It is situated 16 km/10 mi north of Hastings, on the River Rother. **Bodiam Castle** was built by Sir Edward Dalyngruge in 1385, and was one of the last castles to be constructed in England. The towers, walls, gateway, portcullis, and moat of this large rectangular castle remain intact, although the interior is less well-preserved. The castle, attractively set in a large moat, now belongs to the National Trust.

## Bodleian Library
Library of the University of Oxford, England, and one of the oldest libraries in Europe. In terms of the number of volumes held, it is the second largest in England, after the British Library. The Bodleian has had a continuous history since 1602, although it was created from the remains of an earlier library donated by Humphrey, Duke of Gloucester. A room built in 1488 to house this collection can still be seen.

The library is named after Sir Thomas Bodley, a retired diplomat who worked on reestablishing the University's library from 1598. The quadrangle of the original building was built 1613–19. A new library building was added in 1939.

## Bodmin
Market town and tourist centre in Cornwall, southwest England, 48 km/30 mi northwest of

Plymouth; population (1991) 12,500. **Bodmin Moor**, to the northeast, is a granite upland culminating in Brown Willy, the highest point in Cornwall at 419 m/1,375 ft.

## Boer War
The second of the South African Wars 1899–1902, waged between Dutch settlers in South Africa and the British.

---

*There's something wrong with actors. We've always been a suspect breed. Socially, I find myself more admissible now in England because I've written books.*

**Dirk Bogarde** English actor.
*Ritz* April 1983

---

## Bogarde, Dirk stage name of Derek Niven van den Bogaerde (1921–1999)
English actor. He appeared in comedies and adventure films such as *Doctor in the House* (1954) and *Campbell's Kingdom* (1957), before acquiring international recognition for complex roles in Joseph Losey's *The Servant* (1963) and *Accident* (1967), and Luchino Visconti's *Death in Venice* (1971).

His other films include *The Night Porter* (1974), *A Bridge Too Far* (1977), and Bertrand Tavernier's *Daddy nostalgie/These Foolish Things* (1990). He also wrote autobiographical books and novels, including *A Postillion Struck by Lightning* (1977), *Backcloth* (1986), *A Particular Friendship* (1989), and *A Short Walk from Harrods* (1993). He was knighted in 1992.

## Bognor Regis
Seaside resort in West Sussex, on the south coast of England, 105 km/66 mi southwest of London; population (1991) 56,700. Originally a small fishing hamlet dating from the 7th century, Bognor was developed as a purpose-built bathing and health resort in the late 18th century. It was popular with Queen Victoria in the 19th century and the word 'Regis' was added to its name after George V visited nearby Aldwick to convalesce in 1929. There is a large holiday camp on the eastern margin of the town, between Bognor and Middleton-on-Sea.

## Boleyn, Anne (c. 1507–1536)
Queen of England 1533–36 as second wife of Henry VIII. She gave birth to the future Queen

Elizabeth I in September 1533. Although she subsequently produced a still-born son in January 1536, she produced no living male heir to the throne, and was executed on a false charge.

*Anne Boleyn was not a catalyst in the English Reformation; she was an element in the equation.*

**E W Ives**
*Anne Boleyn* (1986)

Having no male heir by his first wife, Catherine of Aragón, Henry broke from Rome and the pope (starting the Reformation) in order to divorce Catherine and marry Anne. Three years after Anne had married Henry she was accused of adultery and incest with her half-brother (a charge invented by Thomas Cromwell), and sent to the Tower of London. She was declared guilty, and was beheaded on 19 May 1536 at Tower Green.

## Bolsover Castle

Castle in Derbyshire, England, situated on a ridge of the Pennines, 10 km/6 mi east of Chesterfield. Originally built by William Peveril in the 11th century, all that remains is a mixture of Gothic and Renaissance styles dating from the 17th century. The castle is now owned by English Heritage.

## Bolton

Industrial town in Greater ◊Manchester, northwest England, 18 km/11 mi northwest of Manchester; population (1994 est) 210,000. Important in the wool trade from medieval times, Bolton expanded in the 18th and 19th centuries as a major centre of the cotton-spinning industry. It was the home of Samuel Crompton, an early industrialist who invented the spinning mule in 1779. Once dominated by mills and smoking chimneys, Bolton has undergone much redevelopment and is now a regional shopping centre with modern facilities alongside refurbished Victorian buildings.

*Features*

Dating from 1251, the Old Man and Scythe is the oldest inn in Bolton, and dominating Victoria Square in the town centre is the imposing Town Hall, opened in 1873. Samuel Crompton is buried in the churchyard of the grand Victorian Gothic parish church, and his former home, Hall I' Th' Wood, a 15th-century manor house, contains a folk museum and relics of Crompton. An example of the spinning mule can be seen at the Textile Museum. Nearby Smithill's Hall, dating from the 14th century, is one of Greater Manchester's oldest manor houses.

## Bolton Priory

Priory situated on the banks of the River Wharfe, in the village of Bolton Abbey near Ilkley, North Yorkshire, England. Its Augustinian community was founded in 1120 by William de Meschines and his wife Cicely de Romily, and moved to Bolton around 1154. The nave survives as the parish church.

## Bond films

Series of films featuring novelist Ian ◊Fleming's creation, the urbane British spy and womanizer James Bond (also known as 007). Blending comedy and drama, gunplay and sex scenes, and deploying every conceivable mode of transport, the series has exerted an enduring appeal for mainstream cinemagoers since *Dr No*, the first instalment, premiered in 1962. The series has

**Bond Films** The Scottish actor Sean Connery was the first to portray the suave secret agent James Bond on screen, in a series of films that helped raise the international profile of the British film industry in the 1960s. So popular are the Bond films that they continue to be made, despite no longer being based on scripts from the original novels of Bond's creator, Ian Fleming. Rex produced such classics of the British cinema as *Goldfinger* (1964) and *On Her Majesty's Secret Service* (1969), and has added a memorable array of evil masterminds to the pantheon of screen villains. Five actors have played the charismatic leading man: Sean Connery, George Lazenby, Roger Moore, Timothy Dalton, and Pierce Brosnan.

## Bond Street

Street and shopping centre in London, running between Piccadilly and Oxford Street. The southern section, known as Old Bond Street, was built in 1686 by Thomas Bond, a member of Queen Henrietta Maria's household, and after whom the street was named. The northern section, New Bond Street, was built around 1721.

The composer Georg Friedrich Handel lived at 25 Brook Street, close to the junction of Brook Street and New Bond Street, from 1723 until his death.

## Bonnie Prince Charlie

Scottish name for ◊Charles Edward Stuart, pretender to the throne.

## Booker Prize for Fiction

British literary prize of £20,000 awarded annually (from 1969) to a Commonwealth writer by the Booker company (formerly Booker McConnell) for a novel published in the UK during the previous year. See below for a list of winners.

## Boole, George (1815–1864)

English mathematician. His work *The Mathematical Analysis of Logic* (1847) established the basis of modern mathematical logic, and his **Boolean algebra** can be used in designing computers.

Boole's system is essentially two-valued. By subdividing objects into separate classes, each with a given property, his algebra makes it possible to treat different classes according to the presence or absence of the same property. Hence it involves just two numbers, 0 and 1 – the binary system used in the computer.

## Booth, William (1829–1912)

British founder of the ◊Salvation Army (1878), and its first 'general'. Booth experienced religious conversion at the age of 15. In 1865 he founded the Christian Mission in Whitechapel, east

## Booker Prize

This UK literary prize of £20,000 is awarded annually in October.

| Year | Winner | Awarded for | Year | Winner | Awarded for |
|------|--------|-------------|------|--------|-------------|
| 1969 | P H Newby | Something to Answer For | 1985 | Keri Hulme | The Bone People |
| 1970 | Bernice Rubens | The Elected Member | 1986 | Kingsley Amis | The Old Devils |
| 1971 | V S Naipaul | In a Free State | 1987 | Penelope Lively | Moon Tiger |
| 1972 | John Berger | G | 1988 | Peter Carey | Oscar and Lucinda |
| 1973 | J G Farrell | The Siege of Krishnapur | 1989 | Kazuo Ishiguro | The Remains of the Day |
| 1974 | Nadine Gordimer | The Conservationist | 1990 | A S Byatt | Possession |
| 1974 | Stanley Middleton | Holiday | 1991 | Ben Okri | The Famished Road |
| 1975 | Ruth Prawer Jhabvala | Heat and Dust | 1992 | Barry Unsworth | Sacred Hunger |
| 1976 | David Storey | Saville | 1992 | Michael Ondaatje | The English Patient |
| 1977 | Paul Scott | Staying On | 1993 | Roddy Doyle | Paddy Clarke Ha Ha Ha |
| 1978 | Iris Murdoch | The Sea, The Sea | 1994 | James Kelman | How Late It Was, How Late |
| 1979 | Penelope Fitzgerald | Offshore | 1995 | Pat Barker | The Ghost Road |
| 1980 | William Golding | Rites of Passage | 1996 | Graham Swift | Last Orders |
| 1981 | Salman Rushdie | Midnight's Children | 1997 | Arundhati Roy | The God of Small Things |
| 1982 | Thomas Keneally | Schindler's Ark | 1998 | Ian McEwan | Amsterdam |
| 1983 | J M Coetzee | The Life and Times of Michael K | 1999 | J M Coetzee | Disgrace |
| 1984 | Anita Brookner | Hotel du Lac | | | |

London, which became the Salvation Army in 1878. 'In Darkest England, and the Way Out' (1890) contained proposals for the physical and spiritual redemption of the many down-and-outs. His wife Catherine (1829–1890, born Mumford), whom he married in 1855, became a public preacher in about 1860, initiating the ministry of women.

## Bootle

Industrial town and seaport in Merseyside, northwest England, at the mouth of the River Mersey, adjoining Liverpool; population (1991) 65,500. Bootle includes the northern section of the docks of the Mersey estuary and extensive areas have been rebuilt following World War II bombing raids.

## Boots

UK's largest pharmacy chain, founded by **Jesse Boot** (1850–1931). In 1863 Boot took over his parents' small Nottingham shop trading in medicinal herbs. Recognizing that the future lay with patent medicines, he concentrated on selling cheaply, advertising widely, and offering a wide range of medicines. In 1892 Boots also began to manufacture drugs. The chain grew rapidly. By 1900 there were 126 shops and more than 1,000 when Jesse Boot died in 1931. The shops now sell photographic and audio equipment, small household wares, and children's clothing, as well as cosmetics and pharmaceuticals.

## Borders, The

Colloquial term for the border between England and Scotland. In 1996 ◊Scottish Borders was created as a unitary authority.

## borough, Old English burg, 'a walled or fortified place'

Urban-based unit of local government which existed from the 8th century until 1974, when it continued as an honorary status granted by royal charter to a district council, entitling its leader to the title of mayor. In England in 1998 there were 32 London borough councils and 36 metropolitan borough councils.

See also ◊local government.

## Boston

Port and market town in Lincolnshire, eastern England, on the River Witham, 50 km/31 mi southeast of Lincoln; population (1991) 34,600. The town is situated in the flat, fertile agricultural district of the Lincolnshire Fens.

St Botolph's Church, dating from the 14th century, is said to be England's largest parish church. Its 83-m/272-ft high tower, known as **Boston stump**, is the highest parish church tower in England and a landmark for sailors.

*History*
Boston was the second-largest port in Britain during the 13th and 14th centuries, and its prosperity was based on the wool trade with Flanders. The town became a centre of Nonconformism in the early 17th century, and a group of pilgrims, later known as the Pilgrim Fathers, were imprisoned in the town in 1607 following their failed attempt to find religious freedom by sailing to Holland. The cells in which the pilgrims were confined can be seen in Boston's Guildhall. In 1630 John Winthrop emigrated to North America on the *Arbella*, and founded a settlement on Massachusetts Bay named Boston after his hometown.

## Boswell, James (1740–1795)

Scottish biographer and diarist. He was a member of Samuel ◊Johnson's Literary Club and the two men travelled to Scotland together in 1773, as recorded in Boswell's *Journal of a Tour to the Hebrides* (1785). His *Life of Samuel Johnson* was published in 1791. Boswell's ability to record Johnson's pithy conversation verbatim makes this a classic of English biography.

## Bosworth, Battle of

Last battle of the Wars of the ◊Roses, fought on 22 August 1485. Richard III, the Yorkist king, was defeated and slain by Henry of Richmond, who became Henry VII. The battlefield is near the village of Market Bosworth, 19 km/12 mi west of Leicester, England.

Richard's oppressive reign ensured that Henry, landing in Wales, gathered an army of supporters as he marched into England to meet Richard's army which was drawn up on a hill at Bosworth. A third, smaller, army led by Lord Stanley stood off from both sides, undecided upon which to join. Henry opened the battle by advancing up the hill and charging into the opposition. Lord Stanley now made his decision and fell on the rear of King Richard's position, causing the king's force to break and flee. Richard was unhorsed in the rush and beaten to death as he lay. As the battle ended, Lord Stanley crowned Henry as king; Henry later married Edward IV's daughter Elizabeth, uniting the houses of York and Lancaster to bring the Wars to an end.

## Bothwell, James, 4th Earl of Bothwell
(c. 1536–1578)

Scottish nobleman. The third husband of ◊Mary Queen of Scots, 1567–70, he was alleged to have arranged the explosion that killed Darnley, Mary's previous husband, in 1567.

Tried and acquitted a few weeks after the assassination, he abducted Mary and married her on 15 May. A revolt ensued, and Bothwell was forced to flee. In 1570 Mary obtained a divorce, and Bothwell was confined in a castle in the Netherlands where he died insane.

## Boudicca (died AD 61)

Queen of the Iceni (native Britons), often referred to by the Latin form of her name, **Boadicea**. Her husband, King Prasutagus, had been an ally of the Romans, but on his death AD 60 the territory of the Iceni was violently annexed. Boudicca was scourged and her daughters raped. Boudicca raised the whole of southeast England in revolt, and before the main Roman armies could return from campaigning in Wales she burned Londinium (London), Verulamium (St Albans), and Camulodunum (Colchester). Later the Romans under governor Suetonius Paulinus defeated the British between London and Chester; they were virtually annihilated and Boudicca poisoned herself.

## Boulting, John (1913–1985) and Roy
(1913–   )

English director–producer team, known as the Boulting brothers, who were successful in the years after World War II. Their films include *Brighton Rock* (1947), *Lucky Jim* (1957), and *I'm All Right Jack* (1959). They were twins.

## Bounty, Mutiny on the

Naval mutiny in the Pacific in 1789 against British captain William ◊Bligh.

## Bournemouth

Seaside resort in southern England, on Poole Bay, 40 km/25 km southwest of Southampton; population (1997) 161,500. Part of the county of Dorset until 1997, Bournemouth is now a unitary authority with an area of 46 sq km/18 sq mi. With its clifftop scenery, long sandy beach, and traditional seaside attractions, Bournemouth is one of the principal resorts on the south coast of England. It is also a conference venue and hosts a variety of annual festivals including the Music Competitions Festival and the Musicmakers Festival.

*History*

The area was undeveloped until the early 19th century when pine trees were planted in the Bourne valley and, with its sheltered position and mild climate, Bournemouth developed as a popular summer and winter resort.

*Features*

Bournemouth has a 10 km/6 mi stretch of sands and two piers, one of which is 305 m/1,000 ft long. Among the town's many public parks and gardens is Compton Acres which includes seven gardens with different themes. The Russell-Cotes Art Gallery and Museum houses a collection of Japanese art and 17th–20th century paintings. Bournemouth University was founded in 1992 (formerly Bournemouth Polytechnic).

## bovine spongiform encephalopathy, BSE or mad cow disease

Disease of cattle, related to scrapie in sheep, which attacks the nervous system, causing aggression, lack of coordination, and collapse. First identified in 1985, it is almost entirely confined to the UK. By 1996 it had claimed 158,000 British cattle.

A government inquiry into BSE and the possibly related, human disease, CJD (Creutzfeldt-Jakob Disease), of which there were 48 definite and probable UK cases reported between 1985 and 1999, was to report at the end of March 2000.

## Bow Bells

The bells of St Mary-le-Bow church, ◊Cheapside, London; a person born within the sound of Bow Bells is traditionally considered a true Cockney. The bells also feature in the legend of Dick ◊Whittington. The church was nearly destroyed by bombs in 1941. The bells, recast from the old metal, were restored in 1961.

## bowls

Outdoor and indoor game played in Britain since the 13th century and popularized by Francis Drake, who is reputed to have played bowls on Plymouth Hoe as the Spanish Armada approached in 1588.

Two popular forms of the game are played in Britain: **lawn bowls**, played on a flat surface, and **crown green bowls**, played on a rink with undulations and a crown at the centre of the green.

## Bowness, or Bowness-on-Windermere

Residential and holiday town in Cumbria, England. It is situated on the eastern shore of Lake

◊Windermere, 13 km/8 mi northwest of Kendal. Bowness is a centre for pleasure trips and water sports on the lake. The Windermere Steamboat Museum is nearby, and there is a regular car ferry service from Bowness to Belle Isle on the lake.

## Bow Street Runners

Informal police force organized in 1749 by the novelist Henry ◊Fielding, chief magistrate at Bow Street in London. The scheme was initially established as a force of detectives to aid the Bow Street Magistrates' court but from 1757 it was funded by the government to cover the rest of London. It formed the basis for the Metropolitan police force established by Robert Peel's government in 1829.

## Box Hill

Wooded hill overlooking the valley of the River Mole near Dorking in Surrey, England; height 170 m/558 ft. The National Trust owns 400 ha/988 acres of woods and chalk downland here. Box Hill is one of the best-known beauty spots in southeast England. Box trees give the area its name.

## Boycott, Charles Cunningham (1832–1897)

English land agent in County Mayo, Ireland, who strongly opposed the demands for agrarian reform by the Irish Land League 1879–81, with the result that the peasants refused to work for him; hence the word **boycott**, meaning to isolate an individual, organization or country, socially or comercially.

## Boyne, Battle of the

Battle fought on 1 July 1690 in eastern Ireland, in which the exiled king James II was defeated by William III and fled to France. It was the decisive battle of the War of English Succession, confirming a Protestant monarch. It took its name from the River Boyne which rises in County Kildare and flows 110 km/69 mi northeast to the Irish Sea.

## BR

Abbreviation for **British Rail**, the nationalized railway system from 1948 (as British Railways) until privatization began in 1992 (completed 1997). See ◊railways and ◊Railtrack.

## Bracknell

Town and, since April 1998, administrative headquarters of ◊Bracknell Forest unitary authority in southern England, 16 km/10 mi southeast of Reading; population (1991 est) 93,800. It was designated a new town in 1949; before 1998 it was part of the county of Berkshire. The headquarters of the Meteorological Office are here. Bracknell is one of the world's two global area forecasting centres which monitor upper-level winds and temperatures for all air traffic; the other is in Washington DC, USA. Industries include engineering, electronics, and the manufacture of biscuits (Burtons).

## Bracknell Forest

Unitary authority (borough status) in central south England, created in 1998 from part of the former county of Berkshire; population (1997) 109,600; area 109 sq km/42 sq mi. Its principal towns are ◊Bracknell (administrative headquarters), ◊Sandhurst, and Crowthorne.

*Physical*

Although it is an area with much new development, Bracknell Forest is partly in the Metropolitan Green Belt and contains 1,052 hectares/2,600 acres of Crown Estate woodland.

*Features*

The Royal Military Academy at Sandhurst was established here in 1799 for officer training. The Meteorological Office at Bracknell is one of two global weather forecasting centres for the world's airlines; the Transport Research Laboratory is also here. The Look Out Discovery Park is south of Bracknell.

*Economy*

The local economy is based on high technology industries, engineering, electronics, and some manufacturing.

## Bradford

Industrial city and metropolitan borough in West Yorkshire, England, 14 km/9 mi west of Leeds; population (1994 est) 357,000. A centre of the woollen trade from the 13th century, Bradford developed rapidly during the industrial revolution and by the mid-19th century it was the world's largest producer of worsted cloth. Since the decline in the textile industry in the 1970s, Bradford's potential as a tourist destination has been developed. Socially and culturally vibrant and diverse, the city is home to a great many immigrant communities.

*Features*

The National Museum of Photography, Film, and Television (opened 1983), includes a giant IMAX cinema screen, $14 \times 20$ m/$46 \times 66$ ft, and also contains the Pictureville Cinerama Screen (opened in 1992) which features the only 1950s-style three-projector format in the world. The Colour Museum and the Bradford Industrial Museum illustrate the history of the city's textile industry. The Alhambra Theatre, an Edwardian music hall, has been restored as a major venue for ballet, opera, and plays. Saltaire, an industrial model village north of the city centre, includes Salt's Mill which houses the 1853 Gallery with a large collection of works by the 20th-century artist David Hockney who was born in Bradford. The city is the site of Bradford University (1966).

## Braemar

Village in Grampian, Scotland, where the most celebrated of the ◊Highland Games, the **Braemar Gathering**, takes place on the first Saturday in September.

## Brancaster

Village in Norfolk, England, 29 km/18 mi northeast of King's Lynn. It stands on the ancient site of the Roman fort of **Branodunum**. The parish of Brancaster includes Brancaster Staithe and Deepdale, a fishing village with a harbour from which boats depart for Scolt Head Island, now a nature reserve belonging to the National Trust.

## Brazil, Angela (1868–1947)

English writer. She founded the genre of girls' school stories, writing over 50; among them are *A Pair of Schoolgirls* (1912), *Captain Peggie* (1924), and *The New School at Scarsdale* (1940).

## breakfast

British culinary institution, nowadays more frequently enjoyed in its traditional form on a weekly, rather than a daily basis. W Somerset Maugham said that 'To eat well in England, you should have breakfast three times a day'. Changing lifestyles mean orange juice, cereals and toast, plus the occasional croissant, have largely replaced eggs and bacon as the morning meal, but a 'full cooked breakfast' is still often found in hotels and guest houses.

Breakfast literally means the meal that 'breaks the fast of the night'. Saxons started the day's work with ale, cold pork, and coarse dark bread; in the Middle Ages the rich breakfasted on boiled beef, mutton, salt herring, and wine, while the poor subsisted on bread, salt pork, and fish on Fridays. This was much the pattern for the next 500 years. In Scotland oatmeal boiled with water became the staple morning food; along with marmalade and kippers, Scotch porridge is now an integral part of the British breakfast repertoire.

In the 17th and 18th centuries tea and coffee began to replace the 'morning draught'; by the end of the 19th century the Edwardians had turned breakfast into an art form. In its heyday the classic breakfast, served on silver dishes on a hotplate, included eggs boiled, scrambled, or fried, bacon, ham, devilled kidneys, sausages, mushrooms, smoked fish, kedgeree, cold meats and game, rolls, and conserves. Such breakfasts were only served in affluent households with plenty of servants – the poor had to make do with stale bread and watery gruel.

## Breakspear, Nicholas

Original name of ◊Adrian IV, the only English pope.

## Brecon Beacons

Group of mountains in the south of Powys, central Wales. Pen y Fan (885 m/2,904 ft) and Corn Du (873 m/2,864 ft) are the major peaks. It is the highest mountain mass of Old Red Sandstone in the British Isles. The area is designated as a National Park. There is a mountain centre near Defynog.

## Brentwood

Market town in Essex, England, about 17 km/11 mi southwest of Chelmsford; population (1991) 67,400. Brentwood is situated in wooded countryside, and has a school founded in 1557 and dedicated to the English martyr St Thomas à Becket.

## brewing

Making of beer, ale, or other alcoholic beverage, from malt and barley by steeping (mashing), boiling, and fermenting.

See ◊public house for a feature on the development of the British pub and with it, brewing.

## Bridgend

Unitary authority in south Wales, created in 1996 from part of the former county of Mid Glamorgan; population (1996) 128,300; area 40 sq km/15 sq mi. Its principal towns are ◊Bridgend (administrative headquarters), Porthcawl (resort and residential area), and ◊Maesteg.
*Physical*
Most of the authority consists of the western end of a lowland plateau, Bro Morgannwg. To the north lie the Cymer Forest and Mynydd Caerau (556 m/1,824 ft).
*Economy*
Bro Morgannwg is a rich agricultural area of mixed farming and large villages. Industries

include civil engineering and chocolate manufacture.

## Bridgend

Industrial and market town in ◊Bridgend unitary authority, south Wales, situated on the River Ogmore 31 km/19 mi west of Cardiff; population (1981) 31,600. A Royal Ordnance factory, established here in 1936, was turned into an industrial estate for a wide variety of light industries in 1945.

## Bridgewater Canal

Canal in northwest England, the first major British canal, initially built to carry coal from the Duke of Bridgewater's mines at Worsley to Manchester and on to the Mersey, a distance of 67.5 km/42 mi. The canal crosses the Irwell Valley on an aqueduct. An underground waterway constructed at the mine simultaneously acted as a mine drain.

The Duke of Bridgewater began its construction, under the direction of James ◊Brindley, in 1759. The canal was sold to the Manchester Ship Canal Company in 1887, and continued to be used for goods traffic until the mid-1970s. It is now used mainly by pleasure craft.

## Bridgwater Carnival

Annual carnival held at Bridgwater, Somerset, on the nearest Thursday to 5th November, in commemoration of the Gunpowder Plot in 1605; its two-hour procession, containing over 130 floats and carts, culminates in a huge fireworks display.

## Bridlington

Seaside resort in the East Riding of Yorkshire, England; population (1991) 31,000. It is situated on Bridlington Bay, 10 km/6 mi southwest of Flamborough Head. The town is the headquarters of the Royal Yorkshire Yacht Club; its harbour accommodates numerous small vessels. Its main industry lies in the entertainment sector.

The lodgings in Bridlington of Queen Henrietta Maria, wife of Charles I, were bombarded by the Parliamentary ships of Admiral Batten in February 1643.

## Brighton

Seaside resort in Brighton and Hove unitary authority, on the south coast of England; population (1994 est) 155,000. Brighton developed as a fashionable spa in the 18th century and was patronized from 1783 by the Prince of Wales (later George IV). The largest seaside resort on the south coast and the closest to London, Brighton is also the home of two universities and many language schools. It is known not only for its fine Regency architecture and its 11 km/7 mi of seafront, but also for its alternative and lively cultural and social scene. Brighton Festival, held in May, is one of England's largest arts festivals.

*Features*

Brighton's attractions include the magnificent ◊Royal Pavilion, extensively remodelled for the Prince Regent by John Nash in a mixture of classical and oriental styles. The Palace Pier, built in 1899, is one of Britain's most visited tourist attractions, with some three million visitors each year. West Pier was closed following storm damage in the 1970s, but in March 1998 the National Lottery Heritage Fund awarded a grant towards the first phase of its restoration. The Lanes area of the town contains 18th-century buildings on the medieval street plan of the original fishing village of **Brightemstone**. Other attractions include the Sea Life Centre, the Marina, and Fishing Museum.

## Brindley, James (1716–1772)

English canal builder. He was the first to employ tunnels and aqueducts extensively, in order to reduce the number of locks on a direct-route canal. His 580 km/360 mi of canals included the ◊Bridgewater (Manchester–Liverpool) and Grand Union (Manchester–Potteries) canals.

## Bristol

Industrial port in southwest England, at the junction of the rivers Avon and Frome; population (1996) 374,300, urban area (1991) 516,500. Part of the former county of Avon to 1996, it is now a unitary authority with an area of 109 sq km/42 sq mi. Once England's second city and long established as a leading port and commercial centre, Bristol flourished in the 17th and 18th centuries as Britain's principal port for transatlantic trade. The city was heavily bombed during World War II but among the historic buildings that survive are a wealth of medieval churches and some fine Georgian houses. The city hosts a varied programme of festivals and is the site of two universities.

*History*

Already an important trading centre in the 12th century, by the 14th century Bristol had links with France, Holland, Portugal, and Spain, trading in wool, leather, wine, and salt. It was from here that in 1497 the Italian seafarer Giovanni Caboto set sail across the Atlantic and reached Newfoundland. Later, in the 17th and 18th centuries, Bristol became the leading British port for trade with the American colonies and the West Indies.

Part of a triangular trading system between West Africa and the West Indian and American plantations, Bristol was especially important in the slave trade. Jamaican sugar and molasses and West African cocoa were brought into Britain along this trade route, leading to the development of sugar and chocolate industries in Bristol. The *Great Western*, Isambard Kingdom ◊ Brunel's first steam ship was launched here in 1838. The importance of the port declined in the 19th century when it was unable to berth increasingly large vessels and new docks were built at the mouth of the Avon in the 1870s.

## Features

The redeveloped city docks are home to Brunel's *SS Great Britain*, the world's first iron ocean-going steam ship, and also include the Bristol Industrial Museum and the Maritime Heritage Centre. A major new visitor attraction in the harbour area, including Science World and Wild-screen World, opens from spring 2000 as a landmark project for the millennium. The city centre is a diverse mixture of medieval, Georgian, Victorian, and contemporary architecture, with Brunel's Temple Meads railway station at its heart. Other attractions include the City Museum and Art Gallery, and the Theatre Royal, home to

the Bristol Old Vic since 1946. One of Bristol's best known landmarks is Brunel's magnificent Clifton Suspension Bridge. Spanning the Avon Gorge, it is 214 m/702 ft long and 75 m/246 ft high. The residential district of Clifton also includes Bristol Zoo and England's longest Georgian crescent, the Royal York Crescent.

## Cathedral and churches

Among the many medieval churches in Bristol is the 13th–14th-century St Mary Redcliffe, described by Queen Elizabeth I as 'the fairest church in England', and with its large 13th-century tower and 87 m/287ft-high spire, it is still considered to be one of the finest of England's medieval churches. The cathedral, originally the abbey church of St Augustine (founded in about 1140), is the only 'hall-church' in England (with aisles, nave, and choir all of the same height). It became a cathedral in 1542 at the time of the Dissolution of the Monasteries when the see of Bristol was created. John Wesley's chapel, dating from 1739, is England's earliest Methodist building.

## Bristol Channel

Inlet in the southwest of England; coastline length 352 km/219 mi. Situated on the Atlantic Ocean,

**Bristol** Clifton Suspension Bridge is one of Bristol's most notable landmarks. Spanning the Avon Gorge, it is a wrought-iron construction designed by the engineer Isambard Kingdom Brunel and completed, after his death, in 1864. In the late 19th century a woman fell from the bridge but was saved when her crinoline and ample skirts acted as a parachute, breaking her fall. Robert Hallmann/Collections

it is an extension of the ◊Severn estuary, and is surrounded by South Wales to the north, and by Devon, Somerset and North Somerset to the south. The Bristol Channel is Britain's largest inlet, with a length of about 128 km/79 mi, a breadth which varies from 8 km/5 mi to 69 km/43 mi, and a depth from 9 m/30 ft to 73 m/240 ft.

## Britannia
The Roman name for Britain, later a national symbol of Great Britain in the form of a seated woman with a trident. Also the name of the royal yacht, decommissioned in 1997.

## British Council
Semi-official organization set up in 1934 (royal charter 1940) to promote a wider knowledge of the UK, excluding politics and commerce, and to develop cultural relations with other countries. It employs more than 6,000 people and is represented in 109 countries, running libraries, English-teaching operations, and resource centres.

## British Empire
Empire covering, at its height in the 1920s, about a sixth of the landmass of the Earth, all of its lands recognizing the United Kingdom as their leader. See feature on pages 54–57 and table of member countries.

---

*Great Britain has lost an empire and has not yet found a role.*

**Dean Acheson** US Democratic politician. Speech at the Military Academy, West Point 5 December 1962

---

## British Legion
Organization to promote the welfare of British veterans of war service and their dependants. Established under the leadership of Douglas Haig in 1921 (royal charter 1925) it became the **Royal British Legion** in 1971; it is nonpolitical. The sale on Remembrance Sunday of Flanders poppies raises much of its funds.

## British Library
National library of the UK. Created in 1973, it comprises the **reference division** (the former library departments of the British Museum, rehoused in Euston Road, St Pancras, London); **lending division** at Boston Spa, Yorkshire, from which full text documents and graphics can be sent by satellite link to other countries; **bibliographic services division** (incorporating the

British National Bibliography); and the **National Sound Archive** in South Kensington, London.

The Humanities Reading Room of the new library at St Pancras was opened in November 1997, with smaller reading rooms 1998–99. The new library holds 12 million volumes, can accommodate 1,200 readers, and includes a conference centre and exhibition facilities.

Construction work on the site began in 1982. Its escalating costs (£511 million in total), delays in completion, and ultra-modern design caused controversy.

## British Museum
Largest museum of the UK. Founded in 1753, it opened in London in 1759. Rapid additions led to the construction of the present buildings (1823–47), and in 1881 the Natural History Museum was transferred to South Kensington. The museum's Great Court, renovated and topped with a glass roof, and the restored reading room open November 2000.

## British Rail
The nationalized railway system, 1948–97. See ◊railways.

## Brittain, Vera (Mary) (1893–1970)
English socialist writer. She was a nurse to the troops overseas from 1915 to 1919, as told in her *Testament of Youth* (1933); *Testament of Friendship* (1940) commemorates English novelist Winifred ◊Holtby.

She married political scientist George Catlin (1896–1979); their daughter is the politician Shirley Williams, aspects of whose childhood are recorded in her mother's *Testament of Experience* (1957).

## Britten, Benjamin (1913–1976)
English composer. He often wrote for the individual voice; for example, the role in the opera *Peter Grimes* (1945), based on verses by George Crabbe, was written for his life companion, the tenor Peter Pears. Among his many works are the *Young Person's Guide to the Orchestra* (1946); the chamber opera *The Rape of Lucretia* (1946); *Billy Budd* (1951); *A Midsummer Night's Dream* (Shakespeare) (1960); and *Death in Venice* (after Thomas Mann) (1973).

By intellectual conviction and personal disposition Britten was an outsider; the themes of lost innocence, persecution, and isolation are constantly repeated in his music, especially the operas.

## broadcasting

Broadcasting is operated in Britain under a compromise system, where a ◊television and ◊radio service controlled by the state-regulated British Broadcasting Corporation (◊BBC) operates alongside commercial channels operating under franchises granted by the Independent Television Commission (known as the Independent Broadcasting Authority before 1991) and the Radio Authority. The franchizing of cable television systems is carried out by the Programme and Cable Division of ITC. See also ◊ITV, ◊Channel 4, ◊Channel 5, and ◊SC4.

## Broadstairs

Seaside resort in east Kent, England, 5 km/3 mi southeast of Margate; population (1991) 24,000. The North Foreland lighthouse is nearby. Broadstairs is closely associated with the novelist Charles ◊Dickens, who wrote *David Copperfield* here. Many places in Broadstairs are mentioned in Dickens's works and the town is now the site of an annual Dickens festival.

A house where the novelist Charles Dickens spent much time in the 1850s and 1860s stands on the cliff above the harbour. The house was renamed Bleak House after Dickens's novel of the same name, and is now the Dickens and Maritime Museum.

## Bromsgrove

Market town in Worcestershire, 20 km/12 mi southwest of Birmingham; population (1991) 88,500. Bromsgrove Museum illustrates the history of the Bromsgrove Guild, an organization of craftsmen founded in 1894. In the early 19th century the Guild designed and produced the gates and railings of Buckingham Palace, London. The poet A E Housman was born near Bromsgrove and attended school here. Music at Bromsgrove is an annual festival held in May featuring international artists, and the Court Leet is a traditional celebration held in the summer which includes a carnival and Elizabethan street market. The Avoncroft Museum of Buildings, a large collection of reconstructed historic buildings, is nearby.

## Brontë Sisters

Three English novelists, daughters of a Yorkshire parson. **Charlotte** (1816–1855), notably with *Jane Eyre* (1847) and *Villette* (1853), reshaped autobiographical material into vivid narrative. **Emily** (1818–1848) in *Wuthering Heights* (1847) expressed the intensity and nature mysticism which also pervades her poetry (*Poems*, 1846). The more modest talent of **Anne** (1820–1849) produced *Agnes Grey* (1847) and *The Tenant of Wildfell Hall* (1848).

The Brontës were brought up by an aunt in their father's rectory (now a museum) at ◊Haworth in Yorkshire. During 1848–49 Emily, Anne, and their brother Patrick Branwell (1817–1848) all died of tuberculosis, aided in Branwell's case by alcohol and opium addiction; his portrait of the sisters survives. Charlotte married her father's curate, A B Nicholls, in 1854, and died during pregnancy. The sisters share a memorial in Westminster Abbey, London.

### Charlotte

Charlotte attended a school for clergymen's daughters at Cowan Bridge with her older sisters, Maria and Elizabeth, and Emily. She suffered intensely, watching her older sisters rapidly fail in health; after their sisters' deaths from consumption the two younger girls were brought home. Throughout her early years, Charlotte was writing and, with Patrick, she created an elaborate imaginary world, described and illustrated in many volumes of verse and prose.

From 1835 to 1838 she worked as a teacher for

**Charlotte Brontë** English novelist Charlotte Brontë, who is best known for her novel *Jane Eyre*, which achieved great success when she published it under the pseudonym Currer Bell in 1847. She lived in Haworth, Yorkshire with her sisters Emily and Anne; all the sisters wrote fiction and worked for brief periods as governesses and teachers. Corbis

# ◆ THE GROWTH AND DECLINE OF THE BRITISH EMPIRE ◆

At its height in the 1920s, the British Empire consisted of the Empire of India, four self-governing countries known as dominions, and dozens of colonies and territories, all recognizing the UK as their leader. After World War II it began to dissolve as colony after colony became independent, and today the UK has only 13 small dependent territories. With 52 other independent countries, it forms the voluntary association of the Commonwealth. Although Britain's monarch is accepted as head of the Commonwealth, most of its member states are republics, and the links are largely cultural and economic.

A major factor in the break-up of the British Empire was that while in its earlier days it brought wealth to the mother country, later it became a liability which Britain could no longer afford. In addition, people's attitudes toward colonies had changed. In the 19th century many Britons believed that they had a mission to improve the lot of other peoples, but on their own terms; this idea is now generally regarded with distaste.

## Early empire

The story of the British Empire began in 1497 when the Italian seafarer John Cabot sailed across the Atlantic Ocean in the service of King Henry VII of England and reached Newfoundland. In 1583 the explorer Sir Humphrey Gilbert took possession of Newfoundland for Elizabeth I. By this time the Portuguese and Spanish had divided between them a considerable part of the Earth's land surface. England was already a formidable power at sea, but its seafarers were mainly freebooters engaged in trade, piracy, and slavery. The defeat of the Spanish Armada in 1588 reinforced English sea power, which continued to be mostly privately organized. Unlike the Spanish and Portuguese, the English in the 16th century were neither missionaries nor colonists. England was a poor country, lacking the wealth of Portugal and Spain; when the English put to sea it was to seek immediate profits.

## 17th century

This pattern began to change in the 17th century. Between 1623 and 1632 English settlers occupied St Kitts, Barbados, St Croix (later lost), Nevis, Antigua, and Montserrat. In 1655 Oliver Cromwell's forces took Jamaica from the Spaniards, who officially ceded it in 1760. British Honduras (now Belize) was governed as part of Jamaica until 1884, and the tiny South Atlantic island of St Helena was annexed in 1673. The attraction of the West Indies for the English lay in the sugar and rum produced there. Virginia, the first permanent English colony in mainland America, was established in 1607 by the Virginia Company, which also took over Bermuda in about 1610. Shortly after this, in 1620, the Pilgrim Fathers landed from the ship *Mayflower* to found the colony of Massachusetts. By 1733 the English had established 13 colonies along the Atlantic seaboard between French Canada and Spanish Florida.

## 18th century

In 1707 England had united with Scotland to form, as Great Britain, the largest free-trade area then existing, and by the late 18th century Britain had become the leading industrial nation. Its main pattern of trade was based on the 'triangular route'; British ships took manufactured goods and spirits to West Africa to exchange them for slaves, whom they landed in the West Indies and the southernmost of the 13 colonies. The ships then returned to Britain with cargoes of cotton, rum, sugar, and tobacco, produced mainly by the labour of the black slaves. Britain's prosperity was bound up with the slave trade until this became illegal in 1807. By that time the importance of the slave trade had diminished and other forms of commerce had become more profitable.

## Seven Years' War

In 1756–63 the Seven Years' War against France brought Britain lands in Canada and India, plus more islands in the West Indies, and Gibraltar. The 13 colonies on the North Atlantic seaboard won independence as the USA 1776–83. Britain acquired the Bahamas in 1783, and the defeat of France in the Napoleonic Wars enabled Britain to add Malta, St Lucia, Grenada, Dominica, St Vincent, Trinidad, Tobago, part of Guiana (now Guyana), Ceylon (now Sri Lanka), the Seychelles, and Cape Colony (now part of South Africa) to its empire.

## Spread of science

In the 17th and 18th centuries the British ruling class developed a great interest in science, which had repercussions on the growth of the British Empire. Between 1768 and 1780 scientific naval expeditions commanded by Captain James Cook explored islands and coasts of the Pacific Ocean, from the entrance to the Arctic Ocean at the Bering Strait to the then unknown coasts of New Zealand and Australia.

Successive British governments showed no more interest in annexing these southern lands than they had in places elsewhere. In most cases they left the building of the empire to private individuals such as William Penn (who founded Pennsylvania) or to chartered companies, the most famous of which was the East India Company (1660–1858). An important exception was in the West Indies, where government intervention was frequent because many members of Parliament had commercial interests there.

## Members of the British Empire

| current name | colonial names and history | colonized | independent |
| --- | --- | --- | --- |
| India | British East India Company | 18th century–1858 | 1947 |
| Pakistan | British East India Company | 18th century–1858 | 1947 |
| Myanmar | Burma | 1866 | 1948 |
| Sri Lanka | Portuguese, Dutch 1602–1796; Ceylon 1802–1972 | 16th century | 1948 |
| Ghana | Gold Coast; British Togoland integrated 1956 | 18th–19th centuries | 1957 |
| Nigeria | | 1861 | 1960 |
| Cyprus | Turkish to 1878, then British rule | 1878 | 1960 |
| Sierra Leone | British protectorate | 1788 | 1961 |
| Tanzania | German East Africa to 1921; British mandate from League of Nations/UN as Tanganyika | 19th century | 1961 |
| Jamaica | Spanish to 1655 | 16th century | 1962 |
| Trinidad & Tobago | Spanish 1532–1797; British 1797–1962 | 1532 | 1962 |
| Uganda | British protectorate | 1894 | 1962 |
| Kenya | British colony from 1920 | 1895 | 1963 |
| Malaysia | British interests from 1786; Federation of Malaya 1957–63 | 1874 | 1963 |
| Malawi | British protectorate of Nyasaland 1907–53; Federation of Rhodesia & Nyasaland 1953–64 | 1891 | 1964 |
| Malta | French 1798–1814 | 1798 | 1964 |
| Zambia | Northern Rhodesia – British protectorate; Federation of Rhodesia & Nyasaland 1953–64 | 1924 | 1964 |
| The Gambia | | 1888 | 1965 |
| Singapore | Federation of Malaya 1963–65 | 1858 | 1965 |
| Guyana | Dutch to 1796; British Guiana 1796–1966 | 1620 | 1966 |
| Botswana | Bechuanaland – British protectorate | 1885 | 1966 |
| Lesotho | Basutoland | 1868 | 1966 |
| Bangladesh | British East India Company 18th century–1858; British India 1858–1947; eastern Pakistan 1947–71 | 18th century | 1971 |
| Zimbabwe | Southern Rhodesia from 1923; UDI under Ian Smith 1965–79 | 1895 | 1980 |
| Belize | British Honduras | 17th century | 1981 |
| Hong Kong | Hong Kong | 1841 | 1997 (returned to China) |

## Convict settlements

One reason for the British government's interest in the 13 American colonies was as a dumping ground for convicts, debtors, and political prisoners, many of whom were sentenced to transportation rather than to gaol or the gallows (at that time the law provided the death sentence for stealing a sheep). American independence posed the problem for Britain of where to send its surplus prison population, so in 1788 a new convict settlement was established in Australia at Botany Bay in New South Wales, near where Sydney is now located. This territory had been recently recorded by the voyages of James Cook.

## 19th century

Britain annexed New Zealand in 1840, Tristan da Cunha in 1816, the Falkland Islands in 1833, and Papua in 1884. In 1878 Turkey handed over Cyprus to a British administration.

## India

At the heart of the British Empire was India, which was controlled not by the government but by the East India Company, whose power extended from Aden (annexed in 1839) in Arabia to Penang (leased in 1786) in Malaya. Both places were vital ports of call for company vessels travelling between Britain, India, and China. Politically, the East India Company was the most powerful private company in history. It controlled India partly by direct rule and partly by a system of alliances with Indian princes, whose powers and security were backed by the company's powerful army. Finally, in 1857, a mutiny by its Indian troops terminated the company's affairs, and in 1858 the British government took over its functions. In 1877 Benjamin Disraeli, then prime minister, made Queen Victoria Empress of India. Her new empire included present-day India, Pakistan, Sri Lanka, Bangladesh, and most of Myanmar (Burma). In 1879 the nearby Maldive Islands were annexed.

## Imperialism

By this time British policy was becoming imperialistic. In the last quarter of the 19th century Britain tended to annex countries not just for commercial gain but for reasons of national prestige. The commercial operations of the East India Company extended into the East Indies, a vast area that had come under Dutch control. When the Netherlands were occupied by the French under Napoleon (1793–1815), parts of the Dutch East Indies were occupied by the East India Company and held until 1824. When the British government took over from the East India Company it also acquired the Straits Settlements. These comprised Penang, Malacca (not returned to the Dutch), and Singapore, founded by Stamford Raffles in 1819. Increasingly the British became involved in the affairs of the Malay Sultanates, several of which sought British protection from the domination of Siam (now Thailand). By 1914 all of Malaya was under British control. Eastward, in Borneo, Sarawak had become the personal possession of James Brooke, a freebooting British ex-soldier of the East India Company. The British North Borneo Company acquired present-day Sabah in 1888. In the same year the once powerful adjoining sultanate of Brunei, which had formerly possessed Sarawak and Sabah, itself came under British protection.

## Hong Kong

The acquisition of Hong Kong was typical of the way in which western countries seized colonies between about 1840 and 1890. In 1839 China stopped the importation by the East India Company of opium, which China complained was having a debilitating effect upon its people. When British and American ships defied the ban, Chinese officials publicly destroyed 20,000 cases of the drug. Faced with the collapse of its Far Eastern operations (for without the opium trade it was not financially viable) the company persuaded the British government, then led by Lord Palmerston, to declare war on China. As a result of the Opium War, Britain gained Hong Kong island. Kowloon was added to the colony after a second Opium War (1856–58) and more mainland territory was taken in 1898.

## Colonizing Africa

Before the 1880s the British showed little interest in Africa apart from Cape Colony. The first large group of British settlers landed in the Cape in 1820. They were bitterly resented by the Boers (Dutch farmers), descendants of Dutch Protestants who had settled in the Cape nearly 200 years earlier. When slavery was ended throughout the British Empire in 1833, the Boers were forced to free their African slaves. Although the British government gave them generous financial compensation, the Boers regarded this further interference by the British as too much to accept. In 1836 they began the 'Great Trek' northward to found the Orange Free State and the South African Republic. By 1856 the British had recognized the independence of these states but had themselves founded a new colony in Natal. After heavy fighting, beginning in 1879, the British conquered the African military state of Zululand and added it to Natal in 1897.

The discovery of diamonds and gold in southern Africa led to disputes between the Boers and the British. Britain annexed the South African Republic, but the Boers struck back. They won the first Boer War (1880–81) and regained the lost territory, which the Boers renamed the Transvaal Republic.

Britain had maintained a few forts in West Africa, where gold and ivory kept their importance after the slave trade ended. An exception was Sierra Leone, where Granville Sharp, an Englishman opposed to slavery, established a settlement of freed American slaves in 1787. This coastal strip of Sierra Leone was made a British colony in 1808. In 1821 the British established a coastal colony around the tiny town of Bathurst on the River Gambia. Only later were colonies established on the coasts of present-day Ghana and Nigeria.

From the 1880s onward Belgium, Britain, France, Germany, Italy, Portugal, and Spain vied with each other to establish colonies in Africa. British protectorates were established to cover roughly the area of present-day Gambia, Sierra Leone, Ghana, and Nigeria. Because of the climate, which gave West Africa its reputation as 'the white man's grave', these colonies attracted very few British settlers.

In East Africa the situation was different, for on high ground the land proved suitable for settlement by white colonists. Private companies under charter from the British government established control over Kenya in 1888 and Uganda in 1890. In 1890 Germany, which had already relinquished its interests in Uganda, ceded Zanzibar (now part of Tanzania) to Britain in exchange for Heligoland, an island off the German coast. By 1900 all Kenya and Uganda was under the control of the British government. Northern Somalia had come under direct control of the British in 1884. By the time the European scramble for Africa ended, Britain held the second-largest share of the continent.

David Livingstone, a Scottish missionary, explored much of the area that is now Botswana, Zambia, and Zimbabwe. Following his journeys, the Free Church of Scotland set up a mission in Nyasaland (now Malawi) in 1875, and the country became a British protectorate in 1891, a year after Bechuanaland (now Botswana). Basutoland (now Lesotho) became a colony in 1884.

In the late 1880s the British South Africa Company, which was largely controlled by Cecil Rhodes, negotiated land mineral rights from African chiefs in Matabeleland and Mashonaland. By 1889 the company had conquered these two territories and united them as Rhodesia, named after Rhodes. The company intervened further northwards, stamping out the slave trade and bringing that area under their control too. They named it Northern Rhodesia (later Zambia).

In 1890 Rhodes became prime minister of Cape Colony, at a time when tension was again mounting between the Boers and the British. The Boers resisted encroachments by British speculators interested in diamonds and gold. After three years of the second Boer War (1899–1902), the two Boer republics, plus Swaziland, were annexed by Britain.

## Dominions and independence

The concept of self-government for the larger and more distant colonies was first formulated in the 'Report on the Affairs of British North America' in 1839 by Lord John Durham, Canada's governor-general. This report recommended that responsible government (the acceptance by governors of the advice of local ministers) should be granted to Upper Canada (Ontario) and Lower Canada (Quebec), which should be merged into one. The merge took place immediately, but responsible government did not come into being until 1847 under the governorship of Lord Elgin, the son-in-law of Lord Durham. This pattern was subsequently applied to the other Canadian provinces and to the Australian colonies. The Australian colonies had attained responsible government by 1859 (except for Western Australia, 1890). New Zealand obtained responsible government in all but native affairs in 1856, and this reservation disappeared by 1870. Cape Colony achieved responsible government in 1872, followed by Natal in 1893.

The British devised a further intermediate stage between colonial status and independence, which came to be called dominion status. Canada became a dominion in 1867, Australia in 1901, New Zealand in 1907, and the Union of South Africa (Cape Colony, Natal, Orange Free State, and Transvaal) by 1910. These constitutional changes were effected without rancour. Eire (southern Ireland), which had been part of the UK, also became a dominion as the Irish Free State in 1922. It did not acknowledge this status, and declared itself independent in 1938. Eire's breakaway was accomplished only with much violence and bitterness.

To improve communications with India, Disraeli purchased for Britain shares in the Suez Canal in 1875. This led to British involvement in Egypt, a country supposedly under Turkish suzerainty, but in fact largely independent. In 1882 Egypt came under British occupation, and shortly after this British and Egyptian troops were jointly involved in Sudan, to the south. By 1899, a protectorate had been established, setting up a condominium called Anglo-Egyptian Sudan. The great dream of Rhodes had been that one day the British Empire in Africa would stretch from the Cape to Cairo. By 1899 this dream was almost a reality; only German East Africa (Tanganyika) stood in the way. The defeat of Germany and Turkey in World War I not only gave Britain a mandate over Tanganyika, but also over Palestine, Transjordan, Iraq, and part of Cameroon. German Southwest Africa (now Namibia) went to South Africa, German New Guinea to Australia, German Samoa to New Zealand, and the Pacific island of Nauru to Britain, Australia, and New Zealand jointly.

## 20th century

By the 1920s the British Empire had reached its zenith. As well as the places already mentioned, it included part of Antarctica and many small territories, mainly Pacific islands. Its continuance depended upon British superiority at sea, upon the ability of Britain to maintain its industrial and financial supremacy, and also upon the psychological acceptance of British (and Western) superiority. However, all three were waning. In the 1920s there had been stirrings in India, where Mahatma Gandhi led unarmed protests, called 'civil disobedience', to British rule. By 1939 the end of all empires was near, and World War II speeded their end. After the war ended the rest of the empire began to break up. India was the first to acquire independence, dividing as it did so into two countries, India and Pakistan. The rest of the colonies then became independent, most of them before 1980. With the return of Hong Kong to China in 1997 Britain was left with only 13 small dependencies.

her former headmistress, but this ended in a quarrel and estrangement. Various posts as governess in private families proved equally uncongenial. Charlotte, however, was ambitious for herself and her sisters, and her aunt agreed to support them in the venture of a small private school. With this scheme in mind, Charlotte lived in Brussels from 1842 to 1844 to improve her French. After her return, Charlotte's letters to her teacher, M Héger, show that she was deeply and unhappily in love with him. Her last novel, *Villette*, embodies her experiences in Brussels.

### Emily

Emily was passionately attached to the wild countryside around her home. In her only novel, the extraordinary *Wuthering Heights*, she portrays the influence of the elements and elemental passions on human souls; the strangeness of the characters contrasts with the realistic description of the bleak moorland setting, yet the two are inseparable. Charlotte was astonished by her poetry and regarded her work as unparalleled. Much of Emily's poetry supposedly describes events in the history of her imaginary country, Gondal. She endured her last illness with the stoic fortitude expressed in the 'Last Lines', written some months before her death from tuberculosis.

### Anne

Anne successfully held posts as a governess in England. She was particularly close to Emily, and shared with her the imaginary world which gave rise to the bulk of Emily's Gondal poetry. Although her reputation has been overshadowed by that of her sisters her two novels, completed when she was already seriously ill, represent a considerable achievement. More than Charlotte's works, they need to be considered as period pieces, but they are notable for their realism and the then advanced and unconventional ideas on such themes as the position of women in society.

## Brooke, Rupert (1887–1915)

English poet. He stands as a symbol of the World War I 'lost generation'. His five war sonnets, including 'The Soldier', were published posthumously. Other notable poems are 'Grantchester' (1912) and 'The Great Lover', written in 1914.

Brooke's war sonnets were published in *1914 and Other Poems* (1915); they caught the prevailing early wartime spirit of selfless patriotism.

Brooke toured America (*Letters from America*, 1916), New Zealand, and the South Seas, and in 1914 became an officer in the Royal Naval Volunteer Reserve. After fighting at Antwerp, Belgium, he sailed for the Dardanelles, but died of blood poisoning on the Greek island of Skyros, where he is buried.

## Brooklands

Former motor racing track near Weybridge, Surrey. One of the world's first purpose-built circuits, it was opened 1907 as a testing ground for early motorcars. It was the venue for the first British Grand Prix (then known as the RAC Grand Prix) in 1926. It was sold to the aircraft-builders Vickers in 1946. The circuit has been rejuvenated, and now houses the Brooklands Museum.

## Brown, Capability (1716–1783)

English landscape gardener and architect. He acquired his nickname because of his continual enthusiasm for the 'capabilities' of natural landscapes. He worked on or improved the gardens of many great houses and estates, including Hampton Court; Kew; Blenheim, Oxfordshire; Stowe, Buckinghamshire; and Petworth, West Sussex.

From about 1740 to about 1749 he collaborated with the architect William ◊Kent, but from 1751 he had his own very large architectural practice.

## Brown, Ford Madox (1821–1893)

English painter, associated with the ◊Pre-Raphaelite Brotherhood through his pupil Dante Gabriel Rossetti. His pictures, which include *The Last of England* (1855; City Art Gallery, Birmingham) and *Work* (1852–65; City Art Gallery, Manchester), are characterized by elaborate symbolism and abundance of realistic detail. His later subject pictures, romantic treatments of scenes from history and literature such as *Christ Washing St Peter's Feet* (Tate Gallery, London), are not always harmonious in design and colour, but as a colourist he excels in some small landscapes.

## Browning, Elizabeth Barrett (1806–1861)

English poet. In 1844 she published *Poems* (including 'The Cry of the Children'), which established her reputation and led to her friendship with and secret marriage to Robert ◊Browning in 1846. She wrote *Sonnets from the Portuguese* (1850), a collection of love lyrics, during their courtship. She wrote strong verse about social injustice and oppression in Victorian England, and she was a learned, fiery, and metrically experimental poet.

She suffered illness as a child, led a sheltered and restricted life, and was from the age of 13 regarded by her father as an invalid. Correspondence from Robert Browning, also a rising poet, led to their meeting and secret marriage. The story of their love, vividly reflected in their own letters, has been retold in many novels and plays.

She was freed from her father's oppressive influence by her marriage and move to Italy, where her health improved and she produced her mature works. She died in Florence, and a volume of *Last Poems* was issued in 1862.

## Browning, Robert (1812–1889)
English poet. His work is characterized by the accomplished use of dramatic monologue (in which a single imaginary speaker reveals his or her character, thoughts, and situation) and an interest in obscure literary and historical figures. It includes *Pippa Passes* (1841) (written in dramatic form) and the poems 'The Pied Piper of Hamelin' (1842), 'My Last Duchess' (1842), 'Home Thoughts from Abroad' (1845), and 'Rabbi Ben Ezra' (1864).

In 1845 he met Elizabeth Barrett; they eloped the following year and went to Italy. There he wrote *Christmas Eve and Easter Day* (1850) and much of *Men and Women* (1855), the latter containing some of his finest love poems and dramatic monologues. He published no further collection of verse until *Dramatis Personae* (1864), which was followed by *The Ring and the Book* (1868–69), based on an Italian murder story.

## Bruce
One of the chief Scottish noble houses. ◊Robert (I) the Bruce and his son, David II, were both kings of Scotland descended from Robert de Bruis (died 1094), a Norman knight who arrived in England with William the Conqueror in 1066. See genealogy on page 60.

## Bruce, Robert
King of Scotland; see ◊Robert (I) the Bruce, and genealogy on page 60.

## Bruce, Robert de, 5th Lord of Annandale (1210–1295)
Scottish noble, one of the unsuccessful claimants to the throne at the death of Alexander II in 1290. His grandson was ◊Robert (I) the Bruce. See genealogy.

## Brummell, Beau (1778–1840)
English dandy and leader of fashion. He introduced long trousers as conventional day and evening wear for men. A friend of the Prince of Wales, the future George IV, he later quarrelled with him. Gambling losses drove him in 1816 to exile in France, where he died in an asylum.

## Brunel, Isambard Kingdom (1806–1859)
English engineer and inventor. In 1833 he became engineer to the Great Western Railway, which adopted the 2.1-m/7-ft gauge on his advice. He built the Clifton Suspension Bridge over the River Avon at Bristol and the Saltash Bridge over the River Tamar near Plymouth. His shipbuilding designs include the *Great Western* (1837), the first steamship to cross the Atlantic regularly; the *Great Britain* (1843), the first large iron ship to have a screw propeller; and the *Great Eastern* (1858), which laid the first transatlantic telegraph cable.

In 1833 he was appointed to carry out improvements on the Bristol docks, and while working on this project his interest in the potential of railways was fired. In all, Brunel was responsible for building more than 2,600 km/1,600 mi of the permanent railway of the west of England, the Midlands, and South Wales. He also constructed two railway lines in Italy, and acted as adviser on the construction of the Victoria line in Australia and on the East Bengal railway in India.

## Brunel, Marc Isambard (1769–1849)
French-born British engineer and inventor, father of Isambard Kingdom Brunel. He constructed the tunnel under the River Thames in London from Wapping to Rotherhithe 1825–43.

## BSE
Abbreviation for ◊bovine spongiform encephalopathy.

## BST
Abbreviation for **British Summer Time**, March to October, when clocks are set an hour ahead of standard UK time to gain benefit of daylight hours.

## Buchan, John (1875–1940)
Scottish writer and politician. His popular adventure stories, today sometimes criticized for their alleged snobbery, sexism, and anti-Semitism, include *The Thirty-Nine Steps*, a tale of espionage published in 1915, *Greenmantle* (1916), and *The Three Hostages* (1924).

He was Conservative member of Parliament for the Scottish universities 1927–35, and governor general of Canada 1935–40. He also wrote historical and biographical works, literary criticism, and poetry.

## Buckingham, George Villiers, 1st Duke of Buckingham (1592–1628)
English courtier, adviser to James I and later Charles I. He was introduced to the court of

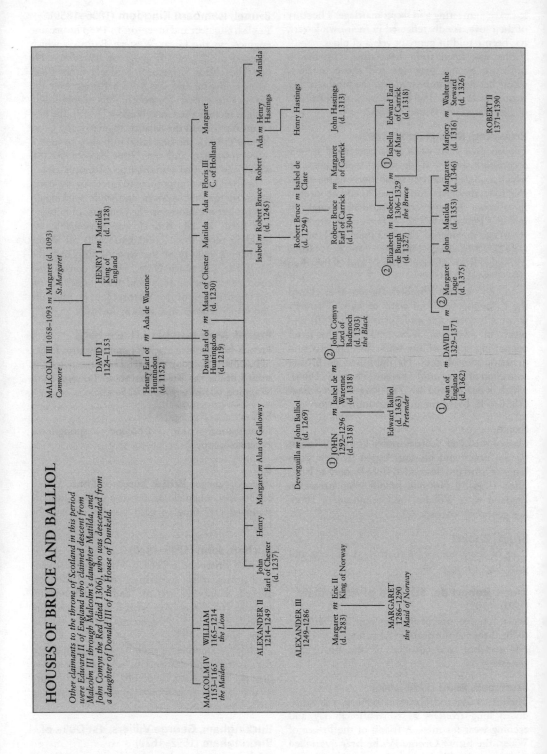

# HOUSES OF BRUCE AND BALLIOL

*Other claimants to the throne of Scotland in this period were Edward II of England who claimed descent from Malcolm III through Malcolm's daughter Matilda, and John Comyn the Red (died 1306), who was descended from a daughter of Donald III of the House of Dunkeld.*

James I in 1614 and soon became his favourite. He failed to cement the marriage of Prince Charles and the Infanta of Spain in 1623, but on returning to England negotiated Charles's alliance with Henrietta Maria, sister of the French king. After Charles's accession, Buckingham attempted to form a Protestant coalition in Europe, which led to war with France; however, he failed to relieve the Protestants (Huguenots) besieged in La Rochelle in 1627. His policy on the French Protestants was attacked in Parliament, and when about to sail for La Rochelle for a second time, he was assassinated in Portsmouth.

## Buckingham Palace

London home of the British sovereign, it stands at the west end of St James's Park. The Queen's Gallery presents exhibitions of portions of the royal collections, and the state rooms and Royal Mews are also open to visitors.

The original Buckingham House, begun in 1703 for the 1st Duke of Buckingham, was sold to George III in 1761. George IV obtained a parliamentary grant for its repair and enlargement, but instead he and the architect, John ◊Nash, began a new building (1821–26). The palace was incomplete at George IV's death in 1830, when Nash was displaced by Edward Blore, who reputedly covered most of Nash's work.

Nash's gateway was removed in 1851 and became Marble Arch. William IV did not like the palace, and it did not become a regular royal residence until the accession of Queen Victoria. In 1914 a new façade by Aston Webb replaced Blore's. The palace retains a park of 17 ha/42 acres.

## Buckinghamshire

County of southeast central England; population (1996) 671,700; area 1,565 sq km/604 sq mi. The county is largely agricultural and partly commuter belt for London. Its principal towns are ◊Aylesbury (administrative headquarters), Beaconsfield, Buckingham, High Wycombe, and Olney. Buckinghamshire is one of the ◊Home Counties, and is divided into eight 'hundreds' (a former division of land): Ashendon, Aylesbury, Buckingham, Burnham Cottesloe, Desborough, Newport, and Stoke; Burnham, Desborough and Stoke are known collectively as the Chiltern Hundreds.

### History

The refusal of the politician John Hampden to pay ship-money in 1636 was instrumental in precipitating the English Civil War; an early skirmish was fought on the outskirts of Aylesbury in 1642.

### Physical

The landscape is predominantly agricultural, with about 75% of the land under cultivation. Notable natural features include the ◊Chiltern Hills in the south, rising to their highest point at Coombe Hill (260 m/852 ft); the central Vale of Aylesbury; and Burnham Beeches in the south, the remains of an ancient forest with a large number of beech trees. Almost one-third of the county is covered by the Metropolitan Green Belt.

### Features

Buckinghamshire contains a number of important country houses, including ◊Chequers (country seat of the prime minister) and ◊Cliveden, a country house designed by Charles Barry (now a hotel; it was once the home of Nancy, Lady Astor). The 16th-century Claydon House, 18th-century Palladian-style West Wycombe House (home of Francis Dashwood of 'Hell-Fire Club' fame), and 19th-century ◊Waddesdon Manor in the style of a French chateau, all contain priceless collections of art treasures. There are lesser houses of interest at Gayhurst (once the home of Everard Digby, one of the Gunpowder Plot conspirators), Nether Winchendon, and Tyringham. Stowe School (1923) now occupies the former residence of the Duke of Buckinghamshire, and Stowe landscape gardens are well known. The county also has the homes of the poets William Cowper at Olney and John Milton at Chalfont St Giles, and of the Tory prime minister Benjamin Disraeli at Hughenden. The grave of William Penn, Quaker founder of Pennsylvania, can be seen at Jordans, near Chalfont St Giles, and the church of the poet Thomas Gray's 'Elegy' at Stoke Poges. ◊Bletchley Park, home of World War II code-breaking activities, now has a privately run museum.

### Economy

The fertile soil produces cereals (barley, wheat, oats) and grazing for cattle, pigs, poultry, and sheep. Agriculture is supplemented by engineering and some manufacturing.

## Bunyan, John (1628–1688)

English writer, author of *The Pilgrim's Progress* (first part 1678, second part 1684), one of the best-known religious allegories in English. A Baptist, he was imprisoned in Bedford 1660–72 for unlicensed preaching and wrote *Grace Abounding* in 1666, which describes his early spiritual life. He started to write *The Pilgrim's Progress* during a second jail sentence 1676–77. Written in straightforward language with fervour and imagination, it achieved immediate popularity and was highly influential.

## Burbage, Richard (c. 1567–1619)

English actor. He is thought to have been Shakespeare's original Hamlet, Othello, and Lear. He also appeared in first productions of works by Ben Jonson, Thomas Kyd, and John Webster. His father **James Burbage** (c. 1530–1597) built the first English playhouse, known as 'the Theatre'; his brother **Cuthbert Burbage** (c. 1566–1636) built the original ◊Globe Theatre in 1599 in London.

---

*Without class differences, England would cease to be the living theatre that it is.*

**Anthony Burgess** English novelist and literary critic.
Sayings of the Week, the *Observer*, May 1985

---

## Burgess, Anthony pen name of John Anthony Burgess Wilson (1917–1993)

English novelist, critic, and composer. A prolific and versatile writer, Burgess wrote about 60 books as well as screenplays, television scripts, and reviews. His work includes *A Clockwork Orange* (1962), made into a film by Stanley Kubrick in 1971, a despairing depiction of high technology and violence set in a future London terrorized by teenage gangs; and the panoramic *Earthly Powers* (1980), a vast survey of the 20th century narrated by a fictional world-famous novelist, which was short-listed for the Booker Prize. Equally ambitious was *The Kingdom of the Wicked* (1985), a spectacular retelling of the biblical Acts of the Apostles.

## Burgess, Guy Francis de Moncy (1911–1963)

British spy, a diplomat recruited by the USSR as an agent. He was linked with Kim ◊Philby, Donald ◊Maclean, and Anthony ◊Blunt.

## burgh

Former unit of Scottish local government, referring to a town enjoying a degree of self-government. Burghs were abolished in 1975; the terms **burgh** and **royal burgh** once gave mercantile (trading) privilege but are now only an honorary distinction.

## Burghley, William Cecil, 1st Baron Burghley (1520–1598)

English politician, chief adviser to Elizabeth I as secretary of state from 1558 and Lord High Treasurer from 1572. He was largely responsible for the Religious Settlement of 1559, by which Elizabeth I enforced Protestantism, and took a leading role in the events preceding the execution of Mary Queen of Scots in 1587.

## Burghley House

House in Cambridgeshire, England, near Stamford, Lincolnshire. Built between 1556 and 1587 by William Cecil, first Lord ◊Burghley, it is now the seat of his descendants, the Marquesses of Exeter. Capability ◊Brown laid out the surrounding park from 1756.

## Burke, Edmund (1729–1797)

British Whig politician and political theorist, born in Dublin, Ireland. In Parliament from 1765, he opposed the government's attempts to coerce the American colonists, for example in *Thoughts on the Present Discontents* (1770), and supported the emancipation of Ireland. However, he denounced the French Revolution, for example in *Reflections on the Revolution in France* (1790), and attacked the suggestion of peace with France in *Letters on a Regicide Peace* (1795–97).

Burke was a skilled orator and is regarded by British Conservatives as the greatest of their political theorists.

## Burke, William (1792–1829)

Irish murderer. He and his partner William Hare, living in Edinburgh, sold the body of an old man,

---

**Anthony Burgess** English writer Anthony Burgess, photographed in 1980. As well as novels including *A Clockwork Orange* (1962), which was made into an Academy Award-nominated film by Stanley Kubrick in 1971, and *Earthly Powers* (1980), he produced criticism, biography, screenplays, and orchestral works. Corbis

who had died from natural causes in their lodging house, to an anatomist as a subject for dissection. After that, they increased their supplies by murdering at least 15 people. Burke was hanged on the evidence of Hare. Hare is said to have died a beggar in London in the 1860s.

## Burne-Jones, Edward Coley (1833–1898)

English painter. In 1856 he was apprenticed to the Pre-Raphaelite painter and poet Dante Gabriel ◊Rossetti, who remained a dominant influence. His paintings, inspired by legend and myth, were characterized by elongated forms and subdued tones, as in *King Cophetua and the Beggar Maid* (1880–84; Tate Gallery, London). He also collaborated with William ◊Morris in designing stained-glass windows, tapestries, and book decorations for the Kelmscott Press. His work influenced both Symbolism and ◊Art Nouveau. He was created a baronet in 1894.

## Burnett, Frances Eliza Hodgson (1849–1924)

English writer. Her novels for children include the rags-to-riches tale *Little Lord Fauntleroy* (1886) and *The Secret Garden* (1911), which has its values anchored in nature mysticism. She emigrated with her family to the USA in 1865.

## Burney, Fanny (Frances) (1752–1840)

English novelist and diarist. She achieved success with *Evelina*, an epistolary novel published in 1778, became a member of Samuel ◊Johnson's circle, and received a post at court from Queen Charlotte. She published three further novels, *Cecilia* (1782), *Camilla* (1796), and *The Wanderer* (1814).

## Burnley

Town in Lancashire, northwest England, on the Leeds and Liverpool Canal, 19 km/12 mi northeast of Blackburn; population (1991) 74,700. Burnley prospered during the Industrial Revolution with the growth of the Lancashire cotton-weaving industry, and numerous mills were established. Since the decline of coalmining and cotton manufacture, Burnley's industries have diversified and the town centre has been redeveloped.
*Features*
Weaving sheds, weavers' cottages, foundries, and mills are preserved in the Weavers' Triangle, and the town's industrial history is illustrated at the Canal Toll House Heritage Centre.

## Burns, Robert (1759–1796)

Scottish poet. He used a form of Scots dialect at a time when it was not considered suitably 'elevated' for literature. Burns's first volume, *Poems, Chiefly in the Scottish Dialect*, appeared in 1786. In addition to his poetry (such as 'To a Mouse'), Burns wrote or adapted many songs, including 'Auld Lang Syne'. **Burns Night** is celebrated on 25 January, his birthday.

Burns is recognized as the culminating figure in two centuries' tradition of folk song and genre poetry and one of the greatest of all writers of love songs. Although not a Romantic himself, the example of his work was one of the vital influences in the coming Romantic movement. He contributed some 300 songs to James Johnson's *Scots Musical Museum* (1787–1803) and Thomson's *Select Collection of Original Scottish Airs* (1793–1841). Whether composing original pieces or, as in the case of 'Auld Lang Syne', revitalizing a song which had already passed through more than one version, he had the touch of lyric genius. To this he added a power of vitriolic satire, shown in such poems as 'Holy Willie's Prayer', and a command of vivid description that appears at its best in 'Tam o' Shanter' and 'The Jolly Beggars'.

Born in Alloway, near Ayr, he became joint tenant with his brother Gilbert of his late father's farm at Mossgiel in 1784, but it was unsuccessful. Burns intended to emigrate to Jamaica with Mary Campbell as his wife, but she died. In 1786, to earn money for his passage, he published *Poems, Chiefly in the Scottish Dialect*. It was an immediate success and contained much of his best work especially in social criticism. Burns was thereafter welcomed among intellectuals and aristocrats and was dissuaded from going abroad.

---

*My heart's in the Highlands, my heart is not here; / My heart's in the Highlands a-chasing the deer; / Chasing the wild deer, and following the roe, / My heart's in the Highlands, wherever I go.*

**Robert Burns** Scottish poet.
'My Heart's in the Highlands'

---

## Burton, Richard stage name of Richard Walter Jenkins (1925–1984)

Welsh stage and screen actor. He had a rich, dramatic voice but his career was dogged by personal problems and an often poor choice of roles. Films in which he appeared with his wife Elizabeth Taylor include *Cleopatra* (1963) and

*Who's Afraid of Virginia Woolf?* (1966). Among his later films are *Equus* (1977) and *Nineteen Eighty-Four* (1984).

Other films include *Beckett* (1964) and *The Spy Who Came in from the Cold* (1966). His rendition of Dylan Thomas's *Under Milk Wood* for radio was another of his career highlights. He won acclaim for his stage performances in both Shakespearean and contemporary dramas throughout his film career.

## Burton upon Trent

Town in Staffordshire, central England, northeast of Birmingham; population (1991) 60,500. Burton has been known since the 11th century for its beer and is still the UK's principal brewing centre, with five major breweries in operation. It is also the home of Marmite, produced here since 1902 from the yeast by-products. Burton's brewing heritage is illustrated at the Bass Museum.

## Bury

Industrial city in Greater ◊Manchester, northwest England, on the River Irwell, 16 km/10 mi north of central Manchester; population (1991) 62,600. Bury prospered during the industrial revolution when cotton and paper-making industries flourished here, using water from the Irwell as a source of power. The town is perhaps best known for its black pudding.

*Features*

The market place includes a statue of Robert ◊Peel, founder of the modern police force, who was born near Bury. Bury Art Gallery includes a collection of paintings by Turner, Constable, and other 19th-century artists.

## Bury St Edmunds

Market town in Suffolk, eastern England, on the River Lark, 43 km/27 mi east of Cambridge; population (1991) 31,200. It was named after St Edmund, the last Saxon king of East Anglia, and there are remains of a large Benedictine abbey.

*History*

Bury St Edmunds was the first planned town in Norman Britain, laid out on a grid pattern by Abbot Baldwin (1065–97). On 14 November 1214 (St Edmund's Day) Cardinal Langton, archbishop of Canterbury, and the barons swore at the high altar of the abbey church to force King John to sign the ◊Magna Carta.

## Busby, Matt (1909–1994)

Scottish football player and manager, synonymous with the success of Manchester United both on and off the field. He was best known as manager of Manchester United 1945–1969. His 'Busby Babes' won the championship in 1952, 1956, and 1957, before eight members were tragically killed in an air crash in Munich in 1958. Busby's reassembled team reached the 1958 FA Cup final, and won the FA Cup in 1963. The team went on to win the European Cup in 1968, the first English side to do so.

## Butler, 'Rab', Baron Butler of Saffron Walden (1902–1982)

British Conservative politician. As minister of education 1941–45, he was responsible for the 1944 Education Act, which established primary, secondary, and further education, and raised the school-leaving age to 15.

---

*Politics is the art of the possible.*

**Richard Austen ('Rab') Butler** British Conservative
politician.
Attributed remark

---

## Butler, Samuel (1835–1902)

English writer. He made his name in 1872 with a satiric attack on contemporary utopianism, *Erewhon* (an anagram of *nowhere*). He is now remembered for his unfinished, semi-autobiographical discursive novel, *The Way of All Flesh*, a study of Victorian conventions, the causes and effects of the clash between generations, and religious hypocrisy (written and frequently revised 1873–84 and posthumously published in 1903).

## Butlin, Billy (1899–1980)

British holiday-camp entrepreneur, born in South Africa. He went in early life to Canada, but later entered the fairground business in the UK and originated a chain of camps (the first at Skegness in 1936) that provided accommodation, meals, and amusements at an inclusive price.

## Buxton

Town and former spa in Derbyshire, central England, 54 km/34 northwest of Derby, on the River Wye, surrounded by the Peak District National Park; population (1991) 19,900. Known from Roman times for its hot springs, it is now a tourist centre and a source for bottled mineral water.

At about 300 m/984 ft above sea level, Buxton is the highest town of its size in England. It has a restored Edwardian opera house, and the **Buxton Festival** of music is held annually.

## History

The Roman settlement of **Aquae Arnemetiae** was founded here in about AD 79, the Romans being attracted by the natural spring water supplied at a constant temperature of 28°C/82°F. In the Middle Ages the town became a centre of pilgrimage, and Mary Queen of Scots was treated for rheumatism at the spa. In the 1780s, under the guidance of the 5th Duke of Devonshire, the Crescent and other buildings were built, modelled on the architecture of the fashionable spa town of Bath.

## Features

**Buxton Country Park**, to the southwest of the town, includes Poole's Cavern, a limestone cave near the source of the Wye, which has large chambers with complex stalactite and stalagmite formations. Other features are St Ann's Hotel in the Crescent; St Ann's Well; and the Micrarium, which displays exhibits as seen through a microscope, situated in the old Pump Room.

## Byrd, William (1543–1623)

English composer. His sacred and secular choral music, including over 200 motets and masses for three, four, and five voices, exemplifies the English polyphonic style.

Byrd studied under Thomas ◊Tallis as one of the children of the Chapel Royal in London. He became organist at Lincoln Cathedral in 1563. He married Juliana Birley there in 1568, and was elected a Gentleman of the Chapel Royal in 1569, but continued his duties at Lincoln until 1572, when he became organist of Queen Elizabeth's Chapel Royal jointly with Tallis. In 1575 Queen Elizabeth granted Byrd and Tallis an exclusive licence for printing and selling music and they dedicated to her their *Cantiones sacrae* published that year.

## Byron, George Gordon, 6th Baron Byron (1788–1824)

English poet. He became the symbol of ◊Romanticism and political liberalism throughout Europe in the 19th century. His poetic strength can be clearly seen in his romantic and self-dramatizing poems which, together with the events of his life, have given rise to the concept of the Byronic hero. His reputation was established with the first two cantos of *Childe Harold* (1812). Later works include *The Prisoner of Chillon* (1816), *Beppo* (1818), *Mazeppa* (1819), and, most notably, the satirical *Don Juan* (1819–24). He left England in 1816 and spent most of his later life in Italy.

Byron published his first volume *Hours of Idleness* in 1807 and attacked its harsh critics in *English Bards and Scotch Reviewers* (1809). Overnight fame came with the first two cantos of *Childe Harold*, which romantically describes his tours in Portugal, Spain, and the Balkans. In 1815 he married mathematician Ann Milbanke (1792–1860), with whom he had a daughter, Augusta Ada Byron, who also became a mathematician and worked with Charles Babbage.

---

*Except for his genius, he was an ordinary nineteenth-century English gentleman, with little culture and no ideas.*

**Matthew Arnold** English writer and critic. On Lord Byron, in *Essays in Criticism*

---

Byron and his wife separated shortly after the birth amid much scandal. He then went to Europe and became friendly with Percy and Mary Shelley. He engaged in Italian revolutionary politics and sailed to Greece in 1823 to further the Greek struggle for independence, but died of fever at Missolonghi.

## caber, tossing the (Gaelic *cabar* 'pole')

Scottish athletic sport, a ◊Highland Games event. The caber (a tapered tree trunk about 6 m/20 ft long, weighing about 100 kg/220 lb) is held in the palms of the cupped hands and rests on the shoulder. The thrower runs forward and tosses the caber, rotating it through 180 degrees so that it lands on its opposite end and falls forward. The best competitors toss the caber about 12 m/40 ft.

## Cadwalader (died *c.* 664)

Semi-mythical British king, the son of ◊Cadwallon, king of Gwynedd, North Wales, described by Geoffrey of Monmouth in his book *Historia Regum Britanniae/History of the Kings of Britain.*

## Cadwallon (lived 6th century), also Caedwalla

King of Gwynedd (*c.* 625–34), in North Wales. He allied with Penda of Mercia and in 632 defeated and killed Edwin of Northumbria at Hatfield Chase. The following year he was himself defeated and killed near Hexham by Edwin's nephew, Oswald.

---

*The only British king of historic times who overthrew an English dynasty, and the British peoples never found an equal leader.*

**F M Stenton**
Referring to Cadwallon, *Anglo-Saxon England*
2nd ed (1947)

---

## Caerleon, Welsh Caerllion

Small town in Newport unitary authority, south Wales, situated on the River Usk 5 km/3 mi northeast of Newport. Formerly a separate settlement, it is now a suburb of ◊Newport. It stands on the site of the Roman fortress of **Isca Silurum**.

There is a legionary museum and remains of an amphitheatre.

### History

Isca Silurum, planned by governor of Britain Sextus Julius Frontinus 74–78, was the headquarters of the Second Legion, which arrived here in about 75 and remained until late in the 3rd century. The place was a focal point from which a network of roads spread west and north into Wales, and was therefore one of the most important points in Roman Britain. The military quarters and amphitheatre had already been excavated when, in 1954 on an adjacent site, there was discovered a large town distinct from, but once dependent on, the fortress. It was occupied, as were similar towns at York and Chester, by the wives and families of the legionaries.

## Caernarfon, or Caernarvon

Administrative centre of ◊Gwynedd, north Wales, situated on the southwest shore of the ◊Menai Strait; population (1991) 9,700. Formerly the Roman station of **Segontium** (Caer Seint), it is now a market town, port, and tourist centre.

**Caernarfon Castle**, one of the finest examples of medieval fortifications in the British Isles, lies to the west of the town. It was built by Edward I in 1284, and is in an excellent state of preservation. It is an irregularly shaped building with 13 polygonal towers; the famous Eagle Tower was built by Edward II. The castle was besieged by Owain Glyndwr in 1402.

The first Prince of Wales (later Edward II) was born in Caernarfon Castle; Edward VIII was invested here in 1911 and Prince Charles in 1969.

## Caerphilly

Unitary authority in south Wales, created in 1996 from parts of the former counties of Mid Glamorgan and Gwent; population (1996) 172,000; area

**Caernarfon** An aerial view of Caernarfon Castle shows the imposing walls and battlements of this medieval fortification, built on a strategic site between the River Seiont and the Menai Strait. Caernarfon was one of several castles constructed by King Edward I in the late 13th century to protect his newly conquered lands in Wales. Michael St Maur Sheil/Collections

270 sq km/104 sq mi. The principal towns are Hengoed (administrative headquarters), ◊Caerphilly, Bargoed, Newbridge, and Rhymney.

*Physical*
The rivers Rhymney and Sirhowy flow through the authority.

*Features*
Caerphilly Castle, built in the 13th century, is considered one of the finest defensive castles in Britain.

*Economy*
Iron and steel production and coalmining have been replaced by a wide range of light industries.

## Caerphilly, Welsh Caerffili

Market town in the unitary authority of Caerphilly, south Wales, 11 km/7 mi north of Cardiff; population (1991) 35,900. **Caerphilly Castle**, built by the Anglo-Norman Earl Gilbert de Clare, mainly between 1268–1271, is one if the finest concentric castles (castle within a castle) in Wales, and has a double moat. The town gives its name to a mild, white cheese.

When the Welsh rebellions ended, the castle started to fall into decay; during Elizabethan times the stone was taken for other building work.

Restoration work began in the 19th century and has continued in the 20th century.

## Cairngorm Mountains

Granite mountain group in Scotland, northern part of the ◊Grampian Mountains, between the River Dee and the upper Spey. The central range includes four out of five of Britain's highest mountains: Ben Macdhui (1,309 m/4,296 ft), Braeriach (1,296 m/4,251 ft), Cairn Toul (1,291 m/4,235 ft), and Cairn Gorm (1,245 m/4,084 ft). Cairn Gorm can be accessed by chair-lift.

The winter snowfall is heavy, and winds are higher than normally encountered in mountain ranges on the exposed and extensive plateau. Mountaineering, rock- and snow-climbing, skiing, deer hunting, grouse shooting, and angling are popular. Large herds of red deer are found in the hills, as are Britain's only herd of reindeer.

## Caledonia

Roman term for the Scottish Highlands, inhabited by the Caledoni. The tribes of the area remained outside Roman control – they were defeated but not conquered by Agricola in AD 83–84 and again by Septimius Severus who reached beyond modern Aberdeen in 208. Since the 18th century, the name has been revived as a romantic alternative for the whole of Scotland.

## Caledonian Canal

Waterway in northwest Scotland, 98 km/61 mi long, linking the Atlantic and the North Sea. Situated between the Moray Firth and Loch Linnhe, the canal was constructed as a transport route to save the long sail around Scotland. It is one of Scotland's largest marina facilities. Of its total length, only a 37 km/22 mi stretch is artificial, the rest being composed of lochs Lochy, Oich, and Ness.

Thomas ◊Telford began construction of the canal in 1803 and it was completed by 1822.

## Callanish, or Calanais, or Challernish

Village on the Isle of ◊Lewis, in the Outer Hebrides group, Western Isles unitary authority, Scotland, situated on the east shore of East Loch Roag, 25 km/16 mi west of Stornoway. The megalithic standing stones of Callanish are regarded as one of the most impressive prehistoric monuments in Britain.

The monument features an alignment of parallel stones culminating at one end in a circle, which contains a large stone cairn and is intersected by a cross.

## Cambrian Mountains

Region of hills, plateaux, and deep valleys in Wales, 175 km/ 110 mi long, linking Snowdonia in the northwest and the Brecon Beacons and Black Mountains in the south.

The Cambrian Mountains are in the heart of Wales, the source of the Severn, Towy, and Wye rivers. The highest peak is Aran Fawddwy (905m/ 2,950 ft) in the Berwyn Mountains in the centre. The area is sparsely populated, with livestock farming the chief occupation.

## Cambridge

Historic city and administrative headquarters of ◊Cambridgeshire, eastern England, on the River Cam, 80 km/50 mi north of London; population (1994 est) 117,000. Lying on the southern edge of the ◊Fens, Cambridge is a thriving agricultural market town and a centre of high-technology and computer-based research industries. The seat of ◊Cambridge University from the 13th century, it is also a major tourist destination known for some of Britain's most outstanding architectural treasures. The city hosts a variety of annual festivals

and events including Strawberry Fair, the Cambridge Folk Festival, and an international arts festival.

*Features*

The Backs, an ancient strip of land by the banks of the Cam overlooking the colleges, command the most famous views of the colleges, King's College Chapel, and the river, with its many bridges and punts. The city centre is compact, and in addition to those of the university, it has a wealth of fine historic buildings. St Benet's church, with a Saxon tower dating from about 1000, is the oldest building in Cambridge.

The Holy Sepulchre or Round Church, dating from about 1130, is the oldest of four round churches in England. Cambridge's theatres and concert venues include the recently refurbished Arts Theatre, the ADC Theatre, and the restored Corn Exchange, a venue for opera, concerts, and musicals.

*Museums and galleries*

The Fitzwilliam Museum's varied collections include Egyptian sarcophagi and mummies as well as Greek and Chinese vases; its collection of paintings includes works by Titian, Hogarth, and Picasso. Other museums include the Cambridge and County Folk Museum, the Museum of Archaeology and Anthropology, and the Sedgwick Museum which includes the oldest geological collection in the world. Kettle's Yard gallery houses a large collection of 20th-century art and sculpture, including works by Henry Moore and Barbara Hepworth.

## Cambridgeshire

County of eastern England, which has contained the unitary authority of ◊Peterborough since April 1998; population (1996) 703,100; area 3,410 sq km/1,316 sq mi. The county is mostly flat with large areas of fenland; it has some of the richest agricultural land in Britain. The principal towns and cities are ◊Cambridge (administrative headquarters), ◊Ely, Huntingdon, March, Wisbech, St Neots, and Whittlesey.

*History*

In Celtic times, the northern part of Cambridgeshire was in the territory of the Iceni, while the remainder was controlled by the Catuvellauni. There are remains of pre-Roman earthworks, while relics of the Roman occupation, such as roads, amphorae, and coins, are common. The inhabitants of the district resisted the Norman invasion stubbornly, and it was at Ely that Hereward the Wake held out against the Normans for some years. The county was later prominent in the bitter struggles under kings Stephen, John, Henry III, and Charles I.

*Physical*

Although the county is generally very flat, there are hills in the south (the Gog Magog Hills), in the southeast (near Weston Colville, West Wickham, and Castle Camps), and in the west. The south is more wooded than the rest of the county. The rivers Nene, Ouse (with tributaries Cam, Lark, and Little Ouse), and Welland travel along largely man-made channels. They overflow to create flood meadows in winter. Bedford Level is a peaty area of the fens in the east.

*Features*

Cambridge has the fine college buildings and chapels of ◊Cambridge University as well as the city's churches and Guildhall. Ely has one of the largest cathedrals in England, with a notable octagonal 'lantern' tower. The monasteries at Thorney and Ramsey were founded before the Norman Conquest. There are outstanding examples of medieval architecture, especially in the county's many fine churches. There are medieval bridges at Huntingdon, Wansford, and St Ives. Country houses include Anglesey Abbey at Lode, a partly medieval, partly Tudor house; the 18th-century Wimpole Hall; and houses at Elton and Hinchingbrooke. Whittlesey has a Straw Bear festival in January, originally a fund-raising entertainment by agricultural labourers,

now a growing folk event. The Imperial War Museum at Duxford houses a collection of military aircraft from both world wars and presents air shows in summer. Wicken Fen, near Ely, is a managed area of ancient fenland, important for wild flowers and butterflies.

*Economy*

Cambridgeshire is one of the chief cereal and sugar-beet producing districts of England; fruit and vegetables are grown, and there is also dairy farming and sheep-rearing. Industries include brewing, paper, electronics, food processing, and mechanical engineering; there are also scientific, medical, pharmaceutical, and technology research and development establishments.

## Cambridge University

English university, one of the earliest in Europe, founded in the 12th century. The university was a centre of Renaissance learning and Reformation theology, and more recently has excelled in scientific research. For colleges, see list, with dates of foundation.

According to tradition the university was founded by scholars who had left Oxford because of conflict with the people of the town.

Some of the colleges of the university back onto the gardens and lawns through which the River Cam flows (known as 'the Backs'). King's College Chapel, dating from 1446, has a richly decorated

## Cambridge University Colleges

| year founded | college | year founded | college |
| --- | --- | --- | --- |
| 1284 | Peterhouse | 1695 | Homerton |
| 1326 | Clare | 1800 | Downing |
| 1347 | Pembroke | 1869 | Girton |
| 1348 | Gonville and Caius | 1871 | Newnham[1] |
| 1350 | Trinity Hall | 1882 | Selwyn |
| 1352 | Corpus Christi | 1885 | Hughes Hall[2] |
| 1441 | King's | 1896 | St Edmund's |
| 1448 | Queen's | 1954 | New Hall[1] |
| 1448 | Christ's | 1960 | Churchill |
| 1473 | St Catharine's | 1964 | Lucy Cavendish[12] |
| 1496 | Jesus | 1964 | Darwin |
| 1511 | St John's | 1965 | Wolfson[2] |
| 1542 | Magdalene | 1966 | Clare Hall |
| 1546 | Trinity | 1966 | Fitzwilliam |
| 1584 | Emmanuel | 1977 | Robinson |
| 1596 | Sidney Sussex | | |

[1] women's colleges [2] colleges for mature students

interior with extravagant fan-vaulting and a carved organ screen which is one of the earliest examples of Italianate Renaissance woodcarving in England. The altarpiece, the *Adoration of the Magi* by Rubens, was donated to King's in 1961. The collection of books in the university library (built 1931–34) includes the first book ever printed in English.

## Camden
Inner borough of northwest Greater London; population (1991) 170,400. It includes the districts of ◊Bloomsbury, Fitzrovia, ◊Hampstead, Highgate, Holborn, and Somers Town.
*Features*
St Pancras station (1868); Highgate Cemetery (1839), burial place of George Eliot, Michael Faraday, Karl Marx, and Herbert Spencer; new British Library (opened 1997); Inns of Court; Hatton Garden, centre of the diamond trade; the London Silver Vaults; Camden Lock street market; Hampstead Heath; the Roundhouse, Chalk Farm (1846), a former engine shed, to be converted into the British Architectural Library; ◊Kenwood House; the ◊British Museum.

## Camden Town Group
School of British painters (1911–13), based in Camden, London, led by Walter ◊Sickert. The work of Spencer Gore (1878–1914) and Harold Gilman (1876–1919) is typical of the group, rendering everyday town scenes in Post-Impressionist style. In 1913 they merged with another group to form the London Group.

## Camelot
Legendary seat of King ◊Arthur and name of the company that operates the National Lottery.

A possible site of Authur's Camelot is the Iron Age hillfort of South Cadbury Castle in Somerset, England, where excavations from 1967 have revealed remains dating from 3000 BC to AD 1100, including those of a large 6th-century settlement, the time ascribed to Arthur.

## Campaign for Nuclear Disarmament, CND
Nonparty-political British organization advocating the abolition of nuclear weapons worldwide. Since its foundation in 1958, CND has sought unilateral British initiatives to help start, and subsequently to accelerate, the multilateral process and end the arms race.

The movement was launched by the philosopher Bertrand Russell and Canon John Collins and grew out of the demonstration held outside the government's Atomic Weapons Research Establishment at Aldermaston, Berkshire, at Easter 1956. CND is part of Abolition 2000, a global network, founded in 1995 and with organized support in 76 countries, to press for the elimination of nuclear weapons.

## Campbell, Donald (1921–1967)
British car and speedboat enthusiast, son of Malcolm Campbell, who simultaneously held the land-speed and water-speed records. In 1964 he set the world water-speed record of 444.57 kph/276.3 mph on Lake Dumbleyung, Australia, with the turbojet hydroplane *Bluebird*, and achieved the land-speed record of 648.7 kph/403.1 mph at Lake Eyre salt flats, Australia. He was killed in an attempt to raise his water-speed record on Coniston Water, England.

## Campbell, Malcolm (1885–1948)
British racing driver who once held both land- and water-speed records. He set the land-speed record nine times, pushing it up to 484.8 kph/301.1 mph at Bonneville Flats, Utah, USA, in 1935, and broke the water-speed record three times, the best being 228.2 kph/141.74 mph on Coniston Water, England, in 1939. His car and boat were both called *Bluebird*. His son Donald ◊Campbell emulated his feats.

## Campbell, Mrs Patrick born Beatrice Stella Tanner (1865–1940)
English actress. Her roles included Paula in Pinero's *The Second Mrs Tanqueray* (1893) and Eliza in *Pygmalion*, written for her by George Bernard Shaw, with whom she had an amusing correspondence.

## Campion, Thomas (1567–1620)
English poet and musician. He was the author of the critical *Art of English Poesie* (1602) and four books of *Ayres* (1601–17), for which he composed both words and music.

The *Art of English Poesie* is an attack on the use of rhyme and a plea for the adoption of unrhymed metres formed on classical models.

He composed masques that are among the best of their kind, including *The Mask of Flowers*, and produced many fine lyrics notable for their metrical finish. The best known of his songs are 'There is a Garden in her Face' and 'My Sweetest Lesbia, Let Us Live and Love', a translation from Catullus.

## canals
The first major British canal was the ◊Bridgewater Canal 1759–61, constructed for the 3rd Duke of

Bridgewater to carry coal from his collieries to Manchester. The engineer, James ◊Brindley, overcame great difficulties in the route. Today many of Britain's canals form part of an interconnecting system of waterways some 4,000 km/2,500 mi long. Many that have become disused commercially have been restored for recreation and the use of pleasure craft. In 1998 167 km/104 mi of canals in the UK were classed as Sites of Special Scientific Interest.

## Canary Wharf

420 thousand-sq m/4.5 million-sq ft office development on the Isle of Dogs in London's ◊Docklands, the first phase of which was completed in 1992, along with the foundations for a further 740 thousand sq m/8 million sq ft. The complex of offices, surrounding landscaped squares, is best known for its central skyscraper, the second tallest in Europe at 244 m/800 ft.

## Canterbury

Historic cathedral city in Kent, southeast England, on the River Stour, 100 km/62 mi southeast of London; population (1991) 36,500. Canterbury developed as one of the main centres of the Christian Church in England from the 6th century, and it is the seat of of the archbishop of Canterbury. ◊Canterbury Cathedral, St Augustine's Abbey, and St Martin's Church are together a World Heritage site, and the cathedral, scene of the murder of Thomas à ◊Becket in 1170, is one of the most visited tourist attractions in the UK. The city hosts a number of annual festivals including the international Canterbury Festival, the largest mixed arts festival in Kent.

*History*

Canterbury was the site of the Roman **Durovernum Cantiacorum**, an important fortress and military station on Watling Street, the Roman road between Dover and London, and in the 6th century the Saxon town, known as **Cantwarabyrig**, was the capital of Ethelbert, king of Kent. St ◊Augustine, sent from Rome to convert England to Christianity, was welcomed here in 597 by Ethelbert, king of Kent, and he made Canterbury his see when he became the first archbishop of England in 601. The shrine of Thomas à Becket became an important place of pilgrimage in the middle ages; the poet Geoffrey Chaucer, who visited the city between 1360 and 1361, portrayed a group of pilgrims on the way to visit the shrine in his *Canterbury Tales*.

*Features*

Much of the city has been rebuilt following heavy bombing during World War II but it still has a wealth of 17th- and 18th-century buildings as well as remains of a Norman castle and the medieval city walls. Among the city's main attractions are the Canterbury Heritage Museum and the Roman Museum. The University of Kent, was established here in 1965.

*St Augustine's Abbey and St Martin's*

The ruins of St Augustine's Abbey, established here in 598, include 7th-century walling. St Martin's, one of the oldest churches in England still in use, is built partly of Roman brick and tile.

## Canterbury Cathedral

Established on the site of previous churches possibly dating back to Roman times, the present cathedral represents the finest work of four centuries, initiated by Archbishop Lanfranc, the first Norman archbishop (1070–89), following a great fire in 1067. It is in the form of a double cross, with a central and two west towers. The total length is 160 m/525 ft, the east transept measuring 47 m/154 ft. Canterbury's Norman crypt remains in its entirety, with exceptionally fine carvings. Its 12th-century choir is the most important specimen of Transitional-Norman work in England in the nascent Gothic style, using both the pointed and the rounded arch, carved capitals, and a ribbed vault. The late 14th-century nave is a masterpiece of Perpendicular style, with lierne vaults (short ribs intersecting the longer),

**Canterbury Cathedral** A view of Canterbury Cathedral from the north-west. Historically and artistically, it is one of the most important buildings in England. The oldest part of the building is the crypt, dating from the late 11th century. Externally, the dominant feature is the majestic central tower (known as 'Bell Harry'), built in the 15th century. Corbis

and strikingly lofty aisles. The cathedral's stained glass is among the finest and oldest surviving in quantity, many specimens dating from around 1200, or earlier.

Until the Reformation (1538) the Trinity Chapel was the site of Thomas à ◊ Becket's shrine, indicated by the marks worn in the stones by many generations of pilgrims. The framework for Chaucer's ◊ *Canterbury Tales* is a group of pilgrims on their way to visit the shrine of Thomas à Becket. Nearby is the tomb of Edward the Black Prince (1376), and facing it the tomb of Henry IV and his consort, Joan of Navarre.

## Canterbury, archbishop of

Archbishop of the Church of England (Anglican), the primate (archbishop) of all England, and first peer of the realm, ranking next to royalty. He crowns the sovereign, has a seat in the House of Lords, and is a member of the Privy Council. He is appointed by the prime minister.

Formerly selected by political consultation, since 1980 the new archbishops have been selected by a church group, the Crown Appointments Commission (formed in 1977). The first holder of the office was St Augustine (601–04). George Carey was appointed in 1991.

The archbishop's official residence is at Lambeth Palace, London, and second residence at the Old Palace, Canterbury.

## Canterbury Tales, The

Unfinished collection of stories in prose and verse (*c.* 1387) by Geoffrey ◊ Chaucer, told in Middle English by a group of pilgrims on their way to Thomas à ◊ Becket's tomb at Canterbury. The tales and preludes are remarkable for their vivid character portrayal and colloquial language, and they were a major influence on the development of English literature.

Each of the thirty or so pilgrims was meant to tell two stories on the way, and two on the return journey. Though it comprises 17,000 lines of prose and verse, including prologues and epilogues, the 24 stories only constitute less than a fifth of the projected work, which was never put into any proper order. They range from the sublimity of the 'Knight's Tale', to the mock heroism of the 'Nun's Priest's Tale', the humour of the 'Merchant's Tale', and the sheer bawdiness of the 'Miller's Tale'.

## Canute (c. 995–1035)

King of England from 1016, Denmark from 1018, and Norway from 1028. Having invaded England in 1013 with his father, Sweyn, king of Denmark, he was acclaimed king on his father's death in 1014 by his ◊ Viking army. Canute defeated Edmund (II) Ironside at Assandun, Essex, in 1016, and became king of all England on Edmund's death. He succeeded his brother Harold as king of Denmark in 1018, compelled King Malcolm to pay homage by invading Scotland in about 1027, and conquered Norway in 1028. He was succeeded by his illegitimate son Harold I.

Under Canute's rule English trade improved, and he gained favour with his English subjects by sending soldiers back to Denmark. The legend of Canute disenchanting his flattering courtiers by showing that the sea would not retreat at his command was first told by Henry of Huntingdon in 1130.

## Cardiff, Welsh Caerdydd

Capital of ◊ Wales, seaport, and administrative centre of Cardiff unitary authority, situated at the mouth of the Taff, Rhymney, and Ely rivers; population (1994 est) 290,000. Once Britain's principal coal-exporting port, Cardiff is now an important political, administrative, and commercial centre which has in recent years undergone a major programme of redevelopment. It is the site of some of Wales's most important historic landmarks as well as some of its newest and most popular tourist attractions. Cardiff Bay is the site of the National Assembly for Wales and the city hosts a variety of festivals including an annual summer festival.

*History*
While the city's history dates back to Roman times and a castle was built here in the Norman period, Cardiff was not a major city until the docks on the Bristol Channel were opened in 1839. It flourished in the late 19th century and early 20th century as a major coal-exporting port. Cardiff became the largest Welsh town in 1881, and the capital city of Wales in 1955.

*Features*
The civic buildings of Cardiff, including the grand City Hall and Civic Centre, reflect the city's prosperity in the Victorian and Edwardian eras. The castle in the centre of the city was the residence of the earls and marquises of Bute from the 18th century and was given to the city in 1947. Originally built on the site of a Roman fort in the late 11th century, the castle was substantially altered in the centuries that followed and it includes lavish Victorian interiors. The Norman keep survives and now includes two regimental

**Cardiff Bay** In common with many other such sites around Britain, changing patterns of manufacture and overseas trade left this former bustling dockland area derelict by the 1980s. In 1999, however, it became the site of the National Assembly for Wales. A new building for the assembly is scheduled to be completed here in 2001. Until then, the assembly meets in Crickhowell House, on the left. Malcolm Bradbury/Skyscan

museums. The National Museum of Wales illustrates the history of Wales and Cardiff, and houses a large collection of Impressionist paintings. Llandaff Cathedral, virtually rebuilt in the 19th century and restored between 1948 and 1957 after air-raid damage in World War II, contains Jacob Epstein's sculpture *Christ in Majesty*. The Cardiff Bay Millennium Waterfront regeneration project has in recent years contributed to the transformation of the docklands area of the city which now includes major attractions such as Atlantic Wharf (a large entertainment complex), Techniquest (an interactive science centre), the Welsh Industrial Maritime Museum, and the Wales Millennium Centre (a showcase for opera, dance, and museum displays). At St Fagan's 5 km/3 mi to the west is the Welsh National Folk Museum, one of the most popular tourist attractions in Wales. Cardiff Arms Park, the home of Welsh rugby, is now the site of the 75,000-seat ◊Millennium Stadium, the venue for the 1999 Rugby World Cup.

## Carisbrooke
Village southwest of Newport, Isle of Wight, England. It was once the capital of the Isle of Wight, and remains traditionally the island's principal town. Charles I was imprisoned in

**Carisbrooke Castle** (established in Roman times) from 1647 to 1648. The castle houses the Isle of Wight County Museum.

## Carlisle
City and administrative headquarters of ◊Cumbria, northwest England; population (1991) 72,400. Lying at the western end of ◊Hadrian's Wall and only 14 km/9 mi south of the Scottish border, Carlisle has a turbulent history dating back to when it was a military stronghold in Roman times. A thriving market centre, the city developed rapidly in the 19th century as a railway hub and, lying on the main line from London to Glasgow, it remains a major railway and service centre. Carlisle is the northern end of the scenic 116 km/72 mi Settle–Carlisle Railway.
### History
The frontier town **Luguvalium**, established here by the Romans in the 1st century, was raided by the Picts and other Scottish tribes. The Saxon town was sacked by the Danes and the Scots and in the 11th century the Norman king William Rufus built a castle here as a stronghold against the Scots. There were frequent border raids and Carlisle remained the scene of much conflict between the English and Scots throughout the

medieval period. The Scots gained control of the town from 1136 to 1157 and during the English Civil War, the town was a surrendered to the Scots after suffering considerable damage during a siege from 1644 to 1645. Carlisle was captured again by the Scots in 1745, during the Jacobite rising led by Charles Edward Stuart, but it was soon recaptured by the Duke of Cumberland.

### Features

Surviving as impressive evidence of Carlisle's strategic importance, **Carlisle Castle**, dating from 1092, underwent many alterations during centuries of military use but it still has its large Norman keep. The Tullie House Museum illustrates the city's history from Roman times onwards.

The cathedral, completed in 1123, was originally the church of an Augustinian priory. Rebuilt and embellished at various stages, it has a fine east window with 14th-century stained glass.

## Carlyle, Thomas (1795–1881)

Scottish essayist and social historian. His works include the partly autobiographical *Sartor Resartus/The Tailor Retailored* (1833–34), reflecting his loss of Christian belief; *The French Revolution* (1837); and the long essay 'Chartism' (1839), attacking the doctrine of *laissez faire*. His prose style was idiosyncratic, encompassing grand, thunderous rhetoric and deliberate obscurity.

Carlyle was born in Ecclefechan, Dumfriesshire. Leaving Edinburgh University without taking a degree, he supported himself by teaching while he devoted several years to intensive study of German literature. In 1826 he married Jane Baillie Welsh (1801–1866) and they moved to her farm at Craigenputtock, where *Sartor Resartus* and many of his most influential essays were written; Jane was a celebrated letter-writer, noted for her vivacity and wit. His reputation was established with *The French Revolution* and in 1834 they moved to London.

After the death of his wife in 1866 he edited her letters (1883) and prepared his *Reminiscences* (1881), which shed an unfavourable light on his character and his neglect of her, for which he could not forgive himself. The house in Cheyne Row, Chelsea, London, where Carlyle and his wife lived from 1834, is a museum.

## Carmarthenshire, Welsh **Sir Gaerfyrddin**

Unitary authority in south Wales, created in 1996; population (1996; 68,900); area 2,390 sq km/923 sq mi. It was formerly a county and then part of Dyfed between 1975 and 1996. The chief towns are ◊Carmarthen (administrative headquarters) and ◊Llanelli.

### Physical

The southern spur of the ◊Cambrian Mountains stretches across the north of the authority, including Mynydd Mallaen (459 m/1,506 ft), and the Black Mountain range is in the east. Carmarthenshire is dominated by the Vale of Tywi, but there are numerous grassy hills, mostly under 300 m/1,000 ft; the southern valleys are fertile and the hillsides afford good pasturage. The main rivers are the Tywi, Taf, and Teifi. The coastline borders the mouth of the Bristol Channel, and includes Carmarthen Bay where the mouths of the Taf and Tywi rivers meet in a beautiful estuarine setting. Along the coast are extensive sands and marshes.

### Features

Part of the ◊Brecon Beacons National Park lies in the east. Carmarthen Castle is the official residence of the Prince of Wales; Kidwelly Castle is a Norman construction to the south of Carmarthen. The Museum of the Welsh Woollen Industry is at Dre-Fach Felindre, near Llandysul, and the Boat House, home of the poet Dylan Thomas, is at Laugharne, 6 km/4 mi southeast of St Clears. The National Botanic Garden of Wales is a Millennium project, in the Regency park of Middleton Hall.

### Economy

The local economy is largely based on agriculture (dairy farming and stock-raising). There is some tourism.

## Caroline of Brunswick (1768–1821)

Queen consort of George IV of Great Britain. King George attempted to divorce her, unsuccessfully, on his accession to the throne in 1820.

Second daughter of Karl Wilhelm, Duke of Brunswick, and Augusta, sister of George III, she married her first cousin, the Prince of Wales, in 1795, but after the birth of Princess Charlotte Augusta a separation was arranged. When her husband ascended the throne in 1820 she was offered an annuity of £50,000 provided she agreed to renounce the title of queen and to continue to live abroad. She returned forthwith to London, where she assumed royal state. In July 1820 the government brought in a bill to dissolve the marriage, but Lord Brougham's brilliant defence led to the bill's abandonment. On 19 July 1821 Caroline was prevented by royal order from entering Westminster Abbey for the coronation. Her funeral a few weeks later was the occasion of popular riots.

## Carrickfergus

Seaport on Belfast Lough, County Antrim, Northern Ireland; population (1991) 32,800. The port has a large marina and a sailing school.

The well-preserved **Carrickfergus Castle** was begun in 1180, and now houses a museum. Carrickfergus was the main port of medieval Ulster but declined from the 17th century onwards, with the development of Belfast.

## Carrington, Dora (1893–1932)

English painter, a member of the ◊Bloomsbury Group. She developed a style which, in its emphasis on design and bold colours, is typical of English Post-Impressionism of the period from World War I to the 1930s. Among her best known works are an elegant portrait of her close friend, the writer Lytton ◊Strachey (1918), and the landscape *The Mill House at Tidmarsh* (1918).

## Carroll, Lewis Pen name of Charles Lutwidge Dodgson (1832–1898)

English author of the children's classics *Alice's Adventures in Wonderland* (1865) and its sequel *Through the Looking-Glass, and What Alice Found There* (1872). Among later works was the mock-heroic narrative poem *The Hunting of the Snark* (1876). He was a lecturer in mathematics at Oxford University 1855–81 and also published mathematical works.

---

*'O frabjous day! Callooh! Callay!'/ He chortled in his joy.*

**Lewis Carroll** English author. *Alice Through the Looking-Glass* (1872) ch 1

---

Dodgson first told his fantasy stories to Alice Liddell and her sisters, daughters of the dean of Christ Church, Oxford University. His two Alice books brought 'nonsense' literature to a peak of excellence, and continue to be enjoyed by children and adults alike. The reasons for their success include the illustrations of John ◊Tenniel, the eminently quotable verse, and the combination of exciting adventures, imaginative punning, and humorous characters,with a more sophisticated level of ingenious imagination which parodies everything from mathematical to literary theories. Dodgson was a prolific letter writer and one of the pioneers of portrait photography (his sitters included John Ruskin, Alfred Tennyson, and Dante Gabriel Rossetti, as well as children). He is said to be, after Shakespeare, the most quoted writer in the English language.

## Carry On films

Series of low-budget, highly profitable British comedies with an emphasis on the unsubtle double entendre. The first was *Carry On Sergeant* (1958) and the series continued for 20 years with such titles as *Carry On Nurse*, *Carry On Spying*, *Carry On Screaming*, and *Carry On Doctor*. *Carry On Columbus* (1992), starring a combination of *Carry On* regulars and contemporary comic talent, was a late and anachronistic addition to the series.

All were produced by Peter Rogers and directed by Gerald Thomas. Regular stars included Kenneth Williams, Charles Hawtrey, Sid James, Joan Sims, Barbara Windsor, and Hattie Jacques.

## Carter, Angela (1940–1992)

English writer of the magic realist school. Her works are marked by elements of Gothic fantasy, a fascination with the erotic and the violent, tempered by a complex lyricism and a comic touch. Her novels include *The Magic Toyshop* (1967; filmed in 1987) and *Nights at the Circus* (1984). She co-wrote the script for the film *The Company of Wolves* (1984), based on one of her stories. Her last novel was *Wise Children* (1991).

*Shaking a Leg: Collected Writings and Journalism*, edited by Jenny Uglow, was published posthumously in 1997.

## Carter, Howard (1873–1939)

English Egyptologist. He discovered the virtually intact tomb of Tutankhamen, an Egyptian king of the 18th dynasty. This important archaeological find was made in 1922 in the Valley of the Kings at Luxor with the British archaeologist Lord Carnarvon, although the sealed door was not opened until February 1923.

Carter worked on numerous Egyptian sites, including the ancient city of Tell el Amarna in Upper Egypt with the archaeological survey led by Flinders Petrie 1891–99, and conducted excavations as an inspector in the antiquities department of the Egyptian government.

The contents of Tutankhamen's tomb included many works of art and his solid-gold coffin, which are now displayed in a Cairo museum. An exhibition in the British Museum in 1972 celebrated the 50th anniversary of the discovery of the royal tomb and attracted a record 1.6 million visitors.

## Casement, Roger (1864–1916)

Irish nationalist. While in the British consular service, he exposed the ruthless exploitation of the

**Howard Carter** British archaeologist Howard Carter (right) at the opening of Tutankhamen's tomb at Luxor, Egypt, in 1922. Carter spent ten years making a detailed record of the tomb; his work here is regarded as the most important single piece of excavation in the history of Egyptology. Corbis

people of the Belgian Congo and Peru, for which he was knighted in 1911 (degraded 1916).

In 1914 Casement went to Germany and attempted to induce Irish prisoners of war to form an Irish brigade to take part in a republican insurrection. He returned to Ireland in a submarine in 1916 (actually to postpone, not start, the Easter Rising), was arrested, tried for treason, and hanged.

## castles
Fortified buildings or group of buildings, characteristic of medieval Britain. Outstanding examples are the 13th-century ◊Caernarfon Castle, with its unique polygonal towers; and the 14th-century ◊Warwick Castle.

The **motte and bailey** castle was introduced to England after the Norman Conquest in 1066. The motte was a mound of earth, topped by a wooden tower, while the bailey was a courtyard below, containing the main dwellings. The first **rectangular stone keep** was the White Tower in the ◊Tower of London, begun in 1078. Entrance was usually at upper first floor level.

During the 12th century more substantial defensive systems were developed, based in part on the Crusaders' experiences of sieges during the First Crusade of 1096. The first **curtain walls** with projecting towers were built at this time, as at Framlingham, Suffolk. In the 13th century **round towers** were introduced, both for curtain walls, as at ◊Pembroke, Wales, and for keeps, as seen at ◊Conisbrough, Yorkshire. **Concentric planning**, with two rings of walls protecting the inner buildings, may be found in the castles built by Edward I in Wales, such as Caernarfon, ◊Beaumaris, and ◊Harlech. **Fortified town walls** became increasingly common during this period.

With the first use of gunpowder in the 14th century, gunports were included in curtain walls, such as those at ◊Bodiam, Sussex, but in the face of this new weapon castles became less defensible, and increases in civil order led to their replacement in the 15th century by unfortified manor houses. Fortified coastal defences, however, continued to be built in the 16th century, as at ◊Falmouth, Cornwall.

In the late 19th and early 20th centuries castlelike buildings were built as residences for the wealthy as part of the Romantic revival in Britain, ◊Castle Drogo, Devon, being a notable example.

## Castle Coole
Classical house southeast of Enniskillen, County Fermanagh, Northern Ireland. It was built 1790–96 by James Wyatt, and contains plasterwork by Joseph Rose (1745–99) and furniture lent by the Earl of Belmore. The 32 ha/79 acre estate was given to the National Trust by the Ulster Land Fund in 1951.

## Castle Drogo
20th-century granite castle near Drewsteignton, Devon, built by Edwin ◊Lutyens between 1910 and 1930 on a 274 m/899 ft rocky outcrop above the River Teign. The castle was given to the National Trust in 1974, together with the Elizabethan Whiddon Deer Park.

## Castlereagh, Robert, Viscount Castlereagh (1769–1822)
British Tory politician. As chief secretary for Ireland 1797–1801, he suppressed the rebellion of 1798 and helped Pitt the Younger secure the union of England, Scotland, and Ireland in 1801. As foreign secretary 1812–22, he coordinated European opposition to Napoleon and represented Britain at the Congress of Vienna 1814–15.

Castlereagh sat in the Irish House of Commons from 1790. When his father, an Ulster landowner, was made an earl in 1796, he took the courtesy title of Viscount Castlereagh. In Parliament he was secretary for war and the colonies 1805–06 and 1807–09, when he had to resign after a duel with foreign secretary George Canning. During his time as foreign secretary, he devoted himself to the overthrow of Napoleon and subsequently to the congress system. His policy abroad favoured the development of material liberalism, but at home he repressed the parliamentary reform movement, and popular opinion held him responsible for the ◊Peterloo massacre of peaceful demonstrators in 1819.

## Castle Rising
Village in Norfolk, England, 6 km/4 mi northeast of King's Lynn. There are the ruins of a large Norman castle here, built around 1150 by William de Albini, Earl of Sussex, and now managed by English Heritage. The keep is one of the largest in England. Isabella of France was exiled to Castle Rising following the murder of Edward II.

Castle Rising is also the site of the 12th-century church of St Lawrence, and of Bede House, founded by Henry Howard in 1614 for poor women. Today Bede House is an almshouse for elderly women, who wear Jacobean costume to attend church on Sundays.

## Castleton
Village in Derbyshire, England, 25 km/16 mi west of Sheffield. It is situated at the foot of a hill, on the summit of which stands Peak Castle, originally built by William Peveril on land granted to him by William (1) the Conqueror in 1068. The keep was built by Henry II in 1176. Today the castle is managed by English Heritage. The castle features in Walter Scott's novel *Peveril of the Peak*. The area around the village contains the Peak, Speedwell, and Treak Cliff Caverns, as well as the ◊Blue John Cavern, which is known for its coloured fluorspar.

## Castle Ward
Imposing 18th-century mansion in County Down, Northern Ireland, 11 km/7 mi northeast of Downpatrick. Castle Ward was reputedly one of the first houses in Ireland to exemplify 'the modern Gothic'. Standing on the southern shore of Strangford Lough, the house boasts an unusual compromise of west and east fronts in both Classical and Neo-Gothic styles. The estate includes a Victorian laundry and a wildfowl collection (the Strangford Lough Wildlife Centre), and was given to the National Trust by the Northern Ireland government in 1953.

## cathedrals
In Britain cathedrals, the principal church of a bishop or archbishop, were formerly distinguished as either monastic or secular, the clergy of the latter not being members of a regular monastic order. Some are referred to as 'minsters', such as Southwell and York, the term originating in the name given to the bishop and cathedral clergy who were often referred to as a *monasterium*. After the ◊Dissolution of the Monasteries by Henry VIII, most of the monastic churches were refounded and called Cathedrals of the New Foundation. Cathedrals of dioceses founded since 1836 include St Albans, Southwark, Truro, Birmingham, and Liverpool.

Most cathedrals were built during the Middle Ages and reflect the many styles of ◊Norman architecture, as at Durham Cathedral, and ◊Gothic architecture as at Ely Cathedral, Exeter Cathedral, Winchester Cathedral, and York Minster. ◊Canterbury Cathedral spans the Norman to Perpendicular periods. Among the few built since medieval times are the 17th-century St Paul's Cathedral and 19th-century Westminster Cathedral, London. The 20th-century saw the construction of the Liverpool (Catholic) and Guildford cathedrals, and the rebuilding of Coventry Cathedral after World War II.

In British ecclesiastical architecture, the enclosed space forming the precinct of a cathedral or monastery is known as the close, as found at Salisbury Cathedral.

## Catherine of Aragón (1485–1536)
First queen of Henry VIII of England, 1509–33, and mother of Mary I. Catherine had married Henry's elder brother Prince Arthur in 1501 and on his death in 1502 was betrothed to Henry, marrying him on his accession. She failed to produce a surviving male heir and Henry divorced her without papal approval, thus creating the basis for the English Reformation.

## Catherine of Braganza (1638–1705)
Queen of Charles II of England, 1662–85. Her childlessness and Catholic faith were unpopular, but Charles resisted pressure for divorce. She was instrumental in Charles II's return to Catholicism on his deathbed. After his death, she returned to Lisbon in 1692.

The daughter of John IV of Portugal (1604–1656), she brought the Portuguese possessions of Bombay and Tangier as her dowry and introduced tea drinking and citrus fruits to England.

## Catherine of Valois (1401–1437)

Queen of Henry V of England, whom she married in 1420; the mother of Henry VI. After the death of Henry V, she secretly married Owen Tudor (*c.* 1400–1461) in about 1425, and their son Edmund Tudor was the father of Henry VII. See genealogy on page 470.

## Catholic Emancipation

In British history, acts of Parliament passed 1780–1829 to relieve Roman Catholics of civil and political restrictions imposed from the time of Henry VIII and the Reformation.

## cavalier

Horseman of noble birth, but mainly used as a derogatory nickname to describe a male supporter of Charles I in the English Civil War (Cavalier), typically with courtly dress and long hair (as distinct from a Roundhead); also a supporter of Charles II after the Restoration.

## Cavell, Edith (Louisa) (1865–1915)

English nurse. As matron of a Red Cross hospital in Brussels, Belgium, in World War I, she helped Allied soldiers escape to the Dutch frontier. She was court-martialled by the Germans and condemned to death. The British government made much propaganda from her heroism and execution, which was cited as an example of German atrocities.

---

*I realize that patriotism is not enough. I must have no hatred or bitterness towards any one.*

**Edith Cavell** English hospital matron in World War I.
Last words 12 October 1915, quoted in *The Times* 23 October 1915

---

## Caxton, William (*c.* 1422–1491)

First English printer. He learned the art of printing in Cologne, Germany, in 1471 and set up a press in Belgium where he produced the first book printed in English, his own version of a French romance, *Recuyell of the Historyes of Troye* (1474). Returning to England in 1476, he established himself in London, where he produced the first book printed in England, *Dictes or Sayengis of the Philosophres* (1477).

The books from Caxton's press in Westminster included editions of the poets Chaucer, John Gower, and John Lydgate (*c.* 1370–1449). He translated many texts from French and Latin and revised some English ones, such as Malory's *Morte d'Arthur*. Altogether he printed about 100 books.

---

*And certaynly our langage now used varyeth ferre from that which was used and spoken when I was borne.*

**William Caxton** The first English printer. 1490

---

## Cecil, Robert, 1st Earl of Salisbury (1563–1612)

Secretary of state to Elizabeth I of England, succeeding his father, Lord Burghley; he was afterwards chief minister to James I (James VI of Scotland) whose accession to the English throne he secured. He discovered the ◊Gunpowder Plot, the conspiracy to blow up the King and Parliament 1605.

## Celt

Member of an Indo-European tribal people that originated in Alpine Europe about 1200 BC and spread throughout Europe and beyond, settling in the British Isles from about the 5th century BC (see ◊Ancient Britain). The Celts had a distinctive religion, led by Druids, and were renowned for their horsemanship, ferocity in battle, and their ritual savagery. They were subjugated by the invading Romans after AD 43, leaving only Ireland unscathed.

There was a resurgence of ◊Celtic art and culture after the end of the Roman era, and a thriving Celtic church. After the 11th century the Celts were gradually absorbed, conquered, and mostly assimilated into English-based culture. The most important legacy of the Celtic presence is in language, both in place names, especially those of rivers, and in Scottish Gaelic, Irish Gaelic, Welsh, Manx, and Cornish. The island of Iona is regarded as the cradle of the Celtic kingdom of Scotland.

## Celtic art

Art of the Celtic peoples of western Europe, emerging about 500 BC, probably on the Rhine, and flourishing only in Britain and Ireland from the 1st century BC to the 10th century AD. In Britain, Celtic art may be divided into two broad

**Celtic Art** The Celtic cross is a distinctive feature of Celtic Christianity. The Celtic religion spread to Britain and Ireland from the 1st century BC, and prevailed until the 10th century AD. The design of this symbol, a cross in a circle, is said to derive ultimately from the ancient Egyptian symbol of life, known as the *ankh*. Corbis

periods: the pre-Christian (from 250 BC) and the Christian (from AD 597); the influence of Anglo-Saxon culture may be found from AD 400.

Pre-Christian metalwork was commonly in bronze or possibly gold (for example, the Ipswich torques, about 50 BC), and weapons, bracelets, and horse harness and trappings were frequently decorated. Repoussé work has been found throughout the British Isles, and the designs are sometimes enriched by yellow, blue, green, and red enamel, millefiori glass, or patches of coloured vitreous pastes. A unique oval bronze shield, recovered from the River Thames, has 27 settings of red enamel. Typical designs were based on animal and plant motifs and formed semi-abstract patterns of divergent spirals of whorls and elliptical curves. Engraved lines or dots filled the pattern, highlighting the plain groundwork.

With the arrival of Christianity and the introduction of new artefacts, many fresh elements of ornament appeared, such as fretwork (geometrical carving), interlaced work, and shaped designs. Sculpture in the form of large stone crosses is also a distinctive feature of this period. The ◊Lindisfarne Gospels (690; British Museum, London), with their intricately illuminated pages, clearly show the flowing designs previously associated with Celtic applied arts. The main collections of Celtic art are in the British Museum.

## Ceredigion

Unitary authority in southwest Wales, created in 1996 from part of the former county of Dyfed, of which it was a district; population (1996) 68,900; area 1,793 sq km/ 692 sq mi. Its western coastline on Cardigan Bay attracts tourists; the east is mountainous. The principal towns are ◊Aberaeron (administrative headquarters), ◊Aberystwyth, Cardigan, Lampeter, Llandyssul, and Tregaron.
*Physical*
Ceredigion extends from the mouth of the River Dovey in the north to the mouth of the Teifi in the south. The interior contains part of the Cambrian Mountains, including Plynlimon Fawr (752 m/2,468 ft). The rivers Teifi, Rheidol, Ystwyth, Aeron, and Tywi flow through Ceredigion.

*Features*
There are remains of Roman roads and military stations, and inscribed stones. The ruins of the 12th-century Strata Florida Abbey are to the southeast of Aberystwyth. Devil's Bridge spans the Rheidol Falls. The National Library of Wales is in Aberystwyth.
*Economy*
The local economy is founded on agriculture, tourism, and small enterprises. In the north and northeast there are large sheep farms, while in the lower parts of the district, milk production is important. There is a large milk-collecting and processing factory at Felinfach. There are a number of small woollen mills, and a considerable amount of tourist traffic at the coastal resorts of Borth, Aberystwyth, Aberaeron, New Quay, Tresaith, Llangranog, and Aberporth. The rivers and lakes are noted for freshwater fishing, while fishing from coracles (an ancient design of boat) still survives on the River Teifi.

## Chamberlain, Neville (1869–1940)

British Conservative politician, son of Joseph Chamberlain. He was prime minister 1937–40; his policy of appeasement toward the Italian fascist dictator Benito Mussolini and German Nazi Adolf Hitler (with whom he concluded the Munich Agreement in 1938) failed to prevent the outbreak of World War II. He resigned in 1940 following the defeat of the British forces in Norway.

## Chamberlain, Lord

The only officer of state whose position survives from Norman times; responsibilities include the arrangements for the opening of Parliament, assisting with the regalia at coronations, and organizing the ceremony when bishops and peers are created. The post is part-time and the symbols of the office are a white staff and key, which are carried on ceremonial occasions. In the Middle Ages the King's Chamberlain often acted as the monarch's spokesman in council and parliament. It remained a political appointment until 1924.

## chamber music

Chamber music, intended for performance in a small room or chamber, rather than in the concert hall, and usually written for instrumental combinations, developed as an instrumental alternative to music for voices such as the madrigal; madrigals published in England in the 16th and 17th centuries were often designed to be playable on instruments. A peculiarly English form was the 'fantasy' or 'fancy' for stringed instruments or keyboard, a free composition not restricted by the structures of dance or variation form. The idea of 'fantasy' chamber music was revived in Britain in the early 20th century, with the establishment of a composition prize for such pieces. William ◊ Byrd also wrote works specifically for instruments, to which texts were set subsequently.

Chamber music continued to develop during the 17th and 18th centuries, through musical clubs (such as those that existed in London and Oxford) and the patronage of royalty – Charles II had a private band of musicians. The expertise of English viol players was much in demand in the courts of Europe at this time. In the mid-18th century, London was an important centre for the publication of 'accompanied keyboard sonatas', works for keyboard with violin or cello accompaniment, that are the direct precursors of intrumental sonatas and piano trios.

In the 19th century few British composers wrote for chamber forces, although works from the Classical repertoire were heard in concert series. In the 20th century the human voice began to be used in chamber music; in Britain chamber works with voice were written by ◊ Vaughan Williams, Maxwell Davies, and ◊ Holst, among others. Chamber operas and symphonies have also been written, the size of their forces partly dictated by commercial considerations. Many British festivals now present concerts of chamber music, and a number of universities have resident chamber ensembles.

## Chancellor, Lord, (Latin cancellarius)

State official, originally the royal secretary, today a member of the cabinet, whose office ends with a change of government. The Lord Chancellor acts as Speaker of the House of Lords, may preside over the Court of Appeal, and is head of the judiciary; the office is now always held by a lawyer.

## chancellor of the Exchequer

Senior cabinet minister responsible for the national economy. The office, established under Henry III, originally entailed keeping the Exchequer seal. The chancellor of the Exchequer has an official residence at 11 Downing Street, although the current chancellor, Gordon Brown, a bachelor, lives in the residential quarters of 10 Downing Street, allowing the prime minister and his family to live in 11 Downing Street, where the residential quarters are more spacious.

## Chanctonbury Ring

Iron Age hillfort on the West Sussex Downs, England; situated 3 km/2 mi west of Steyning; height 250 m/ 820 ft. There are also the remains of two Roman buildings here.

## Channel 4

Britain's fourth national television channel, launched on 2 November 1982 as a wholly-owned subsidiary of the IBA (Independent Broadcasting Authority; now known as the ITC or Independent Television Commission). Its brief was to serve minority interests, encourage innovation through the use of independent producers, and develop a character distinct from the other channels.

The company's financial involvement in film production, both at home and abroad, played a significant part in a revival of the fortunes of filmmaking in the UK. Films it has commissioned include *My Beautiful Laundrette* (1985), *Four Weddings and a Funeral* (1994), and *Trainspotting* (1996). It became a public broadcasting service in 1993. Channel 4 makes very few programmes, typically buying from external production companies. A separate company, ◊ S4C, serves Wales.

## Channel 5

Britain's fifth television channel. Launched on 30 March 1997, it was set up by the 1990 Broadcasting Act, under which the Independent Television Commission (ITC) was required to create a fifth national channel. It was awarded by competitive tender in 1995 to Channel 5 Broadcasting Ltd, a consortium of companies including Pearson, owners of the *Financial Times*, and United News and Media, owners of the *Daily Express* and Anglia Television.

The ITC's aim in launching Channel 5 was to introduce more competition to the advertising market. Early indications were that the channel was to pitch at a downmarket audience. Its stated aim was to include seven hours of live broadcasting, and a feature film, each day, both of which targets were compatible with its low commissioning budget. Channel 5 is the first UK TV channel to display a continuously broadcast on-screen logo.

## Channel Islands

Group of islands in the English Channel, off the northwest coast of France; they are a possession of the British crown. They comprise the islands of ◊Jersey, ◊Guernsey, Alderney, Great and Little Sark, with the lesser Herm, Brechou, Jethou, and Lihou.

**Area** 194 sq km/75 sq mi

**Features** very mild climate, productive soil; financially the islands are a tax haven

**Industries** farming, fishing, and tourism; flowers, early potatoes, tomatoes, butterflies, and dairy cattle are exported

**Currency** English pound, also local coinage

**Population** (1991) 145,600

**Language** official language French (Norman French) but English more widely used

**Religion** chiefly Christian

**Government** the main islands have their own parliaments and laws. Unless specially signified, the Channel Islands are not bound by British acts of Parliament, though the British government is responsible for defence and external relations

**History** originally under the duchy of Normandy, they are the only part still held by Britain. The islands came under the same rule as England in 1066, and are dependent territories of the British crown. Germany occupied the islands June 1940–May 1945, the only British soil to be occupied by the Germans during World War II.

## Channel Tunnel

Tunnel built beneath the ◊English Channel, linking Britain to mainland Europe, from just northwest of Folkestone to Sangatte, west of Calais, France. It comprises twin rail tunnels, 50 km/31 mi long and 7.3 m/24 ft in diameter, located 40 m/130 ft beneath the seabed. Construction began in 1987, and the French and English sections were linked in December 1990. It was officially opened on 6 May 1994. The shuttle train service, Le Shuttle, opened to lorries in May 1994 and to cars in December 1994. The tunnel's high-speed train service, Eurostar, linking London to Paris and Brussels, opened in November 1994. See chronology on page 82.

The estimated cost of the tunnel has continually been revised upwards to a figure of £8 billion (1995). In 1995 Eurotunnel plc, the Anglo-French company that built the tunnel, made a loss of £925 million.

*High-speed link*

The contract to build the London–Dover high-speed rail link was awarded to the London and Continental Railways Consortium in February 1996. The link, due to be completed in 2003, would allow Eurostar trains to maintain their high speeds within Britain; under existing legislation, Eurostar trains that travel at up to 300 kph/186 mph in France are forced to slow to 80 kph/50 mph once in Britain. Transit time between London and Paris is 3 hours, and 2 hours 40 minutes between London and Brussels.

A fire broke out in a freight train in the tunnel on 18 November 1996, involving 34 people who were removed to safety.

## Chaplin, Charlie (1889–1977)

English film actor and director. One of cinema's most popular stars, he made his reputation as a tramp with a smudge moustache, bowler hat, and twirling cane in silent US comedies, including *The Rink* (1916), *The Kid* (1921), and *The Gold Rush* (1925). His work combines buffoonery with pathos, as in *The Great Dictator* (1940) and *Limelight* (1952).

Chaplin was born in London and first appeared on the music-hall stage at the age of five. He joined Mack Sennett's Keystone Company in Los Angeles in 1913. Along with Mary Pickford, Douglas Fairbanks, and D W Griffith, Chaplin formed United Artists in 1919 as an independent company to distribute their films. His other films include *City Lights* (1931), *Modern Times* (1936), and *Monsieur Verdoux* (1947). *Limelight* (1952) was awarded an Academy Award for Chaplin's musical theme. When accused of communist sympathies during the Joe McCarthy witchhunt, he left the USA in 1952 and moved to Switzerland.

## Charge of the Light Brigade

Disastrous attack by the British Light Brigade of cavalry against the Russian entrenched artillery on 25 October 1854 during the ◊Crimean War at the

## Channel Tunnel: Chronology

**1751** French farmer Nicolas Desmaret suggested a fixed link across the English Channel.

**1802** French mining engineer Albert Mathieu-Favier proposed to Napoleon I a Channel tunnel through which horse-drawn carriages might travel. Discussions with British politicians ceased 1803 when war broke out between the two countries.

**1842** De la Haye of Liverpool designed an underwater tube, the sections of which would be bolted together underwater by workers without diving apparatus.

**1851** Hector Horeau proposed a tunnel that would slope down towards the middle of the Channel and up thereafter, so that the carriages would be propelled downhill by their own weight and for a short distance uphill, after which compressed air would take over as the motive power.

**1857** A joint committee of British and French scientists approved the aim of constructing a Channel tunnel.

**1875** Channel-tunnel bills were passed by the British and French parliaments.

**1878** Borings began from the French and British sides of the Channel.

**1882** British government forced abandonment of the project after public opinion, fearing invasion by the French, turned against the tunnel.

**1904** Signing of the Entente Cordiale between France and the UK enabled plans to be reconsidered. Albert Sartiaux and Francis Fox proposed a twin-tunnel scheme.

**1930–40** British prime minister Winston Churchill and the French government supported the digging of a tunnel.

**1955** Defence objections to a tunnel were lifted in the UK by prime minister Harold Macmillan.

**1961** Study Group plans for a double-bore tunnel presented to British government.

**1967** British government invited tunnel-building proposals from private interests.

**1975** British government cancelled project because of escalating costs.

**1984** Construction of tunnel agreed in principle at Anglo-French summit.

**1986** Anglo-French treaty signed; design submitted by a consortium called the Channel Tunnel Group accepted.

**1987** Legislation completed, Anglo-French treaty ratified; construction started in Nov.

**1990** First breakthrough of service tunnel took place in December.

**1991** Breakthrough of first rail tunnel in May; the second rail tunnel was completed in June.

**1994** 6 May: The Queen and President Mitterrand officially inaugurated the Channel Tunnel. November: Limited commercial Eurostar services (for foot passengers) commenced. December: Limited commercial shuttle services (for cars) commenced.

**1995** April: Eurotunnel chairman Alistair Morton warned of the risk of financial collapse. Cost of project reported at £8 billion. Complete service for cars started. September: Eurotunnel suspended interest payments on its £8 billion debt. November: The millionth car was carried through the tunnel.

**1996** 18 November: A fire broke out in a freight train injuring 34 people, and resulting in the tunnel being closed for repair.

**1997** Passenger and freight services resumed fully.

---

Battle of Balaclava. Of the 673 British soldiers who took part, there were 272 casualties. The brigade was only saved from total destruction by French cavalry.

## Charing Cross

District in Westminster, London, around Charing Cross railway station. It derives its name from the site of the last of 12 stone crosses erected by Edward I in 1290 at the resting-places of the coffin of his queen, Eleanor. The present cross was designed by A S Barry in 1865.

Charing Cross is regarded as the centre of London for the purposes of calculating distances from other towns.

## Charles

Two kings of Great Britain and Ireland:

### Charles I (1600–1649)

King of Great Britain and Ireland from 1625, son of James I of England (James VI of Scotland). He accepted the petition of right in 1628 but then dissolved Parliament and ruled without a parliament 1629–40. His advisers were Thomas, Earl of Strafford and William ◊Laud, archbishop of Canterbury, who persecuted the Puritans and provoked the Scots to revolt. The Short Parliament, summoned in April 1640, refused funds, and the Long Parliament of later that year rebelled. Charles declared war on Parliament in 1642 but surrendered in 1646 and was beheaded in 1649. He was the father of Charles II.

Charles was born in Dunfermline, Scotland, and became heir to the throne on the death of his brother Henry in 1612. He married Henrietta Maria, daughter of Henry IV of France. Friction with Parliament began shortly after Charles succeeded his father. Charles dissolved the parliaments of 1625, 1626, and 1629. During his period of rule without parliament, Charles raised money by unpopular expedients, such as ◊ship money, while the ◊Star Chamber suppressed opposition. He caused unrest in 1637 by attempting to force a prayer book on the English model on Presbyterian Scotland. After the Short Parliament, the Scots advanced into England and forced their own terms on Charles. The Long Parliament declared extraparliamentary taxation illegal, abolished the Star Chamber, and voted that Parliament could not be dissolved without its own consent.

Confident that he had support among those who felt that Parliament was becoming too radical, Charles declared war on Parliament on 22 August by raising his standard at Nottingham (see ◊ Civil War, English). Charles was defeated at the Battle of ◊ Naseby, in June 1645. In May 1646 he surrendered to the Scots, who handed him over to Parliament in January 1647.

In November 1647 Charles escaped from Hampton Court Palace, where he had been confined by the army, but was recaptured and held at Carisbrooke Castle on the Isle of Wight. He was tried by a high court of justice set up by the House of Commons in January 1649, and was executed on the 30 January in front of the Banqueting House in Whitehall, London.

## Charles II (1630–1685)

King of Great Britain and Ireland from 1660, when Parliament accepted the restoration of the monarchy after the collapse of Oliver Cromwell's Commonwealth; son of Charles I. His chief minister Edward Clarendon, who arranged Charles's marriage in 1662 with Catherine of ◊ Braganza, was replaced in 1667 with the Cabal of advisers (the initials of its five counsellors coincidentally made up the word Cabal). His plans to restore Catholicism in Britain led to war with the Netherlands 1672–74 in support of Louis XIV of France and a break with Parliament, which he dissolved in 1681. He was succeeded by James II.

During the Civil War, Charles lived with his father in Oxford 1642–45, and after the victory of Cromwell's Parliamentary forces he withdrew to France. Accepting the Scottish Presbyterian Covenanters' offer to make him king, he landed in Scotland in 1650, and was crowned at Scone on 1 January 1651. An attempt to invade England was ended 3 September by Cromwell's victory at Worcester. Charles escaped, and for nine years he wandered through Europe. In April Charles issued the Declaration of Breda, promising a general amnesty and freedom of conscience. Parliament accepted the Declaration and he was proclaimed king on 8 May 1660.

In 1673 Parliament forced Charles to withdraw the Declaration of Indulgence (which had suspended all penal laws against Catholics and Dissenters) and accept a Test Act excluding all Catholics from office. The following year Parliament forced the end of the Dutch War started in 1672. The Test Act was responsible for the end of the Cabal. In 1681 Charles summoned Parliament to Oxford, but dissolved it when compromises failed. He now ruled without a parliament, financed by Louis XIV. Charles was a patron of the arts and science, and had several mistresses.

## Charles (Charles Philip Arthur George) (1948– )

Prince of the UK, heir to the British throne, and Prince of Wales since 1958 (invested 1969). He is the first-born child of Queen Elizabeth II and the Duke of Edinburgh. He studied at Trinity College, Cambridge, 1967–70, before serving in the Royal Air Force and Royal Navy. The first royal heir since 1660 to have an English wife, he married Diana, Princess of Wales (then Lady

**Prince Charles** The heir to the British throne faces pressures unknown to previous generations of the Royal Family. Intense media interest has caused friction between Buckingham Palace and sections of the press. Charles supports a number of contemporary causes, such as organic farming, but will become king in a Britain where many question the role of monarchy in a modern democracy. Jiri Jiru/Rex

Diana Spencer), daughter of the 8th Earl Spencer, in 1981. There are two sons and heirs, William (1982– ) and Henry (1984– ). Amid much publicity, Charles and Diana separated in 1992 and were divorced in 1996. Following the death of Diana, Princess of Wales in 1997 his popularity with the British public seemed in some doubt; however opinion polls in 1998 indicated that public feeling had warmed towards him and to his long-standing relationship with Camilla Parker Bowles (1946– ).

His concern with social issues and environmental issues has led to many projects for the young and underprivileged, of which the Prince's Trust is the best known, and he has been outspoken on the subject of the unsympathetic features of contemporary architecture.

## Charles Edward Stuart, the Young Pretender or Bonnie Prince Charlie (1720–1788)

British prince, grandson of James II and son of James, the Old Pretender. In the Jacobite rebellion of 1745 Charles won the support of the Scottish Highlanders; his army invaded England to claim the throne but was beaten back by the Duke of Cumberland and routed at ♭Culloden on 16 April 1746. Charles fled; for five months he wandered through the Highlands with a price of £30,000 on his head before escaping to France. He visited England secretly in 1750, and may have made other visits. In later life he degenerated into a friendless drunkard. He settled in Italy in 1766.

## Chartism

Radical British democratic movement, mainly of the working classes, which flourished around 1838–48. It derived its name from the People's Charter, a six-point programme comprising universal male suffrage, equal electoral districts, secret ballot, annual parliaments, and abolition of the property qualification for, and payment of, members of Parliament.

Under the leadership of Fergus O'Connor, Chartism became a powerful expression of working class frustration.

## Chartwell

House near Westerham, Kent, England, bought by Winston ♭Churchill in 1922, and where he lived, with the exception of the war years, until his death in 1965. He decided to sell the house after losing the 1945 General Election, but a group of close friends bought Chartwell and gave it to the National Trust on the understanding that he

continued living there undisturbed during his lifetime.

## Chatham

Town in Medway Towns unitary authority, southeast England, on the River Medway, between Rochester to the west and Gillingham to the east; population (1991) 71,700. For four centuries Chatham was the site of England's principal naval dockyard. Following its closure in 1984, with the loss of 7,000 jobs, Chatham became the focus of revival for the whole Medway area. The dockyard was converted to an industrial area, marina, and museum, with part of the docks being preserved as the Chatham Historic Dockyard, covering 34 ha/85 acres and containing 47 ancient monuments. In 1999 the World Naval Base was launched and HMS *Cavalier*, the last surviving World War II destroyer, arrived in Chatham.

### History

First established by Henry VIII, the dockyard was developed by Elizabeth I and it was the largest naval base in England by the reign of Charles II. The *Victory*, later the flagship of Admiral Nelson at the Battle of Trafalgar, was launched here in 1765. Charles Dickens lived at Chatham between 1817 and 1821 when his father worked in the naval offices, and the area is featured in many of his novels.

### Features

Chatham Historic Dockyard includes displays illustrating nautical crafts and the history of the yard. The Lifeboat exhibition includes 15 lifeboats, and the Ropery, the dockyard's ropemaking centre, is the longest brick building in the UK, extending for approximately 402 m/1,320 ft.

## Chatsworth

House and seat of the dukes of Devonshire, 7 km/4 mi west of Chesterfield, Derbyshire, England. It was commenced by William Cavendish (1505–57). Chatsworth was gradually rebuilt in classical style from 1688 to 1707 by William, 1st Duke of Devonshire (1640–1707) with a curved north front. The courtyard plan of the Elizabethan house was retained, but a long wing was added by the 6th Duke from 1820.

The house contains one of the world's finest collection of drawings, as well as outstanding picture and book collections. The landscape architect Joseph Paxton (1801–1865) was gardener here, and some of his work remains.

It was here that Mary Queen of Scots was imprisoned under the care of the Earl of Shrewsbury.

## Chatwin, Bruce (1940–1989)

English writer. His works include *The Songlines* (1987), written after living with Australian Aborigines; the novel *Utz* (1988), about a manic porcelain collector in Prague; and travel pieces and journalism collected in *What Am I Doing Here* (1989).

## Chaucer, Geoffrey (*c.* 1340–1400)

English poet, the most influential English poet of the Middle Ages. *The ◊ Canterbury Tales*, a collection of stories told by a group of pilgrims on their way to Canterbury, reveals his genius for metre and characterization, his knowledge of human nature, and his stylistic variety, from urbane and ironic to simple and bawdy. His *Troilus and Criseyde*, is a substantial narrative poem about the tragic betrayal of an idealized courtly love.

Chaucer presented English society as had never been done before, and he wrote in English rather than in French, the language of the court and of many of his originals. Thus he developed English as a literary medium, and in doing so ensured that the Southeast Midland dialect used in London was the one ultimately to become standard English.

His early work shows formal French influence, as in the dream-poem *The Book of the Duchess* and his adaptation of the French allegorical poem on courtly love, *The Romaunt of the Rose*. More mature works reflect the influence of Italian realism, as in *Troilus and Criseyde*, adapted from Boccaccio.

Chaucer was born in London, the son of a vintner. Taken prisoner in the French wars, he had to be ransomed by Edward III in 1360. In 1366 he married Philippa Roet, becoming in later life the brother-in-law of ◊ John of Gaunt, Duke of Lancaster. He became justice of the peace for Kent in 1385 and knight of the shire in 1386. In 1389 he was made clerk of the king's works, and superintended undertakings at Woolwich and Smithfield. In 1391 he gave up the clerkship and accepted the position of deputy forester of North Petherton, Somerset in 1391. Late in 1399 he moved to Westminster and died the following year; he was buried in the Poets' Corner of Westminster Abbey.

## Cheapside (Old English *ceap*, 'barter')

Street running from St Paul's Cathedral to Poultry, in the City of London. Now a business district, it was the scene of the 13th-century 'Cheap', a permanent fair and chief general market in the city. The church of St Mary-le-Bow in Cheapside, designed by Christopher Wren, has the ◊ Bow Bells.

Various side lanes were named after their services in the market, including Milk Street, Bread Street, and Wood Street, while Cheapside itself was a centre of the goldsmiths and silversmiths trade. In the Middle Ages Cheapside was the scene of ceremonies and pageants and a place of penance and punishment. Royal tournaments were held in the open ground on the northern side, the king and nobility watching from a balcony on Bow Church. An Eleanor Cross, erected by Edward I in memory of his wife, Eleanor of Castile, stood at the junction with Wood Street until its destruction by Parliament in 1643. Cheapside extends to the east as far as Poultry, formerly the poultry-selling area of the market, which was noted for its numerous inns before the Great Fire of London in 1666.

Cheapside suffered severely from bombing in World War II. The halls of the Mercers' and Saddlers' livery companies were destroyed, but have since been restored.

## Cheddar

Village in Somerset, southwest England, in the Mendip Hills, 32 km/20 mi southwest of Bristol. It gives its name to *Cheddar cheese*, a hard variety first produced here around the beginning of the 12th century. Nearby are the limestone **Cheddar Gorge** and caves, owned by the National Trust. Tourism is important.

*Features*

**Cheddar Reservoir**, about 3 km/2 mi in circumference, lies to the west of the village. Archaeological excavations have uncovered evidence of prehistoric, Stone Age, Saxon, and Roman occupation in the area. Roman lead-mines have been found on the Mendip Hills near Cheddar, and in 1962 the site of a Saxon palace was discovered nearby. The 10,000 year-old skeleton of **Cheddar Man**, who lived in the gorge at the end of the last Ice Age, is on display in the museum.

*Cheddar Gorge and caves*

Limestone cliffs rise to nearly 150 m/490 ft on either side of Cheddar Gorge; 274 steps known as Jacob's Ladder lead to the cliff-top. The caves beneath the gorge, including Gough's Cave and Cox's Cave, have complex and richly coloured stalactites and stalagmites. Stone Age communities are believed to have lived in Gough's Cave.

## cheesemaking

Cheesemaking in Britain can be traced back to 2000 BC and the perforated curd strainers discovered on Bronze Age sites. The monks of the

Middle Ages developed cheesemaking as an important way of preserving milk. Cheese became a largely uninterrupted staple of British dairy farms until 1933 when the creation of the Milk Marketing Board provided a dependable market for milk and this, together with wartime rationing, led to a decline in farmhouse cheesemaking.

The decline was nearly fatal as some cheeses came close to extinction. In their place came mass produced block and vacuum-packed cheese. The modern revival in British cheese dates to the imposition of EEC milk quotas which led dairy farmers to diversify again.

At the end of the 20th century there were some 1,000 British cheeses on the market, with new artisan cheesemakers producing some of the best and most distinctive cheese.

## Chelmsford

Market town and administrative headquarters of ◊Essex, southeast England, 48 km/30 mi northeast of London; population (1991) 97,500. The Perpendicular church of St Mary the Virgin became a cathedral in 1914. Originally completed in 1424, it was rebuilt after most of it fell down in the early 19th century. In 1920 the first wireless-telegraph broadcasting service in the world was transmitted from Chelmsford by Marconi. The Chelmsford Cathedral Festival, a ten-day music festival, is held annually in May. The Anglia Polytechnic University was established here in 1992.

## Chelsea

Historic area of the Royal Borough of Kensington and Chelsea, London, immediately north of the Thames where it is crossed by the Albert and Chelsea bridges.

The Royal Hospital was founded 1682 by Charles II for old and disabled soldiers, 'Chelsea Pensioners', and the National Army Museum, founded 1960, covers the history of the British and Commonwealth armies. The Physic Garden for botanical research was established in the 17th century; the home of the essayist Thomas Carlyle in Cheyne Row is a museum. The **Chelsea Flower Show** is held annually by the ◊Royal Horticultural Society in the grounds of the Royal Hospital. Ranelagh Gardens (1742–1804) and Cremorne Gardens (1845–77) were popular places of entertainment.

## Cheltenham

Spa town in Gloucestershire, England, 12 km/7 mi northeast of Gloucester; population (1991) 91,300. Situated at the foot of the ◊Cotswold Hills, Cheltenham is a popular tourist destination known for its elegant Georgian architecture and its festivals. Annual events include the Cheltenham Festival of Literature in October, the International Festival of Music in July, and the National Hunt Festival in March. The steeplechase course in Prestbury Park is the venue for horse-racing's annual Cheltenham Gold Cup.

*History*
Cheltenham was a small village until the early 18th century. After the discovery of mineral spring water here in 1716, the only alkaline spring in the UK, the town gradually developed as a spa and health resort. A pump room was built in 1738 and the town was visited by George III in 1788.

*Features*
The town has much Georgian and Regency architecture, with broad avenues, squares, crescents, and terraces, reflecting the town's development as a fashionable spa. Spa waters can still be taken at the domed Pittville Pump Room. The Art Gallery and Museum includes a collection of furniture, silver, and arts and crafts. Prinknash Abbey, to the southwest, is a Benedictine house that produces pottery. Cheltenham College was founded here in 1841, and Cheltenham Ladies' College in 1853. Cheltenham is the site of the British government's electronic surveillance operations (GCHQ).

## Cheltenham Festival

The premier National Hunt fixture in British horse racing, known formally as the National Hunt Meeting. It has been held at Cheltenham Racecourse in Gloucestershire since 1910. The highlights of the three-day festival are the Cheltenham Gold Cup (first run 1924) and the Champion Hurdle (first run 1927).

## Chepstow, Welsh **Cas-Gwent**

Market town in Monmouthshire, south Wales, on the River ◊Wye near its junction with the Severn. The high tides, sometimes 15 m/50 ft above low level, are the highest in Britain. **Chepstow Castle** was possibly the first stone castle in Britain. The ruins of Tintern Abbey lie 6.5 km/4 mi to the north of the town.

The town lies on a slope between steep cliffs and is surrounded by beautiful scenery; it is a holiday centre for the Wye Valley and the Forest of Dean. The castle was built by William the Conqueror's friend, William FitzOsbern, starting in 1067; it sustained several sieges during the Civil War and is now in ruins. The remains of the town wall lead from the castle through the town. Brunel's 19th-century tubular suspension bridge across the Wye has been replaced by a modern structure.

## Chequers, popular name for Chequers Court
Country home of the prime minister. It is an Elizabethan mansion in the Chiltern hills near Princes Risborough, Buckinghamshire, and was given to the nation by Lord Lee of Fareham under the Chequers Estate Act 1917, which came into effect in 1921.

The mansion dates from 1565 or earlier, but was extensively altered by Lord Lee. It contains a collection of Cromwellian portraits and relics.

## Cheshire
County of northwest England, which has contained the unitary authorities ◊ Halton and ◊ Warrington since April 1998; population (1996) 980,000; area 2,320 sq km/896 sq mi. Cheshire borders Wales to the west. It has a long history of occupation and exploitation, and offers a diversity of historic treasures and sites. The principal towns and cities are ◊ Chester (administrative headquarters), ◊ Crewe, Congleton, and Macclesfield.

### History
Chester was a Roman fortress. From the Norman Conquest to the Tudor period, Cheshire was a county palatine (an area under an overlord that did not send representatives to Parliament).

### Physical
The county consists chiefly of a fertile plain, with the Pennines in the east. The rivers Mersey, Dee, and Weaver flow through it. A sandstone ridge extending south through central Cheshire together with Delamere Forest provide a landscape of woodland and heath.

### Features
There are salt mines and geologically rich former copper workings at Alderley Edge (in use from Roman times until the 1920s). Lindow Man, the remains of an Iron Age man found in Lindow Marsh in 1984, dates from around 500 BC. Beeston Castle dates from the 13th century. Little Moreton Hall is a well-preserved, black-and-white Tudor house near Congleton, the oldest part dating from about 1520. ◊ Tatton Park, at Knutsford, is an 18th–19th century Neo-Classical style building. Notable museums include the cotton-industry museum at Quarry Bank Mill, Styal, and the Boat Museum at Ellesmere Port. In Nantwich there is a fine 14th-century church, and also many houses from the Tudor and Georgian periods. Sandbach has two Saxon crosses and many villages have handsome churches, almost all built in the local red sandstone. ◊ Jodrell Bank is the site of the Nuffield Radio Astronomy Laboratories of the University of Manchester.

### Economy
There is arable farming in the north and cheese (Cheshire cheese) and dairy production in the centre and south of the county. There are also aerospace and motor industries, chemicals, pharmaceuticals, and textiles. Salt is still extracted, and petrochemical industries have developed around Ellesmere Port.

## Chesil Beach (Anglo-Saxon *ceosil*, 'pebble-bank')
Shingle bank extending 18 mi/29 km along the coast of Dorset, England, from Bridport in the west to the Isle of ◊ Portland in the east.

Chesil Beach connects Portland with the mainland and encloses a tidal lagoon known as the Fleet. At the Portland end the bank is about 13 m/43 ft above high water mark, and 183 m/600 ft broad. The pebbles gradually decrease in size from east to west; they are 2.5–7.5 cm/1–3 in in diameter at Portland and reach the size of peas at Bridport. At the western end of the Fleet is the Abbotsbury swannery, a wetland reserve for a breeding herd of mute swans.

The bank was formed 10,000 years ago at the end of the last glacial period, when the rise in sea level and large waves from the southwest pushed vast quantities of rock debris and sediments inshore.

The whole area of Chesil Beach and the Fleet is proposed for designation as a protected site under the European Union's habitats directive.

## Chester
Historic city and administrative headquarters of ◊ Cheshire, England, on the River Dee 26 km/16 mi south of Liverpool; population (1991) 80,100. A centre of trade and commerce, Chester is also a popular tourist destination known for its medieval centre, the most complete city walls in England, and its half-timbered two-tier galleried shops known as the 'Rows'. Chester Summer Music Festival is held annually in July and the city hosts the Chester Mystery Plays, the oldest and most complete of the four surviving mystery play cycles performed in the UK.

### History
Chester was originally established as the Roman **Deva**, a legionary fortress constructed some time between AD 70 and 79 on a sandstone bluff beside the Dee, commanding the route to North Wales.

In the medieval period it was a major port for trade with Ireland, although its importance declined when the Dee estuary began to silt up and traffic transferred to Liverpool. The city prospered during the 19th century when the development of the railway network made it an important trading centre once more.

*Features*

Much evidence of Chester's Roman past survives, the Roman Amphitheatre being the largest stone-built arena to have been discovered in Britain. Parts of the Roman walls remain and many Roman relics are displayed in the Grosvenor Museum. The Deva Roman Experience also includes archaeological finds. The Roodee, once the site of the large Roman harbour, is now the venue for the Chester Races. Chester Cathedral dates originally from the late 11th century, but work of the 14th century is dominant, and restoration was carried out between 1868 and 1876. Chester Zoo is the largest in area in the country, spreading over 324 ha/80 acres.

## Chesterfield

Market town in Derbyshire, central England, on the River Rother, to the east of the ◊ Peak District National Park, 40 km/25 mi north of Derby; population (1991) 71,900. Chesterfield's market was established some 800 years ago and is said to be England's largest. All Saints' Church, dating from the 14th century, is renowned for its twisted 69 m/228 ft-tall spire which leans nearly 3 m/9.5 ft from the true centre. The pioneer locomotive engineer George Stephenson is buried in Trinity Church.

## Chesters

Park containing the site of the Roman station of **Cilurnum**, on the banks of the North Tyne near Chollerford in Northumberland, England. Cilurnum is one of the most important forts of ◊ Hadrian's Wall, since 1987 a World Heritage Site. It was a garrison for 500 troops. The fort site is managed by English Heritage.

Remains of its gateway and streets can still be seen, and its military bathhouse, between the fort and the river, is well preserved. Much excavation work has been carried out. A collection of Roman artefacts is housed in a museum in the park of Chesters.

## Chesterton, G(ilbert) K(eith) (1874–1936)

English novelist, essayist, and poet. He wrote numerous short stories featuring a Catholic priest,

Father Brown, who solves crimes by drawing on his knowledge of human nature. Other novels include the fantasy *The Napoleon of Notting Hill* (1904) and *The Man Who Was Thursday* (1908), a deeply emotional allegory about the problem of evil.

He was also active as a political essayist, and with the writer Hilaire ◊ Belloc advocated a revolt against capitalism in the direction opposite to socialism by discouraging big business.

---

*Before the Roman came to Rye or out to Severn strode, / The rolling English drunkard made the rolling English road.*

**G K Chesterton** English novelist, essayist, and poet.
*The Rolling English Road* (1914)

---

## Cheviot Hills

Range of hills, 56 km/35 mi long, mainly in Northumberland but also extending into the Scottish Borders; they form the border between England and Scotland for some 48 km/30 mi. The Cheviots lie between the Pennines and the Southern Uplands ranges. The highest point is the **Cheviot** at 816 m/2,676 ft. For centuries the region was a battleground between the English and the Scots. The area gives its name to a breed of white-faced sheep.

The range lies in the northern part of the Northumberland National Park. In the 1920s and 1930s a major afforestation scheme was carried out, mainly over areas to the northwest, and this became a national forest park in 1955.

## Chichester

City and market town and administrative headquarters of ◊ West Sussex, southern England, 111 km/69 mi southwest of London; population (1991) 27,100. It lies in an agricultural area, and has a harbour. It was a Roman town, **Noviomagus Regnensium**, and the nearby remains of ◊ Fishbourne Palace (about AD 80) is one of the finest Roman archaeological sites outside Italy.

It has a cathedral which is mainly Norman, and the Chichester Festival Theatre (1962). Chichester has become a cultural centre, with an annual arts festival in July. ◊ Goodwood Park racecourse is nearby to the north.

## Chichester, Francis (1901–1972)

English sailor and navigator. In 1931 he made the first east–west crossing of the Tasman Sea in *Gipsy*

*Moth*, and in 1966–67 circumnavigated the world in his yacht *Gipsy Moth IV*. KBE 1967.

## Childers, Erskine (1870–1922)
British civil servant and, from 1921, Irish Sinn Féin politician; author of the spy novel *The Riddle of the Sands* (1903).

Before turning to Irish politics, Childers was a clerk in the House of Commons in London. In 1921 he was elected to the Irish Parliament as a supporter of the Sinn Féin leader Éamon de Valera, and took up arms against the Irish Free State in 1922. Shortly afterwards he was captured, court-martialled, and shot by the Irish Free State government of William T Cosgrave. His son, Erskine Hamilton Childers (1905–1974), was Irish president from 1973.

## Chiltern Hills
Range of chalk hills extending for some 72 km/45 mi in a curve from a point north of Reading to the Suffolk border. Coombe Hill, near Wendover, 260 m/852 ft high, is the highest point.

## Chippendale, Thomas (1718–1779)
English furniture designer. He set up his workshop in St Martin's Lane, London, in 1753. His trade catalogue *The Gentleman and Cabinet Maker's Director* (1754), was a significant contribution to furniture design, and the first of its type to be published. Although many of his most characteristic designs are Rococo, he also employed Louis XVI, Chinese, Gothic, and Neo-Classical styles. He worked mainly in mahogany, newly introduced from South America.

Chippendale's work is characterized by solidity without heaviness; his ribbon-backed chairs are perhaps his most notable work, followed by his settees of two or three conjoined chairs. His business was carried on by his eldest son, Thomas (1749–1822), until 1813.

## Christchurch
Resort town in Dorset, southern England, at the junction of the Stour and Avon rivers, 8 km/5 mi east of Bournemouth; population (1991) 36,400. The Norman and Early English Holy Trinity church is the longest parish church in England, extending for 95 m/312 ft. The church contains a monument to the poet Percy Bysshe Shelley. North of Holy Trinity are the ruins of **Christchurch Castle**, built in Henry I's reign, with well-preserved remains of a medieval hall. Christchurch is noted for salmon fishing and sailing. Nearby to the south is Hengistbury Head, a nature reserve.

## Christie, Agatha, born Miller (1890–1976)
English detective novelist. She is best known for her ingenious plots and for the creation of the characters Hercule Poirot and Miss Jane Marple. She wrote more than 70 novels, including *The Murder of Roger Ackroyd* (1926) and *The Body in the Library* (1942). Her play *The Mousetrap*, which opened in London in 1952, is the longest continuously running show in the world.

Her first crime novel, *The Mysterious Affair at Styles* (1920), introduced the Belgian detective Hercule Poirot. She often broke purist rules, as in *The Murder of Roger Ackroyd* in which the narrator is the murderer. She was at her best writing about domestic murders in the respectable middle-class world. A number of her books have been filmed, for example *Murder on the Orient Express* (1934), filmed in 1975.

Under the name Mary Westmacott she wrote several successful romantic novels.

## Christmas
Anniversary of the birth of Christ, celebrated on 25 December, though it is unlikely that this was the actual date of Jesus' birth. The day is traditionally spent with family and friends, and marked by present-giving, a practice that can be traced back to the Romans; eating a special **Christmas dinner**, usually roast turkey followed by **Christmas pudding**; and, often, watching television and playing family games. Children are particularly indulged. The day after Christmas is Boxing Day, which may be named after the practice of opening charity boxes hung in churches, to distribute the contents to the poor. This ceased in the early 19th century.

The custom of decorating houses and churches is probably pagan in origin, though the idea of bringing into the house and decorating a **Christmas tree** came from Germany in the reign of Queen Victoria. **Christmas cards**, exchanged in the weeks before Christmas, were introduced in 1846. **Father Christmas**, who supposedly comes down the chimney and places gifts in the children's stockings hanging by the fireplace or at the end of the bed, has a parallel in every European country. **Christmas carols** and the image of the **manger** (attributed to Francis of Assisi) date from the Middle Ages. The beginning of the celebration of Christmas cannot be dated.

## Churchill, Winston (1874–1965)
British politician, prime minister 1940–45 and 1951–55. He was an inspirational wartime leader.

**Winston Churchill** The British politician Winston Churchill had an eventful early career as a war correspondent before entering Parliament. It is as premier of a coalition government during World War II that he is best remembered; his pugnacious attitude and defiant, rousing radio broadcasts typified the nation's 'bulldog spirit' when Britain stood alone in Europe against Nazi Germany. Rex

Churchill was born at Blenheim Palace, Woodstock, Oxfordshire, the eldest son of Lord Randolph Churchill. He was educated at Harrow and Sandhurst and joined the army in 1895. As both soldier and military correspondent he served in India, Egypt, and South Africa.

He entered politics in 1900 as Conservative member of Parliament for Oldham but, disagreeing with Joseph Chamberlain's tariff reform policy, in 1906 he joined the Liberals. He was colonial undersecretary in the Liberal government 1908–10, and in 1910 became president of the Board of Trade, and introduced legislation for the introduction of labour exchanges. As home secretary in 1910, he used the army against rioting miners in Tonypandy, South Wales, and was also involved in dealing with the Sidney Street siege in 1911 (1,000 troops and armed police trapped three anarchists in an East London house, which later burnt down, killing two). He became First Lord of the Admiralty in 1911, but was forced to resign in 1915, taking responsibility for the Dardanelles disaster. He joined the army and served in the trenches in France 1915–16. In 1917 he became minister of munitions in David Lloyd George's cabinet.

He served as secretary for war and air in the coalition government 1919–21. In 1924 he rejoined the Conservatives as member of Parliament for Epping and was chancellor of the Exchequer 1924–29, returning Britain to the gold standard. He edited the government newspaper, the *British Gazette*, during the General Strike in May 1926. Out of office between 1929 and 1939, he was a severe critic of Neville Chamberlain's appeasement policy. On the outbreak of war he returned to the Admiralty, and in May 1940 he replaced Chamberlain as prime minister, leading a coalition government.

Churchill proved an inspirational wartime leader. His close relationship with the US president Franklin D Roosevelt and the signing of the 1941 Atlantic Treaty began Britain's 'special relationship' with the USA. The tripartite meeting with Roosevelt, Churchill, and Stalin in the Crimea at Yalta in 1945 planned the final defeat of Germany and its post-war occupation. In June 1945 Churchill attended the Potsdam Conference in the final stages of the war, but he was replaced by Clement Attlee in July, following the Conservative defeat in the general election.

As opposition leader Churchill was concerned

with the USSR's intentions in Eastern Europe and warned of 'the Iron Curtain' descending on Europe. He promoted the concept of a united Europe – a united Europe that Britain would be allied to but not a member of. In 1951 Churchill again became prime minister until his resignation in 1955. He remained member of Parliament for Woodford until 1964.

Churchill was a keen amateur painter and historian. His books include a six-volume history of World War II (1948–54) and a four-volume *History of the English Speaking Peoples* (1956–58). In 1995 the British government paid Winston Churchill's family £13.25 million for Churchill's pre-1945 writings, the 'Chartwell Papers', to prevent their sale abroad.

---

*The British are unique in this respect: they are the only people who like to be told how bad things are, who like to be told the worst.*

**Winston Churchill** British Conservative prime minister.
Speech, Guildhall, 1921

---

## Church in Wales
The Welsh Anglican church; see ◊Wales, Church in.

## Church of England
Established form of Christianity in England, a member of the Anglican Communion. It was dissociated from the Roman Catholic Church in 1534 under Henry VIII; the British monarch is still the supreme head of the Church of England today. The service book is the Book of Common Prayer.

The Church of England suffered its largest annual decline in Sunday service attendance for 20 years in 1995, according to the annual Church Statistics report. The average attendance was 1,045,000 – a drop of 36,000 from 1994.

In November 1992 the General Synod of the Church of England voted in favour of the ordination of women, and the first women priests were ordained in England in 1994. By 1998 there were some 860 stipendiary women clergy.

### Organization
Two archbishops head the provinces of Canterbury and York, which are subdivided into bishoprics. The Church Assembly (established in 1919) was replaced in 1970 by a General Synod with three houses (bishops, other clergy, and laity) to regulate church matters, subject to Parliament and

the royal assent. A Lambeth Conference (first held in 1867), attended by bishops from all parts of the Anglican Communion, is held every ten years and presided over in London by the archbishop of Canterbury. It is not legislative but its decisions are often put into practice. The **Church Commissioners** for England (dating from 1948) manage the assets of the church and endowment of livings.

### Main groups
The main parties, all products of the 19th century, are: the Evangelical or **Low Church**, which maintains the church's Protestant character; the Anglo-Catholic or **High Church**, which stresses continuity with the pre-Reformation church and is marked by ritualistic practices, the use of confession, and maintenance of religious communities of both sexes; and the Liberal or Modernist movement, concerned with the reconciliation of the church with modern thought. There is also the Pentecostal Charismatic movement, emphasizing spontaneity and speaking in tongues.

## Church of Scotland
Established form of Christianity in Scotland, first recognized by the state in 1560. It is based on the Protestant doctrines of the reformer Calvin and governed on Presbyterian lines.

### History
The church went through several periods of episcopacy (government by bishops) in the 17th century, and those who adhered to episcopacy after 1690 formed the Episcopal Church of Scotland, an autonomous church in communion with the Church of England. In 1843 there was a split in the Church of Scotland (the Disruption), in which almost a third of its ministers and members left and formed the ◊Free Church of Scotland. By an Act of Union of 3 October 1929 the Church of Scotland was united with the United Free Church of Scotland to form the United Church of Scotland. There are over 680,000 members of the Church of Scotland (1998).

### Government
The government of the Church of Scotland is by kirk sessions, presbyteries, synods, and the General Assembly, the supreme court. The kirk session consists of the parish minister and ruling elders, elected by the congregation. The presbyteries consist of all parish ministers in a specified district, with one ruling elder from every congregation. The provincial synods, of which there are 12, comprise three or more presbyteries. The

presbyteries elect the two commissioners who sit in the General Assembly.

## Cibber, Colley (1671–1757)

English actor, dramatist, and poet. He wrote numerous plays, such as *Love's Last Shift, or The Fool in Fashion* (1696) and *The Careless Husband* (1705), and acted in many parts. In 1709 he became a joint proprietor of the Drury Lane Theatre, London, and was the first manager to run a theatre on strictly business lines. He was poet laureate from 1730.

His first play, *Love's Last Shift* (written to provide a bigger part for himself), was so successful that John Vanbrugh wrote a sequel to it, *The Relapse* (1696), in which Cibber played Lord Foppington.

## Cinque Ports

Group of ports in southern England; originally five (◊Sandwich, ◊Dover, ◊Hythe, Romney, and ◊Hastings), later including ◊Rye, ◊Winchelsea, and others. Probably founded in Roman times, they rose to importance after the Norman conquest and until the end of the 15th century were bound to supply the ships and men necessary against invasion. Their importance declined in the 16th and 17th centuries with the development of a standing navy.

The office of lord warden of the Cinque Ports survives as an honorary distinction (Winston Churchill 1941–65, Robert Menzies 1965–78, the Queen Mother from 1979). The official residence is Walmer Castle.

## Cirencester

Market town in Gloucestershire, England, on the River Churn, in the ◊Cotswold Hills, 25 km/16 mi southeast of Gloucester; population (1991) 15,200. The Royal Agricultural College is situated here. Cirencester was the important Roman settlement of **Corinium Dobunnorum**, and flourished in the Middle Ages as the centre of the Cotswold wool trade.

### Features

Cirencester's medieval prosperity is reflected in the 15th-century Perpendicular church of St John the Baptist, one of the largest in England. The church contains a wineglass pulpit dating from about 1450, one of the few surviving pre-Reformation pulpits in England. There are remains of the Hospital of St John, founded by Henry II, and the 15th-century Weavers' Hall. The remains of a Roman amphitheatre seating 8,000 spectators

have been excavated, and the Corinium Museum displays a collection of Roman exhibits, including sections of mosaic pavement.

## Cissbury Hill

Hill in West Sussex 5 km/3 mi north of Worthing, England; height 184 m/604 ft. On the summit of the hill lies **Cissbury Ring**, the largest hillfort on the South Downs, which dates from around 300 BC. The fort has more than 200 pits containing prehistoric flint works.

## City, the

Financial centre of London, England. It is situated on the north bank of the River Thames, between Tower Bridge and London Bridge, in the oldest part of the capital. The ◊Bank of England, Lloyd's, the Royal Exchange, and the head offices of the 'big four' banks (Barclays, Lloyds, Midland, National Westminster) are in the City.

The City also contains the law courts of the ◊Old Bailey (Central Criminal Court) and Royal Courts of Justice.

## civil list

Annual sum provided from public funds to meet the official expenses of the sovereign and immediate dependents; private expenses are met by the privy purse, which is funded by the personal resources of the British Sovereign.

The amount is granted by Parliament on the recommendation of a Select Committee. It has to be renegotiated within the first six months of a new reign. In 1991 a fixed 10-year annual sum of £7.9 million was agreed for all of the royal family but this was changed in 1992 to provide only for the Queen, the Queen Mother, and the Duke of Edinburgh. Outside the Civil List Parliament makes payments for the upkeep of the royal palaces and the Queen's Flight, through the respective government departments. Other payments, such as those to members of the Queen's extended family come from her private income.

Since 1995 the Queen has paid income tax on her private income, the amount of which is not publicly disclosed. Additional royal income has been generated since 1993 by the opening of Buckingham Palace, between August and October each year, to paying public visitors. The income generated has been used to fund the restoration of Windsor Castle. In 1998 the Royal Yacht *Britannia* was decommissioned and the prime minister floated plans for joint use of the royal aircraft.

## civil service

Body of administrative staff appointed to carry out the policy of a government. Members of the UK civil service may not take an active part in politics, and do not change with the government.

---

*With the ascension of Charles I to the throne, we come at last to the Central Period of English History (not to be confused with the Middle Ages, of course), consisting in the utterly memorable Struggle between the Cavaliers (Wrong but Wromantic) and the Roundheads (Right and Repulsive).*

**W C Sellar and R J Yeatman** English writers. *1066 and All That, A Memorable History of England* (1930)

## Civil War, English

Conflict between King Charles I and the Royalists (also called Cavaliers) on one side and the Parliamentarians (also called Roundheads) under Oliver ◊ Cromwell on the other. Their differences centred initially on the king's unconstitutional acts, but later became a struggle over the relative powers of crown and Parliament. Hostilities began in 1642 and a series of Royalist defeats (at Marston Moor in 1644, and then at Naseby in 1645) culminated in Charles's capture in 1647, and execution in 1649. The war continued until the final defeat of Royalist forces at Worcester in 1651. Cromwell then became Protector (ruler) from 1653 until his death in 1658. See chronology and feature on pages 94 and 95.

## Clackmannanshire

Unitary authority in central Scotland, bordering the north side of the Firth of Forth; population (1996) 47,700; area 161 sq km/62 sq mi. A county until 1974, it was a district of Central region 1975–96. The principal towns are Alloa (administrative headquarters) and Tillicoultry.

### *Physical*

Clackmannanshire is a compact geographical area comprising the extensive flat flood plain of the River Devon, which rises dramatically at the Ochil Hills to Ben Cleuch (721 m/2,365 ft).

### *Features*

The authority has five historic castles. The **Clackmannan Tower**, associated with Robert the Bruce, dates from the medieval period, with 17th-century additions. There are ten Sites of Special Scientific Interest and one country park.

### *Economy*

This is based largely on small enterprises in a mixed economy, including brewing, distilling, manufacture of bottles, and knitwear. Agriculture is intensive on the flood plain of the Forth, and less intensive on the Ochil Hills.

## clan (Gaelic *clann*, 'children')

Social grouping based on kinship. In Scotland each Highland clan is theoretically descended from a single ancestor from whom the name is derived – for example, clan MacGregor ('son of Gregor').

Clans played a large role in the ◊ Jacobite revolts of 1715 and 1745, after which their individual

**Civil War battles, 1642–51**

✗ battle, with date
✱ major siege

0     100 mi
0     200 km

ATLANTIC OCEAN

North Sea

Irish Sea

English Channel

Auldern 1645
Tippermuir 1644
Kilsyth 1645
Dunbar 1650
Philiphaugh 1645
Marston Moor 1644
Hull
Preston 1648
Preston
Newark
Nantwich 1644
Chester
Cropredy Bridge 1644
Worcester 1651
Naseby 1645
Edgehill 1642
Oxford
Gloucester
Chalgrove 1643
Bristol
Reading
Newbury 1643, 1644
Lansdown 1643
Cheriton 1644
Stratton 1643
Langport 1645
Portsmouth
Lostwithiel 1644
Plymouth
Roundway Down 1648
Drogheda 1649
Limerick
Kilkenny 1649
Clonmel 1649
Wexford 1649
Ross 1649
Carrick 1649

## Chronology of the English Civil War

**1625** James I died, succeeded by Charles I, whose first Parliament was dissolved after refusing to grant him tonnage and poundage (taxation revenues) for life.

**1627** 'Five Knights' case in which men who refused to pay a forced loan were imprisoned.

**1628** Coke, Wentworth, and Eliot presented the Petition of Right, requesting the king not to tax without Parliamentary consent, not to billet soldiers in private homes, and not to impose martial law on civilians. Charles accepted this as the price of Parliamentary taxation to pay for war with Spain and France. Duke of Buckingham assassinated.

**1629** Parliament dissolved following disagreement over religious policy, tonnage and poundage, beginning Charles' 'Eleven Years' Tyranny'. War with France ended.

**1630** End of war with Spain.

**1632** Strafford made lord deputy in Ireland.

**1633** Laud became archbishop of Canterbury. Savage punishment of puritan William Prynne for his satirical pamphlet 'Histriomastix'.

**1634** Ship money first collected in London.

**1634–37** Laud attempted to enforce ecclesiastical discipline by metropolitan visits.

**1637** Conviction of John Hampden for refusal to pay ship money infringed Petition of Right.

**1638** Covenanters in Scotland protested at introduction of Laudian Prayer Book into the Kirk.

**1639** First Bishops' War. Charles sent army to Scotland after its renunciation of episcopacy. Agreement reached without fighting.

**1640** Short Parliament April–May voted taxes for the suppression of the Scots, but dissolved to forestall petition against Scottish war. Second Bishops' War ended in defeat for English at Newburn-on-Tyne. Scots received pension and held Northumberland and Durham in Treaty of Ripon. Long Parliament called, passing the Triennial Act and abolishing the Star Chamber. High Commission and Councils of the North and of Wales set up.

**1641** Strafford executed. English and Scots massacred at Ulster. Grand Remonstrance passed appealing to mass opinion against episcopacy and the royal prerogative. Irish Catholic nobility massacred.

**1642 January** Charles left Westminster after an unsuccessful attempt to arrest five members of the Commons united both Houses of Parliament and the City against him.

**February** Bishop's Exclusion Bill passed, barring clergy from secular office and the Lords.

**May–June** Irish rebels established supreme council. Militia Ordinance passed, assuming sovereign powers for parliament. Nineteen Propositions rejected by Charles.

**August** Charles raised his standard at Nottingham. Outbreak of first Civil War.

**October** General Assembly of the Confederate Catholics met at Kilkenny. Battle of Edgehill inconclusive.

**1643** Irish truce left rebels in control of more of Ireland. Solemn League and Covenant, alliance between English Parliamentarians and Scots, pledged to establish Presbyterianism in England and Ireland, and to provide a Scottish army. Scots intervened in Civil War.

**1643–49** Westminster Assembly attempted to draw up Calvinist religious settlement.

**1644** Committee of Both Kingdoms to coordinate Scottish and Parliamentarians' military activities established. Royalists decisively beaten at Marston Moor.

**1645** Laud executed. New Model Army created. Charles pulled out of Uxbridge negotiations on a new constitutional position. Cromwell and the New Model Army destroyed Royalist forces at Naseby.

**1646** Charles fled to Scotland. Oxford surrendered to Parliament. End of first Civil War.

**1647 May** Charles agreed with Parliament to accept Presbyterianism and to surrender control of the militia.

**June–August** Army seized Charles and resolved not to disband without satisfactory terms. Army presented Heads of Proposals to Charles.

**October–December** Army debated Levellers' Agreement of the People at Putney. Charles escaped to the Isle of Wight, and reached agreement with the Scots by Treaty of Newport.

**1648 January** Vote of No Addresses passed by Long Parliament declaring an end to negotiations with Charles.

**August** Cromwell defeated Scots at Preston. Second Civil War began.

**November–December** Army demanded trial of Charles I. Pride's Purge of Parliament transferred power to the Rump of independent MPs.

**1649 January–February** Charles tried and executed. Rump elected Council of State as its executive.

**May** Rump declared England a Commonwealth. Cromwell landed in Dublin.

**September–October** Massacres of garrisons at Drogheda and Wexford by Cromwell. Large numbers of native Irish were transplanted.

**1650 September** Cromwell defeated Scots under Leslie at Dunbar

**1651** Scots under Charles II invaded England, but were decisively defeated at Worcester (3 September) by Cromwell. Charles fled to the Continent and lived in exile for 9 years.

# ◆ THE WORLD TURNED UPSIDE DOWN: CIVIL WAR AND REVOLUTION ◆

From 1640 to 1660 the British Isles witnessed some of the most dramatic events of their history. In this period, the English, Scottish, and Irish states all experienced major, and interconnected, internal convulsions.

## Scotland

In the late 1630s the Scots rose in armed insurrection to defend their Calvinist, or presbyterian, church against a new 'popish' prayer book which Charles I was attempting to impose. In 1640 the Scots Covenanters defeated Charles's army at Newburn, precipitating the deep political crisis in England which led to civil war in 1642. In 1643 they entered into a military alliance with the English Parliamentarians, and Scottish forces contributed much to the defeat of the Royalists. The Scots had assumed that Charles's defeat would be followed by the introduction of a Scottish-style church in England, but by 1649 the presbyterian English Parliament had lost power to the soldiers of the New Model Army, most of whom firmly rejected the concept of any national church.

The Scots then transferred their allegiance, backing the attempts of Charles I and then his son to win back the English crown. They were, however, defeated at Preston (1648), Dunbar (1650), and Worcester (1651) by Cromwell, who then brought all of Lowland Scotland under direct English rule for the first time in its history. In 1654 he forced Scotland into a union with England. While this union was overturned at the Restoration in 1660, the English hegemony it had established ensured that England entered the union of 1707 as much the dominant partner.

## Ireland

In Ireland the mid-century crisis erupted with the Ulster Rising of 1641, during which several thousand native Catholics rose up against Protestant colonists planted on their lands earlier in the century. The rebellion quickly spread. A provisional Catholic government was set up at Kilkenny, and in 1643 Charles I recognized its authority in exchange for Irish military assistance in England. The recovery of Ireland was entrusted to Cromwell in 1649. Within nine months he broke the back of the rebellion with an efficiency and ruthlessness for which he has never been forgiven by the Irish people. This military reconquest was swiftly followed by the Cromwellian Land Settlement, which ejected most of the Catholic population from their lands and gave them the famous choice of going to 'Hell or Connaught'. These events laid the foundations for the English Protestant Ascendancy.

## England

It was in England, however, that the revolutionary nature of the 1640s and 1650s was most apparent. Here a full-scale civil conflict resulted in the public trial and execution of a king who many still regarded as divinely appointed, the establishment of a republic, and the emergence of a military junta. In the religious sphere, the established national church was dismembered in favour of a large number of unorthodox radical sects, including the Ranters, who encouraged indulgence in alcohol, tobacco, and casual sex, and the Quakers, whose refusal to defer to social superiors made them especially subversive.

These 20 years were marked by an extraordinary intellectual ferment. Many English men and women began to espouse very radical solutions to a wide range of social and political problems. The Levellers advocated universal male suffrage. Gerrard Winstanley established a short-lived commune on St George's Hill near Weybridge, and argued in print for a communist solution to social inequalities. The poet John Milton sought liberal divorce laws, and other writers debated women's rights, polygamy, and vegetarianism.

England had fallen into civil war in 1642 for want of a peaceful solution to the serious differences between Charles I and some of his most influential subjects. Some of these differences had been political, but more important was a religious struggle manifested in the opposition of many English Calvinists to a clique of anti-Calvinists, or Arminians, who (under Charles's patronage) had gained control of the established church in the 1630s. Parliament's victory in the Civil War owed much to the organizational ability of its early leader John Pym, its access to the financial and demographic resources of London, and the creation of the New Model Army in 1645. After his defeat, Charles's own obstinate refusal to settle with his opponents finally drove the leaders of the army to the desperate expedient of regicide.

From 1649 to 1660, England remained a military state. Cromwell struggled to reconcile the country to his rule, but failed because of his association with the army in a nation now thoroughly fed up with the military. Moreover, Cromwell and his puritan colleagues considered it their duty to impose their own godly culture on the nation. Initiatives such as the introduction of the death penalty for adultery were met with widespread hostility. In restoring the Stuarts in 1660, the English were decisively rejecting this puritan culture in favour of a world once more turned right way up.

by Christopher Durston

tartan Highland dress was banned 1746–82. Rivalry between them was often bitter.

## Clandon Park

House near Guildford, Surrey, England, which was built around 1735 by Giacomo Leoni (1686–1746) for the 2nd Lord Onslow. It was given to the National Trust by the Countess of Iveagh in 1956.

The house contains the Onslow family pictures and furniture, the Gubbay collection of furniture, porcelian and needlework, and the Ivo Forde collection of Meissen Italian comedy figures.

## Clarence House

House in London, residence of HM Queen ◊Elizabeth the Queen Mother. It stands immediately opposite Friary Court, St James's Palace, and was built by John ◊Nash in 1825–29 for William IV when he was Duke of Clarence. It was enlarged by one storey in 1873.

## Claridge's Hotel

Hotel in Brook Street, London, opened in 1855 by William Claridge, a butler from a noble household. It was bought by the Savoy Company in 1895 and rebuilt. It is known as the best-equipped hotel in London to accommodate royalty and the rich.

## Clark, Jim (1936–1968)

Scottish-born motor-racing driver who was twice world champion, 1963 and 1965. He spent all his Formula One career with Lotus. He won 25 Formula One Grand Prix races, a record at the time, before losing his life at Hockenheim, West Germany during a Formula Two race in 1968.

## Clark, Kenneth, Baron Clark (1903–1983)

English art historian, who popularized the history of art through his television series *Civilization* (1969), published as a book in the same year. He was director of the National Gallery, London, from 1934 to 1945 and chair of the Arts Council between 1953 and 1960. His books include *Leonardo da Vinci* (1939), *Landscape into Art* (1949), and *The Nude* (1956).

## classical music

Term used to distinguish 'serious music' from pop music, rock music, folk music, and jazz.

### Middle Ages to the Reformation

One of the earliest English composers of note was John Dunstable (died 1453), a master of vocal polyphony known in Europe whose influence was especially felt in Flanders. Eminent composers of church music in this period were Robert Fayrfax (1464–1521), organist at St Alban's cathedral; William Cornyshe (c. 1468–1523), master of the choristers at Westminster Abbey, who also organized court pageants and masques for Henry VII; and John Taverner (c.1490–1545), who produced masses in a florid style.

### A Golden Age

With the introduction of a new liturgy after the Reformation, church music became relatively restrained and was dominated by Thomas ◊Tallis, William ◊Byrd and Orlando ◊Gibbons. Various secular forms of music also developed: lute music and songs with lute were composed by Thomas ◊Campion and John ◊Dowland; keyboard music by Byrd and John Bull (c.1562–1628); and vocal music of all kinds, especially madrigals, by composers such as Thomas Morley (c.1557–c.1602), Thomas Weelkes (c.1575–1623), and John Wilbye (c.1574–1638). These last three composers all contributed to *The Triumphs of Oriana* (1601), a madrigal collection in honour of Elizabeth I.

There were many continental musicians working in England at this period, but English musicians in their turn made careers for themselves abroad: Dowland in Denmark, for instance, and Bull in the Netherlands. Notable composers in the mid-17th century were Henry Lawes (1596–1662), who wrote mainly vocal music; his brother William (1602–1645), who wrote consort-music; and Matthew Locke (c.1621–1677), who composed instrumental music, and collaborated with Henry Lawes and others on a setting of Davenant's *The Siege of Rhodes* (1656), creating what could be regarded as one of the earliest English operas.

### Restoration

With the Restoration, Locke became court composer to Charles II. Many of the other musicians who found favour with the King were French. A new generation of native composers came to the fore: Pelham Humfrey (1647–74), John Blow (1649–1708), and Jeremiah Clarke (1673–1707) among them, but it was Henry ◊Purcell, a pupil of Blow and Humfrey, who was the greatest force in late 17th-century English music, writing in and enriching a variety of forms.

### Influence of Handel

The gap left by Purcell's early death was filled by the German-born ◊Handel, who lived most of his life in England. His musical roots were German and Italian, and at a time when there was a taste for Italian opera, he wrote several which were well received in London, where the Royal Italian Opera House was opened at Covent Garden in 1732 (a precursor of the ◊Royal Opera House). A native tradition of ballad opera, exemplified by John ◊Gay's *Beggar's Opera* is found throughout the century.

Foreign musicians and composers continued to come to England in large numbers, among them J C Bach (1735–1782), who settled in London in 1762. Public concerts became fashionable. Against this background English composers tended to adopt a style influenced by Handel, although Thomas Arne (1710–1778), William Boyce (1710–1779), and (later) Charles Dibdin (1745–1814), among others, strove to create individual styles of their own. The two Thomas Linleys, father (1733–1795) and son (1756–1778), were theatre composers and contributed to the development of English opera. The 18th century also saw the beginnings of musical scholarship at university level.

## 1780–1880
There are few British figures of note in the field of music from the late 18th and 19th centuries. Cipriani Potter's (1792–1871) symphonies show him to be a composer of individuality and sure orchestral command – even Beethoven acknowledged that Potter was gifted; and Irishman John Field (1782–1837) was a great pianist, and is known principally for the nocturnes he composed for piano. Victorian audiences lionised Mendelssohn and (later) Gounod, but their tastes seem to have been for bland oratorios and sensational operas. Only English operetta flourished, Arthur Sullivan (1842–1900) being its principal exponent (see Gilbert and Sullivan).

## Late-19th century renaissance
The late 1870s and early 1880s witnessed the start of a renaissance in English musical life. Two eminent figures were Hubert Parry (1848–1918) – at once composer, teacher, theorist, and administrator – and Charles Stanford (1852–1924), who founded the ◊Royal College of Music in 1882. The college proved an excellent training-ground for young composers. Two great figures of this renaissance were Edward ◊Elgar and Frederick ◊Delius, both of whom were largely self-taught. Each formulated personal musical languages that were recognisable English, yet exhibited the influence of music being composed on the European continent. The honours gradually paid to Elgar were a measure of the increase in status of music in England.

At the start of the 20th century, research into folk-music was being undertaken by several musicians in Europe, notably by Bartók in Romania and Hungary. The research undertaken in England, notably by Cecil ◊Sharp and later by Ralph ◊Vaughan Williams, provided a nationalist impetus to composition in England. Impetus was also provided by the republication of much early English music, which initiated a tradition of exploring musical resources from the past. By 1914, musical life in Britain was flourishing. Rising talent included Arnold Bax (1883–1953), Frank Bridge (1879–1941), George Butterworth (1885–1916), Ivor Gurney (1890–1937), and Herbert Howells (1892–1983). There was an active musical press and the popularity of orchestral concerts increased, largely on account of the extrovert conductors Thomas ◊Beecham and Henry Wood (1869–1944).

## Post-World War I
World War I dealt musical life in Britain a severe blow. The post-war generation was suspicious of grand designs, real structural complexity, and unabashed expressiveness, the dominant mood being satirical. Stravinsky and French composers were much admired. To the new generation of composers belonged Arthur Bliss (1891–1975), Lennox Berkeley (1903–1989), Constant Lambert (1905–1951), Alan Rawsthorne (1905–1971), William ◊Walton, Havergal Brian (1876–1972), Frank Bridge (1879–1941), and Gustav ◊Holst. The British song tradition was cultivated by Gerald Finzi (1901–1956) and Peter Warlock (1894–1930).

Two composers who came to prominence just before World War II, Benjamin ◊Britten and Michael ◊Tippett went on to dominate the British music scene, though Tippett had to wait many years for official recognition. Britten made several exceptional contributions to the English opera repertoire. The influence of music composed on the European continent continued – the serial procedures of the Viennese School were used by Elisabeth Lutyens (1906–1983).

## Late 20th century
Since the late 1950s, the development of music in England has been closely linked with developments in western classical music around the world. The range of individual compositional styles has increased enormously, as has the number of influences on classical music – for example, the works of John Tavener (1944–       ) show the influence of Greek Orthodox church music. Purely electronic music has been written by several composers (including Jonathan Harvey), and electronic instruments have featured often in new works.

Prominent British composers at the end of the 20th century included Peter Maxwell Davies (1934–    ), Alexander Goehr (1932–    ) and Harrison Birtwistle (1934–    ), whose works have provoked much fertile discussion in the media as to the nature and accessibility of contemporary classical music.

## Claydon House

House in Buckinghamshire, England, 21 km/13 mi northwest of Aylesbury. Claydon was the home of the Verney family from 1463. The present house was built 1752–68, but all that now remains is the west wing, containing magnificent rococo state rooms, including Florence ◊Nightingale's bedroom and museum. She was the sister of Parthenope Verney, and a constant visitor to Claydon. The Verney family gave Claydon to the National Trust in 1956, but continue to live in the house.

## Clee Hills

Range of hills in southern Shropshire, England. The principal summits are Brown Clee Hill (546 m/1791 ft) and Titterstone Clee Hill (533 m/1749 ft). Some coal reserves remain here, although they are no longer mined. A noted hard rock called Dhu stone, which is used mainly for road metal, is quarried here.

## Cleopatra's Needle

Name given to two ancient Egyptian granite obelisks erected at Heliopolis in the 15th century BC by Thutmose III, and removed to Alexandria by the Roman emperor Augustus about 14 BC; they have no connection with Cleopatra's reign. One of the pair was taken to England in 1878 and erected on the Victoria Embankment in London. It is 21 m/68.5 ft high.

## Clevedon

Resort in North Somerset, England; population (1991) 20,800. It is situated on the Severn estuary at the foot of Dial Hill, 17 km/11 mi southwest of Bristol. **Clevedon Court** was built by John de Clevedon in the 14th century, and added to in practically every century since then. It was in the possession of the Elton family from 1709 to 1961, when it was transferred to the National Trust through the Treasury. It has extensive collections of pottery and glass.

Samuel Coleridge lived at nearby Myrtle Cottage in 1795.

## Cliff, Clarice (1899–1972)

English pottery designer. Her Bizarre ware, characterized by brightly coloured floral and geometric decoration on often geometrically shaped china, became increasingly popular in the 1930s and increasingly collectable in the 1970s and 1980s. Contemporary artists such as Laura Knight (1877–1970) and Vanessa ◊Bell also designed for her Bizarre range.

Born in the ◊Potteries, she worked for many years at Wilkinson's Newport factory. By 1929 production was given over exclusively to her work. In 1963 she became art director of the factory, which was part of the Royal Staffordshire Pottery in Burslem.

## Clive, Robert, 1st Baron Clive (1725–1774)

British soldier and administrator who established British rule in India by victories over French troops at Arcot and over the nawab of Bengal at Plassey in 1757. This victory secured Bengal for the East india Company, and Clive was appointed governor of the province from 1757. He returned to Britain on account of ill health in 1760, but was governor for a further year in 1765–6. On his return to Britain in 1766, his wealth led to allegations that he had abused his power. Although acquitted by a Parliamentary enquiry, he committed suicide.

## Cliveden

Large Victorian house near Maidenhead, England, on the Buckinghamshire–Berkshire border. The 2nd Viscount ◊Astor gave Cliveden to the National Trust in 1942, together with its gardens and woods which dominate the Cliveden reach of the Thames. The house is now a privately owned hotel, but the grounds are open to the public.

## Clyde

Third longest river and firth in Scotland, and longest in southern Scotland; 171 km/106 mi long. Formerly one of the world's great industrial waterways, and famed for its shipbuilding, its industrial base has declined in recent years and the capacity of the ports on the Clyde has reduced.

## Coalbrookdale

Village in the Telford and Wrekin unitary authority, England, effectively a suburb of Telford, situated in the Severn Gorge; population (1991) 1,000. Sometimes known as the 'cradle of the Industrial Revolution', Coalbrookdale became the world's most important iron-producing area following Abraham Darby I's successful attempt in 1709 to use coke – rather than coal or charcoal – to smelt iron in a blast-furnace, thereby allowing for a massive increase in production. It is now the site of the Coalbrookdale Museum of Iron which forms part of the ◊Ironbridge Gorge World Heritage Site.

## coalmining

Traditionally one of Britain's key industries. Coal was mined on a small scale from Roman times, but production expanded rapidly between 1550 and 1700. Coal became the main source of energy for the ◊Industrial Revolution; by 1700 over 50% of the country's energy needs was supplied by coal, and Britain became the world's largest coal producer. Under the Coal Industry Nationalization Act (1946) Britain's mines were administered by the National Coal Board, but the industry was privatized in 1994. The York, Derby, and Notts coalfield, which extends north of Selby in Yorkshire, is Britain's chief reserve.

Competition from oil as a fuel, cheaper coal from overseas (USA, Australia), the decline of traditional users (town gas, railways), and the exhaustion of many underground workings resulted in the closure of mines: 850 mines in 1955; 54 in 1992. However, rises in the price of oil, greater productivity, and the discovery of new, deep coal seams suitable for mechanized extraction improved the position of the British coal industry from 1973 to 1990. Britain remains very dependent on the use of coal in electricity generation.

## Cobbett, William (1763–1835)

English Radical politician and journalist, who published the weekly *Political Register* (1802–35). He spent much of his life in North America. His crusading essays on the conditions of the rural poor were collected as 'Rural Rides' (1830).

## Cockcroft, John (1897–1967)

British physicist. In 1932 he and Irish physicist Ernest Walton succeeded in splitting the nucleus of an atom for the first time. For this they were jointly awarded a Nobel prize in 1951.

The voltage multiplier built by Cockcroft and Walton to accelerate protons was the first particle accelerator. They used it to bombard lithium, artificially transforming it into helium. The production of the helium nuclei was confirmed by observing their tracks in a cloud chamber. They

**Coalmining** A cartoon of 1844 from the satrical magazine *Punch*, entitled *Capital and Labour*, contrasts the luxurious life of a mineowner with the harsh working conditions in the pits. Although the Industrial Revolution brought Britain as a whole greater material prosperity, it also caused massive social upheavals. Philip Sauvain Picture Collection

then worked on the artificial disintegration of other elements, such as boron. He was knighted in 1948, and awarded the Order of Merit in 1957.

## cockney

Native of the City of London. According to tradition, cockneys must be born within sound of ◊ Bow Bells in Cheapside. The term cockney is also applied to the dialect of the Londoner, of which a striking feature is rhyming slang.

## coffee house

Alternative to ale-houses as social meeting place, largely for the professional classes, popular in the 17th and 18th centuries. Christopher Bowman opened the first Coffee House in London (later known as the 'Pasqua Rosee') in St. Michael's Alley, Cornhill, in 1652. Others soon followed in both London and Oxford so that by 1708 London alone boasted 3,000 coffee houses. The coffee houses declined in popularity toward the end of the 18th century as coffee itself was largely superseded by the new fashion for tea.

---

*It is folly of too many to mistake the echo of a London coffee house for the voice of the kingdom.*

**Jonathan Swift** Irish satirist and Anglican cleric.
*The Conduct of the Allies* (1711)

---

## Colchester

Town in Essex, eastern England, 80 km/50 mi northeast of London; population (1991) 96,100. As **Camulodunum** it was the first capital of Roman Britain, and it is the oldest recorded town in England. For centuries an important market town, it is still an important centre of trade and commerce and, with a wealth of historic features, including parts of the Roman town walls, a Norman castle, and many half-timbered and Georgian buildings, it is a popular tourist destination. It is also the site of an army base and the University of Essex. The Colchester Oyster Feast, held every October, dates from medieval times.

*History*

Following the Roman invasion in AD 43, the Romans made Camulodunum their headquarters and built the first Roman temple in Britain here, dedicating it to Claudius I. Camulodunum later became a 'colony' for Roman ex-soldiers and, in a rising against the Romans, ◊ Boudicca devastated the town in AD 60. After her defeat a new town was

established, defended by a wall which is thought to have been over 6 m/20 ft high and 3 m/10 ft thick. William (I) the Conqueror built a castle here on the site of the Roman temple and the town flourished as a major centre of the weaving and cloth trade from the 14th to 17th centuries. In 1648, during the English Civil War, the town underwent an 11-week siege before finally surrendering to the Parliamentarians. In the 19th century a large permanent garrison was established which became the principal military base in East Anglia.

*Features*

Remains of the Roman town include parts of the Roman walls, the foundations of the Roman temple, and Balkerne Gate, the largest surviving Roman town gate in Britain. At the heart of the town is the castle, which dates from 1070 and has the largest surviving Norman keep in England, now housing a museum.

## Coleridge, Samuel Taylor (1772–1834)

English poet, critic, and philosopher. A friend of the poets Robert Southey (1774–1843) and William ◊ Wordsworth, he collaborated with the latter on the highly influential collection *Lyrical Ballads* (1798), which was the spearhead of the English Romantic Movement. His poems include 'The Rime of the Ancient Mariner', 'Christabel', and 'Kubla Khan' (all written 1797–98); his critical works include *Biographia Literaria* (1817).

Coleridge was educated at Cambridge University where he became friends with Southey. In 1797 he moved to Nether Stowey, Somerset, and worked closely with Wordsworth on *Lyrical Ballads*, producing much of his finest poetry during this period. In 1798 he went to Germany where he studied philosophy and literary criticism. In 1800 he settled in the Lake District with Wordsworth and from 1808 to 1819 gave a series of lectures on prose and drama. Suffering from rheumatic pain, Coleridge became addicted to opium and from 1816 lived in Highgate, London, under medical care. Here he produced his major prose work *Biographia Literaria* (1817), a collection of autobiographical pieces in which he develops his philosophical and critical ideas.

## Coleridge-Taylor, Samuel (1875–1912)

English composer. He wrote the cantata *Hiawatha's Wedding Feast* (1898), a setting in three parts of Longfellow's poem. The son of a West African doctor and an English mother, he was a student and champion of traditional black music.

## Collins, Michael (1890–1922)

Irish nationalist. He was a ◊Sinn Féin leader, a founder and director of intelligence of the Irish Republican Army (see ◊IRA) in 1919, minister for finance in the provisional government of the Irish Free State in 1922, commander of the Free State forces in the civil war, and for ten days head of state before being killed by Irishmen opposed to the partition treaty with Britain.

## Collins, Wilkie (1824–1889)

English author of mystery and suspense novels. He wrote *The Woman in White* in 1860 (with its fat villain Count Fosco), often called the first English detective novel, and *The Moonstone* (1868), featuring Sergeant Cuff, one of the first detectives in English literature.

Collins was born in London and qualified as a barrister. In 1848 he wrote a life of his father, the painter William Collins, and in 1850 published his first novel, *Antonina*. In 1851 he formed a friendship with the novelist Charles ◊Dickens, with whom he collaborated on a number of works, including the play *A Message from the Sea* (1861).

## Columba, St (Latin form of Colum-cille, 'Colum of the cell') (521–597)

Irish Christian abbot, missionary to Scotland. He was born in County Donegal of royal descent, and founded monasteries and churches in Ireland. In 563 he sailed with 12 companions to Iona, and built a monastery there that was to play a leading part in the conversion of Britain. Feast day 9 June.

## Common Prayer, Book of

The service book of the Church of England and the Episcopal Church, based largely on the Roman breviary.

The first service book in English was known as the *First Prayer Book of Edward VI*, published in 1549, and is the basis of the *Book of Common Prayer* still, although not exclusively, in use. The *Second Prayer Book of Edward VI* appeared in 1552, but was withdrawn in 1553 on Mary's accession. In 1559 the *Revised Prayer Book* was issued, closely resembling that of 1549. This was suppressed by Parliament in 1645, but its use was restored in 1660 and a number of revisions were made. This is the officially authorized *Book of Common Prayer* but an act of 1968 legalized alternative services, and the Worship and Doctrine Measure (1974) gave the church control of its worship and teaching. The church's *Alternative Service Book* (1980), in contemporary language, is also in use.

## Commons, House of

Lower chamber of ◊Parliament, in Westminster, London.

## Commonwealth Games

Multisport gathering of competitors from British Commonwealth countries, held every four years. The first meeting (known as the British Empire Games) was in Hamilton, Canada, August 1930. It has been held in Britain on four occasions: London 1934; Cardiff 1958; Edinburgh 1970 and 1986. Manchester will host the 2002 games.

## Commonwealth, the

Republican rule by Parliament during the Interregnum of 1649–60, more precisely the periods 1649–53 and 1659–60 – in the intervening years Oliver ◊Cromwell ruled by direct personal government under the protectorate. After the abolition of the monarchy in 1649, the Rump Parliament declared England to be a 'Commonwealth or Free State'. The House of Commons held supreme authority, with the former executive powers of the monarchy being vested in a 40-member Council of State. However, Parliament was not sufficiently radical for the army, and was dissolved in May 1653 by Cromwell.

In December, the Barebones Parliament (its name derived from a member, Praise-God Barbon) passed the 'Instrument of Government', placing supreme authority in the hands of Cromwell personally. Cromwell ruled under the terms of the Protectorate until his death in 1659, when he was succeeded briefly by his son Richard. Richard was unable to provide the strong leadership of his father, and in May the army restored the Rump Parliament. Parliament and the army were unable to cooperate any better than in the first phase of the Commonwealth, and the House of Commons began negotiations for the ◊Restoration of Charles II.

## Commonwealth, the British

Voluntary association of 54 countries and their dependencies, the majority of which once formed part of the ◊British Empire and are now independent sovereign states. They are all regarded as 'full members of the Commonwealth'; the newest member being Mozambique, which was admitted in November 1995. Additionally, there are some 20 territories that are not completely sovereign and remain dependencies of the UK or one of the other fully sovereign members, and are regarded as 'Commonwealth countries'. Heads of government meet every two years, apart from those of

## Countries of the British Commonwealth

| country | date joined | constitutional status |
|---|---|---|
| **in Africa** | | |
| Botswana | 1966 | sovereign republic |
| British Indian Ocean Territory | 1965 | British dependent territory |
| Cameroon | 1995 | emergent democratic republic |
| Fiji Islands | 1970, 1997 | sovereign republic |
| Gambia | 1965 | sovereign republic |
| Ghana | 1957 | sovereign republic |
| Kenya | 1963 | sovereign republic |
| Lesotho | 1966 | sovereign constitutional monarchy |
| Malawi | 1964 | sovereign republic |
| Mauritius | 1968 | sovereign republic |
| Mozambique | 1995 | emergent democracy |
| Namibia | 1990 | sovereign republic |
| Nigeria[1] | 1960 | sovereign republic |
| St Helena | 1931 | British dependent territory |
| Seychelles | 1976 | sovereign republic |
| Sierra Leone | 1961 | sovereign republic |
| South Africa | 1910[2] | sovereign republic |
| Swaziland | 1968 | sovereign republic |
| Tanzania | 1961 | sovereign republic |
| Uganda | 1962 | sovereign republic |
| Zambia | 1964 | sovereign republic |
| Zimbabwe | 1980 | sovereign republic |
| **in the Americas** | | |
| Anguilla | 1931 | British dependent territory |
| Antigua and Barbuda | 1981 | sovereign constitutional monarchy[3] |
| Bahamas | 1973 | sovereign constitutional monarchy[3] |
| Barbados | 1966 | sovereign constitutional monarchy[3] |

| country | date joined | constitutional status |
|---|---|---|
| Belize | 1982 | sovereign constitutional monarchy[3] |
| Bermuda | 1931 | British dependent territory |
| British Virgin Islands | 1931 | British dependent territory |
| Canada | 1931 | sovereign constitutional monarchy[3] |
| Cayman Islands | 1931 | British dependent territory |
| Dominica | 1978 | sovereign republic |
| Falkland Islands | 1931 | British dependent territory |
| Grenada | 1974 | sovereign constitutional monarchy[3] |
| Guyana | 1966 | sovereign republic |
| Jamaica | 1962 | sovereign constitutional monarchy[3] |
| Montserrat | 1931 | British dependent territory |
| St Kitts and Nevis | 1983 | sovereign constitutional monarchy[3] |
| St Lucia | 1979 | sovereign constitutional monarchy[3] |
| St Vincent and the Grenadines | 1979 | sovereign constitutional monarchy[3] |
| Trinidad and Tobago | 1962 | sovereign republic |
| Turks and Caicos Islands | 1931 | British dependent territory |
| **in the Antarctic** | | |
| Australian Antarctic Territory | 1936 | Australian external territory |
| British Antarctic Territory | 1931 | British dependent territory |

## Countries of the British Commonwealth (continued)

| country | date joined | constitutional status |
|---|---|---|
| Falkland Islands Dependencies | 1931 | British dependent territories |
| Ross Dependency | 1931 | New Zealand associated territory |
| **in Asia** | | |
| Bangladesh | 1972 | sovereign republic |
| Brunei | 1984 | sovereign monarchy |
| India | 1947 | sovereign republic |
| Malaysia | 1957 | sovereign constitutional monarchy |
| Maldives | 1982 | sovereign republic |
| Pakistan | 1947[4] | sovereign republic |
| Singapore | 1965 | sovereign republic |
| Sri Lanka | 1948 | sovereign republic |
| **in Australasia and the Pacific** | | |
| Australia | 1931 | sovereign constitutional monarchy[3] |
| Cook Islands | 1931 | New Zealand associated territory |
| Norfolk Island | 1931 | Australian external territory |
| Kiribati | 1979 | sovereign republic |
| Nauru | 1968 | sovereign republic |
| New Zealand | 1931 | sovereign constitutional monarchy[3] |
| Niue | 1931 | New Zealand associated territory |
| Papua New Guinea | 1975 | sovereign constitutional monarchy[3] |

| country | date joined | constitutional status |
|---|---|---|
| Pitcairn Islands | 1931 | British dependent territory |
| Solomon Islands | 1978 | sovereign constitutional monarchy[3] |
| Tokelau | 1931 | New Zealand associated territory |
| Tonga | 1970 | sovereign monarchy |
| Tuvalu | 1978 | sovereign constitutional monarchy[3] |
| Vanuatu | 1980 | sovereign republic |
| Western Samoa | 1970 | sovereign republic |
| **in Europe** | | |
| Channel Islands | 1931 | UK crown dependencies |
| Guernsey | | |
| Jersey | | |
| Cyprus | 1961 | sovereign republic |
| Gibraltar | 1931 | British dependent territory |
| Malta | 1964 | sovereign republic |
| Isle of Man | 1931 | UK crown dependency |
| United Kingdom | 1931 | sovereign constitutional monarchy[3] |
| England | | |
| Northern Ireland | | |
| Scotland | | |
| Wales | | |

[1] suspended 1995  [2] withdrew from membership 1961 and readmitted 1994  [3] Queen Elizabeth II constitutional monarch and head of state  [4] left 1972 and rejoined 1989

Nauru and Tuvalu; however, Nauru and Tuvalu have the right to participate in all functional activities. The Commonwealth, which was founded in 1931, has no charter or constitution, and is founded more on tradition and sentiment than on political or economic factors. However, it can make political statements by withdrawing membership; a recent example was Nigeria's suspension in November 1995 because of human-rights abuses. Fiji was readmitted in October 1997, ten years after its membership had been suspended as a result of discrimination against its ethnic Indian community.

## Communist Party of Great Britain, CPGB

British Marxist party founded in 1920, largely inspired by the Russian Revolution of 1917. Its affiliation with the Labour Party (it had originally been intended as a branch of the Labour Party) ended in the late 1920s, when the organization

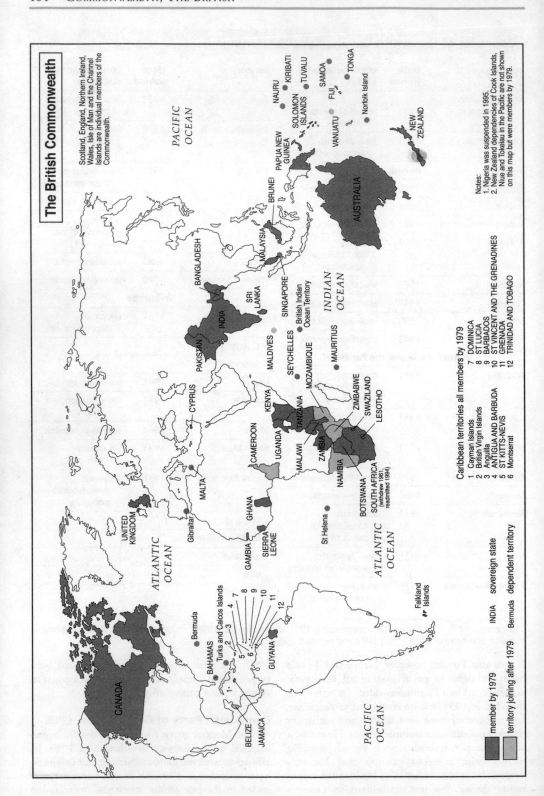

## The British Commonwealth

Scotland, England, Northern Ireland, Wales, Isle of Man and the Channel Islands are individual members of the Commonwealth.

Notes:
1. Nigeria was suspended in 1995.
2. New Zealand dependencies of Cook Islands, Niue and Tokelau in the Pacific are not shown on this map but were members by 1979.

**Caribbean territories all members by 1979**

| | | |
|---|---|---|
| 1 Cayman Islands | 7 DOMINICA | |
| 2 British Virgin Islands | 8 ST LUCIA | |
| 3 Anguilla | 9 BARBADOS | |
| 4 ANTIGUA AND BARBUDA | 10 ST VINCENT AND THE GRENADINES | |
| 5 ST KITTS-NEVIS | 11 GRENADA | |
| 6 Montserrat | 12 TRINIDAD AND TOBAGO | |

INDIA sovereign state

Bermuda dependent territory

member by 1979

territory joining after 1979

was proscribed. The party enjoyed its greatest popularity in the 1930s and 1940s, particularly after Britain allied with the USSR during World War II. It had 18,000 members in 1939 and had two MPs elected in 1945, representing West Fife in Scotland and Mile End in London. The party was riven internally by the Soviet invasion of Hungary in 1956 and moved away from the USSR during the 1960s, particularly after the invasion of Czechoslovakia of 1968. Disbanded in 1991, the party was relaunched as 'Democratic Left', although some splinter factions still lay claim to the old name.

## Compton, Denis (1918–1997)

English cricketer and football player. He played for Middlesex and England, and was a right-handed batsman of prodigious talent and great style, who in 78 tests between 1937 and 1957 scored 5,807 runs at an average of 50.06. In the 1947 English season he scored 3,816 runs (at an average of 90.85) and 18 hundreds, records which are unlikely ever to be surpassed. As a footballer he won Football League and FA Cup winners' medals with Arsenal and played in 12 wartime internationals for England.

## Compton Wynyates

Tudor mansion, once moated, 20 km/12 mi southeast of Stratford-upon-Avon, Warwickshire, England. Begun in 1480, it is built round a courtyard, with the arms of Henry VIII and Catherine of Aragon over the porch.

The house has a number of secret staircases and hiding-places. The great hall is panelled, with two minstrels' galleries, carved screens and a timber roof.

In the grounds is a church, rebuilt in 1665, with many memorials of the Compton family. Compton Wynyates is the seat of the Marquess of Northampton.

## Concorde

The only supersonic airliner, which cruises at Mach 2, or twice the speed of sound, about 2,170 kph/1,350 mph. Concorde, the result of Anglo-French cooperation, made its first flight in 1969 and entered commercial service seven years later. It is 62 m/202 ft long and has a wing span of nearly 26 m/84 ft. Developing Concorde cost French and British taxpayers £2 billion.

## Congreve, William (1670–1729)

English dramatist and poet. His first success was the comedy *The Old Bachelor* (1693), followed by *The Double Dealer* (1694), *Love for Love* (1695), the tragedy *The Mourning Bride* (1697), and *The Way of the World* (1700). His plays, which satirize the social affectations of the time, are characterized by elegant wit and wordplay, and complex plots.

---

*I nauseate walking; 'tis a country diversion, I loathe the country.*

**William Congreve** English dramatist and poet.
*The Way of the World* (1700) IV. iv

---

## Conisbrough

Town in South Yorkshire, England, 8 km/5 mi southwest of Doncaster; population (1991) 14,500. **Conisbrough Castle**, with a fine circular keep, is a Norman castle built by Hamelin, a half-brother of Henry II, in around 1180.

## Coniston Water

Lake in the Cumbrian Lake District, England. It has a length of 8 km/5 mi and a width of 1 km/0.6 mi, which makes it one of the smaller lakes in the area. The village of **Coniston** (population (1991) 1,200) lies 14 km/9 mi west of Bowness, between the lake and **Coniston Old Man**, which is 802 m/2631 ft high.

Donald ⬦Campbell died while attempting to improve his world water-speed record on Coniston Water in 1967.

**Concorde** The Anglo-French *Concorde* supersonic airliner, which made its maiden flight in 1969 and is still operating regular services, is a technological triumph. However, it has not enjoyed great commercial success; its noise levels brought early landing restrictions by US airport authorities, while its high operating costs deterred other airlines from buying it. Corel

Peel Island, one of three small islands on the lake, is the 'Wild Cat Island' of Arthur Ransome's novel *Swallows and Amazons* (1931). Brantwood, once the home of John Ruskin, stands above the eastern shore of Coniston Water; Ruskin is buried in Coniston churchyard.

## Conrad, Joseph pen name of Teodor Józef Konrad Nalecz Korzeniowski (1857–1924)

British novelist, born in Ukraine of Polish parents. His greatest works include the novels *Lord Jim* (1900), *Nostromo* (1904), *The Secret Agent* (1907), and *Under Western Eyes* (1911); the short story *Heart of Darkness* (1902); and the short novel 'The Shadow Line' (1917). These combine a vivid and sensuous evocation of various lands and seas with a rigorous, humane scrutiny of moral dilemmas, pitfalls, and desperation.

The novel *Chance* (1912) was Conrad's first triumphant success. Thereafter he was regarded as one of the greatest modern authors, although his subsequent output was small. His critical reputation and influence have grown steadily since his death.

**Joseph Conrad** English writer Joseph Conrad, photographed in about 1905. Conrad, who first learned English at the age of 21, is regarded as one of the greatest of 20th-century English novelists. His works include the novels *Lord Jim* (1900) and *Nostromo* (1904), and the short story 'Heart of Darkness' (1902). Corbis

Conrad was brought up in Russia and Poland. He landed at Lowestoft, Suffolk, in 1878 with no knowledge of English, but in 1886 he gained his master mariner's certificate and became a naturalized British subject. He retired from the sea in 1894 to write, living in Kent from 1896.

## conservation

Conservation groups in Britain originated in the 1860s; early groups included the Commons Preservation Society (1865), which fought successfully against the enclosure of Hampstead Heath (1865) and Epping Forest (1866) in London; the National Footpaths Preservation Society (1844); and the ◊National Trust (1895). More recently ◊English Heritage (1983), ◊English Nature (1991) (formerly the Nature Conservancy Council), and the Countryside Commission, formed 1968 but since 1999 the ◊Countryside Agency, have become heavily involved.

See appendix for list of Areas of Outstanding Natural Beauty, designated by the Countryside Agency. See also ◊World Heritage Sites.

### Natura 2000

Twelve coastal sites in Great Britain, including five Special Areas of Conservation, have been designated by the European Commission to be part of a network of Natura 2000 sites. The EC will provide funds to help preserve these sites from development, overfishing, and pollution, and to monitor rare plants. They include the north Northumberland coast, with its sea caves, its breeding population of grey seals in the Farne Islands, and Arctic species such as the wolf fish; the Wash and north Norfolk coast, with its population of common seals, waders, and wildfowl, and its extensive salt marshes; and Plymouth Sound and estuaries, with their submerged sandbanks.

### 'Turning the Tide'

A £10 million project, launched in 1997 by the Millennium Commission, to protect and restore Britain's only magnesium limestone cliffs, between Hartlepool and Sunderland, in northeast England. The area is rich in wild flowers, with grassland and denes (steep, wooded valleys). Intensive farming and the use of fertilizers have damaged the flora and fauna of the area. The beaches are polluted as a result of over two centuries of coal mining along the Durham coast. Waste from the mines was dumped into the sea and on to the beaches, leaving heaps of spoil 3.7–4.6 m/12–15 ft high. The restoration project aims to remove spoil from the beaches and return the cliffs to their natural grassland.

## conservation, architectural
Attempts to maintain the character of buildings and historical areas in Britain are subject to a growing body of legislation that has designated around a million listed buildings, the largest number in Western Europe. There are now over 6,000 conservation areas and 500,000 listed buildings throughout England alone. See also ◊ English Heritage.

## Conservative Party
One of the two historic British political parties; the name replaced **Tory** in general use from 1830 onwards. Traditionally the party of landed interests, it broadened its political base under Benjamin ◊ Disraeli's leadership in the 19th century. The present Conservative Party's free-market capitalism is supported by the world of finance and the management of industry. In recent history, the Conservative Party was in power under Margaret Thatcher 1979–90 and John Major 1990–97. After the party's defeat in the 1997 general election, John Major resigned and was succeeded by William Hague. The party's Central Office is located in Smith Square, London.

In the 1980s the party's economic policies increased the spending power of the majority, but also the gap between rich and poor; nationalized industries were sold off (see ◊ privatization); military spending and close alliance with the USA were favoured; and the funding of local government was overhauled with the introduction of the poll tax (levied on each individual without regard to income or property. The Conservative government of John Major 1990–97 repudiated some of the extreme policies of ◊ Thatcherism, notably the poll tax, introduced the Citizen's Charter (a programme aimed at improving public services), and promoted further privatization or market testing.
*History*
Opposed to the *laissez-faire* of the Liberal manufacturers, the Conservative Party supported, to some extent, the struggle of the working class against the harsh conditions arising from the Industrial Revolution. The split of 1846 over Robert ◊ Peel's ◊ Corn Law policy led to 20 years out of office, or in office without power, until Disraeli 'educated' his party into accepting parliamentary and social change, extended the franchise

to the artisan (winning considerable working-class support), launched imperial expansion, and established an alliance with industry and finance. The Irish Home Rule issue of 1886 drove Radical Imperialists and old-fashioned Whigs into alliance with the Conservatives, so that the party had nearly 20 years of office, but fear that Joseph Chamberlain's protectionism would mean higher prices led to a Liberal landslide in 1906. The Conservative Party fought a rearguard action against the sweeping reforms that followed and only the outbreak of World War I averted a major crisis. During 1915–45, except briefly in 1924 and 1929–31, the Conservatives were continually in office, whether alone or as part of a coalition, largely thanks to the break-up of the traditional two-party system by the rise of Labour.

Labour swept to power after World War II, but the Conservative Party formulated a new policy in their Industrial Charter of 1947, visualizing an economic and social system in which employers and employed, private enterprise and the state, work to mutual advantage. Antagonism to further nationalization and postwar austerity returned the Conservatives to power in 1951 with a small majority, and prosperity kept them in office throughout the 1950s and early 1960s. Narrowly defeated in 1964 under Alec Douglas-Home, the Conservative Party from 1965 elected its leaders, beginning with Edward Heath, who became prime minister in 1970. The imposition of wage controls led to confrontation with the unions; when Heath sought a mandate in February 1974, this resulted in a narrow defeat, repeated in a further election in October 1974.

Margaret Thatcher replaced Heath, and under her leadership the Conservative Party returned to power in May 1979. She was re-elected in 1983 and 1987, but was ousted in November 1990 following an intra-party challenge by Michael Heseltine.

## Constable, John (1776–1837)
English artist; one of the greatest landscape painters of the 19th century. He painted scenes of his native Suffolk, including *The Haywain* (1821; National Gallery, London), as well as castles, cathedrals, landscapes, and coastal scenes in other parts of Britain. Constable inherited the Dutch tradition of sombre Realism, in particular the style of Jacob Ruisdael. He aimed to capture the momentary changes of the weather as well as to create monumental images of British scenery, as in *The White Horse* (1819; Frick Collection, New York) and *Salisbury Cathedral from the Bishop's*

*Grounds* (1827; Victoria and Albert Museum, London).

Constable's paintings are remarkable for their atmospheric effects and were admired by many French painters, including Eugène Delacroix. Notable are *The Leaping Horse* (1825; Royal Academy, London); *The Cornfield* (1826; National Gallery, London); and *Dedham Vale* (1828; National Gallery of Scotland, Edinburgh). His many oil sketches are often considered among his best work.

The flat lands, streams, water meadows and cornfields of his native East Anglia, and especially the part of the Stour valley near his home are now known as 'Constable country'.

In England his immediate influence was practically nil; in France, on the other hand, his influence was felt by the Barbizon School, and later by the Impressionists.

## constitution

The UK is one of the few countries not to adopt a written constitution; instead it has an accumulation of customs and precedents, together with a body of laws defining certain of its aspects. See ◊government.

## Continuity IRA

An extremist Irish Republican terrorist group which split away from the ◊IRA in 1995. It was responsible for blowing up Killyhevlin Hotel, near Enniskillen, in July 1996 and car bombings during 1997 and 1998. It is based in the Irish Republic, just south of the border with Northern Ireland, and is aligned with Republican Sinn Fein, which broke away from Sinn Fein proper in 1986 when the latter decided to take a seat in the Irish Parliament. Although its membership was estimated to be below 50, from September 1998 it was the only Republican terrorist body which remained officially active.

## Conwy

Unitary authority in north Wales, created in 1996 from parts of the former counties of Clwyd and Gwynedd; population (1996) 113,000; area 1,107 sq km/427 sq mi. The principal towns are ◊Conwy (administrative headquarters), Abergele, ◊Llandudno, and Llanrwst.

*Physical*
The rivers Conwy and Elwy flow through the area.

*Features*
Part of the ◊Snowdonia National Park extends into Conwy to the west. The coast is lined with sandy beaches, and includes the seaside town of Colwyn Bay, known as 'the garden resort of Wales'.

*Economy*
Tourism is a major activity.

## Conwy

Port, market town and administrative centre of the ◊Conwy unitary authority, north Wales, situated on a steep slope at the estuary of the River Conwy; population (1991) 3,600. It was known until 1972 by the anglicized form **Conway**. Still surrounded by walls, it has the ruins of a castle rebuilt by Edward I in 1284 to subjugate the Welsh. Bodnant Gardens are situated on the east bank of the river.

**Castle Conwy**, one of the finest feudal fortresses of Britain, has very thick walls and eight vast towers. It was held for Charles I in the Civil War. The Cistercian monks who inhabited the abbey, built in 1185 in the same area, were removed by Edward I to Maenan, near Llanwrst; the abbey ruins can still be seen. The ancient church at Conwy, which contains part of the old abbey building, has a magnificent 15th-century rood screen. Plas Mawr, an old Elizabethan mansion, is now the home of the Royal Cambrian Academy of Art. The remains of the Roman fort of **Conovium** (Caerhun) are 8 km/5 mi from Conwy. The site was excavated in 1926–27, showing that it was probably built in about 80 and evacuated about 140.

## Cook, James (1728–1779)

English naval explorer. After surveying the St Lawrence River in North America in 1759, he made three voyages: 1768–71 to Tahiti, New Zealand, and Australia; 1772–75 to the South Pacific; and 1776–79 to the South and North Pacific, attempting to find the Northwest Passage and charting the Siberian coast. He was largely responsible for Britain's initial interest in acquiring colonies in Australasia. He was killed in Hawaii early in 1779 in a scuffle with islanders.

## Cook, Thomas (1808–1892)

Pioneer British travel agent and founder of Thomas Cook & Son. He organized his first tour, to Switzerland, in 1863. He introduced traveller's cheques (then called 'circular notes') in the early 1870s.

## Cookham-on-Thames

Town in Windsor and Maidenhead unitary authority, southern England, on the River Thames, 43 km/27 mi west of London. A memorial gallery of the work of the artist Stanley ◊Spencer, who lived in Cookham for many years, was opened here in 1962. The Keeper of Royal Swans is based here.

## Cookson, Catherine (1906–1998)
English popular novelist. From 1950 she was a prolific author of bestselling fiction set in her native Tyneside, northeast England. Her books, characterized by romance and tragedy, are set in various periods from the 19th century onwards. They include the Mallen trilogy (1973–74) and the Tilly Trotter series (1980–82). More recent novels include *The House of Women* (1992), *A Ruthless Need* (1995), *The Branded Man* (1996), and *The Bonny Dawn* (1996).

## Cooper, Susie (1902–1995)
English pottery designer. Her designs varied from colourful Art Deco to softer, pastel decoration on more classical shapes, with simply-styled patterns of bands, spots, flowers, and animals. She started her own company in 1929 for painting ready-made pottery, and this later became part of the Wedgwood factory, where she was senior designer from 1966.

## Corfe Castle
Village in the Isle of Purbeck, Dorset, southern England, 8 km/5 mi southwest of Poole; population (1981) 1,300. It was built around the ruins of a Norman castle, destroyed during the English Civil War. Industries include electronics and oil, and tourism is important.

The castle is situated on a high ridge, separated from the village by a ravine over which a bridge has been built. It was built in the 11th century on the site of a Saxon stronghold where King ◊Edward the Martyr was murdered in 978. It was captured by the Earl of Devonshire in the reign of Stephen, and during the English Civil War the castle was a Royalist stronghold and the home of John Bankes, chief justice to Charles I. In 1643 his wife defended it for six weeks against 600 Parliamentary troops, but the castle was finally captured and largely destroyed in 1646.

## Cornhill
Street in the City of London, running from the Royal Exchange to Leadenhall Street. It contains the churches of St Michael and St Peter, both built by Christopher ◊Wren, as well as many banks and insurance offices.

The Royal Exchange, situated between Cornhill and Threadneedle Street, was originally built by Sir Thomas Gresham between 1566 and 1571 as a centre for the meetings of merchants and bankers. It was destroyed in the Fire of London in 1666 and rebuilt between 1667 and 1669; it was again destroyed by fire in 1838, and rebuilt between 1842 and 1844.

A Roman basilica used to stand at the eastern end of Cornhill, partly on the site now occupied by Leadenhall Market. A general market appears to have existed here in the 14th century.

## Cornish language
Extinct member of the ◊Celtic languages, a branch of the Indo-European language family, spoken in Cornwall, England, until 1777. In recent years the language has been revived in a somewhat reconstructed form by people interested in their Cornish heritage.

## Corn Laws
In Britain until 1846, laws used to regulate the export or import of cereals in order to maintain an adequate supply for consumers and a secure price for producers. For centuries the Corn Laws formed an integral part of the mercantile system in England; they were repealed because they became an unwarranted tax on food and a hindrance to British exports.

Although mentioned as early as the 12th century, the Corn Laws only became significant in the late 18th century. After the Napoleonic wars, with mounting pressure from a growing urban population, the laws aroused strong opposition because of their tendency to drive up prices. They were modified in 1828 and 1842. The Corn Laws became a hotly contested political issue, as they were regarded by radicals as benefiting wealthy landowners at the expense of the ordinary consumer. The Anti-Corn Law League was formed to campaign for the repeal of the laws in 1838. Partly as a result of the league, and also partly on account of the Irish potato famine, the laws were repealed by prime minister Robert ◊Peel in 1846.

## Cornwall
County in southwest England including the Isles of ◊Scilly (Scillies); population (1996) 483,300; area (excluding Scillies) 3,550 sq km/1,370 sq mi. It occupies the extreme southwest tip of England, ending at ◊Land's End in the far west and ◊Lizard Point to the south, and has rocky cliffs along its coastline and hills and moorland in the interior. A coastal footpath follows most of the dramatic coastline. As a result of its isolated position, it has retained a strong Cornish identity. The ◊Cornish

**Cornwall** Cotehele House, which stands above the River Tamar valley in Cornwall, was built by a prosperous family 1485–1627, largely from the local materials of granite and slatestone. It is one of numerous attractions in the richly varied duchy of Cornwall. Andrew Besley/National Trust Photographic Library

language was widely spoken until the 18th century and many words survive in local names. The principal towns and cities are ⬦Truro (administrative headquarters), Camborne, and Launceston; Bude, ⬦Falmouth, ⬦Newquay, ⬦Penzance, and ⬦St Ives are resorts. The climate is mild, particularly in the south, and vegetation grows prolifically.

### History
Tin was mined in Cornwall from the Bronze Age and traded abroad, as far as Greece and Phoenicia. In 1998 the last mine, at South Crofty, near Camborne, was closed. The Stannary, or Tinners' Parliament, has six members from each of the four Stannary towns: Losthwithiel, Launceston, Helston, and Truro. Established in the 11th century, it ceased to meet in 1752, but its powers were never rescinded at Westminster and it was revived in 1974 as a separatist movement. The flag of St Piran, a white St George's cross on a black ground, is used by separatists.

### Physical
The northern, Atlantic coastline of Cornwall is formed of rugged cliffs, and is famous for its wild scenery. Although it has only two harbours of any importance – one formed by the estuary of the River Camel (where Padstow is situated), the

other at St Ives bay – there are numerous small creeks, formerly used by smugglers. The southern coast is also rocky, but to a lesser degree, and has headlands covered with luxuriant vegetation; the most important harbour is at Falmouth. The surface of Cornwall is extremely irregular; from the River Tamar, which forms the border with Devon, to Land's End it is a series of rugged hills, alternating with wide stretches of moorland and bogs. The highest point is Brown Willy (419 m/1,375 ft) on Bodmin Moor. The Tamar is the county's chief river; it is tidal, and navigable for 30 km/19 mi; other rivers are the Camel, Fal, Fowey, and Tamar. The Scilly Isles are 38 km/24 mi west of Land's End.

### Features
There are several types of prehistoric remains in Cornwall: cromlechs, such as Lanyon, Mulfra, and Zennor (all in the Land's End district); rough monoliths, found in all parts of Cornwall; stone circles, of which the principal one is the Hurlers, near Liskeard; stone avenues, an example being the Nine Maidens near St Colomb Major; and the remains of hut dwellings. Later historic remains include the Romano-Cornish village of Chysauster and many ruined cliff-top and hill-top castles; famous examples are the castles at ⬦Tintagel (the

legendary birthplace of King Arthur) and Launceston, parts of which date from Norman times. Other castles are Henry VIII's Pendennis Castle and St Mawes Castle opposite each other at Falmouth and the remains of the 12th-century Restormel Castle overlooking the River Fowey. St Michael's Mount is a small island in Mount's Bay with a picturesque castle on the summit, linked to Marazion on the mainland by a causeway.

Country houses include ◊Cotehele House, a medieval and Tudor manor; Lanhydrock, dating from the 17th century but rebuilt in the 19th century; and Trerice, an Elizabeth manor. Dosmany Pool is a circular lake on Bodmin Moor into which the knight Sir Bedivere is said to have cast King Arthur's sword Excalibur at his death. The Padstow Hobbyhorse ceremony is held each year on 1 May. Poldhu is the site of the first transatlantic radio signal in 1901. St Ives is associated with the St Ives School of painters, whose work is displayed in a branch of the Tate Gallery here (opened in 1993). The Mineral Tramways Project, which aims to preserve the mining landscape, was once the centre of the world's hard-rock mining industry. The 'Lost' Gardens of Heligan were opened to the public in 1992, after restoration. The Eden Project consists of two 'biomes' (tropical rainforest and Mediterranean) built in a disused china-clay pit near St Austell, scheduled for 2000 as a Millennium Commission Landmark Project.

*Economy*
Cornwall's mines were formerly a great source of wealth, yielding the elements arsenic, bismuth, copper, iron, lead, tin, and zinc. At one time Cornwall supplied half of the world's copper, and all of Britain's tin. Today agriculture and tourism are the main sources of income. Crops are early in some places: fruit, oats, and vegetables, including swedes, turnips, and mangolds. Spring flowers are cultivated and there is cattle and sheep rearing. Mevagissey, Newlyn, and St Ives are the principal fishing ports. Ornaments are produced from serpentine rock, quarried mainly in the Lizard district.

## Coronation Street
Drama serial produced for ITV by Granada since 1961. See ◊soap operas.

## Cotehele
Medieval house near Calstock, Cornwall, England, on the west bank of the River Tamar. The house, which is virtually unaltered, was acquired by the National Trust, together with 520 ha/1,284 acres, through the Treasury in 1947.

The original furniture, fabrics, and armour remain in the house. The estate includes a valley shrub garden with many subtropical plants; **Cotehele Quay** on a bend of the river, 1 km/0.5 mi below the house; and Morden Mill, the manorial water-mill, are now restored to working order.

## Cotman, John Sell (1782–1842)
English landscape painter. With John Crome, he was a founder of the ◊Norwich School. His early watercolours were bold designs in simple flat washes of colour; *Greta Bridge, Yorkshire* (about 1805; British Museum, London) was a classic in the art.

In the simplification of design to broad, expressively silhouetted areas, he was highly original and unlike any of his contemporaries.

Of his two painter sons, **Joseph John Cotman** (1814–1878) and **Miles Edmund Cotman** (1810–1858), the latter is the more distinguished for his river and sea views.

## Cotswold Hills, or Cotswolds
Range of limestone hills in Gloucestershire, South Gloucestershire, and Bath and North East Somerset, England, 80 km/50 mi long, between Bath and Chipping Camden. They rise to 333 m/1,086 ft at Cleeve Cloud, near Cheltenham, but average about 200 m/600 ft. The area is known for its picturesque villages, built with the local honey-coloured stone. Tourism is important.

*History*
Old tracks and evidence of early British forts and Roman camps indicate that the area was important in ancient times. It prospered in the 14th and 16th centuries when the woollen industry flourished. The decline of the area's wool industry was primarily triggered by the industrialization of the 1830s, which led to labour disputes, fluctuating markets, strikes, failing machinery, and mill closures.

The artist William ◊Morris, founder of the Arts and Crafts movement, spent his holidays in Broadway and lived at Kelmscott Manor, Lechlade, from 1871 until his death in 1876; he is buried in the churchyard with his wife Jane. Following his patronization of the town, Broadway quickly became a favourite venue for visiting artists; at one stage Broadway Green was so busy that easel space had to be rented.

*Principal towns and villages*
Among the chief towns in the region are Stroud, ◊Cirencester, Chipping Norton, Chipping Campden, Stow-on-the-Wold, ◊Malmesbury, Bourton-on-the-Water, Northleach, Lechlade,

Burford, and Tetbury. Gloucester, Cheltenham, Tewkesbury, and Evesham are on the periphery of the Cotswolds area. The main villages are Winchcombe, Cleeve-Hill, Upper and Lower Slaughter, Sherborne, Painswick, Bibury, Sapperton, Fairford, and Broadway, which is known as the 'gateway' to the Cotswolds.

## council

In local government in England and Wales, a popularly elected local assembly charged with the government of the area within its boundaries. Under the Local Government Act 1972, they comprise three types: ◊county councils, district councils (a lower unit of administration), and ◊parish councils (the lowest administrative unit).

## Council for the Protection of Rural England

Countryside conservation group founded in 1926 by the architect and town planner Patrick Abercrombie (1879–1957), with interests ranging from planning controls to energy policy. A central organization campaigns on national issues and 42 local groups lobby on regional matters.

The **Campaign for the Preservation of Rural Wales** is the Welsh equivalent.

## country park

Pleasure ground or park, often located near an urban area, providing facilities for the public enjoyment of the countryside. Country parks were introduced in the UK following the 1968 Countryside Act and are the responsibility of local authorities with assistance from the Countryside Commission. They cater for a range of recreational activities such as walking, boating, and horse-riding.

## Countryside Agency

Statutory conservation body established in 1999, when the Countryside Commission was merged with the Rural Development Commission (RDC). The agency, which has an advisory and executive role, works to conserve and enhance the English countryside and to increase the enjoyment derived from it. It also has a commitment to promote social equity and economic opportunity for the people who live in the countryside.

It designates Areas of Outstanding Natural Beauty and National Trails, as well as National Parks, and as part of a Coastal Heritage Forum designates Heritage Coasts in England.

## Countryside Council for Wales

Welsh nature conservation body formed in 1991 by the fusion of the former Nature Conservancy Council and the Welsh Countryside Commission. It is government-funded and administers conservation and land-use policies within Wales.

## county (Latin *comitatus* through French *comté*)

The name given by the Normans to Anglo-Saxon 'shires'; the boundaries of many present-day English counties date back to Saxon times. There are currently 34 English administrative non-metropolitan counties and 6 metropolitan counties, in addition to 34 unitary authorities. Welsh and Scottish counties were abolished in 1996 in a reorganization of local government throughout the UK, and replaced by 22 and 33 unitary authorities respectively. Northern Ireland has 6 geographical counties, although administration is through 26 district councils.

## county council

In England, a unit of local government whose responsibilities include broad planning policy, highways, education, personal social services, and libraries; police, fire, and traffic control; and refuse disposal. The tier below the county council has traditionally been the district council, but with local government reorganization from 1996, there has been a shift towards unitary authorities (based on a unit smaller than the county) replacing both.

## County Hall

Building in central London, on the River Thames opposite the Palace of Westminster. Opened in 1922, it was the headquarters of the governing body for London until the abolition of the Greater London Council (GLC) by the Conservative government in 1986. Part of the building now houses the London Aquarium. The main building was designed by Ralph Knott.

## Courtauld, Samuel (1793–1881)

English industrialist who developed the production of viscose rayon and other synthetic fibres from 1804. He founded the firm of Courtauld's in 1816 in Bocking, Essex, and at first specialized in silk and crepe manufacture.

His great-nephew **Samuel Courtauld** (1876–1947) was chair of the firm from 1921, and in 1931 gave his house and art collection to the University of London as the **Courtauld Institute**.

## Coutts, Thomas (1735–1822)

British banker. He established with his brother the firm of Coutts & Co (one of London's oldest banking houses, founded in 1692 in the Strand), becoming sole head on the latter's death in 1778.

Since the reign of George III an account has been maintained there by every succeeding sovereign.

## Covent Garden

Popular name of the Royal Opera House at Covent Garden, London. The present building was completed in 1858 after two previous ones burnt down. The ◊ Royal Ballet is also in residence here.

In 1997 the Royal Opera House closed for a complete reconstruction, including the provision of a second auditorium. It reopened late 1999, after a series of financial crises.

## Covent Garden

London square (named from the convent garden once on the site) laid out by Inigo Jones in 1631. The buildings that formerly housed London's fruit and vegetable market (moved to Nine Elms, Wandsworth 1973) have been adapted for shops and restaurants. The Royal Opera House, also housing the Royal Ballet, is here; also the London Transport Museum.

The Theatre Museum, opened 1987, is in the Old Flower Market.

## Coventry

Industrial city in the West Midlands, England, 29 km/18 mi southeast of Birmingham; population (1994 est) 303,000. As a centre of armaments manufacture during World War II, it was the target of a massive German air raid in 1940 in which much of the city centre was destroyed, including the medieval cathedral. Comprehensive restoration and redevelopment of the city has since taken place and it is the site of a modern cathedral and two universities.

### History

Long established as one of Britain's principal engineering and manufacturing centres, Coventry has an industrial heritage dating back many centuries. By the 14th century the city was the focus for the wool trade and cloth industry in the Midlands and it later became known for its caps, bonnets, silk ribbons, clocks, and watches. The manufacture of bicycles and motor vehicles began in the late 19th century.

### Features

Post-war architecture dominates most of the city centre and few historic buildings survive. The Herbert Gallery and Museum illustrates the legend of Lady Godiva who is said to have ridden naked through the streets of Coventry to protest against the taxes introduced by her husband Leofric, Earl of Mercia. Every three years the city hosts one of the four surviving mystery play cycles performed in England. Under the Phoenix Initiative, a project to mark the millennium, Coventry is undergoing a programme of regeneration, with parts of the city centre being excavated prior to redevelopment.

### Coventry Cathedral

The impressive modern Coventry Cathedral, built next to the ruins of the medieval cathedral, was designed by the Scottish architect Basil Spence (1907–1976) and consecrated in 1962. On the east side of the porch is Jacob ◊ Epstein's statue *St Michael Overcoming the Devil*. The west wall of the cathedral is made of glass, the nave is inset with a series of long windows, each strikingly different, and the massive baptistry window, by John Piper (1903–1992), is intended to represent the Love of God flowing into the world. Behind the altar hangs Graham ◊ Sutherland's tapestry *Christ in Majesty*, measuring 23×11 m/75×36 ft. Benjamin Britten composed his *War Requiem* for the consecration ceremony.

## Coverdale, Miles (1488–1568)

English Protestant priest whose translation of the Bible, *Coverdale's Bible* (1535), was the first to be printed in English. In 1539 he edited the *Great Bible* which was ordered to be placed in churches. His translation of the psalms is that retained in the Book of Common Prayer.

---

*Mad dogs and Englishmen / Go out in the midday sun.*

**Noël Coward** English dramatist and composer.
'Mad Dogs and Englishmen'

---

## Coward, Noël (1899–1973)

English dramatist, actor, revue-writer, director, and composer. He epitomized the witty and sophisticated man of the theatre. From his first success with *The Young Idea* (1923), he wrote and appeared in plays and comedies on both sides of the Atlantic such as *Hay Fever* (1925), *Private Lives* (1930) with Gertrude Lawrence, *Design for Living* (1933), *Blithe Spirit* (1941), and *A Song at Twilight* (1966). His revues and musicals included *On With the Dance* (1925) and *Bitter Sweet* (1929).

Coward also wrote for and acted in films, including the patriotic *In Which We Serve* (1942) and the sentimental *Brief Encounter* (1945). After World War II he became a nightclub and cabaret entertainer, performing songs like 'Mad Dogs and Englishmen'.

## Cowes

Seaport and resort on the north coast of the Isle of Wight, England, on the Medina estuary, opposite Southampton Water, 14 km/9 mi southwest of Portsmouth; population (1981) 19,600. A major yachting centre, Cowes is the starting point for the Around the World Yacht Race, finishing at Cape Town; and **Cowes Castle** is the headquarters of the Royal Yacht Squadron, which holds the annual **Cowes Week** regatta. Maritime-related industries include boatbuilding, marine engineering, sail-making, hovercraft construction, and the manufacture of radar equipment. Tourism is important; facilities include the island's ferry connection with Southampton.

*Features*

East Cowes is the location of ◊Osborne House, built by Albert, the Prince Consort, and Thomas Cubitt. The house was a seaside residence of Queen Victoria, who died there in 1901. To the south of Osborne House is Whippingham Church (1854–62), reputedly designed by Prince Albert.

## Cowper, William (1731–1800)

English poet. His verse anticipates ◊Romanticism and includes the six books of *The Task* (1785). He also wrote hymns (including 'God Moves in a Mysterious Way').

Cowper's work is important for its directness and descriptive accuracy, and it deals with natural themes later developed in Wordsworth's poetry. Cowper was also among the finest of English letter writers. His letters contain humorous accounts of the trivia of rural life and sensitive descriptions of nature, disrupted from time to time by the expression of irrational fear.

## Cozens, John Robert (1752–1797)

English landscape painter, a watercolourist. His romantic views of Europe, mostly Alpine and Italian views, painted on tours in the 1770s and 1780s, were very popular and greatly influenced the development of English landscape painting.

He was taught painting by his father, the painter Alexander Cozens (*c.* 1717–1786). He became mentally ill in 1794 and was cared for by Dr Thomas Monro (1759–1833), a patron of art. Cozens's drawings in his collection influenced the young Thomas Girtin and J M W Turner, employed by Monro in copying them. John Constable claimed that Cozens was 'the greatest genius who ever touched landscape' and 'all poetry'.

## Craigavon

City in Armagh county, Northern Ireland; population (1990 est) 62,000. It was created by integrating Lurgan and Portadown, with a new town centre and new residential and industrial areas, and was designated a new town in 1965. It was named after James Craig (Viscount Craigavon), the first prime minister of Northern Ireland (1921–40).

## Craigievar Castle

Stately 17th-century castle built on a hillside 5 km/3 mi north of Lumphanan, Aberdeenshire, Scotland, by William Forbes. The castle is little altered, and contains magnificent plasterwork in the Elizabethan style. Craigievar was acquired by the National Trust for Scotland in 1963.

## Cranmer, Thomas (1489–1556)

English clergyman, archbishop of Canterbury from 1533. A Protestant convert, he helped to shape the doctrines of the Church of England under Edward VI. He was responsible for the issue of the Prayer Books of 1549 and 1552, and supported the succession of Lady Jane Grey in 1553.

Condemned for heresy under the Catholic Mary I, he at first recanted, but when his life was not spared, resumed his position and was burned at the stake, first holding to the fire the hand which had signed his recantation.

Cranmer suggested in 1529 that the question of Henry VIII's marriage to Catherine of Aragón should be referred to the universities of Europe rather than to the pope, and in 1533 he declared it null and void. Three years later he annulled the marriage with Anne Boleyn in the same fashion. In 1540 he divorced Henry from Anne of Cleves.

## Crathes Castle

Castle near Crathes, Aberdeenshire, Scotland, built 1546–96 on the north side of the River Dee by the Burnett family. It contains original tempera painted ceilings, and the problem of preserving these has prompted the establishment of a centre for the restoration of tempera in Edinburgh. Crathes was given to the National Trust for Scotland in 1951.

## Crawley

Town in West Sussex, England, northeast of Horsham, 45 km/28 mi south of London; population (1991) 88,200; Crawley urban area 114,600. Originally chartered by King John in 1202, it developed as a new town from 1947. It is a centre of light industry and lies close to London's Gatwick Airport.

## Crewe

Industrial town in Cheshire, England; population (1991) 63,400. Crewe expanded rapidly in the mid-19th century as the hub of a six-point star of railways, and it remains a major railway junction and engineering centre. Britain's last steam engine was constructed here.

## cricket

The exact origins of cricket are unknown, but it certainly dates back to the 16th century. The name is thought to have originated from the Anglo-Saxon word *cricc*, meaning a shepherd's staff. The first players were the shepherds of south-east England, who used their crooks as bats and the wicket gate and movable bail of the sheep pens as a target for the bowlers.

In the 18th century, runs were recorded by notches cut on a stick. The wicket consisted of two stumps and a crosspiece (the third stump was added in the late 1770s). Until about 1773 bats retained the curve akin to a hockey stick, suited to deal with the prevalent under-arm bowling of the time. By about 1780 the straight bat was in almost universal use to counter the advance in bowling technique whereby the ball rose from the pitch on a 'length'.

The first major alteration in the laws for which the Marylebone Cricket Club (MCC) was responsible was the licence given to the bowler in 1835 to raise his arm as high as the shoulder and bowl round-arm. Formerly he was compelled to deliver the ball underarm and the new method had for years been the subject of heated argument. This concession was the prelude to the legalization of overarm bowling in 1864. Modern bat blades are made of willow (*salix coerulea*) with handles of compressed cane and rubber; early bats were in

## British Cricket: Some key dates

**c. 1550** An English court case of 1598 refers to 'crickett' being played at the 'Free School' at Guildford, Surrey, at this time. It is the first certain reference to cricket.

**1646** The first recorded cricket match in England is played at Coxheath, Kent.

**1709** Kent play Surrey in the first 'county' cricket match, at Dartford Brent, England.

**1744** The first known Laws of Cricket, probably a revision of an existing code, are issued by the cricketers of the London Star and Garter Club.

**18 June 1744** Kent defeat All England at the Artillery ground, London, in the first major cricket match of which a full record of the score survives.

**c. 1767** The Hambledon Club, the first great cricket club, is formed near the village of Hambledon in Hampshire.

**1787** The Marylebone Cricket Club (MCC) is founded by Thomas Lord and members of the White Conduit Club, at Thomas Lord's new private ground at Dorset Square, Marylebone, London.

**1814** The Marylebone Cricket Club (MCC) moves Lord's cricket ground to its present site at St John's Wood, London.

**1839** Sussex County Cricket Club, the oldest first-class English county cricket club, is established as the Royal Sussex Cricket Club.

**1871** The English cricketer W(illiam) G(ilbert) Grace and his brothers found the Gloucestershire Cricket Club.

**1890** Surrey wins the first official English County Cricket Championship.

**24 June 1938–27 June 1938** Test Cricket from Lord's is broadcast on British television for the first time.

**1947** In the course of the English first-class cricket season, the English batsman Denis Compton of Middlesex scores a record 3,816 runs, including an unprecedented and unsurpassed 18 centuries.

**27–31 July 1956** In the fourth Cricket Test between England and Australia at Old Trafford, Manchester, the England offspinner Jim Laker becomes the first bowler to take all ten wickets in a Test match innings. His match analysis of 19–90 beats the previous Test record of 17–159 set by S F Barnes in 1913–14.

**16–20 July 1962** The Gentlemen v. Players cricket match, established in 1806, is played for the last time at Lord's, London, as the Marylebone Cricket Club (MCC) votes to abolish the distinction between amateurs ('gentlemen') and professionals ('players').

**7 September 1963** Cricket's first limited-overs competition, sponsored by Gillette, is held in England. In the final at the Lord's ground, Sussex beat Worcestershire by 14 runs.

**21 July 1981** In the third Test at Leeds against Australia, England becomes only the second side in 104 years of Test cricket to win a match after being forced to follow on. Ian Botham saves England from defeat with an innings of 149 not out, then Bob Willis takes 8 for 43 in Australia's second innings to give England victory.

**19 March 1982** Fifteen England cricketers led by Graham Gooch are banned from Test cricket for three years for participating in a cricket tour of South Africa, breaking an international ban on sporting links with that country because of its policy on apartheid.

**September 1998** The Marylebone Cricket Club votes in favour of admitting women members for the first time in its 211 year history.

one piece. The early Victorian period saw the introduction of protective clothing.

*Test cricket*

The first Test match (that is, between countries) held in England was in 1880. In 1882 Australia's victory over England at the Oval inspired a journalist to write a mock obituary notice of English cricket, in which he coined the term the ◊Ashes. The introduction of the six-ball over in England in 1900 aided higher scoring; bowlers countered the batting dominance by the practice of swing bowling (by fast bowlers), and the introduction in the early 1900s of the 'googly', a style quickly adopted around the world.

**Players and grounds**

Great English cricketers have included W G ◊Grace, Jack Hobbs, Len ◊Hutton, and Denis ◊Compton. Major grounds in England include ◊Lord's (London), Kennington ◊Oval (London), ◊Old Trafford (Manchester), Edgbaston (Birmingham), ◊Trent Bridge (Nottingham), and ◊Headingley (Leeds).

---

*It is hard to tell where the MCC ends and the Church of England begins.*

**J B Priestley** English novelist and playwright.
*New Statesman* 20 July 1962

---

## Crimean War

War 1853–56 between Russia and the allied powers of England, France, Turkey, and Sardinia. The war arose from British and French mistrust of Russia's ambitions in the Balkans. It began with an allied Anglo-French expedition to the Crimea to attack the Russian Black Sea city of Sevastopol. The battles of the River Alma, Balaclava (including the ◊Charge of the Light Brigade), and Inkerman 1854 led to a siege which, owing to military mismanagement, lasted for a year until September 1855. The war was ended by the Treaty of Paris in 1856. The scandal surrounding French and British losses through disease led to the organization of proper military nursing services by Florence ◊Nightingale.

## Crippen, Hawley (1861–1910)

US murderer who killed his wife, variety artist Belle Elmore, in 1910. He buried her remains in the cellar of his London home and tried to escape to the USA with his mistress Ethel le Neve (dressed as a boy). He was arrested on board ship following a radio message, the first criminal captured 'by radio', and was hanged.

## Crome, John (1768–1821)

English landscape painter. He was a founder of the ◊Norwich School with John Sell ◊Cotman in 1803. His works, which show the influence of Dutch landscape painting, include *Boy Keeping Sheep* (1812; Victoria and Albert Museum); *Mousehold Heath* (about 1814–16), 'painted for air and space'; *The Poringland Oak* (1818; National Gallery); and *The Slate Quarries* (about 1802–05) and *Moonrise on the Yare* (about 1811–16), both in the Tate Gallery, London.

## Cromer

Seaside resort on the northeast coast of Norfolk, England, 37 km/23 mi north of Norwich; population (1991) 4,800. Apart from tourism, fishing (especially for crabs) is the main activity.

Cromer became popular as a holiday destination because of its favourable location, sheltered on the land side by hills and woods. The sea has greatly encroached on parts of the coast; the cliffs are protected by sea walls at Cromer, but are subject to rapid erosion between Cromer and Overstrand. There is a lifeboat station and a lighthouse, whose light is visible for 37 km/23 mi.

## Crompton, Samuel (1753–1827)

English inventor at the time of the Industrial Revolution. He developed the 'spinning mule' in 1779 in Bolton, combining the ideas of Richard ◊Arkwright and James ◊Hargreaves. This span a fine, continuous yarn and revolutionized the production of high-quality cotton textiles.

Crompton's invention was called the mule because it was a hybrid. It used the best from the spinning jenny and from Richard Arkwright's water frame of 1768. The strong, even yarn it produced was so fine that it could be used to weave delicate fabrics such as muslin, which became fashionable among the middle and upper classes, creating a new market for the British cotton trade. Spinning was taken out of the home and into the factories.

## Cromwell, Oliver (1599–1658)

English general and politician, Puritan leader of the Parliamentary side in the ◊Civil War. He raised cavalry forces (later called Ironsides) which aided the victories at Edgehill in 1642 and Marston Moor in 1644, and organized the New Model Army, which he led (with General Fairfax) to victory at Naseby in 1645. He declared Britain a republic ('the Commonwealth') in 1649, following the execution of Charles I. As Lord Protector (ruler) from 1653, Cromwell established religious

**Oliver Cromwell** Oliver Cromwell, in a painting attributed to Van Dyck. Lord Protector and virtual dictator of England after the execution of Charles I, Cromwell inherited a divided and war-weary nation, to which he forcibly united Scotland and Ireland for the first time in their histories. His rule became associated with an unpopular type of Puritan zeal, and the Stuart Charles II was welcomed back by most of Britain after Cromwell's death. Philip Sauvain Picture Collection

toleration and raised Britain's prestige in Europe on the basis of an alliance with France against Spain.

Cromwell was born at Huntingdon, northwest of Cambridge, the son of a small landowner. He entered Parliament in 1629 and became active in the events leading to the Civil War. Failing to secure a constitutional settlement with Charles I 1646–48, he defeated the 1648 Scottish invasion at Preston. A special commission, of which Cromwell was a member, tried the king and condemned him to death, and a republic, known as 'the Commonwealth', was set up.

The ◊ Levellers demanded radical reforms, but he executed their leaders in 1649. He used terror to crush Irish clan resistance 1649–50, and defeated the Scots (who had acknowledged Charles II) at Dunbar in 1650 and Worcester in 1651. In 1653, having forcibly expelled the corrupt 'Rump Parliament', he summoned a convention ('Barebones Parliament', named after a member, Praise-God Barbon), soon dissolved as too radical, and under a constitution (the 'Instrument of Government') drawn up by the army leaders, became Protector (king in all but name). The Parliament of 1654–55 was dissolved as uncooperative, and after a period of military dictatorship, his last Parliament offered him the crown; he refused because he feared the army's republicanism.

*Take away these baubles.*

    **Oliver Cromwell** English general and politician. Referring to the symbols of Parliamentary power when he dismissed Parliament 1653

### Cromwell, Thomas, Earl of Essex (c. 1485–1540)

English politician who drafted the legislation that made the Church of England independent of Rome. Originally in Lord Chancellor Wolsey's service, he became secretary to Henry VIII in 1534 and the real director of government policy; he was executed for treason.

### Crown jewels, or regalia

Symbols of royal authority, used by royalty on state occasions. The British set (except for the Ampulla and the Anointing Spoon) were broken up at the time of Oliver Cromwell, and the current set dates from the Restoration of the monarchy in 1660. In 1671 Colonel Blood attempted to steal them, but was captured, then pardoned and pensioned by Charles II; Blood's previous association with Protestant Irish rebel groups suggest he may have been a government spy. The Crown Jewels are kept in the Tower of London in the Crown Jewel House.

### Crufts

UK's largest dog show. The first show was organized in 1886 by the dog expert **Charles Cruft** (1852–1938), and from that year annual shows bearing his name were held in Islington, London. In 1948 the show's venue moved to Olympia and in 1979 to Earl's Court. Since 1991 it has been held at the NEC in Birmingham.

### Cruikshank, George (1792–1878)

English painter and illustrator. He is remembered for his political cartoons and illustrations for Charles Dickens' *Oliver Twist* and Daniel Defoe's *Robinson Crusoe*. From 1835 he published the *Comic Almanack*, a forerunner of *Punch*.

Following his father, he began with political and social caricatures in the Gillray and Rowlandson style for *The Scourge* (1811–16) and *The Meteor* (1813–14), but evolved a grotesque and humorous manner of his own in sketches of Victorian London life and in book illustration.

## Crusades, the (French *croisade*)

Series of wars undertaken 1096–1291 by European rulers intended, among other things, to recover Palestine from the Muslims. Motivated by religious zeal, the desire for land, and the trading ambitions of the major Italian cities, the Crusades had varying degrees of success in their aims and effects.

Several expeditions were mounted towards the end of the 1100s in response to the conquests of Saladin, Sultan of Egypt, who had captured Damascus in 1174, Aleppo in 1183, and Jerusalem in October 1187. The most important of these expeditions was the Third Crusade led by Philip II of France, Frederick I Barbarossa of Germany, and ◊Richard I of England in 1189. Richard distinguished himself in the capture of Acre, but quarrelled with his allies, who left him to carry on the war alone. After a year of brilliant but useless exploits, he made a truce with Saladin, and returned to Europe.

Almost a century later, in 1270 Prince Edward of England (later ◊Edward I), led his own followers to Acre, but achieved no results.

## Cuillin Hills

Range of mountains in southern Skye, the largest island of the Inner Hebrides, in Highland unitary authority, Scotland, running southwestwards from Sligachan to Loch Coriusk. The Cuillin Hills have an average height of 895 m/2,936 ft to 965 m/3,166 ft, and their precipitous ridges attract numerous climbers. The highest point is Sgurr Alasdair, which rises to 993 m/3,257 ft.

## Culloden, Battle of

Defeat in 1746 of the ◊Jacobite rebel army of the British prince ◊Charles Edward Stuart (the 'Young Pretender') by the Duke of Cumberland on a stretch of moorland near Inverness, Scotland. This battle effectively ended the military challenge of the Jacobite rebellion.

## Culzean Castle

Castle 6 km/4 mi west of Maybole, South Ayrshire, Scotland. In 1775 Robert ◊Adam was employed to reconstruct the old castle, and to build a brew-house which was replaced a century later by the present west wing. The castle and over 200 ha/494 acres were given to the National Trust for Scotland in 1945, and in 1971 Scotland's first Country Park was established on the estate.

## Cumbria

County of northwest England, created in 1974; population (1996) 490,600; area 6,810 sq km/2,629 sq mi. It includes the ◊Lake District, with the largest English lakes and the romantic, rugged countryside described by the poets William ◊Wordsworth and Samuel Taylor ◊Coleridge. It also has part of the Yorkshire Dales National Park and the North Pennines. The principal towns and cities are ◊Carlisle (administrative headquarters), Barrow, ◊Kendal, Penrith, Whitehaven, and Workington.

Cumbria is divided into six districts, which are (from north to south): Carlisle, the city and its surrounding area up to the border with Scotland; Allerdale, the northwest coastal lowland with the coastal towns of Maryport and Workington, and the inland towns of Cockermouth and ◊Keswick; Eden, from Helvellyn to the boundary in the Pennines with Northumberland, Durham, and North Yorkshire; Copeland, the western valleys and coastlands, including Whitehaven; South Lakeland, stretching from Grasmere and Ambleside to the shores of Morecambe Bay; and Barrow-in-Furness, which covers the town and neighbouring Dalton-in-Furness. Barrow, Carlisle, and Copeland have been given the status of borough.

*History*

In the 7th century Cumbria was part of ◊Northumbria. In the 10th and 11th centuries it alternated between Scottish and English rule, until it was taken by the English in 1157.

*Physical*

Cumbria is the second largest English county (after North Yorkshire) and one of the least populated. ◊Scafell Pike (978 m/3,210 ft), the highest mountain in England, is in Cumbria, also Helvellyn (950 m/3,118 ft). Lake ◊Windermere is the largest lake in England (17 km/10.5 mi long, 1.6 km/1 mi wide); the other lakes include ◊Derwent Water, ◊Grasmere, Haweswater, and ◊Ullswater. The main rivers are the Eden and Derwent. The M6 motorway runs north to south through the centre of the county.

*Features*

Cumbria has a variety of historic remains, including barrows, stone circles, the western section of ◊Hadrian's Wall, and a number of castles. The Lake District National Park is a major attraction

**Cumbria** Castlerigg stone circle near Keswick in Cumbria. Human settlement of this area, with its plentiful fresh water and natural defensive sites, began in Neolithic times. Cumbria is characterized by its lakes and mountain scenery; behind the stone circle is the peak Blencathra, also called Saddleback. Corel

for tourists and walkers. ◊Dove Cottage at Grasmere was Wordsworth's home, and Beatrix ◊Potter's Hilltop Farm is at Sawrey; both are open to the public. Larger-scale country houses include Holker Hall and its fine gardens and the Elizabethan Levens Hall and topiary garden. The Grizedale Forest sculpture project also draws many visitors. Carlisle has an 11th-century castle and 12th-century cathedral, and the 14th-century Naworth Castle at Brampton provided the setting for Walter Scott's novel *The Lay of the Last Minstrel* (1805). The remains of Furness Abbey, founded in 1123 and taken over by the Cistercians in 1147, are on the ◊Furness peninsula; other ecclesiastical sites are Calder Abbey and Lanercost Priory.

*Economy*

Agriculture is important, primarily dairy farming in the north and east; sheep are also reared. The traditional coal, iron, and steel industries of the coast towns have been replaced by newer industries including chemicals, plastics, marine engineering, electronics, steel, and shipbuilding (at Barrow-in-Furness, nuclear submarines and warships). Tourism and salmon fishing are also important. There are controversial nuclear power stations at Calder Hall and Sellafield (formerly Windscale, the first to produce plutonium in the UK). Permission was granted in 1992 to build fifteen 24 m/80 ft-high wind generators. The British Nuclear Fuels' THORP nuclear reprocessing plant began operating in 1994.

## curling

Game played on ice with stones; sometimes described as 'bowls on ice'. One of the national games of Scotland, it has spread to many countries. It can also be played on artificial (cement or tarmacadam) ponds.

## Cuthbert, St (died 687)

English Christian saint. A shepherd in Northumbria, England, he entered the monastery of Melrose, Scotland, after receiving a vision. He travelled widely as a missionary and because of his alleged miracles was known as the 'wonderworker of Britain'.

He became prior of Lindisfarne in 664, and retired in 676 to Farne Island. In 684 he became bishop of Hexham and later of Lindisfarne.

## *Cutty Sark*

British sailing ship, built in 1869, one of the tea clippers that used to compete in the 19th century to see which clippers could bring its cargo most quickly from China to Britain.

The biennial **Cutty Sark International Tall Ships Race** is named after it. The ship is preserved in dry dock at Greenwich, London.

## daffodil

A national symbol of Wales, worn on St David's Day (1 March), which is traditionally the first day it blooms. In the Scilly Isles Prince Charles is paid one daffodil annually as rent. **National Daffodil Day** has been promoted by Marie Curie Cancer Care since 1990 and the daffodil has also been adopted as a symbol by the Irish Cancer Society.

## Dafydd ap Gwilym (c. 1340–c. 1400)

Welsh poet. His work exhibits a complex but graceful style, concern with nature and love rather than with heroic martial deeds, and has references to Classical and Italian poetry.

Some of his themes recall those of the troubadours and perhaps derive indirectly from them.

## Dahl, Roald (1916–1990)

British writer, of Norwegian ancestry. He is celebrated for short stories with a twist, such as *Tales of the Unexpected* (1979), and for his children's books, including *James and the Giant Peach* (1961), *Charlie and the Chocolate Factory* (1964), *The BFG* (1982), and *Matilda* (1988). Many of his works have been successfully adapted for television or film. He also wrote the screenplay for the James Bond film *You Only Live Twice* (1967).

The enormous popularity of his children's books can be attributed to his weird imagination, the success of his child characters in outwitting their elders, and his repulsive detail.

## Dales, or Yorkshire Dales

Series of river valleys in northern England, running east from the Pennines in West Yorkshire; a National Park was established in 1954. The principal valleys are Airedale, Nidderdale, ◊Swaledale, ◊Wensleydale, and ◊Wharfedale. The three main peaks are Ingleborough, Whernside, and Pen-y-Ghent.

Dairy farming is the main agricultural activity, Wensleydale cheese being the most notable product. Tourism is also important; the Dales offer magnificent scenery, and walking and potholing are popular activities. Dry stone walls and barns are regular features of the landscape.

## Danelaw

11th-century name for the area of north and east England settled by the Vikings in the 9th century. It occupied about half of England, from the River Tees to the River Thames. Within its bounds, Danish law, customs, and language prevailed. Its linguistic influence is still apparent.

## Darling, Grace (1815–1842)

British heroine. She was the daughter of a lighthouse keeper on the Farne Islands, off Northumberland. On 7 September 1838 the *Forfarshire* was wrecked, and Grace Darling and her father rowed through a storm to the wreck, saving nine lives. She was awarded a medal for her bravery.

## Darlington

Industrial town in northeast England, 53 km/33 mi south of Newcastle; population (1996) 100,600. Part of the county of Durham until 1997, it is now a unitary authority with an area of 197 sq km/76 sq mi. Lying in the broad gap between the North Yorkshire moors and the Pennines, which forms the east coast passage between England and Scotland, Darlington prospered in the 19th century after the world's first passenger railway was opened between Darlington and Stockton on 27 September 1825. George ◊Stephenson's *Locomotion*, which pulled the first train to run on the line, is displayed at the Darlington Railway Centre and Museum.

## Darnley, Henry, Lord Darnley (1545–1567)

Scottish aristocrat, second husband of Mary Queen of Scots from 1565, and father of James I of England (James VI of Scotland).

On the advice of her secretary, David Rizzio, Mary refused Darnley the crown matrimonial; in revenge, Darnley led a band of nobles who murdered Rizzio in Mary's presence. Darnley was in turn assassinated in 1567.

## Dartford

Industrial town in Kent, southeast England, on the River Darent to the south of the Thames estuary, 27 km/17 mi southeast of London; population (1991) 59,400. Lying at the point where ◊Watling Street crossed the River Darent, Dartford has a history dating back to Roman times, and is now known for the nearby **Dartford Crossing**, including the **Dartford Tunnel** (1963) which runs under the Thames to Purfleet, Essex, and the Queen Elizabeth II bridge which opened in 1991. Dartford lies within the 'Thames Gateway', an area undergoing a programme of economic development and regeneration. Europe's largest regional shopping centre, Bluewater, opened near Dartford in 1999.

## Dartmoor

Plateau of southwest Devon, England; mostly a national park, 956 sq km/369 sq mi in area. Over half the region is around 300 m/1,000 ft above sea level, making it the highest and largest of the moorland areas in southwest England. The moor is noted for its wild aspect and the tors, rugged blocks of bare granite, which crown its loftier points. The highest are Yes Tor, rising to 619 m/2,030 ft; and High Willhays, which climbs to 621 m/2,039 ft.

The region provides grazing for sheep, cattle, and **Dartmoor ponies**, a semi-wild breed probably descended from animals turned out on the moor in the Dark Ages. Dartmoor was the setting for Arthur Conan Doyle's *The Hound of the Baskervilles*.

### Physical features

The slopes beneath the granite tors are covered by gorse and heather, and the low-lying areas are characterized by broad tracts of dark peat and bog with bright green grass. The region has no natural lakes, but Devon's chief rivers, including the, the Tavy, the Plym, the Avon, and the Erme, have their sources on the moor. Eight reservoirs have been constructed, covering a total 209 ha/516 acres.

The main areas of broad-leaved woodland, mainly oak, lie in deep valleys at the southern edge of the moorland, such as the Dart and the Teign valleys. Originally oak and birch forest covered all but the very highest reaches of the moor, but only three ancient upland copses of oak trees survive at Black Tor Beare, Piles Copse, and Wistman's Wood. The valley woodlands were managed until the 20th century, being used for building, fuel, and other local purposes, but these woods are no longer generating naturally because of grazing pressure and lack of management. Tree preservation orders now cover over 1,100 ha/2,500 acres, and the Forestry Commission manages 1,740 ha/4,300 acres of conifer plantations. In 1990 severe storms destroyed 3% of Dartmoor's woodland, about 107,000 trees.

### Historic remains and architectural features

Extensive evidence of the region's prehistoric occupation includes stone rows, cairns, and the remains of hillfort settlements of the Bronze and Iron ages. Several simple clapper bridges, slabs supported on stones, are preserved. Buckfast Abbey, completed in 1938, occupies the site of an 11th-century abbey near Buckfastleigh, in the southeast region of Dartmoor. A Ministry of Defence artillery range lies in the northern part of the moor to the south of Okehampton.

### Mining

Tin, copper, lead, and manganese were mined in the Middle Ages. The tin industry was ruled through the ◊stannaries courts at Ashburton, Tavistock, Chagford, and Plympton. Offenders breaking the laws of the stannaries were imprisoned in ◊Lydford Castle. The last working tin mine on Dartmoor closed in 1930. Hemerdon, just outside the national park boundary, contains reserves of tungsten, and the southwestern area of the moor has china clay deposits.

### Chief towns

Okehampton lies on the northern boundary of the moor, Ashburton and Buckfastleigh in the east, Widecombe-in-the-Moor in the southeast, Ivybridge in the south, Tavistock and Lydford in the west, and Princetown and Postbridge in the centre of the moor. Ashburton, with about 3,500 inhabitants, is the largest settlement within the national park boundary.

## Dartmouth

English seaport and resort at the mouth of the River Dart; 43 km/27 mi east of Plymouth, on the Devon coast; population (1996 est) 6,000. It is a centre for yachting and has an excellent harbour. The Britannia Royal Naval College dates from 1905. Dartmouth Castle (15th century), 1.6

km/1 mi southeast of the town, guards the narrow entrance of the Dart estuary.

## Darwin, Charles (1809–1882)

English naturalist who developed the modern theory of evolution and proposed, with the Welsh naturalist Alfred Russel Wallace (1823–1913), the principle of natural selection.

After research in South America and the Galápagos Islands as naturalist on HMS *Beagle* 1831–36, Darwin published *On the Origin of Species by Means of Natural Selection or the Preservation of Favoured Races in the Struggle for Life* (1859). This book explained the evolutionary process through the principles of natural selection and aroused bitter controversy because it disagreed with the literal interpretation of the Book of Genesis in the Bible.

Darwin's work marked a turning point in many of the sciences, including physical anthropology and palaeontology.

His theory of natural selection concerned the

**Charles Darwin** English naturalist Charles Darwin, author of one of the most influential scientific books ever published, *On the Origin of Species by Means of Natural Selection* (1859). At a time when most people still believed in the literal truth of the *Bible*'s account of creation, Darwin's idea that species had evolved gradually caused a storm of controversy. The first edition of the book sold out on the day of publication. Corbis

variation existing between members of a sexually reproducing population. Those members with variations better fitted to the environment would be more likely to survive and breed, subsequently passing on these favourable characteristics to their offspring. He avoided the issue of human evolution, however, remarking at the end of *The Origin of Species* that 'much light will be thrown on the origin of man and his history'. It was not until his publication of *The Descent of Man and Selection in Relation to Sex* (1871), that Darwin argued that people evolved just like other organisms.

## David, Elizabeth, born Gwynne (1914–1992)

British cookery writer. Her *A Book of Mediterranean Food* (1950) and *French Country Cooking* (1951) helped to spark an interest in foreign cuisine in Britain, and also inspired a growing school of informed, highly literate writing on food and wine.

Her other books include *Italian Food* (1954), *French Provincial Cooking* (1960), and *English Bread and Yeast Cookery* (1977).

## David

Two kings of Scotland.

## David I
(1084–1153)

King of Scotland from 1124. The youngest son of Malcolm III Canmore and St ◊Margaret, he was brought up in the English court of Henry I, and in 1113 married Matilda, widow of the 1st Earl of Northampton and daughter of the Earl of Northumbria.

He invaded England in 1138 in support of Queen ◊Matilda, Henry I's daughter, but was defeated at Northallerton in the Battle of the Standard, and again in 1141.

## David II (1324–1371)

King of Scotland from 1329, son of ◊Robert (I) the Bruce. David was married at the age of four to Joanna, daughter of Edward II of England. In 1346 David invaded England, was captured at the battle of Neville's Cross, and imprisoned for 11 years.

After the defeat of the Scots by Edward III at Halidon Hill in 1333, the young David and Joanna were sent to France for safety. They returned in 1341. On Joanna's death in 1362 David married Margaret Logie, but divorced her in 1370.

## David, St (lived 5th–6th century), or Dewi

Patron saint of Wales, Christian abbot and bishop. According to legend he was the son of a prince of Dyfed and uncle of King Arthur. He was responsible for the adoption of the leek as the national emblem of Wales, but his own emblem is a dove. Feast day 1 March.

## Davy, Humphry (1778–1829)

English chemist. He discovered, by electrolysis, the metallic elements sodium and potassium in 1807, and calcium, boron, magnesium, strontium, and barium in 1808. In addition, he established that chlorine is an element and proposed that hydrogen is present in all acids. He invented the safety lamp for use in mines where methane was present, enabling miners to work in previously unsafe conditions. He was knighted in 1812, and became a baronet in 1818.

## Day-Lewis, Cecil (1904–1972)

Irish poet brought up in England who wrote under the name **C Day Lewis**. With W H Auden and Stephen Spender, he was one of the influential left-wing poets of the 1930s. His later poetry moved from political concerns to a more traditional personal lyricism. He also wrote detective novels under the pseudonym **Nicholas Blake**. He was British poet laureate 1968–1972.

His poetry, which includes *From Feathers to Iron* (1931) and *Overtures to Death* (1938), is marked by accomplished lyrics and sustained narrative power. *The Complete Poems* was published in 1992.

## D-day

6 June 1944, the day of the Allied invasion of Normandy under the command of General Eisenhower to commence Operation Overlord, the liberation of Western Europe from German occupation. The Anglo-US invasion fleet landed on the Normandy beaches on the stretch of coast between the Orne River and St Marcouf. Artificial harbours known as 'Mulberries' were constructed and towed across the Channel so that equipment and armaments could be unloaded on to the beaches. After overcoming fierce resistance the allies broke through the German defences; Paris was liberated on 25 August, and Brussels on 2 September.

## Deal

Port and resort on the east coast of Kent, southeast England; population (1991) 28,500. Industries include fishing, boatbuilding, and tourism. Julius Caesar is said to have landed at nearby ◊Walmer in 55 BC, and Deal became one of the ◊Cinque Ports. The castle, built by Henry VIII, houses the town museum.

**Deal Castle** was one of many fortifications built along the south coast in about 1540, resulting from Henry's fear of invasion by Catholic France after the English Reformation. Together with the castles of Walmer to the south and Sandown to the north (now in ruins), Deal protected the Downs roadstead, an area of safe anchorage between the coast and the hazardous sandbanks known as the ◊Goodwin Sands. The castle has a unique circular form, with a central keep surrounded by two rings of six semi-circular bastions.

In the 18th century Deal gained notoriety as a centre of smuggling.

## Decorated

In architecture, the second period of English Gothic, covering the latter part of the 13th century and the 14th century. Chief characteristics include ornate window tracery, the window being divided into several lights by vertical bars called mullions; sharp spires ornamented with crockets and pinnacles; complex church vaulting; and slender arcade piers.

The reconstruction of Exeter Cathedral (begun about 1270) was in the Decorated style (see ◊Exeter). Other examples include the naves of Lichfield Cathedral, Beverley Minster, and the parish church of Heckington, Lincolnshire; the choirs of Bristol, Lincoln and St Albans cathedrals; the choir, west front and chapterhouse of York; and the chapter-houses of Salisbury, Southwell, and Wells cathedrals.

## Dee

River which flows through Aberdeenshire, Scotland and the city of Aberdeen; length 137 km/85 mi. From its source in the Cairngorm Mountains, it flows east into the North Sea at Aberdeen (by an artificial channel in this latter stage). Near Braemar the river passes through a rock gorge, the **Linn of Dee**. ◊Balmoral Castle is on its banks. It is noted for salmon fishing and is the fifth longest river in Scotland.

## Defoe, Daniel (1660–1731)

English writer. His *Robinson Crusoe* (1719), though purporting to be a factual account of shipwreck and solitary survival, was influential in the development of the novel. The fictional *Moll Flanders* (1722) and the partly factual *A Journal of the Plague Year* (1722) are still read for their concrete realism. A prolific journalist and pamphleteer, he was imprisoned in 1703 for the ironic *The Shortest Way with Dissenters* (1702). He first achieved fame with the satirical poem *The True-Born Englishman* (1701).

Since Defoe's death, an increasing number of works have been attributed to him, bringing the total to more than 600.

---

*Your Roman-Saxon-Danish-Norman English.*

**Daniel Defoe** English writer.
*The True-Born Englishman*

---

## De Havilland, Geoffrey (1882–1965)
English aircraft designer who designed and whose company produced the Moth biplane, the Mosquito fighter-bomber of World War II, and in 1949 the Comet, the world's first jet-driven airliner to enter commercial service.

## Delafield, E M, pen name of Edmée Elizabeth Monica Dashwood, born de la Pasture (1890–1943)
English writer. Her amusing *Diary of a Provincial Lady* (1931) skilfully exploits the foibles of middle-class life. This was so successful that she followed it with three sequels, the last being *The Provincial Lady in War Time* (1940).

## de la Mare, Walter John (1873–1956)
English poet and writer. His works include verse for children, such as *Peacock Pie* (1913), and the novels *The Three Royal Monkeys* (1910), for children; and *The Memoirs of a Midget* (1921), for adults. He excelled at creating a sense of eeriness and supernatural mystery.

*The Listeners* (1912) established his reputation as a writer of delicately imaginative verse in the twin domains of childhood and dreamland.

## Delius, Frederick (1862–1934)
English composer. His haunting, richly harmonious works include the opera *A Village Romeo and Juliet* (1901); the choral pieces *Appalachia* (1903), *Sea Drift* (1904), *A Mass of Life* (1905); orchestral works such as *In a Summer Garden* (1908) and *A Song of the High Hills* (1911); chamber music; and songs.

## Democratic Unionist Party, DUP
Northern Ireland political party, which is orientated towards the Protestant Unionist community and opposes union with the Republic of Ireland.

The DUP originated in 1971 as a breakaway from the Official ♢Ulster Unionist Party. It was co-founded by the Reverend Ian Paisley, a Presbyterian minister and militant Unionist MP for North Antrim, who continues to lead it. At the May 1997 general election the DUP won two of Ulster's 18 seats. The party gained 18.1% of votes in the June 1998 elections to the new 108-seat Belfast assembly.

## Denbighshire, Welsh Sir Ddinbych
Unitary authority in north Wales; population (1996) 91,000; area 844 sq km/326 sq mi. A county until 1974, it was largely merged 1974–96, together with Flint and part of Merioneth, into Clwyd; a small area along the western border was included in Gwynedd. Its principal towns are Ruthin (administrative headquarters), Denbigh, and Llangollen.
*Physical*
The area is rugged and mountainous except for the fertile vales of Llangollen and Clwyd. The Clwydian range of mountains in the east rises to a height of 555 m/1,820 ft, with ♢Offa's Dyke along the main ridge. The rivers Clwyd, Dee, and Elwy flow through it, and it has a stretch of northern coastline on the Irish Sea.
*Features*
The 13th-century Rhuddlan and 14th-century Denbigh castles and the seaside resorts of Rhyl and Prestatyn are important attractions; Bodelwyddan Castle houses a fine collection of paintings, furniture, and sculpture. Ruthin has well preserved half-timbered buildings. The Llangollen International Music Eisteddfodd takes place in July.
*Economy*
The economy is based on agriculture (chiefly dairy farming) and tourism.

## dependent territories
Term used as a means of referring collectively to colonies, protectorates, protected states, and trust territories for which Britain remains responsible.

In 1998 there were 11 inhabited British dependent territories: Anguilla; Bermuda; British Virgin Islands; Cayman Islands; Falkland Islands; Gibraltar; Montserrat; Pitcairn Islands; St Helena; South Georgia and the South Sandwich Islands; and the Turks and Caicos Islands. There were also two offshore crown dependencies: the Channel Islands and the Isle of Man. British Antarctic Territory and British Indian Ocean Territory are uninhabited dependencies.

## Depression, the

The world economic crisis precipitated by the Wall Street crash of 29 October 1929 when millions of dollars were wiped off US share values in a matter of hours. Britain was already weakened by the 1926 General Strike and unemployment rose to over 2 million. International loss of confidence in sterling in 1931 led to a crisis that caused a coalition government to be in power until World War II. The economy was slow to recover, as witnessed by a series of hunger marches, notably the ◊Jarrow Crusade.

## Deptford

District in southeast London, in the Greater London borough of Lewisham, on the River Thames west of Greenwich. It was a major royal naval dockyard (1513–1869), established by Henry VIII to build the flagship *Great Harry*.

Francis Drake was knighted at Deptford, and Peter the Great, tsar of Russia, studied shipbuilding here in 1698. The diarist John Evelyn (1620–1706) lived at Sayes Court near the dockyard and helped Grinling ◊Gibbons establish himself as a woodcarver.

## De Quincey, Thomas (1785–1859)

English writer. His works include *Confessions of an English Opium-Eater* (1821) and the essays 'On the Knocking at the Gate in Macbeth' (1825) and 'On Murder Considered as One of the Fine Arts' (in three parts, 1827, 1839, and 1854). He was a friend of the poets William ◊Wordsworth and Samuel Taylor ◊Coleridge, and his work had a powerful influence on Charles Baudelaire and Edgar Allan Poe, among others.

In the essays 'Suspiria de Profundis' (1845) and 'The English Mail Coach' (1849), he began a psychological study of dreaming, examining how childhood experiences can through symbols in dreams affect the dreamer's personality. In this way he gave lasting expression to the fleeting pictures of his usually macabre dreams, and it could be said that he explored the subconscious before it was formally discovered.

## Derby

Industrial city in north central England, 200 km/124 mi north of London; population (1996) 218,800. Part of the county of Derbyshire until 1997, it is now, as **Derby City**, a unitary authority with an area of 87 sq km/30 sq mi. A centre for the manufacture of porcelain from the 18th century, Derby was established as the headquarters of Rolls-Royce cars in 1908 and is still important for

**Depression** A photograph illustrating poverty in Wigan, England (1939) by Kurt Hutton. He moved to England in 1934 to escape the Nazi regime in Germany and did a good deal of work for the magazine *Picture Post*. He specialized in human interest stories and summed up his attitude in the words: 'A photograph should suggest that behind the face, whatever sort of face it may be: young or old, pretty, plain or ugly, lively or quiet, there is a thinking and feeling human being.' Corbis

the manufacture of cars (Toyota) and aero engines (Rolls-Royce). The University of Derby was established in 1993.

### History

◊Charles Edward Stuart, having invaded England in the Jacobite rebellion of 1745, held his final war council in Derby before retreating to Scotland. The town began to develop as a manufacturing centre at the end of the 17th century, and in 1717 England's first silk mill was established here. Derby expanded with the founding of the Royal Crown Derby works (now part of Royal Doulton) in the 18th century, and grew further in the 19th century as an important railway engineering town and the headquarters of Midland Railway Company. Derby received its city charter in 1977.

### Features

The City Museum and Art Gallery has a collection of Royal Crown Derby porcelain and paintings by

Joseph ◊Wright who was born in Derby in 1734. Derby Industrial Museum, on the site of the first 18th-century silk mill, includes a collection of Rolls-Royce aero engines.

### Cathedrals and churches
Originally built as All Saints' parish church in medieval times, the cathedral was rebuilt in the early 18th century, but the 16th-century tower survives. The cathedral has an unusual wrought-iron screen designed by the local smith Robert Bakewell (died 1752). The church became a cathedral in 1927.

## Derby
Blue riband of the English horseracing season, run over 2.4 km/1.5 mi at Epsom Downs, Surrey, every June. It was established in 1780 and named after the 12th Earl of Derby.

## Derbyshire
County of north central England; population (1996) 962,000; area 2,550 sq km/984 sq mi. The county is mountainous in the north and contains much of the ◊Peak District National Park; its wild landscape, high waterfalls, and beautiful dales attract walkers. The principal towns and cities are ◊Matlock (administrative headquarters), ◊Buxton, ◊Chesterfield, Glossop, Ilkeston, and Long Eaton. Since April 1997 **Derby City** (see ◊Derby) has been a separate unitary authority, contained within Derbyshire.

### History
Cresswell Crags in the northeast is one of the earliest known human settlements in the British Isles. Buxton was a Roman spa town. In 1665–66 the bubonic plague killed 80% of the inhabitants of the village of Eyam. The English pioneering manufacturer Richard Arkwright opened the world's first water-powered cotton spinning mill on the banks of the River Derwent at Cromford, near Matlock, in 1771.

### Physical
The southern part of the county is very fertile, the north very rugged and mountainous. The county's many rivers, the Dane, Derwent, Dove, Goyt, Rother, Trent, and Wye as well as tributaries of the Don, Mersey, and Trent, have their source in the Peak District, at the southern end of the Pennine chain. There are springs near Buxton and Matlock, both of which were fashionable spa towns. The Peak District National Park includes Kinder Scout (636 m/2,088 ft). Kinder Downfall is a spectacular waterfall on Kinder Scout, with a drop of about 120 m/400 ft. The south has a moorland landscape interspersed with beautiful valleys; Dovedale is especially popular with walkers. There are limestone caverns around Castletown, popular with potholers.

### Features
Derbyshire contains numerous antiquities, including the prehistoric stone circle of Arbor Low, the most important in England after Stonehenge and Avebury. There are several ceremonial Bronze Age sites east of the River Derwent. Other places of interest include the ruined abbey of Dale, the Saxon crypt at Repton, and the 17th-century ◊Bolsover Castle. Important country houses include ◊Chatsworth House (seat of the Duke of Devonshire); the castellated ◊Haddon Hall, near Bakewell; ◊Hardwick Hall, commissioned in 1591; Kedleston Hall (designed by Robert Adam); and Calke Abbey, an 18th-century Baroque mansion. Buxton has a fine 18th-century crescent. The National Tramway Museum is at Crich, near Matlock. Well-dressing, the floral decoration of wells at Whitsun, takes place at Tissington, Wirksworth, Eyam, and other villages. The Castleton caverns include the Peak, Speedwell, and Treak Cliff Caverns, as well as the ◊Blue John Cavern, known for its coloured fluorspar. Bakewell tart, a pastry case containing a layer of jam and almond sponge, originated in the village of ◊Bakewell.

### Economy
Tourism and agriculture are important to the local economy. In the south there is cultivation of cereals, root crops, and dairy farming, with sheep farming in the northern hills. There is also car assembly, metalworking, and quarrying.

## Derwent Water
Lake in Cumbria, England, part of the ◊Lake District. Derwent Water stretches for 5 km/3 mi south of Keswick into Borrowdale. The lake was part of the area forming the core of the ◊National Trust when it was founded.

## Design Museum
Museum in London's Docklands dedicated to mass-produced goods with an emphasis on design. Opened in 1989 and supported by the designer-entrepreneur Terence Conran, it sets out to promote 'awareness of the importance of design in education, industry, commerce and culture'.

The museum is unique in exhibiting design outside the traditional contexts of fine art or technology. It houses a permanent study collection, a 'review' section for contemporary products, and temporary exhibits.

## devolution

Movement to decentralize governmental power. The Labour government that took office in May 1997 introduced legislation to establish Scottish and Welsh assemblies and their membership . The ◊Scottish Parliament is located in Edinburgh and the National Assembly for Wales in Cardiff. The ◊Northern Ireland Assembly was proposed in 1998 as part of the Good Friday Agreement, came into operation fully in 1999, but was suspended in February 2000 following stalemate on IRA weapons decommissioning.

## Devon

County of southwest England, between Cornwall and Somerset; population (1996) 1,059,300; area 6,720 sq km/2,594 sq mi. It is a hilly and attractive county, with two large national parks, ◊Dartmoor in the south and part of ◊Exmoor in the north. It has a rugged northern coast and fine harbours on the south coast; with its picturesque thatched cottages in quintessentially English rural settings, it is a popular tourist destination. The principal towns and cities are ◊Exeter (administrative headquarters) and the resorts of ◊Barnstaple, Bideford, ◊Exmouth, Ilfracombe, Sidmouth, ◊Teignmouth, and Tiverton. ◊Plymouth and ◊Torbay have been separate unitary authorities since April 1998.

### History

Devon was one of the last counties to be conquered by the Saxons, and became one of the wealthiest parts of England, with an economy based on farming, fishing, mining, and the tin and woollen trades. There was also a large overseas trade, but this began to decline during the 17th century. Some of the great naval seamen, including Francis ◊Drake and Walter ◊Raleigh, came from Devon.

### Physical

Devon is the third largest county in England and Wales. The surface is hilly, with the rolling uplands of Dartmoor, and its numerous rugged tors (hills or rocky peaks), in the southwest. On the lower slopes of hills the soil is fertile, especially in the lower Exe valley, which has orchards and market gardens. The northern coast on the Bristol Channel is very rugged, with cliffs 122–152 m/400–500 ft high; there are also rocky inlets, the largest of which is Bideford Bay. On the southern coast, on the English Channel, are the headlands Bolt Tail and Start Point, and the harbours Tor Bay and Plymouth Sound, one of the best harbours in Britain. The rivers Dart, Exe, Plym, Tamar, Taw, Teign, and Torridge flow through the county.

### Features

Parts of Devon, particularly Dartmoor, are rich in prehistoric remains. The Dartmoor and Exmoor national parks are important conservation and recreational areas; Dartmoor and Exmoor ponies wander freely there. Castles include the 15th-century harbour fortress at Dartmouth; the 14th-century Powderham Castle was converted to a manor in the 18th century. Exeter has a fine cathedral; Buckfast Abbey was founded in the 11th century and rebuilt in the 20th century; the Cistercian Buckland Abbey, founded in the 13th century, was the last home of Sir Francis Drake. ◊Saltram is a Tudor house with classical façades added in the 18th century, A La Ronde is a unique 16-sided house dating from the 18th century, and ◊Castle Drogo is a 20th-century castle designed by Edwin Lutyens. There is an important naval college at Dartmouth. ◊Lundy Island, 19 km/12 mi northwest of Hartland Point, is the site of a bird sanctuary and marine nature reserve in the Bristol Channel. Devon cream teas (scones, jam, and clotted cream) are a local speciality, and Devon pixies are mischievous characters in the county's folklore.

### Economy

Tourism is important in Devon, and related products include cider, clotted cream, fishing, lace (at Honiton), and Dartington glass. Agriculture comprises mainly sheep and dairy farming, and beef cattle. There is also a kaolin (china clay) industry, quarrying, and mineral extraction, and a defence industry. Axminster carpets are produced in Devon.

## de Wint, Peter (1784–1849)

English landscape painter of Dutch-American descent, born in Staffordshire, USA. He was apprenticed to the painter and engraver John Raphael Smith (1752–1812), but was directed towards watercolour by the advice of the painter John Varley and the example of Thomas Girtin, whose work he greatly admired. From 1806 watercolour was his chief means of expression, his best work being executed with broad washes summarizing natural forms. The city of Lincoln and the lush countryside round it, home of his wife, were his main subjects.

## dialect

Dialect has long been a prominent feature of spoken English in Britain. Today, while vocabulary is becoming increasingly standardized, and 'estuary English', heard in London and the south-east, is widespread, differences of pronunciation are still marked in certain regions.

Among them are the 'flat' vowels of 'Brummie' spoken in the Birmingham area; the substitution of 'f' or 'v' for 'th' and the dropping of initial 'h' in 'Cockney'; the long 'a' in words such as 'talk' and 'walk' and the rising tone in statements, making them sound like questions, in 'Geordie', spoken in northeast England; the short 'a' in both 'gas' and 'grass' in Lancashire and Yorkshire; the 'flat' intonation and adenoidal voice quality in 'Scouse', in the Liverpool area; and the distinctive burr in West Country speech, sometimes known as 'Zummerzet', with 'z' for initial 's' ('zum' for 'some') and 'v' for 'f' ('varm' for 'farm').

Many such dialects and their individual turns of speech become generally familiar through television drama and ◊soap opera, with 'Brummie' heard in *Crossroads*, 'Cockney' in *EastEnders*, 'Geordie' in *Auf Wiedersehen, Pet*, and 'Scouse' in *Bread* and *Brookside*.

Dialects in Scotland fall into four main groups: the Northern Isles (Orkney and Shetland) with 'f' for 'wh' in such words as 'who' and a rounded front vowel 'ui' in such words as 'good' ('guid') and 'school' ('scuil'); Northern Scots with 'ee' for 'oo' in such words as 'moon', 'shoe'; Central Scots with 'ai' or 'i' for 'oo' in those words; and Southern Scots with 'twae' for 'two', 'whae' for 'who' and 'waiter' for 'water'. Speech in Wales often has a distinctive 'sing-song' quality, reflecting that in Welsh itself. Dialects in Northern Ireland are much as south of the border, with a distinctive 'burring' 'r' in such words as 'worse' and 'hard' and phonological features similar to those of American English.

## Diana, Princess of Wales born Diana Frances Spencer (1961–1997)

Daughter of the 8th Earl Spencer, Diana married Prince Charles in St Paul's Cathedral, London, in 1981. She had two sons, William and Harry, before her separation from Charles in 1992. In February 1996 she agreed to a divorce, after which she became known as Diana, Princess of Wales. Her worldwide prominence for charity work, including a campaign against the use of landmines, contributed to a massive outpouring of public grief after her death in a car crash in Paris, France, on 31 August 1997. Her funeral proved to be the biggest British televised event in history. Her brother, Earl Spencer, opened a museum in her memory at ◊Althorp, the Spencer family home, where she is buried.

In 1995 in a landmark BBC *Panorama* interview with Martin Bashir, she said that she would like to be a 'queen of people's hearts, in people's hearts'. Her divorce was settled shortly after.

The investigation into the car crash that killed Diana, Princess of Wales and Dodi Al Fayed, concluded in early January 1999 that no one involved should face criminal charges. The official report, at the end of a 16-month inquiry, absolved staff at the Ritz Hotel in Paris of any blame (the hotel had supplied the car and its driver) and lifted manslaughter charges against nine French press photographers who had been following the car at the time of the crash.

### Diana Memorial Fund

This fund, set up and granted charitable status within four days of Diana's death, raised over £40 million in its first seven months. It is run by a board of trustees, among them Lady Sarah McCorquodale, one of Diana's two sisters, and Christopher Spence, founder of the London Lighthouse AIDS care centre. On March 10 1998 six organizations of which Diana was patron at the time of her death were awarded £2 million each from the fund: Centrepoint, English National Ballet, Great Ormond Street Hospital, the National AIDS Trust, the Royal Marsden NHS Trust, and the Leprosy Mission. Smaller amounts went to a range of arts, health and sports charities.

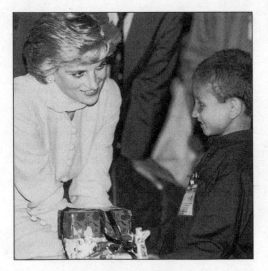

**Diana, Princess of Wales** Diana, Princess of Wales, talking with children at the Khanum Memorial Cancer Hospital in Lahore, Pakistan in February 1996. Diana was well-known for her work supporting charitable organizations. Corbis

## Dickens, Charles (1812–1870)

English novelist. He is enduringly popular for his memorable characters and his portrayal of the social evils of Victorian England. Dickens was born in Portsea, Hampshire, and received little formal education. In 1827 he became a lawyer's clerk, and then a reporter for the *Morning Chronicle*, to which he contributed the *Sketches by Boz*. In 1836 he published the first number of the *Pickwick Papers*. They were originally intended merely as an accompaniment to a series of sporting illustrations, but the adventures of Pickwick outgrew their setting and established Dickens's reputation.

In 1842 he visited the USA, where he was welcomed as a celebrity. After his visit, American feeling was deeply offended by *American Notes* (1842), attacking the pirating of English books by American publishers. On his return home, he satirized US democracy in *Martin Chuzzlewit* (1844). *Dombey and Son* (1848) was largely written abroad. *David Copperfield*, his most popular novel and his own favourite, contains many autobiographical incidents and characters; Mr Micawber is usually recognized as a sketch of his father. Dickens inaugurated the weekly magazine *Household Words* in 1850, reorganizing it in 1859 as *All the Year Round*; many of his later stories were published serially in these periodicals. In 1858 he began giving public readings from his novels, which proved such a success that he was invited to make a second US tour in 1867–68. *Edwin Drood*, a mystery story influenced by the style of his friend Wilkie ◊Collins, was left incomplete on his death.

Dickens's novels are characterized by strong satire, inclining to caricature; the protest against injustice, indignant but too humorous to be shrill; pathos, tending to sentimentality; well-observed characters, and the melodrama. See table for dates of major works and their characters.

## dictionaries

The first dictionaries of English (*glossa collectae*), in the 17th century, served to explain difficult words, generally of Latin or Greek origin, in everyday English. Samuel ◊Johnson's *A Dictionary of the English Language* (1755) was one of the first dictionaries of standard English, and the first to give extensive coverage to phrasal verbs. The many-volume *Oxford English Dictionary*, begun in

## Dickens: Major Works

| title | date | well-known characters |
| --- | --- | --- |
| The Pickwick Papers | 1836 | Mr Pickwick, Sam Weller, Mr Snodgrass, Mr Jingle, Mr and Mrs Bardell |
| Oliver Twist | 1837 | Oliver Twist, Fagin, Mr Bumble, The Artful Dodger |
| Nicholas Nickleby | 1838 | Nicholas Nickleby, Wackford Squeers, Madame Mantalini, Smike, Vincent Crummles |
| The Old Curiosity Shop | 1840 | Little Nell, Dick Swiveller, Daniel Quilp |
| Barnaby Rudge | 1841 | Simon Tappertit (Sim), Miss Miggs, Gashford |
| A Christmas Carol | 1843 | Ebenezer Scrooge, Bob Cratchit, Marley's Ghost, Tiny Tim |
| Martin Chuzzlewit | 1844 | Martin Chuzzlewit (Junior), Mr Pecksniff, Mrs Gamp, Tom Pinch |
| Dombey and Son | 1848 | Dombey, Paul and Florence Dombey, Edith Granger, James Carker, Major Bagstock |
| David Copperfield | 1850 | David Copperfield, Mr Micawber, Mr Dick, Uriah Heep, Little Em'ly, Betsey Trotwood |
| Bleak House | 1853 | John Jarndyce, Esther Summerson, Harold Skimpole, Lady Dedlock, Mrs Jellyby |
| Hard Times | 1854 | Tom and Louisa Gradgrind, Josiah Bounderby Gradgrind, Cissy Jupe Bitzer |
| Little Dorrit | 1857 | Amy Dorrit, Flora Finching, Mr Merille |
| A Tale of Two Cities | 1859 | Dr Manette, Charles Darnay, Sydney Carton, Jerry Cruncher, Madame Defarge |
| Great Expectations | 1861 | Pip, Estella, Miss Havisham, Joe Gargery, Wemmick, Magwitch |
| Our Mutual Friend | 1865 | Noddy Boffin, Silas Wegg, Mr Podsnap, Betty Higden, Bradley Headstone, Reginald Wilfer |
| The Mystery of Edwin Drood (unfinished) | 1870 | Rosa Bud, John Jasper |

1884 and subject to continuous revision (and now computerization), provides a detailed historical record of each word and, therefore, of the English language.

## Dimbleby, Richard (1913–1965)

English broadcaster. He was the leading commentator on royal and state occasions on radio and television and covered the Queen's coronation in 1953, the funeral of President Kennedy in 1963, and the funeral of Sir Winston Churchill in 1965.

## Diplomatic Service, British

Body that represents Britain abroad in regard to its international interests, comprising diplomatic agents and occasionally consuls, although the latter are in general concerned exclusively with the interests of British subjects resident abroad. Diplomatic agents include ambassadors, or envoys, who are officials permanently accredited to a foreign state, and *chargés d'affaires* who either act as deputy for an ambassador or are accredited as the British representative to a foreign country of minor importance.

The Diplomatic Service employs some 5,500 (1998) people for the Foreign and Commonwealth Office and diplomatic missions abroad.

## Disraeli, Benjamin, 1st Earl of Beaconsfield (1804–1881)

British Conservative politician and novelist. Elected to Parliament in 1837, he was chancellor of the Exchequer under Lord Derby 1852,

1858–59, and 1866–68, and prime minister 1868 and 1874–80. His imperialist policies brought India directly under the crown, and he was personally responsible for purchasing control of the Suez Canal. His trilogy of popular, political novels, *Coningsby* (1844), *Sybil* (1845), and *Tancred* (1847), reflect an interest in social reform.

---

*The Continent will not suffer England to be the workshop of the world.*

**Benjamin Disraeli** British Conservative prime minister and novelist.
Speech in House of Commons 15 March 1838

---

## Dissolution of the Monasteries

Closure of the monasteries of England and Wales from 1536 to 1540 and confiscation of their property by Henry VIII. The operation was organized by Thomas ◊Cromwell and affected about 800 monastic houses with the aim of boosting royal income. Most of the property was later sold off to the gentry.

## divine right of kings

Christian political doctrine that hereditary monarchy is the system approved by God, hereditary right cannot be forfeited, monarchs are accountable to God alone for their actions, and rebellion against the lawful sovereign is therefore blasphemous.

### The 17th and 18th centuries

James I of England, in his *Trew Law of Free Monarchies*, insisted on divine right as a principle. This was carried to extremes by the supporters of his son. Charles I's claim to divine right was a direct cause of the Royalist and Parliamentary struggles of the 17th century.

The doctrine was again invoked in the Glorious ◊Revolution of 1688 when James II was replaced in an aristocratic coup by William of Orange. The most influential exposition of divine right in English is to be found in Sir Robert Filmer's *Patriarcha* (1680), which argues by analogy that the powers of God over the universe, of father over family, and sovereign over people, are all divinely ordained and absolute. The success of John Locke's *Two Treatises on Government* (1690),

**Benjamin Disraeli** Twice prime minister, Benjamin Disraeli in 1876 introduced a bill in Parliament which gave Queen Victoria the additional title of 'Empress of India'. Victoria afterwards referred to Disraeli as 'her kind, good and considerate friend'.
Private collection

signalled the decline of the theory of divine right in England.

## Docklands

Urban development area east of St Katherine's Dock, London, occupying the site of the former Wapping and Limehouse docks, the Isle of Dogs, and Royal Docks. It comprises 2,226 ha/5,550 ac of former wharves, warehouses, and wasteland. Distinguished buildings include the Tidal Basin Pumping Station in Royal Docks, designed by Richard Rogers, and the printing plant for the *Financial Times*, designed by Nicholas Grimshaw.

## Doctor Who

Hero of a British science-fiction television series of the same name, created in 1963 by Sidney Newman and Donald Wilson; his space vehicle is the *Tardis* and his most famous enemies are the Daleks, robotlike aliens. The actors who have played Doctor Who include William Hartnell (1908–1975), Patrick Troughton (1920–1987), Jon Pertwee (1919–1996), Tom Baker (1936– ), Peter Davison (1951– ), Colin Baker (1943– ), Sylvester McCoy (1943– ), and Peter Cushing (1913–1994).

## Dogger Bank

Submerged sandbank in the North Sea, about 115 km/70 mi off the coast of Yorkshire, England. It is about 270 km/168 mi long by 110 km/68 mi wide. In places the water is only 11 m/36 ft deep, but the general depth is 18–36 m/60–120 ft; it is a well-known fishing ground.

In World War I, it was the site of the Battle of Dogger Bank, a substantial naval engagement on 24 January 1915 between British and German forces under the commands of Admiral Sir David (later Earl) Beatty and Admiral Franz von Hipper, respectively.

## Dogs, Isle of

District of east London, part of the Greater London borough of Tower Hamlets. It is bounded on three sides by the River Thames, and is part of the Docklands urban development area.

The Isle of Dogs is home to the ◊Billingsgate fish market (based since 1982 in the West India Dock) and the ◊Canary Wharf development. The Blackwall Tunnel provides a road link with the south side of the Thames.

## Dolgellau, formerly Dolgelly

Market town at the foot of the Cadair Idris mountain range in north Wales, situated on the River Wnion, 38 km/24 mi northeast of Aberystwyth; population (1991) 2,400. The town lies within the ◊Snowdonia National Park and is a tourist centre. Nearby are the Gwynfynydd ('White Mountain') and Clogau gold mines; a nugget from the latter has supplied gold for the wedding rings of royal brides since 1923.

## Domesday Book

Record of the survey of England carried out in 1086 by officials of William the Conqueror in order to assess land tax and other dues, ascertain the value of the crown lands, and enable the king to estimate the power of his vassal barons. The name is derived from the belief that its judgement was as final as that of Doomsday.

Northumberland and Durham were omitted, and also London, Winchester, and certain other towns. The Domesday Book is preserved in two volumes at the Public Record Office, London.

## Donald III, Bane ('fair') (c. 1039–c. 1100)

King of Scotland. He came to the throne in 1093 after seizing it on the death of his brother ◊Malcolm III. He was dethroned in 1094 by his nephew, Malcolm's son, ◊Duncan II. He regained power in 1094 but was defeated and captured in 1097 by Edgar, fourth son of Malcolm III, who had him blinded and imprisoned until his death.

## Doncaster

Industrial town in South Yorkshire, England, 56 km/35 mi southwest of York; population (1991) 71,600. With a history dating back to Roman times, Doncaster grew rapidly in the 19th as a railway engineering town and until the 1980s it was an important mining centre. In recent years, as its traditional industries have declined, it has developed its tourism and leisure industries. Its racecourse, one of the best known in Britain, is the venue for the world's oldest classic race, the ◊St Leger (1776).

### History

The Romans established the military station of **Danum** here and the town became an important trading centre in the middle ages and a busy coaching stop in the 18th century. Following the opening of the railway in 1849 and the establishment of the Great Northern Railway works in 1853, it developed rapidly as a railway engineering town, producing many locomotives including the *Flying Scotsman* and the *Mallard*.

### Features

The Mansion House (built 1744–1748) contains a fine banqueting hall and is one of only three civic mansion houses in England (the others being in London and York). At ◊Conisbrough to the southwest of the town, there is a ruined Norman castle with a well-preserved circular keep. The castle features in Walter Scott's novel *Ivanhoe* as Athelstan's stronghold. The Earth Centre, Europe's largest centre for ecological research and display, opened in 1999.

## Donne, John (1572–1631)

English metaphysical poet. His work consists of love poems, religious poems, verse satires, and sermons, most of which were published after his death.

His poems are characterized by the imaginative power of their imagery and the use of irregular meter and colloquial diction. His religious poems show the same passion and ingenuity as his love poetry, and his sermons, written in an elegant prose style, reflect his preoccupation with humanity's place in the universe and its approaching end. His verse was not published in collected form until after his death, and was long out of favour, but he is now recognized as one of the greatest English poets.

Born into a Catholic family, Donne matriculated early at Oxford University. In 1596 he joined a naval expedition against Spain with the Earl of Essex and Walter Raleigh, and on his return became private secretary to Sir Thomas Egerton (about 1540–1617), Keeper of the Seal. This appointment was ended by his secret marriage in 1601 to Ann More (died 1617), niece of Egerton's wife. They endured many years of poverty and had 12 children (of whom seven survived childhood).

In 1610 he made a bid for the patronage of James I with the prose work *Pseudo-Martyr* and in 1615 he was ordained in the Church of England, urged on by the King. From 1621 to his death he was dean of St Paul's, where he is buried.

## Dorchester

Market town and administrative headquarters of ◊Dorset, southern England, on the River Frome, north of Weymouth, 192 km/119 mi southwest of London; population (1991) 15,000. Tourism plays an important role in the town's economy. The hillfort ◊Maiden Castle to the southwest was occupied from about 4000 BC, although the first identifiable settlement dates from 2000 BC. The novelist Thomas ◊Hardy was born nearby; Dorchester featured as 'Casterbridge' in his novel *The Mayor of Casterbridge*.

In 1685 Judge ◊Jeffreys held his 'Bloody

Assizes' here after the Monmouth Rebellion and the ◊Tolpuddle Martyrs were sentenced in the local court house in 1834.

### *Roman remains*

Dorchester occupies the site of the Roman town of **Durnovaria**, established in about 70 AD. The line of the town's Roman walls is marked by avenues known as 'The Walks'. The foundations of a Roman villa with a mosaic floor, discovered in 1937 in the grounds of the county hall, are preserved. Maumbury Rings, a prehistoric earthwork dating back to 2000 BC, was converted into an amphitheatre for the Roman town, seating an audience of about 10,000; later the site was used for public hangings until 1705.

### *History*

In the 17th century the Puritans gained control of the town, using money gained from the town brewhouse monopoly to pay for poor relief from 1622. In 1642 Dorchester was a centre of Parliamentary revolt, but was captured by the Royalists in 1643.

### *Features*

The Dorset County Museum contains collections illustrating the archaeology, natural history, and geology of Dorset. Judge Jeffreys is said to have held his Bloody Assizes in the Oak Room of the Antelope Hotel. In the Shire Hall of 1797, the room where the Tolpuddle Martyrs were tried is preserved.

## Dorchester-on-Thames

Town in Oxfordshire, England, 14 km/9 mi southeast of Oxford; population (1991) 2,100. Traces of Neolithic, Iron, and Bronze Age settlements have been found on the Sinodun Hills southwest of the town. Dorchester was the seat of a bishopric in the early Middle Ages, and has an abbey church dating from the 12th century.

The Dyke Hills just south of Dorchester are an ancient British earthwork. The town was also the site of a Roman station and a Romano-British town.

## Dorset

County of southwest England; population (1996) 681,900; area 2,541 sq km/981 sq mi. Known for its hills and heritage coastline on the English Channel and as the setting for the novels of Thomas Hardy, Dorset is a popular tourist destination. Its chief towns and cities are ◊Dorchester (administrative headquarters), ◊Shaftesbury, ◊Sherborne, ◊Lyme Regis, ◊Weymouth, Poole, and Bridport. Since April 1997 ◊Bournemouth and ◊Poole have been separate unitary authorities.

**Dorset** The coast of Dorset in southern England is characterized by soft limestone cliffs eroded by the action of the waves. One of the most striking formations is the archway pierced through a prominent headland at Durdle Door, just west of the small harbour of Lulworth Cove. Corel

## Physical

The county is characterized by the chalk hills of the Dorset Downs, the clay beds of the north and west, and the limestone cliffs of the coast. Durdle Door is a striking natural archway created by erosion in a headland just west of Lulworth Cove. ◊Chesil Beach, a shingle bank along the coast 19 km/11 mi long, connects the limestone Isle of ◊Portland to the mainland. The lias (Lower Jurassic) rocks near Lyme Regis have yielded significant dinosaur remains. The principal rivers are the River Stour, Frome, and Piddle. Canford Heath is the home of some of Britain's rarest breeding birds and reptiles (including the nightjar, Dartford warbler, sand lizard, and smooth snake).

## Features

The county's prehistoric monuments include ◊Maiden Castle, a huge earthwork near Dorchester, and the hillside chalk carving of a giant near the village of Cerne Abbas. There are many Roman remains including Maumbury Rings, a Roman amphitheatre that originated as a prehistoric earthwork. Other features include the forest of Cranborne Chase; Thomas Hardy's cottage at

Higher Bockhampton; the Dorset County Museum, Dorchester, including a reconstruction of Hardy's study; the Antelope Hotel, Dorchester, where Judge Jeffreys is said to have held his ◊Bloody Assizes; Dorchester's Shire Hall, including the room where the ◊Tolpuddle Martyrs were sentenced in 1834; the Isle of Purbeck, including the ruined ◊Corfe Castle and the holiday resort of Swanage; the Isle of Portland, including Portland Bill lighthouse; the Dorset Coast Path; the Tank Museum at the Royal Armoured Corps Centre, Bovington, where the cottage of the soldier and writer T E Lawrence is a museum; Wimborne Minster (12th century); and the abbey church of Sherborne (12th–15th century). Sherborne Castle was built by Sir Walter Raleigh in the 16th century.

## Economy

Tourism, dairy farming, manufacturing, and commerce are important in the county. Marble and china clay are quarried from the Isle of ◊Purbeck; Portland stone, quarried from the limestone Isle of Portland, has been used for buildings all over the world including St Paul's Cathedral, London. There are ferry services from

Poole and Weymouth to the Channel Islands and France.

## Dove

River in Derbyshire, England, a tributary of the ◊Trent; length 65 km/40 mi. The Dove rises on Axe Edge, 6 km/4 mi from Buxton, and forms the southwestern border between Derbyshire and Staffordshire as it flows south to join the Trent near Burton. Izaak ◊Walton, author of *The Compleat Angler* (1653), fished the Dove.

The valley of **Dovedale**, below Hartington, where the river runs through a rocky, wooded gorge some 3 km/2 mi long, is popular with walkers.

## Dove Cottage

Small house at Grasmere in the English Lake District where the poet William ◊Wordsworth settled with his sister Dorothy in 1799, and later with his wife Mary Hutchinson in 1802. Wordsworth wrote much of his best work here, including 'Ode: Intimations of Immortality', 'Michael', and 'Resolution and Independence', before reluctantly moving to a larger house in 1808. It is now a museum.

## Dover

Market town and seaport in Kent, southeast England, on the coast of the English Channel; population (1991) 34,200. It is Britain's nearest point to mainland Europe, 34 km/21 mi from Calais, France. Dover is the world's busiest passenger port and England's principal cross-channel port, with ferry, hovercraft, and cross-channel train services. Tourism is important.

As Roman **Dubris**, the port was a naval base and the starting point of ◊Watling Street. The Roman beacon or 'lighthouse', dating from about 50 AD, in the grounds of the Norman castle, is one of the oldest Roman buildings in the country. Dover was the largest of the original ◊Cinque Ports.

### Features

Dover is known for its white cliffs, and views from the castle keep, 116 m/380 ft above sea level, can include the French coast from Boulogne to Gravelines, the shoreline from Folkestone to Ramsgate, and many of the fortifications honeycombing the Dover cliffs. The White Cliffs Experience Museum illustrates the history of Dover from Roman times to World War II. The Roman Painted House describes the Roman occupation and includes Roman wall paintings and the remains of an underground Roman heating system. The Duke of York's Royal Military School is located in the town.

### Dover Castle

Dover Castle was built on the cliffs overlooking the town, on the site of earlier fortifications. An important military headquarters and defensive garrison for centuries, it has a massive keep built by Henry II in the 1180s, with walls 5–7 m/17–22 ft thick. The castle was seized by Oliver Cromwell during the English Civil War, and it was strengthened during the Napoleonic Wars. Within the grounds of the castle is the Saxon church of St Mary in Castro.

### 20th-century history

Dover suffered considerable damage from bombing and shelling during World War II, and much of the town and the seafront have since been redeveloped. A network of tunnels underneath the castle known as Hellfire Corner, built originally during the Napoleonic Wars, was used during World War II as the control base for the Dunkirk evacuation. The ◊Channel Tunnel, to the west of Dover, opened in 1994.

## Dowland, John (*c.* 1563–*c.* 1626)

English composer of lute songs. He introduced daring expressive refinements of harmony and ornamentation to English Renaissance style in the service of an elevated aesthetic of melancholy, as in the masterly *Lachrymae* (1605).

## Down

County of southeastern Northern Ireland; population (1981) 339,200; area 2,470 sq km/953 sq mi. The chief towns and cities are ◊Downpatrick (county town), ◊Bangor (seaside resort), Newtownards, Newry, and Banbridge. The northern part of the county lies within the commuter belt for Belfast, and includes part of the city of ◊Belfast, east of the River Lagan.

### Physical

Down is a largely lowland county, although the south is dominated by the Mourne Mountains, the highest point of which is Slieve Donard (852 m/2,796 ft). The coast at Dundrum Bay, where the mountains rise abruptly, is sandy, but elsewhere the coastline is mainly low and rocky. In the east it is penetrated by the long sea inlet Strangford Lough, a noted habitat for birds and grey seals.

### Features

There are a number of fortifications and early ecclesiastical remains in the county, including the prehistoric Giant's Ring earthwork; Legananny Dolmen, a Stone Age monument; the well-preserved tower house Audley's Castle; the 5th-century Nendrum Monastery on Mahee Island in Strangford Lough; Grey Abbey, a Cistercian foundation dating from 1193; Mount Stewart House and Gardens, the 18th-century former home of the Marquess of Londonderry, noted for its statues and carvings dating from the early 20th century; ◊Castle Ward, an 18th-century house; and the Strangford Stone, 10 m/33 ft high, erected on the shores of Strangford Lough on Midsummer's Day, June 1999, to mark the millennium. The Ulster Folk and Transport Museum is at Holywood.

*Economy*
County Down has very fertile land. The principal crops are barley, potatoes, and oats; there is also livestock rearing and dairying. Light manufacturing and technology businesses are also important.

## Downing Street

Street in Westminster, London, leading from Whitehall to St James's Park, named after Sir George Downing (died 1684), a diplomat under Cromwell and Charles II. **Number 10** is the official residence of the prime minister and **Number 11** is the residence of the chancellor of the Exchequer. **Number 12** is the office of the government whips. After his appointment as prime minister in May 1997, Tony Blair chose to use Number 11 to accommodate his family, using Number 10 as his office and for Cabinet meetings. The chancellor of the Exchequer, Gordon Brown, retained his office in Number 11 but used the flat above Number 10 as his residence.

## Downing Street Declaration

Statement, issued jointly by UK prime minister John Major and Irish premier Albert Reynolds on 15 December 1993, setting out general principles for holding all-party talks on securing peace in ◊Northern Ireland.

## Downs, North and South

Two lines of chalk hills in southeast England; see ◊North Downs and ◊South Downs.

## Doyle, Arthur Conan (1859–1930)

Scottish writer. He created the detective Sherlock ◊Holmes and his assistant Dr Watson, who first appeared in *A Study in Scarlet* (1887) and featured in a number of subsequent stories, including *The Hound of the Baskervilles* (1902). Among Doyle's other works is the fantasy adventure *The Lost World* (1912). In his later years he became a spiritualist and wrote a *History of Spiritualism* (1926).

The Sherlock Holmes character featured in several books, including *The Sign of Four* (1890) and *The Valley of Fear* (1915), as well as in volumes of short stories, first published in the *Strand Magazine*.

## Drake, Francis (c. 1540–1596)

English buccaneer and explorer. Having enriched himself as a pirate against Spanish interests in the Caribbean 1567–72, he was sponsored by Elizabeth I for an expedition to the Pacific, sailing round the world 1577–80 in the *Golden Hind*, robbing Spanish ships as he went. This was the second circumnavigation of the globe (the first had been by the Portuguese explorer Ferdinand Magellan). Drake also helped to defeat the ◊Spanish Armada in 1588 as a vice-admiral in the *Revenge*.

When the Spanish ambassador demanded that Drake be punished for robbing Spanish ships on his round the world trip, the Queen knighted him on the deck of the *Golden Hind* at Deptford, London. In a raid on Cádiz in 1587 he burned 10,000 tons of shipping ('singed the King of Spain's beard'), and delayed the invasion of England by the Spanish Armada for a year.

On his last expedition to the West Indies, Drake captured Nombre de Dios on the north coast of Panama but failed to seize Panama City. In January 1596 he died off the coast of Panama.

---

*The advantage of time and place in all practical actions is half the victory; which being lost is irrecoverable.*

**Francis Drake** English buccaneer and explorer.
Letter to Queen Elizabeth I, 1588

---

## drove roads

Trackways for cattle, maintained by constant usage. They were probably established in prehistoric times, when communities moved their livestock from one grazing area to another. They were in continual use until the first half of the 19th century, when enclosures and the advent of the railway made long-distance drove roads obsolete.

## Druidism

Religion of the Celtic peoples of the pre-Christian British Isles and Gaul. The word is probably derived from the Greek *drus* (oak), a tree regarded by the Druids as sacred, though it has also been connected to the Gaelic word *draoi*, meaning 'magician'. One of the Druids' chief rites was the cutting of mistletoe from the oak with a golden sickle. They taught the immortality of the soul and a reincarnation doctrine, and were expert in astronomy. The Druids are thought to have offered human sacrifices.

In Britain the Druids had their stronghold in Anglesey, Wales, until they were driven out by the Roman governor Agricola. They existed in Scotland and Ireland until the coming of the Christian missionaries. What are often termed Druidic monuments – cromlechs and stone circles – are of New Stone Age (Neolithic) origin, though they may later have been used for religious purposes by the Druids.

## Drury Lane

London street connecting Aldwych with High Holborn. It has been a part of the theatre district since the 17th century. Charles II's mistress Nell Gwyn was born here and is traditionally supposed to have sold oranges in the **Drury Lane Theatre** (first opened 1663). The same theatre was leased by the dramatist Richard Brinsley Sheridan from 1776.

Drury Lane takes its name from Drury Place, a 15th-century house owned by the Drury family. It was here that Robert Devereux, 2nd Earl of Essex, planned his rebellion of 1601, which led to his execution.

## Dryburgh Abbey (Gaelic *Darach-bruach* 'bank of oaks')

Monastic ruin in the Scottish Borders region of Scotland, on the River Tweed, near Melrose. It was founded about 1150 for Premonstratensian canons by Hugo de Morville, constable of Scotland. The style is mainly ◊Decorated.

Dryburgh was burned by Edward II (1322), and was partly restored by Robert Bruce. Under Richard II it again suffered (1385), and was reduced to ruins by Bowes and Latoun (1544), and by the Earl of Hertford's expedition (1545).

St Mary's aisle in the north transept has the tombs of the novelist Walter Scott, his biographer, John Gibson Lockhart, and Field Marshal Earl Haig.

## Dryden, John (1631–1700)

English poet and dramatist, one of the leading writers of the Restoration period. He is noted for his satirical verse and for his use of the heroic couplet. His poetry includes the verse satire *Absalom and Achitophel* (1681), *Annus Mirabilis* (1667), and 'A Song for St Cecilia's Day' (1687). Plays include the heroic drama *The Conquest of Granada* (first performed in 1670, printed in 1672), the comedy *Marriage à la Mode* (first performed in 1672, printed in 1673), and *All for Love* (first performed in 1677, printed in 1678). Critical works include the essay 'Of Dramatic Poesy' (1668).

Dryden was born in Northamptonshire, and educated at Cambridge University. In 1657 he moved to London, where he worked for the republican government of Oliver Cromwell. His stanzas commemorating the death of Cromwell appeared in 1659 and *Astraea Redux*, in honour of the Restoration, was published in 1660. He followed this with a panegyric in honour of Charles II's coronation in 1661. Dryden was much involved in the intellectual spirit of the 'new age', and was one of the first to liken the reign of Charles II to that of the Roman emperor Augustus. In 1668 he became the first poet officially to hold the title of poet laureate. He converted to Roman Catholicism following the accession of James II, but lost the post of poet laureate after the Revolution of 1688.

## Dudley

Industrial town and metropolitan borough in the West Midlands, 14 km/9 mi northwest of Birmingham, England; population (1994 est) 141,000. Dudley was an important industrial centre from medieval times, with its abundant resources of coal, ironstone, limestone, and clay. Coalmining existed in the late 13th century, and the coalmining and iron-smelting industries expanded in the 17th century. The handwrought-rail trade flourished in the early 16th century, and the manufacture of glass and bricks began in the early 17th. Dudley now manufactures clothing, glass, and light engineering products.

The Black Country Museum illustrates the area's industrial heritage and includes reconstructed period buildings. There are ruins of a Norman castle, with a zoo in the grounds.

## Dudley, Lord Guildford (died 1554)

English nobleman, fourth son of the Duke of Northumberland. He was married by his father to Lady Jane Grey in 1553, against her wishes, in an attempt to prevent the succession of Mary I to the throne. The plot failed, and he and his wife were executed.

## Dulwich

District of the Greater London borough of Southwark. It includes Dulwich College (1619); the Horniman Museum (1901), with a fine ethnological collection; Dulwich Picture Gallery

(1814), the first public art gallery to be opened in London; Dulwich Park; and Dulwich Village.

## Du Maurier, Daphne (1907–1989)

English novelist. Her romantic fiction includes *Jamaica Inn* (1936), *Rebecca* (1938), *Frenchman's Creek* (1942), and *My Cousin Rachel* (1951), and is set in Cornwall. Her work is made compelling by her storytelling gift.

*Jamaica Inn*, *Rebecca*, and her short story *The Birds* were made into films by the English director Alfred Hitchcock.

## Dumbarton

Administrative headquarters of ◊West Dunbartonshire, Scotland, on the River Leven near its confluence with the Clyde, 23 km/14 mi northwest of Glasgow; population (1991) 22,000.

**Dumbarton Castle**, built on a basalt rock, dates from the 6th century; Dumbarton was then capital of the kingdom of Strathclyde until 1034 when it was absorbed into the kingdom of Scotland. William ◊Wallace was confined within the castle's walls in 1305, and in 1571 it was captured for James VI.

## Dumfries

Administrative headquarters of ◊Dumfries and Galloway unitary authority, Scotland; population (1991) 32,100. It is situated on the River Nith, 53 km/33 mi northwest of Carlisle. The poet Robert Burns is buried in the graveyard of St Michael's church.

The site of a Franciscan friary where ◊Robert (I) the Bruce killed the Red Comyn is now built on; a stone marks the site of the old castle of Dumfries which Robert captured after Comyn's death. This death started the long war of independence.

Sweetheart Abbey, southwest of Dumfries, was founded in 1273 by Devorgilla Balliol in memory of her husband; the couple founded Balliol College, Oxford. Caerlaverock Castle (1290) is situated nearby.

Robert Burns worked at Ellisland Farm, 10 km/6 mi north of the town, from 1788 until 1791, when he moved to Dumfries, where he worked as an exciseman until he died in 1796. The playwright JM Barrie was educated at the town's academy and is understood to have conceived *Peter Pan* at this time.

Two foot bridges and four traffic bridges span the river. Devorgilla's Bridge (1426) is the oldest and is now reserved for pedestrians.

## Dumfries and Galloway

Unitary authority in southwest Scotland, formed in 1996 from the regional council of the same name (1975–96); population (1996) 147,800; area 6,421 sq km/2,479 sq mi. Bordering Cumbria, England, to the southeast, it has a coastline on the Solway Firth and is hilly inland. The chief towns are Annan, ◊Dumfries (administrative headquarters), Kirkcudbright, Stranraer, Castle Douglas, and Newton Stewart.

*Physical*

The area is characterized by an indented coastline, including Luce Bay and Wigtown Bay, backed by a low-lying coastal strip of varying width; it is intensively forested in the Galloways. Much of the inland area is upland: east to west this includes Eskdalemuir (Hart Fell, 808 m/2,651 ft), the Lowther Hills (Green Lowther, 732 m/2,402 ft), and the Galloway Hills (the Merrick, 843 m/2,766 ft). The climate is the mildest in Scotland.

*Features*

There are Neolithic tombs and a wide range of later prehistoric sites at Burnswark; also at Burnswark and Birrens there are Roman artefacts. Early Christian monuments include those at Whithorn and Ruthwell. Many earthen mounds (mottes) for timber castles testify to the Norman penetration of Scotland. Caerlaverock Castle is one of the foremost examples of medieval secular architecture in Scotland. ◊Gretna Green is a village near the English border where, until 1940, runaway couples could be legally married by declaration before witnesses. There are 93 Sites of Special Scientific Interest, five National Nature Reserves, four Ramsars (wetland sites), three Special Protection Areas, three Biosphere Reserves, and three National Scenic Areas.

*Economy*

Agriculture is the most important economic enterprise in the area, with poorer lands being intensively forested and better quality lands being intensively cropped or grazed. Tourism is also important, with many camping and caravan sites along the southern coast. There are also manufacturing and service industries. The shortest ferry route to Ireland is from Stranraer.

## Dunbar, Battles of

Two English victories over the Scots at Dunbar, now a port and resort in Lothian.

**27 April 1296** defeat by John de Warenne, Earl of Surrey, of Scottish king John Balliol. The defeat all but ended Scottish resistance to Edward I. Edinburgh fell shortly after and in July John surrendered his throne to Edward and fled the country.

**3 Sept 1650** crushing defeat by Oliver Cromwell of a Scottish army under David Leslie supporting Charles II. Combined with Charles's defeat at Worcester the following year, it effectively ended Scotland's independence of action.

## Duncan

Two kings of Scotland.

## Duncan I

He succeeded his grandfather, Malcolm II, as king in 1034, but was defeated and killed by ◊Macbeth. He is the Duncan in Shakespeare's play *Macbeth* (1605).

## Duncan II

Son of ◊Malcolm III and grandson of ◊Duncan I. He gained English and Norman help to drive out his uncle ◊Donald III in 1094. He ruled for a few months before being killed by agents of Donald, who then regained power. See genealogy on pages 140–141.

## Dundee

Scotland's fourth-largest city, lying on the north side of the Firth of Tay in eastern Scotland; population (1996) 155,000. It is also a unitary authority; area 62 sq km/24 sq mi. The city developed around the jute industry in the 19th century. Today, the chief industries are fishing, engineering, textiles, electronics, and food processing

*Features*
*Discovery*, the ship used by Robert Falcon Scott on his expedition to the Antarctic 1901–04 is moored on the Tay, to the west of the Tay road bridge. At nearby Broughty Ferry there is a 15th-century castle, with a museum documenting Dundee's 18th-century whaling industry. Other notable buildings include the Albert Institute (1867) and Caird Hall. The university (1967) developed from Queen's College (founded in 1881).

## Dunfermline

Industrial town north of the Firth of Forth in Fife, Scotland; population (1991) 55,100. Industries include engineering, electronics, and textiles. It was the ancient capital of Scotland, with many sites of royal historical significance. Many Scottish kings, including Robert the Bruce and Malcolm Canmore, are buried in **Dunfermline Abbey**. A royal 'square mile' includes a royal palace, a 12th-century abbey, and a royal burial site.

Dunfermline is the birthplace of the industrialist and philanthropist Andrew Carnegie, who presented the city with Pittencrieff Park and Glen, a free library.

## Dungannon

Market town in County Tyrone, Northern Ireland, 64 km/40 mi southwest of Belfast; population (1991) 8,300. It was the main seat of the O'Neill family, former kings of Ulster. Dungannon was a significant scene of conflict with the English crown during the 16th and 17th centuries.

## Dunkeld, House of

Royal house of the kingdom of Scotland 1030–1290. Despite its origins in the struggle between ◊Duncan I and his cousin ◊Macbeth and almost constant pressure from Anglo-Norman and Plantagenet England, the house of Dunkeld provided a series of strong and competent monarchs of Scotland. Among the more successful rulers were ◊Malcolm III Canmore, William I the Lion (1165–1214), and ◊Alexander II and his brother ◊Alexander III, under whom medieval Scotland enjoyed something of a golden age.

See genealogy on pages 140–141.

## Dunlop, John Boyd (1840–1921)

Scottish inventor who founded the rubber company that bears his name. In 1888, to help his child win a tricycle race, he bound an inflated rubber hose to the wheels. The same year he developed commercially practical pneumatic tyres, first patented by Robert William Thomson (1822–1873) in 1845 for bicycles and cars.

## Dunmow, Little

Village in Essex, eastern England, 4 km/2 mi southeast of **Great Dunmow**. It was the original scene of the **Dunmow Flitch** trial (dating from 1111), in which a side of bacon is presented to any couple who 'will swear that they have not quarrelled nor repented of their marriage within a year and a day after its celebration'. Couples are judged by a jury whose members are all unmarried. The trial, which is carried out every four years, now takes place at Great Dunmow.

## Dunoon

Holiday resort and former burgh in Argyll and Bute unitary authority, Scotland, on the Firth of Clyde, at the southwest end of the Cowal peninsula, 45 km/28 mi northwest of Glasgow; population (1991) 9,000. Over 1,000 pipers converge on Dunoon for the annual Cowal Gathering.

## Dunsinane

Elevation of the Sidlaw Hills in Perth and Kinross unitary authority, Scotland, rising 15 km/9 mi northeast of Perth to a height of 308 m/1,010 ft. On its summit lie the remains of 'Macbeth's Castle', where Siward, Earl of Northumbria, is reputed to have defeated ◊Macbeth in 1054. The playwright William Shakespeare produced a dramatic version of the event in his tragedy *Macbeth*.

## Dunstaffnage

Ruined castle in Argyll and Bute unitary authority, Scotland, on Loch Etive, 4 km/2.5 mi northeast of Oban. It is traditionally believed to be the royal seat of the ancient Dalriadan kings of Scotland, and held the Stone of Destiny (the Scottish throne) before its removal to ◊Scone. Dunstaffnage was captured by Robert (I) the Bruce in 1308, and became the stronghold of the Campbells and Macdougals.

During the Jacobite risings of 1715 and 1745 it formed an English military station. Flora Macdonald, the Scottish heroine who rescued Prince Charles Edward Stuart, was imprisoned in the fortress in 1746.

## Dunstanburgh Castle

Ruined castle on the Northumberland coast, England, 11 km/7 mi northeast of Alnwick. It is the largest castle in Northumbria, and served as an outpost of the Lancastrian side during the Wars of the Roses.

Dunstanburgh Castle was built in 1316 by Thomas, Earl of Lancaster, and later enlarged by John of Gaunt. The site is geologically interesting, as the point where the Whin Sill (the rock system on which Hadrian's Wall is built) reaches the coast in basalt cliffs. The quartz crystals found in the area are called 'Dunstanburgh diamonds'.

## Durham

City and administrative headquarters of the county of Durham, northeast England, on the River Wear, 19 km/12 mi south of Newcastle-upon-Tyne; population (1991) 36,900. Durham was an important defensive site and the seat of a powerful bishopric in medieval times, as well as a place of pilgrimage. Its Norman cathedral and castle are situated on a peninsula on a bend in the River Wear, and today are together a World Heritage site. The city was formerly a centre for the coalmining industry.

*Cathedral and castle*

Tradition holds that monks from Lindisfarne brought the body of St Cuthbert here in 995, and

**Durham** The nave of Durham Cathedral, England. Dating from the 12th century, Durham Cathedral is one of the finest examples of Norman architecture. This picture clearly shows two typical features of the Norman style, massive piers, and round arches. Corbis

established a church to serve as St Cuthbert's shrine. Durham thus became a place of pilgrimage for Saxons and Normans. The site was then called **Dunholme**, or 'hill island'. Little remains of the original Saxon cathedral. The present cathedral was built between 1093 and 1133. Its interior is richly ornamented and has the earliest English examples of pointed transverse arches, and ribbed vaulting on a grand scale. The remains of the theologian and historian the Venerable Bede are here, placed in the Lady Chapel in 1370.

In return for defending the northern Marches against Scottish invasions, the bishops of Durham were given important secular powers, holding sway over a county palatine with many royal privileges. They had their own army, courts, councils, and judges. The powers of the 'prince-bishops' were gradually reduced after the 14th century, with their final demise in the mid-19th century.

The castle was built in 1072 by William I. It

# HOUSE OF DUNKELD 1034–1290

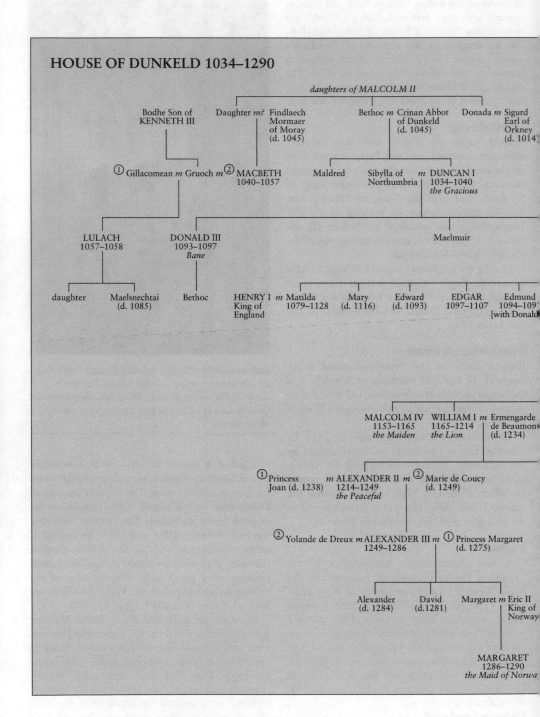

*daughters of MALCOLM II*

Bodhe Son of
KENNETH III

Daughter *m?* Findlaech
Mormaer
of Moray
(d. 1045)

Bethoc *m* Crinan Abbot
of Dunkeld
(d. 1045)

Donada *m* Sigurd
Earl of
Orkney
(d. 1014)

① Gillacomean *m* Gruoch *m* ② MACBETH
1040–1057

Maldred

Sibylla of *m* DUNCAN I
Northumbria | 1034–1040
*the Gracious*

LULACH
1057–1058

DONALD III
1093–1097
*Bane*

Maelmuir

daughter

Maelsnechtai
(d. 1085)

Bethoc

HENRY I *m* Matilda
King of 1079–1128
England

Mary
(d. 1116)

Edward
(d. 1093)

EDGAR
1097–1107

Edmund
1094–109?
[with Donald

MALCOLM IV
1153–1165
*the Maiden*

WILLIAM I *m* Ermengarde
1165–1214 de Beaumon
*the Lion* (d. 1234)

① Princess
Joan (d. 1238)

*m* ALEXANDER II *m* ② Marie de Coucy
1214–1249 (d. 1249)
*the Peaceful*

② Yolande de Dreux *m* ALEXANDER III *m* ① Princess Margaret
1249–1286 (d. 1275)

Alexander
(d. 1284)

David
(d.1281)

Margaret *m* Eric II
King of
Norway

MARGARET
1286–1290
*the Maid of Norwa*

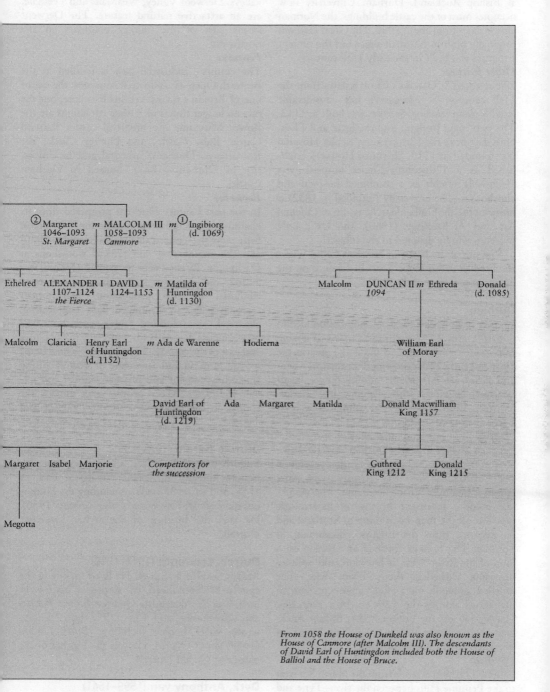

From 1058 the House of Dunkeld was also known as the
House of Canmore (after Malcolm III). The descendants
of David Earl of Huntingdon included both the House of
Balliol and the House of Bruce.

was the palace of the bishops of Durham until 1836, when they moved their home to the palace at Bishop Auckland. Durham University now occupies most of the castle buildings; the Norman chapel dates from about 1080. The Great Hall was originally built in Norman times but the present structure was built in the early 14th century.

*Other features*

The restored St Oswald's Church dates from the 11th century; St Margaret's has considerable late-Norman remains; St Giles was built in 1112. The two main bridges, Framwellgate and Elvet, both date from the 12th century. Kepier Hospital was founded in 1112; Sherburn Hospital, established as a 12th-century leper hospital, was extensively rebuilt as a combined hospital and almshouses. The university (founded in 1832) is home to the the the Gulbenkian Museum of Oriental Art and Archaeology (1960), the UK's only museum wholly devoted to the subject.

The site of the Battle of Neville's Cross, where the English defeated the Scots in 1346, is on the northern outskirts of the city.

## Durham

County of northeast England; population (1996) 608,100; area 2,232 sq km/862 sq mi. It was an important coalmining and industrial area in the 19th and early 20th centuries. Its principal towns and cities are ◊Durham (administrative headquarters), Newton Aycliffe, Peterlee, and Chester-le-Street. Since April 1997, ◊Darlington has been a separate unitary authority.

*History*

Between 1071 and 1836, Durham was a palatinate county, that is the bishop of Durham exercised such jurisdiction over the territory as in other counties belonged to the sovereign. The county was made a palatinate because of its strategic position on the then main route to Scotland and its distance from the English government in London. The bishops fortified an outcrop on a loop of the River Wear at Durham, and built an imposing cathedral there. From here they repelled, generally successfully, a series of Scottish incursions during the 12th to 14th centuries. Hartlepool was the bishops' port, Bishop Auckland their country residence, and the 'forest' of Weardale their hunting ground.

*Physical*

County Durham extends from the North Sea west to the Pennine Hills between the rivers Tyne and Tees. East of the River Wear, it occupies a low plateau (100–120 m/328–394 ft above sea-level) with a coast lined by cliffs. To the west of the Wear, it rises to the Pennines, which pass through the county on its far western side. The river valleys, Derwent Valley, Weardale, and Teesdale, are an attractive natural feature. The Derwent forms part of the county boundary in the northwest.

*Features*

The county's industrial past is recalled in the Beamish Open-air Industrial Museum; the site of one of Britain's richest coalfields is here, but the pits no longer function. Other attractions are the Bowes Museum; the medieval castles Barnard Castle, Raby Castle, and Lumley Castle; the Romanesque Durham Cathedral; and the University of Durham (1832), housed in Durham Castle.

*Economy*

In the past County Durham prospered from its coalmining and industrial production. The largest firms were the Consett steelworks (closed in 1980) and the engineering and railway workshops at Darlington. By the 1920s the demand for coal was falling and post-war rationalization led to a rundown of coal production. Government regional policies encouraged light engineering, electrical, and clothing factories on industrial estates across the coalfields, especially in the centre and east of the county. The economy is now based on hill farming and a mixture of manufacturing (including cement and phamaceuticals) and service industries. Many people work outside the county in the industrial areas of Tyneside and Teesside.

## Durrell, Gerald (1925–1995)

English naturalist, writer, and zoo curator. He became director of Jersey Zoological Park in 1958, and wrote 37 books, including the humorous memoir *My Family and Other Animals* (1956). He was the brother of the writer Lawrence Durrell.

## Durrell, Lawrence (1912–1990)

British novelist and poet. He lived mainly in the eastern Mediterranean, the setting of his novels, including the Alexandria Quartet: *Justine*, *Balthazar*, *Mountolive*, and *Clea* (1957–60). He also wrote travel books, including *Bitter Lemons* (1957) about Cyprus. He was the brother of the naturalist Gerald Durrell.

## Dyck, Anthony van (1599–1641)

Flemish painter. He was an assistant to Rubens from 1618 to 1620, then worked briefly in England at the court of James I before moving to

Italy in 1622. Returning to England in 1632, by invitation of Charles I, he produced numerous portraits of the royal family and English aristocracy, such as *Charles I on Horseback* (about 1638; National Gallery, London). His refinement of style and colour, and dignity of composition, left a profound impression on subsequent portraiture in England. The portrait of Charles I, now in the Louvre, and the many memorable works still in the Royal Collection, are distinct creations and, despite the large extent to which van Dyck employed studio assistants, never fall into superficiality. His landscape studies (British Museum) anticipate John Constable in conveying the atmosphere of the English countryside.

## Ealing Studios

British film-producing company, based in Ealing, West London, headed by Michael ◊Balcon 1937–58. The studio made a distinctive series of comedies, which had an understated, self-deprecating humour, such as *Passport to Pimlico, Kind Hearts and Coronets, Whisky Galore!* (all 1949), *The Man in the White Suit* (1951), and *The Ladykillers* (1955).

The studios also made movies in other genres, such as the crime thriller *The Blue Lamp* (1950) and the war story *The Cruel Sea* (1952). In 1994 film production began again at Ealing after an interval of nearly 40 years.

## Early English

In architecture, the first of the three periods of the English ◊Gothic style, late 12th century to late 13th century. It is characterized by tall, elongated windows (lancets) without mullions (horizontal bars), often grouped in threes, fives, or sevens; the pointed arch; pillars of stone centres surrounded by shafts of black Purbeck marble; and dog-tooth (zig-zag) ornament. Salisbury Cathedral (begun in 1220) is almost entirely Early English.

Most of Wells Cathedral, including the west front, and Lincoln Cathedral, except for the choir and west front, were built in the Early English style. Other examples include the west fronts of Peterborough and Ripon cathedrals; the choirs of Lichfield, Southwark, Southwell and Worcester cathedrals; the nave of York Minster; and the 'Chapel of the Nine Altars' at Durham Cathedral.

The choirs of ◊Westminster Abbey and of the Temple Church in London, and the choir and transepts of Beverley Minster are also Early English.

## Easington

Town in County Durham, England, 14 km/9 mi south of Sunderland; population (1991) 95,700. Easington was a centre of extensive coalmining in the region, beginning in the 1820s and reaching a peak in the early 20th century; the colliery was closed in the 1980s. The mine galleries of Easington pit extended far out under the North Sea.

## East Anglia

Region of eastern England, formerly a Saxon kingdom, including Norfolk, Suffolk, and parts of Essex and Cambridgeshire. ◊Norwich is the principal city of East Anglia. The Sainsbury Centre for Visual Arts, opened in 1978 at the University of East Anglia, has a collection of ethnographic art and sculpture. East Anglian ports such as Harwich and Felixstowe have greatly developed as trade with the rest of Europe has increased.

## East Ayrshire

Unitary authority in southwest Scotland, created in 1996 from two districts of the Strathclyde region; population (1996) 124,000; area 1,269 sq km/490 sq mi. It is a rural area, mountainous in the south, and has associations with the Scottish king Robert (I) the Bruce and the poet Robert Burns, who wrote his early poems in the area. The principal towns are Kilmarnock (administrative headquarters), Cumnock, Stewarton, Galston, and Crosshouse.

*History*

In 1307 Robert (I) the Bruce defeated 6,000 of the Earl of Pembroke's Englishmen with a force of only 600 at Loudoun Hill.

*Physical*

The area is mainly low lying and undulating in the north, becoming mountainous towards the south.

The highest point is Blackcraig Hill (700 m/2,298 ft). The biggest lake is Loch Doon, and the rivers Ayr and Irvine flow through East Ayrshire.

### Features
Principal historical and tourist sites include Burns's House Museum at Mauchline, Loudoun Castle Theme Park, and Dunaskin Heritage Museum. There are 15 Sites of Special Scientific Interest and one country park.

### Economy
Agriculture, especially livestock, is an important industry in a predominantly rural area. Many rural towns have lost their traditional industrial base of mining or textile production and now suffer economic problems. There is engineering and printing.

## Eastbourne
Seaside resort in East Sussex, southeast England, 103 km/64 mi southeast of London; population (1991) 94,800. Originally a small village – comprising the four hamlets of East Bourne, Southbourne, Sea Houses, and Meads – Eastbourne developed in the mid-19th century as a resort and model of town planning. The modern town, which extends along the coast for 5 km/3 mi, has become a popular place for retirement. To the east the South Downs terminate in Beachy Head.

### Features
The resort has terraced promenades, tree-lined streets, theatres, winter gardens, and golfing facilities; tennis tournaments are held at Devonshire Park. Other features include the pier, opened in 1872; a bandstand, built to seat over 3,000 spectators; and the Carpet Gardens. The Transitional Norman St Mary's Church, built in the 12th century in the old village of Eastbourne, lies about 2 km/1 mi inland.

The Lifeboat Museum illustrates the work of Eastbourne's sea-rescue service; the Towner Art Gallery is housed in an 18th-century manor house and includes collections of 19th and 20th-century British art; and Eastbourne Redoubt Fortress, a restored Napoleonic fortress, contains a large military museum.

## East Dunbartonshire
Unitary authority in central Scotland, created in 1996 from two districts of Strathclyde region; population (1996) 110,000; area 175 sq km/67 sq mi. Immediately north of ◊Glasgow, it is an affluent area, home to many commuters. The principal towns are Kirkintilloch (administrative headquarters), Bearsden, and Milngavie.

### Physical
Low-lying lands to the south give way dramatically to the Campsie Fells in the north; Earl's Seat rises to 578 m/1,896 ft, and the River Kelvin flows through the area.

### Features
The Forth and Clyde Canal, linking the Firth of Forth to the east with the mouth of the River Clyde to the west, passes through the area, as does part of the Roman Antonine Wall, the furthest northwest Roman frontier in Britain. There are four Sites of Special Scientific Interest and one country park.

### Economy
The area is largely a commuter belt for the city of Glasgow. Smaller industrialized villages, such as Croy, are also evident.

## EastEnders
Drama serial produced by the BBC. See ◊soap operas.

## Easter Rising, or Easter Rebellion
In Irish history, a republican insurrection that began on Easter Monday, April 1916, in Dublin. It was inspired by the Irish Republican Brotherhood (IRB) in an unsuccessful attempt to overthrow British rule in Ireland. It was led by Patrick Pearse of the IRB and James Connolly of Sinn Féin.

Arms from Germany intended for the IRB were intercepted but the rising proceeded regardless with the seizure of the Post Office and other buildings in Dublin by 1,500 volunteers. The rebellion was crushed by the British Army within five days, both sides suffering major losses: 220 civilians, 64 rebels, and 134 members of the Crown Forces were killed during the uprising. Pearse, Connolly, and thirteen other rebel leaders were subsequently executed in Kilmainham Jail. Others, including Éamon de Valera, were spared due to US public opinion, to be given amnesty in June 1917.

## East India Company (British)
Commercial company (1600–1858) chartered by Queen Elizabeth I and given a monopoly of trade between England and the Far East. In the 18th century the company became, in effect, the ruler of a large part of India, and a form of dual control by the company and a committee responsible to Parliament in London was introduced by Pitt's India Act 1784. The end of the monopoly of China trade came in 1834, and after the Indian Mutiny of 1857 the crown took complete control

of the government of British India. The India Act 1858 abolished the company.

By 1652 there were some 23 English factories in India. Bombay came to the British crown in 1662, and was granted to the East India Company for £10 a year. The British victory in the Battle of Plassey in 1757 gave the company control of Bengal. See also ◊ British Empire.

---

*... establish such a politie of civil and military power and create and secure a large revenue ... as may be the foundation of a large, well-grounded sure English dominion in India for all time to come.*

**East India Company**
Letter from the East India Company, London, to its agent in Surat 1687

---

## East Kilbride
Town in South Lanarkshire, Scotland; population (1991) 70,400. It was designated a new town in 1947 to take overspill from Glasgow, 11 km/7 mi to the northeast. It is the site of the National Engineering Laboratory and headquarters of British Energy.

## East Lothian
Unitary authority in southeast Scotland, created in 1996 from a district of Lothian region; population (1996) 85,500; area 677 sq km/261 sq mi. It has a coastline at the mouth of the Firth of Forth, and its chief towns are Haddington (administrative headquarters), North Berwick, and Dunbar.

### History
Traprain Law (221 m/725 ft), a hill of volcanic origin near East Linton, had the most important native stronghold site of the Iron Age in Scotland. A hoard of 4th-century Roman silver coins was found here in 1919 (now in Edinburgh's Museum of Antiquities).

### Physical
East Lothian is an area of contrasts, with coastal plains of cliffs, beaches, and estuarine marines, the broad river valley of the Tyne, volcanic outcrops (Bass Rock, Traprain Law), and the gentle slopes of the Lammermuir Hills in the south.

### Features
Important historic sites include Traprain Law fort, Tantallon Castle, and Dunbar Castle. There is a fine golf course at Muirfield. The Lammermuir Hills are associated with Walter Scott's *The Bride of Lammermoor* (1819) and Verdi's opera

based on the novel. The area has 21 Sites of Special Scientific Interest, one Special Protection Area, and one country park.

### Economy
East Lothian is an affluent area with a mixed economy. The western towns are within the Edinburgh commuter belt, with agricultural economies to the south, and tourist-based and service sector enterprise by the coast.

## East Renfrewshire
Unitary authority in central Scotland, created in 1996 from part of Renfrew district in Strathclyde region; population (1996) 86,800; area 174 sq km/67 sq mi. It lies to the southwest of ◊ Glasgow and the northeast is home to many commuters. The main towns are Barrhead, Giffnock (administrative headquarters), Newton Mearns, and Clarkston.

### Physical
The area is a low-lying plateau rising from the plain of the River Clyde.

### Features
The conservation village of Eaglesham is an 18th-century experiment in town planning, laid out in the shape of a triangle. The authority has four Sites of Special Scientific Interest.

### Economy
There is a sharp contrast between the northeastern affluent commuter zone, which is bound into Glasgow's economy, and the de-industrializing Barrhead area. The agricultural lands in the south support rough grazing and some dairy farming.

## East Riding of Yorkshire
Unitary authority in northeast England, created in 1996 from part of the former county of Humberside; population (1996) 310,000; area 2,416 sq km/933 sq mi. It has a long coastline on the North Sea and the southern border follows the north bank of the Humber estuary. Its principal towns are ◊ Beverley (administrative headquarters), Driffield, Goole (inland port), Hornsea, and ◊ Bridlington.

### Physical
There are chalk cliffs, notably at ◊ Flamborough Head, and gentle hills (the southern Yorkshire Wolds) running north–south through the centre. The Holderness Peninsula to the south ends in the dynamic spit of Spurn Head at the mouth of the Humber estuary. The main river is the Hull.

### Features
Architectural and historic highlights include the 13th-century Beverley Minster; All Saints Tower (34 m/110 ft) at Driffield; Sledmere House, an 18th-century mansion with grounds laid out by

Capability Brown; Rudstone, with Britain's tallest standing stone (8 m/25 ft); Sewerby Hall, Bridlington, a Georgian mansion including a museum dedicated to the aviator Amy Johnson (1903–1941); and Withernsea Lighthouse (39 m/127 ft) including a museum. Bempton Cliffs, north of Flamborough Head, is home to a gannet colony and many other seabirds.

### Economy
The economy is based on tourism and related businesses, including pottery, as well as agriculture, light industry, and transport and distribution services.

## East Sussex
County of southeast England, created in 1974; population (1996) 734,900; area 1,725 sq km/666 sq mi. It is one of the most wooded counties in England, with the eastern end of the South Downs following the southwest coast. The Norman invasion led by William (I) the Conqueror in 1066 took place here. The principal towns are Lewes (administrative headquarters), Newhaven (cross-channel port), ◊Eastbourne, ◊Rye, and ◊Winchelsea; ◊Bexhill-on-Sea, ◊Hastings, St Leonards, and Seaford are coastal resorts. Since April 1997, ◊Brighton and Hove has been a separate unitary authority.

### History
Two major historical events that took place in the county are the Battle of ◊Hastings (1066), and the Battle of Lewes (1264), when Henry III was defeated and captured by Simon de Montfort, Earl of Leicester, leader of the baronial opposition to the monarchy.

### Physical
Along the South Downs, which lie generally within 15 km/9 mi of the English Channel, runs the South Downs Way, from Beachy Head (the highest headland on the south coast, 180 m/590 ft), through East and West Sussex to the Hampshire border; high points along its path include Ditchling Beacon (248 m/814 ft). The Weald, in the north of the county, is now a dairy farming area; until the 17th century its iron industry was nationally important. Ashdown Forest, in the northwest, was originally a Norman hunting forest; attempts to cultivate the land have failed because of the forest's sterile soil and it is now heathland. The main rivers are the Cuckmere, Ouse, and East Rother (which flows into the sea near Rye).

### Features
The county has a variety of historical monuments and sites, including prehistoric earthworks; an Iron Age hill fort at Mount Caburn, near Lewes; Roman villas; the 'Long Man' chalk ◊hill figure at Wilmington, near Eastbourne; ◊Herstmonceux, with a 15th-century castle (conference and exhibition centre) and adjacent modern buildings, site of the Greenwich Royal Observatory (1958–90); castles at Hastings, Lewes, ◊Pevensey, and ◊Bodiam; Bayham Abbey; ◊Battle Abbey and the site of the Battle of Hastings; Michelham Priory; and Sheffield Park garden. There are the former homes of Henry James at Rye, Rudyard Kipling at Batemans in Burwash, Thomas Sackville at Buckhurst, and Virginia Woolf at Rodmell. The University of Sussex at Falmer, near Brighton, was founded in 1961. The ◊Glyndebourne festival of opera takes place between May and August.

### Economy
Tourism is important to the county. Agricultural products are mainly cereals, hops, fruit, and vegetables, and there is fishing (at Hastings). There is also light engineering.

## Edinburgh
Capital of Scotland and, as the **City of Edinburgh**, a unitary authority, located near the southern shores of the Firth of Forth; area: 263 sq km/122 sq mi; population (1996) 477,600. Historically the cultural and political centre of Scotland, today Edinburgh is also the country's centre of finance, banking, tourism, and law, and home to the new ◊Scottish Parliament. The Old Town and New Town are a World Heritage site.

### History
The site was occupied in Roman times by Celtic peoples. In about 617 it was captured by Edwin of the Angles of Northumbria, and the city took its name from the fortress of Din Eidin. The early settlement, known today as the Old Town, developed around Edinburgh Castle on Castle Rock in the 12th century, while about a mile to the east another burgh, Canongate, grew up around the abbey of Holyrood, founded in 1128 by David I. It remained separate from Edinburgh until 1856. Robert the Bruce, having made Edinburgh the capital in 1325, made Edinburgh a burgh in 1329, and established its port at Leith.

In 1544 and 1547 the town was destroyed by the English. After the union with England in 1707, Edinburgh lost its political importance but remained culturally pre-eminent, and the focus of Scottish national identity. During the 18th century Edinburgh was known as the 'Athens of the North' because of its concentration of intellectual talent, for example, the economist Adam

**Edinburgh** A courtyard in Edinburgh Castle. The castle stands on top of a granite outcrop that dominates the old part of Scotland's capital city. From its gates the 'Royal Mile', the old town's main thoroughfare, descends the hill to the palace of Holyrood. Edinburgh Castle is the scene of a spectacular annual military tattoo. Joe Cornish

◊Smith, the philosopher David Hume (1711–1776), and the chemist Joseph Black (1728–1799), discoverer of carbon dioxide. Development of the area known as New Town started in 1767.

*Features*

Edinburgh is situated in a valley, surrounded on all sides (except the north) by hills, and dominated by the steep basalt cliffs of Castle Rock. The ridge descending from Castle Rock to the Netherbow Port (an old city gateway) constituted the ancient city, and on it the High Street is built. To the north of this ridge was formerly the North Loch. The New Town lies on the ground which rises beyond the valley of the North Loch, and its wide streets and stately Georgian houses stretch down towards the Firth of Forth.

Edinburgh Castle contains St Margaret's chapel, the oldest building in Edinburgh, dating from the 12th century. The Great Hall, built at the beginning of the 16th century, was restored in 1892. The palace of ◊Holyrood House was built in the 15th and 16th centuries on the site of a 12th-century abbey; it is the British sovereign's official Scottish residence.

Edinburgh's principal church, St Giles, was consecrated in 1243 and became a cathedral in 1633. The episcopal cathedral of St Mary, opened in 1879, is in the New Town area. The Royal Observatory has been at Blackford Hill since 1896. The main thoroughfares are Princes Street and the Royal Mile. Parliament Square contains the old Parliament House (1632–40), and John Knox's grave is believed to be here, to the rear of St Giles. Other historic sites along the Royal Mile include the Old Canongate Tolbooth, and Canongate Kirk Church. The Palace of Holyrood House, standing at the lower end of the Royal Mile, was begun by James IV, while the greater portion of it was built in the time of Charles II.

Among other noteworthy public buildings in Edinburgh are the Royal Scottish Academy (1823–1826), the ◊National Gallery of Scotland, the Surgeon's Hall, the Royal Scottish Museum, and the Scottish National War Memorial. A Museum of Scotland was opened in 1998.

The city has three universities: the University of Edinburgh (1583), Heriot-Watt University, and Napier University. The Conference Centre, designed by Terry Farrell, opened in 1995, as did the Edinburgh Festival Theatre. A permanent home for the new Scottish Parliament (elected in

# ◆ HOW THE EDUCATION SYSTEM WORKS ◆

The organization of the modern school system has been a subject of heated debate in the United Kingdom for more than 30 years. Although political interest has now shifted somewhat to the curriculum and assessment, school organization can still arouse fierce passions.

The situation is further confused because although the Department for Education and Employment in London (and its equivalents in Wales, Scotland, and Northern Ireland) has taken an increasingly centralizing role in what goes on in school, actual control still rests with more than one hundred local education authorities (LEAs) based in town and county halls. As a result, the organization of schools may vary from one part of England to another, although the other three constituent parts of the UK have had more uniform – but different – structures.

## Compulsory from age five

Compulsory schooling does not begin for children in the United Kingdom until the age of five, although in practice many children start before that age. Part-time nursery education is widely, although not evenly available, but is not compulsory. The Labour Government elected in 1997 is making places available for all four-year-olds whose parents want it, and intends to extend provision for three year olds.

At five children move from the nursery school or class to primary school, where the emphasis during the early years is very much on the skills of reading, writing, and mathematics. Children generally stay in their primary school until they are eleven (twelve in Scotland) although some local areas provide separate infants and junior schools with a break at seven, or first and middle schools with a break at eight or nine and again at twelve or thirteen, rather than eleven.

Secondary education in the UK is generally 'comprehensive': schools accept children of all abilities without any selective procedure on entry. Only Northern Ireland retains a completely selective system in which children are allocated to grammar (academic) or secondary modern schools on the basis of tests of attainment at the age of eleven. Scotland runs a completely comprehensive secondary system, starting at the age of twelve. In England a few local education authorities have retained some grammar schools, in some cases running them alongside 'comprehensives', which are of course unlikely to be able to recruit the full ability range.

## Specialist schools

Within the comprehensive system, the Labour government is encouraging some schools to specialize by providing grants for subjects such as technology, languages, and the performing arts. These schools will be able to admit a small proportion of children on the basis of their 'aptitude' for the specialist subject.

Another complicating factor is the role of the religious denominations in the provision of education in the UK. Historically the Church of England was responsible for the establishment of many schools, particularly in rural areas. The Roman Catholic Church also established its own schools. In England, Wales, and Scotland most schools are non-denominational 'county' schools, but about a third are run jointly by the local council and a religious denomination.

The former Conservative government allowed parents to vote to transform their existing LEA schools into a new type of school, directly funded by the government and responsible for running their own affairs. The establishment of these grant-maintained schools proved highly controversial in many areas, and they are being brought back into cooperative arrangements with their local authorities under Labour.

There is also a flourishing system of fee-paying private schools which caters for just under 8% of British children. These range from prestigious, academic, and very expensive, boarding schools like Eton and Harrow to small day schools, some of the specializing in the education of children with special needs.

Compulsory education ends at the age of 16, but in practice the majority of young people continue their full-time education at least until the age of 18. At 16 there are four educational options: to remain at school for another one or two years to gain further qualifications such as A Level and GNVQs in a 'sixth form'; to move on to a sixth form college, which will provide mainly the same sort of academic courses offered in a sixth form; to go to a further education college which will provide a range of vocational and prevocational courses; or, in some areas, to go to a tertiary college which will offer academic and vocational courses in one post-16 institution.

After school those who wish to continue their education – and more than one third of the age group now do so – have a choice of higher education courses in almost 200 degree-awarding institutions ranging from international universities of the stature of Oxford and Cambridge, London and Manchester, to new universities which specialize in vocational degree and diploma programmes, and small institutes and colleges which offer a more restricted range of higher education courses.

by Maureen O'Connor

1999) is being built on the Royal Mile, adjacent to Holyrood House, with completion planned for 2001.

The city hosts the **Edinburgh Festival**, an international arts festival and one of the UK's main annual cultural events, which includes music, drama, opera, and art exhibitions. It was founded in 1947 by Rudolph Bing and has been held annually ever since, in August–September. The **Edinburgh Fringe Festival** is held at the same time, and provides a showcase for amateur groups and new talent.

## education
The Department for Education and Employment, established in 1944 as the Ministry of Education and headed by a cabinet minister, is responsible for universities throughout Great Britain, and for school education in England. From 1999 the ◊Scottish Parliament took responsibility for education in these areas; in Wales, primary and secondary education remains the responsibility of the Welsh Education Office.

See page 149 for a feature on the education system today.

## Edward, called the Black Prince (1330–1376)
Prince of Wales, eldest son of Edward III of England. The epithet (probably posthumous) may refer to his black armour. During the ◊Hundred Years' War he fought at the Battle of Crécy in 1346 and captured the French king at Poitiers in 1356. He ruled Aquitaine 1360–71. During the revolt that eventually ousted him, he caused the massacre of Limoges in 1370.

## Edward
Eight kings of England or Great Britain:

## Edward I (1239–1307)
King of England from 1272, son of Henry III. Edward led the royal forces against Simon de Montfort in the Barons' War 1264–67, and was on a crusade when he succeeded to the throne. He established English rule over all Wales, and secured recognition of his overlordship from the Scottish king, although the Scots (under William ◊Wallace and ◊Robert (I) the Bruce) fiercely resisted actual conquest. In his reign Parliament took its approximate modern form with the Model Parliament of 1295. He married ◊Eleanor of Castile in 1254; she died in 1290 and in 1299 he married Margaret, daughter of Philip III of France. He was succeeded by his son Edward II.

## Edward II (1284–1327)
King of England from 1307, son of Edward I. Born at Caernarfon Castle, he was created the first Prince of Wales in 1301. Incompetent and frivolous, and unduly influenced by his favourite, Piers Gaveston, Edward struggled throughout his reign with discontented barons, who attempted to restrict his power through the Ordinances of 1311. His invasion of Scotland in 1314 to suppress revolt resulted in defeat at ◊Bannockburn. When he fell under the influence of a new favourite, Hugh le Depenser, he was deposed in 1327 by his wife Isabella (1292–1358), daughter of Philip IV of France, and her lover Roger de Mortimer, and murdered in Berkeley Castle, Gloucestershire. He was succeeded by his son, Edward III.

## Edward III (1312–1377)
King of England from 1327, son of Edward II. He assumed the government in 1330 from his mother, through whom in 1337 he laid claim to the French throne and thus began the ◊Hundred Years' War. He was succeeded by his grandson Richard II.

Edward improved the status of the monarchy after his father's chaotic reign. He began by attempting to force his rule on Scotland, winning a victory at Halidon Hill in 1333. During the first

**Edward I** A 16th-century manuscript depicting Edward I in Parliament. The king is flanked by Alexander II of Scotland on his right and Llewellyn ap Gruffyd of Wales on his left. In front of him the justices and law officers are sitting on woolsacks. Philip Sauvain Picture Collection

# ◆ THE HAMMER OF THE CELTS: EDWARD I AND WALES ◆

Edward I's conquest of Wales was achieved by the use of force on a scale that the Welsh could not hope to match, and by taking advantage of the divisions within the country. In the early and mid-13th century, the princes of Gwynedd, Llewelyn the Great and his grandson Llewelyn ap Gruffydd, had been remarkably successful in capitalizing on the political difficulties faced in England by King John and then by Henry III. Before he came to the throne, Edward himself had failed to maintain proper control of the lands in Wales granted to him in 1254. Llewelyn ap Gruffydd supported the Crown's opponent Simon de Montfort in the civil war of 1264–65. It was hardly surprising that, when he came to the throne, Edward should wish to take his revenge.

At the same time, Llewelyn's own position in Wales was not secure. His push to achieve dominance over members of his own family, notably his brother Dafydd and the other Welsh princes, had been successful, but left him with dangerous enemies. He overestimated the strength of his position, and his refusal to accept Edward's demands that he acknowledge English overlordship by performing homage left him fatally exposed.

## The campaign of 1277

The conquest was achieved in three major campaigns. The first, in 1277, clearly demonstrated that the Welsh could not resist a substantial English army marching along the north Welsh coast; Llewelyn's support was limited, and he had to sue for peace on humiliating terms. Edward I, however, failed to reward those Welshmen, who even included Llewelyn's own brother Dafydd, who had supported him in 1277. Attempts to introduce English law in Welsh affairs were provocative, and there was widespread rebellion 1282–83. The English campaign to put down the rising was lengthy, and Edward's forces suffered a disaster when knights who had crossed to the mainland from Anglesey were ambushed and slaughtered. However, Llewelyn was slain at the battle of Irfon Bridge in December 1282, and Dafydd's attempts to carry on the fight ended in failure in the next year. He was handed over to Edward by men of his own nation. The Welsh ruling dynasties were ruined and Wales virtually became an English colony.

## The 1294 rebellion

There was a minor rebellion in the south of the country in 1287, followed by a much more serious rising in 1294. The introduction of English methods of taxation, and general oppression by English officials led to the rebellion, which was timed to coincide with the English involvement in war with France. Edward was able to divert the troops intended for France to Wales and an expensive campaign ended in complete success for the English. Edward was capable of putting as many as 30,000 troops in the field against the Welsh. He had heavily armed cavalry in numbers which his opponents could never hope to match, and while he used the traditional feudal obligation as one means of recruitment, the majority of his troops were either paid, or were serving at their own expense. In 1282 he had hoped that the whole army would serve for wages, but this aroused hostility from the baronage, whose independence was threatened by such a move. Infantry were recruited in large numbers, many of them from south Wales, and the majority were armed with the longbow, a devastating weapon. In addition, during the second war he recruited a force of crossbowmen from his overseas dominion of Gascony. Every effort was made to ensure that food supplies for the armies were sufficient, while ships were brought from the south coast of England and Ireland to provide the naval support which was essential if the armies were to be properly provided for. Edward was able to keep his armies in place over the winter months of 1282–83 and 1294–95. The Welsh could not hold out for long against such unremitting pressure.

## The great castles

Edward's campaigns were each marked by a programme of castle-building. New castles on a grand scale were designed to hold down the Welsh. Flint, Rhuddlan, Builth, and Aberystwyth were built after the first Welsh war; after the second Snowdonia was hemmed in much more closely by Conwy, Caernarfon, and Harlech, while after the rebellion of 1294 Beaumaris was founded to establish a secure hold on Anglesey. The castles were largely the work of a single man of genius, Master James of St George, a master mason recruited from Savoy. It was Savoyard, not English, masons who were responsible for much of the design and detail of the castles. Caernarfon was the exception. It was based on the walls of Constantinople, and was built as a grand imperial gesture by a king who wanted to express in stone not only his might, but also legendary connections with the Imperial past of ancient Rome.

by Michael Prestwich

stage of the Hundred Years' War, English victories included the Battle of Crécy in 1346 and the capture of Calais in 1347. In 1360 Edward surrendered his claim to the French throne, but the war resumed in 1369. During his last years his son ◊ John of Gaunt acted as head of government.

## Edward IV (1442–1483)

King of England 1461–70 and from 1471. He was the son of Richard, Duke of York, and succeeded Henry VI in the Wars of the ◊ Roses, temporarily losing the throne to Henry when Edward fell out with his adviser Warwick, but regaining it at the Battle of Barnet 1471. He was succeeded by his son Edward V.

Edward was known as Earl of March until his accession. After his father's death he occupied London in 1461, and was proclaimed king in place of Henry VI by a council of peers. His position was secured by the defeat of the Lancastrians at Towton in 1461 and by the capture of Henry. He quarrelled, however, with Warwick, his strongest supporter, who in 1470–71 temporarily restored Henry, until Edward recovered the throne by his victories at Barnet and Tewkesbury.

## Edward V (1470–1483)

King of England 1483. Son of Edward IV, he was deposed three months after his accession in favour of his uncle (◊ Richard III). He and his brother Richard are the ◊ Princes in the Tower traditionally believed to have been murdered on Richard's orders.

## Edward VI (1537–1553)

King of England from 1547, only son of Henry VIII and his third wife, Jane Seymour. The government was entrusted to his uncle the Duke of Somerset (who fell from power 1549), and then to the Earl of Warwick, later created Duke of Northumberland. He was succeeded by his sister Mary I.

Edward became a staunch Protestant, and during his reign the Reformation progressed. He died of tuberculosis, and his will, probably prepared by Northumberland, set aside that of his father so as to exclude his half-sisters, Mary and Elizabeth, from the succession. He nominated Lady Jane Grey, a granddaughter of Henry VII, who had recently married Northumberland's son. Technically Jane reigned for nine days, and was deposed by Mary I.

## Edward VII (1841–1910)

King of Great Britain and Ireland from 1901. As Prince of Wales he was a prominent social figure,

but his mother Queen Victoria considered him too frivolous to take part in political life. In 1860 he made the first tour of Canada and the USA ever undertaken by a British prince.

Edward was born at Buckingham Palace, the eldest son of Queen Victoria and Prince Albert. After his father's death in 1861 he undertook many public duties, took a close interest in politics, and was on friendly terms with the party leaders. In 1863 he married Princess Alexandra of Denmark, and they had six children. He toured India 1875–76. He succeeded to the throne in 1901 and was crowned in 1902.

Although he overrated his political influence, he contributed to the Entente Cordiale of 1904 with France and the Anglo-Russian agreement of 1907.

## Edward VIII (1894–1972)

King of Great Britain and Northern Ireland from January to December 1936, when he renounced the throne to marry Wallis Warfield Simpson (see ◊ abdication crisis). He was created Duke of Windsor and was governor of the Bahamas 1940–45.

Eldest son of George V, he received the title of Prince of Wales in 1910 and succeeded to the throne 20 January 1936. In November that year a constitutional crisis arose when Edward wished to marry Mrs Simpson; it was felt that, as a divorcee, she would be unacceptable as queen. On 11 December Edward abdicated and left for France, where the couple were married in 1937. He was succeeded by his brother, George VI.

---

*I have found it impossible to discharge my duties as King as I would wish to do without the help and support of the woman I love.*
**Edward VIII**
Abdication speech, broadcast on radio 11 December 1936

---

## Edward the Confessor (c. 1003–1066)

King of the West Saxons from 1042, the son of Ethelred II. He lived in Normandy until shortly before his accession. During his reign power was held by Earl Godwin and his son ◊ Harold, while the king devoted himself to religion, including the rebuilding of Westminster Abbey (consecrated in 1065), where he is buried. His childlessness led ultimately to the Norman Conquest in 1066. He was canonized in 1161.

## Edward the Elder (c. 870–924)

King of the West Saxons. He succeeded his father
◊Alfred the Great in 899. He reconquered southeast England and the Midlands from the Danes,
uniting Wessex and ◊Mercia with the help of his
sister, Athelflad.

By the time Edward died, his kingdom was the
most powerful in the British Isles. He was
succeeded by his son Athelstan (c. 895–939). See
genealogy under House of ◊Wessex.

## Edward the Martyr (c. 963–978)

King of the West Saxons from 975. Son of King
Edgar, he was murdered at Corfe Castle, Dorset,
probably at his stepmother Aelfthryth's instigation (she wished to secure the crown for her son,
Ethelred). He was canonized in 1001.

## eisteddfod, Welsh 'sitting'

Traditional Welsh gathering lasting up to a week
and dedicated to the encouragement of the bardic
arts of music, poetry, and literature. The custom
dates from pre-Christian times.

Towns and rural communities often hold their
own annual eisteddfod. The national eisteddfod
was discontinued from the late 17th century until
the beginning of the 19th century. Since then the
Royal National Eisteddfod has been held annually, at the beginning of August, at a different site
each year. During the meetings bardic degrees are
awarded and the traditional eisteddfod culminates
with the ceremony of 'chairing' the bard (composer of the best verse in strict metre).

## Eleanor of Aquitaine (c. 1122–1204)

Queen of France 1137–51 as wife of Louis VII,
and of England from 1154 as wife of Henry II.
Henry imprisoned her 1174–89 for supporting
their sons, the future Richard I and King John, in
revolt against him.

## Eleanor of Castile (c. 1245–1290)

Queen of Edward I of England, the daughter of
Ferdinand III of Castile. She married Prince
Edward in 1254, and accompanied him on his
crusade in 1270. She died at Harby, Nottinghamshire, and Edward erected stone crosses in towns
where her body rested on the funeral journey to
London. Several **Eleanor Crosses** are still standing, for example, at Northampton.

## Elgar, Edward (1857–1934)

English composer. Although his celebrated oratorio *The Dream of Gerontius* (1900), based on the

**Eisteddfod** Members of the *Gorsedd* gather at the annual
National Eisteddfod, the principal celebration of Welsh traditional
culture. The *Gorsedd* is a society of bards, led by the archdruid
of Wales, that administers and conducts the pageantry of the
festival. Most importantly, it is responsible for crowning and
chairing the winners of the poetry contests, the centrepiece of
the Eisteddfod. Collier's/Collections

written work by theologian John Henry Newman,
was initially unpopular in Britain, its good reception in Düsseldorf (1902) led to a surge of interest
in his earlier works, including the *Pomp and
Circumstance Marches* (1901). His *Enigma Variations* (1899) brought him lasting fame.

Among his later works, which tend to be more
introspective than the earlier ones, are oratorios,
two symphonies, a violin concerto, chamber
music, songs, and the symphonic poem *Falstaff*
(1913), culminating in the poignant cello concerto of 1919. After this piece, Elgar published no
further music of significance. He concentrated on
transcriptions and made some early gramophone
recordings of his own work.

## Elgin marbles

Collection of ancient Greek sculptures, including
the famous frieze and other sculptures from the
Parthenon at Athens, assembled by the 7th Earl of
Elgin. Sent to England 1803–1812, and bought
for the nation in 1816 for £35,000, they are now
in the British Museum. Greece has repeatedly
asked for them to be returned to Athens.

## Eliot, George pen name of Mary Ann (later Marian) Evans (1819–1880)

English novelist. Her works include the pastoral *Adam Bede* (1859); *The Mill on the Floss* (1860), with its autobiographical elements; *Silas Marner* (1861), containing elements of the folk tale; and *Daniel Deronda* (1876). *Middlemarch*, published serially 1871–72, is considered her greatest novel for its confident handling of numerous characters and central social and moral issues. She developed a subtle psychological presentation of character, and her work is pervaded by a penetrating and compassionate intelligence.

George Eliot had a strict evangelical upbringing. In 1841 she was converted to free thought. As assistant editor of the *Westminster Review* under John Chapman 1851–53, she made the acquaintance of Thomas Carlyle, Harriet Martineau, Herbert Spencer, and the philosopher and critic George Henry Lewes (1817–1878). Lewes was married but separated from his wife, and from 1854 he and Eliot lived together in a relationship that she regarded as a true marriage and that continued until his death. Lewes strongly believed in her talent and as a result of his encouragement the story 'Amos Barton' was accepted by *Blackwoods Magazine* in 1857. This was followed by a number of other short stories, and their success persuaded Eliot to embark on writing her full-length novels.

## Eliot, T(homas) S(tearns) (1888–1965)

US-born poet, playwright, and critic, who lived in England from 1915. His first volume of poetry, *Prufrock and Other Observations* (1917), introduced new verse forms and rhythms; subsequent major poems were *The Waste Land* (1922), a long symbolic poem of disillusionment, and 'The Hollow Men' (1925). Eliot's plays include *Murder in the Cathedral* (1935) and *The Cocktail Party* (1950). His critical works include *The Sacred Wood* (1920), setting out his views on poetic tradition. His collection *Old Possum's Book of Practical Cats* (1939) was used for the popular English composer Andrew Lloyd Webber's musical *Cats* (1981).

Eliot was born in St Louis, Missouri, and was educated at Harvard, the Sorbonne, and Oxford University. He married and settled in London in 1917 and became a British subject in 1927. He was for a time a bank clerk, later lecturing and entering publishing at Faber & Faber, where he became a director. As editor of the highly influential literary magazine *Criterion* 1922–39, he was responsible for a critical re-evaluation of metaphysical poetry and Jacobean drama.

Although he makes considerable demands on his readers, he is regarded as the founder of Modernism in poetry: as a critic he profoundly influenced the ways in which literature was appreciated. He won the Nobel Prize for Literature in 1948.

## Elizabeth, the Queen Mother (1900– )

Wife of King George VI of England and mother of Queen Elizabeth II. She was born Lady Elizabeth Angela Marguerite Bowes-Lyon, and on 26 April 1923 she married Albert, Duke of York, who became King George VI in 1936. Their second child is Princess Margaret.

The Queen Mother is the youngest daughter of the 14th Earl of Strathmore and Kinghorne (died 1944), through whom she is descended from Robert Bruce, king of Scotland. When her husband became King George VI she became Queen Consort, and was crowned with him in 1937. She adopted the title Queen Elizabeth, the Queen Mother after his death.

**Elizabeth, the Queen Mother** The widow of the former King George VI, the Queen Mother is held in great public affection. During the wartime Blitz, she and her husband remained in London and visited victims of the intensive bombing of the poor industrial eastern districts of the city. On her birthday, crowds gather outside her London residence of Clarence House to sing 'Happy Birthday'. Corel

## Elizabeth
Two queens of England or the UK:

*I'm glad we've been bombed. It makes me feel I can look the East End in the face.*

**Elizabeth, the Queen Mother** Wife of King
George VI of England.
Remark to a policeman 13 September 1940
following German bombing of Buckingham Palace

## Elizabeth I (1533–1603)
Queen of England 1558–1603, the daughter of Henry VIII and Anne Boleyn. Through her Religious Settlement of 1559 she enforced the Protestant religion by law. She had ◊Mary Queen of Scots executed in 1587. Her conflict with Roman Catholic Spain led to the defeat of the ◊Spanish Armada in 1588. The Elizabethan age was expansionist in commerce and geographical exploration, and arts and literature flourished. The rulers of many European states made unsuccessful bids to marry Elizabeth, and she used these bids to strengthen her power. She was succeeded by James I.

Elizabeth was born at Greenwich, London, 7 September 1533. She was well educated in several languages. During her Roman Catholic half-sister Mary's (◊Mary I) reign, Elizabeth's Protestant sympathies brought her under suspicion, and she lived in seclusion at Hatfield, Hertfordshire, until on Mary's death she became queen.

The arrival in England in 1568 of Mary Queen of Scots and her imprisonment by Elizabeth caused a political crisis, and a rebellion of the feudal nobility of the north followed in 1569. Friction between English and Spanish sailors hastened the breach with Spain. When the Dutch rebelled against Spanish tyranny Elizabeth secretly encouraged them; Philip II retaliated by aiding Catholic conspiracies against her. This undeclared war continued for many years, until the landing of an English army in the Netherlands in 1585 and Mary's execution in 1587, brought it into the open. Philip's Armada (the fleet sent to invade England in 1588) met with total disaster.

The war with Spain continued with varying fortunes to the end of the reign, while events at home foreshadowed the conflicts of the 17th century. Among the Puritans discontent was developing with Elizabeth's religious settlement, and several were imprisoned or executed. Parliament showed a new independence, and in 1601 forced Elizabeth to retreat on the question of the crown granting manufacturing and trading monopolies. Yet her prestige remained unabated, as shown by the failure of Essex's rebellion in 1601.

*Though God hath raised me high, yet this I count the glory of my crown: that I have reigned with your loves.*

**Elizabeth I** Queen of England.
The Golden Speech 1601, quoted in D'Ewes' *Journal*

## Elizabeth II, Elizabeth Alexandra Mary (1926– )
Queen of Great Britain and Northern Ireland from 1952, the head of the British Commonwealth, and queen of Canada, New Zealand, Australia, and several other countries. She is the elder daughter of George VI and married her third cousin, Philip, the Duke of Edinburgh, in 1947. They have four children: Charles, Anne, Andrew, and Edward.

Princess Elizabeth Alexandra Mary was born in

Elizabeth II Queen of Great Britain and Northern Ireland, seen here at the opening of the National Assembly for Wales in 1999. As a constitutional monarch, representing the supreme legal and political authority, the Queen summons and dissolves Parliament, gives her official approval to acts of Parliament, sanctions government judicial appointments, and confers honours and awards. Rex

London on 21 April 1926; she was educated privately, and assumed official duties at 16.

During World War II she served in the Auxiliary Territorial Service, and by an amendment to the Regency Act she became a state counsellor on her 18th birthday. On the death of George VI in 1952 she succeeded to the throne while in Kenya with her husband and was crowned on 2 June 1953.

In her reign the Queen has generally been seen as conscientious and hard-working, taking a serious interest in government. A major change in her time has been the increasing interest of the media and public in the lives of the Royal Family, and in her Christmas TV broadcast of 1992 the Queen admitted it had been an 'annus horribilis', with two of her children experiencing publicly reported marriage difficulties. In 1997 the Royal Family was accused of appearing cold and distant when Diana, Princess of Wales died in a car crash, and since then the Queen has made renewed efforts to appear less aloof.

With an estimated wealth of £5 billion (1994), the Queen is the richest woman in Britain. In April 1993 she voluntarily began paying full rates of income tax and capital gains on her private income, which chiefly consists of the proceeds of a share portfolio and is estimated to be worth around £45 million. See ◊government for the role of the Sovereign, ◊monarchy for the line of succession and House of ◊Windsor for a genealogy.

## Elizabethan playhouse

Open-air theatre in use in England in the late 16th and early 17th centuries. The first playhouse was the Theatre, Shoreditch, London (1576). The ◊Globe Theatre (built in 1599 by the company to which Shakespeare was attached), the Rose (1587), and the Hope (1613) soon followed in Southwark, where the City's strict regulations on entertainment were waived. Elizabethan or Jacobean playhouses could be circular, octagonal, or square in shape, and accommodated a large number of spectators – the Swan Playhouse could reputedly hold 3,000 people. After the discovery of its original site, the Globe Theatre was reconstructed and reopened in 1996.

## Ellesmere Port

Oil port and industrial town in Cheshire, northwest England, on the River Mersey and the Manchester Ship Canal, 11 km/7 mi north of Chester; population (1991) 64,500. It was formerly the biggest transhipment canal port in northwest England. Today, chief industries are engineering and the manufacture of petroleum products and cars.

### History

The Shropshire Union Canal, developed to transport iron ore from the Furness peninsula to the West Midlands, and china clay to the Potteries, reached Ellesmere Port in 1795. A variety of industries were later established, including metal processing, dyestuffs, flour-milling, and paper. From 1894 the opening of the Manchester Ship Canal led to further growth.

The Ellesmere Port Boat Museum (opened 1976) traces the history of canals, with many old narrow boats and a blacksmith's forge.

## Ely

City in the Cambridgeshire ◊Fens, eastern England, on the Great Ouse River, 24km/15 mi northeast of Cambridge; population (1991) 10,300. The cathedral, dating from 1083, is one of the largest in England.

Ely was the chief town of the former administrative district of the **Isle of Ely**, so called because the town originally lay on a low hill, isolated by the surrounding marshland of the Fens before they were drained in the 17th and 18th centuries. The Anglo-Saxon rebel Hereward the Wake had his stronghold against William (I) the Conqueror here, until it was captured in 1071. At the annual feast of St Etheldreda (Audrey), cheap, low-quality souvenirs were sold; the word 'tawdry', a corruption of St Audrey, derives from this practice.

### Ely Cathedral

The cathedral's long nave, high west tower, adjoining transept tower, octagon, and Lady Chapel, make it a completely original composition that stands out from the flat fenland in every direction. The present cathedral was begun by Abbot Simeon, a kinsman of William the Conqueror, in 1083, though it was not the see of a bishop until 1109.

The architecture of the present cathedral is chiefly Norman, of a variety which strikingly foreshadows English Perpendicular, the style of three centuries later. The crossing tower was completely redesigned as an octagon in 1322–28, becoming one of the most celebrated creations of Gothic architecture. Its remarkable lantern, resting apparently on slender wooden rib vaults, was completed in 1342.

## enclosure

Appropriation of common land as private property, or the changing of open-field systems to enclosed fields (often used for sheep). This process began in the 14th century and became widespread in the 15th and 16th centuries. It caused poverty, homelessness, and rural depopulation, and resulted in revolts in 1536, 1569, and 1607. A further wave of enclosures occurred between about 1760 and 1820.

## England

Largest division of the United Kingdom; capital, London; population (1993 est) 48,500,000.

### Religion

Christian, with the Church of England as the established church, 31,500,000; and various Protestant groups, of which the largest is the Methodist 1,400,000; Roman Catholic about 5,000,000; Muslim 900,000; Jewish 410,000; Sikh 175,000; Hindu 140,000

### Government

Returns 529 members to Parliament; a mixture of 2-tier and unitary local authorities, with 34 non-metropolitan counties, 46 unitary authorities, 6 metropolitan counties (with 36 metropolitan boroughs), 32 London boroughs, and the Corporation of London. See map for local government divisions from 1997, and page 159 for the list of **historic counties** that still retain a ceremonial and sporting role.

### History

See chronology of English history, below, and page 160 for a list of sovereigns. For England's union with Wales, Scotland, and Ireland, see Act of ◊Union. See also chronology of British history 1707–1998 at the end of the guide.

## English Channel

Stretch of water between England and France, leading in the west to the Atlantic Ocean, and in the east via the Strait of Dover to the North Sea. The ◊Channel Tunnel, opened in 1994, runs between Folkestone, Kent, and Sangatte, west of Calais.

The English Channel is 560 km/348 mi long west–east; 27 km/17 mi wide at its narrowest (Cap Gris Nez–Dover) and 177 km/110 mi wide at its widest (Ushant–Land's End). The average depth is 40–60 m/131–197 ft, reaching 120 m/394 ft at the entrance to the Strait of Dover and as much as 180 m/590 ft at Hurds Deep, 30 km/19 mi northwest of Guernsey.

## England: Chronology

*For earlier history, see Ancient Britain.*

**AD 43** Roman invasion.

**5th–7th centuries** Anglo-Saxons overran all England except Cornwall and Cumberland, forming independent kingdoms including Northumbria, Mercia, Kent, and Wessex.

*c.* **597** England converted to Christianity by St Augustine.

**829** Egbert of Wessex accepted as overlord of all England.

**878** Alfred ceded northern and eastern England to the Danish invaders but kept them out of Wessex.

**1066** Norman Conquest; England passed into French hands under William the Conqueror.

**1172** Henry II, king of England, also became king of Ireland and established a colony there.

**1215** King John forced to sign Magna Carta.

**1284** Conquest of Wales, begun by the Normans, completed by Edward I.

**1295** Model Parliament set up.

**1338–1453** Hundred Years' War with France enabled Parliament to secure control of taxation and, by impeachment, of the king's choice of ministers.

**1348–49** Black Death killed about 30% of the population.

**1381** Social upheaval led to the Peasants' Revolt, which was brutally repressed.

**1399** Richard II deposed by Parliament for absolutism.

**1414** Lollard revolt repressed.

**1455–85** Wars of the Roses.

**1497** Henry VII ended the power of the feudal nobility with the suppression of the Yorkist revolts.

**1529** Henry VIII became head of the Church of England after breaking with Rome.

**1536–43** Acts of Union united England and Wales after conquest.

**1547** Edward VI adopted Protestant doctrines.

**1553** Reversion to Roman Catholicism under Mary I.

**1558** Elizabeth I adopted a religious compromise.

**1588** Attempted invasion of England by the Spanish Armada.

**1603** James I united the English and Scottish crowns; parliamentary dissidence increased.

**1642–52** Civil War between royalists and parliamentarians, resulting in victory for Parliament.

**1649** Charles I executed and the Commonwealth set up.

**1653** Oliver Cromwell appointed Lord Protector.

**1660** Restoration of Charles II.

**1685** Monmouth's rebellion.

**1688** William of Orange invited to take the throne; flight of James II.

**1707** Act of Union between England and Scotland under Queen Anne, after which the countries became known as Great Britain.

*For history after 1707, see the chronology at the end of the guide.*

England – local government divisions

| | |
|---|---|
| BA | BATH AND NE SOMERSET |
| BE | BEDFORDSHIRE |
| BR | BRACKNELL FOREST |
| BT | BRISTOL |
| BU | BUCKINGHAMSHIRE |
| DA | DARLINGTON |
| DC | DERBY CITY |
| GR | GREATER MANCHESTER |
| HA | HALTON |
| HE | HERTFORDSHIRE |
| LC | LEICESTER CITY |
| LE | LEICESTERSHIRE |
| LU | LUTON |
| MK | MILTON KEYNES |
| NH | NORTHAMPTONSHIRE |
| NL | NORTH LINCOLNSHIRE |
| NS | NORTH SOMERSET |
| NT | NOTTINGHAMSHIRE |
| PB | PETERBOROUGH |
| PT | PORTSMOUTH |
| R | READING |
| RU | RUTLAND |
| SG | SOUTH GLOUCESTERSHIRE |
| SO | SOUTHAMPTON |
| SS | STOCKTON-ON-TEES |
| ST | STOKE-ON-TRENT |
| TW | TELFORD AND WREKIN |
| WA | WARRINGTON |
| WK | WEST BERKSHIRE |
| WM | WEST MIDLANDS |
| WN | WINDSOR AND MAIDENHEAD |
| WO | WOKINGHAM |
| WR | WORCESTERSHIRE |

SCOTLAND

NORTHERN
IRELAND

NORTHUMBERLAND

TYNE AND WEAR

CUMBRIA

DURHAM

HARTLEPOOL
REDCAR AND CLEVELAND
DA   SS
MIDDLESBROUGH

Isle
of Man

NORTH YORKSHIRE

North
Sea

Irish Sea

LANCA-
SHIRE

YORK

THE EAST RIDING
OF YORKSHIRE

BLACKPOOL

WEST
YORKSHIRE

NL

KINGSTON UPON HULL

BLACKBURN
AND DARWEN

MERSEYSIDE

GR

SOUTH
YORK-
SHIRE

NORTH EAST
LINCOLNSHIRE

REPUBLIC
OF
IRELAND

WA
HA
CHESHIRE

ST

DERBY-
SHIRE

DC

NT

LINCOLN-
SHIRE

NOTTINGHAM CITY

STAFFORD-
SHIRE

TW

LE   RU

PB

NORFOLK

SHROP-
SHIRE

WM

LC

ENGLAND

WALES

WR

WARWICK-
SHIRE

NH

CAMBRIDGE-
SHIRE

SUFFOLK

HEREFORD-
SHIRE

MK
BE
LU

GLOUCESTER-
SHIRE

BU

HE

ESSEX

OXFORD-
SHIRE

SOUTHEND

SG
BT
NS   BA

SWINDON

WK

SLOUGH
R   WN
WO   BR

GREATER
LONDON

THURROCK

WILTSHIRE

SURREY

MEDWAY TOWNS

KENT

unitary authority within
another local government area

HAMPSHIRE

WEST
SUSSEX

EAST
SUSSEX

0        50 mi
0        100 km

SOMERSET

SO   PT

POOLE

DEVON

DORSET

ISLE OF
WIGHT

BRIGHTON
AND HOVE

PLYMOUTH

BOURNEMOUTH

CORNWALL

TORBAY

Isles of
Scilly

English Channel

FRANCE

## England: Historic Counties

| | | |
|---|---|---|
| Bedfordshire | Kent | Suffolk |
| Berkshire | Lancashire | East Suffolk |
| Buckinghamshire | Leicestershire | West Suffolk |
| Cambridgeshire and Isle of Ely | Lincolnshire | Surrey |
| Cheshire | Holland | Sussex |
| Cornwall | Kesteven | East Sussex |
| Cumberland | Lindsey | West Sussex |
| Derbyshire | Greater London | Warwickshire |
| Devonshire | Norfolk | Westmorland |
| Dorset | Northamptonshire | Wight, Isle of |
| Durham | Northumberland | Wiltshire |
| Essex | Nottinghamshire | Worcestershire |
| Gloucestershire | Oxfordshire | Yorkshire |
| Hampshire | Rutland | East Riding |
| Herefordshire | Shropshire | North Riding |
| Hertfordshire | Somerset | West Riding |
| Huntingdonshire and Peterborough | Staffordshire | |

## English Heritage

The UK's leading conservation organization, responsible for the conservation of historic remains in England. Under the National Heritage Act 1983, its duties are to secure the preservation of ancient monuments and historic buildings; to promote the preservation and enhancement of conservation areas; and to promote the public's enjoyment and understanding of ancient monuments and historic buildings. All the properties in the care of English Heritage either belong to the nation or are in its guardianship. Most are open to the public.

## English language

Language spoken by more than 300 million native speakers, and between 400 and 800 million foreign users. See feature on page 162 on the development of the English language.

English is the official language of air transport and shipping; the leading language of science, technology, computers, and commerce; and a major medium of education, publishing, and international negotiation. For this reason scholars frequently refer to its latest phase as World English.

## English law

One of the major European legal systems, Roman law being the other. English law has spread to many other countries, including former English colonies such as the USA, Canada, Australia, and New Zealand.

English law has a continuous history dating from the local customs of the Anglo-Saxons, traces of which survived until 1925. After the Norman Conquest there grew up, side by side with the Saxon shire courts, the feudal courts of the barons and the ecclesiastical courts. From the king's council developed the royal courts, presided over by professional judges, which gradually absorbed the jurisdictions of the baronial and ecclesiastical courts. By 1250 the royal judges had amalgamated the various local customs into the system of common law – that is, law common to the whole country. A second system known as equity developed in the Court of Chancery, in which the Lord Chancellor considered petitions.

A unique feature of English law is the doctrine of judicial precedents, whereby the reported decisions of the courts form a binding source of law for future decisions. A judge is bound by decisions of courts of superior jurisdiction but not necessarily by those of inferior courts.

The Judicature Acts 1873–75 abolished a multiplicity of courts, and in their place established the Supreme Court of Judicature, organized in the Court of Appeal and the High Court of Justice; the latter has three divisions – the

## English Sovereigns

Henry II became additionally King of Ireland in 1172; Wales united with England in 1536–43; Scotland and England united in 1603. For genealogies of some houses, see main entries.

| Reign | Name | Relationship |
|---|---|---|
| **West Saxon Kings** | | |
| 899–924 | Edward the Elder | son of Alfred the Great |
| 924–39 | Athelstan | son of Edward the Elder |
| 939–46 | Edmund | half-brother of Athelstan |
| 946–55 | Edred | brother of Edmund |
| 955–59 | Edwy | son of Edmund |
| 959–75 | Edgar | brother of Edwy |
| 975–78 | Edward the Martyr | son of Edgar |
| 978–1016 | Ethelred (II) the Unready | son of Edgar |
| 1016 | Edmund Ironside | son of Ethelred (II) the Unready |
| **Danish Kings** | | |
| 1016–35 | Canute | son of Sweyn I of Denmark who conquered England in 1013 |
| 1035–40 | Harold I | son of Canute |
| 1040–42 | Hardicanute | son of Canute |
| **West Saxon Kings (restored)** | | |
| 1042–66 | Edward the Confessor | son of Ethelred II |
| 1066 | Harold II | son of Godwin |
| **Norman Kings** | | |
| 1066–87 | William I | illegitimate son of Duke Robert the Devil |
| 1087–1100 | William II | son of William I |
| 1100–35 | Henry I | son of William I |
| 1135–54 | Stephen | grandson of William II |
| **House of Plantagenet** | | |
| 1154–89 | Henry II | son of Matilda (daughter of Henry I) |
| 1189–99 | Richard I | son of Henry II |
| 1199–1216 | John | son of Henry II |
| 1216–72 | Henry III | son of John |
| 1272–1307 | Edward I | son of Henry III |
| 1307–27 | Edward II | son of Edward I |
| 1327–77 | Edward III | son of Edward II |
| 1377–99 | Richard II | son of the Black Prince |
| **House of Lancaster** | | |
| 1399–1413 | Henry IV | son of John of Gaunt |
| 1413–22 | Henry V | son of Henry IV |
| 1422–61, 1470–71 | Henry VI | son of Henry V |

| Reign | Name | Relationship |
|---|---|---|
| **House of York** | | |
| 1461–70, 1471–83 | Edward IV | son of Richard, Duke of York |
| 1483 | Edward V | son of Edward IV |
| 1483–85 | Richard III | brother of Edward IV |
| **House of Tudor** | | |
| 1485–1509 | Henry VII | son of Edmund Tudor, Earl of Richmond |
| 1509–47 | Henry VIII | son of Henry VII |
| 1547–53 | Edward VI | son of Henry VIII |
| 1553–58 | Mary I | daughter of Henry VIII |
| 1558–1603 | Elizabeth I | daughter of Henry VIII |
| **House of Stuart** | | |
| 1603–25 | James I | great-grandson of Margaret (daughter of Henry VII) |
| 1625–49 | Charles I | son of James I |
| 1649–60 | the Commonwealth | |
| **House of Stuart (restored)** | | |
| 1660–85 | Charles II | son of Charles I |
| 1685–88 | James II | son of Charles I |
| 1689–1702 | William III and Mary | son of Mary (daughter of Charles I); daughter of James II |
| 1702–14 | Anne | daughter of James II |
| **House of Hanover** | | |
| 1714–27 | George I | son of Sophia (granddaughter of James I) |
| 1727–60 | George II | son of George I |
| 1760–1820 | George III | son of Frederick (son of George II) |
| 1820–30 | George IV (regent 1811–20) | son of George III |
| 1830–37 | William IV | son of George III |
| 1837–1901 | Victoria | daughter of Edward (son of George III) |
| **House of Saxe-Coburg** | | |
| 1901–10 | Edward VII | son of Victoria |
| **House of Windsor** | | |
| 1910–36 | George V | son of Edward VII |
| 1936 | Edward VIII | son of George V |
| 1936–52 | George VI | son of George V |
| 1952– | Elizabeth II | daughter of George VI |

Queen's Bench, Chancery, and Family Divisions. All High Court judges may apply both common law and equity in deciding cases.

From the Court of Appeal there may be a further appeal to the House of Lords.

## English literature

Term commonly applied to all literature in the English language; however what follows is an account of literature in Britain (see also ◊Scottish Gaelic literature, ◊Welsh literature, and ◊Old English literature).

### 12th–15th century: Middle English period

With the arrival of a Norman ruling class at the end of the 11th century, the ascendancy of Norman-French in cultural life began, and it was not until the 13th century that the native literature regained its strength. Prose was concerned chiefly with popular devotional use, but verse emerged typically in the metrical chronicles, such as Layamon's *Brut*, and the numerous romances based on the stories of Charlemagne, the Arthurian legends, and the classical episodes of Troy. First of the great English poets was Geoffrey ◊Chaucer, whose early work reflected the predominant French influence, but later that of Renaissance Italy. Of purely native inspiration in the 14th century was *The Vision of William Concerning Piers the Plowman* (1367–1386) of William Langland in the old alliterative verse, and the anonymous *Pearl, Patience*, and *Gawayne and the Grene Knight*. Chaucer's mastery of versification was not shared by his successors, the most original of whom was John Skelton (c. 1460–1529), tutor to the future Henry VIII. More successful were the anonymous authors of songs and carols, and of the ballads, which (for example, those concerned with the legendary outlaw ◊Robin Hood) often formed a complete cycle. Drama flowered in the form of miracle and morality plays; and prose, although still awkwardly handled by John ◊Wycliffe in his translation of the Bible, rose to a great height with Thomas ◊Malory in the 15th century.

### 16th century: Elizabethan

The Renaissance, which had first touched the English language through Chaucer, came to delayed fruition in the 16th century. Thomas Wyatt and Henry Surrey used the sonnet and blank verse in typically Elizabethan forms and prepared the way for Edmund ◊Spenser, Philip Sidney, Samuel Daniel, Thomas ◊Campion, and others. With Thomas Kyd and Christopher ◊Marlowe, drama emerged into theatrical form; it reached the highest level in the works of

**Charles Dickens** English novelist Charles Dickens, whose immense creative energy made him the most popular novelist of his age. Born into a family on the fringes of gentility, he was always acutely conscious of the social and economic abysses of Victorian society. Corbis

◊Shakespeare and Ben ◊Jonson. Elizabethan prose is represented by Richard Hooker, Thomas North, Roger Ascham, Raphael Holinshed, John Lyly, and others.

### 17th century

English prose achieved full richness in the 17th century, with the Authorized Version of the Bible (1611), Francis ◊Bacon, John ◊Milton, John ◊Bunyan, Jeremy Taylor, Thomas Browne, Izaak ◊Walton, and Samuel ◊Pepys. Most renowned of the 17th-century poets were Milton and John ◊Donne; others include the religious writers George Herbert, Richard Crashaw, Henry Vaughan, and Thomas Traherne, and the Cavalier poets Robert Herrick, Thomas Carew, John Suckling, and Richard Lovelace. In the Restoration period (from 1660) Samuel Butler and John ◊Dryden stand out as poets. Dramatists include Thomas Otway and Nathaniel Lee in tragedy. Comedy flourished with William ◊Congreve, John ◊Vanbrugh, and George Farquhar.

### 18th century: the Augustan Age

Alexander ◊Pope developed the poetic technique of Dryden; in prose Richard Steele and Joseph Addison evolved the polite essay, Jonathan ◊Swift used satire, and Daniel ◊Defoe exploited his journalistic ability. This century saw the development of the novel, through the epistolary style of

# ◆ THE DEVELOPMENT OF THE ENGLISH LANGUAGE ◆

## Origins of English

English is a member of the West Germanic branch of the Indo-European family of languages. As Old English, it was first spoken by the Angles, Saxons and Jutes from Jutland, Schleswig and Holstein respectively who settled in Britain in the 5th and 6th centuries AD. The Jutes went to what is now Kent, southern Hampshire and the Isle of Wight; the Saxons spread out in the rest of England south of the Thames, as well as modern Middlesex and Essex; and the Angles penetrated the remainder of England as far north as the Firth of Forth. The Anglian-speaking region developed two speech groups, Northumbrian, to the north of the River Humber, and Southumbrian, or Mercian, to the south of it. The dialect of the Jutes became known as Kentish, and that of the Saxons as West Saxon in what emerged as the kingdom of Wessex.

In the 8th century Northumbrian led in literature and culture, but its predominance was broken by the Vikings, who sacked Lindisfarne, off the Northumbrian coast, in 793. They landed in strength in 865. The first raiders were Danes, but they were later joined by Norwegians from Ireland and the Western Isles who settled in northwestern England. In the 9th century, thanks to the economic and political influence of the kingdom of Wessex in the reign of Alfred the Great (871–899), the cultural leadership passed from Northumbria to Wessex. Following the arrival of St Augustine in 597 and the subsequent conversion of England to Latin Christianity, the Roman alphabet superseded the original Germanic runes.

The language of the Celts who inhabited Britain at the time of the arrival of the Angles, Saxons and Jutes is chiefly evident today in river names such as Avon, Exe, Esk, Ouse and Wye, which all mean 'river' or 'water'. The first parts of many city names such as Winchester, Salisbury and Lichfield are also of Celtic origin. The Scandinavians gave such common nouns as band, birth, dirt, egg, knife, race, root, seat, skill, sky, and window.

## The effect of the Norman conquest on the English language

The Norman Conquest of 1066 had two chief linguistic consequences. First, it placed all four Old English dialects more or less on a level. Second, it introduced a number of French words to the language. West Saxon lost its supremacy and the centre of culture and learning shifted from Winchester to London. The Northumbrian dialect divided into Lowland Scottish and Northern, and the Mercian dialect was split into East and West Midland. West Saxon slightly decreased in area and became known as South Western, while the Kentish dialect extended and became South Eastern.

England was now essentially bilingual. The ordinary people spoke and wrote the Germanic language that was now known as Middle English. The followers of William the Conqueror, who took over most of the important offices of church and state, spoke Norman French, which thus became the language of the court, parliament, law and education. The result was that the language contained many doublets. The cows, sheep and pigs that the English peasant tended became beef, mutton and pork on his Norman master's table. Doublets also evolved in English from Norman French and Central French, such as the pairs canal and channel, catch and chase, real and royal, wage and gage, warden and guardian. Words for basic concepts and things that have remained from their Old English originals include pairs of opposites such as heaven and earth, love and hate, life and death, beginning and end, day and night, month and year, heat and cold.

## The transition from middle English to modern English

The death of Chaucer at the close of the 14th century marked the beginning of the transition from Middle English to early Modern English. This period saw three major developments: the rise of London English as the dominant form, Caxton's invention of printing in 1476, which reinforced this dominance, and the spread of the new learning, which introduced Latin and Greek words through French or direct from Latin and Greek respectively. Words that had already entered through French were now borrowed again, giving doublets such as benison and benediction, blame and blaspheme, count and compute, dainty and dignity. There were even triplets, such as Anglo-Norman real, Norman French royal, and Latin regal. Borrowings from Latin and Greek produced further doublets, such as the pairs malnutrition and dystrophy, and transfer and metaphor. Printed English, for its part, retained features of written English that no longer reflected the actual pronunciation, and was thus largely responsible for crystallizing the disparity between spelling and pronunciation that is characteristic of English today.

## The development of modern English

Modern English proper is usually dated from the restoration of the monarchy in 1660. Words from languages other than Latin and Greek were now becoming established, including nautical words from Dutch such as buoy, deck, dock, skipper and yacht, and musical terms from Italian such as allegro, cantabile, legato and staccato. Global borrowings have since completed the jigsaw of English.

by Adrian Room

Samuel ◊Richardson to the robust narrative of Henry ◊Fielding and Tobias Smollett, the comic genius of Laurence ◊Sterne, and the Gothic 'horror' of Horace ◊Walpole. The Neo-Classical standards established by the Augustans were maintained by Samuel ◊Johnson and his circle – Oliver ◊Goldsmith, Edmund ◊Burke, Joshua Reynolds, Richard ◊Sheridan, and others – but the romantic element present in the poetry of James Thomson, Thomas ◊Gray, Edward Young, and William Collins was soon to overturn them.

### 19th century

The *Lyrical Ballads* 1798 of William ◊Wordsworth and Samuel Taylor ◊Coleridge were the manifesto of the new Romantic age. Lord ◊Byron, Percy Bysshe ◊Shelley, and John ◊Keats form a second generation of Romantic poets. In fiction Walter ◊Scott took over the Gothic tradition from Mrs ◊Radcliffe, to create the historical novel, and Jane ◊Austen established the novel of the comedy of manners. Criticism gained new prominence with Coleridge, Charles ◊Lamb, William ◊Hazlitt, and Thomas De Quincey. During the 19th century the novel was further developed by Charles ◊Dickens, William Makepeace ◊Thackeray, the ◊Brontës, George ◊Eliot, Anthony ◊Trollope, and others. The principal poets of the reign of Victoria were Alfred ◊Tennyson, Robert and Elizabeth ◊Browning, Matthew ◊Arnold, the ◊Rossettis, William ◊Morris, and Algernon Swinburne. Among the prose writers of the era were Thomas Macaulay, John Newman, John Stuart ◊Mill, Thomas ◊Carlyle, John ◊Ruskin, and Walter Pater. The transition period at the end of the century saw the poetry and novels of George ◊Meredith and Thomas ◊Hardy; the work of Samuel ◊Butler and George Gissing; and the plays of Arthur ◊Pinero and Oscar ◊Wilde. Although a Victorian, Gerald Manley ◊Hopkins anticipated the 20th century with the experimentation of his verse forms.

### 20th century

Poets of World War I include Siegfried ◊Sassoon, Rupert ◊Brooke, Wilfred ◊Owen, and Robert ◊Graves. A middle-class realism developed in the novels of H G ◊Wells, Arnold ◊Bennett, E M ◊Forster, and John ◊Galsworthy while the novel's break with traditional narrative and exposition came through the Modernists D H Lawrence, Virginia ◊Woolf, Somerset ◊Maugham, Aldous ◊Huxley, Christopher ◊Isherwood, Evelyn ◊Waugh, and Graham ◊Greene. Writers for the stage include George Bernard ◊Shaw, John ◊Galsworthy, J B ◊Priestley, Noël ◊Coward, and Terence ◊Rattigan, and the writers of poetic drama, such as T S ◊Eliot, Christopher Fry, W H ◊Auden, Christopher Isherwood, and Dylan ◊Thomas. The 1950s and 1960s produced the 'kitchen sink' dramatists, some also described as 'angry young men', including John ◊Osborne.

Other notable playwrights who emerged in the 1960s and 1970s included John Arden and Robert Bolt, both much concerned with interpreting the present in terms of the past, Alan Ayckbourn, ingeniously exploring situations often from several viewpoints, enfant terrible Joe ◊Orton, Peter Shaffer, extracting drama from concerns of modern psychology and vengeance, and Harold Pinter and Tom Stoppard, both expert manipulators of language and characterization.

### Post-war novelists

Post-war novelists of middle class manners include Kingsley ◊Amis, A S Byatt, Margaret Drabble, Elizabeth Jane Howard, Iris ◊Murdoch, Anthony Powell, and Angus ◊Wilson. Malcolm Bradbury and David Lodge have depicted, with considerable wit, academic life in universities. A new generation of anti-heroes features in the regional novels of Stan Barstow, John Braine, Alan Sillitoe, and David Storey. Chaim Bermant, Dan Jacobson, and Bernice Rubens have extended the scope of the Jewish novel.

Bizarre or futuristic imagination informs much of the fiction of Martin Amis, J G Ballard, Julian Barnes, Anthony ◊Burgess, Angela ◊Carter, Doris Lessing, Ian McEwan, Muriel Spark, Fay Weldon, and Angus ◊Wilson. Lawrence ◊Durrell, John Fowles, and William ◊Golding have written distinguished philosophical novels of action. The detective novel has been enriched by Colin Dexter, Nicolas Freeling, Reginald Hill, P D James, Ian Rankin, and Ruth Rendell.

John ◊Betjeman, T S Eliot, C ◊Day-Lewis, and Stephen ◊Spender were among the notable poets of the 1930s who continued to write after the war, if not so intensively. That poetry can still sell has been demonstrated by Douglas Dunn and Ted ◊Hughes, who have laid bare personal tragedies, and Seamus Heaney, who has written of the political tragedy in Northern Ireland. Other poets of the postwar period who have, each in his or her own way, spoken plainly enough to be appreciated by the general public as well as by critics include George Mackay Brown, Charles Causley, Gavin Ewart, W S Graham, Philip ◊Larkin, Elizabeth Jennings, Norman MacCaig, Roger McGough, Ruth Pitter, Kathleen Raine, John Silkin, and Iain Crichton Smith.

## English National Ballet

Ballet company based in London. Formerly the London Festival Ballet (founded in 1950), it was renamed in 1989. Derek Deane was appointed artistic director in 1993.

## English National Opera

Opera company based at the London Coliseum. The company was founded in 1931 as the Vic-Wells Opera, becoming the English National Opera in 1974. It always performs in English.

## English Nature

Agency created in 1991 from the division of the Nature Conservancy Council into English, Scottish, and Welsh sections.

It is one of the five bodies responsible for countryside policy and nature conservancy. It is also involved through the Joint Nature Conservation Committee (JNCC) with international nature conservation matters and those that affect Great Britain.

## English Stage Company

British theatre company formed in 1956 for the presentation of contemporary drama. It opened at the ◊ Royal Court Theatre in London, its permanent home, under the direction of George Devine. Among dramatists whose plays have been performed are John Arden, Samuel Beckett, Bertolt Brecht, Jean Genet, Eugène Ionesco, John Osborne, and Arnold Wesker. Ian Rickson became the company's artistic director in 1998.

## Enlightenment

European intellectual movement that reached its high point in the 18th century. Enlightenment thinkers were believers in social progress and in the liberating possibilities of rational and scientific knowledge. They were often critical of existing society and were hostile to religion, which they saw as keeping the human mind chained down by superstitition. British intellectuals who played a major role included the philosophers John ◊ Locke and David Hume (1711–1776), Isaac ◊ Newton, the poet and naturalist Erasmus Darwin (1731–1802), politicians Edmund ◊ Burke and Thomas ◊ Paine, and the educationalist Jeremy ◊ Bentham.

## Environment Agency

Government agency that from April 1996 took over the responsibilities of the National Rivers Authority, Her Majesty's Inspectorate of Pollution, and local waste regulation authorities for England and Wales. Scotland has its own Scottish Environmental Protection Agency.

## Environmentally Sensitive Area, ESA

Scheme introduced by the UK Ministry of Agriculture in 1984, as a result of EC legislation, to protect some of the most beautiful areas of the British countryside from the loss and damage caused by agricultural change. The first areas to be designated ESAs were in the Pennine Dales, the North Peak District, the Norfolk Broads, the Breckland, the Suffolk River Valleys, the Test Valley, the South Downs, the Somerset Levels and Moors, West Penwith, Cornwall, the Shropshire Borders, the Cambrian Mountains, and the Lleyn Peninsula.

The total area designated as ESAs was estimated in 1997 at 3,239,000 ha/8,000,000 acres. The scheme is voluntary, with farmers being encouraged to adapt their practices so as to enhance or maintain the natural features of the landscape and conserve wildlife habitat.

## Epping Forest

One of Europe's oldest forests, situated in Essex, southeast England, to the south of the town of Epping. It covers an area of approximately 2,000 ha/5,000 acres. Once part of the ancient forest of Waltham, it originally covered the whole of Essex.

## Epsom

Residential town in Surrey, southeast England, 30 km/19 mi southwest of London; population (1991) 64,400 (with Ewell). In the 17th century it was a spa town producing **Epsom salts**, used as a relaxant and laxative and added to baths to soothe the skin. The ◊ Derby and the Oaks horse races are held annually at **Epsom Downs** racecourse.

## Epstein, Jacob (1880–1959)

US-born British sculptor. Initially influenced by Rodin, he turned to primitive forms after Brancusi and is chiefly known for his controversial muscular nude figures, such as *Genesis* (1931; Whitworth Art Gallery, Manchester).

## Equal Opportunities Commission

Commission established by the UK government in 1975 (1976 in Northern Ireland) to implement the Sex Discrimination Act 1975. Its aim is to prevent discrimination, particularly on sexual or marital grounds.

## Ermine Street

Ancient road of Roman origin, or possibly earlier, running from London to York, and by extension to southern Scotland. The name is also applied to the Silchester to Gloucester route. Ermine Street, along with ◊Watling Street, and the ◊Icknield and ◊Fosse ways, were specially protected by the King's Peace at least from Norman times and probably earlier.

## Eskdale

The valley of the River **Esk**, which rises between Scafell Pike and Bowfell in the ◊Lake District, Cumbria, England, turns west near Hardknott Castle (a Roman fort), and ultimately flows into the Irish Sea at Ravenglass. A narrow-gauge railway from Ravenglass to Dalegarth has become a tourist attraction of the area.

## Essex (Old English **East-Seaxe**)

County of southeast England, which has contained the unitary authorities ◊Southend and ◊Thurrock since April 1998; population (1996) 1,586,100; area 3,670 sq km/1,417 sq mi. The county is situated in the south of rural East Anglia and just to the north of London. It is characterized by extensive farmland, coastal resorts, and river mouths and creeks which attract yachting, and industrial centres. Much of the southern half of the county is now a dormitory area for London commuters. The chief towns and cities are ◊Chelmsford (administrative headquarters), ◊Basildon, ◊Colchester, Harlow, Harwich (port), and Clacton-on-Sea (resort).

### History

The Romans established their first British colony at Colchester. In 991 the Saxons were defeated by the Vikings at the Battle of the Maldon, described in the Anglo-Saxon poem *The Battle of Maldon*.

### Physical

Essex is flat and marshy with numerous river estuaries near the North Sea coastline in the east, and richly wooded in the southwest. Its main rivers are the Blackwater, Crouch, Colne, Lee, Stour, and the Thames, which forms part of its southern boundary.

### Features

The abbey at Waltham is reputedly the oldest Norman building in England. Founded in 1030, it was enlarged by King Harold in 1060, and is traditionally his burial place (1066). Significant buildings include the 11th-century Colchester Castle, 17th-century Tilbury fort, and the fine Jacobean house Audley End. The former royal hunting ground of ◊Epping Forest (2300 ha/

**Essex** The Flemish Cottages, Southfields, Dedham, Essex, southeast England. Throughout the Middle Ages wool was the most important English export. East Anglia was one of the centres of the woollen industry and Dedham was a thriving weaving community. Robert Hallmann/Collections

5680 acres) has been controlled from 1882 by the City of London. Since 1111 at Little ◊Dunmow (and later at Great Dunmow) the Dunmow flitch (a side of cured pork) can be claimed every four years by any couple proving to a jury they have not regretted their marriage within the year (winners are few). Stansted, London's third airport from 1985, has a passenger terminal by Norman Foster, opened in 1991. A new Roman Catholic cathedral at Brentwood, designed by Quinlan Terry, was dedicated in 1991. Colchester hosts an Oyster Feast in October.

*Economy*

Agriculture includes wheat, fruit, sugar beet, livestock rearing, and dairy products. The main industries include engineering (at Dagenham, Chelmsford, and Colchester) and oil products (there are large oil refineries at Shellhaven and Canvey). The Tilbury and Victoria and Albert Docks of the Port of London are on the Thames in the south of the county. Harwich is the port for continental traffic; Essex has forged strong European business links.

## Eton

Town in Windsor and Maidenhead unitary authority, southern England, on the north bank of the River Thames, opposite Windsor; population (1991) 2,000.

*Eton College*

One of the UK's oldest, largest, and most prestigious public (private and fee-paying) schools. It was founded in 1440 by Henry VI as a grammar school and, after a stormy history which included a rebellion by pupils in 1783, became dominated by the sons of the aristocracy and the wealthy middle classes. Of the pupils in 1991, 40% were the sons of Old Etonians (former pupils). It has provided the UK with 19 prime ministers and more than 20% of all government ministers between 1900 and 1998. Prince William became a student at Eton in 1995; Prince Harry followed in 1998.

## European Union, EU; formerly (to 1993) European Community

European political and economic alliance that the UK joined in 1973, following a referendum. The other members are: Belgium, France, Germany, Italy, Luxembourg, the Netherlands, Denmark, the Republic of Ireland, Greece, Spain, Portugal, Austria, Finland, and Sweden.

The aims of the EU include the expansion of trade, reduction of competition, the abolition of restrictive trading practices, the encouragement of free movement of capital and labour within the alliance, and the establishment of a closer union among European people. A single market with free movement of goods and capital was established in January 1993.

On 1 January 1999 the Single European Currency, the euro, came into being. Britain, along with Denmark, Sweden, and Greece opted not to join the European monetary zone at this stage.

## Evans, Arthur (1851–1941)

English archaeologist. His excavations at Knossos on Crete uncovered a vast palace complex, and resulted in the discovery of various Minoan scripts. He proved the existence of a Bronze Age civilization that predated the Mycenean, and named it Minoan after Minos, the legendary king of Knossos.

## Excalibur

The mystic sword of King ◊Arthur, which, according to the promise of Merlin, he received from the Lady of the Lake. At his death it was thrown back into the lake by the knight Bedivere, and was received by a hand which rose from the waters.

## Exeter

City and administrative headquarters of Devon, England, on the River Exe; population (1994 est) 107,000. Founded by the Romans, Exeter later developed into a medieval cathedral town, and today preserves fine examples of medieval, Georgian, and Regency architecture. Its chief industries are brewing, iron and brass founding, light engineering, printing, financial services, and tourism.

*History*

Evidence suggests that a town may have existed here in the 3rd century BC. The Roman settlement of Isca Dumnoniorum was well established by AD 55; it later became the Anglo-Saxon settlement **Escancestre**. During the Middle Ages it twice resisted sieges by the Danes (in 876 and around 894) before being sacked and taken by them in 1003. In 1067 the town initially resisted William (I) the Conqueror, but submitted after an 18-day siege. William built the motte-and-bailey castle of Rougemont – so named from its red masonry and earth – in 1068. In the Tudor period the town became a centre for the wool trade. During the English Civil War Royalist forces had their western headquarters here, until in 1646 the town surrendered to Thomas Fairfax, commander in chief of the Parliamentary forces. The city suffered severe damage during World War II air raids.

### Features

A cathedral was first established at Exeter in 1050, and the Normans rebuilt it between 1107 and 1137. The present building, begun around 1275, is mainly in the ◊Decorated style, but includes two Norman towers; it has a 14th-century west front with many sculptured figures, and its fine ceiling is the longest stretch of Gothic vaulting in the world. The cathedral library contains the Exeter Book, a collection of Anglo-Saxon poetry, as well as the Exeter Domesday Book, the episcopal and chapter archives, and many city archives.

Cathedral Close has buildings dating from medieval to Georgian times, including the Elizabethan Mol's Coffee House. The Guildhall (1330) is one of the oldest surviving civic buildings in England; it has a portico dating from about 1595, and its hall has a fine 15th-century roof. Sections of the Roman and medieval walls survive, and there are some remains of Rougemont Castle. Other features include part of the Benedictine Priory of St Nicholas, the Custom House (1681), and the Maritime Museum at the Quay. The Royal Albert Memorial Museum includes collections illustrating zoology and local archaeology. Exeter University (formerly University College, founded in 1922) was established in 1955.

## Exmoor

Moorland district in north Devon and west Somerset, southwest England, forming (with the coast from Minehead to Combe Martin) a national park since 1954. The park covers an area of around 7,700 ha/19,000 acres, and includes Dunkery Beacon, its highest point at 519 m/1,705 ft; and the Doone Valley.

Exmoor is thinly populated and remains isolated by relatively poor road connections. The principal settlements are the twin coastal resort towns of ◊Lynton and Lynmouth in the north and Dulverton in the southeast; the resort town of ◊Minehead lies just outside the national park to the northeast. Tourism and craft industries are important to the local economy. The moor provides grazing for Exmoor ponies, horned Exmoor sheep, and about 1,000 wild red deer. It is also the habitat of grouse, hawks, and falcons. Stag-hunting in the region attracts widespread controversy. Prehistoric remains, including early stone circles and barrows (burial mounds), are mainly located around the edge of the moor, settlement of the moor occurring around 1800 to 1500 BC. Iron Age hillforts include Shoulsbarrow Castle. Tarr Steps, an ancient packhorse bridge over the River Barle, is a simple, stone-slab clapper construction with 17 spans; it may date from the Bronze Age, although other estimates set it in the medieval period around 1400. Exmoor is the setting for R D Blackmore's romance *Lorna Doone* (1869).

### Physical features

A plateau of red sandstone and slate, Exmoor has a varied landscape, with grassy and marshy moorland as well as heathland, and substantial woodland covering about 10% of the area. The coastal region is characterized by a series of headlands with cliffs and wooded valleys. There are gentle contours in the Brendon Hills to the east, and inland is **Exmoor Forest**, at the heart of the moor, an area reserved for royal hunting until 1819. The River Exe rises in the uplands of the moor.

The area is subject to heavy rainfall. In August 1952 exceptionally intense rains caused the East and West Lyn rivers to flood Lynmouth, resulting in great destruction and several deaths. Its twin town Lynton, located 180 m/600 ft higher on the clifftop, escaped the torrent.

## Exmouth

Resort town and former port in Devon, southwest England, at the mouth of the River Exe, 14 km/9 mi southeast of Exeter; population (1996 est) 31,920. The port was permanently closed to commercial vessels in 1989, but the town remains a yachting and boating centre.

Other tourist facilities include pleasure boat cruises up the Exe to Topsham, just below Exeter, and local angling for salmon and trout. The Exe estuary nature reserve is notable for its bird life.

## Eyam

Village in western Derbyshire, England, 16 km/10 mi northeast of Buxton; population (1991) 1,600. Industries include the manufacture of shoes and the mining of fluorspar and lead.

Eyam lies in a district where many British and Saxon antiquities are found; its churchyard contains a 9th- or 10th-century runic cross, restored in 1788.

In 1665–66, most of the population of Eyam died of plague; this tragedy is commemorated in the annual local ceremony of 'well-dressing': decorating the well with a picture made of moss and flowers in supplication for a clean water supply (also practised in Tissington and Wirksworth).

## Fabian Society

Socialist organization for research, discussion, and publication, founded in London in 1884. Its name is derived from the Roman commander Fabius Maximus, and refers to the evolutionary methods by which it hopes to attain socialism by a succession of gradual reforms. Early members included the playwright George Bernard Shaw and Beatrice and Sidney Webb. The society helped to found the Labour Representation Committee in 1900, which became the Labour Party in 1906.

## FA Cup

Abbreviation for **Football Association Challenge Cup**, the major annual soccer knockout competition in England and Wales, open to all member clubs of the English Football Association. First held in 1871–72, it is the oldest football knockout competition.

## Fair Isle (Old Norse faar, 'sheep')

Small island, one of the ◊Shetland Islands group, isolated midway between the Shetlands and the Orkney Islands, Scotland, 38 km/24 mi southwest of Sumburgh Head; population (1991) 87. Covering an area of 15 sq km/6 sq mi, it has a spectacular rocky coastline of high cliff crags. The principal activities are fishing and the production of multi-coloured knitted goods with characteristic intricate patterns.

A birdwatching station is based on Fair Isle for research into the origins, routes, wintering areas, and feeding habits of spring and autumn migratory birds. The island passed into the care of the National Trust for Scotland in 1954.

## Falkirk

Unitary authority in central Scotland, created in 1996, from part of the former Central region; population (1995) 142,800; area 297 sq km/115 sq mi. The principal towns are Falkirk (administrative headquarters) and Grangemouth.

*Physical*

A low-lying area between Edinburgh and Glasgow, Falkirk borders the southern side of the Firth of Forth; the River Avon flows though.

*Features*

The Forth and Clyde canal, which divides Scotland at its narrowest part, and the Union canal, run through; remains of the Antonine Wall is (about AD 140) can be seen at Rough Castle.

*Economy*

The area is particularly renowned for its chemical industries.

*Other features*

The remains of the Antonine Wall (about AD 140) and a Roman road, can be seen at Rough Castle, west of Falkirk town. The Scottish Railway Preservation Society is at Bo'ness.

*Environment*

There are nine Sites of Special Scientific Interest and one country park.

*Administrative history*

Prior to 1975, the area was part of the county of Stirlingshire.

## Falklands War

War between Argentina and Britain over disputed sovereignty of the ◊Falkland Islands initiated when Argentina invaded and occupied the islands on 2 April 1982. On the following day, the United Nations Security Council passed a resolution calling for Argentina to withdraw. A British task force was immediately dispatched and, after a fierce conflict in which more than 1,000 Argentine and British lives were lost, 12,000 Argentine troops surrendered and the islands were returned to British rule on 14–15 June 1982.

## Falmouth

Port and resort on the south coast of Cornwall, southwest England, on the estuary of the River Fal, 11 km/7 mi southwest of Truro; population (1981) 18,500. It is a major yachting centre and the marine rescue and coastguard centre for the southwest region. Principal industries include tourism, ship-repair at Pendennis shipyard, and the construction of aluminium buildings and naval architecture.

Aluminium fabrications constructed here include the NatWest Media Centre at Lord's cricket ground, London. Trade through the port is less significant now, with some fish wholesaling and a specialist trade in exotic plants for public gardens.

---

*Tuesday 15 June Stanley woke up to find it was back under British rule. The British soldiers didn't look like men who had just walked across the island but they had, every step of the way on their own two feet. Fifty miles they'd come over mountains and bogs in weather that chilled the bone and soaked the skin, and at the end of it they'd fought bravely and well.*

**Brian Hanrahan** English TV and radio correspondent. BBC TV news report of 25 June 1982 on the end of the Falklands War, recorded in *I Counted Them All Out and I Counted Them All Back* (1982)

---

### Features

Falmouth has a temperate climate in which sub-tropical plants flourish. The castles of Pendennis and St Mawes, on opposite sides of the estuary, were built in 1543 to guard the entrance to the natural, deepwater harbour. The town contains the headquarters of the Royal Cornwall Yacht Club and hosts a number of local regattas. From 1998 Falmouth once again became the starting point for the biennial Cutty Sark International Tall Ships Race.

### History

Pendennis Castle was captured during the Civil War by the Parliamentarians after a five-month siege. In 1688 Falmouth became a Mail Packet Station, handling mail destined for North America and the West Indies, and it was an important trading port in the 18th century. The Riot Act (1714) was read for the last time to mutinous crews of packet ships docked at Fal-

mouth. The town developed as a resort after the railway opened in 1863.

## Faraday, Michael (1791–1867)

English chemist and physicist. In 1821, he began experimenting with electromagnetism, and discovered the induction of electric currents and made the first dynamo, the first electric motor, and the first transformer. Faraday isolated benzene from gas oils and produced the basic laws of electrolysis in 1834. He also pointed out that the energy of a magnet is in the field around it and not in the magnet itself, extending this basic conception of field theory to electrical and gravitational systems.

Faraday became a laboratory assistant to Humphry ◊Davy at the Royal Institution in 1813, and in 1833 succeeded him as professor of chemistry. Faraday delivered highly popular lectures at the Royal Institution from 1825–62. His restored laboratory at the Royal Institution is open to visitors.

## farce

Broad popular comedy involving stereotyped characters in complex, often improbable situations frequently revolving around extramarital relationships (hence the term 'bedroom farce').

Originating in the physical knockabout comedy of Greek satyr plays and the broad humour of medieval religious drama, the farce was developed and perfected during the 19th century by Arthur Pinero in England. Two successful English series in the 20th century were Ben ◊Travers' Aldwych farces in the 1920s and 1930s and the Whitehall farces produced by Brian Rix during the 1950s and 1960s.

## Fareham

Market town in Hampshire, southern England, 10 km/6 mi northwest of Portsmouth; population (1996 est) 102,500. Brickmaking, horticulture (notably strawberries), and leisure sailing industries have recently been supplemented by a fast-growing high-tech industrial sector, which includes the manufacture of scientific instruments.

Fareham was formerly a river port above Portsmouth Harbour. The ironmaker Henry Cort lived here at the end of the 18th century. His pioneering work on the manufacture of wrought iron and iron bars was an important contribution to the Industrial Revolution.

# Farnborough

Town in Hampshire, southern England, 4 km/2.5 mi north of Aldershot; population (1996 est) 53,000. It is the headquarters of the UK Defence Evaluation and Research Agency (DERA, until 1995 RAE Farnborough), which carries out research and experimental development in aeronautics and related instrumentation to support the Ministry of Defence. Aeronautical displays are given at the biennial air show.

The mansion of Farnborough Hill, now a convent, was occupied by Napoleon III and the Empress Eugénie of France, and she is buried with her husband and son in a mausoleum at St Michael's Catholic Church (built by the empress in 1887). St Michael's Abbey, adjoining the church, is occupied by a Benedictine community.

# Farne Islands

Group of about 28 rocky islands in the North Sea, close to the mainland of northeast England, 2–8 km/1–5 mi from Bamburgh, Northumberland. The islands are a sanctuary for birds and grey seals.

On Inner Farne, the largest of the group, there is a 14th-century chapel on the site of the hermitage at which St Cuthbert stayed from 676 to 684; he returned to die here in 687. The Longstone lighthouse, on one of the most remote of the islands, was the scene of the rescue of shipwrecked sailors by Grace ◊Darling in 1838.

The group has been owned by the National Trust since 1925. The islands are a nature reserve and sanctuary for many species of seabirds, particularly guillemots, puffins, terns, and kittiwakes. To protect the birds only two of the islands are open to visitors. It is the only breeding station of Atlantic seals on the east coast of Britain.

# Farnham

Town in Surrey, southeast England, on the River Wey; population (1996 est) 36,200. Waverley Abbey (1128), the first Cistercian house in England, lies nearby to the southeast; Walter Scott is said to have named his first novel after the foundation.

**Farnham Castle**, dating from the 12th century, was the palace of the bishops of Winchester until 1925, and then the seat of the bishop of Guildford until 1956. Farnham was formerly the centre of a large hop-growing district and it has many fine Georgian buildings, reflecting its importance as a market centre in the 18th century.

# Farrell, J(ames) G(ordon) (1935–1979)

English historical novelist. His work includes *Troubles* (1970), set in Ireland just after World War I, the *The Siege of Krishnapur* (1973) (Booker Prize), describing the Indian Mutiny, and *The Singapore Grip* (1978) which describes the fall of Singapore to the Japanese. His novel *The Hill Station* (1981) was unfinished when Farrell died.

# farthing

Formerly the smallest English coin, a quarter of a penny. It was introduced as a silver coin in Edward I's reign. The copper farthing became widespread in Charles II's reign, succeeded by the bronze farthing in 1860. It was dropped from use in 1961.

# Faversham

Town in Kent, England, 15 km/9 mi northwest of Canterbury; one of England's best-preserved historic towns. It has prehistoric, Roman, and Anglo-Saxon associations, and was an important medieval river port, situated on Faversham Creek.

Abbey Street in Faversham has been restored as a complete period piece from before the 19th century, and there are many ancient buildings in the town, including those in Market Place, the Norman church of St Mary of Charity, and the old grammar school.

The former village of Ospringe, now within the town, has the Maison Dieu museum, containing Roman finds. A large abbey – erected by King Stephen in the 12th century, originally for the Cluniac order and later for the Benedictines – was excavated at Faversham in 1965.

# Fawcett, Millicent born Garrett (1847–1929)

English ◊suffragette and social reformer, younger sister of Elizabeth Garrett ◊Anderson. A nonmilitant, she rejected the violent acts of some of her contemporaries in the suffrage movement. She joined the first Women's Suffrage Committee in 1867 and became president of the Women's Unionist Association in 1889. She was president of the National Union of Women's Suffrage Societies 1897–1919.

She was also active in property reform and campaigned for the right of married women to own their own property, and the higher education and employment of women.

# Fawkes, Guy (Guido) (1570–1606)

English conspirator in the ◊Gunpowder Plot to blow up King James I and the members of both Houses of Parliament. Fawkes, a Roman Catholic convert, was arrested in the cellar underneath the House on 4 November 1605, tortured, and subsequently executed. The event is still commemorated in Britain every 5 November with bonfires, fireworks, and the burning of the 'guy', an effigy.

## Felbrigg Hall

House in Norfolk, England, 3 km/2 mi southwest of Cromer, the home of the Windham family from the mid-15th century. The present house was built in the 17th century and remains outwardly unaltered; the rooms also retain their original furniture and pictures. The house, contents and estate were left to the National Trust in 1969 by Robert Wyndham Ketton-Cremer, the last squire of Felbrigg.

---

*Guido's composure was astonishing. Yes, he had intended to blow up the King and the Lords. No, he had no regrets – except the fact that he had not succeeded. 'The devil and not God', he said firmly, was responsible for the discovery of the Plot. No, he had not sought to warn the Catholic peers, he would have contented himself with praying for them.*

**Antonia Fraser** English writer.
Describing the questioning of Guido (Guy) Fawkes in *The Gunpowder Plot: Terror and Faith in 1605* (1996)

---

## Fenian movement

Irish-American republican secret society, founded in 1858 and named after the ancient Irish legendary warrior band of the Fianna. The collapse of the movement began when an attempt to establish an independent Irish republic by an uprising in Ireland in 1867 failed, as did raids into Canada in 1866 and 1870, and England in 1867.

## Fens, the

Level, low-lying tracts of reclaimed marsh in eastern England, west and south of the Wash, covering an area of around 40,000 sq km/15,500 sq mi, about 115 km/70 mi north–south and 55 km/34 mi east–west. They fall within the counties of Lincolnshire, Cambridgeshire, and Norfolk. Formerly a bay of the North Sea, they are now crossed by numerous drainage canals and form some of the most fertile and productive agricultural land in Britain. The southern peat portion of the Fens is known as the Bedford Level.

*Ecology*
Northeast of Cambridge, attempts have been made to preserve the raised bogs of **Burwell Fen** and **Wicken Fen** undrained as nature reserves, but agriculture in the surrounding area has affected water levels, partially destroying their ecology. Areas such as **Lopham Fen** and **Redgrave Fen** are also recognized as having important ecological value for specific animal and plant life, including otters, great raft spiders, rare birds, and the marsh hellibore orchid, although their existence is considerably threatened by land drainage and groundwater draw-down for public supplies. Wildfowl and fish remain abundant in the rivers and marshlands, but ecological problems have been caused by the introduction of fish species such as the zander, a voracious predator.

## Ferguson, Harry George (1884–1960)

Northern Irish engineer who pioneered the development of the tractor, joining forces with Henry Ford in 1938 to manufacture it in the USA. He also experimented in automobile and aircraft development.

## Fermanagh

County of Northern Ireland; population (1991) 50,000; area 1,680 sq km/648 sq mi. It occupies the southwestern corner of Northern Ireland and is characterized by hills in the west and Lough Erne, which has many wooded islands and is used for fishing and sailing. The main towns are ◊Enniskillen (county town), Lisnaskea, and Irvinestown.

*Physical*
Upper and Lower Lough Erne bisect the county, the southwest portion of which consists of a series of scenic hills that rise to 663 m/2,175 ft in Mount Cuilcagh, and contain several remarkable cave systems, notably at Marble Arch. In the centre is a broad trough of low-lying land, and in the east there are low hills.

*Features*
Fermanagh has a number of fine castles and tower houses dating from the plantation period, most notably the well-preserved remains of Monea Castle. On Devenish Island, Lower Lough Erne, are the extensive ruins of a monastery, originally founded in the 6th century by St Molaise. Florence Court, a Georgian mansion and forest park, was the home of the Earl of Enniskillen. Castle Coole is a neoclassical, late 18th-century house, and was the home of the Earls of Belmore. Tully Castle is a 17th-century fortified house, and White Island is the site of a 10th-century monastery and 12th-century church. Crom Castle Estate, on the shores of Upper Lough Erne, is an important wetland conservation area and has 770 ha/1,903 acres of woodland and parkland, and the ruins of a castle built in 1611 stand in the grounds.

### Economy

Agriculture and tourism provide the main occupations in the county, with clothing and tweeds being produced alongside some light engineering.

### Ferranti, Sebastian Ziani de (1864–1930)

British electrical engineer who established the principle of a national grid and an electricity-generating system based on alternating current (AC) (successfully arguing against Thomas Edison's proposal). He brought electricity to much of central London. In 1881 he made and sold his first alternator.

### Ferrier, Kathleen (1912–1953)

English contralto. She brought warmth and depth of conviction to English oratorio roles during wartime and subsequently to opera and lieder (songs), including Gluck's *Orfeo ed Euridice*, Mahler's *Das Lied von der Erde/The Song of the Earth*, and the role of Lucretia in Benjamin Britten's *The Rape of Lucretia* (1946).

### Festival of Britain

Artistic and cultural festival held in London May–September 1951 both to commemorate the 100th anniversary of the Great Exhibition and to boost morale after years of post-war austerity. The South Bank of the Thames formed the focal point of the event and the Royal Festival Hall built specially for the festival is a reminder of the modernist style of architecture promoted at the time.

### feudalism (Latin *feudem* 'fief', coined 1839)

The main form of social organization in medieval Europe, including Britain. A system based primarily on land, it involved a hierarchy of authority, rights, and power that extended from the monarch downwards. An intricate network of duties and obligations linked royalty, nobility, lesser gentry, free tenants, villeins, and serfs. Feudalism was reinforced by a complex legal system and supported by the Christian church. With the growth of commerce and industry from the 13th century, feudalism gradually gave way to the class system as the dominant form of social ranking.

### field

Enclosed area of land used for farming.

In Britain, regular field systems were functioning before the Romans' arrival. The open-field system was in use at the time of the Norman Conquest. Enclosure began in the 13th century and continued into the 19th century.

In the Middle Ages, the farmland of an English rural community was often divided into three large fields (the **open-field system**). These were worked on a simple rotation basis of one year wheat, one year barley, and one year fallow. The fields were divided into individually owned strips of the width that one plough team with oxen could plough (about 20 m/66 ft). At the end of each strip would be a turning space, either a road or a **headland**. Through repeated ploughing a **ridge-and-furrow** pattern became evident; ridges can still be seen, for instance, in Nottinghamshire and Cumbria. A farmer worked a number of strips, not necessarily adjacent to each other, in one field.

The open-field communities were subsequently reorganized, the land enclosed, and the farmers' holdings redistributed into individual blocks which were then divided into separate fields. This enclosure process reached its peak during the 18th century. Twentieth-century developments in agricultural science and technology encouraged farmers to amalgamate and enlarge their fields, often to as much as 40 hectares/100 acres.

**Henry Fielding** A 1754 portrait of the 18th-century English novelist, Henry Fielding. He broke away from the prevailing epistolary and moralizing tradition of novels to a comic and satiric realism, and frequently wrote parodies of the literary successes of the day. Concern for social justice, seen in his best-known novel *Tom Jones* (1749), was also a feature of his term as a magistrate. Corbis

## Fielding, Henry (1707–1754)

English novelist. His greatest work, *The History of Tom Jones, a Foundling* (1749) (see ◊ *Tom Jones*), which he described as 'a comic epic poem in prose', was an early landmark in the development of the English novel, realizing for the first time in English the form's potential for memorable characterization, coherent plotting, and perceptive analysis. The vigour of its comic impetus, descriptions of high and low life in town and country, and its variety of characters made it immediately popular.

Fielding gave a new prominence to dialogue in his work, which was to have a marked influence on the development of the English novel.

## Fields, Gracie stage name of Grace Stansfield (1898–1979)

English comedian and singer. Much loved by the public, her humorously sentimental films include *Sally in Our Alley* (1931), *Sing as We Go* (1934), *We're Going to be Rich* (1938), and *Holy Matrimony* (1943).

## Fife

Unitary authority in eastern Scotland, north of the Firth of Forth, created in 1996 from the former region of Fife; population (1996) 351,200; area 1,321 sq km/510 sq mi. It has coastline on three sides, and was settled very early on in Scottish history. It was the home and burial place of several Scottish kings, and has the world-famous St Andrews golf courses. The chief towns are Cupar, Dunfermline, ◊Glenrothes (administrative headquarters), Kirkcaldy, and St Andrews.

*Physical*

The coastal area is predominantly low lying, with an undulating interior and dramatic escarpment at Lomond Hills; the rivers Eden and Leven flow through the area.

*Features*

Tentsmuir, a coastal sand-dune area in the north, is possibly the earliest settled site in Scotland. The ancient palace of the Stuarts (16th century) was at Falkland, and eight Scottish kings were buried at Dunfermline. The Rosyth naval base and dockyard, used for nuclear submarine refits, is at St Margaret's Hope. The Old Course at St Andrews is considered the 'home of golf'. There are 53 Sites of Special Scientific Interest, three National Nature Reserves, one Ramsar (wetland site), two Special Protection Areas, one regional park, and three country parks.

*Economy*

At one time Fife's economy was dominated by the coalmining industry; this is less important now, although some of the most modern and mechanized pits in Scotland are located in the area. It has a mixed economy. St Andrews has a thriving service sector and tourist base, Glenrothes (New Town) has contemporary electronics industries, and much of the northeast is predominantly agricultural.

## Financial Times Index, FT Index

Indicator measuring the daily movement of 30 major industrial share prices on the London Stock Exchange, issued by the UK *Financial Times* newspaper. Other FT indices cover government securities, fixed-interest securities, gold mine shares, and Stock Exchange activity.

## Fingal's Cave

Cave on the island of Staffa, Inner Hebrides, Argyll and Bute, Scotland. It is lined with volcanic basalt columns, and is 70 m/230 ft long and 20 m/65 ft high. Visited by the German Romantic composer Felix Mendelssohn in 1829, the cave was the inspiration of his *Hebridean* overture, otherwise known as *Fingal's Cave*.

## Fire of London

Fire on 2–5 September 1666 that destroyed four fifths of the City of London. It broke out in a bakery in Pudding Lane and spread as far west as the Temple. It destroyed 87 churches, including St Paul's Cathedral (prompting Christopher ◊Wren's redesign), and 13,200 houses, although fewer than 20 people lost their lives.

Monument underground station is named after the monument erected to commemorate the fire and the huge task of rebuilding the City.

---

*This fatal night about ten, began that deplorable fire near Fish Street in London ... all the sky were of a fiery aspect, like the top of a burning oven, and the light seen above 40 miles round about for many nights.*

**John Evelyn** English diarist and author.
*Diary* 23 Sept 1666

---

## Fishbourne Palace

Romano-British villa, near Chichester in West Sussex, dating from the 1st century AD; it has some of the best-preserved Roman mosaics in Britain. The villa may have been built for the Roman client king, Tiberius Claudius Cogidubnus who ruled in that area. It was largely destroyed by fire in the 3rd century.

## Fisher, John, St (c. 1469–1535)

English cleric, created bishop of Rochester in 1504. He was an enthusiastic supporter of the revival in the study of Greek, and a friend of the humanists Thomas More and Desiderius Erasmus. In 1535 he was tried on a charge of denying the royal supremacy of Henry VIII and beheaded.

## Fishguard, Welsh Abergwaun

Seaport and holiday centre at the mouth of the River Gwaun on the south side of Fishguard Bay, Pembrokeshire, southwest Wales, 30 km/19 mi southwest of Cardigan; population about 5,000. There is a ferry service to Rosslare in the Republic of Ireland.

## Fitzherbert, Maria Anne born Smythe (1756–1837)

Wife of the Prince of Wales, later George IV. She became Mrs Fitzherbert by her second marriage in 1778 and, after her husband's death in 1781, entered London society. She secretly married the Prince of Wales in 1785 and finally parted from him in 1803.

## Flamborough Head (from 'Flein's burg')

Prominent headland on the coast of the East Riding of Yorkshire, England, 3 km/2 mi east of the village of Flamborough. Flamborough Head is composed of chalk cliffs, which rise in places to a height of 120 m/394 ft. Formerly, beacons were lit on the clifftop; now a lighthouse, whose beam is visible at a distance of 34 km/21 mi, stands 65 m/213 ft above the high-water mark.

An ancient British earthwork, misleadingly called Danes' Dyke, runs across Flamborough peninsula, culminating at the Head.

## Flamsteed, John (1646–1719)

English astronomer. He began systematic observations of the positions of the stars, Moon, and planets at the Royal Observatory he founded at Greenwich, London in 1676. His observations were published in *Historia Coelestis Britannica* (1725).

As the first Astronomer Royal of England, Flamsteed determined the latitude of Greenwich, the slant of the ecliptic, and the position of the equinox. He also worked out a method of observing the absolute right ascension (a coordinate of the position of a heavenly body) that removed all errors of parallax, refraction, and latitude.

## Flanagan, Bud (1896–1968)

English comedian. He was the leader of the 'Crazy Gang' from 1931 to 1962. He played in variety theatre all over the world and, with his partner Chesney Allen, popularized such songs as 'Underneath the Arches'.

## Flatford

Location on the River Stour, in Suffolk, England. Flatford Mill and Dedham Mill (on the Essex bank of the Stour) formed the sites for paintings by John ◊Constable. Flatford Mill now belongs to the ◊National Trust, which administers the property as a field study centre.

## Fleet Street

Street in London (named after the subterranean River Fleet). It runs from Temple Bar eastwards to Ludgate Circus. Traditionally the centre of British journalism, it contained (with adjoining streets) the offices and printing works of many leading British newspapers until the mid-1980s, when most moved to sites farther from the centre of London. The earliest extant reference to the street is in about 1188.

Up to the mid-15th century it was, apart from Thames Street, the only paved street in the city and its immediate vicinity. It became celebrated for its taverns, and later became the centre of London's newspaper industry. The *Daily Courant*, Britain's first daily paper, started here in 1702, as did *Punch* magazine, devised in 1841.

## Fleetwood

Port and seaside resort in Lancashire, England, at the mouth of the River Wyre, 13 km/8 mi from Blackpool; population (1991) 27,200.

The Fleetwood Harbour Village retail park has been developed in the docks area. Tourism and the service sector also provide significant employment.

Fleetwood was formerly one of the chief fishing ports in Britain and, although the industry has declined, it remains England's major west coast fishing centre.

## Fleming, Alexander (1881–1955)

Scottish bacteriologist who discovered the first antibiotic drug, penicillin, in 1928. In 1922 he had discovered lysozyme, an antibacterial enzyme present in saliva, nasal secretions, and tears. While studying this, he found an unusual mould growing on a culture dish, which he isolated and grew into a pure culture; this led to his discovery of penicillin. It came into use in 1941. In 1945 he won the Nobel Prize for Physiology or Medicine with Howard Florey and Ernst Chain, whose research had brought widespread realization of the value of penicillin.

### Fleming, Ian Lancaster (1908–1964)
English author. His suspense novels feature the ruthless, laconic James Bond, British Secret Service agent 007. The first novel in the series was *Casino Royale* (1953); others include *From Russia with Love* (1957), *Goldfinger* (1959), and *The Man with the Golden Gun* (1965). Most of the novels were made into a successful series of ◊ Bond films.

During World War II he worked for British Intelligence where he had the opportunity to give full rein to his vivid imagination in disseminating false information and rumours.

### Fletcher, John (1579–1625)
English dramatist. He is remarkable for his range, which included tragicomedy and pastoral dramas, in addition to comedy and tragedy. He collaborated with Francis ◊ Beaumont in some 12 plays, producing, most notably, the tragicomedy *Philaster* (1610) and *The Maid's Tragedy* (about 1611). He is alleged to have collaborated with ◊ Shakespeare on *The Two Noble Kinsmen* and *Henry VIII* (1613).

### Flint, Welsh Fflint
Town in Flintshire, northeast Wales, situated on the Dee estuary, 20 km/12 mi from Chester; population (1991) 11,600. **Flint Castle** was built between 1277 and 1284. It was here that Richard II was betrayed to Henry of Bolingbroke (Henry IV) in 1399.

### Flintshire, Welsh Sir y Fflint
Unitary authority in northwest Wales, created in 1996 from part of Clwyd; population (1996) 144,000; area 437 sq km/167 sq mi. It has a northern coastline on the Irish Sea, and its main towns are ◊ Mold (administrative headquarters), Flint, Holywell, Buckley, and Connah's Quay.
*Physical*
Flintshire is bounded by the Irish Sea to the north, the Dee estuary to the east, and the Clwydian Range, which rises to 555 m/1,820 ft, to the southwest. The rivers Dee and Alyn flow through it.
*Features*
Flint Castle dates from the 13th century. Greenfield Valley was in the forefront of the Industrial

Revolution before the advent of steam, and now has a museum of industrial archaeology.
*Economy*
The local economy is based on manufacturing of artificial silk, chemicals, and optical glass, and there is dairy farming and stock-raising. There is an airport at Hawarden.

### Flodden, Battle of
Defeat of the Scots by the English under the Earl of Surrey on 9 September 1513 on a site, 5 km/3 mi southeast of Coldstream, in Northumberland, England. ◊ James IV of Scotland, declaring himself the active ally of France, crossed the border to England with an invading army of 30,000. The Scots were defeated, suffering heavy losses, and James himself was killed.

### Florence Court
Mid-18th-century house in County ◊ Fermanagh, Northern Ireland, standing 11 km/7 m south of Enniskillen, near the Cuilcagh Mountains which form the Northern Ireland–Eire border. One of the most important historic houses in Northern Ireland, it contains some outstanding Rococo plasterwork and 18th-century furniture. The house was given to the National Trust in 1954. It was designed by John Cole, father of the 18th Earl of Enniskillen.

### folk dancing
Folk dancing once formed an important part of many ancient rituals, but it has tended to die out since industrialization. The English ◊ morris dance and the dance round the fertility 'totem' ◊ maypole (linked with regeneration rituals) on the village green are derived from ceremonies of the pre-Christian era. In the early 20th century, the folk historian Cecil ◊ Sharp made extensive researches to record English country music and dances, which helped to reactivate interest and encourage revivals where some traditions had been lost. Other English folk dances include the hornpipe, jig, clog dancing, and the sword dance.

The **jig**, mainly associated with Scotland and Ireland (but also found in Wales) and generally identifiable from the 16th century onwards, was usually a solo dance, a forerunner of the galliard. The Frenchified version, the **gigue**, was toned down and assimilated into courtly entertainment and also staged dance (for example, 'Kemps's Jigge', named after the Shakespearean comic actor William Kemp (died 1603) who was celebrated for his jigs at the close of a performance).

**Folk dancing** Sword dancers from the Hampshire town of Farnborough perform outside a pub. Folk dances with swords are of ancient origin, and are thought to have been originally performed to ward off evil spirits or to mime human and animal sacrifice. They are related to the more widespread practice of Morris dancing. Brian Shuel/Collections

**Scottish folk dancing**, including the Highland fling and the sword dance (to be differentiated from the English version), is generally categorized as the faster reels (almost certainly of northern origin) or the slower Strathspey, and often accompanied by the bagpipes.

**Irish folk dancing** includes the jig (often accompanied by bagpipes, the harp, or the fiddle); céilidhs (social dance gatherings, also popular in Scotland) usually feature jigs, reels, and hornpipes. Irish clog dances are often performed in wooden clogs and are among the most complex versions known of clog dancing (made popular in the mid-1990s by the hit show *Riverdance*).

**Welsh folk dancing** includes reels with three or four dancers, jigs, and clog dances to a harp or hornpipe, but the dancing tradition was subdued by Welsh Presbyterianism or Chapel from the 16th century.

## Folkestone

Port and resort on the southeast coast of Kent, England, 10 km/6 mi southwest of Dover; population (1991) 46,200. There are passenger ferry and hovercraft connections with Boulogne, and to the northwest of the town is the British terminal of Eurotunnel, which offers a high-speed train link through the ▷Channel Tunnel to Paris and Brussels for private and haulage traffic.

The physician William Harvey, who discovered the circulation of blood, was born here in 1578; his statue stands on the cliff top.

### Features

The Eurotunnel Exhibition Centre illustrates the building of the Channel Tunnel. To the east of the town is the East Cliff and the Warren, a chalk landslip basin between high cliffs, rich in fossil remains. Many of the town's buildings date from the 19th century, reflecting its development as a resort following the arrival of the railway in the mid 19th century. The Leas is a long promenade above the beach along the cliff top. The original fishing quarter and harbour has some of the town's oldest buildings, and is now a popular yachting and cruising venue. There is a racecourse, and the Leas Cliff Hall (1927) is used for concerts and conferences. The town suffered considerable damage during World War II.

The first nunnery in England was established here in 630 by St Eanswythe, grand-daughter of Ethelbert, the first Christian king of Kent. The Early English and Perpendicular church of St

Mary and St Eanswythe was built just to the west of the site of the nunnery.

## folk music

Traditional music, especially from rural areas, which is passed on by listening and repeating, and is usually performed by amateurs. The term is used to distinguish it from ◊classical music, and from urban popular or commercial music. Most folk music exists in the form of songs, or instrumental music to accompany folk dancing, and is usually melodic and rhythmic rather than harmonic in style.

### Different national styles

Recognizably different styles of folk music can be seen within the countries of the British Isles: English, Scottish, Irish, and Welsh folk music all have distinctive characteristics.

In England, folk song is generally in the ballad tradition, either unaccompanied or with a simple concertina or melodeon accompaniment, and, typically for a maritime nation, there is also a large number of shanties. The two folk-dance traditions, ◊morris dancing and country dance and their many regional variations, each have their own associated tunes, usually played on a pipe and drum, fiddle, or concertina.

Scottish folk music can be divided roughly into two styles: Highland (associated with the Gaelic language), and Lowland (associated with the Scots language). Unusually for a true oral folk tradition, most Scottish folk songs are by known composers and poets whose names have been passed down with their songs, which are mainly in the form of unaccompanied ballads. Instrumental music includes dance music for fiddle and concertina, and a uniquely Scottish genre, the pibroch, a form of theme and variations specifically for the bagpipes.

Irish folk song can similarly be divided according to language, with distinct musical traditions for both Irish and English lyrics. Dances such as the jig and the reel are typical in Irish instrumental music, and are played on the fiddle and pipe, and Irish versions of the harp and bagpipes, almost invariably with the rhythmic accompaniment of the bodhrán, a kind of drum. Much of the traditional repertoire has been preserved and played in the latter part of the 20th century by groups such as the Chieftains.

Although there is a long tradition of musical culture in Wales, very little true folk music has survived. Welsh traditional music, like Scottish folk music, is mostly by known poets and composers, but because of its association with the Bardic culture, this is perhaps more accurately regarded as a classical rather than a folk culture.

### History

It was not until the late 19th century that there was any systematic collection of folk music. In England, this was seen in the transcription and preservation of folk tunes by such people as the Rev Sabine Baring-Gould and Cecil ◊Sharp. The Folk Song Society was founded in 1898 and became the English Folk Dance and Song Society in 1911. In true Victorian fashion, they bowdlerized much of the material they collected, and edited out much of the sophisticated ornamentation and rhythmic complexity, which they felt to be 'primitive', or simply poor performance. The collection of folk music continued through the first half of the 20th century, with important contributions made by Ralph ◊Vaughan Williams (whose collections not only influenced his own music but have been a significant source to the present day), A L Lloyd, and Ewan MacColl; and a unique and invaluable collection gathered by several generations of the Copper family of Sussex.

### Folk revival in the 20th century

The post-World War II folk revival in the USA had a counterpart in the UK, with both a renewed interest in traditional folk music and a new generation of songwriters and performers in a folk style. The 1960s saw the appearance of performers in many different folk styles: the Watersons, who popularized traditional unaccompanied folk singing; groups such as Pentangle and the Incredible String Band, and the singer Donovan produced new music in a folk style; and folk-rock bands such as Fairport Convention and Steeleye Span brought some of the folk repertoire to a new audience by performing using the instruments of the rock band, as well as introducing new songs in a folk idiom. This folk revival continued through the 1980s, and was furthered by rock guitarist Richard ◊Thompson and such groups as the Pogues (formed 1983), while the singer/songwriter Billy Bragg continued in the tradition of the political protest song. In recent years, there has been a growing interest in roots, or world, music, encompassing traditional as well as modern music from many cultures.

## Fonteyn, Margot stage name of Peggy Hookham (1919–1991)

English ballet dancer. She made her debut with the Vic-Wells Ballet in *Nutcracker* (1934) and first appeared as Giselle in 1937, eventually becoming prima ballerina of the Royal Ballet, London. Renowned for her perfect physique, clear line, musicality, and interpretive powers, she created many roles in Frederick ◊Ashton's ballets and formed a legendary partnership with Rudolf Nureyev. She retired from dancing in 1979.

Fonteyn's first major role was in Ashton's *Le Baiser de la fée* (1935); other Ashton ballets include *Symphonic Variations* (1946), *Ondine* (1958, filmed 1959), and *Marguerite and Armand* (1963, filmed 1972). She also appeared in Macmillan's *Romeo and Juliet* (1965, filmed 1966) with Nureyev. She was made a DBE in 1956.

## food and drink
See chronology of some food and drink highlights below.

## football, association, or soccer
Form of football originating in the UK, played in the UK according to the rules laid down by the home countries' football associations. Slight amendments to the rules take effect in certain competitions and international matches as laid down by the sport's world governing body, Fédération Internationale de Football Association (FIFA, 1904). FIFA organizes the competitions for the World Cup, held every four years since 1930.

See chronology of some key football dates, on page 180.

---

*But the English – what passion.*

**Daniel Passarella** Argentina's national football coach.
After his team's torrid World Cup quarter-final victory over England in 1998

---

## Ford, John (*c.* 1586–*c.* 1640)
English poet and dramatist. His play *'Tis Pity She's a Whore* (performed in about 1626, printed in

---

## Food and Drink: Some key dates

*c.* **1400** The use of spices and sauces becomes widespread in cooking in England in an effort to improve the repetitive diet of dried and salted foods.

**1609** Tea is returned to Europe from China by the Dutch East India Company. It reaches Britain by 1615.

**1657** Coffee is sold for the first time in London, England. It is promoted as a patent medicine, capable of curing a variety of ailments.

**1741** English doctor William Brownrigg creates the first artificially carbonated mineral water at Whitehaven, Cumberland.

**1762** John Montagu, Earl of Sandwich, invents the sandwich (meat between two slices of bread) to stave off hunger while he is at the gaming table in London.

**1797** James Keiller starts to manufacture the first orange marmalade, in Dundee, Scotland.

**1824** George Smith opens Glenlivet, in Scotland, the first licensed whisky distillery.

**1824** English Quaker John Cadbury opens a tea and coffee shop in Birmingham, England, the beginnings of the Cadbury confectionery company.

**1831** Edward Adcock of Melton Mowbray, Leicestershire, England, begins to sell the now world-famous pork pies.

**1837** Using a recipe from Sir Marcus Sandys, British chemists John Lee and William Perrins produce Worcester Sauce.

**1839** Tea from India reaches the British market and quickly becomes more popular than the unfermented green Chinese tea.

**1840** James Pimm, of Pimm's Oyster Bar in London, develops Pimms No.1, a mixture of gin, liqueurs, herbs, and spices made to an undisclosed recipe. From 1859 it is available in bottled form.

*c.* **1870** Fish and chip shops start to become popular in the north of England.

**1875** The British confectionery company Fry's introduces chocolate Easter eggs.

**1876** The British confectionery company Slater & Bullock creates lettered rock; they will soon use the names of towns, the first being Blackpool.

**1919** The first Indian cuisine restaurant in London, England, opens.

**23 October 1933** Lyons opens its 'Corner House' fast-food restaurant with seats for 2,000 in London.

**21 January 1937** Marcel Boulestin shows how to cook an omelette in *Cook's Night Out*, and becomes the first television chef in the UK.

**12 January 1948** The London Co-operative Society opens the first supermarket in Britain, at Manor Park in London.

**31 December 1971** The Campaign for Real Ale (CAMRA) is founded in Britain.

**1974** McDonalds opens its first UK outlet, in London.

**1995** Sainsbury's is the UK's largest supermarket chain, with 355 stores.

**25 March 1996** The European Union bans the export of British beef abroad following anxiety over the potential for transmission of the BSE (bovine spongiform encephalopathy) infection to humans as CJD (Creuzfeld Jakob disease).

**September 1999** Legislation is passed in the UK to make compulsory the labelling of genetically modified (GM) foods by all establishments selling food, including supermarkets, restaurants, and fast-food outlets.

**December 1999** The European Union finally lifts its ban on the export of British beef.

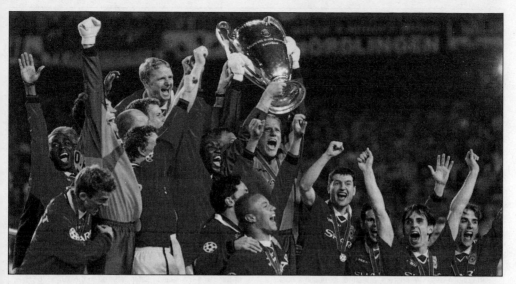

**Football** Manchester United celebrate with the European Cup after beating Bayern Munich 2–1 in Barcelona in May 1999, having scored both goals in three minutes of injury time. The win completed an historic treble: the team had already won the English Premiership and the FA Cup. Glyn Kirk/Actionplus

1633) is a study of incestuous passion between brother and sister. His other plays include *The Lover's Melancholy* (1629), *The Broken Heart* (1633), *Love's Sacrifice* (1633), in which Bianca is one of Ford's finest psychological studies of women, and *The Chronicle History of Perkin Warbeck* (1634). Dwelling on themes of pathos and frustration, they reflect the transition from a general to an aristocratic audience for drama.

## Foreign and Commonwealth Office, or FCO

Government department established in 1782 as the Foreign Office. It is responsible for the conduct of foreign policy, representation of British interests abroad, relations with other members of the ◊Commonwealth, and overseas aid policy and administration. Robin Cook was appointed foreign secretary in 1997.

## Forester, C(ecil) S(cott) (1899–1966)

English novelist. He is best known for a series of historical novels set in the Napoleonic era that, beginning with *The Happy Return* (1937), cover the career – from midshipman to admiral – of Horatio Hornblower. One of the series, *A Ship of the Line* (1939), won the James Tait Black Memorial Prize.

His first novel, *Payment Deferred* (1926), was a subtle crime novel, and he also wrote *The African Queen* (1935), filmed in 1952 with Humphrey Bogart and Katharine Hepburn.

## Forestry Commission

Government department responsible for forestry in Britain. Established in 1919, it is responsible for over 1 million hectares/2.7 million acres of land, and is funded partly by government and partly by sales of timber. In Northern Ireland responsibility for forestry lies with the Department of Agriculture's forestry service.

Between 1945 and 1980 the Forestry Commission doubled the forest area in the UK, planting, for example, Kielder Forest, Cumbria. In 1991 woodland cover was estimated at 2.3 million hectares, around 10% of total land area. This huge increase has been achieved mainly by planting conifers for commercial use on uplands or on land difficult to farm. In spite of such massive afforestation, around 90% of the UK's timber needs are imported at an annual cost of some £4 billion.

## Formby, George (1904–1961)

English comedian. He established a stage and screen reputation as an apparently simple Lancashire working lad, and sang such songs as 'Mr Wu' and 'Cleaning Windows', accompanying himself on the ukulele. His father was a music-hall star of the same name.

## Forster, E(dward) M(organ) (1879–1970)

English novelist, short-story writer, and critic. He was concerned with the interplay of personality and the conflict between convention and instinct.

## Football: Some key dates

**1349** Football and other games are banned in England by King Edward III because they interfere with archery practice. The ban is repeated in 1389 and 1401, but with limited effect.

**1848** The first football rules are drawn up by students at Cambridge University, most of whom are Old Etonians who object to the Rugby form of the game with its emphasis on handling, mauling, and hacking. Along with the rules of Harrow football they will form the basis of the Football Association's first code of rules in 1863.

**1862** Notts County, the oldest club in the English Football League, is founded.

**26 October 1863** The Football Association is founded in London, by the representatives of 11 clubs. Their purpose is to establish 'a definite code of rules for the regulation of the game'. All clubs are from the London area.

**16 March 1872** A crowd of 2,000 at the Oval cricket ground in London watch Wanderers, a team of ex-public school players, defeat the Royal Engineers 1–0 to win the inaugural Football Association (FA) Cup final.

**30 November 1872** At the West of Scotland cricket ground at Patrick, near Glasgow, England and Scotland draw 0–0 in the first-ever official international association football match.

**13 March 1873** The decision to form the Scottish Football Association is made at a meeting of eight Scottish clubs called by Queen's Park Football Club to organize a cup competition similar to the English Football Association Cup.

**20 July 1885** The Football Association in England legalizes professionalism.

**1888** The English Football League is founded on the initiative of William MacGregor, a member of Aston Villa Football Club. Twelve teams, all from the Midlands and the north of England, contest the first championship.

**28 April 1923** The English Football Association (FA) Cup final is held at Wembley Stadium, London, for the first time. An estimated 200,000 spectators see Bolton Wanderers beat West Ham United 2–0.

**1931** Arsenal is the first London team to win the English Football League championship.

**25 November 1953** England's footballers lose at Wembley in London, for the first time to an overseas team, beaten 6–3 by Hungary. Six months later, Hungary confirms its overwhelming superiority over England with a 7–1 victory in Budapest, Hungary.

**6 February 1958** Eight members of the Manchester United football side from England are killed in an air crash in Munich, West Germany, while returning from a European Cup tie in Belgrade, Yugoslavia.

**1961** The maximum wage of £20 a week for English Football League players is abolished; Johnny Haynes of Fulham becomes the first English player to earn £100 a week.

**1961** Tottenham Hotspur becomes the first side to win the English League and the Football Association (FA) Cup 'double' since Aston Villa in 1897.

**30 July 1966** England wins football's World Cup, beating West Germany in the final at Wembley, 4–2 after extra time. The England forward Geoff Hurst scores the first-ever hat trick in a World Cup final.

**25 May 1967** Glasgow Celtic becomes the first British football team to win the European Cup, beating the Italian team Inter Milan 2–1 in Lisbon, Portugal.

**27 November 1972** The English Football Association decides to abolish amateur status. It announces that from the start of the 1974–75 season (later deferred to the 1975–76 season) all footballers will be known simply as 'players'.

**29 November 1978** Viv Anderson of Nottingham Forest becomes the first black footballer to play for England.

**26 May 1982** Aston Villa football club defeats Bayern Munich of West Germany 1–0 in the European Cup final in Rotterdam, in the Netherlands; it is the sixth successive year that an English club has won the competition.

**11 May 1985** Fifty-five people die when fire destroys the main stand at Bradford City's Valley Parade ground, in Bradford, during a Football League match.

**29 May 1985** Thirty-nine people are killed at the Heysel stadium in Brussels, Belgium, following a riot by Liverpool fans before the European Cup Final between Liverpool and Juventus of Italy; as a consequence, English football clubs are banned from all European competitions for five years.

**15 April 1989** Ninety-six Liverpool fans die in a crush during the Football Association (FA) Cup semifinal against Nottingham Forest at Hillsborough, Sheffield.

**1991** Twenty-two soccer clubs break away from the English Football League, under the auspices of the Football Association (FA), to form the FA Premier League. Play commences in August 1992.

**11 May 1996** Manchester United defeats Liverpool 1–0 in the English Football Association (FA) Cup final to complete an unprecedented second league championship and FA Cup double, having first achieved the feat two years earlier.

**1999** Manchester United score an historic treble, winning the English Premiership, the FA Cup, and the European Cup.

His novels include *A Room with a View* (1908), *Howards End* (1910), and *A Passage to India* (1924). Collections of stories include *The Celestial Omnibus* (1911) and *Collected Short Stories* (1948), and of essays and reviews 'Abinger Harvest' (1936). His most lasting critical work is *Aspects of the Novel* (1927).

Forster published his first novel, *Where Angels Fear to Tread*, in 1905. He enhances the superficial situations of his plots with unexpected insights in *The Longest Journey* (1907), *A Room with a View*, and *Howards End*. These three novels explore Forster's preoccupation with the need to find intellectual and spiritual harmony in a world dominated by narrow social conventions. His many years spent in India and as secretary to the Maharajah of Dewas provided him with the material for his best-known work *A Passage to India*, which explores the relationship between the English and the Indians with insight and wisdom. It is considered to be one of the most influential of modern English novels. *Maurice*, written in 1914 and published 1971, has a homosexual theme. Many of his works have been successfully adapted for film.

## Forth
River in central Scotland, with its headstreams, Duchray Water and Avondhu, rising on the northeast slopes of Ben Lomond. It flows east approximately 105 km/65 mi to Kincardine where the **Firth of Forth** begins. The Firth is approximately 80 km/50 mi long, and is 26 km/16 mi wide where it joins the North Sea.

The Forth is the seventh longest river in Scotland. At South Queensferry near Edinburgh are the Forth rail (1890) and road (1964) bridges. The **Forth and Clyde Canal** crosses the lowlands of Scotland and links the east coast and the Firth of Forth to the west coast and the River Clyde, from Grangemouth to Bowling. It was built between 1768 and 1790 and stretches for some 61 km/38 mi. A new coalfield was located beneath the Firth of Forth in 1976. There are salmon and white fisheries in the Forth's basin.

Places of historical interest on the river's banks include Stirling (once a royal residence), Cambuskenneth, Alloa, Kincardine, and Aberfoyle.

## Fortnum and Mason
High-class store in Piccadilly, London, famous for its exotic range of foods. It was founded in 1707 by William Fortnum, a footman to Queen Anne, and Hugh Mason, a local shopkeeper.

## Fort William
Town in Highland unitary authority, Scotland, near the head of Loch Linnhe, at the southern end of the ◊Caledonian Canal, 90 km/56 mi southeast of Inverness; population (1991) 10,400. Straddling a natural route to the Highlands and Great Glen, the provision of tourist services has become a major industry.

## Fosse Way, or Fosseway
Roman military road in England, from Lincoln in the north to Exeter, Devon, on the south coast. It intersected the Roman ◊Watling Street at a point known as the 'centre of England', and effectively

divided the 'barbarian' north and west from the southeast.

The road probably functioned as a frontier in the early years of the Roman conquest and may have been intended as the final limit of the province until fighting spread to Wales. Its route ran through the Celtic territories of the Durotiges, Dobunni, and Corieltauvi, passing through Newark, Leicester, High Cross, Cirencester, Bath, and the hills near Chard, Axminster, and Honiton.

The Fosse Way continued in use until modern times and was one of the four 'royal roads' of 11th-century Britain. It was named after the foss, or ditch, constructed on either side to keep the road well drained.

## Fountains Abbey
Cistercian abbey in North Yorkshire, England, situated 13 km/8 mi north of Harrogate. Celebrated as the greatest monument to English monasticism and its architecture, it was founded about 1132, and closed in 1539 at the Dissolution of the Monasteries. The ruins were incorporated into a Romantic landscaped garden (1720–40) with a lake, formal water garden, temples, and a deer park.

## fourth estate
Term for the press, coined in the 18th century by the British politician Edmund Burke. It derived from a medieval theory that there were usually three estates – the **nobility**, the **clergy**, and the **commons** – whose functions were, respectively, defending society from foreign aggression and internal disorder, attending to its spiritual needs, and working to produce the base with which to support the other two orders.

## Fowey
Port and resort on the south coast of Cornwall, southwest England, on the west bank of the Fowey estuary, 45 km/28 mi southwest of Devonport; population (1995 est) 2,100. It is administered with ◊St Austell. Fowey is the principal outlet for the Cornish china clay mining industry based at St Austell, and is also a centre for recreational sailing.

The port has a deep, sheltered harbour and a lifeboat station. Ferries operate to Brodinnick and Polruan across the Fowey river.
### History
Fowey was once an important seaport which fitted out ships for the Crusades. During the reign of Edward III the town equipped a fleet of 47 vessels

and supplied about 800 men for the siege of Calais in 1347, and Fowey's seafarers continued to raid the coast of France throughout the Hundred Years' War. The inhabitants were later convicted of piracy by Edward IV, and deprived of their vessels.

Daphne Du Maurier's locally based work, including *Rebecca*, is celebrated at an annual arts and literature festival based in Fowey. Her first novel, *The Loving Spirit* (1931), was written while she lived at Brodinnick.

## fox-hunting

The pursuit of a fox across country on horseback, aided by a pack of foxhounds specially trained to track the fox's scent. The aim is to catch and kill the fox. In drag-hunting, hounds pursue a prepared trail rather than a fox.

Described by the playwright Oscar Wilde as 'the unspeakable in pursuit of the uneatable', fox-hunting attracted highly charged debate at the end of the 20th century. Animal-rights activists condemn it as involving excessive cruelty, and in Britain groups of hunt saboteurs disrupt it. Fox-hunting dates from the late 17th century, when it arose as a practical method of limiting the fox population which endangered poultry farming, but by the early 19th century it was indulged in as a sport by the British aristocracy and gentry who ceremonialized it.

English 'hunts' (organized groups of hunters) include the Quorn, Pytchley, Belvoir, and Cottesmore. The recognized fox-hunting season runs from the first Monday in November until the following April. An estimated 12,500 foxes are killed in the UK by hunting each year, and another 100,000 killed by other means. In 1997 there were approximately 200 packs of foxhounds in the UK.

In 1998 the Labour government postponed debate on an anti-fox-hunting bill due to lack of parliamentary time, despite considerable popular support.

## Franciscan order

Catholic order of friars, **Friars Minor** or **Grey Friars**, founded in 1209 by the Italian monk Francis of Assisi. The first Franciscans to establish themselves in England arrived in 1224 and settled at Canterbury, London, and Oxford. By the middle of the 13th century they had established around 50 friaries with over 1,200 friars. Many friaries subsequently closed, but since the

**Foxhunting** Riders and hounds assemble for a hunt in Northumberland. The hunting with dogs of wild animals such as foxes and stags excites great passions. While its supporters defend it as a legitimate country pursuit that helps control overpopulation of wild animals and protects livestock, its opponents regard it as a cruel, unnecessary sport practised by a privileged few. Corel

mid-19th century many Franciscan houses have reopened.

An Anglican Franciscan community was established near Batcombe (Cerne Abbas), Dorset, England, in 1921 and is active in evangelistic work. A small Anglican community for women has also been started with headquarters at Freeland, Oxford.

The British scholars Duns Scotus, Roger Bacon, and William of Ockham were members of the Franciscan order.

## Free Church of Scotland
Body of Scottish Presbyterians who seceded from the Established Church of Scotland in the Disruption of 1843. In 1900 all but a small section that retains the old name (known as the **Wee Frees**) combined with the United Presbyterian Church to form the United Free Church of Scotland. Most of this reunited with the Church of Scotland in 1929, although there remains a continuing United Free Church of Scotland. It has 6,000 members, 110 ministers, and 140 churches.

## freehold
In England and Wales, ownership of land for an indefinite period. It is contrasted with a leasehold, which is always for a fixed period. In practical effect, a freehold is absolute ownership.

## freemasonry
Beliefs and practices of a group of linked national organizations open to men over the age of 21, united by a common code of morals and certain traditional 'secrets'. Modern freemasonry began in 18th-century Europe. Freemasons do much charitable work, but have been criticized in recent years for their secrecy, their male exclusivity, and their alleged use of influence within and between organizations (for example, the police or local government) to further each other's interests.
*History*
Freemasonry is descended from a medieval guild of itinerant masons, which existed in the 14th century and by the 16th was admitting men unconnected with the building trade. The term 'freemason' may have meant a full member of the guild or one working in freestone, that is, a mason of the highest class. There were some 25 lodges in 17th-century Scotland, of which 16 were in centres of masonic skills such as stonemasonry.

The present order of **Free and Accepted Masons** originated with the formation in London of the first Grand Lodge, or governing body, in 1717, and during the 18th century spread from Britain to the USA, continental Europe, and elsewhere.

In 1994 there were 359,000 masons registered in England and Wales; there were also an estimated 100,000 in Scotland and 60,000 in Ireland. There are approximately 6 million members worldwide.

## friendly society
Association that makes provisions for the needs of sickness and old age by money payments. In 1995 there were 1,013 orders and branches (17 orders, 996 branches), 18 collecting societies, 294 other centralized societies, 72 benevolent societies, 2,271 working men's clubs, and 131 specially authorized societies in the UK. Among the largest are the National Deposit, Odd Fellows, Foresters, and Hearts of Oak.

In the UK the movement was the successor to the great medieval guilds, but the period of its greatest expansion was in the late 18th and early 19th centuries, after the passing in 1797 of the first legislation providing for the registration of friendly societies. In the 20th century the Friendly Societies Act 1992 allowed friendly societies to become companies and offer a wider range of financial services.

## Friends of the Earth, FoE, or FOE
Largest international network of environmental pressure groups, established in the UK in 1971, that aims to protect the environment and to promote rational and sustainable use of the Earth's resources. It campaigns on such issues as acid rain; air, sea, river, and land pollution; recycling; disposal of toxic wastes; nuclear power and renewable energy; the destruction of rainforests; pesticides; and agriculture. FoE is represented in 52 countries.

FoE is one of the leading environmental pressure groups in the UK. It operates as a charity, commissioning detailed research and providing extensive information and educational materials. Over the years FoE has achieved bans on ozone-destroying chlorofluorocarbons (CFCs), reduced trade in rainforest timber and increased support for cleaner energy technologies. FoE was the first environmental pressure group in the UK to start campaigns for whales, endangered species, and tropical rainforests, and against acid rain, ozone depletion, and climate change.

## Friends, Society of, or Quakers
Christian Protestant sect founded by George ◊Fox in England in the 17th century. They were

persecuted for their nonviolent activism, and many emigrated to form communities elsewhere; for example, in Pennsylvania and New England. In 1997 there were about 19,000 members in Great Britain and Ireland, and about 219,800 members worldwide. Their worship stresses meditation and the freedom of all to take an active part in the service (called a meeting, held in a meeting house). They have no priests or ministers.

The name 'Quakers' may originate in Fox's injunction to 'quake at the word of the Lord'. Originally marked out by their sober dress and use of 'thee' and 'thou' to all as a sign of equality, they incurred penalties by their pacifism and refusal to take oaths or pay tithes. In the 19th century many Friends were prominent in social reform, for example, Elizabeth ◊ Fry.

## Frink, Elisabeth (1930–1993)

English sculptor. She created rugged, naturalistic bronzes, mainly based on human and animal forms; for example, the *Alcock Brown Memorial* (1962) for Manchester airport, *In Memoriam* (heads), and *Running Man* (1980).

## Frogmore

Royal residence in the Home Park, Windsor, England, about 2 km/1 mi southeast of the castle. The estate has long been the property of the Crown. The central block of the house dates from the early 18th century, but there have been many later alterations and additions.

Frogmore has two mausolea adjacent, and the bodies of Queen Victoria and Albert, Prince Consort lie here.

## Frome

Market town in Somerset, England, 40 km/25 mi southeast of Bristol; population (1991) 22,400. A medieval shopping street (Cheap Street) survives in Frome. The town was once the centre of a prosperous wool trade.

## Fry, Elizabeth born Gurney (1780–1845)

English Quaker philanthropist. From 1813 she began to visit and teach the women in Newgate Prison who lived with their children in terrible conditions. She formed an association for the improvement of conditions for female prisoners in 1817, and worked with her brother, **Joseph Gurney** (1788–1847), on an 1819 report on prison reform. She was a pioneer for higher nursing standards and the education of working women.

## Fry, Roger (1866–1934)

English artist and art critic. An admirer of the French painter Paul Cézanne, he championed Post-Impressionism in Britain, expounding the theory of 'significant form' and colour as the criteria for true art. He was a member of the Bloomsbury Group and founded the ◊ Omega Workshops to improve design and to encourage young artists. His critical essays, which were very influential in the 1920s and 1930s, are contained in *Vision and Design* (1920).

## Furness

Peninsula in northwest England, between the Irish Sea and Morecambe Bay, formerly a detached northern portion of Lancashire, separated from the main part by Morecambe Bay. In 1974 it was included in the new county of ◊ Cumbria.

The peninsula is associated with the Cistercian monks of **Furness Abbey**, who planted trees to provide charcoal for the iron industry, and began the reclamation of the nearby marshes. The abbey lies to the northeast of Barrow-in-Furness. It was originally founded in 1123 by Savignac monks and was absorbed by the Cistercian order in 1147. The foundation acquired extensive property in Cumbria, the Isle of Man, and Ireland, and became the second most wealthy Cistercian monastery in Britain after Fountains Abbey. In 1537 the abbey was the first large foundation to be closed in the Dissolution of the Monasteries and it fell into disrepair. Remains include one end of the church, late Norman arches of the cloisters, and the adjoining Early English chapter house.

## Gaelic language

Member of the Celtic branch of the Indo-European language family, spoken in Ireland, Scotland, and (until 1974) the Isle of Man. Gaelic has been in decline for several centuries, though efforts are being made to keep it alive, for example by means of the government's Gaelic Broadcasting Fund, established in 1993, which subsidises television and radio programmes in Gaelic for transmission in Scotland.

In Scotland in 1991 there were about 70,000 speakers of Gaelic (1.4% of the population), concentrated in the Western Isles and in parts of the northwest coast. See also ◊Scottish Gaelic literature.

## Gainsborough, Thomas (1727–1788)

English landscape and portrait painter. In 1760 he settled in Bath, where his elegant and subtly characterized society portraits brought great success. In 1774 he went to London, becoming one of the original members of the Royal Academy and the principal rival of Joshua Reynolds. He was one of the first British artists to follow the Dutch example in painting realistic landscapes rather than imaginative Italianate scenery, as in *Mr and Mrs Andrews* (about 1750; National Gallery, London).

Although he learned painting and etching in London, Gainsborough was largely self-taught. His method of painting – what Reynolds called 'those odd scratches and marks ... this chaos which by a kind of magic at a certain distance assumes form' – is full of temperament and life. The portrait of his wife (Courtauld Institute, London) and *The Morning Walk* (National Gallery) show his sense of character and the elegance of his mature work. His *Blue Boy* (San Marino, California) is a homage to van Dyck. The landscapes he painted for his own pleasure took on

an imaginary look; rhythmic in movement, the *Harvest Wagon* (Birmingham) already has this Utopian character. A foundation member of the Royal Academy and elected to its Council in 1774, Gainsborough moved that year to Schomberg House in London. Influenced in landscape by Rubens now, rather than by Ruisdael as in his youth, he produced the massing and play of light seen in *The Market Cart* (1786; National Gallery).

## Galsworthy, John (1867–1933)

English novelist and dramatist. His work examines the social issues of the Victorian period. He wrote *The Forsyte Saga* (1906–22) and its sequel,

## Irish Gaelic Words Borrowed into English

| leprechaun | 17th century | ('small body') a small and often mischievous supernatural creature |
|---|---|---|
| banshee | 18th century | ('fairy woman') a supernatural female being who wails under the windows of a house where death is imminent |
| blarney | 18th century | flattering or cajoling talk; to talk in such a way, named after a village near Cork |
| céilidh | 19th century | ('companion'; also in Scotland) an informal social gathering, with conversation, music, dancing and story-telling |
| smithereens | 19th century | (unknown origin) small fragments |

the novels collectively entitled *A Modern Comedy* (1929). His plays include *The Silver Box* (1906). He won the Nobel Prize for Literature in 1932.

Galsworthy first achieved recognition with *The Silver Box* and *The Man of Property* (1906), the first instalment of the *Forsyte Saga* series, which also includes *In Chancery* (1920) and *To Let* (1921). Soames Forsyte, the central character, is the embodiment of Victorian values and feeling for property, and the wife whom he also 'owns' – Irene – was based on Galsworthy's wife.

## garden city

Town built in a rural area and designed to combine town and country advantages, with its own industries, controlled developments, private and public gardens, and cultural centre. The idea was proposed by Ebenezer ◊Howard, who in 1899 founded the Garden City Association, which established the first garden city: Letchworth in Hertfordshire.

A second, Welwyn, 35 km/22 mi from London, was started in 1919. The New Towns Act 1946 provided the machinery for developing ◊new towns on some of the principles advocated by Howard (for example Stevenage, begun in 1947).

## gardening

A national obsession, pride in one's garden being perhaps linked to the ethos 'an Englishman's home is his castle'. See ◊leisure, for a feature on The British at Play, giving statistics on gardening, and a chronology of some key dates, below.

---

*Our England is a garden, and such gardens are not made / By singing:– 'Oh, how beautiful!' and sitting in the shade.*

**Rudyard Kipling** English writer.
*The Glory of the Garden* (1911)

---

## Garrick, David (1717–1779)

English actor and theatre manager. From 1747 he became joint licensee of the Drury Lane Theatre, London, with his own company, and instituted a number of significant theatrical conventions including concealed stage lighting and banishing spectators from the stage. He played Shakespearean characters such as Richard III, King Lear, Hamlet, and Benedick, and collaborated with George Colman (1732–1794) in writing the play *The Clandestine Marriage* (1766). He retired from the stage in 1766, but continued as a manager.

## Gardens and Gardening: Some key dates

**1621** The Oxford Physic Garden is opened. The first botanical garden in Britain, it also contains the first rudimentary greenhouse in Britain, a stone greenhouse for the preservation of delicate plants.

**1662** Greenwich Park in London, designed by the French garden designer André Le Nôtre, is completed.

*c.* **1700** Dutch garden designs are fashionable in England.

**1724** Horticulturalist Stephen Switzer constructs the first all-glass hothouse in Britain, for the growing of grapes on the Duke of Rutland's estate.

**1733** The Serpentine, a curving lake in Hyde Park, London, is laid out for Queen Caroline.

**1734** The gardens and garden buildings of Rousham in Oxfordshire, designed by the English architect William Kent, are completed.

**1750** The English artist Francis Hayman completes his decoration of the pavilions at Vauxhall Gardens, a fashionable pleasure park in London.

*c.* **1750** The English landscape gardener Lancelot 'Capability' Brown lays out Warwick Castle Gardens in Warwickshire.

**1759** The Botanical Gardens are founded at Kew, near London.

**1787** William Curtis sets up the first gardening magazine, the monthly *Botanical Magazine*, in London.

**1838** Regent's Park opens in London.

**1841** Kew Gardens, London, are opened to the public.

**1843** Sir Charles Isham starts the British affection for garden gnomes when he imports them from Nuremberg, Germany.

**1845** The tax on glass is dropped in Britain, enabling conservatories to become a feature of suburban houses.

**1895** The National Trust is founded in Britain to preserve country houses, parks, gardens, and areas of natural beauty.

**20–22 May 1913** The Royal Horticultural Society holds the first Chelsea Flower Show, in London.

**21 November 1936** *In Your Garden*, broadcast by the BBC, is the first regular gardening programme.

**1942** The 'Dig for Victory' campaign is started in the UK, encouraging the cultivation of gardens and public space to increase food production.

**1955–1967** *Gardening Club*, a practical guide for gardeners presented by Percy Thrower, is shown on British television.

**March 1979** *Gardening with Michael Barrett* is the first general interest programme to be made for sale on video in the UK.

**1992** The 'lost' gardens of Heligan, southern Cornwall are opened to the public, following restoration.

**Elizabeth Gaskell** English novelist Elizabeth Gaskell lived in Manchester. Set in the slums of the industrial towns of the region, her novels were among the first to portray the moral and social evils of industrialization. Corbis

## Gaskell, Elizabeth born Stevenson (1810–1865)

English novelist. Her most popular book, *Cranford* (1853), is the study of a small, close-knit circle in a small town, modelled on Knutsford, Cheshire, where she was brought up. Her other books, which often deal with social concerns, include *Mary Barton* (1848), *North and South* (1855), *Sylvia's Lovers* (1863–64), and the unfinished *Wives and Daughters* (1866). She wrote a frank and sympathetic biography of her friend Charlotte ◊Brontë (1857).

The success of *Mary Barton* established her as a novelist; in this work she describes with insight and sympathy the life and experiences of working-class people.

## Gateshead

Port in Tyne and Wear, northeast England; population (1994 est) 127,000. Situated on the south bank of the River Tyne, opposite Newcastle upon Tyne, it was formerly a port for the Tyne coalfields and a railway workshop centre. Today it manufactures chemicals, plastics, and glass, with industries also in engineering, printing, and tourism.

*History*

The town received its first charter in 1164. It developed as a thriving port and centre of heavy industry during the 19th century. In 1849 a high-level bridge, 34 m/112 ft above river level, was built to carry road and rail traffic between the high ground on either bank of the Tyne. The town was severely damaged by fire in 1854.

*Features*

Metroland, in the Metro Centre shopping complex, is a major tourist attraction. As part of the Tyneside South Bank development (partly funded by the National Lottery), the Baltic Flour Mills are undergoing conversion into an international centre for the visual arts, the New International Art Gallery, scheduled to open in 2000. *The Angel of the North*, a steel sculpture 20 m/65 ft high overlooking Gateshead, by English sculptor Anthony Gormley, was erected in 1998. It is sited 5 km/3 mi from the town, and is Britain's largest sculpture.

## Gatwick

Site of Gatwick Airport, West Sussex, England, situated 42 km/26 mi south of central London. Designated as London's second airport in 1954, it is now one of the city's three international airports. Nearly 30 million passengers a year pass through its two terminals. A rail connection links Gatwick to Victoria Station, London.

*Life is a jest; and all things show it. I thought so once; but now I know it.*

**John Gay** English poet and dramatist. 'My Own Epitaph'

## Gay, John (1685–1732)

English poet and dramatist. He wrote *Trivia* (1716), a verse picture of 18th-century London. His *The Beggar's Opera* (1728), a 'Newgate pastoral' using traditional songs and telling of the love of Polly for highwayman Captain Macheath, was an extraordinarily popular success. Its satiric political touches led to the banning of *Polly*, a sequel. Bertolt Brecht (1898–1956) based his *Threepenny Opera* (1928) on the story of *The Beggar's Opera*.

## General Strike

Nationwide strike called by the Trade Union Congress (TUC) on 3 May 1926 in support of striking miners.

The immediate cause of the 1926 general strike was the report of a royal commission on the coalmining industry (*Samuel Report* 1926) which, among other things, recommended a cut in wages. The mine-owners wanted longer hours as well as lower wages. The miners' union, under the leadership of A J Cook, resisted with the slogan 'Not a penny off the pay, not a minute on the day'. A coal strike started in early May 1926 and the miners asked the TUC to bring all major industries out on strike in support of the action; eventually it included more than 2 million workers. The Conservative government under Stanley Baldwin used troops, volunteers, and special constables to maintain food supplies and essential services, and had a monopoly on the information services, including BBC radio. After nine days the TUC ended the general strike, leaving the miners, who felt betrayed by the TUC, to remain on strike, unsuccessfully, until November 1926. The Trades Disputes Act of 1927 made general strikes illegal.

## Geoffrey of Monmouth (c. 1100–1154)

Welsh writer and chronicler. While a canon at Oxford, he wrote *Historia Regum Britanniae/ History of the Kings of Britain* in about 1139, which included accounts of the semi-legendary kings Lear, Cymbeline, and Arthur. He is also thought by some to be the author of *Vita Merlini*, a life of the legendary wizard. He was bishop-elect of St Asaph, North Wales, in 1151 and ordained a priest in 1152.

## George

Six kings of Great Britain:

## George I (1660–1727)

King of Great Britain and Ireland from 1714. He was the son of the first elector of Hannover, Ernest Augustus (1629–1698), and his wife Sophia, and a great-grandson of James I. He succeeded to the electorate in 1698, and became king on the death of Queen Anne. He attached himself to the Whigs, and spent most of his reign in Hannover, never having learned English.

Parliament, seeking to ensure a Protestant line of succession to oppose the claim of the Catholic ◊James Edward Stuart, made George third in line after Queen Anne and his mother. He was supported upon his succession by the Whigs,

especially Stanhope, Charles Townshend, and Robert Walpole. The king grew more and more dependent upon his advisers as scandal surrounded him; his supporters turned against him, demanding freedom of action as the price of reconciliation.

## George II (1683–1760)

King of Great Britain and Ireland from 1727, when he succeeded his father, George I. His victory at Dettingen in 1743, in the War of the Austrian Succession, was the last battle to be commanded by a British king. He married Caroline of Anspach in 1705, and was succeeded by his grandson, George III.

Under Queen Caroline's influence, Robert Walpole retained his ministry, begun during the reign of George I, and until his resignation in 1742, managed to keep Britain at peace. The Jacobite rebellion of 1745 was successfully put down by George's favourite son, William Augustus, Duke of Cumberland.

## George III (1738–1820)

King of Great Britain and Ireland from 1760, when he succeeded his grandfather George II. His rule was marked by intransigence resulting in the loss of the American colonies, for which he shared the blame with his chief minister Lord North, and the emancipation of Catholics in England. Possibly suffering from ◊porphyria, he had repeated attacks of insanity, permanent from 1811. He was succeeded by his son George IV.

He married Princess Charlotte Sophia of Mecklenburg-Strelitz in 1761.

---

*The King's party and mine are like two rival inns on the road, the George and the Angel.*
**Caroline of Brunswick** Queen of George IV of Great Britain.
Remark made during her final attempt to be accepted as Queen, 1821

---

## George IV (1762–1830)

King of Great Britain and Ireland from 1820, when he succeeded his father George III, for whom he had been regent during the king's period of insanity 1811–20. In 1785 he secretly married a Catholic widow, Maria ◊Fitzherbert, but in 1795 also married Princess ◊Caroline of Brunswick, in return for payment of his debts. He was a patron of the arts. His prestige was undermined by his treatment of Caroline (they separated in 1796), his dissipation, and his extravagance. He was succeeded by his brother, the duke of Clarence, who became William IV.

### George V (1865–1936)
King of Great Britain from 1910, when he succeeded his father Edward VII. He was the second son, and became heir in 1892 on the death of his elder brother Albert, Duke of Clarence. In 1893, he married Princess Victoria Mary of Teck (Queen Mary), formerly engaged to his brother. During World War I he made several visits to the front. In 1917 he abandoned all German titles for himself and his family. The name of the royal house was changed from Saxe-Coburg-Gotha (popularly known as Brunswick or Hannover) to Windsor.

### George VI (1895–1952)
King of Great Britain from 1936, when he succeeded after the abdication of his brother Edward VIII, who had succeeded their father George V. Created Duke of York in 1920, he married in 1923 Lady Elizabeth Bowes-Lyon (1900–    ), and their children are Elizabeth II and Princess Margaret. During World War II he visited the Normandy and Italian battlefields.

### George, St (died c. 303)
Patron saint of England. The story of St George rescuing a woman by slaying a dragon, evidently derived from the Greek Perseus legend, first appears in the 6th century. The cult of St George was introduced into western Europe by the Crusaders. Feast day 23 April.

He is said to have been martyred at Lydda in Palestine in 303, probably under the Roman emperor Diocletian, but the other elements of his legend are of doubtful historical accuracy.

### Georgian
Period of English architecture, furnituremaking, and decorative art between 1714 and 1830. The architecture is mainly Classical in style, although external details and interiors were often rich in Rococo carving. Furniture was frequently made of mahogany and satinwood, and mass production became increasingly common; designers included Thomas Chippendale, George Hepplewhite, and Thomas Sheraton. The silver of this period is particularly fine, and ranges from the earlier, simple forms to the ornate, and from the Neo-Classical style of Robert Adam to the later, more decorated pre-Victorian taste.

Buildings of the period include many vast aristocratic mansions such as Holkham, Kedleston, Harewood, ◊Kenwood, and ◊Chatsworth; many Georgian houses; many churches of the new 'Protestant' type and Nonconformist meeting-houses; and important public buildings such as Chelsea Hospital and Somerset House.

There was keen rivalry during the second half of the 18th century between William Chambers, the upholder of Palladianism, and Robert ◊Adam, the practitioner of a more original style inspired by Greek and Roman archaeology.

John ◊Nash introduced **Regency** style, so-called because of its patronization by the Prince of Wales (later George IV) during his years as Prince Regent (1811–20). Decorous and refined, it is associated with an extensive use of stucco, and may be seen at Hove, Brighton, Weymouth, Cheltenham, Clifton and Tunbridge Wells, as well as in the terraces and mansions around 'the Regent's Park' in London. Examples of **Greek Revival**, which lasted for several decades abreast of the **Regency** style, include the Athenaeum Club, London (1827–30) by Decimus Burton; and several buildings in Edinburgh by William Henry Playfair.

### Giant's Causeway
Stretch of basalt columns forming a headland on the north coast of Antrim, Northern Ireland. It was formed by an outflow of lava in Tertiary times

**Giant's Causeway** The strikingly unusual rock formations to be seen at the promontory of Giant's Causeway, in County Antrim, Northern Ireland, are the result of molten basalt cooling rapidly some 60 million years ago. Their name derives from the legend that they are stepping stones used by a giant to cross the Irish Sea. Corel

which has solidified in polygonal columns. The Giant's Causeway and Causeway Coast became a World Heritage Site in 1986.

According to legend, the causeway was built to enable the giants to cross between Ireland and Scotland.

### Gibbon, Edward (1737–1794)
English historian. He wrote one major work, arranged in three parts, *The History of the Decline and Fall of the Roman Empire* (1776–88), a continuous narrative from the 2nd century AD to the fall of Constantinople in 1453.

He began work on it while in Rome in 1764. Although it was immediately successful, he was compelled to reply to attacks on his account of the early development of Christianity by a 'Vindication' in 1779.

### Gibbon, Lewis Grassic pen name of James Leslie Mitchell (1901–1935)
Scottish novelist. He was the author of the trilogy *A Scots Quair*, comprising *Sunset Song*, *Cloud Howe*, and *Grey Granite* (1932–34), set in the Mearns, south of Aberdeen, where he was born and brought up. Under his real name he wrote anthropological works and novels, which included *Stained Radiance* (1930) and *Spartacus* (1933). It was under his pseudonym, however, that he made his major contribution to Scottish literature in *A Scots Quair*. Ostensibly a story of a Scots peasant's education, series of marriages, and her son's involvement in the working-class struggle, it is also an analysis of the transition from a rural to an industrial economy, with its social consequences, and, at a third level, an allegory of Scottish history with the heroine personifying Scotland.

### Gibbons, Grinling (1648–1720)
Dutch woodcarver who settled in England around 1667. He produced delicately carved wooden panels (largely of birds, flowers, and fruit) for St Paul's Cathedral, London, and for many large English country houses including Petworth House, Sussex, and Hampton Court, Surrey. He was carpenter to English monarchs from Charles II to George I.

Features of his style include acanthus whorls in oak, and trophies of musical instruments in oak and limewood. Works in marble and bronze include a statue of James I (Whitehall).

### Gibbons, Orlando (1583–1625)
English composer. He wrote many sacred works for the Anglican church; *Cries of London* for voices and strings; instrumental fantasias and other works; and madrigals including *The Silver Swan* for five voices (1612). From a family of musicians, he became organist at Westminster Abbey, London, in 1623.

### Gilbert and Sullivan
Musical partnership of William Schwenk Gilbert (1836–1911) and Arthur Sullivan (1842–1900), often abbreviated to 'G & S'. Of their 13 light operas, many are still performed, often by amateur groups. Among the most popular are *HMS Pinafore* (1878), *The Pirates of Penzance* (1879), and *The Mikado* (1885). The operettas are marked by their catchy and memorable music by Sullivan, ranging from ballads to stirring choruses, and acute, timeless observation of social types and institutions from librettist Gilbert, sometimes using outrageous rhyming, and recitative required to be delivered at breakneck speed.

Encouraged to write together by theatrical entrepreneur Richard D'Oyly Carte, Gilbert and Sullivan found their collaboration met with immediate success, which led directly to the forming of the D'Oyly Carte Opera Company in 1878, and the commissioning of the series of light operas known today. The company still exists, albeit after some changes, not least its departure from the Savoy Theatre in London, which was built by D'Oyly Carte; 'the Savoy operas' is an alternative name for the G & S canon.

### Gill, Eric (1882–1940)
English sculptor, graphic designer, engraver, and writer. He designed the typefaces Perpetua in 1925 and Gill Sans (without serifs) in 1927, and created monumental stone sculptures with clean, simplified outlines, such as *Prospero and Ariel* (1929–31) on Broadcasting House, London.

He studied lettering at the Central School of Art in London, and began his career carving inscriptions on tombstones. Gill was a leader in the revival of interest in lettering and book design. He engraved for his own press, St Dominic, and for the Golden Cockerell Press. His views on art combined Catholicism, socialism, and the Arts and Crafts tradition.

### Gillingham
Largest of the Medway towns, in Kent, England; population (1991) 92,100. The town, which includes the former village of Rainham within its boundaries, merges with ◊Chatham. Gillingham was closely associated with the Royal Navy until the closure of the dockyard at Chatham in 1994.

The Corps of Royal Engineers, with its military museum (founded in 1912), is attached to the town. There is a Norman church in the old centre of Rainham village.

## Gillingham

Town in north Dorset, England, 6 km/4 mi northwest of Shaftesbury; population (1991) 6,700. Features of interest include the nearby Neoloithic Longbury Barrow; Lime Tree House, dating from the early 18th century; and Wyke Hall, a Tudor building that has been largely rebuilt. The annual Gillingham and Shaftesbury agricultural show is held at Motcombe, halfway between the two towns. Glove-making is an important local industry.

### History

In the Middle Ages Gillingham was the seat of a royal hunting lodge used by Henry I, Henry II, Henry III, and King John. The lodge was destroyed by Edward III in 1369 after it had fallen into disrepair. From 1769, Gillingham developed as a mill town for silk. With the arrival of the railway at the end of the 1850s, industries – including brick-making, printing, and cheese and soap production – brought local prosperity. The painter John Constable visited Gillingham several times in the 1820s and painted a number of pictures there, including *Old Gillingham Bridge* (the bridge has since been demolished).

## Gillray, James (1757–1815)

English caricaturist. Creator of over 1,500 cartoons, his fierce, sometimes gross caricatures satirized George III, the Prince of Wales, politicians, and the social follies of his day, and later targeted the French and Napoleon.

Initially a letter engraver and actor, he was encouraged to become a caricaturist by the works of William Hogarth, and he was celebrated for his coloured etchings, directed against the French and the English court. Gillray's works form a brilliant if unconventional history of the late Georgian and Napoleonic period. He became insane in later life.

## Giraldus Cambrensis, Welsh Gerallt Gymro (c. 1146–c. 1220)

Welsh historian, born in Pembrokeshire. He studied in Paris, took holy orders in about 1172, and soon afterwards became archdeacon of Brecknock. In 1184 he accompanied Prince John to Ireland. He was elected bishop of St Davids in 1198, but failed to gain possession of his see. He wrote a history of the conquest of Ireland by Henry II.

## Girl Guides

Female equivalent of the ◊Scout organization, founded in 1910 in the UK by Robert Baden-Powell and his sister Agnes. There are three branches: Brownie Guides (age 7–11); Guides (10–16); Ranger Guides (14–20); they are led by Guiders (adult leaders). The World Association of Girl Guides and Girl Scouts (as they are known in the USA) has some 9 million members (1998).

In the UK there are some 660,000 members of the Guide Association (1998).

## Girtin, Thomas (1775–1802)

English landscape painter, one of the most important watercolourists of the 18th century. His work is characterized by broad washes of strong colour and bold compositions, for example *The White House at Chelsea* (1800; Tate Gallery, London). He was a friend of J M W Turner.

In addition to scenes of the English countryside, such as *View on the Wharfe*, he created some excellent views of Paris (1801–02) which were subsequently made into soft-ground etchings, and on his return from France worked on a vast panorama of London (the *Eidometropolis*). Six sketches for this work are preserved in the British Museum. Though he died of tuberculosis at the age of 27, he made an important contribution to the development of English watercolour painting.

## Gladstone, William Ewart (1809–1898)

British Liberal politician, four times prime minister. He entered Parliament as a Tory in 1833 and held ministerial office, but left the party in 1846 and after 1859 identified himself with the Liberals. He was chancellor of the Exchequer 1852–55 and 1859–66, and prime minister 1868–74, 1880–85, 1886, and 1892–94. He introduced elementary education in 1870 and vote by secret ballot in 1872 as well as many reforms in Ireland, although he failed in his efforts to get a Home Rule Bill passed.

In his first term as prime minister he carried through a series of reforms, including the disestablishment of the Church of Ireland, the Irish Land Act, and the abolition of the purchase of army commissions and of religious tests in the universities.

## Glamis Castle

Fortress near Glamis village, Angus, Scotland, 20 km/12 mi north of Dundee. It has been the seat of the Lyon family, later earls of Strathmore, since 1372. Its central tower dates from the 15th century, but the castle was greatly enlarged from 1650 to 1696. Glamis is the legendary setting of Shakespeare's *Macbeth*.

The castle is also famed for the legend of a secret chamber, supposedly known only to each heir.

## Glasgow

Largest city in Scotland, and, as **Glasgow City**, a unitary authority, formed in 1995 from part of Strathclyde region; population (1996) 618,400. Lying on both sides of the River Clyde surrounded by hills, Glasgow is a major commercial centre which expanded rapidly with the growth of its heavy industry in the 19th century. After an extensive programme of redevelopment, the city has more recently been successfully promoted as a centre of culture and tourism. It was the 1990 European City of Culture and the 1999 UK City of Architecture and Design.

### History

The history of the city stretches back to a settlement on the Clyde which existed before St Mungo arrived in the 6th century to convert the Strathclyde Britons. Glasgow developed as an ecclesiastical and academic centre and became a successful merchant trading city in the 16th and 17th centuries. Situated in the west of Scotland, Glasgow was ideally placed when opportunities opened up in the 18th century for trade across the Atlantic and it prospered as an important port, handling large quantities of tobacco, sugar, and cotton. The city's iron, steel, and shipbuilding industries were the basis of its 19th-century growth. Large public buildings, parks, and libraries were established reflecting the city's rank as one of the world's foremost industrial cities, but at the same time large tenement estates emerged to accommodate the rapidly expanding population, and Glasgow became known for some of Britain's worst slum housing. The city suffered economic decline as the importance of its manufacturing and shipbuilding industries diminished after World War I, but a programme of slum clearance and regeneration in the 1970s and 1980s changed the face of the city which now boasts not only fine Victorian architecture but also some of Scotland's most important arts and cultural venues.

### Features

At the heart of the city are George Square and the redeveloped 18th-century Merchant City. The area to the west of the centre is the location of many of Glasgow's art galleries and museums,

**Glasgow** The skyline of Glasgow, Scotland's largest and most populous city. Glasgow was once famous as a centre of heavy industry, shipbuilding, and engineering, and infamous as the site of some of Britain's worst slum tenement housing. With the decline of manufacturing and the clearance of the slums, the city has successfully marketed itself since the 1980s as a tourist centre, with attractions such as the eclectic Burrell Collection of art treasures. Hamish Williamson/Collections

while south of the city is Pollock Country Park. The city is home to many performing arts organizations including the Royal Scottish National Orchestra, Scottish Opera, and Scottish Ballet. It has many concert venues including The Glasgow Royal Concert Hall, and its theatres include the Theatre Royal, the City Hall, and the King's Theatre. Glasgow is the site of three universities: the University of Glasgow, established in 1451, Strathclyde University (1964), and Glasgow Caledonian University. The city is also home to the Royal Scottish Academy of Music. There are over 70 parks and three football stadia, including the new National Stadium at Hampden Park, a Millennium Commission landmark project.

*Art galleries and museums*

Glasgow's many galleries include the outstanding Burrell Collection in Pollock Park, which opened in 1984. Kelvingrove Art Gallery and Museum is noted for its collection of European painting from the 15th century onwards. The Hunterian Art Gallery has an important collection of work by James McNeill Whistler (1834–1903), as well as a large collection of prints and modern Scottish art. The Glasgow School of Art (1897–1909) is considered to be the finest architectural work of Charles Rennie Mackintosh. Other galleries include the Glasgow Gallery of Modern Art in Stirling's Library. Provand's Lordship (1475) is the oldest house in the city and Tenement House and the People's Palace (1898) reflect Glasgow's social history.

*Glasgow Cathedral*

Built on the site of a chapel built by St Mungo in the 6th century, the present cathedral, situated northeast of the city centre, dates mainly from the 13th century. Built in the Early English style, the cathedral is designed in the form of a Latin cross. It was used after the Reformation as three separate churches: the Inner High, occupying the choir; the Outer High, occupying the nave; and the Laigh (Low) or Barony, occupying the crypt. The rood screen and the unfinished south transept were added in the 15th century. St Mungo is buried in the lower church.

## Glasgow School

Either of two distinct groups of Scottish artists. The earlier of the two groups, also known as the **Glasgow Boys**, was a loose association of late-19th-century artists influenced by the Barbizon School and Impressionism. Leading members were James Guthrie and John ◊Lavery. The later, more important group was part of the Art

Nouveau movement, and included Charles Rennie ◊Mackintosh.

## Glasse, Hannah (1708–1770)

British cookery writer whose *The Art of Cookery made Plain and Easy*, first published in 1747 and in print until 1824, is regarded as the first classic recipe book in Britain.

She was the most influential British cookery writer before ◊Mrs Beeton.

## Glastonbury

Market town in Somerset, southwest England, on the River Brue, 8 km/5 mi southwest of Wells; population (1996 est) 8,100. Tourism is important. **Glastonbury Tor**, a hill crowned by a ruined 14th-century church tower, rises to 159 m̄/522 ft. ◊Glastonbury lake village, occupied from around 150 BC to AD 50, lies 5 km/3 mi to the northwest.

**Glastonbury Abbey**, originally established in the 4th or 5th century, is thought to be on the site of the earliest Christian foundation in England, traditionally established by St Joseph of Arimathaea in about AD 63. Glastonbury has been associated with ◊Avalon, said in Celtic mythology to have been the burial place of the legendary King Arthur and Queen Guinevere. The **Glastonbury Festival** is a pop music festival held outside the town most Junes.

## Glastonbury lake village

English Iron Age settlement near Godney, 5 km/3 mi northwest of Glastonbury, Somerset, in the Somerset Levels. Occupied from around 150 BC to AD 50, the lake dwelling was sited in the former marshy seas around **Glastonbury Tor,** and constructed on an artificial island of wooden piles. At its greatest extent the village contained 18 round houses, supporting about 200 people.

Peaty wetland soils have preserved numerous artefacts indicating a prosperous Celtic society; finds include jewellery, pottery, cooking utensils, and farming, hunting, fishing, and weaving implements, many exhibiting the influences of La Tène culture. The Glastonbury Lake Village Museum is housed in the 15th-century Tribunal, Glastonbury.

The settlement was discovered in 1892 by Arthur Bulleid, and a couple of smaller satellite sites have also been identified.

## glebe

Landed endowment of a parish church, designed to support the priest. It later became necessary to supplement this with taxation.

## glee

Part song, usually for male voices, in not less than three parts, much cultivated by English composers in the 18th and early 19th centuries. The word is derived from the Anglo-Saxon *gliw* ('entertainment'), particularly musical entertainment. Webbe, Stevens, Callcott, Horsley, Attwood, Battishill, Cooke, and others cultivated the glee.

## Glencoe

Valley in the Highland unitary authority, Scotland, extending 16 km/10 mi east from Rannoch Moor to Loch Leven. The mountains rise steeply on either side to over 1,000 m/3,300 ft, and the River Coe flows through the valley. Thirty-eight members of the Macdonald clan were massacred in Glencoe on 13 February 1692 by government troops led by Robert Campbell of Glenlyon; 300 escaped.

The area is popular for winter sports and rock-climbing. The Glencoe chair-lift and ski area lies just beyond the glen on the western side of Rannoch Moor.

## Glendower, Owen Welsh **Owain Glyndwr** (c. 1359–c. 1416)

Welsh nationalist leader of a successful revolt against the English in North Wales, who defeated Henry IV in three campaigns 1400–02, although Wales was reconquered 1405–13. Glendower disappeared in 1416 after some years of guerrilla warfare.

## Gleneagles

Glen in Perth and Kinross, Scotland, 2 km/1 mi south of Auchterarder, famous for its golf courses, hotel, and for the **Gleneagles Agreement**, formulated in 1977 at the Gleneagles Hotel by Commonwealth heads of government, that 'every practical step (should be taken) to discourage contact or competition by their nationals' with South Africa, in opposition to apartheid.

## Globe Theatre

17th-century London theatre, octagonal and open to the sky, near Bankside, Southwark, where many of Shakespeare's plays were performed by Richard Burbage and his company. It was burned down in 1613, rebuilt in 1614, and pulled down

**Globe Theatre** In 1989, excavations on the south bank of the River Thames at Bankside in London unearthed the foundations of the Globe Theatre, where most of William Shakespeare's plays were performed during his lifetime. This replica theatre was built on a site close to the original, with the help of funds from the National Lottery. It was completed in 1997, and plays are now regularly staged there. Richard Kalina/Shakespeare's Globe

in 1644. The reconstructed Globe Theatre was opened to the public in August 1996, largely due to the campaigning efforts of actor Sam Wanamaker. Mark ◊Rylance was appointed the first artistic director of the Globe in 1995.

The original theatre was built in 1599 by Cuthbert Burbage. It was burned down after a cannon, fired during a performance of *Henry VIII*, set light to the thatch. The site was rediscovered in October 1989 near the remains of the contemporaneous Rose Theatre.

## Glorious Revolution
Events surrounding the removal of James II from the throne in 1689; see ◊Revolution, the Glorious, for a feature on the impact of William III's accession to the throne.

## Gloucester, Roman Glevum
City, port, and administrative headquarters of Gloucestershire, southwest England, on the River Severn, 67 km/42 mi northeast of Bristol; population (1996 est) 106,800. It is a finance and insurance centre; timber mills and salmon fisheries in the Severn are important resources.

*History*
Situated to the west of the Cotswold Hills, at the lowest crossing point of the Severn, the Roman settlement of **Glevum**, founded in the late 1st century AD, became one of the four *coloniae* of Roman Britain. In the 7th century it became the capital of the Anglo-Saxon kingdom of Mercia. Already a borough with a royal residence before the Norman Conquest, the town was granted its first charter by Henry II in the 12th century. Henry III was crowned in the cathedral in 1216. Supporting the Parliamentarians in the Civil War, Gloucester withstood a siege in 1643. The city became an important inland port after the opening of the Gloucester and Sharpness Canal in 1827, which linked the city to the Bristol Channel.

*Features*
The docks have been redeveloped and include the Robert Opie Museum of Advertising and Packaging (opened in 1984) and the National Waterways Museum. The City Museum and Art Gallery includes Roman relics found in the city, and the Folk Museum illustrates the social history of the area. The 12th-century church of St Mary-de-Crypt contains the tomb of Robert Raikes, who founded the Sunday School movement in Gloucester in 1780. Some 9 km/6 mi from Gloucester lies Prinknash Abbey, on the site of a former residence of the abbots of Gloucester, occupied since 1928 by Benedictine monks.

The Three Choirs Music Festival is held in Gloucester every three years, in turn with Hereford and Worcester.

## Gloucester Cathedral
A Benedictine abbey was built here in the second half of the 11th century on the site of an earlier Saxon abbey. Edward II was buried here in 1327 and his shrine became an important centre of pilgrimage. The wealth gained from the pilgrims funded the reconstruction of the abbey and church. From 1337 much of the church was remodelled in the Perpendicular style, although the Norman core was preserved. The cathedral's south transept is an early example of the Perpendicular style, and the cloisters (about 1370–1410) include the earliest example of fan vaulting in England. The cathedral's east window is the largest medieval stained-glass window in England, dating from the mid-14th century. The church received cathedral status from Henry VIII.

## Gloucestershire
County of southwest England, bordering Wales; population (1996) 556,300; area 2,640 sq km/1,019 sq mi. Known for its fertile countryside and the rolling Cotswold Hills with their honey-coloured stone villages, rural Gloucestershire is memorably described by Laurie Lee in *Cider with Rosie* (1959). The chief towns and cities are ◊Gloucester (administrative headquarters), Cheltenham, Cirencester, Stroud, and Tewkesbury.

*History*
Gloucestershire was important in Roman times. Camps were established at Gloucester, and also at Cirencester, a station on the Fosse Way known as Corinium, which became the second city of Roman Britain. There are Roman and early British remains, mainly in the Cotswolds. The county is mentioned in the Anglo-Saxon Chronicle of 1016.

*Physical*
The county falls into three distinct parts: the uplands of the Cotswolds in the east; the Severn valley with its rich pastures, known as the Vale; and to the west the historic Forest of Dean, which lies between the Severn and the River Wye on the border with Monmouthshire, Wales. The River Severn runs in a southwesterly direction through the western part of the county and is navigable as far as Sharpness, and between Gloucester and Stourport.

*Features*
Historic sites include the Roman villa at Chedworth; Berkeley Castle, where Edward II was murdered; Sudeley Castle, home of Catherine

Parr after the death of Henry VIII; the pre-Norman churches at Cleeve and Cheltenham, also known for its regency architecture; Gloucester Cathedral; Tewkesbury Abbey, with an early 12th-century nave; and Prinknash Abbey, where pottery is made. The Cotswold Farm Park, near Stow-on-the-Wold, has rare and ancient breeds of farm animals. There is a large arboretum at Westonbirt, established in 1829. Some parts of the Cotswolds, including Dover Hill and land around Chipping Campden, were bought by public subscription in the 20th century to ensure their preservation.

*Economy*

Agricultural products include cereals, fruit (apples and pears), cider, dairy products ('double Gloucester' cheese was formerly made here), and there is sheep farming. Woollen cloth, previously an important product, is now manufactured only in the Stroud Valley and at Dursley. Gloucestershire also has an aerospace industry, light engineering, manufacturing, and an expanding service sector.

## Glyndebourne

Site of an opera house in East Sussex, England, established in 1934 by John Christie (1882–1962). Operas are staged at an annual summer festival and a touring company is also based there. It underwent extensive rebuilding work in the early 1990s.

## Godden, Rumer (1907–1999)

English novelist, poet, and writer of children's books. Her first popular success was the romantic novel *Black Narcissus* (1939; filmed in 1946). Like several of her finest books it is set in India, where she lived for many years. Among her works of children's fiction is *The Story of Holly and Ivy* (1958).

## God Save the King/Queen

British ◊national anthem (see that entry for words). The melody resembles a composition by John Bull and similar words are found from the 16th century. It has also been attributed to Henry Carey. In its present form it dates from the Jacobite Rebellion of 1745, when it was used as an anti-Jacobite Party song.

## Gog Magog Hills

Chalk hills 6 km/4 mi southeast of Cambridge, England. At some 72 m/236 ft high, they are the most elevated point in the flat landscape of Cambridgeshire. They are named after two biblical figures. There are remains of an Iron Age fort at Wandlebury, on the crest of the hills, and traces of a Roman road.

## Golding, William (Gerald) (1911–1993)

English novelist. His work is often principally concerned with the fundamental corruption and evil inherent in human nature. His first book, *Lord of the Flies* (1954; filmed in 1962), concerns the degeneration into savagery of a group of English schoolboys marooned on a Pacific island after their plane crashes; it is a chilling allegory about the savagery lurking beneath the thin veneer of modern 'civilized' life. *Pincher Martin* (1956) is a study of greed and self-delusion. Later novels include *The Spire* (1964). He was awarded the Nobel Prize for Literature in 1983.

Golding's novels deal with universal themes and anxieties: evil, greed, guilt, primal instincts, and unknown forces. *Darkness Visible* (1979) is a disturbing book full of symbolism. The Sea Trilogy – *Rites of Passage* (1980) (Booker Prize), *Close Quarters* (1987), and *Fire Down Below* (1989) – tells the story of a voyage to Australia in Napoleonic times through the eyes of a callow young aristocrat.

Conceived as a parody of R M Ballantyne's idealistic classic *Coral Island* (1858), *Lord of the Flies* was initially turned down by 15 publishers; it sold over 2 million copies in the first ten years. It became a cult book and remains a prescribed text for many English-literature courses. The film version by Peter Brook (1962) was also highly successful.

## Goldsmith, Oliver (1728–1774)

Irish playwright, novelist, poet, and essayist. His works include the novel *The Vicar of Wakefield* (1766), an outwardly artless and gentle story which is also social and political satire, and in which rural honesty, kindness, and patience triumph over urban values; it became one of the most popular works of English fiction. Other works include the poem 'The Deserted Village' (1770) and the play *She Stoops to Conquer* (1773). In 1761 Goldsmith met Samuel ◊Johnson and became a member of his circle.

Johnson found a publisher for *The Vicar of Wakefield* to save Goldsmith from imprisonment for debt at the instigation of his landlady. With that book Goldsmith's reputation was secured. In 1768 his comedy *The Good Natur'd Man* had considerable success.

In 1773 he produced *She Stoops to Conquer*, also with great success. His last works were *Retaliation*, *The History of Greece*, and *An History of the Earth and Animated Nature*, all published in 1774.

## golf

Outdoor game in which a small rubber-cored ball is hit with a wooden- or iron-faced club into a series of holes using the least number of shots. On the first shot for each hole, the ball is hit from a tee, which elevates the ball slightly off the ground; subsequent strokes are played off the ground. Most courses have 18 holes and are approximately 5,500 m/6,000 yd in length. Golf developed in Scotland in the 15th century.

The ruling body of golf is the Royal and Ancient Golf Club (1754), at ◊St Andrews; the town has six golf courses. The British Golf Open competition began in 1860.

## Goodwin Sands

Sandbanks off the coast of Kent, England, about 10 km/6 mi east of Deal, exposed at low tide, and famous for wrecks. According to legend, they are the remains of the island of Lomea, owned by Earl Godwin in the 11th century.

They are divided into the North and South Goodwins, between which is the deep inlet of Trinity Bay. There are three lightships off the Goodwin Sands, and numerous lighted and unlighted buoys.

## Goodwood

Racecourse northeast of Chichester, West Sussex, England founded in 1802 by the third Duke of Richmond. Its races include the Goodwood Cup and Sussex Stakes, held in July/August. A motor-racing track used between 1948 and 1966 was reopened in 1998 for historic car and motor cycle racing, and since 1993 Goodwood has hosted the Festival of Speed, an annual celebration of classic motor-racing. Among the drivers and riders taking part at the reopening was Stirling ◊Moss, who had made his circuit racing debut at Goodwood in 1948.

## Gosport

Town and naval base opposite Portsmouth, Hampshire, southern England; borough population (1996 est) 76,000. Industries include engineering focused on defence research for the maritime industries. Following Ministry of Defence cutbacks in the late 1990s, some associated industries have closed and high-tech computer companies have become more important.

A ferry service connects Gosport with Portsmouth, 400 m/1,300 ft across the mouth of Portsmouth Harbour. The construction of a light, rapid-transport system link to Fareham and Portsmouth is backed by funds from the Millennium Commission.

### Features

The town centre is surrounded by fortifications developed in the 19th century, and its historic buildings include the 19th-century sea defences of Fort Brockhurst. The Royal Navy's Submarine World Museum reflects Gosport's historic association with naval operations.

### Naval base

Gosport was an important naval supply base, with ships' anchors, cables, powder magazines, chains, and sails being produced in the town. Priddy's Hard, established in 1770 as a powder magazine, became the Royal Navy's principal armaments depot; it continued to supply the navy until the 1990s, but is now scheduled to become a museum and leisure centre. Gosport naval base was one of the main D-Day embarkation points for troops in 1944.

## Gothic architecture

English architecture of the period beginning around 1200 to the mid-16th century. It is usually divided into the following styles: ◊Early English, or Early Pointed (about 1220–about 1300); ◊Decorated, or Middle Pointed (about 1300–about 1370); and ◊Perpendicular, or Late Pointed (about 1370–about 1540).

There was no abrupt line of change between these various periods, each merging into the next as new structural or decorative features were introduced. They demonstrate a gradual development of window design and vaulting and buttressing, whereby the thick walls and heavy barrel-vaults, the flat buttresses, and the narrow windows of the 12th century came to be replaced by bolder buttresses with thinner walls between them, thinner vaults supported on stone ribs, and much larger windows filled with tracery.

Gothic architecture died out very slowly, especially in Oxford, but from about 1640 onwards up to about 1830 all architecture was based on that of Rome, save for a few exceptions that led to the ◊Gothic Revival towards the end of that period.

## Gothic novel

Literary genre established by Horace ◊Walpole's *The Castle of Otranto* (1764) and marked by mystery, violence, and horror; other exponents were the English writers Anne ◊Radcliffe, Matthew 'Monk' Lewis, Mary ◊Shelley, and Bram ◊Stoker. In the 20th century elements of the genre are found in popular horror fiction and in the 'Neo-Gothic' works of Emma Tennant (1938– ) and Angela ◊Carter.

## Gothic Revival

The resurgence of interest in Gothic architecture, as displayed in the late 18th and 19th centuries. Gothic Revival buildings include Charles Barry and Augustus Pugin's Houses of Parliament (1836–65) and Gilbert Scott's St Pancras Station Hotel (1868–74) in London.

The growth of Romanticism led some writers, artists, and antiquaries to embrace a fascination with Gothic forms that emphasized the supposedly bizarre and grotesque aspects of the Middle Ages. During the Victorian period, however, a far better understanding of Gothic forms was achieved, and this resulted in some impressive Neo-Gothic architecture, as well as some desecration of genuine Gothic churches in the name of 'restoration'.

## government

The United Kingdom is a classic example of a constitutional monarchy based on a system of parliamentary government. There is no written constitution, the main features being contained in individual pieces of legislation and certain practices followed by successive governments which are regarded as constitutional conventions. Cabinet government, by which the ministers holding the highest executive offices decide government policy, is at the heart of the system, and is founded on convention; the relationship between the monarch, as head of state, and the prime minister, as head of government, is similarly based.

In theory this makes the unwritten constitution extremely flexible. In practice, however, it is as rigid as if it were written, and more rigid than many that have been formally set down. The features that provide this rigidity, as well as ensuring political stability, are the fact that Parliament is sovereign, in that it is free to make and unmake any laws that it chooses, and the concept of the rule of law, which says that all governments are subject to the laws which Parliament makes, as interpreted by the courts.

The Queen is one part of the trinity of Parliament, the other parts being the two legislative and debating chambers, the House of Lords and the House of Commons. Since becoming a member of the European Union (EU) the supremacy of the UK Parliament has been challenged by the superior laws of the EU and it has become clear that, as long as it continues in membership, domestic legislation can in certain circumstances be overridden by that of the EU as a whole. Since 1997 control over the setting of interest rates has been conceded to the independent Bank of England, while other powers have been devolved to the new 'national assemblies' in Scotland, Wales, and Northern Ireland (though the latter was suspended in February 2000 after a stalemate over IRA weapons decommissioning).

### The House of Commons

The House of Commons has 659 members, elected by universal adult suffrage (all people over 18 having the vote), from single-member geographical constituencies, each constituency containing on average about 65,000 electors. Although the House of Lords (see below) is termed the Upper House, its powers, in relation to those of the Commons, have been steadily reduced so that now it has no control over financial legislation and merely a delaying power of a year over other bills.

Before an act of Parliament becomes law it must pass through a five-stage process in each chamber – first reading, second reading, committee stage, report stage, and third reading – and then receive the formal royal assent. Bills, other than financial ones, can be introduced in either House, but most begin in the Commons.

The monarch appoints the prime minister on

## UK Government Departments

| | |
|---|---|
| Agriculture, Fisheries, and Food (Ministry of) | International Development (formerly the Overseas Development Agency – ODA) |
| Cabinet Office (Office of Public Service) | Lord Chancellor's Department |
| Culture, Media, and Sport | Northern Ireland Office |
| Defence | Scotland Office |
| Education and Employment | Social Security |
| Environment, Transport and the Regions | Trade and Industry |
| Foreign and Commonwealth Office | HM Treasury |
| Health | Wales Office |
| Home Office | |

the basis of support in the House of Commons and he or she, in turn, chooses and presides over a cabinet. The simple voting system favours two-party politics and both chambers of Parliament are physically designed to accommodate two parties, the government, sitting on one side of the presiding speaker, and the opposition on the other. No matter how many parties are represented in Parliament only one, that with the second largest number of seats in the Commons, is recognized as the official opposition, and its leader is paid a salary out of public funds and provided with appropriate office facilities within the Palace of Westminister, as the Houses of Parliament are called.

### The House of Lords

The House of Lords has historically had three main kinds of members: those there by accident of birth into the peerage, known as hereditary peers; those there because of some office they hold; and those who are appointed to the House to serve for life, known as the life peers.

In 1997 the newly elected Labour government announced plans for a major reform of the House of Lords, in the interest of greater democracy; the long-term aim is to create a democratically elected second chamber. Accordingly, in 1999 the House of Commons voted to remove the voting rights of hereditary peers, who were for the most part Conservatives or independent 'cross-benchers'. Around 630 hereditary peers and peeresses included dukes, marquesses, earls, viscounts, and barons, and they effectively left the House immediately.

Among those sitting in the House of Lords because of the position they hold are two arch-bishops and 24 bishops of the Church of England and nine senior judges, known as the law lords. The rest, numbering over 470, are the appointed life peers, who include about 100 women, or peeresses. Around 150 life peers align with the Labour Party; most of the rest support the Conservatives, or are independent.

## Gower Peninsula, Welsh Penrhyn Gwyr

Peninsula in ◊Swansea unitary authority, south Wales, situated between Swansea Bay and the Burry Inlet and extending into the Bristol Channel. Much of the coastline is the property of the National Trust, and there is tourism on the south coast; the north is marshy.

In the 11th century the area was overrun by the Normans, who built castles and churches; it was thoroughly anglicized in the west and south. It has notable scenery and contains picturesque ruins. As the coastline is principally composed of limestone, there are numerous caves, including Paviland Cave, the site of the important discovery of a skeleton of an old Stone Age man. The old Welsh kingdom of **Gwyr** was much more extensive and included land to the north.

## Grace, W(illiam) G(ilbert) (1848–1915)

English cricketer. By profession a doctor, he became the most famous sportsman in Victorian England. A right-handed batsman, he began playing first-class cricket at the age of 16, scored 152 runs in his first Test match, and scored the first triple century in 1876. Throughout his career, which lasted nearly 45 years, he scored 54,896 runs and took 2,876 wickets.

## Grahame, Kenneth (1859–1932)

Scottish-born writer. The early volumes of sketches of childhood, *The Golden Age* (1895) and *Dream Days* (1898), were followed by his master-piece *The Wind in the Willows* (1908) which became a children's classic. Begun as a bedtime story for his son, it is a charming tale of life on the river bank, with its blend of naturalistic style and fantasy, and its memorable animal characters, the practical Rat, Mole, Badger, and conceited, bombastic Toad. It was dramatized by A A Milne as *Toad of Toad Hall* (1929) and by Alan Bennett (1990).

Grahame was secretary of the Bank of England from 1898 to 1908.

## Grampian Mountains

Range that includes Ben Nevis, the highest mountain in the British Isles at 1,343 m/4,406 ft, and the Cairngorm Mountains, which include the second highest mountain, Ben Macdhui 1,309 m/4,295 ft. The region includes Aviemore, a winter holiday and sports centre.

The mountains are composed of granite, gneiss, quartzite, marble, and schists. The chief river flowing from the watershed north is the Spey; those flowing east are the Don and the Dee; those flowing south are the Esk and the Tay.

## Grand National

Horse-race held in March or April at ◊Aintree, Liverpool, England. The most famous steeple-chase race in the world, it was inaugurated in 1839 as the Grand Liverpool Steeple Chase, adopting its present name in 1847. The current course is 7,242 m/4.5 mi long, with 30 formidable jumps. The highest jump is the Chair at 156 cm/5 ft 2in. Grand National steeplechases based on the Aintree race are held in Scotland, Wales, and Ireland at Ayr, Chepstow, and Fairyhouse respectively.

## Grant, Duncan (1885–1978)

Scottish painter and designer. A pioneer of Post-Impressionism in the UK, he was influenced by Paul Cezanne and the Fauves, and became a member of the ◊Bloomsbury Group. He lived with the painter Vanessa Bell from about 1914 and worked with her on decorative projects, such as those at the ◊Omega Workshops. One of his finest portraits is *Vanessa Bell* (1942; Tate Gallery, London).

## Grasmere

English lake and village in the Lake District, Cumbria, associated with many writers. William Wordsworth and his sister Dorothy lived at Dove Cottage (now a museum) from 1799 to 1808, Thomas de Quincey later made his home in the same house, and both Samuel Coleridge and Wordsworth are buried in the churchyard of St Oswald's.

## Graves, Robert (1895–1985)

English poet and writer. He was severely wounded on the Somme in World War I, and his frank autobiography *Goodbye to All That* (1929) contains outstanding descriptions of the war. *Collected Poems* (1975) contained those verses he wanted preserved. His fiction includes two historical novels of imperial Rome, *I Claudius* and *Claudius the God* (both 1934). His most significant critical work is *The White Goddess: A Historical Grammar of Poetic Myth* (1948, revised 1966).

## Gravesend

Town in Kent, southeast England, 35 km/22 mi east of London, on the River Thames opposite Tilbury, with which it is linked by ferry; borough population (1991) 95,000. Gravesend is the site of the Thames pilot station, at the point where the Thames estuary narrows and river pilots take control of ships using the Port of London. Local industries include engineering, printing, and the manufacture of electrical goods and paper goods.

The town is mentioned in the Domesday Book of 1086 as **Gravesham**. The American Indian Matoaka Pocahontas died here in 1617 and was buried in St George's Church.

## Gray, Thomas (1716–1771)

English poet. His *Elegy Written in a Country Churchyard* (1751), a dignified contemplation of death, was instantly acclaimed and is one of the most quoted poems in the English language. Other poems include *Ode on a Distant Prospect of Eton College* (1747), *The Progress of Poesy*, and *The Bard* (both 1757). He is now seen as a forerunner of ◊Romanticism.

A close friend of Horace ◊Walpole at Eton, Gray made a continental tour with him from 1739 to 1741, an account of which is given in his vivid letters. His first poem, *Ode on a Distant Prospect of Eton College*, was published anonymously in 1747 and again in 1748 with *Ode on the Spring* and *Ode on the Death of a Favourite Cat* in *A Collection of Poems By Several Hands*, edited by Robert Dodsley (1703–1764). *Poems by Mr Gray* was published in 1768.

The *Elegy Written in a Country Churchyard*, begun in 1741, was immediately appreciated for its exquisite expression and natural pathos. Gray's works are few in number, yet he was a pioneer, a key figure in a transitional period, and the forerunner of Oliver Goldsmith and William Cowper in developing a style markedly different from that of the poetically dominant Alexander Pope; he was one of the first to celebrate the glories of mountain scenery and in this he was a precursor of the Romantics.

## Great Britain

Official name for ◊England, ◊Scotland, and ◊Wales, and the adjacent islands (except the Channel Islands and the Isle of Man) from 1603, when the English and Scottish crowns were united under James I of England (James VI of Scotland). With ◊Northern Ireland it forms the ◊United Kingdom.

## Great Exhibition

World fair held in Hyde Park, London, in 1851, proclaimed by its originator Prince Albert as 'the Great Exhibition of the Industries of All Nations'. In practice, it glorified British manufacture: over half the 100,000 exhibits were from Britain or the British Empire. Over 6 million people attended the exhibition. The exhibition hall, popularly known as the ◊**Crystal Palace**, was constructed of glass with a cast-iron frame, and designed by Joseph Paxton.

## Great Glen, or Glenmore

Valley in Scotland following a coast-to-coast geological fault line, which stretches over 100 km/62 mi southwest from Inverness on the North Sea to Fort William on the Atlantic Ocean. The ◊Caledonian Canal, constructed by connecting Loch Ness and the lochs Oich and Lochy, runs the length of the glen.

The Great Glen is a rift valley formed approximately 400 million years ago by volcanic activity and deepened by glacial activity around 10,000 years ago. Movement along the fault has made the rocks particularly susceptible to erosion, and the line is marked by a number of deep lochs.

## Great Yarmouth

Holiday resort and largest port in Norfolk, eastern England, at the mouth of the River Yare, 32 km/20 mi east of Norwich; population (1991) 56,200. Formerly a major fishing port, it is now a container port and a base for North Sea oil and gas. Tourism is important.

### History

Great Yarmouth was significant as a port in medieval times, and prospered in the 19th century from the herring-fishing industry and from its growth as a holiday resort. The town was attacked by German warships during World War I, and it suffered heavy damage from air raids during World War II; much reconstruction has since taken place.

### Features

The Rows in the old part of Great Yarmouth are narrow parallel alleys arranged on a medieval grid pattern. The area includes the 17th-century Old Merchant's House, and the 13th-century Tolhouse, once the town's court house and jail, and now housing a museum. The Fishermen's Hospital almshouses date from the early 18th century. The parish church of St Nicholas, founded in 1101, is one of the largest parish churches in England. There are remains of the 13th-century Greyfriars cloisters, and some parts of the medieval town walls survive, including some of the town-wall towers. Other features include the Elizabethan House Museum, Maritime Museum, and the Nelson Monument (1819). There are Roman remains at Burgh Castle nearby to the west. Great Yarmouth includes Gorleston on the other side of the River Yare.

## Greek Revival

Architectural style that arose in the late 18th-century with the opening up of Greece and its ancient architectural heritage to the West; until then Roman architecture had been considered the only true Classical style. British architects associated with Greek Revival include John Soane, John Nash, Charles Cockerell, Robert Smirke, and William Henry Playfair.

The publication of *Antiquities of Athens* (1762 and 1789) by Nicholas Revett (1725–1804) and James Stuart, and the arrival in London of the Parthenon sculptures (the ◊Elgin marbles) were major catalysts of the movement.

## Greenaway, Kate (Catherine) (1846–1901)

English illustrator. She specialized in drawings of children. In 1877 she first exhibited at the Royal Academy, London, and began her collaboration with the colour printer Edmund Evans (1826–1905), with whom she produced a number of children's books, including *Mother Goose*.

Since 1955 the **Library Association Greenaway Medal** has been awarded annually to an outstanding illustrated book for children published in the UK.

## green belt

Area surrounding a large city, officially designated not to be built on but preserved where possible as open space for agricultural and recreational use. The first green belts were established from 1938 around conurbations such as London in order to prevent urban sprawl. New towns were set up to take the overspill population.

The term generally refers to the 'outer ring' proposed in the Greater London Plan by Patrick ◊Abercrombie; Abercrombie envisaged a static population in this ring, with new towns beyond it.

## Greene, Graham (1904–1991)

English writer. His novels of guilt, despair, and penitence are set in a world of urban seediness or political corruption in many parts of the world. They include ◊*Brighton Rock* (1938), *The Power and the Glory* (1940), *The Heart of the Matter* (1948), *The Third Man* (1949), *The Honorary Consul* (1973), and *Monsignor Quixote* (1982).

Greene worked as a journalist on *The Times*, and in 1927 was converted to Roman Catholicism. When his first novel, *The Man Within*,

---

*God ... created a number of possibilities in case some of his prototypes failed – that is the meaning of evolution.*

**Graham Greene** English novelist.
*Travels With My Aunt* pt 2, ch 7

---

was published in 1929, he gave up journalism to write full time, but attained success only with his fourth novel, the thriller *Stamboul Train* (1932) which proved the success of a format used by Greene with equal skill in other works. They include *A Gun for Sale* (1936), *The Confidential Agent* (1939), and *The Ministry of Fear* (1943). *Brighton Rock*, about the criminal underworld, is in fact a religious novel, while *The Power and the Glory* explores the inner struggles of a weak, alcoholic priest in Mexico. A World War II period of service for the Foreign Office in Sierra Leone is reflected in the setting of *The Heart of the Matter*. Greene also wrote lighter, comic novels, including *Our Man in Havana* (1958) and *Travels with My Aunt* (1969).

He was one of the first English novelists both to be influenced by, and to recognize, the literary potential of the cinema. His work is marked by an almost cinematic technique and great visual power. Many of his novels have been filmed, and he wrote several screenplays.

## Greenham Common

Site of a continuous peace demonstration (1981–90) on public land near Newbury (then in Berkshire), outside a US airbase. The women-only camp was established in September 1981 in protest against the siting of US cruise missiles in the UK. The demonstrations ended with the closure of the base. Greenham Common reverted to standby status, and the last US cruise missiles were withdrawn in March 1991.

## Green Man, or Jack-in-the-Green

In English folklore, a figure dressed and covered in foliage, associated with festivities celebrating the arrival of spring.

His face is represented in a variety of English church carvings, in wood or stone, often with a protruding tongue. Similar figures also occur in French and German folklore, the earliest related carvings being in Trier, France, on the River Mosel (about AD 200).

## Greenock

Port and administrative headquarters of ◊ Inverclyde, western Scotland, on the southern shore of the part of the Firth of Clyde which runs northwest to southeast to meet the River Clyde; population (1991) 50,000. Traditionally associated with industries such as shipbuilding, engineering, chemicals, and sugar refining, the area now has computer and electronics enterprises. It was the birthplace of the engineer and inventor James Watt, who gave his name to the measurement of power.

The town's public buildings include the custom house (1818). The McLean Museum and Art Gallery houses items relating to the career of James Watt and to the shipping history of the town. The resited (in 1920) Old West Kirk, dating from 1591, contains windows by William Morris, Edward Burne-Jones, and Dante Gabriel Rossetti, and was the first church built after the Reformation.

The Free French naval base was at Greenock (1940–45); there is a memorial at Lyle Hill to the men of the Free French forces who died in the Battle of the Atlantic.

The town stretches along the river front for nearly 6 km/4 mi. The deep-water facilities of Greenock stimulated the movement of the centre of shipping activity downstream from Glasgow. The Clydeport authority plan to convert the former Scott Lithgow shipyard at nearby Port Glasgow into a retail and residential complex. Shipbuilding capacity is still retained via Clydeport container terminal.

## Green Party

Environmentalist party, founded in 1973 as the Ecology Party, and led, initially, by Jonathon ◊ Porrit. It adopted its current name in 1985 and campaigns for protection of the environment and the promotion of social justice.

The 'greening' of the larger political parties since 1989 has also been a factor in the Greens' failure to make an electoral breakthrough. In the 1992 general election the party lost almost 200 deposits and attracted only 1% of the national vote. In 1997 it contested fewer than 80 seats.

## Greenwich

Outer London borough of southeast Greater London, to the south of the River Thames; population (1991) 205,000. It includes the districts of ◊ Woolwich and Eltham.

*Features*

The ◊ Millennium Dome (1999); Queen's House (1637, designed by Inigo Jones), the first Palladian-style building in England; the **Royal Naval College**, designed by Christopher Wren in 1694 as a naval hospital, and used from 1873 as a college – the Naval College has now closed and the building is occupied by the National Maritime Museum and the University of Greenwich; the **Old Royal Observatory** (see ◊ Royal Greenwich Observatory) in Greenwich Park, founded in 1675 by Charles II. The source of ◊ Greenwich Mean Time, the observatory was moved to Herstmonceux, East Sussex, in 1958, and then to Cambridge in 1990, but the Greenwich meridian (0°) remains unchanged. The *Cutty Sark*, built in 1869 and one of the great tea clippers, is preserved as a museum of sail and the *Gipsy Moth IV*, in which Francis Chichester circumnavigated the world in 1966–67, is also here. In 1997 Greenwich was designated a World Heritage Site.

The Royal Naval College was built on the site

**The Dome** The Millennium Dome, opened to the public on 1 January 2000, has changed the skyline of Greenwich, at least temporarily. Built on a tract of derelict land, the vast arena is thirteen times the size of the Albert Hall, and is linked to central London by the extended Jubilee Line underground service. The Dome exhibition is scheduled to close on 31 December 2000. Simon Hazelgrove/Collections

of a former palace (the birthplace of Henry VIII, Mary, and Elizabeth I). Queen's House was designed for Anne of Denmark, the wife of James I, and it was completed in 1637 for Queen Henrietta Maria, wife of Charles I. Part of the buildings of the Old Royal Observatory have been named Flamsteed House after the first ◊ Astronomer Royal; other buildings of the observatory are the Meridian Building and the Great Equatorial Building. Greenwich Park, originally a part of Blackheath, was enclosed by Humphrey, Duke of Gloucester for his palace and later laid out for Charles II by André Le Nôtre, the French landscape gardener who planned the gardens at Versailles. Eltham Palace was built in about 1300; it was a royal residence from the time of Edward II until the reign of Henry VIII. The Great Hall, built during the reign of Edward IV, has a fine 15th-century hammerbeam roof. Occupied in the 1930s by members of the Courtauld textiles family, it has been faithfully restored in Art Deco style and is open to visitors.

## Greenwich Mean Time, or GMT
Local time on the zero line of longitude (the **Greenwich meridian**), which passes through the Old Royal Observatory at Greenwich, London. It was replaced in 1986 by coordinated universal time (UTC), but continued to be used to measure longitudes and the world's standard time zones.

## Gretna Green
Village in Dumfries and Galloway region, Scotland, where runaway marriages were legal after they were banned in England in 1754; all that was necessary was the couple's declaration, before witnesses, of their willingness to marry. From 1856 Scottish law required at least one of the parties to be resident in Scotland for a minimum of 21 days before the marriage, and marriage by declaration was abolished in 1940.

## Grey, Lady Jane (1537–1554)
Queen of England for nine days, 10–19 July 1553, the great-granddaughter of Henry VII. She was married in 1553 to Lord Guildford Dudley (died 1554), son of the Duke of Northumberland. Edward VI was persuaded by Northumberland to set aside the claims to the throne of his sisters Mary and Elizabeth. When Edward died on 6 July 1553, Jane reluctantly accepted the crown and was proclaimed queen four days later. Mary, although a Roman Catholic, had the support of the populace, and the Lord Mayor of London announced that she was queen on 19 July. She was executed on Tower Green.

## Grierson, John (1898–1972)

Scottish film producer, director, and theoretician. He pioneered the documentary film in Britain in the 1930s when he produced a series of information and publicity shorts for the General Post Office (GPO). The best known is *Night Mail* (1936), an account of the journey of the London–Glasgow mail train, directed by Basil Wright (1907–1987) and Harry Watt (1906–1987), with a score by Benjamin Britten and a commentary written by poet W H Auden.

## Grimaldi, Joseph (1779–1837)

English clown. Born in London, he was the son of an Italian actor. He appeared on the stage at two years old. He gave his name 'Joey' to all later clowns, and excelled as 'Mother Goose', performed at Covent Garden in 1806.

## Grimsby

Fishing port and administrative headquarters of North East Lincolnshire, England, on the River Humber, 24 km/15 mi southeast of Hull; population (1995) 89,400. It is one of Britain's major fishing ports and an important food-processing centre. The ports of Grimsby and Immingham, 10 km/6 mi up river, are managed jointly from Grimsby. The commercial dock at Immingham handles crude oil, iron ore, processed steel, coal, cars, fish, and container traffic.

### History

There is evidence of Roman occupation in the area. It is thought that by the late 12th century Grimsby was the main port on the Humber, however during the Middle Ages, and in Tudor and Stuart times, the prosperity of the town declined due to the silting up of the harbour. In 1800 a new dock was opened, in 1848 the Sheffield and Lincolnshire Railway Company extended the line to Grimsby, and in 1852 the Royal Dock opened. Through the rest of the 19th century Grimsby's prosperity grew rapidly, and it became one of the foremost fishing ports in the world. In 1912 a new commercial dock was opened at Immingham to relieve the congestion at Grimsby docks; and a new fish dock was opened in 1934. The National Fishing Heritage Centre is housed in the redeveloped Alexandra Dock area.

## groat ('great penny')

English coin worth four pennies. Although first minted in 1279, the groat only became popular in the following century, when silver groats were produced. Half groats were introduced in 1351.

## Gruffydd ap Cynan (c. 1054–1137)

King of Gwynedd 1081–1137. He was raised in Ireland, but came to claim the throne of Gwynedd in 1075 and helped halt Norman penetration of Wales. Although defeated and exiled by the Normans in 1098, he returned and was allowed to establish his kingdom after paying homage to Henry I. He led a rising against English dominance in 1135 until his death two years later. He is traditionally regarded as a patron of music and the arts and helped codify much of the previously chaotic bardic tradition.

## Gruffydd ap Llewellyn (died 1063)

King of Gwynedd. He had gained control of Gwynedd and Powys by 1039, Deheubarth by 1044, and extended his influence to Gwent by 1055. By the middle of the 11th century, most of Wales was either under his direct control or subject to his wishes, but his successors were unable to retain this dominance after his death. He conducted a series of raids across the English border and formed alliances with dissatisfied elements in Mercia and other English border areas. The English moved against him and defeated him at Rhuddlan in 1063, and he was killed by his own supporters.

## Guernsey

Second largest of the ◊Channel Islands; area 63 sq km/24.3 sq mi; population (1991) 58,900. The capital is St Peter Port. Products include electronics, tomatoes, flowers, and butterflies; since 1975 it has been a major financial centre. Guernsey cattle, which are a distinctive pale fawn colour and give rich, creamy milk, originated here.

Guernsey has belonged to the English crown since 1066, but was occupied by German forces 1940–45.

The island has no jury system; instead, it has a Royal Court with 12 jurats (full-time unpaid jurors appointed by an electoral college) with no legal training. This system dates from Norman times. Jurats cannot be challenged or replaced.

## Guildford

Cathedral city and county town of Surrey, southeast England, on the River Wey, 48 km/30 mi southwest of London; urban population (1991) 60,000; borough population (1996 est) 124,600.

### History

In about 880 Alfred the Great bequeathed the town to his nephew Ethelwold, and it began to develop as a defensive and commercial centre. Guildford was a royal mint town until 1100, and the earliest known charters of Guildford date to 1257. In medieval times Guildford prospered as an important centre of the wool trade, introduced by the Cistercians, and it was an important staging post in the 17th century – the railway replaced this service in 1845.

*Features*

Only the ruined 12th-century Norman keep remains of the castle, once a royal residence. The Guildhall has a 17th-century facade and a gilded clock dating from 1683. An inscription over the gate of the Royal Grammar School attributes its foundation to Edward VI in 1552, and the present building was begun about 1557. The Abbot's Hospital was founded in 1619 by George Abbot, archbishop of Canterbury. Battersea College of Advanced Technology was granted a charter as the University of Surrey in 1966. The Yvonne Arnaud Theatre, built on the banks of the Wey, was named after the French actress who lived in Guildford for many years and died here in 1958.

The Tudor mansion Sutton Place, 3 km/2 mi to the northeast of the city, was the 17th-century home of Richard Weston, a noted agricultural innovator and instigator of the 25 km/15.5 mi-long Wey Navigation (1651–53), built to transport grain, timber, gunpowder, and chalk. Sutton Place later became the home of J Paul Getty, the 20th-century US oil millionaire. Loseley House, an Elizabethan manor house, lies 2 km/1 mi to the southwest.

*Cathedral*

The modern brick-built cathedral (1936–68) is situated on Stag Hill, to the northwest of the city centre. Designed by Edward Maufe, it was the first entirely new Anglican cathedral to have been built in southern England since the Reformation.

## Guildhall

Council hall of the Corporation (governing body) of the City of London. The Great Hall of the present building dates from 1954, designed by Giles Gilbert ◊Scott, and is the venue for ceremonial banquets held by the lord mayor of London. A reference library of books, manuscripts, maps, and prints relating to London is housed in a separate building.

## guinea

English gold coin, notionally worth 21 shillings (£1.05). It has not been minted since 1817, when it was superseded by the gold sovereign, but was used until 1971 in billing professional fees. Expensive items in shops were often priced in guineas.

## Guinevere, Welsh **Gwenhwyfar**

In British legend, the wife of King ◊Arthur. Her adulterous love affair with the knight ◊Lancelot of the Lake led ultimately to Arthur's death.

## Guinness

Irish brewing family who produced the dark, creamy stout of the same name. In 1752 Arthur Guinness (1725–1803) inherited £100 and used it to set up a brewery in Leixlip, County Kildare, which was moved to Dublin in 1759. The business grew under his son Arthur (1767–1855) and under Arthur's son Benjamin (1798–1868), who developed an export market in the USA and Europe.

In the 1980s the family interest in the business declined to no more than 5% as the company expanded by taking over large and established firms such as Bells in 1985 and Distillers in 1986 (the takeover of the latter led to a trial in 1990).

## Gulf War

War between Iraq and a coalition led by the USA, of 28 nations, including the UK, 16 January–28 February 1991. Iraq had invaded and annexed Kuwait on 2 August 1990 on account of a dispute over a shared oilfield, and the price of oil, provoking a build-up of US troops in Saudi Arabia, eventually totalling over 500,000.

An air offensive lasting six weeks destroyed about one-third of Iraqi equipment and inflicted massive casualties. A 100-hour ground war followed, which effectively destroyed the remnants of the 500,000-strong Iraqi army in or near Kuwait. The UK deployed 42,000 troops during the war.

*Gulf War Syndrome*

Mystery illness suffered by over a thousand British soldiers who fought in the Gulf War. In 1999, a US virologist discovered antibodies to squalene in the blood of 95% of sick veterans tested. Squalene is a component of many experimental vaccines, indicating that troops may have reacted to untested vaccines.

## Gunn, Neil (1891–1974)

Scottish novelist. His first novel, *Grey Coast* (1926), at once brought him recognition and was followed by a series of others including *The Lost Glen* (1932), *Butcher's Broom* (1934), *Wild Geese Overhead* (1939), *Highland River* (1937) (Tait Black Memorial Prize), and *The Silver Darlings* (1941).

Gunn excelled in depicting the ordinary life and social and economic history of the Scottish

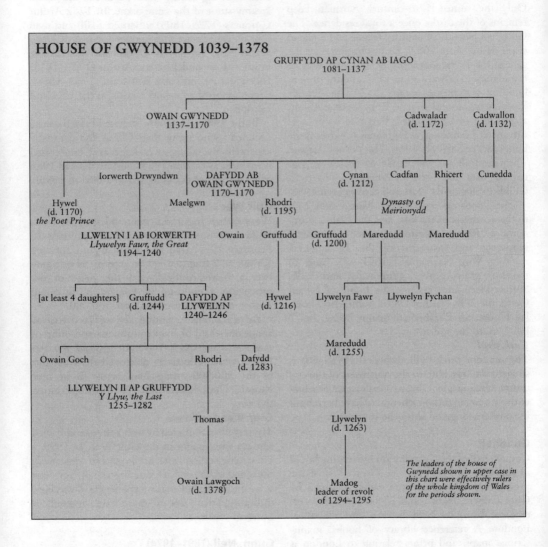

**HOUSE OF GWYNEDD 1039–1378**

GRUFFYDD AP CYNAN AB IAGO
1081–1137

OWAIN GWYNEDD
1137–1170

Cadwaladr
(d. 1172)

Cadwallon
(d. 1132)

Iorwerth Drwyndwn

DAFYDD AB
OWAIN GWYNEDD
1170–1170

Cynan
(d. 1212)

Cadfan

Rhicert

Cunedda

Hywel
(d. 1170)
*the Poet Prince*

Maelgwn

Rhodri
(d. 1195)

*Dynasty of
Meirionydd*

LLWELYN I AB IORWERTH
*Llywelyn Fawr, the Great*
1194–1240

Owain

Gruffudd

Gruffudd
(d. 1200)

Maredudd

Maredudd

[at least 4 daughters]

Gruffudd
(d. 1244)

DAFYDD AP
LLYWELYN
1240–1246

Hywel
(d. 1216)

Llywelyn Fawr

Llywelyn Fychan

Owain Goch

Rhodri

Dafydd
(d. 1283)

Maredudd
(d. 1255)

LLYWELYN II AP GRUFFYDD
*Y Llyw, the Last*
1255–1282

Thomas

Llywelyn
(d. 1263)

Owain Lawgoch
(d. 1378)

Madog
leader of revolt
of 1294–1295

*The leaders of the house of
Gwynedd shown in upper case in
this chart were effectively rulers
of the whole kingdom of Wales
for the periods shown.*

Highlands, and in interpreting the folk wisdom and psychology of the Celts.

## Gunpowder Plot

Catholic conspiracy to blow up James I and his parliament on 5 November 1605. It was discovered through an anonymous letter. Guy ◊Fawkes was found in the cellar beneath the Palace of Westminster, ready to fire a store of explosives. Several of the conspirators were killed as they fled, and Fawkes and seven others were captured and executed.

In 1604 the conspirators, led by Robert Catesby, took possession of a vault below the House of Lords where they stored barrels of gunpowder. Lord Monteagle, a Catholic peer, received the anonymous letter warning him not to attend Parliament on 5 November. A search was made, and Guy Fawkes was discovered in the vault and arrested.

The event is commemorated annually in England on 5 November by fireworks and burning 'guys' (effigies) on bonfires, and also by a ceremonial searching of the vaults before each State Opening of Parliament.

## Gwyn or Gwynn, Nell (Eleanor) (1650–1687)

English comedy actress from 1665. She was formerly an orange-seller at Drury Lane Theatre, London. The poet Dryden wrote parts for her, and from 1669 she was the mistress of Charles II.

## Gwynedd

Unitary authority in northwest Wales, created in 1996 from part of the former county of Gwynedd; population (1996) 116,000; area 2,546 sq km/983 sq mi. Most of the authority lies within Snowdonia National Park; it has a long coastline and the highest mountain in Wales, Snowdon. Many tourists visit Gynedd for walking and the coastal resorts of the Lleyn Peninsula. The main town is ◊Caernarfon (administrative headquarters).

*Physical*

A large part of the area is mountainous. Snowdon rises to 1,085 m/3,560 ft. Other mountains include Carnedd Llywelyn (1,062 m/3,484 ft), Carnedd Dafydd (1,044 m/3,425 ft), Glyder Fawr (999 m/3,278 ft), Aran Mawddwy (926 m/3,038 ft) and Cadair Idris (892 m/2,928 ft). There are several attractive river valleys, including the Dyfi (Dovey), Mawddach, and Maentwrog. There are over 50 lakes among the mountains, including the largest Welsh lake, Llyn Tegid (Bala Lake), and several waterfalls. The River Dee drains Bala Lake before passing out of the authority. The rural Lleyn Peninsula juts out into the Irish Sea and forms the northern limit of Cardigan Bay.

*Features*

Off the tip of the Lleyn Peninsula is the former pilgrimage centre of Bardsey Island, with its 6th-century ruined abbey. In Tremadog Bay is the fantasy Italianiate resort of Portmeirion, built by Clough Williams-Ellis. A rack railway to the top of Snowdon can be taken from the village of Llanberis, which also houses the Welsh Slate Museum. Other tourist centres and seaside resorts in the area include Aberdaron, Abersoch, Barmouth, Criccieth, Dolgellau, Harlech, and Pwllheli. Features of Pen y Bryn manor house at Aber, near Bangor, have been identified as surviving from the royal palace of Llewellyn I and Llewellyn II. The castles and town walls of King Edward I in the unitary authority are a World Heritage Site. The area includes Caernarfon, Criccieth, and Harlech castles. Caernarfon also includes the Sergontium Roman Fort Museum.

*Economy*

In addition to tourism, it is generally a region of mixed farming with sheep rearing on the hills and dairy and beef cattle on the lowland fringes. Quarrying for slate and granite were major occupations but have now declined, and light industries are found in the small towns. The Clogau mine at Bontddu supplies the gold for royal wedding rings. Lead, copper, and manganese have been worked near Dolgellau in the past.

## Gwynedd, kingdom of

Medieval Welsh kingdom comprising north Wales and Anglesey. It was the most powerful kingdom in Wales during the 10th and 11th centuries: its king ◊Gruffydd ap Llewellyn dominated Wales in the mid-11th century and nearly succeeding in uniting the Welsh. When the Normans invaded England, Gwynedd led Welsh resistance against Norman efforts to extend their dominance over the border, with mixed success. Llewellyn ap Gruffydd styled himself Prince of Wales in 1258, and the English king Henry III was forced to acknowledge him as such in 1267. Edward I rightly recognized Gwynedd as the key to subduing the Welsh and he launched a major offensive against Llewellyn in 1277, ultimately destroying the kingdom. Gwynedd was subsequently broken up and the lands of the ruling dynasty passed to the English Prince of Wales. See genealogy on page 206.

## Hackney, formerly St John at Hackney

Inner borough of north-central Greater London.
It includes the districts of Shoreditch and Stoke
Newington; population (1994) 192,500.

### Features

**Hackney Downs** and **Hackney Marsh**, formerly
the haunt of highwaymen, now a leisure area; the
Theatre, Shoreditch, site of England's first theatre
(1576); the Geffrye Museum, housed in early
18th-century almshouses and opened as a
museum in 1914; early 16th-century Sutton
House, housing the Early Music Centre; early
Georgian Christ Church, designed by Nicholas
Hawksmoor; Spitalfields market, moved here in
1991. The **hackney carriage**, originally a horse-
drawn carriage for hire, is so named because
harness horses were bred here in the 14th century.

### History

Proximity to the City of London and the railway
brought rapid development from the mid 19th
century and for a time it was a fashionable
residential area. Industries subsequently became
established, particularly along the River Lee.

In the 16th century Shoreditch was already a
suburb of London, and by the mid-18th century
its population was about 10,000. Industrialization
in the 19th century led to rapid development, and
before World War II it was one of the most
overcrowded areas in London. Since World War
II there has been a large increase in the ethnic
minority population, especially of Afro-Caribbean origin; ethnic minorities now form one third
of the total population.

## Haddon Hall

Castellated house, standing on the River Wye,
England, 3 km/2 mi southeast of Bakewell,
Derbyshire. The first house was fortified around
1195, but little of the Norman structure remains.

The main building periods were the years
around 1370 (the hall and parlour), early 15th
century to early 16th century (the chapel and
lower courtyard), and 1600 (the long gallery).
Between 1700 and the careful restoration of the
20th century, the building remained untouched.

Before the Norman Conquest, Haddon was the
property of the Crown, but William I granted it to
William Peveril. It has been successively in the
families of Avenell, Vernon, and Manners. The
house is now seasonally open to the public.

## Hadrian's Wall

Roman frontier system built AD 122–26 to mark
England's northern boundary and abandoned in
about 383; its ruins run 185 km/115 mi from
Wallsend on the River Tyne to Maryport, West
Cumbria. In some parts, the wall was covered with
a glistening, white coat of mortar. It was defended
by 16 forts and smaller intermediate fortifications.
It was breached by the Picts on several occasions
and finally abandoned in about 383.

In 1985 Roman letters (on paper-thin sheets of
wood), the earliest and largest collection of Latin
writing, were discovered at Vindolanda Fort.
Other sites with plenty of visible remains include
Chesters and Housesteads. Hadrian's Wall was
declared a World Heritage Site in 1987.

## Haggard, H(enry) Rider (1856–1925)

English novelist. He used his experience in the
South African colonial service in his romantic
adventure tales, including *King Solomon's Mines*
(1885) and *She* (1887), the best of which also
illuminate African traditions and mythology.

His first book, *Cetewayo and his White Neighbours*, appeared in 1882. In 1884 he published
*Dawn*, the first of his novels, and followed it with
others, most of which were very successful.

Haggard was deeply interested in agricultural
and rural questions; *Rural England* (1902) was a
valuable study. He was knighted in 1912.

**Hadrian's Wall** Marking the northernmost limit of the Roman colonization of Britain, Hadrian's Wall was constructed to prevent tribes such as the Scots and Picts from launching raids into northern England. Skilfully built to take advantage of the lie of the land, and guarded by troops stationed in small forts, the wall was an effective defence, though it was breached in AD 197, 296, and 367–68. Graeme Peacock/Collections

## haggis

Scottish dish made from a sheep's or calf's heart, liver, and lungs, minced with onion, oatmeal, suet, spices, and salt, mixed with stock, and traditionally boiled in the animal's stomach for several hours.

Haggis is traditionally served at Hogmanay (New Year's Eve) and on Burns' Night (25 January).

## Haig, Douglas, 1st Earl Haig (1861–1928)

Scottish army officer, commander in chief in World War I. His Somme offensive in France in the summer of 1916 made considerable advances only at enormous cost to human life, and his Passchendaele offensive in Belgium from July to November 1917 achieved little at a similar loss. He was created field marshal in 1917 and, after retiring, became first president of the ♭British Legion in 1921.

A national hero at the time of his funeral, Haig's reputation began to fall after Lloyd George's memoirs depicted him as treating soldiers' lives with disdain, while remaining far from battle himself.

## Halifax

Town in West Yorkshire, northern England, on the River Calder, 13 km/8 mi northwest of Huddersfield; population (1991) 91,100. Important in the woollen cloth trade since medieval times, the town prospered with the growth of the textile industry in the 18th and 19th centuries, and its museums and architecture reflect its industrial heritage. The town still produces textiles as well as carpets, clothing, and confectionery.

### History

It is likely that the cloth trade was established here in the late 13th century; local records for that period refer to 'websters' (weavers), 'walkers' (fullers), and 'litsters' (dyers). In the 15th century the parish of Halifax produced more cloth than anywhere else in Yorkshire. The street named Woolshops was once the site of the woolstaplers' (dealers) warehouses. The local weavers began making worsteds in the mid-18th century, the area expanded, and associated industries developed. With the arrival of the railways, Bradford became the chief textile-marketing centre for the area.

*Features*
The restored Piece Hall, built in 1779 as a cloth market, has 315 rooms and a colonnaded courtyard, and is now used for shops and a market. Shibden Hall, in Shibden Park, is a timbered mansion dating partly from the 15th century; it houses a museum containing 17th-century furniture, a collection of manuscripts relating to the district, early printed books, and court rolls. The Bankfield Museum (opened in 1887) contains art, textiles, archaeology, and natural history collections. Other features include the Calderdale Industrial Museum; the Perpendicular Gothic St John's Church; All Souls' (1857–59), designed by Gilbert Scott; and the town hall (1859–62), designed by Charles Barry, architect of the Houses of Parliament. Part of the original Halifax gibbet (a predecessor of the guillotine), used to behead cloth stealers (1541–1650), is preserved. Eureka! is an interactive hands-on museum of technology designed for children.

Open spaces include Shroggs Park, overlooking Wheatley Valley; Saville Park, with Albert Promenade overlooking Copley Valley; the People's Park; West Vale Park (with Clare House); Shibden Hall and Park; Akroyd Park; Belle Vue Park; and Manor Heath.

## Hall, Radclyffe pen name of Marguerite Radclyffe-Hall (1880–1943)
English novelist. *The Well of Loneliness* (1928) brought her notoriety because of its lesbian theme. It was successfully prosecuted for obscenity and banned in the UK, but republished in 1949. Her other works include the novel *Adam's Breed* (1926; Femina Vie Heureuse and Tait Black Memorial prizes) and five early volumes of poetry.

## Halley, Edmond (1656–1742)
English astronomer. He not only identified the comet that was later to be known by his name, but also compiled a star catalogue, detected the proper motion of stars using historical records, and began a line of research that, after his death, resulted in a reasonably accurate calculation of the astronomical unit.

Halley calculated that the comet sightings reported in 1456, 1531, 1607, and 1682 all represented reappearances of the same comet. He reasoned that the comet would follow a parabolic path and announced in 1705 in his *Synopsis Astronomia Cometicae* that it would reappear in 1758. When it did, public acclaim for the astronomer was such that his name was irrevocably attached to it.

He made many other notable contributions to astronomy, including the discovery of the proper motions of Aldebaran, Arcturus, and Sirius, and working out a method of obtaining the solar parallax by observations made during a transit of Venus. He was Astronomer Royal from 1720.

## hallmark
Official mark stamped on British gold, silver, and (from 1913) platinum, instituted in 1327 (royal charter of London Goldsmiths) in order to prevent fraud. After 1363 personal marks of identification were added. Now tests of metal content are carried out at authorized assay offices in London, Birmingham, Sheffield, and Edinburgh; each assay office has its distinguishing mark, to which is added a maker's mark, date letter, and mark guaranteeing standard.

## Hallowe'en
Evening of 31 October, immediately preceding the Christian feast of Hallowmas or All Saints' Day. Customs associated with Hallowe'en include children wearing masks or costumes, and 'trick or treating' – going from house to house collecting sweets, fruit, or money.

Hallowe'en is associated with the ancient Celtic festival of **Samhain**, which marked the end of the year and the beginning of winter. It was believed that on the evening of Samhain supernatural creatures were abroad and the souls of the dead were allowed to revisit their former homes.

## Halton
Unitary authority in northwest England, created in 1998 from part of Cheshire (principally Widnes and Runcorn); population (1996) 122,300; area 74 sq km/29 sq mi. Its chief towns and cities are Runcorn, ◊Widnes (administrative headquarters), and Ditton.
*Physical*
The River Mersey divides Runcorn from Widnes and Ditton.
*Features*
The Manchester Ship Canal and Bridgewater Canal reach the Mersey at Runcorn and St Helen's Canal joins the Mersey via a series of locks at Widnes. Catalyst, the world's first museum of the chemical industry, is at Spike Island, Widnes. Norton Priory Museum (Runcorn) is on the site of a 12th-century priory.
*Economy*
The local economy is based on industrial manufacturing, including chemicals, pharmaceuticals,

and plastics. There is also light engineering and production of scientific instruments.

## Ham House
Jacobean-style house at Petersham, near Richmond, Surrey, situated on the south bank of the Thames and owned by the National Trust. It was built in 1660 to an H-shaped Jacobean plan, and is notable for its historic contents, which are under the care of the Victoria and Albert Museum. These include Elizabethan furniture, and some portraits by Peter ◊Lely in the Long Gallery.

## Hamilton
Administrative headquarters of South Lanarkshire, Scotland, on the Clyde, 17 km/10.5 mi southeast of Glasgow; population (1991) 50,000. A declining industrial town, its industries include textiles, electronics, and engineering.

There is a racecourse, and between Hamilton and Motherwell is Strathclyde Country Park which is an extensive recreational area, with a theme park, recreational and sporting facilities. The artificial loch in the park was the site of **Hamilton Palace**, one of the largest palaces ever built in Scotland, which was finally demolished in 1927.

The ruins of Cadzow Castle (1744) lie 1.6 km/1 mi south of Hamilton in Chatelherault Country Park and are home to a breed of wild white cattle.

## Hamilton, Emma, Lady born Amy Lyon (c. 1761–1815)
English courtesan who in 1782 became the mistress of Charles Greville and in 1786 of his uncle Sir William Hamilton (1730–1803), the British envoy to the court of Naples, who married her in 1791. After Admiral ◊Nelson's return from the Nile in 1798 during the Napoleonic Wars, she became his mistress and their daughter, Horatia, was born in 1801.

## Hammersmith and Fulham
Inner borough of west central Greater London, north of the Thames; population (1991) 136,500.
*Features*
Hammersmith Terrace, 18th-century houses on riverside; Parish Church of St Paul (1631); Lyric Theatre (1890); Fulham Palace, residence of the bishops of London from the 12th century until 1973, one of the best medieval domestic sites in London, with buildings dating from the 15th century; Riverside studios; Olympia exhibition centre (1884); 18th-century Hurlingham Club; Wormwood Scrubbs prison.

## Hampden Park
Scottish football ground, opened 1903, home of the Queen's Park club and the national Scottish team. It plays host to the Scottish FA Cup and League Cup final each year, as well as semifinals and other matches.

Extensive rebuilding work began at the stadium in the early 1990s, to create a capacity of approximately 52,000. The Scottish National Museum of Football is scheduled to open here in 2000.

Hampden Park recorded a crowd of 149,547 for the Scotland versus England game in 1937, the largest official attendance for a football match in Britain.

## Hampshire
County of southern England; population (1996) 1,627,400; area 3,679 sq km/1,420 sq mi. The ◊New Forest, originally a Saxon royal hunting ground, attracts walkers and wildlife enthusiasts while the Solent, a sea channel between the mainland and the Isle of Wight, is a centre for yachting. The main towns and cities are ◊Winchester (administrative headquarters), Aldershot, Andover, Basingstoke, Eastleigh, Gosport, Romsey, and Lymington. Since April 1997 ◊Portsmouth and ◊Southampton have been separate unitary authorities.
*Physical*
The county is divided by Southampton Water, which opens into the Solent opposite the Isle of Wight. The South Downs end south of Petersfield at Butser Hill (271 m/889 ft). There are also hills in the northern part of the county along the boundary, which are some of the highest chalk downs in England; the highest point is Sidown Hill (286 m/938 ft). There are the remains of the minor forests at Bere, Woolmer, Alice Holt, and Waltham Chase. The New Forest (area 373 sq km/144 sq mi) is in the southeast of the county. The main rivers are the Avon, Ichen, and Test, which has trout fishing.
*Features*
In addition to the 2,500-year-old Celtic hill fort at Danebury, there are early fortified hilltop refuges at Old Winchester Hill; St Catherine's Hill, Winchester; Ladle Hill, Sydmonton; Beacon Hill, Burghclere; and Quarley Hill. The site of the Roman town of Silchester is to the north of Basingstoke. There are convent ruins at Netley, Beaulieu, and Titchfield; notable monastic churches still in use are Winchester Cathedral and Romsey Abbey. More recent features include Beaulieu (including the National Motor

Museum); Broadlands (home of the late Lord Mountbatten); Highclere Castle (home of the Earl of Carnarvon, with gardens by Capability Brown); Hambledon, where the first cricket club was founded in 1750; and Jane Austen's cottage at Chawton (1809–17), now a museum. New Forest ponies wander freely through villages and over roads in the New Forest.

*Economy*

Britain has onshore and offshore oil in the Hampshire Basin, and oil is refined at Fawley. There is high-technology engineering, a developed service sector, and retail and leisure industries. The Royal Navy has an establishment at Gosport, and the army has important military depots and training areas at Aldershot and Bordon in the northeast, and at Tidworth in the northwest.

## Hampstead

District in the Greater London borough of ◊Camden. It is the site of Primrose Hill, Hampstead Heath, and Parliament Hill (on which Boudicca is said to have been buried in a barrow); Hampstead Garden suburb was begun in 1907. Notable buildings include Kenwood (about 1616, remodelled by Robert Adam in 1764), containing the Iveagh Bequest of paintings; Fenton House (1693), with a large collection of early keyboard instruments; and Keats House (1815–16), home of the poet John Keats, now a museum. John Constable is buried in the churchyard. Many famous people lived here, including Martin Frobisher, John Galsworthy, Edward Elgar, Ramsay Macdonald, and Anna Pavlova.

## Hampton Court Palace

Former royal residence near Richmond, England, 24 km/15 mi west of central London. Hampton Court is one of the greatest historical monuments in the UK, and contains some of the finest examples of Tudor architecture and of Christopher ◊Wren's work. It was built in 1515 by Cardinal Wolsey and presented by him to Henry VIII who subsequently enlarged and improved it. In the 17th century William (III) and Mary (II) made it their main residence outside London, and the palace was further enlarged by Wren. Part of the building was extensively damaged by fire in 1986.

The last monarch to live at Hampton Court was George II, who died in 1760. During his life many of the Tudor apartments were pulled down and replaced. The palace was opened to the public, free of charge, by Queen Victoria in 1838 (though visitors now pay an admission fee).

Hampton Court has a remarkable collection of pictures housed in the Hampton Court Gallery.

## Hancock, Tony (1924–1968)

English lugubrious radio and television comedian. His radio show *Hancock's Half Hour* (1951–53) showed him famously at odds with everyday life; it was followed by a television show of the same name in 1956. He also appeared in films, including *The Rebel* (1961) and *The Wrong Box* (1966).

On radio he teamed up with other British comics including Hattie Jacques, Kenneth Williams, Bill Kerr, and Sid James. The latter would co-star with him in his television show, offering a more upbeat worldview than Hancock's pessimistic vision. Other film credits are *Orders are Orders* (1954), *The Punch and Judy Man* (1963), and *Those Magnificent Men in Their Flying Machines* (1965). He committed suicide.

## Handel, George Frideric originally Georg Friedrich Händel (1685–1759)

German composer, a British subject from 1726. His first opera, *Almira*, was performed in Hamburg in 1705. In 1710 he was appointed Kapellmeister to the elector of Hanover (the future George I of England). In 1712 he settled in England, where he established his popularity with such works as the *Water Music* (1717), written for George I, and, later *Music for the Royal Fireworks*, first performed in London in 1749. His great choral works include the *Messiah* (1742) and the later oratorios *Samson* (1743), *Belshazzar* (1745), *Judas Maccabaeus* (1747), and *Jephtha* (1752).

---

*What the English like is something they can beat time to, something that hits them straight on the drum of the ear.*

**George Frideric Handel** German-born British composer.
Quoted in Schmid *C W von Gluck* 1854

---

Visits to Italy 1706–10 inspired a number of operas and oratorios, and in 1711 his opera *Rinaldo* was performed in London. *Saul* and *Israel in Egypt* (both 1739) were unsuccessful, but his masterpiece, the oratorio *Messiah*, was acclaimed on its first performance in Dublin in 1742. Other works include the pastoral *Acis and Galatea* (1718) and a set of variations for harpsichord that were later nicknamed 'The Harmonious Blacksmith'.

## Hanover, House of

German royal dynasty that ruled Great Britain and Ireland from 1714 to 1901. Under the Act of ▷Settlement of 1701, the succession passed to the ruling family of Hannover, Germany, on the death of Queen Anne. On the death of Queen Victoria, the crown passed to Edward VII of the house of Saxe-Coburg. See the Hanover and Stuart genealogy on page 214.

## Hansard

Official report of the proceedings of the British Houses of Parliament, named after Luke Hansard (1752–1828), printer of the House of Commons *Journal* from 1774. It is published by Her Majesty's Stationery Office. The name *Hansard* was officially adopted in 1943. Hansard can now be consulted on the Internet.

## hansom cab

Two-wheeled horse-drawn carriage in which the driver's seat is outside behind the body, the reins passing over the hooded top. Originally called the 'patent safety cab', it was designed in 1834 by Joseph Hansom (1803–1882), who received £300 for his invention.

## Hardwick Hall

House in Derbyshire, England, given to the National Trust by the Treasury in 1959, with over 7,200 ha/17,783 acres, including the 6,500 ha/16,055 acre Hope Woodlands Estate. Elizabeth, Dowager Countess of Shrewsbury (Bess of Hardwick), commissioned the Hall in 1591, and many of her furnishings remain in the house. Hardwick has an unusually large expanse of window, and is built entirely of local materials.

## Hardy, Thomas (1840–1928)

English novelist and poet. His novels, set in rural 'Wessex' (his native West Country), portray intense human relationships played out in a harshly indifferent natural world. They include *Far From the Madding Crowd* (1874), *The Return of the Native* (1878), *The Mayor of Casterbridge* (1886), *The Woodlanders* (1887), *Tess of the d'Urbervilles* (1891), and *Jude the Obscure* (1895). His poetry includes the *Wessex Poems* (1898), the blank-verse epic of the Napoleonic Wars *The Dynasts* (1903–08), and several volumes of lyrics. Many of his books have been successfully dramatized for film and television.

Hardy was born in Dorset and trained as an architect. His first success was *Far From the Madding Crowd* and *Tess of the d'Urbervilles*,

**Thomas Hardy** English writer Thomas Hardy, photographed in the late 19th century. Now remembered chiefly for his novels, including *Tess of the d'Urbervilles* and *Jude the Obscure*, Hardy also wrote eight volumes of poetry and more than 40 short stories. Corbis

subtitled 'A Pure Woman', outraged public opinion by portraying as its heroine a woman who had been seduced. *Jude the Obscure* received an even more hostile reception, which reinforced Hardy's decision to confine himself to verse in his later years.

In his novels Hardy dramatizes with uncompromising directness a belief in the futility of fighting against the cruelties of circumstance, the inevitability of each individual's destiny, and the passing of all beauty. His poems, many of which are now rated as highly as the best of his prose fiction, often contain a compressed version of the same theme, either by seeing ahead from a happy present to a grim future or else looking back from the bitterness of the present to a past that was full of promise.

## Hargreaves, James (c. 1720–1778)

English inventor who co-invented a carding machine for combing wool in 1760. About 1764 he invented his 'spinning jenny' (patented in 1770), which enabled a number of threads to be spun simultaneously by one person.

The spinning jenny multiplied eightfold the output of the spinner and could be worked easily by children. It did not entirely supersede the

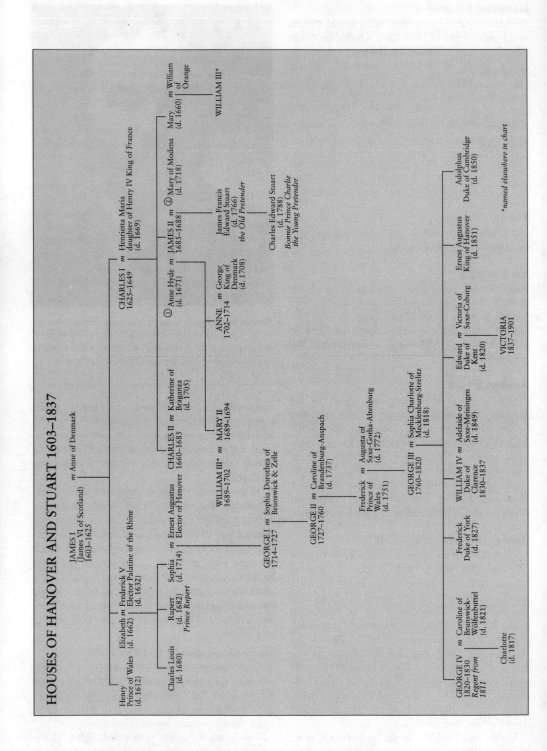

# HOUSES OF HANOVER AND STUART 1603–1837

JAMES I
(James VI of Scotland)
1603–1625 *m* Anne of Denmark

Henry
Prince of Wales
(d. 1612)

Elizabeth *m* Frederick V
(d. 1662)   Elector Palatine of the Rhine
            (d. 1632)

CHARLES I *m* Henrietta Maria
1625–1649    daughter of Henry IV King of France
             (d. 1669)

Rupert
(d. 1682)
*Prince Rupert*

Sophia *m* Ernest Augustus
(d. 1714)  Elector of Hanover

Charles Louis
(d. 1680)

CHARLES II *m* Katherine of
1660–1685    Braganza
             (d. 1705)

① Anne Hyde *m* JAMES II *m* ② Mary of Modena
(d. 1671)      1685–1688      (d. 1718)

Mary *m* William
(d. 1660)   of
            Orange

WILLIAM III*

James Francis
Edward Stuart
(d. 1766)
*the Old Pretender*

Charles Edward Stuart
(d. 1788)
*Bonnie Prince Charlie
the Young Pretender*

WILLIAM III* *m* MARY II
1689–1702      1689–1694

ANNE *m* George
1702–1714   King of
            Denmark
            (d. 1708)

GEORGE I *m* Sophia Dorothea of
1714–1727    Brunswick & Zelle

GEORGE II *m* Caroline of
1727–1760    Brandenburg-Anspach
             (d. 1737)

Frederick *m* Augusta of
Prince of    Saxe-Gotha-Altenburg
Wales        (d. 1772)
(d. 1751)

GEORGE III *m* Sophia Charlotte of
1760–1820      Mecklenburg-Strelitz
               (d. 1818)

GEORGE IV *m* Caroline of
1820–1830    Brunswick-
*Regent from*  Wölfenbüttel
*1811*        (d. 1821)

Frederick
Duke of York
(d. 1827)

WILLIAM IV *m* Adelaide of
Duke of        Saxe-Meiningen
Clarence       (d. 1849)
1830–1837

Edward *m* Victoria of
Duke of     Saxe-Coburg
Kent
(d. 1820)

Ernest Augustus
King of Hanover
(d. 1851)

Adolphus
Duke of Cambridge
(d. 1850)

Charlotte
(d. 1817)

VICTORIA
1837–1901

*named elsewhere in chart

spinning wheel in cotton manufacturing (and was itself overtaken by Samuel ◊Crompton's mule). However, for woollen textiles the jenny could be used to make both the warp and the weft.

## Haringey

Inner borough of north Greater London. It includes the suburbs of Wood Green, Tottenham, and Hornsey; population (1991) 202,200.

*Features*

Bruce Castle, Tottenham, an Elizabethan manor house (said to stand on the site of an earlier castle built by Robert the Bruce's father); Alexandra Palace (1873), with park; Finsbury Park (1869), one of the earliest municipal parks.

## Harlech

Coastal town in Gwynedd, north Wales, 16 km/10 mi from Barmouth; population (1991) 1,230. **Harlech Castle**, now in ruins, was built by the English king Edward I between 1283 and 1289. It was taken by the Welsh chieftain Owen ◊Glendower from 1404 to 1408, and by the Yorkists, in the Wars of the ◊Roses, in 1468. Harlech is now a centre for visitors to ◊Snowdonia National Park. There is a championship golf course here.

The Welsh war song 'March of the Men of Harlech' originated in the Yorkist siege.

During the Civil War the castle held out for Charles I, but eventually became the last one to fall to Parliament. Its ruins overlook the sea and offer impressive views of ◊Lleyn Peninsula, Tremadog Bay, and Snowdonia.

## Harley Street

Road in central London, famed for having many private doctors and other medical specialists. Originally Harley Street was a smart residential area until the doctors moved in, around 1845. It was named after Edward Harley, 2nd Earl of Oxford, the ground landlord.

## Harold

Two kings of England:

## Harold I (1016–1040)

King of England from 1035. The illegitimate son of Canute, known as **Harefoot**, he claimed the throne in 1035 when the legitimate heir Hardicanute was in Denmark. He was elected king in 1037.

## Harold II (c. 1020–1066)

King of England from January 1066. He succeeded his father Earl Godwin in 1053 as earl of Wessex. In 1063 William of Normandy (◊William the Conqueror) tricked him into swearing to support his claim to the English throne, and when the Witan (a council of high-ranking religious and secular men) elected Harold to succeed Edward the Confessor, William prepared to invade. Meanwhile, Harold's treacherous brother Tostig (died 1066) joined the king of Norway, Harald Hardrada (1015–1066), in invading Northumbria. Harold routed and killed them at Stamford Bridge on 25 September. Three days later William landed at Pevensey, Sussex, and Harold was killed at the Battle of Hastings on 14 October 1066.

## Harrison, John (1693–1776)

English horologist and instrumentmaker. He made the first chronometers that were accurate enough to allow the precise determination of longitude at sea, and so permit reliable (and safe) navigation over long distances. In 1996 Dava Sobel's book about Harrison, *Longitude*, became a bestseller.

## Harrods

Department store in Brompton Road, London, the largest store in the UK and one of the biggest in the world, with about 5,000 staff.

In 1849 Henry Charles Harrod (1800–1885), a wholesale tea merchant, bought a grocer's shop in Knightsbridge. From 1861 his son Charles Digby Harrod gradually expanded the store to cater for his increasingly fashionable clientele. After the premises were destroyed by fire in 1883, C D Harrod designed an even bigger shop, the nucleus of the present store, whose main frontage was built 1901–05. In 1959 it was bought by the House of Fraser, and in the 1980s by the Egyptian Al-Fayed brothers.

## Harrogate

Resort and spa town in North Yorkshire, northern England, about 24 km/15 mi north of Leeds; population (1996 est) 69,800. The town developed as a spa after the discovery of Tewit Well in 1571, and it became a fashionable resort and the leading spa in the north of England in Victorian and Edwardian times. The town formerly had over 80 springs, used for drinking and bathing and in the treatment of rheumatic, skin, and heart complaints. Today, the main industries are in the service sector, particularly related to conferences and tourism.

*Features*

Victorian spa facilities include the Royal Baths (1897) and Assembly Rooms; and the Royal Pump Room (1841–42), designed by Isaac

**Harrods** Britain's most famous department store occupies a large Edwardian building in the fashionable London district of Knightsbridge. Its most notable features are the imposing terracotta facade on the Brompton Road illuminated by thousands of lightbulbs, and a lavish food hall with decorative tilework. Since 1985, the store has been owned by the flamboyant Egyptian businessman Mohammed Al-Fayed. Corel

Thomas Shutt, and now housing a museum of local history. Turkish baths, sauna, and massage treatments are still available at the Royal Baths. Parks and open spaces include the Stray, a large common to the south of the town centre; and the Harlow Car Gardens of the Royal Horticultural Society to the west of the town. The resort has many hotels and a large exhibition hall (a centre for trade fairs). Annual events include the Great Yorkshire Agricultural Show held in July and an International Festival of Music and Arts in July/August. The North of England Horticultural Society organizes annual flower shows here.

## Harrow school

Fee-paying independent school in North London, founded in 1571 and opened in 1611; it became a leading public school for boys during the 18th century, and among its former pupils are the writers Byron and Sheridan and the politicians Peel, Palmerston, and Churchill.

## Hartlepool

Town and port in northeast England; population: (1996) 90,400. It is also a unitary authority, formed in 1996 from part of the county of Cleveland; area 94 sq km/36 sq mi. An important port in the 19th century, it now mainly services North Sea oil fields. The redeveloped dock area includes the Museum of Hartlepool (opened in 1995); the Gray Art Gallery and Museum; remains of the medieval town walls; and the Early English church of St Hilda.

### History

A settlement was established here in the 7th century when a monastery was founded on the headland north of the harbour. It became a local market centre in the 11th century, and in the 12th century the harbour was improved and Hartlepool became the official port for the Palatinate bishopric of Durham. Town walls were built in medieval times.

The industrialization of Hartlepool began with the building of a railway linking it with the South Durham coalfield in 1835. In 1847 a rival railway reached the coast just south of Hartlepool, and docks were built at its terminus. A new town, West Hartlepool, was established to the south and east of the docks, and the two settlements remained administratively separate until 1969.

Due to the town's importance as a centre for ship-owning companies in the early part of the 20th century, the first hostile action taken by Germany against Britain in World War I was the bombardment of Hartlepool from the sea in 1914. Shipbuilding and steel manufacture were the town's main industries until after World War II, when heavy industry declined in the town. The last ship was built here 1960–61.

## Hartnell, Norman (1901–1979)

English fashion designer. He was known for his ornate evening gowns and tailored suits and coats. He worked for the designer Lucille from 1923 before founding his own studio. Appointed dressmaker to the British royal family in 1938, he created Queen Elizabeth II's wedding dress, when she was Princess Elizabeth, in 1947, and her coronation gown in 1953. The Hartnell fashion house closed in 1992. Knighted 1977.

## Harvey, William (1578–1657)

English physician who discovered the circulation of blood. In 1628 he published his book *De motu cordis/On the Motion of the Heart and the Blood in Animals*. He also explored the development of chick and deer embryos.

Harvey's discovery marked the beginning of the end of medicine as taught by Greek physician Galen, which had been accepted for 1,400 years.

# Hastings

Resort and fishing town in East Sussex, southeast England, on the English Channel; population (1996) 85,000. A leading port in medieval times, it is also the site of the Battle of Hastings (1066), where William the Conqueror defeated Harold II and established Norman rule over England. Today, the town has Britain's largest fleet of beach-launched fishing boats and a new wholesale fish market.

## History

The settlement became prominent after the Saxon period, and by the 12th century Hastings was the leading member of the ◊Cinque Ports, with William I's castle dominating the town. With the silting-up of the harbour and use of larger ships, the importance of the town declined, and it was known in the early 18th century as a smugglers' haunt. It became a fashionable resort in the early 19th century, but its popularity declined in the later part of the century, and it suffered extensive bomb damage during World War II.

## Features

The old town in the east part of Hastings is surrounded by high cliffs, and includes the 13th-century St Clement's Church; the old town hall, now housing a museum of local history; and the Perpendicular All Saints' Church. The castle ruins include a museum that tells the story of the invasion of 1066 and the history of the castle. The Fisherman's Museum, housed in a building that was once the fishing community's church, and the Shipwreck Heritage Centre depicts the town's fishing and maritime history. St Clement's Caves, a labyrinth of sandstone caves, contain a museum illustrating the importance of smuggling to the town's economy in the late 18th century. The western part of the town, which developed as a resort in the early 19th century, has a promenade and a pier. Battle Abbey, built on the site of William the Conqueror's victory, lies 10 km/6 mi to the northwest. The wreck of the Dutch East Indiaman *Amsterdam* (1748) lies buried in mud on the beach near Hastings. The annual **Hastings International Chess Congress**, England's leading international chess tournament, is held here in December/January.

# Hastings, Battle of

Battle on 14 October 1066 at which William, Duke of Normandy ('the Conqueror') defeated King Harold II of England, and himself took the throne. The site is actually 10 km/6 mi inland from Hastings, at Senlac, Sussex; it is marked by Battle Abbey.

Both sides suffered heavy losses but the decimation of the English army and Harold's death left England open to Norman rule.

The English were attacked by Norman archers, foot soldiers, and finally cavalry with no result. Then some of Harold's personal guard left their places to pursue some stragglers, and William ordered part of his force to simulate panic and flight. The strategy worked – many of the English troops broke ranks to run down the hill after the Normans, who then turned and cut them down. William then resumed his attack on the hill, with his archers shooting into the air. With arrows falling about them, the English opened up, allowing the Norman foot soldiers to get among them. Harold and his two brothers were killed and his army totally destroyed.

# Hastings, Warren (1732–1818)

English colonial administrator. A protégé of Lord Clive, who established British rule in India, Hastings carried out major reforms, and became governor general of Bengal in 1774. Impeached for corruption on his return to England in 1785, he was acquitted in 1795.

# Hatfield House

Jacobean house in Hertfordshire, England, standing in a park 16 km/10 mi in circumference. It is the residence of the Marquess of Salisbury and is one of the best examples of Jacobean architecture in Britain. A surviving wing of the Old Palace of the bishops of Ely, built about 1496 by Cardinal Morton, Henry VII's principal minister, stands in the grounds.

The palace was seized by Henry VIII and inhabited by Edward VI and Elizabeth I before their accession. In James I's reign it was given to Robert ◊Cecil, 1st Earl of Salisbury, in exchange for Theobalds. Three wings of the palace were then pulled down and the materials used for the foundations of Hatfield, which was built between 1607 and 1611, Robert Lyminge being the master carpenter.

# Hathaway, Anne (1556–1623)

Englishwoman, daughter of a yeoman farmer, who married William ◊Shakespeare in 1582. She was born at Shottery, near Stratford, where her cottage can still be seen.

# Havant

Town in Hampshire, England, at the head of Langstone Harbour, 8 km/5 mi northeast of Portsmouth; population (1991) 115,400. The town is largely residential, with some light industry. Hayling Island in Langstone Harbour is a popular holiday centre.

## Hawksmoor, Nicholas (1661–1736)

English architect. He was assistant to Christopher ◊Wren in designing various London churches and St Paul's Cathedral, and joint architect of Castle Howard and Blenheim Palace with John ◊Vanbrugh. His genius is displayed in a quirky and uncompromising style incorporating elements from both Gothic and Classical sources.

After 1712 Hawksmoor completed six of the 50 new churches planned for London under the provisions made by the Fifty New Churches Act of 1711: St Alphege, Greenwich (1712–14); St Anne, Limehouse (1712–24); St George-in-the-East (1714–34); St Mary Woolnoth (1716–27); St George, Bloomsbury (1720–30); and Christ Church, Spitalfields (1714–29).

## Haworth

Moorland village in West Yorkshire, England, 5 km/3 mi south of Keighley. The writers Charlotte, Emily, and Anne ◊Brontë lived at the parsonage here from their earliest years. The old church of Haworth has been restored, and contains the graves of Charlotte and Emily Brontë. The parsonage is now the Brontë museum.

Vivid descriptions of the local moorland scenery are to be found in their novels, notably *Wuthering Heights* (1847) by Emily Brontë.

## Hay-on-Wye, Welsh Y Gelli

Market town in Powys, Wales, situated 24 km/15 m northeast of Brecon on the south bank of the River ◊Wye. It is an angling and walking centre. It is known as the 'town of books' because of the huge second-hand book shop started here in 1961 by Richard Booth; it was followed by others. The town hosts an annual children's festival of the arts.

## Hazlitt, William (1778–1830)

English essayist and critic. His work is characterized by invective, scathing irony, an intuitive critical sense, and a gift for epigram. His essays include 'Characters of Shakespeare's Plays' (1817), 'Lectures on the English Poets' (1818–19), 'English Comic Writers' (1819), and 'Dramatic Literature of the Age of Elizabeth' (1820).

## Headingley

Leeds sports centre, home of the Yorkshire County Cricket Club and Leeds Rugby League Club. The two venues are separated by a large stand. The cricket ground has been a centre for Test matches since 1899.

The crowd of 158,000 for the five-day England Australia Test match at Headingley in 1948 is an English record. Britain's first official Rugby League Test match against New Zealand was at Headingley in 1908. The rugby ground is one of the best in the country and has excellent turf. It was the first club to install undersoil heating. The main stand is one of the biggest in Rugby League.

## health care

See ◊NHS, Department of ◊Health, ◊Health Education Authority, and chronology of medicine and health care.

## Heathrow

Major international airport to the west of London in the Greater London borough of Hounslow, approximately 24 km/14 mi from the city centre. Opened in 1946, it is one of the world's busiest airports, with four terminals. It was linked with the London underground system in 1977. A government decision on whether to build a fifth terminal was due in early 2000.

## Hebrides

Group of more than 500 islands (fewer than 100 inhabited) off the west coast of mainland Scotland; total area 2,900 sq km/1,120 sq mi. The Hebrides were settled by Scandinavians during the 6th–9th centuries and passed under Norwegian rule from about 890 to 1266.

The **Inner Hebrides** are divided between Highland and Argyll and Bute authorities, and include Raasay, ◊Rum, Muck, Eigg, Scalpay, ◊Skye (Highland) and ◊Mull, ◊Jura, ◊Islay, ◊Iona, Coll, Tiree, Colonsay, and uninhabited Staffa (Argyll and Bute). The **Outer Hebrides** form the islands area of the ◊Western Isles authority, separated from the **Inner Hebrides** by the Little Minch. They include Harris/Lewis, North Uist, South Uist, Benbecula, ◊Barra, and ◊St Kilda.

The island of Eigg, which has been in private ownership since 1308, was bought by its residents in April 1997 after an eight-month ownership battle. In December 1996, an initial bid by the islanders of £1.2 million was rejected by the then owner, a German artist; a month later the Trustees of the Heritage Lottery Fund turned down their appeal for financial help. Finally, an English millionairess, who has remained anonymous, was believed to have given them around £900,000—the bulk of the £1.5 million purchase price.

## hedgerows

A feature of the landscape since Roman times. There is an estimated total of 450,600 km/280,000 miles of hedgerows in Britain, sheltering more than 600 plant species, 1,500 types of insect, 65 birds, and 20 different mammals. Among this diverse flora and fauna are 13 species which are either in very rapid decline or endangered globally. Ancient and species-rich hedgerows were among 14 key wildlife habitats on which the government and leading wildlife charities agreed rescue plans as a follow-up to the 1992 Rio Earth Summit. In 1996 the government estimated that more than 16,000 km/10,000 mi of hedgerows were disappearing each year because of neglect, 'grubbing out', and the spray drift of pesticides. New laws were introduced in 1997 to help combat this decline.

Hedgerows are frequently mentioned in Anglo-Saxon charters, the earliest reference in England to planting a hedge being in Wiltshire in 940. During the period of ◊enclosures, an estimated 321,800 km/200,000 mi of hedges were planted. However, between 1984 and 1990, nearly 25% of Britain's hedgerows were destroyed.

## Helensburgh

Holiday resort and residential town in Argyll and Bute unitary authority, Scotland, situated on the Firth of Clyde at the mouth of Gare Loch, 40 km/25 mi northwest of Glasgow; population (1991) 22,600. With neighbouring Rhu, it is a centre for dinghy sailing.

Founded in the 18th century, the town has villas built by wealthy Glaswegians. The most outstanding example is Hill House, designed by Charles Rennie ◊Mackintosh and built in 1902–3.

## Hell-Fire Club

18th-century club devoted to hedonism and debauchery established by Sir Francis Dashwood (1708–1781) in the village of Medmenham, Buckinghamshire, England. The club reputedly engaged in wild orgies, including devil worship, in caves under the village church. Most of these rumours were later proved to be untrue, but the club revelled in the notoriety they caused and it spawned a series of imitators.

## Helston

Market town in Cornwall, England, 16 km/10 mi southwest of Falmouth. Helston was made a borough by King John in 1201.

The traditional **Helston Furry** or 'Floral' Dance is performed in processional formation through the streets and houses. The steps are in the ◊morris dance tradition, and the dance takes place in May in order to welcome spring and drive away evil spirits from the area.

'Furry' is derived from an ancient word 'fer', a fair or festivity. There are many theories regarding the dance's origin, one being that it honours the goddess Flora. Local legend tells of a dragon threatening the town, and the borough seal shows a dragon being slain by St Michael, Helston's patron saint.

## Helvellyn

Peak of the ◊Lake District in Cumbria, northwest England; height 950 m/3,118 ft.

The summit is the highest point of the ridge which separates the the valleys containing Thirlemere and Ullswater lakes. The peak may be climbed from Wythburn at the head of Thirlemere on the western side, and from Patterdale or Glenridding on Ullswater to the east. Two sharp ridges, Striding Edge and Swirrell Edge, on the east side, provide more challenging routes. Helvellyn forms part of an annual Three Peaks charity event held in the Lake District; the other peaks are Skiddaw (930 m/3,052 ft) and Scafell Pike (978 m/3,210 ft).

## Hemel Hempstead

Town in Hertfordshire, southeast England, 37 km/23 mi northwest of London, on the River Gade; population (1997) 80,800. It was designated a new town in 1946. It was formerly a centre of the straw-plaiting industry.

The mainly Norman church of St Mary's dates from the 12th century. Remains of a Roman villa have been discovered at nearby Boxmoor.

## Hengist (died c. 488)

Legendary leader, with his brother **Horsa**, of the Jutes, who originated in Jutland and settled in Kent in about 450, the first Anglo-Saxon settlers in Britain.

## Henley-on-Thames

Town in Oxfordshire, south-central England, 56 km/35 mi west of London; population (1996 est) 10,000. The ◊**Henley Royal Regatta**, held here annually since 1839, is in June/July. Henley Management College, established in 1946, was the first in Europe. A River and Rowing museum opened in 1998.

A fine five-arched bridge, built in 1786, spans the River Thames.

## Henley Royal Regatta

Rowing festival on the River Thames at Henley, Oxfordshire, inaugurated in 1839. It is as much a social as a sporting occasion. The principal events are the solo *Diamond Challenge Sculls* and the *Grand Challenge Cup*, the leading event for eight-oared shells. The regatta is held in June/July. From 1998 professional rowers were allowed to compete at Henley after the Regatta's stewards had dropped the amateur definition from their rules.

## Henrietta Maria (1609–1669)

Queen of England 1625–49. The daughter of Henry IV of France, she married Charles I of England in 1625. By encouraging him to aid Roman Catholics and make himself an absolute ruler, she became highly unpopular and was exiled 1644–60. She returned to England at the Restoration but retired to France in 1665.

## Henry

Eight kings of England:

## Henry I (1068–1135)

King of England from 1100. Youngest son of William the Conqueror, he succeeded his brother William II. He won the support of the Saxons by granting them a charter and marrying a Saxon princess, Matilda, daughter of Malcolm III of Scotland. An able administrator, he established a professional bureaucracy and a system of travelling judges.

His only legitimate son, William, was drowned in 1120, and Henry tried to settle the succession on his daughter ◊Matilda's son Henry (later Henry II). However, Matilda was unpopular and the throne was taken by Henry's nephew Stephen, who, towards the end of his reign, agreed to adopt Matilda's son as his heir.

## Henry II (1133–1189)

King of England from 1154. The son of ◊Matilda and Geoffrey of Anjou (1113–1151), and the first of the Angevin kings, he succeeded ◊Stephen. He brought order to England after the chaos of Stephen's reign, curbing the power of the barons and reforming the legal system. His attempt to bring the church courts under control had to be abandoned after the murder of Thomas à ◊Becket. During his reign the English conquest of

**Henley Royal Regatta** Held every summer on a long, straight stretch of the River Thames at Henley-on-Thames in Oxfordshire, the Royal Regatta is both a major international rowing festival and a principal event in the British upper-class social calendar. The Regatta was inaugurated in 1839. Gerry Gavigan/Collections

Ireland began. Henry was succeeded by his son Richard I.

### Henry III (1207–1272)

King of England from 1216, when he succeeded John, but the royal powers were exercised by a regency until 1232, and by two French nobles, Peter des Roches and Peter des Rivaux, until the barons forced their expulsion in 1234, marking the start of Henry's personal rule. His financial commitments to the papacy and his foreign favourites antagonized the barons who issued the Provisions of Oxford in 1258, limiting the king's power. Henry's refusal to accept the provisions led to the second Barons' War in 1264, a revolt of nobles led by his brother-in-law Simon de ◊Montfort. Henry was defeated at Lewes, Sussex, and imprisoned, but restored to the throne after the royalist victory at Evesham in 1265. He was succeeded by his son Edward I.

### Henry IV, (Bolingbroke) (1367–1413)

King of England from 1399, the son of ◊John of Gaunt. In 1398 he was banished by ◊Richard II for political activity but returned in 1399 to head a revolt and be accepted as king by Parliament. He was succeeded by his son Henry V.

He had difficulty in keeping the support of Parliament and the clergy, and had to deal with baronial unrest and Owen ◊Glendower's rising in Wales. In order to win support he had to conciliate the church by a law for the burning of heretics, and to make many concessions to Parliament.

### Henry V (1387–1422)

King of England from 1413, the son of Henry IV. Invading Normandy in 1415 (during the Hundred Years' War), he captured Harfleur and defeated the French at ◊Agincourt. He invaded again in 1417–19, capturing Rouen. His military victory forced the French into the Treaty of Troyes (1420), which gave Henry control of the French government. He married ◊Catherine of Valois in 1420 and gained recognition as heir to the French throne by his father-in-law Charles VI, but died before him. He was succeeded by his son Henry VI.

### Henry VI (1421–1471)

King of England from 1422, son of Henry V. He assumed royal power in 1442 and sided with the party opposed to the continuation of the Hundred Years' War with France. After his marriage in 1445, he was dominated by his wife, ◊Margaret of Anjou. He was deposed in 1461 in the Wars of the

◊Roses; was captured in 1465, temporarily restored in 1470, but again imprisoned in 1471 and then murdered.

Henry was eight months old when he succeeded to the English throne, and shortly afterwards, by the death in 1422 of his maternal grandfather, Charles VI, he became titular king of France. Unlike his father, Henry was disinclined to warfare, and when Joan of Arc revived French patriotism the English gradually began to lose their French possessions. By 1453 only Calais remained of his father's conquests.

The unpopularity of the government, especially after the loss of the English conquests in France, encouraged Richard, Duke of ◊York, to claim the throne, and though York was killed in 1460, his son Edward IV proclaimed himself king in 1461.

### Henry VII (1457–1509)

King of England from 1485, when he overthrew Richard III at the Battle of ◊Bosworth. A descendant of ◊John of Gaunt, Henry, by his marriage to Elizabeth of York in 1486, united the houses of York and Lancaster. Yorkist revolts continued until 1497, but Henry restored order after the Wars of the Roses by the ◊Star Chamber and achieved independence from Parliament by amassing a private fortune through confiscations. He was succeeded by his son Henry VIII.

Born in Pembroke, Wales, the son of Edmund Tudor, Earl of Richmond (c. 1430–1456), Henry lived in Brittany, France, from 1471 to 1485, when he landed in Britain to lead the rebellion against Richard III. Henry succeeded in crushing the independence of the nobility by means of a policy of forced loans and fines. His chancellor, Cardinal Morton, was made responsible for the collection of these fines, and they were enforced by the privy councillors Empson and Dudley. This form of taxation became known as **Morton's Fork**, the dilemma being that, if a subject liable for taxation lived an extravagant lifestyle, obviously they could afford to pay the fine; if they lived austerely they should have sufficient funds saved with which to pay. To further curb the pretensions of the nobility, there were no unions of his children with the baronage. He married his son Henry to Catherine of Aragón, daughter of the joint sovereigns of Spain, his daughter Margaret to James IV of Scotland, and his youngest daughter Mary to Louis XII of France.

### Henry VIII (1491–1547)

King of England from 1509, when he succeeded his father Henry VII and married Catherine of Aragón, the widow of his brother.

During the period 1513–29 Henry pursued an active foreign policy, largely under the guidance of his Lord Chancellor, Cardinal Wolsey, who shared Henry's desire to make England stronger. Wolsey was replaced by Thomas More in 1529 for failing to persuade the pope to grant Henry a divorce. After 1532 Henry broke with papal authority, proclaimed himself head of the church in England, dissolved the monasteries, and divorced Catherine. His subsequent wives were Anne Boleyn, Jane Seymour, Anne of Cleves, Catherine Howard, and Catherine Parr.

Henry divorced Catherine of Aragón in 1533 because she was too old to give him an heir, and married Anne Boleyn, who was beheaded in 1536, ostensibly for adultery. Henry's third wife, Jane Seymour, died in 1537. He married Anne of Cleves in 1540 in pursuance of Thomas Cromwell's policy of allying with the German Protestants, but rapidly abandoned this policy, divorced Anne, and beheaded Cromwell. His fifth wife, Catherine Howard, was beheaded in 1542, and the following year he married Catherine Parr, who survived him. Henry never completely lost his popularity, but wars with France and Scotland towards the end of his reign sapped the economy, and in religion he not only executed Roman Catholics, including Thomas More, for refusing to acknowledge his supremacy in the church, but also Protestants who maintained his changes had not gone far enough.

### Henry's legacy

Henry ended his reign with the reputation of a tyrant, despite the promise of his earlier years – in 1536 the rebellion known as the ◊Pilgrimage of Grace was viciously suppressed, and advisers of the calibre of More and Bishop John Fisher had died rather than sacrifice their own principles to Henry's will. But the power of the crown had been considerably strengthened by Henry's ecclesiastical policy, and the monastic confiscations gave impetus to the rise of a new nobility which was to become influential in succeeding reigns.

He was succeeded by his son Edward VI.

---

*You have sent me a Flanders mare.*

**Henry VIII** King of England.
Attributed remark on seeing Anne of Cleves for the first time

---

### Hepplewhite, George (died 1786)

English furnituremaker associated with Neo-Classicism. His reputation rests upon his book of designs *The Cabinetmaker and Upholsterer's Guide*, published posthumously in 1788, which contains over 300 designs, characterized by simple elegance and utility. No piece of furniture has been identified as being made by him.

Hepplewhite's designs were mainly in mahogany or satinwood, delicately inlaid or painted with decorations of feathers, shells, or ears of wheat. He favoured heart- and shield-backs for chairs, and used 'Marlboro' (square-tapered) legs on tables and sideboards. His workshop was in St Giles, Cripplegate, London.

### Hepworth, Barbara (1903–1975)

English sculptor. She developed a distinctive abstract style, creating slender upright forms reminiscent of standing stones or totems; and round, hollowed forms with spaces bridged by wires or strings, as in *Pelagos* (1946; Tate Gallery, London). Her preferred medium was stone, but she also worked in concrete, wood, and aluminum, and many of her later works were in bronze.

Hepworth was an admirer of Henry ◊Moore, Constantin Brancusi, and Hans Arp. She married first the sculptor John Skeaping and in 1933 the painter Ben ◊Nicholson, whose influence encouraged her interest in abstract forms. In 1939 she moved to St Ives, Cornwall (where her studio is now a museum). She was made DBE in 1965.

Her public commissions included *Winged Figure* (1962) for the John Lewis Building, London and *Single Form* (1962– 63; United Nations, New York).

### heraldry

The science of armorial bearings. In England it developed rapidly during the 13th and 14th centuries, reaching a climax in the reigns of Edward III and Richard II. There was a revival in the 19th century. The English College of Arms, founded in 1484, is the world's oldest heraldic court, and it continues to exercise its function; in Scotland the equivalent body is the Court of the Lord Lyon. In 1672 all older registers in Scotland were superseded by the 'Public Register of All Arms and Bearings in Scotland'.

### Hereford

City in the county of Herefordshire, west-central England, on the River Wye, 34 km/21 mi southwest of Worcester; population (1996 est) 48,900. It is an agricultural centre, with a livestock market noted for its white-faced Hereford cattle. The city has the UK's largest cider industry. Other activities include brewing, food processing, tourism, and the manufacture of non-ferrous alloys and components.

## History

The site of Hereford was seized from the Welsh by the Mercians in about AD 600, and it became the capital of West Mercia and a garrison against the Welsh. King Offa of Mercia later established the Wye as border between Wales and England, and built Offa's Dyke in about 785 to mark the border. Hereford's first castle, built by Ralph, the nephew of Edward the Confessor, was destroyed (along with the original Saxon cathedral) following a defeat by the Welsh in 1055. In Norman times the city was an important garrison, and it received its first charter from Richard I in 1189. It prospered in the Middle Ages as a centre of the wool trade, but it continued to be the scene of warfare until after the English Civil War.

## Hereford Cathedral

Much altered since it was built in the 12th century, the cathedral exhibits a mixture of architectural styles, including Norman arches at the eastern end of the nave, a 13th-century northern transept, and a 14th-century central tower. The elaborate *Mappa Mundi* (map of the world) is one of the largest medieval maps in Europe; it was made in England around 1285 by Richard of Haldingham, with the Welsh castles added in 1289. The Chained Library – a library where each book is attached to the bookcase by a chain – is the largest of its kind in the world, housing almost 1,500 books, both handwritten and printed.

## Features

The Old House is a 17th-century black-and-white timbered residence, now housing a museum. The river is spanned by the Wye Bridge, dating from 1490, and Greyfriars Bridge, opened in 1966. Other features include Castle Green on the site of the old castle; the Coningsby Hospital (1614) almshouses; the Cathedral School, which had its first known headmaster in 1384; St Ethelbert's Hospital; All Saints' Church, with 14th-century carved stalls and a chained library; and the 12th–14th-century church of St Peter's. The Wye is an excellent salmon river.

The Three Choirs Festival is held in the cathedral every third year, in turn with Gloucester and Worcester.

# Herefordshire

Unitary authority in west England, on the border with Wales, created in 1998; population (1996) 166,100; area 2,288 sq km/884 sq mi. Herefordshire existed as a county until 1974, when it was amalgamated with Worcestershire to form the single county of Hereford and Worcester; in 1998 this was divided back into Herefordshire and ◊Worcestershire, which regained their pre-1974 boundaries. The authority's main towns and cities

**Herefordshire** Symond's Yat on the border between Gloucestershire and Herefordshire is a well-known site of outstanding natural beauty. Here, the River Wye loops through a narrow gorge surmounted by a steep rocky outcrop that commands panoramic views of the surrounding countryside. Joe Cornish

are ◊Hereford (administrative headquarters), Leominster, Ross-on-Wye, and Ledbury.

*Physical*

The area is largely agricultural, with the River Wye flowing through it. The Black Mountains are in the southwest and the Malvern Hills in the east.

*Features*

The authority contains a variety of historic sites, including the Herefordshire Beacon (340 m/1,115 ft) Iron Age fort. Part of Offa's Dyke, an 8th-century fortification against the Welsh, is in the county, and border castles include Croft Castle. The 11th-century Hereford Cathedral houses the late 13th/early 14th-century Mappa Mundi, and the Chained Library, with over 1,400 chained books and 200 manuscripts dating from the 8th to 12th centuries. The Waterworks Museum, also in Hereford, is accommodated in a restored Victorian pump house. Other notable sites are Croft Castle, Leominster; St Mary's Church, Kempley, with its medieval wall paintings; The Prospect, a walled clifftop garden in Ross-on-Wye designed by John Kyrle in the 17th century; and Norman Church, Kilpeck, with fine carvings.

*Economy*

A significant part of the local economy derives from agriculture, including beef cattle (Red Herefordshire bulls are bred here) and dairying, orchards and the cider industry, and agricultural services and machinery. There is also manufacturing and commerce in high-technology products.

## Hereward the Wake (lived 11th century)

English leader of a revolt against the Normans in 1070. His stronghold in the Isle of Ely was captured by William the Conqueror in 1071. Hereward escaped, but his fate is unknown.

## Herne Bay

Resort on the north coat of Kent, southeast England, 11 km/7 mi north of Canterbury; population (1991) 32,800.

Herne Bay's pier, formerly the second-longest in England, is storm-severed; its inshore portion remains with an associated sports centre, but the offshore section is inaccessible. A large breakwater contains a viewing gallery.

The coastal area developed in the 19th century. The old village of **Herne** inland has a 13th-century church.

## Heron, Patrick (1920–1999)

English painter, designer, and writer on art. Most of his work is abstract and vibrantly coloured. He was art critic for several journals, including the *New Statesman*, and wrote several books on art.

Heron was born in Leeds, the son of a textiles manufacturer, for whom he made designs in the 1930s and 1940s. In 1956 he settled in Cornwall and was considered a leading figure of the ◊St Ives School of painters.

## Herrick, Robert (1591–1674)

English poet and cleric. He published *Hesperides: or the Works both Humane and Divine of Robert Herrick* (1648), a collection of verse admired for its lyric quality, including the well-known poems 'Gather ye rosebuds' and 'Cherry ripe'.

The 'divine' poems are, on the whole, unremarkable, but the 'humane' works are rich and varied, owing much to Roman models such as Catullus and Martial and to native influences such as Ben ◊Jonson and popular ballads. They range in scale from couplets to Horatian odes and verse epistles, and cover such subjects as religion, politics, love, erotic fantasy, the value of poetry, and the changing cycles of life in the countryside.

## Herriot, James pen name of James Alfred Wight (1916–1995)

English writer. A practising veterinary surgeon in Yorkshire from 1939, he wrote of his experiences in a series of humorous books which described the life of a young vet working in a Yorkshire village in the late 1930s. A World of James Herriot Centre opened in Thirsk, North Yorkshire, in 1999.

He wrote his first book, *If Only They Could Talk*, when he was in his 50s. This was quickly followed by *It Shouldn't Happen To A Vet*, and *Let Sleeping Vets Lie*; all three were published as a compilation under the title *All Creatures Great and Small* (1972).

The success of Herriot's novels was based on their warm humour, their colourful, larger-than-life characters, and an implicit nostalgia for the pre-war way of life in which there was a strong and enduring sense of community. By the 1980s his books had been translated into every major language, including Japanese, and a long-running television series was being sold world-wide.

## Herstmonceux

Village in East Sussex, southeast England, 11 km/7 mi north of Eastbourne; population (1996 est) 2,300. The Royal Greenwich Observatory was sited alongside the 15th-century castle from 1958 until 1990, when it relocated to Cambridge. The Isaac Newton telescope was moved to the Canary Islands in 1979.

In 1995, the Herstmonceux Science Centre opened in the former Observatory buildings.

The name derives from the 11th-century Norman lord of the manor. **Herstmonceux Castle**, a fortified manor house, is one of the earliest brick buildings in England; fortification was added in 1441. The castle was restored in the 20th century, and is now used as an international study centre for Queen's University, Canada. All Saints' Church dates from the late 12th century and **Herstmonceux Place** was built in the early 18th century with bricks from the castle.

## Hertfordshire
County of southeast England; population (1996) 1,015,800; area 1,630 sq km/629 sq mi. It is a hilly county with parks and woods, although it borders Greater London to the south. The principal towns and cities are ◊ Hertford (administrative headquarters), Bishop's Stortford, Hatfield, Hemel Hempstead, Letchworth (1903, the first garden city, followed by Welwyn in 1919), Stevenage (the first new town, designated in 1946), St Albans, Watford, and Hitchin.

### History
St Albans was the Roman town of Verulanium, destroyed by Boadicea during the revolt of the Iceni. In 896 a battle took place in Hertfordshire between Alfred the Great and the Danes. During the Wars of the Roses the battles of St Albans and Barnet were fought here. Elizabeth I was at Hatfield palace when she heard of her accession.

### Physical
The county is hilly in the northwest, containing part of the Chiltern Hills. The south is gently undulating and the main rivers are the Lea, Stort, and Colne. The Grand Union Canal passes through part of the county.

### Features
Hertfordshire has a Norman castle at Berkhamsted. Its country houses include the 17th-century Hatfield House, Knebworth House, home of Lord Lytton, dating from the 15th century and redecorated in Gothic style in the 19th century, and Brocket Hall (home of the prime ministers Lord Palmerston and Lord Melbourne). The home of George Bernard Shaw is at Ayot St Lawrence. The Elstree film studios are in Hertfordshire. St Albans hosts the British Rose Festival in July.

### Economy
There is a combination of agriculture and horticulture (barley is grown for the brewing industry), and space equipment, aircraft, computer, electronics, and engineering industries.

## Hever Castle
Castle in Kent, England, 3 km/2 mi east of Edenbridge. It was the Boleyn family home in Tudor times but sank into obscurity with the family's decline after the dissolution of Anne ◊ Boleyn's marriage to Henry VIII. In the early 20th century it was modernized by William Waldorf ◊ Astor and includes an entire Tudor-style village built to augment the castle's accommodation, and magnificent gardens.

## Hexham
Market town in Northumberland, northeast England, 34 km/21 mi west of Newcastle upon Tyne; population (1991) 11,342. Woodchip board is the principal manufacture. The town is a tourist centre for ◊ Hadrian's Wall, a Roman frontier system and World Heritage Site lying 13 km/8 mi to the north. **Hexham Abbey** dates from the 12th century.

## Heyer, Georgette (1902–1974)
English novelist. She wrote her first historical novel *The Black Moth* in 1921, to amuse a sick brother. Her best works, such as *These Old Shades* (1926) and *Regency Buck* (1935), are Regency romances based on considerable research, a fictional form she can be said to have invented.

## Heywood, Thomas (c. 1570–c. 1650)
English actor and dramatist. He wrote or adapted over 220 plays, including the domestic tragedy *A Woman Kilde with Kindnesse* (1602–03). He also wrote an *Apology for Actors* (1612), in answer to attacks on the morality of the theatre.

## Hickstead
English equestrian centre built in 1960 at the Sussex home of Douglas Bunn (1928–  ), a leading figure and administrator in the horse world. The British Show Jumping Derby has been held there since 1961, as well as many other national and international events.

## High Force
Waterfall 21 m/69 ft high, where the River ◊ Tees crosses the Whin Sill (the rock system on which Hadrian's Wall is built), near Middleton-in-Teesdale, Durham, England.

## Highland
Unitary authority in northern Scotland, created in 1996 from the region bearing the same name; population (1996) 207,500; area 26,157 sq km/10,100 sq mi (one-third of Scotland). This

huge area occupying the northernmost part of Scotland is largely rural, with hills and mountains, including Ben Nevis, Britain's highest peak. The islands off the west coast, including Skye, the fine salmon fishing and grouse and deer hunting, and winter sports facilities draw tourists. Loch Ness is legendary for its reputed 'monster'. The main towns are ◊Inverness (administrative headquarters), Thurso, Wick, Fort William, and Aviemore.

*History*
Many key historical moments in Scottish history have occurred in Highland, including the massacre of ◊Glencoe, the Battle of ◊Culloden, and the 19th-century Highland clearances, when landowners drove tenants off the land.

*Physical*
The mainland area consists of a series of high plateaus cut through by narrow glens and straths (valleys); in the northeast (Caithness), the landscape is softer and lower. The Grampian Mountains along the southern border include Ben Nevis (1,343 m/4,406 ft) and the Cairngorm Mountains, with Ben Macdhui (1,309 m/4,295 ft). Highland includes many islands of the Inner ◊Hebrides. The highest point of the Cuillin Hills on Skye is Sgurr Alasdair (993 m/3,257 ft). The most northerly and most westerly points of the British mainland are in Highland.

*Features*
The Caledonian Canal cuts across Highland from the Moray Firth in the east to Loch Linnhe in the west, passing through lochs Ness, Oich, and Lochy. John O'Groats is a village at Britain's northernmost point. The privately financed Skye Bridge was completed in 1995; users pay a toll to cross. Dunvegan Castle on Skye dates from the 13th century. The West Highland Museum is at Fort William. The authority has 356 Sites of Special Scientific Interest, 27 National Nature Reserves, eight Ramsars (wetland sites), 16 Special Protection Areas, three Biosphere Reserves, and 16 National Scenic Areas.

*Economy*
Highland is a predominantly rural area, although much of the land is not amenable to crops or forestry. Subsistence economies in the form of crofting still characterize the least accessible parts of the area. More accessible parts are exploiting their tourist potential and the opportunities afforded by mountain sports, for example, Aviemore and Fort William. Traditional industries, such as whisky distilling and crafts, are sustained by the tourist industry.

## Highland Clearances
Forced removal of tenants from large estates in Scotland during the early 19th century, as landowners 'improved' their estates by switching from arable to sheep farming. It led ultimately to widespread emigration to North America.

## Highland fling
Scottish dance step, rather than a dance itself, although it is often so called. The music is that of the strathspey and the step is a kick of the leg backwards and forwards.

## Highland Games
Traditional Scottish outdoor gathering that includes tossing the caber, putting the shot, running, dancing, and bagpipe playing.

The most celebrated is the Braemar Gathering, held annually in August.

## highwayman
In English history, a thief on horseback who robbed travellers on the highway (those who did so on foot were known as **footpads**). Highwaymen continued to flourish well into the 19th century.

With the development of regular coach services in the 17th and 18th centuries, the highwaymen's activities became notorious, and the ◊Bow Street Runners were organized to suppress them.

## High Wycombe
Town in Buckinghamshire, southern England, on the River Wye, between London and Oxford; population (1991) 62,500. RAF Strike Command has underground headquarters (1984) beneath the Chiltern Hills nearby.

*Features*
The church of All Saints dates from about 1275, but it was considerably altered and enlarged in the 15th and 16th centuries. The Local History and Chair Museum illustrates the tradition of furniture-making in the town. The Little Market House was built in 1761, and the Guildhall dates from 1757. The ruined hospital of St John dates from about 1180; it was converted into a grammar school in 1550. Hughenden Manor, home of Benjamin Disraeli from 1847 until his death in 1881, is nearby to the north.

## Hill, Graham (1929–1975)
English motor-racing driver. He won the Dutch Grand Prix in 1962, progressing to the world driver's title in 1962 and 1968. In 1972 he became the first Formula One World Champion

**Highland Games** Contestants in the sword dancing competition at a Highland Games meeting in Scotland. Highland Games are celebrations of clan membership and Scottish identity, and include a number of different athletic events, such as tossing the caber and sword (or Highland) dancing, in which the contestants must perform a sequence of complicated steps and leaps over a pair of crossed swords. Brian Shuel/Collections

to win the Le Mans Grand Prix d'Endurance (Le Mans 24-Hour Race). He was also the only driver to win the Formula One world championship, Le Mans 24-Hour Race, and the Indianapolis 500 Race in his career as a driver. Hill started his Formula One career with Lotus in 1958, went to BRM 1960–66, returned to Lotus 1967–69, moved to Brabham 1970–72, and formed his own team, Embassy Shadow, 1973–75. He was killed in an air crash. His son Damon won his first Grand Prix in 1993, making them the first father and son to both win a Grand Prix.

### Hill, Rowland (1795–1879)
English Post Office official who invented adhesive stamps. His pamphlet *Post Office Reform* (1837) prompted the introduction of the penny prepaid post in 1840 (previously the addressee paid, according to distance, on receipt).

He was secretary to the Post Office 1854–64, and made a KCB in 1860.

### hill figure
Any of a number of figures, often human or animal, cut from the turf to reveal the underlying chalk. Their origins are variously attributed to Celts, Romans, Saxons, Druids, or Benedictine monks, although most are of modern rather than ancient construction. Examples include 17 ◊White Horses, and giants such as the Cerne Abbas Giant, near Dorchester, Dorset, associated with a prehistoric fertility cult.

Nearly 50 hill figures are known in Britain, of which all but four are on the southern chalk downs of England. Some are landmarks or memorials; others have a religious or ritual purpose. It is possible that the current figures are on the site of, or reinforce, previous ones. There may have been large numbers of figures dotted on the landscape in the Iron Age, which were not maintained. The White Horse at Uffington, on the Berkshire Downs, used to be annually 'scoured' in a folk ceremony.

Other hill-figure designs include the Long Man of Wilmington on Windover Hill, East Sussex; crosses, such as the Bledlow and Whiteleaf crosses on the Chiltern Hills; a collection of military badges made at Fovant Down, Wiltshire (1916); an aeroplane, and a crown. A stag at Mormond Hill, Aberdeenshire, Scotland, is cut into white quartz.

## Cerne Abbas Giant

This male figure, 55 m/180 ft in height, is ithyphallic (with an erect penis) and holds a great club in his right hand, his left hand being outstretched as though in the act of grasping. He is represented in outline, marked by a 60 cm/2 ft trench. The figure lies in an area rich in prehistoric remains. Just beyond his head is a small four-sided earthwork, probably of the early Iron Age. The foundations of the Benedictine abbey of Cerne lie nearby.

A number of theories have been postulated concerning the origins of the giant. A traditional annual maypole celebration (involving an intricate weaving dance around a pole, possibly linked to ancient fertility rites) took place in the early Iron Age earthwork until quite recent years, adding weight to the suggestion that the site may be identified with a fertility cult. One theory identifies the giant with Hercules, who is associated with a fertility cult, or Priapus worship, revived by the Roman emperor Commodus in the later 2nd century AD.

## Long Man of Wilmington

The Long Man is 70.4 m/231 ft in height and holds a staff in each hand. The figure is outlined by trenches defined by white-painted bricks. Nothing is known of the giant's early history, but there has been a mass of mostly fanciful conjecture associating it with Celts, Romans, Saxons, and Druids as well as various mythological characters, astronomers, and the Benedictine monks of the priory of Wilmington, dissolved in 1414. One recent theory is that the figure may have served as a giant advertisement for the priory, where travellers would receive rest and refreshment.

## hillfort

Type of site with massive banks and ditches for defence, used as both a military camp and a permanent settlement, dating from the European Iron Age. Hillforts are found across Europe, and examples in Britain include ◊Maiden Castle, Dorset, England; Danebury in Hampshire; and Navan Fort near Armagh, Northern Ireland. There are several others in the hill country of Wales and the north. Many of these hillforts were occupied well into the Roman era and can sometimes be linked with the establishment of a Roman town nearby.

## Hilliard, Nicholas (c. 1547–1619)

English miniaturist and goldsmith. Court artist to Elizabeth I and James I, his sitters included Francis Drake, Walter Raleigh, and Mary Queen of Scots. A fine collection of his brilliant, highly detailed portraits, set in gold cases, including *An Unknown Young Man Amid Roses* (about 1590), is in the Victoria and Albert Museum, London.

He wrote a treatise on miniature painting, *The Arte of Limninge*, in 1593. After 1600 he was gradually superseded by his pupil Isaac ◊Oliver, and in 1617 was imprisoned for debt. His son **Lawrence Hilliard** (1582–after 1640) was also a miniaturist.

## Hitchcock, Alfred (1899–1980)

English film director, a US citizen from 1955. A master of the suspense thriller, he was noted for his meticulously drawn storyboards that determined his camera angles and for his cameo walk-ons in his own films. His *Blackmail* (1929) was the first successful British talking film. *The Thirty-Nine Steps* (1935) and *The Lady Vanishes* (1938) are British suspense classics. He went to Hollywood in 1940, and his work there included *Rebecca* (1940), *Notorious* (1946), *Strangers on a Train* (1951), *Rear Window* (1954), *Vertigo* (1958), *North by Northwest* (1959), *Psycho* (1960), and *The Birds* (1963).

## Hobbes, Thomas (1588–1679)

English political philosopher and the first thinker since Aristotle to attempt to develop a comprehensive theory of nature, including human behaviour. In *Leviathan* (1651), he advocates absolutist government as the only means of ensuring order and security; he saw this as deriving from the ◊social contract.

## Hogarth, William (1697–1764)

English painter and engraver. He produced portraits and moralizing genre scenes, such as the story series of prints *A Rake's Progress* (1735; Soane Museum, London). His portraits are remarkably direct and full of character, for example *Heads of Six of Hogarth's Servants* (about 1750–55; Tate Gallery) and his oil sketch masterpiece *The Shrimp Girl* (National Gallery).

Hogarth was born in London and apprenticed to an engraver. He published *A Harlot's Progress*, a series of six engravings, in 1732. Other story series followed, including *Marriage à la Mode* (1745), *Industry and Idleness* (1749), and *The Four Stages of Cruelty* (1751). A stern critic of 'phizmongering' (traditional portrait painting), his book *The Analysis of Beauty* (1753) also attacked the uncritical appreciation of the arts, advocating the double curved line and serpentine spiral as a key to visual beauty (both traceable in the composition of his own work). Hogarth's house in Chiswick is now a museum, and the artist is buried nearby, in St Nicholas's churchyard.

## Hogmanay

Scottish name for New Year's Eve. A traditional feature is first-footing, visiting the homes of friends and neighbours after midnight to welcome in the new year with salt, bread, whisky, and other gifts. Children may also go from house to house singing and receiving oatmeal cakes.

## Hog's Back

Narrow part of the North ◊Downs between Guildford and Farnham in Surrey, England. At its highest point, the Hog's Back has an elevation of over 150 m/492 ft, and from it there are panoramic views to both north and south.

The ancient royal hunting ground of Windsor Forest used to extend as far as the Hog's Back.

## Holbein, Hans, the Younger (1497–1543)

German painter and woodcut artist, who from 1536 was court painter to Henry VIII. He created a remarkable and unparalleled evocation of the English court in a series of graphic, perceptive portraits. He also travelled in Europe to paint some of Henry's prospective wives, including the Duchess of Milan in Brussels and Anne of Cleves (Louvre). One of his best known works is *The (French) Ambassadors* (1533; National Gallery), remarkable in technical skill and curious detail.

A dynastic group for the Privy Chamber at Whitehall was destroyed by fire in 1698, but one of his numerous portrayals of Henry VIII survives in the Thyssen Collection, Madrid. Other works in England included ornamental designs, such as the drawing for the *Jane Seymour Cup* (Bodleian Library), and the miniatures which inspired Nicholas ◊Hilliard, examples of which are in the Victoria and Albert Museum. He was also one of the finest graphic artists of his age; he designed the title page of Thomas More's *Utopia*.

## Holinshed or Hollingshead, Raphael (c. 1520 – c. 1580)

English historian. He published two volumes of the *Chronicles of England, Scotland, and Ireland* (1578), which are a mixture of fact and legend. The *Chronicles* were used as a principal source by Elizabethan dramatists for their plots. Nearly all Shakespeare's historical plays (other than the Roman histories), as well as *Macbeth, King Lear*, and *Cymbeline*, are based on Holinshed's work.

## Holkham Hall

House in Norfolk, England, 13 km/8 mi north of Fakenham. One of the masterpieces of the Palladian style, it was designed by William ◊Kent, advised by Richard ◊Burlington, and built between 1734 and 1759. Capability ◊Brown laid out the grounds in 1762.

Its grey brick exterior contrasts with a palatial interior, the chief feature of which is its pillared, apsidal entrance hall and staircase.

## Holmes, Sherlock

Fictitious private detective, created by the English writer Arthur Conan ◊Doyle in *A Study in Scarlet* (1887) and recurring in novels and stories until 1927. Holmes' ability to make inferences from slight clues always astonishes the narrator, Dr Watson.

The criminal mastermind against whom Holmes repeatedly pits his wits is Professor James Moriarty. Holmes is regularly portrayed at his home, 221b Baker Street, London (since 1990 a Sherlock Holmes museum), where he plays the violin and has bouts of determined action interspersed by lethargy and drug-taking. His characteristic pipe and deerstalker hat were the addition of an illustrator.

## Holst, Gustav (1874–1934)

English composer of distant Swedish descent. He wrote operas, including *Sávitri* (1908) and *At the Boar's Head* (1924); ballets; choral works, including *Hymns from the Rig Veda* (1908–12) and *The Hymn of Jesus* (1917); orchestral suites, including *The Planets* (1914–16); and songs. He was a lifelong friend of Ralph ◊Vaughan Williams, with whom he shared an enthusiasm for English folk music. His musical style, although tonal and drawing on folk song, tends to be severe. He was the father of Imogen Holst (1907–  ), musicologist and his biographer. His home in Cheltenham is a museum.

## Holtby, Winifred (1898–1935)

English novelist and journalist. She was an ardent advocate of women's freedom and of racial equality. Her novel *South Riding* (1936), set in her native Yorkshire, was awarded the Tait Black Memorial Prize and was subsequently filmed and televised. Her other works include an analysis of women's position in contemporary society, *Women in a Changing Civilization* (1934).

## Holy Grail

In medieval Christian legend, the dish or cup used by Jesus at the Last Supper, supposed to have supernatural powers. Together with the spear with which he was wounded at the Crucifixion, it was an object of quest by King Arthur's knights in certain stories incorporated in the Arthurian legend.

According to one story, the blood of Jesus was collected in the Holy Grail by Joseph of Arimathaea at the Crucifixion, and he brought it to Britain where he allegedly built the first church, at Glastonbury. At least three churches in Europe possess vessels claimed to be the Holy Grail.

## Holy Island, or Lindisfarne

Island in the North Sea, 3 km/2 mi off the coast of Northumberland, northeast England, with which it is connected by a causeway at low tide; area 10 sq km/4 sq mi; population (1991) 179. It is the site of a monastery founded by St ◊Aidan in 635.

*Features*

The northern part of the island is mostly sandy, but the rest is fertile. To the southwest of the island is a small village with a harbour. Nothing has survived of the original monastery but there are remains of the 11th-century Benedictine priory. In the 16th century stones from the priory were used to construct **Lindisfarne Castle**, which was converted into a private house by Edwin Lutyens in 1903, and is now the property of the National Trust.

*History*

The Celtic manuscript known as the ◊Lindisfarne Gospels, dating from about 698, was written here as a memorial to St Cuthbert (prior of Lindisfarne from 664 to 676). The manuscript is now in the British Museum. Following his death on Farne Island in 687, St Cuthbert's body was returned to Lindisfarne, and the monastery became a place of pilgrimage until the monks were driven from the island by the Danes in 875. According to tradition, the monks took with them the remains of St Cuthbert and finally settled in Durham in 995. Benedictine monks from Durham returned to the island in 1082, renamed it Holy Island, and established a Benedictine priory here.

## Holy Island, or Holyhead Island, Welsh Ynys Gybi

Rocky and barren island west of the Isle of Anglesey, northwest Wales; length 13 km/8 mi, width 6 km/4 mi. It is connected to Anglesey by a sandy causeway. The island is a centre for surfing and sea angling, and Trearddur on Penrhos Bay is a seaside resort. Holy Island is designated as an Environmentally Sensitive Area.

The island is one of the oldest sites of human settlement in Wales, and has numerous prehistoric and Roman remains including an Iron-Age hillfort and a Roman watchtower on Holyhead Mountain (Welsh *Mynydd Twr*), 200 m/656 ft.

## Holyrood House

Royal residence in Edinburgh, Scotland. The palace was built from 1498 to 1503 on the site of a 12th-century abbey by James IV. It has associations with Mary Queen of Scots, and Charles Edward, the Young Pretender. Holyrood was the royal palace of the Scottish kings until the Union, and is now a palace of the British monarchy, used during state visits but otherwise open to the public.

One wing remains from the original building begun by James IV, but everything else was burnt in 1544. The main part of the palace was built between 1671 and 1679 for Charles II, to the designs of William Bruce (*c.* 1630–1710).

Adjoining the palace are the ruins of Holyrood Abbey, founded in 1128 by David I.

## Home Counties

Counties in close proximity to London: Hertfordshire, Essex, Kent, Surrey, Buckinghamshire, and formerly Berkshire and Middlesex.

## home front

Organized sectors of domestic activity in wartime, mainly associated with World Wars I and II. Features of the UK home front in World War II included the organization of the black-out, evacuation, air-raid shelters, the Home Guard, rationing, and distribution of gas masks. With many men on active military service, women were called upon to carry out jobs previously undertaken only by men.

## Home Guard

Unpaid force formed in Britain in May 1940 to repel the expected German invasion, and known until July 1940 as the Local Defence Volunteers. It consisted of men aged 17–65 who had not been called up, formed part of the armed forces of the Crown, and was subject to military law. Over 2 million strong in 1944, it was disbanded on 31 December 1945, but revived in 1951, then placed on a reserve basis in 1955. It ceased activity in 1957. The long-running television comedy series *Dad's Army* was based on the Home Guard.

## Home Office

Government department established in 1782 to deal with all the internal affairs of England except those specifically assigned to other departments. Responsibilities include the police, the prison service, immigration, race relations, and broadcasting. Including the HM Prisons Service, which had 38,000 staff in 1998, it employs more than 50,000 people. The home secretary holds cabinet rank.

There is a separate secretary of state for Scotland and another for Wales. The home secretary has certain duties in respect of the Channel Islands and the Isle of Man.

## Home Rule, Irish

Movement to repeal the Act of ◊Union of 1801 that joined Ireland to Britain, and to establish an Irish Parliament responsible for internal affairs. In 1870 Isaac Butt (1813–1879) formed the Home Rule Association and the movement was led in Parliament from 1880 by Charles ◊Parnell. After 1918 the demand for an independent Irish republic replaced that for home rule.

Gladstone's Home Rule bills of 1886 and 1893 were both defeated. A third bill was introduced by the Liberals in 1912, which aroused opposition in Ireland where the Protestant minority in Ulster feared domination by the Catholic majority. Ireland appeared on the brink of civil war but the outbreak of World War I rendered further consideration of Home Rule inopportune.

In 1920 the Government of Ireland Act introduced separate Parliaments in the North and South and led to the treaty of 1921 that established the Irish Free State.

## Honiton

Market town in Devon, southwest England, on the River Otter, 27 km/17 mi northeast of Exeter; population (1996 est) 9,700. Honiton's handmade pillow-lace industry, introduced by Flemish settlers during the reign of Elizabeth I, is undergoing a revival of interest.

Tourism is significant locally; the River Otter is renowned for its trout fishing.

## honours list

Military and civil awards approved by the sovereign of the UK and published on New Year's Day and on her official birthday in June. Many Commonwealth countries, for example, Australia and Canada, also have their own honours list.

The Political Honours Scrutiny Committee is a group of privy councillors established after Lloyd George's extravagant abuse of the honours system to reward party benefactors. Names are considered for honours in four ways: (1) from senior government officials; (2) nominated personally by the Queen; (3) directly from the major political parties, through the chief whip; and (4) through the prime minister who can add to or subtract from all the above lists. It became a criminal offence to misuse the honours system in the UK in 1925.

## Hood, Robin

Hero of English legend; see ◊Robin Hood.

## Hood, Samuel, 1st Viscount Hood (1724–1816)

English admiral. A masterly tactician, he defeated the French at Dominica in the West Indies in 1783, and in the ◊Revolutionary Wars captured Toulon and Corsica.

## Hopkins, Frederick (1861–1947)

English biochemist whose research into diets revealed the necessity of certain trace substances, now known as vitamins, for the maintenance of health. Hopkins shared the 1929 Nobel Prize for Physiology or Medicine with Christiaan Eijkman, who had arrived at similar conclusions.

## Hopkins, Gerard Manley (1844–1889)

English poet and Jesuit priest. His works are marked by originality of diction and rhythm and include 'The Wreck of the Deutschland' (1876), and 'The Windhover' and 'Pied Beauty' (both 1877). His collected works was published posthumously in 1918 by his friend the poet Robert Bridges. His employment of 'sprung rhythm' (the combination of traditional regularity of stresses with varying numbers of syllables in each line) greatly influenced later 20th-century poetry.

His poetry is profoundly religious and records his struggle to gain faith and peace, but also shows freshness of feeling and delight in nature.

## Horniman, Annie Elizabeth Fredericka (1860–1937)

English pioneer of repertory theatre. She subsidized the Abbey Theatre, Dublin (built 1904), and founded the Manchester company at the Gaiety Theatre 1908.

## hornpipe

English dance popular between the 16th and 19th centuries, associated especially with sailors. During the 18th century it changed from triple time

(3/4) to common time (4/4). Examples include those by Purcell and Handel.

## Horse Guards
The Household Cavalry, or **Royal Horse Guards**, formed in 1661; also their headquarters in Whitehall, London. The building was erected in 1753 by John Vardy (1718–65) to a design by William ◊Kent, on the site of the Tilt Yard of Whitehall Palace. To the rear lies Horse Guards Parade, a large exercise ground where the ceremony of Trooping the Colour takes place annually in early June to mark the sovereign's official birthday.

Horseguards is the centre for two United Kingdom army commands: the London District, responsible for military administration in the City of London, and the Household Division, which has guard, escort, and ceremonial duties.

## horse racing
Sport of racing mounted or driven horses. Two forms in Britain are **flat racing**, for Thoroughbred horses over a flat course, and **National Hunt racing**, in which the horses have to clear obstacles.
*History*
Racing took place in Stuart times and with its royal connections became known as the 'sport of kings'. Early racecourses include Chester, Ascot, and Newmarket. The English classics were introduced in 1776 with the St Leger (run at Doncaster), followed by the Oaks in 1779 and Derby in 1780 (both run at Epsom), and 2,000 Guineas in 1809 and 1,000 Guineas in 1814 (both run at Newmarket). The first governing body for the sport was the Jockey Club, founded about 1750; it still has a regulatory role, but the British Horseracing Board became the governing body in 1993. The National Hunt Committee was established in 1866.
*Types of race*
**Steeplechasing** is a development of foxhunting, of which **point-to-point** is the amateur version, and **hurdling** a version with less severe, and movable, fences. Outstanding steeplechases are the Grand National (1839; at Aintree, Liverpool), and the Cheltenham Gold Cup (1924; at Cheltenham). The leading hurdling race is the Champion Hurdle (1927; at Cheltenham).
*Race horses, UK and Ireland*
There are approximately 8,000 Thoroughbred racehorses born each year in Britain and Ireland. The births occur mostly between February and May, but all Thoroughbred foals are registered as being 1 year old on 1 January of the following year. The next autumn, aged 18–20 months, they

begin training for racing in the coming spring. Horses are raced between two and eight years old.

## hospice
Residential facility specializing in palliative care for terminally ill patients and their relatives.

The first research and teaching hospice in the UK was St Christopher's Hospice in London, founded in 1967 by Cicely ◊Saunders.

## Housman, A(lfred) E(dward) (1859–1936)
English poet and classical scholar. His *A Shropshire Lad* (1896), a series of deceptively simple, nostalgic, ballad-like poems, has been popular since World War I. This was followed by *Last Poems* (1922), *More Poems* (1936), and *Collected Poems* (1939).

As a scholar his great work was his edition of the Roman poet Manilius, which is a model of textual criticism and marks him as one of the greatest English Latinists.

## Hove
Residential town and seaside resort, and from 1998 the administrative headquarters of ◊Brighton and Hove unitary authority, on the south coast of England, adjoining Brighton to the west; population (1996 est) 93,400. One of the world's pioneering filmmaking centres at the beginning of the 20th century, it was home to a group of British filmmakers known as the Brighton School.

Hove developed as a resort in the 19th century and includes Regency-style squares and terraces, as well as many parks and public gardens. The Sussex county cricket ground is here. It was the home of English novelist Ivy Compton-Burnett from 1892 to 1916.

## Howard, Catherine (c. 1520–1542)
Queen consort of ◊Henry VIII of England from 1540. In 1541 the archbishop of Canterbury, Thomas Cranmer, accused her of being unchaste before marriage to Henry and she was beheaded in 1542 after Cranmer made further charges of adultery.

## Huddersfield, Anglo-Saxon Oderesfelt
Industrial town in West Yorkshire, on the River Colne, between Leeds and Manchester; population (1991) 119,000. A thriving centre of woollens manufacture by the end of the 18th century, it now produces textiles and related products.
*History*
A village in Anglo-Saxon times, Huddersfield was mentioned in the Domesday Book of 1086 as

**Oderesfelt**, and in Subsidy Rolls, dated 1297, as Huddersfield. Nearby Almondbury (now a suburb to the south of the town) had a weekly market from 1272, and Huddersfield market was established in 1672. It was an important centre by the end of the 18th century, and developed rapidly in the 19th century as mills grew up along the river.

*Features*

Castle Hill, at the medieval settlement of Almondbury, was the site of an Iron Age camp and is crowned by the Victoria Tower (1897), built to commemorate the diamond jubilee of Queen Victoria. Ravensknowle Park and Hall (1860) includes the Tolson Memorial Museum, illustrating the development of the cloth industry, and some restored parts of the original Cloth Hall (built in 1776 and demolished in 1930). The Library and Art Gallery includes a collection of 20th-century art. To the west of the town is Slack, where excavations have revealed evidence of the Roman camp of **Cambodunum**. Nearby at Kirklees Park is the reputed grave of Robin Hood. The University of Huddersfield (formerly Huddersfield Polytechnic) was established in 1992.

### Hudson, Henry (c. 1565–1611)

English explorer. Under the auspices of the Muscovy Company 1607–08, he made two unsuccessful attempts to find the Northeast Passage to China. In September 1609, commissioned by the Dutch East India Company, he reached New York Bay and sailed 240 km/150 mi up the river that now bears his name, establishing Dutch claims to the area. In 1610 he sailed from London in the *Discovery* and entered what is now **Hudson Strait**. After an icebound winter, he was turned adrift by a mutinous crew in what is now **Hudson Bay**.

### Hughes, Ted (Edward James) (1930–1998)

English poet, poet laureate from 1984. His work is characterized by its harsh portrayal of the crueller aspects of nature, by its reflection of the agonies of personal experience, and by the employment of myths of creation and being, as in *Crow* (1970) and *Gaudete* (1977). His free-verse renderings, *Tales from Ovid* won the 1997 Whitbread Book of the Year prize.

Collections include *The Hawk in the Rain* (1957), *Lupercal* (1960), *Wodwo* (1967), *Wolfwatching* (1989), and *Winter Pollen: Occasional*

*Prose* (1994). His novels for children include *The Iron Man* (1968).

Hughes worked in various jobs as a gardener, security guard, film reader, and teacher. *Birthday Letters* (1998), a collection of poems written at various times, following the course of his seven-year marriage to the US poet Sylvia Plath, who committed suicide in 1963, won the 1998 Forward Prize and the 1998 Whitbread Book of the Year Award.

### Huguenot

French Protestant, particularly a Calvinist, persecuted in the 16th and 17th centuries under Francis I and Henry II. In 1598, under Henry IV, the Huguenots were granted toleration by the Edict of Nantes. This edict was revoked by Louis XIV in 1685, prompting large-scale emigration. Some 40,000 Huguenots settled in Britain, bringing their industrial skills with them.

Some were expert craftsmen in silver, an area in which they set new standards. In the next generation Paul de Lamerie (1688–1751) became the best known of English silversmiths. Other craftsmen secured the success of Spitalfields silk. Well-known descendants of the Huguenot immigrants include the actor David Garrick and the textile manufacturer Samuel Courtauld.

### Hull

Shortened name of ◊**Kingston upon Hull**, a city and unitary authority on the north bank of the Humber estuary, northeast England.

### Humber Bridge

Suspension bridge with twin towers 163 m/535 ft high, which spans the estuary of the River

**Humber Bridge** When completed in 1981, the Humber Bridge in northeast England was the world's longest suspension bridge, with a centre span of 1,410 m/4,628 ft. British Steel

Humber in northeast England. When completed in 1981, it was the world's longest bridge with a span of 1,410 m/4,628 ft.

Built at a cost of £150 million, toll revenues over the following 15 years proved inadequate to pay even the interest on the debt.

## Hundred Years' War

Series of conflicts between England and France 1337–1453. Its origins lay with the English kings' possession of Gascony (southwest France), which the French kings claimed as their fief, and with trade rivalries over Flanders. The two kingdoms had a long history of strife before 1337, and the Hundred Years' War has sometimes been interpreted as merely an intensification of these struggles. It was caused by fears of French intervention in Scotland, which the English were trying to subdue, and by the claim of England's ◊Edward III (through his mother Isabella, daughter of Philip IV of France) to the crown of France. See chronology below.

## hunger march

Procession of the unemployed, a feature of social protest in interwar Britain.

The first took place in 1922 from Glasgow to London and another in 1929. In 1932 the National Unemployed Workers' Movement organized the largest demonstration, with groups converging on London from all parts of the country, but the most emotive was probably the Jarrow Crusade of 1936, when 200 unemployed shipyard workers marched to the capital.

## Hunt, Leigh (1784–1859)

English essayist and poet. He influenced and encouraged the Romantics. His verse, though easy and agreeable, is little appreciated today, and he is best remembered as an essayist. He recycled parts of his *Lord Byron and Some of his Friends* (1828), in which he criticized Byron's character, as *Autobiography* (1850). The character of Harold Skimpole in Charles Dickens's *Bleak House* was allegedly based on him.

## Hunt, James (1947–1993)

English motor-racing driver who won his first Formula One race at the 1975 Dutch Grand Prix. He went on to win the 1976 world driver's title. Hunt started his Formula One career with Hesketh in 1973 and moved to Maclaren 1976–79, finishing in 1979 with Wolf. He later took up commentating for the BBC's Grand Prix coverage until his sudden death of a heart attack in June 1993.

## Hunt, Holman (1827–1910)

English painter, one of the founders of the ◊Pre-Raphaelite Brotherhood in 1848. His paintings, characterized both by a meticulous attention to detail and a clear moral and religious symbolism, include *The Awakening Conscience* (1853; Tate Gallery, London) and *The Light of the World* (1854; Keble College, Oxford).

## hunting

See ◊fox-hunting.

## Hurst Castle

Coastal fortification in Hampshire, England, about 6 km/4 mi southwest of the port of Lymington, at the mouth of the western arm of the ◊Solent. The castle lies at the end of a long shingle spit, and was originally erected by Henry VIII for the purpose of defending the Solent.

---

## Chronology of the Hundred Years' War

**1340** The English were victorious at the naval Battle of Sluis.

**1346** Battle of Crécy, a victory for the English.

**1347** The English took Calais.

**1356** Battle of Poitiers, where Edward the Black Prince defeated the French. King John of France was captured.

**late 1350s–early 1360s** France had civil wars, brigandage, and the popular uprising of the Jacquerie.

**1360** Treaty of Brétigny. France accepted English possession of Calais and of a greatly enlarged duchy of Gascony. John was ransomed for £500,000.

**1369–1414** The tide turned in favour of the French, and when there was another truce in 1388, only Calais, Bordeaux, and Bayonne were in English hands. A state of half-war continued for many years.

**1415** Henry V invaded France and won a victory at Agincourt, followed by conquest of Normandy.

**1420** In the Treaty of Troyes, Charles VI of France was forced to disinherit his son, the Dauphin, in favour of Henry V, who was to marry Catherine, Charles's daughter. Most of northern France was in English hands.

**1422–28** After the death of Henry V, his brother, the duke of Bedford, was generally successful.

**1429** Joan of Arc raised the siege of Orléans, and the Dauphin was crowned Charles VII at Rheims.

**1430–53** Even after Joan's capture and death the French continued their successful counteroffensive, and in 1453 only Calais was left in English hands.

**Hyde Park** Cyclists in Hyde Park, central London, England, in 1898. Hyde Park was traditionally a meeting place for fashionable people, and it was not until 1895 that cyclists were allowed in the park. At that time cycling was becoming a socially acceptable activity for women, and contributed to changes towards less restrictive styles of dress for women. Private collection

## Hutton, James (1726–1797)

Scottish geologist, known as the 'founder of geology', who formulated the concept of uniformitarianism. In 1785 he developed a theory of the igneous origin of many rocks.

His *Theory of the Earth* (1788) proposed that the Earth was incalculably old. Uniformitarianism suggests that past events could be explained in terms of processes that work today. For example, the kind of river current that produces a certain settling pattern in a bed of sand today must have been operating many millions of years ago, if that same pattern is visible in ancient sandstones.

## Hutton, Len (1916–1990)

English cricketer, born in Pudsey, West Yorkshire. A right-handed opening batsman, he captained England in 23 test matches 1952–56 and was England's first professional captain. In 1938 at the Oval he scored 364 against Australia, a world-record test score until beaten by Gary Sobers 1958. He was knighted for services to the game in 1956.

## Huxley, Aldous (1894–1963)

English writer of novels, essays, and verse. From the disillusionment and satirical eloquence of *Crome Yellow* (1921), *Antic Hay* (1923), and *Point Counter Point* (1928), Huxley developed towards the Utopianism exemplified by *Island* (1962). His most popular work, the science fiction novel ◊ *Brave New World* (1932) shows human beings mass-produced in laboratories and rendered incapable of freedom by indoctrination and drugs.

Huxley's later devotion to mysticism led to his experiments with the hallucinogenic drug mescalin, recorded in *The Doors of Perception* (1954). His other works include the philosophical novel *Eyeless in Gaza* (1936), and *After Many a Summer* (1939; Tait Black Memorial Prize).

## Huxley, Julian (1887–1975)

English biologist, first director general of UNESCO, and a founder of the World Wildlife Fund (now the World Wide Fund for Nature). He wrote popular science books, including *Essays of a Biologist* (1923). He was the brother of Aldous Huxley.

## Hyde Park

One of the largest open spaces in London, occupying over 138 ha/340 acres in Westminster, and adjoining Gardens to the west. It includes the Serpentine, a boating lake; and Rotten Row, a riding track. Open-air meetings are held at Speakers' Corner, in the northeast corner near Marble Arch. In 1851 the Great Exhibition was held here. The southeast corner of the park is known as **Hyde Park Corner**.

### History

The park was originally part of the **Manor of Hyde**, owned by Westminster Abbey, until it was taken by Henry VIII in 1536 at the time of the Dissolution of the Monasteries. It then became a royal deer park until it was opened to the public by Charles I. It was sold by Parliament in 1652, but reverted to the Crown at the Restoration. It became a fashionable coach- and horse-racing track, a rendezvous for duellists, and from its northwest corner crowds used to watch executions at Tyburn. The Serpentine (1730–33) was formed on the course of the old Westbourne River. The Great Exhibition of 1851 was housed in the ◊Crystal Palace, a glass and iron construction moved to Sydenham Hill in 1854, where it burned down in 1936. In 1855 a large number of people gathered illegally in the northeast corner of the park to demonstrate against the Sunday Trading Bill. There were further demonstrations, and the right of assembly in the park was recognized in 1872, the site becoming Speakers' Corner.

## Hythe

Seaside resort (one of the original ◊Cinque Ports) in the Romney Marsh area of Kent, southeast England; population (1996 est).

### Features

The Royal Military Canal (constructed 1804–06) was built as a defence against the threatened Napoleonic invasion, and is now a recreation area and scene of an annual water festival. The terminus of the Romney, Hythe, and Dymchurch narrow-gauge railway is here. Said to be the smallest public railway in the world, it runs for 23 km/14 mi from Hythe to Dungeness. Saltwood Castle, dating mainly from the 14th century, lies nearby to the north.

## Hywel Dda, Hywel the Good

Welsh king. He succeeded his father Cadell as ruler of Seisyllwg (roughly former Cardiganshire and present Towy Valley), at first jointly with his brother Clydog c. 910–920 then alone 920–950. He had extended his realm to Dyfed, Gwynedd, and Powys by 942, creating a larger Welsh kingdom than any before. His reign was peaceful, mainly because he was subservient to the English kings. He is said to have codified Welsh laws, but there is no contemporary record of this.

## Icknield Way

Major pre-Roman trackway traversing southeast England. It runs from Wells-next-the-Sea on the Norfolk coast in a generally southwesterly direction, passing first through Cambridgeshire and Hertfordshire. The Icknield Way then runs through Luton in Bedfordshire, skirts the Chiltern Hills, crosses the River Thames at Goring and follows the line of the Berkshire Downs to the source of the River Kennet in Wiltshire.

## Ickworth

House and 730 ha/1803 acre estate in Suffolk, England, 1 km/0.5 mi southwest of Bury St Edmunds. Ickworth was built by Frederick Augustus Hervey (1730–1803), 4th Earl of Bristol and bishop of Derry, around 1794, and was presented to the National Trust by the Treasury in 1956.

Its unusual design comprises an elliptical rotunda with two curved corridors leading to flanking wings. The rotunda was designed to contain the living accommodation, while the wings were designed to house the bishop's collections of furniture, silver, pictures, and sculpture. The collections are now on display in the house, which is open to the public.

## Ilkley, Roman Olicana

Spa town in West Yorkshire, northern England, on the River Wharfe, 16 km/10 mi north of Bradford; population (1996 est) 13,900. The largest town in Wharfedale, it is mainly residential, acting as a dormitory town for Leeds and Bradford. It is a popular centre for touring the Yorkshire Dales. **Ilkley Moor** lies to the south of the town.

Originally the site of an Iron Age settlement, it was later the Roman station of **Olicana**. An Elizabethan manor house, built on the site of the Roman fort, has been restored and now houses the Manor House Museum. All Saints' Church includes three Anglo-Saxon crosses in the churchyard. White Wells, on Ilkley Moor, is the site of a spring and small bath-house. Other features nearby are Bolton Abbey (founded 1151), 8 km/5 mi to the northwest of the town; and the Cow and Calf Rocks to the south. The dialect ballad 'On Ilkla Moor baht'at' (on Ilkley Moor without a hat) was reputedly composed by a church choir from Halifax during the course of a picnic beneath the rocks.

## immigration

Major subject of political debate in the UK in the 20th century. Following World War II Britain welcomed immigrants from the Commonwealth to help rebuild the economy with cheap labour; see ◊*Empire Windrush*. However the size of the immigrant population became a matter for concern in the 1960s, leading to Commonwealth Immigration Acts, passed 1962 and 1968, subsequently replaced by a single system of control under the Immigration Act of 1971. The British Nationality Act 1981 further restricted immigration by ruling that only a British citizen has the right to live in the United Kingdom.

There are five different categories of citizenship, with varying rights. Under the British Nationality Act 1981, amended by the British Nationality (Falkland Islands) Act 1983 and the Hong Kong Act 1985, only a person designated as a **British citizen** has a right of abode in the UK; basically, anyone born in the UK to a parent who is a British citizen, or to a parent who is lawfully settled in the UK. Four other categories of citizenship are defined: **British dependent territories citizenship**, **British overseas citizenship**, **British subject**, and **Commonwealth citizen**. Rights of abode differ widely for each.

See also ◊population, ◊Afro=Caribbean, and

◊ Muslim community for a feature detailing Muslim immigration over the past 300 years.

## Imperial War Museum

British military museum, founded in 1917. It includes records of all operations fought by British forces since 1914. Its present building (formerly the Royal Bethlehem, or Bedlam, Hospital) in Lambeth Road, London, was opened in 1936; it was rebuilt and enlarged in 1989.

## inch

Imperial unit of linear measure, a twelfth of a foot, equal to 2.54 centimetres. It was defined in statute by Edward II of England as the length of three barley grains laid end to end.

## Industrial Revolution

Sudden acceleration of technical and economic development that began in Britain in the second half of the 18th century. The traditional agrarian economy was replaced by one dominated by machinery and manufacturing, made possible through technical advances such as the steam engine. This transferred the balance of political power from the landowner to the industrial capitalist and created an urban working class. From 1830 to the early 20th century, the Industrial Revolution spread throughout Europe and the USA and to Japan and the various colonial empires. See chronology below, and feature on the Industrial Revolution, opposite.

The new working conditions led to political changes as wealth moved away from the land and towards the new manufacturing classes and there were massive social changes brought about by internal migration, a rising population, and the growth of urban areas.

### Textile industry

The textile industry saw most of the early benefits of these innovations. The flying shuttle was invented in 1738, rendering the old process of carrying the weft through the threads of the warp obsolete and enabling the weaver to double output. This in turn led spinners to seek mechanical aids to meet the increased demand for yarn. These innovations were swiftly followed by

## Chronology of the Industrial Revolution in Britain

**1701** The seed drill was invented by Jethro Tull. This was a critical point of the agricultural revolution which freed labour from the fields and lowered crop prices.

**1709** Abraham Darby introduced coke smelting to his ironworks at Coalbrookdale in Shropshire.

**1712** The first workable steam-powered engine was developed by Thomas Newcomen.

**1740** Crucible steelmaking was discovered by Benjamin Huntsman, a clockmaker of Doncaster.

**1759** The first Canal Act was passed by the British Parliament; this led to the construction of a national network of inland waterways for transport and industrial supplies. By 1830 there were 6,500 km/4,000 mi of canals in Britain.

**c. 1764** The spinning jenny, which greatly accelerated cotton spinning, was invented by James Hargreaves in Blackburn.

**1764** Pierre Trosanquet, a French engineer, developed a new method of road building. Similar techniques were used by Thomas Telford in Britain to build modern roads from 1803.

**1769** James Watt patented a more reliable and efficient version of the Newcomen engine.

**1779** The spinning mule, which made the production of fine yarns by machine possible, was developed in Bolton by Samuel Crompton.

**1785** The power loom marked the start of the mechanised textile industry.

**1797** The first true industrial lathe was invented, virtually simultaneously, by Henry Maudslay in England and David Wilkinson in the USA.

**1802** The first electric battery capable of mass production was designed by William Cruickshank in England.

**1811–16** Textile workers known as Luddites staged widespread protests against low pay and unemployment in Nottinghamshire, which involved destroying new machines.

**c. 1812** The population of Manchester passed 100,000.

**c. 1813** Industrial employment overtook agricultural employment in England for the first time.

**1825** The first regular railway services started between Stockton and Darlington in northeast England.

**1826** The Journeymen Steam Engine Fitters, the first substantial industrial trade union, was established in Manchester.

**1829** With his steam locomotive *Rocket*, English engineer George Stephenson won a contest to design locomotives for the new Manchester–Liverpool railway.

**1831–52** British industrial production doubled.

**1832** The Reform Act concerning elections to the British Parliament gave representation to the industrial cities.

**1833** The first effective Factory Act was passed in Britain regulating child labour in cotton mills.

**1842** Cotton-industry workers in England staged a widespread strike.

**1846** Repeal of the Corn Law in Britain reduced agricultural prices, thereby helping industry.

**1851** Britain celebrated its industrial achievements in the Great Exhibition.

**1852–80** British industrial production doubled again.

**1858** The 'great stink' of London dramatized the increasing pollution in the cities.

# ◆ DARK SATANIC MILLS: THE INDUSTRIAL REVOLUTION ◆

The British economy changed dramatically in the late 18th and early 19th centuries. Technological innovation, agricultural development, communications improvements, growing trade, and the increased consumer demand and labour supply afforded by a rising population took Britain to the forefront of economic progress. These changes had a profound impact on the lives and the mental outlook of contemporaries.

## Technological development

Though the rate of industrialization in Britain in the late 18th century was less impressive than used to be believed, and was restricted to only a few sectors (notably cotton textiles and metallurgy), a sense of economic change and the possibilities of progress was powerfully obvious to many contemporary observers. A popular metaphor was that of Prometheus Unbound, of extraordinary opportunities offered by technological innovation.

John Kay's flying shuttle of 1733, which was in general use in Yorkshire by the 1780s, increased the productivity of hand-loom weavers. James Hargreaves' spinning jenny (c. 1764), Richard Arkwright's 'spinning frame' (1768), and Samuel Crompton's mule (1779) revolutionized textile spinning. Arkwright and his partners built a number of cotton mills in Lancashire and the Midlands with all the characteristic features of factory system, including the precise division of labour and the co-operation of workers in different manufacturing processes. Cotton production grew by nearly 13% in the 1780s.

In 1769 James Watt patented a more energy-efficient use of steam engines. Steam pumps removed water from deep coal mines, and steam-powered winding engines were introduced in the early 1790s. Coal production increased rapidly, allowing a similar increase in the production of iron and lead. Canals and waggon-ways built to move coal prompted a wider revolution in transportation: for example, the 4th Duke of Portland built a new harbour at Troon on the west coast of Scotland in 1808, linked to his coal pits at Kilmarnock by a waggon-way which during 1839 carried over 130,000 tons of coal.

The coalfields attracted new, heavy industry, particularly in South Wales, Strathclyde, Northeast England, West Yorkshire, South Lancashire, the Vale of Trent, and the West Midlands. The smelting of iron and steel using coke, rather than charcoal, freed a major industry from dependence on wood supplies, while technological development spurred by Britain's wars and the demands of an Empire revolutionized the secondary metallurgical industries, especially gun founding. The percentage of the male labour force employed in industry rose from 19 in 1700 to 30 in 1800.

## The social dimension

The strains of industrialization in the early 19th century caused much social and political tension. Improvements in working conditions brought about by technological changes were very gradual, with the result that general living standards only began to rise noticeably after mid-century. The social – and indeed biological – pressure placed on the bulk of the population by the emergence of industrial work methods and economics is indicated by a marked decline in the height of army recruits in the second quarter of the century. Working conditions were often unpleasant and hazardous with, for example, numerous fatalities in mining accidents. The Factory Acts regulating conditions of employment in the textile industry still left work there both long and arduous. The 1833 Act established a factory inspectorate and prevented the employment of under-9s, but 9–13 year olds could still work 8-hour days, and 13–17 year olds 12 hours. The 1844 Act cut that of under-13s to 6 and a half hours, and of 18-year olds and all women to 12; those of 1847 and 1850 reduced the hours of women and under-18s to 10 hours. Despite such legislation, there were still about 5,000 half-timers under 13 in the Bradford worsted industry in 1907. If the bulk of the working population faced difficult circumstances, the situation was even worse for those more marginal to the new economy. 'Hell is a city much like London – A populous and a smoky city;' wrote the poet Shelley in *Peter Bell the Third* (1819). Fast-expanding towns became crowded and polluted, a breeding ground for disease. In 1852, 8,032 of the 9,453 houses in Newcastle lacked toilets.

## Britain the world leader

The Industrial Revolution gave Britain a distinctive economy. It became the world leader in industrial production and foreign trade. The annual averages of coal and lignite production, in million metric tons, for 1820–24 were 18 for Britain, compared with 2 for France, Germany, Belgium, and Russia combined. The comparable figures for 1855–59 were 68 and 32, and for 1880–84 159 and 108. The annual production of pig-iron in million metric tons in 1820 was 0.4 for Britain and the same for the rest of Europe, in 1850 2.3 and 0.9, and in 1880 7.9 and 5.4. Raw cotton consumption in thousand metric tons in 1850 was 267 for Britain and 162 for the rest of Europe. Britain was the workshop of the world.

by Jeremy Black

others, notably James Hargreaves's 'spinning jenny' about 1764, Richard Arkwright's water-frame spinning roller in 1768, and Samuel Crompton's 'spinning mule', a combination of Hargreaves's jenny and Arkwright's water-frame, in 1779. Edmund Cartwright's power loom was not perfected for another 25 years but by that time his Doncaster factory was equipped with a steam engine and a year or two later hundreds of his looms were selling to Manchester firms. Gradually the power loom began to be used in the woollen industry as well as the cotton trade for which it had been invented.

## Inveraray

Former county town and royal burgh in Argyll and Bute unitary authority, Scotland, situated on Loch Fyne, 37 km/23 mi northwest of Greenock; population (1991) 500. A popular tourist centre, the town was originally laid out on a grand scale in 1743 by Archibald, 3rd Duke of Argyll; it was sited close to **Inveraray Castle**, his ancestral seat.

The castle, initially constructed in the 15th century as the stronghold of the 1st Earl of Argyll, head of the clan Campbell, was also redesigned in 1745 by the 3rd duke to provide a stately home.

## Inverclyde

Unitary authority in western Scotland, created in 1996 from Inverclyde district in Strathclyde region; population (1996) 90,000; area 161 sq km/62 sq mi. It is situated on the Firth of Clyde, near Glasgow, and the chief towns are ◊Greenock (administrative headquarters), Port Glasgow, and Gourock. The area played a key part in the industrial history of Scotland as a port and a heavy engineering centre.
*Physical*
Inverclyde is characterized by coastal lowland on the Firth of Clyde estuary, rising sharply to an inland plateau of 305 m/1,000 ft.
*Features*
The area has the Inverkip Marina, four Sites of Special Scientific Interest and one regional park.
*Economy*
It is predominantly a de-industrializing urban area with more affluent villages in the south and low-quality agricultural land away from the coastal plain. Regeneration has been led by high technology.

## Inverness

Main town in, and the administrative centre of, Highland unitary authority, Scotland, at the head of the Moray Firth, lying in a sheltered site at the mouth of the River Ness; population (1991)

41,200. It is the administrative, commercial, and tourist centre of the ◊Highlands, and has services and manufacturing related to offshore oil exploration.
*History*
Inverness was the capital of the Pictish kingdom of King Brude, who was visited and converted by St Columba in the mid-6th century. A medieval burgh by the 12th century, the town was a royal residence and fortress – which it remained for centuries – with a castle attributed to King Malcolm III Canmore (*c.* 1031–1093).
*Features*
The present castle dates from the 19th century. Of the surviving earlier buildings there are the old Town Cross (1685), the Town Steeple, the old High Church (1769–72), and St Andrew's Cathedral (1866–71) Culloden Moor, scene of the massacre of clansmen loyal to Charles Edward Stuart by the English Army in April 1746, is to the east of Inverness.

## Iona

Island in the Inner Hebrides; area 850 hectares/2,100 acres. A centre of early Christianity, it is the site of a monastery founded 563 by St ◊Columba. It later became a burial ground for Irish, Scottish, and Norwegian kings. It has a 13th-century abbey.

## Ipswich, Saxon Gyppeswyk

River port and administrative headquarters of Suffolk, eastern England, on the Orwell estuary, 111 km/69 mi northeast of London; population (1996 est) 113,000. It was an important wool port in the 16th century.
*History*
Originally the site of a small Roman settlement, **Gyppeswyk** prospered as a port and agricultural centre throughout the Saxon period. The Danes were defeated at sea off the mouth of the Orwell in 885 by King Alfred, but in 991 and 1010 they invaded the town and set fire to it. In 1200 King John granted Ipswich its first charter. During the reign of Edward III weavers and wool workers from the Netherlands settled in the area and the Suffolk wool industry grew rapidly. In 1518 Henry VIII granted a charter confirming the corporation's jurisdiction over the Orwell estuary as far as what is now the port of Harwich.
*Features*
At the centre of the town is Cornhill, formerly the site of the Saxon market. In the Butter Market is the Ancient House, or Sparrowe's House (1567), which includes a fine example of pargeting (ornamental carving of the plasterwork on its façade).

To the north of the centre is Christchurch Mansion (1548–50), which now houses a museum with paintings by the Suffolk artists John Constable and Thomas Gainsborough. Ipswich Museum includes geological and archaeological exhibits. The library was built in 1924, and is an important repository for Suffolk records. **Ipswich School** (now a private school) was established in 1477 or earlier in the precincts of the Blackfriars monastery; it moved to its present site in 1851.

The town has many medieval churches: St Margaret's dates from the early 13th century; the Perpendicular St Peter's was renovated and extended in 1878 under Gilbert Scott; and the church of St Nicholas has a 14th-century nave and aisles. Other churches include St Mary-le-Tower, where King John's charter was received in 1200 by the bailiffs and burgesses; the 15th-century St Mary-at-the-Quay; and St Lawrence, a lofty Perpendicular church.

### IRA, or Irish Republican Army

Militant Irish nationalist organization formed in 1919, the paramilitary wing of ◊ Sinn Féin. Its aim has been to create a united Irish socialist republic including Ulster. To this end, the IRA has habitually carried out bombings and shootings in Ireland, mainland Britain, and in British military bases in continental Europe. Despite its close association with Sinn Féin, it is not certain that the politicians have direct control of the military, the IRA usually speaking as a separate, independent organization. The chief common factor shared by Sinn Féin and the IRA is the aim of a united Ireland.

In 1969 the IRA split into two wings, one 'official' and the other 'provisional'. The official wing sought reunification by political means, while the **Provisional IRA**, or Provos, carried on with terrorist activities, their objective being the expulsion of the British from Northern Ireland. It is this wing, of younger, strongly sectarian Ulster Catholics, who are now generally regarded and spoken of as the IRA.

In February 2000 the new ◊ Northern Ireland Assembly was suspended after continuing refusal by the IRA to decommission weapons.

### Ireland

One of the British Isles, lying to the west of Great Britain, from which it is separated by the Irish Sea. It comprises the provinces of Ulster, Leinster, Munster, and Connacht, and is divided into the Republic of Ireland (which occupies the south, centre, and northwest of the island) and ◊ Northern Ireland (which occupies the northeastern corner and forms part of the United Kingdom). See page 242 for a chronology of Ireland's history.

### Ireland, Northern

See ◊ Northern Ireland.

### Irish Free State

Former name (1922–37) of Southern Ireland, now the Republic of Ireland.

### Irish National Liberation Army, or INLA

Guerrilla organization committed to the end of British rule in Northern Ireland and the incorporation of Ulster into the Irish Republic. The INLA was a 1974 offshoot of the Irish Republican Army (IRA). Among the INLA's activities was the killing of British politician Airey Neave in 1979. The INLA initially rejected the IRA's call for a ceasefire in 1994; its assassination in 1997 of loyalist leader Billy Wright threatened to destabilize the peace process and bomb attacks occurred in London in 1998. However, after the Omagh bomb atrocity in 1998 the INLA became the first republican subversive group to explicitly state that the war was over and voice strong support for the peace process.

### Irish Sea

Arm of the North Atlantic Ocean separating England and Wales from Ireland; area 103,600 sq km/39,990 sq mi. Its greatest width, between Morecambe Bay, Lancashire, and Dundalk Bay, Louth, is 240 km/150 mi. It joins the Atlantic to the south by St George's Channel and to the north by the North Channel.

### Ironbridge Gorge

Site in the Telford and Wrekin unitary authority, England, on the River Severn, south of Telford; it is the site of the Iron Bridge (1777–79) designed by Abraham Darby III (1750–89). The bridge was the world's first iron bridge, and is one of the first and most striking products of the Industrial Revolution in Britain. Designated a British National Monument, it forms the centrepiece of the Ironbridge Gorge World Heritage Site, a series of museums of industrial archaeology in and near the villages of Ironbridge (population (1991) 2,200) and ◊ Coalbrookdale.

Abraham Darby III constructed the Iron Bridge from castings made in his pioneering iron foundry at nearby Coalbrookdale. It was here that Abraham Darby I had first used coke rather than the more expensive charcoal in the iron smelting process, so allowing for increased production. Abraham Darby II (1711–63) later succeeded in

# Ireland: Chronology

**432 or 456** St Patrick's mission to Ireland.
**563** St Columba founds the monastery at Iona.
**585** St Columba sails to France.
**795** First Viking raids on Ireland.
**840** Vikings found Dublin.
**1002** Brian Boru acknowledged High King of Ireland.
**1014** Brian Boru killed as he defeats Norsemen at Battle of Clontarf.
**1169** Norman invasion of Ireland begins.
**1172** Henry II lands at Waterford.
**1315** Edward Bruce invades Ireland.
**1318** Edward Bruce killed at Battle of Dundalk.
**1394** First visit of Richard II to Ireland.
**1399** Second visit of Richard II to Ireland.
**1491** Poyning's law makes Irish legislature dependent on England.
**1541** Irish parliament confirms Henry VIII as king of Ireland.
**1569** First Desmond rebellion against Protestant 'plantations' or settlements.
**1579** Second Desmond rebellion.
**1586** Plantation of Munster by English and Scottish settlers.
**1594** Rebellion of Hugh O'Neill, Earl of Tyrone.
**1598** Battle of the Yellow Ford, supported by Spanish troops, O'Neill annihilates an English force.
**1601** Battle of Kinsale; O'Neill defeated by Lord Mountjoy.
**1603** Treaty of Mellifont; a general amnesty follows.
**1607** Flight of the Earls; the earls of Tyrone and Tyrconnell flee to Spain.
**1609** Plantation of Ulster by Protestant English settlers.
**1633** Sir Thomas Wentworth becomes Lord Deputy of Ireland.
**1641** Ulster rising begins; Ulster Protestants are massacred.
**1642** Confederation of Kilkenny formed; an independent Irish parliament.
**1646** Owen Roe O'Neill defeats a Scottish army led by Robert Monro at the Battle of Benburb.
**1649** Oliver Cromwell captures Drogheda and Wexford.
**1652** English confiscation of land from Irish begins.
**1681** Irish Jesuit and Primate of Ireland Oliver Plunkett executed in London.
**1689** Unsuccessful siege of Londonderry by the forces of James II.
**1690** William III wins the Battle of the Boyne.
**1691** Treaty of Limerick, followed by land confiscation.
**1695** Penal laws introduced against Catholics.
**1720** Act declaring British parliament's right to legislate for Ireland passed.
**1791** Society of United Irishmen formed.
**1792** Catholic Relief Acts ease penal laws against Catholics.
**1795** Protestant Orange Order founded in Co Armagh.
**1798** United Irishmen's rising fails; a prominent member, Wolfe Tone, commits suicide.
**1800** Act of Union establishes United Kingdom of Great Britain and Ireland; effective 1801.
**1823** Catholic Association founded by Daniel O'Connell to campaign for Catholic political rights.

**1828** O'Connell elected for County Clare; forces granting of rights for Catholics to sit in Parliament.
**1829** Catholic Emancipation Act.
**1838** Tithe Act (abolishing payment) removes a major source of discontent.
**1840** Franchise in Ireland reformed. 'Young Ireland' formed.
**1846–51** Potato famine results in widespread death and emigration. Population reduced by 20%.
**1850** Irish Franchise Act extends voters from 61,000 to 165,000.
**1858** Fenian Brotherhood formed.
**1867** Fenian insurrection fails.
**1869** Church of Ireland disestablished.
**1870** Land Act provides greater security for tenants but fails to halt agrarian disorders. Protestant Isaac Butt forms Home Government Association (Home Rule League).
**1874** Home Rule League wins 59 Parliamentary seats and adopts a policy of obstruction.
**1880** Charles Stuart Parnell becomes leader of Home Rulers, dominated by Catholic groups. 'Boycotts' against landlords unwilling to agree to fair rents.
**1881** Land Act greeted with hostility. Parnell imprisoned. 'No Rent' movement begins.
**1882** 'Kilmainham Treaty' between government and Parnell agrees conciliation. Chief Secretary Cavendish and Under Secretary Burke murdered in Phoenix Park, Dublin.
**1885** Franchise Reform gives Home Rulers 85 seats in new parliament and balance between Liberals and Tories. Home Rule Bill rejected.
**1886** Home Rule Bill rejected again.
**1890** Parnell cited in divorce case, which splits Home Rule movement.
**1893** Second Home Rule Bill defeated in House of Lords; Gaelic League founded.
**1900** Irish Nationalists reunite under Redmond. 82 MPs elected.
**1902** Sinn Féin founded by Arthur Griffith.
**1906** Bill for devolution of power to Ireland rejected by Nationalists.
**1910** Sir Edward Carson leads Unionist opposition to Home Rule.
**1912** Home Rule Bill for whole of Ireland introduced. (Protestant) Ulster Volunteers formed to resist.
**1913** Home Rule Bill defeated in House of Lords but overridden. (Catholic) Irish Volunteers founded in the South.
**1914** Nationalists persuaded to exclude Ulster from Bill for six years but Carson rejects it. Curragh 'mutiny' casts doubt on reliability of British troops against Protestants. Extensive gun-running by both sides. World War I defers implementation of Home Rule.
**1916** Easter Rising by members of Irish Republican Brotherhood. Suppressed by troops and leaders executed.
**1919** Irish Republican Army (IRA) formed.
**1921** Partition of Ireland; creation of Irish Free State.

making iron suitable for forging as well as casting. The area fell into decline in the 20th century until it was restored as an open-air museum, a major tourist attraction which recreates the heyday of this 'cradle of the Industrial Revolution'. Features include the Coalbrookdale Museum of Iron, Blists Hill Museum, Coalport China Museum, and Jackfield Tile Museum.

## Irving, Henry stage name of John Henry Brodribb (1838–1905)

English actor. He established his reputation from 1871, chiefly at the Lyceum Theatre in London, where he became manager in 1878. He staged a series of successful Shakespearean productions, including *Romeo and Juliet* (1882), with himself and Ellen ◊Terry playing the leading roles. He was the first actor to be knighted, in 1895.

## Isherwood, Christopher (William Bradshaw) (1904–1986)

English novelist. He lived in Germany from 1929–33 just before Hitler's rise to power, a period that inspired *Mr Norris Changes Trains* (1935) and *Goodbye to Berlin* (1939), creating the character of Sally Bowles, the basis of the musical *Cabaret* (1968). Returning to England, he collaborated with W H ◊Auden in three verse plays.

Isherwood was born in Disley, Cheshire, and educated at Cambridge University. After temporary employment as a private secretary and tutor, he went to Berlin. His first novel, *All the Conspirators*, was published in 1928, and was followed by *The Memorial* (1932). His next novel, *Mr Norris Changes Trains*, established his reputation, consolidated by *Goodbye to Berlin*.

In 1938 he went with Auden to China to write a book with him about conditions there, *Journey to a War* (1939). Isherwood afterwards lived in California, becoming a US citizen in 1946.

## Isis

Local name for the River ◊Thames around Oxford.

## Islandmagee

Peninsula on the coast of Antrim, Northern Ireland, near Larne; area 11 km/7 mi by 3 km/2 mi. There are large basalt cliffs on the east side, a section of which is known as the Gobbins.

There is a dolmen (Neolithic stone chamber) known as the Druid's Chair, at which a number of ornaments and funeral urns have been found.

In 1642 the inhabitants of Islandmagee were killed by forces from Carrickfergus, some reputedly by being thrown off the cliffs. Slaughterford Bridge commemorates this event.

## Isle of Anglesey

see ◊Anglesey, Isle of.

## Isle of Man

See ◊Man, Isle of.

## Isle of Wight

See ◊Wight, Isle of.

## Isles, Lord of the

Title adopted by successive heads of the MacDonald clan to assert their dominance over the Scottish highlands and the Western Isles, and independence from the king of Scots. James IV acquired their rights in 1493 and today the title is held by the Prince of Wales as heir to the monarch in Scotland.

## Islington

Inner borough of north Greater London. It includes the suburbs of Finsbury, Barnsbury, and Holloway; population (1991) 164,700.

*Features*

Sadler's Wells music hall, built in 1638 when Clerkenwell springs were exploited and Islington Spa became famous; present Sadler's Wells theatre (1927–31), where opera and ballet companies were established under direction of Lilian ◊Baylis; 16th-century St John's Gate at Clerkenwell; 17th-century houses at Newington Green; 18th-and 19th-century squares and terraces in Canonbury, Highbury, and Barnsbury; Wesley's Chapel (1777, restored 1978), with museum of Methodism and John Wesley's house; Regents Canal, with 886 m/2,910 ft-long tunnel; Tower Theatre (1952) in early 16th-century Canonbury Tower; Kings Head, pioneer of public-house theatres in the late 1960s; Almeida Theatre; Business Design Centre; Chapel Market; Camden Passage (antiques centre).

## ITV, or Independent Television

Independent television in the UK, paid for by advertising, dating from 1955. In 1998 there were 16 ITV licensees: Anglia, Border, Carlton, Central, Channel, GMTV, Grampian, Granada, HTV, London Weekend, Meridian, Scottish, Tyne Tees, Ulster, West Country, and Yorkshire. Their 10-year licences were granted from January 1993. Independent television companies are regulated by the ◊Independent Television Commission (ITC), and are required to provide quality, independent productions, with provision for viewers with disabilities.

See also ◊television and ◊comedy.

## Jack the Ripper

Popular name for the unidentified mutilator and murderer of at least five women prostitutes in the Whitechapel area of London in 1888.

The murders understandably provoked public outrage; the police were heavily criticized, which later led to a reassessment of police procedures. Jack the Ripper's identity was never discovered, although several suspects have been proposed, including members of the royal household.

## Jacobean

Style in the arts, particularly in architecture and furniture, during the reign of James I (1603–25) in England. Following the general lines of Elizabethan design, the Jacobean period was one of transition, using classical features with greater complexity and with more profuse ornamentation, and adopting many motifs from Italian Renaissance design.

An extreme example is the 'Tower of the Five Orders' (1613–18) at the Bodleian Library, Oxford, where the Classical Orders decorate a building with mullioned windows, battlements, and pinnacles.

A sudden change to full-blown Italian Renaissance architecture occurred early in the 17th century with the arrival of the Classical architect Inigo Jones, designer of the Queen's House, Greenwich (1617–35), and the Banqueting House, Whitehall (1619–22). Other notable Jacobean buildings include ◊Hatfield House, Hertfordshire (1607–12), and Blicking Hall, Norfolk (completed 1628), both by Robert Lyminge.

The most important example of ecclesiastical building is St John's Church, Leeds (1634), which is entirely Gothic in structure and general design, but contains magnificent Jacobean (strictly 'Carolean') interior woodwork fittings.

## Jacobite

Supporter of the royal house of Stuart after the deposition of James II in 1688. They include the Scottish Highlanders, who rose unsuccessfully under ◊Claverhouse in 1689; and those who rose in Scotland and northern England in 1715 under the leadership of ◊James Edward Stuart, the Old Pretender, and followed his son ◊Charles Edward Stuart in an invasion of England from 1745 to 1746 that reached Derby. After their final defeat at ◊Culloden, Jacobitism disappeared as a political force. The two risings are known as the **Jacobite Rebellions**.

## Jaguar

British car manufacturer that has enjoyed a long association with motor racing; owned by Ford from 1989. One of the most successful companies in the 1950s, Jaguar won the Le Mans 24-hour race five times in 1951–58. They enjoyed a comeback at Le Mans in the late 1980s winning in 1988 and 1990.

The legendary XK120 was built in 1949. In the 1960s Jaguar were unable to compete with the more powerful Ferrari sports cars and did not make a comeback until the 1980s. In 1989 the company was bought by Ford for £1.6 billion.

## James

Two kings of Britain:

### James I (1566–1625)

King of England from 1603 and Scotland (as **James VI**) from 1567. The son of Mary Queen of Scots and her second husband, Lord Darnley, he succeeded to the Scottish throne on the enforced abdication of his mother and assumed power in 1583. He established a strong centralized authority, and in 1589 married Anne of Denmark (1574–1619). As successor to Elizabeth I in England, James alienated the Puritans by his High

**James I** The son of Mary, Queen of Scots, James I of England was already King of Scotland when he came to the throne in England in 1603. Private collection

Church views and Parliament by his assertion of ◊divine right, and was generally unpopular because of his favourites, such as George Villiers, 1st Duke of ◊Buckingham, and his schemes for an alliance with Spain. He was succeeded by his son Charles I.

As king of Scotland, he curbed the power of the nobility, although his attempts to limit the authority of the Kirk (Church of Scotland) were less successful.

James thwarted Guy Fawkes's plot to blow up Parliament during its opening in 1605. The ◊gunpowder plot, with its anti-Catholic reaction, gave James a temporary popularity which soon dissipated. His foreign policy, aimed primarily at achieving closer relations with Spain, was also disliked.

### James II (1633–1701)
King of England and Scotland (as **James VII**) from 1685. The second son of Charles I, he succeeded his brother, Charles II. In 1660 James married Anne Hyde (1637–1671, mother of Mary II and Anne) and in 1673 ◊Mary of Modena (mother of James Edward Stuart). He became a Catholic in 1671, which led first to attempts to exclude him from the succession, then to the rebellions of ◊Monmouth and Argyll, and finally to the Whig and Tory leaders' invitation to William of Orange to take the throne in 1688. James fled to France, then led an uprising in Ireland in 1689, but after being defeated at the Battle of the Boyne (1690) he fled to France and remained in exile.

### James
Seven kings of Scotland:

### James I (1394–1437)
King of Scotland in 1406–37, who assumed power in 1424. He was a cultured and strong monarch whose improvements in the administration of justice brought him popularity among the common people. He was assassinated by a group of conspirators led by the Earl of Atholl, and was succeeded by his son James II.

### James II (1430–1460)
King of Scotland from 1437, who assumed power in 1449. The only surviving son of James I, he was supported by most of the nobles and parliament. He sympathized with the Lancastrians during the Wars of the ◊Roses, and attacked English possessions in southern Scotland. He was killed while besieging Roxburgh Castle.

Almost continual civil war raged during the period of his minority; the prize of the victors was custody of the king. In 1449 he married Mary, daughter of the Duke of Gueldres. He was succeeded by his son James III.

### James III (1451–1488)
King of Scotland from 1460, who assumed power in 1469. His reign was marked by rebellions by the nobles, including his brother Alexander, Duke of Albany. He was murdered during a rebellion supported by his son, who then ascended the throne as James IV.

Eldest son of James II, he became king at the age of nine. In 1469 he married Margaret, daughter of King Christian I of Denmark.

### James IV (1473–1513)
King of Scotland from 1488. He came to the throne after his followers murdered his father, James III, at Sauchieburn. His reign was internally peaceful, but he allied himself with France against England, invaded in 1513, and was defeated and killed at the Battle of ◊Flodden. James IV was a patron of poets and architects as well as a military leader.

In 1503 he married Margaret Tudor (1489–1541, daughter of Henry VII), which eventually led to his descendants succeeding to the English crown. He was succeeded by his son James V.

## James V (1512–1542)
King of Scotland from 1513, who assumed power in 1528. During the long period of his minority, he was caught in a struggle between pro-French and pro-English factions. When he assumed power, he allied himself with France and upheld Catholicism against the Protestants. Following an attack on Scottish territory by Henry VIII's forces, he was defeated near the border at Solway Moss in 1542.

Son of James IV and Margaret Tudor, he succeeded his father at the age of one year. His first wife, Madeline, daughter of King Francis I of France, died in 1537; the following year he married Mary of Guise. Their daughter, Mary Queen of Scots, succeeded him.

## James VI
Of Scotland. See ◊ James I of England.

## James VII
Of Scotland. See ◊ James II of England.

## James Francis Edward Stuart (1688–1766)
British prince, known as the **Old Pretender** (for the ◊ Jacobites, he was James III). Son of James II, he was born at St James's Palace and after the revolution of 1688 was taken to France. He landed in Scotland in 1715 to head a Jacobite rebellion but withdrew through lack of support. In his later years he settled in Rome.

## Jarrow Crusade
March in 1936 from Jarrow in Tyne and Wear, northeast England to London, protesting at the high level of unemployment following the closure of Palmer's shipyard in the town.

The march was led by Labour MP Ellen Wilkinson, and it proved a landmark event of the 1930s Depression. In 1986, on the fiftieth anniversary of the event, a similar march was held to protest at the high levels of unemployment in the 1980s.

## Jedburgh
Small town in the Scottish Borders unitary authority, Scotland, on **Jed Water**, 77 km/48 mi south of Edinburgh; population (1991) 4,100. It has the remains of a 12th-century abbey. Jedburgh is a woollen manufacturing centre.

The town's medieval castle was destroyed in 1409, and a prison built on its site in 1823. The fortified town house where Mary Queen of Scots stayed in 1566 is now a museum. The abbey was originally a church attached to an Augustinian priory founded by David I. The Spread Eagle is reputed to be the oldest hotel in Scotland and the fourth oldest in the British Isles.

## Jeffreys of Wem, George, 1st Baron Jeffreys of Wem (1644–1689)
Welsh judge, popularly known as 'the hanging judge'. He became Chief Justice of the King's Bench in 1683, and presided over many political trials, notably those of Philip Sidney, Titus Oates, and Richard Baxter, becoming notorious for his brutality.

Jeffreys was born in Denbighshire. In 1685 he became Lord Chancellor and, after ◊ Monmouth's rebellion, conducted the 'bloody assizes' during which 320 rebels were executed and hundreds more flogged, imprisoned, or transported. He was captured when attempting to flee the country after the revolution of 1688, and died in the Tower of London.

## Jekyll, Gertrude (1843–1932)
English landscape gardener and writer. She created over 300 gardens, many in collaboration with the architect Edwin ◊ Lutyens. In her books, she advocated colour design in garden planning and natural gardens of the cottage type, with plentiful herbaceous borders.

Originally a painter and embroiderer, she took up landscape design at the age of 48 when her eyesight deteriorated. Her home at Munstead Wood, Surrey, was designed for her by Lutyens.

## Jenner, Edward (1749–1823)
English physician who pioneered vaccination. In Jenner's day, smallpox was a major killer. His discovery in 1796 that inoculation with cowpox gives immunity to smallpox was a great medical breakthrough.

Jenner observed that people who worked with cattle and contracted cowpox from them never subsequently caught smallpox. In 1798 he published his findings that a child inoculated with cowpox, then two months later with smallpox, did not get smallpox. He coined the word 'vaccination' from the Latin word for cowpox, *vaccinia*.

## Jerome, Jerome K(lapka) (1859–1927)
English journalist and writer. His works include the novel *Three Men in a Boat* (1889), a humorous account of a trip on the Thames from Kingston to Oxford; the humorous essays 'Idle Thoughts of an Idle Fellow' (1889); and the play *The Passing of the Third Floor Back* (story 1908, dramatized version 1910).

*Three Men in a Boat* was followed by *Three Men on the Bummel* (1900), a less entertaining account of a tour in Germany.

## Jersey

Largest of the ◊Channel Islands; capital St Helier; area 117 sq km/45 sq mi; population (1991) 58,900. It is governed by a lieutenant governor representing the English crown and an assembly. Jersey cattle were originally bred here. Jersey gave its name to a woollen garment.

The island was occupied from 1940 until 1945 by German forces. Jersey zoo (founded in 1959 by Gerald Durrell) is engaged in breeding some of the world's endangered species.

## Jervaulx Abbey

Ruined Cistercian monastery in North Yorkshire, England, on the banks of the River Ure, 8 km/5 mi southeast of Leyburn. The abbey was founded in 1156. The remains of the cruciform church, the cloistral courts, chapter-house, refectory, and nine-windowed dormitory, belong to the Transitional Norman or Early English period.

The last abbot was hanged in 1537 because he was implicated in the Pilgrimage of Grace (1536–37), a rebellion against Henry VIII.

## Jewish community

The Jewish community in Britain numbers about 285,000 (1998); it is the largest in western Europe after that in France. The main groups are in Greater London (183,000), Manchester and Salford (28,000), Leeds (10,000), and Brighton and Hove (6,000). About 70% are affiliated to synagogues.

Jews first settled in Britain at the time of the Norman Conquest and remained until 1290, when they were banished by a royal decree. The present-day community was founded by Jews of Spanish and Portuguese origin, known as the Sephardim, who arrived in Britain in 1656; these now account for some 3% of the community. Later, more settlers came from Germany and eastern Europe. These are known as the Ashkenazim.

Most Ashkenazi Jews (63%) acknowledge the authority of the Chief Rabbi, while the more strictly observant (7%) have their own spiritual leaders, as do the Separdhim. There are about 360 Jewish congregations in Britain, and the officially recognized representative body for all groups is the Board of Deputies of British Jews, founded in 1760.

**Reform Judaism**, a branch of Judaism, has some 40 affiliated synagogues in the UK, collectively known as the Reform Synagogues of Great Britain. Their chief executive is Tony Bayfield, and in 1998 Mark Weiner was appointed Rabbi at the West London Synagogue.

**Jewish community** A Jewish elementary school. Certain areas of Britain are strongly identified with the Jewish community, for example the Golders Green and Mansion House districts of North London (with sizeable numbers of orthodox Hassidic Jews). As tailoring was a traditional Jewish profession, communities also developed in centres of the garment industry such as Manchester and Leeds. Jewish leaders are concerned that numbers may dwindle as more Jews marry and raise children outside the faith. Liba Taylor/Collections

## jig

Dance popular in the British Isles during the 16th century, which is thought to have developed into the **gigue**, later commonly used as the last movement of a Baroque suite.

## jingoism

Blinkered, war-mongering patriotism. The term originated in 1878, when the British prime minister Disraeli developed a pro-Turkish policy, which nearly involved the UK in war with Russia. His supporters' war song included the line 'We don't want to fight, but by jingo if we do ...'.

## Jockey Club

Governing body of English ◊horse racing until 1993, when the British Horseracing Board was formed. The Jockey Club still oversees licensing and regulation. It was founded about 1750 at the Star and Garter, Pall Mall, London.

## Jodrell Bank

Site in Cheshire, England, of the Nuffield Radio Astronomy Laboratories of the University of Manchester. Its largest instrument is the 76 m/250 ft radio dish (the Lovell Telescope), completed in 1957 and modified in 1970. A 38 × 25 m/125 × 82 ft elliptical radio dish was introduced in 1964, capable of working at shorter wave lengths.

## John, Augustus (1878–1961)

Welsh painter. He is known for his vivacious portraits, including *The Smiling Woman* (1910; Tate Gallery, London), portraying his second wife, Dorelia McNeill. His sitters included such literary figures as Thomas Hardy, Dylan Thomas, W B Yeats, T E Lawrence, and James Joyce.

From 1910 to 1919 John led a nomadic existence in Ireland, Dorset, and Wales, producing many poetic small oil paintings of figures in landscape. His cartoon for a mural decoration, *Galway* (1916; Tate Gallery), shows an inclination for large-scale work which was never fully realized. During World War I he was an official artist to the Canadian Corps.

## John, Gwen(dolen Mary) (1876–1939)

Welsh painter. She lived in France for most of her life. Many of her paintings depict young women or nuns (she converted to Catholicism in 1913), but she also painted calm, muted interiors.

Her style was characterized by a sensitive use of colour and of tone.

## John (I) Lackland (1167–1216)

King of England from 1199 and acting king from 1189 during his brother Richard the Lionheart's absence on the Third Crusade.

He lost Normandy and almost all the other English possessions in France to Philip II of France by 1205. His repressive policies and excessive taxation brought him into conflict with his barons, and he was forced to seal the ◊Magna Carta in 1215. Later repudiation of it led to the first Barons' War, 1215–17, during which he died. He was succeeded by his son Henry III.

## John Bull

Imaginary figure who is a personification of England. He is represented in cartoons and caricatures as a prosperous farmer of the 18th century.

The name was popularized by Dr John ◊Arbuthnot's political satire *History of John Bull* (1712), advocating the Tory policy of peace with France.

## John of Gaunt (1340–1399)

English noble and politician, fourth (and third surviving) son of Edward III, Duke of Lancaster from 1362. He distinguished himself during the Hundred Years' War. During Edward's last years, and the years before Richard II attained the age of majority, he acted as head of government, and Parliament protested against his corrupt rule.

In 1359 he married Blanche, daughter of Henry, Duke of Lancaster (died 1361), whose title passed to John of Gaunt in 1362; their son became Henry IV of England.

Later, John of Gaunt married his mistress of long standing, Katharine Swynford (*c*. 1350–1403), with whom he already had four children; they were legitimized in 1397 by charter of Richard II, and founded the house of Beaufort, from whom Henry VII was descended.

## John o' Groats

Village in the northeast of Highland unitary authority, Scotland, about 3 km/2 mi west of Duncansby Head, Britain's northernmost point. It is the furthest point from Land's End on the British mainland.

It is named after the Dutchman John de Groot, who built a house there in the 16th century. There are ferry connections to Burwick on South Ronaldsay.

## Johnson, Amy (1903–1941)

English aviator. She made a solo flight from England to Australia in 1930, in 9 ½ days, and in 1932 made the fastest-ever solo flight from England to Cape Town, South Africa. Her plane disappeared over the English Channel in World War II while she was serving with the Air Transport Auxiliary.

## Johnson, Samuel Dr Johnson (1709–1784)

English lexicographer, author, and critic. He was also a brilliant conversationalist and the dominant figure in 18th-century London literary society. His *Dictionary* (1755), provided in its method the pedigree for subsequent lexicography and remained authoritative for over a century. In 1764 he founded, at the suggestion of the painter Joshua Reynolds, a club, known from 1779 as the Literary Club, whose members at various times included the political philosopher Edmund Burke, the dramatist Oliver Goldsmith, the actor David Garrick, and James ◊Boswell, Johnson's biographer.

Johnson's first meeting with Boswell was in 1763. A visit with Boswell to Scotland and the Hebrides in 1773 was recorded in *A Journey to the*

*Western Isles of Scotland* (1775). Other works include a satire imitating Juvenal, *The Vanity of Human Wishes* (1749), the philosophical romance *Rasselas* (1759), an edition of Shakespeare (1765), and the classic *Lives of the English Poets* (1779–81).

Johnson's prose style is balanced, judicious, and sometimes ponderous, and as a critic he displayed great creative insight. His edition of Shakespeare is the forerunner of modern scholarly editions and his 'Preface to Shakespeare' remains a classic critical essay of permanent value. His well-known wit and humanity are documented in Boswell's classic *The Life of Samuel Johnson LL.D*, published in 1791, after Johnson's death.

---

Oats A grain, which in England is generally given to horses, but in Scotland supports the people.

**Samuel Johnson** English lexicographer, author, and critic.
*Dictionary of the English Language* (1755)

---

## Jones, Inigo (1573–1652)

English Classical architect. He introduced the ◊Palladian style to England. He was employed by James I to design scenery for Ben ◊Jonson's masques and was appointed Surveyor of the King's Works from 1615 to 1642. He designed the Queen's House, Greenwich (1616–35), and his English Renaissance masterpiece, the Banqueting House, Whitehall (1619–22). His work was to provide the inspiration for the Palladian Revival a century later.

Jones travelled a great deal, notably in Italy. Through his designs for masques and plays presented at Court, he introduced Italian perspective scenery into England, developing his own system of movable backcloths, and the proscenium arch.

## Jonson, Ben(jamin) (1572–1637)

English dramatist, poet, and critic. *Every Man in his Humour* (1598) established the English 'comedy of humours', in which each character embodies a 'humour', or vice, such as greed, lust, or avarice. This was followed by *Cynthia's Revels* (1600) and *The Poetaster* (1601). His first extant tragedy is *Sejanus* (1603), with Burbage and Shakespeare as members of the original cast. His great comedies are *Volpone, or The Fox* (1606), *The Alchemist* (1610), and *Bartholomew Fair* (1614). Jonson wrote extensively for court entertainment in the form of masques produced with scenic designer Inigo ◊Jones.

Jonson had a unique comic vision and a remarkable technical mastery of form. His work has had a profound influence on English drama and literature, for example on the Restoration dramatists and on novelists such as Henry ◊Fielding and Tobias ◊Smollett. As an outspoken and biting critic of folly, particularly those aspects associated with a materialistic society, Jonson's work continues to be influential and popular.

He was born in Westminster, London, and entered the theatre as an actor and dramatist in 1597. In 1598 he narrowly escaped the gallows for killing a fellow player in a duel; his goods were confiscated and he was imprisoned. In prison he became a Catholic, but 12 years later reverted to Protestantism. He was buried in Westminster Abbey.

## judge

Person invested with power to hear and determine legal disputes.

In the UK, judges are chosen from barristers of long standing, but solicitors can be appointed circuit judges. Judges of the High Court, the crown courts, and the county courts are appointed at the advice of the Lord Chancellor, and those of the Court of Appeal and the House of Lords at the advice of the prime minister, although all judges are appointed by the crown. The independence of the higher judiciary is ensured by the principle that they hold their office during good behaviour and not at the pleasure of the crown. They can be removed from office only by a resolution of both houses of Parliament.

## Julian of Norwich (c. 1342–after 1413)

English mystic. She lived as a recluse, and recorded her visions in *The Revelation of Divine Love* (1403), which shows the influence of neo-Platonism.

## Jura

Island of the Inner ◊Hebrides, Argyll and Bute; area 380 sq km/147 sq mi; population (1991) 196. It is separated from the Scottish mainland by the **Sound of Jura**. The whirlpool Corryvreckan (Gaelic 'Brecan's cauldron') is off the north coast. It has a range of mountains known as the 'Paps of Jura', the highest of which is Beinn an Oir at 784 m/2,572 ft.

Jura is the only major Scottish island without a direct link to the mainland.

## Kean, Edmund (1787–1833)

English tragic actor. He was noted for his portrayal of villainy in the Shakespearean roles of Shylock, Richard III, and Iago. He died on stage, playing Othello opposite his son as Iago.

## Keats, John (1795–1821)

English Romantic poet. He produced work of the highest quality and promise before dying at the age of 25. *Poems* (1817), *Endymion* (1818), the great odes (particularly 'Ode to a Nightingale' and 'Ode on a Grecian Urn' written in 1819, published in 1820), and the narratives 'Isabella; or the Pot of Basil' (1818), 'Lamia' (1819), and 'The Eve of St Agnes' (1820), show his lyrical richness and talent for drawing on both classical mythology and medieval lore.

Born in London, Keats studied at Guy's Hospital from 1815–17, but then abandoned medicine for poetry. In 1819 he fell in love with Fanny Brawne (1802–1865). Suffering from tuberculosis, he sailed to Italy in 1820 in an attempt to regain his health, but died in Rome. Valuable insight into Keats's poetic development is provided by his *Letters*, published in 1848.

Keats's poetry often deals with the relationship between love and death, beauty and decay. While 'The Eve of St Agnes', with its sensuous, pictorial language and romantic narrative, had immense influence on later 19th-century poetry, it is the odes which are Keats's most distinctive achievement, reflecting his feelings about human mortality. 'Ode to a Nightingale' is a symbol of beauty's power to surmount death, a theme which reappears in 'Ode on a Grecian Urn', where the figures on the vase are seen to epitomize an enduring truth, while 'Ode to Autumn' asserts the fulfilment of complete fruition and ripeness.

## Kells, Book of

8th-century illuminated manuscript of the Gospels produced at the monastery of Kells in County Meath, Ireland. It is now in Trinity College library, Dublin.

## Kempe, Margerie born Brunham (*c.* 1373–*c.* 1439)

English Christian mystic. She converted to religious life after a period of mental derangement, and travelled widely as a pilgrim. Her *Boke of Margery Kempe* (about 1420) describes her life and experiences, both religious and worldly. It has been called the first autobiography in English.

**John Keats** English romantic poet John Keats, who wrote most of his best-known poems during a concentrated spell in 1818. At this time he fell in love with Fanny Brawne, with whom he remained infatuated until his death. Today his letters, which are witty, warm, and insightful, are almost as highly regarded as his poetry. Corbis

## Kendal

Town in Cumbria, northwest England, on the River Kent, 35 km/22 mi north of Lancaster; population (1991) 24,900. The town is a tourist centre for visitors to the ◊Lake District.

Kendal was an important woollen textile centre from the 14th century. **Kendal mint cake**, made from sugar and peppermint oil, comes from here. The town was the birthplace of Catherine Parr, the sixth wife of Henry VIII.

Features include the remains of a Norman castle and Abbot Hall Art Gallery and Museum of Lakeland Life and Industry. The restored Sizergh Castle lies to the south of the town. **Kendal green**, mentioned in William Shakespeare's *Henry IV*, was a woollen cloth worn by English archers.

## Kenilworth

Town in Warwickshire, central England, 8 km/5 mi north of Warwick; population (1991) 21,000. The Norman castle, celebrated in Walter Scott's novel *Kenilworth*, became a royal residence. Edward II relinquished his crown here in 1327. The castle was enlarged by John of Gaunt and later by the Earl of Leicester – who entertained Elizabeth I here in 1575 – but was dismantled after the English Civil War.

There are some remains of an Augustinian priory dating from about 1122. The ruins of the castle were given to the British nation by the first Lord Kenilworth in 1937.

## Kenneth

Two kings of Scotland:

## Kenneth I called MacAlpin (died 860)

King of Scotland from about 844. Traditionally, he is regarded as the founder of the Scottish kingdom (Alba) by virtue of his final defeat of the Picts about 844. He invaded Northumbria six times, and drove the Angles and the Britons over the River Tweed.

## Kenneth II (died 995)

King of Scotland from 971, son of Malcolm I. He invaded Northumbria several times, and his chiefs were in constant conflict with Sigurd the Norwegian over the area of Scotland north of the River Spey. He is believed to have been murdered by his subjects.

## Kensington and Chelsea

Inner borough of central Greater London; population (1991) 138,400.

*Features*

◊Holland House (about 1606) and Holland Park; Camden House (about 1612); Kensington Palace, Jacobean house redesigned by Christopher ◊Wren for ◊William and Mary (1689); Kensington Gardens, with statue of Peter Pan; Leighton House (1866); Imperial College of Science and Technology (1907); Kensington and Chelsea Town Hall (1976) designed by Basil ◊Spence; museums – Victoria and Albert, Natural History, Science, and Geology; Royal College of Music; Royal College of Art; annual Notting Hill Carnival, held each August, is the largest street carnival in Europe.

## Kensington Palace

Palace in London, part of the royal household. Formerly Nottingham House, the home of Heneage Finch (1621–82), 1st Earl of Nottingham, it was purchased in 1689 by William III. The latter had it remodelled by Christopher ◊Wren, whose work survives mainly in the south front and northeast wing. Under George I there was further reconstruction by William Benson (1682–1754) and William Kent (northeast and southeast wings). George II was the last sovereign to use the palace.

Diana, Princess of Wales, lived at Kensington Palace and had her offices here following her separation from Prince Charles.

## Kent

County occupying the southeast tip of England, known as the 'garden of England'; population (1996) 1,557,300; area 3,730 sq km/1,440 sq mi. It is a county of great geographical contrast, with the rolling North Downs, white cliffs of Dover, wooded hills of the Weald, and fertile fruit farms. Circular oast houses with conical roofs, traditional buildings for drying hops, are characteristic. Kent is the arrival point in England for thousands of foreign visitors each year, and the Channel Tunnel opened just to the west of Dover in 1994. The principal towns and cities are ◊Maidstone (administrative headquarters), Ashford, ◊Canterbury, Deal, ◊Dover (ferry terminus), Gravesend, Hythe, New Ash Green (a new town), Sevenoaks, and Royal Tunbridge Wells; the main resorts are Folkestone, Margate, and Ramsgate. Parts of northwest Kent have now been absorbed into the southern outskirts of London, or lie within the commuter belt. Since April 1998 ◊Medway has been a separate unitary authority.

*History*

Kent's proximity to Europe and to London has meant that many historically important events have taken place in the county. It was on the coast of Kent that Caesar landed in 55 BC; to which

Hengist and Horsa brought their Saxon mercenaries; and to which St Augustine led his followers. The archbishop of Canterbury traces his descent as Primate of all England from St Augustine. St Thomas à Becket was murdered in Canterbury Cathedral, and his shrine became a place of pilgrimage until the Reformation. Canterbury is of great antiquity and evidence has been found here for continuity of settlement from Roman to Jute and Frankish times. The influences of these groups are reflected in Kent's language, custom, and settlement pattern, which contrast with those of the more predominantly Saxon Surrey and Sussex. Parts of Kent are open countryside, which could easily be invaded, and the former Royal Military Canal was cut across Romney Marsh as a defence against Napoleon.

*Features*

The Roman occupation is represented by Lullingstone Villa, which has fine mosaics. Canterbury continues to be an important centre for pilgrims and tourists alike. Historic castles include those at Dover (Roman, Saxon, and Norman) and Deal, a coastal defence fort built by Henry VIII. The county's most magnificent castles and country houses include Leeds Castle (converted to a palace by Henry VIII); Ightham Mote; Hever Castle (where Henry VIII courted Anne Boleyn); Chartwell (Winston Churchill's country home); Knole; and Sissinghurst Castle and gardens, home of the writer Vita Sackville-West. Walmer Castle is the official residence of the Lord Warden of the ◊Cinque Ports. The Brogdale Horticultural Trust, based outside Faversham, has the world's finest collection of apple and other fruit trees, and is open to the public. The former RAF Manston became Kent International Airport in 1989. Dungeness has a nuclear power station and a garden created by film-maker Derek Jarman (1942–1994).

*Economy*

Kent contains about half the orchards in England and Wales, providing half their hops, and one-fifth of their soft fruit. Tourism and travel to and from Europe is important to the local economy, and there is also mineral extraction and cement production, oil refining, and shipbuilding. The Bluewater shopping centre is a major retail development.

## Kent, William (1685–1748)

English architect, landscape gardener, and interior designer. Working closely with Richard ◊Burlington, he was foremost in introducing the ◊Palladian style to Britain from Italy, excelling in richly carved, sumptuous interiors and furnishings, as at ◊Holkham Hall, Norfolk, begun in 1734.

Immensely versatile, he also worked in a Neo-Gothic style, and was a pioneer of Romantic landscape gardening, for example, the grounds of Stowe House, Buckinghamshire, and Rousham Park, Oxfordshire (1738–40). Horace Walpole called him 'the father of modern gardening'.

## Kenwood House

Mansion on the east side of ◊Hampstead Heath, London. It was enlarged by the Earl of Mansfield after he received the estate in 1765. Robert ◊Adam designed two façades and the superb library, with lesser rooms, around 1766.

The house contains the art collection of the 1st Earl of Iveagh, including works by Rembrandt, Vermeer, Hals, ◊Gainsborough, Reynolds, Turner, and Stubbs. English Heritage now manage the house and art collection, which were bequeathed to the nation in 1927.

## Keswick

Market town and tourist centre in Cumbria, England, 35 km/22 mi southwest of Carlisle; population (1991) 4,600. The town is in the centre of the ◊Lake District and offers accommodation for walkers and holidaymakers. Another industry is the manufacture of pencils.

Derwent Water is adjacent to the town and a number of high hills are within easy reach. Skiddaw (930 m/3,052 ft), immediately north of Keswick, gives fine views.

## Kettering

Market town in Northamptonshire, England, 20 km/12 mi northeast of Northampton; population (1991) 73,800. Its principal industries are the manufacture of footwear and clothing, and engineering.

## Kew Gardens

Popular name for the Royal Botanic Gardens, Kew, Surrey, England. They were founded in 1759 by Augusta of Saxe-Coburg (1719–1772), the mother of King George III, as a small garden and were passed to the nation by Queen Victoria in 1840. By then they had expanded to almost their present size of 149 hectares/368 acres and since 1841 have been open daily to the public. They contain a collection of over 25,000 living plant species and many fine buildings. The gardens are also a centre for botanical research.

The herbarium is the biggest in the world, with

**Kew Gardens** The large glass Palm House of Kew Gardens in London, England, covers 24,000 sq ft and houses a collection of palm trees and waterlilies. Kew Gardens has an area of 300 acres and contains plants from all over the world. Liz Stares/Collections

over 5 million dried plant specimens. Kew also has a vast botanical library, the Jodrell Laboratory, and three museums. The buildings include the majestic Palm House (1848), the Temperate House (1862), both designed by Decimus Burton, and the Chinese Pagoda, some 50 m/165 ft tall, designed by William Chambers in 1761. More recently, two additions have been made to the glasshouses: the Alpine House (1981) and the Princess of Wales Conservatory, a futuristic building for plants from ten different climatic zones, built in 1987. Much of the collection of trees at Kew was destroyed by a gale in 1987.

Since 1964 there have been additional grounds at Wakehurst Place, Ardingly, West Sussex. Kew received £21 million from the Millennium Commission in December 1995 to construct a new seed bank here; it aims to house seeds of 10% of the world's flowers by 2010.

## Keynes, John Maynard, 1st Baron Keynes (1883–1946)

English economist. His *General Theory of Employment, Interest, and Money* (1936) proposed the prevention of financial crises and unemployment by adjusting demand through government control of credit and currency. He is responsible for that part of economics which studies whole economies, now known as macroeconomics.

Keynes led the British delegation at the Bretton Woods Conference in 1944, which set up the International Monetary Fund.

His theories were widely accepted in the aftermath of World War II, and he was one of the most influential economists of the 20th century. His ideas are today often contrasted with monetarism, the theory that economic policy should be based on control of the money supply.

## Kidd, 'Captain' William (c. 1645–1701)

Scottish pirate. He spent his youth privateering for the British against the French off the North American coast, and in 1695 was given a royal commission to suppress piracy in the Indian Ocean. Instead, he joined a group of pirates in Madagascar. In 1699, on his way to Boston, Massachusetts, he was arrested, taken to England, and hanged.

His execution marked the end of some 200 years of semi-official condoning of piracy by the British government.

## Kidderminster

Market town in Worcester, England, on the River Stour, 22 km/14 mi north of Worcester; population (1991) 54,600. Its carpet industry dates from about 1735, and associated activities include the manufacture of woollen and worsted yarns, and dyeing. Other industries include steel forging, pleasure boat building, and the manufacture of plastic and ceramic products, sugar, and chemicals. Small high-tech businesses are proliferating.

*History*

From the early 13th century the town was important for cloth weaving. Its charter of incorporation, granted by Charles I in 1636, describes it as 'an ancient borough of great commerce for the making and manufacture of cloth'.

*Features*
The Perpendicular church of St Mary and All Saints dates mainly from about 1450. The Staffordshire and Worcestershire Canal passes through the town, and it is also the southern terminus of the Severn Valley Railway. Kidderminster is known for the manufacture of Wilton, Axminster, Brussels, and tufted carpets.

*Famous people*
Rowland ◊ Hill, originator of the penny post, was born here in 1795, and the Nonconformist cleric Richard Baxter (1615–91) was a lecturer (minister) in the town from 1639 to 1662.

## Killiecrankie, Battle of

During the first ◊ Jacobite uprising, defeat on 7 May 1689 of General Mackay (for William of Orange) by John Graham of ◊ Claverhouse, a supporter of James II, at Killiecrankie, Scotland. Despite the victory, Claverhouse was killed and the revolt soon petered out; the remaining forces were routed on 21 August.

## Kilmainham Treaty

In Irish history, an informal secret agreement in April 1882 that secured the release of the nationalist Charles Stewart ◊ Parnell from Kilmainham jail, Dublin, where he had been imprisoned for six months for supporting militant Irish tenant farmers who had joined the Land League's campaign for agricultural reform. In particular, they were demanding lower rates to reflect the downturn in agriculture.

The British government realized that Parnell could quell the violence more easily out of prison than in it. In return for his release, he agreed to accept the Land Act of 1881. The Kilmainham Treaty marked a change in British policy in Ireland from confrontation to cooperation, with the government attempting to conciliate landowners and their tenants. This strategy was subsequently threatened by the ◊ Phoenix Park Murders.

## Kilmartin

Village in Argyll and Bute unitary authority, Scotland, situated near the southern end of Loch Awe, straddling the natural route to Oban, 11 km/7 mi north of Lochgilphead. Some of Scotland's most important prehistoric sites are found in the vicinity, including chambered cairns, sculptured slabs and crosses, and Bronze Age cairns.

The capital of the ancient Dalriada kingdom, established around AD 500, was situated at nearby Dunadd Fort.

## Kinder Scout

Mountain in Derbyshire, central England; height 636 m/2,087 ft. It is the highest point in the ◊ Peak District. The summit is an extensive peat-covered plateau.

## Kingsley, Charles (1819–1875)

English author. A rector, he was known as the 'Chartist clergyman' because of such social novels as *Yeast* (1848) and *Alton Locke* (1850). His historical novels include *Westward Ho!* (1855) and *Hereward the Wake* (1866). He also wrote, for children, *The ◊ Water Babies* (1863).

He was deeply interested in social questions, and threw himself wholeheartedly into the schemes of social relief which were supported under the name of Christian Socialism, writing many tracts and articles as 'Parson Lot'.

## King's Lynn formerly Bishop's Lynn

Port and market town in Norfolk, eastern England, at the mouth of the River Great Ouse, 56 km/35 mi northeast of Peterborough; population (1996) 40,200. It was a thriving port in medieval times, named **Bishop's Lynn** until it became royal property during the reign of Henry VIII.

*Features*
St George's Guildhall, dating from the early 15th century, has been restored as a theatre, annual festival centre, and art gallery; it is believed to be the oldest surviving guildhall in England. Other features include Trinity Guildhall, dating from 1421; the Saturday Market Place and the Tuesday Market Place; the Old Gaol House (1784), now housing a museum; and Thoresby College (1500), originally a monastic house. Merchant buildings include Hampton Court, originally a 14th-century warehouse; the Hanseatic Warehouse (1428); Greenland Fishery House (1605); Clifton House (12th–18th centuries), with fine 14th-century tiled floors and a five-storey brick watchtower, constructed in about 1600; and Custom House, built in 1683.

## Kingston upon Hull, or Hull

City, port, and unitary authority created in 1996 from part of the former county of Humberside, situated where the River Hull flows into the north side of the Humber estuary, northeast England; area: 71 sq km/27 sq mi; population: (1996) 265,000. It is one of the UK's major seaports, with 11 km/7 mi of modern docks located on the Humber estuary, handling timber, grain, oilseeds, wool, and the export and import of manufactured goods. There are ferries from here to Rotterdam and Zeebrugge.

*History*
The site of the present city was held at the end of the 12th century by Cistercian monks. Their settlement, then known as Wyke, was acquired by Edward I in 1293, who changed its name to Kingston upon Hull. In 1299 its first charter made the town a free borough, and it grew into a flourishing seaport. New quays were built, internal communications improved, a ferry to the southern shore of the Humber established, and in 1322 the town was enclosed and fortified. In 1440 a charter of Henry VI incorporated the town. During the reign of Henry VIII new fortifications to protect the harbour were built.

During the Civil War the first forcible resistance to Charles I was the closing of the gates of Hull against him in 1642, and the town sustained two Royalist sieges. It continued to maintain its position as a port and thriving commercial centre, and between 1774 and 1829 three docks were built to make a ring of water around the old town. The largest dock in Hull, the King George, was opened by George V in 1914. The town was made a city in 1897. During World War II the central area of Hull was severely damaged in bombing raids, and much reconstruction subsequently took place.

*Features*
The large parish church of Holy Trinity dates to the 13th century. The city is home to several museums and galleries, including the Maritime Museum, housed in the old Town Docks offices; Wilberforce House (birthplace of the reformer William Wilberforce); Streetlife, the Hull Museum of Transport, which includes among its exhibits rare trams; and the Ferens Art Gallery, which houses an eclectic collection ranging from 16th-century Dutch masters to the present day. The old Grammar School has also been converted into a museum, with collections dedicated to Victorian Britain and the history of Hull and its people. The town has two universities: the University of Hull (1954) and the University of Lincolnshire and Humberside, which has a campus here (1992, formerly Humberside Polytechnic).

The Humber Bridge, linking the town with the south bank of the estuary, was the world's longest single-span suspension bridge when it opened in 1981. Built at a cost of £150 million, far higher than intended, the toll bridge was refinanced in 1998, and the loans for its construction are expected to be repaid by 2032.

## Kingston upon Thames

Outer borough of southwest Greater London; administrative headquarters of ◊Surrey, although not in the county; population (1997 est) 144,600

*Features*
Seven Saxon kings, from Edward the Elder in 900 to Ethelred the Unready in 979, were crowned at Kingston; their coronation stone is preserved here, set with seven silver pennies; oldest of the three Royal Boroughs of England, with the ancient right to elect its own High Steward and Recorder; Kingston Grammar School, founded by Elizabeth I in 1561.

*History*
Athelstan, king of the Mercians and West Saxons, was crowned king here in 925. In medieval times Kingston was an important Thames crossing place and market centre. The present bridge was opened in 1828, but a bridge existed here in the 13th century, providing the furthest downstream access across the river above London Bridge until 1750. The earliest surviving town charter is dated 1200, and it was granted a fair by Henry III and market charters by James I and Charles II.

---

*There's a whisper down the field where the year has shot her yield, / And the ricks stand grey to the sun, / Singing: 'Over then, come over, for the bee has quit the clover, / And your English summer's done.'*

**Rudyard Kipling** English writer. 'The Long Trail'

---

## Kipling, Rudyard (1865–1936)

English writer, born in India. *Plain Tales from the Hills* (1888), about Anglo-Indian society, contains the earliest of his masterly short stories. His books for children, including *The Jungle Book* (1894–95), *Just So Stories* (1902), *Puck of Pook's Hill* (1906), and the picaresque novel *Kim* (1901), reveal his imaginative identification with the exotic. Poems such as 'If–', 'Danny Deever', and 'Gunga Din', express an empathy with common experience, which contributed to his great popularity, together with a vivid sense of 'Englishness' (sometimes denigrated as a kind of jingoist imperialism).

Born in Bombay, Kipling was educated at the United Services College at Westward Ho!, Devon, England, which provided the background for *Stalky and Co* (1899). He worked as a journalist in India from 1882 to 1889 and lived largely in the USA from 1892 to 1899, where he produced the two *Jungle Books* and *Captains Courageous* (1897). Settling in Sussex, southeast England, he published *Kim*, usually regarded as his greatest work of fiction; the *Just So Stories*; *Puck of Pook's Hill*; and *Rewards and Fairies* (1910).

## Kirkoswald

Village in South Ayrshire unitary authority, Scotland, 6 km/4 mi southwest of Maybole; population (1991) 300. The poet Robert Burns studied here briefly and two of his ⬦fictional characters, Tam o'Shanter and Souter Johnnie, are supposed to be modelled on people he met: Douglas Graham of Shanter Farm and John Davidson the shoemaker (souter). Their graves are in Kirkoswald churchyard. Souter Johnnie's cottage now belongs to the National Trust of Scotland and is open to the public.

## Kirkwall

Administrative headquarters and port of the ⬦Orkney Islands, Scotland, on the north coast of the largest island, Mainland; population (1991) 6,700. The main industry is distilling. The Norse cathedral of St Magnus dates from 1137. The Bishop's Palace is also 12th-century, and the Earl's Palace was completed in 1606.

Every Christmas and New Year's Day, a unique football match, known as the Ba', is played. The match can involve 200 players and last for seven hours.

---

*I don't mind your being killed, but I object to your being taken prisoner.*

**Horatio Herbert Kitchener, Earl Kitchener of Khartoum**
Irish soldier and administrator.
To the Prince of Wales (later Edward VIII) when he asked to go to the Front in World War I, quoted in Viscount Esher's *Journal* 18 December 1914

---

## Kitchener, Horatio, 1st Earl Kitchener of Khartoum (1850–1916)

Irish soldier and administrator. He defeated the Sudanese at the Battle of Omdurman in 1898 and reoccupied Khartoum. In South Africa, he was commander in chief 1900–02 during the Boer War, and he commanded the forces in India 1902–09. Appointed war minister on the outbreak of World War I, he was successful in his campaign calling for voluntary recruitment.

## kitchen-sink movement

Loose-knit group of British painters, active in the late 1940s and early 1950s. They depicted drab, everyday scenes with an aggressive technique and often brilliant, 'crude' colour. The name was coined in 1954 by the art critic David Sylvester.

The best known were John ⬦Bratby, Derrick Greaves (1927–   ), Edward Middleditch (1923–1987), and Jack Smith (1928–   ). These painters had something in common with the 'Angry Young Men' writers of the same time, and playwrights such as John Osborne are sometimes described as 'kitchen sink dramatists'.

## Knaresborough

Market town in North Yorkshire, northern England, on the River Nidd, 6 km/4 mi northeast of Harrogate; population (1991) 13,600. There is an outstanding railway viaduct, and the remains of a castle first established around 1070.

Most of the castle ruins date from the 14th century, and there is a well-preserved dungeon. To the south of the town is a 'dropping well' where the water has petrifying qualities, immersed items becoming coated with calcium carbonate. Nearby is the cave where the prophet Mother Shipton is said to have lived. St Robert's Cave, or Eugene Aram's Cave, is where the convicted murderer Eugene Aram is said to have hidden the corpse of Daniel Clark, a local shoemaker, in 1745. The chapel of Our Lady in the Crag lies near St Robert's Cave.

## Knights of the Round Table

In British legend, the knights of King Arthur; see ⬦Round Table.

## Knole

House in Kent, England, situated 1.5 km/1 mi from Sevenoaks. One of the largest private houses in England, it was begun by Thomas Bourchier (*c.* 1404–1486), archbishop of Canterbury, in 1456, but greatly extended around 1603 by Thomas Sackville, to whom it was granted by Queen Elizabeth I. It was given in 1946 by the 4th Lord Sackville to the National Trust.

The state rooms contain a large number of historic pictures, rare furniture (including the Knole settee), rugs, and tapestries.

## Knox, John (*c.* 1505–1572)

Scottish Protestant reformer, founder of the Church of Scotland. He spent several years in exile for his beliefs, including a period in Geneva where he met John Calvin. He returned to Scotland in 1559 to promote Presbyterianism. His books include *First Blast of the Trumpet Against the Monstrous Regiment of Women* (1558).

**John Knox** The 16th-century Scottish Protestant reformer and founder of Presbyterianism, John Knox. Originally a Roman Catholic, Knox spent some years in exile after the accession of Mary Queen of Scots and met Calvin in Geneva. Knox was an outspoken and zealous preacher, and his influence on the Scottish Reformation was seminal. Corbis

Originally a Roman Catholic priest, Knox is thought to have been converted by the reformer George Wishart. When Wishart was burned for heresy, Knox went into hiding, but later preached the reformed doctrines.

Captured by French troops in Scotland in 1547, he was imprisoned in France, sentenced to the galleys, and released only by the intercession of the British government in 1549. In England he assisted in compiling the Prayer Book, as a royal chaplain from 1551. On the accession of Mary I in 1553 he fled the country and in 1557 was, in his absence, condemned to be burned. In 1559 he returned to Scotland. He was tried for treason but acquitted in 1563. He wrote a *History of the Reformation in Scotland* (1586).

### Korda, Alexander (1893–1956)

Hungarian-born British film producer and director. He was a dominant figure in the British film industry during the 1930s and 1940s. His films as director include *Marius* (1931), in France, and *The Private Life of Henry VIII* (1933), in England. He was the producer of *The Scarlet Pimpernel* (1935), *The Thief of Bagdad* (1940), *The Third Man* (1949), and *Richard III* (1956), among many others.

Korda formed London Film Productions in 1932, later linking his company with Metro-Goldwyn-Mayer to form MGM-British Productions. He did much to make British films the equal of the Hollywood product.

## Labour Party

Political party based on socialist principles, originally formed to represent workers. It was founded in 1900 and first held office in 1924. The first majority Labour government in 1945–51 introduced nationalization and the National Health Service, and expanded ◊social security. Labour was again in power in 1964–70, 1974–79 and from 1997. The party leader (Tony ◊Blair from 1994) is elected by an electoral college, with a weighted representation of the Parliamentary Labour Party (30%), constituency parties (30%), and trade unions (40%).

In 1900 a conference representing the trade unions, the Independent Labour Party (ILP), and the ◊Fabian Society, founded the Labour Party, known until 1906, when 29 seats were gained, as the Labour Representation Committee. All but a pacifist minority of the Labour Party supported World War I, and in 1918 a socialist programme was first adopted, with local branches of the party set up to which individual members were admitted. By 1922 the Labour Party was recognized as the official opposition.

From 1936 to 1939 there was internal dissension on foreign policy; the leadership's support of nonintervention in Spain was strongly criticized and Stafford Cripps, Aneurin Bevan, and others were expelled for advocating an alliance of all left-wing parties against the government of Neville Chamberlain. The Labour Party supported Winston Churchill's wartime coalition, but then withdrew and took office for the first time as a majority government under Clement Attlee, party leader from 1935, after the 1945 elections. The welfare state was developed by nationalization of essential services and industries, a system of national insurance was established in 1946, and the National Health Service was founded in 1948. Defeated in 1951, Labour was split by disagreements on further nationalization, and unilateral or multilateral disarmament, but achieved unity under Hugh Gaitskell's leadership in 1955–63.

---

*We are not here just to manage capitalism but to change society and to define its finer values.*

**Tony Benn** British Labour politician.
Speech, Labour Party Conference 1975

---

Under Harold Wilson the party returned to power 1964–70 and, with a very slender majority, 1974–79. James Callaghan, who had succeeded Wilson in 1976, was forced to a general election in 1979 and lost. Michael Foot was elected to the leadership in 1980; Neil Kinnock succeeded him in 1983 after Labour had lost another general election. The party adopted a policy of unilateral nuclear disarmament in 1986 and expelled the left-wing faction Militant Tendency, but rifts remained. Labour lost the 1987 general election, a major reason being its non-nuclear policy. In spite of the Conservative government's declining popularity, Labour was defeated in the 1992 general election, following which Neil Kinnock stepped down as party leader; John Smith succeeded him July in 1992 but died suddenly in May 1994. Tony Blair was elected to succeed him in July 1994, in the first fully democratic elections to the post, and launched a campaign to revise the party's constitution by scrapping Clause 4, concerning common ownership of the means of production, and ending trade union direct sponsorship of MPs; a new charter was approved in April 1995.

Under the title **New Labour**, Blair sought to move the party nearer to the 'middle ground' of

LAMB, CHARLES · 259

politics to secure the 'middle England' vote. By 1996 Labour Party membership was 365,000 and rising and it led the Conservatives in the opinion polls by more than 20 points. The Labour Party returned to power after a landslide victory in the May 1997 general election. Membership peaked in January 1998, at 405,000, and began to gradually decline for the first time since Blair became leader, amid concerns among traditionalist members that control over the party had become too centralized.

The Labour Party's anthem is 'The Red Flag', written by the Irish socialist Jim Connell (1850–1929) during the London strike in 1889.

## Lacock

Village in Wiltshire, England, mostly owned by the National Trust, including **Lacock Abbey**, Manor Farm, and Bewley Common, about 130 ha/321 acres in all. Lacock Abbey was a nunnery for Augustinian canonesses, and the 13th-century cloisters, sacristy, chapter-house, and nuns' parlour remain. After the Reformation, around 1540, William Sharrington built a Tudor mansion around these monastic ruins, the chief features of which are the octagonal tower overlooking the River Avon and the large courtyard with half-timbered gables and clock-house.

It was at Lacock that William Henry Fox ◊Talbot pioneered his photographic process, and a museum of his work is now open at the Abbey.

## Lake District

Region in Cumbria, northwest England. It contains the principal English lakes, separated by wild uplands rising to many peaks, including ◊Scafell Pike (978 m/3,210 ft), the highest peak in England. The area was made a national park in 1951, covering 2,292 sq km/882 sq mi, and is a popular tourist destination.

The Lake District has associations with the writers William ◊Wordsworth, Samuel Taylor ◊Coleridge, Robert ◊Southey, Thomas De Quincey, John ◊Ruskin, and Beatrix ◊Potter. The principal lakes are ◊Windermere, the largest lake in England; ◊Ullswater; ◊Derwent Water; ◊Coniston Water; Bassenthwaite; and Thirlmere. Peaks include Helvellyn (950 m/3,118 ft) and Great Gable (899 m/2,949 ft). The main tourist centres are Windermere, ◊Keswick, ◊Ambleside, and ◊Grasmere. The overall population is 41,600, and growing slowly.

Thirlmere, Hawes Water, and some other smaller lakes are managed as reservoirs to supply some of England's major conurbations, including Manchester.

The Lake District has a radial system of valleys, deepened by glaciers. Windermere, in the southeast, is connected with Rydal Water and Grasmere. The westerly Scafell range extends south to the Old Man of Coniston overlooking Coniston Water, and north to Wastwater. Ullswater lies in the northeast of the district, on the east side of Helvellyn peak, with Hawes Water and Thirlmere nearby. The River Derwent flows north through Borrowdale forming Derwentwater and Bassenthwaite. West of Borrowdale lie Buttermere, Crummock Water, and, beyond, Ennerdale Water. Woodland includes broadleaf species, partly naturally occurring; and the plantations (mainly coniferous) of the Forestry Commission. Much of the scenery is relatively wild and very attractive.

### Conservation

There are 100 Sites of Special Scientific Interest, and 82 regionally important geological or geomorphological sites, making the area of enormous conservation interest. There are also nearly 2,000 listed buildings. Much of the land in the area is owned by the National Trust, and the National Park owns 8,600 ha/3,481 acres of the land under their jurisdiction.

### Economy

Agriculture (particularly sheep farming), forestry, and fishing employ about 10% of the working population, with a further 5% employed in energy, water, and mining. Manufacturing industries employ about 10%, and the construction industry another 8%, but almost 38% of the population is supported by retailing, tourism, and catering, with another 30% in general service industries.

## Lamb, Charles (1775–1834)

English essayist and critic. He collaborated with his sister **Mary Lamb** (1764–1847) on *Tales from Shakespeare* (1807), and his *Specimens of English Dramatic Poets Contemporary with Shakespeare, with Notes* (1808) revealed him as a penetrating critic and helped to revive interest in Elizabethan plays. As 'Elia' he contributed essays to the *London Magazine* from 1820 (collected 1823 and 1833).

Lamb's essays are still widely read and admired; they include 'A Dissertation on Roast Pig', 'Mrs Battle's Opinions on Whist', 'Dream Children', and 'The Supernatural Man'.

As a friend of Coleridge, some of his poems were included in the second edition of *Poems on Various Subjects* (1797). He was a clerk with the East India Company at India House 1792–1825, when he retired to Enfield. His sister Mary stabbed their mother to death in a fit of insanity in 1796, and Charles cared for her between her periodic returns to an asylum.

## Lambeth

Inner borough of south central Greater London. It includes the districts of Waterloo, Kennington, Clapham, Stockwell, and Brixton; population (1991) 244,800.

*Features*

Lambeth Palace, chief residence of the archbishop of Canterbury since 1200, with brick Tudor gatehouse (1495); Tradescant museum of gardening history; the ◊South Bank, including Royal Festival Hall, Hayward Gallery, National Theatre, the Art Deco Oxo Wharf Tower (1928), now converted into mixed-use development; the Oval (headquarters of Surrey County Cricket Club from 1846) at Kennington, where the first England–Australia test match was played 1880; Old Vic theatre (1816–18); Brixton Prison; Anti-Slavery Archive in Brixton; Channel Tunnel rail terminal at Waterloo; London Aquarium opened 1997 in part of the converted County Hall.

## Lambeth Palace

London residence of the archbishops of Canterbury, situated by Lambeth Bridge in the London borough of Lambeth. Building was begun by Archbishop Hubert ◊Walter at the end of the 12th century, although Stephen ◊Langton was the first archbishop to live here. The chapel dates from around 1230 with stalls erected byArchbishop Laud in 1634, and beneath it is a crypt built around 1200.

## Lammermuir Hills

Range of hills dividing East Lothian and Scottish Borders, Scotland, running northeast from Gala Water to St Abb's Head on the North Sea. The highest summits are Meikle Says Law (535 m/1,755 ft) and Lammer Law (527 m/1,730 ft).

## Lancashire

County of northwest England; population (1996) 1,424,700; area: 3,040 sq km/1,173 sq mi. It was formerly a world centre of cotton manufacture. Its principal towns and cities are ◊Preston (administrative headquarters), which since 1970 has formed part of Central Lancashire New Town (together with Fulwood, Bamber Bridge, Leyland, and Chorley); Lancaster, Accrington, and Burnley; Fleetwood and Heysham are ports; and Morecambe and Southport are seaside resorts. Since April 1998 ◊Blackpool and ◊Blackburn have been separate unitary authorities.

*Physical*

Lancashire has a coastline on the Irish Sea. The ◊Pennine Hills pass down the east side of the county and the River Ribble flows down from the Pennines, past Preston, to the sea. Bowland Fells is

---

**Lancashire Cotton Mill** Male factory workers spinning yarn in a Lancashire cotton mill in the 1890s. Along with the metal industries, textile manufacturing had been central to the industrial revolution, a consequence of which had been a steep increase in population during the 19th century. Private collection

an area of moorland and farming valleys in the north, and the Forest of Bowland and Ribble Valley are in the east.

*Economy*

Cotton manufacturing has been replaced with high-technology aerospace, nuclear fuels, and electronics industries. There is also dairy farming and market gardening.

## Lancaster

City in Lancashire, northwest England, on the River Lune; population (1991) 44,500. The city's castle was originally established in the 11th century on the site of a Roman fort. Lancaster has an established annual literary festival.

*Features*

The Norman keep was built in about 1170 and restored in the late 16th century. The castle was enlarged by John of Gaunt, Duke of Lancaster from 1362, and father of Henry IV. It was a parliamentary stronghold during the Civil War. Now much altered it is used as a court and prison. Some of the early structure survives, including the 13th-century Hadrian's Tower. The priory church of St Mary was founded as a Benedictine priory in 1094. It has a Saxon doorway, but dates mainly from the 15th century. Many of the city's buildings are Georgian, reflecting the period of prosperity in the 18th century when Lancaster was an important port for trade with the West Indies. The River Lune Millennium Park is being created by the City Council.

## Lancaster, House of

English royal house, a branch of the Plantagenets.

It originated in 1267 when Edmund (died 1296), the younger son of Henry III, was granted the earldom of Lancaster. Converted to a duchy for Henry of Grosmont (died 1361), it passed to John of Gaunt in 1362 by his marriage to Blanche, Henry's daughter. John's son, Henry IV, established the royal dynasty of Lancaster in 1399, and he was followed by two more Lancastrian kings, Henry V and Henry VI.

See genealogy on page 262.

## Lancelot of the Lake

In British legend, one of King Arthur's knights, the lover of Queen Guinevere. Originally a folk hero, he first appeared in the Arthurian cycle of tales in the 12th century.

## Land Acts, Irish

Series of 19th-century laws designed to improve the lot of the Irish peasantry. The first act in 1870 awarded tenants compensation for improvements they had made to land, but offered no protection against increased rents or eviction. The second act in 1881 introduced the 'three f's' – fair rents, fixity of tenure, and freedom of sale. The third act in 1885, part of Gladstone's abortive plans for Home Rule, provided £5 million for tenants to buy out their landlords. This scheme was further strengthened by the Wyndham Act of 1903 which offered inducements to landlords to sell. Before the end of the Union with Britain in 1921, some 11 million acres were purchased with government assistance.

## Land League

Irish peasant-rights organization, formed in 1879 by Michael ◊Davitt and Charles ◊Parnell to fight against tenant evictions. Through its skilful use of the boycott against anyone who took a farm from which another had been evicted, it forced Gladstone's government to introduce a law in 1881 restricting rents and granting tenants security of tenure.

## landscape painting

British landscape painting was much influenced by the Dutch, and attained its great development in the 18th and early 19th centuries. Wilson, Crome, the Norwich School, ◊Gainsborough, ◊Constable, and Turner appear in succession and their work in oils is paralleled by that of the watercolour landscapists – Paul Sandby, John Cozens, Cotman, Girtin, Bonington, and a host of others.

At the end of the 19th century and beginning of the 20th century, Impressionism and Post-Impressionism influenced British landscape painting, notably in the work of Philip Wilson Steer and several of the members of the Camden Town Group. In the period between the two world wars, Paul Nash and Graham Sutherland were among the artists who maintained the English romantic landscape tradition whilst responding to modern currents, infusing their work with a sense of Surrealist strangeness. Victor Pasmore and John Piper were among the other leading modern exponents of landscape. In the 1950s there was a fashion for gritty realism in landscape, paralleling the work of the 'kitchen sink' school, but a more lyrical approach has prevailed in, for example, the work of Roger de Grey.

## Landseer, Edwin Henry (1802–1873)

English painter, sculptor, and engraver of animal studies. Much of his work reflects the Victorian

# HOUSE OF LANCASTER 1399–1471

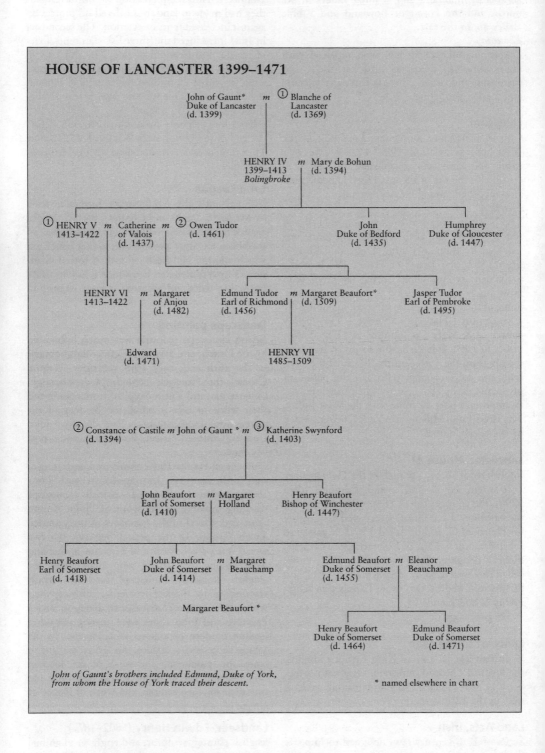

taste for sentimental and moralistic pictures, for example *Dignity and Impudence* (1839; Tate Gallery, London). His sculptures include the lions at the base of Nelson's Column in Trafalgar Square, London (1857–67).

His works show close knowledge of animal forms and he established a vogue for Highland animal and sporting scenes, much encouraged by Queen Victoria's patronage. Among his best-known works are *The Old Shepherd's Chief Mourner* (1837); *Monarch of the Glen* (1851), painted for the House of Lords; and *The Stag at Bay* (1846). He was knighted in 1850.

## Land's End

Promontory of southwest Cornwall, 15 km/9 mi southwest of Penzance, the westernmost point of England.

A group of dangerous rocks, the Longships, extend 0.6 km/1 mi out beyond Land's End; and are marked by a lighthouse (1793).

Land's End is a turf slope ending in a granite cliff about 18 m/59 ft high. A natural tunnel pierces the headland, and there are caves which are accessible at low tide. The Longships include the Carn Bras, Meinek, Tal-y-maen, Kettle's Bottom, and Armed Knight rocks.

The area has been under private ownership since 1987.

## Langtry, Lillie stage name of Emilie Charlotte le Breton (1853–1929)

English actress. She was the mistress of the future Edward VII. She was known as the 'Jersey Lily' from her birthplace in the Channel Islands and considered to be one of the most beautiful women of her time.

She was the daughter of a rector, and married Edward Langtry (died 1897) in 1874. She first appeared professionally in London in 1881, and had her greatest success as Rosalind in Shakespeare's *As You Like It*. In 1899 she married Sir Hugo de Bathe.

## Lanhydrock House

House in Cornwall, England, 3 km/2 mi southeast of Bodmin. The original 17th-century house was largely destroyed by fire in 1881, but the north wing and detached granite gatehouse survived, and the house was rebuilt within four years. Gilbert ◊Scott laid out the formal gardens in 1857. The 7th Viscount Clifden gave the house and 220 ha/543 acres to the National Trust in 1953.

## Largs

Town and resort in North Ayrshire unitary authority, Scotland, situated on the Firth of Clyde, 19 km/12 mi southwest of Greenock; population (1991) 10,900. A busy tourist centre, its services include sailing facilities and car ferries to the island of Great Cumbrae.

## Larkin, Philip (1922–1985)

English poet. His perfectionist, pessimistic verse appeared in *The Less Deceived* (1955), and in the later volumes *The Whitsun Weddings* (1964), and *High Windows* (1974) which confirmed him as one of the most powerful and influential of 20th-century English poets. After his death, his letters and other writings, which he had instructed should be destroyed, revealed an intolerance and misanthropy not found in his published material. From 1955 until his death he was librarian at the University of Hull.

He edited *The Oxford Book of 20th-Century English Verse* (1973). *Collected Poems* was published in 1988.

## Larne

Seaport and industrial town of County Antrim, Northern Ireland, on **Lough Larne**, 30 km/19 mi north of Belfast; population (1991) 17,500. It is the terminus of sea routes to Stranraer, Liverpool, and Dublin.

The Curran is a raised gravel beach running south from Larne, on which many Neolithic flint implements have been found. The Norse used Lough Larne in the 10th and 11th centuries as a port. Edward Bruce (brother of Robert) landed at Larne with his army in 1315; his campaign was supported by the Bissett family whose castle (Olderfleet, dating from the 13th century) and lands were confiscated by the British crown as a result. The ruins of Olderfleet Castle can still be seen on the Curran.

> Be of good comfort, Master Ridley, and play the man; we shall this day light such a candle, by God's grace, in England as I trust shall never be put out.
>
> **Hugh Latimer** English church reformer and bishop. Attributed remark, to Nicholas Ridley as they were about to be burned at the stake

## Latimer, Hugh (c. 1485–1555)

English Christian church reformer and bishop. After his conversion to Protestantism in 1524 he was imprisoned several times but was protected by

Cardinal Wolsey and Henry VIII. After the accession of the Catholic Mary I, he was burned for heresy.

## Laud, William (1573–1645)

English priest; archbishop of Canterbury from 1633. Laud's High Church policy, support for Charles I's unparliamentary rule, censorship of the press, and persecution of the Puritans all aroused bitter opposition, while his strict enforcement of the statutes against enclosures and of laws regulating wages and prices alienated the propertied classes. His attempt to impose the use of the Prayer Book on the Scots precipitated the English ◊Civil War. Impeached by Parliament in 1640, he was imprisoned in the Tower of London, summarily condemned to death, and beheaded.

## Lavenham

Village in Suffolk, England, 16 km/10 mi south of Bury St Edmunds; population (1991) 1,600. It is much visited by tourists. In the 16th century Lavenham had a thriving woollen industry, and the surviving medieval buildings reflect the prosperity of that period. The village has streets of timbered houses, a late 15th-century guildhall, and a church which is a fine example of the late Perpendicular style.

## law courts

Bodies that adjudicate in legal disputes.

In England and Wales the court system was reorganized under the Courts Act (1971). The higher courts are: the **House of Lords** (the highest court for the whole of Britain), which deals with both civil and criminal appeals; the **Court of Appeal**, which is divided between criminal and civil appeal courts; the **High Court of Justice**, dealing with important civil cases; **crown courts**, which handle criminal cases; and **county courts**, which deal with civil matters. **Magistrates' courts** deal with minor criminal cases and are served by ◊justices of the peace or stipendiary (paid) magistrates; and **juvenile courts** are presided over by specially qualified justices. There are also special courts, such as the Restrictive Practices Court and the Employment Appeal Tribunal.

The courts are organized in six circuits. The towns of each circuit are first-tier (High Court and circuit judges dealing with both criminal and civil cases), second-tier (High Court and circuit judges dealing with criminal cases only), or third-tier (circuit judges dealing with criminal cases only). Cases are allotted according to gravity among High Court and circuit judges and recorders (part-time judges with the same jurisdiction as circuit judges). In 1971 solicitors were allowed for the first time to appear in and conduct cases at the level of the crown courts, and solicitors as well as barristers of ten years' standing became eligible for appointment as recorders, who after five years become eligible as circuit judges. In Scotland, the supreme civil court is the **Court of Session**, with appeal to the House of Lords; the highest criminal court is the **High Court of Justiciary**, with no appeal to the House of Lords. See also ◊legal system for a table of courts and glossary of the legal system.

## Lawrence, D(avid) H(erbert) (1885–1930)

English writer. His work expresses his belief in emotion and the sexual impulse as creative and true to human nature, but his ideal of the complete, passionate life is seen to be threatened by the encroachment of the modern and technological world. His writing first received attention after the publication of the semi-autobiographical *The White Peacock* (1911) and *Sons and Lovers* (1913). Other novels include *The Rainbow*

**D H Lawrence** English writer D H Lawrence, photographed in the early 20th century. Controversy surrounded him for much of his creative life; the frankly sexual novel *Lady Chatterley's Lover* was banned in England until 1960; *The Rainbow* (1915) was also accused of obscenity. As well as his novels, Lawrence wrote short stories, travel books, and poetry. Corbis

(1915), *Women in Love* (1921), and ◊*Lady Chatterley's Lover*, printed privately in 1928.

Lawrence tried to forge a new kind of novel, with a structure and content so intense that it would reflect emotion and passion more genuinely than ever before. This often led to conflict with official and unofficial prudery, and his interest in sex as a life force and bond was often censured. *The Rainbow* was suppressed for obscenity, and *Lady Chatterley's Lover* could only be published in an expurgated form in the UK in 1932. Not until 1960, when the obscenity law was successfully challenged, was it published in the original text.

The son of a Nottinghamshire miner, Lawrence studied at University College, Nottingham. He became a clerk and later a teacher. On going to London in 1908, he wrote under the pseudonym of Lawrence H Davidson. His first novel, *The White Peacock*, was published on the recommendation of Ford Madox ◊Ford. In 1914 he married Frieda von Richthofen, ex-wife of his university professor. Lawrence's travels resulted in a series of fine travel essays, including *Sea and Sardinia* (1921) and *Mornings in Mexico* (1927). Lawrence suffered from tuberculosis, from which he eventually died near Nice, France.

---

*Curse the blasted jelly-boned swines, the slimy belly-wriggling invertebrates, the miserable sodding rotters, the flaming sods, the snivelling, dribbling, dithering, palsied pulseless lot that make up England today. ... Why, why, why was I born an Englishman?*

**D H Lawrence** English writer.
Letter to Edward Garnett, 3 July 1912

---

## Lawrence, T(homas) E(dward) known as Lawrence of Arabia (1888–1935)

British soldier, scholar, writer, and translator. Appointed to the military intelligence department in Cairo, Egypt, during World War I, he took part in negotiations for an Arab revolt against the Ottoman Turks, and in 1916 attached himself to the emir Faisal. He became a guerrilla leader of genius, combining raids on Turkish communications with the organization of a joint Arab revolt, described in his book *The Seven Pillars of Wisdom* (1926). At the end of the war he was awarded the DSO for his services, and became adviser to the Foreign Office on Arab affairs. Disappointed by the Paris Peace Conference's failure to establish Arab independence, he joined the Royal Air Force in 1922 as an aircraftman under the name Ross, transferring to the tank corps under the name T E Shaw in 1923 when his identity became known. In 1935 he was killed in a motorcycle accident.

## Leach, Bernard (1887–1979)

English potter. His simple designs of stoneware and *raku* ware, inspired by a period of study in Japan from 1909 to 1920, pioneered a revival of studio pottery in Britain. In 1920 he established the Leach Pottery, a communally-run workshop at St Ives, Cornwall, with the Japanese potter Shoji Hamada (1894–1978).

Having worked with trailed slip designs on *raku* ware in Japan, he also revived the 17th-century technique of moulding plates with slip decorations.

## Leamington, officially Royal Leamington Spa

Town and former health resort in Warwickshire, England, adjoining Warwick, on the River Leam, southeast of Birmingham; population (1991) 42,300. The Royal Pump Room still offers spa treatment.

With mineral springs (saline, chalybeate) first recorded in 1586, Leamington developed as a spa in the late 18th century, and it became a royal spa after Queen Victoria visited the town in 1838. Leamington has extensive parks, gardens, and spacious avenues with Regency-style terraces.

## Lean, David (1908–1991)

English film director. His films, painstakingly crafted, include early work codirected with the playwright Noël Coward, such as *Brief Encounter* (1946). Among his later films are such accomplished epics as *The Bridge on the River Kwai* (1957; Academy Award), *Lawrence of Arabia* (1962; Academy Award), and *Dr Zhivago* (1965).

The unfavourable reaction to *Ryan's Daughter* (1970) caused him to withdraw from filmmaking for over a decade, but *A Passage to India* (1984) represented a return to form. He was knighted in 1984.

## Lear, Edward (1812–1888)

English artist and humorist. His *Book of Nonsense* (1846) popularized the limerick (a five-line humorous verse). His *Nonsense Songs, Botany and Alphabets* (1871), includes two of his best-known poems, 'The Owl and the Pussycat' and 'The Jumblies'.

He first attracted attention by his paintings of birds, and later turned to landscapes. He travelled to Italy, Greece, Egypt, and India, publishing books on his travels with his own illustrations, and spent most of his later life in Italy.

Born in Holloway, London, of Danish descent, Lear was the 20th of 21 children and was brought up by an elder sister. His father was declared bankrupt when he was four, he had only five years of schooling, and he was both epileptic and asthmatic. He gave drawing lessons to Queen Victoria in 1846.

---

*They dined on mince, and slices of quince, /
Which they ate with a runcible spoon; / And
hand in hand, on the edge of the sand, / They
danced by the light of the moon.*

**Edward Lear** English artist and humorist.
*Nonsense Songs*, 'The Owl and the Pussy-Cat'

---

## Lee, Laurie (1914–1997)

English writer. His autobiographical *Cider with Rosie* (1959) is a classic evocation of childhood: subsequent volumes are *As I Walked Out One Summer Morning* (1969), and *A Moment of War* (1991), in which he describes the horrors of the Spanish Civil War in 1936. His travel writing includes *A Rose for Winter* (1955). *Selected Poems* was published in 1983.

## Leeds

Industrial city and metropolitan borough in West Yorkshire, England, 40 km/25 mi southwest of York, on the River Aire; population (1991) 424,200 (city), 680,700 (district). It is the industrial capital of Yorkshire and a major hub of communications and transport for road, rail, and canals. An important wool-producing centre in the 16th century, the city still has a clothing industry.

### History

The town has its origins in Anglo-Saxon times, but its early history is obscure. In the 12th century, local Cistercian monks traded in wool here, and in the 14th century Flemish immigrants introduced weaving and cloth manufacture; by the 16th century the town was as important as York in the wool-producing trade. The first royal charter, which made the town and parish into a municipal borough, was granted by Charles I in 1626.

Leeds owes its modern development to its industries. The city benefited from its communication with Liverpool (via the Leeds and Liverpool Canal, completed in 1816), and with the Humber (via the Aire and Calder Navigation system). The proximity of the great coal-and iron-fields, developed during the Industrial Revolution, was a major factor in establishing the city's prosperity. Engineering developed during the 19th century, in particular railway engineering, due to the city's central position on the national rail network. Leeds was made a county borough in 1889 and a city in 1893.

### Features

St John's Church (1634) is a fine example of 17th-century Gothic architecture, and contains a famous English Renaissance screen. The parish church of St Peter (rebuilt 1841) has a pre-Conquest cross, the oldest monument in Leeds. Other churches include St Anne's Roman Catholic cathedral near Park Row, and Holy Trinity church (1727). The City Museum, in Park Row, contains an Egyptian mummy, Roman artefacts, and zoological specimens. Leeds Industrial Museum in Armley Mill (once the largest textile mill in the world) is now a museum of the textile, clothing, and engineering industries. There is also a folk museum at Abbey House, Kirkstall. The Leeds City Art Gallery (founded 1888), with the adjoining Henry Moore Institute (1993), is the largest gallery in Europe devoted solely to sculpture. The Royal Armouries Museum opened in 1996, housing a national collection of arms and armour formerly in the White Tower at the Tower of London.

The opera company Opera North is based here, and the city hosts the Leeds Music Festival and the Leeds International Pianoforte Competition every three years. The City of Leeds Open Brass Band Championships take place each May. There is a famous cricket ground at Headingley. The city has two universities, the University of Leeds and Leeds Metropolitan University.

## leek

A national symbol of Wales, appearing on pound coins and worn on St David's Day (1 March). The reason for its choice as an emblem is uncertain. It was reputedly adopted in the 7th century, when the Welsh, under Cadwalader, wore leeks in their caps to distinguish their forces from the Saxon invaders. Folklore also tells of a Welsh victory in some battle in a garden of leeks, a legend referred to by Shakespeare in *Henry V*. The growing of giant leeks for competition, as part of agricultural shows, has been a popular pastime in England since the 1880s.

## legal system
See ◊English law and ◊Scottish law.

## Leicester
Industrial city in central England, on the River Soar; population (1996) 270,500. Formerly part of the county of Leicestershire, it became a separate unitary authority in 1997; area 73 sq km/28 sq mi.

### History
Leicester was founded in AD 50 as the Roman **Ratae Coritanorum**, and flourished as a wealthy town in the Roman period. The town was called Legerceastre by the Saxons, and was the seat of the East Mercian bishopric until 874. In the 12th century the castle was built, and Henry II besieged and partly destroyed the town. In 1201 a meeting of barons took place, a forerunner to the meeting in 1215 at Runnymede, when King John signed the Magna Carta. Three parliaments were held in Leicester in the 15th century. During the Civil War Leicester supported the Parliamentarians; it was captured by the Royalist Prince Rupert but it was retaken by Oliver Cromwell after the Battle of Naseby.

### Features
Places of note are the 14th-century Guildhall; St Martin's Cathedral, dating from Norman times but substantially modified in the 19th century; and the 15th-century Bradgate House, the home of Lady Jane Grey, located in Bradgate Park, 10 km/6 mi northwest of Leicester. Bradgate Park contains part of Charnwood Forest, and was a hunting ground in the 12th century. There are remains of the medieval castle, which was built in the 12th century – the Turret Gateway dates from 1423 and there are remains of the original Great Hall.

There are two universities: the University of Leicester, established in 1957, and De Montfort University, formerly Leicester Polytechnic, established in 1992. The Jain Centre in Leicester contains one of the few Jain temples in Western Europe.

### Museums and galleries
The Leicestershire Museum and Art Gallery includes a large collection of German expressionist paintings, and an Egyptian Gallery. The Jewry Wall and Archaeology Museum illustrates the history of the city to the Middle Ages; exhibits include sections of mosaic pavement, wall paintings, and milestones from the Fosse Way (the

**Leicester** Although it is now forms part of a museum of industry and technology and is no longer in regular use, the richly ornamented Abbey pumping station in Leicester bears witness to the industrial past that saw the city boom during the 19th century. Leicester became known particularly for manufacturing hosiery and footwear. McQuillan & Brown/Collections

main Roman road that traversed Britain). Newarke Houses Museum, situated in an early 17th-century house, traces the industrial and social history of Leicestershire from the 16th century to the present. Other museums include a costume museum housed in Wygston House, and the Museum of Technology.

## Leicester, Robert Dudley, Earl of Leicester
(c. 1532–1588)
English courtier. Son of the Duke of Northumberland, he was created Earl of Leicester in 1564. He led the disastrous military expedition in 1585–87 sent to help the Netherlands against Spain. Despite this failure, he retained the favour of Queen Elizabeth I, who gave him command of the army prepared to resist the threat of Spanish invasion in 1588.

His father was executed in 1553 for supporting Lady Jane Grey's claim to the throne, and Leicester was himself briefly imprisoned in the

Tower of London. His good looks attracted Queen Elizabeth, who made him Master of the Horse in 1558 and a privy councillor in 1559. He was a supporter of the Protestant cause.

Elizabeth might have married him if he had not been already married to Amy Robsart. When his wife died in 1560 after a fall downstairs, Leicester was suspected of murdering her. In 1578 he secretly married the widow of the Earl of Essex.

## Leicestershire

County of central England; population (1996) 927,500; area 2,084 sq km/804 sq mi. Its chief towns and cities are Loughborough, Melton Mowbray, and Market Harborough (its administrative headquarters are at Glenfield, Leicester). Since April 1997 ◊Leicester City and ◊Rutland have been separate unitary authorities.

### History

There is only slight evidence of prehistoric settlement in the county. The Roman occupation gave rise to three great roads, the Great North Road, Watling Street, and the Fosse Way, which pass through Leicestershire. In the 9th century the district was in the hands of the Danish invaders, and there are many place-names of Scandinavian origin. Richard III was defeated by Henry VII at the Battle of ◊Bosworth in 1485.

### Physical

The broad valley of the River Soar is one of the county's chief physical features, running from south to north, and separating the Charnwood Forest area from the uplands of the east. The Wreake valley, which runs from east to west, cuts through these eastern uplands. The highest point in the county is Bardon Hill (278 m/912 ft), in the Charnwood Forest. There are large coal deposits under the Vale of Belvoir.

### Features

The county contains Belvoir Castle, the seat of the Dukes of Rutland since the time of Henry VIII, which was rebuilt by James Wyatt in 1816. Other sites include the Snibston Discovery Park at Coalville, the Battlefield Centre near Market Bosworth, and Stanford Hall, which has a motorcycle museum. The county has the Donington Park motor-racing circuit at Castle Donington, and has traditionally had several fox-hunts, including the Quorn hunt. Loughborough University of Technology was founded in 1966.

### Economy

The county has good pasture with horses, cattle, and sheep (especially the New Leicester breed, first bred by Robert Bakewell in the 18th century at Dishley). Dairy products include Stilton

cheese, produced at Melton Mowbray, also associated with pork pies. Leicestershire has an industrial past; it was famous for its wool as early as 1343, and in the 17th century established itself as the main area for hosiery manufacture in the country (hosiery continues to be made at Earl Shilton, Hinckley, and Loughborough). There is also engineering and quarrying of coal (Ashfordby), limestone, and granite.

## leisure

See feature on the British at play.

---

*England is the paradise of individuality, eccentricity, heresy, anomalies, hobbies, and humours.*

**George Santayana** Spanish-born US philosopher and critic.
*Soliloquies in England* (1922)

---

## Leith

Port in City of Edinburgh unitary authority, Scotland, south of the Firth of Forth, which was incorporated into Edinburgh in 1920. Leith was granted to Edinburgh as its port by Robert the Bruce in 1329. By the 15th century, Leith dominated the maritime commerce of the Lothian area, and several times served as a military strongpoint. The port is now a zone for service sector development.

## Lely, Peter adopted name of Pieter van der Faes (1618–1680)

Dutch painter. He was active in England from 1641, painting fashionable portraits in the style of van Dyck. His subjects included Charles I, Cromwell, and Charles II. He painted a series of admirals, *Flagmen* (National Maritime Museum, London), and one of *The Windsor Beauties* (Hampton Court, Richmond), fashionable women of Charles II's court.

## Lennon, John Winston (1940–1980)

Rock singer, songwriter, and guitarist; a founder member of the ◊Beatles. He lived in the USA from 1971. Both before the band's break-up in 1970 and in his solo career, he collaborated intermittently with his wife Yoko Ono (1933– ). 'Give Peace a Chance', a hit in 1969, became an anthem of the peace movement. His solo work alternated between the confessional and the political, as on the album *Imagine* (1971). He was shot dead by an obsessed fan.

# ◆ THE BRITISH AT PLAY ◆

'In order to form a just estimation of the character of any particular people, it is absolutely necessary to investigate the Sports and Pastimes most generally prevalent among them.'

So wrote Joseph Strutt in 1801 in his introduction to *The Sports and Pastimes of the People of England*. While Strutt then went on to give an authoritative account of the various ways in which the British have amused themselves at play from Roman times onwards, neither he nor any subsequent researcher has truly succeeded in describing the British at play.

With competitions covering everything from soccer to worm-charming, games from conkers to gut-barging, and clubs ranging from the noble values of the Queen's English Society to the somewhat more esoteric interests of the International Correspondence of Corkscrew Addicts, the breadth of our leisure activities makes the task formidable. Even the question of what is Britain's favourite pastime is impossible to answer. In recent years, chess, bridge, darts, and fishing have all claimed around three million adherents, though such a figure begs the question of how committed a participant one needs to be in order to be included. In chess, for example, distinct surveys have shown that about eight million homes have chess sets, about three million people say they play occasionally, up to 50,000 are members of chess clubs, but only a little over 10,000 participate frequently in organized events. Bridge, darts, and fishing would produce comparable figures to these, but they are all probably beaten by the armies of crossword solvers whom no-one has ever succeeded in quantifying.

## Walking tops the chart

The most thorough recent account of what Britons do in their spare time is to be found in the 'General Household Survey' for 1996 (published in 1998 by the Office for National Statistics). This revealed high rates of participation in sporting activities with 64% of adults having taken part in some sport or physical activity in the four-week period prior to the survey and 81% having done so at some time in the previous 12 months. Those figures dropped to 46% and 66%, however, if the single most popular activity, walking (which specifically was defined as taking a leisure walk of two miles or more), was excluded from consideration.

A long way behind walking (which 45% of adults claimed to have done in the month before the survey), indoor swimming was the next most popular activity (at 13%), followed by keep fit or yoga classes (12%), pool, snooker, or billiards (11%) and cycling (11%). Over the same four-week period, 71% of men and 58% of women took part in some physical activity, with more women participating in keep fit classes, but more men in every other area.

For men, the most common leisure activities involving some element of physical exertion were: 1. Walking; 2. Snooker (or other cue game); 3. Indoor swimming; 4. Cycling; 5. Golf; 6–7. Tenpin bowling and soccer; 8. Outdoor swimming; 9. Weight training; 10. Running or jogging. For women the top ten were: 1. Walking; 2. Indoor swimming; 3. Keep fit or yoga; 4. Cycling; 5. Outdoor swimming; 6. Tenpin bowling; 7. Snooker (or other cue game); 8–10. Weight training, badminton and tennis.

Over a whole year, the average adult went cycling 11.6 times, went to a keep fit or yoga class 10.8 times, went for 8.2 swims, played 6.6 games of snooker, lifted weights 5.3 times jogged or ran 3.5 times and took to the soccer pitch 3.3 times.

The 'General Household Survey' also investigated the participation rates over a range of non-physical leisure activities. The most popular activity was watching television, which 99% of respondents had done in the four weeks prior to their interview. Almost as many (96%) had visited or entertained friends or relations, while 88% had listened to the radio, 78% had listened to records or tapes, and 65% had read books. Those were the only categories included in the survey which topped 50%, though gardening, at 48%, only narrowly failed to be among those things that more than half the country do in an average month.

## Bee-keeping to knot-tying

Yet all the above figures do no more than scratch the surface of the Great British public at leisure, for they neglect the many minor sports and activities which individually may appear negligible, yet taken together add up to a mountain of unclassified leisure. Looking, for example, at the clubs and societies in Hampshire – a county that includes only about 2% of the population – we find clubs for battle reenactments, beekeepers and bellringers, groups to cater for anyone interested in rabbits, railways or rambling, cigarette cards or computing. The official web site for the county lists 21 dance groups, including seven troupes of Morris Dancers. There are three groups specializing in arts and crafts, including a branch of the International Guild of Knot Tyers. Stamp collectors may choose between two clubs, while anyone wanting to join a knitting circle has three from which to select. The British are without doubt a playful nation, and especially skilled at the game of frustrating leisure researchers.

by Bill Hartston

## leprechaun (Old Irish 'small body')

In Irish folklore, a fairy in the shape of an old man, sometimes conceived as a cobbler, with a hidden store of gold. If caught by a human he can be forced to reveal his treasure, but he is usually clever enough to trick his captor into looking away, enabling him to vanish.

## Levellers

Democratic party in the English Civil War. The Levellers found wide support among Cromwell's New Model Army and the yeoman farmers, artisans, and small traders, and proved a powerful political force in 1647–49. Their programme included the establishment of a republic, government by a parliament of one house elected by male suffrage, religious toleration, and sweeping social reforms.

Cromwell's refusal to implement this programme led to mutinies by Levellers in the army, which, when suppressed by Cromwell in 1649, ended the movement. They were led by John ◊Lilburne.

**True Levellers** (also known as ◊Diggers) were denounced by the Levellers because of their more radical methods.

## Leven, Loch

Lake in Perth and Kinross, Scotland; area 16 sq km/6 sq mi. The River Leven flows from Loch Leven. It has six islands; Mary Queen of Scots was imprisoned on Castle Island until she escaped in 1568. The whole loch has been a National Nature Reserve since 1964. The loch is known for its trout fisheries.

St Serf's, the largest island in the loch, contains the ruins of an old priory.

## Lewis, or Lewis-with-Harris

Largest and most northerly island in the Outer ◊Hebrides, Western Isles; area 2,220 sq km/857 sq mi; population (1991) 21,700. Its main town is Stornoway. It is separated from northwest Scotland by the Minch. The island is 80 km/50 mi long from north to south, and its greatest breadth is 45 km/28 mi. There are many lochs and peat moors. The Callanish standing stones on the west coast are thought to be up to 5,000 years old, second only to Stonehenge in archaeological significance in the UK.

Harris and Lewis are often assumed to be two separate islands, but they are linked by a narrow neck of land.

The coast is indented on the east and west coasts. The most northerly point is the **Butt of Lewis**. Much of the south and southwest of the island is rugged and mountainous, while northern and central Lewis are dominated by an undulating peat bog.

The chief occupations are crofting and fishing. Oats and potatoes are grown, and sheep and cattle are raised. There are many archaeological remains; the standing stones at Callanish, a circle of 47 stones 24 km/15 mi west of Stornaway, are thought to date from between 3,000 and 1,500 BC. **Lewis Castle** (1856–63) was presented to the town by Lord Leverhulme, and now houses a technical college.

Daily flights link the island with Inverness and Glasgow. A car ferry service connects Stornaway to Ullapool on the mainland.

## Lewis, C(live) S(taples) (1898–1963)

English academic and writer, born in Belfast. He became a committed Christian in 1931 and wrote the Chronicles of Narnia, a series of seven novels of Christian allegory for children set in the magic land of Narnia, beginning with *The Lion, the Witch, and the Wardrobe* (1950).

Lewis was a fellow of Magdalen College, Oxford, from 1924–54 and professor of Medieval and Renaissance English at Cambridge from 1954–63.

## Lewis, Wyndham (1882–1957)

English writer and artist. He pioneered ◊Vorticism, which, with its feeling of movement, sought to reflect the age of industry. He had a hard and aggressive style in both his writing and his painting. His literary works include the novel *The Apes of God* (1930); the essay collection *Time and Western Man* (1927); and an autobiography, *Blasting and Bombardiering* (1937). In addition to paintings of a semi-abstract kind, he made a number of portraits; among his sitters were the poets Edith Sitwell, Ezra Pound, and T S Eliot.

## Lewisham

Inner borough of southeast Greater London. It includes the suburbs of ◊Blackheath, Sydenham, Catford, and ◊Deptford; population (1991) 215,300.

### Features

Deptford shipbuilding yard (1512–1869); Armoury Mill produced steel for armour in the 16th century, musket barrels in the Napoleonic Wars, and gold and silver thread for Victorian uniforms.

## Liberal Democrats

In politics, common name for the ◊ Social and Liberal Democrats.

## Liberal Party

British political party, the successor to the ◊ Whig Party, with an ideology of liberalism. In the 19th century it represented the interests of commerce and industry. Its outstanding leaders were Lord Palmerston, William Gladstone, and Lloyd George. From 1914 it declined, and the rise of the Labour Party pushed the Liberals into the middle ground. The Liberals joined forces with the Social Democratic Party (SDP) as the Alliance for the 1983 and 1987 elections. In 1988 a majority of the SDP voted to merge with the Liberals to form the ◊ Social and Liberal Democrats.

The term 'Liberal', used officially from about 1840 and unofficially from about 1815, marked a shift of support for the party from aristocrats to include also progressive industrialists, backed by supporters of the utilitarian reformer Jeremy ◊ Bentham, Nonconformists (especially in Welsh and Scottish constituencies), and the middle classes. During the Liberals' first period of power, from 1830 to 1841, they promoted parliamentary and municipal government reform and the abolition of slavery, but their *laissez-faire* theories led to the harsh Poor Law of 1834. Except for two short periods, the Liberals were in power from 1846 to 1866, but the only major change was the general adoption of free trade. Liberal pressure forced Peel to repeal the Corn Laws of 1846.

### Gladstone's reforms

Extended franchise (1867) and Gladstone's emergence as leader began a new phase, dominated by the Manchester school with a programme of 'peace, retrenchment, and reform'. Gladstone's 1868–74 government introduced many important reforms, including elementary education and vote by ballot. The party's left, mainly composed of working-class Radicals and led by Charles ◊ Bradlaugh (a lawyer's clerk) and Joseph ◊ Chamberlain (a wealthy manufacturer), repudiated *laissez faire* and inclined towards republicanism, but in 1886 the Liberals were split over the policy of Home Rule for Ireland, and many became Liberal Unionists or joined the Conservatives.

Except for the period 1892 to 1895, the Liberals remained out of power until 1906, when, reinforced by Labour and Irish support, they returned with a huge majority. Old-age pensions, National Insurance, limitation of the powers of the Lords, and the Irish Home Rule Bill followed.

Lloyd George's alliance with the Conservatives from 1916 to 1922 divided the Liberal Party between him and his predecessor Asquith, and although reunited in 1923 the Liberals continued to lose votes. They briefly joined the National Government (1931–32). After World War II they were reduced to a handful of members of Parliament.

A revival began under the leadership (1956–67) of Jo Grimond and continued under Jeremy Thorpe, who resigned after a period of controversy within the party in 1976. After a caretaker return by Grimond, David Steel became the first party leader in British politics to be elected by party members who were not MPs. Between 1977 and 1978 Steel entered into an agreement to support Labour in any vote of confidence in return for consultation on measures undertaken. He resigned in 1988 and was replaced by Paddy Ashdown, who in turn stepped down in 1999, replaced as leader by Charles Kennedy.

## Liberty, Arthur (1843–1917)

English shopkeeper and founder of a shop of the same name in London in 1875. Originally importing Oriental goods, it gradually started selling British Arts and Crafts and Art Nouveau furniture, tableware, and fabrics. Art Nouveau is still sometimes called *stile Liberty* in Italy.

A draper's son, Liberty trained at Farmer & Rogers' Cloak and Shawl Emporium. He was knighted in 1913.

## libraries

In 1998 there were some 5,000 public libraries in Britain, nearly 700 libraries in higher and further education, and over 3,000 specialized libraries in other organizations, as well as three national libraries. Altogether they employ around 42,500 people. In England about 60% of adults are members of their local library, half of these borrowing books at least once a month. See chronology of some key dates on page 272.

Lending or circulating libraries became widespread in the 19th century. The first documented free public library in the UK was established in Manchester in 1852, after the 1850 Public Library Act. See also ◊ British Library.

## licensing laws

Legislation governing the sale of alcoholic drinks; in Britain, sales can only be made by pubs, restaurants, shops, and clubs which hold licences obtained from licensing justices. The hours during which alcoholic drinks can be sold are

## Libraries: Some key dates

**1608** The first municipal public library in England is established in Norwich. It contains mainly religious works.

**1653** English merchant Humphrey Chetham establishes the Chetham Library in Manchester, England. It is the first library to be fully open to the public and soon carries books in a broad range of subjects.

**1682** The Advocates Library in Edinburgh is founded by the Scottish jurist George MacKenzie. It opens in 1698, and later forms the nucleus of the National Library of Scotland.

**1684** Trinity College Library at Cambridge University, designed by the English architect Christopher Wren, is completed.

**1689** The Advocates Library in Edinburgh, opens. It was founded in 1682.

**1697** The English scholar and bibliographer Edward Bernard publishes *Catalogi Librorum Manuscriptorum Angliae et Hiberniae/Catalogue of English and Scottish Books and Manuscripts*, a library catalogue of English and Scottish manuscripts.

**1726** The Scottish poet Allan Ramsay opens the first commercial lending library in Britain, in Edinburgh.

**1729** The Doctor William's Library is founded in London in memory of the nonconformist minister Daniel Williams, for students of religion and philosophy.

**1749** The Radcliffe Camera in Oxford, a library designed by the English architect James Gibbs, is completed. It is one of the finest examples of English Baroque architecture.

**1753** The extensive library of Sir Robert Bruce Cotton is transferred to the British Museum Library.

**1768** Britain's first privately owned library open to the public is set up, in Liverpool, with members paying an annual subscription to borrow books. Libraries in Sheffield, Hull, Bristol, and Birmingham soon follow.

**1823** The English educationalist and doctor George Birkbeck founds the Mechanics' Institute in Britain to provide libraries, reading rooms, and other educational facilities for workers.

**5 May 1841** The London Library opens as a private-subscription circulating library in England.

**1842** The English bibliophile Charles Edward Mudie's popular circulating library is founded in London.

**1850** The English politician William Ewart sponsors an act of Parliament in Britain to establish the first public libraries.

**1851** The rates are increased for the funding of public library facilities in England and Wales.

**1852** The Manchester Free Library opens, the first free public library in Britain.

**1859** The Warrington Mechanics' Institution start the first mobile library in Britain.

**1862** The first children's library in Britain opens at the Campfield Reference Library in Manchester.

**24 October 1946** King George VI opens the New Bodleian Library in Oxford.

**1973** The British Library is created.

**1984** Public lending right (PLR) comes into operation in Britain, where authors are paid a fee based on the number of loans of their books by libraries.

**1997–99** The reading rooms of the new British Library building at St Pancras, London, open in stages.

restricted: licensed premises can sell alcohol between 11am and 11pm Monday to Saturday, and 12 noon to 3pm and 7pm to 10.30pm on Sundays. These hours may be extended for special occasions, by application to the licensing justices.

From the late 19th century, temperance and nonconformist movements lobbied for tighter restrictions on the consumption of alcohol. In Wales Sunday closing was enforced from 1881, and in 1913 Scotland was permitted to hold local referenda on licensing issues. Restrictions on pub hours in England were initially introduced as a temporary war measure in World War I, not as a morality act, but to improve efficiency on the home front, but the regulations were retained after the war.

## Lichfield

Cathedral city in Staffordshire, central England, in the Trent Valley, 25 km/16 mi northeast of Birmingham; population (1996 est) 31,800. The writer and dictionary compiler Samuel Johnson was born in Lichfield in 1709.

The Early English and Decorated-style cathedral contains the *Lichfield Gospels* (a manuscript dating from the 8th century) and *The Sleeping Children* (1817) statute by Francis Chantrey. The birthplace of Samuel Johnson is now a museum. On the edge of Stowe Pool is the church and well of St Chad, who settled here in 669 and became the first bishop of Lichfield. There is a statue to Capt Edward Smith of the *Titanic* in the city park.

## Limehouse

District in east London; part of ◊Tower Hamlets. It takes its name from the kilns which preceded shipping as the main industry. In the 1890s it was the home of Chinese sailors working from the West India Docks. Bomb damage during World War II led to a decline in population, especially after closure of the docks. The Limehouse docks now form part of the Docklands urban development area. The Limehouse Link motorway and tunnel, linking Tower Hill and Canary Wharf, opened in 1993.

## limerick

Five-line humorous verse, often nonsensical and with a strict rhyme scheme, which first appeared in England in about 1820 and was popularized by Edward ◊ Lear. An example is: 'There was a young lady of Riga, Who rode with a smile on a tiger; They returned from the ride With the lady inside, And the smile on the face of the tiger.'

## Lincoln

Industrial and cathedral city, administrative headquarters of Lincolnshire, England, situated on the River Witham, 210 km/130 mi north of London; population (1991) 80,300. It was a major centre for the wool trade in the Middle Ages. Today it is the market centre for a large agricultural area.

### History

The first settlement on the site of Lincoln was the ancient British settlement of Lindos (meaning marsh or pool); the Romans latinized the name as **Lindum**. The Roman presence dates from AD 48 and continued into the 5th century; the title of *colonia* was conferred on the town in about AD 96. At the time of the Norman Conquest Lincoln was one of the six largest towns in the kingdom, with a considerable trade in wool. Under the Danish settlement Lincoln was one of the five boroughs of the ◊ Danelaw. William the Conqueror decided to build a castle here, and the town was chosen as the seat of a bishopric.

Lincoln received its first royal charter in 1154. The prosperity of medieval Lincoln was based on the wool trade. The raw wool was brought to Lincoln mainly along the waterways, and was there made up for export to Flanders and the Hanseatic towns. Cloth was being made in Lincoln by 1157, at which date there was a guild of weavers. From 1369 Boston became the centre of the wool trade, and Lincoln declined in importance until improved fen drainage in the 19th century made it an important agricultural centre. The first railway line to reach Lincoln was opened in 1846, and industry soon developed. Initially, agricultural machinery was manufactured, and later, heavy engineering products.

### Lincoln Castle

The castle was built by William the Conqueror in 1068 to supplement the defences of the city, whose Roman walls and gates had for the most part survived. The upper town was annexed to the new castle as a kind of outer bailey, which gave rise to the modern name 'Bailgate'. Lincoln Castle departs from the usual Norman plan in having two mounds instead of one; both stand on the south side of the castle yard, their bases being only about 60 m/197 ft apart. The castle houses one of the four surviving copies of the Magna Carta.

### Other features

The 11th–15th-century cathedral has the earliest Gothic work in Britain, while its surrounding close has the earliest English example of a polygonal Chapter House (1225). The 12th-century High Bridge, which spans the Witham, is the oldest in Britain still to have buildings on it (half-timbered houses dating to about 1540). The area known as the Jewish quarter contains a number of preserved medieval buildings.

Among Lincoln's religious houses are Monks Abbey, a cell of the Benedictine abbey of St Mary of York; St Catherine's priory of the order of St Gilbert of Sempringham; and the friars' houses, the only remaining example being Grey Friars (founded in 1090), which was later used as the grammar school and is now the museum; it preserves a chapel built in about 1230. The three most interesting medieval parish churches, St Benedict, St Mary-le-Wigford, and St Peter-at-Gowts, are all south of the river. St Mary-le-Wigford and St Peter-at-Gowts both possess notable Saxon towers.

The Usher Art Gallery contains important permanent collections, including the Usher and Tennyson collections and a collection of works by Peter de Wint, the water-colourist.

In 1996 a campus was opened in Lincoln for the newly formed University of Lincolnshire and Humberside.

## Lincolnshire

County of eastern England, bounded by the Wash and the North Sea to the east; population (1996) 615,900; area 5,890 sq km/2,274 sq mi. Much of the county is flat, with Lincoln Edge and the Lincolnshire Wolds providing more hilly landscapes; there are sandy beaches and coastal resorts (Skegness, Mablethorpe, Sutton) which draw holidaymakers in summer. The principal towns and cities are ◊ Lincoln (administrative headquarters), Skegness, Boston, and Stamford.

### History

The Pilgrims sailed from the port of Boston in 1630 and founded the city of Boston in America.

### Physical

There are fens in the southeast and the coastline is marshy, with long stretches of fine sand. Lincoln Edge (also known as the Heights, or the Cliff) runs from Grantham to Lincoln, and on to the River Humber; the Wolds in the northeast run from Spilsby to Barton-upon-Humber, rising to over 152 m/500 ft. The southwest is wooded. The county's major rivers are the Trent, Welland, and Witham.

*Features*

Lincoln has Roman remains, the second largest cathedral in England, a Norman castle, and a Jewish quarter. The poet laureate Alfred, Lord Tennyson spent his youth in Lincolnshire and there is a museum and statue in Lincoln. The Boston Stump (83 m/272 ft), the tower of St Botolph's church in Boston, is the highest parish church tower in England. The 16th-century Burghley House, near the greystone town of Stamford, has a lake and deer park by Capability Brown and hosts the annual Burghley Horse Trials. Belton House is a notable Restoration mansion. Spalding holds an annual flower parade with floats created from tulip heads processing through the town. There are nature reserves at Gibraltar Point and Saltfleetby.

*Economy*

Lincolnshire's economy is largely based on agriculture and flower bulbs; it has the largest bulb-growing industry in the UK, around Spalding.

## Lindisfarne

Site of a monastery off the coast of Northumberland, England; see ◊Holy Island.

## Lindisfarne Gospels, or St Cuthbert's Evangelistarium

Celtic manuscript conceived as a memorial volume to St Cuthbert, who died in 687, held in the British Museum, London. It was produced at the Anglo-Irish monastery of Lindisfarne on ◊Holy Island, Northumberland. Its decorative interlaced ornament is similar in style to that of the Book of ◊Kells, now in Trinity College, Dublin.

Under Ethelwold, bishop of Lindisfarne, the manuscript was enriched early in the 8th century by an elaborate painting of an evangelist to each of the four Gospels and by illuminated capital letters at the commencement of each book.

## lion

The most important heraldic animal, associated with valour and strength. The **lion rampant** (standing on hind legs) in the arms of Scotland derives from the earls of Northumberland and Huntingdon, from whom some Scottish monarchs were descended. Two of the three **lions passant gardant** (walking, full-faced) in the shield of England derive from William the Conqueror, and Henry II added the third. The lion and the unicorn have been supporters of the royal arms since 1603.

## Lisburn

Town in County Antrim, Northern Ireland, on the River Lagan, 14 km/9 mi from Belfast; population (1991) 27,400. Lisburn was founded in the 17th century and planted with English settlers and French Huguenot refugees. The development of the linen industry, which came to be important in the town, owed much to the Huguenot settlers. The Church of Ireland cathedral was built in 1623.

## Lister, Joseph, 1st Baron Lister (1827–1912)

English surgeon. He was the founder of antiseptic surgery, influenced by Louis Pasteur's work on bacteria. He introduced dressings soaked in carbolic acid and strict rules of hygiene to combat wound sepsis in hospitals.

The number of surgical operations greatly increased following the introduction of anaesthetics, but death rates were more than 40%. Under Lister's regime they fell dramatically.

Lister was born in Upton, Essex, and studied at University College, London. He was professor of surgery at Glasgow 1860–69, at Edinburgh 1869–77, and at King's College, London 1877–92. In 1891 he became chair of the newly formed British Institute of Preventive Medicine (later the Lister Institute).

## Little John

In English legend, a companion of ◊Robin Hood.

## Little Moreton Hall

Outstanding black-and-white Tudor house near Congleton, Cheshire, England. It was built in stages throughout the 16th century, the oldest part dating from about 1520. The somewhat random structure is surrounded by a moat, while inside the hall and gallery are decorated with carving and plasterwork. The Hall was presented to the National Trust in 1938.

## Liverpool

City, seaport, and metropolitan borough in Merseyside, northwest England; population (1991) 481,800. Liverpool is the UK's chief Atlantic port with miles of specialized, mechanized quays on the River Mersey, and 2,100 ha/5,187 acres of dockland. Imports include crude oil, grain, ores, edible oils, timber, and containers. There are ferries to Ireland and the Isle of Man. Traditional industries, such as ship-repairing, have declined.

*History*

Liverpool became a county borough in 1207, when it was granted a charter by King John. From its beginnings as a port it was associated with the transport of soldiers and military supplies to Ireland, and with general trade. The original port was probably a sheltered creek, the 'Pool', long since filled in, and the early town was clustered around the church of St Nicholas and a former castle. By 1445 Liverpool's trade was challenging the prosperity of Chester as a port, but the town remained small. It developed under Charles II (1630–85), with the growing trade with America and the West Indies, and it became the chief centre of the slave trade. In 1715 the 'Old Dock' was opened, on the site of the Custom House (since filled up).

During the 18th century Liverpool grew rapidly. By then, its port had long since eclipsed Chester and the surrounding area was also growing in importance, with industrial areas to the north (including the Cheshire salt deposits), the textile areas of the Pennines and their fringes, and the metallurgical areas of the Midlands. The city's position was strengthened by the building of canals to the River Mersey, including the Sankey Canal from St Helens (1757), the Bridgewater from Manchester to Runcorn (1773), the Trent and Mersey (1777), and the Leeds and Liverpool (which reached Wigan in 1774 but Liverpool only in 1816). At the same time, the dock area was expanded, at first from 1715 to 1797, when several docks south of the Pier Head were built (the Pier Head is the great river focus of Liverpool, as the Mersey narrows here to a mere 915 m/3,000 ft), and then again from 1821, when docks were built to the north of Pier Head.

### Features

Landmarks include the Bluecoat Chambers (1717); the Town Hall (1754); St George's Hall (1838–54), a good example of classical architecture; the Brown Library and Museum (1860); the Picton Library (1879); the Walker Art Gallery (1877); the Anglican Cathedral (begun 1904, completed 1980); and the Roman Catholic Metropolitan Cathedral of Christ the King (consecrated in 1967). The historic waterfront is now a major tourist attraction, and the restored Albert Dock includes the Merseyside Maritime Museum as well as the Tate Gallery in the North.

Notable buildings include the 16th-century Speke Hall, the Victoria Building of the University of Liverpool, the Dock Offices, the Port of Liverpool building (1907), the Royal Liver Building (1911), and the Cunard Building (1916) on Pier Head.

The Central Libraries (a conglomerate of several libraries) constitute one of the best public libraries in the country. There are two universities: the University of Liverpool (1903) and John Moores University (1992).

The members of the Beatles were born here. The Liverpool Institute for the Performing Arts, set up by former Beatle Paul McCartney and opened in 1995, occupies the old Liverpool Institute for Boys, where Paul McCartney and George Harrison went to school.

The city is also home to the Liverpool Philharmonic Orchestra (founded in 1840, the Royal LPO since 1957). The Grand National steeplechase (first instituted in 1839) takes place at nearby Aintree every year in March or April.

## livery companies

Guilds (organizations of traders and artisans) of the City of London. Their role is now social rather than industrial. Many administer charities, especially educational ones. Each livery company is governed by an annually elected court, typically composed as follows: The Master (elected from the Wardens); Upper Warden; Middle Warden; Lower Warden (elected from the Court assistant); between 10 and 20 Court Assistants (elected from the Livery); a Clerk (to keep the records); a Beadle (to keep order).

After years of dispute, an order of precedence for livery companies was settled in 1515, starting with Mercers at number 1 and so on down to number 48. Merchant Taylors and Skinners, however, continued to alternate between numbers 6 and 7 in alternate years, following a compromise reached some 30 years earlier. Numbers 1 to 12 inclusive are known as the Great Twelve. Through choice, the companies of Parish Clerks and Watermen and Lightermen remain City Guilds without grant of livery.

## Livingstone, David (1813–1873)

Scottish missionary explorer. In 1841 he went to Africa, reaching Lake Ngami in 1849. He followed the Zambezi to its mouth, saw the Victoria Falls in 1855, and went to East and Central Africa 1858–64, reaching Lakes Shirwa and Nyasa. From 1866, he tried to find the source of the River Nile, and reached Ujiji in Tanganyika in November 1871. British explorer Henry Stanley joined Livingstone in Ujiji.

Livingstone not only mapped a great deal of the African continent but also helped to end the Arab slave trade.

He died in Old Chitambo (now in Zambia) and was buried in Westminster Abbey, London.

**David Livingstone,** Scottish missionary and explorer David Livingstone hoped to abolish the slave trade in Africa by spreading Christianity, and during his travels he discovered the Zambesi River (1851) and Victoria Falls (1855). He became a national hero in Britain and played a major role in shaping European attitudes towards Africa. Corbis

## Lizard Point

Southernmost point of mainland England in Cornwall. The coast is broken into small bays, overlooked by two cliff lighthouses. The point is notable for Cornish heath and other plants similar to those found in southwest Europe. The Lizard Countryside Centre at Trelowarren displays material on all aspects of the Lizard peninsula.

## Llanberis

Village in Gwynedd, northwest Wales, situated 5 km/3 mi east of Caernarfon. It is the point of departure for the ascent of Mount ◊Snowdon (1,085 m/3,560 ft), either on foot or using the mountain railway which starts here.

There are two lakes in the vicinity, and Llanberis is also a resort for fishermen.

## Llandaff, Welsh Llandaf

Town in south Wales, 5 km/3 mi northwest of Cardiff, of which it forms part. The 12th-century cathedral, heavily restored, contains Jacob Epstein's sculpture *Christ in Majesty*, crowning a 20th-century arch of reinforced concrete.

## Llandrindod Wells

Administrative centre of ◊Powys, east Wales; population (1991) 4,400. Situated on the River Ithon, it is a popular health resort possessing medicinal springs.

## Llandudno

Seaside resort in Gwynedd, north Wales, situated on Conwy Bay. Lying on the Creuddyn Peninsula, it has two sandy beaches and is a touring centre. Great Orme's Head is a spectacular limestone headland encircled by a marine 'drive'.

## Llanfair P G

Village in Anglesey, northwest Wales, 24 km/15 mi east of Holyhead; full name **Llanfairpwllgwyngyllgogerychwyrndrobwllllantysiliogogogoch** (St Mary's church in the hollow of the white hazel near the rapid whirlpool of St Tysillio's church, by the red cave), the longest place name in the UK.

## Llangollen

Town in Denbighshire, northeast Wales, on the River Dee, 15 km/9 mi southwest of Wrexham; population (1991) 3,300. It is a summer resort. The annual international musical ◊eisteddfod (festival) is held here. The Vale of Llangollen includes places of historic interest, such as the ruins of Valle Crucis Abbey. Other local features include the Llangollen Canal and the scenic Llangollen Railway.

## Llewelyn

Two princes of Wales:

### Llewelyn I (1173–1240)

Prince of Wales from 1194. He extended his rule to all Wales not in Norman hands, driving the English from northern Wales in 1212, and taking Shrewsbury in 1215. During the early part of Henry III's reign, he was several times attacked by English armies. He was married to Joanna, the illegitimate daughter of King John.

### Llewelyn II ap Gruffydd (c. 1225–1282)

Prince of Wales from 1246, grandson of Llewelyn I. In 1277 Edward I of England compelled Llewelyn to acknowledge him as overlord and to surrender southern Wales. His death while leading a national uprising ended Welsh independence.

## Lleyn Peninsula, Welsh Llŷn

Westward-extending peninsula in north Wales, between Cardigan Bay and Caernarfon Bay. Its coastline is designated as a National Heritage Coastline and an Area of Outstanding Natural Beauty. It includes the resort of ◊Pwllheli. ◊Bardsey Island, at its tip, is reputedly the burial place of saints.

It is a low plateau with a number of mountains, of which Yr Eifl (564 m/1,850 ft) is the highest. The area is rural with a predominantly Welsh-speaking population. Other resorts along the coast include Criccieth, Abersoch, Aberdaron, and Nefyn. Activities include surfing, sailing, and sea angling.

## Lloyd George, David, 1st Earl Lloyd-George of Dwyfor (1863–1945)

British Liberal politician, prime minister of Britain from 1916 to 1922. A pioneer of social reform and the welfare state, as chancellor of the Exchequer (1908–15) he introduced old-age pensions in 1908 and health and unemployment insurance in 1911. High unemployment, intervention in the Russian Civil War, and use of the military police force, the ◊Black and Tans, in Ireland eroded his support as prime minister, and the creation of the Irish Free State in 1921 and his pro-Greek policy against the Turks caused the collapse of his coalition government.

## Lloyd's of London

International insurance market and centre of shipping intelligence, based in London. Lloyd's was established in 1688 and named after Edward Lloyd, whose coffee-house was a meeting place for those interested in shipping. Lloyd's accounts for half of all international insurance premiums underwritten in the London market. Lloyd's moved into a new building in the City of London, designed by the architect Richard Rogers, in 1986.

Members of Lloyd's (known as 'names') are organized into syndicates, and pledge personal fortunes in return for premiums. There is no limit to a name's liability, but risks are spread among the members of a syndicate, so that no individual takes too great a personal risk. However, during the late 1980s and early 1990s, Lloyd's suffered a series of losses (Piper Alpha, Hurricane Hugo, the *Exxon Valdez* oil spill, European storms in 1990), and many names faced large bills to meet the insurance cover; a financial settlement was reached in 1996.

## local government

See ◊England, ◊Scotland, ◊Wales, and ◊Northern Ireland for details of the local government divisions.

## Locke, John (1632–1704)

English philosopher. His *Essay concerning Human Understanding* (1690) maintained that experience is the only source of knowledge (empiricism), and that 'we can have knowledge no farther than we have ideas' prompted by such experience. *Two Treatises on Government* (1690) helped to form contemporary ideas of liberal democracy.

## Lockerbie

Town and former burgh in Dumfries and Galloway unitary authority, Scotland, 19 km/12 mi northeast of Dumfries; population (1991) 4,000. It hosts the largest lamb fair in Scotland, held annually in August. On 21 December 1988 the bombing over Lockerbie of Pan-Am Flight 103 to New York killed 270 people, including 11 on the ground.

## Lollard

Follower of the English religious reformer John ◊Wycliffe in the 14th century. The Lollards condemned the doctrine of the transubstantiation of the bread and wine of the Eucharist, advocated the diversion of ecclesiastical property to charitable uses, and denounced war and capital punishment. They were active from about 1377; after the passing of the statute *De heretico comburendo* ('The Necessity of Burning Heretics') in 1401 many Lollards were burned, and in 1414 they raised an unsuccessful revolt in London, known as Oldcastle's Rebellion.

The name is derived from the Dutch *lollaert* (mumbler).

## Lomond, Loch

Largest freshwater Scottish lake, 37 km/21 mi long, area 70 sq km/27 sq mi. It is overlooked by the mountain **Ben Lomond** (973 m/3,192 ft) and is linked to the Clyde estuary.

---

*The people of London with one voice would say to Hitler: ... You do your worst – and we will do our best.*

**Winston Churchill** British Conservative prime minister.
Speech at County Hall, London 14 July 1942

---

## London

Capital of England and the United Kingdom, located on the River Thames.

Since 1965 its metropolitan area has been known as ◊ Greater London, consisting of the City of London and 32 boroughs; total area 1,580 sq km/610 sq mi; combined population (1995) for 31 boroughs, excluding the cities of London and Westminster, 7,001,900. London is the world's leading international financial centre, with banking and insurance concentrated in the **City of London** (known as the 'square mile'). Tourism, retail, printing and publishing, and media-related businesses are also important sectors of the city's economy.

### Boroughs

The inner London boroughs of Greater London are Camden, Hackney, Hammersmith and Fulham, Haringey, Islington, Kensington and Chelsea, Lambeth, Lewisham, Newham, Southwark, Tower Hamlets, Wandsworth, and the City of Westminster. The outer boroughs of Greater London are Barking and Dagenham, Barnet, Bexley, Brent, Bromley, Croydon, Ealing, Enfield, Greenwich, Harrow, Havering, Hillingdon, Hounslow, Kingston upon Thames, Merton, Redbridge, Richmond upon Thames, Sutton, and Waltham Forest.

London has not had a city-wide strategic authority since 1986; however, following proposals for local government reform in the late 1990s, London was scheduled to elect its own mayor in May 2000.

### Inner city landscape

The **City of London**, the oldest part of the capital, lies on the north bank of the Thames between Tower Bridge to the east and London Bridge to the west. It is the financial and business heart of the capital, and contains the law courts of the Old Bailey and Royal Courts of Justice. The 11th-century ◊ Tower of London stands just outside the City, and houses the crown jewels and the royal armouries; it is a World Heritage Site. ◊ St Paul's Cathedral (1675–1710) is in the centre of the City; and the Barbican residential and arts complex (1982) lies to the north.

West of the City the Strand runs southwest towards the administrative and government centres of the City of ◊ Westminster and Whitehall. It terminates in Trafalgar Square, site of Nelson's Column and the National Gallery. The Houses of Parliament (1840–60), with the bell tower of Big Ben (1858), line the riverfront. ◊ Westminster Abbey (1050–1745), the coronation and burial place of many of Britain's monarchs, lies nearby. Westminster is also the London seat of the royal court, whose chief residences are ◊ Buckingham Palace and St James's Palace. Slightly northwards, but on the south side of the river is the South Bank arts and culture complex, and the London Eye – the world's largest observational ferris wheel, built in 1999 as one of the city's millennial projects and offering panoramic views of the city and beyond.

To the west of the City, London's West End contains most of the capital's hotels, shops, restaurants, and theatres. The area incorporates Soho and Covent Garden, notable for their nightlife and restaurants, and Marylebone, Piccadilly, and Mayfair. Further west, the Royal Borough of ◊ Kensington and Chelsea extends from Notting Hill in the north to the riverfront of Chelsea. Many of the capital's museums are concentrated in South Kensington. Northwest of the City, the historic neighbourhood of Bloomsbury is home to the British Museum and parts of London University.

---

*This is a London particular. ... A fog, miss.*

**Charles Dickens** English novelist.
*Bleak House* ch 3

---

### Museums and galleries

London's oldest museums are the British Museum (1759), the largest in the UK; the ◊ Natural History Museum (1856); the ◊ Science Museum (1853); the ◊ Victoria and Albert Museum (1852), housing one of the world's largest collections of the decorative arts; and the waxworks of Madame ◊ Tussaud (1802). The ◊ National Gallery (1824) houses pre-20th-century art and the most comprehensive collection of Italian Gothic and Renaissance works outside Italy, and the

◊National Portrait Gallery (1856) is devoted to distinguished British figures. Modern art from the 17th century to the present is displayed at the ◊Tate Gallery (1897), while the Courtauld Institute (1931) has fine Impressionist and post-Impressionist collections. Other museums include the Museum of London, the Museum of the Moving Image, the Imperial War Museum, and the National Army Museum. The National Maritime Museum in Greenwich incorporates the Old Royal Observatory, the point from which Greenwich Mean Time was originally established.

*Music and the performing arts*

London has been a leading international venue of music and the performing arts since the 18th century. Today, the city has five professional symphony orchestras and is home to the English National Opera and English National Ballet. The refurbished Royal Opera House in Covent Garden reopened at the end of 1999. Classical and contemporary dance is performed at Sadler's Wells. London's many concert halls include the Royal Festival Hall in the South Bank complex; the Barbican arts centre, the Wigmore Hall recital rooms, and the Royal Albert Hall, home to the annual Proms from 1895.

Most of London's theatres are located in and around Piccadilly, Shaftesbury Avenue, and Leicester Square. Historic West End theatres include the Haymarket (1821), Criterion (1874), Drury Lane (1663), and Her Majesty's (1897). Others include the Old Vic (1818), in south London; the Garrick Theatre (1889), in Charing Cross; and the west London playhouses of the Lyric (1870) and the Royal Court (1898). Modern theatres include the National Theatre (1963) in the South Bank complex, and the Barbican. In-the-round stages are found at the New Vic and the reconstructed Elizabethan-period ◊Globe Theatre at Bankside (1996).

*Parks and events*

Many of London's lakes and parks were former royal preserves; today, the eight royal parks are official public open spaces, belonging to the crown. The main central parks are Regent's Park, site of London Zoo; Hyde Park, with the Serpentine Lake and Serpentine Gallery; Holland Park; and St James's Park. Richmond Park is the largest urban park in Britain. ◊Kew Gardens (or the Royal Botanic Gardens) were founded in 1759 and are also a centre for botanical research (Kew received £21 million from the Millennium Commission to construct a new seed bank).

London is host to many international sports events, most famously lawn tennis at Wimbledon,

**London** Two classic images of London: 'bobbies' on patrol stand in front of 'Big Ben' at the Houses of Parliament. The nickname for the police derives from their founder, Sir Robert Peel; the popular name for the clocktower only refers, strictly speaking, to the bell inside it, but has come to be applied to the whole structure. Corel

and Test matches at the Lord's and Oval cricket grounds. Among the major annual cultural events are the Notting Hill Carnival, a Caribbean-style street festival held in August; the Boat Race, on the Thames between Putney and Mortlake, held since 1829 between the universities of Oxford and Cambridge; the London Marathon, established in 1981; and the New Year's Eve celebrations in Trafalgar Square.

*History to 1700*

Roman **Londinium** was established soon after the Roman invasion in AD 43. By the 11th century it was the main city of England and was officially linked with the originally separate town of Westminster. In the medieval period, London was controlled largely by the city guilds – chartered associations controlling a craft or trade – that arose from the 12th century. During the Tudor period the power of the crown increased at the expense of the church and the guilds, but industrial progress was maintained from the medieval period, and the merchant classes flourished with the opening of shipping routes to America, Africa,

**London** Looking east over Regent's Park, which lies to the north of Oxford Street, one of the city's key east–west thoroughfares. Laid out in the early nineteenth century by John Nash for the Prince Regent (later George IV), the park is over 450 acres in size. To the right, the golden dome of the Regent's Park Mosque (completed 1977) is visible. Simon Hazelgrove/ Collections

roads, and railways, and the world's largest enclosed dock system was built to the east of the city. Communications and transport developed rapidly with the extension of canal networks and the growth of the railways. The world's first underground steam railway opened in London in 1863, and the world's first tube steam railway, the Tower Subway, in 1870. By 1901 the population of greater London had reached over 6.5 million.

After World War II, in the aftermath of extensive devastation caused to London by heavy bombing, the first concerted efforts were made to provide overall planning for the metropolitan region. Provision was made for open spaces, and suburbs and residential schemes were greatly expanded, measures which eased the city's congestion. The importance of the docks declined, and by the early 1980s most of them had closed, opening the way for extensive riverside development.

*Educational institutions*

University College was founded in 1826 and King's College in 1828. The University of London was established in 1836 to set examinations and grant degrees to students from both these colleges. The University of London now incorporates 26 colleges, including the Imperial College of Science, Technology, and Medicine, the London School of Economics (LSE), and the School of Oriental and African Studies (SOAS). Other universities in the Greater London area include the City University (1966), the University of Greenwich (1992), the University of North London (1992), the South Bank University (1992), Thames Valley University (1992), the University of East London (1992), and the London Guildhall University (1993).

*When a man is tired of London, he is tired of life; for there is in London all that life can afford.*
**Samuel Johnson** English lexicographer, author, and critic.
Boswell's *Life of Johnson* vol III

and Asia. About 90% of England's overseas trade was conducted through the port of London. The economy also expanded with the continuing growth of London as a centre of national government and royal administration.

Soon after the ◊ Restoration of the monarchy in 1660, two major disasters struck London: in 1665 the Great Plague killed over 80,000 people, about one-sixth of the city's population; and in 1666 the Fire of London destroyed most of the City. London's economic prosperity soon recovered, and by 1700 it was the largest city in western Europe, with a population of around 575,000.

*The world's largest city*

When the first official census was taken in 1801, the population of London was about 1 million; over the next 30 years numbers doubled. During the 19th century London was the world's largest city in both population size and area. London's physical expansion was rapid and enormous; thousands of acres were turned over to housing,

*London's millennium celebrations*

London's official millennium party began on the morning of 31 December and continued through the following day. Highlights of the celebrations were the opening of the Millennium Dome in Greenwich on New Year's Eve, attended by Tony Blair and the Queen, and a 15-minute fireworks display over the river – the biggest ever – as Big Ben chimed midnight.

**Londonderry**, also known as **Derry** (Irish 'oakwood'); until the 10th century known as **Derry-Calgaich**, 'the oak wood of Calgaich' (a fierce warrior)

Historic city and port on the River Foyle, 35 km/22 mi from Lough Foyle, county town of County ◊ Londonderry, Northern Ireland; population (1991) 95,400. Industries include the manufacture of textiles, chemicals, food processing, shirt manufacturing, and acetylene from naphtha.

*Features*

The Protestant Cathedral of St Columba dating from 1633; the Gothic revival Roman Catholic Cathedral of St Eugene (completed in 1833); the Guildhall (rebuilt in 1912), containing stained glass windows presented by livery companies of the City of London; the city walls, on which are modern iron statues by Anthony Gormley; four gates into the city still survive.

*History*

Londonderry dates from the foundation of a monastery there by St Columba in AD 546. The city was subject to a number of sieges by the Danes between the 9th and 11th centuries, and by the Anglo-Normans in the 12th century; however, these were unsuccessful until James I of England captured the city in 1608. The king granted the borough and surrounding land to the citizens of London. The Irish Society was formed to build and administer the city and a large colony of English Protestants was established. The city, then governed by Major Henry Baker and the Reverend George Walker, was unsuccessfully besieged in 1689 by the armies of James II, who had fled England when William of Orange was declared joint sovereign with James' daughter Mary. James' army was led by Richard Talbot, Earl of Tyrconnell, in a conflict known as the **Siege of Derry**, when 13 Derry apprentices and citizens loyal to William of Orange locked the city gates against the Jacobite army. The siege lasted 15 weeks, during which many of the inhabitants died of starvation and disease because of the blockade.

*Topography*

The old city walls that still surround Londonderry extend for over 1 km/0.5 mi and include seven gates and several bastions. The waterside, the part of the city on the right bank of the Foyle, is connected to the old city by the Craigavon Bridge (opened in 1933), which carries a roadway 360 m/1,180 ft long. The original eight bells in the

tower of the Cathedral of St Columba were recast in 1929 and another five were added. Among the parks are Brooke Park in which is situated the municipal library, St Columba's Park, and Meenan Park.

*From Derry to Londonderry*

The town of Derry was fortified and garrisoned by the English, and made a city in 1608. In 1609, during the ◊ Plantation of Ireland, James I granted Derry, Coleraine, and a large tract of land between to the City of London. The land was distributed among the London ◊ livery companies, but in order to avoid jealousy among the companies, the City of London Corporation retained the boroughs of Londonderry and Coleraine. The Irish Society was formed in 1613 to administer the boroughs; its members were appointed from within the City of London Corporation. The Society was incorporated by royal charter in 1613 and was trustee for the Corporation. Its court consisted of a governor, a deputy governor, and 24 assistants, in addition to the Recorder of London. It was on account of the connection with the City of London Corporation that the name of the city was changed from Derry to Londonderry.

The port was a major naval base during World War II, but has declined in importance since.

**Londonderry**, also known as **Derry**

County of Northern Ireland; population (1981) 187,000; area 2,070 sq km/799 sq mi. Its principal towns and cities are ◊ Londonderry (county town), Coleraine, Portstewart, and Limavady.

*Physical*

Londonderry is bounded on the north by the Atlantic, and is dominated by the Sperrin Mountains which run in an arc from southwest to northeast, dividing the lowlands fringing the River Bann in the east from those of the River Foyle in the west. Mount Sawell (670 m/2,198 ft) in the Sperrin Mountains is the county's highest peak. The Roe and the Faughan are the main westward flowing streams, while the Bann forms the eastern border for most of its length.

*Features*

The county has Ireland's longest beach, Magilligan Strand. The ruined Downhill Castle estate contains the clifftop Mussenden Temple built in classical style to accommodate a bishop's library.

*Economy*

Farming is hindered by the very heavy rainfall; flax is cultivated and there is moorland grazing and salmon and eel fisheries on the Bann. Industries include textiles, light engineering, and stone and lime quarrying.

## London, Greater
Metropolitan area of ◊London, comprising the City of London, which forms a self-governing enclave, and 32 surrounding boroughs; population (1991) 6,679,700; area 1,580 sq km/610 sq mi. The population of Inner London is 2,504,500 and that of Outer London 4,175,200.

## London Underground
First underground rail line in the world, opened in 1863. At first it was essentially a roofed-in trench. The London Underground is still the world's longest subway, with over 250 mi/400 km of routes.

## longbow
Longer than the standard bow, made of yew, introduced in the 12th century. They were favoured by English archers in preference to the cross bow, as the longer bow allowed arrows of greater weight to be fired further and more accurately. They were highly effective in the Hundred Years' War, to the extent that the French took to removing the first two fingers of prisoners so that they would never again be able to draw a bow.

## Longleat
Estate in Wiltshire between Warminster and Frome, best known for its safari park, the first of its kind in England. The Elizabethan house is the seat of the Marquess of Bath. Begun in 1568 by John Thynne (died 1580), it was revolutionary in its classic symmetry and simplicity, and allocation of most of the wall to window space. Only the exterior survives intact: the interior decoration is now mainly 19th century. Stables were added by Jeffrey Wyatville (1807–11), and the park was laid out by Capability Brown.

## Lord Chancellor
State official; see ◊Chancellor, Lord.

## Lord Lieutenant
The sovereign's representative in a county, who recommends magistrates for appointment. It is an unpaid position and the retirement age is 75.

## Lord's
Cricket ground in St John's Wood, London. One of England's test-match grounds and the headquarters of one of cricket's governing bodies, the Marylebone Cricket Club (MCC), since 1788 when the MCC was formed following the folding of the White Conduit Club.

The ground is named after Yorkshireman **Thomas Lord** (1757–1832) who developed the first site at Dorset Square in 1787. He moved the ground to a field at North Bank, Regent's Park, in 1811, and in 1814 developed the ground at its present site at St John's Wood. Lord's is also the home of the Middlesex Cricket Club.

On 28 September 1998, the MCC voted in favour of admitting women for the first time in its 211-year history.

## Lords, House of
See ◊government.

## lottery
See ◊National Lottery.

## Loughborough
Industrial town in Leicestershire, central England, 18 km/11 mi northwest of Leicester, on the River Soar; population (1995 est) 55,300.

A grammar school was founded here in 1495. Great Paul, the bell of St Paul's Cathedral, London, was cast in Loughborough. Loughborough University of Technology was established in 1966 (formerly the College of Technology, and incorporating the college of education).

## Lowestoft Old Norse Hloover's Toft 'dwelling belonging to Hloover'
Resort town and port in Suffolk, England, 62 km/38 mi northeast of Ipswich, the most easterly town in Britain; population (1996 est) 66,300. Offshore oil and gas fields provide significant employment related to production and exploration. Historically a fishing port, the industry is still active but has declined dramatically. Tourism is also important. **Lowestoft Ness** is the most easterly point in England.

The older part of Lowestoft is built on the cliff overlooking the sea, while later development – after the opening of the railway in 1847 – is further south.

*History*

The name Lowestoft appears in the Domesday Book of 1086 as **Lothu Wistoft**, derived from the Old Norse **Hloover's Toft**, an Old Norse name. During World War I the town was attacked by German warships, and it was damaged during World War II. Kirkley was incorporated in Lowestoft in 1854 and Oulton Broad in 1921. Lowestoft china was made here from 1757 to 1802.

The harbour was formed by linking Lake

Lothing, now known as the Inner Harbour, with the sea in 1831. The construction of Trawler Basin in 1846, Waveney Basin in 1883, and Hamilton Dock in 1906 greatly extended the quay space. Large coastal protection schemes have been carried out to the north and south of the harbour.

## Lowry, L(aurence) S(tephen) (1887–1976)

English painter. His works depict life in the industrial towns of the north of England. In the 1920s he developed a naive style characterized by matchstick figures, often in animated groups, and gaunt simplified factories and terraced houses, painted in an almost monochrome palette. *The Pond* (1950; Tate Gallery, London) is an example.

Born in Manchester, he spent the rest of his life in nearby Salford, earning his living as a rent collector. Although he was a legend in his lifetime, he remained an elusive, retiring figure, rarely venturing beyond his native towns.

A waterfront arts complex, called the Lowry Centre, was scheduled to open in Salford in April 2000, as a Millennium Commission Landmark Project.

## Lucan, Richard John Bingham, 7th Earl of Lucan (1934–1999)

English aristocrat and professional gambler. On 7 November 1974 his wife was attacked and their children's nanny murdered. No trace of Lucan has since been found, and there has been no solution to the murder. He was officially declared dead in 1999.

## Luddite

One of a group of people involved in machine-wrecking riots in northern England 1811–16. The organizer of the Luddites was referred to as **General Ludd**, but may not have existed. Many Luddites were hanged or transported to penal colonies, such as Australia.

The movement, which began in Nottinghamshire and spread to Lancashire, Cheshire, Derbyshire, Leicestershire, and Yorkshire, was primarily a revolt against the unemployment caused by the introduction of machines in the Industrial Revolution.

## Ludlow

Market town in Shropshire, England, on the rivers Teme and Corve, near the Welsh border, 42 km/26 mi south of Shrewsbury; population (1991) 9,000. Tourism is important.

*Features*

**Ludlow Castle**, on a hill overlooking the rivers Teme and Corve, was built as a stronghold of the Welsh Marches (border) in about 1086 and has a large Norman keep. John Milton's masque *Comus* was first presented in the castle in 1634, and an arts festival is held here each year. The large 15th-century St Laurence's Church, with its 41-m/135-ft tower, reflects the town's prosperity as a centre of the wool trade in the Middle Ages. The poet A E Housman is buried in the churchyard. The town has many half-timbered buildings, notably the Jacobean Feathers Hotel.

## Lulworth, West and East

Two villages in Dorset, southwest England. **West Lulworth** is 12 km/7 mi east of Wareham. Nearby are **Lulworth Cove**, a bay about 450 m/1,500 ft across, almost enclosed by hills, and the natural rock arch known as Durdle Door. **East Lulworth** includes the restored 17th century Lulworth Castle. The Roman Catholic chapel in East Lulworth, built in 1786, was the first to be built by royal permission after the Reformation (apart from those attached to foreign embassies).

## Lundy Island

Rocky, granite island at the entrance to the Bristol Channel; 19 km/12 mi northwest of Hartland Point, Devon, southwest England; area 9.6 sq km/3.7 sq mi; population (1975) 40. Formerly used by pirates and privateers as a lair, it is now the site of a bird sanctuary and the first British Marine Nature Reserve (1986). It has Bronze and Iron Age field systems, which can be traced by their boundaries which stand up above the surface.

Contact with the Devon mainland is mainly by ferry from Bideford or Ilfracombe.

## Luton

Industrial town in south-central England, 48 km/30 mi north of London; population (1996) 181,400. Formerly part of the county of Bedfordshire, it became a unitary authority in 1997; area 43 sq km/17 sq mi. The straw and fashion hat industry was responsible for Luton's prosperity in the 19th century. Luton airport is a secondary airport for London.

*History*

Luton was known as **Lygetune** by the Saxons, and in the Domesday Book of 1086 it was called **Loitoine**. The town was incorporated as a municipal borough in 1876, and became a county borough in 1964, with extended boundaries. In 1974 it became a district of the county of Bedfordshire.

*Features*

The Luton Hoo mansion (1767), designed and built by Robert Adam and with a park laid out by

Capability Brown, is to the south of the town; the church of St Mary (13th–15th centuries) is a cruciform building largely in the Decorated and Perpendicular styles.

## Lutyens, Edwin (1869–1944)

English architect. His designs ranged from the picturesque, such as ♭Castle Drogo (1910–30), Devon, to Renaissance-style country houses, and ultimately evolved into a Classical style as seen in the Cenotaph, London (1919). His complex use of space, interest in tradition, and distorted Classical language have proved of great interest to a number of Post-Modern architects, especially Robert Venturi.

His first commission was a country cottage, Munstead Wood (1896), for Gertrude ♭Jekyll, who greatly influenced his earlier work. His later designs displayed a more formal Georgian or Queen Anne style, a particularly dignified example being Heathcote, Ilkley (1906). Lutyens was President of the Royal Academy from 1938 to 1944.

## Lydford

Village in Devon, England, 18 km/11 mi east of Launceston; population (1991) 1,700. It was a walled town before the Norman Conquest, and Jeffreys of Wem (the 17th-century 'hanging judge') held his assizes at the castle. For many years it was the capital of Devonshire stannary (see ♭stannaries), because of its important position on the edge of the great tin-mining district of Dartmoor.

## Lyme Park

House in Disley, Cheshire, England. It is partly Elizabethan with 18th- and 19th-century additions by Giacomo Leoni (c. 1686–1746) and Lewis Wyatt (1814–17). The house stands in 530 ha/1309 acres of park and moorland, and was given to the National Trust in 1947. The largest house in Cheshire, it displays period interiors from four centuries.

Its collections include tapestries, carvings by Grinling Gibbons, and a collection of clocks. The house is set in gardens with an orangery by Wyatt, a lake, and a Dutch garden.

## Lyme Regis

Seaport and resort in Dorset, southern England; population (1993 est) 3,600. Tourism and fishing are the main industries. The town was formerly a major port, and the rebel Duke of Monmouth,

claimant to the English crown, landed here in 1685. The Cobb (a massive stone pier) features in Jane Austen's *Persuasion* (1818) and John Fowles's *The French Lieutenant's Woman* (1969).

The Lias (Lower Jurassic) rocks nearby are rich in fossils and have yielded remains of ichthyosaur and plesiosaur dinosaurs. The first ichthyosaur was found by Mary Anning in 1819; and in 1995 the fossilized end of an ichthyosaur's body and tail was recovered, containing petrified traces of soft tissues, including the outline of the tail fin.

### *History*

The Cobb was first mentioned in the mid-13th century, when it formed an artificial harbour. Edward I gave Lyme Regis its charter in 1284 and it was incorporated by Elizabeth I. The port's most prosperous historical period was between 1500 and 1700 when trade flourished with the Mediterranean, West Indies, and Americas; even as late as 1780 it was larger than the port of Liverpool. During the English Civil War Lyme Regis withstood a Royalist siege, and 23 rebels were later hung and quartered on the beach.

## Lymington

Port and yachting centre in Hampshire, southern England, on the River Lymington, 19 km/12 mi southwest of Southampton; population (1998 est) 14,300. There is a ferry link to Yarmouth on the Isle of Wight.

## Lynton and Lynmouth

Twin resort towns on the north coast of Devon, southwest England, on the Bristol Channel, 19 km/12 mi east of Ilfracombe; population (est 1995) 1,700. The fishing village of Lynmouth, on the shore, is linked by a steep road and cliff railway (1890) to Lynton, 152 m/500 ft above at the top of a cliff.

In August 1952, 22.5 cm/9 in of rainfall within 24 hours on Exmoor caused disastrous flooding at Lynmouth, leaving 31 people dead and the harbour and over 100 buildings severely damaged.

## Lytes Cary

Medieval manor house in Somerset, England, 10 km/6 mi north of Yeovil. Additional buildings were added to the house in almost every century from the 14th. Walter Jenner designed the Elizabethan-style garden, and left the house, contents and 145 ha/358 acres to the National Trust in 1949. The house includes a 14th-century chapel, a 15th-century hall, and a 16th-century 'great chamber'.

## McAdam, John (1756–1836)

Scottish engineer, inventor of the **macadam** road surface. It originally consisted of broken granite bound together with slag or gravel, raised for drainage. A camber, making the road slightly convex in section, ensured that rainwater rapidly drained off the road and did not penetrate the foundation. By the end of the 19th century, most of the main roads in Europe were built in this way.

McAdam was also responsible for reforms in road administration, and advised many turnpike trusts. He ensured that public roads became the responsibility of the government, financed out of taxes for the benefit of everyone.

## Macbeth (c. 1005–1057)

King of Scotland from 1040. The son of Findlaech, hereditary ruler of Moray and Ross, he was commander of the forces of Duncan I, King of Scotland, whom he killed in battle in 1040. His reign was prosperous until Duncan's son Malcolm III led an invasion and killed him at Lumphanan in Aberdeenshire.

Shakespeare's play, *Macbeth* (1605), was based on a version of Macbeth's life told in the 16th-century historian ♦Holinshed's *Chronicles*.

## MacCaig, Norman (1910–1996)

Scottish poet. He began as a poet in revolt against the influence of W H ♦Auden in *Far Cry* (1943); in *The Inward Eye* (1946) there was a change to a poetic, metaphysic standpoint. He compensated for what seemed to be a lack of deep feeling with wit, wordplay, and lavish imagery. His many works included *Riding Lights* (1957), *Measures* (1965), *A Man in My Position* (1969), *The White Bird* (1973), *The Equal Skies* (1980), and *Voice-Over* (1988).

## Macclesfield

Industrial town in Cheshire, northwest England, on the River Bollin on the edge of the Pennines, 28 km/17 mi south of Manchester; population (1991, est) 69,700. Formerly the centre of the English silk industry, it has two working silk museums, one producing silk for sale.

## MacDiarmid, Hugh pen name of Christopher Murray Grieve (1892–1978)

Scottish poet. A nationalist and Marxist, he was one of the founders in 1928 of the National Party of Scotland. His works include *A Drunk Man looks at the Thistle* (1926) and the collections *First Hymn to Lenin* (1931) and *Second Hymn to Lenin* (1935), in which poetry is made relevant to politics. He was the leader of the Scottish literary renaissance of the 1920s and 1930s. He also edited *The Golden Treasury of Scottish Poetry* (1941), and after 1940 wrote in English. *Complete Poems 1920–1976* was published in 1978 and *Selected Poems* in 1992.

## Macdonald, Flora (1722–1790)

Scottish heroine. She rescued Prince Charles Edward Stuart, the Young Pretender, after his defeat at Culloden in 1746. Disguising him as her maid, she escorted him from her home on South Uist in the Hebrides, to France. She was arrested and imprisoned in the Tower of London, but released in 1747.

## MacDonald, Ramsay (1866–1937)

British politician, first Labour prime minister January–October 1924 and 1929–31. Failing to deal with worsening economic conditions, he left the party to form a coalition government in 1931, which was increasingly dominated by Conservatives, until he was replaced by Stanley Baldwin in 1935.

## Macintosh, Charles (1766–1843)

Scottish manufacturing chemist who invented a waterproof fabric, lined with rubber, that was used for raincoats – hence **mackintosh**.

## Mackintosh, Charles Rennie (1868–1928)

Scottish architect, designer, and painter, whose highly original work represents a dramatic break with the late Victorian style. He worked initially in the ◊Art Nouveau idiom but later developed a unique style, both rational and expressive.

Influenced by the ◊Arts and Crafts movement, he designed furniture and fittings, cutlery, and lighting to go with his interiors. Mackintosh was initially influential, particularly on Austrian architects such as Joseph Maria Olbrich and Josef Hoffman. However, he was not successful in his lifetime, and has only recently come to be regarded as a pioneer of modern design.

Mackintosh was born and educated in Glasgow, and also travelled in Italy. In 1896 he won the competition for the Glasgow School of Art (completed 1909). Other major works include the Cranston tea rooms, Glasgow (1897–1909); and Hill House, Helensburgh (1902–03). After 1913

**Charles Rennie Mackintosh** The Scottish architect and designer Charles Rennie Mackintosh was a leading exponent of the international style known as Art Nouveau. He believed that all elements within a building, including furniture and even cutlery, should be integrated into the overall design. This principle is embodied in the Willow Tea Rooms in Glasgow's main thoroughfare, Sauchiehall Street. George Wright/ Collections

he devoted himself to painting and eventually abandoned architecture and design altogether.

## McLaren

British racing-car manufacturer, which made its debut in Formula One in 1970. The team won the Constructors' championship seven times between 1974 and 1991, and the Driver's title nine times within the same years. From 1988 to 1991 it dominated the sport, winning both titles for four consecutive years. Notable drivers for McLaren have included Ayrton Senna, Alain Prost, and James ◊Hunt. Mika Hakkinen won the Driver's title in 1998 in a McLaren, securing the constructors' title for the company as well.

## Maclean, Donald (1913–1983)

English spy who worked for the USSR while in the UK civil service. He defected to the USSR in 1951 together with Guy ◊Burgess.

Maclean, was educated at Cambridge University, where he was recruited by the Soviet KGB. He worked for the UK Foreign Office in Washington in 1944 and then Cairo in 1948 before returning to London, becoming head of the American Department at the Foreign Office in 1950.

## Macmillan, Harold, 1st Earl of Stockton (1894–1986)

British Conservative politician, prime minister 1957–63; foreign secretary 1955 and chancellor of the Exchequer 1955–57. In 1963 he attempted to negotiate British entry into the European Economic Community (EEC), but was blocked by the French president Charles de Gaulle. Much of his career as prime minister was spent defending the retention of a UK nuclear weapon, and he was responsible for the purchase of US Polaris missiles in 1962.

Macmillan was MP for Stockton 1924–29 and 1931–45, and for Bromley 1945–64. As minister of housing 1951–54 he achieved the construction of 300,000 new houses a year. He became prime minister on the resignation of Anthony Eden after the ◊Suez Crisis, and led the Conservative Party to victory in the 1959 elections on the slogan 'You've never had it so good' (the phrase was borrowed from a US election campaign). Internationally, his realization of the 'wind of change' in Africa advanced the independence of former colonies. Macmillan's nickname **Supermac** was coined by the cartoonist Vicky.

## MacNeice, Louis (1907–1963)

Northern Irish poet, born in Belfast. He made his debut with *Blind Fireworks* (1929) and developed a polished ease of expression, reflecting his classical training, as in the autobiographical and topical *Autumn Journal* (1939). He is noted for his low-key, socially committed but politically uncommitted verse; and his ability to reflect the spirit of his times in his own emotional experience earned him an appreciative public.

Later works include the play *The Dark Tower* (1947), written for radio (he was employed by the BBC features department from 1941–61); a verse translation of Goethe's *Faust* (1949); and the collections *Springboard* (1944) and *Solstices* (1961). *Collected Poems* (1966) was revised in 1979 and *Selected Plays* appeared in 1993.

## Madame Tussaud's

See ◊Tussaud, Madame.

## magazines

At the end of the 20th century, two main types of magazine dominated: those giving details of television times, with the monthly *SkyTVGuide* reaching an average 5.7 million readers in 1998, and the weekly *What's On TV* reaching 4.2 million; and general weeklies aimed at women, such as *Take a Break*, which attracted over 4.5 million readers. Women's magazines were a big growth area of the 1990s.

### History

The first magazine in Britain was a penny weekly, the *Athenian Gazette*, better known later as the *Athenian Mercury* (1690–97). This was produced by a London publisher, John Dunton, to resolve 'all the most Nice and Curious Questions'. It was soon followed by the *Gentleman's Journal* (1692–94), started by the French-born Peter Anthony Motteux, with a monthly blend of news, prose, and poetry.

The earliest illustrations were wood engravings; the half-tone process was invented in 1882 and photogravure was used commercially from 1895. Printing and paper-manufacturing techniques progressed during the 19th century, making larger print runs possible. Advertising began to appear in magazines around 1800; it was a significant factor by 1850 and crucial to most magazines' finances by 1880. Specialist magazines for different interests and hobbies, and comic books, appeared in the 20th century.

## Magazines: Some key dates

**1690** The *Athenian Gazette* is Britain's first magazine, aiming to resolve 'Nice and Curious Questions'.

**1701** A Baldwin publishes *Memoirs for the Curious* in London, England, the first illustrated magazine.

**3 March 1770** *Trysorfa Gwybodaeth neu Eurgrawn Cymraeg*, the first Welsh language magazine to enjoy ongoing publication, is published.

**April 1771** The *Ladies Magazine* features the first colour fashion plate, 'Spring Dress', in London, England.

**July 1828** The *Spectator*, a weekly magazine covering politics and the arts, is launched in London, with Robert S Rintoul as editor.

**1832** The *Penny Magazine* is launched by Charles Knight in London. The first mass-circulation magazine, it quickly reaches sales in excess of 100,000.

**1841** Henry Mayhew launches the weekly comic magazine *Punch*, in London, with Mark Lemon as editor and John Leech as chief illustrator.

**May 1842** The *Illustrated London News* is launched by Herbert Ingram, in London.

**September 1843** The *Economist* magazine is launched, with James Wilson as editor, in London.

**1852** Publisher Samuel Orchart Beeton launches the first mass-market women's magazine, the *Englishwoman's Domestic Magazine*. Its popularity is partly due to the contributions of his wife, Isabella Beeton, on domestic management.

**1855** Samuel Orchart Beeton launches the *Boy's Own Magazine*. The first children's magazine to be concerned with entertainment rather than education, its main subjects are adventure stories and sports, and it is very successful.

**1893** The *Phonogram* is the first record magazine in Britain.

**1904** The *Optical Lantern and Cinematograph Journal*, the first cinema magazine in Britain, is launched.

**1916** A British edition of the US magazine *Vogue* is published.

**1922** A British edition of the US magazine *Good Housekeeping* is published.

**1923** The *Radio Times*, a listeners' guide to radio programmes, is launched.

**1926** The magazine *Melody Maker* is founded: it plays an important role in promoting the spread of jazz in the country.

**1929** *The Listener*, a magazine reprinting talks from BBC radio programmes, is launched.

**1938** Edward Hulton founds the illustrated news magazine *Picture Post*.

**14 November 1952** The popular music magazine *New Musical Express* publishes Britain's first pop singles chart.

**1978** The music magazine *Smash Hits* is launched; it will become the most successful magazine for the teenage market in the UK.

**1979** The scurrilous magazine *Viz* begins publication.

**September 1996** The magazine *Punch*, originally published 1841–1992, is resurrected.

The 1930s saw the introduction of colour printing. The development of cheap offset litho printing made possible the flourishing of the **underground press** in the 1960s, although it was limited by unorthodox distribution methods such as street sales. Prosecutions and economic recession largely killed the underground press; the main survivors in Britain are the satirical *Private Eye* (1961), and the London listings guide *Time Out* (1968).

*Women's magazines*

From the *Ladies' Mercury* (1693) until the first feminist publications of the late 1960s, the content of mass-circulation women's magazines in Britain was largely confined to the domestic sphere – housekeeping, recipes, beauty and fashion, advice columns, patterns – and gossip. In the late 18th century, women's magazines reflected society's temporary acceptance of women as intellectually equal to men, discussing public affairs and subjects of general interest, but by 1825 the trend had reversed. Around 1900 publications for working women began to appear, lurid weekly novelettes known as 'penny dreadfuls'. The first colour magazine for women in Britain, *Woman*, appeared in 1937. By the 1990s women's magazines were an extremely strong part of the whole magazine market, with several weeklies reaching between 1.5 and 3 million readers, and over a dozen monthlies reaching between 1 and 2 million readers.

## Magna Carta (Latin 'great charter')

In English history, the charter granted by King John in 1215, traditionally seen as guaranteeing human rights against the excessive use of royal power. As a reply to the king's demands for excessive feudal dues and attacks on the privileges of the church, Archbishop Langton proposed to the barons the drawing-up of a binding document in 1213. John was forced to accept this at Runnymede (now in Surrey) on 15 June 1215.

Magna Carta begins by reaffirming the rights of the church. Certain clauses guard against infringements of feudal custom: for example, the king was prevented from making excessive demands for money from his barons without their consent. Others are designed to check extortions by officials or maladministration of justice: for example, no freeman to be arrested, imprisoned, or punished except by the judgement of his peers or the law of the land. The privileges of London and the cities were also guaranteed.

As feudalism declined, Magna Carta lost its significance, and under the Tudors was almost forgotten. During the 17th century it was rediscovered and reinterpreted by the Parliamentary party as a democratic document. Four original copies exist, one each in Salisbury and Lincoln cathedrals and two in the British Library.

## Maiden Castle

Prehistoric hillfort with later additional earthworks 3 km/1.8 mi southwest of Dorchester in Dorset, England. The site was occupied from 4000 BC, although the first identifiable settlement is late Neolithic (New Stone Age, about 2000 BC). The fort was stormed by the Romans in AD 43. The site was systematically excavated 1934–37 by the English archaeologist Mortimer Wheeler.

*History of occupation*

The first identifiable settlement existed in the late Neolithic period, with earthen banks and ditches built on top of a long series of earlier remains. There is evidence of further occupation by late Neolithic cultures and ◊ Beaker people of the early Bronze Age, but it was not until about 350 BC, in the early Iron Age, that the hillfort was extensively developed. Initially an enclosure was built at the east end to encompass a small settlement. During the Iron Age the settlement area extended west, and the east and west entrances to the hillfort were given additional protection in the form of projecting earthworks.

The most impressive phase of the site was in the 2nd century BC, with circular houses in rows and extensive areas given over to grain silos, suggesting a large population. By the time of the Roman occupation, the eastern entrance had one of the largest cemeteries in southern England, including graves of those who had met a violent death. The ramparts were about 18 m/60 ft high.

## Maidenhead

Town in southern England, on the River Thames, 40 km/25 mi west of London; it became the administrative headquarters of ◊ Windsor and Maidenhead unitary authority in April 1998; population (1991) 59,600. It is a major centre for the telecommunications industry. The leisure industry is more limited than in nearby Windsor, but the river is a focus for some tourism.

Two bridges cross the River Thames at Maidenhead, a seven-arched road bridge completed in 1777, and a railway bridge (1838), designed by Isambard Kingdom Brunel. The town is bounded on the west by **Maidenhead Thicket**, once part of Windsor Forest and now preserved by the National Trust.

**maid of honour**
The closest attendant on a queen. They are chosen generally from the daughters and granddaughters of peers, but in the absence of another title bear that of Honourable.

The appointment dates from the Plantagenet kings and included a mistress of the robes (almost invariably a duchess) and ladies-in-waiting (officially styled 'ladies and women of the bedchamber').

**Maidstone**
Town and administrative headquarters of ◊Kent, southeast England, on the River Medway; population (1991) 90,900.
*History*
The town appointed its first mayor in 1549. When the town supported Sir Thomas Wyatt's Protestant uprising in 1554, its Charter of Incorporation was withdrawn, and was not granted again until 15 years later, when the town was made into a borough by Elizabeth I. The town supported the royalist cause during the Civil War.
*Features*
Among the town's medieval buildings are the parish church of All Saints', the late 14th-century Archbishop's Palace (a former residence of the archbishops of Canterbury), and the College of Priests (1395–98). A range of 18th-century buildings include Sir John Banks' Almshouses (1700), a Unitarian church, and the Town Hall (1762–63). The Palace stables and tithe barn house the Tyrwhitt-Drake Carriage Museum, containing a collection of 17th–19th-century carriages. The Elizabethan Chillington Manor is an art gallery and museum.

**Mainland**
Largest of the ◊Orkney Islands, situated about 30 km/19 mi off the north coast of Scotland, population (1991) 15,100. Extending over an area of 380 sq km/146 sq mi, it is divided from the southern islands of Hoy, Flotta, and South Ronaldsay by ◊Scapa Flow. Agriculture, trout-fishing, and sea-fishing are the principal occupations. The main harbour towns are ◊Kirkwall, the island capital, and Stromness.

The terrain is hilly, with extensive lowland tracts and lochs, and the climate windy but relatively frost-free (unlike the western Highlands, Mainland benefits from the warm North Atlantic Drift ocean current, which keeps frost to a minimum).

Evidence of prehistoric settlement includes the Neolithic (Stone Age) village of ◊Skara Brae on the Bay of Skaill, 13 km/8 mi from Stromness, and the megalithic monuments of the Ring of Brodgar, Stenness Standing Stones, and Maes Howe burial chamber. This last contains a wealth of later Viking runic inscriptions.

**Malcolm**
Four Celtic kings of Scotland:

**Malcolm I** (943–954)
King of Scotland, who succeeded his father Donald II.

**Malcolm II** (c. 954–1034)
King of Scotland from 1005. The son of Kenneth II, he was succeeded by his grandson ◊Duncan I.

**Malcolm III**, called **Canmore** (c. 1031–1093)
King of Scotland from 1058, the son of Duncan I. He fled to England in 1040 when the throne was usurped by ◊Macbeth, but recovered southern Scotland and killed Macbeth in battle in 1057. In 1070 he married Margaret (c. 1045–1093), sister of Edgar Atheling of England; their daughter Matilda (d. 1118) married Henry I of England. Malcolm was killed at Alnwick while invading Northumberland, England.

**Malcolm IV** the Maiden (1141–1165)
King of Scotland from 1153. The son of Henry, eldest son of ◊David I, he was succeeded by his brother William the Lion.

**Malham**
Village in North Yorkshire, England, 10 km/6 mi east of Settle on the River Aire. The Craven Fault, a displacement of limestone, forms two amphitheatres of rock, Malham Cove and Gordale Scar, 2 km/1 mi from the village. The cliffs of **Malham Cove** are nearly 100 m/328 ft high; the River Aire rises at their foot. **Malham Tarn**, north of the cove, is an upland lake.

**Mallaig**
Fishing port on the west coast of Highland unitary authority, Scotland, 50 km/31 mi northwest of Fort William; population (1991) 900. Winter herring and prawns are the major catches. The town, lying at the end of the 'Road to the Isles', is the terminus of the scenic West Highland railway.

A car ferry crosses the Sound of Sleat from here to Armadale on the Isle of Skye. Loch Morar, Scotland's deepest loch, lies southeast of Mallaig.

The local heritage centre houses exhibitions focusing on the history and culture of the West Highlands of Scotland.

## Mall, The

Road in London extending from the Victoria Memorial in front of Buckingham Palace to Admiralty Arch. The Mall in its present form was designed by Aston Webb 1903–04. It is London's main processional route, being the first stage of the monarch's journey to the Houses of Parliament, Westminster Abbey, or Horse Guards Parade.

The Mall was first laid out as a fashionable avenue in the 1660s.

## Malmesbury

Ancient hill-top market town in Wiltshire, southwest England, on the River Avon, 30 km/19 mi northwest of Bath; population (1991) 4,700. Tourism is a key source of income. The 12th-century church was built on the site of a Saxon abbey church, founded in the 7th century; it was the burial place of Athelstan, grandson of Alfred the Great and king of the Mercians and West Saxons in the 10th century.

The church's elaborate 12th-century south porch includes some of the finest Romanesque sculpture in Britain, depicting scenes from the Bible. The interior has stained glass by William Morris and Edward Burne-Jones. The town's market cross dates from around 1490.

## Malory, Thomas (c. 1410–1471)

English author. He is known for the prose romance ◊ Le Morte D'Arthur written in about 1470, printed in 1485. It is the fullest version of the legends of King ◊ Arthur, the knights of the Round Table and the quest for the ◊ Holy Grail, and it is a notable contribution to English prose.

Malory's identity is uncertain. He is thought to have been the Warwickshire landowner of that name who was member of Parliament for Warwick in 1445 and was subsequently charged with rape, theft, and attempted murder. If that is so, he must have compiled Le Morte D'Arthur during his 20 years in and out of prison. He became a knight of the shire in 1445.

## Malvern

English spa town in Worcester, on the east side of the **Malvern Hills**, which extend for about 16 km/10 mi and have their high point in Worcester Beacon 425 m/1,395 ft; population (1991) 31,500. The **Malvern Festival** 1929–39, associated with the playwright G B Shaw and the composer Edward Elgar, was revived in 1977. Elgar lived and was buried here.

## Manchester

Metropolitan district of Greater Manchester, and city in northwest England, on the River Irwell, 50 km/31 mi east of Liverpool; population (1991) 402,900. It was Britain's second city by the mid-19th century, due to its growth and importance as a cotton-manufacturing centre, and the first huge urban conurbation to develop after the industrial revolution. Although the textile trade has declined, Manchester still produces cotton and synthetic textiles. It is linked to the River Mersey and the Irish Sea by the **Manchester Ship Canal**, opened in 1894. The city will host the Commonwealth Games in 2002.

### History

Originally a Roman camp (**Mancunium** or **Mamucium**), Manchester is mentioned in the Domesday Book, and by the 13th century was already a centre for the wool trade. Its damp climate and many waterways made it ideal for the production of cotton, introduced in the 16th century, and from the mid-18th century onwards the Manchester area was a world centre of manufacture, using cotton imported from North America and India.

Numerous canals were opened in the area from the 18th century. Though the canals through central Manchester are now hidden by buildings or partially filled in, maps of the early 19th century show that they dominated much of the central area and were surrounded by numerous factories, warehouses, timber yards, and other industrial areas.

Manchester attracted railways as readily as canals. In 1830 the Liverpool and Manchester line was built to a terminus in Liverpool Road that is still in use. In 1838 a line was opened to Bolton, and in 1839 the Manchester and Leeds railway was built from a station in Oldham Road, completed in 1841. The London link was made in 1842 by the Manchester and Birmingham railway through Stockport and Crewe, and in 1845 the Sheffield and Lincolnshire railway was opened. As early as 1842, Manchester had four terminal stations, one each for Liverpool, Bolton, Leeds, and London. The network of canal and railway links contributed greatly to Manchester's rapid expansion and population growth throughout the 19th century.

In 1801 Manchester's population, with Salford, was 84,000, more than Liverpool (78,000) or Birmingham (74,000); by 1851 its population

**Manchester** In an attempt to solve the problem of inner-city traffic congestion, Manchester inaugurated the Metrolink in 1992. This integrated urban transit system reintroduced the tram as a viable means of public transport. Here, a tram arrives in St Peter's Square in the heart of the city. Liz Stares/Collections

was 303,382. Its growth, however, was not in isolation from the surrounding area that was eventually (in 1951) defined as the Manchester conurbation, which had 322,000 inhabitants in 1801, and 1,063,000 in 1851. The 19th century a time of large-scale immigration, and in 1851 more than one tenth of Manchester's population had been born in Ireland.

The late 19th century saw the growth of suburbs, and by 1901 the city of Manchester was part of a conurbation that had a population of 2,150,000.

*Features*
The cathedral dates from the 15th century. Of 18th-century Manchester there remains the church of St Ann, and St John Street with two fairly complete Georgian terraces. The Town Hall, designed by Alfred Waterhouse, dates to 1877; the Free Trade Hall to 1856. Liverpool Road station is the world's oldest surviving passenger station. Also of note are the Whitworth Art Gallery, the Cotton Exchange (now a leisure centre), the Central Library designed by Frank Lloyd Wright (1934, the world's largest municipal library), and the John Rylands Library (1900). Manchester is the home of the Hallé Orchestra, the Royal Northern College of Music, Manchester Grammar School (1515), four universities (the University of Manchester, UMIST, Manchester Metropolitan University, and the University of

Salford); and Manchester United Football Club. The Castlefield Urban Heritage Park includes the Granada television studios, including the set of the soap opera *Coronation Street*, open to visitors, and also the Museum of Science and Industry.

## Manchester, Greater
Metropolitan county of northwest England, created in 1974; population (1991) 2,499,400; area 1,290 sq km/498 sq mi. In 1986 most of the functions of the former county council were transferred to metropolitan district councils. The chief towns and cities are ◊Manchester, Bolton, Oldham, Rochdale, Salford, Stockport, and Wigan.

*Physical*
The Manchester Ship Canal links the county with the River Mersey and the Irish Sea.

*Features*
The Old Trafford cricket ground is at Stretford and Manchester has the football ground of Manchester United.

*Economy*
There is considerable industry and manufacturing, including textiles and textile machinery, chemicals, plastics, electrical goods and electronic equipment, paper, printing, and rubber.

## Manchester Ship Canal
Waterway that links the city of Manchester with the River Mersey and the sea; length 57 km/35.5

mi, width 14–24 m/45–80 ft, depth 9 m/28.3 ft. It has five locks. The canal was opened in 1894, linking Manchester to Eastham in Merseyside.

The canal transformed Lancashire's economy by making Manchester accessible to ocean-going craft. In particular, it led to the development of the cotton industry as raw cotton was transported east along the canal to Manchester and the finished textile products were shipped west to the Merseyside ports. Although the area has suffered industrial decline, the canal is still in effect the 'port of Manchester'.

## Man, Isle of Gaelic Ellan Vannin
Island in the Irish Sea, a dependency of the British crown, but not part of the UK
**Area** 570 sq km/220 sq mi
**Capital** Douglas
**Towns and cities** Ramsey, Peel, Castletown
**Features** Snaefell 620 m/2,035 ft; annual TT (Tourist Trophy) motorcycle races; gambling casinos, tax haven; tailless Manx cat
**Currency** the island produces its own coins and notes in UK currency denominations
**Population** (1991) 69,800
**Language** English (Manx, nearer to Scottish than Irish Gaelic, has been almost extinct since the 1970s)
**Government** crown-appointed lieutenant-governor, a legislative council, and the representative House of Keys, which together make up the Court of Tynwald, passing laws subject to the royal assent. Laws passed at Westminster only affect the island if specifically so provided
**History** Norwegian until 1266, when the island was ceded to Scotland; it came under UK administration in 1765.

## Manning, Olivia (1908–1980)
English novelist. Among her books are the semi-autobiographical series set during World War II. These include *The Great Fortune* (1960), *The Spoilt City* (1962), and *Friends and Heroes* (1965), forming the 'Balkan trilogy', and a later 'Levant trilogy'.

## manor
Basic economic unit in ◊feudalism in Europe, established in England under the Norman conquest. It consisted of the lord's house and cultivated land, land rented by free tenants, land held by villagers, common land, woodland, and waste land.

Here and there traces of the system survive in England – the common land may have become an area for public recreation – but the documents sometimes sold at auction, entitling the owner to be called 'lord of the manor', seldom have any rights attached to them.

## Mansfield
Industrial town in Nottinghamshire, England, on the River Maun, 22 km/14 mi north of Nottingham; population (1991) 71,900. Formerly a coalmining area, Mansfield no longer has any active collieries. Sherwood Forest lies to the east.

## Mansion House
Official residence of the Lord Mayor of London, opposite the Bank of England. It was built in 1739–53 by George Dance the Elder on the site of the old Stocks Market.

## Mappa Mundi
14th-century symbolic map of the world. It is circular and shows Asia at the top, with Europe and Africa below and Jerusalem at the centre (reflecting Christian religious rather than geographical belief). It was drawn by David de Bello, a canon at Hereford Cathedral, England, who left the map to the cathedral, where it was used as an altarpiece.

## Marble Arch
Triumphal arch in London in the style of the Arch of Constantine. It was designed by John ◊Nash and John Flaxman (1755–1826) in 1828 to commemorate Nelson's and Wellington's victories, and was originally intended as a ceremonial entry to ◊Buckingham Palace. In 1851, after the completion of Buckingham Palace, it was moved by Edward Blore to the northeast corner of Hyde Park at the end of Oxford Street.

## Marcher Lords
Semi-independent nobles on the Welsh–English border ◊(Marches), granted special privileges in return for protecting the border area. In William the Conqueror's reign, strong lords were placed in Chester, Shrewsbury, and Hereford to protect England from Celtic or Saxon incursions. They began to usurp power in their own right, making wars of their own, particularly in the valleys of South Wales, and claiming rights of conquest. After Edward I subjugated Wales, the Marcher Lords no longer played a vital role in the protection of the realm and Edward sought to restrict their independence. By the end of the 15th century most of the lordships had come into the possession of the crown and the last independent lordship, Brecon, was taken by the crown in 1521.

## Marches

Boundary areas of England with Wales, and England with Scotland. For several centuries from the time of William the Conqueror, these troubled frontier regions were held by lords of the Marches, those on the Welsh frontier called ◊Marcher Lords, sometimes called *marchiones*, and those on the Scottish border known as earls of March. The first Marcher Lord was Roger de Mortimer (about 1286–1330); the first earl of March, Patrick Dunbar (died in 1285).

## Maree, Loch

Large lake in Wester Ross, Highland unitary authority, Scotland, extending over a length of 22 km/14 mi and widening to 3 km/2 mi. Its outflow is the River Ewe, which joins the sea-inlet of Loch Ewe. Studded with islands, and bordered by soaring mountain peaks, including Slioch (980 m/3,215 ft), it is considered to be one of Scotland's most beautiful lochs.

## Margaret (1283–1290)

Queen of Scotland from 1285. Known as the **the Maid of Norway**, she was the daughter of Eric II, King of Norway, and Princess Margaret of Scotland. When only two years old she became queen of Scotland on the death of her grandfather, Alexander III, but died in the Orkneys on the voyage from Norway to her kingdom.

## Margaret of Anjou (1430–1482)

Queen of England from 1445, wife of ◊Henry VI of England. After the outbreak of the Wars of the ◊Roses 1455, she acted as the leader of the Lancastrians, but was defeated and captured at the battle of Tewkesbury 1471 by Edward IV.

Her one object had been to secure the succession of her son, Edward (born 1453), who was killed at Tewkesbury. After five years' imprisonment Margaret was allowed in 1476 to return to her native France, where she died in poverty.

## Margaret, St (c. 1045–1093)

Queen of Scotland, the granddaughter of King Edmund Ironside of England. She went to Scotland after the Norman Conquest, and soon after married Malcolm III. The marriage of her daughter Matilda to Henry I united the Norman and English royal houses.

Through her influence, the Lowlands, until then purely Celtic, became largely anglicized. She was canonized in 1251 in recognition of her benefactions to the church.

## Margate

Town and resort on the north coast of Kent, southeast England, on the Isle of ◊Thanet; population (1991) 38,500. It was one of the original ◊Cinque Ports, and developed in the late 18th century as one of the earliest coastal resorts in England.

Benjamin Beale, a Quaker from Margate, invented the bathing machine in the mid-18th century.

## Marks & Spencer

Chain store. The company was founded in 1884 by **Michael Marks** (1863–1907). In 1894 he was joined by **Thomas Spencer** (1852–1905), cashier at one of his suppliers. The founder's son Simon Marks, from 1961 1st Baron Marks of Broughton, became chairman in 1916 and with his brother-in-law, Israel (later Lord) Sieff (1899–1972), developed the company from a 'Penny Bazaar' to a national and international chain store.

The company's first stores outside the UK were opened in the 1970s. In 1998 there were 289 stores in the UK, 90 in Europe, 33 in the Far East, and 260 in North America.

## Marlborough

Market town in Wiltshire, southwest England, on the River Kennet, 41 km/25 mi northeast of Salisbury; population (1991) 6,800. **Marlborough College** (1843), a co-educational private school, is in the centre of the town.

Nearby are the ancient sites of Avebury, West Kennet, and Silbury Hill.

## Marlborough, John Churchill, 1st Duke of Marlborough (1650–1722)

English soldier, created a duke in 1702 by Queen Anne. He was granted the ◊Blenheim mansion in Oxfordshire in recognition of his services, which included defeating the French army outside Vienna in the Battle of Blenheim in 1704, during the War of the Spanish Succession.

In 1688 he deserted his patron, James II, for William of Orange, but in 1692 fell into disfavour for Jacobite intrigue.

He had married Sarah Jennings (1660–1744), confidante of the future Queen Anne, who created him a duke on her accession. He achieved further victories in Belgium at the battles of Ramillies (1706) and Oudenaarde (1708), and in France at Malplaquet in 1709. However, the return of the Tories to power and his wife's quarrel with the queen led to his dismissal in 1711, and his flight to Holland to avoid charges of corruption. He returned in 1714.

## Marlowe, Christopher (1564–1593)

English poet and dramatist. His work includes the blank-verse plays *Tamburlaine the Great* in two parts (1587–88), *The Jew of Malta* (about 1591), *Edward II* (about 1592), and *Dr Faustus* (about 1594); the poem 'Hero and Leander' (1598); and a translation of parts of Ovid's *Amores*. Marlowe transformed the new medium of English blank verse into a powerful, melodic form of expression.

He was born in Canterbury and educated at Cambridge University, where he is thought to have become a government agent. His life was turbulent, with a brief imprisonment in connection with a man's death in a brawl (of which he was cleared), and a charge of atheism (following statements by the dramatist Thomas Kyd under torture). He was murdered in a Deptford tavern, allegedly in a dispute over the bill, but it may have been a political killing.

## Martello tower

Circular tower for coastal defence. Formerly much used in Europe, many were built along the English coast, especially in Sussex and Kent, in 1804, as a defence against the threatened French invasion. The name is derived from a tower on Cape Mortella, Corsica, which was captured by the British with great difficulty in 1794, and was taken as a model. They are round towers of solid masonry, sometimes moated, with a flat roof for mounted guns.

## Marvell, Andrew (1621–1678)

English metaphysical poet and satirist. In 'To His Coy Mistress' (1650–52) and 'An Horatian Ode

upon Cromwell's Return from Ireland' (1650) he produced, respectively, the most searching seduction and political poems in the language. He was committed to the Parliamentary cause, and was Member of Parliament for Hull from 1659. He devoted his last years mainly to verse satire and prose works attacking repressive aspects of the state and government.

His reputation in his own day was as a champion of liberty and toleration, and as a polemicist. Today his reputation rests mainly on a small number of skilful and graceful but perplexing and intriguing poems, which were published posthumously as *Miscellaneous Poems* (1681). His prose works include *An Account of the Growth of Popery and Arbitrary Government* (1677), a scathing review of Charles II's reign.

---

*But at my back I always hear / Time's wingèd chariot hurrying near. / And yonder all before us lie / Deserts of vast eternity.*

**Andrew Marvell** English poet and satirist.
'To His Coy Mistress'

---

## Mary Queen of Scots (1542–1587)

Queen of Scotland 1542–67. Also known as **Mary Stuart**, she was the daughter of James V. Mary's connection with the English royal line from Henry VII made her a threat to Elizabeth I's hold on the English throne, especially as she represented a champion of the Catholic cause. She was married three times. After her forced abdication she was imprisoned but escaped in 1568 to England. Elizabeth I held her prisoner, while the Roman Catholics, who regarded Mary as rightful queen of England, formed many conspiracies to place her on the throne, and for complicity in one of these she was executed.

Mary's mother was the French Mary of Guise. Born in Linlithgow (now in Lothian region, Scotland), Mary was sent to France, where she married the dauphin, later Francis II. After his death she returned to Scotland in 1561, which, during her absence, had become Protestant. She

**Andrew Marvell** English metaphysical poet and satirist Andrew Marvell. He was unofficial poet laureate to Oliver Cromwell and took the post of Latin secretary to the Council of State on Milton's retirement. His 'Upon the Death of his Late Highness the Lord Protector' (1658) mourns the death of Cromwell. After the Restoration, Marvell continued to anonymously publish tracts that were anti-royalist or which attacked courtly corruption.
Corbis

married her cousin, the Earl of ◊Darnley, in 1565, but they soon quarrelled, and Darnley took part in the murder of Mary's secretary, ◊Rizzio. In 1567 Darnley was assassinated as the result of a conspiracy formed by the Earl of ◊Bothwell, possibly with Mary's connivance, and shortly after Bothwell married her. A rebellion followed; defeated at Carberry Hill, Mary abdicated and was imprisoned. She escaped in 1568, raised an army, and after its defeat at Langside fled to England, only to be imprisoned again. A plot against Elizabeth I devised by Anthony Babington led to her trial and execution at Fotheringay Castle in 1587.

## Mary, Queen (1867–1953)
Consort of George V of Great Britain and Ireland. She was the only daughter of the Duke and Duchess of Teck, the latter a grand-daughter of George III. In 1891 she was engaged to marry Prince Albert Victor (born 1864), Duke of Clarence and eldest son of the Prince of Wales (later Edward VII), but he died in 1892, and in 1893 she married his brother George, Duke of York, who succeeded to the throne in 1910.

## Mary
Two queens of England:

## Mary I called Bloody Mary (1516–1558)
Queen of England from 1553. She was the eldest daughter of Henry VIII by Catherine of Aragón. When Edward VI died, Mary secured the crown without difficulty in spite of the conspiracy to substitute Lady Jane Grey. In 1554 Mary married Philip II of Spain, and as a devout Roman Catholic obtained the restoration of papal supremacy and sanctioned the persecution of Protestants. She was succeeded by her half-sister Elizabeth I.

## Mary II (1662–1694)
Queen of England, Scotland, and Ireland from 1688. She was the Protestant elder daughter of the Catholic ◊James II, and in 1677 was married to her cousin ◊William of Orange. After the 1688 revolution she accepted the crown jointly with William.

During William's absences from England she took charge of the government, and showed courage and resource when invasion seemed possible in 1690 and 1692.

## Mary Rose
English warship, built for Henry VIII of England, which sank off Southsea, Hampshire, on 19 July

1545, with the loss of most of the 700 on board. The wreck was located in 1971, and raised for preservation in dry dock in Portsmouth harbour (where it had originally been built) in 1982. Preserved in the accumulated silt were over 25,000 objects, including leather and silk items, a unique record of Tudor warfare and daily life. The cause of the disaster is not certain, but the lower gun ports were open after firing, and that, combined with overcrowding, may have caused the sinking.

## Masefield, John (1878–1967)
English poet and novelist. His early years in the merchant navy inspired *Salt Water Ballads* (1902) and two further volumes of poetry, and several adventure novels; he also wrote children's books, such as *The Midnight Folk* (1927) and *The Box of Delights* (1935), and plays. *The Everlasting Mercy* (1911), characterized by its forcefully colloquial language, and *Reynard the Fox* (1919) are long verse narratives. He was poet laureate from 1930.

---

*Dirty British coaster with a salt-caked smoke stack, / Butting through the Channel in the mad March days, / With a cargo of Tyne coal, / Road-rail, pig-lead, / Firewood, iron-ware, and cheap tin trays.*

**John Masefield** English poet and novelist.
'Cargoes'

---

## masque
Spectacular court entertainment with a fantastic or mythological theme in which music, dance, and extravagant costumes and scenic design figured larger than plot. Originating in Italy, where members of the court actively participated in the performances, the masque reached its height of popularity at the English court between 1600 and 1640, with the collaboration of Ben Jonson as writer and Inigo Jones as stage designer. John Milton also wrote masque verses. Composers included Thomas Campion, John Coperario, Henry Lawes, William Byrd, and Henry Purcell.

The masque had great influence on the development of ballet and opera, and the elaborate frame in which it was performed developed into the proscenium arch.

## Matilda, the Empress Maud (1102–1167)
Claimant to the throne of England. On the death of her father, Henry I, in 1135, the barons elected her cousin Stephen to be king. Matilda invaded

England in 1139, and was crowned by her supporters in 1141. Civil war ensued until Stephen was finally recognized as king in 1153, with Henry II (Matilda's son) as his successor.

Matilda was recognized during the reign of Henry I as his heir. She married first the Holy Roman emperor Henry V and, after his death, Geoffrey Plantagenet, Count of Anjou (1113–1151).

## Matlock

Spa town and administrative headquarters of ◊Derbyshire, central England, on the River Derwent, 19 km/12 mi northwest of Derby; population (1996 est) 9,400. It is a centre of tourism on the edge of the Peak District National Park.

Matlock is set in picturesque scenery among gritstone and limestone hills, and the Derwent Gorge extends to the south. The village of **Matlock Bath**, about a mile to the south, has caverns, petrifying wells, thermal water, and illuminations; it is dominated by the High Tor (205 m/673 ft) and the Heights of Abraham.

Nearby to the south is Bonsall, noted for its well-dressing ceremony and its ancient lead mines. Cromford to the south has imposing Black Rocks and in 1771 Richard Arkwright founded his water-powered cotton mill here, the original mill can still be visited.

## Maugham, Somerset (1874–1965)

English writer. His work includes the novels *Of Human Bondage* (1915), *The Moon and Sixpence* (1919), and *Cakes and Ale* (1930); the short-story collections *Ashenden* (1928) and *Rain and Other Stories* (1933); and the plays *Lady Frederick* (1907) and *Our Betters* (1917). There were new editions of *Collected Stories* in 1900 and *Selected Plays* in 1991. A penetrating observer of human behaviour, his writing is essentially anti-romantic and there is a vein of cynicism running through his work.

## Maxwell, James (1831–1879)

Scottish physicist. His main achievement was in the understanding of electromagnetic waves: **Maxwell's equations** bring together electricity, magnetism, and light in one set of relations. He studied gases, optics, and the sensation of colour, and his theoretical work in magnetism prepared the way for wireless telegraphy and telephony.

## May Day

First day of May. Traditionally the first day of summer, in parts of England it is still celebrated as a pre-Christian magical rite; for example, the dance around the maypole (an ancient fertility symbol).

## Mayfair

District of Westminster, London, vaguely defined as lying between Piccadilly and Oxford Street, and including Park Lane; formerly a fashionable residential district, but increasingly taken up by offices, hotels, and nightclubs.

Mayfair is bounded to the west by Hyde Park and to the south and east by St James's Park, two of London's largest green areas. Mayfair derives its name from a fair held here in May from Charles II's time until 1809; part of the site is now occupied by Shepherd Market, built in about 1735.

## Mayflower

Ship in which the Pilgrims sailed in 1620 from Plymouth, England, to found Plymouth plantation and Plymouth colony in present-day Massachusetts.

The *Mayflower* was one of two ships scheduled for departure in 1620. The second ship, the *Speedwell*, was deemed unseaworthy, so 102 people were crowded into the 27-m/90-foot *Mayflower*, which was bound for Virginia. Tension between Pilgrim and non-Pilgrim passengers threatened to erupt into a mutiny. Blown off course, the ship reached Cape Cod, Massachusetts, in December. The **Mayflower Compact** was drafted to establish self-rule for the Plymouth colony and to protect the rights of all the settlers.

## mayor

Title of head of urban administration. In England, Wales, and Northern Ireland, the mayor is the principal officer of a district council that has been granted district-borough status under royal charter. In 1996 the Labour Party floated proposals for directly elected mayors in Britain, which it confirmed when it came into power in 1997. London is scheduled to elect a mayor in 2000.

## maypole

Tall pole with long ribbon streamers attached to the top. It is used for traditional ◊May Day dances to celebrate the arrival of spring.

The maypole probably represents the sacred tree which formed the centrepiece of pagan spring festivals. In modern survivals of the ceremony two circles of dancers, all holding streamers, move in opposite directions, weaving the streamers into a pattern.

## Medway Towns

Unitary authority in southeast England, created in 1998 by combining the former city council of Rochester upon Medway with Gillingham borough council, both formerly in the county of Kent; population (1995) 240,000; area 194 sq km/75 sq mi. The area has associations with Charles Dickens, who lived in Rochester. The chief towns are ◊Rochester, Chatham, Gillingham, and ◊Strood (administrative headquarters).

*Physical*

The River Thames forms the northern border of the authority and the River Medway flows through Rochester. Reclaimed estuarine mudflats form the Isle of Grain. Rural areas include the Hoo Peninsula, Capstone Valley, and Gillingham Riverside.

*Features*

Historic and literary sites include the 16th-century Upnor Castle, the Charles Dickens Centre in Rochester, housed in a 16th-century mansion, and the Royal Engineers Museum at Gillingham. There is a Royal Naval Dockyard and the World Naval Base museum at Chatham. Rochester hosts a Dickens Festival in summer and a Dickensian Christmas weekend in December.

*Economy*

There are oil refineries on the Isle of Grain, and the authority has heavy and maritime industries and engineering. Thamesport is a privately owned deep-water container port. There are also financial services and information technology.

## Mee, Margaret (1909–1988)

English botanical artist. In the 1950s she went to Brazil, where she accurately and comprehensively painted many plant species of the Amazon basin.

She is thought to have painted more species than any other botanical artist.

## Melford Hall

House in Suffolk, England, 5 km/3 mi north of Sudbury. It was built in the second half of the 16th century, and incorporates the remains of the manor house of the abbots of St Edmunds. It was given by the Treasury with some contents to the National Trust in 1960. A turreted brick Tudor mansion, it has changed little since it was built in 1578; the interior includes an original panelled banqueting hall.

Later additions include an 18th-century drawing-room, a regency library and a Victorian bedroom. The house has collections of English furniture and Chinese porcelain.

## Melrose (Celtic mao ros 'bare moor')

Town in Scottish Borders, Scotland, 59 km/37 mi southeast of Edinburgh; population (1991) 2,300. Melrose is on the River Tweed at the foot of the Eildon Hills, a range of volcanic origin with three peaks, the highest of which is 450 m/1,476 ft. The heart of Robert I the Bruce is buried here. The ruins of **Melrose Abbey** (1136) are commemorated in verse by Sir Walter Scott.

**Old Melrose**, 4 km/2.5 mi to the east, is the site of a Columban monastery, established in about 640 by St Aidan. Triumontium, the site of a Roman camp, is 2 km/1 mi to the east at Newstead. About 5 km/3 mi west of Melrose is Abbotsford, home of Walter Scott.

## Melton Mowbray

Market town in Leicestershire, central England, on the River Eye, 24 km/15 mi northeast of Leicester; population (1995 est) 24,800. A fox-hunting centre, it is known for pork pies and Stilton cheese.

## Menai Bridge, Welsh Porth Aethwy

Small town on the Isle of Anglesey, northwest Wales, on the ◊Menai Strait; population (1991) 3,200. It is a suburb of Bangor, to which it is linked by the suspension bridge across the strait. Its English name is derived from the bridge, which was completed in 1825 to a design by Thomas Telford. The town is a centre for angling and fishing. An annual fair, held in October, dates from 1691.

The bridge was the world's first example of a large iron suspension bridge.

## Mendip Hills, or Mendips

Range of limestone hills in southern England, stretching nearly 40 km/25 mi southeast–northwest from Wells in Somerset towards the Bristol Channel. There are many cliffs, scars, and caverns, notably ◊Cheddar Gorge. The highest peak is Blackdown (326 m/1,068 ft).

The range includes Burrington Coombe, and Wookey Hole caves. The hills are mainly composed of carboniferous limestone, with old red sandstone.

## Menuhin, Yehudi, Baron Menuhin (1916–1999)

US-born British violinist and conductor. His solo repertoire extended from Vivaldi to George Enescu. He recorded the Elgar *Violin Concerto* in 1932 with the composer conducting, and commissioned the *Sonata* for violin solo in 1944 from an ailing Bartók. He appeared in concert with sitar virtuoso Ravi Shankar, and with jazz violinist Stephane Grappelli. In March 1997 he was awarded Germany's highest honour, the Great Order of Merit. He first played in Berlin in 1928, and was the first Jewish artist to play with the Berlin Philharmonic after World War II.

He made his debut with an orchestra at the age of 11 in New York. A child prodigy, he achieved great depth of interpretation, and was often accompanied on the piano by his sister **Hephzibah** (1921–1981). In 1959 he moved to London, becoming a British subject in 1985. He founded the **Yehudi Menuhin School of Music**, at Stoke d'Abernon, Surrey, in 1963.

## Merchants Adventurers
English trading company founded in 1407, which controlled the export of cloth to continental Europe. It comprised guilds and traders in many northern European ports. In direct opposition to the Hanseatic League, it came to control 75% of English overseas trade by 1550. In 1689 it lost its charter for furthering the traders' own interests at the expense of the English economy. The company was finally dissolved in 1806.

## Mercia
Anglo-Saxon kingdom that emerged in the 6th century. By the late 8th century it dominated all England south of the Humber, but from about 825 came under the power of ◊Wessex. Mercia eventually came to denote an area bounded by the Welsh border, the River Humber, East Anglia, and the River Thames.

## Meredith, George (1828–1909)
English novelist and poet. His realistic psychological novel *The Ordeal of Richard Feverel* (1859) engendered both scandal and critical praise. His best-known novel, *The Egoist* (1879), is superbly plotted and dissects the hero's self-centredness with merciless glee. The sonnet sequence *Modern Love* (1862) reflects the failure of his own marriage to the daughter of Thomas Love ◊Peacock. Other novels include *Evan Harrington* (1861), *Diana of the Crossways* (1885), and *The Amazing Marriage* (1895). His verse also includes *Poems and Lyrics of the Joy of Earth* (1883).

## Mersey
River in northwest England; length 112 km/70 mi. Formed by the confluence of the Goyt and Tame rivers at Stockport, it flows west through the south of Manchester, is joined by the Irwell at Flixton and by the Weaver at Runcorn, and enters the Irish Sea at Liverpool Bay. The Mersey is linked to the Manchester Ship Canal.

The Mersey became an artery of communications from the 18th century. Boats for passengers and goods used the river, with its major tributary the Irwell, between Liverpool and Manchester from 1720; the Bridgewater Canal acquired this traffic in the late 18th century. The Mersey had passenger services until the development of the railway in the middle of the 19th century.

## Mersey beat
Pop music of the mid-1960s that originated in the northwest of England. It was also known as the Liverpool sound or beat music in the UK. It was almost exclusively performed by all-male groups, the most popular being the Beatles.

## Merseyside
Metropolitan county of northwest England, created in 1974; population (1996) 1,420,400; area 650 sq km/251 sq mi. The principal towns and cities are ◊Liverpool, Bootle, Birkenhead, St Helens, Wallasey, and Southport. Merseyside has a long industrial past, and in the second half of the 20th century it became famous as the home of the Beatles. In 1986 most of the functions of the former county council were transferred to metropolitan borough councils (The Wirral, Sefton, Liverpool, Knowsley, and St Helens).
*Physical*
The River Mersey and its wide estuary and mouth dominates the south of the county; it has a western coastline on the Irish Sea.
*Features*
Liverpool's Albert Dock has the Merseyside Maritime Museum, the Beatles Story, and the Tate Gallery in the North. The Merseyside Innovation Centre (MIC) is linked with Liverpool and John Moores Universities; Prescot has a museum of clock- and watch-making. Country houses include Speke Hall, notable for its Tudor half-timbering and plasterwork, and Croxteth Hall and Country Park (a working country estate open to the public). Knowsley originally grew up around Knowsley Hall, the home of the Stanley family (Earls of Derby) since 1835.
*Economy*
Glassmaking in St Helens dates back more than 200 years, and coal has been mined since the 16th century; in 1757 the Sankey Canal was constructed to carry coal to Liverpool, Warrington,

and also Northwich for the then growing salt industry. The chemical and copper industries left large areas of derelict land in St Helens, which have now cleared. There are a variety of local industries today, including brewing, chemicals and pharmaceutical products, electrical goods, glassmaking and metal-working, and vehicle production.

## Merthyr Tydfil
Unitary authority in south Wales, created in 1996 from part of the former county of Mid-Glamorgan; population (1996) 60,000; area 111 sq km/43 sq mi. The principal town is Merthyr Tydfil (administrative headquarters).
*Physical*
The authority is in the upper valley of the River Taff and includes part of the Brecon Beacons National Park. It has featured the largest land-reclamation scheme in Europe.
*Economy*
Formerly a centre of the Welsh coal and steel industries, the area now has light engineering and electrical goods manufacturing.

## Meteorological Office, or Met Office
Organization based at Bracknell, producing weather reports for the media and conducting specialist work for industry, agriculture, and transport. It was established in London in 1855. Kew is the main meteorological observatory in the British Isles, but other observatories are at Eskdalemuir in the southern uplands of Scotland, Lerwick in the Shetlands, and Valentia in southwest Ireland.

## Methodism
Evangelical Protestant Christian movement that was founded by John ◊Wesley in 1739 within the Church of England, but became a separate body in 1795.

The itinerant, open-air preaching of John and Charles Wesley and George Whitefield drew immense crowds and led to a revival of faith among members of the English working and agricultural classes who were alienated from the formalism and conservatism of the Church of England. Methodist doctrines are contained in Wesley's sermons and 'Notes on the New Testament'. A series of doctrinal divisions in the early 19th century were reconciled by a conference in London in 1932 that brought Wesleyan Methodists, Primitive Methodists, and United Methodists into the Methodist Church.

## metropolitan county
In England, a group of six counties established under the Local Government Act of 1972 in the largest urban areas outside London: Tyne and Wear, South Yorkshire, Merseyside, West Midlands, Greater Manchester, and West Yorkshire. Their elected assemblies (county councils) were abolished in 1986 when most of their responsibilities reverted to metropolitan borough councils.

## MI5
Abbreviation for **Military Intelligence, section five**, the counter-intelligence agency of the British intelligence services. Its role is to prevent or investigate espionage, subversion, and sabotage.

## MI6
Abbreviation for **Military Intelligence, section six**, the secret intelligence agency of the British intelligence services which operates largely under Foreign Office control.

## Middle English
The period of the ◊English language from about 1050 to 1550.

## Middlesbrough
Industrial town and port on the estuary of the River Tees, northeast England, population (1996) 146,000. It became a unitary authority in 1996, created from part of the former county of Cleveland (of which it was the administrative headquarters until 1996); area 54 sq km/21 sq mi. It is the commercial centre of the Teesside industrial area, which also includes Stockton-on-Tees, Redcar, Billingham, Thornaby, and Eston.
*History*
Middlesbrough developed rapidly in the 19th century, after it was decided in 1828 to extend the Stockton and Darlington railway by 6 km/4 mi to reach deeper anchorage on the river. A wet dock was built and trade began in 1830. The original town, between the railway and river, proved too small and the main commercial centre was extended to the south of the docks, in a strictly rectangular layout.
*Features*
Transporter Bridge (1911) takes cars and passengers across the Tees to Hartlepool in a cable car; Newport Bridge (1934) was the first vertical lift bridge in England; the Captain Cook Birthplace Museum commemorates the life of the naval explorer James Cook; the 18th-century National

**MI6** With the end of the Cold War in the 1990s, the British intelligence services adopted a policy of greater openness, revealing the names of their operational heads for the first time. MI6 also moved into these high-profile new offices at Vauxhall Bridge in London. None the less, many feel that a culture of official secrecy still holds sway in Britain, which has no Freedom of Information Act. Simon Shepheard/Impact

Trust-owned Ormesby Hall is located nearby. The University of Teesside, formerly Teesside Polytechnic, was established in 1992.

## Midlands
Area of central England corresponding roughly to the Anglo-Saxon kingdom of ◊Mercia. The **East Midlands** comprises Derbyshire, Leicestershire, Northamptonshire, and Nottinghamshire. The **West Midlands** covers the metropolitan district of ◊West Midlands created from parts of Staffordshire, Warwickshire, and Worcestershire, and split into the metropolitan boroughs of Dudley, Sandwell, Coventry, Birmingham, Walsall, Solihull, and Wolverhampton; and (often included) the **South Midlands** comprising Bedfordshire, Buckinghamshire, and Oxfordshire.

## Midlothian
Unitary authority in southeast Scotland, south of Edinburgh and the Firth of Forth, which was previously a county (until 1974) and a district within Lothian region (1975–96); population

(1996) 79,900; area 363 sq km/140 sq mi. Historically it was an important mining area. The principal towns are ◊Dalkeith (administrative headquarters), Penicuik, and Bonnyrigg.
*Physical*
An inland area, it rises toward the Moorfoot Hills in the south. The River Esk flows through it.
*Features*
Crichton Castle, now in ruins, is 19 km/12 mi east of Edinburgh. The 14th-century tower house, mentioned by Walter Scott in his story *Marmion* (1808), was rebuilt in 1585 in Italianate style by Francis Stuart, 5th Earl of Bothwell. The 15th-century chapel at Roslin, built by William Sinclair, has intricate stone carvings and sculptures, including the allegorical 'Dance of Death', and the Late Gothic 'Prentice Pilar'. The Scottish Mining Museum at Lady Victoria Colliery, near Newtongrange, was a working mine from 1890 until its closure in 1981. It contains the 'Grant-Richie' winding engine which could lift coal from almost 500 m/1,640 ft below the surface. There are 14 Sites of Special Scientific Interest, two

Ramsars (wetland sites), one regional park, and three country parks.

*Economy*
The area is diversifying as it adjusts to the demise of the coal industry. Development is on a small to medium scale. Products include glass and crystal, light manufacturing, and food processing. There is productive arable and dairy farming in the north. The biotechnology industry is becoming increasingly important to the authority.

## Mildenhall treasure
Hoard of 4th-century Romano-British silverware discovered in 1942 at Mildenhall in Suffolk, England. The hoard consisted of 34 pieces of silver kitchenware, ornamented with hunting scenes and embossed figures. Some pieces contain Christian motifs. The hoard was probably buried by a wealthy family as protection against the Saxon raids. It is now housed in the British Museum.

## Mill, John Stuart (1806–1873)
English philosopher and economist who wrote *On Liberty* (1859), the classic philosophical defence of liberalism, and *Utilitarianism* (1863), a version of the 'greatest happiness for the greatest number' principle in ethics.

*On Liberty* moved away from the Utilitarian notion that individual liberty was necessary for economic and governmental efficiency and advanced the classic defence of individual freedom as a value in itself and the mark of a mature society. In *Utilitarianism*, he states that actions are right if they bring about happiness and wrong if they bring about the reverse of happiness. His progressive views inspired *On the Subjection of Women* (1869).

Mill was born in London, the son of the Scottish philosopher **James Mill**, from whom he received a rigorously intellectual education. He sat in Parliament as a Radical 1865–68 and introduced a motion for women's suffrage.

## Millais, John Everett (1829–1896)
English painter, a founder member of the ◊**Pre-Raphaelite Brotherhood** in 1848. Among his best known works are *Ophelia* (1852; National Gallery, London) and *Autumn Leaves* (1856; City Art Galleries, Manchester). By the late 1860s he had left the Brotherhood, developing a more fluid and conventional style which appealed strongly to Victorian tastes.

Precocious in talent, he was a student at the Royal Academy Schools at the age of 11. Early acquaintanceship with Holman ◊Hunt and Dante Gabriel ◊Rossetti led to the founding of the Pre-Raphaelite Brotherhood and, inspired by its doctrine of 'truth to nature', he produced some of his best works during the 1850s, among them the painting of Miss Siddell as Ophelia and *Christ in the House of His Parents* (1850; Tate Gallery, London); the latter caused an outcry on its first showing, since its realistic detail was considered unfitting to a sacred subject.

## Millennium Commission
Organization set up in 1993 to receive money from the ◊National Lottery, and give it to projects and awards to mark the millennium and beyond. Money has gone towards capital projects, to smaller community projects, and to the **Millennium Experience Festival**, of which the **New Millennium Experience** at ◊Greenwich is the centrepiece. The Commission is chaired by Chris Smith, secretary of state for culture, media, and sport. The Commission is partly funding the British Museum Great Court Project, by which the museum's Great Court is being renovated and roofed to create a new public space in the capital, and the creation of the Tate Gallery of Modern Art, a national gallery that will display the ◊Tate Gallery's modern collection on a permanent basis.

Capital projects funded by the Commission include: rebuilding of ◊Cardiff Arms Park stadium; further development of ◊Portsmouth docks as a maritime museum; development work in ◊Sheffield city centre; the Eden project in ◊Cornwall; and reopening the Forth and Clyde Canal and the Union Canal, to link Glasgow and Edinburgh.

## Millennium Dome
Giant structure serving as the centrepiece of Great Britain's Millennium Festival and Experience celebrating the year 2000. Located on a 732,483 sq m/181-acre festival site in Greenwich, southeast London, the Dome is on the Greenwich Prime Meridian (0° longitude). The Dome is 320 m/1,050 ft in diameter, 50 m/164 ft in height, and covers an area of 80,425 sq m/19.86 acres. It was designed by the Richard Rogers Partnership (architects of another London landmark, the Lloyd's Building), and is twice as big as the world's former largest dome, the Georgia Dome in Atlanta, USA. It opened on 31 December 1999.

Inside the Dome 14 exhibition areas are arranged around a central performance arena with a seating capacity of 12,500. Situated next to the Dome is a 6,000-seat amphitheatre. The Millennium Commission, set up in 1993 and benefiting from ◊national lottery funds, is responsible for financing the Millennium Festival and Experience as well as several other projects in the UK. The Millennium Dome and Experience are run by the New Millennium Experience Company, which is wholly owned by the government.

### The site
The 732,483 sq m/181-acre Greenwich Peninsula site is on former waste land, in a bend of the River Thames. Work began on cleaning up the site in July 1996 and construction started on 23 June 1997. Access to the site includes a new Underground station (the largest in Europe) at North Greenwich on the Jubilee Line, river boats from the site to central London and Greenwich and park and ride (and 'sail and ride') facilities.

### Dome facts
With a circumference of 1.005 km/0.6 mi, the Dome has a floor area of 80,425 sq m/19.86 acres, equivalent to 13 Albert Halls or two Wembley Stadiums. It holds 37,000 people. Facilities were planned for up to 70,000 people per day. The dome canopy is made of panels of teflon-coated PTFE, supported by 12 steel masts, each 100 m/328 ft long.

## Millennium Stadium
Welsh rugby ground, formerly known as Cardiff Arms Park, or the National Stadium, situated in Cardiff. The stadium became the permanent home of the Welsh national team in 1964 and had a capacity of 64,000. It was demolished and replaced by the 73,000-seater Millennium Stadium in time for the 1999 Rugby World Cup.

## Milne, A(lan) A(lexander) (1882–1956)
English writer. He is best known as the author of ◊ Winnie-the-Pooh (1926) and The House at Pooh Corner (1928), based on the teddy bear and other toys of his son Christopher Robin, with illustrations by E H Shepard. He also wrote children's verse, including When We Were Very Young (1924) and Now We Are Six (1927). He was an accomplished dramatist whose plays included Wurzel-Flummery (1917), Mr Pim Passes By (1920), The Dover Road (1922), and Toad of Toad Hall (1929), an adaptation of Kenneth ◊Grahame's The Wind in the Willows.

## Milton, John (1608–1674)
English poet and prose writer. His epic ◊ Paradise Lost (1667) is one of the landmarks of English literature. Early poems, including Comus (a masque performed 1634) and Lycidas (an elegy, 1638), showed Milton's superlative lyric gift. He also wrote many pamphlets and prose works, including Areopagitica (1644), which opposed press censorship, and he was Latin secretary to Oliver ◊Cromwell and the Council of State from 1649 until the restoration of Charles II.

Born in Cheapside, London, and educated at St Paul's School and Christ's College, Cambridge, Milton was a scholarly poet, ambitious to match the classical epics, and with strong theological views. Of polemical temperament, he published prose works on republicanism and church government. His middle years were devoted to the Puritan cause and writing pamphlets, including The Doctrine and Discipline of Divorce (1643), which may have been based on his own experience of marital unhappiness. During his time as secretary to Cromwell and the Council of State his assistants, as his sight failed, included Andrew ◊Marvell. Paradise Lost and the less successful sequel Paradise Regained (1671) were written when he was blind and in some political danger (after the restoration of Charles II), as was the dramatic poem Samson Agonistes (1671).

Milton's early poems have a baroque exuberance, while his later works are more sober, the blank verse more measured in its mixture of classical and English diction. His stated intention in writing Paradise Lost was to 'assert eternal Providence/And justify the ways of God to men'.

## Milton Keynes
Unitary authority in central England, formerly part of Buckinghamshire; area 311 sq km/120 sq mi; towns and cities Milton Keynes (administrative headquarters), Newport Pagnell, Olney, Bletchley, Stony Stratford, Woburn Sands, Wolverton; population of Milton Keynes town (1995) 192,900.

### Features
Grand Union Canal; River Great Ouse; River Tove; Open University (established in Milton Keynes 1971); Milton Keynes National Bowl (venue for outdoor events); National Badminton Centre (Milton Keynes); Bletchley Park, government centre of code-breaking during World War II; Ouse Valley Park with wetland habitats; Peace Pagoda (Milton Keynes), first to be built in northern hemisphere and surrounded by a thousand cherry and cedar trees planted in memory of all war victims; Milton Keynes' famous concrete cows, constructed in 1978 by a community artist and local school children.

### Industries
Financial services, telecommunications, soft drinks, high technology industries, motor vehicle

parts and manufacture (Aston Martin-Lagonda, Mercedes-Benz, Volkswagen-Audi), education (Open University and De Montfort University campuses), vellum and parchment.

## Minehead

Seaside resort in Somerset, England, 4 km/2.5 mi northwest of Dunster; population (1991) 6,200. It is situated within the Exmoor National Park, of which it is the main tourist centre. Minehead harbour is used for boating and sailing.

The West Somerset steam railway runs along the coast from Minehead.

## Mini

Originally called the **Mini-Minor**, best-selling car designed by Alec Issigonis in 1959. It was made by the British Motor Corporation.

## Minton, Thomas (1765–1836)

English potter. After an apprenticeship as an engraver for transfer printing at Caughley and working for the potter Josiah Spode, he established himself at Stoke-on-Trent as an engraver of designs in 1789. The Chinese-style blue and white 'willow pattern' was reputedly originated by Minton. In 1796 he founded a pottery, producing a cream-base blue-decorated earthenware and (from 1798) high-quality porcelain and bone china, decorated with flowers and fruit. Chinaware became the chief production under his son Herbert Minton (1792–1858).

## Mitford sisters

The six daughters of British aristocrat 2nd Lord Redesdale, including: **Nancy** (1904–1973), author of the semi-autobiographical *The Pursuit of Love* (1945) and *Love in a Cold Climate* (1949), and editor and part author of the satirical essays collected in *Noblesse Oblige* (1956) elucidating 'U' (upper-class) and 'non-U' behaviour; **Diana** (1910– ), who married Oswald ◊Mosley; **Unity** (1914–1948), who became an admirer of Hitler; and **Jessica** (1917– ), author of the autobiographical *Hons and Rebels* (1960) and *The American Way of Death* (1963).

## mod

British youth subculture that originated in London and Brighton in the early 1960s; it was revived in the late 1970s. Mods were smart, fashion-conscious, speedy, and upwardly mobile; they favoured scooters and soul music.

Mods and rockers (motorcycle gangs) have traditionally fought pitched battles at certain English seaside resorts on summer bank holidays.

## monarchy

The monarchy is the oldest institution of British government; only at the time of 'the ◊Commonwealth' (republic) 1649–60, declared by Cromwell, was there no King or Queen. The Queen, head of state, appoints the prime minister, according to support in the House of Commons; see ◊government for more on the monarch's role.

See overleaf for a table showing the succession to the throne; see also ◊Elizabeth II, and House of ◊Windsor, for genealogy.

## Monmouth, James Scott, 1st Duke of Monmouth (1649–1685)

Claimant to the English crown, the illegitimate son of Charles II and Lucy Walter. After James II's accession in 1685, Monmouth landed in England at Lyme Regis, Dorset, claimed the crown, and raised a rebellion, which was crushed at Sedgemoor in Somerset. He was executed with 320 of his accomplices. Created duke 1663.

## Monmouth, Welsh Trefynwy

Market town in Monmouthshire, southeast Wales, 25 km/16 mi north of Chepstow at the confluence of the Rivers Wye and Monnow; population (1991) 75,000. It is a tourist and fishing centre. Henry V was born in Monmouth Castle in 1388.

**The Mini** One of the most successful small cars in the history of motoring, the Mini was the brainchild of the engineer Alec Issigonis. He anticipated the needs of the city driver by designing a practical runabout vehicle that was manoeuvrable in traffic and easy to park. The Mini's clean lines and urban chic made it an instant hit in the 1960s, and it has remained popular ever since. Corel

## The Succession to the Throne

British succession rules were determined following the end of the Commonwealth in the 17th century by the Bill of Rights of 1689. This was amended by the Act of Settlement in 1701 which laid down that only Protestant descendants of Princess Sophia – the Electress of Hanover, granddaughter of James I – can succeed. Sons of the Sovereign and their descendants have precedence over daughters, in succeeding to the Throne. Daughters take precedence over the Sovereign's brothers. When a daughter succeeds, she becomes Queen Regnant and has the same powers as a King. In 1998, however, it was announced that Queen Elizabeth II supports plans to remove gender bias from the succession.

| Order of succession | Relationship |
|---|---|
| The Prince of Wales | Eldest son of Her Majesty The Queen |
| Prince William of Wales | Eldest son of The Prince of Wales |
| Prince Henry of Wales | Second son of The Prince of Wales |
| The Duke of York | Second son of Her Majesty The Queen |
| Princess Beatrice of York | Eldest daughter of The Duke of York |
| Princess Eugenie of York | Second daughter of The Duke of York |
| The Prince Edward | Third son of Her Majesty The Queen |
| The Princess Royal | Only daughter, second child of Her Majesty The Queen |
| Peter Phillips | Only son, eldest child, of The Princess Royal |
| Zara Phillips | Only daughter of The Princess Royal |

A picturesque bridge, unique in its two-storeyed fortified gatehouse, crosses the Monnow. There are still some remains of the 12th-century castle, one of a number built by William Fitz Osbern after the Norman Conquest. The castle keep collapsed in 1647 and was replaced, in 1673, by Great Castle House, which became the headquarters of the Royal Monmouthshire Engineer Militia (now the Royal Monmouthshire Regiment) in 1875.

## Monmouthshire, Welsh Trefynwy

Unitary authority in southeast Wales, with a southern coastline on the River Severn and bordering England to the east; population (1996) 80,400; area 851 sq km/328 sq mi. Formerly a county in its own right, it became the county of Gwent (except for a small area on the border with Mid-Glamorgan) 1974–96. Its principal towns are ◊Cwmbran (administrative headquarters) and Chepstow.

### History

Medieval Monmouthshire was undoubtedly Welsh. The Act of Union of 1536 created the original county out of 'divers Lordships Marchers within the said Country or Dominion of Wales'. Later in the Tudor period it was brought under the jurisdiction of the courts of Westminster in certain matters, while separate courts were provided for the rest of Wales. It has been included in

Wales since 1964 when the descrption Wales and Monmouthshire was dropped.

### Physical

The coast is exposed to high spring tides which rush up the Severn in a 'bore' from the Bristol Channel, rising at Chepstow sometimes to 18 m/60 ft. The southern part, east and west of the River Usk, comprises the Caldecot and Wentloog levels, which are protected from the sea by sea walls. North of the Caldecot level, between the Usk and the Wye rivers, the surface is undulating. The north of the county is more mountainous, and the northwest is within the Brecon Beacons National Park. About 7 km/4.3 mi from Abergavenny is the peaked mountain called Pen-y-Fal or Sugar Loaf (596 m/1,955 ft), over 8.1 sq km/3.1 sq mi of which have been presented to the National Trust. Skirrid Fawr (486 m/1,595 ft), known locally as the Holy Mountain, has views of the Black Mountains, the Usk valley, and the Sugar Loaf.

### Features

During the Roman occupation the only Roman town in Wales was built at Caerwent. There are also ruins of feudal strongholds at Chepstow, Caldicot, Raglan, and elsewhere, and the remains of Tintern Abbey and the Cistercian abbey of Llanthony are here. Between Abergavenny and Usk is the wooded hill-fort of Coed-y-Bonedd, one of several Monmouthshire camps.

### Economy
The lowlands have rich mixed farming, and there is good salmon and trout fishing. There is also a strong service sector.

## Monopolies and Mergers Commission, or MMC
Government body re-established in 1973 under the Fair Trading Act and, since 1980, embracing the Competition Act. Its role is to investigate and report when there is a risk of creating a monopoly by a company merger or takeover, or when a newspaper or newspaper assets are transferred. It also investigates companies, nationalized industries, or local authorities that are suspected of operating in a noncompetitive way.

## Montacute House
Elizabethan house in Somerset, England, 6 km/4 mi west of Yeovil. It was begun in 1588 by Thomas Phelips, and completed about 1601 by his son, Edward Phelips, Speaker of the House of Commons and master of the rolls under James I. The property was presented to the National Trust through the Society for the Protection of Ancient Buildings in 1931. It contains a collection of period furniture, pictures and tapestries.

### Features
Montacute House has an H-shaped ground plan and includes contemporary plasterwork, chimney pieces, and other Renaissance features (curvilinear and finialled gables, an open balustraded parapet, and fluted angle columns). The interior has fine 17th- and 18th-century furniture and Elizabethan and Jacobean paintings from the National Portrait Gallery in the Long Gallery and adjoining rooms.

## Montfort, Simon de Montfort, 1st Earl of Leicester (c. 1208–1265)
English politician and soldier. From 1258 he led the baronial opposition to Henry III's misrule during the second ◊Barons' War, and in 1264 defeated and captured the king at Lewes, Sussex. In 1265, as head of government, he summoned the first parliament in which the towns were represented; he was killed at the Battle of Evesham during the last of the Barons' Wars.

## Montgomery, Bernard Law, 1st Viscount Montgomery of Alamein (1887–1976)
English field marshal. In World War II he commanded the 8th Army in North Africa in the Second Battle of El ◊Alamein in 1942. As commander of British troops in Northern Europe from 1944, he received the German surrender in 1945.

In 1948 he became permanent military chair of the Commanders-in-Chief Committee for Western European defence, and 1951–58 was deputy Supreme Commander Europe. He was created 1st Viscount Montgomery of Alamein in 1946.

---

*In defeat, unbeatable; in victory, unbearable.*
**Winston Churchill** British Conservative prime minister.
Attributed remark, referring to Field Marshal Montgomery

---

## Moore, Henry (1898–1986)
English sculptor. His subjects include the reclining nude, mother-and-child groups, the warrior, and interlocking abstract forms. Many of his post-1945 works are in bronze or marble, such as *Reclining Figure* (1957–58), outside the UNESCO building in Paris, and are often designed to be placed in landscape settings.

Moore claimed to have learned much from archaic South and Central American sculpture, and this is reflected in his work of the 1920s which laid stress on truth to material and the original block, as in *Reclining Figure* (1929; Leeds City Art Gallery). By the early 1930s most of his main themes had emerged, and the Surrealists' preoccupation with organic forms in abstract works proved a strong influence.

Born in Castleford, Yorkshire, Moore studied at Leeds and the Royal College of Art (1921–24). As an official war artist during World War II, he made a series of drawings of people in London's air-raid shelters. Many of his works are now exhibited in the gardens and fields overlooking his home in Hertfordshire, looked after by the Henry Moore Foundation (set up by the artist, his wife, and daughter in 1977).

## Moray
Unitary authority in northeast Scotland, created in 1996 from the Moray district of Grampian region; population (1996) 85,000; area 2,224 sq km/859 sq mi. Mountainous in the south, it slopes towards the mouth of the Moray Firth and the North Sea in the north. Moray has numerous royal residences as well as Gordonstoun school, where Prince Philip and Prince Charles were educated; it also is the setting for Shakespeare's *Macbeth*. The principal towns are ◊Elgin (administrative headquarters), Forres, Buckie, and Lossiemouth.

## Physical

The land descends gradually from the Grampian Mountains in the south (Cairn Gorm 1,245 m/4,085 ft); extensive coastal lowlands fringe an area of sand-dune formation; part of this land was reclaimed from the sea and is now covered by the Culbin forest. The River Spey reaches the North Sea near Buckie.

## Features

Elgin has the remains of a 13th-century cathedral. Brodie Castle, 5 km/3 mi west of Forres, was built in about 1567 for the Brodie family; it was extended in the early 17th and 19th centuries. Duffus Castle, 8 km/5 mi northwest of Elgin, is a good example of a Norman motte and bailey castle, with a water-filled moat. There are 33 Sites of Special Scientific Interest, one National Nature Reserve, three Ramsars (wetland sites), two Special Protection Areas, and one National Scenic Area.

## Economy

The area has a rural economy, and still produces traditional food and whisky.

## More, (St) Thomas (1478–1535)

English politician and author. From 1509 he was favoured by ◊Henry VIII and employed on foreign embassies. He was a member of the privy council from 1518 and Lord Chancellor from 1529 but resigned over Henry's break with the pope. For refusing to accept the king as head of the church, he was executed. The title of his political book *Utopia* (1516) has come to mean any supposedly perfect society.

Son of a London judge, More studied Greek, Latin, French, theology, and music at Oxford, and law at Lincoln's Inn, London, and was influenced by the humanists John Colet and Erasmus, who became a friend. In Parliament from 1504, he was made Speaker of the House of Commons in 1523. He was knighted in 1521, and on the fall of

Cardinal Wolsey became Lord Chancellor, but resigned in 1532 because he could not agree with the king on his ecclesiastical policy and marriage with Anne Boleyn. In 1534 he refused to take the oath of supremacy to Henry VIII as head of the church, and after a year's imprisonment in the Tower of London he was executed. More was canonized in 1935.

## Morecambe

Town and seaside resort in Lancashire, northwest England, on Morecambe Bay, joined with the port of Heysham, which has a ferry service to the Isle of Man; joint population (1991) 46,700. Tourism is important.

The town developed from the end of the 18th century as people started visiting the villages of Poulton-le-Sands, Torrisholme, and Bare. During the 19th century the arrival of the railway enabled people from the nearby Lancashire mill towns to reach the coast easily. The name Morecambe was adopted in 1889. The town has increasingly drawn more day-visitors than those staying for a holiday; there are illuminations in the autumn, and the ecology and birdlife of **Morecambe Bay** are an attraction. There are dangerous quicksands in the bay and tides advance very quickly.

## Morecambe and Wise

Comedy partnership of Eric Morecambe (1926–1984) and Ernie Wise (1925–1999). At its peak in the 1970s, the *Morecambe and Wise Show* was the lynchpin of the BBC's Christmas schedule, attracting an audience of 29 million – over half the nation – in 1977.

Eric Morecambe, tall, with glasses, was the funny man, with 'little Ern', whom Eric constantly ridiculed on screen for having 'short, fat, hairy legs', as his foil. They began to work as a duo in the late 1940s, performing in clubs and on radio before moving into commercial television in 1961. From 1968 until 1978 they worked for the BBC, subsequently moving back to ITV, where their career was cut short by Eric's death from a heart attack.

Finely tuned as a partnership, with established on-screen personae and character quirks,

**Morecambe and Wise** One of the most celebrated double-acts in British comedy. Eric Morecambe was famous for debunking the pretensions of his pompous 'straight man' Ernie Wise (left). Both crafted their comedy with great attention to detail, but overwork brought on a heart attack that caused Eric Morecambe's untimely death in 1984. Rex

Morecambe and Wise would invite actors and celebrities, none of them associated with comedy, to be guests on their shows and with a mix of exaggerated respect and ridicule, reveal new sides to their guests' abilities, not least their good-humour. An invitation to be on the show was seen as an accolade.

## Morpeth

Town and administrative headquarters of the county of ◊Northumberland, England, 22 km/14 mi north of Newcastle; population (1991) 13,700. Morpeth has a small iron foundry and a thriving cattle-market. There are remains of a medieval castle; and the town has an ancient chantry and clock tower. Newminster Abbey dates from the 12th century and the parish church of St Mary from the 14th century.

The town hall was designed by John Vanbrugh in 1714. The Chantry Bagpipe Museum includes pipes from Northumberland, the Borders, Ireland, Greece, and Italy.

## Morris, William (1834–1896)

English artist, designer, socialist, and writer. A founder of the ◊Arts and Crafts movement, he condemned 19th-century mechanization and sought a revival of traditional crafts. He linked this to a renewal of society based on Socialist principles.

Morris was born in London and educated at Oxford University, where he formed a lasting friendship with the Pre-Raphaelite artist Edward ◊Burne-Jones and was influenced by the art critic John Ruskin and the painter and poet Dante Gabriel ◊Rossetti. He abandoned his first profession, architecture, to study painting. In 1861 he cofounded Morris, Marshall, Faulkner and Company ('the Firm') which designed and produced stained glass, furniture, fabric, carpets, and decorative wallpapers; many of the designs, inspired by medieval, classical, and oriental sources, are still produced today. His Kelmscott Press, set up in 1890 to print beautifully designed books, influenced printing and book design.

Kelmscott Manor, his home near Lechlade, Gloucestershire, is open to visitors.

## Morris dance

Old English folk dance. It derived its name from the Moorish *Moresca* (old English 'morys', 'Moorish'), introduced into England about the 15th

**Morris Dancing** Morris men from Bampton in Oxfordshire. The precise origins of this ritual folk dance are unclear, but it is believed to derive from a pagan custom. In rural England, the tradition was revived in the 19th century after centuries of neglect. Morris men can often to be seen at country fairs and pubs. Brian Shuel/Collections

century, and may have originated in pre-Christian ritual dances. It was danced in various kinds of fancy dress, with jingles tied to the dancers' legs. In early times it was usually performed by six men, one of whom wore girl's clothing while another portrayed a horse. In some districts elements of the Sword Dance were introduced into it. The music, a great variety of tunes, was played by a pipe and tabor, or more rarely by a bagpipe or violin. Morris dancing is still popular.

## Mosley, Oswald (1896–1980)

British politician, founder of the British Union of Fascists (BUF) 1932. He was a member of Parliament 1918–31, then led the BUF until his internment 1940–43 during World War II. In 1946 Mosley was denounced when it became known that Italy had funded his prewar efforts to establish fascism in Britain, but in 1948 he resumed fascist propaganda with his Union Movement, the revived BUF.

His first marriage was to a daughter of the Conservative politician Lord Curzon, his second to Diana Freeman-Mitford, one of the ◊Mitford sisters.

## Motherwell

Industrial town and administrative headquarters of North Lanarkshire, Scotland, southeast of Glasgow; population (1991) 60,500. The two burghs of Motherwell and Wishaw were amalgamated in 1920, but the towns retain distinct identities. Formerly a coalmining, iron, and engineering town, Motherwell has a Eurofreight terminal. The town is named after an old well, reputedly with healing waters, dedicated to the Blessed Virgin.

## Mottisfont Abbey

Abbey in Hampshire, England, 15 km/9 mi west of Winchester. The 660 ha/1630 acre estate, which includes most of **Mottisfont village**, the abbey itself, and 162 ha/400 acres of woodland, was given to the National Trust in 1957. The abbey has early 13th-century origins and was an Augustinian priory until the Dissolution of the Monasteries in the 1530s, when it was acquired by Lord Chancellor Sandys and converted into a Tudor mansion. Other major changes were made in the early 18th century.

The house contains 'Gothic' trompe l'oeil paintings by Rex Whistler in the Whistler Room.

A tributary of the River Test flows through the garden, which together with walled gardens and a collection of old-fashioned types of roses, creates a superb setting.

## Mountbatten, Louis, 1st Earl Mountbatten of Burma (1900–1979)

English admiral and administrator, a great-grandson of Queen Victoria. In World War II he became chief of combined operations in 1942 and commander in chief in southeast Asia in 1943. As last viceroy and governor general of India 1947–48, he oversaw that country's transition to independence. He was killed by an Irish Republican Army (IRA) bomb aboard his yacht at Mullaghmore, County Sligo, in the Republic of Ireland.

## Mourne Mountains, or Mountains of Mourne

Mountain range in the south of County Down, Northern Ireland, extending from above Newcastle to Carlingford Lough. The highest summit is Slieve Donard; height 852 m/2795 ft. The mountains are of granite.

## MP

Member of ◊Parliament.

## Much Wenlock

Town in Shropshire, England, on the River Severn, 19 km/12 mi southeast of Shrewsbury; population (1991) 3,100. Wenlock dates from the Middle Ages. To the southwest of the town is the limestone ridge of **Wenlock Edge** (240 m–290 m/800–950 ft).

The town includes the ruins of Wenlock Priory, originally founded as a convent in the 7th century and later a priory for Cluniac monks. There is also a 16th-century half-timbered guildhall and the church of Holy Trinity, parts of which are Norman.

## Mull

Second largest island of the Inner ◊Hebrides, Argyll and Bute, Scotland; area 950 sq km/367 sq mi; population (1991) 2,700. It is mountainous, and is separated from the mainland by the **Sound of Mull** and the Firth of Lorne; it lies 11 km/7 mi west of Oban. The main town is Tobermory, from which there are ferry connections to Oban; Craignure is also connected by ferry to Oban. The economy is based on fishing, forestry, tourism, and stock rearing.

The west coast of Mull is indented with sea

lochs, of which the main ones are Loch-na-Keal and Loch Scridain. The highest peak is Ben More (966 m/3,171 ft). On the south coast of the island, the Carsaig Arches are a series of columnar black basalt caves and arches, said to have been used as a hiding-place by nuns during the Reformation.

## Munnings, Alfred James (1878–1959)
English painter. He excelled in racing and hunting scenes, and painted realistic everyday scenes featuring horses, such as horsefairs or horses grazing. *Epsom Downs* is a notable example. As president of the Royal Academy (1944–51) he was outspoken in his dislike of 'modern art'.

## Murdoch, Iris (1919–1999)
English novelist and academic, born in Dublin. Her novels combine philosophical speculation with often outrageous situations and tangled human relationships. They include *The Sandcastle* (1957), *The Bell* (1958), *The Sea, The Sea* (1978; winner of the Booker Prize), *Nuns and Soldiers* (1980), *The Message to the Planet* (1989), *The Green Knight* (1993), and *Jackson's Dilemma* (1995).

From 1948–63 she was a fellow and tutor in philosophy at St Anne's College, Oxford. Her first work was a philosophical study, *Sartre, Romantic Rationalist* (1953). Her first novel was *Under The Net* (1954), which, with *The Flight from the Enchanter* (1956), made her reputation as a writer of high seriousness of purpose and great wit.

In 1999, *Iris: a Memoir*, by her husband, John Bayley, described her illness with Alzheimer's disease, and became a best-seller.

## Murrayfield
Scottish rugby football ground in west Edinburgh, home of the national team. It staged its first international in 1925 when Scotland beat England 14–11. The capacity is approximately 70,000.

## music
See ◊classical music, ◊chamber music, ◊folk music, ◊pop music, ◊musical, ◊orchestras, ◊ballet, ◊opera, also individual entries.

## musical
20th-century form of dramatic musical performance, combining elements of song, dance, and the spoken word, often characterized by lavish staging and large casts. It developed from the operettas and musical comedies of the 19th century.

### Operetta
The operetta is a light-hearted entertainment with extensive musical content: such as the light operas by W S ◊Gilbert and A S ◊Sullivan.
### Musical comedy and revue
The musical comedy is an anglicization of the French *opéra bouffe*, of which the first was *A Gaiety Girl* (1893), mounted by George Edwardes (1852–1915) at the Gaiety Theatre, London. Noël Coward's revues and musicals included *On With the Dance* (1925) and *Bitter Sweet* (1929), while Ivor Novello wrote *Glamorous Night* (1925), and *The Dancing Years* (1939).
### Musical
Sandy Wilson's *The Boy Friend* (1953) revitalized the British musical and was followed by hits such as Lionel Bart's *Oliver!* (1960). Musicals began to branch into religious and political themes with *Oh, What a Lovely War* (1963), produced by Joan Littlewood and Charles Chiltern, and the Andrew Lloyd Webber musicals *Jesus Christ Superstàr* (1971) and *Evita* (1978). Another category of musical, substituting a theme for conventional plotting, is exemplified by Lloyd Webber's *Cats* (1981), using verses by T S Eliot. In the 1980s 19th-century melodrama was popular, for example the long-running *Les Misérables* (first London performance 1985) and *The Phantom of the Opera* (1986). In the 1990s Willy Russell's *Blood Brothers* and Lloyd Webber's *Starlight Express* were popular, as was *Buddy*, on the life on Buddy Holly, and the film-derived *Grease* and *Saturday Night Fever*. See ◊theatre for table showing the musical's dominance of London's West End in the 1990s.

## music hall
Light theatrical entertainment, in which singers, dancers, comedians, and acrobats perform in 'turns'. The music hall's heyday was at the beginning of the 20th century, with such artistes as Marie Lloyd, Harry Lauder, and George Formby.

Many performers had a song with which they were associated, such as Albert Chevalier (1861–1923) ('My Old Dutch'), or a character 'trademark', such as Vesta Tilley's immaculate masculine outfit as Burlington Bertie. Later stars of music hall included Sir George Robey, Gracie Fields, the Crazy Gang, Ted Ray, and the US comedian Danny Kaye.
### History
Music hall originated in the 17th century, when tavern-keepers acquired the organs that the Puritans had banished from churches. On certain

**Muslim Community** Muslims leaving a mosque in Dalston, northeast London. The Muslim community increased greatly from the 1950s onwards, as immigration from the Indian subcontinent was encouraged, to supplement Britain's workforce. Bangladeshis in the East End of London have replaced earlier generations of immigrants who lived there, such as Jews from eastern Europe. Giles Askham/Impact

nights organ music was played, and this resulted in a weekly entertainment known as the 'free and easy'. Certain theatres in London and the provinces then began to specialize in variety entertainment. With the advent of radio and television, music hall declined, but in the 1960s and 1970s there was a revival in working men's clubs and in pubs.

## Muslim community
Second largest religious community in the UK, with between 750,000 and 2 million followers in Britain (1998). Recent estimates, based on the 1991 census, suggest the population is between 1 million and 1.5 million, while estimates within the Muslim community itself suggest the figure is between 1.5 and 2 million. Most Muslims originate from Pakistan and Bangladesh, while others come from India, Cyprus, the Arab states,

Malaysia, and parts of Africa. There are increasing numbers of British-born Muslims, mainly the children of immigrant parents.

There are over 600 mosques and many prayer centres in Britain. The first mosque was established in Woking, Surrey, in 1889. The Central Mosque in Regent's Park, London, has the largest congregation in Britain; during festivals it can number over 30,000. The Islamic Cultural Centre attached to the Central Mosque is one of the most important Muslim institutions in the West. Other important mosques and cultural centres are in Liverpool, Manchester, Leicester, Birmingham, Bradford, Cardiff, Edinburgh, and Glasgow.

Both the Sunni and the Shi'a traditions are represented in Britain, and members of some of the major Sufi traditions have also developed branches.

# Nantwich

Town in Cheshire, England, 7 km/4 mi from Crewe; population of Crewe and Nantwich (1991) 99,500. A market town in the heart of a fertile region, Nantwich was formerly a centre of the salt industry. The 14th-century parish church, much restored, dominates the town centre.

After a disastrous fire in 1583 the town was rebuilt with money provided by a national subscription sponsored by Elizabeth I. Some houses, and the Crown Hotel, date from the period immediately after the fire. Churche's Mansion, a Tudor manor house built in 1577, is on the edge of the town.

Salt deposits here were known to the Romans, and the town's brine springs were noted in the Domesday Book of 1087. Nantwich's salt industry was at its most productive in medieval and Tudor times but declined from the 17th century onwards.

# Napier, John, 8th Laird of Merchiston (1550–1617)

Scottish mathematician who invented logarithms in 1614 and 'Napier's bones', an early mechanical calculating device for multiplication and division.

It was Napier who first used and then popularized the decimal point to separate the whole number part from the fractional part of a number.

Napier was born in Merchiston Castle, near Edinburgh, and studied at St Andrews. He never occupied any professional post.

# Napoleonic Wars

Series of European wars (1803–15) conducted by Napoleon I of France against an alliance of Britain, the German states, Spain, Portugal, and Russia, following the ◊Revolutionary Wars, and aiming for French conquest of Europe. At one time nearly all of Europe was under Napoleon's domination. He was finally defeated at the ◊Battle of Waterloo in 1815.

During the Napoleonic Wars, the annual cost of the British army was between 60% and 90% of total government income. About half of Napoleon's army was made up of foreign mercenaries, mainly Swiss and German.

# Naseby, Battle of

Decisive battle of the English Civil War on 14 June 1645, when the Royalists, led by Prince Rupert, were defeated by the Parliamentarians ('Roundheads') under Oliver Cromwell and General Fairfax. It is named after the nearby village of Naseby, 32 km/20 mi south of Leicester.

# Nash, John (1752–1835)

English architect. His large country-house practice, established about 1796 with the landscape gardener Humphry ◊Repton, used a wide variety of styles, and by 1798 he was enjoying the patronage of the Prince of Wales (afterwards George IV). Later he laid out Regent's Park, London, and its approaches, as well as Trafalgar Square and St James's Park. Between 1811 and 1821 he planned Regent Street (later rebuilt), repaired and enlarged ◊Buckingham Palace (for which he designed Marble Arch), and rebuilt the Royal Pavilion, Brighton, in flamboyant oriental style.

For himself he built East Cowes Castle (1798) which greatly influenced the early Gothic Revival.

# Nash, Paul (1889–1946)

English painter. He was an official war artist in world wars I and II. In the 1930s he was one of a group of artists promoting avant-garde style, and was deeply influenced by Surrealism. Two works

**Paul Nash** English artist. A leading figure in English avant-garde art in the 1930s and 1940s, Nash used French Surrealism to revitalize the British landscape tradition. Corbis

which illustrate the visionary quality of his paintings are *Totes Meer/Dead Sea* (1940–41; Tate Gallery), London; and *Solstice of the Sunflower* (1945; National Gallery of Canada, Ottawa). In his pictures of World War I, such as *The Menin Road* (Imperial War Museum), he created strange patterns out of the scorched landscape of the Western Front.

### Nash, 'Beau' (1674–1762)
Welsh dandy. As master of ceremonies at Bath from 1705, he made the town a fashionable spa resort, and introduced a polished code of manners into polite society.

### national anthem
'God Save the King/Queen'. The melody resembles a composition by John Bull and similar words are found from the 16th century. In its present form it was arranged by Dr Thomas Arne, under the title 'Song for Two Voices'. This version was first performed at Drury Lane Theatre in London on 28 September 1745, following the news of the defeat of the army of King George II by the 'Young Pretender' to the British Throne, Prince Charles Edward Stuart, at the battle of Prestonpans. The song immediately became popular as an anti-Jacobite Party song during the 1745 Jacobite Rebellion.

The words shown opposite are those sung in 1745, substituting 'Queen' for 'King' where appropriate. On official occasions, only the first verse is usually sung. 'Land of Hope and Glory' is considered an unofficial national anthem of England. See ◊Scotland and ◊Wales for their national anthems.

### National Assembly for Wales
60-seat devolved body, based in Cardiff, that has taken over the functions of the Welsh Office, spending its £7 billion budget. Narrowly approved in a September 1997 referendum, the assembly implements Westminster laws and does not have primary law-making powers, even in respect to the Welsh language. However, it oversees quangos (quasi-autonomous non-governmental organizations), which proliferated during the Conservative years, making them more accountable. The assembly was elected in 1999, with a third of its seats being selected by proportional representation. Labour won 28 seats (three short of an outright majority), Plaid Cymru won 17, the Conservatives won 9 and the Liberal Democrats 6. In October 1998, a design concept put forward by the Richard Rogers Partnership was chosen for the National Assembly for Wales building, to be located at Cardiff Bay.

### National Galleries of Scotland, the
Three Scottish galleries administered by one director under a single board of trustees. They are the ◊National Gallery of Scotland, the ◊Scottish National Portrait Gallery, and the ◊Scottish National Gallery of Modern Art.

### National Gallery
London art gallery housing the British national collection of pictures by artists no longer living, founded in 1824. Its collection covers all major pre-20th-century periods and schools, but it is unique in its collection of Italian Gothic and Renaissance works, which is more comprehensive than any other collection outside Italy.

The present building in Trafalgar Square was designed by William Wilkins and opened in 1838. There have been several extensions, including the Sainsbury Wing, designed by US architect Robert Venturi, which opened in July 1991.

### National Gallery of Scotland
Edinburgh art gallery housing the Scottish national collection of old master paintings, opened in 1859. It consists of European and English works from the period 1400–1900,

## 'God Save The Queen'

God save our gracious Queen, Long live our noble
  Queen
God save the Queen!
Send her victorious, Happy and Glorious
Long to reign over us
God save the Queen!

O Lord our God arise, Scatter her enemies
And make them fall
Confound their politics, Frustrate their knavish tricks
On Thee our hopes we fix
Oh, save us all!

Thy choicest gifts in store, On her be pleased to pour
Long may she reign
May she defend our laws, And ever give us cause
To sing with heart and voice
God save the Queen!

Not in this land alone, But be God's mercies known
From shore to shore!
Lord make the nations see, That men should brothers
  be
And form one family
The wide world over.

From every latent foe, From the assassins blow
God save the Queen!
O'er her thine arm extend, For Britain's sake defend
Our mother, prince, and friend
God save the Queen!

## 'Land of Hope and Glory'

Although this anthem can identify with the whole of
the UK by references to the empire 'wider and still
wider, shall thy bounds be set', it is also the unofficial
national anthem of England, and is used for the English
teams at the Commonwealth Games, although the
English national football and rugby teams use 'God
Save the Queen'.

Words by A C Benson, music by Sir Edward Elgar from
'Pomp & Circumstance March No. 1'.

Dear Land of Hope, thy hope is crowned.
God make thee mightier yet!
On Sov'ran brows, beloved, renowned, Once more thy
  crown is set.
Thine equal laws, by Freedom gained, Have ruled thee
  well and long
By Freedom gained, by Truth maintained, Thine Empire
  shall be strong.

Land of Hope and Glory, Mother of the Free
How shall we extol thee, who are born of thee?
Wider still and wider shall thy bounds be set
God, who made thee mighty, make thee mightier yet
God, who made thee mighty, make thee mightier yet.

Thy fame is ancient as the days, As Ocean large and
  wide
A pride that dares, and heeds not praise, A stern and
  silent pride
Not that false joy that dreams content With what our
  sires have won
The blood a hero sire hath spent, Still nerves a hero son.

together with a representative collection of Scottish paintings. An important loan of pictures from the Duke of Sutherland includes works by Raphael, Titian, and Rembrandt. The Department of Prints and Drawings contains the Vaughan Bequest, a notable group of Turner watercolours.

## National Health Service
See ◊NHS.

## national insurance
State social-security scheme that provides child allowances, maternity benefits, and payments to the unemployed, sick, and retired, and also covers medical treatment. It is paid for by weekly or monthly contributions from employees and employers.

## National Lottery
Lottery launched by the British government in November 1994 to raise money for the arts, sports, charities, national heritage, and the Millennium Fund, set up to celebrate the year 2000. Its operators are the Camelot Consortium, led by

Cadbury Schweppes plc. Of the weekly takings, 50% is used as prize money, 28% goes to the above causes, 12% is taken in taxes, and the remaining 10% is split between Camelot and an estimated 10,000 retail outlets that sell tickets. An estimated 80% of the adult population play the national lottery, each spending a weekly average of £2.50. From 1997 lottery draws were held twice a week, on Wednesdays and Saturdays.

## National Museum of Wales, Welsh Amgueddfa Genedlaethol Cymru
Museum in Cardiff, with outlying museums, namely the Museum of Welsh Life at St Fagans, the Welsh Slate Museum at Llanberis, and the Industrial and Maritime Museum at Cardiff's Bay development.

## National Museums of Northern Ireland
Organization that in 1998 brought together the three main museums in Northern Ireland: the Ulster Museum in Belfast, the Ulster Folk and Transport Museum in County Down, and the Ulster–American Folk Park in County Tyrone.

## National Museums of Scotland
Collective body made up of the Royal Museum of Scotland, the Scottish United Services Museum, the Scottish Agricultural Museum (all in Edinburgh), the Museum of Flight near North Berwick, and the Museum of Costume near Dumfries. A purpose-built new Museum of Scotland opened next to the Royal Museum in 1998.

## national park
Land set aside and conserved for public enjoyment. National parks include not only the most scenic places, but also places distinguished for their historic, prehistoric, or scientific interest, or for their superior recreational assets. They range from areas the size of small countries to pockets of just a few hectares.

In England and Wales under the National Park Act (1949) ten national parks were established including the Peak District, the Lake District, and Snowdonia. National parks are protected from large-scale development, but from time to time pressure to develop land for agriculture, quarrying, or tourism, or to improve amenities for the local community means that conflicts of interest arise between land users.

Other protected areas include Areas of Outstanding Natural Beauty (see ◊conservation) and ◊Sites of Special Scientific Interest (SSSIs). See the end of the guide for a list of national parks.

## National Portrait Gallery
London art gallery containing portraits of distinguished British men and women. It was founded in 1856 and moved to its present building in St Martin's Place, Trafalgar Square, in 1896.

Overall the collection has over 8,000 original paintings, drawings, and sculptures, and photographs of noted figures from Tudor times onwards, together with an archive and reference library.

## National Theatre, Royal
National theatre company established in 1963, and the complex, opened in 1976, that houses it on London's South Bank. From 1988 it has been formally called the Royal National Theatre of Great Britain.

## National Trust
British trust founded in 1895 for the preservation of land and buildings of historic interest or beauty, incorporated by an act of Parliament in 1907. It is the largest private landowner in Britain. The National Trust for Scotland was established in 1931.

Under the terms of the 1907 Act, the Trust holds property 'inalienably', meaning that it cannot sell or develop property given to it except by an act of Parliament. In 1934 the Trust set up its Country House Scheme, and in 1947 a gardens fund. In 1997 the Trust in England, Wales, and Northern Ireland opened 300 of its properties to the public and it owned 909 km/565 mi of coastline.

## Natural History Museum
Museum in South Kensington, London, housing 68 million specimens relating to the life and earth sciences. First opened on this site in 1881, it was originally part of the British Museum in Bloomsbury. The original collection had been donated by Hans Sloane (1660–1753), the physician who founded London's Chelsea Physic Garden. A new Darwin Centre, displaying aspects of scientific research, as well as specimens, is scheduled to open in 2002.

## nature reserve
Area set aside to protect a habitat and the wildlife that lives within it, with only restricted admission for the public. Under the National Parks Act (1949), the (now defunct) Nature Conservancy Council (NCC) was given the power to designate such areas in Britain; this is now under the control of the Joint Nature Conservation Committee (JNCC). There are both officially designated nature reserves – managed by ◊English Nature, the ◊Countryside Council for Wales, and ◊Scottish Natural Heritage – and those run by a variety of voluntary conservation organizations. In 1997 there were 343 National Nature Reserves (covering more than 490,000 acres); 3 Marine Nature Reserves; over 500 Local Nature Reserves; and nearly 6,2000 ◊Sites of Special Scientific Interest (SSSIs).

## Neagh, Lough
Lake in Northern Ireland, 25 km/15 mi west of Belfast; area 396 sq km/153 sq mi. It is the largest lake in the British Isles and Ireland, being 27 km/17 mi long, 16 km/10 mi wide, with an average depth of 12 m/39 ft. The shores are mostly flat and marshy; there are a few islands of which Ram's Island is the largest, on which is an early round tower. The lake is famous for trout and eel fishing, and breeding waterbirds.

## Neath, Welsh Castell-nedd
Town in Neath Port Talbot unitary authority, south Wales, 11 km/7 mi northeast of Swansea

near the mouth of the River Neath; population (1991) 46,000. The Roman fort of Nidum was discovered nearby in 1949; there are also remains of a 13th-century Norman castle and Neath Abbey, founded in 1130.

## Neath Port Talbot

Unitary authority in south Wales, created in 1996 from part of the former county of West Glamorgan; 442 sq km/171 sq mi in area; administrative headquarters ◊Port Talbot. Population (1996) 139,400.

*Physical*

The terrain is dominated by the alternation of river valleys and high moorland interfluves.

*Features*

Roman fort of Nidum is near ◊Neath

*Economy*

The county is mainly industrial with coal mining predominating, including anthracite in the upper valleys and metallurgical industries at coastal sites.

## Needles, the

Group of white rocks standing in the sea, rising to 30 m/100 ft, off the western extremity of the Isle of Wight, southern England.

The origin of the rocks is attributable to the erosion of the steep cliffs which form the western point of the Isle of Wight. The largest of the rocks, which was 36 m/118 ft high, was undermined and fell during a storm in 1764. The rocks are black at their bases, and streaked throughout with black strata of flints. There is a lighthouse on the outermost rock.

## Nelson, Horatlo, 1st Viscount Nelson (1758–1805)

English admiral. He joined the navy in 1770. During the Revolutionary Wars against France he lost the sight in his right eye in 1794 and lost his right arm in 1797. He became a rear admiral and a national hero after the victory off Cape St Vincent, Portugal. In 1798 he tracked the French fleet to Aboukir Bay where he almost entirely destroyed it. In 1801 he won a decisive victory over Denmark at the Battle of ◊Copenhagen, and in 1805, after two years of blockading Toulon, he defeated the Franco-Spanish fleet at the Battle of ◊Trafalgar, near Gibraltar.

Nelson was almost continuously on active service in the Mediterranean 1793–1800; he lingered at Naples for a year, during which he helped to crush a democratic uprising, and fell completely under the influence of Lady ◊Hamilton. In 1800 he returned to England and soon after separated from his wife, Frances Nisbet (1761–1831). He was promoted to vice admiral in 1801, and sent to the Baltic to operate against the Danes, nominally as second in command; in fact, it was Nelson who was responsible for the victory of Copenhagen and for negotiating peace with Denmark. On his return to England he was created a viscount. In 1803 he received the Mediterranean command and for nearly two years blockaded Toulon. When in 1805 his opponent, the French admiral Pierre de Villeneuve (1763–1806), eluded him, Nelson pursued him to the West Indies and back, and on 21 October defeated the combined French and Spanish fleets off Cape Trafalgar, capturing 20 of the enemy ships; Nelson himself was mortally wounded. He is buried in St Paul's Cathedral, London.

---

*I have only one eye, I have a right to be blind sometimes: ...*
*I really do not see the signal!*

**Horatio Nelson** British admiral.
At the Battle of Copenhagen 1801

---

## Neo-Classicism

Movement in art, architecture, and design in Europe and North America, from about 1750 to 1850, characterized by a revival of Classical Greek and Roman styles. In Britain leading figures of Neo-Classicism were the architects Robert Adam, John Soane, Charles Cockerell, James Gibbs, and William Playfair; the painters Angelica Kauffman and Frederic Leighton; the sculptors John Flaxman, Thomas Banks and John Gibson; and the designers Josiah Wedgwood, George Hepplewhite, and Thomas Sheraton.

Neo-Classicism was inspired both by the excavation of the Roman towns of Pompeii and Herculaneum and by the cultural studies of the German art historian Johann J Winckelmann. Neo-Classical artists sought to capture the 'noble simplicity and calm grandeur' of Classical art by conscious emulation of Classical styles and subject matter. They took themes from Homer and Plutarch and were influenced by John Flaxman's austere linear illustrations for the *Iliad* and *Odyssey*.

## Nesbit, E(dith) (1858–1924)

English author of children's books. She wrote *The Story of the Treasure Seekers* (1899) and *The Railway Children* (1906). Her stories often have a humorous magical element, as in *Five Children and It* (1902) and *The Phoenix and the Carpet*

(1904). *The Treasure Seekers* is the first of several books about the realistically squabbling Bastable children; it was followed by *The Would-be Goods* (1901) and *The New Treasure Seekers* (1904). Nesbit was a Fabian socialist and supported her family by writing. Her stories struck a new note with their naturalistic portrayal of children.

## Ness, Loch

Lake in the Highland unitary authority, Scotland, extending northeast to southwest. Forming part of the Caledonian Canal, it is 36 km/22.5 mi long, 2 km/1 mi wide (on average), 229 m/754 ft deep. There have been unconfirmed reports of a **Loch Ness monster** since the 15th century.

Loch Ness, Loch Lochy and Loch Oich are connected by the ◊Caledonian Canal, and together provide the only navigable channel between the east and west coasts of Scotland.

## Newcastle-under-Lyme

Market and industrial town in Staffordshire, west-central England, on the River Lyme, 3 km/2 mi west of Stoke-on-Trent; population (1996) 60,000.

A castle was built at Newcastle-under-Lyme between 1142 and 1146, of which only the excavated boundaries now remain. St Giles's Church dates from the 13th century, but was largely rebuilt between 1873 and 1876. Keele University (established 1962) is nearby to the west.

---

*Geordies tell you that the skyline has changed in these parts. The pit-heads have gone. The cranes of the shipyards have disappeared into the history books. The yards that once built a quarter of the world's ships – including the world's first oil tanker at Jarrow – are now almost silent apart from some modest resurgence of ship repair work on the Tyne. The Newcastle that made a living by getting its hands dirty has been allowed to die.*

**Tony Parsons** English journalist.
*Daily Mirror*, 1997

---

## Newcastle upon Tyne

City and metropolitan borough in Tyne and Wear in northeast England on the north bank of the River Tyne opposite Gateshead, 17 km/10 mi from the North Sea; population city (1991) 189,150, metropolitan district (1994) 274,000. It is the administrative centre of Tyne and Wear and

regional centre for retail, commerce, communications, and the arts. Only 1% of the workforce is now employed in heavy industry, with 80% working in the public or service sectors.

The town first began to trade in coal in the 13th century, and was an important centre for coal and ship-building until the 1980s. In 1826 ironworks were established by the English engineer, George Stephenson, and the first engine used on the Stockton and Darlington railway was made in Newcastle.

The Town Moor and associated parks, occupying an area of 375 ha/937 acres, separate the commercial town from its northern suburbs in Gosforth. Newcastle is connected with Gateshead by eight bridges and a tunnel.

### History

Newcastle stands on the site of a Roman settlement, **Pons Aelius**. In 1080 the Normans built a castle near the site of the original Roman bridge, and the town grew along the riverside and northwards across the plateau above the river; there are traces of the medieval street pattern, though few buildings remain from this period. From the 13th to 18th centuries, Newcastle was walled and traces of the wall and towers remain. Newcastle provided a military base for English troops during intermittent wars with Scotland and was occupied by the Scots in 1640 and 1644–47. In times of peace Newcastle became a regional trading centre, but its chief importance was as a supplier of coal to London and North Sea towns. The Newcastle merchants or Hostmen maintained a monopoly of the trade from 1220 until the 18th century.

During the early 19th century the section of the town on the plateau was drastically rebuilt, and there are some fine examples of Regency architecture from this period, such as the curvilinear Grey Street (1834–39).

### The castle, cathedral, and churches

Although nothing of the Norman castle itself survives, remains of the Norman wall are still to be seen. The keep was built by Henry II between 1172 and 1177. The original appearance of the building has been entirely altered by battlements constructed in 1810. The great hall of the castle has a modern roof, but the chapel is a fine example of late Norman architecture.

St Nicholas Cathedral was formerly the parish church of Newcastle. Tradition has it that the church of St Nicholas was founded in 1091, but it is believed that a church was standing on the site long before then. The Norman church was destroyed by fire in 1216 and was replaced by a building in the Early English style. The church as it is today is mainly the work of 14th-century builders, with the exception of the Perpendicular tower and steeple, built about 1430.

St Mary's Roman Catholic cathedral was built in 1844 to a design by Augustus Pugin, and its tall, graceful spire was added in 1872. Other churches include All Saints' church, completed in 1796 on the site of an earlier church; St Andrew's church, dating from the middle of the 12th century; the church of St John the Baptist, dating mainly from the 14th and 15th centuries; and St Ann's church, built in 1768 with stones from part of the town wall.

### Other features

Parts are preserved of a castle built by Henry II (1172–77) on the site of the first castle (1080). There is evidence that a guildhall existed as early as the 13th century, though most of the interior of the present building dates from 1658. Nearby are Elizabethan houses of note.

The high-level bridge designed by Robert Stephenson (1849), which carries the railway and road over the river, was the largest bridge in the world at the time of its construction. The quayside with its historic buildings has been restored. Millennium Bridge – a steel footbridge that will open like the visor on a motorcycle helmet – will link the quay with the Baltic Flour Mills development at Gateshead. Newcastle's museums include the Laing Art Gallery, the Newcastle Discovery Museum, and the Hancock Museum. A genetics institute, called the International Centre for Life, was scheduled to open in the spring of 2000 in a building designed by Terry Farrell, as a Millennium Commission landmark project. The University of Newcastle was established in 1963 and the University of Northumbria in 1992.

### Newcomen, Thomas (1663–1729)

English inventor of an early steam engine. His 'fire engine' of 1712 was used for pumping water from mines until James ◊Watt invented one with a separate condenser.

### New Forest

Ancient forest in southwest Hampshire, southern England, and the largest stretch of semi-natural vegetation in lowland Britain. Lying between the River Avon on the west and Southampton Water on the east, its legal boundary encloses 38,000 ha/93,898 acres (1995). Of this area 8,400 ha/20,756 acres is enclosed plantation, and 20,000 ha/49,420 acres is common land, including ancient woodland, heath, grassland, and bog. The remainder is privately owned land and villages. More than six million tourists visit annually.

At least 46 rare plants are found in the New Forest, as well as more than half of Britain's species of butterflies, moths, and beetles.

### Features

The principal trees in the forest are oak and beech, with large patches of holly as undergrowth. The area provides a habitat for many breeds of birds, as well as badgers, foxes, and deer. New Forest ponies, a small breed said to have descended from small Spanish horses, graze in the forest. Much of the grazing is unfenced and managed as common land. Natley and Denny is a nature reserve.

The principal town in the New Forest is ◊Lyndhurst. Villages include Brockenhurst, Minstead, and ◊Beaulieu. Other features include the Knightwood Oak, with a circumference of about 7 m/22 ft, and the Rufus Stone, marking the place where William (II) Rufus is thought to have been killed in 1100.

### History

A hunting ground in Saxon times, the New Forest was reserved as Crown property in 1079 and William the Conqueror extended its area. His sons William (II) Rufus and Richard were both killed here while hunting. The forest became important as a source of timber for the building of ships in the 17th–19th centuries.

### Newham

Inner borough of east Greater London, north of the River Thames. It includes the districts of East and West Ham and the northern part of Woolwich; population (1991) 200,200

### History

From 1671 onwards the borough was associated with the Quakers – from 1704 there was a meeting house in Plaistow, which the Gurneys, Frys, and Barclays attended; it was closed in 1924.

### Features

Site of former Royal Docks: Victoria (1855), Albert (1880), and King George V (1921); post-war tower blocks (the collapse of Ronan Point in 1968 led to an official enquiry).

### Newlyn

Working seaport near Penzance, Cornwall, southwest England; population (est 1995) 4,200. The town gave its name to the **Newlyn School** of artists from 1880–90, who included Stanhope Forbes (1857–1947).

### Newmarket

Town in Suffolk, eastern England, 21 km/13 mi northeast of Cambridge; population (est 1996)

**Newmarket** The Suffolk town of Newmarket is the centre of horse racing in Britain. The headquarters of the Jockey Club were established here in 1752, in a building known as the 'Coffee Room'. The Jockey Club was formerly the governing body of flat racing in the country, but ceded control to a new body, the British Horseracing Board, in the 1990s. Bill Weils/Collections

17,100. A centre for horse racing since the reign of James I, it is the headquarters of the Jockey Club and the National Stud, and site of the National Horseracing Museum (1983). There are two racecourses, the July course and the Rowley Mile Racecourse, both owned by the Jockey Club, and lying to the southwest. The most important races held at Newmarket are the 1,000 and 2,000 Guineas, the Cambridgeshire, and the Cesarewitch.

## Newport

Unitary authority in south Wales, created in 1996 from part of the former county of Gwent; 190 sq km/73 sq mi in area; administrative headquarters ◊Newport; Population (1996) 133,300.
*Physical*
Rivers ◊Usk Ebbw, Afon Llwyd
*Features*
Legionary Museum and Roman amphitheatre at ◊Caerleon

*Industries*
Steel and aluminium production, engineering, chemicals, fertilizers, electronics.

## Newport, Welsh **Casnewydd**

Seaport and administrative centre of ◊Newport unitary authority, southeast Wales, situated on the River ◊Usk 30 km/19 mi northwest of Bristol; population (1994 est) 111,000. There is a steelworks at nearby Llanwern, and a high-tech complex at Cleppa Park. Other industries include engineering, and the manufacture of chemicals, fertilizers, aluminium, and electronics.

The Newport Transporter Bridge was built 1906.

It was formerly a walled town defended by a castle, the ruins of which still stand. St Woolos' church, the cathedral of the diocese of Monmouth, dates from Saxon times. The poet W H Davies was born here in 1871.

## Newquay

Holiday resort on the Atlantic coast of Cornwall, England, about 18 km/11 mi north of Truro; population (1991) 15,200. It is a leading centre for surfing.

## newspapers

Nearly 60% of the British public over the age of 15 reads a daily paper, over 65% read a Sunday paper, and about 90% read a regional or local paper. The oldest national newspaper currently printed in the UK is the ◊*Observer* (1791); the highest circulation UK newspaper is the Sunday ◊*News of the World* (nearly 5 million copies weekly).
*History*
The first English newspaper appeared in 1622, the *Weekly News*, edited by Nicholas Bourne and Thomas Archer. By 1645 there were 14 news weeklies on sale in London, but the first daily was the subsidized progovernment *Daily Courant* (1702). Arrests, seizure of papers, and prosecution for libel or breach of privilege were employed by the government against opposition publications, and taxes and restrictions were imposed 1700–1820 in direct relation to the growth of radical opinion. The last of these taxes, stamp duty, was abolished in 1855.

Improved printing (steam printing in 1814, the rotary press in 1857), newsprint (paper made from woodpulp, used in the UK from the 1880s), and a higher literacy rate led to the growth of newspapers throughout the 19th century. A breakthrough in printing technology was the

## Newspapers: Some key dates

**1500** English printer Wynkyn de Worde establishes the first press in Fleet Street, London. The street will become synonymous with printing and newspapers.

**1590** The first regular newspaper, the *Mercurius Gallobelgicus*, is printed in London, carrying reports of news from continental Europe.

**23 November 1646** The first advertisement in an English newspaper appears in Samuel Pecke's *Perfect Diurniall*. It is for books and Pecke charges 6d per advert.

**1701** Francis Burgess founds the *Norwich Post*, the first newspaper in England published outside London.

**2 March 1702** E Mallet launches the *Daily Courant*, the first successful daily newspaper published in England.

**1730–1807** The *Daily Advertiser* is launched in London. With its dependence on advertisements, this may be regarded as the first modern newspaper.

**1751** John Hill, writing as 'The Inspector', begins the first regular newspaper column, in the *London Advertiser and Literary Gazette*.

**25 January 1762** Anna Maria Smart is the first British woman to edit a newspaper when she becomes the editor and publisher of the *Reading Mercury* in Britain.

**1778** The *Whitehall Evening Post* in London is the first newspaper to carry regular sports reports.

**26 March 1780** The *British Gazette and Sunday Monitor* is the first Sunday newspaper in the country.

**1 January 1814** The first Welsh language newspaper, *Seren Gomer*, is launched.

**1842** The first photograph to be printed in a newspaper appears in the London paper *The Times*.

**1875** *The Times* starts publishing the first generally available daily weather forecasts.

**25 October 1881** *The Evening Illustrated Newspaper*, the first illustrated newspaper in Britain, is launched.

**1900** Cyril Arthur Pearson publishes the *Express* in Britain; one of the paper's innovations is to have news on the front page.

**1904** The British newspaper the *Daily Illustrated Mirror* is the first in the world to employ photographers on its staff and to publish photographs of news events.

**1915** The first British comic strip appears in the *Daily Mail*, Charles Folkard's 'Adventures of Teddy Tail'.

**1920** The Press Association leases telegraph wires for news distribution in Britain.

**1967** The *London Daily Express* is transmitted electronically, via telephone lines and satellite, to Puerto Rico. It is the first newspaper to be printed simultaneously in another part of the world.

**1969** The Australian businessman Rupert Murdoch buys the *Sun*, which is relaunched as a tabloid.

**1977** *Gay News* (launched 1972) is prosecuted for blasphemy in a private case brought by Mary Whitehouse.

**1981** Rupert Murdoch's News International buys *The Times*.

**August 1989** The Associated Newspapers group – *Evening Standard*, *Daily Mail* and *Mail on Sunday* – are the first to print newspapers in nonsmudge ink in Britain.

**13 December 1990** The *Northern Echo* in Darlington, England is the first British newspaper to appear on CD-ROM.

**1994** The *Daily Telegraph* launches an electronic version of the paper on the Internet.

---

Linotype machine that cast whole lines of type, introduced in Britain in 1896; and better train services made national breakfast-time circulation possible. There were nine evening papers in the London area at the end of the 19th century, and by 1920, 50% of British adults read a daily paper; by 1947, just before the introduction of television, the average adult read 1.2 daily papers and 2.3 Sunday papers.

Newspapers in the first half of the 20th century reinforced the traditional model of British society, being aimed at upper, middle, or working-class readers. During World War II and until 1958, newsprint rationing prevented market forces from killing off the weaker papers. Polarization into 'quality' and 'tabloid' newspapers followed. Sales of national newspapers that have closed, such as the *News Chronicle*, were more than 1 million; they were popular with the public but not with advertisers. Papers with a smaller circulation, such as *The Times* (founded 1785; 1998 circulation

700,000) and the *Independent* (launched 1986; 1998 circulation 250,000), survive because their readership is comparatively well off, so advertising space can be sold at higher rates. The *Guardian*

> I don't think the British public are sanctimonious. They love to read humbug, their appetite for it is limitless, but I don't believe they are actually humbugs themselves.
>
> **Lord Rothermere** British newspaper proprietor. Interviewed a month before his death in the *Daily Telegraph*, August 1998

(launched as a daily, 1855; 1998 circulation 400,000) is owned by a nonprofit trust. Colour supplements have proliferated since their introduction by some Sunday papers in the 1960s. The sales of the mass-circulation papers are boosted by lotteries and photographs of naked women; their news content is small. Some claim not to be newspapers in the traditional sense; their editorial policy is to entertain rather than inform. The daily tabloid with the highest circulation in 1998 was the *Sun*, selling 3.8 million copies.

---

*Journalism is to England what bullfighting is to Spain: a daring national sport that offers youngsters with the guts for it a chance to pull themselves up out of pedestrian destinies.*

**Irma Kurtz** US-born journalist.
*Dear London* (1997)

---

## Newstead

Village in Nottinghamshire, England, 14 km/9 mi north of Nottingham, situated in Sherwood Forest; population (1991) 1,900. A colliery lies within the village. **Newstead Abbey**, founded by Henry II in the 12th century, was granted by Henry VIII to the Byron family, who held it until 1818 when the 6th Lord Byron (the poet) sold it. The house and gardens have since been restored.

## Newton, Isaac (1642–1727)

English physicist and mathematician who laid the foundations of physics as a modern discipline. During 1665–66, he discovered the binomial theorem, differential and integral calculus, and that white light is composed of many colours. He developed the three standard laws of motion and

---

*I do not know what I may appear to the world, but to myself I seem to have been only a boy playing on the sea-shore, and diverting myself in now and then finding a smoother pebble or a prettier shell than ordinary, whilst the great ocean of truth lay all undiscovered before me.*

**Isaac Newton** English physicist and mathematician.
Quoted in L T More's *Isaac Newton*

---

the universal law of gravitation, set out in *Philosophiae naturalis principia mathematica* (1687), usually referred to as the *Principia*.

Newton's greatest achievement was to demonstrate that scientific principles are of universal application. He clearly defined the nature of mass, weight, force, inertia, and acceleration.

In 1679 Newton calculated the Moon's motion on the basis of his theory of gravity and also found that his theory explained the laws of planetary

motion that had been derived by German astronomer Johannes Kepler on the basis of observations of the planets.

Newton was born at Woolsthorpe Manor, Lincolnshire, and studied at Cambridge, where he became professor at the age of 26. He resisted James II's attacks on the liberties of the universities, and sat in the parliaments of 1689 and 1701–02 as a Whig. Appointed warden of the Royal Mint in 1696, and master in 1699, he carried through a reform of the coinage. Most of the last 30 years of his life were taken up by studies of theology and chronology, and experiments in alchemy.

Newton began to investigate the phenomenon of gravitation in 1665, inspired, legend has it, by seeing an apple fall from a tree. But he was also active in algebra and number theory, classical and analytical geometry, computation, approximation, and even probability.

## NHS, or National Health Service

One of the biggest public health organizations in the world, set up in 1948 to provide free health care for everybody in Britain. The hopes of its founders, that it would so improve public health that its cost could be easily contained, have proved in vain. Better and more expensive treatments have sent costs soaring, though it has succeeded in its basic aims. The Labour government elected in 1997 announced that it would cut waiting lists, reduce the running costs of the service, and would end the internal market introduced by the previous government.

*History and structure*

When the NHS began there were a number of counties without even one consulting physician, surgeon, or obstetrician, and many other specialities were also lacking. Now all parts of the country have good medical facilities. In spite of the existence of the NHS, some people prefer to pay into private health schemes, such as BUPA, to avoid long waiting lists for treatment.

The National Health Service Act (1946) was largely the work of Aneurin Bevan, Labour minister of health. It instituted a health service from July 1948 that sought to provide free medical, dental, and optical treatment. Successive governments, both Labour and Conservative, introduced charges for some services. The NHS offers free hospital care, but limited fees are made for ordinary doctors' prescriptions, eye tests and spectacles, and dental treatment, except for children and people on very low incomes.

In 1998 the NHS was administered by 100

health authorities in England, five in Wales, 15 health boards in Scotland and four health and social services boards in Northern Ireland. The devolution of central government power to the ◊Northern Ireland Assembly, ◊National Assembly for Wales, and ◊Scottish Parliament will have an impact on the organization of health care in these areas.

*Vital statistics*

The NHS employs about 1 million people, including part-timers. In 1996–97 it spent £34,900 million. It offers free health care to the population at a cost of 5.8% of the GDP (gross domestic product), compared with an average cost among developed countries of 7.6% of GDP. However, the number of available hospital beds in public hospitals decreased by 25% between 1971 and 1987, while the number of private hospital beds increased by 157%. On average, 317,000 beds are occupied in NHS hospitals.

## Nicholson, Ben (1894–1982)

English abstract artist. After early experiments influenced by Cubism and the Dutch De Stijl group, Nicholson developed an elegant style of geometrical reliefs, notably a series of white reliefs (1933–38). He won the first Guggenheim Award in 1957.

Son of artist William ◊Nicholson, he studied briefly at the Slade School of Art, London, and travelled in Europe and in California from 1912 to 1918. He married the sculptor Barbara ◊Hepworth in 1934 and was a leading member of the ◊St Ives School.

## Nightingale, Florence (1820–1910)

English nurse, the founder of nursing as a profession. She took a team of nurses to Scutari (now Üsküdar, Turkey) in 1854 and reduced the ◊Crimean War hospital death rate from 42% to 2%. In 1856 she founded the Nightingale School

**Florence Nightingale** A 19th-century lithograph of the English nurse, hospital reformer, and philanthropist, Florence Nightingale, known as 'the Lady of the Lamp'. She organized the barracks hospital at Scutari during the Crimean War, greatly reducing the mortality rate of wounded soldiers by improvements in nursing discipline and sanitation. Corbis

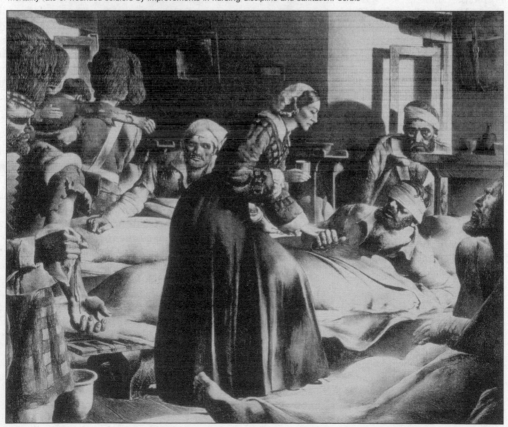

and Home for Nurses in London. A Florence Nightingale Museum occupies part of St Thomas's Hospital, in Lambeth, London.

Born in Florence, Italy, she trained in Germany and France. Florence Nightingale was involved with philanthropic and social work in England from an early age, and in 1844 she visited many hospitals and reformatories in Europe. In 1851 she trained as a nurse at an institution of the Protestant Deaconesses at Kaiserswerth, on the River Rhine, Germany, and on her return to England devoted herself to the Governesses' Sanatorium in connection with the London Institute.

At the beginning of the Crimean War, appalled by the sufferings of the wounded, Florence Nightingale volunteered her services and sailed in 1854 with a party of 38 nurses, including Sisters of Mercy from England and Ireland. Her self-sacrificing services to the wounded made her name famous throughout Europe. She wrote several pamphlets on nursing and hospitals, and established a fund in 1857 for the purpose of training nurses at the St Thomas's and King's College hospitals, London. She was the author of the classic *Notes on Nursing* (1860), the first textbook for nurses. In 1907 she was awarded the Order of Merit.

---

*It may seem a strange principle to enunciate as the very first requirement in a Hospital that it should do the sick no harm.*

**Florence Nightingale** English founder of nursing.
*Notes on Hospitals*

---

## Ninian, St (*c.* 360–432)

First Christian missionary to Scotland. He appears to have been the son of a Cumbrian chief, but was educated in Rome. He was made a bishop by the pope in 394 and sent to convert Britain. According to Bede, he converted the Picts of southern Scotland, and founded the monastery at Whithorn in about 397.

## Norfolk

County of eastern England; population (1996) 777,000; area 5,360 sq km/2,069 sq mi. It is a flat county known for the Norfolk Broads (a series of lakes famous for fishing and waterfowl, and for boating) and its windswept sandy coastline. Windmills and fine village churches feature in the rural landscape, and holiday makers and bird-watchers are drawn to the coastal resorts and nature reserves. The principal towns and cities are

◊Norwich (administrative headquarters), King's Lynn, and Great Yarmouth (the latter two are both ports); Cromer and Hunstanton are the chief resorts.

### History

The earliest record of the term 'North Folk' is dated 1040, but the county's division from Suffolk is almost certainly earlier. Norfolk suffered many incursions from the Danes.

### Physical

The whole county is low-lying, with the Broads in the east and a part of the Fens known as the Bedford Level in the west. Thetford Forest is in the south. The coastline has suffered from widespread erosion, though much land has been reclaimed from the Wash around King's Lynn. There are long stretches of sand, and few inlets; the coast is dangerous owing to numerous sandbanks. Norfolk's main rivers are the Bure, Ouse, Waveney, and Yare.

### Features

Among the oldest manmade remains in Norfolk are the Neolithic flint mines known as Grime's Graves. Notable country houses include Blickling Hall (Jacobean, built 1619–24, situated 14 km/7 mi south of Cromer), and Sandringham House (built 1869–71), the private country residence of Elizabeth II. There are many fine churches around the county, the best known being the Norman cathedral at Norwich. The village churches in the marshland areas are notable for both their grandness of scale and length of nave. The most notable examples are at Emneth, Walsoken, and West Walton (all near Wisbech); at Terrington St Clement and Tilney All Saints (near King's Lynn); at Cley, and at Walpole St Peter, which is also remarkable for its battlement-like parapets and gargoyles. At Castle Rising there is a fine Norman church and the ruins of a Norman castle. Other feudal and monastic ruins are the well-preserved castle at Norwich; Castle Acre; Bacton Abbey; and the ruins of the Augustinian priory at Walsingham containing the shrine of Our Lady of Walsingham, a medieval and present-day centre of pilgrimage. Cromer is known for its crabs, sunshine, and a pier with a theatre at the end. The north Norfolk coast is protected and nature reserves include Halvergate Marshes, Cley Marshes, and Blakeney Point, which has a seal colony. Just outside Norwich is the University of Anglia and Norwich Research Park (plant and food research).

### Economy

Norfolk is traditionally a rural county, and continues to produce cereals, root crops, turkeys, geese, and cattle. Fishing is centred on Great

Yarmouth. 'Gingerbread stone', the local building stone, is quarried near Snettisham, and limestone at Marham. Clay is dug for bricks and tiles at Hunstanton and Snettisham; flints are worked for facing walls. The marshy reedbeds supply materials for thatching. Tourism is important and many people are employed in the service sector.

## Norfolk Broads

Area of interlinked shallow freshwater lakes in East Anglia, eastern England, between Norwich, Sea Palling, and Lowestoft. The area has about 200 km/125 mi of navigable waterways, and the region is a popular tourist destination for boating and fishing.

The lakes formed some 600 years ago when medieval peat diggings were flooded as a result of a rise in the water level. They are connected by 'dykes' to the six rivers which intersect the region: the Bure, Yare, Waveney, Thurne, Ant, and Chet. The Upper Bure is where motorcruising developed and many of the smaller broads open out from here. It is an important wetland region supporting a rich variety of wildlife, including swallowtail butterflies and many breeds of birds. Reeds which grow around the margins of the lakes are used for thatching; Thurne has the most extensive reedbeds. Much of the water has been affected by excessively high levels of phosphates and nitrates draining off from agricultural land, and sewage pollution.

### Principal lakes

Hickling Broad (about 3 km/2 mi long) is the largest of the Norfolk Broads. Others include South Walsham, Wroxham, Barton, Salhouse, Blackhorse, Malthouse, Surlingham, Rockland, Horsey (the nearest to the coast in the northeast), Ormesby, Rollesby, Filby, and Somerton. Oulton is the largest of the Suffolk Broads, to the south. Breydon Water and Oulton Broad are segments of estuaries that have been converted into tidal lakes.

### Nature reserves

There are nature reserves at Hickling, Horsey, and Strumpshaw Fen, with huge wildfowl populations, including ducks, waders, and geese, and at Upton fen where wild flora are important.

## Norman

Any of the descendants of the Norsemen (to whose chief, Rollo, Normandy was granted by Charles III of France in 911) who adopted French

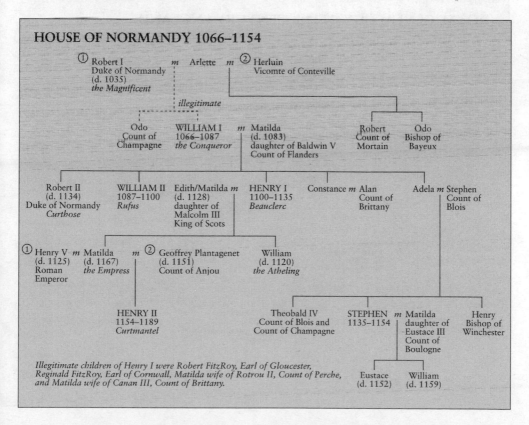

HOUSE OF NORMANDY 1066–1154

① Robert I — Duke of Normandy (d. 1035) *the Magnificent* — m Arlette — m ② Herluin Vicomte of Conteville

*illegitimate*

Odo Count of Champagne

WILLIAM I 1066–1087 *the Conqueror* — m Matilda (d. 1083) daughter of Baldwin V Count of Flanders

Robert Count of Mortain

Odo Bishop of Bayeux

Robert II (d. 1134) Duke of Normandy *Curthose*

WILLIAM II 1087–1100 *Rufus*

Edith/Matilda m (d. 1128) daughter of Malcolm III King of Scots

HENRY I 1100–1135 *Beauclerc*

Constance m Alan Count of Brittany

Adela m Stephen Count of Blois

① Henry V — m Matilda (d. 1167) *the Empress* — m ② Geoffrey Plantagenet (d. 1151) Count of Anjou
(d. 1125) Roman Emperor

William (d. 1120) *the Atheling*

HENRY II 1154–1189 *Curtmantel*

Theobald IV Count of Blois and Count of Champagne

STEPHEN 1135–1154 — m Matilda daughter of Eustace III Count of Boulogne

Henry Bishop of Winchester

*Illegitimate children of Henry I were Robert FitzRoy, Earl of Gloucester, Reginald FitzRoy, Earl of Cornwall, Matilda wife of Rotrou II, Count of Perche, and Matilda wife of Canan III, Count of Brittany.*

Eustace (d. 1152)

William (d. 1159)

language and culture. During the 11th and 12th centuries they conquered England in 1066 (under William the Conqueror), Scotland in 1072, and parts of Wales and Ireland.

They introduced feudalism, Latin as the language of government, and Norman French as the language of literature. Church architecture and organization were also influenced by the Normans, although they ceased to exist as a distinct people after the 13th century. See feature on their impact on Britain, and genealogies.

## Norman architecture

Style of architecture used in England in the 11th and 12th centuries, also known as Romanesque. Norman buildings are massive, with round arches (although trefoil arches are sometimes used for small openings). Buttresses are of slight projection, and vaults are barrel-roofed. Examples include the Keep of the Tower of London and parts of the cathedrals of Chichester, Gloucester, and Ely.

The so-called 'Jews' Houses' at Lincoln, built of stone, are among the few remaining examples of domestic architecture.

## Norman Conquest

Invasion and settlement of England by the ◊Normans, following the victory of ◊William the Conqueror at the Battle of ◊Hastings in 1066.

William, Duke of Normandy, claimed that the English throne had been promised to him by his maternal cousin Edward the Confessor (died January 1066), but the Witan (Parliament) elected Edward's brother-in-law Harold as king. Harold was killed at the Battle of Hastings in October 1066, and Edgar Atheling was immediately proclaimed king; he was never crowned, renouncing his claim in favour of William. There were several rebellions against William's rule, especially from the north, which he ruthlessly suppressed.

Under Norman rule the English gradually lost their landed possessions and were excluded from administrative posts. In 1085 William instigated the compilation of the ◊Domesday Book, a

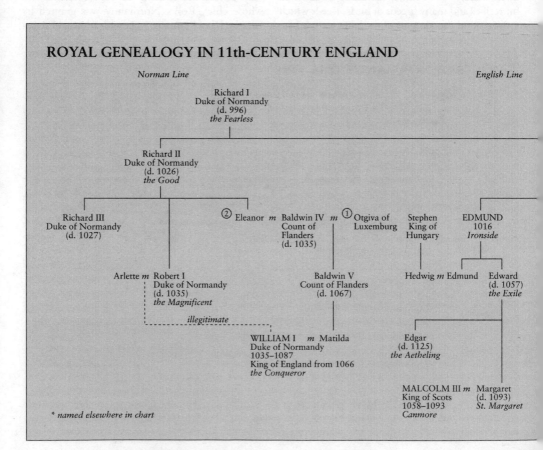

**ROYAL GENEALOGY IN 11th-CENTURY ENGLAND**

*Norman Line*                                                                                          *English Line*

Richard I
Duke of Normandy
(d. 996)
*the Fearless*

Richard II
Duke of Normandy
(d. 1026)
*the Good*

Richard III          ② Eleanor *m* Baldwin IV *m* ① Otgiva of      Stephen        EDMUND
Duke of Normandy                 Count of          Luxemburg        King of        1016
(d. 1027)                        Flanders                           Hungary        *Ironside*
                                 (d. 1035)

Arlette *m* Robert I                          Baldwin V             Hedwig *m* Edmund   Edward
           Duke of Normandy                   Count of Flanders                        (d. 1057)
           (d. 1035)                          (d. 1067)                                *the Exile*
           *the Magnificent*

                 ---- *illegitimate* ----

           WILLIAM I    *m* Matilda                  Edgar
           Duke of Normandy                          (d. 1125)
           1035–1087                                 *the Aetheling*
           King of England from 1066
           *the Conqueror*

                                          MALCOLM III *m* Margaret
                                          King of Scots    (d. 1093)
                                          1058–1093        *St. Margaret*
                                          Canmore

*\* named elsewhere in chart*

recorded survey of land and property in the English shires.

## Norman French

Form of French used by the Normans in Normandy from the 10th century, and by the Norman ruling class in England after the Conquest in 1066. It remained the language of the English court until the 15th century, the official language of the law courts until the 17th century, and is still used in the Channel Islands.

## Northampton

Market town and administrative headquarters of Northamptonshire, central England, on the River Nene, 108 km/67 mi northwest of London; population (1996 est) 192,400. The manufacture of boots and shoes was historically important. Northampton was designated a new town in 1968.

### History

Northampton was held by the Danes at the beginning of the 10th century, and they burned down the town in 1010. After the Norman Conquest, Simon de Senlis, 1st Earl of Northampton, built a castle here (now destroyed) which became a favourite resort of the Norman and Angevin kings. The town became important for shoe- and bootmaking during the Civil War, when it provided boots for Parliamentary troops. Many of Northampton's buildings were destroyed in a fire of 1675. The town expanded greatly in the 19th century with the development of road and rail links, and with the growth of the footwear industry.

### Features

St Peter's church is a fine example of late Norman work, and the church of St Sepulchre, dating from the 12th century, is one of only four surviving round churches in England. All Saints church was rebuilt following the fire of 1675. The Central Museum and Art Gallery traces the town's industrial history and includes a large collection of shoes. Other features include the County Hall (1682), the Victorian Gothic Guildhall (1864), and the Roman Catholic Cathedral, designed by Augustus Pugin.

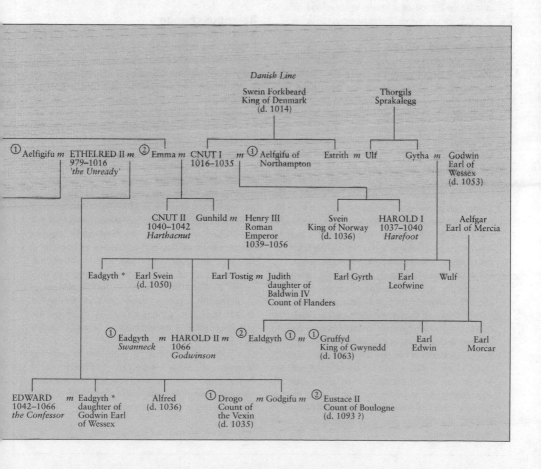

# ◆ THE NEW ORDER: THE IMPACT OF THE NORMANS ◆

Of all dates, 1066 is probably the best remembered in English history. But exactly what impact the Norman Conquest really had has always been controversial. Did it represent a clear break in the history of Anglo-Saxon England, or were the Normans quickly assimilated, simply hastening developments already underway, and even learning from them?

In a more nationalistic age than ours, many English historians felt instinctively that the virtues and institutions long thought to be characteristically English ought somehow to be traceable to a purely English past – a past that predated the arrival of the 'French' Normans. Detailed research into the survival of pre-Conquest institutions such as shire- and hundred-based local government, the common law, an efficient royal administration, and a national taxation system (Danegeld), led to the argument that the Norman Conquest did little to change an already highly sophisticated society. A less nationalistic view, however, reveals the Norman Conquest as a manifestation of wider changes in Western Europe as a whole, in social and cultural terms, in military terms, and in religious terms.

## Society and culture

Changes already taking place in Anglo-Saxon society by 1066 made it less 'English' than was previously thought. As recently as 1042, England had been ruled by a Danish king. The Danes had brought new types of landholding (and therefore social status) to parts of England, and the Anglo-Saxon term 'thane' had been replaced by the Scandinavian 'housecarl' for the warrior class, perhaps also reflecting a social change. Scandinavian influence in the east and north of the country contributed to the lukewarm support which some chroniclers noted in those regions for Harold II, the former Earl of Wessex. A surviving legal case from the reign of William I features a landowner dispossessed in the Conquest who argues that his land should be returned as he is a Dane, and was therefore neutral in the struggle between Normans and Anglo-Saxons.

The Norman Conquest brought the wholesale replacement of the Anglo-Saxon nobility, but it also brought changes in the way English society was conceived. Above all, the ancient Germanic concept of the free peasant owing personal military service to his king was finally brought to an end: after the Conquest, the Anglo-Scandinavian free peasants were reduced to the status of feudal villeins, bound to the land and excluded from military service. Elsewhere in western Europe this new conception of society, central to what we call feudalism, had developed since the 10th century; in England, the older conceptions were only swept away by the Normans.

## Military change

The events of 1066 can be seen as part of a wider colonization of the borderlands of Europe by a military elite from Western Europe. The Battle of Hastings was one of the key points of conflict between two of the three distinct military systems of 11th-century Europe. In Scandinavia and Anglo-Scandinavian England the heavy infantryman had dominated the battlefield, armed with the two-handed axe. On the Celtic fringe, mobile light infantrymen, expert with bows, were characteristic. And in feudal Western Europe the warrior par excellence was the heavy horseman, the knight. The knight's charge, with his lance held firm (couched) so as to focus the whole weight of man and charging horse at its point, was the classic tactical device of medieval warfare. Its use at Hastings can be seen in the Bayeux Tapestry. The *Anglo-Saxon Chronicle* confirms the novelty in post-Conquest England of both knights and castles, the two defining features of feudal warfare.

## Religious change

Some of the most obvious changes in post-Conquest England were in the church. Most notably, church lands exempt from taxation or military service to the Anglo-Saxon kings were brought within the feudal system of knight-service. Under Lanfranc, appointed archbishop of Canterbury in 1070, the English church itself was thoroughly reorganized. He enforced unity and discipline within the church and the monasteries under the authority of Canterbury, established regular councils and synods, and introduced a whole system of canonical law and separate courts for the church. Above all, the bishops and abbots brought in to replace Anglo-Saxon prelates re-integrated England into the cultural and intellectual mainstream of Northern France.

The ideological importance of these changes cannot be stressed enough. The late Anglo-Saxon church, despite significant reform, had become moribund in a way that was obvious to many of its members; the Norman church in post-Conquest England was perceived even by those nostalgic for the old ways as a positive, dynamic influence. Changes in the church impressed contemporaries as much as the spread of castles or the organization of the Domesday survey.

In many respects, then, it is possible to view the Norman Conquest as a reintegration of the kingdom of England into the cultural, intellectual, military, and religious world of Western Europe, itself on the verge of great changes in the 12th century.

by Simon Hall

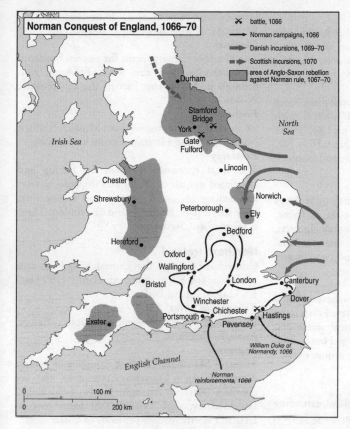

**Norman Conquest of England, 1066–70**

✗ battle, 1066
→ Norman campaigns, 1066
➤ Danish incursions, 1069–70
➤ Scottish incursions, 1070
▓ area of Anglo-Saxon rebellion against Norman rule, 1067–70

Durham

Stamford Bridge
York
Gate Fulford

North Sea

Irish Sea

Lincoln

Chester

Shrewsbury

Peterborough

Norwich

Ely

Bedford

Hereford

Oxford

Wallingford

London

Canterbury

Bristol

Winchester

Dover

Portsmouth
Chichester
Hastings
Pevensey

Exeter

William Duke of Normandy, 1066

English Channel

Norman reinforcements, 1066

0   100 mi
0   200 km

## Northamptonshire

County of central England; population (1996) 604,300; area 2,370 sq km/915 sq mi. It is a gently undulating county, beginning to rise up from the eastern flatlands of Cambridgeshire. There are many historic and attractive traditional villages. The principal towns and cities are ◊Northampton (administrative headquarters), Kettering, Corby, Daventry, and Wellingborough.

### History
At Draughton there is evidence of occupation in the early Iron Age. Prehistoric and Roman remains have been found, and Watling Street and Ermine Street both cross the county. Northamptonshire was part of the Anglo-Saxon kingdom of Mercia, and in the 11th century was part of the earldom of Tostig. In 1215 the barons besieged Northampton Castle, held by King John, and in 1264 the castle was taken from Simon de Montfort, leader of the baronial opposition to the king, by Henry III. Henry VI was defeated at Northampton during the Wars of the Roses. The Battle of Naseby, the decisive battle of the English

Civil War in 1645, in which Oliver Cromwell defeated the Royalists, was fought at Naseby 32 km/20 mi south of Leicester.

### Physical
The surface of the county is fairly level, with occasional low hills and woodland. The main rivers are the Avon, Cherwell, Leam, Nene, Ouse, and Welland, and the Grand Union Canal crosses the county.

### Features
Northamptonshire has few monastic remains, but there are Norman churches. There are market crosses at Brigstock, Helpston, Higham Ferrers, and Irthlingborough, and at Hardingstone and Geddington are two of the crosses built by Edward I in memory of his wife, Queen Eleanor. The ruins of Fotheringhay Castle, where Mary Queen of Scots was executed, are also in the county. Mansions include Althorp Park, the Spencer family home and burial place of Diana, Princess of Wales; Rushton Hall, Rockingham Castle, Castle Ashby, Dingley Hall, Deene Park, and the ruined Kirby Hall. Churches in the county typically have broached spires (an octagonal spire on a square tower). The World Conker Championships are held each autumn at Ashton, near Oundle.

### Economy
Rich pasture in the Nene and Welland valleys supports cattle rearing, and cereals and sugar beet are grown throughout the county; some 80% of the land is used for agriculture. There is a range of industries, including engineering, food processing, and printing, and Northampton is the centre of the leather trade in England. Ironstone is quarried in large quantities, also Weldon stone (a type of building stone), limestone, and clay.

## North Ayrshire

Unitary authority in western Scotland, including the Isle of Arran and smaller islands, created in 1996 from Cunninghame district in Strathclyde region; population (1996) 139,200; area 889 sq km/343 sq mi. The chief towns are ◊Irvine (administrative headquarters), Kilwinning, Saltcoats, Largs, and Kilbirnie.

## History
The Battle of Largs took place in 1263, when the Scots captured the Hebrides from the Norwegians. The Eglinton Tournament was held here in the 19th century.

## Physical
The mainland area is low-lying coastal plain rising inland to a plateau of over 305 m/1,000 ft, with Goat Fell the highest point at 874 m/2,867 ft; the islands of the Firth of Clyde are Arran, Holy Isle, and the Cumbraes. The rivers Irvine and Garnock reach the sea at Irvine.

## Features
Noteworthy are the Pencil Monument at Largs and the Scottish Maritime Museum at Irvine. There are 27 Sites of Special Scientific Interest, one National Nature Reserve, one National Scenic Area, one regional park, and two country parks.

## Economy
The towns of the Garnock Valley have suffered from de-industrialization. Irvine New Town is the focus for electronics and chemical industries. There is a nuclear power station at Hunterston. The area is within the Glasgow commuter zone.

# North Downs
Line of chalk hills in southeast England, extending from Salisbury Plain across Hampshire, Surrey, and Kent. They face the ◊ South Downs across the Weald of Kent and Sussex and are used for sheep pasture.

The downs run from Andover (on the edge of Salisbury Plain) in the west to the cliffs of South Foreland in the east. The North Downs Way is a long-distance footpath (length 227 km/141 mi) which runs along the crest of the North Downs, coinciding in places with the Pilgrims' Way (an ancient track running from Winchester to Canterbury). The Surrey Hills and the Kent Downs are both designated areas of outstanding natural beauty, and at Wye and Crundale Downs there is a national nature reserve. The rivers Stour, Medway, Darent, Mole, and Wey cut through the chalk creating natural routes and important centres, as at Guildford, Reigate, Maidstone, Ashford, and Canterbury.

# North East Lincolnshire
Unitary authority in eastern England, created in 1996 from part of the former county of Humberside; population (1996) 164,000; area 192 sq km/74 sq mi. Its principal towns and cities are ◊ Grimsby (administrative headquarters), Immingham, Cleethorpes, Humberston, New Waltham, Waltham, Healing, and Laceby.

## Physical
The Humber Estuary forms the eastern border of the authority, and the River Freshney runs through it. It contains part of the Lincolnshire Wolds.

## Features
Of interest are the Immingham Museum and the National Fishing Heritage Centre at Grimsby.

## Economy
The local economy is based on fishing and associated industries, docks and shipping services at Immingham and Grimsby, and engineering, manufacturing, chemicals, and oil refining. There is tourism at Cleethorpes.

# Northern Ireland
Constituent part of the United Kingdom; area 13,460 sq km/5,196 sq mi; population (1993 est) 1,632,000; capital Belfast.

## Towns and cities
Londonderry, Enniskillen, Omagh, Newry, Armagh, Coleraine

## Features
Mourne Mountains, Belfast Lough and Lough Neagh; Giant's Causeway; comprises the six counties (Antrim, Armagh, Down, Fermanagh, Londonderry, and Tyrone) that form part of Ireland's northernmost province of Ulster

## Exports
Engineering, shipbuilding, textile machinery, aircraft components; linen and synthetic textiles; processed foods, especially dairy and poultry products; rubber products, chemicals

## Language
English; 5.3% Irish-speaking

## Religion
Protestant 51%, Roman Catholic 38%

## Government
Direct rule from the UK from 1972, though the ◊ Northern Ireland Assembly was to have devolved

## Northern Ireland: Counties

| County | County town | Area (sq km) | (sq mi) | Population (1991) |
|--------|-------------|------|------|------------|
| Antrim | Belfast | 2,830 | 1,092 | 44,500 |
| Armagh | Armagh | 1,250 | 482 | 51,800 |
| Down | Downpatrick | 2,470 | 953 | 58,000 |
| Fermanagh | Enniskillen | 1,680 | 648 | 54,000 |
| Londonderry | Londonderry | 2,070 | 799 | 95,400 |
| Tyrone | Omagh | 3,136 | 1,211 | 158,500 |

**Northern Ireland – local government divisions**

| | |
|---|---|
| A | ANTRIM |
| AR | ARMAGH |
| BA | BALLYMENA |
| BL | BALLYMONEY |
| BN | BANBRIDGE |
| BT | BELFAST |
| C | CARRICKFERGUS |
| CA | CASTLEREAGH |
| CL | COLERAINE |
| CO | COOKSTOWN |
| CR | CRAIGAVON |
| DE | DERRY |
| DU | DUNGANNON |
| LI | LIMAVADY |
| L | LISBURN |
| MA | MAGHERAFELT |
| MO | MOYLE |
| N | NEWTOWNABBEY |
| NM | NEWRY AND MOURNE |
| NO | NORTH DOWN |

ATLANTIC OCEAN

NORTHERN IRELAND

REPUBLIC OF IRELAND

Unionist Party, as its 'First Minister', was charged with establishing, with the Irish government, a joint North–South ministerial council to cooperate and take decisions on matters of mutual interest.

## North Lanarkshire

Unitary authority in central Scotland, created in 1996 from three districts of Strathclyde region; population (1995) 326,700; area 475 sq km/183 sq mi. It is a heavily urbanized area. The chief towns are Airdrie, Coatbridge, Cumbernauld, and ◊Motherwell (administrative headquarters).

*Physical*

The land is low-lying, with the River Clyde flowing through it.

*Features*

The eight Sites of Special Scientific Interest and three country parks are important recreational areas.

*Economy*

It is an area of contrasting economic fortunes. To the north in Cumbernauld New Town, prestige industrial estates attract high technology investment, while to the south, the impacts of de-industrialization are felt, despite concerted efforts to regenerate the area. It is overwhelmingly an urban economy.

## North Lincolnshire

Unitary authority in eastern England, created in 1996 from part of the former county of Humberside; population (1996) 153,000; area 850 sq km/328 sq mi. The main towns are ◊Scunthorpe (administrative headquarters), Brigg, Barton-upon-Humber, and Epworth.

*Physical*

The Humber Estuary, containing the Isle of Axholme, forms the northern border of the authority. The Trent and Tome are the chief rivers; the Stainforth and Keadby Canal flows through North Lincolnshire.

*Features*

The southern end of the Humber Bridge is near Barton-upon-Humber. Julian's Bower, near Alkborough, is a medieval maze cut in turf; other sites of interest include Sandtoft Transport Centre with 60 trolley buses running on the centre's own circuit, and the Old Rectory at Epworth where John Wesley, founder of Methodism, was born.

powers. Northern Ireland is entitled to send 18 members to the Westminster Parliament. Local government: 26 district councils. The province costs the UK government £3 billion annually.

Under the terms of the 1998 Good Friday Agreement, Northern Ireland gained the 108-member Northern Ireland Assembly, elected by proportional representation, to exercise devolved executive and legislative authority in areas including health, social security, education and agriculture. The assembly was suspended in February 2000 following stalemate over decommissioning of weapons by the ◊IRA.

See feature on the history of Northern Ireland.

## Northern Ireland Assembly

Power-sharing assembly based in Belfast and created by the 1998 Good Friday Agreement between leaders of the contending Unionist and Irish Nationalist communities in ◊Northern Ireland. It was first elected in June 1998, came into full operation in December 1999, and in February 2000 was suspended following stalemate over decommissioning of weapons by the ◊IRA. The Assembly comprised 108 members, elected by proportional representation, and was to exercise devolved executive and legislative authority in areas including health, social security, education and agriculture.

The assembly was effectively to take over much of the work of the Northern Ireland Office; the post of Secretary of State for Northern Ireland remains. In addition, the Assembly, which has elected David ◊Trimble, leader of the Ulster

# ◆ THE ORIGINS AND HISTORY OF NORTHERN IRELAND ◆

Variously described as Ulster, the 'six counties', or 'the North', Northern Ireland is a political entity created under the UK's Better Government of Ireland Act (1920). However Northern Ireland does not correspond to the historic nine-county province of Ulster, to natural geographical boundaries, to a pre-existing administrative unit, or to a clear religious divide. The chief factor in the separation of Northern Ireland was the existence of Protestant-majority populations in Armagh, Down, Fermanagh, Londonderry, and Tyrone, who were generally opposed to inclusion in a Roman Catholic-dominated all-Ireland state. However, although leading unionist politicians persisted in calling the province 'a Protestant state for a Protestant people', from the outset it contained a substantial one-third Catholic minority which now exceeds 40%. Protestants are a considerable majority in the northern and eastern parts of Northern Ireland; Catholic pluralities exist in the west and south. In many districts, especially in rural areas, Protestants and Catholics reside in close physical proximity. However, in cities, notably Londonderry (Derry) and Belfast, residential segregation is the norm.

## Partition

The formation of Northern Ireland was controversial, as nationalists working towards home rule for Ireland as a whole rejected the concept of two Irelands. In 1912 almost half a million men and women signed the Ulster covenants, pledging armed resistance to home rule. In 1914, despite unionist opposition, the third home rule bill was passed. However, its enactment was suspended following the outbreak of World War I and superseded in the south by demands for a republic. Ulster unionists never sought a separate parliament, but the 1920 Better Government of Ireland Act, passed by a Conservative-dominated coalition government, established two subsidiary jurisdictions of Northern and Southern Ireland with an overarching Council of Ireland (moribund from its inception).

In 1921 the Anglo-Irish Treaty, which set up the Irish Free State within the British Commonwealth, confirmed the separation of the six northern Protestant-majority counties. Ironically, although bitterly opposed to home rule, Northern Ireland became the only part of Ireland to be given this form of government.

Partition was not accepted by nationalists, and in southern Ireland articles of the Irish constitution (1937), which renamed the Irish Free State as Éire, staked its territorial claim over the whole of the island. Following the declaration of the Republic of Ireland in 1948, the UK's Ireland Act (1949), recognized the Republic of Ireland but also declared that Northern Ireland would continue to remain a part of the UK until its parliament decided otherwise. Since then this assurance has been reiterated in various forms. Attempts to force unification by the militant nationalist Irish Republican Army (IRA) and its offshoots led to bombing campaigns in the 1920s, late 1930s, and mid-1950s, and finally led to the eruption of the 'Troubles' in 1968.

Northern Ireland enjoyed a considerable degree of stability between the beginning of the 1920s and the late 1960s. Yet, underneath the surface, the region experienced political and economic problems. Its chief industries, shipbuilding, engineering, textile production, and agriculture, suffered during the inter-war years. After 1945 Northern Ireland's economy was relatively buoyant until the later 1960s and its people benefited from the UK's social welfare schemes. The confluence of structural changes in the economy and the 'Troubles' led to high levels of unemployment, especially in the western, more Catholic, portion of the province but Northern Ireland had higher per capita standards of living than the Republic of Ireland until the mid-1980s, after which the gap closed rapidly and the relative positions were reversed.

## Civil rights movement

Ulster Unionists never felt entirely secure as London governments seem to temporize about the future of the province; in.1940 Winston Churchill offered to end partition if Éire dropped its neutrality and entered World War II. Terence O'Neill, prime minister of Northern Ireland 1963–69, gave the regime a more conciliatory image through his overtures to the Republic of Ireland, and unsuccessful attempts to extend the franchise of Catholics. Although these gestures were welcomed in London, they met with criticism within Ulster Unionism. However, the real challenge to the Protestant regime came from the Northern Ireland Civil Rights Association (NICRA), founded in 1967, which wanted the government's good intentions translated into positive actions for the improvement of Catholic rights. It demanded reforms such as 'one person, one vote' in local government elections, equal rights in the allocation of council housing, and an end to discrimination in the public employment sector.

## The 'Troubles' begin

Unionist reluctance to redress grievances prompted the NICRA to stage a series of marches 1968–69; these were disrupted by hostile Protestant mobs, sometimes abetted by the police. On 25 August 1969 the British cabinet responded to the unrest by sending peace-keeping troops to Northern Ireland. De-stabilization followed rapidly. The UK government attempted to defuse the civil disorder, creating commissions to investigate the riots and their underlying causes.

In mid-1971 the republican movement revived its military campaign against partition, and the UK government responded with the implementation of internment, imprisoning suspected terrorists without trial; open warfare on the streets of Belfast followed. On 24 March 1972 the Northern Ireland parliament was suspended, and government passed directly to Westminster through the secretary of state for Northern Ireland, and the Northern Ireland Office. IRA attacks in Northern Ireland and mainland Britain expanded. The UK government attempted to conciliate Catholic opinion in 1972 by introducing 'special category' status for some prisoners, holding secret talks in London with IRA representatives, and guaranteeing the constitutional position of Northern Ireland while recognising an 'Irish dimension'. Meanwhile opposition to the republican movement had emerged in the shape of the Protestant paramilitary Ulster Defence Association. Now both communities possessed an armed, potentially aggressive force and a wave of sectarian, reprisal killings followed.

## London–Dublin initiatives

In December 1973 the Sunningdale Agreement between the UK and Irish governments, and the Northern Ireland executive, provided for a devolved power-sharing executive. The executive, composed of Ulster Unionists, the Alliance Party, and the mainly Catholic Social Democratic and Labour Party (SDLP), was established on 1 January 1974 and headed a new Northern Ireland assembly. However a general strike on 14 May by the Ulster Workers' Council, opposed to the Sunningdale Agreement, forced the executive to resign on 28 May and control returned to Westminster.

After Margaret Thatcher became prime minister of the UK in May 1979, regular meetings began between the prime ministers of the UK and the Republic of Ireland, which formed frameworks for cooperation, largely by-passing the political leaders, particularly unionists, in Northern Ireland. However, this process received a setback in the spring and summer of 1971 when republican prisoners staged a hunger strike over the refusal to grant new prisoners 'special category' status, ending with several deaths and retaliation by republican paramilitaries on mainland Britain. In November 1985 the Anglo-Irish Agreement, which gave the Republic a consultative role in the affairs of Northern Ireland, heralded a new era of cooperation between London and Dublin. It also caused the mass resignation of Ulster Unionist members of Parliament.

## Progress towards peace

In December 1993 another increment in the London–Dublin relationship was reached with the Downing Street Declaration, which set out general principles for holding all-party talks on securing peace in Northern Ireland. IRA ceasefires followed in August 1994 and in May 1997. Multi-party talks from February 1998, culminated in the 1998 Good Friday (Belfast) agreement. Its terms included the devolution of a wide range of executive and legislative powers to a Northern Ireland Assembly, in which executive posts would be shared on a proportional basis; the establishment of a North/South Ministerial Council, accountable to the assembly and the Dáil (Irish parliament); and a British-Irish Council to bring together the two governments and representatives of devolved administrations in Northern Ireland, Scotland, and Wales. The agreement, which was overwhelmingly endorsed by polls in the north and south, was coupled to paramilitary decommissioning of weapon arsenals, and the relinquishing of the Republic of Ireland's territorial claims on the north.

The apparent spirit of cooperation was marred by a large measure of acrimony, differences of interpretation concerning the articles of the agreement, the timetable for implementation, and the persistence of violence. In late November 1999 an understanding was reached between the main parties, with the exception of the Democratic Ulster Unionists led by Ian Paisley, and devolution of ministerial powers from Westminster to Northern Ireland was enacted on 2 December. Unusually in liberal-democratic tradition, the executive consists of members committed to the abolition of Northern Ireland and those who are unwilling to countenance any change of political status. Perhaps the outcome warrants Northern Ireland's characterization as 'a place apart'. But the existence of a devolved executive hinged on a number of matters, including prominently 'de-commissioning' which remains a problem that at the time of publication had led to a suspension of the Executive and resumption of direct rule from Westminster.

by Alan O'Day

There are wetland nature reserves at Barton Waterside and Blackroft Sands.

### Economy

Local industries include steelworks, oil refining, computer equipment and electronics, and food processing.

## North Sea

Sea to the east of Britain and bounded by the coasts of Belgium, The Netherlands, Germany, Denmark, and Norway; part of the Atlantic Ocean. The Dogger Bank extends east to west with shallows of as little as 11 m/36 ft, forming a traditionally well-stocked fishing ground. In the northeast the North Sea joins the Norwegian Sea, and in the south it meets the Strait of Dover. It has 300 oil platforms, 10,000 km/ 6,200 mi of gas pipeline (gas was discovered in 1965), and fisheries (especially mackerel and herring). Overfishing is a growing problem.

### Rising sea level

A gradual lowering of the British coastline since the Ice Age has meant a gradual rise in the sea level, producing floods in 1881, 1928, 1953, and 1978. It is believed that the melting of the polar ice cap as a result of the greenhouse effect will increase this rise in sea level.

### North Sea oil

There has been a large growth in production of oil. UK reserves stand at 2 billion tonnes, which is as much as has been produced since the early 1970s. Oil reserves are forecast to last until 2020.

## North Somerset

Unitary authority in southwest England, created in 1996 from part of the former county of Avon; population (1996) 177,000; area 372 sq km/144 sq mi. It is situated southwest of ◊Bristol. The principal towns are ◊Weston-super-Mare (administrative headquarters and resort), Clevedon, Portishead, Yatton, and Congresbury.

### Physical

The Severn estuary forms the northwest border of the authority and the River Avon the northeast border. The west end of the Mendips, including Bleadon Hill (134 m/440 ft) are within the authority.

### Features

Weston Woods and Worlebury Hill are Iron Age sites near Weston-super-Mare. Clevedon Court is a fine 14th–15th-century manor house owned by the Elton family. There is an international helicopter museum at Weston-super-Mare.

### Economy

The local economy is based largely on manufacturing automotive components and rubber and plastics; tourism on the coast is also important, and an increasing number of companies are relocating to this area.

## North Uist

Island of the Outer ◊Hebrides, Western Isles, Scotland. Lochmaddy is the main port and town. There is a Royal Society for the Protection of Birds reserve at Balranald.

North Uist is connected to Benbecula to the south by the island of Grimsay and two stone causeways. The crofting population is found on the north and west coasts. The interior consists of peat bogs and many lochs. Eaval (347 m/1,138 ft), on the southeast coast, rises abruptly from the generally lowland landscape.

There are many important Iron Age sites, especially on the Machair lands of the north and west coasts. In the southwest, at Carinish, there are the ruins of a 13th-century monastery and college, Trinity Temple (1203). Balranald is home to the corncrake, one of Europe's most endangered species.

North Uist is served by car ferries to Berneray (from Otternish), Uig on Skye (from Lochmaddy), and Leverburgh on Harris.

## Northumberland

County of northeast England; population (1996) 307,400; area 5,030 sq km/1,942 sq mi. Situated on the border with Scotland, the county has a turbulent history which is reflected in its ruined castles and historic sites. With its remote and rugged landscape, its forests and moors, and its dramatic coastline, Northumberland is popular with walkers. Its chief towns and cities are ◊Morpeth (administrative headquarters), Berwick-upon-Tweed, and Hexham.

### Physical

The greater part of the county, comprising the districts of Berwick, Alnwick, and Tynedale, is rural. The Cheviot Hills, along the Anglo-Scottish border, rise to 810 m/2,657 ft; further east there are uplands rising to a height of 250–450 m/820–1,476 ft above sea-level. They dip towards a low coastal plateau, meeting the North Sea in low cliffs and shallow bays backed by sand dunes. The chief rivers are the Aln, Coquet, Rede, Till, Tweed, and upper Tyne. Kielder Water (1982) is the largest artificial lake in northern Europe. There are extensive forests in the west of Northumberland, and much of the upland is used by the army. South of the River Coquet, coal is found underneath the coastal plateau in the districts of Wansbeck, Blyth, and Castle Morpeth.

## Features

Northumberland National Park, including part of the ◊Pennine Way, lies in the west. The ◊Farne island group 8 km/5 mi east of Bamburgh is home to seal and bird colonies. Remains of Hadrian's Wall (a World Heritage site) are preserved, including Housesteads Fort, Chesters Fort, and Corbridge, the site of a Roman town; there are castles at Alnwick, Bamburgh, and Dunstanburgh. Other features include ◊Holy Island (Lindisfarne), the Thomas Bewick museum, Hexham Abbey, the walls of Berwick-upon-Tweed, Warkworth Castle with its 14th-century hermitage, and the Longstone Lighthouse from which Grace Darling rowed to rescue the crew of the *Forfarshire*. The wild white cattle of Chillingham are famous.

## Economy

Coalmining and shipbuilding have declined; tourism, agriculture (sheep, cattle, fishing), and light industries are now the basis of the county's economy.

# Northumbria

Anglo-Saxon kingdom that covered northeast England and southeast Scotland. Comprising the 6th-century kingdoms of Bernicia (Forth–Tees) and Deira (Tees–Humber), united in the 7th century, it accepted the supremacy of Wessex in 827 and was conquered by the Danes in the late 9th century. It was not until the reign of William the Conqueror that Northumbria became an integral part of England.

Influenced by Irish missionaries, it was a cultural and religious centre until the 8th century with priests such as Bede, Cuthbert, and Wilfrid.

# North Yorkshire

County of northeast England, created in 1974; population (1996) 734,700; area 8,037 sq km/3,102 sq mi. It is England's largest county. With its attractive coastline, the Yorkshire Dales and North York Moors national parks, and fine ruined abbeys, it is an important centre for tourism and walkers. The chief town is ◊Northallerton (administrative headquarters); the main resorts are Harrogate, Scarborough, and Whitby. Since April 1996 ◊York has been a separate unitary authority.

## History

Yorkshire as a whole formed part of the Brigantian kingdom with the Parisii on the Wolds and in Holderness. It was conquered by the Romans in the 1st century AD, and by the Danes in the 9th century, and came under the rule of Harold of England in 1066 after the Battle of Stamford Bridge. Large areas were devastated by the Normans. Since then the county has been the scene of many battles. During the Wars of the Roses one of the bloodiest battles ever to have been fought in Britain took place at Towton Field. During the Civil War the county was divided, and the principal battle was fought at Marston Moor, where the Royalists were defeated.

## Physical

North Yorkshire is divided into eight districts. The Pennines are in the west part of the county. There are several beautiful dales, which together constitute the Yorkshire Dales National Park, the principal ones being Swaledale, Wensleydale, Nidderdale, Airedale, and Ribblesdale. To the northeast are the Cleveland Hills and the valley of the River Esk, which flows to the North Sea; south of Esk lies Fylingdales Moor, the Hambleton Hills, and the North Yorkshire Moors, which form a national park (within which is Fylingdales radar station to give early warning – 4 minutes – of nuclear attack). From these moors, several valleys, such as Bilsdale and Farndale, run down to the Vale of Pickering, through which runs the River Derwent, which flows southwest from near the coast to join the Ouse between Selby and Goole. The county extends south of the Vale of Pickering to the Yorkshire Wolds (an area of moorland). The coast from Runswick Bay in the north to Filey Bay in the south is varied; the stretch between Whitby and Scarborough, with its high cliffs, is especially attractive.

## Features

Important monuments in the county include the great Iron Age camp at Stanwix and the Roman town at Aldborough. Among many castles the best known are Richmond, Bolton, Skipton, Knaresborough, and Scarborough. Middleham Castle was a residence of Warwick 'The King Maker'. Of the ecclesiastical remains the most important are the Cistercian abbeys of Fountains (with Studley Royal Gardens), Rievaulx, and Jervaulx; the Augustinian priories of Bolton and Kirkham; and the Premonstratensian House at Easby. Whitby has the remains of a 13th-century abbey on a 7th-century monastic site. Castle Howard, designed by Vanbrugh, has Britain's largest collection of 18th–20th-century costume. Harrogate was a fashionable spa town in the 18th century. The Battlefield Chamber at Ingleton is the largest accessible cavern in Britain.

## Economy

Alongside agriculture (cereals, dairy products, wool and meat from sheep), there is coalmining and fast-growing high-technology industries. Tourism is increasingly important, to the coastal resorts at Scarborough and Whitby, the numerous small market towns and villages within the two National Parks, and nearby towns, particularly Richmond, Ripon, Harrogate, and Pickering.

## Norwich

Historic cathedral city and administrative headquarters of ◊Norfolk, eastern England, on the River Wensum, 160 km/100 mi northeast of London; population (1991) 172,600. One of the most important of English provincial towns until the industrial revolution, Norwich has a fine Norman cathedral and castle, and more than 30 medieval churches. It preserves the most complete medieval street pattern in England, including cobbled streets and many historic buildings within its large walled centre. Known for the manufacture of mustard, it is also a market and tourist centre, with high-tech and light industries. The Millennium Commission has part-funded the creation of a new complex in the heart of the city centre, to include a library, a business and education centre, a multimedia auditorium, and a range of bars and restaurants.

### History

First fortified by the Saxons in the 9th century, Norwich was settled in medieval times by Flemish weavers and it became the centre of the worsted trade in the 14th century. As northern manufacturing towns expanded during the Industrial Revolution, Norwich saw its importance decline.

### Norwich Cathedral

The largely Norman cathedral was begun in 1096 by Bishop Losinga. It has a 15th-century octagonal spire (96 m/315 ft high), the second highest in England after that of Salisbury Cathedral. The Cathedral's cloisters, dating from 1297, are the only two-storey monastic cloisters surviving in England.

### Castle and castle museum

The imposing 12th-century castle keep stands on a mound which existed before 1100. The originally Norman structure, built soon after the Norman Conquest to dominate East Anglia, was destroyed in the Earl of Norfolk's rebellion against William I, and the present building, an almost cubic block, dates from about 1120. It was captured by Flemish forces in 1174 and by French troops in the reign of King John I. It was given to the county of Norfolk by George III and was used as a jail until 1887. Refaced in 1834–39, the keep was opened in 1894 as the Norwich Castle Museum. It contains a large collection of ceramic

teapots and the art gallery houses paintings by the **Norwich School** (John Sell Cotman and John Crome).

### Other features

The city has an irregular street plan dating from Saxon times, and some cobbled streets are preserved. Fragments of the ancient walls, which were 6 km/4 mi in circuit, remain. The Guildhall, a flint-and-stone building, dates from 1407–1413. Norwich's many medieval churches are mostly built of flint in late Decorated or Perpendicular style. The largest is St Peter Mancroft, built in 1430–1455. It has an elaborate tower and its east window contains 15th-century glass.

The 15th-century St Andrew's Hall and Blackfriars' Hall were originally the nave and chancel of the church of the Dominicans. The fine Georgian Assembly House was restored in 1950 as an arts centre. Other features include Tombland, the marketplace of the original Anglo-Saxon settlement of Norwich; the Stranger's Hall, a 14th-century merchant's house, now a folk museum; Suckling House, a 16th-century banqueting hall; the Bridewell, built in 1370, now a museum of local industries; and the 13th-century Bishop's Bridge, one of the oldest bridges in England.

The University of East Anglia (established in 1963) includes the Sainsbury Centre for Visual Arts (1978), designed by Norman Foster, which houses a collection of paintings and ethnographic art. The building was designed to display openly its steel structure, one of the first examples of its kind.

## Norwich School

English regional school of landscape painters, inspired by the 17th-century Dutch realist tradition of landscape painting, notably the work of Ruisdael. Founded in 1803, the school was made up of both professional and amateur artists and flourished until the 1830s. Its leading members were John Sell ◊Cotman and John ◊Crome.

They constituted a local school of landscape unique in the history of British art. The many minor but interesting artists of the school included Crome's son John Berney Crome, George Vincent, James Stark, Joseph and Alfred Stannard, John Thirtle, Thomas Lound, Henry Ninham, and Samuel David Colkett.

## Nostell Priory

Outstanding Palladian house in West Yorkshire, England, 8 km/5 mi east of Wakefield. It was built in 1733 by James Paine for Rowland Winn, 4th Baronet, on the site of a 12th-century priory.

Later in the century the 5th Baronet commissioned Adam to add four large wings to the house. Of these only the northeast was built, as the work was curtailed when the 5th Baronet died. Nostell was given to the National Trust in 1955 by the 4th Lord St Oswald.

The state rooms, decorated by Robert Adam, Joseph Rose (1745–99), and Zucchi (1726–95), contain notable pictures and ⟡Chippendale furniture that was made especially for the house. It is thought that Chippendale began his career at Nostell.

## Nottingham

Industrial city and, as Nottingham City, a unitary authority in central England, on the River Trent, 200 km/124 mi northwest of London; unitary authority area 74 sq km/29 sq mi; population (1994 est) 285,000. It was the administrative headquarters of the county of Nottinghamshire to April 1998. Industries include tourism, engineering, and the manufacture of bicycles, textiles, knitwear, pharmaceuticals, tobacco, lace, hosiery, and electronics. The English Civil War began here in 1642, and the city expanded rapidly in the late 18th century as a centre of the lace industry.

### Features

Among the city's cultural attractions are the Nottingham Playhouse (1963), the Theatre Royal (1866), the Royal Concert Hall (1982), and the Castle Museum. There are two universities, the University of Nottingham (1881) and the Nottingham Trent University (1992), formerly the Trent Polytechnic. The Goose Fair, dating from the Middle Ages, is held here every October. The National Water Sports Centre is located to the east of the city, near the village of Holme Pierrepont. A Tudor mansion, Holme Pierrepont Hall, is also situated in the village. Nottingham has a racecourse, and test matches are played on the Trent Bridge cricket ground. The Harvey Haddon sports stadium opened in 1964.

### Nottingham Castle

The heavily restored 13th-century gatehouse is all that remains of the original castle. Built on Castle Rock 40 m/130 ft above the city soon after the Norman Conquest, the castle became a royal palace and fortress, but it was dismantled after the Civil War in 1651. A mansion was built on the site during 1674–78, but was burned during riots in 1831. It was restored and opened as a museum in 1878 as England's first provincial museum and art gallery. The collections include examples of Nottingham alabaster carving, a local industry of the 14th and 15th centuries.

### Architectural features and museums

The 'Trip to Jerusalem' Inn, below the castle, is said to be the oldest inn in England. The church of St Mary dates from the 15th century; St Peter's church is partly 12th and partly 15th century; and the church of St Nicholas was built in 1678. The Roman Catholic cathedral of St Barnabas was designed by Augustus Pugin. Other features include the old Lace Market with 19th-century warehouses, the Lace Hall museum, the Costume Museum, and the restored Green's Mill, where the mathematician George Green was once a miller. Wollaton Park (300 ha/741 acres) includes Wollaton Hall, an Elizabethan mansion, now a natural history museum. The former home of the writer D H Lawrence is located nearby at Eastwood. Newstead Abbey, to the north of the city, was once the home of the poet George Byron. The remains of ⟡Sherwood Forest, formerly a royal forest and the legendary home of Robin Hood, also lie to the north of the city.

### Early history

From the 6th century Nottingham was a Saxon settlement known as 'Snotingham'. It was occupied by the Danes in 868, and William the Conqueror occupied the town in 1086. Richard III had his headquarters at Nottingham Castle before the Battle of Bosworth. Charles I raised his standard here in 1642, and in 1643 the town and castle were taken by the Parliamentarians.

### Industrial history

In 1589 the Reverend William Lee invented the first stocking-frame in Nottingham. Richard Arkwright introduced his first spinning-frames here in the late 18th century and James Hargreaves set up his spinning jenny in a small Nottingham cotton mill after being driven from his family home in Blackburn in the late 1760s. From the late 18th century the city's population grew rapidly with the expansion of the lace and hosiery industries. ⟡Luddite riots, caused by the introduction of machinery, took place in 1811–12 and 1816–17. In 1863 Jesse Boot, the pharmacist, took over his father's shop selling medicinal herbs, and began the manufacture of drugs in 1892.

## Nottinghamshire

County of central England, which has contained the separate unitary authority ⟡Nottingham City since April 1998; population (1996) 1,031,800; area 2,160 sq km/834 sq mi. The county contains the remains of Sherwood Forest, home of the legendary ⟡Robin Hood. Situated in England's industrial heartland, it was formerly an important centre of coal mining and industrial development, the setting for the novels of the Nottinghamshire writer D H Lawrence. The principal towns are ◊West Bridgford (administrative headquarters), Mansfield, Newark, and Worksop.

**History**
The remains of prehistoric humans have been found at Cresswell Crags. In Saxon times Nottinghamshire was part of the kingdom of Mercia, and after the Danish invasions it formed part of the Danelaw. At the time of the dissolution of the monasteries there were 16 religious houses in Nottinghamshire.

**Physical**
The county forms part of the extensive lowland to the east of the southern Pennines, the greater part being between 30 and 120 m (98 and 427 ft) above sea-level. Only in the west, around Mansfield, is there hilly country, which reaches a height of 180 m (591 ft). The coalfield belt is in the northwest. The main rivers are the Erewash Idle, Soar, and Trent.

**Features**
The remaining areas of Sherwood Forest are included in the Dukeries, an area of estates; originally 32 km/20 mi long and 12 km/7 mi wide, the forest was formerly a royal hunting ground. Newstead Abbey has the best preserved remains of the former religious houses. The

county has some fine churches, including Southwell Minster, of Norman construction. There is a D H Lawrence commemorative walk from Eastwood, where he lived, to Old Brinsley Colliery. Sporting facilities include the Nottingham Forest soccer ground and Trent Bridge cricket ground.

**Economy**
Coalmining is in decline; the local economy is based on quarrying, light engineering, and a range of manufacturing together with agriculture, orchards, and market gardening. During World War II Nottinghamshire produced the only oil out of U-boat reach, and drilling was revived in the 1980s.

## Notting Hill Carnival
Largest street festival in Europe, held in the Notting Hill area of London each August. Traditionally a celebration of the end of slavery in the West Indies, the Carnival began among the West Indian community in London in the early 1960s and today involves 70–100 bands in masquerade. Over one million people attend each year.

## Novello, Ivor stage name of Ivor Novello Davies (1893–1951)
Welsh composer and actor-manager. He wrote popular songs, such as 'Keep the Home Fires Burning', in World War I, and musicals in which he often appeared as the romantic lead, including *Glamorous Night* (1925), *The Dancing Years* (1939), and *Gay's the Word* (1951).

## Nuffield, William, 1st Viscount Nuffield (1877–1963)
English manufacturer and philanthropist. Starting with a small cycle-repairing business, in 1910 he designed a car that could be produced cheaply, and built up **Morris Motors Ltd** at Cowley, Oxford.

He endowed **Nuffield College**, Oxford, in 1937 and the **Nuffield Foundation** for medical, social, and scientific research in 1943. Baronet 1929, Baron 1934, Viscount 1938.

**Notting Hill Carnival** The principal annual festival of Britain's Afro-Caribbean community is the carnival that takes place in Notting Hill, a district of west London once heavily settled by immigrants from the West Indies. This huge event involves detailed planning, and the many music and dance troupes work for months to perfect their elaborate costumes and routines. Javed A Jafferji/Impact

# ◆ NURSERY RHYMES – ROBUST AND IRREVERENT SURVIVORS ◆

Nursery rhymes are one of the glories of children's literature, as sparky, irreverent and irrepressible today as they have always been in the past. But paradoxically few were composed with children specifically in mind. Because babies particularly like the sound of the human voice, mothers and other adults involved with looking after infants have always talked and sung to them, sometimes in order to soothe, at other times to entertain. The songs and rhymes used on these occasions have varied from family to family. Today they might include television jingles, football chants, and pop songs, chosen, as in the past, because they are the first things that come to mind rather than because they are particularly suitable for young children.

> *Curly locks, curly locks,*
> *Wilt thou be mine?*
> *Thou shalt not wash dishes,*
> *Nor yet feed the swine*
> *But sit on a cushion*
> *And sew a fine seam*
> *And dine upon strawberries,*
> *Sugar and cream.*

Historically, such scraps came from different sources. To quote Peter and Iona Opie, the world's leading authorities on this topic, nursery rhymes originated from 'unrelated snatches of worldly songs, adult jests, lampoons, proverbial maxims, charms, and country ballads.' Infants usually forget most early songs and chants over the years, but sometimes particular family favourites will stick in the memory. The sole reason why today's nursery rhymes dating from the remote past managed to survive in a pre-print culture was because enough parents remembered them from their own childhood and passed them to the next generation. To quote Andrew Lang, a collector of nursery rhymes, they are like 'smooth stones from the brook of time, worn round by constant friction of tongues long silent.'

> *Jack Spratt could eat no fat*
> *His wife could eat no lean*
> *And so between them both*
> *you see*
> *They licked the platter clean*

## The move into print

When nursery rhymes eventually made their way into print they were not always of the best quality. The earliest anthology *Tom Thumb's Pretty Song Book*, published in 1744, contained two versions still too indelicate to publish for children today. The first really comprehensive nursery rhyme anthology had to wait till 1842, when it was assembled by a folklorist named James Halliwell. But he had not reckoned on the enthusiasm with which child readers would greet his collection, even though it was not addressed to them in the first instance. In the succeeding editions he quickly brought out in order to satisfy demand, he was forced to alter some of the more racy rhymes originally included. Extra-violent rhymes and a couple with anti-Semitic themes were also dropped or cut. Subsequent anthologists generally chose from Halliwell's collection in its final edition.

Eventually every anthology was concentrating on the same old popular favourites, from 'Jack and Jill' to 'Mary had a little lamb'. But in the 1960s a new generation of tough-minded illustrators like Raymond Briggs brought back some of those older rhymes once thought too outspoken for modern children into the anthologies coming out at the time. In the public mind, however, a fixed cannon of nursery rhyme favourites had by now become well established. Since no-one was collecting any new ones from whatever modern parents were choosing to sing to infants, further developments stopped altogether.

## Still thriving in the electronic age

Having survived attacks from Puritans in the past, who did not approve of teaching nonsense to infants in place of hard common sense, nursery rhymes still seem strong enough to continue to thrive in a world of video and computers. Their long-term appeal is not based on any far-fetched theory, like the idea that nursery rhymes once offered coded glimpses from British history (the notion that 'Ring-a-ring o' roses' marks a folk memory of dying from the Great Plague has long been discredited). Nursery rhymes survive because children have always liked them, whether the rhyme concerned makes sense or not (no-one for example has ever worked out what exactly 'Pop goes the weasel' is really about). As the poet Dylan Thomas wrote, 'The first poems I knew were nursery rhymes, and before I could read them for myself I had come to love just the words of them... 'Ride a cock-horse to Banbury Cross' was haunting to me who did not know then what a cock horse was or cared a damn where Banbury Cross might be.' For nursery rhymes have been chosen by, as well as for, children: a marked contrast to other literature written by adults for children, whether young readers always like it or not.

by Nicholas Tucker

## Nuneaton

Industrial town in Warwickshire, central England, on the River Anker, 15 km/9 mi northeast of Coventry; population (1991) 65,900.

The church of St Nicholas is Early English and Perpendicular, and has a square embattled tower and pinnacles. The church of St Mary the Virgin (1877) was built on the site of the ruins of a Benedictine nunnery founded in 1150, from which the town derives its name. Arbury Hall, to the southwest of the town, is a fine example of Gothic Revival architecture. The novelist George Eliot was born nearby at Astley in 1819.

## nursery rhyme

Short traditional poem or song for children. Usually limited to a couplet or quatrain with strongly marked rhythm and rhymes, nursery rhymes have often been handed down by oral tradition.

Some of the oldest nursery rhymes are connected with a traditional tune and were sung as accompaniment to ancient ring games, such as 'Here we go round the mulberry bush', which was part of the May Day festivities. See feature on the previous page on the origins of nursery rhymes.

## oak

Unofficial emblem of England, appearing as a 'national' plant on pound coins. Its folklore is confined to three areas: weather rhymes, such as 'Oak before ash, We'll have a splash'; legends concerning individual trees, for instance the **Major Oak** of Sherwood Forest where Robin Hood reputedly hid; and the wearing of an oakleaf or oakapple on **Oak Apple Day** (29 May) to commemorate the restoration of the monarchy in 1660 – Charles II had hidden in an oak at Boscobel after his defeat at the Battle of Worcester (1651).

## Oaks

Horse race, one of the English classics, run at Epsom racecourse in June, now run two days before the ♢Derby, for three-year-old fillies only. The race is named after the Epsom home of the 12th Earl of Derby.

## oast house

Traditional building containing kilns for drying hops. The hops were placed on horse-hair covered floors, which were heated from below, and the oast house was constructed to allow a constant draught of warm air to pass through and out at the top. Circular oast houses with conical roofs are seen in hop-growing districts, for example Kent, England.

## Oates, Laurence (1880–1912)

English Antarctic explorer who accompanied Robert Falcon ♢Scott on his second expedition to the South Pole. On the return journey, suffering from frostbite, he went out alone into the blizzard to die rather than delay the others.

---

*I am just going outside and may be some time.*

**Laurence Oates** English Antarctic explorer.
Last words, quoted in R F Scott's *Diary* 16–17 March 1912

---

## Oates, Titus (1648–1705)

English conspirator. A priest, he entered the Jesuit colleges at Valladolid, Spain, and St Omer, France, as a spy in 1677–78, and on his return to England announced he had discovered a 'Popish Plot' to murder Charles II and re-establish Catholicism. Although this story was almost entirely false, many innocent Roman Catholics were executed during 1678–80 on Oates's evidence.

In 1685 Oates was flogged, pilloried, and

**Oast House** With their conical roofs surmounted by wooden cowls, oast houses (kilns in which hops for beer-making were dried) are a familiar sight in the southeastern county of Kent. As local breweries declined and drinking habits changed in the 1960s, with foreign hop varieties being imported to make lager, many oast houses became redundant and were converted into highly distinctive living spaces. Corel

imprisoned for perjury. He was pardoned and granted a pension after the revolution of 1688.

## Oban

Seaport and resort in Argyll and Bute, western Scotland; population (1991) 8,200. It is an important service, tourist, and communications centre to the Hebridean islands. The main industries are whisky distilling and tweed manufacture; fishing is also carried on.

The island of Kerrera shelters Oban's harbour from the Atlantic gales. The unfinished folly McCaig's Tower is a conspicuous landmark, which overlooks the harbour.

Car and passenger ferries sail to the islands of Islay, Colonsay, Gigha, Coll, Tiree, Mull, Lismore, Barra, and South Uist and to Kennacraig, Argyll, and Bute on the mainland.

## Occam or Ockham, William of (c. 1300–1349)

English philosopher and scholastic logician who revived the fundamentals of nominalism (the theory that denies that universals really exist). The principle of reducing assumptions to the absolute minimum is known as **Occam's razor**. He was imprisoned in Avignon, France, on charges of heresy in 1328 but escaped to Munich, Germany, where he died.

## O'Connell, Daniel (1775–1847)

Irish politician, called 'the Liberator'. Although ineligible, as a Roman Catholic, to take his seat (there had been a ban on Catholics holding public office since the 'Popish Plot' allegedly discovered by Titus ◊Oates in 1678), he was elected member of Parliament for County Clare in 1828 and was instrumental in forcing the UK government to grant Catholic emancipation. In Parliament he cooperated with the Whigs in the hope of obtaining concessions until 1841, when he launched his campaign for repeal of the 1801 union with Great Britain.

In 1823 O'Connell founded the Catholic Association to press Roman Catholic claims. His reserved and vacillating leadership and conservative outlook on social questions alienated his most active supporters, who broke away and formed the nationalist Young Ireland movement.

## Offa's Dyke

Defensive earthwork dyke along the English–Welsh border, of which there are remains from the mouth of the River Dee to that of the River ◊Severn. It was built about AD 785 by King Offa of Mercia, England, and represents the boundary secured by his wars with Wales.

The dyke covered a distance of 240 km/149 mi, of which 130 km/81 mi are still standing. It consists of a large rampart and ditch, the latter usually on the Welsh side, and was laid out to take advantage of natural physical features.

## Ogham

Early Celtic alphabet, comprising in its basic form 20 letters made up of straight lines at a right angle or an oblique angle to a base line. It has been found in Cornwall, Wales, and Scotland, and dates from the 4th century AD.

## Old Bailey

Popular name for the Central Criminal Court in London, situated in a street of that name in the City of London, off Ludgate Hill.

## Old English

General name for the range of dialects spoken by Germanic settlers in England between the 5th and 12th centuries AD, also known as Anglo-Saxon.

Old English written records may be divided into three or four dialectal groups: the southern English dialects and the Anglian dialects, divided into Northumbrian (being dialects of the Angles north of the Humber) and Mercian (the dialects of the Angles of the Midlands). There were probably also East Anglian dialects, but nothing is known of their early form. Of the southern dialects the most important by far is that of Wessex, or West Saxon, which became dominant for literary purposes during the early 10th century and maintained its supremacy until the close of the Old English period. See also ◊Old English literature.

## Old English literature

Poetry and prose in the various dialects of Old English written between AD 449 and 1066. Poetry (alliterative, without rhyme) was composed and delivered orally; much has therefore been lost. What remains owes its survival to monastic scribes who favoured verse with a Christian motivation or flavour. Prose in Old English was a later achievement, essentially beginning in the reign of Alfred the Great.

The greatest surviving epic poem is ◊ *Beowulf* (c. 700), which recounts the hero's battles with mythical foes such as the man-eating Grendel and his mother. *Widsith/The Wanderer*, *Finnsburgh* (about a tragic battle), and *Waldhere* (fragments of a lost epic), all written in the mid-7th century, also belong to the earlier centuries and express the bleakness and melancholy of life. *The Battle of Maldon*, written soon after the event in 991, extols heroic values of courage in defeat.

One of the earliest attributed short poems consists of six lines by ◊Caedmon the herder, reputedly inspired to sing about the Creation by a vision. 'The Dream of the Rood' (about 698) shows the cult of the Cross, as does ◊Cynewulf's 'Elene'. Elegies, including 'The Seafarer', written before 940, express the sense of loneliness in exile and an inflexible Fate.

Prose in Old English dates from Alfred the Great's translations of St Gregory, Boethius, and Bede's *History of the English Peoples* (first published in Latin in 731, translated between 871 and 899). Historical writing began with the ◊*Anglo-Saxon Chronicle*, at first brief notes of yearly events but later a dignified and even poetic narrative. Dating from the 10th and 11th centuries are sermons by ◊Aelfric, a Dorset monk who also translated the Old Testament, and those by the prelate Wulfstan (died 1023). Some spells and riddles have also survived.

## Oldham

Industrial town in Greater Manchester, England, 10 km/6 mi northeast of Manchester, on the lower slopes of the Pennine upland; population (1991) 102,300. It was traditionally a cotton-spinning town.

In 1900 Winston Churchill was elected Conservative member of Parliament for Oldham, his first constituency.

## Old Moore's Almanac

Annual publication in the UK containing prophecies of the events of the following year. It was first published in 1700 under the title *Vox Stellarum/ Voices of the Stars*, by Francis Moore (1657–c. 1715).

## Old Sarum

Iron Age fortified hill settlement north of Salisbury, Wiltshire. Used as a fortress in Roman, Saxon, and Norman times, the settlement gained importance on the completion of a cathedral under St Osmund in 1092. A new cathedral was built in the valley in 1220 (using stones from the original), and Old Sarum was eventually abandoned.

## Old Trafford

Two sporting centres in Manchester, England. **Old Trafford football ground** is the home of Manchester United FC and was opened in 1910. The record attendance was 76,692 at an FA Semifinal match in March 1939; the capacity was later reduced to 55,800. It was used for the 1966 World Cup competition and the 1996 European Championships and has also hosted one FA Cup Final and two FA Cup Final replays. A rugby union international was staged at the stadium for the first time in November 1997 when England played New Zealand. **Old Trafford cricket ground** was opened in 1857 and has staged Test matches regularly since 1884. The ground capacity is approximately 21,000.

## Old Vic

Theatre in south London, former home of the National Theatre (1963–76). It was founded in 1818 as the Coburg. Taken over by Emma Cons in 1880 (as the Royal Victoria Hall), it became a popular centre for opera and drama, and was affectionately dubbed the Old Vic.

In 1898 Lilian ◊Baylis, niece of Emma Cons, assumed the management, and in 1914 began a celebrated series of Shakespeare productions. Badly damaged in air raids in 1940, the Old Vic reopened 1950–81. In 1963 it became the home of the National Theatre until the latter moved to its South Bank building in 1976. In 1983 the Old Vic was bought by Ed Mirvish, a Canadian entrepreneur, and was refurbished in 1985.

## Olivier, Laurence, Baron Olivier (1907–1989)

English actor and director. For many years associated with the Old Vic Theatre, he was director of the National Theatre company 1962–73 (see ◊National Theatre, Royal). His stage roles include Henry V, Hamlet, Richard III, and Archie Rice in John Osborne's *The Entertainer* (1957; filmed 1960). He directed and starred in filmed versions of Shakespeare's plays; for example, *Henry V* (1944) and *Hamlet* (1948) (Academy Award).

---

*What is acting but lying and what is good acting but convincing lying?*

**Laurence Olivier** English actor and director.
*Autobiography*

---

Olivier appeared in many films, including *Wuthering Heights* (1939), *Rebecca* (1940), *Sleuth* (1972), *Marathon Man* (1976), and *The Boys from Brazil* (1978).

The Olivier Theatre (part of the National Theatre on the South Bank, London) is named after him. He was married to the actress Vivien Leigh 1940–60, and to the actress Joan Plowright from 1961 until his death.

## Omagh

County town of County ◊Tyrone, Northern Ireland, in the foothills of the Sperrin Mountains, on the River Strule, 48 km/30 mi south of Londonderry; population (1991) 17,300.

Omagh was the scene of a terrorist attack when a republican car bomb exploded on 15 August 1998 in a busy shopping area, killing 29 people and injuring scores of others. The breakaway republican group, the Real IRA, claimed responsibility for the bombing. This tragic incident appeared to have a bonding and strengthening effect which spurred the Northern Ireland peace process forward.

## Omega Workshops

Group of early 20th-century English artists (1913–20), led by Roger ◊Fry, who brought them together to design and make interiors, furnishings, and craft objects. The workshops included members of the ◊Bloomsbury Group, such as Vanessa Bell, Duncan Grant, Wyndham Lewis, and Henri Gaudier-Brzeska.

The articles they made were often primitive – both in design and execution – and brightly coloured. Some members moved to Charleston, a house in the South Downs which they decorated and fitted out with their creations.

## Open College

A network launched in 1987 by the Manpower Services Commission (now the Training Agency) to enable people to gain and update technical and vocational skills by means of distance learning, such as correspondence, radio, and television.

## Open University

Institution established in the UK in 1969 to enable mature students without qualifications to study to degree level without regular attendance. Open University teaching is based on a mixture of correspondence courses, TV and radio lectures and demonstrations, personal tuition organized on a regional basis, and summer schools.

Announced by Harold Wilson in 1963 as a 'university of the air', it was largely created by Jennie Lee, minister for the arts, from 1965.

## opera

Italian opera became very popular among the upper classes in London at the start of the 18th century, with Handel its most prominent exponent. *The Beggar's Opera*, a ballad opera (a play interspersed with popular tunes that did not disturb the flow of the plot), had a huge success in 1728. The influence of this form continued to be felt long after, with ballads being included in various types of drama and even opera. The form was revived in the 20th century by ◊Vaughan Williams, ◊Holst, ◊Tippett, and ◊Bush.

Italian opera maintained its position and cachet throughout most of the 19th century. Opera in German began to gain ground after the first London performance of Wagner's Ring cycle in 1882. Very little opera (in the sense of drama entirely set to music) in English had been composed in the later 18th and 19th centuries, although the ballad opera did develop in complexity, with the introduction of finales, and arias borrowed from foreign opera; plots were also often borrowed from foreign sources. Several attempts were made by various companies in the mid-19th century to commission and perform full-length operas in English; however, a lack of patronage from the upper classes meant that these ventures did not last long.

In 1875 opera companies were founded by both Carl Rosa and Richard D'Oyly Carte, who produced many operas by Gilbert and ◊Sullivan. These operas had English elements (ballads and ◊glees for example), as well as elements of French operetta (which had been performed in London from the 1860s) and influences from Mendelssohn and Schubert.

English opera at the start of the 20th century was influenced by Wagner, and Ethyl Smyth's *The Wreckers* (1906) is a notable work. The changes in social conditions after World War I were partly responsible for the advent of chamber and one-act operas, as well as works written specifically for amateurs. ◊Sadler's Wells opened in 1931, presenting opera in English; the company moved to the Coliseum in 1968, and became the ◊English National Opera in 1974. The company has supported new work by British composers, and important English opera composers in the latter half of the 20th century included ◊Britten, ◊Goehr, Maxwell ◊Davies, ◊Tippett, and ◊Birtwistle.

Among the first operas produced in Scotland were those brought by the Carl Rosa company after 1877. ◊Scottish Opera was founded in 1962, and ◊Welsh National Opera in 1946.

## Opium Wars

Two wars, the First Opium War 1839–42 and the Second Opium War 1856–60, waged by Britain against China to enforce the opening of Chinese ports to trade in opium. Opium from British India paid for Britain's imports from China, such as porcelain, silk, and, above all, tea.

The **First Opium War** resulted in the cession of Hong Kong to Britain and the opening of five treaty ports. Other European states were also subsequently given concessions. The **Second Opium War** followed with Britain and France in alliance against China, when there was further Chinese resistance to the opium trade. China was forced to give the European states greater trading privileges, at the expense of its people.

## Opposition

Party in opposition to the government, usually the second largest party in the House of Commons. The leader of this party has the official title of leader of Her Majesty's Opposition and is assisted by the 'shadow cabinet', which consists of colleagues appointed by the leader to be spokesmen for the party in various policy areas. Since 1989 the leader of the Opposition has received a government salary, starting at £98,000 (from 1997). William Hague has been leader of the Opposition since 1997.

In presenting itself as an alternative government the Opposition does not normally expect to defeat the government in the House of Commons, although it sometimes seeks to do so in a 'snap' vote, but so to damage the government's credibility that the electorate will be persuaded to elect the opposition party to power at the next general election. The Opposition also seeks and sometimes succeeds in securing the modification of government policy and may resort to obstructive tactics in Parliament to demonstrate the strength of its feeling.

## Orangeman

In Northern Ireland, a member of the Ulster Protestant **Orange Society** established in 1795 in opposition to the United Irishmen and the Roman Catholic secret societies. It was a revival of the Orange Institution (founded in 1688), formed in support of William (III) of Orange, whose victory over the Catholic James II at the Battle of the Boyne in 1690 is commemorated annually by Protestants in parades on 12 July.

## Orange Prize

British literary prize of £30,000. The controversial award, established in January 1996, is open to women only, of any nationality. In its first year, it was won by British author Helen Dunmore for *A Spell of Winter*.

## Ordnance Survey, OS

Official body responsible for the mapping of Britain. It was established in 1791 as the **Trigonometrical Survey** to continue work initiated in 1784 by Scottish military surveyor General William Roy (1726–1790). Its first accurate maps appeared in 1830, drawn to a scale of 1 in to the mile (1:63,000). In 1858 the OS settled on a scale of 1:2,500 for the mapping of Great Britain and Ireland (higher for urban areas, lower for uncultivated areas).

Subsequent revisions and editions include the 1:50,000 Landranger series of 1971–86. In 1989, the OS began using a computerized system for the creation and continuous revision of maps. Customers can now have maps drafted to their own specifications, choosing from over 50 features (such as houses, roads, and vegetation). Since 1988 the OS has had a target imposed by the government to recover all its costs from sales.

## Orkney Islands

Island group and unitary authority off the northeast coast of Scotland; population (1996) 19,600; area 1,014 sq km/391 sq mi. There are over 70

**Orkney Islands** The Ring of Brogar is one of several ancient monuments on Mainland, in the Orkney Islands. It comprises a great circle of 60 prehistoric standing stones, some 27 of which remain upright. Nearby is another circle known as the stones of Stenness and the gigantic burial mound of Maes Howe. Corel

low, treeless islands in the group, several with remains of prehistoric and Norse settlements. The chief towns are ◊Kirkwall (administrative headquarters) and Stromness, both on Mainland (Pomona). The declining native population is of Scandinavian descent; in recent years the islands' remoteness from the rest of the world has attracted new settlers.

## History

The Orkneys, under the name 'Orcades', are mentioned by ancient geographical writers, including Pliny and Ptolemy. In 876 Harold I (Harald Haarfager) of Norway conquered the islands. During most of the 10th century the Orkney Islands were ruled by independent Scandinavian jarls (earls), but in 1098 became subject to the Norwegian crown and remained Scandinavian until 1468, when they were given to James III of Scotland as security for the dowry of his wife, Margaret of Denmark. In 1590, on the marriage of James VI with the Danish princess Anne, Denmark formally resigned all pretensions to the sovereignty of the Orkneys. In the mid-19th century there was a big influx of farmers from Aberdeenshire and other parts of northeast Scotland, and two world wars also brought many others to reside permanently in Orkney. Scapa Flow, between Mainland and Hoy, was a naval base in both world wars, and the German fleet scuttled itself here on 21 June 1919.

---

*Scotland is a foreign country, from their point of view.*

**Jo Grimond** British Liberal politician. On the people in his constituency of Orkney and Shetland, who voted 'no' in the Scottish devolution referendum of 1979

---

## Physical

The islands are separated from the Scottish mainland by the 11-km/7-mi-wide Pentland Firth. The surface of the islands is irregular and indented by many arms of the sea. Next to Mainland, the most important of the islands are North and South Ronaldsay, Hoy, Rousay, Stronsay, Flotta, Shapinsay, Eday, Sanday, and Westray. The highest peak is Ward Hill in Hoy, which has an elevation of 479 m/1,572 ft. The Old Man of Hoy is an isolated stack of red sandstone 137 m/450 ft high, off Hoy's northwest coast. The climate of the Orkney Islands is mild, owing to the Gulf Stream. At the season of the longest day, there is almost no darkness for about six weeks,

and during the summer solstice photographs can be taken at midnight.

## Features

Many brochs, chambered cairns, and burial mounds remain – the Neolithic dwellings of Skara Brae and the Maes Howe burial chamber, both on Mainland, are important examples. Kirkwall has the 12th-century Norse cathedral of St Magnus. Modern environmental technology is represented by the world's most productive wind-powered generator at Burgar Hill; a 300 kW wind turbine with blades 60 m/197 ft in diameter, capable of producing 20% of the islands' energy needs. There are 34 Sites of Special Scientific Interest, five Special Protection Areas, and one National Scenic Area.

## Economy

The islands have a buoyant mixed economy. While the predominant industry is agriculture (beef stock and Orkney cheese) and other 'community' industries, such as fishing, crafts, and knitwear, are important, the economic vitality of the islands is largely attributable to the development of the oil industry in the 1980s.

## Orme's Head

Limestone promontories near Llandudno, in Conwy county borough, north Wales. **Great Orme's Head**, lying to the west of Llandudno, rises to 207 m/680 ft above the Irish Sea. A cable tramway runs to the summit. The lighthouse has been converted to a hotel and there is a country park with nature trails. Bronze-Age copper mines are open to visitors. **Little Orme's Head**, 141 m/463 ft, lies to the east of Llandudno.

## Orton, Joe (1933–1967)

English dramatist. In his black comedies, surreal and violent action takes place in genteel and unlikely settings. Plays include *Entertaining Mr Sloane* (1964), *Loot* (1966), and *What the Butler Saw* (1968). His diaries deal frankly with his personal life. He was murdered by his lover Kenneth Halliwell.

## Orwell, George pen name of Eric Arthur Blair (1903–1950)

English writer. His books include the satirical fable ◊*Animal Farm* (1945) (an attack on the Soviet Union and its leader Stalin), which included such slogans as 'All animals are equal, but some are more equal than others', and the prophetic ◊*Nineteen Eighty-Four* (1949) (targeting Cold War politics), which portrays the catastrophic excesses of state control over the individual. He also wrote numerous essays. Orwell was distrustful of all political parties and ideologies and a deep sense of social conscience and antipathy towards political dictatorship characterize his work.

*Life*

Orwell was born in India, and served in Burma with the Indian Imperial Police from 1922–27, an experience reflected in the novel *Burmese Days* (1934). In horrified retreat from imperialism, he moved towards socialism and even anarchism. A period of poverty, during which he was successively tutor, teacher, dishwasher, tramp, and bookshop assistant, is described in *Down and Out in Paris and London* (1933), and also provided him with material for *The Road to Wigan Pier* (1937) and *Keep the Aspidistra Flying* (1936). In 1936 he fought on the Republican side in the Spanish Civil War and was wounded; these experience are related in *Homage to Catalonia* (1938). During World War II, Orwell worked for the BBC, writing and monitoring propaganda.

---

*A family with the wrong members in control – that, perhaps, is as near as one can come to describing England in a phrase.*

**George Orwell** English author.
*The Lion and the Unicorn* (1941)

---

## Osborne, John (1929–1994)

English dramatist. He became one of the first ◊Angry Young Men (anti-establishment writers of the 1950s) of British theatre with his debut play, *Look Back in Anger* (1956), which caught the mood of a generation disillusioned by the gulf between their expectations and the drab reality of a postwar Britain in decline. Other plays include *The Entertainer* (1957), *Luther* (1960), *Inadmissible Evidence* (1964), and *A Patriot for Me* (1965).

Osborne's plays are first and foremost character studies, although they also reflect broader social issues. Other works include *Hotel in Amsterdam* (1968), *West of Suez* (1971), *Watch It Come Down* (1976), and *Too Young to Fight, Too Old to Forget* (1985). With *Déjà-Vu* (1992) he returned unsuccessfully to Jimmy Porter, the hero of the epochmaking *Look Back in Anger*.

Osborne also formed a film company with the director Tony ◊Richardson and made highly acclaimed versions of *Look Back in Anger*, starring Richard Burton, and *The Entertainer*, starring Laurence Olivier. His adaptations for cinema include *Tom Jones* (1963), which brought him an Oscar for best screenplay, *Hedda Gabler* (1972), and *The Picture of Dorian Gray* (1973).

## Osborne House

House on the Isle of Wight, England, 1.6 km/1 mi southeast of Cowes. It was the preferred residence of Queen Victoria, for whom it was built in 1845. The house was designed by Prince Albert and Thomas Cubitt. Queen Victoria died there in 1901, and the estate passed to the Prince of Wales who, on his coronation as Edward VII in 1902, made a gift of the building and grounds to the nation, to be used as a convalescent home for officers of the Army and Navy. The state apartments are now open to the public.

## Osterley Park

House and 16 ha/40 acre estate in western Greater London, 5 km/3 mi northwest of Richmond; one of the last great houses with its estate intact in the London area. The house is Elizabethan, but was extensively remodelled into an 18th-century villa with Neo-Classical interiors by Robert ◊Adam around 1760–80.

The interior includes the Etruscan Room and the sumptuous Tapestry Room, the latter hung with 18th-century Gobelins tapestries after designs by François Boucher (1769). Osterley Park was given to the National Trust in 1949 by the 9th Earl of Derby.

## Oswald, St (c. 605–642)

King of Northumbria from 634, after killing the Welsh king Cadwallon. He became a Christian convert during his exile on the Scottish island of Iona. With the help of St ◊Aidan he furthered the spread of Christianity in northern England. Feast day 9 August.

## Ottery St Mary

Town in Devon, England, 19 km/12 mi east of Exeter, on the River Otter; population (1991) 8,100. The church of St Mary dates from 1061 and has a Norman font. The poet Samuel Coleridge was born in Ottery St Mary. The Vale of Otter is noted for its scenery and trout fishing.

Examples of Elizabethan architecture are found in the area at Cadhay and Knightstone. Escot Grange was the 'Fairoaks' of *Pendennis* by William Thackeray. An annual carnival, said to have originated in 1688, is held on 5 November.

## Oughtred, William (1575–1660)

English mathematician, credited as the inventor of the slide rule in 1622. His major work *Clavis mathematicae/The Key to Mathematics* (1631) was a survey of the entire body of mathematical knowledge of his day. It introduced the 'x' symbol for multiplication, as well as the abbreviations 'sin' for sine and 'cos' for cosine.

## Oval, the

Cricket ground in Kennington, London, the home of Surrey County Cricket Club. In 1880 it was the venue for the first Test match to be held in England (between England and Australia).

## Owen, Wilfred (1893–1918)

English poet. His verse, owing much to the encouragement of Siegfried ◊Sassoon, is among the most moving of World War I poetry; it shatters the illusion of the glory of war, revealing its hollowness and cruel destruction of beauty. Only four poems were published during his lifetime; he was killed in action a week before the Armistice. After Owen's death Sassoon collected and edited his *Poems* (1920). Among the best known are 'Dulce et Decorum Est' and 'Anthem for Doomed Youth', published in 1921. Benjamin ◊Britten used several of the poems in his *War Requiem* (1962).

In technique Owen's work is distinguished by the extensive use of assonance in place of rhyme,

**Wilfred Owen** English poet Wilfred Owen (left). Admired for the bleak realism of his World War I poetry, Owen's work exemplifies his horror at the brutalities of warfare. He fought on the Somme, won the Military Cross, and was killed in action in 1918, one week before the Armistice. Corbis

anticipating the later school of W H ◊Auden and Stephen ◊Spender.

## Oxbridge

Generic term for Oxford and Cambridge universities, the two oldest universities in the UK. They are still distinctive because of their academic and social prestige, their ancient collegiate structure, their separate entrance procedures, and their high proportion of students from private schools compared to all other higher education.

## Oxford

University city and administrative centre of ◊Oxfordshire in south central England, at the confluence of the rivers Thames (called the Isis around Oxford) and Cherwell, 84 km/52 mi northwest of London; population (1994 est) 121,000. ◊Oxford University has 36 colleges, the oldest being University College (1249). Industries include motor vehicles at Cowley, steel products, electrical goods, publishing (Oxford University Press, Blackwells), and English language schools. Tourism is important.

### Features

These include Christ Church cathedral (12th century); the Divinity School and Duke Humphrey's Library (1488); the Sheldonian Theatre, designed by Christopher ◊Wren 1663–69; the Ashmolean museum (1845); and the 17th-century Bodleian Library. Other museums include the University Museum (1855–60), designed by Benjamin Woodward, the Pitt-Rivers Museum, and the Museum of Modern Art. Features of the colleges include the 14th-century Mob Quad and library at Merton College; the Canterbury Quad (1636) and gardens laid out by 'Capability' Brown at St John's College; and Holman Hunt's *The Light of the World* in Keble College. The Bate Collection of Historical Instruments is housed at the Faculty of Music. The Botanic Gardens (laid out in 1621) are the oldest in Britain. On 1 May (May morning) madrigals are sung at the top of Magdalen College tower. St Giles fair takes place every September.

### History

The town was first occupied in Saxon times as a fording point, and is first mentioned in written records in the Anglo-Saxon Chronicle of 912. The University of Oxford, the oldest in England, is first mentioned in the 12th century, when its growth was encouraged by the influx of English students expelled from Paris in 1167. The fame of the university grew steadily, until by the 14th century it was the equal of any in Europe. As the university grew, there was increasing antagonism between it and the town. Most of the university's buildings were built during the 15th, 16th, and 17th centuries. Oxford's earliest colleges were University College (1249), Balliol (1263), and Merton (1264).

During the Civil War, the university supported the Royalist cause while the city declared for Parliament. Oxford became the headquarters of the king and court in 1642, but yielded to the Parliamentary commander in chief, Gen Fairfax, in 1646.

By the beginning of the 20th century, the city had experienced rapid expansion and industrialization, and printing and publishing industries had become firmly established. In the 1920s the English industrial magnate William Morris (1877–1963), later Lord ◊Nuffield, began a motor-car industry at Cowley, just outside the city, which became the headquarters of the Austin-Rover group.

### City layout and landmarks

The old town of Oxford is built almost entirely in the angle formed by the Cherwell and the Thames, here called the Isis. The four main roads of the town meet at the place known as Carfax (derived from Latin *quadrifurcus*, 'four-forked'). Carfax Tower, said to have been built in the reign of Edward III, may have been built at a much earlier date. It was renovated in 1896, and the curious 'Quarter Boys', a relic of the past, restored to use. Some fragments of the old city wall still remain, notably as part of the wall of Merton Gardens. West from Carfax runs Queen Street, continued as New Road. In Cornmarket Street is St Michael's church, the tower of which dates to the late 11th-century. Not far from it is the church of St Mary Magdalene, an interesting building of various dates. Nearby is the Martyrs' Memorial, a monument commemorating the martyrdom of bishops Ridley, Latimer, and Cranmer (1556), designed by Sir Gilbert Scott. South runs St Aldate's as far as Folly Bridge. Until near the end of the 18th century, an ancient water-tower, known as Friar Bacon's Study, rose over the old bridge.

Eastwards from Carfax runs the High Street, off which is the university church of St Mary the Virgin, built between the 13th and 15th centuries, except for the Baroque porch, erected by the Laud's chaplain, Dr Morgan Owen, in 1637. It was to St Mary's that the remains of Amy Robsart, wife of Robert Dudley, Earl of Leicester, were brought from Cumnor in 1560 – Dudley was suspected of murdering her; and from St Mary's

pulpit the Anglican priest and religious poet John Keble preached his sermon on national apostasy in 1833.

High Street passes over Magdalen Bridge, which commands fine views north and south, the former toward the wooded heights of Headington Hill, with St Clement's church (1828) in the middle distance, the latter toward Magdalen College School playing fields and a section of the botanic gardens. In High Street are the examination schools, used in the world wars as a military hospital, designed by Sir Thomas Graham Jackson, who also designed Oxford's 'Bridge of Sighs' (1913–14), connecting the two sections of Hertford College.

Christ Church cathedral, the smallest, but one of the most beautiful of English cathedrals, is a good example of English church architecture. The pier arches are early 12th-century work, as are the transepts and choir aisles. Originally the church of St Frideswide's Priory, it was incorporated by the English cleric and politician Thomas Wolsey into his collegiate foundation in the 16th century, and later designated the cathedral of Oxford by Henry VIII. Tom Tower contains the famous bell from which the tower gets its name; the upper part of the tower (1681–82) was designed by Christopher Wren.

## Oxford and Asquith, Earl of

Title of British Liberal politician Herbert Henry ◊Asquith.

## Oxford English Dictionary, The, OED

Multi-volume English ◊dictionary, which provides a detailed historical record of each word, with usage and senses illustrated by quotations. It is subject to continuous revision (and now computerization). Originally called the *New English Dictionary on Historical Principles*, it was first conceived by the Philological Society in 1858. The first part appeared in 1884 under the editorship of James ◊Murray and the final volume appeared in 1928.

## Oxfordshire

County of south central England; population (1996) 603,100; area 2,610 sq km/1,007 sq mi. Its gentle landscape is home to ◊Oxford, the city of 'dreaming spires', world famous for its university, the oldest in England, and fine architecture; Oxford is the administrative headquarters of the county. The other main towns are Abingdon, Banbury, Goring, Henley-on-Thames, Wallingford, Witney, Woodstock, Wantage, Chipping Norton, and Thame.

## Oxford University Colleges

### full colleges

| date[1] | college | note |
|---|---|---|
| 1249 | University | |
| 1263–8 | Balliol | |
| 1264 | Merton | |
| c. 1278 | St Edmund Hall | |
| 1314 | Exeter | |
| 1326 | Oriel | the last men-only college to go mixed, in 1984 |
| 1340 | The Queen's | |
| 1379 | New | |
| 1427 | Lincoln | |
| 1438 | All Souls | has no students – for fellows only |
| 1458 | Magdalen | |
| 1509 | Brasenose | |
| 1517 | Corpus Christi | the smallest college in terms of number of students |
| 1546 | Christ Church | |
| 1554–5 | Trinity | |
| 1555 | St John's | |
| 1571 | Jesus | |
| 1612 | Wadham | |
| 1624 | Pembroke | |
| 1714 | Worcester | |
| 1740 | Hertford | |
| 1786 | Manchester | for mature students |
| 1870 | Keble | |
| 1878 | Lady Margaret Hall | |
| 1879 | Somerville | women only up until Oct 1994 |
| 1886 | Mansfield | |
| 1886 | St Hugh's | |
| 1893 | St Anne's | |

### full colleges

| date[1] | college | note |
|---|---|---|
| 1893 | St Hilda's | women only |
| 1929 | St Peter's | |
| 1953 | St Anthony's | graduate college |
| 1958 | Nuffield | graduate college |
| 1962 | Linacre | graduate college |
| 1963 | St Catherine's | the largest college in terms of numbers of students |
| 1965 | St Cross | graduate college; date of establishment given as no charter yet granted |
| 1979 | Green | graduate college; date of establishment given as no charter yet granted |
| 1981 | Wolfson | graduate college |
| 1984 | Templeton | graduate college for management studies |
| 1990 | Kellogg College | graduate college for part-time students |

### permanent private halls

*Not affiliated to the University as full colleges, but students study for the same degrees.*

| date[1] | college | note |
|---|---|---|
| 1221 | Blackfriars | mainly for members of the Dominican Order |
| 1810 | Regent's Park | |
| 1896 | Campion Hall | mainly for members of the Society of Jesus |
| 1897 | St Benet's Hall | mainly for members of the Benedictine community |
| 1910 | Greyfriars | mainly for members of the Franciscan Order |

[1]date of college's foundation or of recognition as a full college; for permanent private halls the date of foundation is given.

## Physical

The Cotswold Hills are in the northwest of the county, the Chiltern Hills in the southeast, and part of the White Horse Hills in the southwest, containing the large Thames basin with the city of Oxford at its centre. The River Thames and its tributaries the Cherwell, Evenlode, Ock, Thame, and Windrush flow through the county.

## Features

There are several prehistoric remains in Oxfordshire, including the Rollright stones, and the Devil's Quoits. There are also several Roman villas, such as North Leigh. Few old monastic buildings or castles remain, the most important being the abbey church at Dorchester-on-Thames, and the castles at Shirburn and Broughton, near Banbury. There are remains of famous houses at Greys Court, Minster Lovell, and Rycote. Churches of note include those in Oxford itself, and those at Adderbury, Iffley, and Minster Lovell.

Other features include the Vale of the White Horse (with a chalk hill figure 114 m/374 ft, below the hill camp known as Uffington Castle); Blenheim Palace (the birthplace of Winston Churchill); Woodstock (started in 1705 by Vanbrugh with help from Nicholas Hawksmoor, completed in 1722), with landscaped grounds by Capability Brown; the early 14th-century Broughton Castle; Rousham Park (1635), remodelled by William Kent (1738–40), with landscaped garden; Ditchley Park, designed by James Gibbs in 1720; and the Manor House, Kelmscott (country house of William Morris, leader of the Arts and Crafts Movement). Winston Churchill is buried in the village of Bladon. Europe's major fusion project JET (Joint European Torus) is at the UK Atomic Energy Authority's fusion laboratories at Culham. Henley Royal Regatta is an important sporting and social event held on the River Thames each summer.

## Economy

Oxfordshire supports agriculture (cereals, sheep, dairy farming) and a variety of industries. Agricultural implements and aluminium are produced at Banbury and cars at Cowley; there are high technology and biotechnology industries, nuclear research (Harwell and Culham), printing and publishing, English-language teaching, and tourism (concentrated in Oxford).

## Oxford Street

A main road in central London; one of the capital's principal shopping thoroughfares, containing department stores such as Selfridges and John Lewis. It forms the boundary between the City of Westminster and the former borough of St Marylebone. It is crossed halfway along its length by Regent Street. Oxford Street follows the site of a Roman road that ran from London to Silchester.

The street has been known at different times as 'the way from Uxbridge', 'the road to Oxford', and 'Tyburn road' (as it led to the gallows at ◊Tyburn). It was eventually named after Edward Harley, 2nd Earl of Oxford, who married the daughter of the Duke of Newcastle, who owned land in St Marylebone.

## Oxford University

Oldest British university, established during the 12th century, the earliest existing college being founded in 1249. After suffering from land confiscation during the Reformation, it was reorganized by Elizabeth I in 1571. In 1996–97 there were 15,641 undergraduates in residence. All colleges, with the exception of St Hilda's (women only), are now coeducational. See table.

Besides the colleges, notable academic buildings are the Bodleian Library (including the New Bodleian, opened in 1946, with a capacity of 5 million books), the Divinity School, the Radcliffe Camera, and the Sheldonian Theatre.

## Packwood House

Mid-16th-century timber-framed house with 17th-century additions in Warwickshire, England, 8 km/5 mi southeast of Solihull. Packwood was given to the National Trust in 1941 and contains collections of tapestries, needlework, and furniture.

The yew topiary in the garden was designed by

**Thomas Paine** The title page of Thomas Paine's pamphlet *Common Sense*. Written in America in 1776, it advocated independence and resistance to Britain and encouraged the American Revolution. Corbis

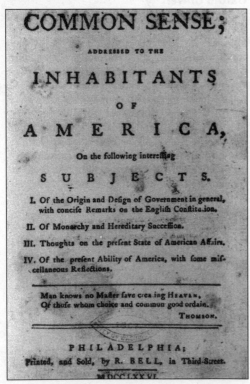

John Fetherston in the 17th century to represent the Sermon on the Mount.

## Paine, Thomas (1737–1809)

English left-wing political writer. He was active in the American and French revolutions. His pamphlet *Common Sense* (1776) ignited passions in the American Revolution; others include *The Rights of Man* (1791) and *The Age of Reason* (1793). He advocated republicanism, deism, the abolition of slavery, and the emancipation of women.

Paine, born in Thetford, Norfolk, was a friend of US scientist and politician Benjamin Franklin and went to America in 1774, where he published several republican pamphlets and fought for the colonists in the revolution. In 1787 he returned to Britain. *The Rights of Man* is an answer to the conservative theorist Burke's *Reflections on the Revolution in France*. In 1792, Paine was indicted for treason and escaped to France, to represent Calais in the National Convention. Narrowly escaping the guillotine, he regained his seat after the fall of Robespierre. Paine returned to the USA in 1802 and died in New York.

## Paisley (Roman Vanduara)

Town in Scotland and administrative headquarters of ◊Renfrewshire, 11 km/7 mi southwest of Glasgow; population (1991) 75,500. In the 19th century the town became known for its woollen shawls, with their distinctive Paisley patterns based on Indian designs, and for the production of linen, cotton, and silk. A collection of shawls is displayed in the Paisley Museum and Art Gallery. Other features include the remains of an abbey church originally established in 1163 and rebuilt in the 14th century. Glasgow airport (Abbotsinch) is nearby and the University of Paisley was established in 1992.

# Palladian

Style of revivalist architecture influenced by the work of the Italian Renaissance architect Andrea Palladio. Inigo Jones introduced Palladianism to England with his Queen's House, Greenwich (1616–35), but the true Palladian revival began in the early 18th century when Richard Boyle ◊Burlington and Colen ◊Campbell 'rediscovered' the Palladio–Jones link. Campbell's Mereworth Castle, Kent (1722–25), is an example of the style.

# Pall Mall

Main road in London, running from the southern end of St James's Street to the southern end of Haymarket. It is a centre of social clubs, including the Athenaeum, the Reform, the Travellers, and the Royal Automobile Club. The street derives its name from the French game of *paille maille* (from which croquet is believed to have developed), played here at least as early as 1635, when Pall Mall was part of St James's Park. The game was discontinued during the rule of Oliver Cromwell, and there was a considerable increase of building in the area. Pall Mall was the first London street lit by gas, in 1807.

Former inhabitants of Pall Mall include the actress (and mistress of Charles II) Nell Gwyn, the 1st Duke of Marlborough, the historian Edward Gibbon, and the painter Thomas Gainsborough.

# Palmer, Samuel (1805–1881)

English landscape painter and etcher. He was largely self-taught as an artist, though given some instruction by John Linnell, whose daughter he married. His early works, small pastoral scenes mostly painted in watercolour and sepia, have an intense, visionary quality, greatly influenced by a meeting with the aged William Blake, and the latter's engravings for Thornton's *Virgil*. From 1826 to 1835 he lived in Shoreham, Kent, with a group of artists who followed Blake, styling themselves 'the Ancients'.

His works from this period, now highly regarded, have had a distinct influence on the imaginative treatment of landscape in modern English art, and fine examples may be found in the Tate Gallery and the Victoria and Albert Museum, London, and the Ashmolean Museum, Oxford.

# Palmerston, Henry, 3rd Viscount Palmerston (1784–1865)

British politician. He was prime minister from 1855–58 (when he rectified Aberdeen's mismanagement of the Crimean War, suppressed the Sepoy Rebellion, and carried through the Second Opium War) and 1859–65 (when he almost involved Britain in the American Civil War on the side of the South). Initially a Tory, in Parliament from 1807, he was secretary-at-war 1809–28. He broke with the Tories in 1830 and sat in the Whig cabinets of 1830–34, 1835–41, and 1846–51 as foreign secretary. Palmerston became home secretary in the coalition government of 1852, and prime minister on its fall. He was popular with the people and made good use of the press, but his high-handed attitude annoyed Queen Victoria and other ministers.

# Pankhurst, Emmeline born Goulden (1858–1928)

English ◊suffragette. Founder of the Women's Social and Political Union (WSPU) in 1903, she launched the militant suffragette campaign in 1905. In 1926 she joined the Conservative Party and was a prospective Parliamentary candidate.

In 1879 she married **Richard Marsden Pankhurst** (died 1898), a lawyer, and they served together on the committee that promoted the Married Women's Property Act. From 1906, as a militant, she was frequently arrested and in 1913 was sentenced to three years' penal servitude in connection with the blowing up of Lloyd George's house at Walton.

She was supported by her daughters **Christabel Pankhurst** (1880–1958), political leader of the movement, and **Sylvia Pankhurst** (1882–1960). The latter was imprisoned nine times under the 'Cat and Mouse Act' (1913), by which women prisoners on hunger strike could be released to regain their health and then rearrested, and was a pacifist in World War I.

---

*We women suffragists have a great mission – the greatest mission the world has ever known. It is to free half the human race, and through that freedom save the rest.*
**Emmeline Pankhurst** English women's rights campaigner.
Speech, published in *Votes for Women* 25 October 1912

---

# pantomime

In the British theatre, a traditional Christmas entertainment. It has its origins in the harlequin spectacle of the 18th century and burlesque of the 19th century, which gave rise to the tradition of the principal boy being played by an actress and the dame by an actor. The harlequin's role diminished altogether as themes developed on folk tales such as 'The Sleeping Beauty' and 'Cinderella', and with the introduction of additional material such as popular songs, topical comedy, and audience participation. Popular television stars regularly feature in modern pantomime.

After World War II, pantomimes on ice became popular. The term 'pantomime' was also applied to Roman dumbshows performed by a masked actor, to 18th-century ballets with mythical themes, and, in 19th-century France, to the wordless Pierrot plays from which modern mime developed.

---

*There's no other country in the world where you have pantomime with men dressed as women and women dressed as men and everyone thinks this is perfectly suitable entertainment for children.*
**Angela Carter** English writer.
Interviewed in *New Writing* (1992)

---

## pargeting
Fine, relief-patterned plasterwork used for the external decoration of timber-framed buildings. Originating in the Elizabethan period, it is commonly found on 16th- and 17th-century buildings in East Anglia. The design was modelled on wet plaster and then colour-washed.

## parish council
Lowest, neighbourhood, unit of local government in England and Wales, based on church parishes. They developed as units for local government with the introduction of the Poor Law in the 17th century. In Wales and Scotland they are commonly called **community councils**. In England approximately 8,200 out of the 10,000 parishes have elected councils. There are 730 community councils in Wales and about 1,000 in Scotland, which, unlike their English and Welsh counterparts, do not have statutory powers.

Parish councils provide and maintain monuments, playing fields, footpaths, and churchyards, administer local charities, are elected every four years, and function in parishes of 200 or more electors. Parish councils were established by the Local Government Act 1894, but most of their legal powers were abolished by the 1972 Local Government Act.

## Park, Mungo (1771–1806)
Scottish explorer who traced the course of the Niger River 1795–97. He disappeared and probably drowned during a second African expedition from 1805–06. He published *Travels in the Interior of Africa* (1799).

Park spent 18 months in the Niger Basin while tracing the river. Even though he did not achieve his goal of reaching Timbuktu, he proved that it was feasible to travel through the interior of Africa.

## Parkinson, Norman adopted name of Ronald Smith (1913–1990)
English fashion and portrait photographer. He caught the essential glamour of each decade from the 1930s to the 1980s. Long associated with the magazines *Vogue* and *Queen*, he was best known for his colour work, and from the late 1960s took many official portraits of the royal family.

## Parkinson's law
Formula invented by the English political analyst Cecil Northcote Parkinson (1909–1993), which states that 'work expands so as to fill the time available for its completion'.

## Parliament (French 'speaking')
The supreme legislature, meeting in the Palace of Westminster, comprising the House of Commons and the House of Lords; see also ◊government.

The origins of Parliament are in the 13th century, but its powers were not established until the late 17th century. The powers of the Lords were curtailed in 1911, and the duration of parliaments was fixed at five years, but any parliament may extend its own life, as happened during both world wars.

### *History*
Parliament originated under the Norman kings as the Great Council of royal tenants-in-chief, to which in the 13th century representatives of the shires were sometimes summoned. The Parliament summoned by Simon de Montfort in 1265 (as head of government in the Barons' War) set a precedent by including representatives of the boroughs as well as the shires. Under Edward III the burgesses and knights of the shires began to meet separately from the barons, thus forming the House of Commons.

By the 15th century Parliament had acquired the right to legislate, vote, and appropriate supplies, examine public accounts, and impeach royal ministers. The powers of Parliament were much diminished under the Yorkists and Tudors but under Elizabeth I a new spirit of independence appeared. The revolutions of 1640 and 1688 established parliamentary control over the executive and judiciary, and finally abolished all royal claim to tax or legislate without parliamentary consent. During these struggles the two great parties (Whig and Tory) emerged, and after 1688 it became customary for the sovereign to choose ministers from the party dominant in the Commons. The English Parliament was united with the Scottish in 1707, and with the Irish from 1801–1922. The ◊franchise was extended to the middle classes in 1832, to the urban working classes in 1867, to agricultural labourers in 1884, and to women in 1918 and 1928. The duration of parliaments was fixed at three years in 1694, at seven in 1716, and at five in 1911. Payment of MPs was introduced in 1911. A **public bill** that has been passed is an ◊act of Parliament.

## Parliament, Houses of

Building where the legislative assembly meets. The present Houses of Parliament in London, designed in Gothic Revival style by the architects Charles ◊Barry and A W N ◊Pugin, were built in 1840–60, the previous building having burned down in 1834. It incorporates portions of the medieval Palace of Westminster.

The House of Commons debating chamber was destroyed by incendiary bombs in 1941: the rebuilt chamber (opened in 1950) is the work of architect Giles Gilbert ◊Scott and preserves its former character.

### House of Commons

The Speaker's chair is at the northern end. The benches on his or her right are occupied by the members of the party in power, those on the left by the party in opposition, the front benches being occupied by cabinet ministers and Opposition leaders respectively. In front of the Speaker's chair is the clerk's table, upon which the Mace (symbol of the Speaker's authority from the sovereign) is placed when the House sits as a house, but below which the Mace is put when the House goes into committee. Above are the public galleries. When the House is sitting a light shows at night from the clock tower.

### House of Lords

The thrones for the sovereign and consort, designed by Pugin, stand at its southern end, and in front of them is the Lord Chancellor's ◊woolsack. In front of the chancellor's woolsack are two other woolsacks on which the judges sit at the opening of Parliament. At the other end of the chamber is the bar, at which the members of

the Commons attend to hear the speech from the throne at the opening of Parliament and to hear the royal assent to acts of Parliament. See ◊government, for an outline of how the two houses operate, and for details of the reform of the House of Lords at the end of the 20th century.

## Parnell, Charles Stewart (1846–1891)

Irish nationalist politician. He supported a policy of obstruction and violence to attain ◊Home Rule, and became the president of the Nationalist Party in 1877. In 1879 he approved the ◊Land League, and his attitude led to his imprisonment in 1881. His career was ruined in 1890 when he was cited as co-respondent in a divorce case.

Parnell, born in County Wicklow, was elected member of Parliament for Meath in 1875. He welcomed Gladstone's Home Rule Bill, and continued his agitation after its defeat in 1886. In 1887 his reputation suffered from an unfounded accusation by *The Times* of complicity in the murder of Lord Frederick ◊Cavendish, chief secretary to the Lord Lieutenant of Ireland. Three years later came the adultery scandal, and for fear of losing the support of Gladstone, Parnell's party deposed him. He died suddenly of rheumatic fever at the age of 45.

---

*No man has a right to fix the boundary of the march of a nation; no man has a right to say to his country – thus far shalt thou go and no further.*

**Charles Stewart Parnell** Irish politician.
Speech in Cork 1885

---

## Parr, Catherine (1512–1548)

Sixth wife of Henry VIII of England. She had already lost two husbands when in 1543 she married Henry. She survived him, and in 1547 married the Lord High Admiral Thomas Seymour of Sudeley (1508–1549).

## Paston Letters

Correspondence of a Norfolk family, together with state papers and other documents, covering the period 1422–1509. They form an invaluable source of information on 15th-century life and manners, and on conditions during the Wars of the Roses, as well as giving vivid portraits of some members of the Paston family.

## Paycocke's

Early 16th-century merchant's house in Essex, England, 13 km/8 mi west of Colchester. It is half-timbered, and remarkable for the richness of the panelling and wood-carving inside. Lord Noel-Buxton gave Paycocke's to the National Trust in 1924, and it is now furnished with 16th- and 17th-century furniture from the Grigsby Collection.

It is thought that John Paycocke (after whom the house was named) was, in addition to being a butcher, also a clothier. There was a flourishing cloth industry in the area at the time, and the Buxton family, who later owned the house, were also clothiers.

### Peacock, Thomas Love (1785–1866)

English satirical novelist and poet. His unique whimsical novels are full of paradox, prejudice, curious learning, and witty dialogue, interspersed with occasional poems, and he satirizes contemporary ideas, outlooks, and attitudes in a prevailing comic tone. They include *Headlong Hall* (1816), *Melincourt* (1817), and *Nightmare Abbey* (1818), which has very little plot, consisting almost entirely of conversation expressing points of view on contemporary controversies and society.

### Peak District

Elevated plateau of the south ◊Pennines in northwest Derbyshire, central England; area 1,438 sq km/555 sq mi. It is a tourist region and part of it forms a national park. The highest point is Kinder Scout (636 m/2,087 ft), part of High Peak. In the surrounding area the main cities are Manchester, Sheffield, and Derby, and the town of Bakewell is located within the Peak District.

The Peak District National Park, established in 1951, was Britain's first national park. Britain's first long-distance footpath, the Pennine Way (opened in 1965), traverses much of the region, from north to south. In addition to tourism, which includes rock climbing, exploring caverns, and grouse hunting, industries include sheep farming and mineral extraction. Limestone is quarried, particularly in the vicinity of Buxton, and the area also produces potter's clay and Blue John (a type of fluorspar).

The Peak District covers the plateau north of Buxton. The rocks are formed of millstone grit and shale grit, underlain by limestone. The northern area, with underlying gritstone, is sometimes known as **Dark Peak**, while the southern part, predominantly limestone, is known as **White Peak**. High Peak is the highest elevation in the south Pennines; other peaks include Axe Edge (566 m/1,857 ft) and Mam Tor (518 m/1,699 ft), and approximately half of the **Derbyshire Dales** lie within the Peak District. The rivers Derwent,

Dove, and Wye rise in the area. The village of Chapel-en-le-Frith is known as 'the capital of the Peak'. The Peak Cavern nearby goes 450 m/1,476 ft into the limestone. Rock-climbing edges are found at Laddow in the Woodhead valley, Stanage near Sheffield, Windgather, Castle Naze, Black Rocks, and Cratcliffe Tor.

### Peake, Mervyn (1911–1968)

English writer and illustrator. His novels include the grotesque fantasy trilogy *Titus Groan* (1946), *Gormenghast* (1950), and *Titus Alone* (1959), together creating an allegory of the decline of modern civilization. He illustrated most of his own work and produced drawings for an edition of *Treasure Island* (1949), and other works. Among his collections of verse are *The Glassblowers* (1950) and the posthumous *A Book of Nonsense* (1972). He also wrote a play, *The Wit to Woo* (1957).

### Peasants' Revolt

The rising of the English peasantry in June 1381, the result of economic, social, and political disillusionment. It was sparked off by the imposition of a new poll tax, three times the rates of those imposed in 1377 and 1379. Led by Wat ◊Tyler and John ◊Ball, rebels from southeast England marched on London and demanded reforms. The authorities put down the revolt by deceit and force.

Following the plague of the Black Death, a shortage of agricultural workers resulted in higher wages. The Statute of Labourers (1351), attempted to return wages to pre-plague levels. When the third poll tax was enforced in 1381, riots broke out all over England, especially in Essex and Kent. Wat Tyler and John Ball emerged as leaders and the rebels went on to London, where they continued plundering, burning John of Gaunt's palace at the Savoy, and taking the prisons at Newgate and Fleet. The young king Richard II attempted to appease the mob, who demanded an end to serfdom and feudalism. The rebels then took the Tower of London and murdered Archbishop Sudbury and Robert Hales. Again the king attempted to make peace at Smithfield, but Tyler was stabbed to death by William Walworth, the Lord Mayor of London. The king made concessions to the rebels, and they dispersed, but the concessions were revoked immediately.

### Peel

Fishing port in the Isle of Man, 19 km/12 mi northwest of Douglas. Peel Castle was the seat of the rulers of the Norse kingdom of Mann and the Isles in the 11th century.

Within the castle walls are the ruins of an 11th-century church and round tower, a Viking palace, and a 13th-century cathedral. A causeway links the town with St Patrick's Isle, where the castle stands.

## Peel, Robert (1788–1850)
British Conservative politician. As home secretary (1822–27 and 1828–30), he founded the modern police force and in 1829 introduced Roman Catholic emancipation. He was prime minister 1834–35 and 1841–46.

Peel, born in Lancashire, entered Parliament as a Tory in 1809. After the passing of the Reform Bill of 1832, which he had resisted, he reformed the Tories under the name of the Conservative Party, on a basis of accepting necessary changes and seeking middle-class support. He fell from prime ministerial office because his repeal of the ◊Corn Laws in 1846 was opposed by the majority of his party. He and his followers then formed a third party standing between the Liberals and Conservatives; the majority of the Peelites, including Gladstone, subsequently joined the Liberals.

## peerage
The high nobility; in the UK, holders, in descending order, of the titles of duke, marquess, earl, viscount, and baron. Most hereditary peerages pass on death to the nearest male relative, but some of these titles may be held by a woman in default of a male heir; no title can be passed on to the untitled husband of a woman peer.

## Pembroke, Welsh Penfro ('land's end')
Seaport and engineering centre in Pembrokeshire, southwest Wales; population (1991) 8,650. Henry VII was born in Pembroke Castle in 1457. Tourism is a growing industry. A car ferry operates between here and Rosslare in the Republic of Ireland.

Originally founded in 1090 by the Norman Lord Grimley de Montgomery, the castle was completely rebuilt around 1207 by William Marshall, the greatest English knight of the Middle Ages, and remains largely unaltered today. There is a bridge crossing the River Cleddau, an arm of Milford Haven.

## Pembrokeshire, Welsh Sir Benfro
Unitary authority occupying the southwest tip of Wales, formerly a county (until 1974) and part of the county of Dyfed from 1974–96; population

(1996) 117,700; area 1,588 sq km/613 sq mi. It has a long coastline, much of which is protected as the Pembrokeshire Coast National Park. The main towns are ◊Haverfordwest (administrative headquarters) and Milford Haven.

*Physical*
Pembrokeshire is bounded on the south by the Bristol Channel and on the west and north by St George's Channel, into which protrudes St David's Head. The chief bays are Milford Haven and St Bride's, the coast of which is part of the national park; smaller bays include Fishguard and Newport. All have good anchorage. A number of islands lie off the coast, including Skokholm, Skomer, Caldey, Ramsey, and Grassholm, as well as many rocky islets, including the group known as the Bishops and Clerks, which has a lighthouse. The south coast is wild and precipitous, fronted by high cliffs. Inland, Pembrokeshire is undulating, consisting of green hills alternating with fertile valleys. The main relief is the Preseli Hills in the northeast; the most important rivers are the East and West Cleddau, which unite and form a navigable portion of Milford Haven.

*Features*
There are several prehistoric monuments in the authority. Other historic sites are St David's Cathedral, containing the relics of the patron saint of Wales, and Pembroke Castle, rebuilt in the 13th century.

*Economy*
There is an important oil refinery at Milford Haven; otherwise, agriculture and tourism support the local economy, with some fishing and woollen milling. Ferries sail to Ireland from Fishguard and Pembroke Dock.

## Penda (c. 577–654)
King of Mercia, an Anglo-Saxon kingdom in England, from about 632. He raised Mercia to a powerful kingdom, and defeated and killed two Northumbrian kings, Edwin in 632 and ◊Oswald in 642. He was killed in battle by Oswy, King of Northumbria.

## Penguin Books
Publishing house founded in 1935 by Allen Lane (1902–1970) and his two brothers, John and Richard, to produce paperback reprints of fiction, with a distinctive penguin logo. Within two years over 100 Penguin titles had been published at sixpence a volume (equivalent to 2.5p in decimal currency).

Early Penguins, with their characteristic orange-banded covers, have become collectors' items.

## Peninsular War

War of 1808–14 caused by the French emperor Napoleon's invasion of Portugal and Spain. British expeditionary forces under Sir Arthur Wellesley (Duke of ◊ Wellington), combined with Spanish and Portuguese resistance, succeeded in defeating the French at Vimeiro in 1808, Talavera in 1809, Salamanca in 1812, and Vittoria in 1813. The results were inconclusive, and the war was ended by Napoleon's forced abdication in 1814.

## Penn, William (1644–1718)

English member of the Society of Friends (Quakers), born in London. He joined the Society in 1667, and in 1681 obtained a grant of land in America (in settlement of a debt owed by the king to his father) on which he established the colony of Pennsylvania as a refuge for persecuted Quakers.

## Pennines, the

Range of hills in northern England, known as the 'the backbone of England'; length (from the Scottish border to the Peaks in Derbyshire) 400 km/250 mi. The highest peak in the Pennines (which are sometimes referred to as mountains rather than hills) is Cross Fell (893 m/2,930 ft). It is the watershed for the main rivers of northeast England. The rocks are carboniferous limestone and millstone grit, the land high moorland and fell.

The **Pennine Way**, Britain's first long-distance footpath (opened in 1965), extends along the length of the range.

## penny

Basic coin of English currency from about the 6th century, apparently named after Penda, King of Mercia. The penny was the only coin in general circulation until the 13th century and was defined in terms of a pound (libra) of silver, the equivalent of 240 pennies. One side showed the king's head, the other displayed the mark of the mint.

## penny post

First prepaid postal service, introduced in 1840. Until then, postage was paid by the recipient according to the distance travelled. Rowland ◊ Hill of Shrewsbury suggested a new service which would be paid for by the sender of the letter or package according to its weight. The **Penny Black** stamp was introduced in May 1840, and bore the sovereign's portrait in the manner of coins.

## Penrhyn Castle

Huge neo-Norman castle near Bangor, Gwynedd, north Wales, designed 1820–40 by Thomas Hopper (1776–1856). Penrhyn was given to the National Trust in 1951 by the Treasury, with the 17,000 ha/41,989 acre Ysbyty Estate. The castle contains 'Norman' furniture, panelling, and plasterwork designed by Hopper, and one of the best private collections of paintings in Wales.

There are also collections of dolls, stuffed birds, and animals; a railway museum in the grounds; and a Victorian walled garden.

The keep is said to have been inspired by Castle Hedingham in Essex.

## Penshurst

Village in Kent, England, northwest of Tunbridge Wells; population (1991) 1,400. **Penshurst Place**, a 14th-century manor house, was the birthplace of the Elizabethan poet Philip Sidney. The house has a Barons' Hall, Elizabethan Long Gallery, and many portraits. The village church has an ancient lych-gate.

## Pentland Firth

Channel separating the Orkney Islands from the northern mainland of Scotland. It is 20 km/12 mi long and 8–13 km/5–8 mi wide. Ferries cross the Firth, but strong tidal currents and whirlpools render navigation dangerous.

The **Pentland Skerries**, 8 km/5 mi northeast of Duncansby Head, include two islets, one of which has a lighthouse.

## Pentland Hills

Mountainous ridge in southeast Scotland running from Carnwath in South Lanarkshire unitary authority, 30 km/19 mi northeast to the city of Edinburgh. Its average height is above 300 m/985 ft, and its breadth is 6–10 km/4–6 mi. Scald Law, rising to 579 m/1,900 ft, and Carnethy Hill, at 576 m/1,890 ft, are the highest points.

A large dry ski-slope has been established at Hillend at the northern end of the ridge. Significant archaeological remains are located on the slopes of Castlelaw, height 486 m/1,594 ft.

## Penzance

Seaport and resort in Cornwall, southwest England, on Mount's Bay 38 km/24 mi southwest of Truro; population (1991) 19,700. The most westerly town in England, it has a ferry link with the Scilly Isles. It is the centre of a market-gardening and agricultural area, and early fruit, flowers, and vegetables are produced. It now incorporates the seaport of ◊Newlyn. It is known as the 'Cornish Riviera'.

### Features
Penzance has a mild climate in which palm trees flourish, and subtropical plants are grown in Morrab Gardens. There is a museum of the Royal Geological Society of Cornwall, and Penlee Park includes an art gallery and museum containing a natural history collection and paintings by members of the Newlyn School. The town overlooks St Michael's Mount in the bay.

### History
In 1332 Edward III granted Penzance a weekly market and an annual fair of seven days. In 1512 Henry VIII gave Penzance a charter granting it ship dues on condition that the town maintained the quays in repair. Another grant of a market was received in 1592 from Elizabeth I. Penzance was burned by the Spanish in 1595 and was incorporated by James I in 1614. Formerly important in the tin trade, it developed with the growth of tourism from the early 19th century, and further expansion followed the arrival of the railway in the 1850s.

The occasional pirate raids that Penzance experienced during the 17th century, due to its location on a sheltered bay on England's south-west point, made it the location for Gilbert and Sullivan's operetta *The Pirates of Penzance*.

## Pepys, Samuel (1633–1703)
English naval administrator and diarist. His *Diary* (1660–69) is a unique record of the daily life of the period, the historical events of the Restoration, the manners and scandals of the court, naval administration, and Pepys's own interests, weaknesses, and intimate feelings. Written in shorthand, it was not deciphered until 1825.

Pepys entered the Navy Office in 1660 and was secretary to the Admiralty from 1672–79. He was imprisoned in 1679 in the Tower of London on suspicion of being connected with the Popish Plot (see Titus ◊Oates). He was reinstated as secretary to the Admiralty in 1684, but was finally deprived of his post after the 1688 Revolution. He published *Memoires of the Navy* in 1690. Pepys abandoned writing his diary because he believed, mistakenly, that his eyesight was about to fail – in fact, it continued to serve him for 30 or more years of active life.

The original manuscript of the *Diary*, preserved in Cambridge together with other papers, is in six volumes, containing more than 3,000 pages. It is closely written in cipher (a form of shorthand), which Pepys probably used in case his journal

**Samuel Pepys** Portrait of the English diarist Samuel Pepys in 1679 by an unnamed artist. The private diaries of Pepys, who was an energetic public servant, express a relish for life and its full range of experiences. His account of the last great plague epidemic in 1665 and of the Fire of London in 1666 are particularly valuable as social history. Mary Evans Picture Library

should fall into unfriendly hands during his life or be rashly published after his death. Highlights include his accounts of the Great Plague of London in 1665, the Fire of London in 1666, and the sailing up the Thames of the Dutch fleet in 1667.

> *But Lord! to see the absurd nature of Englishmen, that cannot forbear laughing and jeering at everything that looks strange.*
>
> **Samuel Pepys** English diarist.
> *Diary* 27 November 1662

## Percival, or Perceval
In British legend, one of King Arthur's knights, particularly associated with the quest for the ◊Holy Grail. Based on the Welsh hero Peredur, he first appeared in Chrétien de Troyes's *Perceval, ou le conte du Graal* about 1190.

Brought up in a Welsh forest by his widowed mother, a chance meeting with some knights prompts his departure for Arthur's court. Later he is knighted, falls in love with Blanchefleur, and encounters the wounded Fisher King. His failure to ask about the lance and Holy Grail, which he sees during dinner with the Fisher King, leads to destruction and suffering.

## Percy, Henry 'Hotspur' (1364–1403)
English soldier, son of the 1st Earl of Northumberland. In repelling a border raid, he defeated the Scots at Homildon Hill, Durham, in 1402. He was killed at the Battle of Shrewsbury while in revolt against Henry IV.

## Percy, Thomas (1729–1811)
English scholar; bishop of Dromore, Ireland, from 1782. He was given a manuscript collection of songs, ballads, and romances, which became the basis of the *Reliques of Ancient English Poetry* (1765). The Percy collection renewed interest in ballads and was influential in the Romantic revival as well as inspiring Walter ◊Scott's *Minstrelsy of the Scottish Border*.

## Perpendicular
Period of English Gothic architecture lasting from the end of the 14th century to the mid-16th century. It is characterized by window tracery consisting chiefly of vertical members, two or four arc arches, lavishly decorated vaults, and the use of traceried panels. Examples include the choir, transepts, and cloister of Gloucester Cathedral (about 1331–1412); and King's College Chapel, Cambridge, built in three phases: 1446–61, 1477–85, and 1508–15.

## Perry, Fred (1909–1995)
English lawn-tennis player, the last Briton to win the men's singles at Wimbledon, in 1936. He also won the world table-tennis title in 1929. Perry later became a television commentator and a sports-goods manufacturer.

## Perth
Town and administrative headquarters of ◊Perth and Kinross, central Scotland, on the River Tay, 70 km/43 mi northwest of Edinburgh; population (1991) 41,500. It is known as the 'fair city'. Industries include whisky distilling. It was the capital of Scotland from the 12th century until 1452. James I of Scotland was assassinated here in 1437.

Reputed to have been founded by Agricola in AD 70, Perth is believed to have been occupied by the Romans for 320 years.

## Perth and Kinross
Unitary authority in central Scotland, created in 1996 from the district bearing the same name in Tayside region; population (1996) 131,800; area

5,388 sq km/2,080 sq mi. The attractive scenery of mountains and lochs, fishing, and winter sports facilities such as the Glenshee Ski Development draw visitors. The chief towns are Blairgowrie, Crieff, Kinross, ◊Perth (administrative headquarters), Pitlochry, and Aberfeldy.

*History*
Major historical events include the defeat of Macbeth at Dunsinane in 1054, the victory of the Scots under Viscount Dundee over the English at Killiecrankie in 1689, and the escape of Mary Queen of Scots from Loch Leven Castle in 1568.

*Physical*
The geological fault that gives the distinctive character to lowland and highland Scotland passes southwest–northeast through the area. The population is largely centred in the lowlands, along wide fertile valleys such as Strathearn, and the Carse of Gowrie, in the Tay river basin. To the north and west are the Grampians intersected by narrow glens with lochs in their valley floors. Among the highest elevations in the Grampians are Ben Lawers (1,214 m/3,984 ft) and Schiehallion (1,083 m/3,554 ft); in the south are the lower Ochil and Sidlaw Hills. The main rivers are the Tay, with its large estuary in the east, and the Earn, Almond, and their tributaries.

*Features*
There are many remains of prehistoric stone circles and standing stones, and several Roman sites of great interest, notably Ardoch Roman Camp, near Braco. Dunkeld Cathedral was founded in 1107, and the church of St John, Perth, in 1126. The area is particularly rich in fine mansions, such as Kinross House (17th century), designed by William Bruce, and Scone Palace (1803–08); there are also many good examples of castles, such as Grandtully (1560) and Blair (1269). Highland Games are held annually at Pitlochry. There are 111 Sites of Special Scientific Interest, six National Nature Reserves, three Ramsars (wetland sites), one Special Protection Area, and five National Scenic Areas.

*Economy*
To the north, there is afforestation and 14 hydroelectric power installations, and the natural scenery has made tourism an important part of northern Perth and Kinross' economy. In the south, agriculture plays a more central role in the local economy. Woollen manufacture and whisky distilling and blending continue.

## Peterborough
Unitary authority in eastern England, created in 1998 from part of Cambridgeshire; area 334 sq

km/129 sq mi; the main towns are ◊ Peterborough (administrative headquarters), Wittering, Old Fletton, Thorney, Glinton, Northborough, Peakirk; population (1995) 159,300

*Features*
River Nene; western margins of the Fens; St Peter's Cathedral (Peterborough), 12th century, containing Catherine of Aragon's tomb; Wildfowl and Wetlands Centre at Peakirk

*Industries*
Aluminium founding and manufacture, electronics, domestic appliances, plastics and rubber manufacture, precision engineering, telecommunications equipment, food manufacture and processing.

## Peterborough
Industrial city in eastern England, 64 km/40 mi northeast of Northampton; population (1994 est) 139,999. Part of the county of Cambridgeshire until April 1998, it now also forms part of a unitary authority of the same name. Long established as a market town on the edge of the ◊Fens, Peterborough became a major railway junction in the 19th century, with important engineering and brick industries. Since 1967 when it was declared a ◊new town, the city has grown rapidly and has undergone much urban development. Still expanding, it is a thriving engineering, business, and regional shopping centre. It also has a rich historical heritage and its fine 12th-century cathedral of St Peter is one of the most important examples of Norman architecture in Britain. Excavations at nearby Flag Fen have revealed well-preserved remains of a Bronze Age settlement. The University of Peterborough was established in 1998.

*Cathedral of St Peter*
Established on the site of two earlier monastic churches, the present cathedral was begun in 1117. The cathedral's magnificent painted wooden ceiling dates from 1220 and its impressive three-arched west front was completed in the 13th century. The cathedral contains the tomb of Catherine of Aragon, first wife of Henry VIII. In 1541 it was one of only six monastic churches to be refounded as cathedrals by Henry VIII.

## Peterloo massacre
The events in St Peter's Fields in Manchester, England, on 16 August 1819, when an open-air meeting in support of parliamentary reform was charged by yeomanry and hussars. Eleven people were killed and 500 wounded. The name was given in analogy with the Battle of Waterloo.

## Petworth House
Late 17th-century mansion in West Sussex, England, 21 km/13 mi northeast of Chichester. It was rebuilt 1688–96 by the 6th Duke of Somerset. The west front of the house is 98 m/321 ft long. In 1947 the 3rd Lord Leconfield gave the house and 300 ha/740 acres of park to the National Trust.

Much of the furniture and contents of the house was lent to the Trust by the Treasury, including many paintings by J M W Turner who was a friend of the 3rd Lord Egremont and often stayed at Petworth. There are also paintings here by Van Dyck, Claude, and Poussin, a large collection of antique and 18th-century sculpture, and a room carved by Grinling ◊Gibbons.

## Pevensey
English village in East Sussex, 8 km/5 mi northeast of Eastbourne, the site of the Norman king William the Conqueror's landing in 1066. The walls remain of the Roman fortress of Anderida, later a Norman castle, which was prepared against German invasion in World War II.

## Pevsner, Nikolaus (1902–1983)
Anglo-German art historian. Born in Leipzig, he fled from the Nazis to England. He became an authority on architecture, especially English. His *Outline of European Architecture* was published in 1942, followed by numerous other editions. In his series *The Buildings of England* (46 volumes; 1951–74), he built up a first-hand report on every notable building in the country.

## Philby, Kim (1912–1988)
British intelligence officer from 1940 and Soviet agent from 1933. He was liaison officer in Washington 1949–51, when he was confirmed to be a double agent and asked to resign. Named in 1963 as having warned Guy Burgess and Donald Maclean (also double agents) that their activities were known, he fled to the USSR and became a Soviet citizen and general in the KGB. A fourth member of the ring was Anthony Blunt.

## Phiz pseudonym of Hablot Knight Browne (1815–1882)
English artist who illustrated the greater part of the *Pickwick Papers* and other works by Charles Dickens.

## Phoenix Park Murders
The murder of several prominent members of the British government in Phoenix Park, Dublin, on 6

May 1882. The murders threatened the cooperation between the Liberal government and the Irish nationalist members at Westminster which had been secured by the ◊Kilmainham Treaty.

The murders began with the stabbing of Thomas Burke, the permanent under-secretary for Ireland, and Lord Frederick Cavendish, chief secretary to the viceroy. A murderous campaign was continued by the Irish National Invincibles until some members gave evidence against their accomplices.

The British government responded to the killings in Ireland with the Prevention of Crimes Act which suspended trial by jury and gave the police exceptional powers for three years.

## phoney war

The period in World War II between September 1939, when the Germans had occupied Poland, and April 1940, when the invasions of Denmark and Norway took place. During this time there were few signs of hostilities in Western Europe; indeed, Hitler made some attempts to arrange a peace settlement with Britain and France.

## photography

Britain has produced a number of pioneers in the development and application of photography, the most significant advances occurring in the first half of the 19th century.

### Development

As early as 1790 Thomas Wedgewood made **photograms** on leather sensitized with silver nitrate, and in 1807 William Wollaston (1766–1828) developed the *camera lucida* for copying drawings, using light reflected through a prism to create an image. These inventions proved inspirational to William ◊Fox Talbot, one of the foremost pioneers of photography. By 1841 he had patented the **calotype** process, the first multi-copy method of photography using a negative/positive process, and in 1851 he used a one-thousandth per second exposure to demonstrate high speed photography. The first three-colour photograph was produced in 1861 by Scottish physicist James Clerk Maxwell (1831–1879), and the first twin-lens reflex camera made in London in 1880. One of the greatest landmarks of the 20th century was the demonstration of the principles of holography (three-dimensional photography) by physicist Dennis ◊Gabor in 1947.

### Application

The first book illustrated with photographs was Fox Talbot's *The Pencil of Nature* (1844–46). Notable pioneers of photographic portraiture were David Hill (1802–1870) and Robert Adamson (1821–1848) who worked together in Edinburgh between 1843 and 1848, producing some 2,500 calotypes. In 1855 photographer Roger Fenton (1819–1861) comprehensively documented the Crimean War from a specially constructed caravan with a portable darkroom. Early innovators in photographic technique included Henry Robinson (1830–1901), who from 1851 produced images which closely imitated Victorian painting by combining several negatives in one print; and Julia Cameron (1815–1879), who used long lenses for her dramatic portraits of the Victorian intelligentsia. Differential focusing was used by English landscape photographer Peter Emerson (1856–1936) to produce naturalistic images in which only part of the picture was sharply focused. *Picture Post*, introduced in 1938, was the first UK magazine devoted to photojournalism. Notable photographers of the 20th century include the war photographer Don McCullin; fashion photographers David Bailey and Norman Parkinson; and Anthony Snowdon, who is especially known for his portraits.

Photographic processes found early application in the field of astronomy. Warren de la Rue invented the first heliographic photograph, and took the first photograph of a solar eclipse in 1860, and William Huggins (1824–1910) pioneered the use of photography in stellar spectography. The cataloguing of stars through photography was led by Scottish astronomer David Gill in 1882. In archaeology Kenneth St Joseph (1912–1994) pioneered the use of aerial photography, discovering thousands of previously unknown sites.

### Collections

In 1851 the Great Exhibition in London contained one of the first public displays of photography. The Photographers Gallery was established in London in 1971, and in 1983 the National Museum of Photography, Film, and Television opened in Bradford.

## Piccadilly

A main road in London, running between Piccadilly Circus and the southeast corner of Hyde Park. In Piccadilly are St James's Church, designed by Christopher Wren; Burlington House, home of the Royal Academy of Arts; and the Ritz Hotel. In Piccadilly Circus, at the eastern end of Piccadilly, is a fountain with a statue, popularly known as Eros, erected in memory of the 7th Earl of Shaftesbury.

Piccadilly was extensively developed and made

fashionable in the late 17th century, when the life of the court centred on nearby St James's Palace.

## Pict

Roman term for a member of the peoples of northern Scotland, possibly meaning 'painted' (tattooed). Of pre-Celtic origin, and speaking a Celtic language which died out in about the 10th century, the Picts are thought to have inhabited much of England before the arrival of the Celtic Britons. They were united with the Celtic Scots under the rule of Kenneth MacAlpin in 844. Their greatest monument is a series of carved stones, whose symbols remain undeciphered.

## pidgin English

Originally a trade jargon developed between the British and the Chinese in the 19th century, but now commonly and loosely used to mean any kind of 'broken' or 'native' version of the English language.

*Pidgin* is believed to have been a Chinese pronunciation of the English word *business*. There have been many forms of pidgin English, often with common elements because of the wide range of contacts made by commercial shipping. The original pidgin English of the Chinese ports combined words of English with a rough-and-ready Chinese grammatical structure. Melanesian pidgin English (also known as Tok Pisin) combines English and the syntax of local Melanesian languages. For example, the English pronoun 'we' becomes both *yumi* (you and me) and *mifela* (me and fellow, excluding you).

## pier

Structure built out into the sea from the coastline for use as a landing place or promenade.

The first British pier was built at Ryde, Isle of Wight, in 1814. Eugenius Birch (1818–1883) designed the West Pier, Brighton, in 1866 (339 m/1,115 ft); Margate Pier 1856; and the North Pier, Blackpool, 1863.

## Pilgrimage of Grace

Rebellion against Henry VIII of England 1536–37, originating in Yorkshire and Lincolnshire. The uprising was directed against the policies of the monarch (such as the dissolution of the monasteries and the effects of the enclosure of common land).

At the height of the rebellion, the rebels controlled York and included the archbishop there among their number. A truce was arranged in December 1536 and the rebels dispersed, but their demands were not met, and a further revolt broke out in 1537, which was severely suppressed, with the execution of over 200 of the rebels, including the leader, Robert Aske.

## Pilgrims

Emigrants who sailed from Plymouth, Devon, England, in the *Mayflower* on 16 September 1620 to found the first colony in New England, North America, at New Plymouth, Massachusetts. Of the 102 passengers about a third were Puritan refugees.

The Pilgrims originally set sail for Virginia in the *Mayflower* and *Speedwell* from Southampton on 5 August 1620, but had to put into Dartmouth when the *Speedwell* needed repair. Bad weather then drove them into Plymouth Sound, where the *Speedwell* was abandoned. They landed at Cape Cod in December and decided to stay, moving on to find New Plymouth harbour and founding the Massachusetts colony. Considerable religious conflict had erupted between the 35 Puritans and the other, largely Anglican, passengers. Open mutiny was averted by the Mayflower Compact, which established the rights of the non-Puritans. About half of the Pilgrims died over the winter before they received help from the Indians; the survivors celebrated the first Thanksgiving in the autumn of 1621.

## Pilgrims' Way

Track running from Winchester to Canterbury, England, which was the route taken by medieval pilgrims visiting the shrine of Thomas à Becket. It was some 195 km/120 mi long, and can still be traced for most of its length.

## Pinero, Arthur Wing (1855–1934)

English dramatist. A leading exponent of the 'well-made' play, he enjoyed great contemporary success with his farces, beginning with *The Magistrate* (1885). More substantial social drama followed with *The Second Mrs Tanqueray* (1893), and comedies including *Trelawny of the 'Wells'* (1898). He was knighted in 1909.

## Pitt, William, the Elder, 1st Earl of Chatham (1708–1778)

British Whig politician, 'the Great Commoner'. As paymaster of the forces from 1746–55, he broke with tradition by refusing to enrich himself; he was dismissed for attacking the Duke of Newcastle, the prime minister. He served effectively as prime minister in coalition governments in 1756–61 (successfully conducting the Seven Years' War) and 1766–68.

**Pilgrims' Way** Medieval pilgrims on their way to the shrine of St Thomas à Becket at Canterbury. Pilgrimage, immortalized by Geoffrey Chaucer, was a remarkably common activity throughout medieval Europe, at all social levels. Canterbury was the most important English pilgrimage site, attracting pilgrims from elsewhere in Europe too. Philip Sauvain Picture Collection

## Pitt, William, the Younger (1759–1806)

British Tory prime minister 1783–1801 and 1804–06. He raised the importance of the House of Commons, clamped down on corruption, carried out fiscal reforms, and effected the union with Ireland. He attempted to keep Britain at peace but underestimated the importance of the French Revolution and became embroiled in wars with France from 1793; he died on hearing of Napoleon's victory at Austerlitz. The son of William Pitt the Elder, he entered Cambridge University at age 14 and Parliament at age 22.

---

*Necessity is the plea for every infringement of human freedom. It is the argument of tyrants; it is the creed of slaves.*

**William Pitt the Younger** British Tory prime minister.
Speech, House of Commons 18 November 1783

---

## plague

See ◊Black Death.

## Plaid Cymru (Welsh 'Party of Wales')

Welsh nationalist political party established in 1925, dedicated to an independent Wales. In the 1999 elections to the National Assembly for Wales Plaid Cymru gained 17 of the 60 seats.

Plaid Cymru has campaigned for separation from and independence of the United Kingdom in order to safeguard the culture, language, and economic life of Wales. Founded in 1925, Plaid Cymru has contested parliamentary elections in Wales since 1929, but did not gain representation in Westminster until 1966, when it won the Carmarthen by-election. This seat was lost in 1970, but in the two general elections of February and October 1974 Plaid Cymru won two and three seats respectively. In 1997 it gained four seats.

## Plaidy, Jean pen name of Eleanor Hibbert (c. 1910–1993)

English historical novelist. A prolific writer, she produced popular historical novels under three different pseudonyms: Jean Plaidy, Victoria Holt, and Philippa Carr.

## Plantagenet

English royal house, reigning 1154–1399, whose name comes from the nickname of Geoffrey, Count of Anjou (1113–1151), father of Henry II, who often wore in his hat a sprig of broom, *planta genista*. In the 1450s, Richard, Duke of York, took 'Plantagenet' as a surname to emphasize his superior claim to the throne over that of Henry VI. See genealogy.

## Plantation of Ireland

Colonization and conquest of Ireland by English and Scottish settlers from 1556 to 1660. There were several rebellions against the plantation by the Irish and the Anglo-Irish aristocracy. The final stages of the conquest took place under ◊Cromwell.

## Plymouth

City, seaport, and resort in southwest England; population 257,000. Part of the county of Devon until April 1998, it is now a unitary authority with an area of 79 sq km/31 sq mi. Lying at the head of the spacious bay of Plymouth Sound, the city is a thriving commercial and regional shopping centre and holiday resort, with a dockyard, naval base, and ferry links with France and Spain. Plymouth

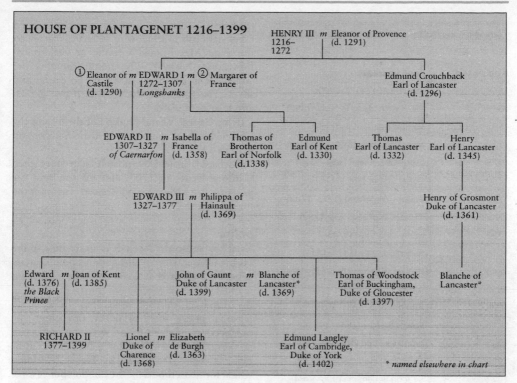

**HOUSE OF PLANTAGENET 1216–1399**

HENRY III *m* Eleanor of Provence
1216–1272 (d. 1291)

① Eleanor of *m* EDWARD I *m* ② Margaret of France
Castile 1272–1307 France
(d. 1290) *Longshanks*

Edmund Crouchback
Earl of Lancaster
(d. 1296)

EDWARD II *m* Isabella of France
1307–1327 (d. 1358)
*of Caernarfon*

Thomas of Brotherton
Earl of Norfolk
(d.1338)

Edmund
Earl of Kent
(d. 1330)

Thomas
Earl of Lancaster
(d. 1332)

Henry
Earl of Lancaster
(d. 1345)

EDWARD III *m* Philippa of Hainault
1327–1377 (d. 1369)

Henry of Grosmont
Duke of Lancaster
(d. 1361)

Edward *m* Joan of Kent
(d. 1376) (d. 1385)
*the Black Prince*

John of Gaunt *m* Blanche of Lancaster*
Duke of Lancaster (d. 1369)
(d. 1399)

Thomas of Woodstock
Earl of Buckingham,
Duke of Gloucester
(d. 1397)

Blanche of
Lancaster*

RICHARD II
1377–1399

Lionel *m* Elizabeth
Duke of de Burgh
Charence (d. 1363)
(d. 1368)

Edmund Langley
Earl of Cambridge,
Duke of York
(d. 1402)

*\* named elsewhere in chart*

also has a rich maritime history dating back to when it became an important naval garrison in the 15th century. Much of the city centre was destroyed during World War II bombing raids and has since been rebuilt.

### History

It was from Plymouth that Sir Francis ◊Drake and Sir John Hawkins set out on many of their expeditions and Drake set sail from here to defeat the Spanish Armada in 1588. Tradition has it that he played bowls on the Hoe, an esplanade overlooking Plymouth Sound, as the Armada approached. The *Mayflower* Pilgrims sailed from here to North America in 1620.

### Features

Dominating the city are the ramparts of the 17th-century citadel, built to guard the harbour soon after the long sieges when Plymouth successfully withstood Royalist attacks during the Civil War. The Hoe has many monuments including a statue of Sir Francis Drake, and Smeaton's Tower, originally erected in 1759 on the ◊Eddystone Rocks and replaced in 1882. Other attractions include Plymouth Aquarium, Plymouth Dome, which illustrates Plymouth's past and present using high-tech displays, and the Mayflower Stone and Steps. While much of the city centre is modern, many historic buildings survive in the Barbican harbour area. Plymouth University,

formerly South West Polytechnic, was established in 1992.

### Plymouth Brethren

Fundamentalist Christian Protestant sect characterized by extreme simplicity of belief, founded in Dublin about 1827 by the Reverend John Nelson Darby (1800–1882). The Plymouth Brethren have no ordained priesthood, affirming the ministry of all believers, and maintain no church buildings. They hold prayer meetings and Bible study in members' houses. In the UK, the Plymouth Brethren are mainly found in the fishing villages of northeast Scotland.

### Plymouth Sound

Arm of the English Channel between Devon and Cornwall, covering an area of 2,226 ha/5,500 acres. It provides good anchorage. Its inlets include the Catwater (or 'Cattewater'), Sutton Pool, Mill Bay, Stonehouse Pool, the Hamoaze (a naval harbour at the estuary of the River Tamar), and Cawsand Bay. A long breakwater was completed 4 km/2.5 mi south of the Hoe in 1845, to provide shelter from southwesterly gales.

### poet laureate

Poet of the British royal household, so called because of the laurel wreath awarded to eminent poets in the Graeco-Roman world. Early UK

## Poets Laureate

| Appointed | Poet Laureate |
| --- | --- |
| 1668 | John Dryden (1631–1700) |
| 1689 | Thomas Shadwell (c 1642–1692) |
| 1692 | Nahum Tate (1652–1715) |
| 1715 | Nicholas Rowe (1674–1718) |
| 1718 | Laurence Eusden (1688–1730) |
| 1730 | Colley Cibber (1671–1757) |
| 1757 | William Whitehead (1715–1785) |
| 1785 | Thomas Warton (1728–1790) |
| 1790 | Henry James Pye (1745–1813) |
| 1813 | Robert Southey (1774–1843) |
| 1843 | William Wordsworth (1770–1850) |
| 1850 | Alfred, Lord Tennyson (1809–1892) |
| 1896 | Alfred Austin (1835–1913) |
| 1913 | Robert Bridges (1844–1930) |
| 1930 | John Masefield (1878–1967) |
| 1968 | Cecil Day-Lewis (1904–1972) |
| 1972 | Sir John Betjeman (1906–1984) |
| 1984 | Ted Hughes (1930–1998) |
| 1999 | Andrew Motion (1952–  ) |

poets with unofficial status were John Skelton, Samuel Daniel, Ben ◊Jonson, and William Davenant. John ◊Dryden was the first to receive the title by letters-patent in 1668 and from then on the post became a regular institution.

There is a stipend of £70 a year, plus £27 in lieu of the traditional butt of sack (cask of wine). See table above.

### point-to-point
A form of horse racing over fences, organized by local hunts in Britain. It is open only to amateurs riding horses that have been regularly used in hunts. The point-to-point season lasts January to May.

### Poitevin
In English history, relating to the reigns of King John and King Henry III. The term is derived from the region of France south of the Loire (Poitou), which was controlled by the English for most of this period.

### Polesden Lacey
Villa near Dorking, Surrey, England. Originally an elegant 1820s villa, the house was extensively remodelled after 1906, and bequeathed to the National Trust in 1942, with 365 ha/902 acres, by the Hon Mrs Ronald Greville (a well-known Edwardian hostess). The house contains her collection of paintings, furniture, porcelain, and silver. The gardens include a walled rose garden and tree-lined walks.

King George VI and Queen Elizabeth (now the Queen Mother) spent part of their honeymoon here in 1923.

Richard Brinsley ◊Sheridan bought the original Caroline house in 1797, and his son sold the property in 1818 to Joseph Bonsor, who built the present house.

### police
Civil law-and-order force. It is responsible to the Home Office, with 56 autonomous police forces, generally organized on a county basis; mutual aid is given in circumstances such as mass picketing in the 1984–85 miners' strike, but there is no national police force or police riot unit. The predecessors of these forces were the ineffective medieval watch and London's Bow Street runners, introduced in 1749 by Henry ◊Fielding which formed a model for the London police force established by Robert ◊Peel's government in 1829 (hence the nickname 'bobbies'); the system was introduced throughout the country from 1856.

### Poole
Industrial town and port in southern England, 8 km/5 mi west of Bournemouth; population (1996) 138,100. Part of the county of Dorset until 1997, it is now a unitary authority with an area of 64 sq km/25 sq mi. The town is known for its pottery and for **Poole Harbour**, Europe's largest natural harbour, which is a centre for yachting.
*Features*
Brownsea Island, in Poole Harbour, may be reached by passenger ferry from Poole Quay. The first Scout camp was held on the island in 1907, and it is now the site of an important nature reserve and bird sanctuary. The historic buildings in the quay area of the town reflect the town's importance as a major port in medieval times, and the Waterfront Museum, housed in a 15th-century warehouse, illustrates the history of the town and the Scout Movement.

### Pop art
Movement in modern art that took its imagery from the glossy world of advertising and from popular culture such as comic strips, films, and

television; it developed in the 1950s and flourished in the 1960s. The term was coined by the British critic Lawrence Alloway (1926–1990) in about 1955, to refer to works of art that drew upon popular culture. Richard Hamilton, one of the leading British pioneers and exponents of Pop art, defined it in 1957 as 'popular, transient, expendable, low-cost, mass-produced, young, witty, sexy, gimmicky, glamorous, and Big Business'. In its eclecticism and sense of irony and playfulness, Pop art helped to prepare the way for the Post-Modernism that has been a feature of Western culture since the 1970s.

Pop art was an expression of a time of relative affluence that followed a period of austerity after World War II. It was often comical in mood, sometimes deliberately debunking the values of the art world.

Leading British figures included Peter Blake, David Hockney, Allen Jones, and Eduardo Paolozzi. For some of these artists, such as Hockney, Pop art represented a brief stage in their career, but others have solidly committed themselves to the style.

## Pop design

Design movement of the 1960s which was characterized by its use of bright colours, expressive forms, synthetic materials, and throwaway objects.

Pop design centred on fashion – exemplified by the work of Mary ◊ Quant and John Stephen who opened a number of boutiques in Carnaby Street – and graphics, as in the work of the psychedelic poster artists Michael English (1942– ) and Nigel Weymouth. In essence, Pop design set out to challenge and subvert establishment design values.

## Pope, Alexander (1688–1744)

English poet and satirist. He established his poetic reputation with the precocious *Pastorals* (1709) and *An Essay on Criticism* (1711), which were followed by a parody of the heroic epic, *The Rape of the Lock* (1712–14), *The Temple of Fame* (1715), and 'Eloisa to Abelard' (1717). The highly Neo-Classical translations of Homer's *Iliad* and *Odyssey* (1715–26) were very successful but his edition of Shakespeare (1725) attracted scholarly ridicule, which led Pope to write a satire on scholarly dullness, *The Dunciad* (1728). His finest mature works are his *Imitations of the Satires of Horace* (1733–38) and his personal letters.

Pope had a biting wit, expressed in the heroic couplet, of which he was a master. His couplets

have an epigrammatic quality ('True wit is nature to advantage dressed/What oft was thought, but ne'er so well expressed'), and many of his observations have passed into the language as proverbs, for example 'A little learning is a dang'rous thing'.

## pop festival

Outdoor concert usually spanning a weekend and featuring a number of bands; pop, rock, heavy-metal, and world-music festivals have become regular events in many countries since the 1960s. British pop festivals include Glastonbury (established in 1970) and Reading (1971).

## pop music

A major British industry at the end of the 20th century. See chronology of some key dates on page 366.

## population

The UK's population at the end of the 20th century was 59 million. 1996 projections suggest that it will reach over 64 million by 2021.

## Porteous riots

Riots in Edinburgh, Scotland on 14 April 1736, after Lieutenant John Porteous, captain of the

## Population by Ethnic Group in Great Britain

(Average over the period Summer 1997 to Spring 1998.)
Source: *Annual Abstract of Statistics, 1999*, Office for National Statistics, © Crown copyright 1999

| Ethnic group | | Number |
|---|---|---|
| Black | Caribbean | 531,000 |
| | African | 351,000 |
| | other (non-mixed) | 127,000 |
| | mixed | 177,000 |
| Indian | | 929,000 |
| Pakistani | | 580,000 |
| Bangladeshi | | 208,000 |
| Chinese | | 162,000 |
| Other | Asian (non-mixed) | 199,000 |
| | other (non-mixed) | 142,000 |
| | mixed | 215,000 |
| **All ethnic minority groups** | | 3,623,000 |
| White | | 52,963,000 |
| **All ethnic groups**[1] | | 56,602,000 |

[1] Figure includes ethnic groups not stated.

## Pop Music: Some key dates

**1952** *Hit Parade* is the first television pop music show on British television.

**14 November 1952** The popular music magazine *New Musical Express* publishes Britain's first pop singles chart.

**1956** Rock 'n' roll music dominates dance floors in Britain.

**1957** The US rock singer Elvis Presley's single 'All Shook Up' becomes his first number one in Britain.

**3 March 1957** *The Eurovision Song Contest*, which started in 1956, is shown for the first time on British television.

**1960–69** The Beatles' song 'She Loves You' is the best-selling single of the 1960s in Britain. The Beatles are responsible for five out of the top six singles in Britain in the 1960s.

**1961** The British rock group the Rolling Stones is formed.

**1961** The Shadows become the first British rock group to top the UK album charts, with *The Shadows*.

**1963** Rhythm and blues music becomes popular in Britain, with key acts including Chuck Berry and Bo Diddley.

**1964** *Top of the Pops*, to date the longest-running rock and pop music programme on British television, starts broadcasting. It has a significant influence on sales.

**29 March 1964** Radio Caroline, the first offshore 'pirate' radio station broadcasting to Britain, begins transmissions from a ship in the North Sea. Modelled on Radio Luxembourg with its nonstop diet of pop music, it is Britain's first pop music station.

**1966** Soul is fashionable in Britain, with the music of James Brown, Wilson Pickett, Otis Redding, and Stevie Wonder very popular.

**30 September 1967** The BBC launches a national pop music station, Radio 1. The first programme is *The Breakfast Show*, presented by Tony Blackburn, and the first record played is 'Flowers in the Rain' by the Move.

**1969** The British rock group the Beatles make their last-ever public appearance on the roof of the Apple Records building in London, England. It is recorded as part of their film *Let It Be*.

**1971** Glam rock emerges. A reaction against progressive rock, it is characterized by elaborate costumes, makeup, and stage posturing, as exemplified by British bands such as T Rex and the Sweet.

**1971** The first Glastonbury music festival takes place.

**1972** Groups such as the Bay City Rollers mark the era of 'Teenybop', with the bands appealing particularly to teenage girls.

**1972** The first rock concert at Wembley Stadium in London, England, takes place. Artists appearing include Bill Haley and Chuck Berry and a film of the event, *The London Rock and Roll Show*, is released.

**20 December 1975** The British pop group Queen promotes its song 'Bohemian Rhapsody', from the album *A Night at the Opera*, with the first pop video. The video, produced by Bruce Gowers on a £4,500 budget, debuts on the television programme *Top of the Pops*.

**1977** Punk music comes to prominence in the UK, with the emergence of bands such as the Sex Pistols, the Clash, the Buzzcocks, the Damned, and the Stranglers.

**1978** The music magazine *Smash Hits* is launched; it will become the most successful magazine for the teenage market in the UK.

**1982** *The Tube*, Britain's most influential television music programme of the 1980s, starts on BBC2, with presenters Paula Yates and Jools Holland.

**13 July 1985** Live Aid, organized by Band Aid to raise funds for famine relief in Africa, is a day-long concert held simultaneously at Wembley Stadium in London and JFK Stadium in Philadelphia, USA. Over $70 million is raised worldwide.

**20 September 1997** The English pop star Elton John releases the single 'Candle in the Wind 1997' as a tribute to Diana, Princess of Wales. It goes immediately to number one and becomes the best-selling single of all time.

Edinburgh militia, ordered his men to open fire on a crowd rioting in protest at the execution of smugglers. Six members of the crowd were killed and Porteous was sentenced to death but was later reprieved. The prison in which Porteous was being held was stormed on 8 September by an angry mob which dragged him out and lynched him. The city was fined £2,000 and the Lord Provost was dismissed. As a result of the affair Walpole lost the crucial support of the Duke of Argyll, who led Scottish peers in the House of Lords.

### Portland, Isle of

Limestone peninsula on the coast of Dorset, southern England, joined to the mainland by the bank of shingle, ◊Chesil Bank; length 7 km/4 mi. The naval base, founded here in 1845, closed in 1995. Portland stone, used for St Paul's Cathedral, London, is still quarried locally. Portland harbour is Europe's largest artificial harbour. Portland Castle was built by Henry VIII in 1539–40.

The principal villages on the peninsula are Easton and Fortuneswell. Portland Harbour is enclosed by Portland Breakwater, built from Portland stone by convicts in 1849–72. At the southernmost tip of the peninsula, known as **Portland Bill**, is a lighthouse (1906). With a height of 35 m/115 ft, the lighthouse was designed to send out a 30-km/18-mi beam of light. It is now a bird-watching station.

## Portmeirion

Holiday resort in Gwynedd, north Wales, built by the architect Clough Williams-Ellis in Italianate fantasy style on a private headland overlooking Tremadoc Bay. It was the setting of the 1967 cult television series *The Prisoner*, but the name is also associated with Portmeirion Potteries, started in the 1960s by Susan Clough-Ellis, to supply the gift shop in the village.

## portraiture

The secular spirit of art after the Reformation helped to to give portraiture special importance in Britain from the 16th century onwards, as exemplified by the work of Hans Holbein the Younger while painter to Henry VIII. Holbein also introduced the art of miniature painting to England. In the 17th century Anthony van Dyck produced numerous portraits of royalty and aristocrats, such as *Charles I on Horseback* (about 1638; National Gallery, London).

This long tradition found its greatest expression in the 18th century with William Hogarth, Thomas Gainsborough, Joshua Reynolds, George Romney, Allan Ramsay, Henry Raeburn, Thomas Lawrence, and others. A special area of growth was the intimate 'conversation piece'.

The decline of portraiture began in the 19th century. The invention of photography was obviously a contributory factor, and artists were becoming preoccupied with ideas and styles that paid a decreasing attention to likeness of the sitter. However, the tradition was maintained into the 20th century by artists such as John Singer Sargent, who brilliantly depicted affluent late-Victorian and Edwardian society, Augustus ◊John, and Wiliam Orpen. Their kind of traditional society portraiture had become something of an anachronism by the second half of the 20th century, although it still had distinguished practitioners such as Gerald Kelly. Other artists produced portraits in a more modern and subjective vein, for example Graham Sutherland, Lucian Freud, Francis Bacon, and later David Hockney. Artists who have broken further away from the conventional idea of portraiture include Marc Quinn, whose *Self* (1991; Saatchi Collection, London) is a cast of his head made from his own frozen blood (it is displayed in a refrigerated cabinet).

## Portsmouth

City and naval port in southern England, 118 km/73 mi southwest of London; population (1996) 189,300. Part of the county of Hampshire until 1997, it is now a unitary authority with an area of 42 sq km/16 sq mi. Lying on the peninsula of Portsea Island, opposite the Isle of Wight, Portsmouth is the site of Britain's principal naval station and it has ferry links with France, the Isle of Wight, and the Channel Islands. It is also a major centre of tourism with a wealth of attractions reflecting its rich maritime heritage and long history as a naval dockyard. Work is underway on 'The Renaissance of Portsmouth Harbour', a landmark millennium project redeveloping the historic waterfront, creating a major maritime leisure complex.

### History

Portsmouth was established as a royal dockyard and garrison when the first dry dock was built here during the reign of Henry VII. It was from Portsmouth that Admiral Horatio ◊Nelson and his fleet departed for Trafalgar in September 1805. An important military target, it was heavily bombed during World War II and it was a principal embarkation point in the ◊D-day operation.

### Features

The Historic Ships complex in the Royal Naval Base is home to HMS *Warrior* (1860), Britain's first armoured battleship, the Tudor warship *Mary Rose*, and Nelson's flagship HMS *Victory*. Also within the complex is the Royal Naval Museum which illustrates the city's maritime history. Many of the city's older buildings were destroyed during World War II bombing raids, but some Georgian and Tudor buildings survive in Old Portsmouth around the harbour. The building where Charles Dickens was born now houses a museum. Portsmouth University, formerly Portsmouth Polytechnic, was established in 1992.

## Port Sunlight

Housing estate built as a model village in 1888 by W H Lever (1851–1925) for workers at the Lever Brothers (now Unilever) soap factory on the Wirral Peninsula at Birkenhead, near Liverpool, northwest England. It is now part of ◊Bebington, Merseyside. A model example of a village created by philanthropic industrialists, it has nearly 900 houses, set in gardens with extensive open spaces. It was designed for a population of 3,000 and includes the Lever art gallery, a church, library, and social hall.

## postal service

Regular permanent postal systems were not created in Britain until the emergence of the modern nation state. Henry VIII in 1516 appointed Sir Brian Tuke as Master of the Posts, to maintain a regular service on the main roads from London. Postmasters (usually innkeepers) passed the mail to the next post, and supplied horses for the royal couriers. In 1635 a royal proclamation established the first public service. Private services were discouraged to avoid losing revenue for the state service and assisting treasonable activities, the latter point being stressed by the act establishing the Post Office, passed under Oliver ◊Cromwell in 1657. Mail coaches first ran in 1784, and in 1840 Rowland ◊Hill's prepaid penny postage stamp, for any distance within the UK, led to a massive increase in use. Services were extended to registered post in 1841; post boxes in 1855; savings bank in 1861; postcards in 1870; postal orders in 1881; parcel post in 1883; air mail in 1911; telephone in 1912; data processing by computer in 1967; and giro in 1968. In 1969 the original General Post Office ceased to be a government department, and in 1981 it split into two, the Post Office and the telecommunications corporation ◊British Telecom (privatized in 1984). The Post Office lost its monopoly in 1987. International cooperation is through the Universal Postal Union (1875) at Bern, Switzerland.

## poster art

Ancestors of the modern poster were handbills with woodcut illustrations. One of the first English posters by a distinguished artist, Frederick Walker's design announcing *The Woman in White*

(1871), was engraved on wood. The 1890s were the classic age of the poster, exponents being the Art Nouveau illustrator Aubrey Beardsley, and the 'Beggarstaff Brothers' (William Nicholson and James Pryde), whose strikingly simple designs evolved from cut-paper shapes, subsequently lithographed. In the early 20th century Frank Brangwyn, Duncan Grant, Graham Sutherland, and Paul Nash, and patrons such as London Transport and Shell-Mex, contributed to the development of poster design. The advent of Psychedelic art, especially in the work of Michael English (1942–  ), popularized poster art in the 1960s.

## potato famine

Famine in Ireland 1845–48 caused by the failure of the potato crop, the staple of the Irish diet. Nearly a million people died from malnutrition-related diseases such as cholera, dysentery, and typhus and at least the same number again emigrated, mainly to America. The former Irish population of 8 million had thus fallen by at least 2 million. The famine devastated Ireland for many years after. The British government was slow to provide relief and provoked Irish hostility in consequence.

## Potter, Beatrix (1866–1943)

English writer and illustrator of children's books. Her first book was *The Tale of Peter Rabbit* (1900), followed by *The Tailor of Gloucester* (1902), based on her observation of family pets and wildlife. Other books in the series include *The Tale of Mrs Tiggy-Winkle* (1904), *The Tale of Jeremy Fisher* (1906), and a sequel to Peter Rabbit, *The Tale of the Flopsy Bunnies* (1909). Her tales are told with a childlike wonder, devoid of sentimentality, and accompanied by delicate illustrations.

Potter was also an accomplished mycologist. She was the first person to report the symbiotic relationship between lichen and fungi, and to catalogue the fungi of the British Isles. She was excluded from professional scientific societies because of her sex.

She had a quiet and restrained childhood in London, relieved by holidays in Scotland, Wales,

**Beatrix Potter** The author of a series of children's classic stories about animals, Beatrix Potter was also an accomplished watercolourist, who illustrated all her own works, and a gifted natural scientist. Her books continue to have a wide appeal, and have been adapted for both stage and screen. Seen here, from the film version of her tales, is the frog, Jeremy Fisher. Ronald Grant

and the Lake District, during which she studied and painted the countryside and its animals and plants. From 1905 she lived in the Lake District, where she bred hill-sheep and was an active conservationist. Her diaries, written in a secret code, were translated and published in 1966. She left her extensive estate to the National Trust, and her Lake District home at Sawrey is now a museum.

## Potter, Dennis (1935–1994)

English dramatist and journalist. His most important work was written for television, extending the boundaries of the art form. Serials include *Pennies from Heaven* (1978) (feature film 1981), and *The Singing Detective* (1986); *Brimstone and Treacle* (1976) (transmitted 1987, feature film 1982), was a play.

Potter's television dramas exhibit a serious concern for social issues, and are characterized by a marked avoidance of euphemism or delicacy. Highly inventive in form, they explore the medium's technical possibilities, employing devices such as overlap, fantasy sequences, and flashback. Two TV scripts were produced posthumously, *Cold Lazarus* and *Karaoke* (both 1995). Potter often incorporated popular music into his works, for example in *Pennies from Heaven*, in which the action is interrupted by songs lip-mimed by the characters.

## Potteries, the

Home of the china and earthenware industries, in central England. Wedgwood and Minton are factory names associated with the Potteries.

The Potteries lie in the upper Trent basin of north Staffordshire, covering the area around Stoke-on-Trent, and include the formerly separate towns of Burslem, Hanley, Longton, Fenton, and Tunstall.

## pound

British standard monetary unit, issued as a gold sovereign before 1914, as a note from 1914–83, and as a circular yellow metal-alloy coin from 1983.

The edge inscriptions on the pound coin are: 1983 *Decus et tutamen* 'An ornament and a safeguard'; 1984 (Scottish) *Nemo me impune lacessit* 'No one injures me with impunity'; 1985 (Welsh) *Pleidiol wyf i'm gwlad* 'True am I to my country', from the national anthem. A new £2 coin, the UK's first bi-coloured coin, was introduced in 1998.

## Powell, Enoch (1912–1998)

British Conservative politician. He was minister of health 1960–63, and contested the party leadership in 1965. In 1968 he made a speech against immigration that led to his dismissal from the shadow cabinet. He resigned from the party in 1974, and was Official Unionist Party member for South Down, Northern Ireland, 1974–87.

---

*All political lives, unless they are cut off in midstream at a happy juncture, end in failure, because that is the nature of politics and of human affairs.*

**Enoch Powell** British Conservative politician. *Joseph Chamberlain*, epilogue

---

## Powis Castle

Medieval castle in Welshpool, Powys, Wales, owned by the National Trust. The late 13th-century walls and bastions remain, but the castle was adapted in Elizabethan times and again in the latter half of the 17th century. It became the home of Robert Clive, created Earl of Powis, and contains many of his relics. The house contains the Clive Museum; the garden has late 17th-century terraces.

The 4th Earl remodelled the interior, and made further modifications to the castle before giving it to the National Trust in 1952.

## Powys

Unitary authority in central Wales, created in 1996 from the former county of Powys; population (1996) 123,600; area 5,179 sq km/1,999 sq mi. It is mainly mountainous with wooded valleys towards the English border in the east. It includes the Brecon Beacons National Park in the south. The principal towns are ◊Llandrindod Wells (administrative headquarters), Brecon, Builth Wells, Newtown, and Welshpool.

### Physical

The north is almost wholly mountainous, a large portion consisting of bleak elevated moorland, but with several open, fertile, and well-wooded valleys towards the east. The Cambrian Mountains run along the western border. Over one-half of the central district is 300 m/1,000 ft or more above sea-level, the highest point being at 660 m/2,165 ft in Radnor Forest. The highest peaks of the area are Pen y Fan (885 m/2,904 ft) in the Brecon Beacons, and Waun Fach (811 m/2,660 ft) and Carmarthen Van (802 m/2,630 ft) in the Black Mountain range in the southeast. The main rivers are the Wye, Severn, Dovey, Taff, Tawe, Teme, and Usk; the Wye and Severn valleys are especially beautiful. Near Rhayader are the Elan Valley and Claerwen reservoirs. Lake Vyrnwy in the north is an artificial reservoir supplying Liverpool and Birmingham.

*Features*
Some 5 km/3 mi west of Brecon is Y Gaer, the Roman Bannium, an excavated walled fort. The 14th-century fortified manor house of Tretower Court and the adjacent Norman tower 5 km/3 mi from Crickhowell are ancient monuments. In the Vale of Ewyas are the ruins of Llanthony Abbey, which was founded early in the 12th century. The Centre for Alternative Technology, Celtica, is near Machynlleth. The Royal Welsh Show is an annual event.

*Economy*
Agriculture is the main occupation of the area. Much arable and dairy farming is undertaken on the lower valley lands, especially on the fertile alluvial soils of the Usk and Wye region. A pure breed of Welsh ponies is reared in the central district. The River Teme has good trout fishing. Afforestation has been undertaken extensively in the north; forestry and quarrying are undertaken in the south; and limestone is worked in the central areas.

## Powys, House of
Ancient kingdom in Wales, bordering England in the east. It was frequently threatened from the east, and lands in the present English counties of Herefordshire, Worcestershire, and Shropshire were lost following the incursion of the Mercians in the period leading up to the construction in the late 8th century of Offa's Dyke between the two countries. The rulers of Powys often fought those of neighbouring Gwynedd. The last ruler of Powys as an intact kingdom was Madog ap Maredudd (*d.* 1160). His successors ruled over a Powys divided into north and south. The name was restored for the county of Powys, formed in 1974 from the counties of Breconshire, Mongomeryshire, and Radnorshire.

## Pre-Raphaelite Brotherhood
Group of British painters (1848–53); Dante Gabriel ◊Rossetti, John Everett ◊Millais, and Holman Hunt – at this time young students at the Royal Academy – were the leading figures among the seven founders. They aimed to paint serious subjects, to study nature closely, and to return to the sincerity of spirit of painters before the time of Raphael Sanzio (1483–1520). Their subjects were mainly biblical and literary, painted with obsessive naturalism and attention to detail. The group was short-lived but added a new realism to the art of the 1850s, and influenced many painters including W H Deverell, W L Windus, John Brett, W S Burton, and Robert Martineau.

In his later work only Hunt remained true to Pre-Raphaelite ideals, but the name stuck to Rossetti, the least committed of the original group, and was applied to his later dreamily romantic pictures although these had moved away from the movement's founding ideas. A 'second wave' of Pre-Raphaelitism in the late 19th century, stimulated by Ruskin and Rossetti, was associated with the revival of handicrafts and the art of design. William Morris and Edward Burne-Jones were among the many artists influenced at this time.

## Presbyterianism
System of Christian Protestant church government, expounded during the Reformation by John Calvin, which gives its name to the established Church of Scotland, and is also practised in England, Wales, Ireland, Switzerland, North America, and elsewhere. There is no compulsory form of worship and each congregation is governed by presbyters or elders (clerical or lay), who are of equal rank.

Congregations are grouped in presbyteries, synods, and general assemblies.

## Preseli Hills, or Prescelly Mountains, Welsh Mynydd Preseli
Range of hills in Pembrokeshire, southwest Wales, rising to 536 m/1,759 ft (at Foel Cwmcerwyn) and crossed by a primitive trackway. A site of Neolithic settlement, the eastern section of these hills is thought to have provided the bluestone of ◊Stonehenge; this is the only known place in Britain where bluestone is found.

## press gang
Method used to recruit soldiers and sailors into the British armed forces in the 18th and early 19th centuries. In effect it was a form of kidnapping carried out by the services or their agents, often with the aid of armed men.

## Preston
Industrial town and administrative headquarters of ◊Lancashire, northwest England, on the River Ribble, 34 km/21 mi south of Lancaster, at the highest navigable point of the Irish Sea estuary; population (1991) 126,100. Since the decline of

its traditional cotton industry, Preston's role as an administrative, commercial, and regional shopping centre has developed. It is the site of the University of Central Lancashire (1992).

*History*

The first cotton mills in England were established here in the 18th century and by 1835 Preston had 40 factories spinning cotton. The town was the birthplace of the manufacturing pioneer Richard Arkwright, inventor of the water frame.

*Features*

Although Preston is mentioned in the Domesday Book and received its first charter in 1179, there are few visual traces of its early history. Much of the 19th-century housing has been cleared and the town centre and the former dock area have been redeveloped. Known in Lancashire as 'Proud Preston', the town has imposing public buildings, including the neo-classical Harris Museum and Art Gallery, and its skyline is dominated by the fine slender spire of St Walburge's, over 92 m/302 ft high. The Preston Guild Festival, a fair dating back to 1179, is celebrated every 20 years.

## pretender

Claimant to a throne. In British history, the term is widely used to describe the Old Pretender (◊James Edward Stuart) and his son, the Young Pretender (◊Charles Edward Stuart).

## Priestley, J(ohn) B(oynton) (1894–1984)

English novelist and dramatist. His first success was a novel about travelling theatre, *The Good Companions* (1929). He followed it with a realist novel about London life, *Angel Pavement* (1930). His career as a dramatist began with *Dangerous Corner* (1932), one of several plays in which time is a preoccupation. His best-known plays are the enigmatic *An Inspector Calls* (1945) and *The Linden Tree* (1948), a study of postwar social issues.

Priestley had a gift for family comedy; for example, the play *When We Are Married* (1938). He was also known for his wartime broadcasts and literary criticism, such as *Literature and Western Man* (1960).

## priest's hole

Hiding place, in private homes, for Catholic priests in the 16th–17th centuries when there were penal laws against them in Britain. Many priest's holes still exist, for example at Speke Hall, near Liverpool.

## prime minister, or premier

Head of the parliamentary government. The first prime minister in Britain is usually considered to have been Robert ◊Walpole, but the office was not officially recognized until 1905. In the late 20th century, the office became increasingly presidential, with the prime minister being supported by a large private office and the No 10 Policy Unit. Tony ◊Blair became Britain's prime minister in 1997.

The prime minister is appointed by the sovereign, but in asking someone to form a government the sovereign is constitutionally bound to invite the leader of the party with a majority of seats in the House of Commons (see ◊Commons, House of), a situation which is normally determined by a general election. If no party has a majority then the sovereign normally invites the leader of the party with the largest number of seats to form a government, and, failing this, may consult various party leaders and elder statesmen. If the prime minister dies or resigns between elections the sovereign waits until the party concerned has elected a new leader. All governmental appointments are made by the sovereign on the advice of the prime minister.

While Robert Walpole is widely regarded as the first prime minister, his career set a precedent for the post rather than establishing it firmly as part of the machinery of government. The first prime minister in the modern sense was probably William Pitt the Younger (see ◊Pitt, William, the Younger), who clearly established the role of the prime minister as the dominant figure in the cabinet.

The post of prime minister is largely the product of constitutional convention, although the office was recognized in formal precedence in 1905 and has been mentioned in various acts of Parliament since 1918. The prime minister normally holds the post of First Lord of the Treasury, and, in the past, sometimes held a major departmental portfolio.

## Princes in the Tower

Popular name for King ◊Edward V and his younger brother Richard, Duke of York (1472–1483). They are said to have been murdered in the Tower of London by order of their uncle, the Duke of Gloucester, so that he could succeed to the throne as ◊Richard III.

## Princess Royal

Title borne only by the eldest daughter of the British sovereign, granted by royal declaration. It was first borne by Mary, eldest daughter of Charles I, probably in imitation of the French court, where the eldest daughter of the king was

## ◆ THE PUB – A NATIONAL INSTITUTION ◆

The word 'pub' is instantly and universally recognized, a term of verbal shorthand. On the 'must-do' list of every visitor to Britain, alongside a ride on a red London bus or in a black taxi, will be a visit to a pub. Other countries have bars, cafés, and kellers, but only Britain has its public houses, over 70,000 of them in towns, cities, villages, and hamlets, with names that express the deep roots the institution has in the country's history, community, and culture. Many attempts have been made to export 'the English pub', often with risible results, but it flourishes only on its native soil.

### Ale-houses and taverns

The public house is a comparatively modern term, dating from Victorian times, when large and imposing new licensed premises were built by rich brewers with government backing to offer a relatively sober alternative to sordid gin shops. Until the development of the

photo: Corel

public house, people drank in ale houses, inns, and taverns, an overlapping and interconnected system of drinking places as old as the island race. Brewing for centuries was a domestic activity, usually carried out by women who made ale for home consumption as naturally as they made bread. The Roman invaders built their *tabernae* where wine was drunk, but such establishments were not open to the natives, though they duly noted the name and later adopted it for their own use. The Danes, Vikings, and Saxons who followed the Romans brought with them a passion for ale drinking that became deeply embedded in the way of life of the emerging nation. Gradually the ale wives or brewsters

who made the best beer would offer it to others in their local communities: when a fresh brew was ready, a pole with a garland of evergreens on the end would emerge from a window. These rudimentary drinking places were forced to grow, with additional rooms added to accommodate willing customers. The ale house was born.

With the spread of Christianity, brewing came under the control of the church. Monasteries had their own large breweries and the monks built adjoining inns to provide accommodation for pilgrims and travellers. Innkeepers gave their houses names, often taken from the coats of arms of the local nobility. As towns and cities grew, inns were built to refresh the urban masses, and often took as their inn signs the names of the guilds and associations formed by city craftsmen, such as the Baker's Arms, Lamb and Flag (merchant tailors), Three Compasses (carpenters), and the Elephant and Castle (master cutlers). It also became the custom to name inns after the monarch of the day, which is why Britain still has a profusion of Queen's and King's Head pubs bearing the visage of the chosen monarch.

The types of drinking establishments were strictly codified in medieval England: an ale house could sell only beer, while a tavern had to serve food as well as drink, and an inn offered accommodation as well, an important consideration as a network of roads developed and coaches took people on long journeys that required regular stops for refreshment and sleep.

## The growth of breweries

During the Tudor period, commercial or 'common' brewers appeared who supplied ale to casual callers and to innkeepers. But most innkeepers made their own ale in tiny brewhouses, a habit that did not start to decline until the 18th century when the spread of vast cities created a demand for beer that innkeepers could not meet. Commercial brewing became big business and the owners bought pubs to create a captive market for their products. In spite of government efforts to stop the spread of brewery-owned pubs in the 19th century, by the turn of that century the 'tied house' system was deeply entrenched, with the biggest and wealthiest brewers building large estates of houses.

For most of the 20th century the pub scene remained largely unaltered, divided between tied houses owned by brewers and 'free houses' run by independent small businessmen. The system worked well as long as there were several hundred breweries offering choice and diversity in their houses. Choice declined rapidly from the 1970s onward as a series of mergers and takeovers created half a dozen giant national companies, each owning thousands of pubs and restricting them to a handful of beers. Efforts by successive governments in the 1980s and 1990s to break the stranglehold of the national brewers had only limited success. Rather than improve choice as a result of government diktat, the brewers sold off most of their tied estates, creating new quasi-independent pub groups. In some, the choice of beer has improved; in others, the same old national brands dominate.

Restricted choice goes hand in hand with the tunnel vision of both brewers and pub owners who think that young people are the only customers worthy of note. The late 1990s saw a rash of 'circuit pubs' and 'theme pubs' that allowed teenagers and those in their early twenties to roam the streets in search of strong alcohol and high-decibel entertainment. Deafening music, strobe lights, and bouncers on the door make a mockery of the notion of a public house open to all. But there are signs that even younger people are tiring of the excesses of circuit drinking; the public house, that most enduring of institutions, seems set to survive in the 21st century, once again providing good beer, simple food, and the opportunity for people to throw off the stresses of modern life. In the pub, heaven knows, even the English talk to one another.

by Roger Protz

styled 'Madame Royale'. The title is currently held by Princess Anne.

## Princes Street

Main street in central Edinburgh, Scotland, which has many shops and restaurants. It was named after the young sons of George III. The gardens along its south side are a memorial to Sir Walter Scott.

## privatization

Policy or process of selling or transferring state-owned or public assets and services (notably nationalized industries) to private investors. Privatization of services involves the government contracting private firms to supply services previously supplied by public authorities. The policy of privatization has been pursued by the post-1979 Conservative and Labour administrations.

Supporters of privatization argue that the public benefits from theoretically greater efficiency of firms already in the competitive market, and the release of resources for more appropriate use by government. Those against privatization believe that it transfers a country's assets from all the people to a controlling minority, that public utilities such as gas and water become private monopolies, and that a profit-making state-owned company raises revenue for the government.

**Industries in the UK privatized since 1979** include British Telecom, British Gas Corporation, British National Oil Corporation, British Airways, British Airports Authority, British Aerospace, British Shipbuilders, British Steel, British Transport Docks Board, British Water Board, National Freight Company, Enterprise Oil, Jaguar, National Freight Company, Rover Group, Water Supply, Electricity and gas companies, and British Rail.

## Proms, the

Popular name for the Henry Wood Promenade Concerts held annually between July and September in the Royal Albert Hall, London. The Proms were launched by the English conductor Henry ◊Wood at Queen's Hall, London, in 1895; they have been held at the Albert Hall since 1941. The concerts have been sponsored and broadcast by the BBC since 1927. A proportion of the audience stands during performances.

The eight-week concert season features mainly classical music, with regular premieres of new works. Henry Wood conducted the Proms 1895–1944; he was succeeded by Malcolm ◊Sargent

1944–67. The **Last Night of the Proms** is a traditionally patriotic occasion, with Elgar's *Land of Hope and Glory*, Henry Wood's *Fantasia on British Sea Songs*, Thomas Arne's *Rule, Britannia!*, and Hubert Parry's *Jerusalem* stirringly performed by the BBC Symphony Orchestra. The audience, particularly those standing – the 'Promenaders' – wave flags, bob up and down, and participate enthusiastically.

## Provisional IRA

Radical faction of the ◊IRA.

## public house, or pub

Building licensed for consumption of liquor. In Britain a pub is either 'free' (when the licensee has free choice of suppliers) or, more often, 'tied' to a brewery company owning the house. There are some 77,100 pubs in Britain (1998), many of which also serve food. Legal opening hours are 11.00–23.00 Monday to Saturday and 12.00–22.30 on Sunday. See feature on page 372.

## public inquiry

In English law, a legal investigation where witnesses are called and evidence is produced in a similar fashion to a court of law. Inquiries may be held as part of legal procedure, or into a matter of public concern.

Inquiries that are part of certain legal procedures, such as where planning permission is disputed, or where an inquiry is required by an act of Parliament, are headed by an inspector appointed by the secretary of state concerned, who then makes a decision based on the inspector's report (although this report is not binding). Inquiries into a matter of public concern are usually headed by a senior judge. Examples include the Scarman inquiry following inner-city riots in 1981, an inquiry into child abuse in Cleveland in 1988, and the BSE inquiry, from 1996.

## public lending right, PLR

Method of paying a royalty to authors when books are borrowed from libraries, similar to a royalty on performance of a play or piece of music. Payment to the copyright holder for such borrowings was introduced in the UK in 1984.

## public school

In England and Wales, a prestigious fee-paying independent school. In Scotland a 'public' school is a state-maintained school, and independent schools are generally known as 'private' schools.

Some English public schools (for example Eton, Harrow, Rugby, Winchester) are ancient foundations, usually originally intended for poor male scholars; others developed in the 18th–19th centuries. Among those for girls are Roedean and Benenden. Many public schools are coeducational in the sixth form, and some schools now admit girls at 13. Some discipline (less than formerly) is in the hands of senior boys and girls (prefects).

Originally, UK public schools stressed a classical education, character training, and sports, but the curriculum is now closer allied to state education, although with generally a wider range of subjects offered and a lower pupil-to-teacher ratio.

---

*It is not that the Englishman can't feel – it is that he is afraid to feel. He has been taught at his public school that feeling is bad form.*

**E M Forster** English novelist.
*Abinger Harvest*, 'Notes on English Character'

---

## puddings

Most British puddings trace their origin back to one of two ancient confections; the 'pye' or pudding filled with dried fruit and nuts plus shredded meat (hence the term 'mincemeat'), or a soft, jellied milk pudding, made from wheat or barley, called 'frumenty'. As available ingredients increased, so did the fashion for encasing the pudding in a thick pastry crust or 'coffyn'.

Pies grew increasingly spectacular, but by the end of the 17th century tastes became more rustic and regionalized. Batter and steamed puddings and plate pies were all popular, and local fairs or 'junkets' gave their name to a popular dish that could be made on the spot with milk warm from the cow. This fondness for sweet creamy things still manifests itself in desserts such as gooseberry fool, Trinity or burnt cream, Eton Mess, and the Scottish cranachan made with oatmeal, whisky, and raspberries, as well as the brown bread ice cream that was an Edwardian favourite.

In the late 20th century traditional 'nursery' puddings enjoyed something of a revival (Queen of puddings, spotted dick, Sussex pond pudding, and sticky toffee pudding) but the greatest, Christmas pudding, has never fallen out of favour since it first decorated tables in the 18th century.

## Pugin, Augustus (1812–1852)

English architect and designer. He collaborated with Charles ◊Barry in the detailed design of the

New Palace of Westminster (Houses of Parliament). He did much to instigate the ◊Gothic Revival in England, largely through his book *Contrasts* (1836). Pugin believed in a close connection between Christianity and Gothic architecture, and attacked what he held to be the 'pagan' method of Classical architecture. He became a Roman Catholic, and designed many Roman Catholic churches, including the cathedral of St George at Southwark (severely damaged during World War II).

## Punch and Judy

Traditional puppet play in which Punch, a humpbacked, hooknosed figure, fights with his wife, Judy.

Punch generally overcomes or outwits all opponents. The play is performed by means of glove puppets, manipulated by a single operator concealed in a portable canvas stage frame, who uses a squeaky voice for Punch. Punch originated in Italy, and was probably introduced to England at the time of the Restoration.

## punk

Movement of disaffected youth of the late 1970s, manifesting itself in fashions and music designed to shock or intimidate. **Punk rock** began in the UK and stressed aggressive performance within a three-chord, three-minute format, as exemplified by the Sex Pistols. The punk aesthetic continued to be revived periodically with the nostalgia boom of the 1990s, supported by the growth of a neo-punk movement in the USA and by groups such as the Clash being accorded the status of rock 'n' roll 'classics'.

## Purbeck, Isle of

Peninsula in southeast Dorset, southern England, between Poole Harbour and the English Channel, terminating at St Aldhelm's Head (or St Alban's Head). Purbeck marble and china clay are obtained from the area, which includes the villages of Corfe Castle and Swanage.

The northern ridge of the chalk Purbeck Hills traverses the peninsula from east to west. Purbeck was once a deer forest, but the land is now mainly heath and downs.

## Purcell, Henry (c. 1659–1695)

English Baroque composer. His music balances high formality with melodic expression of controlled intensity, for example, the opera *Dido and Aeneas* (1689) and music for Dryden's *King Arthur* (1691) and for *The Fairy Queen* (1692). He wrote more than 500 works, ranging from secular operas and incidental music for plays to cantatas and church music.

Born at Westminster, he became a chorister at the Chapel Royal, and subsequently was a pupil of Dr John Blow. In 1677 he was appointed composer to the Chapel Royal, and in 1679 organist at Westminster Abbey. As composer to the king, Purcell set odes or anthems to music.

## Quaker
Popular name, originally derogatory, for a member of the Society of ◊Friends.

## Quantock Hills, or the Quantocks
Range of hills in northwest Somerset, England, extending 13 km/8 mi between Taunton and the Bristol Channel. They form a series of irregular ridges, chiefly of greywacke (dark sandstone or grit) and limestone. The highest point is Willsneck (387 m/1,270 ft).

## Queen, the
See ◊Elizabeth II, ◊government, and ◊monarchy.

## Queen Anne style
Decorative art style in England (1700–20), characterized by plain, simple lines, mainly in silver and furniture.

## Queensberry, John Sholto Douglas, 8th Marquess of Queensberry (1844–1900)
British patron of boxing. In 1867 he gave his name to a new set of boxing rules. Devised by the pioneering British sports administrator John Chambers (1841–1883), the **Queensberry Rules** form the basis of today's boxing rules.

He was the father of Lord Alfred ◊Douglas and it was his written insult to Oscar Wilde that set in motion the events leading to the playwright's imprisonment. He became Marquess in 1858.

### rackets, or racquets

Indoor game played on an enclosed court. Although first played in the Middle Ages, rackets developed in the 18th century and was played against the walls of London buildings. It is considered the forerunner of many racket and ball games, particularly squash.

The game is played on a court usually 18.3 m/60 ft long by 9.1 m/30 ft wide, by two or four persons each with a racket about 75 cm/2.5 ft long, weighing 255 g/9 oz. The ball is 25 mm/1 in in diameter and weighs 28 g/1 oz. Play begins from a service box – one is marked at each side of mid-court – and the ball must hit the end wall above a 2.75 m/9 ft line high. After service it may be played anywhere above a line 68.5 cm/27 in high on the end wall, the general rules of tennis applying thereafter.

### Rackham, Arthur (1867–1939)

English illustrator. Influenced by ◊Art Nouveau, he developed an ornate and delicate style. He illustrated a wide range of books, but is best remembered for his illustrations for children's classics, including *Peter Pan* (1906) and *Andersen's Fairy Tales* (1932).

### Radcliffe, Ann born Ward (1764–1823)

English novelist. An exponent of the Gothic novel or 'romance of terror', she wrote, for example, *The Mysteries of Udolpho* (1794). She excelled in depicting scenes of mystery and terror, and was one of the first novelists to include vivid descriptions of landscape and weather.

Her other novels include *A Sicilian Romance* (1790), *The Romance of the Forest* 1791, and *The Italian* (1797). Her work was extremely popular in her day.

### radio

Radio channels, both national and local, are run by the ◊BBC and by a mix of independent commercial companies who play on-air advertising. The five BBC national radio stations are Radio 1 (pop), Radio 2 (mainstream music), Radio 3 (predominantly classical music and some talk), Radio 4 (mostly speech: news and current affairs, features, drama), and Radio 5 Live (sport and news). In addition the BBC runs a range of local radio stations and the World Service, which in 1998 broadcasted in 47 languages, including English.

In the independent sector the national stations are Virgin (music), Talk Radio, and Classic FM (music), while the local commercial stations include Capital, in London. Commercial radio stations are licensed by the Radio Authority, created in 1991 to take on radio responsibilities from the Independent Broadcasting Authority.

### Raeburn, Henry (1756–1823)

Scottish painter. One of the leading portrait painters of the 18th century, his technique of painting with broad brush-strokes directly on the canvas, without preparatory drawing, gave his works an air of freshness and spontaneity. *The Reverend Robert Walker Skating* (about 1784; National Gallery of Scotland, Edinburgh) is typical.

Raeburn was active mainly in Edinburgh, his subjects being the notable figures of literature and law, and the chieftains of the Highland clans. He excelled in male rather than female portraits, his style being well adapted to convey their rugged dignity. He was knighted in 1822 and appointed painter to George IV in 1823.

## Raffles, Stamford (1781–1826)

British colonial administrator, born in Jamaica. He served in the British ◊East India Company, took part in the capture of Java from the Dutch in 1811, and while governor of Sumatra 1818–23 was responsible for the acquisition and founding of Singapore in 1819. Knighted 1817.

## Railtrack

Company responsible for the commercial operation of the railway network (track and stations) in Britain. In May 1996, as part of privatization, the 20 British Rail service companies that had previously provided Railtrack's infrastructure support functions were sold into the private sector.

Railtrack does not operate train services, but is responsible for timetabling and signalling, and owns the freehold of stations. Following privatization, passenger services were divided into 25 train-operating units to be franchised to private sector operators, enabling the private sector to eventually run completely new services. The three subsidiary companies that were responsible for British Rail's passenger rolling stock were privatized in February 1996.

## railways

Following the work of British steam pioneers such as Scottish engineer James ◊Watt, English engineer George ◊Stephenson built the first public steam railway, from Stockton to Darlington, England, in 1825. This heralded extensive railway building in Britain, continental Europe, and North America, providing a fast and economical means of transport and communication. After World War II, steam engines were replaced by electric and diesel engines. At the same time, the growth of road building, air services, and car ownership destroyed the supremacy of the railways.

### Growth years

Four years after building the first steam railway, Stephenson opened the first steam passenger line, inaugurating it with his locomotive *Rocket*, which achieved speeds of 50 kph/30 mph. The railway construction that followed resulted in 250 separate companies in Britain, which resolved into four systems in 1921 and became the nationalized British Railways in 1948, known as British Rail from 1965.

**Railways** *Over London by Rail* (1872), an engraving by the French artist Gustave Doré. Though most of his works are book illustrations, in the 1870s Doré engraved a series depicting the grim realities of slum life in London. His images were so powerful they were used in British government reports on the conditions of the poor. Corbis

## Gauge

Railway tracks were at first made of wood but later of iron or steel, with ties wedging them apart and keeping them parallel. The distance between the wheels is known as the gauge. Since much of the early development of the railway took place in Tyneside, England, the gauge of local coal wagons, 1.24 m/4 ft 8.5 in, was adopted in 1824 for the Stockton–Darlington railway, and most other early railways followed suit. The main exception was the Great Western Railway (GWR) of Isambard Kingdom ◊Brunel, opened in 1841, with a gauge of 2.13 m/7 ft. The narrow gauge won legal backing in the UK in 1846, but parts of GWR carried on with Brunel's broad gauge until 1892.

## Decline of railways

With the increasing use of private cars and government-encouraged road haulage after World War II, and the demise of steam, rising costs on the railways meant higher fares, fewer passengers, and declining freight traffic. In the UK many rural rail services closed down on the recommendations of the Beeching Report of 1963, reducing the size of the network by more than 20% between 1965 and 1970, from a peak of 24,102 km/14,977 mi.

The process of rail privatization in Britain, begun in 1992, was formally completed in April 1997 when the British Rail chairman signed papers handing over ScotRail to National Express. National Express, with five of the 25 franchises, extending from London to the Highlands, became the biggest single buyer of BR.

Railtrack is now responsible for the track and infrastructure. There are three rolling stock companies that lease locomotives and passenger coaches; 25 train operating companies; four freight service providers; seven infrastructure maintenance companies and six track renewal companies.

## Raj, the

The period of British rule in India before independence in 1947.

## Raleigh, or Ralegh, Walter (c. 1552–1618)

English adventurer, writer, and courtier to Queen Elizabeth I. He organized expeditions to colonize North America in 1584–87, all unsuccessful, and made exploratory voyages to South America in 1595 and 1616. His aggressive actions against Spanish interests, including attacks on Spanish ports, brought him into conflict with the pacific James I. He was imprisoned for treason from 1603–16 and executed on his return from an unsuccessful final expedition to South America. He is traditionally credited with introducing the potato to Europe and popularizing the use of tobacco.

Born in Devon, Raleigh became a confidant of Queen Elizabeth I and was knighted in 1584. After initiating several unsuccessful attempts in 1584–87 to establish a colony in North America, he led a gold-seeking expedition to the Orinoco River in South America in 1595 (described in his *Discoverie of Guiana* 1596). He distinguished himself in expeditions against Spain in Cádiz in 1596 and the Azores in 1597.

After James I's accession to the English throne in 1603, Raleigh was condemned to death on a charge of conspiracy, but was reprieved and imprisoned in the Tower of London, where he wrote his unfinished *History of the World*. Released in 1616 to lead a second expedition to the Orinoco, which failed disastrously, he was beheaded on his return under the charges of his former sentence.

## Rambert, Marie adopted name of Cyvia Myriam Rambam (1888–1982)

Polish-born British ballet dancer and teacher. One of the major innovative and influential figures in modern ballet, she worked with Vaslav Nijinsky on *The Rite of Spring* for the Diaghilev ballet in Paris from 1912–13, opened the Rambert School in London in 1920, and in 1926 founded the Ballet Rambert which she directed. It became a modern-dance company from 1966 and was renamed the Rambert Dance Company in 1987.

## Ramblers' Association

Society founded in Britain in 1935 to conserve the countryside and ensure that footpaths remain open.

## Ramsey, Alf(red) (1920–1999)

English football player and manager. England's most successful manager ever, he won the World Cup in 1966. Of the 123 matches in which he was in charge of the national side between 1963 and 1974, England had 78 victories and only 13 defeats. Shrewd, pragmatic and single-minded, he was not afraid to go against traditional football wisdom, most notably in 1966 when he decided to play without wingers, a step that was greeted with widespread scepticism, but subsequently hailed as a masterstroke when England won the World Cup. He led England to the quarter-finals of the 1970 World Cup, but was sacked four years later after the team failed to qualify for the 1974 finals.

## Ramsgate

Seaside resort and cross-Channel port in the Isle of Thanet, northeast Kent, southeast England; population (1991) 37,100. It is a centre for yachting and fishing, and became popular as a resort following George IV's visit in 1827. There are ferry links with France and Belgium.

St Augustine, sent by the Pope to convert England to Christianity, is said to have landed here in 597.

## Rank, J(oseph) Arthur, 1st Baron Rank (1888–1972)

English film magnate. Having entered films in 1933 to promote the Methodist cause, by the mid-1940s he controlled, through the Rank Organization, half the British studios and more than 1,000 cinemas. The Rank Organization still owns the Odeon chain of cinemas, although film is now a minor part of its activities. He was created a baron in 1957.

## Ransome, Arthur (1884–1967)

English writer of adventure stories for children. His children's novels feature sailing and include ◊ Swallows and Amazons (1930) and Peter Duck (1932). A journalist, he was correspondent in Russia for the Daily News during World War I and the Revolution.

He was also a student of folklore, and the stories he collected while working in Russia were published in 1916 as Old Peter's Russian Tales.

## Rathlin Island

Island in Northern Ireland, 10 km/6 mi off the north coast of County Antrim, opposite Ballycastle. Its main industries are fishing and tourism.

The Kebble national nature reserve is a breeding ground for such seabirds as razorbills and puffins. There is also a scuba-diving centre here.

Rathlin Island has had a long history of conflict: it was raided by Vikings in 790 and later by the Campbells of Scotland; later still, English forces slaughtered the inhabitants in 1597. In 1617 Rathlin Island was subject to a legal dispute over ownership between Scotland and Ireland which finally settled it as Irish.

The island was the refuge of Robert ◊ Bruce, King of Scotland, in 1306. Legend has it that this is where the exiled king learned his lesson in perseverance from watching a spider weave its web in a basalt cave now known as Bruce's Cave.

## rationing

Food rationing was introduced in Britain during World War I. During World War II food rationing, organized by the government, began in Britain in 1940. Each person was issued with a ration book of coupons. Bacon, butter, and sugar were restricted, followed by other goods, including sweets, petrol, clothing, soap, and furniture. All food rationing finally ended in Britain in 1954. During the Suez Crisis of 1956, petrol rationing was reintroduced.

## Rattigan, Terence (1911–1977)

English dramatist. His play Ross (1960) was based on the character of T E Lawrence (Lawrence of Arabia). Rattigan's work ranges from the comedy French Without Tears (1936) to the psychological intensity of The Winslow Boy (1946). Other plays include The Browning Version (1948) and Separate Tables (1954).

## Reading

Industrial town in southern England, on the River Thames where it meets the Kennet, 61 km/38 mi west of London; population (1996) 131,000. Part of the county of Berkshire until April 1998, it is now a unitary authority with an area of 37 sq km/14 sq mi. Reading expanded during the 19th century with the growth of its factories, becoming known for its biscuits, beer, and bulbs. It is now a centre of light industry and commerce, a residential town, and a regional shopping centre.

*Features*

While much of the town's architecture reflects its Victorian industrial heritage, the town was extensively rebuilt after World War II. Little visible evidence of Reading's early history survives, but there are remains of the 12th-century Benedictine abbey where Henry I was buried. The Museum of Reading includes Roman and Saxon relics and a full-size Victorian reproduction of the Bayeaux Tapestry. Oscar Wilde was imprisoned in Reading gaol from 1895 to 1897. Reading hosts an annual rock festival and it is the site of the University of Reading (1926).

## Real IRA

An extremist Irish Republican terrorist group which split away from the ◊ IRA in 1997. Based in the Republican stronghold of Dundalk, County Louth, in the Irish Republic, close to the border with Northern Ireland, its political mouthpiece has been the 32 County Sovereignty Committee. On 15 August 1998 it was responsible for the deadliest terrorist atrocity in Northern Ireland's history, when 28 innocent bystanders were killed by a car bomb detonated in the shopping centre of Omagh, County Tyrone. Following condemnation of the attack by ◊Sinn Féin and revulsion within Dundalk, the Real IRA apologized for the deaths and claimed that the warnings given had not been misleading, as the media and police claimed. Soon afterwards, it announced a suspension to its military operations.

## Record Office, Public
Government office containing the English and Welsh national records since the Norman Conquest, brought together from courts of law and government departments, including the Domesday Book, the Gunpowder Plot papers, and the log of HMS *Victory* at Trafalgar. It was established in 1838 in Chancery Lane, London; records dating from the 18th century onwards have been housed at Kew, London, since 1976.

The Scottish Records Office is situated in Edinburgh and the Public Record Office of Northern Ireland is in Belfast. Scotland's national archives were established in the 13th century, with the appointment of a Clerk of the Rolls. There are also Public Record Offices for each county.

## Redcar and Cleveland
Unitary authority in northeast England created in 1996 from part of the former county of Cleveland; it has an area of 240 sq km/93 sq mi; population (1996) 144,000; and its towns and cities include Redcar (administrative headquarters), Skelton, Guisborough, Marske-by-the-Sea, Saltburn-by-the-Sea, Brotton, and Loftus.
*Features*
North Sea coast; River Tees forms northwest border; Boulby Cliffs are highest cliffs on England's east coast (203 m/666 ft); 12th-century Priory at Guisborough; Cleveland Way long-distance path reaches coast at Saltburn; RNLI Zetland Lifeboat Museum (Redcar); Ironstone Mining Museum (Saltburn-by-the-Sea).
*Industries*
Manufacture of steel products (British Steel), engineering, fertilizers and potash products, textiles.

## Redditch
Industrial town in Worcestershire, 19 km/12 mi south of Birmingham; population (1991) 72,700. Formerly a needle-making centre, it was designated a new town in 1964 to take overspill population from Birmingham.

## Redgrave, Michael (1908–1985)
English actor. His stage roles included Hamlet and Lear (Shakespeare), Uncle Vanya (Chekhov), and the schoolmaster in Terence Rattigan's *The Browning Version* (filmed 1951). On screen he appeared in *The Lady Vanishes* (1938), *The Importance of Being Earnest* (1952), and *Goodbye Mr Chips* (1969).

He was the father of the actresses Vanessa and Lynn Redgrave.

## Red Rum
Racehorse whose exploits in the ◊Grand National at ◊Aintree won him national fame. The only horse to win the race three times, with victories in 1973, 1974, and 1977, he also finished second in 1975 and 1976. He died in 1995 at the age of 30, and is buried at Aintree near to the winning post.

## Reed, Oliver (1938–1999)
English actor. He appeared in a range of films, including *Oliver!* (1968), *Women in Love* (1969), *The Devils* (1971), and *Castaway* (1987). He was the nephew of the director Carol ◊Reed.

## Reed, Carol (1906–1976)
English film producer and director. He was an influential figure in the British film industry of the 1940s. His films include *Odd Man Out* (1946), *The Fallen Idol* (1948), *The Third Man* (1949), *Our Man in Havana* (1959), and the Academy Award-winning musical *Oliver!* (1968).

## reel
A Scottish, Irish, and Scandinavian dance, either of Celtic or Scandinavian origin. It is performed with the dancers standing face to face and the music is in quick 2–4 or 4–4, occasionally 6–8, time and divided into regular eight-bar phrases. A musical characteristic of many reels is a drop into the triad of the subdominant unprepared by modulation.

## Reform Acts
Acts of Parliament in 1832, 1867, and 1884 that extended voting rights and redistributed parliamentary seats; also known as ◊Representation of the People Acts.

The 1832 act abolished the pocket, or ◊rotten borough, which had formed unrepresentative constituencies, redistributed seats on a more equitable basis in the counties, and formed some new boroughs. The franchise was extended to male householders in property worth £10 a year or more in the boroughs and to owners of freehold property worth £2 a year, £10 copyholders, or £50 leaseholders in the counties. The 1867 act redistributed seats from corrupt and small boroughs to the counties and large urban areas. It also extended the franchise in boroughs to adult male heads of households, and in counties to males who owned, or held on long leases, land worth £5 a year, or who occupied land worth £12 on which they paid poor rates. The 1884 act extended the franchise to male agricultural labourers.

## Reformation

Religious and political movement in 16th-century Europe to reform the Roman Catholic Church, which led to the establishment of Protestant churches. Anticipated from the 12th century by the Waldenses, Lollards, and Hussites, it was set off by German priest Martin Luther in 1517, and became effective when the absolute monarchies gave it support by challenging the political power of the papacy and confiscating church wealth. See feature opposite.

*The Reformation was the greatest revolution in English history. It meant that England was suddenly separated from the Europe of western Christendom, of which it had formed an important part for more than a millennium. This was the first element in the establishment of an independent nation-state which was to be isolated from Europe until 1973.*
**Edwin Jones** English historian.
*The English Nation: the Great Myth* (1998)

## Reformation Parliament

English parliament of November 1529–April 1536 which passed Thomas Cromwell's antipapal legislation. It acknowledged the sovereign as head of the Church in place of the pope, and empowered Henry VIII to abolish payments to Rome of the first year's income of all newly installed bishops, as had hitherto been the practice. It sanctioned the installation of Thomas Cranmer as primate of the English church, and enabled Henry to divorce Catherine of Aragón in 1533 and have Anne Boleyn executed in 1536, so that he at last had a male heir (Edward) in 1537 by Jane Seymour. The dissolution of the monasteries followed 1636–40. The Parliament lasted an unprecedented seven years and altogether enacted 137 statues, 32 of which were of vital importance.

### Regency

The years 1811–20 during which ◊George IV (then Prince of Wales) acted as regent for his father ◊George III.

### Regency style

Style of architecture and interior furnishings popular in England during the late 18th and early 19th centuries. It is characterized by restrained simplicity and the imitation of ancient classical elements, often Greek.

Architects of this period include Decimus Burton (1800–1881), Henry Holland (1746–1806), and John ◊Nash.

### regent

Person who carries out the duties of a sovereign during the sovereign's minority, incapacity, or lengthy absence from the country. In England since the time of Henry VIII, Parliament has always appointed a regent or council of regency when necessary.

Regencies were established during the minorities of Henry III, Edward III, Richard II, Henry VI, Edward V, and Edward VI, and during the insanity of Henry VI. The most recent period of prolonged regency occurred during the reign of George III, whose mental illness in 1788 and after 1810 led to the nomination of the Prince of Wales as regent.

Legislation was passed to deal with particular contingencies during the reigns of William IV, Victoria, and George V, but comprehensive provision for the incapacity, illness, or absence of the sovereign was not passed until 1937. The Regency Acts 1937–53 now provide for the delegation of royal function to counsellors of state, who may be the wife or husband of the sovereign, the four people next in succession to the throne, and, since 1953, Queen Elizabeth the Queen Mother. Counsellors of state may not, however, dissolve Parliament nor grant peerages. The same legislation also provides for the establishment of a regency where the sovereign is under 18 years of age and in the event of the mental or physical incapacity of the sovereign.

### Regent's Park

Park in London, covering 188 ha/464 acres. It contains London Zoo. Regent's Canal runs through the park, which was laid out by John Nash for the Prince Regent, later George IV. Grand terraced residences, which overlook the park, were designed by Nash and by Decimus Burton (1800–81).

# ◆ SOVEREIGNS AND PURITANS: THE BRITISH REFORMATION ◆

The conventional history of the British Reformation, written by the victorious Protestants, is a tale of how a decaying, corrupt, and unpopular medieval Church was bowled over by an irresistible movement of reform and renewal. Recent research has destroyed this picture completely. Historians are now certain that in 1520 the Church in Britain was a thriving, dynamic, and well-loved institution. Parish churches were the foci of intense local devotion, ecclesiastical courts were respected and much in demand, and there were more applicants for the priesthood than there were jobs. To be sure, there were also problems: too many religious houses, clashes with the growing numbers of common lawyers, and the persistence of small groups of people in southern England, collectively called Lollards, who privately rejected aspects of the official religion. None of these, however, represented a serious weakness.

## Royal involvement

The real issue after 1520 was not that the old Church was going wrong, but that an increasing number of people started to think that it had never been right. It depended upon the doctrine that Christians could best get to heaven by performing ritual works: by joining in ceremonies, by beautifying churches, and by revering saints as personal divine patrons. Over the centuries this behaviour had become ever more elaborate, intense, and expensive. The argument of Protestantism, as first preached by Martin Luther in Germany in 1517, was that it was all a confidence trick, for the Bible suggested that none of it was necessary. Indeed, to Protestants it was actually evil, for it diverted attention from direct concern with God and Scripture.

Nonetheless, popular Protestantism was so weak in Britain before 1550 that it would have made little impact had not the English Crown embraced the new ideas. All over Europe in this period monarchs were increasing their control over the Church within their realms. This could be accomplished perfectly well by allying with it against Protestantism, and such a line was taken by Henry VIII of England during the 1520s. In 1529, however, he quarrelled with the Pope over the latter's refusal to grant him a divorce, and resolved to take over the Church in England himself. His avowed aim was to reform it within a Catholic tradition, but he came increasingly to rely upon Protestant advisers and the latter took control when Henry died, on behalf of his young son Edward VI.

## Counter-Reformation

Under Henry the monasteries were dissolved and the cult of the saints destroyed, while Edward's regime removed the old ornaments and rituals altogether. Both encountered fierce resistance, Henry provoking the huge northern rising known as the Pilgrimage of Grace and Edward's ministers facing the Western Rebellion in 1549. The first was defeated by trickery and the second in pitched battles. By early 1550 a majority of the English, especially in the southeast, had probably ceased to believe in the old Church, but only a minority had acquired any active commitment to the new faith. In Scotland, the association of Protestantism with England, the old enemy, had kept the traditional religion in power even though a growing number of Scots were turning against it.

There was therefore a real potential for the Reformation to be reversed, and so it was when Edward died in 1553 and was succeeded by his Catholic sister Mary. She restored her Church, with more streamlining and central control than before, and persecuted Protestants with a savagery unique in British religious history, burning about 300. It seems likely that had she lived for a further 20 years then Britain would be Catholic to this day, but she died after only 5 years and left her Protestant sister, Elizabeth, to take over.

## The Elizabethan compromise

The English Catholics were demoralized by the lack of any alternative heir but comforted by promises of good treatment. The Scottish Protestants now chose their moment to rebel and Elizabeth sent an English army to help them into power. Another English expeditionary force in 1573 secured their position, and the young king of the Scots, James VI, was brought up in the Protestant tradition and inherited England when Elizabeth died in 1603.

It was the sheer length of Elizabeth's reign which allowed the Reformation to triumph in Britain, so that by the 1580s the majority of its people had been so thoroughly re-educated in the new faith that they genuinely identified with it. It never, however, achieved the unity of the old one. The Church of England reflected Elizabeth's wish for compromise, yoking Protestant doctrine to a Catholic structure of bishops, cathedrals, and festivals. Many Protestants remained deeply unhappy with it. The Church of Scotland, formed in revolution, made a more radical departure, to a presbyterian structure and a complete abolition of the old festivals and vestments. The defeat of Catholicism in Britain made certain a future struggle between the different strands of Protestantism.

by Ronald Hutton

The park was developed on the site of Marylebone Gardens and pasture land. It formed part of a scheme, begun in 1812, to connect the Prince's residence (Carlton House) in the Mall, via Regent Street, with another residence (never built) in the new park. The park was opened to the public in 1838.

Bedford College (now part of Royal Holloway College) was located here from 1909–85. There is an open-air theatre in the Inner Circle of the park.

## Regent Street

Shopping street in London, running from Pall Mall to Langham Place, crossing Piccadilly Circus and Oxford Street. It was designed by John Nash between 1813 and 1820 for the Prince Regent, later George IV, to connect the Prince's residence (Carlton House) in the Mall with another residence (never built) in Regent's Park. Since then it has been completely rebuilt.

The curved area north of Piccadilly Circus, known as the Quadrant, was redesigned in 1925–26 by Reginald Blomfield (1856–1942).

The Café Royal in Regent Street was the haunt of many literary and artistic figures in the late 19th century and early 20th century; among them were Augustus John, Aubrey Beardsley, and Max Beerbohm. The Liberty shop, with its mock Tudor facade, was designed in 1924 by E T and E S Hall. On the Great Marlborough Street side of the building (north) is a public clock on which St George and the Dragon appear each hour.

## Reith, John (1889–1971)

Scottish broadcasting pioneer, the first general manager 1922–27 and director general 1927–38 of the British Broadcasting Corporation (BBC). He was enormously influential in the early development of the BBC and established its high-minded principles of public service broadcasting. He held several ministerial posts in government during World War II, including minister of information in 1940, transport in 1940, and minister of works from 1940–42.

## Remembrance Sunday, Armistice Day until 1945

National day of remembrance for those killed in both world wars and later conflicts, on the second Sunday of November. Remembrance Sunday is observed by a two-minute silence at the time of the signature of the armistice with Germany that ended World War I: 11:00 am, 11 November 1918 (although since 1956 the day of commemoration has been the Sunday). There are ceremonies at the Cenotaph in Whitehall, London, and elsewhere. 'Flanders poppies', symbolic of the blood shed, are sold in aid of war invalids and their dependants.

## Renfrewshire

Unitary authority in west central Scotland, with its northern border on the Firth of Clyde, created in 1996 from the northern and western parts of Renfrew district in Strathclyde region, which in turn was formed from the former county of Renfrewshire (until 1974); population (1995) 178,300; area 260 sq km/100 sq mi. The principal towns are ◊Paisley (administrative headquarters), Renfrew, Johnstone, and Erskine.
*Physical*
The area is mainly low lying, but hilly in the west, rising to the Hill of Stake (525 m/1,723 ft). The rivers are the Clyde, Gryfe, White Cart, and Black Cart.
*Features*
There are interesting sculptural stones at Inchinnan, near Erskine. Paisley has an abbey from the 13th century and a museum with a notable collection of paisley shawls. The authority has seven Sites of Special Scientific Interest, one regional park, and three country parks.
*Economy*
While dominated by large industrial and de-industrializing towns, the area also covers an affluent belt of small towns and villages that are within the Glasgow commuter belt. Industries include engineering, computers, electronics, and food and drink products; service industries are growing. Glasgow International Airport is in Renfrewshire.

## reply, right of

Right of a member of the public to respond to a media statement. A statutory right of reply, enforceable by a Press Commission, as exists in many Western European countries, failed to reach the statute book in the UK in 1989. There is no legal provision in the UK that any correction should receive the same prominence as the original statement and legal aid is not available in defamation cases, so that only the wealthy are able to sue. However, the major newspapers signed a Code of Practice in 1989 that promised some public protection.

## Repton, Humphry (1752–1818)

English garden designer. He worked for some years in partnership with English architect John ◊Nash. Repton preferred more formal landscaping than his predecessor Capability ◊Brown, and was responsible for the landscaping of some 200 gardens and parks. He coined the term 'landscape gardening'.

He laid out Russell Square and Bloomsbury Square in London around 1800, and published many books on landscape.

## Restoration

In English history, the period when the monarchy, in the person of Charles II, was re-established after the English Civil War and the fall of the Protectorate in 1660.

## Restoration comedy

Style of English theatre, dating from the Restoration (1660). It witnessed the first appearance of women on the English stage, most notably in the 'breeches part', specially created in order to costume the actress in male attire, thus revealing her figure to its best advantage. The genre placed much emphasis on wit and sexual intrigues. Examples include Wycherley's *The Country Wife* (1675), Congreve's *The Way of the World* (1700), and Farquhar's *The Beaux' Stratagem* (1707).

## Revolutionary Wars

Series of wars from 1791 to 1802 between France and the combined armies of England, Austria, Prussia, and others, during the period of the French Revolution and Napoleon's campaign to conquer Europe.

## Revolution, the Glorious

Events surrounding the removal of James II from the throne and his replacement in 1689 by his daughter Mary and William of Orange as joint sovereigns (◊Mary II and ◊William III), bound by the ◊Bill of Rights. See feature.

James had become increasingly unpopular on account of his unconstitutional behaviour and Catholicism. Various elements in England, including seven prominent politicians, plotted to invite the Protestant William to invade. Arriving at Torbay on 5 November 1688, William rapidly gained support and James was allowed to flee to France after the army deserted him. Support for James in Scotland and Ireland was forcibly suppressed 1689–90. William and Mary accepted in 1689 a new constitutional settlement, the Bill of Rights, which assured the ascendancy of parliamentary power over sovereign rule. The Act of ◊Settlement of 1701 ensured future Protestant succession to the throne, and William was succeeded by Anne, second daughter of James II.

## Reynolds, Joshua (1723–1792)

English painter. One of the greatest portraitists of the 18th century, he displayed a facility for striking and characterful compositions in the 'Grand Manner', a style based on Classical and Renaissance art. He often borrowed Classical poses, for example *Mrs Siddons as the Tragic Muse* (1784; San Marino, California). His elegant portraits are mostly of wealthy patrons, though he also painted such figures as the writers Laurence Sterne and Dr Johnson, and the actor David Garrick. Active in London from 1752, he became the first president of the Royal Academy in 1768 and founded the Royal Academy schools.

Reynolds was particularly influenced by Classical antiquity and the High Renaissance masters, Michelangelo, Raphael, Titian, and Leonardo da Vinci. In his *Discourses on Art*, based on lectures given at the Royal Academy from 1769 to 1791, he argued that art should be of the Grand Manner, presenting the ideal rather than the mundane and realistic. Some of his finest portraits, however, combine Classical form with a keen awareness of individuality, as in his *Lord Heathfield* (1787; National Gallery, London) and *Admiral Keppel* (1753–54; National Maritime Museum, London). Certain works – such as his *Self-Portrait* (about 1773; Royal Academy, London) – appear closer to Rembrandt than to Renaissance artists. He was knighted in 1769.

## Rhondda

Industrial town in ◊Rhondda Cynon Taff, south Wales, situated 26 km/16 mi northwest of Cardiff; population (1991) 59,900. Lying at the heart of the Rhondda Valley, it was one of the most important coalmining towns in Britain and supplied 90 per cent of the Royal Navy's ships in World War I. The closure of the Maerdy mine in 1990 ended mining in the valley. The Rhondda Heritage Park recreates a 1920s-style mining village for visitors.

## Rhondda Cynon Taff

Unitary authority in south Wales, created in 1996 from part of the former county of Mid Glamorgan; population (1996) 232,600; area 440 sq km/170 sq mi. It takes its name from the rivers Fhondda Fawr and Rhondda Fach, Cynon, and Taff, and consists of a series of linear settlements along the river valleys. The chief town is ◊Clydach Vale (administrative headquarters).

*Physical*

The southern part of the ◊Brecon Beacons is in the north of the authority. To the south is the lowland plateau, or Bro Morgannwg, a rich agricultural area of mixed farming and large villages which is traversed by the M4 motorway.

*Features*
The Royal Mint is at Llantrisant.

*Economy*
The south was formerly an important coal mining area. More recently, a variety of new light industries have been attracted here, and there are two major industrial estates, one at Treforest near Pontypridd and the other at Hirwaun near Aberdare.

## Ribble

River in northern England, formed by the confluence of the Gayle and Cam; length 120 km/75 mi. From its source in the Pennine hills, North Yorkshire, it flows south and southwest past Preston, Lancashire, to join the Irish Sea.

The Ribble Estuary National Nature Reserve is the largest in England. It is a wintering ground for migrating waterfowl. It has salt marshes and sandflats.

The river is contaminated with radioactive waste from the British Nuclear Fuels plant at Springfield. Monitoring takes place every two months.

## Richard

Three kings of England:

## Richard (I) the Lionheart (French *Coeur-de-Lion*) (1157–1199)

King of England from 1189. He spent all but six months of his reign abroad. He was the third son of Henry II, against whom he twice rebelled. In the third Crusade (1191–92) he won victories at Cyprus, Acre, and Arsuf (against Saladin), but failed to recover Jerusalem. While returning overland he was captured by the Duke of Austria, who handed him over to the emperor Henry VI, and he was held prisoner until a large ransom was raised. He then returned briefly to England, where his brother John had been ruling in his stead. His later years were spent in warfare in France, where he was killed.

Himself a poet, he became a hero of legends after his death. He was succeeded by his brother John I.

## Richard II, or Richard of Bordeaux (1367–1400)

King of England from 1377, effectively from 1389, son of Edward the Black Prince. He reigned in conflict with Parliament; they executed some of his associates in 1388, and he executed some of the opposing barons in 1397, whereupon he made himself absolute. Two years later, forced to abdicate in favour of ◊ Henry IV, he was jailed and probably assassinated.

In 1381 the young Richard was faced with the ◊ Peasants' Revolt, a result of the imposition of the Poll Tax in 1380. The leader of the Revolt, Wat Tyler, was stabbed and killed at Smithfield by the Lord Mayor of London, fearing for the safety of the king. Richard's apparent courage in facing the mobs gathered at Mile End and Smithfield also contributed to the failure of the uprising.

Richard was born in Bordeaux. He succeeded his grandfather Edward III when only ten, the government being in the hands of a council of regency. His fondness for favourites resulted in conflicts with Parliament, and in 1388 the baronial party, headed by the Duke of Gloucester, had many of his friends executed. Richard recovered control in 1389, and ruled moderately until 1397, when he had Gloucester murdered and his other leading opponents executed or banished, and assumed absolute power. In 1399 his cousin Henry Bolingbroke, Duke of Hereford (later Henry IV), returned from exile to lead a revolt; Richard II was deposed by Parliament and imprisoned in Pontefract Castle, where he died mysteriously.

**Richard (I) The Lion-Heart** The Great Seal of King Richard I who spent most of his reign away from England. He was a notable soldier who fought in the third Crusade 1191–92, defeating the Muslim leader Saladin and capturing Acre. Philip Sauvain Picture Collection

## Richard III (1452–1485)

King of England from 1483. The son of Richard, Duke of York, he was created Duke of Gloucester by his brother Edward IV, and distinguished himself in the Wars of the ◊Roses. On Edward's death in 1483 he became protector to his nephew Edward V, and soon secured the crown for himself on the plea that Edward IV's sons were illegitimate. He proved a capable ruler, but the suspicion that he had murdered Edward V and his brother undermined his popularity. In 1485 Henry, Earl of Richmond (later ◊Henry VII), raised a rebellion, and Richard III was defeated and killed at ◊Bosworth.

Scholars now tend to minimize the evidence for his crimes as Tudor propaganda.

## Richardson, Ralph (1902–1983)

English actor. He played many stage parts, including Falstaff (Shakespeare), Peer Gynt (Ibsen), and Cyrano de Bergerac (Rostand). He shared the management of the Old Vic Theatre with Laurence ◊Olivier from 1944–50. In later years he revealed himself as an accomplished deadpan comic.

Later stage successes include David Storey's *Home* (1970) and Harold Pinter's *No Man's Land* (1976). His films include *Things to Come* (1936), *Richard III* (1956), *Our Man in Havana* (1959), *The Wrong Box* (1966), *The Bed-Sitting Room* (1969), and *O Lucky Man!* (1973).

## Richardson, Samuel (1689–1761)

English novelist. He was one of the founders of the modern novel. *Pamela* (1740–41), written in the form of a series of letters and containing much dramatic conversation, was sensationally popular all across Europe, and was followed by *Clarissa* (1747–48) and *Sir Charles Grandison* (1753–54).

He set up his own printing business in London in 1719, becoming printer to the House of Commons.

## Richmond

Market town in North Yorkshire, northern England, on the River Swale, 17 km/11 mi southwest of Darlington; population (1991) 7,800. It is the centre of the surrounding farming district and is also the main tourist centre of the Yorkshire Dales National Park. Features include a restored Georgian theatre (1788).

It has the remains – only the keep – of a Norman castle, built in 1071 on a promontory overlooking the River Swale. To the southeast of Richmond are the ruins of Easby Abbey (1152). Also nearby is Catterick Camp, a large military camp.

## Richmond-upon-Thames

Outer borough of southwest Greater London; population (1991) 160,700. The only London borough with land on both sides of the River Thames, it includes the districts of Kew, Teddington, ◊Twickenham, and Hampton. With strong royal associations dating back to the time of Edward III, Richmond became a fashionable residential area in the 17th and 18th centuries and includes many historic houses as well as some of Britain's most visited attractions, including ◊Kew Gardens and ◊Hampton Court Palace.

### Features

Richmond Green, surrounded by 17th and 18th century houses, Richmond Hill, with its beautiful view of meadows, hills, and woods, and the vast Richmond Park, with its deer and ancient oaks, make this one of London's most attractive suburbs. Originally enclosed as a royal hunting ground by Charles I, Richmond Park covers 1,000 hectares/2,470 acres and is the largest urban park in Britain. There are remains of a Tudor royal palace where Elizabeth I died in 1603 and near these remains, forming one side of Richmond Green, is Maids of Honour Row, built to house the ladies of the court during George I's reign. To the south of Richmond Park is Ham House, built in 1610, which has an ornate Stuart interior. Marble Hill House, in Twickenham is a fine example of an English Palladian-style villa. The house was built by the Duchess of Suffolk, the mistress of George II. Twickenham is perhaps best known for its Rugby ground, the headquarters of the Rugby Football Union. Teddington is the highest tidal point on the Thames, and its lock (built in 1811) is the largest (198 m/650 ft by 7.6 m/25 ft) on the river. The former homes of David Garrick, Christopher Wren, and Michael Faraday, can be seen in Hampton, while Twickenham includes the former home of Horace Walpole, Strawberry Hill (1748–77), an early example of Gothic revival architecture.

## Ridley, Nicholas (c. 1500–1555)

English Protestant bishop. He became chaplain to Henry VIII in 1541, and bishop of London in 1550. He took an active part in the Reformation and supported Lady Jane Grey's claim to the throne. After Mary's accession he was arrested and burned as a heretic.

## Ridolfi Plot

Conspiracy of 1571 led by the Italian banker Roberto Ridolfi with Spanish and papal backing to replace Elizabeth I with Mary Queen of Scots. Spanish troops in the Netherlands were to invade England and lead a Catholic uprising against Elizabeth. The plot was discovered before it became a serious threat. Ridolfi was overseas at the time but another conspirator, Thomas Howard, Duke of Norfolk, was executed the following year. Mary was placed in stricter confinement as a result of the plot.

## Rievaulx Abbey

Ruined Cistercian foundation situated near Helmsley, North Yorkshire, England. It dates from 1131, and has a magnificent chancel date from around 1230 and extensive remains among the monastic buildings.

The word means 'valley of the Rye' from a small river that flows by the ruins. There is also a village of Rievaulx.

## Ripon

Small cathedral city and market centre in ◊ North Yorkshire, northern England; population (1991) 14,200. Ripon's history is said to date back to 886 when it was granted its first charter by King Alfred, and the town later became known for its markets and fairs. The large market place still lies at the heart of the city, dominated by a 28 m/90 ft obelisk (1780). Each evening at nine o'clock a horn is blown in the market square, an ancient custom which is said to date from before the 11th century. Ripon's cathedral (1154–1520) was built on the site of an earlier Saxon church, established by St Wilfrid in 672, and the original crypt survives below the present tower. St Wilfrid's Feast is celebrated annually in August with a large procession through the streets. Nearby is the World Heritage Site, Studley Royal Park including the 12th-century ruins of ◊ Fountains Abbey, among the finest monastic ruins in Europe.

## Ritz Hotel

Hotel in Piccadilly, London, opened in 1906 to the specifications of Swiss hotelier César Ritz (1850–1918) and named after him. The hotel is renowned for its rich and opulent interior; the word 'ritzy' derives from it, meaning 'showily smart'.

## rivers

See table opposite for the UK's longest rivers.

## Rizzio, David (c. 1533–1566)

Italian adventurer and musician. He arrived at the court of Mary Queen of Scots in 1561 in the train of the ambassador of the Duke of Savoy. Mary appointed him her French secretary in 1564, and he soon acquired great influence and to some degree directed her policy. This angered her husband ◊ Darnley, and, on suspicion of being the Queen's lover, Rizzio was seized in her presence and murdered by Darnley and his friends.

## Robert

Three kings of Scotland:

## Robert (I) the Bruce (1274–1329)

King of Scotland from 1306, and grandson of Robert de ◊ Bruce. He shared in the national uprising led by William ◊ Wallace and, after Wallace's execution in 1305, rose once more against Edward I of England and was crowned at Scone in 1306. He defeated Edward II at ◊ Bannockburn in 1314. In 1328 the Treaty of Northampton recognized Scotland's independence and Robert as king.

---

*They glory in their warhorses and equipment.*
*For us the name of the Lord must be our hope*
*of victory in battle.*

**Robert (I) the Bruce** King of Scotland.
Addressing his troops before the Battle of
Bannockburn 1314

---

## Robert II (1316–1390)

King of Scotland from 1371. He was the son of Walter (1293–1326), steward of Scotland, and Marjory, daughter of Robert the Bruce. He acted as regent during the exile and captivity of his uncle David II, whom he eventually succeeded. He was the first king of the house of Stuart.

## Robert III (c. 1340–1406)

King of Scotland from 1390, son of Robert II. He was unable to control the nobles, and the government fell largely into the hands of his brother, Robert, Duke of Albany (c. 1340–1420).

## Robin Hood

In English legend, an outlaw and champion of the poor against the rich, said to have lived in Sherwood Forest, Nottinghamshire, during the reign of Richard I (1189–99). He feuded with the sheriff of Nottingham, accompanied by Maid Marian and a band of followers traditionally known as his 'merry men', including Little John (so called because of his huge stature), Friar Tuck

## Longest Rivers in the UK

| Name | Source | Outlet | Length km | mi |
|---|---|---|---|---|
| Severn | Ceredigion/Powys border | Bristol Channel | 354 | 220 |
| Thames | Gloucestershire | North Sea | 346 | 215 |
| Trent | Staffordshire/Cheshire border | Humber estuary | 297 | 185 |
| Great Ouse | Northamptonshire | The Wash | 230 | 143 |
| Wye | Ceredigion | River Severn | 215 | 135 |
| Tay | Highland | Firth of Tay | 188 | 117 |
| Nene | Northamptonshire | The Wash | 161 | 100 |
| Clyde | South Lanarkshire | Firth of Clyde | 158 | 98 |
| Spey | Highland | Moray Firth | 157 | 98 |
| Tweed | Scottish Borders | North Sea | 156 | 97 |
| Dee (Scotland) | Aberdeenshire | North Sea | 137 | 85 |
| Usk | Carmarthenshire/Powys border | Bristol Channel | 137 | 85 |
| Avon (Upper Avon or Warwickshire Avon) | Northamptonshire | River Severn | 136 | 85 |
| Don | Aberdeenshire | North Sea | 133 | 83 |
| Tees | Cumbria | North Sea | 130 | 80 |
| Witham | Leicestershire | The Wash | 129 | 80 |
| Bann | Co Down | Atlantic | 122 | 76 |
| Avon (Bristol Avon) | Gloucestershire | River Severn | 121 | 75 |
| Ribble | North Yorkshire | Irish Sea | 120 | 75 |
| Teifi | Ceredigion | Cardigan Bay | 118 | 73 |
| Dee (Wales) | Bala Lake, Gwynedd | Irish Sea | 112 | 70 |
| Mersey | Stockport, Greater Manchester | Irish Sea | 112 | 70 |
| Nith | East Ayrshire | Solway Firth | 112 | 70 |
| Towy (Welsh Tywi) | Ceredigion/Powys border | Carmarthen Bay | 111 | 69 |
| Welland | Leicestershire | The Wash | 110 | 68 |
| Aire | North Yorkshire | River Ouse | 110 | 68 |
| Wear | Durham | North Sea | 107 | 67 |
| Eden | Cumbria | Solway Firth | 104 | 65 |
| Deveron | Moray | North Sea | 100 | 63 |
| Tamar | Cornwall | Plymouth Sound | 97 | 60 |
| Swale | North Yorkshire | River Ure | 97 | 60 |

(a jovial cleric), and Alan a Dale. He appears in many popular ballads from the 13th century, but his first datable appearance is in William Langland's *Piers Plowman* in the late 14th century.

To judge from the references to him and his legendary associates in ballads and other popular literature, and in records of ritualistic summer games, his name became well known both in England and Scotland in the 15th century.

Traditionally he is a nobleman who remained loyal to Richard during his exile and opposed the oppression of King John. There may be some historical basis for the legend. He has been identified both as an earl of Huntingdon born in about 1160 and as the defendant in a court case in 1354 awaiting trial on a charge of the theft of foliage and venison from a forest in Northamptonshire, but many of the customs and practices associated with his name suggest that he is a character of May Day celebrations. He is claimed to have been buried at Kirklees Hall, Yorkshire.

## Robin Hood's Bay
Village on a wide bay on the coast of North Yorkshire, England, between Scarborough and Whitby. It is an example of a large wave-cut platform. The village is surrounded by moorland.

## Robinson, W(illiam) Heath (1872–1944)
English cartoonist and illustrator. He made humorous drawings of bizarre machinery for performing simple tasks, such as raising one's hat. A clumsily designed apparatus is often described as a 'Heath Robinson' contraption.

## Rob Roy nickname of Robert MacGregor (1671–1734)
Scottish Highland ◊Jacobite outlaw. After losing his estates, he lived by cattle theft and extortion. Captured, he was sentenced to transportation but pardoned in 1727. He is a central character in Walter Scott's historical novel *Rob Roy* (1817). A film of *Rob Roy* was made in 1995, starring Liam Neeson.

## Robson, Flora (1902–1984)

English actress. A stalwart of both stage and screen, she excelled as Queen Elizabeth I in the film *Fire Over England* (1937) and as Mrs Alving in *Ghosts* (1958), a film adaptation of the play by the Norwegian dramatist Henrik Ibsen.

## Rochdale

Industrial town in ♦Greater Manchester, northwest England, 16 km/10 mi northeast of Manchester; population (1994 est) 138,000. Rochdale is an ancient market town which was traditionally associated with the wool trade. It developed in the Victorian era as an important cotton-spinning town and much of its architecture, including the large Gothic-style town hall (1871), reflects the town's prosperity in this period. The Rochdale Pioneers founded the Cooperative Society in England here in 1844 and the Rochdale Pioneers Museum is housed in the building in Toad Lane where the first Co-operative Society shop was established.

## Rochester

City in southeastern England, on the Medway estuary, in Medway Towns unitary authority; population (1991) 24,000. Rochester upon Medway district joined with Gillingham to form the Medway Towns unitary authority in April 1998. Rochester was a Roman town, **Durobrivae**. It has a 12th-century Norman castle keep (the largest in England), a 12th–15th-century cathedral (containing a memorial to Charles Dickens), and many timbered buildings. Industries include aeronautical, electrical, and mechanical engineering; cement; paper; and paint and varnish. The Charles Dickens Centre (1982) commemorates the town's links with the novelist Charles Dickens, whose home was at Gad's Hill.

## Rockall

British islet in the Atlantic, 24 m/80 ft across and 22 m/65 ft high, part of the Hatton-Rockall bank, and 370 km/230 mi west of North Uist in the Hebrides. The bank is part of a fragment of Greenland that broke away 60 million years ago. It is in a potentially rich oil/gas area. A party of British marines landed in 1955 formally to annex Rockall, but Denmark, Iceland, and Ireland challenge Britain's claims for mineral, oil, and fishing rights. The **Rockall Trough** between Rockall and Ireland, 250 km/155 mi wide and up to 3,000 m/10,000 ft deep, forms an ideal marine laboratory.

A 1995 study by the Natural History Museum of 17 seabed sites (including the Great Barrier Reef and the San Diego Trough) revealed that the Rockall Trough had more species than any other site, and greater biodiversity than a coral reef. In 4 cubic metres/5 cubic yards of sediment there were 325 species of worm.

## Rockingham

Village in Northamptonshire, England, 5 km/3 mi northwest of Corby. It was formerly the centre of a royal forest. **Rockingham Castle**, built by William (I) the Conqueror on the site of earlier earthworks, dominates the Welland valley. The village has many 17th-century and 18th-century houses.

## Rolls-Royce

Industrial company manufacturing cars and aeroplane engines, founded in 1906 by Henry ♦Royce and Charles Rolls. The Silver Ghost car model was designed in 1906, and produced until 1925, when the Phantom was introduced. In 1914 Royce designed the Eagle aircraft engine, used extensively in World War I. Royce also designed the Merlin engine, used in Spitfires and Hurricanes in World War II. Jet engines followed, and became an important part of the company.

From 1994, BMW of Germany were to build a percentage of the engines for Rolls-Royce and Bentley cars, as well as providing engineering consultation.

## Roman architecture

Building erected during the Roman occupation (AD 43–around 410). Features were similar to Roman architecture in other provinces of the Empire, being less ambitious and elaborate than those of the city of Rome.

Most examples are to be found in the larger Roman towns: Camulodunum (Colchester), Verulamium (St Albans), Aquae Sulis (Bath), Calleva Atrebatum (Silchester), Viroconium (Wroxeter), and Isca Silurum (Caerwent). Other important towns such as Londinium (London), Eboracum (York), Ratae (Leicester), Lindum (Lincoln), Glevum (Gloucester), and Corinium (Cirencester) have yielded comparatively few remains; usually because later building has smothered or destroyed the Roman work, or because they have not yet been thoroughly excavated.

Public buildings were generally grouped round the forum or market-place, as at St Albans. Notable remains include the amphitheatre at Caerwent; the theatre at St Albans; secular basilicas at Cirencester, Silchester, Wroxeter, and Caerwent; the largest basilica north of the Alps, found under Gracechurch Street, London; and public baths, especially at Bath, but also at Leicester, Silchester, and Wroxeter. No temples remain above ground but the foundations of a large construction have been found at Colchester, and there are numerous temples to the oriental deity Mithras, such as that in Walbrook, London. A fragment of a small basilican church at Silchester, dating from about 410, is the only surviving Christian church of the period.

Domestic town-houses are best studied at St Albans; the streets form a chess-board pattern and contain centrally heated houses, baths, and mosaic floors. Larger dwellings include palaces, such as Fishbourne near Chichester, villas, and farmhouses, some of them having over 50 rooms. They are chiefly situated south and east of a line from York to Exeter, the best examples being at Bignor, Sussex; Brading, Isle of Wight; Chedworth, Gloucestershire; Folkestone, Kent; and Northleigh and Woodchester in Oxfordshire.

## Roman Britain

Period in British history from the two expeditions by Julius Caesar in 55 and 54 BC to the early 5th century AD. Roman relations with Britain began with Caesar's expeditions, but the actual conquest was not begun until AD 43. During the reign of the emperor Domitian, the governer of the province, Agricola, campaigned in Scotland. After several unsuccessful attempts to conquer Scotland, the northern frontier was fixed between the Solway and the Tyne at ◊Hadrian's Wall.

The process of Romanization was enhanced by the establishment of Roman colonies and other major urban centres. Most notable was the city of Colchester (Camulodunum), which was the location of the temple dedicated to the Divine Claudius, and the focus of the revolt of Boudicca. Other settlements included London, York, Chester, St Albans, Lincoln, and Gloucester, as well as the spa at Bath, dedicated to the worship of Sulis Minerva, a combination of local and Roman deities. England was rapidly Romanized, but north of York few remains of Roman civilization have been found.

The province was garrisoned by three Roman legions based at Caerleon in South Wales, Chester, and York. These troops were supplemented by auxiliaries placed on the frontier regions such as Wales and northern Britain, especially along Hadrian's Wall. The development of the province was aided by the creation of a network of roads. These still form the basis of some of the main routes of the country, such as ◊Watling Street from London to Wroxeter (near Shrewsbury), the Fosse Way which runs southwest through places such as Cirencester, and Ermine Street from London to Lincoln and York.

During the 4th century Britain was raided by the Saxons, Picts, and Scots. The Roman armies were withdrawn in 407, and the emperor Honorius wrote a famous letter telling the province to look to its own defence, but there were partial reoccupations from 417 to about 427 and about 450.

## Roman Catholicism

Religion professed by about 10% of the British population. Roman Catholicism is one of the main divisions of the Christian religion, separate

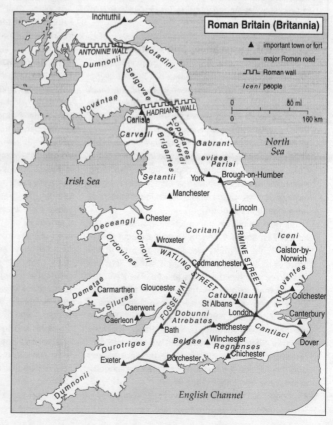

Roman Britain (Britannia)

▲ important town or fort
— major Roman road
⌐⌐ Roman wall
*Iceni* people

# THE EDGE OF THE WORLD: BRITAIN AND THE COMING OF ROME

The expeditions of Julius Caesar and the conquest under Claudius brought most of Britain (but not Ireland) within the political, cultural, and economic system of the Mediterranean-based empire of Rome. But the Roman conquest of Britain was a long process, and cultural domination, at first no more than superficial, was established only slowly.

## Britain before the conquest

The *Cassiterides* or 'Tin Islands' known to Greek writers are generally identified with southwest Britain. During his conquest of Gaul, Julius Caesar crossed to Britain in 55 and 54 BC. This was more for the propaganda effect at Rome of invading the mysterious island in the Ocean than with any serious intent to conquer the island. For the next hundred years the peoples of the southeast of Britain were increasingly influenced by the Romans, and native kings such as Cunobelin (Shakespeare's Cymbeline) maintained diplomatic relations with them. In AD 43 the new emperor Claudius rewarded the army which had placed him on the throne by taking up the work of his ancestor Caesar and invading Britain with a view to conquest.

## Conquest, resistance, and domination

The initial invasion of AD 43 under its commander Aulus Plautius soon overran the southeast of Britain, taking Camulodunum (Colchester) the centre for the most powerful tribe. Its leader, Caractacus, escaped to the Silures of south Wales, where he stirred up resistance until his defeat and capture in AD 51, when he was sent to Rome. Resistance continued in Wales, particularly inspired by the Druids, the priests and law-givers of the Celtic peoples. The Romans depict them as practising barbarous rites such as human sacrifice, but this may be more of an attempt to blacken the image of leaders of resistance than the truth.

The next serious resistance to Rome came from the Iceni of East Anglia. When their king Prasutagus died in 60 or 61, their territory was forcibly annexed to the province of Britannia and Prasutagus' widow Boudicca (Boadicea) and her daughters abused. The Iceni and their southern neighbours the Trinovantes of Essex rose in revolt and sacked the now Roman-style towns at Colchester, London, and Verulamium (St Albans) before being slaughtered in battle by Roman troops under the governor Suetonius Paullinus. This was the last concerted effort to shake off Roman rule, though it was not until the 70s that the Romans completed the conquest of what are now England and Wales.

## Scotland and the walls

In the early 80s Roman power was advanced into Scotland under the governor Gnaeus Julius Agricola, the best-known governor of Britain as the biography by his son-in-law the historian Tacitus has survived. Agricola defeated the Caledonian tribes under their leader Calgacus at the battle of Mons Graupius in northeastern Scotland, but over the next 40 years the Romans gradually gave up their conquests in Scotland. In 122 the emperor Hadrian visited Britain and commanded the construction of a wall from sea to sea. Hadrian's Wall ran from Newcastle to west of Carlisle. With a gate (milecastle) every mile as well as watch-towers and forts, it was designed to control movement across the frontier, supervise the tribes to the north, and stand as a great monument to the might of Hadrian and Rome. At Hadrian's death in 138, his successor Antoninus Pius abandoned the newly completed Wall and advanced to a new line from the Forth to the Clyde, the Antonine Wall. But with the death of its originator in 161 the Antonine Wall was abandoned, and thereafter Hadrian's Wall marked the northern boundary of Rome in Britain.

## The development of Britannia

The initial conquest was long, drawn out, and occasionally bloody, and the Romans never succeeded in subduing all the island. Thus there was always a substantial military garrison in Britain and resistance by unconquered tribes. But the great majority of the people of Britain soon settled down to Roman rule and adapted to the style of their conquerors. Under Roman influence, towns appeared in Britain, including colonies for military veterans such as Colchester, Gloucester, and Lincoln, the great port of London, and other towns which have remained important to the present such as Canterbury and York. Roman fashions could also be seen in the introduction of temples, altars, and sculpture for the worship of native gods, new burial practices, the construction of Roman-style country residences (villas), and the importation of luxuries such as spices or glass from elsewhere in the empire. This 'Romanization' of Britain principally affected the aristocracy, who used Roman manners to please their overlords and to impress the rest of the populace. But the great majority of the people continued to live on the land and eke out a living as peasants, relatively little touched by the forms of Roman civilization.

by Simon Esmonde Cleary

from the Eastern Orthodox Church from 1054, and headed by the pope, currently John Paul II, based in Rome. The head of the Roman Catholic Church in Britain is Cardinal Basil Hume.

### Organization
In Great Britain the Roman Catholic Church is organized into seven provinces and 30 dioceses (22 in England and Wales, 8 in Scotland), each of which is headed by a bishop responsible to the pope. Within the dioceses there are 3,319 parishes and about 4,800 priests. Northern Ireland has six dioceses.

### History
The Protestant churches separated from the Catholic with the Reformation in the 16th century. In England, for more than two centuries after the Reformation, scattered Catholics were served by missionary priests, whose activities were subject to penal laws. Toleration was officially extended to Catholics by the Catholic Emancipation Act 1829, and a Roman Catholic episcopate was restored in England and Wales in 1850, and in Scotland in 1878.

Irish immigration (chiefly as a result of the potato famine in the mid-19th century) played a major role in determining the subsequent development and character of English Roman Catholicism. Today, its demonstrative worship and apostolic fervour contrast forcibly with the sober and unobtrusive English Catholicism of penal times.

## Roman roads
Network of well-built roads constructed across Britain by the Romans, to facilitate rapid troop movements and communications, as well as trade. The best known are Ermine Street, Watling Street, and Fosse Way. Many Roman roads were constructed afresh; others, such as the Icknield Way, were based on ancient routes. The roads were usually as straight as possible to aid speed of travel, and were built from large kerb stones between smaller stones covered with river gravel, often accompanied by drainage ditches. Many of the roads continued in use throughout the Middle Ages.

## Romanticism
Late-18th- and early-19th-century cultural movement which emphasized the imagination and emotions of the individual, in a reaction against the restraint of 18th-century Classicism and Neo-Classicism. Major themes included a love of atmospheric landscapes; nostalgia for the past,

particularly Gothic forms (leading to ◊Gothic Revival architecture); the cult of the hero figure; romantic passion; mysticism; and a fascination with death. The poets Thomas Gray, William Cowper, and William Bowles, and the landscape painters Paul Sandby and Thomas Girtin, are regarded as forerunners of the movement in Britain. Romanticism also gained inspiration from the medieval poetry and short life of Thomas Chatterton, Thomas Percy's manuscript collection of ballads and romances, and James Macpherson's poetry, attributed to the 3rd-century Gaelic bard Ossian.

In **literature**, leading figures of full-blown Romanticism were William Wordsworth, Samuel Taylor Coleridge, Percy Bysshe Shelley, John Keats, and Walter Scott. Byron became a symbol of British Romanticism and political liberalism throughout 19th-century Europe. The movement also led to the rise of English melodrama, marked by Thomas Holcroft's *A Tale of Mystery* (1802).

In **art**, J M W Turner was an outstanding landscape painter of the Romantic tradition, while the poet, artist, and visionary William Blake represented a mystical and fantastic trend. Other leading Romantic artists of the period were John Martin and Thomas Lawrence. The movement was also influenced by John Constable, his paintings, such as *The Haywain*, epitomizing a Wordsworthian return to nature and the study of natural phenomena.

The Romantic tradition of British art continued into the 20th century with the work of James Pryde, and John Piper's dramatic views of landscape and architecture. Piper was part of a movement called **Neo-Romanticism** (around 1935–55), in which British artists revived the spirit of 19th-century Romanticism in a more modern idiom, particularly in landscapes. Other leading figures of the movement were Graham Sutherland and Keith Vaughan.

## Romney Marsh
Stretch of drained marshland on the Kent coast, southeast England, between ◊Hythe and Rye, used for sheep pasture. From Hythe in the north it extends to the ◊Dungeness promontory in the south, and includes Denge Marsh and Walland Marsh. Reclamation of the land began in Roman times. The principal settlement in the area is ◊New Romney.

The Romney, Hythe, and Dymchurch narrow-gauge railway, one of the world's smallest public railways, was opened in 1927. The Rhee Wall, between Appledore and New Romney, is thought to be Roman in origin.

Romney Marsh was formerly a bay extending from Hythe in Kent and to Fairlight in Sussex, England. Shingle spits grew outwards from the headlands to form a bar behind which sedimentation took place. There is an area of shingle, Dungeness Foreland, in which old shorelines can be found, and an area of former marshland which had been almost completely reclaimed by the 17th century to give rich pasture for Romney Marsh sheep.

## rose

A symbol of England, where it is occasionally worn on St George's Day (23 April), and a symbol of love. The rose has been associated with England since the Wars of the Roses of the 15th century, when the Yorkists bore the white rose and the Lancastrians the red. The badges were united by the marriage of Henry VII to Elizabeth of York to form the **Tudor rose**, which remains an English royal emblem. The **red rose** was also adopted in 1986 as a symbol of the Labour Party.

## Roses, Wars of the

Civil wars in England from 1455 to 1485 between the houses of ◊Lancaster (badge, red rose) and ◊York (badge, white rose), both of whom claimed the throne through descent from the sons of Edward III. As a result of ◊Henry VI's lapse into insanity in 1453, Richard, Duke of York, was installed as protector of the realm. Upon his recovery, Henry forced York to take up arms in self-defence. The name Wars of the Roses was given in the 19th century by novelist Walter Scott.

## Rose Theatre

Former London theatre near Southwark Bridge where many of Shakespeare's plays were performed. The excavation and preservation of the remains of the theatre, discovered in 1989, caused controversy between government bodies and archaeologists.

The theatre was built in 1587 by the impresario Philip Henslowe (c. 1550–1616), who managed it until 1603; it was the site of the first performances of Shakespeare's plays *Henry VI* and *Titus Andronicus*.

## Rossetti, Christina (1830–1894)

English poet and a devout High Anglican (see ◊Oxford movement). Her best-known work is *Goblin Market and Other Poems* (1862); among others are *The Prince's Progress* (1866), *Annus Domini* (1874), and *A Pageant* (1881). Her verse expresses unfulfilled spiritual yearning and frustrated love. She was a skilful technician and made use of irregular rhyme and line length. She was the sister of Dante Gabriel ◊Rossetti.

Her first recorded poem was completed at the age of 12. In 1847 a volume of her verses was privately printed, and in 1850, using the pseudonym Ellen Alleyne, she contributed to the famous but short-lived Pre-Raphaelite periodical *The Germ*. The sadness that pervades her writing may be due to an unhappy love affair in her youth, and to the ill health she constantly suffered.

## Rossetti, Dante Gabriel (1828–1882)

English painter and poet. Although a founding member of the ◊**Pre-Raphaelite Brotherhood** in 1848, he produced only two deliberately Pre-Raphaelite pictures: *The Girlhood of Mary Virgin* (1849) and *Ecce Ancilla Domini* (1850), both in the Tate Gallery, London. He went on to develop a broader romantic style and a personal subject matter related to his poetry, but the term Pre-Raphaelite continued to be applied to his painting.

Rossetti was a friend of the critic John ◊Ruskin and William Morris, with whom he initiated a second phase of Pre-Raphaelitism associated with the Arts and Crafts movement.

Between 1850 and 1860 he produced many of his best pictures, mainly in watercolour; his subjects were mainly from Dante or the *Morte D'Arthur* and his chief model was the painter Elizabeth Siddal (1834–1862), who became his wife in 1860. His later works concentrated on single studies of allegorical females such as the *Beata Beatrix* (1864), *Proserpine* (Tate Gallery, London), *Astarte Syriaca* (Manchester City Art Gallery), and *The Day Dream* (Victoria and Albert Museum), his most important model being William Morris's wife, Jane, who became his lover.

Rossetti's early verse includes 'The Blessed Damozel' (1850). His *Poems* (1870) were disinterred from the grave of Elizabeth Siddal, but were attacked as being of 'the fleshly school of poetry'. After this he became addicted to the use of chloral; he attempted suicide in 1872 and suffered from partial paralysis from 1881. His sister was the poet Christina ◊Rossetti.

## Rotherham

Industrial town in ◊South Yorkshire, northern England, 10 km/6 mi northeast of Sheffield; population (1994) 154,000. The town developed as a major centre of heavy industry with important

steelworks. In recent years there has been investment in town-centre improvements and the Magna Centre is a major visitor attraction, due to open in 2001, which is being developed on the site of a former steelworks in Rotherham. A millennium project, it will illustrate all elements of steelmaking and other aspects of British industry.
*Features*
The Chapel of Our Lady, built in about 1483 on the old Rotherham Bridge, is one of only four surviving bridge chapels in England.

## rotten borough
English parliamentary constituency, before the Great Reform Act of 1832, that returned members to Parliament in spite of having small numbers of electors. Such a borough could easily be manipulated by those with sufficient money or influence.

## Roundhead
Member of the Parliamentary party during the English Civil War 1640–60, opposing the royalist Cavaliers. The term referred to the short hair then worn only by men of the lower classes.

## Round Table
In British legend, the table of the knights of King ◊Arthur's court. According to tradition, they quarrelled for precedence and a round table was designed so that all could sit equally. It had one vacant place, the 'Siege Perilous', or 'dangerous seat', awaiting the arrival of the Grail hero Galahad.

The Great Hall in Winchester, Hampshire, contains a Round Table which was presented to Henry VIII; it was known to have existed in Henry III's reign; it has seats for the king and 24 knights. It is probably the relic of a joust, as the Round Table gave its name, from the 12th century, to a form of tournament where knights may have played the part of Arthurian characters.

## Rowlandson, Thomas (1757–1827)
English painter and illustrator. One of the greatest caricaturists of 18th-century England, his fame rests on his humorous, often bawdy, depictions of the vanities and vices of Georgian social life. He illustrated many books, including *Tour of Dr Syntax in Search of the Picturesque* (1809), which was followed by two sequels between 1812 and 1821.

Born in London, Rowlandson studied at the Royal Academy schools and in Paris and in 1777 settled in London as a portrait painter. Impoverished by gambling, he turned to caricature around 1780. Other works include *The Dance of Death* (1815–16) and illustrations for works by the writers Tobias Smollett, Oliver Goldsmith, and Laurence Sterne.

## Rowntree, B(enjamin) Seebohm (1871–1954)
English entrepreneur and philanthropist. He used much of the money he acquired as chair (1925–41) of the family firm of confectioners, H I Rowntree, to fund investigations into social conditions. His writings include *Poverty, A Study of Town Life* (1900), a landmark in empirical sociology. The three **Rowntree Trusts**, which were founded by his father **Joseph Rowntree** (1836–1925) in 1904, fund research into housing, social care, and social policy, support projects relating to social justice, and give grants to pressure groups working in these areas.

## Rowse, A(lfred) L(eslie) (1903–1997)
English historian. He published a biography of Shakespeare in 1963, and in *Shakespeare's Sonnets: The Problems Solved* (1973) controversially identified the 'Dark Lady' of Shakespeare's sonnets as Emilia Lanier, half-Italian daughter of a court musician, with whom the Bard is alleged to have had an affair in 1593–95.

His other works include the scholarly *Tudor Cornwall: Portrait of a Society* (1941, 1969) and *Shakespeare the Man* (1973). He was also a minor poet of Celtic themes and traditional forms of verse: he published *A Life: Collected Poems* in 1981.

## Royal Academy of Arts, RA
British society founded by George III in London in 1768 to encourage painting, sculpture, and architecture; its first president was Joshua ◊Reynolds. It is now housed in Old Burlington House, Piccadilly. There is an annual summer exhibition for contemporary artists, and tuition is provided at the Royal Academy schools.

## Royal Academy of Dramatic Art, RADA
British college founded by Herbert Beerbohm Tree in 1904 to train young actors. Since 1905 its headquarters have been in Gower Street, London. A royal charter was granted in 1920.

## Royal Academy of Music, RAM
Conservatoire of international standing in London, founded in 1822 by John Fane, Lord Burghesh, later 11th Earl of Westmorland. It was

granted a royal charter in 1830. Based in Marylebone Road, it provides full-time training leading to performing and academic qualifications. The current principal is Curtis Price.

## Royal Aeronautical Society
Oldest British aviation body, formed in 1866. Its members discussed and explored the possibilities of flight long before its successful achievement.

## Royal Agricultural Society of England
Premier association in England for the agricultural industry. Founded in 1839, the society is based at the National Agricultural Centre, Stoneleigh, Warwickshire, where it holds a four-day agricultural show every July.

## Royal Air Force, RAF
See ◊armed forces.

## Royal Albert Hall
Large oval hall situated south of Kensington Gardens, London, opposite the ◊Albert Memorial. It was built 1867–71 from the surplus of funds collected for the Albert Memorial. The architect was Francis Fowke (1823–1865). It is usually referred to as the Albert Hall. It holds 6,800 people and is used for concerts, meetings, boxing-matches and other events. It has one of the largest organs in the world.

## Royal Ballet
Leading British ballet company and school, based at the Royal Opera House, Covent Garden, London. Until 1956 it was known as the Sadler's Wells Ballet. It was founded in 1931 by Ninette ◊de Valois, who established her school and company at the Sadler's Wells Theatre. It moved to Covent Garden in 1946. Frederick ◊Ashton became principal choreographer in 1935, providing the company with its uniquely English ballet style. Leading dancers included Margot Fonteyn, Rudolf Nureyev, Alicia Markova, and Antoinette Sibley. Anthony ◊Dowell became artistic director of the company in 1986.

In 1997–98, due to the redevelopment of the Royal Opera House, the company performed at a range of London venues.

## Royal College of Music, RCM
Conservatoire of international standing in London, founded in 1882 in Kensington. It provides full-time training leading to performing and academic qualifications. The current principal is Dr Janet Ritterman.

## royal commission
A group of people appointed by the government (nominally by the sovereign) to investigate a matter of public concern and make recommendations on any actions to be taken in connection with it, including changes in the law. In cases where agreement on recommendations cannot be reached, a minority report can be submitted by dissenters.

## Royal Court Theatre
Theatre in Sloane Square, London. As the home of the ◊English Stage Company from 1956, it is associated with productions of new work.

**Royal Albert Hall** The Royal Albert Hall in Kensington, London, was built as a memorial to Queen Victoria's royal consort Prince Albert, who died prematurely in 1861. It is most famous as the venue (since 1941) of the annual Sir Henry Wood promenade concerts, or 'Proms', a two-month season of classical concerts that attracts a devoted following. Corel

The Royal Court had its first success with Arthur Pinero's *Trelawny of the 'Wells'* in 1898. It thrived under the managing partnership of John Vedrenne (1867–1930) and Harley ◊Granville-Barker (1904–07), with productions of plays by Shakespeare, George Bernard Shaw, John Galsworthy, and others, and under George Devine (1956–64).

## Royal Family
See ◊monarchy.

## Royal Greenwich Observatory
The national astronomical observatory of the UK, founded in 1675 at Greenwich, southeast London, to provide navigational information for sailors. After World War II it was moved to Herstmonceux Castle, Sussex; in 1990 it was transferred to Cambridge. It also operates telescopes on La Palma in the Canary Islands, including the 4.2-m/165-in William Herschel Telescope, commissioned in 1987.

In 1998 the Particle Physics and Astronomy Research Council decided to return some of the Royal Observatory's work back to the original Greenwich site from Cambridge (other technical work goes to a new UK Astronomy Technology Centre in Edinburgh).

The observatory was founded by King Charles II. The eminence of its work resulted in Greenwich Time and the Greenwich Meridian being adopted as international standards of reference in 1884.

## Royal Horticultural Society, RHS
British society established in 1804 for the improvement of horticulture. The annual Chelsea Flower Show, held in the grounds of the Royal Hospital, London, is also a social event, and another flower show is held at Vincent Square, London. There are gardens, orchards, and trial grounds at Wisley, Surrey, and the Lindley Library has one of the world's finest horticultural collections.

## royal household
Personal staff of a sovereign. In Britain the chief officers are the Lord Chamberlain, the Lord Steward, and the Master of the Horse. The other principal members of the royal family also maintain their own households. The civil list, an annual sum provided from public funds, meets the official expenses of the sovereign and their immediate dependents; personal expenditure for the household comes from the sovereign's own resources.

## Royal Institution of Great Britain
Organization for the promotion, diffusion, and extension of science and knowledge, founded in London in 1799 by the Anglo-American physicist Count Rumford (1753–1814). In 1998 it appointed Susan Greenfield (1951– ) as its first woman director.

English chemists Michael ◊Faraday and Humphry ◊Davy were among its directors.

## Royal Mail
Department of the UK Post Office that handles the collection and delivery of letters. The Royal Mail delivers to 26 million addresses in Britain, handling over 2 million letters a day. Collections are made from over 120,000 sites.

## Royal Marines
British military force trained for amphibious warfare.

## Royal Military Academy
British officer training college popularly known as ◊Sandhurst.

## Royal National Institute for the Blind, RNIB
Charity, founded in 1868, providing specialized services for blind and partially-sighted people.

## Royal National Institute for the Deaf, RNID
Charity, founded in 1911, providing specialized services for deaf and hearing-impaired people.

## Royal National Lifeboat Institution, RNLI
Charity, founded in 1824, operating a 24-hour lifeboat rescue service around the coasts of Britain and Ireland. In 1998 it had 2,000 fundraising branches and 100,000 members.

## Royal Opera
Opera company based at the ◊Royal Opera House in Covent Garden, London. The opera was granted its royal charter in 1968.

## Royal Opera House
Britain's leading opera house, sited at Covent Garden, London.

The original theatre opened in 1732, was destroyed by fire in 1808 and reopened in 1809. It was again destroyed by fire in 1856, and the third and present building dates from 1858. It has been the home of the Royal Opera and the Royal Ballet since 1946.

After suffering severe financial difficulties, the Opera House closed from January to December

1999, reopening after financial and managerial restructuring and a major refurbishment.

## Royal Pavilion, or Brighton Pavilion

Palace in Brighton, England, built in 1784 and bought in the early 19th century for the Prince Regent (the future George IV) who had it extensively rebuilt in a mix of classical and Indian styles. Queen Victoria was the last monarch to use it and it is now municipal property.

## royal prerogative

Powers, immunities, and privileges recognized in common law as belonging to the crown. Most prerogative acts in the UK are now performed by the government on behalf of the crown. The royal prerogative belongs to the Queen as a person as well as to the institution called the crown, and the award of some honours and dignities remain her personal choice. As by prerogative 'the king can do no wrong', the monarch is immune from prosecution.

The royal prerogative is traceable to the days before Parliament existed. Examples include the conduct of foreign relations, making war and peace, the dissolution of Parliament, assent to bills, and the choice of ministers.

## Royal Scottish Academy of Music and Drama

Institution in Scotland training musicians, actors, and other professionals in music and drama. Based in state-of-the-art premises in Glasgow, it is the only conservatoire in Scotland.

## Royal Scottish National Orchestra

Orchestra based in Glasgow and regularly touring to other locations in Scotland, England, and beyond.

## Royal Shakespeare Company, RSC

British professional theatre company that performs Shakespearean and other plays. It was founded in 1961 from the company at the Shakespeare Memorial Theatre (1932, now the Royal Shakespeare Theatre) in Stratford-upon-Avon, Warwickshire, England, and produces plays in Stratford and the Barbican Centre in London.

The RSC initially presented mainly Shakespeare at Stratford; these productions were usually transferred to the Aldwych Theatre, London, where the company also performed modern plays and non-Shakespearean classics. In 1982 it moved into a permanent London headquarters at the Barbican. A second large theatre in Stratford, the Swan, opened in 1986 with an auditorium similar to theatres of Shakespeare's day.

The first director of the RSC was Peter Hall. In 1968 Trevor Nunn replaced him, and in 1986 Nunn was succeeded by Terry Hands. Adrian Noble has been director since 1990.

## Royal Society

Oldest and premier scientific society in Britain, originating in 1645 and chartered in 1662; Robert Boyle, Christopher ◊Wren, and Isaac ◊Newton were prominent early members. Its Scottish equivalent is the **Royal Society of Edinburgh** (1783).

## Royal Society for the Protection of Birds, RSPB

UK charity, founded in 1889, aiming to conserve and protect wild birds, both in the UK and overseas. It has a network of reserves in all types of habitat (73,000 ha/180,000 acres), and is the largest voluntary wildlife-conservation body in Europe, with a membership of 827,000 (1990).

## Royal Worcester porcelain

English porcelain, before 1862, Worcester Porcelain. A factory was founded in Worcester in 1751 and produced a hard-wearing type of softpaste porcelain, mainly as tableware and decorative china and also white Parian ware figures. It employed advanced transfer printing techniques on a variety of shapes often based on Chinese porcelain.

## Royston

Town in Hertfordshire, England, 21 km/13 mi southwest of Cambridge; population (1991) 13,600. It is situated on the pre-Roman ◊Icknield Way. The **Royston Cave**, a Roman burial place and oratory, was discovered in 1742. It is dug out of the chalk, is 8 m/26 ft high and 5 m/16 ft in diameter, and contains rough figures and coloured reliefs of saints, kings, and queens. Most figures were made at the time of the Crusades (12th and 13th centuries).

## RSPCA, Royal Society for the Prevention of Cruelty to Animals

British organization formed in 1824 to safeguard the welfare of animals; it promotes legislation, has an inspectorate to secure enforcement of existing laws, and runs clinics. In 1997 it had 43,000 members, 1,200 paid staff, an income of £43.4 million, and annual expenditure of £40.8 million.

## rugby

Contact sport that is traditionally believed to have originated at Rugby School, England, in 1823 when a boy, William Webb Ellis, picked up the ball and ran with it while playing football (now soccer). Rugby is played with an oval ball. It is now played in two forms: ◊**Rugby League** and ◊**Rugby Union**.

## Rugby

Market town and railway junction in ◊Warwickshire, central England, 19 km/12 southeast of Coventry; population (1991) 60,500. A small village until the early 19th century, Rugby expanded with the advent of the London–Birmingham railway in 1838. Dominating the southern end of the town centre is **Rugby School** (1567), a private school for boys, which established its reputation under headmaster Thomas Arnold; it was described in Thomas Hughes' semi-autobiographical classic *Tom Brown's Schooldays*. Rugby football originated at the school in 1823.

## Rugby League

Professional form of rugby football founded in England in 1895 as the Northern Union when a dispute about pay caused northern clubs to break away from the Rugby Football Union. The game is similar to ◊Rugby Union, but the number of players was reduced from 15 to 13 in 1906, and other rule changes have made the game more open and fast-moving.

Major events include the Challenge Cup final, first held in 1897 and since 1929 staged at Wembley Stadium, and the Premiership Trophy, introduced at the end of the 1974–75 season, which is a knockout competition involving the top eight clubs in the first division. In March 1996 the game was played during the summer season for the first time, when the Super League began in the UK comprised of 12 teams, including Paris. In 1997 a world club championship between teams from the British and Australian Super League (which includes teams from New Zealand) was inaugurated.

## Rugby Union

Form of rugby in which there are 15 players on each side. Points are scored by 'tries', scored by 'touching down' the ball beyond the goal line or by kicking goals from penalties. The Rugby Football Union was formed in 1871 and has its headquarters in England (Twickenham, Middlesex). Formerly an amateur game, the game's status was revoked in August 1995 by the International Rugby Football Board, which lifted restrictions on players moving between Rugby Union and Rugby League.

Major events include the International Championship (Six Nations), instituted in 1884, a tournament between England, France, Ireland, Scotland, and Wales and from 2000 including Italy; the Tetley Bitter Cup, the SWALEC Cup, and the Tennents Cup, the club knockout tournaments of the English, Welsh, and Scottish rugby unions. Each of the home countries also stage league championships. Rugby Union (along with cricket) was introduced to the Commonwealth Games for the first time at Kuala Lumpur, Malaysia, in September 1998.

## 'Rule, Britannia'

A patriotic song with music by Thomas Arne, now almost a second British national anthem. It was originally part of the masque *Alfred*, produced on 1 August 1740, at Cliefden (now Cliveden) House near Maidenhead, the residence of Frederick, Prince of Wales. See below for words.

## Rum, or Rhum

Island of the Inner ◊Hebrides, Highland unitary authority, Scotland, area 110 sq km/42 sq mi, a nature reserve since 1957. Askival is 810 m/2,658 ft high.

The island is owned by Scottish National Heritage, known as the Nature Conservatory

### Rule Britannia

Words by James Thomson.

When Britain first, at heaven's command
Arose from out the azure main
This was the charter, the charter of the land
And guardian Angels sung this strain:

Rule, Britannia, rule the waves
Britons never will be slaves.

The nations, not so blest as thee
Must, in their turns, to tyrants fall
While thou shalt flourish great and free
The dread and envy of them all.

Still more majestic shalt thou rise
More dreadful, from each foreign stroke
As the loud blast that tears the skies
Serves but to root thy native oak.

Thee haughty tyrants ne'er shall tame
All their attempts to bend thee down
Will but arouse thy generous flame
But work their woe, and thy renown.

To thee belongs the rural reign
Thy cities shall with commerce shine
All thine shall be the subject main
And every shore it circles thine.

The Muses, still with freedom found
Shall to thy happy coast repair
Blest isle! with matchless beauty crowned
And manly hearts to guard the fair.

Council when it was purchased in 1957. It is served by passenger ferries from the port of Kinloch to Muck, Canna, Eigg, and Mallaig on the mainland.

## Runcorn

Industrial town in ◊Cheshire, northwest England, on the River Mersey and the Manchester Ship Canal, 24 km/15 mi from Liverpool; population (1991) 63,000. Designated a new town in 1964, it has received overspill population from Merseyside.

## Runnymede

Meadow on the south bank of the River Thames near Egham in Surrey, England, where on 15 June 1215 King John put his seal to the ◊Magna Carta.

## Ruskin, John (1819–1900)

English art and social critic. Much of his finest art criticism appeared in two widely influential works, *Modern Painters* (1843–60) and *The Seven Lamps of Architecture* (1849). He was a keen advocate of painters considered unorthodox at the time, such as J M W ◊Turner and members of the ◊Pre-Raphaelite Brotherhood. His later writings were concerned with social and economic problems.

Ruskin was one of the major figures of 19th-century British intellectual life. Like his contemporaries Thomas ◊Carlyle and Matthew ◊Arnold, he was an outspoken critic of Victorian society, and, like them, called for a renewal of British moral, intellectual, and artistic life. His early works were concerned with architecture and painting: his support both for the Pre-Raphaelite Brotherhood and the ◊Gothic Revival had a profound effect on Victorian art, architecture, and crafts.

From these aesthetic concerns he increasingly drew social and moral views, and from the 1860s he devoted himself to political and economic problems, condemning *laissez-faire* economics, and extolling both the dignity of labour and the moral and aesthetic value of 'craftsmanship'. His beliefs took a practical turn, and he played a leading role in providing education and decent housing for working people.

## Russell, Bertrand, 3rd Earl Russell (1872–1970)

English philosopher and mathematician. He contributed to the development of modern mathematical logic and wrote about social issues. His works include *Principia Mathematica* (with A N Whitehead, 1910–13), in which he attempted to show that mathematics could be reduced to a branch of logic; *The Problems of Philosophy* (1912); and *A History of Western Philosophy* (1946). He was an outspoken liberal pacifist.

---

*The British are distinguished among the nations of modern Europe, on the one hand by the excellence of their philosophers, and on the other hand by their contempt for philosophy. In both respects they show their wisdom.*

**Bertrand Russell** English philosopher and mathematician.
*Unpopular Essays* (1950)

---

## Russell, Dora born Black (1894–1986)

English feminist who married Bertrand Russell in 1921. The 'openness' of their marriage (she subsequently had children by another man) was a matter of controversy. She was a founding member of the National Council for Civil Liberties in 1934.

**John Ruskin** English art critic John Ruskin, photographed in old age. He was an enormously prolific writer and was far and away the most influential British writer on art in the 19th century. He was also a talented watercolour painter, but he devoted much of his later life to social reform rather than art. His personal life was wretched, marked by disappointment in love and later by mental illness. Corbis

## Rutherford, Ernest, 1st Baron Rutherford of Nelson (1871–1937)

New Zealand-born British physicist. He was a pioneer of modern atomic science. His main research was in the field of radioactivity, and he discovered alpha, beta, and gamma rays. He was the first to recognize the nuclear nature of the atom in 1911. He was awarded a Nobel prize in 1908. Knighted 1914, Baron 1931.

Rutherford produced the first artificial transformation, changing one element to another (1919), bombarding nitrogen with alpha particles and getting hydrogen and oxygen. After further research he announced that the nucleus of any atom must be composed of hydrogen nuclei; at Rutherford's suggestion, the name 'proton' was given to the hydrogen nucleus in 1920. He speculated that uncharged particles (neutrons) must also exist in the nucleus.

In 1934, using heavy water, Rutherford and his co-workers bombarded deuterium with deuterons and produced tritium. This may be considered the first nuclear fusion reaction.

## Rutherford, Margaret (1892–1972)

English film and theatre actress. She specialized in formidable yet jovially eccentric roles. She played Agatha Christie's Miss Marple in four films in the early 1960s and won an Academy Award for her role in *The VIPs* (1963).

## Rutland

Unitary authority in central England, formerly the smallest English county, which was part of ◊Leicestershire 1974–97; population (1996) 34,600; area 394 sq km/152 sq mi. The main towns are ◊Oakham (administrative headquarters) and Uppingham.

### Physical

The landscape is one of low hills forming valleys, the main one being the Vale of Catmose. Between Oakham and Uppingham the county was at one time covered by Lyfield or Leafield Forest, part of which formed the hunting land of Beaumont Chase. The rivers flowing through the county are the Chater, Eye, Gwash, and Welland. Rutland Water is an artificial reservoir in the valley of the Gwash at Empingham; it is a major feature of the county today.

### Features

Rutland's motto is 'Multum in parvo' (so much in so little), and there are numerous historic villages and churches, including Tickencote, Brooke, Braunston-in-Rutland, Preston, Wing, and Exton. Rutland Water has outdoor leisure facilities, including sailing, cycling, and birdwatching

(ospreys have been introduced here). The Normanton Church Museum is on the shore of the reservoir. Oakham has a Norman castle and a display of horseshoes collected from visiting royalty and aristocracy. Shakespeare plays are performed at the open-air Tolethorpe Hall during the summer.

### Economy

The economy is largely based on agriculture (cereals, sugar beet, potatoes; sheep and cattle reared, and Stilton cheese). There are some light industries, and limestone and ironstone are quarried. Tourism is being actively promoted.

## Rye

Town in East Sussex, southeast England; population (1991) 3,700. It was formerly a flourishing port (and one of the ◊Cinque Ports), but silt washed down by the River Rother has left it 3 km/2 mi inland. Rye has a pottery, but there are no major industries.

### History

In medieval times Rye was a major port, handling iron and timber and the cross-Channel trade. It suffered many naval attacks and was burned by the French in 1377. It became a full member of the Cinque Ports confederation in 1350, but its importance declined as the Rother began to silt up in the 16th century.

### Features

Rye has picturesque cobbled streets and medieval, Tudor, and Georgian buildings. Ypres Tower, built as a fort in about 1250, now houses a museum of local history. The Mermaid Inn, in the cobbled Mermaid Street, dates from the early 15th century. St Mary's church, of Norman to Perpendicular origins, includes a clock which is said to have the oldest functioning pendulum in England (dating from about 1560). The 18th-century Lamb House was once the home of the US novelist Henry James, and it was later the residence of the writer E F Benson (mayor of Rye 1934–37). Peacock's School was established in 1636. To the south are the remains of Camber Castle, built by Henry VIII.

## Rye House Plot

Conspiracy of 1683 by English Whig extremists against Charles II for his Roman Catholic leanings. They intended to murder Charles and his brother James, Duke of York, at Rye House, Hoddesdon, Hertfordshire, but the plot was betrayed. The Duke of ◊Monmouth was involved, and alleged conspirators, including Lord William Russell and Algernon Sidney, were executed for complicity.

# S

## S4C, Sianel Pedwar Cymru (Channel Four Wales)

Welsh television station with a duty to transmit programmes in Welsh, especially in the evening. At other times it shows Channel 4 programmes. Based in Cardiff, it began broadcasting in 1982 and is financed by a government grant and income from advertising. S4C is regulated by the Welsh Fourth Channel Authority, whose members are appointed by government.

## Saatchi Collection

Large UK collection of contemporary art, including much British art. It was formed by the businessman Charles Saatchi (1943– ) and

opened to the public in 1985 in a converted warehouse in north London. Saatchi's huge wealth enabled him to become a major British patron of contemporary art. He has been praised for supporting artists, but also criticized for helping to create an art market based on superficial trends and the investment value of works rather than on serious aesthetic merit.

The controversial Sensation exhibition of avant-garde British art at the Royal Academy, London, in 1997 was drawn from works in the Saatchi Collection.

## Sackville-West, Vita (Victoria Mary) (1892–1962)

English writer. Her novels include *The Edwardians* (1930) and *All Passion Spent* (1931); she also wrote the long pastoral poem *The Land* (1926). The fine gardens around her home at Sissinghurst, Kent, were created by her and her husband Harold Nicolson.

Virginia ◊Woolf was a close friend and based the novel *Orlando* (1928) on her.

## Sadler's Wells

Theatre in Islington, north London, built in the 17th century. Originally a music hall, it was developed by Lilian Baylis as a northern annexe to the ◊Old Vic in 1931. For many years it housed the Sadler's Wells Opera Company (relocated to the London Coliseum in 1969 and known as the English National Opera Company from 1974) and the Sadler's Wells Ballet, which later became the ◊Royal Ballet.

---

**Vita Sackville-West** English novelist and poet Vita Sackville-West. One of the most colourful and flamboyant figures of English literary life in the 1920s and 1930s, she was the model for the central character in the novel *Orlando* (1928) by her close friend Virginia Woolf. Corbis

## Saffron Walden

Town in Essex, England, 26 km/16 mi southeast of Cambridge, and 74 km/46 mi northeast of London; population (1991) 13,400. Its church, the largest in Essex, dates from the 15th century and has a spire that was added in 1832. Nearby are the remains of a Norman keep. The town takes its name from the saffron crocus, which was once cultivated here.

The Sun Inn was the headquarters of Oliver Cromwell and Thomas Fairfax in 1647. The grammar school, endowed in 1525, was re-established by Edward VI. A museum, built in 1834, houses local and other antiquities.

About 2 km/1 mi from Saffron Walden is Audley End, a 16th-century house with 40 ha/98 acres of parkland and gardens. It was enlarged in the reign of James I, and takes its name from Thomas Audley, Speaker of the Commons from 1529 to 1532, and later lord chancellor, to whom in 1538 Henry VIII granted the manor of Walden. The property is now in the care of English Heritage.

## St Albans

City in ◊Hertfordshire, England, 40 km/25 mi northwest of London; population (1991) 80,400. Now a business and retail centre and home to many London commuters, St Albans is also a major tourist centre with ancient origins and historic attractions, including the ruins of the Roman city of ◊Verulamium and a large cathedral dating from the 11th century.

### History

Verulamium was one of the first cities established by the Romans in Britain. It was devastated by ◊Boudicca and the Iceni in AD 62 but it was rebuilt and continued to flourish until the early 5th century.

The city of St Albans developed around a Saxon abbey founded in 793. The abbey is said to have been established by Offa, King of Mercia, on the spot where St Alban, a Christian Roman from Verulamium, was executed in AD 209, becoming Britain's first recorded Christian martyr.

### Features

The ruins of the ancient Verulamium include the foundations of a Roman theatre and fragments of the city walls. The Verulamium Museum includes one of the largest collections of Roman archaeological finds in Britain, including some fine mosaics. Other features include the Clock Tower in the High Street, dating from 1411, and Ye Olde Fighting Cocks which is said to be one of the oldest inns in Britain.

### The cathedral

The abbey church, which became a cathedral in 1877, was built in 1077 on the site of the original Saxon abbey. The cathedral has the longest medieval nave in Britain and its massive Norman tower is built partly of thin Roman bricks taken from the ruined buildings of Verulamium. The series of wall paintings on the west and south sides of the Norman piers in the north arcade of the nave date from the early 13th century.

## St Andrews

Town in Fife, Scotland, 19 km/12 mi southeast of Dundee; population (1991) 11,100. Its university (1411) is the oldest in Scotland. It is considered to be the 'home of golf', with a famous Old Course. The Royal and Ancient Club (1754) is the ruling body of golf. There is a cathedral, founded in 1160 and consecrated in 1318.

There are six golf courses, four of which, the Old, New, Eden, and Jubilee, are owned by the Links Trust; the Old Course dates from the 16th century. The Royal and Ancient Golf Club was so named in 1834, 80 years after its inception as the Society of St Andrews Golfers.

The town is named after St Andrew, the patron saint of Scotland. There are ruins of a castle (originally built in 1200). A fragment of wall and some archways are the only remnants of a wealthy Augustinian priory which Bishop Robert founded here in 1144.

The cathedral suffered iconoclastic damage provoked by a sermon by John Knox in the town's parish church Holy Trinity in 1559. In the 9th century, St Andrews was a bishopric.

## St Austell

Market town in Cornwall, southwest England, 22 km/14 mi northeast of Truro; population (1991, with Fowey, with which it is administered) 21,600. It is the centre of the china-clay industry, which supplies the Staffordshire potteries.

The Eden Project, due to open in 2000, will create two 'biomes' (miniature ecosystems) – tropical rainforest and Mediterranean – in a giant greenhouse in a disused china-clay pit near St Austell; it is a Millennium Commission Landmark Project.

St Austell was formerly the centre of a tin- and copper-mining district.

## St David's, Welsh Tyddewi

Small town in Pembrokeshire, southwest Wales, situated on the River Alun just 2 km/1.2 mi from the sea. Its cathedral, founded by ◊St David, the

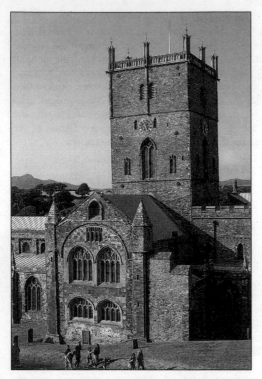

**St David's** Situated in Pembrokeshire, west Wales, St David's is remarkable for being the smallest cathedral city in the British Isles. The cathedral itself is a huge building constructed mainly of sandstone, but with a highly ornate flat timber ceiling dating from the late 15th century. John D. Beldom/Collections

patron saint of Wales, was rebuilt between 1180 and 1522. Formerly the resort of pilgrims, the town is now a summer tourist centre.

St David settled here in the 6th century. His relics are preserved in the sandstone cathedral, which contains the stone screen of Bishop Gower (died 1347), the carved stalls of Bishop Tully (died 1481), and the fan-vaulting of Bishop Vaughan (died 1522). There are also splendid ruins of Bishop Gower's 14th-century palace.

## St Helens

Industrial town in ◊Merseyside, northwest England, 19 km/12 mi northeast of Liverpool; population (1991) 104,700. A former coalmining town, connected to the River Mersey by canal, St Helens has a reputation dating back to the late 18th century for the manufacture of glass, and the town's heritage is illustrated at the Pilkington Glass Museum. The Sankey Canal was constructed in 1757 to carry coal from St Helens to Liverpool, Warrington, and to Northwich for the growing salt industry.

## St Helier

Resort and capital of Jersey, Channel Islands; population (1991) 28,100. The 'States of Jersey', the island legislature, sits here in the *salle des états*.

## St Ives

Fishing port and resort in Cornwall; population (1991) 10,100. Its artists' colony, founded by Walter Sickert and James Whistler, later included Naum Gabo, Barbara ◊Hepworth (a museum and sculpture gardens commemorate her), and Ben Nicholson. A branch of the Tate Gallery opened here in 1993, displaying works of art from the Tate's collection by artists connected with St Ives.

## St James's Palace

Palace in London. It was commissioned by Henry VIII in 1530 on the site of a hospital for leprous women founded at about the time of the Norman Conquest. Of Henry's palace only the imposing gateway survives, since much was destroyed by fire in 1809. It became the official residence of the sovereign from 1698, after Whitehall Palace was destroyed by fire, until 1837 when Queen Victoria chose Buckingham Palace.

The British Court is still officially styled 'the Court of St James'; the palace is now used for apartments for court officials. **St James's Park** (enlarged by Charles II) formed the palace grounds.

Charles I spent his last night here. Adjacent is the Queen's Chapel (1623–27) by Inigo Jones.

## St Kilda

Archipelago of four islands, sea stacks, and skerries, the most westerly of the Outer ◊Hebrides, Western Isles, 200 km/124 mi west of the Scottish mainland. They were populated from prehistory until 1930, and now form a National Nature Reserve belonging to the National Trust of Scotland. They have the world's largest colony of gannets, the oldest and largest colony of fulmars in the British Isles, and a large population of puffins. St Kilda is a World Heritage Site.

St Kilda is also a Biosphere Reserve (1976), a National Scenic Area (1981), a Site of Special Scientific Interest (1984) and a European Community Special Protection Area (1992).

## St Leger

Horse race held at Doncaster, England, every September. It is a flat race over 2.8 km/3,060 yd, and is the last classic of the season. First held in 1776, it is the oldest of the English classic races.

## St Michael's Mount

Small island in Mount's Bay, Cornwall, southwest England; population (1981) 26. It is linked to Marazion on the mainland by a causeway which is submerged at high tide

St Michael's Mount, owned by the National Trust, is formed of granite and slate rock. There is a castle on the summit (76 m/250 ft) which includes a 14th-century chapel. It is thought that a church was built here in the 5th century, and it was the site of a Celtic monastery in the 8th century. In the 11th century the island was given by Edward the Confessor to the Benedictine abbey of Mont St Michel off the coast of northwest France. It remained a priory of this abbey until the reign of Henry V.

## St Paul's Cathedral

Cathedral church of the City of London, the largest Protestant church in England, and a national mausoleum second only to Westminster Abbey. An earlier Norman building, which had replaced the original 7th-century Saxon church, was burned down in the Great Fire of 1666. The present cathedral, a magnificent combination of Gothic plan and Classic detail, was designed by Christopher ◊Wren and built from 1675 to 1711. His assistants included Nicholas Hawksmoor, Grinling Gibbons, Caius Gabriel Cibber, and Jean Tijou, the Huguenot iron worker.

The lantern of the dome is ingeniously supported on a brick cone, concealed between the inner dome and the outer, and curves almost hemispherically. Its ceiling is decorated with scenes from the life of St Paul by James ◊Thornhill. Wren's chapter-house was destroyed in the German raids of 1940–41, which also damaged the choir and high altar.

The **Old St Paul's**, completed in 1287, had the tallest spire and was probably the largest church in Christendom.

## Saki pen name of H(ector) H(ugh) Munro (1870–1916)

Burmese-born British writer. He produced ingeniously witty and bizarre short stories, often with surprise endings. He also wrote two novels, *The Unbearable Bassington* (1912) and *When William Came* (1913).

He served with the Military Police in Burma, and was foreign correspondent of the *Morning Post* 1902–08. He was killed in action on the western front in World War I.

## Salford

Industrial city in ◊Greater Manchester, northwest England, on the west bank of the River Irwell and the Manchester Ship Canal; population (1991) 80,600. A former cotton manufacturing and engineering city, it was once the site of one of Britain's largest ports. Following the decline of the city's traditional industries, the waterfront has been converted to provide leisure and business facilities as well as attractions including a heritage centre.

### Features

The world's largest public collection of works by L S Lowry, who lived in Salford for much of his life, is housed in the city's Museum and Art Gallery. The Lowry Project in Salford Quays is a landmark millennium project, contributing to the regeneration of the area. Designed to bring together both the visual and performing arts, it will also provide a new home for the city's Lowry collection.

The city is home to the Lancashire Mining Museum which vividly portrays working life underground, and it is the site of Salford University (1966), originally founded in 1896 as the Royal Technical Institute.

## Salisbury

City and market town in Wiltshire, south England, on the edge of Salisbury Plain 135 km/84 mi southwest of London; population (1991) 39,300. Salisbury is an agricultural centre, and industries include brewing and engineering. The nearby Wilton Royal Carpet factory closed in 1995. The cathedral of St Mary, built 1220–66, is an example of Early English architecture; its decorated spire 123 m/404 ft is the highest in England; its clock (1386) is one of the oldest still working. The cathedral library contains one of only four copies of the *Magna Carta*.

Another name for the modern city of Salisbury is **New Sarum**, Sarum being an abbreviated form of the medieval Latin corruption ('Sarisburiensis') of the ancient Roman name Sorbiodonum. **Old Sarum**, site of an Iron Age fort, cathedral, and town on a 90-m/300-ft hill to the north, was abandoned in 1220. Old Sarum was the most famous of the 'rotten boroughs' prior to the 1832 Reform Act.

### Location

The city lies amid level meadowlands, at the confluence of the Avon with three small rivers, the Nadder, Bourne, and Wylye, and surrounded by hills.

## Salisbury Cathedral

With the exception of its crowning tower and spire, it is a building of uniform ◊Early English design, built to one plan between 1220 and 1258 (unlike any other English cathedral except Exeter). The cathedral was dedicated to the Virgin Mary on completion. Its 123-m/404-ft spire is the tallest in England.

The **cathedral close** is surrounded on three sides by a great wall, built partly of stone from the cathedral church of Old Sarum; the River Avon completes the boundary. The close is entered by the four old gates: the High Street, St Ann's Gate, Harnham Gate, and the private gate to the bishop's palace. It contains several colleges and some beautiful houses, including the college of matrons, provided by Bishop Seth Ward in 1682 for the widows of priests of the diocese.

### Features

Salisbury was moved from Old Sarum at the beginning of the 13th century, and built on a settled plan 3 km/1.8 mi below the old citadel by Bishop Poore. The planning is indicated by the many straight and wide streets running north to south and east to west, forming 'chequers' or 'squares', with a fine open marketplace in the centre. Audley House, once owned by Mervin, Lord Audley, is a beautiful building, now used as the church house. 'The Hall of John Halle' was built in 1407 by the wool merchant John Halle. Poultry Cross is believed to have been erected in the early 16th century by a nobleman as an act of penance.

The Shoemakers' Guildhall, built in 1638, was added to the timber-framed house left to the Shoemakers' Company by one Philip Crewe, a schoolmaster. This house still overhangs the highway as it did centuries ago. In St Ann Street is the Salisbury, Southern Wiltshire, and Blackmore Museum, containing a large and representative collection of local exhibits. The finely timbered Joiners' Hall, also in St Ann Street, is one of the old halls of the ancient trade guilds of the city. It is Elizabethan, and was purchased by the National Trust in 1898. The Salisbury diocesan training college is on the site of the old deanery in the Close. Salisbury is the 'Melchester' of Thomas Hardy novels and the 'Barchester' of Anthony Trollope's.

## Salisbury Plain

Undulating plateau between Salisbury and Devizes in Wiltshire, southwest England; area 775 sq km/300 sq mi. It rises to 235 m/770 ft in Westbury Down. Since the mid-19th century it has been a military training area. ◊Stonehenge stands on Salisbury Plain.

### Features

A tract of open chalk downs, Salisbury Plain is rich in prehistoric burial mounds and earthworks, particularly of the Bronze and Early Iron Ages. There are extensive remains of Celtic field systems and of Roman settlements.

### Military training

Salisbury Plain has been used as an army training area since the time of the Napoleonic Wars. A permanent camp was started at Tidworth in 1902. During World War I and World War II many training camps were established in the area, and soldiers were prepared for active service here. The airfields at Upavon and Netheravon have been in use since 1912 and are amongst the oldest in Britain. The main army establishments are the Royal Armoured Corps camp at Tidworth, the Royal Artillery camp at Larkhill, the School of Infantry at Warminster, and the Research Centre at Porton Down, Britain's centre for chemical and biological warfare.

## Saltaire

Model town in West Yorkshire, England, on the River Aire near Shipley. Saltaire was founded in 1853 by the manufacturer Titus Salt (1803–1876), who owned large worsted works. One of Salt's mills now houses a large collection of works by Bradford-born artist David Hockney.

## Saltram

House owned by the National Trust in Devon, England, 5 km/3 mi east of Plymouth. Classical façades were added to the original Tudor house around 1750, and Robert ◊Adam designed the saloon and dining-room in 1768. The house is set in a landscaped park and has gardens with an orangery and summer-house. The large picture collection includes 14 portraits by Joshua Reynolds, a frequent visitor. The Parker family lived here from 1712 until 1962.

## Salvation Army

Christian evangelical, social-service, and social-reform organization, originating in 1865 in London, with the work of William ◊Booth. Originally called the Christian Revival Association, it was renamed the East London Christian Mission in 1870 and from 1878 has been known as the Salvation Army, now a worldwide organization. It has military titles for its officials, is renowned for its brass bands, and its weekly journal is the *War Cry*.

## Sandby, Paul (1725–1809)

English painter and etcher. He is often called 'the father of English watercolour'. He specialized in Classical landscapes, using watercolour and gouache, and helped to introduce the technique of aquatint to England.

Working as a topographical surveyor for the Army, he travelled widely in Britain, painting Scottish scenes following the survey of the Scottish Highlands after the 1745 rebellion, and being one of the first to depict Welsh scenery. Subsequently he often stayed in Windsor with his brother, **Thomas Sandby** (1721–1798), who was appointed Deputy Ranger of Windsor Forest, and some of his best work (Royal Collection) is of Windsor Castle and its environs. He was a founder-member of the Royal Academy in 1768. The romantic features in his paintings, such as ruined castles and stormy skies, paved the way for the full-bodied Romanticism of ◊Girtin and ◊Turner.

## Sandhurst

Town in Bracknell Forest unitary authority, southern England, 14 km/9 mi north of Aldershot; population (1981) 13,500. Nearby are the Royal Military Academy (the British military officer training college), founded in 1799, the National Army Museum, and also the military camp of Aldershot.

## Sandringham House

Private residence of the British sovereign in Norfolk, England, 13 km/8 mi northeast of King's Lynn. In 1862 King Edward VII, then Prince of Wales, bought an estate here, and in 1867–70 built a house which is still a private country residence of the royal family.

## Sandwich

Resort and market town in Kent, southeast England, 18 km/11 mi east of Canterbury; population (1981) 4,200. It has many medieval buildings and was one of the original ◊Cinque Ports. Industries include pharmaceutical research and manufacture, and also market gardening. Features include the Guildhall (1578) which now houses a museum, and two town gates, the Barbican and Fisher Gate.

Silting up of the River Stour left the harbour useless by the 16th century. From the 16th century Sandwich prospered as a centre of the cloth industry established by refugee Huguenot cloth workers. It is a golfing centre, with the Royal St George's Golf Club nearby. To the north of the town is the Gazen Salts Nature Reserve, and also nearby to the north are the remains of Richborough Castle, a 3rd-century Roman fort.

## Sargent, Malcolm (1895–1967)

English conductor. He was professor at the Royal College of Music from 1923, chief conductor of the BBC Symphony Orchestra 1950–57, and continued as conductor in chief of the annual Henry Wood promenade concerts at the Royal Albert Hall.

## Sark

One of the ◊Channel Islands, 10 km/6 mi east of Guernsey; area 5 sq km/2 sq mi; population (1991) 575.

There is no town or village. It is divided into Great and Little Sark, linked by an isthmus, and is of great natural beauty. The Seigneurie of Sark was established by Elizabeth I, the ruler being known as Seigneur/Dame, and has its own parliament, the Chief Pleas.

There is no income tax or divorce, cars are forbidden, and immigration is controlled.

## Sassoon, Siegfried (1886–1967)

English poet. His anti-war poems which appeared in *The Old Huntsman* (1917), *Counter-Attack* (1918), and later volumes, were begun in the trenches during World War I and express the disillusionment of his generation. His later poetry tended towards the reflective and the spiritual. His three fictionalized autobiographical studies (including *Memoirs of a Fox-Hunting Man*, 1928, *Memoirs of an Infantry Officer*, 1930, and *Sherston's Progress*, 1936) were published together as *The Complete Memoirs of George Sherston* (1937).

Educated at Cambridge, Sassoon enlisted in the army in 1915, serving in France and Palestine. Decorated and then wounded in France, he published a manifesto severely criticizing the authorities, 'A Soldier's Declaration' (1917). He was diagnosed as suffering from shell-shock and returned to duty.

He wrote volumes of genuine autobiography, *The Old Century and Seven More Years* (1938), *The Weald of Youth* (1942), and *Siegfried's Journey* (1945). He also wrote a biography of the novelist George Meredith (1948) and *Collected Poems 1908–1956* (second edition) was published in 1961.

## Saul

Village in County Down, Northern Ireland, 3 km/2 mi northeast of Downpatrick. St Patrick is reputed to have landed at Saul in 432. Sliabh Padraig Hill (126 m/415 ft) west of Saul is a pilgrimage site; there is an altar and on the summit a granite statue of the saint.

Some 4 km/2 mi from Saul are the ruins of Raholp church said to have been founded by St Tassach, and 2 km/1 mi south of Saul are the ruins of a church, well, and bathhouses, known as St Patrick's Wells, another site of pilgrimage.

Above the village of Saul is a modern Protestant church dedicated to St Patrick.

## Savernake Forest

Large area of woodland in Wiltshire, England, lying about 5 km/3 mi southeast of Marlborough. Covering 1,620 ha/4,000 acres, it is wooded primarily with beech trees, and abounds in deer and game.

## Savery, Thomas (c. 1650–1715)

British engineer who invented the steam-driven water pump in 1696. It was the world's first working steam engine, though the boiler was heated by an open fire.

The pump used a boiler to raise steam, which was condensed (in a separate condenser) by an external spray of cold water. The partial vacuum created sucked water up a pipe; steam pressure was then used to force the water away, after which the cycle was repeated. Savery patented his invention in 1698, but it appears that poor-quality work and materials made his engines impractical.

## Savile Row

Street in London, situated north of Piccadilly. It is a centre of the tailoring trade and synonymous with fine-quality work. It was built in about 1735 by the 3rd Earl of Burlington, and named after his wife, Dorothy Savile, who died in 1717. For many years it was the favoured business location for leading members of the medical profession.

The playwright Richard Sheridan died in Savile Row in 1816.

## Savoy Hotel

Hotel in the Strand, London, opened in 1889. It is next to the Savoy Theatre and is noted for its rich, famous, and idiosyncratic guests. The first manager was César Ritz (subsequent founder of the ◊Ritz Hotel), and its Grill Room is one of the leading traditional restaurants in London.

## Saxon

Member of a Germanic tribe once inhabiting the Danish peninsula and northern Germany. The

Saxons migrated from their homelands in the early Middle Ages, under pressure from the Franks, and spread into various parts of Europe, including Britain (see ◊Anglo-Saxon). They also undertook piracy in the North Sea and the English Channel.

According to the English historian Bede, the Saxons arrived in Britain in 449, and the archaeological evidence and sparse literary sources suggest the years around 450 as marking the end of their piratical raids, and the establishment of their first settlements in southern England.

Saxon cemeteries that have been located show a wide settlement in eastern England, stretching roughly from the Tees to the Thames, penetrating deeply into the Midlands and the upper Thames, and in the south from Kent to north Hampshire and east Wiltshire. Settlers heading inland from the coast sailed up the rivers Thames, Trent, and Ouse; they also travelled along some Roman roads, particularly in Leicestershire, Warwickshire, and Yorkshire. By the end of the 6th century much of England was in Anglo-Saxon hands. Kent, East Anglia, Wessex, Bernicia, Deira, and finally Mercia had all developed into separate kingdoms.

The name Saxon is said to be derived from their national weapon, the *seax*, a short thrusting sword, in the same way that the Franks, the spearmen, took their name from the Old English *franca*, a javelin.

## Sayers, Dorothy L(eigh) (1893–1957)

English writer of detective fiction, playwright, and translator. Her books, which feature the detective Lord Peter Wimsey and the heroine Harriet Vane, include classics of the detective fiction genre such as *Strong Poison* (1930), *Murder Must Advertise* (1933), *The Nine Tailors* (1934), and *Gaudy Night* (1935).

## Scafell Pike

Highest mountain in England, in the ◊Lake District, Cumbria, northwest England; height 978 m/3,210 ft. It is separated from Scafell (964 m/3,164 ft) by a ridge called Mickledore.

The summit of Scafell Pike was presented to the National Trust by the third Lord Leconfield, as a war memorial, in 1919.

## Scarborough

Spa and holiday resort on the North Sea coast of North Yorkshire, northern England, 56 km/35 mi northeast of York; population (1991) 38,900. It is a touring centre for the Yorkshire Moors, and is

# ◆ THE SAXON SHORE: THE END OF ROMAN BRITAIN ◆

In the 3rd century AD the European provinces of the Roman Empire suffered greatly from barbarian invasion and political turmoil. Although Britain was relatively immune, these events set in motion the longer-term dissolution of the Western Roman Empire.

## The sea wolves

The 3rd century AD was a time of peace on the northern frontier of Roman Britain. Treaties and the garrisons of Hadrian's Wall held the northern tribes in check, but at the same time Gaul and Germany were afflicted by invasions, and the fringes of the storm reached Britain. From across the North Sea came Saxon raiders, threatening the villas and settlements of the southeastern coasts. To fend them off a series of strong, new forts, the forts of the Saxon Shore, were built in the late 3rd century around the coasts of East Anglia and the southeast, from Brancaster in Norfolk via the Straits of Dover to Portchester in Hampshire. They show the high walls and towers of late Roman defences and were associated with both land and sea forces to intercept and repel invaders.

By the 4th century the northern frontier was again giving concern, with the Picts and powerful new peoples such as the Scots menacing Hadrian's Wall, which was refurbished to meet the threat. Occasionally the defensive system based on the Wall failed, most notably in the great 'Barbarian Conspiracy' of 367. In this year the Picts, Scots, and Saxons combined to attack Britain from all sides and the army in Britain temporarily collapsed, having to be restored by the general Theodosius (father of the emperor of the same name).

## Britain in the 4th century

A 4th-century writer refers to Britain as 'a very wealthy island' and its importance to the politics and economy of the late Roman west are clear. The island spawned a succession of claimants to the imperial throne, starting successfully with Constantine I, proclaimed the first Christian emperor, at York in 306. Less successful were Magnentius (350–53) and Magnus Maximus (383–88), both of whom may have removed troops to the continent, and whose suppression brought reprisals upon Britain.

Nonetheless, excavations on the towns and villas of Britain have shown that the first half of the 4th century was their heyday and the time of greatest prosperity and stability for Roman Britain. The villas in particular were at their most numerous and elaborate, with palatial residences such as Bignor (Sussex) or Woodchester (Gloucestershire). Both villas and town-houses were embellished with mosaics whose designs drew on themes from Greco-Roman mythology or the newly fashionable Christianity. The well-to-do proprietors of these villas enjoyed a Roman lifestyle comparable with their peers in Gaul, Spain, or Italy. Finds of silver plate such as that from Corbridge (Northumberland) and Mildenhall (Suffolk) or of jewellery from Hoxne and Thetford (both Suffolk) attest to the wealth and the artistic and religious tastes of British aristocrats.

## Decline and fall

By the late 4th century the archaeological evidence shows that the glory days of Roman Britain were passing. Villas were becoming dilapidated or were abandoned, damaged mosaics went unpatched, and the streets and services of the towns fell into decay. The critical moment came early in the 5th century. In 406 the army in Britain proclaimed another claimant to the imperial purple, Constantine III. He took part of the army with him to Gaul, where he was defeated and killed in 411. At the time Gaul was in turmoil through barbarian invasions, and the central Roman authorities were unable to re-establish control or re-garrison Britain.

Though the Romans never formally abandoned Britain (the famous letter of the emperor Honorius in 410 urging the British to look to their own defences may actually refer to Bruttium in southern Italy), it slipped from their grasp in the early 5th century and was never recovered. Despite the level of success of Roman civilization among the British upper classes, the removal of military protection and the imperial system dealt this way of life a body-blow which it could not withstand, and the decay and dilapidation of the late 4th century hastened the final collapse of the Roman life-style in the early 5th century.

## The Dark Ages

There is an almost total lack of contemporary historical sources for the mid- and late 5th centuries. Yet it is in this time that the Anglo-Saxons became established in Britain. One story has it that some were brought over by a post-Roman ruler in Kent, Vortigern, to protect his kingdom against other raiders. Because of Vortigern's treachery they turned against him and took the kingdom for themselves. This has also been seen as the time of the 'historical' King Arthur, a post-Roman war-leader rallying the Britons against the Anglo-Saxon invaders, the last standard-bearer of Rome in Britain.

by Simon Esmonde Cleary

also centre for fishing. A ruined 12th-century Norman castle overlooks the town.

The playwright Alan Ayckbourn has a long association with Scarborough as artistic director of the Stephen Joseph Theatre, and many of his plays have been premiered in the theatre in the round.

### History
During the Civil War the castle surrendered to Parliamentary forces after a siege in 1645. George Fox, the founder of the Society of Friends, was imprisoned in the castle from 1665 to 1666. Scarborough developed as a resort after the discovery of mineral spring water in 1620.

### Features
The Norman castle was built on a rocky headland (87 m/285 ft high) which separates Scarborough's north and south bays. Bronze Age and Iron Age relics have been recovered from the site and in the castle yard are the remains of a Roman signal station. Remains of the Norman castle include the 12th-century keep and the 13th-century barbican. Other features include St Mary's church dating from about 1180; a house where King Richard III is said to have stayed; and Wood End, formerly a home of the Sitwell family, which now houses a museum.

### Famous people
Scarborough was the birthplace of the poet Edith Sitwell. The novelist Anne Brontë is buried in the churchyard of St Mary's church.

## Science Museum
British museum of science and technology in South Kensington, London. Founded in 1853 as the National Museum of Science and Industry, it houses exhibits from all areas of science.

## Scilly, Isles of, or Scilly Isles/Islands, or Scillies
Group of 140 islands and islets lying 40 km/25 mi southwest of Land's End, England; administered by the Duchy of Cornwall; area 16 sq km/6.3 sq mi; population (1991) 2,050. The five inhabited islands are **St Mary's**, the largest, on which is ♢Hugh Town, capital of the Scillies; **Tresco**, the second largest, with subtropical gardens; **St Martin's**, noted for its beautiful shells; **St Agnes**; and **Bryher**.

Products include vegetables and early spring flowers, and tourism is important. The islands have remains of Bronze Age settlements. The numerous wreck sites off the islands include many of Cloudesley Shovell's fleet (1707). The islands are an important birdwatching centre with breeding sea birds in the summer and rare migrants in the spring and autumn.

### Climate
Frost and snow are a rare occurrence. The climate is an important factor in the islands' main industry, the growing of spring flowers for market.

### Transport
There is an air service between Penzance airport on the mainland and St Mary's, and a boat service between St Mary's and Penzance.

### Early history
The islands are crowded with prehistoric burial chambers, menhirs (upright stone monuments), middens, and hut villages. The stone-chambered barrows evidently represent a provincial extension of the great megalithic culture of Brittany, as might be inferred from the geographical setting of the islands. It is thought possible that they may have been the special home of the dead, known in Celtic mythology. The English antiquary William Camden (1551–1623) identified the Scilly Isles with the fabled islands called the Cassiterides, to which came the Phoenician traders, but there is no proof. Tin was worked in Cornwall in the early Iron Age and in Roman times, but there is no trace of tin workings in the Scilly Isles. Some, at least, of the villages belong to the Bronze Age, and to this time also may be attributed the ancient walls of an early field system, examples of which are occasionally to be seen below present sea level.

## Scone
Site of the ancient **Scone Palace** (destroyed in 1559), near the village of New Scone, Perth and Kinross, where many of the Scottish kings were crowned on the Stone of Destiny. The coronation stone was removed to Westminster Abbey, London, by Edward I in 1297, but was returned to Scotland in 1996 and is on display at Edinburgh Castle.

---

*Scotland, land of the omnipotent No.*

**Alan Bold** Scottish poet.
*A Memory of Death* (1969)

---

## Scotland, Roman Caledonia
The northernmost part of Britain, formerly an independent country, now part of the UK.

*Area* 78,470 sq km/30,297 sq mi
*Capital* Edinburgh
*Cities* Glasgow, Dundee, Aberdeen
*Features* The Highlands in the north (with the ♢Grampian Mountains); central Lowlands, including valleys of the Clyde and Forth, with most of the country's population and industries; Southern Uplands (including the ♢Lammermuir

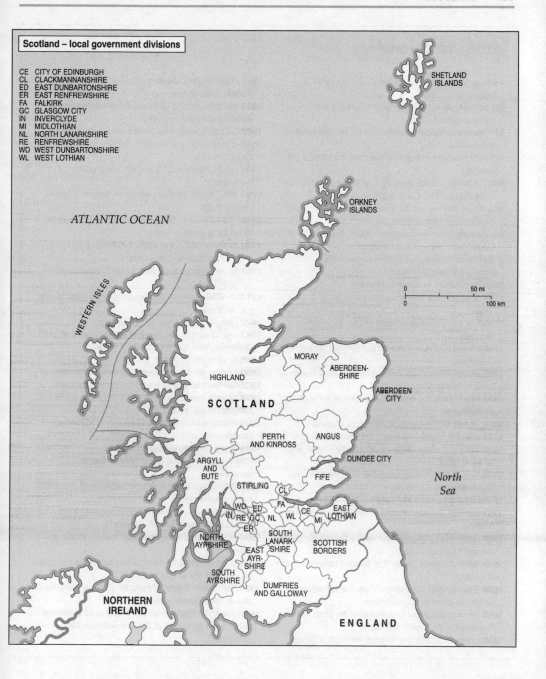

Scotland – local government divisions

CE  CITY OF EDINBURGH
CL  CLACKMANNANSHIRE
ED  EAST DUNBARTONSHIRE
ER  EAST RENFREWSHIRE
FA  FALKIRK
GC  GLASGOW CITY
IN  INVERCLYDE
MI  MIDLOTHIAN
NL  NORTH LANARKSHIRE
RE  RENFREWSHIRE
WD  WEST DUNBARTONSHIRE
WL  WEST LOTHIAN

ATLANTIC OCEAN

SHETLAND ISLANDS

ORKNEY ISLANDS

WESTERN ISLES

HIGHLAND

MORAY

ABERDEEN-SHIRE

ABERDEEN CITY

SCOTLAND

PERTH AND KINROSS

ANGUS

DUNDEE CITY

North Sea

ARGYLL AND BUTE

STIRLING

CL

FA

FIFE

WD
IN
RE
GC
ER
ED
NL
WL
CE
MI

EAST LOTHIAN

NORTH AYRSHIRE

SOUTH LANARK-SHIRE

SCOTTISH BORDERS

EAST AYR-SHIRE

SOUTH AYRSHIRE

DUMFRIES AND GALLOWAY

NORTHERN IRELAND

ENGLAND

0  50 mi
0  100 km

## Scotland: Chronology

**3,000 BC** Neolithic settlements include Beaker people and Skara Brae on Orkney.

**1st millennium BC** The Picts reached Scotland from mainland Europe.

**1st century AD** Picts prevented Romans from penetrating far into Scotland.

**122–128** Hadrian's Wall built to keep northern tribes out of England.

**500** The Scots, a Gaelic-speaking tribe from Ireland, settled in the Kingdom of Dalriada (Argyll).

**563** St Colomba founded the monastery on Iona and began to convert the Picts to Christianity.

**9th century** Norsemen conquered Orkney, Shetland, Western Isles, and much of Highlands.

**c. 843** Kenneth McAlpin unified the Scots and Picts to become first king of Scotland.

**1040** King Duncan murdered by Macbeth.

**1263** Scots defeated Norwegian invaders at Battle of Largs.

**1295** First treaty between Scotland and France (the Auld Alliance).

**1296** Edward I of England invaded and declared himself King of Scotland.

**1297** William Wallace and Andrew Moray defeated English at Battle of Stirling Bridge.

**1314** Robert the Bruce defeated the English at Battle of Bannockburn.

**1328** Scottish independence recognized by England.

**1371** Robert II became first king of the House of Stuart.

**1513** Battle of Flodden: Scots defeated by the English and James IV killed.

**1542** Mary Queen of Scots succeeded to throne when less than a week old.

**1540s** John Knox introduced Calvinism to Scotland.

**1557** The First Covenant established the Protestant faith in Scotland.

**1567** Queen Mary abdicated, later fleeing to England, where she was beheaded in 1587.

**1603** Union of crowns: James VI of Scotland became James I of England.

**1638** Scots rebelled after National Covenant condemned Charles I's changes to church ritual.

**1643** Solemn League and Covenant allied the Scots with Parliament in the English Civil War.

**1650** Cromwell invaded and defeated the Scots at Dunbar.

**1679** Presbyterian Covenanters defeated by Episcopalians at Battle of Bothwell Brig.

**1689** Jacobite victory at Killiecrankie, but rebellion against William III collapsed soon after.

**1692** Campbells massacred the Macdonalds at Glencoe.

**1698** Unsuccessful Scottish colony founded at Darien in Central America.

**1707** Act of Union united the Scottish and English Parliaments.

**1715** 'The Fifteen': Jacobite rebellion in support of James Edward Stuart.

**1745** 'The Forty-Five': Charles Edward Stuart led Jacobite rebels as far south as Derby.

**1746** Jacobites defeated at Battle of Culloden by English forces under Duke of Cumberland.

**1747** Act of Prescription banned Highland costume until repeal in 1782.

**c. 1780–1860** Highland clearances: crofters evicted to make way for sheep.

**1822** George IV made state visit to Scotland.

**1843** The Disruption: 400 ministers left the Church of Scotland to form the Free Church of Scotland.

**1885** Scottish Office created.

**1886** Crofters Act provided security of tenure for crofters.

**1926** Scottish Secretary upgraded to Secretary of State.

**1928** National Party of Scotland formed (became Scottish National Party in 1932).

**1939** Headquarters of Scottish Office moved from London to Edinburgh.

**1945** First Scottish Nationalist MP elected.

**1970s** Aberdeen became centre of North Sea oil development.

**1979** Referendum failed to approve devolution of power to a Scottish Assembly.

**1990** 'Constitutional Convention' of Labour and Liberal Parties demanded a Scottish Parliament.

**1994** Scottish Grand Committee of MPs given additional powers.

**1996** Local government reform: unitary authorities replaced regional and district councils.

**1997** Referendum supported plans for a Scottish Parliament and its tax-varying powers.

**1999** The first Scottish Parliament in 292 years is officially convened in the Church of Scotland Assembly Hall, Edinburgh.

Hills); and islands of the Orkneys, Shetlands, and Western Isles; the world's greatest concentration of nuclear weapons are at the UK and US bases on the Clyde, near Glasgow; 8,000-year-old pinewood forests once covered 1,500,000 ha/3,706,500 acres, now reduced to 12,500 ha/30,900 acres; there were at least 104,876 ha/259,150 acres of native woodlands remaining in the Highlands in 1994, covering only 2% of the total area. The 1995 Millennium Commission award will fund the creation of the Millennium Forest, and double Scotland's forests.

*Industry* Electronics, marine and aircraft engines, oil, natural gas, chemicals, textiles, clothing, printing, paper, food processing, tourism, whisky, coal, computer industries (Scotland's 'Silicon

## Scottish Monarchs 1005–1603

This table covers the period from the unification of Scotland to the union of the crowns of Scotland and England.

| Reign | Name | Reign | Name |
|---|---|---|---|
| **Celtic Kings** | | **English Domination** | |
| 1005–34 | Malcolm II | 1292–96 | John Baliol |
| 1034–40 | Duncan I | 1296–1306 | annexed to England |
| 1040–57 | Macbeth | **House of Bruce** | |
| 1057–93 | Malcolm III Canmore | 1306–29 | Robert I the Bruce |
| 1093–94 | Donald III Donalbane | 1329–71 | David II |
| 1094 | Duncan II | **House of Stuart** | |
| 1094–97 | Donald III (restored) | 1371–90 | Robert II |
| 1097–1107 | Edgar | 1390–1406 | Robert III |
| 1107–24 | Alexander I | 1406–37 | James I |
| 1124–53 | David I | 1437–60 | James II |
| 1153–65 | Malcolm IV | 1460–88 | James III |
| 1165–1214 | William the Lion | 1488–1513 | James IV |
| 1214–49 | Alexander II | 1513–42 | James V |
| 1249–86 | Alexander III | 1542–67 | Mary |
| 1286–90 | Margaret of Norway | 1567–1625 | James VI |
| | | 1603 | union of crowns |

Glen' produces over 35% of Europe's personal computers.)
*Currency* Pound sterling
*Population* (1993 est) 5,120,000
*Languages* English; Scots, a lowland dialect (derived from Northumbrian Anglo-Saxon); Gaelic spoken by 1.3%, mainly in the Highlands
*Religions* Presbyterian (Church of Scotland), Roman Catholic
*Famous people* Robert Bruce, Walter Scott, Robert Burns, Robert Louis Stevenson, Adam Smith

*At no period of its history has Scotland ever stood as high in the scale of nations.*

**Hume Brown**
on David's reign in *History of Scotland* 1899. vol i

*Government* Scotland sends 72 members to the UK Parliament at Westminster. The Local Government (Scotland) Bill of 1994 abolished the two-tier system of local government. Since 1996 there have been 32 unitary authorities; see map (page 797) and list (page 796). See also table of historic counties (page 802). There is a differing legal system to England (see ◊Scottish law).

Scots voted overwhelmingly in favour of a Scottish parliament and the beginning of devolution in a referendum held in September 1997.

*In Scotland there is no shadow even of representation. There is neither a representation of property for the counties, nor of population for the towns.*

**Charles James Fox** English Whig politician.
Quoted in *Parliamentary History of England* by William Cobbett (1763–1835)

Scotland's last legislature vanished with the Union of 1707. The ◊Scottish Parliament was backed by 75% of the 2.4 million people who voted in the two-question referendum and 63% agreed that it should have tax-varying powers. There was a 61.4% turnout.

Elections to the 129-member assembly were planned for spring 1999, with the Parliament coming into being on a site in Edinburgh to be

## Scotland The Brave

Hark where the night is falling
Hark hear the pipes a calling
Loudly and proudly calling down thru the glen
There where the hills are sleeping
Now feel the blood a leaping
High as the spirits of the old highland men

Towering in gallant fame
Scotland my mountain hame
High may your proud standards gloriously wave
Land of my high endeavour
Land of the shining river
Land of my heart forever, Scotland the Brave

High in the misty mountains
Out by the purple highlands
Brave are the hearts that beat beneath Scottish skies
Wild are the winds to meet you
Staunch are the friends that greet you
Kind as the love that shines from fair maidens' eyes

## The Scottish National Anthem: 'Flower of Scotland'

*Although modern, this anthem commemorates the Battle of Bannockburn in 1314 when the Scottish Army under Robert (I) the Bruce King of Scots defeated Edward II, King of England.*

O Flower of Scotland, When will we see Your like again
That fought and died for, Your wee bit Hill and Glen
And stood against him, Proud Edward's Army
And sent him homeward, Tae think again.

The Hills are bare now, and Autumn leaves lie thick and still
O'er land that is lost now, Which those so dearly held
That stood against him, Proud Edward's Army
And sent him homeward, Tae think again.

Those days are past now, And in the past they must remain
But we can still rise now, And be the nation again
That stood against him, Proud Edward's Army
And sent him homeward, Tae think again.

Flower of Scotland, When will we see Your like again
That fought and died for, Your wee bit Hill and Glen
And stood against him, Proud Edward's Army
And sent him homeward, Tae think again.

decided by the turn of the millennium. It will have charge over most of Scotland's domestic affairs, including education, the health service, local government, and agriculture, and will be headed by a First Minister.

*History* See page 412 for a chronology of Scotland's history, and page 413 for a list of monarchs 1005–1603.

---

*Fully 83% said they feel no dislike of the English.*

**David MacCrone** Professor at Edinburgh University. On the findings of an opinion poll in Scotland; the *Sunday Times*, June 1998

---

## Scotland Yard, New

Headquarters of the ◊Criminal Investigation Department (CID) of Britain's London Metropolitan Police, established in 1878. It is named from its original location in Scotland Yard, off Whitehall.

## Scots language

The form of the English language as traditionally spoken and written in Scotland, regarded by some scholars as a distinct language. Scots derives from the Northumbrian dialect of Anglo-Saxon or Old English, and has been a literary language since the 14th century.

It is also known as **Inglis** (now archaic, and a variant of 'English'), ◊**Lallans** ('Lowlands'), **Lowland Scots** (in contrast with the Gaelic of the Highlands and Islands), and '**the Doric**' (as a rustic language in contrast to the 'Attic' or 'Athenian' language of Edinburgh's literati, especially in the 18th century). It is also often referred to as Broad Scots in contrast to the anglicized language of the middle classes.

Scots has been spoken in southeast Scotland since the 7th century. During the Middle Ages it spread to the far north, blending with the Norn dialects of Orkney and Shetland (once distinct varieties of Norse). Scots has a wide range of poetry, ballads, and prose records, including two national epic poems: John Barbour's *Brus* and Blind Harry's *Wallace*. With the transfer of the court to England upon the Union of the Crowns in 1603 and the dissemination of the King James Bible, Scots ceased to be a national and court language, but has retained its vitality among the general population and in various literary and linguistic revivals.

Words originating in Scots that are now widely used in English include *bonnie* (= good-looking), *glamour*, *raid*, and *wee* (= small). In Scotland a wide range of traditional Scots usage intermixes with standard English.

## Scott, (George) Gilbert (1811–1878)

English architect. As the leading practical architect of the mid-19th-century ◊Gothic Revival in England, Scott was responsible for the building or restoration of many public buildings and monuments, including the Albert Memorial (1863–72), the Foreign Office in Whitehall (1862–73), and the St Pancras Station Hotel (1868–74), all in London.

Scott established himself as a restoration architect; his work began in earnest with Ely Cathedral in 1847, and was followed by many other restorations, some 40 cathedrals and 'minsters' in all.

## Scott, Giles Gilbert (1880–1960)

English architect. He was the grandson of Gilbert ◊Scott. He designed Liverpool Anglican Cathedral (begun 1903; completed 1978), Cambridge University Library (1931–34), and Waterloo Bridge, London (1939–45). He also designed and supervised the rebuilding of the House of Commons chamber at the Palace of Westminster in a modern Gothic style after World War II.

His design for Battersea Power Station (1932–34) set the pattern for British power stations and his red telephone boxes in London became a part of British tradition.

## Scott, Peter (1909–1989)

English naturalist, artist, and explorer, founder of the Wildfowl Trust at Slimbridge, Gloucestershire, England, in 1946, and a founder of the World Wildlife Fund (now World Wide Fund for Nature). Knighted 1973.

He was the son of Antarctic explorer Robert Falcon Scott; he studied at Cambridge, in Germany, and at the Royal Academy School, London. In 1936 he represented Britain in the Olympic Games, gaining a bronze medal for the single-handed sailing event. During World War II he served with the Royal Navy. In 1949 he led his first expedition, which was to explore the uncharted Perry River area in the Canadian Arctic. Scott also led ornithological expeditions to Iceland, Australasia, the Galápagos Islands, the Seychelles, and the Antarctic. He was the first president of the World Wildlife Fund 1961–67.

## Scott, Robert Falcon, known as Scott of the Antarctic (1868–1912)

English explorer who commanded two Antactic expeditions, 1901–04 and 1910–12. On 18 January 1912 he reached the South Pole, shortly after the Norwegian Roald Amundsen, but on the return journey he and his companions died in a blizzard only a few miles from their base camp. His journal was recovered and published in 1913.

Born in Devonport, he entered the navy in 1882. With Scott on the final expedition were Edward Wilson (1872–1912), Laurence ◊Oates, H R Bowers, and E Evans. The Scott Polar Research Institute in Cambridge was founded in 1920 out of funds donated by the public following Scott's death, as a memorial to him and his companions.

The *Discovery*, the ship in which Scott made his first Antarctic expedition, is moored at St Katharine's Dock, London, and is a museum of exploration.

## Scott, Walter (1771–1832)

Scottish novelist and poet. His first works were translations of German ballads and collections of Scottish ballads, which he followed with narrative poems of his own, such as *The Lay of the Last Minstrel* (1805), *Marmion* (1808), and *The Lady of the Lake* (1810). He gained a European

**Walter Scott** Scottish novelist and poet Sir Walter Scott, whose early romantic ballads made him the most popular author of his day after Byron. *Waverley* (1814) was the first in a long series of historical novels which Scott wrote anonymously until 1827. He was created a baronet in 1820. Corbis

reputation for his historical novels such as *Waverley* (1814), *Rob Roy* (1817), *The ◊Heart of Midlothian* (1818), and *Ivanhoe* (1819), all published anonymously.

Scott exerted a strong influence on the imaginative life of his country. He stimulated an interest in Scottish history and materially affected the literary movement of his time: his unconventional manner of writing and his total freedom from the academic point of view were largely instrumental in arousing the French Romantic movement. Scott was also the creator of the historical novel, combining naturalness and realism with the historical and romantic element of adventure and the marvels of superstition.

Scott was crippled for life following an early attack of poliomyelitis. Educated at Edinburgh University, he became a lawyer, and in 1799 was appointed a sheriff-depute of Selkirkshire. His *Minstrelsy of the Scottish Border* appeared in 1802–03, and from then he combined writing with his legal profession. He supplied half the capital for starting the publishing house of Ballantyne & Co, and purchased and rebuilt the house of Abbotsford on the Tweed. In 1820 he was elected president of the Royal Society of Scotland. His last years were marked by frantic writing to pay off his debts after the bankruptcy of the printing and publishing business, and continuous overwork ended in a nervous breakdown.

## Scottish Ballet

Ballet company founded in 1956 as the Western Theatre Ballet, based in Glasgow. It tours Scotland and northern England.

## Scottish Borders

Unitary authority in southeast Scotland, created in 1996 to replace the former Borders region; population (1996) 105,300; area 4,733 sq km/1,827 sq mi. It borders the English counties of Northumberland and Cumbria in the south. A series of stone-built castles testify to the insecurity of the border area well into the 16th century. The chief towns are Galashiels, Hawick, Jedburgh, Kelso, ◊Newtown St Boswells (administrative headquarters), Peebles, and Selkirk.

### History

The area has been occupied since early hunter-gatherers moved into Scotland. Through the years there was often unrest over the England–Scotland border. The Raid of the Redeswire (1575), an English defeat at the hands of Jedburgh's provost and townspeople, was the last major engagement of this kind. In another significant battle in the area, the Covenanter General David Leslie

defeated the royalist Marquis of Montrose at Philiphaugh on Yarrow Water in 1645.

### Physical

Much of the western part of the area is upland (Lammermuir, Moorfoot and Pentland Hills); Broad Law (840 m/2,756 ft), near Tweedsmuir, is the highest point. The principal river, the Tweed, traverses the region west–east; its tributaries include the River Teviot. The largest loch is St Mary's, and the only substantial area of low-lying agricultural land is the Merse in the southeast, near the English border. The coast is generally precipitous.

### Features

Early monuments include many hill-forts, of which Eildon Hill North, near Melrose, is the most impressive. There are medieval abbeys at Melrose, Jedburgh, Dryburgh (Field Marshal Haig and Walter Scott are buried here), and Kelso. Hermitage in Liddesdale (c. 13th century) is one of the castles guarding the border area. Later buildings include Abbotsford, created by Walter Scott (1822), and Floors Castle, built by William Adam (1721–25) and altered by Playfair in the 1840s. There are 88 Sites of Special Scientific Interest, three National Nature Reserves, three Ramsars (wetland sites), three Special Protection Areas, and two National Scenic Areas.

### Economy

Lacking coal, the border area was largely bypassed in the industrialization which took place during the 19th century. The tweed industry, however, contributed to the expansion of the mill towns. The area is essentially rural; limited afforestation is now taking place. Agriculture, tourism, and textiles are the mainstays of the modern ecomomy.

## Scottish Gaelic literature

The earliest examples of Scottish Gaelic prose belong to the period 1000–1150, but the most significant early original composition is the history of the MacDonalds in the Red and Black Books at Clanranald. The first printed book in Scottish Gaelic was a translation of Knox's Prayer Book (1567). Prose Gaelic is at its best in the folk tales, proverbs, and essays by writers such as Norman MacLeod in the 19th and Donald Lamont in the 20th century.

Scottish Gaelic poetry falls into two main categories. The older, syllabic verse was composed by professional bards. The chief sources of our knowledge of this are the Book of the Dean of Lismore (16th century), which is also the main early source for the Ossianic ballads; the panegyrics in the Books of Clanranald; and the

Fernaig manuscript. Modern Scottish Gaelic stressed poetry began in the 17th century but reached its zenith during the Jacobite period with Alexander MacDonald, Duncan Macintyre, Rob Donn, and Dugald Buchanan. Only William Livingstone (1808–1870) kept alive the old nationalistic spirit in the 19th century. During and after World War II a new school emerged, including Somhairle MacGilleathain, George Campbell-Hay, and Ruaraidh MacThómais.

## Scottish law

The legal system of Scotland. Owing to its separate development, Scotland has a system differing from the rest of the UK, being based on civil law. Its continued separate existence was guaranteed by the Act of Union with England in 1707.

In the latter part of the 20th century England adopted some features already existing in Scottish law, for example, majority jury verdicts and the replacement of police prosecution by a system of public prosecution (see ◊procurator fiscal). There is no separate system of ◊equity. The supreme civil court is the House of Lords, below which comes the ◊Court of Session, and then the sheriff court (in some respects similar to the English county court, but with criminal as well as civil jurisdiction). More serious criminal cases are heard by the High Court of Justiciary which also sits as a Court of Criminal Appeal (with no appeal to the Lords). Juries have 15 members, and a verdict of 'not proven' can be given. There is no coroner, inquiries into deaths being undertaken by the procurator fiscal.

## Scottish National Gallery of Modern Art

Edinburgh gallery housing the Scottish national collection from 1900 to the present day, founded in 1960. It comprises the most concentrated collection of international modern art in Britain outside London, together with a representative display of modern Scottish art. The collection is especially rich in sculpture, with works by Bourdelle, Moore, Arp, and Giacometti. The permanent collection is constantly supplemented by temporary exhibitions.

## Scottish National Party, SNP

Nationalist party, advocating the separation of Scotland from the UK as an independent state within the European Union. It was formed by the amalgamation of several early nationalist parties in 1934 and at first advocated only autonomy within the UK. It is second only to the Labour Party in

Scotland, having forced the Conservatives into third place.

The party gained its first parliamentary victory in 1945 but did not make serious headway in parliament until the 1970s when it became an influential bloc at Westminster, and its support was crucial to James Callaghan's Labour government. At the 1983 general election, SNP support in Scotland fell back to 12%. However, after subsequently adopting the stance of 'independence within a federal Europe', its support climbed steadily, reaching 22% of the Scottish vote in May 1997, when it won six of Scotland's 72 seats. Led since 1990 by Alex Salmond, the SNP advocates separation by 2007, the 300th anniversary of the Act of Union with England, and is expected to poll strongly in the 1999 elections to the new devolved Scottish parliament.

## Scottish National Portrait Gallery

Edinburgh art gallery, founded in 1882. It aims to illustrate Scottish history with portraits of Scots distinguished in any activity, and paintings which illustrate the history of Scottish dress and other historical developments such as topographical changes. The sequence of portraits starts in the 16th century with Mary Queen of Scots, and continues without serious breaks to the present day (though living people are excepted).

## Scottish Natural Heritage

Conservation body in Scotland formed in 1991. It is government-funded and designates Sites of Special Scientific Interest, National Scenic Areas (the equivalent of Areas of Outstanding Natural Beauty in England; see Countryside Agency for list), National Nature Reserves, Ramsar (wetland) sites, and other protected areas.

## Scottish Opera

Scottish opera company founded in 1962 and based in Glasgow. Richard Armstrong became its music director in 1993. It tours in Scotland and northern England.

## Scottish Parliament

129-member devolved body, approved overwhelmingly in a September 1997 Scottish referendum, when it was agreed the parliament would be based in Edinburgh. The first elections to the parliament were held on 6 May 1999 and the parliament opened on 1 July 1999.

Its temporary base is the Church of Scotland General Assembly Hall and City of Edinburgh Council buildings, in the Lawnmarket and on

George VI Bridge, in Edinburgh. A permanent home is being built on the Royal Mile, next to ◊Hollyrood House, by a design team led by the architect Enric Miralles (1955–　) of Barcelona, with completion planned for the autumn of 2001.

Donald Dewar was elected the country's first minister in 1999. Of the Scottish Parliament's 129 MSPs, 48 are women; only Sweden and Denmark have more women members of parliament.

The parliament has law-making powers in all areas, except those of defence, foreign affairs, the constitution, social security, company regulation, economic management, and taxation. It has, however, the authority to vary the basic rate of income tax in Scotland by up to 3p to supplement a block grant equivalent to the current Scottish Office budget of £14 billion.

## Scouts

Worldwide youth organization that emphasizes character, citizenship, and outdoor life. It was founded (as the Boy Scouts) in England in 1908 by Robert ◊Baden-Powell. His book *Scouting for Boys* (1908) led to the incorporation in the UK of the Boy Scout Association by royal charter in 1912. There are some 25 million members of the World Organization of the Scout Movement (1998).

There are four branches: Beaver Scouts (aged 6–8), Cub Scouts (aged 8–10½), Scouts (10½–15½), and Venture Scouts (15½–20). Girls were admitted to the Venture Scouts in 1976 and to the other branches in 1991 (see also ◊Girl Guides). In 1966 the rules of the Boy Scout Association (now the Scout Association) were revised to embody a more adult and 20th-century image, and the dress was updated; for example, the traditional shorts were exchanged for long trousers. There are over 607,000 members of the Scout Association in the UK (1998).

## sculpture

Historically sculpture has been mainly religious or monumental in purpose, the large Celtic stone crosses of the early Christian period (from AD 597) being among the earliest sculptures in Britain. During the medieval period sculpture was epitomized by niche figures carved in stone for churches and by delicate ivory carvings. Following the Reformation, sculpture became increasingly secularized along with the other visual arts. In the late 17th and early 18th centuries Baroque design favoured relief rather than free-standing sculptures, Grinling Gibbons producing carved wooden panels (mainly birds, flowers, and fruit) for St

Paul's Cathedral and many large country houses. The Neo-Classical sculptors of the 18th century concentrated on smooth perfection of form and surface. Leading Neo-Classicists were Thomas Banks, John Flaxman, and John Gibson.

In the late 19th century the English 'New Sculpture' movement (1890–1915) was characterized by naturalistic modelling and the influence of Symbolism. One of its leading figures was George Frampton, sculptor of *Peter Pan* in Kensington Gardens, London.

In the 20th century various techniques for 'constructing' sculptures were developed, for example metal welding and assemblage. Sculptors such as Henry Moore, Barbara Hepworth, and Jacob Epstein used traditional materials and techniques to create forms inspired by 'primitive' art and nature. Followers of the non-representational school included Reg Butler and Anthony Caro. Traditional sculpture continued, as represented by Frank Dobson (1888–1963), whose work powerfully expresses the Modernist idiom.

Other sculptors have broken with the past entirely, rejecting both carving and modelling. Today the term sculpture applies to the mobiles of Lynn Chadwick and Kenneth Martin, assemblages of various materials, 'environment sculpture' and earthworks, and 'installations'. Contemporary sculptors who work in a variety of unconventional techniques include Damien ◊Hirst and Rachel Whiteread. Another development has been the sculpture garden or park, for example the Grizedale Forest sculpture project in the Lake District.

## Scunthorpe

Industrial town and administrative headquarters of ◊North Lincolnshire, England, 39 km/24 mi west of Grimsby; population (1991) 74,700. Lying on large ironstone deposits, Scunthorpe was a centre of iron production from 1864. Steelmaking began in the town in 1890 and the town remains one of Europe's largest centres of iron and steel production.

## SDLP

Abbreviation for ◊**Social Democratic Labour Party**, a Northern Ireland political party.

## seaside

Favourite destination for many Britons, especially for day-trips. The seaside became especially popular with the advent of direct travel by rail. See chronology 419 for some seaside highlights.

## The Seaside in Britain: Some key dates

**1620** The discovery of a mineral spring leads Scarborough to develop as a spa resort.

**1750s** 'Beale's bathing machines', wagons pulled by horses into the sea at Margate, allow bathers of either sex to enter the water discreetly, from under the cover of a large hood. Similar wagons are still in use over a century later.

**1870s** Having hitherto bathed in the sea naked, men are expected to wear drawers or long bathing costumes.

**18 September 1879** The first illuminations at the seaside resort of Blackpool, Lancashire, are switched on.

**1889** Southend pier is opened. Extended in 1929, it becomes the longest pier in the world.

**1894** The first holiday camp on a permanent site is opened near Douglas, Isle of Man, by Joseph Cunningham. The campers are all male and no alcohol is allowed.

**1903** The first mixed bathing in Britain is introduced, at Bexhill-on-Sea, Sussex.

***c.* 1903** Postcards become very popular in Britain as more people go to the seaside for holidays. Donald McGill begins producing a series of saucy seaside postcards.

**1929** The resort of Bognor adds 'Regis' to its name after George V convalesces nearby at Aldwick.

**1935** Skegness becomes the site of the first Butlin's holiday camp.

**1963** Tony Hancock's film *The Punch and Judy Man* shows traditional seaside entertainments in decline.

**30 March 1964** Fights between rival Mods and Rockers break out in Clacton, Essex, and other seaside resorts during the Easter weekend.

**9 August 1979** Brighton, East Sussex, is the first British seaside resort to provide an area designated for nudists.

**1988** Following concern for the conditions of bathing beaches, the subject of a directive from the European Economic Community on water quality, beaches in the UK that are free of industrial pollution, litter, and sewage, and with water of the highest quality, have the right to fly a blue flag.

## Sedgefield

Town in County ◊Durham, northeast England, 13 km/8 mi northwest of Stockton; population (1991) 88,400. It is known for its nearby racecourse, and Tony Blair, UK Prime Minister from 1997, became MP for the Sedgefield parliamentary constituency in 1983.

## Sedgemoor, Battle of

In English history, a battle on 6 July 1685 in which ◊Monmouth's rebellion was crushed by the forces of James II, on a tract of marshy land 5 km/3 mi southeast of Bridgwater, Somerset.

## Sellafield

Site of a nuclear power station on the coast of Cumbria, northwest England. It was known as **Windscale** until 1971.

## Sellers, Peter stage name of Richard Henry Sellers (1925–1980)

English comedian and film actor. He was particularly skilled at mimicry. He made his name in the madcap British radio programme *The Goon Show* (1949–60). His films include *The Ladykillers* (1955), *I'm All Right Jack* (1960), *Dr Strangelove* (1964), five *Pink Panther* films (1964–78) (as the bumbling Inspector Clouseau), and *Being There* (1979).

## Settlement, Act of

A law passed in 1701 during the reign of King William III, designed to ensure a Protestant succession to the throne by excluding the Roman Catholic descendants of James II in favour of the Protestant House of Hanover. Elizabeth II still reigns under this act.

## Sevenoaks

Town in Kent, southeast England, 32 km/20 mi southeast of London, population (1991) 24,000. Nearby are the houses of Knole (1456) and Chevening (17th century).

Most of the oak trees from which the town derives its name were blown down in the gales which struck southern England in October 1987.

Sevenoaks prospered in the 15th century with the building of the Archbishop of Canterbury's palace at Knole, southeast of the town. The mansion became the property of the crown in 1532, and in 1566 Elizabeth I presented it to her cousin, Thomas Sackville, later Earl of Dorset. In 1946 the fourth Lord Sackville presented it to the National Trust. Knole is set in a park of about 405 ha/1,000 acres.

## Severn, Welsh Hafren

River in Britain, which rises on the slopes of Plynlimon, in Ceredigion, west Wales, and flows east and then south, finally forming a long estuary leading into the Bristol Channel; length 336 km/208 mi. The Severn is navigable for 290 km/180 mi, up to Welshpool (Trallwng) on the Welsh border. The principal towns on its course are Shrewsbury, Worcester, and Gloucester.

England and South Wales are linked by two road bridges and a railway tunnel crossing the Severn (see ◊ Severn Bridge). A remarkable feature of the river is a tidal wave known as the 'Severn Bore' that flows for some miles upstream and can reach a height of 2 m/6 ft.

## Severn Bridge

Bridge linking England with south Wales across the Severn estuary, constructed 1961–66 at a cost of £8 million. A second bridge was built 1992–96, crossing from Severn Beach to New Passage. The construction of the second bridge followed a 63% increase in traffic across the original bridge from 1982 to 1992.

## Sewell, Anna (1820–1878)

English writer. Her only published work, the novel ◊ Black Beauty (1877), tells the life story of a horse. It was a bestseller and became a children's classic. Her aim in writing the book was 'to induce kindness, sympathy, and understanding treatment of horses'.

## Sex Pistols, the

Punk-rock group (1975–78) that became notorious under the guidance of their manager Malcolm McLaren (1946–    ). Their first singles, 'Anarchy in the UK' (1976) and 'God Save the Queen' (1977), unbridled attacks on contemporary Britain, made the Pistols into figures the media loved to hate.

## Seymour, Jane (c. 1509–1537)

English noble, third wife of Henry VIII, whom she married in 1536. She died soon after the birth of her son Edward VI.

Daughter of John Seymour and sister of Edward, Duke of Somerset, she was a lady-in-waiting to Henry VIII's first two wives, Catherine of Aragón and Anne Boleyn. She married Henry a few days after Anne's execution.

## Shackleton, Ernest (1874–1922)

Irish Antarctic explorer. In 1907–09, he commanded an expedition that reached 88° 23′ S latitude, located the magnetic South Pole, and climbed Mount Erebus. Knighted 1909.

He was a member of Scott's Antarctic expedition 1901–04, and also commanded the expedition 1914–16 to cross the Antarctic, when he had to abandon his ship, the *Endurance*, crushed in the ice of the Weddell Sea. He died on board the *Quest* on his fourth expedition 1921–22 to the Antarctic.

## shadow cabinet

The chief members of the British parliamentary opposition, each of whom is responsible for commenting on the policies and performance of a government ministry.

## Shaftesbury

Town in Dorset, southwest England, 30 km/19 mi southwest of Salisbury; population (1991) 6,200. Industries include tourism. King Alfred is said to have founded an abbey on the site in 880 (consecrated in 888); King Canute died at Shaftesbury in 1035. The picturesque, sloping main street has been used for television adverts depicting a rosy past.

*Features*

Excavations have revealed the foundations of the abbey and the plan of the abbey church. The earliest part of St Peter's church dates from the 14th century (and an even older building is underneath); other parts date largely from the 15th century. Gold Hill Wall is part of the old town wall, built in Saxon times and later buttressed.

*History*

It is said that King Alfred's second daughter Ethelgiva was the first abbess of the Benedictine abbey. In 979 the remains of Edward the Martyr (who died in 978 and was initially buried at Wareham) were re-interred at the abbey, and a shrine was built in 1001. This became an important place of pilgrimage, and the town became known for a time as St Edwardstowe. The abbey was demolished soon after its dissolution in 1539. Shaftesbury is mentioned as a borough in the Domesday Book of 1086, being then more important than Exeter or Dorchester.

## Shakespeare, William (1564–1616)

English dramatist and poet. He is considered the greatest English dramatist. His plays, written in blank verse with some prose, can be broadly divided into lyric plays, including *Romeo and Juliet* and *A Midsummer Night's Dream*; comedies, including *The Comedy of Errors*, *As You Like It*, *Much Ado About Nothing*, and *Measure For Measure*; historical plays, such as *Henry VI* (in three parts), *Richard III*, and *Henry IV* (in two parts), which often showed cynical political wisdom; and tragedies, including ◊ *Hamlet*, *Othello*, ◊ *King Lear*, and *Macbeth*. He also wrote numerous sonnets.

Born in Stratford-on-Avon, the son of a wool dealer, he was educated at the grammar school, and in 1582 married Anne ◊ Hathaway. They had a daughter, Susanna, in 1583, and in 1585 twins, Hamnet (died 1596) and Judith. By 1592 Shakespeare was established in London as an actor and a dramatist, and from 1594 he was an important member of the Lord Chamberlain's Company of actors. In 1598 the Company tore down their regular playhouse, the Theatre, and used the timber to build the ◊ Globe Theatre in Southwark. Shakespeare became a 'sharer' in the venture, which entitled him to a percentage of the profits. In 1603 the Company became the King's Men. By this time Shakespeare was the leading playwright of the company and one of its business directors; he also continued to act. He retired to Stratford about 1610, where he died on 23 April 1616. He was buried in the chancel of Holy Trinity, Stratford.

*Follow your spirit; and, upon this charge / Cry 'God for Harry! England and Saint George!'*
**William Shakespeare** English dramatist and poet.
*Henry V* III. i 33

### Early plays
In the plays written around 1589–94, Shakespeare may be regarded as a young writer learning the techniques of his art and experimenting with different forms. These include the three parts of *Henry VI*; the comedies *The Comedy of Errors*, *The Taming of the Shrew*, and *The Two Gentlemen of Verona*; the Senecan revenge tragedy *Titus Andronicus*; and *Richard III*. About 1593 he came under the patronage of the Earl of Southampton, to whom he dedicated his long poems *Venus and Adonis* (1593) and *The Rape of Lucrece* (1594); he also wrote for him the comedy *Love's Labour's Lost*, satirizing the explorer Walter Raleigh's circle, and seems to have dedicated to him his sonnets written around 1593–96, in which the mysterious 'Dark Lady' appears.

### Lyric plays
The lyric plays *Romeo and Juliet*, *A Midsummer Night's Dream*, and *Richard II* (which explores the relationship between the private man and the public life of the state) 1594–97 were followed by *King John* (again exploring the ironies and problems of politics) and *The Merchant of Venice* 1596–97. The Falstaff plays of 1597–1600 – *Henry IV* (parts I and II, juxtaposing the comic world of the tavern and the dilemmas and

**William Shakespeare** English dramatist and poet William Shakespeare. This portrait appeared on the title page of the edition of his works published in 1623. Philip Sauvain Picture Collection

responsibilities attending kingship and political ambition), *Henry V* (a portrait of King Hal as the ideal soldier-king), and *The Merry Wives of Windsor* (said to have been written at the request of Elizabeth I, to show Falstaff in love) – brought his fame to its height. He wrote *Julius Caesar* in 1599 (anticipating the great tragedies in its concentration on a central theme and plot: the conspiracy to assassinate Caesar, and the confrontation between political rivals, in which the more ruthless win). The period ended with the lyrically witty *Much Ado About Nothing*, *As You Like It*, and ◊ *Twelfth Night*, about 1598–1601.

### Tragedies and late plays
With *Hamlet* begins the period of the great tragedies, 1601–08: *Othello*, *King Lear*, *Macbeth*, *Timon of Athens*, ◊ *Antony and Cleopatra*, and *Coriolanus* (the hero of which comes into disastrous conflict with the Roman people through his overriding sense of personal honour). This 'darker' period is also reflected in the comedies *Troilus and Cressida* (a sardonic exploration of the

## Shakespeare's Plays

| Title | Performed/written (approximate) |
|---|---|
| **Early Plays** | |
| Henry VI Part I | 1589–92 |
| Henry VI Part II | 1590–91 |
| Henry VI Part III | 1590–92 |
| The Comedy of Errors | 1591–93 |
| The Taming of the Shrew | 1593–94 |
| Titus Andronicus | 1593–94 |
| The Two Gentlemen of Verona | 1590–95 |
| Love's Labour's Lost | 1593–95 |
| Romeo and Juliet | 1594–95 |
| **Histories** | |
| Richard III | 1592–93 |
| Richard II | 1595–97 |
| King John | 1595–97 |
| Henry IV Part I | 1596–97 |
| Henry IV Part II | 1596–97 |
| Henry V | 1599 |
| **Roman Plays** | |
| Julius Caesar | 1599 |
| Antony and Cleopatra | 1606–07 |
| Coriolanus | 1608 |

| Title | Performed/written (approximate) |
|---|---|
| **The 'Great' or 'Middle' Comedies** | |
| A Midsummer Night's Dream | 1594–95 |
| The Merchant of Venice | 1596–98 |
| Much Ado About Nothing | 1598 |
| As You Like It | 1599–1600 |
| The Merry Wives of Windsor | 1597 |
| Twelfth Night | 1600–02 |
| **The Great Tragedies** | |
| Hamlet | 1601–02 |
| Othello | 1604 |
| King Lear | 1605–06 |
| Macbeth | 1606 |
| Timon of Athens | 1607–08 |
| **The 'Dark' Comedies** | |
| Troilus and Cressida | 1601–02 |
| All's Well That Ends Well | 1602–03 |
| Measure for Measure | 1604 |
| **Late Plays** | |
| Pericles | 1606–08 |
| Cymbeline | 1609–10 |
| The Winter's Tale | 1611 |
| The Tempest | 1611 |
| Henry VIII | 1613 |

concept of chivalric honour in relation to sexual conduct and the war between Greece and Troy), *All's Well That Ends Well*, and *Measure for Measure* around 1601–04. It is thought that Shakespeare was only part author of *Pericles*, which is grouped with the other plays of around 1608–11 – *Cymbeline* (set in ancient Britain, when Augustus Caesar ruled in Rome and Christ was born in Palestine), *The Winter's Tale* (a refashioning of a romance by an envious rival, Robert Greene), and *The Tempest* – as the mature romance or 'reconciliation' plays of the end of his career. It is thought that *The Tempest* may have been based on the real-life story of William Strachey, who was shipwrecked off Bermuda in 1609. During 1613 it is thought that Shakespeare collaborated with John ◊ Fletcher on *Henry VIII* (in which the theme of reconciliation and regeneration after strife is played out in historical terms, so that the young

child who represents hope for the future is none other than Elizabeth I) and *The Two Noble Kinsmen*.

For the first 200 years after his death, Shakespeare's plays were frequently performed in cut or revised form (Nahum Tate's *King Lear* was given a happy ending), and it was not until the 19th century, with the critical assessment of Samuel ◊ Coleridge and William ◊ Hazlitt, that the original texts were restored.

Appreciation of Shakespeare's plays in the 20th century became analytical, examining in detail such aspects as language, structure, contemporary theatrical conditions, and the social and intellectual context of his work. His plays were collected and edited by John Hemige and Henry Condell, two of Shakespeare's former colleagues from the King's company, into the *First Folio* (1623). Later editions were published in 1632, 1664, and 1685 as the *Second*, *Third*, and *Fourth Folios*, respectively.

## Sharp, Cecil (1859–1924)

English collector and compiler of folk songs and dances. He visited the USA 1916–18 to collect songs in the Appalachian mountains, where many English songs were still preserved in their early form by descendants of 17th-century emigrants. His work ensured that the English folk-music revival became established throughout the English-speaking world.

He led a movement to record a threatened folk-song tradition for posterity, publishing *English Folk Song* (1907; two volumes).

## Shaw, George Bernard (1856–1950)

Irish dramatist. He was also a critic and novelist, and an early member of the socialist ◊Fabian Society. His plays combine comedy with political, philosophical, and polemic aspects, aiming to make an impact on his audience's social conscience as well as their emotions. They include *Arms and the Man* (1894), *Devil's Disciple* (1897), *Man and Superman* (1903), *Pygmalion* (1913), and *St Joan* (1923).

Shaw was born in Dublin, and went to London in 1876, where he became a brilliant debater and supporter of the Fabians, and worked as a music and drama critic. He wrote five unsuccessful novels before his first play, *Widowers' Houses*, was privately produced in 1892. Attacking slum landlords, it allied him with the realistic, political, and polemical movement in the theatre, pointing to people's responsibility to improve themselves and their social environment. His first public production was *Arms and the Man*, a cynical view of war.

The volume *Plays: Pleasant and Unpleasant* (1898) also included *The Philanderer*, *Mrs Warren's Profession*, dealing with prostitution and banned until 1902, and *Arms and the Man*. *Three Plays for Puritans* (1901) contained *The Devil's Disciple*, *Caesar and Cleopatra* (a companion piece to Shakespeare's *Antony and Cleopatra*), and *Captain Brassbound's Conversion*, written for the actress Ellen ◊Terry. *Man and Superman* expounds his ideas of evolution by following the character of Don Juan into hell for a debate with the devil.

The 'anti-romantic' comedy *Pygmalion*, first performed in 1913, was written for the actress Mrs Patrick ◊Campbell (and after Shaw's death converted to a musical as *My Fair Lady*). Later plays included *Heartbreak House* (1920), *Back to Methuselah* (1922), and the historical *St Joan*.

Altogether Shaw wrote more than 50 plays and became a byword for wit. He was awarded the Nobel prize in 1925.

*How can what an Englishman believes be heresy? It is a contradiction in terms.*

**George Bernard Shaw** Irish dramatist.
*St Joan* IV

## Sheffield

Industrial city and metropolitan borough in ◊South Yorkshire, England; population of metropolitan district (1991) 501,200. England's fourth largest city, with a long-established reputation for the production of cutlery and tools, Sheffield is still a major centre for the manufacture of steel and an important commercial, retail, sporting, and education centre. Lying amid some of Britain's most attractive scenery close to the ◊Peak District National Park, it is also a touring centre for the southern Pennines. In recent years the city has undergone extensive redevelopment. The National Centre for Popular Music opened in 1999 and, as part of a millennium project designed to contribute to the revitalization of the centre of Sheffield, a new Millennium Gallery and Museum is being built and is due to open in 2001.

### History

Iron was worked here in the 12th century and Sheffield was famed for its knives from the 14th century. The invention of crucible steel and Sheffield plate led to great expansion in the late 18th and early 19th centuries, and by 1850 Sheffield was producing 90 per cent of Britain's steel. The city's cutlery industry expanded further following the invention of stainless steel in 1913.

### Features

The Sheffield Supertram, Britain's most modern light rail system, opened in 1995 and the Meadowhall shopping centre, one of the the UK's largest shopping centres, is in a former steelworking area. The city's cultural attractions include Graves Art Gallery, the Ruskin Gallery, the Mappin Art Gallery, and the City Museum. The Crucible Theatre is the venue for the annual World Professional Snooker Championship, and other theatres include the restored Lyceum. Attractions reflecting the industrial heritage of Sheffield include Kelham Island Industrial Museum and Abbeydale Industrial Hamlet, on the River Sheaf. In 1997 Sheffield was chosen as the site for the new National Sports Institute and the city has two universities, the University of Sheffield, and Sheffield Hallam University.

### Shelley, Mary Wollstonecraft born Godwin (1797–1851)

English writer. She is best known as the author of the Gothic horror story ◊ *Frankenstein* (1818), which is considered to be the origin of modern science fiction, and her other novels include *The Last Man* (1826) and *Valperga* (1823). In 1814 she eloped to Switzerland with the poet Percy Bysshe Shelley, whom she married in 1816 on the death of his first wife Harriet. She was the daughter of Mary Wollstonecraft and William Godwin.

### Shelley, Percy Bysshe (1792–1822)

English lyric poet and critic. With his skill in poetic form and metre, his intellectual capacity and searching mind, his rebellious but constructive nature, and his notorious moral nonconformity, he is a commanding figure of the Romantic movement. He fought all his life against religion and for political freedom. This is reflected in his

---

**Shelley, Percy Bysshe** English Romantic poet Percy Bysshe Shelley, whose creativity was fuelled by his radical thinking and eccentric behaviour. Shelley attempted to establish radical communes in Devon and Wales, then eloped with 16-year-old Harriet Westbrook. His second marriage to Mary Wollstonecraft Godwin was marked by tragedy – two of his children died in infancy and Mary suffered a nervous breakdown. Corbis

early poems such as *Queen Mab* (1813). He later wrote tragedies including *The Cenci* (1818), lyric dramas such as *Prometheus Unbound* (1820), and lyrical poems such as 'Ode to the West Wind'.

Born near Horsham, Sussex, he was educated at Eton and Oxford, where his collaboration in a pamphlet *The Necessity of Atheism* (1811) caused his expulsion. While living in London he fell in love with 16-year-old Harriet Westbrook, whom he married in 1811. He visited Ireland and Wales, writing pamphlets defending vegetarianism and political freedom, and in 1813 published privately *Queen Mab*, a poem with political freedom as its theme. Meanwhile he had become estranged from his wife and in 1814 left England with Mary Wollstonecraft Godwin, whom he married after Harriet drowned herself in 1816. By 1818 Shelley was living in Italy where he produced *The Cenci*; the satire on Wordsworth, *Peter Bell the Third* (1819); and *Prometheus Unbound*. Other works of the period are 'Ode to the West Wind' (1819); 'The Cloud' and 'The Skylark' (both 1820); the lyric drama *Hellas* (1822); and the prose *Defence of Poetry* (1821). In July 1822 Shelley was drowned while sailing near Viareggio, and his ashes were buried in Rome.

### Shepard, E(rnest) H(oward) (1879–1976)

English illustrator and cartoonist. He worked for *Punch*, but is best remembered for his illustrations for children's classics, including A A Milne's *Winnie-the-Pooh* (1926) and Kenneth Grahame's *The Wind in the Willows* (1908).

### Sheraton, Thomas (1751–1806)

English designer of elegant inlaid Neo-Classical furniture. He was influenced by his predecessors ◊ Hepplewhite and ◊ Chippendale. He published the *Cabinet-maker's and Upholsterer's Drawing Book* in 1791.

### Sherborne

Town in Dorset, southwest England, 10 km/6 mi east of Yeovil; population (1991) 7,200. It is a tourist centre. Features include Sherborne Castle, built by the 16th-century adventurer Walter Raleigh, and the ruins of a Norman castle. The abbey church of St Mary the Virgin, founded in the 8th century, contains traces of Anglo-Saxon work.

### Sheridan, Richard Brinsley (1751–1816)

Irish dramatist and politician. His social comedies include *The Rivals* (1775), celebrated for the character of Mrs Malaprop, and *The School for*

*Scandal* (1777). He also wrote a burlesque, *The Critic* (1779). In 1776 he became lessee of the Drury Lane Theatre. He became a member of Parliament in 1780.

---

*Mr Speaker, I said the honourable member was a liar it is true and I am sorry for it. The honourable member may place the punctuation where he pleases.*

**Richard Brinsley Sheridan** Irish dramatist and politician.
Attributed remark, when asked to apologize for calling a fellow Member of Parliament a liar

---

**sheriff** (Old English *scīr* 'shire', *gerēfa* 'reeve')
In England and Wales, the crown's chief executive officer in a county for ceremonial purposes; in Scotland, the equivalent of the English county-court judge, but also dealing with criminal cases.

In England, the office (elective until Edward II) dates from before the Norman Conquest. The sheriff, who is appointed annually by royal patent, and is chosen from the leading landowners, acts as returning officer for parliamentary elections, and attends the judges on circuit. The duties of keeping prisoners in safe custody, preparing panels of jurors for assizes, and executing writs, are supervised by the under-sheriff. The City of London has two sheriffs elected by members of the ◊ livery companies.

### Sherwood Forest

Hilly stretch of parkland in west Nottinghamshire, central England; area about 520 sq km/200 sq mi. Formerly an ancient royal forest extending from Nottingham to Worksop, it is associated with the legendary outlaw ◊ Robin Hood. According to the Forestry Commission, Sherwood Forest is over 1,000 years old.

It was once a vast royal forest of oak, birch, and bracken, covering all of west Nottinghamshire. The great 'Shire Wood' stretched 32 km/20 mi from Nottingham north to Worksop, and was up to 13 km/8 mi wide. Kings and queens of England used it as a hunting ground from medieval times. It was cleared in the 18th century, although parts of it remain from Nottingham to Mansfield and to Worksop.

### Shetland Islands (Old Norse **Hjaltland** 'high land' or 'Hjalte's land')

(Old Norse Hjaltland 'high land' or 'Hjalte's land')
Group of islands and unitary authority off the north coast of Scotland, 80 km/50 mi northeast of the Orkney Islands; population (1996) 22,500; area 1,452 sq km/560 sq mi. The Shetlands are the most northerly part of the UK. There are over 100 islands, 15 of which are inhabited. The Shetlands are an important centre of the North Sea oil industry. The chief town is ◊ Lerwick (administrative headquarters), on Mainland, the largest of the inhabited islands.

*History*
Shetland is rich in archaeological sites, proving that the islands were occupied from the Bronze Age. They were a Norse dependency from the 9th century until 1472 when they were annexed by Scotland.

*Physical*
The islands are mostly bleak, hilly, and clad in moorland. The climate is moist, cool, and windy; in summer there is almost perpetual daylight, whilst winter days are very short. On clear winter nights, the aurora borealis ('northern lights') can frequently be seen in the sky.

*Features*
The best known archaeological sites are Jarlshof, Mousa, and Clickhimin Broch. The settlement site at Jarlshof dates from the Bronze Age. At Mousa, the Picts successfully sought refuge from Roman slave hunters. Clickhimin Broch forms an island at the end of a causeway near Lerwick and was inhabited from c. 6 BC to AD 5. Shetland ponies are a small and sturdy native breed. There are 78 Sites of Special Scientific Interest, three National Nature Reserves, nine Special Protection Areas, and one National Scenic Area.

*Economy*
Shetland enjoys a buoyant mixed economy which prospered with the development of the North Sea oil industry. There are large oil and gas fields west of Shetland; Europe's largest oil port is Sullom Voe, Mainland; and there is production at Foinaven oilfield, the first to be developed in Atlantic waters. Traditional sectors, including fishing and fish processing, cattle and sheep farming, and handknits from Fair Isle and Unst, still play an important part in the economy, and there is some tourism (walking, birdwatching, fishing, and sailing).

### shilling

English coin worth 12 pennies (there were 20 shillings to one pound), first minted under Henry VII. Although the denomination of a shilling was abolished with the advent of decimalization in 1971, the coins remained in circulation as fivepence pieces.

## shinty, Gaelic *camanachd*

Stick-and-ball game resembling Irish hurling, popular in the Scottish Highlands. It is played between teams of 12 players each, on a field 132–183 m/144–200 yd long and 64–91 m/70–99 yd wide. A curved stick (*caman*) is used to propel a leather-covered cork and worsted ball into the opposing team's goal (*hail*). The premier tournament, the Camanachd Cup, was instituted in 1896.

## ship money

Tax for support of the navy, levied on the coastal districts of England in the Middle Ages. Ship money was declared illegal by Parliament in 1641.

Charles I's attempts to levy it on the whole country in 1634–36, without parliamentary consent and in time of peace, aroused strong opposition.

## ships

Building ships has historically been a major concern for Britain, surrounded as it is by sea. See chronology on page 427 for some key dates in the history of British ships. The earliest ships were rafts or dug-out canoes, and date from prehistoric times.

### Development of sailing ships

The invention of the stern rudder during the 12th century, together with the developments made in sailing during the Crusades, enabled the use of sails to almost completely supersede that of oars. Following the invention of the compass, the development of sailing ships advanced quickly during the 14th century. In the 15th century Henry VIII built the *Great Harry*, the first double-decked English warship.

In the 16th century ships were short and high-sterned, and despite Pett's three-decker in the 17th century, English ships did not bear comparison with the Spanish and Dutch until the early 19th century. In the 1840s iron began replacing wood in shipbuilding, pioneered by British engineer Isambard Kingdom ◊Brunel's *Great Britain* in 1845. Throughout the 19th century, improvements were made in warships, including the evolution of the elliptical stern. However, increased rivalry between US and British owners for possession of the Chinese and Indian tea trade led to improvements also being made to the merchant vessel.

The first clipper, the *Ann McKim*, was built in Baltimore in 1832, and Britain soon adopted this type of fast-sailing ship.

### Steamships

Early steamers depended partly on sails for auxiliary power. In 1802 the paddle-wheel steamer *Charlotte Dundas*, constructed by William Symington, was launched on the Forth and Clyde Canal, Scotland. However, the effort was halted amid fears that the wash produced by the paddle would damage the canal banks. In 1812 the *Comet*, built in Scotland in 1804 by Bell, Napier, and Robertson, was launched. This ship, which had a paddle on each side, was a commercial success, and two others were built for service from Glasgow. From this time the steamship-building industry rapidly developed on the banks of the Clyde.

The first steamship to cross the Atlantic was the Dutch vessel *Curaçao*, a wooden paddler built at Dover in 1826, which left Rotterdam in April 1827, and took one month to cross. The next transatlantic steamer, the *Royal William*, crossed from Quebec to London in 17 days in 1833. Britain's entry into the transatlantic efforts began with ◊Brunel's *Great Western* paddle-steamer, which achieved recognition when it completed the journey from Bristol to New York in 15 days – three days faster than a clipper.

### SS Great Britain

The first great iron steamship, *Rainbow*, was launched in 1838. In the following year, Pettit Smith designed the *Archimedes*, the first steamer to use a screw propeller, followed quickly by Brunel's *Great Britain*, which crossed from Liverpool to New York in 14.5 days in 1845.

In 1862 the Cunard Company obtained permission to fit mail steamers with propellers, which suffered less from the rolling of the ship, and the paddle-wheel was relegated to comparatively smooth water. The opening of the Suez Canal in 1869, together with the simultaneous introduction of the compound engine, raised steamships to superiority over sailing ships. In 1902 the turbine engine was employed on passenger steamers on the Clyde, and in 1905 was applied to the transatlantic service. This was followed by the introduction of the internal combustion engine.

### Tankers

Following World War II, when reconstruction and industrial development created a great demand for oil, the tanker was developed to carry supplies to the areas of consumption. Shipyards were flooded with orders for increasingly large tankers. The prolonged closure of the Suez Canal after 1967 and the great increase in oil consumption led to the development of the very large tanker, or 'supertanker'.

## Ships and Shipbuilding: Some key dates

**1647** The Royal Navy adopts a flag code for communication between ships.

**1715** The first dock is built at Liverpool, a city that will become one of the world's most important ports in the coming industrial revolution.

**1726** The English coffee house owner Edward Lloyd first issues the twice-weekly *Lloyd's List*, a list of shipping news for the merchants and ship owners who frequent his establishment.

**1802** Scottish engineer William Symington launches the world's first paddlewheel steamer, the *Charlotte Dundas*, which acts as a tug on the Forth and Clyde Canal. The 17-m/56-ft long steam-driven vessel runs at 13 kph/8 mph and uses a piston rod connected directly to the crankshaft.

**1812** Scottish engineer Henry Bell's steamship *Comet* plies the Clyde River. The first commercially successful steamship in Europe, it heralds the era of steam navigation in Europe.

**1821** The world's first iron-hulled steamship, the *Aaron Manby*, steams from Birmingham, England, to Paris, France, where it enters service on the Seine.

**23 April 1838** The *Great Western* and *Sirius*, both built by the English engineer Isambard Kingdom Brunel, are the first steamships to cross the Atlantic entirely under steam, arriving in New York only hours apart. The *Sirius*, which arrives first, uses a condenser to recover fresh water from the boiler, and the *Great Western* is a wooden paddle steamer driven by two engines.

**19 July 1843** Isambard Kingdom Brunel's ship *Great Britain* is launched. It is the world's largest ship (98 m/322 ft long; weighing 3,332 tonnes/3,270 tons), with six masts and a screw propeller, and becomes the first propeller-driven iron ship to cross the Atlantic.

**1860** British engineer John Russel builds the *Warrior*, the world's first iron-hulled battleship.

**1869** The British clipper ship *Cutty Sark* is launched. It is one of the largest sailing ships at 65 m/212 ft long.

**1877** The Royal Navy's first torpedo boat, the *Lightning*, is completed by British engineer John Isaac Thornycroft.

**1886** The British submarine *Nautilus* is launched. The first electric-powered submarine, it uses two electric 50- horsepower motors powered by a 100-cell storage battery to achieve a speed of 6 knots. The need for frequent battery recharges limits its range to 130 km/80 mi.

**1893** The first British destroyers begin to be built.

**1899** The first icebreaker, the *Ermak*, is built in Britain for the Russian government. It has 38 mm/1.5 in steel plating on its hull, and serves as the prototype for all other icebreakers.

**14–15 April 1912** The British luxury liner *Titanic*, carrying 2,224 people on its maiden transatlantic voyage, hits an iceberg 640 km/400 mi off the coast of Newfoundland and sinks causing the deaths of between 1,503 and 1,517 people (estimates vary). The accident leads to the first international convention for safety at sea, held in London the following year, which draws up safety standards.

**September 1918** The Royal Navy launches the first aircraft carrier, the *Argus*. A converted merchant ship, it has a flight deck measuring 170.7 m/560 ft and a hangar that can house 20 aeroplanes.

**1919** The British ship *Hermes* is launched. It is the first purpose-built aircraft carrier.

**1939** English archaeologists discover the remains of a 7th-century Anglo-Saxon ship burial at Sutton Hoo, Suffolk. The ship is 27 m/88.6 ft long and was crewed by 28–40 oarsmen.

**1948** Radar is installed at Liverpool Docks to supervise shipping approaches in fog.

**18 March 1967** The Liberian-registered tanker *Torrey Canyon* strikes a submerged reef off the coast of Cornwall, England, and spills 860,000 barrels of crude oil into the sea. It is the biggest oil spill to date.

**20 September 1967** The Queen launches the Cunard liner *Queen Elizabeth II*.

**16 March 1977** The British government nationalizes the shipbuilding industry.

**11 October 1982** The *Mary Rose*, King Henry VIII's flagship which was sunk by the French on 19 July 1545, is raised from the bottom of Portsmouth harbour.

**11 December 1997** The British royal yacht, the *Britannia*, is formally retired at a decommissioning ceremony in Portsmouth, England.

More recently ◊hovercraft and hydrofoil boats have been developed for specialized purposes, particularly as short-distance ferries – for example, the catamarans introduced in 1991 by Hoverspeed cross the English Channel from Dover to Calais in 35 minutes, cruising at a speed of 35 knots (84.5 kph/52.5 mph).

Sailing ships in automated form for cargo purposes, and maglev ships (using *mag*netic *levi*tation), were in development in the early 1990s. See chronology of some key dates, above.

### shire

Administrative area formed in Britain for the purpose of raising taxes in Anglo-Saxon times. By AD 1000 most of southern England had been divided into shires with fortified strongholds at their centres. The Midland counties of England are still known as **the Shires**; for example Derbyshire, Nottinghamshire, and Staffordshire.

### Shrewsbury

Historic market town on the River Severn, ◊Shropshire, England, 244 km/152 mi northwest of London; population (1991) 64,200. An important stronghold of the Welsh ◊Marches in Norman times, Shrewsbury prospered with the growth of its wool trade in the middle ages and Tudor period, and is now a regional shopping centre with light industries. It is also a major tourist destination with a wealth of well-preserved medieval, Tudor, and Jacobean buildings. Shrewsbury holds an annual International Music Festival in July and a flower festival in August.

### History
Lying on two hills overlooking a loop of the River Severn, in the border region between England and the Welsh Marches, Shrewsbury had strategic importance from Saxon times. In the 5th century, as **Pengwern**, it was capital of the kingdom of Powys, and as **Scrobbesbyrig** it became part of Offa's kingdom of ◊Mercia at the end of the 8th century. It was frequently raided by the Welsh in the Saxon and Norman periods and a castle and Benedictine monastery were established here in 1083. Edward I made Shrewsbury his seat of government from 1283 to 1287 and the castle remained a royal fortress until the time of Charles II.

### Features
Shrewsbury's red sandstone castle, built to guard the only land approach to the town, now houses the Shropshire Regimental Museum. Shrewsbury Abbey has become known in recent years as the setting for the chronicles of the fictional detective Brother Cadfael, in the bestselling medieval mysteries by Ellis ◊Peters. The town retains much of its medieval character, particularly in the centre with its narrow streets and black and white timber-framed buildings, including Ireland's Mansion (1575) and Owen's Mansion (1592). Rowley's House (1595), another 16th-century timber-framed building, houses a museum which includes relics from the Roman city of Viroconium at nearby Wroxeter. Other features include Clive House Museum, the 18th-century residence of Robert Clive (of India) and the church of St Mary with its remarkable 14th-century Jesse window.

## Shropshire
County of western England, which has contained the separate unitary authority of ◊Telford and Wrekin since April 1998; population (1996) 421,200; area 3,490 sq km/1,347 sq mi. Sometimes abbreviated to Salop (from Salopesberia, a variant of the Saxon name for the town Shrewsbury), Shropshire was officially known by this name from 1974 until local protest reversed the

decision in 1980. The principal towns are ◊Shrewsbury (administrative headquarters), Ludlow, and Oswestry.

### History
On the evidence of its numerous hill-top forts, Shropshire had a considerable population in the early Iron Age. It was settled by the Romans, who established at Wroxeter the third-largest city of Roman Britain (Viroconium), and was subsequently added to the Saxon kingdom of Mercia by Offa in the 8th century. There are several sections of Offa's Dyke, marking the boundary between Mercia and Wales, in the west of the county. During the Middle Ages, it was part of the Welsh Marches and saw persistent conflict between the lords of the Marches and the Welsh. Near Shrewsbury the battle was fought between Henry IV and the Percys (1403) at which Henry 'Hotspur' Percy was killed; the place is now marked by the church and village of Battlefield.

### Physical
Shropshire is bisected northwest–southeast by the River Severn, which enters across the Welsh border; the River Teme also flows through the county. In the south and west it is hilly – the Clee Hills rise to about 610 m/1,800 ft (Brown Clee); other features are the Stiperstones (527 m/1,729 ft), the Long Mynd plateau (517 m/1,696 ft), the Caradoc range, and Wenlock Edge. The north and east is an undulating plain.

Geologically the county displays a greater variety of rocks than any other county in England; this diversity gives rise to great variety of landscape and scenery.

### Features
The county contains many beautiful ruins, such as Haughmond, Buildwas, and Lilleshall abbeys and Much Wenlock Priory. There are a large number of castles, of which only fragments generally remain; Ludlow is the finest. Stokesay House is perhaps the best example in the country of a fortified manor house of the 13th century.

Shropshire's churches display a range of architectural styles: Heath Chapel, Edstaston, and Holgate are Norman; Acton Burnell is a perfect example of Early English; and the church at Tong is in the Perpendicular style. Market Drayton is famous for its gingerbread, and Wem for its sweet peas. There are 16 country parks and nature reserves.

### Economy
Shropshire is the principal iron-producing county of England. There is also agriculture, dairy farming (Shropshire sheep and cattle), and forestry,

and some industry, engineering, and manufacturing (machine tools, agricultural implements, carpets and radio receivers, and clocks).

## Shugborough

House in Staffordshire, England, 9 km/6 mi southeast of Stafford. It has been the home of the Anson family, later to become Earls of Lichfield, from 1624 until the present day. The present late 17th-century house, with 18th-century alterations, contains plasterwork by Vassali and Joseph Rose (1745–99). Shugborough was acquired by the National Trust.

## Sickert, Walter (1860–1942)

English artist. His works, broadly Impressionist in style, capture subtleties of tone and light, often with a melancholic atmosphere, their most familiar subjects being the rather shabby cityscapes and domestic and music-hall interiors of late Victorian and Edwardian London. *Ennui* (about 1913; Tate Gallery, London) is a typical interior painting.

Sickert learned his craft from James Whistler in London and then from Degas in Paris. Though often described as an Impressionist, he was only so to the same limited extent as Degas, constructing pictures from swift notes made on the spot, and never painting in the open air.

He worked in Dieppe from 1885 to 1905, with occasional visits to Venice, and produced music-hall paintings and views of Venice and Dieppe in dark, rich tones. In his 'Camden Town' period (1905–14), he explored the back rooms and dingy streets of North London. His zest for urban life and his personality drew together a group of younger artists who formed the nucleus of the ⟐Camden Town Group, which played a leading role in bringing Post-Impressionism into English art.

His later work became broader in treatment and lighter in tone, a late innovation being the 'Echoes', in which he freely adapted the work of Victorian illustrators.

## Sidney, Philip (1554–1586)

English poet and soldier. In about 1580 he began an unfinished prose romance, known as *Arcadia*, published in a shortened version in 1590, and more fully in 1593. At the same time he wrote an essay on the state of English poetry, published in 1595 both as 'The Defence of Poesie' and 'An Apologie for Poetrie', one of the earliest examples of English literary criticism to be published and the best at least until Dryden. In about 1581 he

composed to a lost love the first major sonnet sequence in English, published as *Astrophel and Stella* (1591).

## Silbury Hill

Artificial mound of the Neolithic (New Stone Age) period, around 2800 BC, situated just south of ⟐Avebury in Wiltshire, England. Steep and rounded, it towers 40 m/130 ft high with a surrounding ditch approximately 6 m/20 ft deep, made when quarrying for the structure. It is the largest ancient artificial mound in Europe.

Local legend suggested that the hill contained a lifesize statue of King Sil and his horse, but no significant finds have ever been made.

## Silchester

Archaeological site, a major town in Roman Britain. It is 10 km/6 mi north of Basingstoke, Hampshire.

## Silverstone

Britain's oldest motor-racing circuit, opened on 2 October 1948. It is situated near Towcester, Northamptonshire, and was built on a disused airfield after World War II. It staged the first officially-titled British Grand Prix in 1948 and on 13 May 1950 hosted the inaugural Grand Prix of the Formula 1 World Drivers' Championship. In 1987 it became the permanent home of the British Grand Prix. Celebrations took place on the weekend of 3 October 1998 to mark the racetrack's 50th anniversary.

---

*Sinn Féin believe the violence we have seen must be for all of us now a thing of the past – over, done with and gone.*

**Gerry Adams** President of Sinn Féin and member of the Northern Ireland Assembly.
A statement – approved by the British, Irish, and US governments – issued on the eve of President Clinton's visit to Ireland, September 1998

---

## Sinn Féin (Gaelic 'we ourselves')

Irish political party founded in 1905, whose aim has been the creation of a united republican Ireland. The driving political force behind Irish nationalism between 1916 and 1921, Sinn Féin returned to prominence with the outbreak of violence ('the Troubles') in ⟐Northern Ireland in the late 1960s, when it split into 'Provisional' and 'Official' wings at the same time as the ⟐Irish Republican Army (IRA), with which it is closely associated. In 1998, the party won 18 seats in the new 108-seat, ◊Northern Ireland Assembly, which took over some executive and legislative powers from the Secretary of State for Northern Ireland.

## Sissinghurst

Village in Kent, southeast England, south of Maidstone, near Cranbrook. The Elizabethan mansion **Sissinghurst Castle**, nearby to the northeast of the village, was the home from 1930 of the writer Vita Sackville-West. Together with her husband Harold Nicolson, she restored the mansion and created extensive gardens in the grounds. The gardens are among the most popular gardens in England; they have been in the care of the National Trust since 1966.

## Site of Special Scientific Interest, SSSI

Land that has been identified as having animals, plants, or geological features that need to be protected and conserved. From 1991 these sites were designated and administered by English Nature, Scottish Natural Heritage, and the Countryside Council for Wales.

Numbers fluctuate, but in 1998 Britain had almost 5,000 SSSIs, two-thirds of which were privately owned. Although SSSIs enjoy some legal protection, this does not in practice always prevent damage or destruction; during 1992, for example, 40% of SSSIs were damaged by development, farming, public access, and neglect. A report by English Nature estimated that a quarter of the total area of SSSIs, over 1 million acres, had been damaged by acid rain. Around 1% of SSSIs are irreparably damaged each year. In 1995–96 7% of Welsh SSSIs and 4.2% of English SSSIs experienced damage.

## Sittingbourne

Town in Kent, England, between Gillingham and Canterbury; population (1991) 56,300. It is in a fruit-growing area, and local industries include fruit packing and preserving; it also manufactures paper, cement, bricks, and clothing. There is also a large agricultural research station here.

---

*The British Bourgeoisie / Is not born, / And does not die, / But, if it is ill, / It has a frightened look in its eyes.*

**Osbert Sitwell** English writer and poet.
'At the House of Mrs Kinfoot'

---

## Sitwell, Osbert (1892–1969)

English poet and author. He was the elder brother of Edith and Sacheverell Sitwell. He published

volumes of verse, including *Selected Poems* (1943); art criticism; and novels including *Miracle on Sinai* (1933). His greatest literary achievement is a series of autobiographical memoirs (1944–62).

## Sitwell, Edith (1887–1964)

English poet, biographer, and critic. Her verse has an imaginative and rhythmic intensity. Her series of poems *Façade* (1922) was performed as recitations to the specially written music of William ◊Walton (1923).

Her *Collected Poems* appeared in 1930 (new edition 1993). Her prose works include *Aspects of Modern Poetry* (1934) and *The Queens and the Hive* (1962).

Sitwell edited the poetry journal *Wheels* (1916–21), a showcase for young poets fighting an artistic revolt against pastoral Georgian verse. The visual imagery and verbal music of her verse influenced T S Eliot and W B Yeats. She was the sister of Osbert and Sacheverell Sitwell.

## Sizergh Castle

Castle in Cumbria, England, 5 km/3 mi southwest of Kendal. The 14th-century pele tower (square fortified tower typical of the Border counties) was built for defence against Border raids, but the castle is largely Tudor, containing panelling, old English furniture, and Stuart and Jacobite relics. The castle was given to the National Trust with 632 ha/1,562 acres by the Hornyold-Strickland family in 1950.

## Sizewell

Nuclear power station in Suffolk, eastern England, 3 km/2 mi east of Leiston. Sizewell A, a Magnox nuclear power station, came into operation in 1966. Sizewell B, Britain's first pressurized-water nuclear reactor (PWR) and among the most advanced nuclear power stations in the world, reached full load in June 1995. Plans to build Sizewell C were abandoned by the British government in December 1995.

## Skara Brae

Preserved Neolithic village built of stone slabs on ◊Mainland in the Orkney Islands, Scotland.

## Skegness

Holiday resort on the North Sea coast of Lincolnshire, eastern England; population (1998) 16,400. It was the site of the first ◊Butlin holiday camp in 1936. An annual carnival is held here in the summer.

## skiffle

British popular music style, introduced by singer and banjo player Lonnie Donegan (1931– ) in

**Skara Brae** The ancient Pictish settlement at Skara Brae on Mainland in the Orkney Islands dates from the Stone Age. It was preserved after a storm buried it in sand; once uncovered, in around 1850, the one-room houses of the village were found to contain a wealth of stone artefacts and furniture, such as cupboards and tables.
Robert Hallmann/Collections

the mid-1950s, using improvised percussion instruments such as tea chests and washboards. Donegan popularized US folk songs like 'Rock Island Line' (1953; a UK hit in 1955 and US hit in 1956) and 'Cumberland Gap' (1957). Skiffle gave way to beat music in the early 1960s.

## Skye

Largest island of the Inner ◊Hebrides, Highland region, off the west coast of Scotland; area 1,740 sq km/672 sq mi; population (1991) 8,900. It is separated from the mainland to the southeast by the Sound of Sleat and by the islands of Raasay and Scalpay to the northeast. The chief port and town is Portree. The economy is based on crofting, craft industries, tourism, and livestock. The **Skye Bridge**, a privately financed toll bridge to Kyleakin on the island from the Kyle of Lochalsh, was completed in 1995. The island has a Gaelic college.

Bonnie Prince Charlie (◊Charles Edward Stuart) took refuge here after the Battle of ◊Culloden.

Much of the island is underlain by Tertiary volcanic rocks, and the scenery of the central part is very mountainous; Sgurr Alasdair (993 m/3,257 ft) in the Cuillin Hills is the highest point. The coastline is deeply indented by numerous sea lochs, and most of the settlements are coastal. Large areas of the northern and central western parts of the island have now been planted as forest. The island is 75 km/47 mi long and 25 km/16 mi wide.

Numerous car ferries serve the island: Armadale is connected to Mallaig on the mainland; Uig to Tarbert (Harris); Uig to Lochmaddy (North Uist); and Sconser to Raasay.

Dunvegan Castle (13th–14th centuries) in the west of the island, is home to the chiefs of the Scottish clan Macleod.

## Slough

Industrial town in southern England, near Windsor, 32 km/20 west of London; population (1996) 105,000. It was part of the county of Berkshire to 1998, when it became a unitary authority; area 28 sq km/11 sq mi.

*History*

A small market town until the beginning of the 20th century, Slough developed into a large residential and industrial area following the conversion of a government mechanical transport depot into a trading estate of 280 ha/692 acres, containing some 290 factories; it was the first of its kind to be established in England. It was granted a borough charter in 1938.

The home of astronomer William Herschel is now a museum; the history of the town is recorded in Slough Museum.

## Smith, Adam (1723–1790)

Scottish economist. He is often regarded as the founder of political economy. His *The Wealth of Nations* (1776) defined national wealth in terms of consumable goods and the labour that produces them, rather than in terms of bullion, as prevailing economic theories assumed. The ultimate cause of economic growth is explained by the division of labour – dividing a production process into several repetitive operations, each carried out by different workers, is more efficient. Smith advocated the free working of individual enterprise, and the necessity of 'free trade'.

In *Theory of Moral Sentiments* (1759), Smith argued that the correct way to discern the morally right is to ask what a hypothetical impartial spectator would regard as fitting or proper. The Adam Smith Institute, an organization which studies economic trends, is named after him.

## Smithfield

Site of a meat market from 1868 and poultry and provision market from 1889, in the City of London. The market now handles fruit and fish in addition to meat and poultry. Formerly an open space used as a tournament ground and cattle market, it was the scene of the murder of Wat Tyler, leader of the Peasants' Revolt in 1381, and the execution of many Protestant martyrs in the 16th century under Mary I.

The annual Bartholomew Fair, a major London market, was held here from 1614 to 1855.

## Smith, W H

Chain of newsagent, book, and record shops developed from a newspaper and stationery business set up in London 1820 by two newsvendor's sons, Henry Edward Smith and William Henry Smith. In 1999 W H Smith acquired internet and publishing businesses and set up its own portal Web site in a bid to move into the forefront of the growth in e-commerce. W H Smith supplied about a third of all newspapers and magazines in the UK in 1996, and had 33,625 employees.

## Snowdon, Welsh Eryri

Highest mountain in Wales, 1,085 m/3,560 ft above sea level. Situated 16 km/10 mi southeast of the Menai Strait, it consists of a cluster of five peaks. At the foot of Snowdon are the Llanberis, Aberglaslyn, and Rhyd-ddu passes. A rack railway ascends to the summit from ◊Llanberis. ◊Snowdonia, the surrounding mountain range, was made a national park in 1951. It covers 2,188 sq km/845 sq mi of mountain, lakes, and forest land.

The five main peaks are Y Wyddfa (1,085 m/3,560 ft), Carnedd Ungain (1,065 m/3,494 ft), Crib Goch (921 m/3,022 ft), Y Lliwedd (898 m/2,946 ft), and Llechog (884 m/2,900 ft). Shaped roughly like an octopus, the massif extends six tentacles or arms around 12 lakes. It is extremely popular for both family walkers and mountaineers.

## Snowdonia

Mountainous region of north Wales, comprising three massifs above 1,000 m/3,280 ft divided by the passes of Llanberis and Nant Ffrancon: ◊Snowdon, the Glyders, and the Carnedds (including Carnedd Dafydd and Carnedd Llewelyn). Snowdonia was designated a National Park in 1951. The park area of 2,188 sq km/845 sq mi dominates Gwynedd and extends eastwards into Conwy county borough.

## Snowshill Manor

Tudor Cotswold manor house in Gloucestershire, England, 10 km/6 mi southeast of Evesham. The house has an early 18th-century façade, but is primarily of interest because it belonged to Charles Paget Wade, an inveterate collector of anything and everything that appealed to him, including clocks, toys, bicycles, orientalia, musical instruments, craft tools, and bygones. Wade left Snowshill and its contents to the National Trust in 1951.

## Soane, John (1753–1837)

English architect. His refined Neo-Classical designs anticipated contemporary taste. Soane was a master of the established conventions of Classical architecture, he also developed a highly individual style based on an elegantly mannered interpretation of Neo-Classicism. He designed his own house in Lincoln's Inn Fields, London (1812–13), now **Sir John Soane's Museum**, which he bequeathed to the nation in 1835, together with his collection of antiques, architectural elements and casts, papers, and drawings. Little remains of his extensive work at the Bank of England, London (rebuilt 1930–40).

## soap operas

On-going TV dramas, a mainstay of British TV schedules, drawing large audiences. At the end of the 1990s the home-grown stalwarts were *Coronation Street* (began 1961), *Emmerdale* (began 1972 as *Emmerdale Farm*), *Brookside* (began 1982), and *EastEnders* (began 1985). *Brookside* was the first soap to be made entirely on location, and has dabbled the most in new ways of presentation: in 1987 a deliberately short-lived soap 'bubble' story, *Damon and Debbie*, 'floated off' from the main story, and extended programmes have covered dramatic storylines.

Not all long-running soaps survive indefinitely: the *Crossroads* Motel closed its doors 23 years after the series began in 1964. Shorter-lived successes have included *Emergency Ward Ten* (from 1957), while *Eldorado* (began 1992), set in Spain, lasted just a year.

*Take the High Road* (began 1981), later

**Soap Operas** Some of the cast of the long-running soap opera *Coronation Street*. This programme, produced by Granada Television in Manchester, along with its rivals, such as the BBC's *EastEnders*, attracts huge audiences. The British viewing public's fascination with soaps is fuelled by extensive coverage in the tabloid press of the stars' private lives. Julian Makey/Rex

renamed *High Road*, is a Scottish soap; *Pobol y Cwm* is Welsh.

## Social and Liberal Democrats
Official name for the British political party formed in 1988 from the former Liberal Party and most of the Social Democratic Party. The common name for the party is the **Liberal Democrats**. Its leader (from 1999) is Charles Kennedy.

## Social Democratic and Labour Party, SDLP
Northern Ireland left-of-centre political party, formed in 1970. It aims ultimately at Irish unification, but has distanced itself from violent tactics, adopting a constitutional, conciliatory role. Its leader, John ◊Hume, played a key role in the negotiations which ended in the 1998 Good Friday Agreement on power-sharing. It secured 24 of the 108 seats in the new Northern Ireland Assembly, elected in June 1998; the party's deputy leader, Seamus Mallon, was voted deputy first minister (to Ulster Unionist David Trimble) by the first meeting of the Assembly.

In October 1998 John Hume was, jointly with David Trimble, awarded the Nobel Peace Prize for his part in the Northern Ireland Peace Process.

## Soho
District of central London, in the City of Westminster, which houses publishing, film, and recording companies; restaurants; nightclubs; and a decreasing number of sex shops. There is a flourishing Chinese community in the area around Gerrard Street.

## Solihull
Industrial and residential town in the county of West Midlands, England, 11 km/7 mi southeast of Birmingham; population (1991) 192,200. The area includes Birmingham Airport and the National Exhibition Centre.

## Somerset
County of southwest England, with a northern coastline on the Bristol Channel; population (1996) 482,600; area 3,460 sq km/1,336 sq mi. It is a lush green and hilly county, known for its apple orchards and rich dairy products, bounded by the Mendip Hills in the northeast, the Quantock Hills and Exmoor in the west, and the Blackdown Hills in the southwest. The coastline is lined with pretty villages, which attract tourists.

The principal towns are ◊Taunton (administrative headquarters), Bridgwater, Frome, Glastonbury, Wells, and Yeovil; Burnham-on-Sea and Minehead are the main coastal resorts.

### History
Somerset was originally part of the kingdom of Wessex, and figured largely in King Alfred's struggle against the Danes. A battle was fought at Allermoor in 1645 during the Civil War. At the Battle of Sedgemoor in 1685, James II defeated the Duke of Monmouth, a claimant to the English crown who had been proclaimed king at Taunton that year.

### Physical
The Quantock Hills, the highest point of which is Willsneck (387 m/1,270 ft), extend from Taunton northwest towards the sea. In the centre of the county is the second-largest area of fen country in England, the Somerset Levels, which includes the area known as Sedgemoor; peat was formerly cut here. The wild forest and moorland of Exmoor National Park lies partly in the extreme west of the county and partly in Devon. Dunkery Beacon (518 m/1,700 ft), the highest point in the county,

is on the northern edge of Exmoor. There are low cliffs along the coast, which has long sandy beaches and mud tracts at low tide, particularly in the northwest. Bridgwater Bay is the chief inlet; the only important harbour is at the mouth of the River Parret. The other rivers are the Avon, Axe, Brue, Exe, and Yeo.

### Features
There are many notable Roman remains in Somerset, including a large mosaic pavement near Langport, and many later Saxon stone carvings in the church at Milborne Port. The Iron Age hillfort of South Cadbury Castle is a possible site of King Arthur's Camelot. The county contains several abbeys, and castles, notably at ◊Glastonbury and Dunster, and an important cathedral at ◊Wells. Country houses include the Elizabethan Montacute House, near Yeovil. Glastonbury has been associated with St Joseph of Arimathaea and King Arthur, who is said to have been buried here. Glastonbury lake village is an important Iron Age settlement in the Somerset Levels. Cheddar Gorge is a dramatic limestone gorge with caves, the original home of Cheddar cheese. At Wookey Hole, a series of limestone caves, Stone Age flint implements and bones of extinct animals have been found. Exmoor ponies are a hardy breed peculiar to the Exmoor district.

### Economy
Somerset's agriculture encompasses dairy farming and related dairy products, notably Cheddar cheese, apples and cider, cereals, vegetables, sheep rearing, and willows (withies) for wickerwork. Industries include agricultural implements, bricks, engineering, and mineral working and stone quarrying. Tourism plays an important role in the local economy.

## Southampton
Industrial city and seaport in southern England, at the head of Southampton Water, 20 km/12 mi southwest of Winchester; population (1996) 207,100. It was part of the county of Hampshire to 1997, when it became a unitary authority; area 52 sq km/20 sq mi. It is a major passenger and container port, and has a ferry link to the Isle of Wight.

### History
There was a settlement here in Roman times (Clausentum), followed by the Saxon Hamtun. A walled town was established on the peninsula between the Test and the Itchen after the Norman Conquest. A charter of incorporation was granted to the town by Henry II (c. 1154–55), and it was created a county by Henry VI in 1447. In the

Southampton A sailing ship moored at the south coast port of Southampton. The quayside she is lying alongside, in the Old Docks area, was once the Cunard Line's Ocean Terminal, serving liners such as the Queen Elizabeth and Queen Mary. Though the transatlantic passenger trade is long gone, Southampton continues to thrive as one of Britain's main ports for containerized freight. Robert Hallmann/Collections

Middle Ages, the town became one of England's major ports, trading especially with France and other Mediterranean countries. In the early 19th century Southampton developed as a spa and, following the arrival of the railway and building of the docks in the 1840s, the city enjoyed another period of prosperity.

### Features

Parts of the medieval town wall survive, including four of the town-wall towers, and Bargate, the elaborate old north gateway to the city. Norman House and Canute's Palace are among the oldest examples of Norman domestic architecture in Britain. The partly Norman St Michael's Church has an 18th-century spire 50 m/164 ft high. Tudor House Museum is situated in a half-timbered 15th-century building, and the 14th-century Wool House now houses a maritime museum. The hospital of God's House was originally founded in 1185 for pilgrims going either to the shrine of St Swithin at Winchester, or to Canterbury; the 15th-century God's House Tower houses a museum of archaeology. Southampton University was established in 1952. The headquarters of the Ordnance Survey are here.

### Docks

The building of the modern system of docks began in 1838. The Old Docks, covering some 80 ha/198 acres, contain three large tidal basins, known as the Ocean, Empress, and Outer Docks. The New Docks, facing the River Test, were completed in 1934. At the western end of the New Docks is the King George V graving (dry) dock, built primarily for the *Queen Mary*. The Princess Alexandra Dock has been redeveloped as a marina and shopping centre. The *Mayflower* originally set sail from here en route to North America in 1620 (bad weather forced it to stop at Plymouth), as did the *Titanic* on its fateful maiden voyage in 1912.

## South Ayrshire

Unitary authority in southwest Scotland, created in 1996 from Kyle and Carrick district (1975–96), Strathclyde region, and prior to that part of the county of Ayrshire; population (1996) 114,000; area 1,245 sq km/480 sq mi. It has a coastline on the Firth of Clyde. It is the birthplace of the poet Robert Burns (Alloway, near Ayr) and Robert the Bruce. The chief towns are ◊Ayr (administrative headquarters), Prestwick, Girvan, Troon, and Maybole.

### Physical

The area comprises a coastal plain which rises to higher ground inland (500 m/1,640 ft). The rivers Ayr, Stinchar, and Water of Girvan run through

it. Natural features include Brown Carrick Hill (287 m/942 ft) and Ailsa Craig. The coastline has many beaches interspersed with cliffs and caves.

### Features

Culzean Castle, 19 km/12 mi south of Ayr, was built by Robert Adam in the late 18th century for the 10th Earl of Cassillis. The ruins of Crossraguel Abbey (1244), a Cluniac monastery, lie near Maybole. There is a Burns National Heritage Park. The Royal Troon and Turnberry championship golf courses and Ayr racecourse are here. The authority has 31 Sites of Special Scientific Interest, one Special Protection Area, and one country park.

### Economy

South Ayrshire is an affluent area with a diverse and prosperous agricultural sector, particularly to the south. The north is dominated by the buoyant economy of Ayr, which combines service sector, tourist, aerospace, technology, and traditional (fishing) enterprise; Glasgow Prestwick Airport supports this enterprise.

## South Bank

Area of London south of the River Thames, between Waterloo Bridge and Hungerford Bridge. It was the site of the Festival of Britain in 1951, and is now a cultural centre. Buildings include the Royal Festival Hall (1951, Robert Matthew and Leslie Martin), the Queen Elizabeth Hall and the Purcell Room (1967), the National Theatre (1976, Denys Lasdun), the Hayward Gallery (1967), the National Film Theatre (1970), and the Museum of the Moving Image (1988), all connected by a series of walkways.

## South Downs

Line of chalk hills in southeast England, running from near Petersfield, Hampshire, across Sussex to the south coast at Beachy Head near Eastbourne. They face the ◊North Downs across the Weald and are used as sheep pasture.

The South Downs long-distance footpath traverses the area. In the west of the range Butser Hill, the highest point, rises to 271 m/887 ft and Duncton Down to 255 m/836 ft; in the east Ditchling Beacon rises to 248 m/813 ft. The rivers Cuckmere, Ouse, Adur, and Arun cut transversely through the chalk, and there are towns at the crossing points such as Lewes and Arundle.

## Southend

Resort town in eastern England, on the Thames estuary, 60 km/37 mi east of London, the nearest seaside resort to London; population (1996)

171,000. It was part of the county of Essex to 1998, when it became a unitary authority; area 42 sq km/16 sq mi. The chief industries are tourism, financial services, light engineering, and boat-building. The Southend unitary authority includes the neighbouring villages of Westcliff, Leigh, Thorpe Bay, Shoeburyness, Southchurch, Eastwood, Cambridge Town, and Prittlewell. Southend attracts nearly 3 million visitors a year.

*History*
The area was successively occupied by Celts, Romans, Saxons, and Danes. The Saxons settled in the area from 500 to 650, and in 894 King Alfred defeated the Danes at Benfleet, driving them across the site of modern Southend to Shoeburyness, where they formed a settlement. The name 'Southende' was first used in a legal document during the reign of Henry VIII. The rise of the town as a health resort dates from about 1794, when it became a fashionable place for sea-bathing. After the arrival of the railway in the 19th century, Southend developed rapidly as a seaside resort, popular with holidaymakers from London.

*Features*
A pier at Southend, 2 km/1.25 mi long, is said to be the longest in the world; there are 11 km/7 mi of seafront, an aquarium, amusement facilities, and many public parks and gardens, including the Cliff Gardens; the town is well known for its flowers, including carpet bedding displays and a Floral Trail Tour. Nearly a third of all land in the area is managed for nature conservation, including Belfairs Wood Nature Reserve and Leigh National Nature Reserve on Two Tree Island.

## South Gloucestershire
Unitary authority in southwest England, created in 1996 from part of the former county of Avon; population (1996) 220,000; area 497 sq km/192 sq mi. It contains the northeastern urban fringe of ◊Bristol. The main towns are ◊Thornbury (administrative headquarters), Patchway, Yate, and Chipping Sodbury.

*Physical*
The authority is bordered by the River Severn to the northwest, and is mainly rural from the Severn Vale to the Cotswold Hills in the east. It contains the Vale of Berkeley.

*Features*
Historic buildings include the 13th-century church of St Peter (Dyrham) and the late 17th-century Dyrham Park Mansion. Marshfield has one of Britain's longest village streets with 17th-century almshouses. Badminton House, home of the Dukes of Beaufort from the 17th century, hosts the annual Badminton Horse Trials. The Severn Road Bridge crosses into Wales from South Gloucestershire.

*Economy*
The local economy is based on agriculture and aerospace and motor industries. The Ministry of Defence Procurement Executive is now located to South Gloucestershire.

## South Lanarkshire
Unitary authority in south central Scotland, created in 1996 from three districts of Strathclyde region, and prior to 1975, part of the county of Lanarkshire; population (1996) 307,100; area 1,772 sq km/684 sq mi. The chief towns are ◊Hamilton (administrative headquarters), Lanark, Rutherglen, East Kilbride, Carluke, and Cambuslang.

*Physical*
It is an area of stark contrast, predominantly rural to the south and urban to the north. The River Clyde flows through the area. Tinto (707 m/2,320 ft) is a key landmark to the south.

*Features*
Historic sites include Craignethan Castle and New Lanark village, a World Heritage site, significant for the attempt to improve living conditions for workers and their families. Carstairs State Hospital is in New Lanark. The authority has 38 Sites of Special Scientific Interest, two National Nature Reserves, and three country parks.

*Economy*
The northern part contains de-industrializing towns, towns within the Glasgow economic system, and the new town of East Kilbride. To the south, a more rural economy prevails, focused around the market town of Lanark.

## Southport
Resort town on the Irish Sea coast in Merseyside, northwest England, 25 km/16 mi north of Liverpool; population (1981) 98,000. Tourism is important and other industries include engineering and the manufacture of clothing and food. Southport pier (1859) was the first pier to be built for pleasure rather than as a landing stage.

The town is built mainly on old sand dunes, and the peat mosslands away from the coastal belt are used for market gardening. A large area has been reclaimed for gardens, a marine lake, swimming pools, and other recreational facilities.

Southport was laid out in a rectangular pattern of tree-lined streets. It acquired its first hotel for visitors in the 18th century, but the town did not expand greatly until the railway to Liverpool was built in 1848, and the line to Wigan and Manchester in 1855. At 1,100 m/1,200 yd, the pier is the second longest in England.

## South Shields

Manufacturing port in Tyne and Wear, northeast England, on the south side of the Tyne estuary opposite North Shields and east of Gateshead; population (1991) 82,400. Shipbuilding has declined and industries now include electrical goods, cables, chemicals, and paint.

It was the site of the Roman fort **Arbeia**, and the Roman Museum displays relics excavated from the site. South Shields was founded by the Convent of Durham in the 13th century. A river port in medieval times, South Shields was a centre of the salt and glass industries in the 17th and 18th centuries, and developed as a resort and coal port in the 19th century.

## South Uist

Second largest island in the Outer ◊Hebrides, Western Isles, Scotland, separated from North Uist by the island of Benbecula. The main town and port with connections to the mainland is Lochboisdale. Most of the population live in crofting townships on the west coast. There are hundreds of lochs in the central area of the island; the east coast is mountainous and dissected by sea lochs.

The island is connected by car ferries from Lochboisdale to Castlebay (Barra), Eriskay, and Mallaig and Oban on the mainland.

## Southwark

Inner borough of south Greater London. It includes the districts of Camberwell, ◊Dulwich, and Walworth. It is the oldest borough in London (after the City of London) and was the first to send representatives to Parliament; population (1991) 218,500.

### Features

Large Roman baths complex, about AD 120, and fine wall paintings have been excavated; Southwark Cathedral (1220), earliest Gothic church in London, with nave built in the 1890s (formerly a parish church, it became a cathedral in 1905); inns and alehouses, including the Tabard Inn, where Chaucer's pilgrims met, and the George Inn (1677), the last galleried inn in London; formerly seven prisons, including the Clink and the Marshalsea; site of Globe Theatre (built on Bankside in 1599 by Burbage, Shakespeare, and others,

burned down in 1613, rebuilt in 1996); the International Shakespeare Globe Centre, adjacent; Imperial War Museum; Dulwich Picture Gallery; Horniman Museum; Elephant and Castle public house, Walworth; Labour Party headquarters in Walworth Road; the Tate Gallery of Modern Art (Swiss architects Herzog and de Meuron), scheduled to open May 2000 in the former Bankside power station.

### Famous people

John Harvard (1607–1638), founder of Harvard College, Massachusetts, USA is commemorated in Harvard Chapel.

## Southwell

Small town in Nottinghamshire, England, 24 km/15 mi northeast of Nottingham; population (1991) 6,600. The main industries are lacemaking, milling, and agriculture. The town is dominated by Southwell Minster (begun about 1110), which was designated a cathedral in 1884.

It is claimed that a church was first established here in 630 by Paulinus, the second bishop of York. The present church shows architectural styles from Norman (the nave) to Perpendicular Gothic, with 13th-century foliage carving in the chapter house, and a 14th-century screen.

## South Yorkshire

Metropolitan county of northeast England, created in 1974; population (1996) 1,304,800; area 1,560 sq km/602 sq mi. The chief towns are Barnsley, Doncaster, Rotherham, and the city of Sheffield (all administrative centres for the districts of the same name). In 1986, most of the functions of the former county council were transferred to the metropolitan borough councils.

### Physical

South Yorkshire contains part of Peak District National Park. There is a rich diversity of rural landscapes between the barren Pennine moors in the southwest and the very low, flat carr-lands (a mixture of marsh and copses) in the east. The River Don flows through it, from southwest to northeast; its main tributaries are the Dearne and the Rother.

### Economy

There is a high level of unemployment; most employed people are engaged in coal-mining, steel manufacturing and processing, and in the glass, brass, wire, and various engineering industries. Sheffield is especially noted for its high-quality alloy steels, machine tools, heavy engineering, and cutlery.

## sovereign

British gold coin, introduced by Henry VII, which became the standard monetary unit in 1817. Minting ceased for currency purposes in the UK in 1914, but the sovereign continued to be used as 'unofficial' currency in the Middle East. It was minted for the last time in 1987 and has now been replaced by the **Britannia**.

The value is notionally £1, but the actual value is that of the weight of the gold at current rates. Sovereigns are bought by investors suspicious of falling values of paper currencies.

## Spaghetti Junction

Nickname for a complex system of motorway flyovers and interchanges at Gravelly Hill, north Birmingham, in West Midlands, central England. It was opened in May 1972.

## Spanish Armada

Fleet sent by Philip II of Spain against England in 1588. Consisting of 130 ships, it sailed from Lisbon, Portugal, and carried on a running fight up the Channel with the English fleet of 197 small ships under Howard of Effingham and Francis ◊ Drake. The Armada anchored off Calais, France, but fire ships forced it to put to sea, and a general action followed off Gravelines. What remained of the Armada escaped around the north of Scotland and west of Ireland, suffering many losses by storm and shipwreck on the way. Only about half the original fleet returned to Spain.

## Speke Hall

House in Merseyside, England, 10 km/6 mi southeast of Liverpool. The manor of Speke was mentioned in the Domesday Book and was therefore in existence in 1066. The present 16th-century house is notable for its Tudor half-timbering and plasterwork. Speke Hall was given to the National Trust in 1944.

## Spencer, Stanley (1891–1959)

English painter. He was born and lived in Cookham-on-Thames, Berkshire, and recreated the Christian story in a Cookham setting. Typically his dreamlike compositions combine a dry, meticulously detailed, and often humorous depiction of everyday life with an elaborate religious symbolism, as in *The Resurrection, Cookham* (1924–26; Tate Gallery, London).

## Spender, Stephen (1909–1995)

English poet and critic. His early poetry has a left-wing political content. With Cyril Connolly he founded the magazine *Horizon* (of which he was co-editor 1939–41), and Spender was co-editor of *Encounter* 1953–66. His *Journals 1939–83* and *Collected Poems 1928–1985* were published in 1985.

In the late 1920s and 1930s he was closely associated with the writers W H Auden, Christopher Isherwood, Louis MacNeice, and Cecil Day-Lewis, sharing their concern with socialism. Later his work became more personal and introspective, and increasingly his public literary activities were as an editor and critic. Knighted 1983.

## Spenser, Edmund (c. 1552–1599)

English poet. His major work is the moral allegory *The Faerie Queene*, of which six books survive (three published in 1590 and three in 1596). Other works include *The Shepheardes Calender* (1579), an excursion into pastoral verse which echoes the language of Chaucer, the sonnet sequence *Amoretti*, and the magnificent wedding hymn 'Epithalamion' (1595) celebrating his own courtship and marriage. He is with Shakespeare the greatest poet of the Elzabethan age, and is a link between the poetry of the Middle Ages and that of Milton and beyond to the Romantics.

Other important works include 'Prothalamion' (1596), a wedding song commissioned for the double marriage of the daughters of the Earl of Worcester. He has been called the 'poet's poet' because of his rich imagery and command of versification.

## Spey

Second longest river in Scotland. It flows through Highland and Moray, rising 14 km/8 mi southeast of Fort Augustus, for 172 km/107 mi to the Moray Firth between Lossiemouth and Buckie. It has salmon fisheries at its mouth.

The upper river augments the Lochaber hydroelectric scheme. Whisky is distilled in the Spey valley.

## spinning jenny

Machine invented in Britain by James Hargreaves about 1764 which allowed several threads to be spun simultaneously. The machine was named after his wife.

## Spitalfields

District in the Greater London borough of ◊ Tower Hamlets. It was once the home of Huguenot silk weavers.

## Spode, Josiah (1754–1827)

English potter. Around 1800, he developed bone porcelain (made from bone ash, china stone, and china clay), which was produced at all English factories in the 19th century. He became potter to King George III in 1806.

He succeeded the Spode factory, founded by his father, Josiah Spode the elder (1733–1797) in 1797, and added porcelain and, in 1805, stone-china to its production. The Spode works were taken over by W T Copeland in 1833.

## Spooner, William (1844–1930)

English academic after whom the phenomenon of spoonerism is named. He was an Anglican cleric and warden of New College, Oxford, from 1903–24, with a tendency to transpose the initial sounds of words, as in 'Let us drink to the queer old Dean' (dear old Queen). Most spoonerisms are apocryphal.

Spooner was elected a fellow of New College in 1867, and lectured on ancient history, philosophy, and divinity. 'You have tasted two whole worms, hissed all my mystery lectures, and been caught fighting a liar in the quad. You must leave Oxford by the next town drain' is often cited as an example of a spoonerism, though he probably never said it.

## Stafford

County town of ◊Staffordshire, England, population (1991) 113,400. Stafford lies on the River Sow, in the green belt between Wolverhampton and Stoke-on-Trent; it is a rail centre, and is served by the M6 motorway. Its chief industries include electrical engineering, shoemaking, salt, adhesives, grinding wheels, concrete reinforcement, and other engineering products. Staffordshire University is located here.

The town dates from the 10th century. The writer Izaak ◊Walton was born in Stafford.

### History

Stafford is mentioned in the Anglo-Saxon Chronicle of AD 913 as Betheney. A royal mint existed on the site in about 940. In the Domesday Book the town appears as Stadford. Stafford's first town charter was granted by King John in 1206. In 1643, during the English Civil War, Parliamentary forces destroyed the town walls and Stafford Castle after their victory at Hopton Heath. A later castle built on the same site has also been demolished. The High House is said to have been built in 1555. Chetwynd House, now the head post office, has associations with the Irish dramatist Richard ◊Sheridan, who was member of Parliament for the town 1780–1806.

## Staffordshire

County of west central England; population (1996) 555,700; area 2,720 sq km/1,050 sq mi. The chief towns are ◊Stafford (administrative headquarters), Newcastle-under-Lyme, Lichfield, Tamworth, Leek, and Uttoxeter. ◊Stoke-on-Trent, the heart of the Potteries manufacturing district, has been a separate unitary authority since April 1997.

### History

There is evidence of pre-Roman and Roman occupation of the county, and Wall (Letocetum) was a Roman station on Watling Street near Lichfield. In Anglo-Saxon times, Staffordshire formed part of the kingdom of Mercia; the Mercian kings had their residence at Tamworth.

### Physical

The county is largely flat, with hilly regions in the north (part of the Peak District National Park) and southwest and rolling farmland in the southeast. The River Trent and its tributaries, the Churnet, Dove, Penk, Sow, and Tame, flow

**Staffordshire** The county of Staffordshire has long been famous as the centre of the British pottery industry, concentrated in the 'five towns' of Tunstall, Hanley, Burslem, Stoke-upon-Trent, and Longton (which merged into Stoke-on-Trent in 1910). Here, gilders are seen putting the final touches to some of the porcelain tableware produced at the Minton factory. McQuillan & Brown/ Collections

through it, and the Staffordshire and Worcestershire canal crosses the county. The ancient woodland of Cannock Chase is a large green area in the centre.

*Features*

There are notable castles at Chartley, Tamworth, and Tutbury. Lichfield has a 13th–14th-century cathedral; Shugborough Hall (17th century) is the seat of the Earls of Lichfield. The Wedgwood Visitor Centre and Bass Brewery Museum provide insights into the county's traditional industries. Keele University was established in 1962. Staffordshire bull terriers are bred here.

*Economy*

There is dairy farming and associated manufacturing of tractors and agricultural equipment. Industries include brewing and china and earthenware in the Potteries and the upper Trent basin (including Wedgwood).

## Staines

Residential town in Surrey, southeast England, at the junction of the rivers Thames and Colne, 29 km/18 mi west of London; population (1991) 53,000. A bridge across the River Thames existed here in the 13th century and a more recent bridge was completed in 1962. Heathrow Airport is nearby.

## Stamford

Market town on the River Welland in Lincolnshire, east-central England, 20 km/12 mi northwest of Peterborough; population (1991) 4,800. Agriculture, engineering, plastics, and the timber and stone trades are important.

Founded by the Danes in the 7th century, Stamford became an important town in the wool trade in the Middle Ages. Its many old buildings include 17th–19th-century houses and public buildings, and medieval churches. Part of the earthworks of a Norman castle may still be seen.

Burghley House, south of the town, was begun in 1575 by Elizabeth I's adviser William Cecil ♢Burghley. During the Middle Ages a number of monasteries were founded; the Benedictine priory of St Leonard retains a Norman arcade and a fine west front. Browne's Hospital, dating from the time of Edward IV (late 15th century), is noteworthy for its glass and screen in the chapel.

The *Lincoln, Rutland, and Stamford Mercury* is one of the oldest newspapers in the country, and is said to have been established in 1695.

## stannaries

Tin mines in Devon and Cornwall, England, which belonged to the Duchy of Cornwall. The workers had the right to have their cases heard in their own stannaries court and the administration of the area was largely delegated to the court under a special privilege granted by Edward I in 1305. In recent times, attempts have been made to impede legislation from Westminster on the grounds that the ancient rights of the stannaries have been ignored. They have been unsuccessful.

## Stansted

London's third international airport, in Essex, southeast England.

As a civilian airport from 1957, offering a limited international service, it featured in three government inquiries before the 1985 decision to make it London's third airport. The passenger terminal, designed by Norman Foster and opened in March 1991, is the centrepiece of a £400 million development, which has taken the airport's annual capacity to 5.5 million passengers (in 1998).

The original runway was built by US forces during World War II and became operational in 1944.

## Stark, Freya (1893–1993)

English traveller, mountaineer, and writer. Often travelling alone in dangerous territories, she described her explorations in the Middle East in many books, including *The Valley of the Assassins* (1934), *The Southern Gates of Arabia* (1936), and *A Winter in Arabia* (1940).

In her 70s and 80s she travelled to Afghanistan, Nepal, and again to Iraq for a journey on a raft down the River Euphrates. The first volume of her autobiography, *The Traveller's Prelude*, which she began soon after World War II, was published in 1950, followed by *Beyond Euphrates* (1951), *The Coast of Incense* (1953), and *Dust in the Lion's Paw* (1961). Her last book, *Rivers in Time*, appeared in 1982.

## Stationery Office

Organization established in 1786 to supply books and stationery to British government departments, and to superintend the printing of government reports and other papers, and books and pamphlets on subjects ranging from national works of art to industrial and agricultural processes. Formerly His/Her Majesty's Stationery Office, HMSO.

## Stenness

Prehistoric site on Mainland, in the Orkney Islands, Scotland, 17 km/11 mi northwest of

Kirkwall. Its ancient monuments include the Ring of Brodgar, the largest stone circle in Scotland, which comprises 27 stones and has a diameter of 104 m/3,431 ft, and the Stenness Standing Stones, comprising 12 slabs, the tallest of which stands at 1.8 m/6 ft.

Maes Howe, a chambered tomb with dry stone walling, and associated with the Boyne megalithic culture of Ireland, lies 4 km/2.5 mi to the east.

### Stephen (c. 1097–1154)
King of England from 1135. A grandson of William the Conqueror, he was elected king in 1135, although he had previously recognized Henry I's daughter ◊Matilda as heiress to the throne. Matilda landed in England in 1139, and civil war disrupted the country until 1153, when Stephen acknowledged Matilda's son, Henry II, as his own heir.

### Stephenson, George (1781–1848)
English engineer. He built the first successful steam locomotive. He also invented a safety lamp independently of Humphrey ◊Davy in 1815. He was appointed engineer of the Stockton and Darlington Railway, the world's first public railway, in 1821, and of the Liverpool and Manchester Railway in 1826. In 1829 he won a prize with his locomotive *Rocket*.

Experimenting with various gradients, Stephenson found that a slope of 1 in 200, common enough on roads, reduced the haulage power of a locomotive by 50% (on a completely even surface, a tractive force of less than 5 kg/11 lb would move a tonne). Friction was virtually independent of speed. It followed that railway gradients should always be as low as possible, and cuttings, tunnels, and embankments were therefore necessary. He also advocated the use of malleable iron rails instead of cast iron. The gauge for the Stockton and Darlington Railway was set by Stephenson at 1.4 m/4 ft 8 in, which became the standard gauge for railways in most of the world.

### Stephenson, Robert (1803–1859)
English civil engineer. He constructed railway bridges such as the high-level bridge at Newcastle-upon-Tyne, England, and the Menai and Conway tubular bridges in Wales. He was the son of George ◊Stephenson. The successful *Rocket* steam locomotive was built under his direction in 1829, as were subsequent improvements to it.

### Sterne, Laurence (1713–1768)
Irish writer. He took orders in 1737 and became vicar of Sutton-in-the-Forest, Yorkshire, the following year. He created the comic anti-hero Tristram Shandy in *The Life and Opinions of Tristram Shandy, Gent* (1759–67), an eccentrically whimsical and bawdy novel in which associations of ideas on the principles of John Locke, and other devices, foreshadow in part some of the techniques associated with the 20th-century novel such as stream-of-consciousness. His other works include *A Sentimental Journey through France and Italy* (1768).

### Stevenage
Town in Hertfordshire, southeast England, 45 km/28 mi north of London; population (1991) 75,000. The town dates from medieval times. In 1946 Stevenage was the first place in England to be designated a new town (to accommodate population overspill).

Stevenage has an annual fair dating from 1280.

### Stevenson, Robert Louis (1850–1894)
Scottish novelist and poet. He wrote the adventure stories ◊*Treasure Island* (1883), *Kidnapped* (1886) and *The Master of Ballantrae* (1889), notable for their characterization as well as their action. He was a master also of shorter fiction such as *The Strange Case of Dr Jekyll and Mr Hyde* (1886), and of stories of the supernatural such as *Thrawn Janet* (1881).

In depth of character and power, his unfinished novel *Weir of Hermiston* might have exceeded all his other works. *A Child's Garden of Verses* (1885) is a collection of nostalgic poetry reflecting childhood.

Stevenson was born in Edinburgh. He studied at the university there and qualified as a lawyer, but never practised. Early works include *An Island Voyage* (1878) and *Travels with a Donkey* (1879). In 1879 he met the American Fanny Osbourne in France and they married in 1880.

### Stilton
High-fat cheese (30–50% fat) with an internal blue mould; it is made from ripened whole milk and contains 33–35% water. It has a mellow flavour and is cured for four to six months. Stilton cheese is still made in and around Melton Mowbray in Leicestershire, England, where it originated, but takes its name from a village in Cambridgeshire, 10 km/6 mi southwest of Peterborough; the cheeses were taken there in coaching days for transport to London.

The name 'Stilton Cheese' was registered as a trademark in 1966 and can only be used for Stilton cheeses produced in Leicestershire, Derbyshire, or Nottinghamshire.

## Stirling

Unitary authority in central Scotland, created in 1996 from Stirling district, Central region; population (1995) 82,300; area 2,196 sq km/848 sq mi. The chief towns are Dunblane, ◊Stirling (administrative headquarters), Aberfoyle.

*Physical*
Mountainous to the north, including the forested Trossachs, and the open moorland north and west of Breadalbane, within the flood plain of the River Forth to the south around Sterling. The area contains many famous Scottish lochs (Tay, Katrine, Lomond) and Scotland's only lake (Lake of Menteith). Peaks include Ben More (1,174 m/3,852 ft) and Ben Venue (727 m/2,385 ft).

*History*
William Wallace won Battle of Stirling Bridge in 1297; English defeated at Bannockburn by Robert the Bruce in 1314; Battle at Sheriffmuir in 1715 between Jacobites and Hanoverians.

*Features*
There are many fine examples of early religious establishments, including Dunblane Cathedral (13th century with a 12th-century tower), Cambuskenneth Abbey (12th century), and the Church of the Holy Rude in Stirling town (15th century). **Stirling Castle**, whose main buildings date from the 15th and 16th centuries, and Doune Castle, dating from the 14th century, are good examples of castle-building of that period. There are 68 Sites of Special Scientific Interest, four National Nature Reserves, one Special Protection Area, three National Scenic Areas, one regional park, and one country park.

*Economy*
Large-scale afforestation has occurred in Breadalbane and the Trossachs, and the attraction of the natural scenery of loch, mountain, and river, has led to the development of a considerable tourist industry concentrated on Aberfoyle and Callander. The Stirling area benefits from the presence of the university and from tourism.

## Stirling

Town and administrative headquarters of Stirling unitary authority, Scotland, on the River Forth, 43 km/27 mi northeast of Glasgow; population (1991) 30,500. The Stirling skyline is noted for its castle, standing on a high plug of volcanic rock, which guarded a key crossing of the river, and the William Wallace Monument, erected in 1870 to commemorate the Scots' victory over the English at nearby **Stirling Bridge** in 1297. Edward I of England (in raising a Scottish siege of the town) went into battle at Bannockburn in 1314 and was defeated by Robert I (the Bruce), in the Scots' greatest victory over the English.

The castle predates the 12th century and was a Scottish royal residence.

The Augustinian abbey at Cambuskenneth, east of Stirling, was founded by David I *c.* 1140; in 1326 Robert the Bruce held his parliament in the abbey, and James III and his queen, Margaret, are buried there. At St Ninians there is the site of the 'Borestone Rotunda' on which it is claimed Robert the Bruce's standard was set up after the Battle of Bannockburn. A university was established at Stirling in 1967.

## Stockport

Industrial town in Greater Manchester, northwest England, 10 km/6 mi southeast of Manchester; population (1991) 130,800. The rivers Tame and Goyt join here to form the Mersey.

*History*
The old town was built on a sandstone ridge overlooking the Mersey. It was granted a charter in 1220 and thrived as a market town, becoming a centre of cotton textiles and hat manufacture in the 19th century. Although the production of hats has now declined, one manufacturer remains.

*Features*
A large railway viaduct across the Mersey, built in 1841 (0.5 km/0.3 mi across the town centre, with 27 arches), dominates the town. The riverside area, once lined with mills, has been redeveloped. The church of St Mary, dating originally from the 12th century, was rebuilt in the early 19th century but retains a 14th-century chancel. The nave and tower were rebuilt in 1813 after a partial collapse which was blamed on an extended bell-ringing session to celebrate Nelson's victory at the Battle of Trafalgar (1805). Nearby to the south is Bramall Hall, a well-preserved black-and-white mansion dating mainly from the 16th century.

## Stockton-on-Tees

Unitary authority in northeast England created in 1996 from part of the former county of Cleveland; population (1996) 176,600; area 200 sq km/77 sq mi. The chief towns are ◊Stockton-on-Tees (administrative headquarters), Billingham, Yarm, Longnewton.

*Features*
River Tees forms east border; Tees Barrage; Yarm viaduct; Preston Hall Museum and Park (Stockton); Castlegate Quay (Stockton) includes a full-scale replica of the *HMS Endeavour*.

## Stockton-on-Tees

Town, port, and administrative headquarters of ◊ Stockton-on-Tees metropolitan borough, on the River Tees, 5 km/3 mi west of Middlesbrough, northeast England; population (1991) 82,400. There are ship-repairing, steel, and chemical industries. It was the starting point for the Stockton–Darlington railway, the world's first passenger railway, which opened in 1825.

The town received its charter of incorporation as a borough between 1201 and 1208, and its first market charter was granted in 1310. The town hall dates from 1735. Stockton's railway station building is the oldest in the world, and the town has many Georgian buildings.

## Stoke-on-Trent

City in central England, on the River Trent, 23 km/14 mi north of Stafford; population (1996) 254,200. It was part of the county of Staffordshire until 1997 when it became a unitary authority; area 93 sq km/36 sq mi. Stoke is the heart of the Potteries, a major ceramic centre, and the largest clayware producer in the world; the ceramics factories of Minton, Wedgwood, Spode, and Royal Doulton are all based here.

An industrial museum at Etruria houses a steam-powered potters' mill. The Gladstone Working Pottery Museum gives demonstrations and lets visitors throw pots.

## Stoke Poges

Village in Buckinghamshire, southern England, 3 km/2 mi north of Slough; population (1991) 4,900. Stoke Poges inspired Thomas ◊ Gray to write his 'Elegy in a Country Churchyard'; the poet is buried in St Giles church.

## Stoker, Bram (1847–1912)

Irish novelist, actor, theatre manager, and author. A civil servant from 1866–78, he subsequently became business manager to the theatre producer Henry Irving at the Lyceum Theatre in London from 1878 to 1905. His novel *Dracula* (1897) crystallized most aspects of the traditional vampire legend and became the source for all subsequent fiction and films on the subject.

Stoker wrote a number of other stories and novels of fantasy and horror, such as *The Lady of the Shroud* (1909).

## Stonehenge (Old English 'hanging stones')

Megalithic monument on Salisbury Plain, 3 km/1.9 mi west of Amesbury in Wiltshire,

**Stonehenge** The stone circle of Stonehenge in southern England. The earliest erections at Stonehenge date from about 3000 BC. The Stonehenge complex, which includes a long avenue and other nearby circles, is thought to have been used to predict various astronomical events and to have been important in worship of the sky and the sun. The building of the main part, about 2000 BC, would have required complex organization, and coincided with the beginnings of chiefdoms in Britain. Corbis

England. The site developed over various periods from a simple henge (earthwork circle and ditch), dating from about 3000 BC, to a cōmplex stone structure, from about 2100 BC, which included a circle of 30 upright stones, their tops linked by lintel stones to form a continuous circle about 30 m/100 ft across. It has been suggested that Stonehenge was constructed as an observatory.

Within the sandstone or sarsen circle (**peristyle**) was a horseshoe arrangement of five sarsen **trilithons** (two uprights plus a lintel, set as five separate entities), and the so-called 'Altar Stone' – an upright pillar – on the axis of the horseshoe at the open, northeast end, which faces in the direction of the rising sun. A further horseshoe and circle within the sarsen peristyle were constructed from bluestone relocated from previous outer circles.

Local sandstone, or sarsen, was used for the uprights, which measure 5.5 by 2 m/18 by 7 ft and weigh some 26 tonnes each. The bluestone was transported from the Prescelly Mountains, Pembrokeshire, Wales.

Stonehenge is one of the best-known archaeological sites in the world. Its conservation poses problems and the decision to close the circle to the public has caused controversy, in particular with regard to the Midsummer solstice ceremony held there. Whatever the original intention of the builders, it has been given ritual significance in later years and is regarded as a 'sacred site'. Stonehenge, Avebury and associated sites were named a World Heritage site in 1986.

---

*I wish I could bring Stonehenge to Nyasaland to show there was a time when Britain had a savage culture.*
**Hastings Banda** Malawi politician and physician. *Observer* 10 March 1963

---

## Stopes, Marie (1880–1958)
Scottish birth-control campaigner. With her second husband H V Roe (1878–1949), an aircraft manufacturer, she founded Britain's first birth-control clinic in London in 1921. In her best-selling manual *Married Love* (1918) she urged women to enjoy sexual intercourse within their marriage, a revolutionary view for the time. She also wrote plays and verse.

She was a palaeontologist (a student of extinct forms of life) and taught at the University of Manchester from 1905 to 1911, the first woman to be appointed to its science staff.

## Stormont
Former village, now part of Belfast, Northern Ireland. It is the site of the new Northern Ireland Assembly, elected as a result of the Good Friday Agreement in 1998. It was the seat of the government of Northern Ireland 1921–72.

## Stourbridge
Town in West Midlands, central England, on the River Stour, 19 km/12 mi southwest of Birmingham; population (1991) 54,700. It is part of the Black Country, and the Stourbridge Canal was formerly used for the transportation of coal. Although industrial activity has declined, allowing more space for housing, warehousing, and parks, some manufacturing remains, including glass-making, an industry established here by Hungarian immigrants in about 1557. There is some tourism, including canal-boating.

## Stourhead
House in Wiltshire, England, 13 km/8 mi south of Frome. Henry Hoare, the banker, commissioned Colen ◊Campbell to build the house in 1722, and the landscaped gardens were laid out 1741–50. The house and its contents, and the estate of 1,000 ha/2,470 acres, including the gardens and the villages of Stourton and Kilmington, were given to the National Trust by Lord Hoare in 1946.

The house contains works of art and furniture by Thomas Chippendale the Younger.

## Strachey, Lytton (1880–1932)
English critic and biographer. He was a member of the ◊Bloomsbury Group of writers and artists. His *Landmarks in French Literature* was written in 1912. The mocking and witty treatment of Cardinal Manning, Florence Nightingale, Thomas Arnold, and General Gordon in *Eminent Victorians* (1918) won him recognition. His biography of *Queen Victoria* (1921) was more affectionate.

## Strand, the
Street in central London, between ◊Charing Cross and ◊Fleet Street. It was originally a track along the strand, or margin, of the River Thames, connecting the cities of London and Westminster.

The road does not appear to have been paved before the time of Richard II (1367–1400). From early times, but especially in the Tudor and Stuart periods, it was lined with mansions. There are two churches in the Strand: St Clement Danes and St Mary-le-Strand, the former by Christopher Wren 1680–82 and James Gibbs 1719, and the latter wholly by Gibbs 1714–17. There are also banks, theatres, and hotels, including the Savoy 1889. Somerset House 1776–86 by William Chambers, at the foot of Waterloo Bridge, houses the Courtauld art collection. The ◊Adelphi 18th-century housing development is off the Strand.

## Strangford Lough
Island-dotted inlet in the east of County Down, Northern Ireland. The entrance to the lough lies between Strangford and Portaferry in the south, and it is bounded from the sea on the east by the Ards Peninsula, 32 km/20 mi long by 8 km/5 mi.

Violent tides enter the lough through the narrow inlet. Strangford Lough is an important habitat for wildlife, especially for overwintering Arctic birds. Queen's University, Belfast, has a marine biological research station and sea-water aquarium at Portaferry on the south of Ards Peninsula. There are many monastic and castle ruins along the shores of Strangford Lough. On Mahee Island, reached by a causeway, are the ruins of Nendrum monastery founded in the 5th century. The Nendrum Bell is now in Belfast Museum.

## Stratfield Saye House
House in Hampshire, England, 11 km/7 mi south of Reading. The central portion of the present house was built about 1630. It is the seat of the Duke of Wellington. The first Duke of Wellington chose Stratfield Saye when Parliament voted him a country estate, following his defeat of Napoleon at Waterloo, and after 1817 he filled the house with his acquisitions from Paris, Spain, and contemporary London. The house contains a collection of French and English furniture and Roman mosaic pavements from Silchester.

## Stratford-upon-Avon
Market town on the River Avon, in Warwickshire, England, 35 km/22 mi southeast of Birmingham; population (1991) 22,200. It is the birthplace of William ◊Shakespeare and has the Royal Shakespeare Theatre (1932), the Swan Theatre, and The Other Place. Stratford receives over 2 million tourists a year. Industries include canning, aluminium ware, and boat building.

The Royal Shakespeare Theatre replaced an earlier building (1877–79) that burned down in 1926. Shakespeare's birthplace contains relics of his life and times. His grave is in the parish church; his wife Anne ◊Hathaway's cottage is nearby.
### Shakespeare landmarks
Shakespeare's reputed birthplace is in Henley Street, purchased for the nation in 1847 for £3,000, (it is administered by the Shakespeare Birthplace Trust, which also runs the adjoining library and study centre, opened in 1964, and several other Shakespeare-related buildings); Anne Hathaway's cottage, 1.5 km/1 mi from the centre of the town; the graves of the poet and his wife in the chancel of Holy Trinity; 'The Cage', which was for 36 years the home of Judith, Shakespeare's younger daughter, wife of Thomas Quiney, vintner; Hall's Croft, old-timbered residence of Susanna, the poet's elder daughter, who married Dr John Hall, his executor, which now houses the offices of the British Council and a Festival Club; Wilmcote, the house of Shakespeare's mother Mary Arden, a fine timbered farmhouse of the Tudor period, 5 km/3 mi outside the town; Nash's House, restored in 17th-century style, with the adjoining vacant site of Shakespeare's house, New Place, and its Elizabethan garden; and King Edward VI Grammar School, endowed in 1482 by Rev Thomas Jolyffe, MA, of Stratford, and re-endowed by Edward VI.
### Royal Shakespeare Theatre and surroundings
The original theatre built by public subscription as the Shakespeare Memorial Theatre, a redbrick building which opened in 1879 for annual summer seasons of Shakespeare's plays, was destroyed by fire in 1926. The present building, which changed its name in 1961 to the Royal Shakespeare Theatre, was designed by Elizabeth Scott and opened in 1932. The buildings adjoining the theatre were not seriously damaged by the fire. They include the library, which, mainly donated by C E Flower (1830–1892) and his wife, contains some 10,000 volumes of Shakespeare editions and dramatic literature, and a number of pictures, including the 'Droeshout' portrait. There is also the art gallery and museum, containing pictures and exhibits illustrating the history of the theatre and Shakespeare productions. Mason Croft, once the home of Marie Corelli, is now the Institute of Shakespeare Studies, run by the University of Birmingham.

## Street
Town in Somerset, England, 3 km/2 mi southwest of Glastonbury; population (1991) 9,200. Shoes, leather, and sheepskin goods are made here, and there is a retail park of factory outlets.

## Stuart, or Stewart
Royal family who inherited the Scottish throne in 1371 and the English throne in 1603, holding it until 1714, when Queen Anne died without heirs; the house of Stuart was replaced by the house of ◊Hanover. See pages 446 and 447 for a genealogy.

# HOUSE OF STEWART 1309–1625

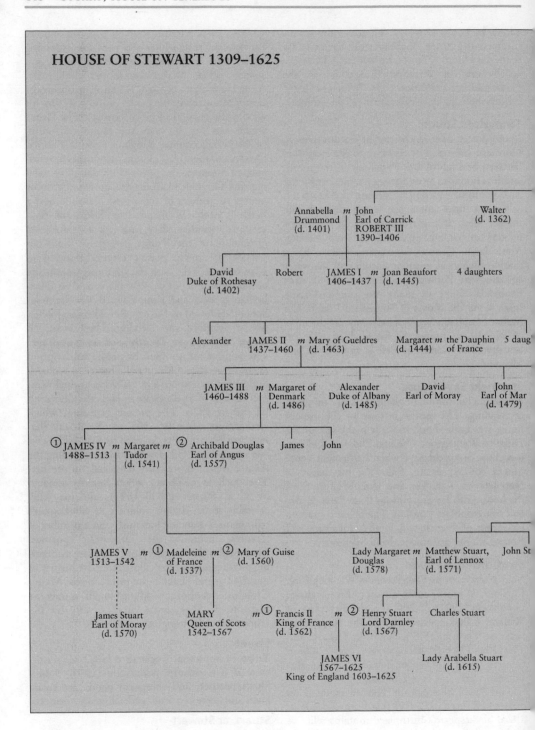

Annabella *m* John      Walter
Drummond | Earl of Carrick      (d. 1362)
(d. 1401) | ROBERT III
       1390–1406

David     Robert     JAMES I *m* Joan Beaufort     4 daughters
Duke of Rothesay          1406–1437 (d. 1445)
(d. 1402)

Alexander    JAMES II *m* Mary of Gueldres     Margaret *m* the Dauphin   5 daug
          1437–1460 | (d. 1463)         (d. 1444)   of France

JAMES III *m* Margaret of    Alexander     David      John
1460–1488 | Denmark    Duke of Albany   Earl of Moray   Earl of Mar
         (d. 1486)     (d. 1485)                  (d. 1479)

① JAMES IV *m* Margaret *m* ② Archibald Douglas   James    John
1488–1513    Tudor        Earl of Angus
        (d. 1541)      (d. 1557)

JAMES V   *m* ① Madeleine *m* ② Mary of Guise        Lady Margaret *m* Matthew Stuart,   John St
1513–1542     of France     (d. 1560)            Douglas     Earl of Lennox
           (d. 1537)                        (d. 1578)     (d. 1571)

James Stuart     MARY       *m* ① Francis II    *m* ② Henry Stuart   Charles Stuart
Earl of Moray    Queen of Scots     King of France     Lord Darnley
(d. 1570)        1542–1567       (d. 1562)       (d. 1567)

JAMES VI          Lady Arabella Stuart
1567–1625         (d. 1615)
King of England 1603–1625

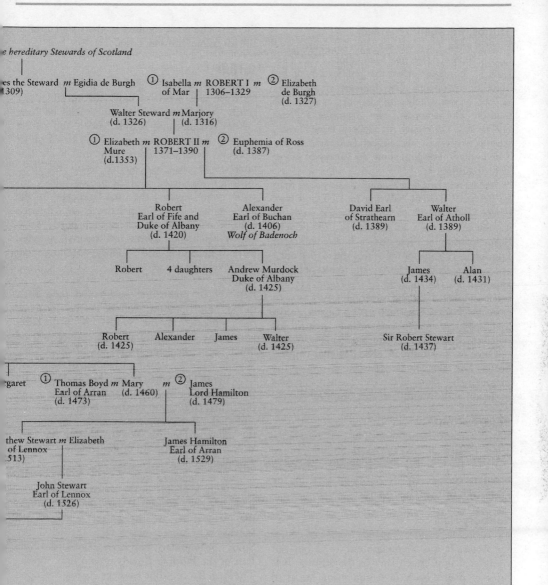

*the hereditary Stewards of Scotland*

James the Steward  *m*  Egidia de Burgh    ① Isabella  *m*  ROBERT I  *m*  ② Elizabeth
(d. 1309)                                            of Mar      1306–1329         de Burgh
                                                                                               (d. 1327)

Walter Steward  *m* Marjory
(d. 1326)                (d. 1316)

① Elizabeth  *m*  ROBERT II  *m*  ② Euphemia of Ross
Mure            1371–1390              (d. 1387)
(d.1353)

Robert                 Alexander              David Earl             Walter
Earl of Fife and    Earl of Buchan       of Strathearn       Earl of Atholl
Duke of Albany        (d. 1406)             (d. 1389)            (d. 1389)
(d. 1420)          *Wolf of Badenoch*

Robert    4 daughters    Andrew Murdock                          James          Alan
                              Duke of Albany                        (d. 1434)     (d. 1431)
                              (d. 1425)

Robert        Alexander      James        Walter              Sir Robert Stewart
(d. 1425)                                  (d. 1425)              (d. 1437)

Margaret   ① Thomas Boyd  *m* Mary    *m*  ② James
              Earl of Arran      (d. 1460)    Lord Hamilton
              (d. 1473)                        (d. 1479)

Mathew Stewart  *m* Elizabeth          James Hamilton
of Lennox                                  Earl of Arran
(d.1513)                                    (d. 1529)

John Stewart
Earl of Lennox
(d. 1526)

*The House of Stewart changed the spelling of
their name to Stuart during the reign of James V,
in recognition of the difficulty their French
allies found in pronouncing the letter W.*

## Stubbs, George (1724–1806)

English artist. He is renowned for his paintings of horses, such as *Mares and Foals* (about 1763; Tate Gallery, London). After the publication of his book of engravings *The Anatomy of the Horse* (1766), he was widely commissioned as an animal painter. The dramatic *Lion Attacking a Horse* (1770; Yale University Art Gallery, New Haven, Connecticut) and the peaceful *Reapers* (1786; Tate Gallery, London) show the variety of mood in his painting.

Stubbs was largely self-taught. As a young man he practised portrait painting in York and elsewhere in the north of England while studying human and animal anatomy, and in 1754 went to Rome, continuing these studies. Before settling in London in 1759 he rented a farm and carried out a series of dissections of horses, the results of which appeared in *The Anatomy of the Horse*. He was often employed by the sporting aristocracy to paint racehorses, *Gimcrack with a Groom, Jockey and Stable-lad on Newmarket Heath*, painted for Viscount Bolingbroke, being a notable example.

Once seen as only an expert animal painter, Stubbs has come to be regarded as one of the major English artists of the 18th century in power of design and composition and all-round ability.

## Stud, National

British establishment founded in 1915, and since 1964 located at ◊Newmarket, Suffolk, where stallions are kept for visiting mares in order to breed racehorses. It is now maintained by the Horserace Betting Levy Board.

## Sudbury Hall

House in Derbyshire, England, 7 km/4 mi east of Uttoxeter. It was begun around 1613 but not completed until much later in the century. It is built of diaper brick (a design using bricks of different colours), and contains plaster ceilings painted by Louis Laguerre (1663–1721), a staircase carved by Edward Pierce (1630–1695), and an overmantel by Grinling Gibbons. Sudbury Hall was transferred to the National Trust through the Treasury in 1967.

## Suez Crisis

Military confrontation from October to December 1956 following the nationalization of the Suez Canal by President Nasser of Egypt. In an attempt to reassert international control of the canal, Israel launched an attack, after which British and French troops landed. Widespread international censure forced the withdrawal of the British and French. The crisis resulted in the resignation of British prime minister Eden.

## Suffolk

County of eastern England; population (1996) 661,600; area 3,800 sq km/1,467 sq mi. It is a gently undulating rural county and its long eastern coastline has seaside resorts and nature reserves. It has a prosperous history based on its medieval wool and cloth trade, and many fine houses and churches survive from this time. Suffolk is associated with the painter John Constable, who depicted the rural landscapes of the Stour valley. The principal towns are ◊Ipswich (administrative headquarters and port), Lowestoft, Felixstowe (ports and resorts), Beccles, Bury St Edmunds, and Sudbury; Aldeburgh and Southwold are seaside resorts.

### History

Remains of prehistoric occupation have been found near Brandon. Suffolk derives its name from settlement by the 'South Folk' in the latter part of the 5th century AD. The county suffered much from the later incursions of the Danes. Walton was the scene of the landing of the Earl of Leicester in 1173 when he marched against Henry II. During the 14th century Suffolk became one of the richest counties in England, based on its wool and cloth production, the latter developing with the influx of Flemish weavers. During the Civil War it was a stronghold of Parliament.

### Physical

Suffolk is England's most easterly county. There are rolling lowlands in the south and west. The River Waveney forms the boundary with Norfolk; the other rivers are the Alde, Deben, Orwell (navigable by large vessels as far as Ipswich dock), Stour (the boundary with Essex), and Little Ouse. Part of the Norfolk Broads extend into Suffolk. The long, flat coastline has been encroached upon by the sea in places, notably at Dunwich. In the extreme northwest, near Mildenhall, is a small area of fenland, and southeast of Mildenhall, at Rede, is the highest point (128 m/420 ft) in the county. Around Brandon, in the northwest, is an area known as the Breckland, which was an ancient heath, but is now largely covered in forest or reclaimed for agriculture.

### Features

Sutton Hoo, near Woodbridge, is the site of a Saxon burial, excavated in 1939. There are monastic remains at Bury St Edmunds (Benedictine); Leiston (Premonstratensian); Kersey, Butley, and Ixworth (Augustinian); Sibton (Cistercian); and Clare (Austin Friary). There are

**Suffolk** The magnificent 15th century Church of the Holy Trinity in Long Melford, Suffolk, is built in the Perpendicular style of architecture (the final stage of development of the English Gothic). Such imposing parish churches are typical of the county; other fine examples can be seen at Blythburgh and Southwold. Liz Stares/Collections

castles at Framlingham and Orford; a Roman fort, known as Burgh Castle, near Great Yarmouth; and fortified manor houses at Mettingham and Wingfield. The many large churches are frequently ornamented with patterns in flint work, and over 40 of them have round towers, many of which date from the 12th century. The wool town of Lavenham is probably unrivalled in Britain in its wealth of medieval buildings; Long Melford and Clare are also fine. Minsmere is an important marshland bird reserve, near Aldeburgh (avocets, bitterns) and the Sandlings is an area of heathlands and bird habitat. There is bloodstock rearing and horse racing at Newmarket, and the National Horseracing Museum. The Aldeburgh Festival, founded by the composer Benjamin Britten, is held every June at Snape Maltings.

*Economy*
Much of Suffolk supports agriculture, including cereals and sugar beet; cattle, sheep, and pig rearing; and fishing (for which Lowestoft is the main centre). Industries include agricultural machinery, chemicals, electronics, fertilizers, food processing, motor vehicle components, printing, and telecommunications research. There is North Sea oil and gas exploration, and Sizewell B at Leiston is Britain's first pressurized-water nuclear reactor plant. Felixstowe is Britain's largest container port.

## suffragette, or suffragist

Woman fighting for the right to vote. Women's suffrage bills were repeatedly introduced and defeated in Parliament between 1886 and 1911, and a militant campaign was launched in 1906 by Emmeline ◊Pankhurst and her daughters. In 1918 women were granted limited franchise; in 1928 it was extended to all women over 21.

Suffragettes (the term was coined by a *Daily Mail* reporter) chained themselves to railings, heckled political meetings, refused to pay taxes, and in 1913 bombed the home of Lloyd George, then chancellor of the Exchequer. One woman, Emily ◊Davison, threw herself under the king's horse at the Derby horse race in 1913 and was killed. Many suffragettes were imprisoned and were force-fed when they went on hunger strike; under the notorious 'Cat and Mouse Act' of 1913 they could be repeatedly released to regain their health and then rearrested. The struggle was called off on the outbreak of World War I.

## Sulgrave Manor

House in Northamptonshire, England, 11 km/7 mi northeast of Banbury. It was built by Lawrence Washington in 1560 on the site of a dissolved priory. The present house, altered and restored, was bought by the British public in 1914 to commemorate the Treaty of Ghent.

John Washington, a descendant of the first owner, emigrated to Virginia in 1656, and his great-grandson, George Washington, became the first president of the USA. The house was later endowed in perpetuity by the Society of the Colonial Dames of America. It is open to the public, and contains portraits of Washington and some of his possessions.

## Sunderland

City and port in Tyne and Wear, northeast England, at the mouth of the River Wear; population (1991) 183,200. A former coalmining and shipbuilding centre, Sunderland now has various industries, including electronics, plus some tourism.

### History

The town of Sunderland developed around the villages of Monkwearmouth, Bishopwearmouth, and Sunderland. Churches were first built at Monkwearmouth on the north bank of the Wear in 674 and at Sunderland on the south bank later in the 7th century. Sunderland developed as a port during the Middle Ages, with a charter dating from 1154. During the Civil War Sunderland was held by the Parliamentarians.

Records of shipbuilding in Sunderland go back to 1346. The first shipyard was established in 1775 and the wet dock was built in 1840. During the 19th century several shipyards were built on the river frontage, and Sunderland became the world's largest shipbuilding town at the time. The shipbuilding industry was hit by the depression of the 1930s and declined further after World War II, ceasing completely in the 1990s. Coal mining, which had taken place at Sunderland from the 14th century onwards, similarly declined, and ceased by 1990.

Sunderland was granted city status by Royal Charter in 1992. The University of Sunderland (formerly Sunderland Polytechnic) was established in 1992.

## Surrey

County of southern England; population (1996) 1,047,100; area 1,660 sq km/641 sq mi. It is densely populated, particularly in the northeast and along the main commuter road and rail links to London. There are beautiful rural areas south of the North Downs, and most of the county is now protected from further urban encroachment; the National Trust has 32 sites in Surrey. The main towns are ◊Kingston upon Thames (administrative headquarters), Farnham, Guildford, Leatherhead, Reigate, Woking, Epsom, and Dorking.

### History

An important event that took place in Surrey was the signing of the Magna Carta by King John at Runnymede in 1215.

### Physical

The western end of the North Downs extends into Surrey, bordering Greater London. Part of the Weald, formerly wooded but now agricultural, lies to the south of the Downs. There are large areas of heath and common land, especially in the west. The county's landmarks include Newlands Corner (164 m/538 ft), near Guildford; the Devil's Punch Bowl, near Hindhead; Box Hill (183 m/600 ft); Gibbet Hill (277 m/909 ft); and Leith Hill (299 m/981 ft) 5 km/3 mi south of Dorking, the highest hill in southeast England. The rivers Mole, Thames, and Wey flow through Surrey. Undeveloped areas are either National Trust land, or have been designated as 'open space', common land, areas of outstanding natural beauty, or metropolitan green belt. In total about 14,500 ha/35,800 acres are open to the public, including the North Downs footpath.

### Features

Archaeologically, Surrey is of national importance for finds of flints near Farnham, dating to the Palaeolithic period, and other finds from the Thames gravels and elsewhere, dating to the Mesolithic period. There are pre-Roman earthworks at Hascombe and Holmbury Hills, and remains from the Roman period include many villas, such as those at Ashtead, Farnham, Rapsley, and Titsey.

A royal castle was established at Guildford after the Norman conquest, and there were others at Abinger, Bletchingley, Farnham, and Reigate. Of the many royal and ecclesiastical palaces built in Surrey, Farnham Castle, now a college, is one of the few surviving examples still in use; Henry VIII's palace at Nonsuch Park (begun 1538) was demolished in 1687. Major religious sites include Waverley Abbey, near Farnham, (the first Cistercian foundation in England), and successful excavations have been carried out at the Dominican friary site at Guildford.

In the Tudor period, many London professional and business men had a country home in Surrey; Sutton Place, Great Tangley Manor, and Loseley Park, all near Guildford, are examples. Other great houses of later date are Clandon Park (1731), Hatchlands (1759), Nonsuch Park (1802–06), and Polesden Lacey, a Regency villa near Dorking. There are also many outstanding examples of humbler dwellings, ranging from typical 17th-century tile-hung and timber-framed

Surrey cottages, to dignified Georgian brick houses, examples of which can be seen in Farnham. Surrey became increasingly residential with the coming of the railway, and many houses by well-known architects were built, such as Goddards, near Dorking, designed by Edwin Lutyens.

Notable gardens are the Royal Botanic Gardens at Kew, the Royal Horticultural Society gardens at Wisley, Painshill Park, and Savill Garden. The Yehudi Menuhin School at Stoke d'Abernon is one of four specialist music schools in England, and Epsom is the home of the Derby horse race.

### Economy

Surrey is home to many wealthy London commuters. The local economy also depends on agriculture (vegetables, sheep rearing, dairy farming, horticulture), service industries, quarrying of sand and gravel, and fuller's earth extraction (near Reigate). The picturesque landscape and wealth of historic houses attract walkers and tourists.

## Sutherland, Graham (1903–1980)

English painter, graphic artist, and designer. He was active mainly in France from the 1940s. A leading figure of the Neo-Romantic movement (1935–55), which revived the spirit of 19th-century Romanticism in a more modern idiom, he executed portraits, landscapes, and religious subjects, often using a semi-abstract style.

Sutherland first studied engraving and etching, his early prints showing some affinity with the work of Samuel ◊Palmer. He began to paint from 1930, and during that decade acquired a Surrealist appreciation of the strangeness and metaphorical suggestion of natural form. This developed into the characteristic thorns, sinister tree shapes, and distillations of his Neo-Romantic landscapes of the 1940s. An official war artist from 1941, his sense of strangeness found vivid expression in paintings of bomb devastation. In the late 1940s he turned increasingly to portraiture.

Varied aspects of his work are shown in his *Crucifixion* (1946; the church of St Matthew, Northampton); his *Origins of the Land* (1951; Tate Gallery, London), for the Festival of Britain; his characterful portrait of the writer *Somerset Maugham* (1949; Tate Gallery, London); and his *Christ in Glory* tapestry (1962; Coventry Cathedral).

Sutherland's portrait of Winston Churchill (1954) was disliked by its subject and eventually burned on the instructions of Lady Churchill (studies survive). He also created designs for posters, stage costumes, and theatre sets. He was awarded the OM in 1960.

## Sutton Coldfield

Residential part of the West Midlands conurbation around ◊Birmingham, central England; population (1991) 103,900.

Sutton Coldfield was incorporated in the city of Birmingham in 1974. Sutton Park, to the west of the town, is a large open space (approximately 1,000 ha/2,400 acres) including woodland, lakes, heathland, and wetland. The park is a remnant of an extensive forest that formerly covered much of the Midlands region. The ancient Roman Rykmild Street runs through it.

## Sutton Hoo

Archaeological site in Suffolk, England, where in 1939 a Saxon ship burial was excavated. It may be the funeral monument of Raedwald, King of the East Angles, who died about 624 or 625. The jewellery, armour, and weapons discovered were placed in the British Museum, London.

## Swaledale

River valley extending from Keld to Richmond, in the Yorkshire ◊Dales national park, North Yorkshire, England; length 32 km/20 mi. It is the narrowest of the northwest dales. A former lead-mining area, Swaledale is now chiefly agricultural, though tourism is also a major industry. It gives its name to a breed of horned sheep. Buttertubs Pass (526 m/1, 726 ft) connects Swaledale and Wensleydale.

Arkengarthdale, a branch dale, starts from the village of Reeth and leads to Tan Hill Inn, England's highest inn (527 m/1,728 ft). Below Reeth are the ruined nunneries of Marrick and Ellerton.

## Swansea, Welsh Abertawe

Port and administrative centre of ◊Swansea unitary authority, south Wales, at the mouth of the River Tawe 70 km/43 mi west of Cardiff; population (1994 est) 172,000. It is the second-largest city in Wales. It has oil refineries, chemicals, metallurgical industries, and tin plate manufacturing, and has produced stained glass since 1936. It is the vehicle-licensing centre of the UK.

Swansea received its first charter in 1210 and a new charter in 1655; it was made a city in 1970. The University College of Swansea, a constituent college of the University of Wales, was established here in 1920. The scientific process of refining copper ore was initiated in the Swansea region.

### Development

Swansea grew up around the Norman castle of **Swinesaye**, which no longer exists, but the ruins of a castle built next to it do still stand. The latter was built by Henry Gower, Bishop of St David's, between 1328 and 1347. The town suffered greatly from air raids in 1941 and much of the town centre has been rebuilt. The industrial and maritime activities of Swansea are carried on to the east of the High Street, the works and wharves being in the valleys beyond and down at the mouth of the Tawe. The residential parts of Swansea, with their wide streets and parkland, have spread along the bay and over the hills behind. The residential and holiday area of The Mumbles is 8 km/5 mi to the southwest.

*Features*

The old guildhall or town hall, built in 1847 near the docks, is in the Italian style. The civic building, with its lofty central tower, in Victoria Park, embraces the new guildhall, law courts, and Brangwyn Hall. Other notable buildings are the Royal Institution of South Wales, with a museum and a library; the public library, which includes the corporation art gallery; the Glynn Vivian Art Gallery; and the Exchange Buildings or Chamber of Commerce. Some educational institutions have been combined into a West Glamorgan Institute of Higher Education. The poet Dylan Thomas was born here in 1914.

*Industry and commerce*

Long recognized as the chief metal port of Great Britain, Swansea is now also a large oil port, while remaining the leading centre of the tin-plate trade. The largest docks are the Queen's, opened in 1920 (0.61 sq km/0.24 sq mi), and the King's (0.29 sq km/0.11 sq mi), the former being used for the oil trade. There is also a municipal dry dock for vessels up to 2,000 tons, and a number of privately-owned dry docks. Swansea's metallurgical importance was founded on copper ore, and copper works multiplied from the early 18th century. The oil-refining industry yields a wide range of products.

## Swansea

Unitary authority in south Wales, created in 1996 from part of the former county of West Glamorgan; population (1996) 232,000; area 377 sq km/156 sq mi. The principal town is Swansea.

*Physical*

The western boundary of the authority is determined by the River Loughor and its estuary. The main river is the Tawe. The Gower Peninsula (an area of outstanding natural beauty) remains mainly rural and its coastal scenery makes it a tourist area, but the suburbs of Swansea have spread west into Gower. The whole complex of

urban-industrial development in the area is sometimes referred to as Swansea Bay City.

*Economy*

The main industries are tinplate manufacture, chemicals, and oil refining. The area has natural resources in limestone, silica, brick-earth, shale, and sand. Its metallurgical importance was founded on copper ore, and the scientific process of refining the ore was initiated in the region.

## Swift, Jonathan (1667–1745)

Irish satirist and Anglican cleric. He wrote ◊ *Gulliver's Travels* (1726), an allegory describing travel to lands inhabited by giants, miniature people, and intelligent horses. His other works include *The Tale of a Tub* (1704), attacking corruption in religion and learning and the satirical pamphlet *A Modest Proposal* (1729), which suggested that children of the poor should be eaten. His lucid prose style is simple and controlled and he imparted his views with fierce indignation and wit.

Swift, born in Dublin, became secretary to the diplomat William Temple (1628–1699) at Moor Park, Surrey, where his friendship with the child 'Stella' (Esther Johnson 1681–1728) began in 1689. Returning to Ireland, he was ordained in the Church of England in 1694, and in 1699 was made a prebendary of St Patrick's, Dublin. He made contributions to the Tory paper *The Examiner*, of which he was editor from 1710–11. He obtained the deanery of St Patrick in 1713. His *Journal to Stella* is a series of intimate letters (1710–13), in which he described his life in London. From about 1738 his mind began to fail.

## Swindon

Town and administrative headquarters of Swindon unitary authority in southwest England, 124 km/77 mi west of London; population (1996) 170,000; it was part of the county of Wiltshire until 1997. The site of a major railway engineering works from 1841–1986 on the Great Western Railway, the town diversified after 1950; the electronics industry is now a key employer.

There is a railway museum, and the White Horse of Uffington, an ancient hill figure on the chalk downs, is nearby.

## Swithun, or Swithin, St (c. 800–c. 862)

English priest, chancellor of King Ethelwolf and bishop of Winchester from 852. According to legend, the weather on his feast day (15 July) determines the weather for the next 40 days.

## Talbot, William Henry Fox (1800–1877)

English pioneer of photography. He invented the paper-based calotype process in 1841, the first negative/positive method. Talbot made photograms several years before Louis Daguerre's invention was announced.

In 1851 he made instantaneous photographs by electric light and in 1852 photo engravings. *The Pencil of Nature* (1844–46) by Talbot was the first book illustrated with photographs to be published.

A museum of his work was opened at ◊Lacock Abbey, Wiltshire, in 1975.

## Tallis, Thomas (c. 1505–1585)

English composer. He was a master of counterpoint. His works include *Tallis's Canon*, 'Glory to thee my God this night', (1567) and the antiphonal *Spem in alium non habui* (about 1573) for 40 voices. He published a collection of 34 motets, *Cantiones sacrae* (1575), of which 16 are by Tallis and 18 by William ◊Byrd. He was one of the earliest composers to write for the Anglican liturgy (1547–53) but some of his most ornate music, including the Mass *Puer natus est nobis*, dates from the brief Catholic reign of Mary Tudor (1553–58). A tune written for Archbishop Parker's

**William Henry Fox Talbot** Pioneering English photographer William Henry Fox Talbot (far right) at work. He was a gentleman scientist with the financial means to pursue his intellectual interests and he was more concerned with solving technical problems than in the artistic potential of photography. Corbis

Psalter of 1567 was used by Vaughan Williams in his *Fantasia on a Theme of Thomas Tallis*.

## Tamworth

Town in Staffordshire, central England, at the junction of the rivers Tame and Anker, 24 km/15 mi northeast of Birmingham; population (1991) 67,500.

### History

Once the capital of the Anglo-Saxon kingdom of Mercia, Tamworth was the site of a palace and mint of Offa, King of Mercia, in the 8th century. King Athelstan held councils here in the early 10th century, and Ethelfleda, daughter of King Alfred, fortified the town.

The Conservative politician and prime minister Robert Peel represented Tamworth from 1830 until his death in 1850. His election address in 1834, the **Tamworth Manifesto**, was adopted as the blueprint for Tory party philosophy.

### Features

The castle has a Norman keep and a Jacobean great hall, and includes a museum of local history. The tower of the 14th-century church of St Editha contains an unusual double spiral staircase. The town hall was built in 1701 by Thomas Guy (*c*.1644–1724), founder of Guy's Hospital and also member of Parliament for Tamworth 1695–1707.

## tartan

Woollen cloth woven in specific chequered patterns individual to Scottish clans, with stripes of different widths and colours crisscrossing on a coloured background; it is used in making skirts, kilts, trousers, and other articles of clothing.

Developed in the 17th century, tartan was banned after the 1745 ◊Jacobite rebellion, and not legalized again until 1782.

## Tate Gallery

Art gallery in London that has housed British art from the late 16th century and international art from 1810. Endowed by the sugar merchant Henry Tate (1819–1899), it was opened in 1897. A Liverpool branch of the Tate Gallery opened in 1988, and a St Ives branch in 1993. In March 2000 the Tate's Millbank site became Tate Britain, and a new display space, the Tate Gallery of Modern Art at Bankside, London, was scheduled to open on the opposite side of the River Thames in May 2000.

The Tate Gallery has unique collections of the work of J M W Turner and William Blake, also one of the best collections of Pre-Raphaelite painting. The Clore Gallery extension for Turner's paintings opened in 1987.

## Tattersall's

British auctioneers of racehorses based at Knightsbridge Green, southwest London, since 1864. The firm is named after Richard Tattersall (1724–1795), who founded Tattersall's at Hyde Park Corner in 1766.

## Tatton Park

House in Cheshire, England, 5 km/3 mi north of Knutsford. Originally built in the 17th century, Tatton Park was rebuilt from 1780 to 1813 by Samuel (1737–1807) and Lewis William Wyatt (1777–1853). The house, furniture, silver, and paintings, as well as a 22 ha/54 acre garden, were bequeathed to the National Trust by the 4th Lord Egerton of Tatton, and subsequently the 800 ha/1,976 acre estate came to the Trust through the Treasury, in 1960. Humphry ◊Repton designed the park and garden.

## Taunton

Market town and administrative headquarters of ◊Somerset, southwest England, 50 km/31 mi northeast of Exeter, on the River Tone; population (1991) 56,400. Situated in the heart of the fertile valley of Taunton Deane, Taunton is the main market centre for west Somerset and east Devon.

### History

Taunton existed as a West Saxon stronghold in the early 8th century, and had a market before the Norman Conquest. It received its first charter in the reign of King Stephen (1135–1154). During the Civil War Taunton was held by the Parliamentarians and its castle held out against a Royalist siege. In 1685 the Duke of Monmouth (the illegitimate son of King Charles II) was proclaimed king here, in rebellion against King James II (his Roman Catholic uncle). Following the abortive rebellion, Judge ◊Jeffreys presided over the Bloody Assizes and inhabitants of Taunton were among the many rebels executed.

### Features

Taunton Castle is a Norman and Edwardian building built on the site of a Saxon fort; it now houses the county museum. The large Perpendicular 15th-century church of St Mary Magdalene has double aisles and an elaborately sculptured tower. Other features include Priory Barn, a 12th–13th-century leper hospital, which formed part of a 12th-century Augustinian priory, and Gray's Almshouses (1635).

## Tay

Longest river in Scotland; length 193 km/120 mi. It flows northeast through **Loch Tay**, then east and southeast past Perth to the **Firth of Tay**, crossed at Dundee by the **Tay Bridge**, before joining the North Sea. The Tay has salmon fisheries; its main tributaries are the Tummel, Isla, Earn, Braan, and Almond.

The first Tay Bridge, opened in 1878, on the then longest span over water in the world, was blown into the river in 1879, along with a train which was passing over it. The bridge was rebuilt 1883–88, and a road bridge, from Newport-on-Tay to Dundee, was completed in 1966.

## Tees

River flowing from the Pennines in Cumbria, northwest England, to the North Sea via Tees Bay, Middlesbrough, in northeast England; length 130 km/80 mi. Its port, **Teesport**, handles in excess of 42 million tonnes per annum, with port trade mainly chemical-related.

Although much of the river is polluted with industrial waste, sewage, and chemicals, the Tees Barrage (opened in 1985, cost of construction £50 million) enables a 16-km/10-mi stretch of the river to provide clean, non-tidal water. This is used for white-water sports, including canoeing.

## Teesside

Industrial area at the mouth of the River Tees, northeast England; population (1994 est) 323,000. It includes the towns of ◊Stockton-on-Tees, ◊Middlesbrough, Billingham, and Thornaby.

## Teignmouth

Port and resort in south Devon, southwest England, 20 km/13 mi from Exeter, at the mouth of the River Teign; population (1991) 13,400. Leisure industries here include a yachting centre.

Teignmouth extends onto the tongue of land between the Teign and the sea, and it has a sea-wall 3 km/2 mi long. It developed as a resort at the end of the 18th century.

## television

See also ◊BBC, ◊ITV, ◊Channel 4, ◊Channel 5, and ◊SC4.

Since television began in Britain in 1936 it has had a huge impact on the nation, providing a shared experience of programmes that has created a talking-point and a common cultural understanding. Significant television 'moments' are remembered long after the event, whether favourite comedy sketches, a tough interview, a shocking documentary, or a sporting win. Live coverage of ceremonies, particularly the 1953 coronation and the funerals of key figures – Churchill; Kennedy; Diana, Princess of Wales, the latter reaching a record worldwide audience – have united the country. A few programmes have prompted action or change: the 1966 Wednesday Play *Cathy Come Home* broke new ground showing something of what it is like to be homeless, and helped Shelter on its way to becoming a major charity and campaigning group. Television has also raised millions of pounds for charities, either via single appeals, or an evening of special programmes to benefit a range of themed charities. Successful examples of the latter are the BBC's annual *Children in Need* appeal, and *Comic Relief*.

---

*The culture that brought us the warmth, skill and benevolent didacticism of David Attenborough is being subsumed by a new, democratised, 'interactive' fashion where TV executives can shrug their shoulders and say 'I don't know what they want. Why don't we give them all a camera and they can film what they want?'*

**Rory Bremner** British comedian. Writing in the *New Statesman*, September 1998, describing a 'karaoke' culture where participation is valued over ability and popularity over excellence

---

### Programmes

◊Soap operas, films, comedies, and sport dominate the ratings. Most costly to produce are drama and comedy, which has encouraged broadcasters to repeat popular programmes alongside new material. As the satellite and digital age of television gets underway, the vast bank of quality programmes produced when only three channels existed is reaching a new audience in addition to those who can remember them first time round.

### History

The first practical demonstration of television was given by the Scottish engineer J L ◊Baird in London on 27 January 1926, and the world's first public television service was started from the BBC station at Alexandra Palace in North London, on 2 November 1936.

### Colour television

Baird gave a demonstration of colour TV in London 1928, but it did not arrive in the UK until the start of BBC2, in 1964.

**Television** Cable television, delivered via underground cables, began in earnest in Britain in the 1980s, and can now potentially be received by some 80 percent of homes. Consumers pay by subscription, and can access between 30 and 65 television channels (including satellite broadcasts) as well as a wide range of telecommunications services, such as home shopping, e-mail, and Internet access. Piers Cavendish/Impact

### Satellite television
Direct broadcasting by satellite began in the UK in February 1989 with the introduction of Rupert Murdoch's Sky Television service; its rival British Satellite Broadcasting (BSB) was launched in April 1990, and they merged in November of the same year, becoming British Sky Broadcasting (BSkyB).

### Digital television
At the end of 1998 the two main operators in the UK digital market were Sky Digital, promising up to 200 digital channels available by satellite, and paid for either by subscription or pay-per-view, and ONdigital, a terrestrial digital operator, owned by two ITV companies, Carlton and Granada, operated largely by subscription, though some pay-per-view services may be included. This was offering some 30 channels.

## Telford
Town and administrative headquarters of ◊ Telford and Wrekin unitary authority, in west-central England, 52 km/32 mi northwest of Birmingham; population (1991) 100,000. Founded as Dawley New Town in 1963, it was extended and renamed Telford in 1968. ◊ Ironbridge Gorge is nearby.

## Telford and Wrekin
Unitary authority in west England, created in 1998 from part of Shropshire; population (1995) 144,600; area 291 sq km/112 sq mi. The principal towns are ◊ Telford (administrative headquarters) and Newport.

### Physical
The Wrekin is an isolated hill rising to 407 m/1,334 ft. The River Severn flows through the area, passing through the ◊ Ironbridge Gorge.

### Features
Ironbridge Gorge, a World Heritage Site, includes the world's first iron bridge, built across the Severn in 1779 by Abraham Derby. The Ironbridge Gorge Museum Trust encompasses seven industrial museums, including Museum of the River, Museum of Iron, Blists Hill Open-Air Museum, and the Coalport China Museum.

### Economy
Activities include dairy farming, food processing (confectionery), iron founding, high tech industries (electronics, software, audio material), and clothing manufacture.

## Telford, Thomas (1757–1834)

Scottish civil engineer. He opened up northern Scotland by building roads and waterways. He constructed many aqueducts and canals, including the ◊ Caledonian Canal (1802–23), and erected the Menai road suspension bridge between Wales and Anglesey 1819–26, a type of structure scarcely tried previously in the UK. In Scotland he constructed over 1,600 km/1,000 mi of road and 1,200 bridges, churches, and harbours.

## Temple Bar

Former western gateway of the City of London, between Fleet Street and the Strand (site marked by a stone griffin); the heads of traitors were formerly displayed above it on spikes. Temple Bar was rebuilt by Christopher Wren in 1672, and moved to Theobald's Park, Hertfordshire, in 1878.

## Tenby, Welsh Dinbych-y-pysgod

Coastal resort in Pembrokeshire, southwest Wales, 15 km/9 mi east of Pembroke; population (1991) 5,600. It is situated on a narrow promontory jutting out into Carmarthen Bay. By the late 15th century Tenby was a prosperous small port. Part of the castle and most of the 13th-century town walls still exist.

## Tenniel, John (1820–1914)

English illustrator and cartoonist. He is known for his cartoons for *Punch* magazine and for his illustrations for Lewis Carroll's *Alice's Adventures in Wonderland* (1865) and *Through the Looking-Glass* (1872).

## tennis, or lawn tennis

Racket-and-ball game invented towards the end of the 19th century, derived from real (or 'royal') tennis.

Although played on different surfaces (grass, wood, shale, clay, concrete), it is also called 'lawn tennis'. The aim of the two or four players is to strike the ball into the prescribed area of the court, with oval-headed rackets (strung with gut or nylon), in such a way that the ball cannot be returned.

The leading UK event is the annual All England Tennis Club championships (originating in 1877), an open event for players of both sexes at ◊ Wimbledon, one of the world's four Grand Slam events.

## Tennyson, Alfred, 1st Baron Tennyson (1809–1892)

English poet. He was poet laureate from 1850 to 1892. His verse has a majestic, musical quality, and few poets have surpassed his precision and delicacy of language. His works include 'The Lady of Shalott' (1833), 'The Lotus Eaters' (1833), 'Ulysses' (1842), 'Break, Break, Break' (1842), and 'The Charge of the Light Brigade' (1854); the longer narratives *Locksley Hall* (1832) and *Maud* (1855); the elegy *In Memoriam* (1850); and a long series of poems on the Arthurian legends, *The Idylls of the King* (1859–89).

Tennyson's poetry is characterized by a wide range of interests; an intense sympathy with the deepest feelings and aspirations of humanity; an exquisite sense of beauty; and a marvellous power of vivid and minute description, often achieved by a single phrase, and heightened by the perfect matching of sense and sound.

## Terry, Ellen (1847–1928)

English actress. She was leading lady to Henry ◊ Irving from 1878. She excelled in Shakespearean roles, such as Ophelia in *Hamlet*. She was a correspondent of longstanding with the dramatist George Bernard Shaw. She was awarded the GCBE in 1925.

## Test match

Sporting contest between two nations, the most familiar being those played between the nine nations that play Test cricket (England, Australia, West Indies, India, New Zealand, Pakistan, South Africa, Sri Lanka, and Zimbabwe). Test matches can also be found in Rugby League and Rugby Union. A cricket Test match lasts a maximum of five days and a Test series usually consists of four to six matches. The first cricket Test match was between Australia and England in Melbourne, Australia, 1877.

## Tewkesbury

Town in Gloucestershire, southwest England, between Cheltenham and Worcester; population (1991) 67,700. It is situated on the River Avon, close to its juncture with the Severn, 16 km/10 mi northeast of Gloucester. The site was settled in Roman times, and in 1087 was a borough and market. The 'Bloody Meadow' on the southern side of the town was the site of the Battle of Tewkesbury in the Wars of the Roses.

Tewkesbury's abbey church, begun in 1092, was part of a Benedictine abbey erected here on an Anglo-Saxon foundation. Monuments of the church include the Beauchamp Chantry (1422) and the tomb of Hugh Le Despenser, Earl of Winchester (d. 1349). Prince Edward, son of Henry VI, is reputed to be buried under the tower. In Tudor times the town produced mustard.

## Thackeray, William Makepeace (1811–1863)

English novelist and essayist. He was a regular contributor to *Fraser's Magazine* and *Punch*. His first novel was *Vanity Fair* (1847–48), significant for the breadth of its canvas as well as for the depth of the characterization. This was followed by *Pendennis* (1848), *Henry Esmond* (1852) (and its sequel *The Virginians*, 1857–59), and *The Newcomes* (1853–55), in which Thackeray's tendency to sentimentality is most marked.

## Thames

River in south England, flowing through London; length 338 km/210 mi. The longest river in England, it rises in the Cotswold Hills above Cirencester and is tidal as far as Teddington. Below London there is protection from flooding by means of the ◊**Thames barrier**. The head-streams unite at Lechlade. The **Thames Path**, a

**Thames** Swans on the River Thames. Swans throughout Britain came to be regarded as royal property in around 1100, but some birds on the Thames were granted to two city livery companies, the Vintners and the Dyers. They still catch and mark their quota of swans in an ancient annual ceremony that takes place on the river between Sunbury and Abingdon and is known as 'swan-upping'. Corel

footpath running the length of the Thames, opened in 1997.

Tributaries from the north are the Windrush, Evenlode, Cherwell, Thame, Colne, Lea, and Roding; and from the south, the Kennet, Loddon, Wey, Mole, Darent, and Medway. Around Oxford the river is sometimes poetically called the Isis.

### Source, course, and estuary

The Thames rises near Cirencester in the Cotswold Hills and follows a course of 330 km/205 mi to the Nore, where it flows into the North Sea. At Gravesend, the head of the estuary, it has a width of 1 km/0.6 mi, gradually increasing to 16 km/10 mi at the Nore. Lying some 5 km/3 mi southwest of the Nore is the mouth of the Medway estuary, at the head of which lie ◊Chatham with important naval dockyards, ◊Gillingham, and ◊Rochester. ◊Gravesend on the south bank of the river, some 40 km/25 mi from the Nore, developed at a point where vessels used to await the turn of the tide. Tidal waters reach Teddington, 100 km/62 mi from its mouth, where the first lock from the sea (except for the tidal lock at Richmond) is located. There are in all 47 locks, St John's Lock, Lechlade, being nearest the source.

### The London Thames

The normal rise and fall of the tide is from 4.5 m/15 ft to 7 m/23 ft at London Bridge and from 4 m/13 ft to 6 m/20 ft at Tilbury. Until Tower Bridge was built, London Bridge was the lowest in the course; the reach between these two bridges is known as the 'Pool of London'. ◊Tilbury Fort and Docks, once important as the main London container terminal, lies opposite Gravesend on the northern bank. At ◊Woolwich, some 30 km/19 mi above Tilbury, was the arsenal; ◊Greenwich, a little farther upriver, has the Royal Naval College. Between Tilbury and London Bridge (some 40 km/ 25 mi upstream) stretches the London dock System (see also ◊Docklands). The Thames has been frozen over at various times, the earliest recorded occasion being 1150.

The embankments of the Thames in London were the work of Joseph Bazalgette (1819–1891), chief engineer of the Metropolitan Board of Works. The Albert Embankment on the south side was completed in 1869, the Victoria Embankment from Westminster to Blackfriars in 1870, and the Chelsea Embankment from the Royal Hospital to Battersea Bridge in 1874. In January 1949 work was started on a new embankment, designed by J Rawlinson, chief engineer of the former London County Council, on the south side from County Hall to Waterloo Bridge. These embankments were raised after 1974. There are walkways (formerly towpaths) from Teddington to Cricklade.

### London bridges
The river is spanned by 20 road and 9 rail bridges between Hampton Court and the Tower of London. These include Tower Bridge (which has a drawbridge mechanism to enable large vessels to pass) and a suspension bridge at Hammersmith. The Queen Elizabeth II Bridge, opened in 1991, joins the counties of Essex and Kent. The Millennium Bridge, a footbridge linking St Paul's Cathedral to the new Tate Gallery on the south bank of the Thames, is to be built by May 2000; its designers are sculptor Anthony Caro and architect Norman Foster.

### London tunnels
The chief tunnels under the Thames are the Thames Tunnel, completed by Marc Isambard Brunel in 1843, the first underwater tunnel in the world, now used by the East London Line of the London Underground; the Blackwall Tunnel (1897) from East India Dock Road to East Greenwich, the Rotherhithe Tunnel (1918) from Shadwell to Rotherhithe, and the Dartford tunnel completed in 1963.

### Upstream
There are regular boats from Kingston to Folly Bridge, Oxford, during the summer. There is some beautiful scenery along this part of the river, for example at ◊Cliveden, ◊Cookham, Sonning, and Pangbourne. There are fine bridges at ◊Richmond-upon-Thames, ◊Hampton Court, Chertsey, Maidenhead, and Shillingford. ◊Henley, Wallingford, Dorchester, ◊Abingdon, Eton, and ◊Windsor are attractive. Along the 80 km/50 mi from its source beneath a tree in 'Trewsbury Mead' to Oxford, the Thames glides through meadows, its course interrupted only by the small towns of Lechlade and Cricklade and the pretty stone-built hamlets of Kelmscott and Ashton Keynes. In these upper reaches there are two medieval bridges, New Bridge and Radcot Bridge. Motor launches can reach Lechlade; beyond that point it is possible to canoe up to Cricklade, but the final 16 km/10 mi to the source of the Thames is best done on foot. One particularly attractive section is the steep-sided valley through the chalk hills between Goring and Reading, known as the Goring Gap.

### Thames barrier
Movable barrier built across the River Thames at Woolwich, London, as part of the city's flood defences. Completed in 1982, the barrier comprises curved flood gates which are rotated 90° into position from beneath the water to form a barrier when exceptionally high tides are expected. It is 520 m/1,706 ft long, with steel gates 20 m/66 ft high.

### Thatcherism
Political outlook comprising a belief in the efficacy of market forces, the need for strong central government, and a conviction that self-help is preferable to reliance on the state, combined with a strong element of nationalism. The ideology is named after Margaret Thatcher, UK prime minister 1979–90, but stems from an individualist view found in Britain's 19th-century Liberal and 20th-century Conservative parties, and is no longer confined to Britain. Since leaving public office, Baroness Thatcher has established her own 'Foundation'.

Elements of Thatcherism, particularly the emphasis on controlling public expenditure and promoting opportunities for personal achievement, have been incorporated into the policy approach of the 'New Labour' government of Tony Blair, from 1997. However, it has sought to include a greater emphasis on social justice and assistance for the socially excluded, in what has been termed the 'third way'.

---

*State socialism is totally alien to the British character.*

**Margaret Thatcher** British Conservative prime minister.
*The Times* 1983

---

### thatching
Method of roofing using reeds or straw, fixed to the roof timbers with hazel pegs and metal hooks. Heather and gorse may also be used. Thatch was the main roofing material in rural areas until the 18th–19th centuries, particularly in England and Wales, and remained the common finish for buildings constructed with cob (sun-baked clay and straw).

**Reed** thatch, such as that found in Norfolk, has a sharply angled appearance with a heavy ridge. **Wheat straw** appears softer and more rounded. In Kent, Essex, and parts of Sussex it is traditionally laid with the heads and butt-ends randomly, then raked to give a flowing surface and ridged with criss-cross stitching. Alternatively it is arranged with the butt-end downwards to give a neatly cropped appearance, a method known as combed wheat reed, or Dorset or Devon reed after its areas of origin. In exposed regions, such as the Isle of Man and the Atlantic coast of Scotland, thatched roofs are held down by a lattice of ropes.

## theatre

One of the earliest known forms of drama in Europe was the Christian **liturgical drama**. The earliest English example was written by Ethelwold, bishop of Winchester, in about 970. The staging of liturgical plays, which were sung, was governed by the physical restrictions of the church or cathedral in which they were performed. Visual symbols, such as the Christmas crib or everyday objects, were endowed with or used for their spiritual significance.

### Secularization of drama

Religious cycle-plays performed in English may have developed from liturgical drama, but their informal conventions, such as the scurrying of 'devils' around the acting area and into the audience, were probably influenced by popular performance techniques. Priests were forbidden to appear on a public stage after 1210, which led to a secularization of drama. Simple plays or farces

Theatre English actor and director Laurence Olivier, unparalleled in British theatre in the 20th century, pictured here in the title role of a 1948 production of *Hamlet*. During a career that spanned nearly 60 years, Olivier played both Shakespearean and modern roles and was director of the Old Vic, London, the Chichester Festival Theatre, and the National Theatre, London, which he helped found. Corbis

were probably performed by itinerant secular actors on rudimentary booth stages.

Miracle play cycles, morality plays, and saints' plays conformed in general to the conventions of liturgical drama, but were performed in one of two ways: either in 'station-to-station' form, in which moveable pageant wagons, which were richly decorated and had sophisticated machinery, were used for performances at different locations in the town; or on stationary 'place-and-scaffold' structures, one for every scene, set up in churches and market squares.

Religious plays continued to be staged regularly in England until the end of the 16th century, while professional itinerant actors performed on stages erected against the hall-screens of Tudor halls and on curtained booth stages wherever they could find an audience.

### Commedia dell'arte

This popular form of knockabout improvised comedy, which emerged from Italy in the 16th century, quickly won widespread popularity. Performed by trained troupes of actors and involving stock characters and situations, it influenced the later genres of harlequinade (popular in the 18th and 19th centuries) and ◊pantomime, a traditional Christmas entertainment in the 20th century.

### Elizabethan theatre

The Elizabethan age witnessed a great advance in the development of drama in London, and saw the advent of the open-air ◊Elizabethan playhouse (see the ◊Globe Theatre). William ◊Shakespeare was attached as actor/writer to the Lord Chamberlain's Men, a theatre company formed in 1594 and renamed the King's Men in 1603. Rather than being characterized by almost bare stages in soberly timbered playhouses, Elizabethan theatre was probably sumptuously decorated, with coloured architecture, and stages occupied by the same impressive scenic emblems used in contemporary court entertainments and religious and civic pageantry. A list of properties (dated 1598) survives in the papers of Philip Henslowe (died 1616), owner of the Fortune, Rose, and Hope theatres.

### New ideas from Italy

During the 17th century Italian innovations such as perspective scenery, the use of elaborate machinery to create spectacular effects, and the proscenium-arch stage, were introduced in England. The architect Inigo Jones, who had trained in Italy, was employed by James I to design scenery for Court masques and plays in collaboration with Ben ◊Jonson. Jones developed a system of flats moving in grooves in and above the stage, the backcloth being formed of two shutters which could open to reveal another elaborate scene behind.

At this time Jonson established the English 'comedy of humours', notably in *Volpone* (1606) and *St Bartholomew's Fair* (1614), which was to have a profound influence on Restoration drama.

### Theatre banned

At the outbreak of the Civil War in 1642, Parliament banned all plays and theatre ceased for almost 20 years. On the reopening of the English theatres at the Restoration (1660), the tradition of Elizabethan open-air theatre was superseded by ◊Restoration comedy and other European-style drama performed in indoor playhouses. Women were finally admitted to the stage.

### Developments in staging

Perspective scenery and proscenium stages were used, though at first a traditional apron stage protruded in front of the proscenium arch. The apron stage diminished in size gradually, although it did not disappear entirely until the middle of the 19th century. Towards the end of the 18th century there was a movement towards greater historical realism in costume and scenery.

### 19th-century melodrama

The influence of ◊Romanticism was responsible for the rise of English melodrama in the 19th century, with its emphasis on the imagination and emotions. Spectacle was also the keynote, and elaborate machinery was invented to reproduce such sensational effects as train crashes, horse races, and ships in storm-tossed seas. There were many technical advances: elevator platforms, sliding stages, and revolving platforms were developed.

Sentimental problem drama (as in the work of James Knowles) enjoyed great popularity in the middle of the century. The movement towards greater historical accuracy continued, and the pageantry of historical spectacles attracted large audiences.

### Box sets and new lighting

The box set arrangement of painted flats joined together to form three walls, with realistic doors, windows, fireplaces, and other items, was introduced by Thomas Robertson (1829–1871) in his domestic melodramas of the 1860s.

During the second half of the 19th century, first limelight and then electric lighting were introduced. As a result, the darkened auditorium and the illuminated and realistically decorated stage became entirely separate entities. Naturalism in scenery, costume, and acting was the logical

## Top Ten Longest-Running West End Theatre Productions at June 1999

| Rank | Production | Category | Years | Months |
|------|------------|----------|-------|--------|
| 1 | The Mousetrap | whodunnit | 46 | 7 |
| 2 | Cats | musical | 18 | 1 |
| 3 | Starlight Express | musical | 15 | 3 |
| 4 | Les Misérables | musical | 13 | 8 |
| 5 | The Phantom of the Opera | musical | 12 | 8 |
| 6 | Blood Brothers | musical | 10 | 11 |
| 7 | The Woman in Black | thriller | 10 | 4 |
| 8 | Miss Saigon | musical | 9 | 9 |
| 9 | Buddy | musical | 9 | 8 |
| 10 | Grease | musical | 5 | 11 |

Source: Society of London Theatre

culmination of the lengthy movement in the 19th century towards a more convincing illusion of reality.

### Experiment and innovation

British theatre in the 20th century has been characterized by experiment and innovation, as much in staging methods as in artistic and intellectual terms. The early reaction against naturalism is linked with director and stage-designer Gordon Craig (1872–1966), who rejected illusion and advocated a theatre of romantic 'mood', in which dance and mime would be prominent. European influences included the work of French director Jacques Copeau during and after World War I, who placed emphasis on the art of acting. His productions used only lighting and a few key props to establish the setting, and his style heavily influenced that of theatre director Peter Brook (1925– ).

### Repertory

Repertory theatres, running a different play every few weeks, proliferated throughout Britain until World War II, the ◊Old Vic in London being an example. Although the repertory movement declined from the 1950s with the spread of cinema and television, a number of regional community theatres did subsequently develop.

### 1950s and 1960s

In 1953 Sandy Wilson's *The Boyfriend* marked a revival of the British ◊musical, a form subsequently taken up by Andrew Lloyd Webber and

## Some Important Regional Theatres

**Birmingham Repertory Theatre** Centenary Square, Broad Street, Birmingham; artistic director: Bill Alexander

**Theatre Royal** King Street, Bristol; artistic director: Andy Hay

**Royal Lyceum Theatre** Grindlay Street, Edinburgh; artistic director: Kenny Ireland

**Citizen's Theatre** Gorbals, Glasgow; artistic director: Giles Havergal

**West Yorkshire Playhouse** Playhouse Square, Quarry Hill, Leeds; artistic director: Jude Kelly

**Haymarket Theatre** Belgrave Gate, Leicester; artistic director: Paul Kerryson

**Royal Exchange Theatre** St Ann's Square, Manchester; artistic directors: Braham Murray, Greg Hersov, Matthew Lloyd

**Nottingham Playhouse** Wellington Circus, Nottingham; artistic director: Giles Croft

**Theatre Royal** Royal Parade, Plymouth, Devon; chief executive Adrian Vinken

**Stephen Joseph Theatre** Westborough, Scarborough; artistic director: Alan Ayckbourn

Tim Rice, who produced a series of successful musicals from the late 1960s. The 1950s also saw the advent of the realistic dramas of the working classes, typified by *Look Back in Anger* written by John ◊Osborne, performed in 1956 by the ◊English Stage Company at the Royal Court Theatre. He, Arnold Wesker, and Alan Sillitoe, were dubbed ◊'Angry Young Men'. At much the same time, Harold Pinter's long writing career was beginning.

In 1968 Edward Bond's *Early Morning* was the last play to be banned by the Lord Chamberlain, whose powers of censorship under the Theatres Act ended that year. From then laws relating to obscenity, blasphemy, and libel acted as a form of censorship.

### *1970s to the late 1990s*
In counterpoint to the founding of the Royal Shakespeare Company and the opening of the ◊National Theatre, the 1970s saw the growth of **alternative theatre** functioning outside the commercial mainstream, usually in an anti-establishment or experimental style and in unconventional venues (converted warehouses and pubs, for example). The movement is also known as **fringe theatre**, a term originating in the 1960s from performances on the 'fringe' of the Edinburgh Festival. One facet of alternative theatre in the

1970s was **women's theatre**, performed by women and about women's lives.

Many of the playwrights who dominated the mainstream theatre in the 1970s and 1980s continued to write and be performed in the 1990s, among them Michael Frayn, Tom Stoppard, Alan Ayckbourn, Peter Shaffer, and Willy Russell. Plays by John Godber, artistic director Hull Truck theatre company were especially popular. Musicals, however, tended to dominate London's West End, as the table below shows.

### *Staging in the late 20th century*
Numerous theatres have been built which dispense with the proscenium arch and combine features associated with medieval and Elizabethan stages together with the facilities offered by modern technology. Alternative types of performing space include open stage, thrust stage, theatre in the round, and studio theatre. Theatres are often associated with a university or are part of a larger cultural centre. Staging conventions in commercial theatre which were once regarded as experimental are now regularly employed in a suitably adapted form, though traditional naturalistic settings are still much in evidence. See table on page 461 for the longest-running West End productions at June 1999; see table on this page for some important regional theatres.

## Theatre Museum
Museum housing memorabilia from the worlds of the theatre, opera, ballet, dance, circus, puppetry, pop, and rock and roll. It opened in Covent Garden, London, in 1987.

## theme parks
There are some 15 theme parks in the UK, attracting more than 15 million visitors a year. The three largest, all multi-themed, are Alton Towers in Staffordshire (1979), which attracted 2.7 million visitors in 1997, and Thorpe Park (1980) and Chessington World of Adventures (1987), both in Surrey.

## thistle
Emblem of Scotland, appearing on pound coins. The history of the emblem and the identity of the species of thistle are confused. It is said to date from the 8th century, after Stirling Castle was saved from a Danish night assault when one of the attackers cried out as he trod on the plant, though it is not recorded as a royal emblem until the 15th century. The name Scottish or Scotch thistle has been given to *Onopordum acanthium*, also known as the cotton thistle. The association of this thistle

with Scotland dates particularly from George IV's visit to the country in 1822, when a wealth of Scottish pageantry was generated.

## Thomas, Dylan (1914–1953)

Welsh poet. His poems, characterized by complex imagery and a strong musicality, include the celebration of his 30th birthday 'Poem in October' and the evocation of his youth 'Fern Hill' (1946). His 'play for voices' *Under Milk Wood* (1954) describes with humour and compassion a day in the life of the residents of a small Welsh fishing village, Llareggub. The short stories of *Portrait of the Artist as a Young Dog* (1940) are autobiographical.

He was born in Swansea, the son of the English teacher at the local grammar school where he was educated. He worked as a reporter on the *South Wales Evening Post*, then became a journalist in London and published his first volume *Eighteen Poems* in 1934. He returned periodically to Wales, to the village of Laugharne, from 1938, with his wife Caitlin (born Macnamara, 1913–1994), moving into the Boat House in 1949. Here he wrote most of *Under Milk Wood*, several major poems, and some short stories. A notorious drinker, he collapsed and died during a lecture tour of the USA.

---

*The land of my fathers. My fathers can have it.*

**Dylan Thomas** Welsh poet.
On Wales; quoted in *Dylan Thomas*, by John Ackerman

---

## Threadneedle Street

Street in the City of London, England, running eastwards from the ◊Bank of England. The name of the street probably indicates that the property once belonged to the Needlemakers' Company. The dramatist Richard Sheridan gave the Bank of England the nickname 'the Old Lady of Threadneedle Street'.

At the east end where Threadneedle Street joins Old Broad Street is the Stock Exchange Building.

## Thurrock

Unitary authority in southeastern England, created in 1998 from part of the county of Essex; population (1996) 130,600; area 163 sq km/63 sq mi. Its southern border runs along the north bank of the River Thames. It is largely industrial and residential, with some rural areas. The main towns are Grays (administrative headquarters), Purfleet,

◊Tilbury, Chadwell, St Mary, Stanford-le-Hope, Corringham, and South Ockendon.

### Physical

Thurrock is located on the north bank of the River Thames, and includes Tilbury and Mucking marshes; Holehaven Creek forms the eastern border.

### Features

Historic features include the 17th-century Tilbury Fort, with three moats, and Alexandra Lake. The Dartford Tunnel (1963, northbound) and Queen Elizabeth II Bridge (1991, southbound) enable traffic to cross the Thames between Kent and Thurrock. The Lakeside shopping centre, alongside the M25, is a major attraction.

### Economy

There are oil refineries and a power station at west Tilbury Marshes, also sand and gravel extraction, and cement works. Retail trade is important at Lakeside.

## Thurso

Port in the Highland unitary authority, Scotland, 140 km/87 mi northeast of Inverness; population (1991) 8,500. It is the principal town of Scotland's north coast. The experimental nuclear reactor site of Dounreay, 14 km/8 mi to the west, was decommissioned in 1994 and replaced by a nuclear waste reprocessing plant. Ferries operate between Scrabster, on **Thurso Bay**, and Stromness in the Orkney Islands.

Thurso was the centre of Norse power on the mainland in the 11th century until it integrated with the rest of Scotland after the Battle of Largs in 1263.

## Tilbury

Port in Thurrock unitary authority, eastern England, on the north bank of the River Thames 42 km/26 mi downstream from London Bridge, opposite Gravesend; population (1991) 11,700. Greatly extended in 1976, it became London's largest container port.

### Tilbury fort

Built for Henry VIII in 1539, the fort was rebuilt under Charles II in 1670–83 as a defence against the Dutch and French. The troops raised in anticipation of a Spanish invasion were reviewed here by Elizabeth I in 1588. The fort is now in the care of English Heritage.

### Docks

The docks were opened in 1886; they originally belonged to the London and East India Dock Company but came under the control of the Port of London Authority in 1909. From 1917 to 1929 the Port of London Authority extended the main dock 442 m/1,450 ft, enabling London to compete for large ocean-liner traffic.

## Times, The

The UK's oldest surviving daily national newspaper, founded in 1785 as the *Daily Universal Register* by the publisher John Walter. Walter intended to establish himself as a book publisher by promoting a more economic method of typesetting, using units of words or groups of letters as well as single letters. The 'logographic' invention was a failure, but the news-sheet printed as an advertisement was a success, and on 1 January 1788 it was retitled *The Times*.

In 1803 the management, and in 1812 the ownership, passed to his second son, John Walter, under whom the paper maintained its independence and secured a leading position. In 1817 Thomas Barnes was appointed editor. He became the outstanding journalist of the century, and, as the champion of middle-class opinion, won for *The Times* the nickname of 'The Thunderer'. The third John Walter succeeded his father as proprietor in 1847. His editor, John Delane, claimed for the press a responsibility in national affairs that was demonstrated by the newspaper's successful agitation for the proper equipment and care of troops in the Crimea.

The competition of cheaper journals after the repeal of the Stamp Act of 1855 was severe, but John Walter refused to endanger the independence or inclusiveness of the paper. In 1887 *The Times* suffered a serious setback to its reputation when it mistakenly indicted Irish politician Charles ◊Parnell on the basis of a letter which turned out to be forged. In 1908 the paper was publicly sold; though the Walter interest was retained, the paper came under the control of Lord Northcliffe. On Northcliffe's death in 1922 control was acquired by J J Astor (later Lord Astor), in association with the fourth John Walter.

---

*Every morning I read the obits in* The Times. *If I'm not there, I carry on.*

**William Douglas-Home** Scottish playwright.
Quoted in the *Observer* 16 August 1987

---

In 1966, in an attempt to increase circulation, *The Times* modernized its layout and news replaced classified advertisements on the front page. But these efforts failed to overcome the paper's financial difficulties and in 1967 it was taken over by Lord Thomson of Fleet who brought it under the control of Times Newspapers Limited, part of the Thomson organization. It was bought by News International, led by Rupert Murdoch, in 1981. In 1986 Murdoch moved production to new premises at Wapping, east London, dispensing with traditional print labour, which led to mass protests.

## Tintagel

Village resort on the coast of north Cornwall, southwest England. There are castle ruins, and legend has it that King ◊Arthur was born and held court here.

Formerly known as Trevena, Tintagel has been associated with King Arthur since medieval times. The castle ruins stand on Tintagel Head, a promontory 91 m/299 ft high on the Atlantic coast. It was a Norman stronghold from the mid-12th century, and the keep dates from the 13th century. Excavations have revealed evidence of a Celtic monastery on the site. It is thought that this may have existed from AD 350 to 850. The Old Post Office building dates from the 14th century.

## Tintern Abbey

Ruined abbey in Monmouthshire, Wales, beautifully situated on the Wye River, 7 km/4 mi north of Chepstow. The ruins date from 1131, when Walter de Clare founded a Cistercian house which became one of the wealthiest foundations in England. The building was mainly erected between 1269 and 1287 by Roger Bigod, Earl of Norfolk, but work continued until 1320.

The chief remains are the ruins of the magnificent cruciform church, the chapter-house, and refectory. The great west window is one of the finest examples of curvilinear tracery. The site was purchased by the crown in 1901.

## Tippett, Michael (1905–1998)

English composer. One of the foremost English composers of his generation, his works include the operas *The Midsummer Marriage* (1952), *The Knot Garden* (1970), and *New Year* (1989); four symphonies; *Songs for Ariel* (1962); and choral music including *The Mask of Time* (1982).

Tippett was very deliberate and highly self-critical, so that his works appeared in slow succession, but always showed closely concentrated craftsmanship and great originality. Amidst many contemporaries whose music could be described as static, one gains above all from Tippett's music a sense of movement.

## Titanic

British passenger liner, supposedly unsinkable, that struck an iceberg and sank off the Grand Banks of Newfoundland on its first voyage 14–15 April 1912; estimates of the number of lives lost, largely due to the inadequate provision of lifeboats, vary between 1,503 and 1,517. In 1985 it was located by robot submarine 4 km/2.5 mi down in an ocean canyon, preserved by the cold environment. In 1987 salvage operations began.

In August 1996 salvage divers eased a 15-tonne section of the liner's steel hull away from the sea floor and raised it more than 2 mi/3.2 km from the seabed using flotation balloons. The high-tech expedition appeared to be on the verge of success when the balloons lost pressure and the liner returned to the ocean floor. By 1996 the cost of the project to raise the wreck stood at £3.3 million.

The results of the first ultrasonic scan of the front of the *Titanic*, much of which is buried in mud, showed that a series of six short slits was the only damage inflicted on the ship by the iceberg, and not, as has always been thought, a gaping 91-m/300-ft gash. The total area of openings was found to be only about 1.1 or 1.2 sq m/12 or 13 sq ft.

In 1997 the film *Titanic* reconstructed the ship's last voyage.

## tithe

Formerly, payment in money or produce exacted from the inhabitants of a parish for the maintenance of the church and its incumbent; some religious groups continue the practice by giving 10% of members' incomes to charity.

It was originally the grant of a tenth of all agricultural produce made to priests in Hebrew society. In the Middle Ages the tithe was adopted as a tax in kind paid to the local parish church, and stored in a special tithe barn. A few tithe barns survive, for instance at Great Coxwell, Oxfordshire.

## Toby jug

Mug or jug shaped like an old man wearing a tri-cornered hat. Originally made in Staffordshire, England, it is reputedly named after **Toby Philpot**, a character in an 18th-century ballad.

## Tolkien, J(ohn) R(onald) R(euel) (1892–1973)

English writer and scholar. To express his theological and philosophical beliefs, and as a vehicle for his linguistic scholarship, he created a complete mythological world of 'Middle Earth', on which he drew for his children's fantasy *The Hobbit* (1937), and the trilogy *The Lord of the Rings* (1954–55), nominated in a UK bookselling chain's survey in 1997 as the 'greatest book of the 20th century'. His work developed a cult following in the 1960s and had many imitators. At Oxford University he was professor of Anglo-Saxon from 1925–45 and Merton professor of English from 1945–59.

## Tolpuddle Martyrs

Six farm labourers of Tolpuddle, a village in Dorset, southwest England, who were transported to Australia in 1834 after being sentenced for 'administering unlawful oaths' – as a 'union', they had threatened to withdraw their labour unless their pay was guaranteed, and had been prepared to put this in writing. They were pardoned two years later, after nationwide agitation. They returned to England and all but one migrated to Canada.

*My Lord, if we have violated any law it was not done intentionally. We have injured no man's reputation, character, person or property. We were meeting together to preserve ourselves, our wives, and our children from utter degradation and starvation.*

**George Loveless** One of the Tolpuddle Martyrs. At their trial March 1833

## Tonbridge

Town on the River Medway in Kent, southeast England, between Tunbridge Wells and Sevenoaks; population (1991) 99,100. The town is a market centre. The ruins of the castle, which has Norman origins, include a large 14th-century gatehouse.

## Torbay

Urban area and unitary authority in southwest England, created in April 1998 from part of the county of Devon; population (1994 est) 128,000; area 627 km/242 sq mi. The chief towns are ◊Torquay, Paignton, and Brixham.

*Physical*

Bordering on the English Channel, it coastline includes Tor Bay and 23 beaches, including Goodrington Sands. The area has been named 'the English Riviera' because of its mild climate and exotic flora.

*Features*

Notable buildings are Oldway Mansion, Paignton, partly modelled on the Palace of Versailles,

France; 12th-century Torre Abbey, Torquay; and the 17th–18th century Abbey Mansion. A replica of Francis ◊Drake's *Golden Hind* is moored at Bixham. Paignton Zoo is a popular attraction.

## Torfaen

Unitary authority in south Wales, created in 1996 from part of the former county of Gwent; population (1996) 90,700; area 98 sq km/38 sq mi. The chief towns are ◊Pontypool (administrative headquarters) and Cwmbran (the first new town in Wales).

### Physical

The authority features rugged mountains in the north, including Coity Mountain, and the River Afon Llwyd (ancient name Torfaen, 'Rock Breaker') flows through the long valley from Blaenavon in the north to Cwmbran in the south.

### Economy

Mining and the iron and tin-plate industries of the past have given way to alternative new industries including electronics, automotive industries, and engineering.

## Torquay

Resort and administrative headquarters of ◊Torbay unitary authority in southern England, 41

**Tower Bridge** Tower Bridge across the Thames stands just downstream of the Tower of London. Its Gothic towers are façades hiding the steel framework and opening mechanism. A distinctive landmark, it is sometimes misidentified; popular rumour maintains that, when US entrepreneurs purchased the old London Bridge in the 1960s, it was in the mistaken belief that they were buying Tower Bridge. Simon Hazelgrove/ Collections

km/25 mi south of Exeter; population (1991) 59,600. It is a sailing centre and has an annual regatta in August. Torquay lies in the area known as the English Riviera on account of its mild climate and exotic plants (including palm trees); tourism is very important.

### History

Archaeological evidence from Kent's Cavern, in the Ilsham valley, shows occupation in prehistoric times; a fine collection of remains is exhibited at the Museum of the Torquay Natural History Society.

The Domesday survey identifies part of the site of Torquay with the Norman period. In 1196 a Roman Catholic monastic order founded Torre Abbey, the ruins of which, together with the restored Monastic Barn and the Mansion House (dating in some parts from about the 15th century), are a conspicuous feature today on the seafront.

The development of Torquay as a modern seaside resort dates from the end of the 18th century when 'Tor Kay' or 'Tor Key' was just a cluster of fishermen's huts on the shore, with the village of Tor (or Torre) a short way inland. To counter the threat of invasion by Napoleon, ships of the fleet constantly used Torbay as an anchorage, and houses were built on the shores of the bay for the accommodation of officers' families.

## Tory Party

Name applied colloquially to the Conservative Party, but originally the forerunner of the British ◊Conservative Party, about 1680–1830. It was the party of the squire and parson, as opposed to the Whigs (supported by the trading classes and Nonconformists).

## tournament

In medieval England, martial competition between knights. Until the accession of the Stuarts to the English throne, chivalric contests were a feature of court life. Jousting and hand-to-hand combat took place, and a lord might dedicate himself to one of the ladies present. In the early part of his reign, Henry VIII participated in tournaments personally, much to the consternation of his counsellors.

## Tower Bridge

Bridge over the River ◊Thames in London, between the Tower of London and Bermondsey. Designed by Horace Jones and John Wolfe Barry, it was built in 1886–94. The central span between two towers consists of two drawbridges which can be raised to allow vessels to pass to and from the Pool of London.

Tower Bridge is the most easterly of the London Thames bridges. It has two high Gothic Revival towers 70 m/200 ft apart, and is connected with each bank by single-span suspension bridges.

## Tower Hamlets

Inner borough of east Greater London. It includes the districts of ◊Limehouse, Spitalfields, Bethnal Green, ◊Wapping, Poplar, Stepney, and the Isle of ◊Dogs. Large parts of the borough's dockland areas have been redeveloped for business and residential use; population (1991) 161,000.

### History
Richard II met the Essex rebels at Mile End Green (now Stepney Green) during the Peasants' Revolt in 1381. In the 17th century the name Tower Hamlets referred to the East London military district of 21 hamlets from which the Lieutenant of the Tower of London had the right to muster militia.

### Features
Tower of London; the Isle of Dogs, bounded on three sides by the Thames; ◊Docklands redevelopment area (including ◊Canary Wharf); site of ◊Billingsgate fish market; Limehouse, the main centre of 18th- and 19th-century shipbuilding, which in the 1890s became a focal point for Chinese sailors working from West India Docks; Spitalfields, which derives its name from the priory and hospital of St Mary's Spital (1197), where silk weaving developed following the influx of Huguenot refugees to the area after 1685 (the industry collapsed in the mid-19th century); Spitalfields Market (formerly a fruit and vegetable market) has been developed by Norman Foster for LIFFE (London International Financial Futures Exchange); Bethnal Green Museum of Childhood (1872); Victoria Park (1840s)

### Historical landmarks
Settlement in the area dates from the time of the Romans. Stepney was a London suburb as early as the composition of the Domesday Book, when it had a population of about 800. The Royal Mint and the Tower of London both lay just outside the City of London and within the borough. Another early foundation was the Royal Hospital of St Katherine by the Tower, which, founded by Queen Matilda in 1148, has always had queens as its patrons. It was founded for the sick and elderly, and in the 1820s, when the site was used for St Katherine's Dock, it was moved to Regent's Park.

In the 1950s it moved back to Stepney and is now located in Butcher Row, partly housed in an 18th-century merchant's house. The chapel still has medieval stalls and carvings. St Dunstan's church dates from the Middle Ages, and the manor house at Bromley from the 15th century. Ratcliff, a Stepney hamlet, was a dock area and it was from here in the 16th century that the explorers Frobisher and Willoughby sailed to Russia while searching for the northwest passage. Later this section of riverside became notorious for its rowdy public houses.

Wapping, an adjacent hamlet, was the site of execution docks, where people such as Captain Kidd were executed for crimes on the high seas. The Thames tunnel, built between 1824 and 1843, links Wapping and Rotherhithe. Blackwall docks were built in 1612–14, followed by the West India Docks in 1799–1802, the East India Docks in 1803–06, and Milwall Docks in 1868. The area of the West India and Millwall docks is a peninsula known as the Isle of Dogs. Ships were built here, one of the most famous being the *Great Eastern*, which was launched in 1858.

Limehouse, an area adjacent to the docks, received the name from the lime kilns which were in use from the Middle Ages until the 19th century. Bow had a porcelain factory in the 18th century producing 'Bow China'. Bethnal Green was mostly farmland in the 18th century until it became largely residential. Bells have been cast at Whitechapel Bell Foundry for over 400 years, and these hang in many famous churches including Westminster Abbey. The Liberty Bell, which was rung to mark the acceptance by the US Congress of the Declaration of Independence, was cast in Whitechapel in 1752.

## Tower of London

Fortress on the bank of the River Thames to the east of the City of London. The keep, or White Tower, was built in about 1078 by Bishop Gundulf on the site of British and Roman fortifications. It is surrounded by two strong walls and a moat (now dry), and was for centuries a royal residence and the principal state prison.

Thomas More, Anne Boleyn, Catherine Howard, Lady Jane Grey, earls Essex and Strafford, Bishop Laud, and the Duke of Monmouth were among those imprisoned and executed at the Tower. Today it is a barracks, an armoury, and a museum. In 1994 the crown jewels, traditionally kept in a bunker in the keep, were moved to a specially designed showcase, the Jewel House, situated above ground level.

## Toynbee, Arnold (1852–1883)
English economic historian who coined the term 'industrial revolution' in his 'Lectures on the Industrial Revolution', published in 1884. Toynbee Hall, an education settlement in the east end of London, was named after him.

## Tradescant, John (1570–c. 1638)
English gardener and botanist who travelled widely in Europe and is thought to have introduced the cos lettuce to England from the Greek island of that name. He was appointed gardener to Charles I and was succeeded by his son, **John Tradescant the Younger** (1608–1662). The younger Tradescant undertook three plant-collecting trips to Virginia in North America.

The Tradescants introduced many new plants to Britain, including the acacia, lilac, and occidental plane. Tradescant senior is generally considered the earliest collector of plants and other natural-history objects.

## Trafalgar, Battle of
During the ◊Napoleonic Wars, victory of the British fleet, commanded by Admiral Horatio Nelson, over a combined French and Spanish fleet on 21 October 1805; Nelson was mortally wounded during the action. The victory laid the foundation for British naval supremacy throughout the 19th century. It is named after Cape Trafalgar, a low headland in southwest Spain, near the western entrance to the Straits of Gibraltar.

## Trafalgar Square
London square commemorating the victory of the British fleet, led by Admiral Nelson, over a combined French and Spanish force at the Battle of ◊Trafalgar. Its centrepiece is Nelson's Column bearing a statue by Edward Baily (1788–1867); four lions by Edwin Landseer recline at the base. The square and its fountains have become the London focus for New Year's Eve and other national celebrations.

Trafalgar Square is London's only metric square, laid out as one hectare.

## transportation
Punishment of sending convicted persons to overseas territories to serve their sentences. It was introduced in England towards the end of the 17th century and although it was abolished in 1857 after many thousands had been transported, mostly to Australia, sentences of penal servitude continued to be partly carried out in Western Australia up until 1867.

The first British convict ship to reach Australia arrived at Sydney Cove, New South Wales, in January 1788 with 736 convicts surviving the journey. The last convict ship to arrive in Australia was the *Hougoumont* which brought 279 prisoners to Fremantle, Western Australia, in 1868. In all, about 137,000 male and 25,000 female convicts were transported to Australia.

## Trent
Third longest river of England; length 275 km/170 mi. Rising in the south Pennines (at Norton in the Moors) by the Staffordshire–Cheshire border, it flows south and then northeast through Derbyshire, along the county boundary of Leicestershire, and through Nottinghamshire and Lincolnshire, joining the Ouse east of Goole to form the Humber estuary, and entering the North Sea below Spurn Head.

## Trent Bridge
Test-cricket ground in Nottingham, home of the Nottinghamshire county side. One of the oldest cricket grounds in Britain, it was opened in 1838.

The ground covers approximately 2.5 hectares/6.2 acres and the present-day capacity is around 30,000. It has staged Test cricket since 1899. A crowd of 101,886 watched the England–Australia Test match in 1948.

## Trollope, Anthony (1815–1882)
English novelist. He delineated provincial English middle-class society in a series of novels set in or around the imaginary cathedral city of Barchester. *The Warden* (1855) began the series, which includes *Barchester Towers* (1857), *Doctor Thorne* (1858), and *The Last Chronicle of Barset* (1867). His political novels include *Can You Forgive Her?* (1864), *Phineas Finn* (1867–69), and *The Prime Minister* (1875–76).

Trollope became a post office clerk in 1834, introduced the pillar box in 1853, and achieved the position of surveyor before retiring in 1867.

## Trossachs ('bristled terrain')
Woodland glen between lochs Katrine and Achray in Stirling unitary authority, Scotland, 3 km/2 mi long. Overlooking it are Ben Venue (727 m/2,386 ft) and Ben A'an (369 m/1,211 ft), a popular climbing venue, which rests against Meall Gainmheich (564 m/1,851 ft). Featured in the novels of Walter Scott, it has become a favoured tourist spot.

## Truro
Market town in Cornwall, England, and administrative headquarters of the county, on the River

**Anthony Trollope,** English novelist Anthony Trollope, who produced a remarkable quantity of fine novels, biographies, and travel books while pursuing a successful career as a civil servant in the Post Office. Trollope introduced the pillar box for letters to Britain and stood unsuccessfully for Parliament in 1868. Corbis

Truro, a branch of the Fal, 14 km/9 mi north of Falmouth; population (1991) 19,000.

Truro was the traditional meeting place of the ◊Stannaries (local parliament; see ◊Cornwall), and was formerly a centre and port for the now defunct tin-mining industry. The cathedral, designed by J L Pearson (1817–1897) dates from 1880–1910, and the museum and art gallery has works by the portrait painter John Opie (1761–1807).

## Tudor and Elizabethan architecture
English architecture during the reign of the Tudor dynasty, from 1485 to 1603. The first stage of transition from Gothic to Renaissance is referred to as **Tudor**, the period 1558–1603 is commonly known as **Elizabethan**. The Renaissance movement in Italy began to influence English architecture early in the 16th century, but at first was confined to small ornamental details imported from Italy (for example the terracotta busts of Roman emperors at Hampton Court, about 1520) or carried out by imported Italian craftsmen (for example Torrigiano's tomb for Henry VII in Westminster Abbey, 1512). Italian ornamental features soon came to be copied by English craftsmen, and books of engravings of the 'Orders of Architecture' and other Roman architectural details were compiled, mainly in Germany and the Netherlands, and were studied in England.

The period saw a great boom and revolution in the building of houses and of grammar schools and colleges. The castlelike silhouettes, symmetry, and large gridded windows of ◊Longleat (1568–75), Wollaton Hall (1580–88), and ◊Hardwick Hall (1590–97), built by Robert Smythson, display a uniquely romantic English version of Classicism.

## Tudor dynasty
English dynasty 1485–1603, founded by Henry VII, who became king by overthrowing Richard III (the last of the York dynasty) at the Battle of Bosworth. Henry VII reigned from 1485 to 1509, and was succeeded by Henry VIII (reigned 1509–47); Edward VI (reigned 1547–53); Mary (reigned 1553–58); and Elizabeth I (reigned 1558–1603). Elizabeth died childless and the

throne of England passed to her cousin James VI of Scotland, who thus became James I of England and the first of the Stuart line. See page 470 for a genealogy.

The dynasty was descended from the Welsh adventurer Owen Tudor (*c.* 1400–1461), who fought on the Lancastrian side in the Wars of the Roses. Owen Tudor later became the second husband of Catherine of Valois (widow of Henry V of England). Their son Edmund, Earl of Richmond, married Margaret Beaufort (1443–1509), the great-granddaughter of ◊John of Gaunt, who was the fourth son of Edward III. Henry VII, the founder of the Tudor dynasty, was the son of Edmund, Earl of Richmond, and Margaret Beaufort.

The dynasty's symbol, the **Tudor rose**, combines the red and white roses of the Lancastrian and Yorkist houses, and symbolizes the union of the two factions which was cemented by Henry VII in January 1486 when he married Elizabeth of York, the eldest daughter of Edward IV.

## Tull, Jethro (1674–1741)
English agriculturist who about 1701 developed a drill that enabled seeds to be sown mechanically and spaced so that cultivation between rows was possible in the growth period. His chief work, *Horse-Hoeing Husbandry,* was published in 1733. Tull also developed a plough with blades set in

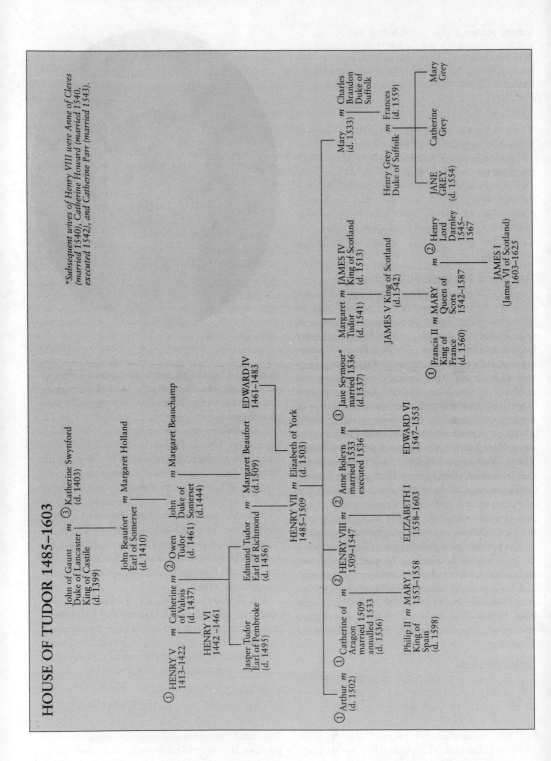

HOUSE OF TUDOR 1485–1603

*Subsequent wives of Henry VIII were Anne of Cleves (married 1540), Catherine Howard (married 1540, executed 1542), and Catherine Parr (married 1543).

① HENRY V *m* Catherine of Valois (d. 1437)
1413–1422

John of Gaunt Duke of Lancaster King of Castile (d. 1399) *m* ③ Katherine Swynford (d. 1403)

John Beaufort Earl of Somerset (d. 1410) *m* Margaret Holland

John Duke of Somerset (d.1444) *m* Margaret Beauchamp

HENRY VI 1442–1461

② Owen Tudor (d. 1461)

Edmund Tudor Earl of Richmond (d. 1456) *m* Margaret Beaufort (d.1509)

Jasper Tudor Earl of Pembroke (d. 1495)

HENRY VII *m* Elizabeth of York (d. 1503)
1485–1509

EDWARD IV 1461–1483

① Arthur (d. 1502)

① Catherine of Aragon married 1509 annulled 1533 (d. 1536) *m* ② HENRY VIII *m* ② Anne Boleyn married 1533 executed 1536
1509–1547

③ Jane Seymour* married 1536 (d.1537)

Philip II King of Spain (d. 1598) *m* MARY I 1553–1558

ELIZABETH I 1558–1603

EDWARD VI 1547–1553

Margaret Tudor (d. 1541) *m* JAMES IV King of Scotland (d. 1513)

Mary (d. 1533) *m* Charles Brandon Duke of Suffolk

JAMES V King of Scotland (d.1542)

① Francis II King of France (d. 1560) *m* MARY Queen of Scots 1542–1587 *m* ② Henry Lord Darnley 1545–1567

JAMES I (James VI of Scotland) 1603–1625

Henry Grey Duke of Suffolk *m* Frances (d. 1559)

JANE GREY (d. 1554)

Catherine Grey

Mary Grey

such a way that grass and roots were pulled up and left on the surface to dry. Basically the design of a plough is much the same today.

Tull was born in Berkshire, studied at Oxford and qualified as a barrister, but took up farming about 1700.

## Tunbridge Wells, Royal

Spa and commuter town in Kent, southeast England, between London and Hastings; population (1991) 60,300. The town developed after the discovery of iron-rich springs here in 1606. The Pantiles shopping parade (paved with tiles in the reign of Queen Anne), was a fashionable attraction; visited by Queen Victoria, the town has been named 'Royal' since 1909.

Following the discovery of the chalybeate (containing iron salts) springs in the area, visitors at first stayed at Tonbridge or Southborough to the north, but in the 1630s large houses were built near the springs and shaded walks were laid out. **Tunbridge ware**, wooden boxes whose mosaic lids are decorated with rural scenes and ornamental borders, was produced here from the 17th century. A fine collection of Tunbridge ware is housed in the museum and art gallery. There was an Iron Age hill-fort at High Rocks nearby.

## Turing, Alan (1912–1954)

English mathematician and logician. In 1936 he described a 'universal computing machine' that could theoretically be programmed to solve any problem capable of solution by a specially designed machine. This concept, now called the **Turing machine**, foreshadowed the digital computer.

Turing is believed to have been the first to suggest (in 1950) the possibility of machine learning and artificial intelligence. During World War II he worked for Britain's code-breaking operations at Bletchley Park, Buckinghamshire.

## Turner, J(oseph) M(allord) W(illiam) (1775–1851)

English painter. He was one of the most original artists of his day. He travelled widely in Europe, and his landscapes became increasingly Romantic, with the subject often transformed in scale and flooded with brilliant, hazy light. Many later works anticipate Impressionism, for example *Rain, Steam and Speed* (1844; National Gallery, London).

A precocious talent, Turner entered the Royal Academy schools in 1789. In 1792 he made the first of several European tours from which numerous watercolour sketches survive. His early oil

paintings show Dutch influence (such as that of van de Velde), but by the 1800s he had begun to paint landscapes in the 'Grand Manner', reflecting the Italianate influences of Claude Lorrain and Richard ◊Wilson.

Many of his most dramatic works are set in Europe or at sea, for example, *Shipwreck* (1805), *Snowstorm: Hannibal Crossing the Alps* (1812), and *Destruction of Sodom* (1805), all at the Tate Gallery, London; and *The Slave Ship* (1839; Museum of Fine Arts, Boston, Massachusetts). Turner was also devoted to literary themes and mythologies, such as *Ulysses Deriding Polyphemus* (1829; Tate Gallery, London).

In his old age he lived as a recluse in Chelsea, London, under an assumed name. He died there, leaving to the nation more than 300 paintings, nearly 20,000 watercolours, and over 19,000 drawings. In 1987 the Clore Gallery extension to the Tate Gallery, London, was opened to display his bequest.

## Turner Prize

Annual prize established in 1984 to encourage discussion about new developments in contemporary British art. £20,000 is awarded to a British artist under the age of 50 for an outstanding exhibition or other presentation of his or her work in the preceding 12 months; the winner is usually announced in November or early December. The Turner Prize has often attracted criticism for not celebrating what is traditionally considered to be art.

The prize was established by the Patrons of New Art, and is named after the British artist J M W ◊Turner. Artists are shortlisted by a jury and their work is exhibited at the Tate Gallery, London. Originally sponsored by an individual, it is now sponsored by Channel 4, which televises the award.

## Turpin, Dick (1705–1739)

English highwayman. The son of an innkeeper, he turned to highway robbery, cattle-thieving, and smuggling, and was hanged at York, England.

His legendary ride from London to York on his mare Black Bess is probably based on one of about 305 km/190 mi from Gad's Hill to York completed in 15 hours in 1676 by highwayman John Nevison (1639–1684).

## Tussaud, Madame born Anne Marie Grosholtz (1761–1850)

French wax-modeller. In 1802 she established an exhibition of wax models of celebrities in London.

It was destroyed by fire in 1925, but reopened in 1928. The exhibition was transferred to Baker Street in 1883 and to its present site in Marylebone Road in 1884, where it remains, one of London's top fee-paying attractions.

Born in Strasbourg, she went to Paris as a young girl in 1766 to live with her wax-modeller uncle, Philippe Curtius, whom she soon surpassed in working with wax. During the French Revolution they were forced to take death masks of many victims and leaders (some still exist in the Chamber of Horrors).

### tweed
Cloth made of woollen yarn, usually of several shades, but in its original form without a regular pattern and woven on a hand loom in the more remote parts of Ireland, Wales, and Scotland. **Harris tweed** is made on the island of Harris in the Outer Hebrides; it is highly durable and largely weatherproof.

### Twickenham
Stadium in southwest London, the ground at which England play home Rugby Union internationals. It first staged an international match in 1910. The Rugby Football Union has its headquarters at Twickenham, and the Harlequins club used to play some of its home matches there. The ground was extensively rebuilt in the 1990s and holds 75,000.

### Tyburn gallows
Gallows in London at the junction of the present Oxford Street and Edgware Road, from the 12th century until 1783. The first recorded execution using the Tyburn gallows took place in 1196. After 1783 the place of execution was moved to Newgate Prison. Among those executed here was Perkin Warbeck and, in the 16th and 17th centuries, many English Catholics.

### Tyler, Wat (died 1381)
English leader of the ◊Peasants' Revolt of 1381. He was probably born in Kent or Essex, and may have served in the French wars. After taking Canterbury, he led the peasant army to Blackheath, outside London, and went on to invade the city. King Richard II met the rebels at Mile End and promised to redress their grievances, which included the imposition of a poll tax. At a further conference at Smithfield, London, Tyler was murdered.

### Tynan, Kenneth (1927–1980)
English theatre critic and author, a leading cultural figure of the radical 1960s. A strong opponent of censorship, he devised the nude revue *Oh Calcutta!* (1969), first staged in New York, USA. His publications include *A View of the English Stage 1944–63* (1975).

### Tyndale, William (c. 1492–1536)
English translator of the Bible. The printing of his New Testament (the basis of the Authorized Version) was begun in Cologne, Germany, in 1525 and, after he had been forced to flee, completed in Worms. Tyndale introduced some of the most familiar phrases to the English language, such as 'filthy lucre', and 'God forbid'. He was strangled and burned as a heretic at Vilvorde in Belgium.

### Tyne
River of northeast England formed by the union of the North Tyne (rising in the Cheviot Hills) and South Tyne (rising near Cross Fell in Cumbria) near Hexham, Northumberland, and reaching the North Sea at Tynemouth; length 72 km/45 mi. Kielder Water (1980) in the North Tyne Valley is Europe's largest artificial lake, 12 km/7.5 mi long and 0.8 km/0.5 mi wide, and supplies the industries of Tyneside, Wearside, and Teesside. As well as functioning as a reservoir, it is a major resource for recreational use.

### Tyne and Wear
Metropolitan county of northeast England, created in 1974; population (1996) 1,127,300; area 540 sq km/208 sq mi. The rivers Tyne and Wear flow through this almost entirely urban county. From the 13th century they facilitated the shipping of locally mined coal to London and Europe; the coal industry dominated the area until the 20th century. In 1986 most of the functions of the former county council were transferred to the metropolitan borough councils. The principal towns and cities are ◊Newcastle upon Tyne, ◊Gateshead, ◊Sunderland (administrative centres for the districts of the same name), ◊South Shields (administrative centre of South Tyneside district), and North Shields (administrative centre of North Tyneside district).

*History*
Several of the towns of Tyne and Wear originated as Anglo-Saxon settlements from the 7th century. These include the fortified monastery at Tynemouth, the monastery at Jarrow, Gateshead at the southern end of the Tyne crossing, North and South Shields by the sheltered waters upstream of the Tyne River mouth, and Monkwearmouth and Sunderland, respectively north and south of the

Wear gorge. The Normans built a castle in 1080 at the easiest crossing point of the Tyne (Newcastle upon Tyne), 16 km/10 mi inland, and later built a bridge at the same place on Roman foundations. This site remained the crossing point of the Tyne nearest to sea-level until the construction of the Tyne Tunnel in 1967.

### Industrial history

The success of the coal industry enabled other industrial development on riverside sites in the 19th century. The banks were soon lined with shipyards; the chemical industry thrived, and there was heavy engineering and armaments above Newcastle upon Tyne. The population of the Tyne and Wear area rose from about 178,000 in 1821 to 1,170,000 in 1921. Dense terrace housing was built close to the mines, shipyards, and factories. Building and chemical pollution took their toll on the local environment. Growth of the local economy could not be sustained in the 20th century, and government aid from 1935 led to the establishment of a number of industrial trading estates and the start of diversification.

### Physical

The Tyne and Wear rivers enter the North Sea within 11 km/7 mi of each other. The Tyne is tidal for 30 km/19 mi, the Wear for 13 km/8 mi; both have relatively narrow, steep-sided valleys with river banks rising to 30–50 m/98–160 ft. The Tyne cuts across a mainly sandstone plateau; both rivers cut gorges through a magnesian limestone plateau at their mouths.

### Features

Part of ◊Hadrian's Wall is in the county. Newcastle and Gateshead are linked with each other and with the coast on both sides by the Tyne and Wear Metro (a light railway using existing suburban lines, extending 54 km/34 mi). The Tyneside International Film Festival is hosted here.

### Economy

Once a centre of heavy industry, Tyne and Wear's industry is being redeveloped and diversified, with car manufacturing on Wearside, electronics, offshore technology (floating production vessels), automobile components, pharmaceuticals, and computers. The rivers remain important. Both have general merchandise quays; the Tyne also has fishing berths, a wet dock, and roll-on/roll-off berths for ferries to ports between Bergen and Esbjerg. Newcastle upon Tyne has become the major office centre of the northern region of England and one of the chief shopping centres in the county.

## Tyrone

County of Northern Ireland; population (1991) 158,500; area 3,160 sq km/1,220 sq mi. It is largely rural, with evidence of the once flourishing linen industry. Many Americans trace their family roots to Tyrone. The chief towns are ◊Omagh (county town), Dungannon, Strabane, and Cookstown.

### Physical

Lough Neagh is in the east and the Sperrin Mountains in the north. The main rivers in the county are the Derg, Blackwater, and Foyle.

### Features

The county contains several Neolithic graves and stone circles, notably at Beaghmore, west of Cookstown. The Ulster Park, north of Omagh, presents history from Neolithic times, with reconstructions of typical historic buildings. Many Tyrone villages have heritage centres, describing the linen industry, and linen polishing is demonstrated at Wellbrook Beetling Mill. The Peatlands Park east of Dungannon preserves an ancient Irish bog. The family home of the US president Woodrow Wilson is at Dergalt, near Strabane, and no fewer than 11 US presidents have had ancestors in Tyrone. The Ulster-American Folk Park, north of Omagh, was endowed by the Mellon banking family of Pittsburgh.

### Economy

The economy is based mainly on agriculture. There is also brickmaking, and production of linen, hosiery, and shirts.

## Tyrrell

British motor-racing team founded by Ken Tyrrell in 1970. He formed a partnership with Jackie Stewart and the celebrated driver won all three of his world titles in Tyrrell-run teams. The team won the Formula One World Constructors' title in 1971.

## Ullswater

Second largest lake in the Cumbrian ◊Lake District, northwest England, on the east side of ◊Helvellyn ridge; length 13 km/8 mi, width 1 km/0.6 mi. The former lead-mining and quarrying villages of Patterdale and Glenridding to the south of the lake now consist mainly of hotels and guesthouses for tourists.

## Ulster

A former kingdom and province in the north of Ireland, annexed by England in 1461; from Jacobean times a centre of English, and later Scottish, settlement on land confiscated from its owners; divided in 1921 into Northern Ireland (counties Antrim, Armagh, Down, Fermanagh, Londonderry, and Tyrone) and the Republic of Ireland (counties Cavan, Donegal, and Monaghan).

## Ulster Unionist Party, UUP, also known as the Official Unionist Party (OUP)

The largest political party in Northern Ireland. Right-of-centre in orientation, it advocates equality for Northern Ireland within the UK and opposes union with the Republic of Ireland. The party has the broadest support of any Ulster party, and has consistently won a large proportion of parliamentary and local seats. Its central organization, dating from 1905, is formally called the Ulster Unionist Council. Its leader from 1995 is David Trimble. It secured 28 of the 108 seats in the new Northern Ireland Assembly, elected in June 1998, and Trimble was elected Northern Ireland's first minister at the Assembly's first meeting on 1 July.

## unicorn

Heraldic animal represented as a horse with a twisted horn, a deer's hooves, a goat's beard, and a lion's tail. When James VI of Scotland became James I of England in 1606, one of the two supporting unicorns on the Scottish arms replaced the Welsh dragon on the English shield, the other supporter being the lion. The legendary animosity between the lion and the unicorn relates to former rivalry between England and Scotland.

## Union, Acts of

Acts of Parliament that accomplished the joining of England with Wales (1536), England and

## Acts of Union

### Act of Union of 1536
The Act of Union passed in 1536, during the reign of King Henry VIII, the second English monarch descended from the Welsh House of Tudor, formally united England and Wales. By its terms, the Welsh Marches, estates held for centuries by semi-independent Marcher lords, became several new counties or were added to older counties. Counties and boroughs in Wales were granted representation in the English Parliament.

### Act of Union of 1707
The Act of Union passed in 1707 by the parliaments of England and Scotland created the Kingdom of Great Britain. Although Scotland retained its judicial system and its Presbyterian church, its parliament was joined with that of England. The crowns of the two countries had been united in 1603 when James Stuart (James VI of Scotland) succeeded Elizabeth I as James I of England, but the kingdoms otherwise remained separate.

### Act of Union of 1800
The Act of Union, which was passed in 1800 and went into effect on 1 January 1801, joined the Kingdom of Great Britain and all of Ireland into the United Kingdom of Great Britain and Ireland. The act was revoked when the Irish Free State was constituted in 1922.

Wales with Scotland (1707), and Great Britain with Ireland (1800). See display text opposite for detail.

## Union Jack
Popular name for the British national flag, properly called the **Union flag**. Strictly speaking, the term Union Jack should be used only when the flag is flown on the jackstaff of a warship. The flag unites the crosses of St George, St Andrew, and St Patrick, representing England, Scotland, and Ireland. The union flag was introduced after the union of England and Scotland in 1707, and at first bore the crosses of St George and St Andrew. At the union with Ireland in 1801, St Patrick's cross – a red diagonal cross on a white ground – was added, forming what has ever since been the UK national flag.

## unitary authority
Administrative unit of Great Britain. Since 1996 the two-tier structure of local government has ceased to exist in Scotland and Wales, and in some parts of England, and has been replaced by unitary authorities, responsible for all local government services.

## United Kingdom, UK
Official name for ◊England, ◊Scotland, ◊Wales, and ◊Northern Ireland, colloquially referred to as Britain or Great Britain. See Acts of ◊Union for when the constituent parts were joined. For history, see constituent parts, also the chronology from 1707, at the end of the guide.

## Uppark
Late 17th-century house in West Sussex, England, 8 km/5 mi south of Petersfield. Uppark was given to the National Trust in 1954 and retains much of the original decorations and furnishings, including flock wallpapers and damask curtains. However, a high proportion of this was destroyed by fire in August 1989. The house was reopened in 1995 following a complete restoration.

It was the home of the Fetherstonhaugh family from 1747, and its many famous visitors included Emma Hart (later Lady Hamilton and Nelson's mistress), Charles Greville, the Prince Regent, and H G Wells, whose mother was housekeeper there for several years.

The restoration of the house was revolutionary in that it attempted to restore the house to its exact state the day before the fire. Modern reproductions and replacements of features such as wallpaper were 'aged' by the incorporation of original fragments.

---

*Here is a country that fought and won a noble war, dismantled a mighty empire in a generally benign and enlightened way, created a far-seeing welfare state – in short, did nearly everything right – and then spent the rest of the century looking on itself as a chronic failure. The fact is that this is still the best place in the world for most things.*

**Bill Bryson** US writer.
*Notes From a Small Island* (1995)

---

## Usk, Welsh Wysg
River in south Wales, rising in the Black Mountain on the boundary between Carmarthenshire and Powys; length 137 km/85 mi; catchment area 1,358 sq km/524 sq mi. It flows south through Powys and Monmouthshire, passing through the towns of Abergavenny, Usk, and Caerlon, and enters the Bristol Channel at Newport.

The Usk valley, of which the upper half is in the ◊Brecon Beacons National Park, has fine scenery and good fishing.

## Vale of Glamorgan

Unitary authority in southeast Wales, created in 1996 from parts of the former counties of Mid Glamorgan and South Glamorgan; population (1996) 119,500; area 337 sq km/130 sq mi. It is situated to the west of ◊Cardiff. The main towns are ◊Barry (administrative headquarters) and Penarth. Barry Island is a tourist resort.

*Physical*

It is a lowland area with a southern coastline on the Bristol Channel.

*Economy*

There is sheep farming and varied agriculture. Barry has a chemical industry. Cardiff International Airport is situated near the coast at Roose, west of Barry. Service staff and civilians are employed in the maintenance of RAF and Royal Navy aircraft at RAF St Athan.

## Vanbrugh, John (1664–1726)

English Baroque architect, dramatist, and soldier. Although entirely untrained as an architect, he designed the huge mansions of Castle Howard (1699–1726), Blenheim (1705–16; completed by Nicholas Hawksmoor 1722–25), Seaton Delaval (1720–29), and many others, as well as much of Greenwich Hospital (1718 onwards). He also wrote the comic dramas *The Relapse* (1696) and *The Provok'd Wife* (1697).

He was imprisoned in Paris 1688–93 as a political hostage during the war between France and the Grand Alliance (including Britain). In

---

**John Vanbrugh** Castle Howard, North Yorkshire, England. It was designed by John Vanbrugh and Nicholas Hawksmoor for the Earl of Carlisle in 1699. Corbis

1704 Vanbrugh built his own theatre, the Queen's Theatre or Italian Opera House in the Haymarket, London (now destroyed). From this point play-writing displaced architecture as his principal activity.

## Vancouver, George (1757–1798)

English navigator who made extensive exploration of the west coast of North America. The Canadian city of Vancouver was named after him. He accompanied James ◊Cook on two voyages, and served in the West Indies. He also surveyed parts of Australia, New Zealand, Tahiti, and Hawaii.

## Vaughan Williams, Ralph (1872–1958)

English composer. His style was tonal and often evocative of the English countryside through the use of folk themes. Among his works are the orchestral *Fantasia on a Theme by Thomas Tallis* (1910); the opera *Sir John in Love* (1929), featuring the Elizabethan song 'Greensleeves'; and nine symphonies (1909–57).

The English pastoral tradition was revived in his 3rd symphony (1921), and the complementary, visionary source of his inspiration was renewed in such sacred works as the Mass in G minor, *Sancta Civitas*, and *Benedicite*. His two best-known symphonies, nos. 4 and 5, were composed between 1934 and 1943; the angularity and fierce accents of the earlier work lead to the repose and serenity of its companion. The last four symphonies continue the composer's spiritual quest, already begun in *The Pilgrim's Progress*. Although Vaughan Williams' compositions are usually classified broadly as pastoral, making use of folk melodies, or at least the lyrical and often model aspects of such melodies, he was conscious of contemporary musical developments and often involved a greater degree of dissonance in his later works.

## Verulamium

Romano-British town near St Albans, Hertfordshire, occupied until about AD 450. Verulamium superseded a nearby Belgic settlement and was first occupied by the Romans in 44–43 BC. The earliest English martyr, St Alban, was martyred here, perhaps during the reign of Septimus Severus. A fragmentary inscription from the site of the forum records the name of the Roman governor Agricola. The site became deserted in the late 5th or 6th century.

## Victoria (1819–1901)

Queen of the UK from 1837, when she succeeded her uncle William IV, and Empress of India from 1877. In 1840 she married Prince ◊Albert of Saxe-Coburg and Gotha. Her relations with her prime ministers ranged from the affectionate (Melbourne and Disraeli) to the stormy (Peel, Palmerston, and Gladstone). Her golden jubilee in 1887 and diamond jubilee in 1897 marked a waning of republican sentiment, which had developed with her withdrawal from public life on Albert's death in 1861.

The only child of Edward, Duke of Kent, fourth son of George III, she was born on 24 May 1819 at Kensington Palace, London. She and Albert had four sons and five daughters. After Albert's death she lived mainly in retirement. Nevertheless, she kept control of affairs, refusing the Prince of Wales (Edward VII) any active role. From 1848 she regularly visited the Scottish Highlands, where she had a house at Balmoral built to Prince Albert's designs. She died at ◊Osborne House, her home in the Isle of Wight, on 22 January 1901, and was buried at Windsor. See also ◊Victorian period.

## Victoria and Albert Museum, V & A

Museum of decorative arts in South Kensington, London, founded in 1852. It houses prints, paintings, and temporary exhibitions, as well as one of the largest collections of decorative arts in the world.

Originally called the Museum of Ornamental Art, it had developed from the Museum of Manufacturers at Marlborough House, which had been founded in the aftermath of the Great Exhibition of 1851. In 1857 it became part of the South Kensington Museum, and was renamed the Victoria and Albert Museum in 1899. The museum was inspired by Prince ◊Albert and Henry Cole (1808–1882), English industrial designer and writer on decorative arts. He selected the museum's first acquisitions and became its first director. In 1990 the Nehru Indian Gallery was opened, displaying a selection of the museum's Indian collection, which derives from the East India Company's Museum, acquired in 1858.

## Victorian period

Mid- and late 19th century in England, covering the reign of Queen Victoria from 1837 to 1901. This period was one of significant industrial and urban development in Britain, and also saw a massive expansion of the ◊British Empire. In domestic politics the period is particularly notable for the rivalry between the Conservative prime minister Benjamin ◊Disraeli and his Liberal successor William Ewart ◊Gladstone.

# ◆ THE SCOURGE OF THE NORTH: THE VIKINGS IN BRITAIN ◆

The Viking Age in the British Isles began in the late 8th century with a series of raids by Scandinavian pirates on coastal monasteries such as Lindisfarne (sacked 793) and Iona (sacked 795). These hit-and-run raids were virtually impossible to prevent: by the time an army had gathered to counterattack, the Vikings had taken their plunder and set sail for home.

In the 840s Viking activity intensified. The Vikings came in larger numbers and founded permanent bases, such as Dublin in 841, from which they could campaign all year round. They were now interested as much in settlement as in plunder. The first areas to be settled were Scotland's northern and western isles, but the largest settlements took place in eastern and northern England after the Danes overran the Anglo-Saxon kingdoms of East Anglia, Northumbria, and Mercia in 865–74. The Vikings were greatly aided in this period by the disunity of the native kingdoms in Britain and Ireland, which failed absolutely to bury their differences and unite against the common enemy.

As the 9th century drew to a close, Viking activity declined. This was partly because many Vikings had now settled down as farmers and partly because of stiffening native resistance, such as that of Wessex under the leadership of Alfred the Great. Once the Vikings had settled down they lost their main advantage over the natives: their mobility. Between 912 and 954 Wessex conquered the Danelaw, as the Viking-settled area of eastern England was known, and the Viking kingdom of York. In Ireland the Vikings of Dublin struggled to maintain their independence and often paid tribute to Irish kings.

The late 10th century saw a resumption of large-scale Viking raiding, directed mostly at England. At first the raiders were content to extract Danegeld (protection money) but as English defences crumbled, the Danish king Sweyn I Forkbeard conquered the country in 1014. A resurgence of English resistance was put down by his son Canute in 1016 and England remained under Danish rule until 1042. The last major Viking invasion of the British Isles was Norwegian King Harald Hardrada's attempt to seize the English throne in 1066: he was defeated and killed by Harold I Godwinson at Stamford Bridge just days before William the Conqueror launched his own successful invasion.

## The cultural impact

Most of our historical sources for Viking Age Britain were written by monks. Monasteries were the main cultural centres of early medieval Britain and Ireland: they were also wealthy and unprotected and this made them a favourite target of Viking raids. Not surprisingly therefore, monastic chroniclers dwelt mainly on the violence and destruction wrought by the Vikings. Some modern historians have argued that these chroniclers were prejudiced against the Vikings because of their paganism and greatly exaggerated the violence of their raids. However, contemporary accounts of Viking raids from Francia, the Byzantine Empire, and the Islamic lands, and Viking poetry, all agree that Viking raiders were extremely violent and destructive. Much of the damage caused by Viking raids was temporary, but their attacks on monasteries were devastating for cultural life: works of art and literature were destroyed, and the communities of learned monks were dispersed. In England, monasticism made a strong recovery in the 10th century, but the brilliant monastic civilization of early Christian Ireland, which had produced masterpieces like the *Book of Kells*, never recovered from the Viking raids.

Perhaps the most important effect of the Viking invasions was that they broke up the existing power structures of the British Isles. Viking raids on western Scotland encouraged the Scots to expand inland, conquering the Picts, thus creating the kingdom of Scotland. By destroying their rivals the Vikings also greatly aided the creation of a unified English kingdom by the kings of Wessex in the 10th century.

## The abiding influence

The Vikings were not only warriors and pirates, however, but also merchants, farmers and settlers, and skilled craftsmen. Viking traders stimulated the growth of trading centres like York and the foundation of new towns like Dublin. Viking art styles influenced and enriched Celtic and Anglo-Saxon art. The English language was also greatly enriched by Danish loan words, including 'sky', 'egg', and 'sister'. After the initial violence of conquest, the Viking settlers farmed peacefully alongside their Celtic or Anglo-Saxon neighbours and, through conversion to Christianity and intermarriage, were quickly assimilated.

The Viking settlements have left few physical remains, but their locations and density can be inferred from the distribution of Scandinavian placenames. For example, Danish placenames (typically ending in '-by' or '-thorpe') are common in much of eastern England, while Norwegian placename elements (such as 'fell') are common in northwest England and the Hebrides. In Orkney and Shetland almost all placenames are of Scandinavian origin, pointing to a particularly dense Viking settlement.

by John Haywood

## Queen Victoria

Victoria became queen on 20 June 1837, and enjoyed the longest reign of any British monarch. In domestic affairs and politics she relied initially on the shrewd advice of her Whig prime minister Lord Melbourne, but later clashed with his Tory successor Robert ◊Peel, the founder of the modern police force. She was also strongly influenced by the views of her husband, Prince ◊Albert of Saxe-Coburg-Gotha, whom she married in 1840. The high point of her reign came in 1851 with the opening of the ◊Great Exhibition in Hyde Park, London, which was organized by Albert. The exhibition was designed in order to display 'the Industries of all Nations', but in fact came to symbolize the technological and industrial achievements of Victorian England.

### Colonial expansion

During Queen Victoria's reign the British Empire was extended significantly, and often by means of military force, in Asia, Africa, and the Middle East. Hong Kong, for example, became part of the Empire as a result of the first ◊Opium Wars of 1839 to 1842, and Kowloon was later added to the colony after a second Opium War of 1856 to 1858. Other additions to the Empire made in the same period include New Zealand (1840), Northern Somalia (1884), Burma (1886), and Egypt, which became a British protectorate after the opening of the Suez Canal in 1869. The centre of the Empire, however, was India, which was controlled by the ◊East India Company until 1858. Control of India eventually passed to the British crown after the Indian Mutiny of 1857, and, in 1877, Benjamin Disraeli's government conferred the title of Empress of India upon Queen Victoria.

## Victorian style

Style of architecture, furnituremaking, and decorative art of the reign of Queen Victoria.

Victorian style was often very ornate, markedly so in architecture, where there was more than one 'revival' of earlier styles, beginning with a lengthy competition between the Classic and Gothic schools. ◊Gothic Revival drew on the original Gothic architecture of medieval times. The Gothic boom had begun in 1818, when Parliament voted a million pounds for building 214 new Anglican churches. No less than 174 of them were constructed in a Gothic or near-Gothic style, and for nearly a century, most churches in England were Gothic in design. Despite the popularity of extravagant decoration, Renaissance or Classic styles were also favoured for public buildings, examples being St George's Hall, Liverpool (1815), and Birmingham Town Hall (1832–50).

Many people, such as John ◊Ruskin, believed in designing objects and architecture primarily for their function, and not for mere appearance. Increasing mass production by machines threatened the existence of craft skills, and encouraged the development of the ◊Arts and Crafts movement, with its nostalgia for the medieval way of life. In the last quarter of the century there were revivals of **Jacobean** and finally of **Queen Anne** architecture.

## Victory

British battleship, the flagship of Admiral ◊Nelson at the Battle of Trafalgar (1805). Weighing 2,198 tonnes/2,164 tons, it was launched in 1765; it is now in dry dock in Portsmouth harbour, England.

## Viking, or Norseman

Inhabitant of Scandinavia in the period 800–1100. The Vikings traded with, and raided, much of Europe, and often settled there. In their narrow, shallow-draught, highly manoeuvrable longships, the Vikings penetrated far inland along rivers.

See feature on page 478 on the Vikings in Britain.

### Viking art

In Britain Viking art did not replace contemporary ◊Celtic art and Anglo-Saxon art of the 8th to 11th century, and made no marked influence until the latter part of the 10th century. It is noted for its woodcarving and finely wrought ornaments in gold and silver, and for an intricate interlacing decorative style similar to Celtic art. A dragonlike creature, known as the 'Great Beast', is a recurring motif; an early 11th-century rune-inscribed sculpture of a Great Beast and serpent (now in the Guildhall (City of London) Museum) was found on a tomb in St Paul's Cathedral churchyard in 1852 .

The three styles of Viking art are all represented in Britain: Jellinge, based on heavy animal designs, as found on a 2-m/6.5-ft-high standing cross in Gosforth, Cumberland; Ringerike, characterized by elaborate foliage ornament and interlacing, as seen in the Winchester school of illuminated manuscripts; and Urnes, notable in English Christian carving.

## Viroconium, or Uriconium

Roman-British town, the remains of which have been excavated at Wroxeter, Shropshire, England.

It was the fourth largest town in Roman Britain, and was founded in about AD 48 as a legionary camp fortress during Roman campaigns against the Welsh.

Viroconium became a town in about 80, when the Cornovii were forced to leave their own hill city on the Wrekin. It became the tribal capital of the Cornovii. A forum and basilica were built by 130, and baths and other public buildings followed. Much of the town was destroyed by fire in about 300, but the site was occupied until the 4th century.

## Vyne, the

House in Hampshire, England, 6 km/4 mi north of Basingstoke. It was built by the Sandys family 1500–20, and a classic portico (large porch with a pediment) was added around 1654 (the earliest added to a country house in England). The house has a 16th-century oak gallery and chapel with Renaissance glass, a Palladian staircase, and some 18th-century Rococo rooms. The Vyne was acquired by the National Trust, together with 445 ha/1,099 acres, in 1956.

## Waddesdon Manor

Late Victorian Renaissance-style house in Buckinghamshire, England, 8 km/5 mi northwest of Aylesbury. It was built for Baron Ferdinand de Rothschild, and was bequeathed to the National Trust in 1957, with a collection of pictures, furniture, and china. The grounds contain an 18th-century aviary.

---

*It's cool to be Welsh these days – well, almost.*
**Patrick Hannan** Welsh broadcaster.
*Daily Telegraph*, September 1998

---

## Wakefield

Industrial city in West Yorkshire, northern England, on the River Calder, south of Leeds; population (1991) 73,600. A medieval town of some importance, Wakefield became a prominent centre for the cloth trade in the 16th century. It became a municipal borough in 1848, and a city in 1888, when a diocese was created and the parish church of All Saints became a cathedral.

### Features

All Saints' cathedral was founded in the 13th century, but dates largely from the 15th; it is chiefly Perpendicular, with a spire of 75 m/246 ft. On the bridge over the Calder stands the chapel of St Mary, one of only four surviving bridge chapels in England; it dates originally from the 14th century and was rebuilt in 1847 in a rich Decorated style. Queen Elizabeth Grammar School, said to be the successor to a 13th-century school, was founded here by a royal charter of Elizabeth I in 1591. The National Coal Mining Museum is here.

Lancastrian forces defeated and killed Richard of York here in 1460, during the Wars of the Roses.

## Wales, Welsh **Cymru**

Principality of; constituent part of the UK, in the west between the British Channel and the Irish Sea.
*Area* 20,780 sq km/8,021 sq mi
*Capital* Cardiff
*Towns and cities* Swansea, Wrexham, Newport, Carmarthen
*Features* Snowdonia Mountains (Snowdon 1,085 m/3,560 ft, the highest point in England and Wales) in the northwest and in the southeast the Black Mountains, Brecon Beacons, and Black Forest ranges; rivers Severn, Wye, Usk, and Dee

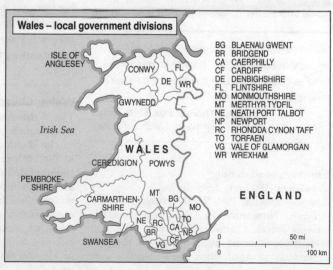

**Wales – local government divisions**

BG BLAENAU GWENT
BR BRIDGEND
CA CAERPHILLY
CF CARDIFF
DE DENBIGHSHIRE
FL FLINTSHIRE
MO MONMOUTHSHIRE
MT MERTHYR TYDFIL
NE NEATH PORT TALBOT
NP NEWPORT
RC RHONDDA CYNON TAFF
TO TORFAEN
VG VALE OF GLAMORGAN
WR WREXHAM

## Wales: Chronology

*For ancient history, see also Ancient Britain.*

**c. 400 BC** Wales occupied by Celts from central Europe.

**AD 50–60** Wales became part of the Roman Empire.

**c. 200** Christianity adopted.

**c. 450–600** Wales became the chief Celtic stronghold in the west since the Saxons invaded and settled in southern Britain. The Celtic tribes united against England.

**8th century** Frontier pushed back to Offa's Dyke.

**9th–11th centuries** Vikings raided the coasts. At this time Wales was divided into small states organized on a clan basis, although princes such as Rhodri (844–878), Howel the Good (c. 904–949), and Griffith ap Llewelyn (1039–1063) temporarily united the country.

**11th–12th centuries** Continual pressure on Wales from the Normans across the English border was resisted, notably by Llewelyn I and II.

**1277** Edward I of England accepted as overlord by the Welsh.

**1284** Edward I completed the conquest of Wales that had been begun by the Normans.

**1294** Revolt against English rule put down by Edward I.

**1350–1500** Welsh nationalist uprisings against the English; the most notable was that led by Owen Glendower.

**1485** Henry Tudor, a Welshman, became Henry VII of England.

**1536–43** Acts of Union united England and Wales after conquest under Henry VIII. Wales sent representatives to the English Parliament; English law was established in Wales; English became the official language.

**18th century** Evangelical revival made Nonconformism a powerful factor in Welsh life. A strong coal and iron industry developed in the south.

**19th century** The miners and ironworkers were militant supporters of Chartism, and Wales became a stronghold of trade unionism and socialism.

**1893** University of Wales founded.

**1920s–30s** Wales suffered from industrial depression; unemployment reached 21% 1937, and a considerable exodus of population took place.

**post-1945** Growing nationalist movement and a revival of the language, earlier suppressed or discouraged.

**1966** Plaid Cymru, the Welsh National Party, returned its first member to Westminster.

**1979** Referendum rejected a proposal for limited home rule.

**1988** Bombing campaign against estate agents selling Welsh properties to English buyers.

**1997** Referendum endorsed devolution proposals by a narrow margin of 50.3%.

**1999** The National Assembly for Wales is convened at a temporary location at the Cardiff University Council Chamber. A new building is to be built at Cardiff Bay and is due to be completed in 2001.

---

*Industries* traditional industries have declined, but varied modern and high-technology ventures are being developed. There are oil refineries and open-cast coal mining. The last deep coal mine in north Wales closed in 1996. Wales has the largest concentration of Japanese-owned plants in the UK. It also has the highest density of sheep in the world and a dairy industry; tourism is important.

---

*I have never felt truly at ease or at home anywhere but in Wales. I fell in love with the land as I believe people are expected to fall in love with other people.*

**Alice Thomas Ellis** British writer.
*A Welsh Childhood* (1990)

---

*Currency* pound sterling

*Population* (1993 est) 2,906,000

*Language* English, 19% Welsh-speaking

*Religion* Nonconformist Protestant denominations; Roman Catholic minority

*Government* returns 40 members to the UK Parliament; in April 1996, the 8 counties were replaced by 22 county and county borough unitary authorities (see map on page 481).

See above for chronology of key dates, and page 484 for a list of sovereigns and princes.

---

*The thing I value about Wales and Welsh background is that it has always been a genuinely more classless society than many people present England as being.*

**Geoffrey Howe** British Conservative politician.
Remark in 1986

---

## Wales, Church in

The Welsh Anglican Church, independent from the ◊Church of England.

The Welsh church became strongly Protestant in the 16th century, but in the 17th and 18th centuries declined from being led by a succession of English-appointed bishops. Disestablished by an act of Parliament in 1920, with its endowments appropriated, the Church in Wales today comprises six dioceses (with bishops elected by an electoral college of clergy and lay people) with an archbishop elected from among the six bishops.

## Wales: Historic Counties

Anglesey
Brecknockshire
Caernarvonshire
Cardiganshire
Carmarthenshire
Denbighshire
Flintshire
Glamorgan
Merioneth
Monmouthshire
Montgomeryshire
Pembrokeshire
Radnorshire

The six dioceses are: St David's, Llandaff, Bangor, St Asaph, Monmouth, and Swansea and Brecon (a diocese which, with Monmouth, was formed after 1920). Until the Welsh Church Acts of 1914 and 1919, Wales was included in the province of Canterbury; the Welsh archbishopric was formed on disestablishment.

## Wales, Prince of

Title conferred on the eldest son of the UK's sovereign. Prince ⚤Charles was invested as 21st prince of Wales at Caernarfon in 1969 by his mother, Elizabeth II.

The conferment is sometimes accompanied or followed by a ceremony of investiture at Caernarfon Castle, north Wales. Edward (afterwards King Edward II), son and heir apparent, was summoned to and sat in Parliament as Prince of Wales; his presentation at Caernarfon in 1301 is legendary. The earliest documented grantee was Edward II's grandson, Edward the Black Prince, with limitation 'to him and his heirs the kings of England'. Consequently, when a Prince of Wales succeeds to the throne, his title merges in the crown and requires a new creation for its separate existence. See table above.

*Liberty is the best of all things;
never live beneath the noose of a
servile halter.*

**William Wallace** Scottish nationalist.
From a medieval proverb

## Wales, Princes of (since 1301; date given is when title was conferred)

| | |
|---|---|
| 1301 | Edward (II) |
| 1343 | Edward (the Black Prince) |
| 1376 | Richard (II) |
| 1399 | Henry of Monmouth (V) |
| 1454 | Edward of Westminster |
| 1471 | Edward of Westminster (V) |
| 1483 | Edward |
| 1489 | Arthur Tudor |
| 1504 | Henry Tudor (VIII) |
| 1610 | Henry Stuart |
| 1616 | Charles Stuart (I) |
| c. 1638 | Charles (II) |
| 1688 | James Francis Edward (Old Pretender) |
| 1714 | George Augustus (II) |
| 1729 | Frederick Lewis |
| 1751 | George William Frederick (III) |
| 1762 | George Augustus Frederick (IV) |
| 1841 | Albert Edward (Edward VII) |
| 1901 | George (V) |
| 1910 | Edward (VIII) |
| 1958 | Charles Philip Arthur George |

## Wallace, William (1272–1305)

Scottish nationalist who led a revolt against English rule in 1297, won a victory at Stirling, and assumed the title 'governor of Scotland'. Edward I defeated him at Falkirk in 1298, and Wallace was captured and executed. He was styled Knight in a charter of 1298.

## Wallace Collection

Collection of paintings and art objects on display in Hertford House, Manchester Square, London. The works were collected by Richard Wallace (1818–1890), and donated to the nation in 1897. It is one of the finest collections of 18th-century French art.

Much of the collection comes from the royal châteaux, and includes sculpture, furniture, and small *objets d'art*, as well as paintings by Watteau, Boucher, Fragonard, and others. There are also many fine paintings of various national schools, including *Lady with a Fan* by Velázquez and *The Laughing Cavalier* by Frans Hals, and collections of European and Oriental armour.

## Wales: Sovereigns and Princes 844–1282

| | |
|---|---|
| 844–78 | Rhodri the Great |
| 878–916 | Anarawd |
| 915–50 | Hywel Dda (Hywel the Good) |
| 950–79 | Iago ab Idwal |
| 979–85 | Hywel ab Ieuaf (Hywel the Bad) |
| 985–86 | Cadwallon |
| 986–99 | Maredudd ab Owain ap Hywel Dda |
| 999–1008 | Cynan ap Hywel ab Ieuaf |
| 1018–23 | Llywelyn ap Seisyll |
| 1023–39 | Iago ab Idwal ap Meurig |
| 1039–63 | Gruffydd ap Llywelyn ap Seisyll |
| 1063–75 | Bleddyn ap Cynfyn |
| 1075–81 | Trahaern ap Caradog |
| 1081–1137 | Gruffydd ap Cynan ab Iago |
| 1137–70 | Owain Gwynedd |
| 1170–94 | Dafydd ab Owain Gwynedd |
| 1194–1240 | Llywelyn Fawr (Llywelyn the Great) |
| 1240–46 | Dafydd ap Llywellyn |
| 1246–82 | Llywellyn ap Gruffydd ap Llywellyn |

## Wallington

House and estate in Northumberland, England, 18 km/11 mi west of Morpeth. The house contains collections of porcelain, paintings and furniture. There is a conservatory in the walled garden. The 5,250 ha/12,967 acre estate was given to the National Trust by Charles Trevelyan in 1942. The estate includes 16 farms and most of the village of Cambo besides the late 17th-century house which was largely redesigned around 1740.

## Wallis, Barnes (1887–1979)

British aeronautical engineer who designed the airship R-100, and during World War II perfected the 'bouncing bombs' used by the Royal Air Force Dambusters Squadron to destroy the German Möhne and Eder dams in 1943. He also assisted in the development of the Concorde supersonic airliner and developed the swing wing aircraft. He was knighted in 1968.

## Wallsend

Town in Tyne and Wear, northeast England, on the River Tyne at the east end of Hadrian's Wall; population (1991) 44,500. The Swan Hunter shipyards were closed in 1994 following the launch of the last ship to be built in the northeast.

Wallsend was the site of the Roman fort of **Segedunum**; relics excavated from the site are displayed in a heritage centre. The 19th-century engineer George Stephenson, and his son Robert who was also an engineer, lived here.

## Walmer

Resort in Kent, southeast England, south of Deal; population (1991) 2,300. Its castle, built for Henry VIII in about 1539, has been the official residence of the Lord Warden of the ◊Cinque Ports since the 18th century. The Duke of Wellington died here in 1852. Walmer is a reputed landing place of Julius Caesar in 55 BC.

## Walpole, Horace, 4th Earl of Orford (1717–1797)

English novelist, letter writer and politician, the son of Robert Walpole, Britain's first prime minister. He was a Whig member of Parliament 1741–67.

He converted his house at Strawberry Hill, Twickenham (then a separate town southwest of London), into a Gothic castle; his *The Castle of Otranto* (1764) established the genre of the Gothic, or 'romance of terror', novel. More than 4,000 of his letters have been published.

## Walsall

Industrial town in West Midlands, central England, 13 km/8 mi northwest of Birmingham; population (1991) 172,600. Walsall's prosperity from early times was due to local deposits of coal and iron ore, and by the 17th century the town was an important industrial centre.

The town has a canal museum and a leather museum. Walsall's art gallery contains the Garman-Ryan collection, over 350 paintings including works by Jacob Epstein. The writer Jerome K Jerome was born here in 1859.

## Walsingham

Village in Norfolk, England, 8 km/5 mi north of Fakenham; population (1991) 1,300. There are ruins of an Augustinian priory founded in 1153, which was a centre of pilgrimage until the time of the Reformation. Pilgrimages to Walsingham were revived in 1921; they centre on the Slipper Chapel (Roman Catholic) 2 km/1 mi from the village, and on an Anglican shrine in the village.

According to tradition, the Virgin Mary appeared before the lady of the manor in 1061, and a shrine was built to 'Our Lady of Walsingham', later incorporated in the church of the

Augustinian priory. The shrine, priory, and a Franciscan friary, dating from the late 13th century, were destroyed at the time of the Reformation.

## Walton, Izaak (1593–1683)
English writer. He is known for his classic fishing compendium *The Compleat Angler, or the Contemplative Man's Recreation* (1653). He also wrote lives of the poets John Donne (1658) and George Herbert (1670) and the theologian Richard Hooker (1665).

*The Compleat Angler* is an autobiographical and philosophical study in the form of a dialogue between an angler, a fowler, and a hunter, with verses, anecdotes, and extracts from folklore.

## Walton, William (1902–1983)
English composer. Among his works are *Façade* (1923), a series of instrumental pieces designed to be played in conjunction with the recitation of surrealist poems by Edith Sitwell; the oratorio *Belshazzar's Feast* (1931); and *Variations on a Theme by Hindemith* (1963).

## Wandsworth
Inner borough of southwest central Greater London; population (1991) 252,400.
### Features
Made famous for hats in the 18th century by influx of Huguenot refugees who were skilled hatters (Roman cardinals ordered their hats from here); mills on River Wandle; Wandsworth Prison (1857); brewing industry (important since the 16th century); Battersea Park and Putney Heath are both in the borough; Battersea Power Station (1937, designed by Giles Gilbert Scott).

## Warrington
Industrial town and administrative headquarters of Warrington unitary authority in northwest England, on the River Mersey, 25 km/16 mi from both Liverpool and Manchester; population (1994 est) 151,000. It was part of the county of Cheshire to 1998, when it became a unitary authority with an area of 176 sq km/68 sq mi. A trading centre since Roman times, it was designated a new town in 1968.

The industrial tradition of Warrington dates back to the medieval period, when it was important for the production of textiles and tools. Industrial expansion took place after the Mersey was made navigable in the 18th century and the ◊Manchester Ship Canal opened in 1894.

The town hall (1750) was designed by the Scottish architect James Gibbs. Warrington Museum and Art Gallery includes over 1,000 paintings. Nearby Risley Moss bog and woodland has nature trails and a visitors' centre.

## Warwick
Market town and administrative headquarters of ◊Warwickshire, central England, 33 km/21 mi southeast of Birmingham, on the River Avon; population (1991) 22,300.
### Warwick Castle
Considered one of the finest medieval castles in England, Warwick contains state rooms, a fine collection of armour, silver vault, dungeon, and ghost tower. It has a reputation for its vivid reconstructions of life in the past.

The first defences were erected here in Saxon times, and a wooden castle with a ditch built around 1065–67 by the Earl of Warwick. The fortifications were strengthened in 1068 by William (I) the Conqueror, and construction of the present stone castle began in 1345. The interior was completely rebuilt in the 17th century, and the Avon-side grounds landscaped in the 18th century by Capability ◊Brown.

## Warwick, Richard Neville, 1st Earl of Warwick (1428–1471)
English politician, called the Kingmaker. During the Wars of the ◊Roses he fought at first on the Yorkist side against the Lancastrians, and was largely responsible for placing Edward IV on the throne. Having quarrelled with him, he restored Henry VI in 1470, but was defeated and killed by Edward at Barnet, Hertfordshire.

## Warwickshire
County of central England; population (1996) 500,600; area 1,980 sq km/764 sq mi. It is described as 'the heart of England' and is associated with William Shakespeare, who was born here. The chief towns and cities are ◊Warwick (administrative headquarters), ◊Nuneaton, Royal ◊Leamington Spa, ◊Rugby, and ◊Stratford-upon-Avon (the birthplace of Shakespeare).
### Physical
The landscape is undulating but the highest point, Ebrington Hill, is only 260 m/853 ft. The rivers Avon, Stour, and Tame flow through it. There are the remains of the 'Forest of Arden' (portrayed by Shakespeare in *As You Like It*).
### Features
Historic sites include ◊Kenilworth and Warwick castles, the latter considered one of the finest medieval castles in England. Edgehill is the site of

**Warwickshire** Stoneleigh Park in Warwickshire, six miles south of the city of Coventry, is the permanent site of the Royal Agricultural Society's annual show. This gathering features the showing of prize livestock, exhibitions of farming machinery, and a showjumping competition. Corel

the Battle of Edgehill in 1642, during the English Civil War. The Beauchamp Chapel of St Mary's church, Warwick, is noteworthy, and there are the remains of a Cistercian monastery at Coombe Abbey, with remains of other religious houses at Kenilworth, Maxstoke, Merevale, Stoneleigh, and Wroxall. Stratford-upon-Avon has Shakespeare's birthplace, Anne Hathaway's cottage (his wife's home), and their graves in Holy Trinity Church. Notable houses include the 17th-century Ragley Hall. The annual Royal Agricultural Show is held at Stoneleigh Park.

*Economy*
Tourism is important in Stratford-upon-Avon and Warwick. The economy also depends on agriculture and the motor industry and electrical and general engineering. Ironstone and lime are worked in the east and south.

## Wash, the
Bay of the North Sea between Norfolk and Lincolnshire, eastern England; 24 km/15 mi long, 40 km/25 mi wide. The rivers Nene, Ouse, Welland, and Witham drain into the Wash. In 1992, 10,120 ha/25,000 acres of the mudflats, marshes, and sand banks on its shores were designated a national nature reserve.

Much of the land adjacent to the Wash has been reclaimed. King John is said to have lost his baggage and treasure while crossing it in 1216.

## Washington
Town in Tyne and Wear, northeast England, 8 km/5 mi southeast of Newcastle upon Tyne, on the River Wear; population (1991) 55,800. Industries include electronics and car assembly. It was designated a new town in 1964.

From 1113 to 1613 Washington Old Hall was the home of the ancestors of George Washington, first president of the United States. The hall was originally built in the 12th century, and rebuilt in the 17th. There is a Wildfowl and Wetlands Trust reserve nearby, established in 1975, whose wildlife includes swans, geese, ducks, and flamingos. Beamish Open-Air Museum is nearby to the west.

## watercolour painting
The art of painting with pigments mixed with water, as practised today, began in England in the 18th century with the work of Paul ◊ Sandby, and was developed by Thomas ◊ Girtin, John Sell ◊ Cotman, and J M W ◊ Turner. The technique, which was was known in China as early as the 3rd century, requires great skill since its transparency rules out overpainting. Artists excelling in watercolour include J R ◊ Cozens, Peter ◊ de Wint, John

◊Constable, David Cox (1783–1859), John Singer Sargent (1856–1925), and Philip Wilson ◊Steer. Paul ◊Nash and John Piper (1903–1992) were among the greatest 20th-century exponents, and in his celebrated World War II drawings of Londoners sheltering in the Underground, Henry ◊Moore used a novel combination of ink, watercolour, and wax. More recently, David Hockney and R B Kitaj have made memorable use of the medium.

The Royal Society of Painters in Water Colours was founded in 1804.

## Waterloo, Battle of

Final battle of the Napoleonic Wars on 18 June 1815 in which a coalition force of British, Prussian, and Dutch troops under the Duke of Wellington defeated Napoleon near the village of Waterloo, 13 km/8 mi south of Brussels, Belgium. Napoleon found Wellington's army isolated from his allies and began a direct offensive to smash them, but the British held on until joined by the Prussians under Marshal Gebhard von Blücher. Four days later Napoleon abdicated for the second and final time.

## Watford

Industrial town in Hertfordshire, southeast England, on the River Colne, 24 km/15 mi northwest of London; population (1991) 110,500. It is a commuter town for London.

St Mary's Church, dating from the 13th century, includes a 16th-century Essex chapel. Other features include almshouses dating from 1590; Monmouth House (17th century); Free School (1704); and Frogmore House (1715).

## Watling Street

Roman road running from London to Wroxeter (*Viroconium*) near Shrewsbury, in central England. Its name derives from *Waetlingacaester*, the Anglo-Saxon name for St Albans, through which it passed.

## Watt, James (1736–1819)

Scottish engineer who developed the steam engine in the 1760s, making Thomas ◊Newcomen's engine vastly more efficient by cooling the used steam in a condenser separate from the main cylinder. He eventually made a double-acting machine that supplied power with both directions of the piston and developed rotary motion. He also invented devices associated with the steam engine, artistic instruments and a copying process, and devised the horsepower as a description of an engine's rate of working. The modern unit of power, the watt, is named after him.

Watt was born in Greenock (now in Strathclyde) and trained as an instrument-maker. Between 1767 and 1774, he made his living as a canal surveyor. In 1775 Boulton and Watt went into partnership and manufactured Watt's engines at the Soho Foundry, near Birmingham. Watt's original engine of 1765 is now in the Science Museum, London.

## Waugh, Evelyn (1903–1966)

English novelist. His humorous social satires include *Decline and Fall* (1928), *Vile Bodies* (1930), *Scoop* (1938), and *The Loved One* (1948). He developed a serious concern with religious issues in *Brideshead Revisited* (1945), successfully dramatized for television in the 1980s. *The Ordeal of Gilbert Pinfold* (1957) is largely autobiographical.

Waugh was born in London and studied at Oxford University. In 1927 he published a life of the Pre-Raphaelite Dante Gabriel Rossetti, and in 1928 the first of his satirical novels, *Decline and Fall*; others are *Black Mischief* (1932), *A Handful of Dust* (1934), and *Put Out More Flags* (1942). These novels are witty and at the same time biting attacks on contemporary society.

After World War II his writing took a more intentionally serious turn, and he produced the trilogy *Men at Arms* (1952), *Officers and Gentlemen* (1955), and *Unconditional Surrender* (1961), in which he attempted to analyse the war as a struggle between good and evil.

## Weald, the, or the Kent Weald (Old English 'forest')

Area between the North and South Downs, England, a raised tract of forest 64 km/40 mi wide. It forms part of Kent, Sussex, Surrey, and Hampshire. Once thickly wooded, it is now an agricultural area producing fruit, hops, and vegetables. In the Middle Ages its timber and iron ore made it the industrial heart of England.

The village of ◊Penshurst, 8 km/5 mi northwest of Tunbridge Wells, is a tourist centre. Features include ◊Hever Castle and Penshurst Place. Other villages in the Weald include Forrest Row, Cranbrook, Mayfield, Hawkhurst, and Tenterden. Ashdown Forest, originally a Norman hunting forest, is a tourist destination.

## weather

The climate of Britain is notoriously variable and changeable from day to day. Weather is generally cool to mild with frequent cloud and rain, but occasional settled spells of weather occur at all seasons. Visitors are often surprised by the long summer days, which are a consequence of the northerly latitude; in the north of Scotland in midsummer the day is 18 hours long and twilight lasts all night. Conversely, winter days are short.

While the south is usually a little warmer than the north and the west wetter than the east, the continual changes of weather mean that, on occasions, these differences may be reversed. Extremes of weather are rare but they do occur. For example, in December 1981 and January 1982, parts of southern and central England experienced for a few days lower temperatures than central Europe and Moscow. During the long spells of hot, sunny weather in the summers of 1975 and 1976 parts of Britain were drier and warmer than many places in the western Mediterranean.

The greatest extremes of weather and climate occur in the mountains of Scotland, Wales, and northern England. Here at altitudes exceeding 600 m/2,000 ft conditions are wet and cloudy for much of the year with annual rainfall exceeding 1,500 mm/60 in and in places reaching as much as 5,000 mm/200 in. These are among the wettest places in Europe. Winter conditions may be severe with very strong winds, driving rain, or snow blizzards.

In spite of occasional heavy snowfalls on the Scottish mountains, conditions are not reliable for skiing and there has been only a limited development of winter sports resorts. Because of the severe conditions which can arise very suddenly on mountains, walkers and climbers who go unprepared face the risk of exposure or even frostbite. Conditions may be vastly different from those suggested by the weather at lower levels.

### Settlement level

Virtually all permanent settlement in Britain lies below 300 m/1,000 ft, and at these levels weather conditions are usually much more congenial. As a general rule the western side of Britain is cloudier, wetter, and milder in winter, than the east, with cooler summers. The eastern side of Britain is

## British Weather: Some key dates and extreme conditions

**1703** A great storm sweeps across Britain, devastating the countryside, killing thousands of people, and destroying the Eddystone Lighthouse at Plymouth.

**1869** English meteorologist Alexander Buchan produces the first weather maps showing the average monthly and annual air pressure for the world. They provide information about the atmosphere's circulation.

**1875** *The Times* newspaper starts publishing the first generally available daily weather forecasts.

**1922** The British meteorologist Lewis Fry Richardson publishes *Weather Prediction by Numerical Process*, in which he applies the first mathematical techniques to weather forecasting.

**26 March 1923** The BBC begins broadcasting daily weather forecasts in Britain.

**1947** Severe winter weather badly disrupts the sporting programme in Britain. All racing fixtures between 22 January and 15 March are called off, and the English Football League season is not concluded until 14 June.

**29 July 1949** The first weather forecast is broadcast on British television: it consists of a voice-over only.

**December 1952** Smog hits London: weather conditions and industrial and domestic pollution combine to produce a haze of toxic pollutants, which limit visibility to a few feet. It lasts for three weeks, and over 4,000 people, mostly elderly, die from respiratory problems caused by poor air quality. The disaster leads to antipollution legislation.

**August 1952** 22.5 cm/9 in of rainfall within 24 hours on Exmoor causes disastrous flooding at Lynmouth, leaving 34

people dead and the harbour and over 100 buildings severely damaged.

**11 January 1954** George Cowling of the Meteorological Office becomes the first weather forecaster to appear on British television.

**May 1961** The Atlas computer, the world's largest (with one megabyte of memory), is installed at Harwell, Oxfordshire; as well as undertaking atomic research, it aids weather forecasting.

**15 January 1962** British weather reports start giving temperatures in centigrade as well as Fahrenheit.

**1973–82** The Thames flood barrier in London, England, is constructed.

**16 October 1987** A great storm, which weather forecasters fail to predict, sweeps across southeast England, killing 17 people and felling 15 million trees. Reckoned to be the worst storm in Britain for 300 years, it does £1.7 billion of damage.

**24–26 December 1997** A fierce storm with winds up to 130 kph/80 mph hits southern England, killing 13 people and leaving thousands of homes without electricity.

**3–4 January 1998** Violent storms sweep through Britain and Ireland, bringing winds up to 160 kph/100 mph and claiming two lives.

**10–11 April 1998** The eastern and central regions of England experience the worst flooding in 50 years, resulting in five deaths and estimated damage of up to £500 million.

drier, with a tendency for summer rain to be heavier than that of winter. Much of central England has very similar weather to that of the east and south of the country. Southwestern England shares the greater summer warmth of southern England but experiences rather milder and wetter winters than the east of the country.

*Northern Ireland*

Northern Ireland shares with the rest of the British Isles a mild, changeable climate with very rare extremes of heat or cold. Ireland is even more influenced by the warm waters of the North Atlantic than England and, consequently, its climate is a little wetter the year round, milder in winter and cooler and cloudier in summer. This mild, rainy climate is particularly favourable to the growth of grass and moss and for this reason Ireland has been called the Emerald Isle.

## Webster, John (c. 1580–c. 1625)

English dramatist. His reputation rests on two tragedies, *The White Devil* (1612) and *The Duchess of Malfi* (c.1613). Though both show the preoccupation with melodramatic violence and horror typical of the Jacobean revenge tragedy, they are also remarkable for their poetry and psychological insight. He collaborated with a number of other dramatists, notably with Thomas Dekker (c.1572–c.1632) on the comedy *Westward Ho* (c.1606).

Born in London, he was the son of a tailor and was apprenticed to the same trade, becoming a freeman of the Merchant Taylors' Company in 1603. But he was also active in the theatre by 1602, working on collaborations and perhaps also acting. His first independent work was *The White Devil*, printed (and probably first performed) in 1612.

## Wedgwood, Josiah (1730–1795)

English pottery manufacturer. He set up business in Staffordshire in the early 1760s to produce his agateware as well as unglazed blue or green stoneware (jasper) decorated with white neo-Classical designs, using pigments of his own invention.

Wedgwood was born in Burslem, Staffordshire, and worked in the family pottery. Eventually he set up in business on his own at the Ivy House Factory in Burslem, and there he perfected cream-colonial earthenware, which became known as queen's ware because of the interest and patronage of Queen Charlotte in 1765. In 1768 he expanded the company into the Brick House Bell Works Factory. He then built the Etruria

Factory, using his engineering skills in the design of machinery and the high-temperature beehive-shaped kilns, which were more than 4 m/12 ft wide.

## Wellington, Arthur Wellesley, 1st Duke of Wellington (1769–1852)

British soldier and Tory politician. As commander in the ◊Peninsular War, he expelled the French from Spain in 1814. He defeated Napoleon Bonaparte at Quatre-Bras and ◊Waterloo in 1815, and was a member of the Congress of Vienna. As prime minister 1828–30, he was forced to concede Roman Catholic emancipation. His home in London was ◊Apsley House; Parliament also granted him an estate at ◊Stratfield Saye following his victory at Waterloo.

## Wells

Cathedral city and market town in Somerset, southwest England, at the foot of the Mendip Hills; population (1991) 9,900. Tourism is the economic mainstay. The cathedral, built near the site of a Saxon church in the 12th and 13th centuries, has a west front with 386 carved figures. Wells was made the seat of a bishopric about 909 (Bath and Wells from 1244) and has a 13th-century bishop's palace.

Ine, king of Wessex, is said to have founded the first church in Wells in 704. The bishop's palace, the residence of the Bishop of Bath and Wells, is moated and surrounded by a defensive wall. It includes the natural wells from which the town derives its name. Other features include the 15th-century deanery and Vicar's Close, a well-preserved medieval street.

*Wells Cathedral*

Begun in the late 12th century, the central parts of the building are in the Transitional ◊style of that period. Jocelin, bishop from 1206 to 1242, built the rest of the nave, the west front, and the north porch, all of which are superb examples of ◊Early English architecture.

The west front, once painted, has a gallery of medieval statuary unrivalled in England;. The cathedral also contains excellent 14th-century stained glass, misericord seats of around 1340, and a clock of around 1390.

## Wells, H(erbert) G(eorge) (1866–1946)

English writer. He was a pioneer of science fiction with such novels as *The Time Machine* (1895) and *The War of the Worlds* (1898), which describes a Martian invasion of Earth and brought him nationwide recognition. His later novels had an anti-establishment, anti-conventional humour remarkable in its day, for example *Kipps* (1905) and *Tono-Bungay* (1909).

---

*In England we have come to rely upon a comfortable time lag of fifty years or a century intervening between the perception that something ought to be done and a serious attempt to do it.*

**H G Wells** English writer.
'The Work, Wealth and Happiness of Mankind'
(1932)

---

Wells was a prophet of world organization. His theme was the need for humans to impose their mastery upon their own creations and to establish benevolent systems and structures by which to rule themselves, and in pursuing this concept he became a leading advocate of social planning. A number of prophecies described in fictional works such as *The First Men in the Moon* (1901) and *The Shape of Things to Come* (1933), as well as in *The Outline of History* (1920) and other popular nonfiction works, have been fulfilled; among them, the significance of aviation, tank warfare,

World War II, and the atomic bomb. He also wrote many short stories.

His social novels explored with humour and sympathy the condition of ordinary lower middle- and working-class people. They include *Love and Mr Lewisham* (1900), *Ann Veronica* (1909), a feminist novel, *The History of Mr Polly* (1910), and *Marriage* (1912).

## Welsh assembly

See ◊National Assembly for Wales.

## Welsh language, in Welsh, Cymraeg

Member of the Celtic branch of the Indo-European language family, spoken chiefly in the rural north and west of Wales. Spoken by 18.7% of the Welsh population, it is the strongest of the surviving ◊Celtic languages.

Welsh has been in decline in the face of English expansion since the accession of the Welsh Henry Tudor (as Henry VII) to the throne of England in 1485. Nowadays few Welsh people speak only Welsh; they are either bilingual or speak only English.

During the late 20th century the decline of Welsh slowed: from about 900,000 speakers at the

---

**Welsh Language** Welsh is spoken by around 500,000 inhabitants of the principality, mainly in the north and west. To promote Welsh as a vigorous living language, it was made a compulsory element of the National Curriculum for Wales, and bilingual education is encouraged in schools. Bruce Stephens/Impact

turn of the century, the number had shrunk to half a million in 1995. However, due to vigorous campaigning and efforts to promote the language, made by the ◊S4C (Sianel Pedwar Cymru) television network, and the Welsh Language Society, and to some extent elsewhere in literature and the media, the numbers speaking Welsh has stabilized. According to a survey, in 1995 21% of the Welsh population spoke the national tongue; of that number, it was the mother tongue of 55%. Use of the language among young people increased as a result of its inclusion in the national curriculum; in 1993–94, 78.4% of Welsh pupils learnt it as either first or second language. See table of Welsh words borrowed into English, on page 492.

## Welsh literature

The prose and poetry of Wales, written predominantly in Welsh but also, more recently, in English. Characteristic of Welsh poetry is the bardic system. In the 18th century the ◊eisteddfod (literary festival) movement brought a revival of classical forms.

### Ancient literature

The chief remains of early Welsh literature are contained in the Four Ancient Books of Wales – the *Black Book of Carmarthen*, the *Book of Taliesin*, the *Book of Aneirin*, and the *Red Book of Hergest* – anthologies of prose and verse of the 6th–14th centuries. The bardic system ensured the continuance of traditional conventions; most celebrated of the 12th-century bards was Cynddelw Brydydd Mawr (active 1155–1200).

### Literature after the English conquest

The English conquest of 1282 involved the fall of the princes who supported these bards, but after a period of decline a new school arose in South Wales with a new freedom in form and sentiment, the most celebrated poet in the 14th-century being ◊Dafydd ap Gwilym, and in the next century the classical metrist Dafydd ap Edmwnd (active 1450–1459). With the Reformation, biblical translations were undertaken, and Morgan Llwyd (1619–1659) and Ellis Wynne (1671–1734) wrote religious prose. Popular metres resembling those of England developed – for example, the poems of Huw Morys (1622–1709).

### Classical revival

Goronwy Owen revived the classical poetic forms in the 18th century, and the ◊eisteddfod movement began: popular measures were used by the hymn writer William Williams Pantycelyn (1717–1791).

### Second revival

The 19th century saw few notable figures, but the foundation of a Welsh university and the work there of John Morris Jones (1864–1929) produced a 20th-century revival, including T Gwynn Jones (1871–1949), W J Gruffydd (1881–1954), and R Williams Parry (1884–1956). Later writers included the poet J Kitchener Davies (1902–1952), the dramatist and poet Saunders Lewis (1893–1985), and the novelist and short-story writer Kate Roberts (1891–1985). Among writers of the period after World War II are the poets Waldo Williams (1904–1971), Euros Bowen (1904– ), and Bobi Jones (1929– ), and the novelists Islwyn Ffowc Elis (1924– ) and Jane Edwards (1938– ).

### Welsh writers in English

Those who have expressed the Welsh spirit in English include the poets Edward Thomas (1878–1917), Vernon Watkins (1906–67),

## The Welsh National Anthem: 'Wlad Fy Nhadau/Land Of My Fathers'

The words are given in Welsh and English.

### Wlad Fy Nhadau

Mae hen wlad fy nhadau yn annwyl i mi
Gwlad beirdd a chantorion, enwogion o fri
Ei gwrol ryfelwyr, gwladgarwyr tra mad
Tros ryddid collasant eu gwaed.
Gwlad, gwlad, pleidiol wyf i'm gwlad
Tra mor yn fur i'r bur hoffbau
O bydded i'r heniaith barhau.
Hen Gymru fynyddig, paradwys y bardd
Pob dyffryn, pob clogwyn i'm golwg sydd hardd
Trwy deimlad gwladgarol, mor swynol yw si
Ei nentydd, afonydd, i mi.
Os treisiodd y gelyn fy ngwlad tan ei droed
Mae hen iaith y Cymry mor fyw ag erioed
Ni luddiwyd yr awen gan erchyll law brad
Na thelyn berseiniol fy ngwlad.

### Land of My Fathers

The land of my fathers is dear unto me
Old land where the minstrels are honoured and free
Its warring defenders so gallant and brave
For freedom their life's blood they gave.
Home, home, true am I to home
While seas secure the land so pure
O may the old language endure.
Old land of the mountains, the Eden of bards
Each gorge and each valley a loveliness guards
Through love of my country, charmed voices will be
Its streams, and its rivers, to me.
Though foemen have trampled my land 'neath their feet
The language of Cambria still knows no retreat
The muse is not vanquished by traitor's fell hand.

## Welsh Words Borrowed into English

| | | |
|---|---|---|
| cromlech | 17th century | ('arched stone') a megalithic chamber tomb or dolmen; standing stone(s) |
| englyn | 17th century | a four-line stanza of prescribed form written in *cynghanedd* metre |
| flummery | 17th century | (unknown origin) a pudding made with coagulated wheatflour or oatmeal; mere flattery or nonsense |
| gorsedd | 18th century | ('throne') a meeting of bards and druids, preliminary to an *eisteddfod* |
| cynghanedd | 19th century | a complex form of alliterative metre |
| cwm | 19th century | a valley; a deep rounded hollow with a steep side formed by a glacier; a cirque |
| eisteddfod | 19th century | ('session') a festival of poetry, singing, and music; a congress of Welsh bards and minstrels |
| hwyl | 19th century | emotional fervour, characteristic of poetry recitation |
| corgi | 20th century | ('dwarf-dog') either of two breeds of short-legged dogs, originally from Wales |

Dylan ♢Thomas, R S Thomas (1913– ), and Dannie Abse (1923– ), and the novelist Emyr Humphreys (1919– ).

**Welsh National Opera**, Opera Cenedlaethol Cymru
Welsh opera company founded in 1946 and based in Cardiff. It tours regularly in Wales and England.

### Wembley Stadium
Sports ground in north London, completed in 1923 for the British Empire Exhibition 1924–25 and now undergoing complete rebuilding, due to be finished in 2003. The ground has been the scene of the annual Football Association (FA) Cup final since 1923. The 1948 Olympic Games and many concerts, including the Live Aid concert of 1985, were held here. Adjacent to the main stadium, which will hold 99,000 people, all seated, are the Wembley indoor arena (which holds about 10,000, depending on the event) and conference centre.

The largest recorded crowd at Wembley is 126,047 for its first FA Cup final; the capacity has since been reduced by additional seating. England play most of their home soccer matches at Wembley. Other sports events over the years have included show jumping, American football, Rugby League, Rugby Union, hockey, Gaelic football, hurling, and baseball.

### Wensleydale
Upper valley of the River Ure in North Yorkshire, England, within the Pennine highlands. It lies largely in the Yorkshire ♢Dales national park, beginning southeast of Middleham and extending to near the source of the river northwest of Hawes,

one of the area's largest towns. The dale gives its name to a type of cheese and a breed of sheep with long wool.

The village of **Wensley** has a 15th-century bridge across the Ure and a 13th-century church. Bolton Castle nearby is a 14th-century fortified mansion, where Mary Queen of Scots was imprisoned in 1568.

### Wesley, John (1703–1791)
English founder of ♢Methodism. When the pulpits of the Church of England were closed to him and his followers, he took the gospel to the people. For 50 years he rode about the country on horseback, preaching daily, largely in the open air. His sermons became the doctrinal standard of the Wesleyan Methodist Church.

Wesley went to Oxford University together with his brother Charles, where their circle was nicknamed Methodists because of their religious observances. He was ordained in the Church of England in 1728 and in 1735 he went to Georgia, USA, as a missionary. On his return he experienced 'conversion' in 1738, and from being rigidly High Church developed into an ardent Evangelical.

### Wessex
The kingdom of the West Saxons in Britain, said to have been founded by Cerdic about AD 500, covering present-day Hampshire, Dorset, Wiltshire, Berkshire, Somerset, and Devon. In 829 Egbert established West Saxon supremacy over all England. See genealogy opposite.

Thomas ♢Hardy used the term Wessex in his novels for the southwest counties of England;

drawing on England's west country, the heartland was Dorset but its outlying boundary markers were Plymouth, Bath, Oxford, and Southampton. He gave fictional names to such real places as Dorchester (Casterbridge), Salisbury (Melchester) and Bournemouth (Sandbourne) but mixed these with a sprinkling of real names such as Stonehenge, the River Frome, and Nettlecombe Tout.

## West, Rebecca pen name of Cicily Isabel Fairfield (1892–1983)

English journalist and novelist, an active feminist from 1911. Her novels, of which the semi-autobiographical *The Fountain Overflows* (1956) and *The Birds Fall Down* (1966) are regarded as the best, demonstrate a social and political awareness.

*The Meaning of Treason* (1947) was reissued as *The New Meaning of Treason* in 1964, which included material on the spies Guy ◊Burgess and Donald ◊Maclean.

## West Berkshire

Unitary authority in southeast England, created in 1998 from part of the former county of Berkshire; population (1996) 142,600; area 705 sq km/272 sq mi. It is known particularly for horseracing. The chief towns are ◊Newbury (administrative headquarters), Hungerford, and Lambourn.

### Physical

The rivers Kennet and Lambourn flow through the authority, which is also crossed by the Kennet and Avon Canal. The area has the highest chalk hills in England, Inkpen Hill (291 m/854 ft) and Walbury Hill (297 m/974 ft).

### Features

Inkpen Hill has a Stone Age tomb and Walbury Hill an Iron Age fort. Newbury has an important racecourse. Snelsmore Common Country Park covers 59 ha/146 acres including wetland habitats; Thatcham Moors reedbeds are designated Sites of Special Scientific Interest. ◊Greenham Common Women's Peace Camp has been the site

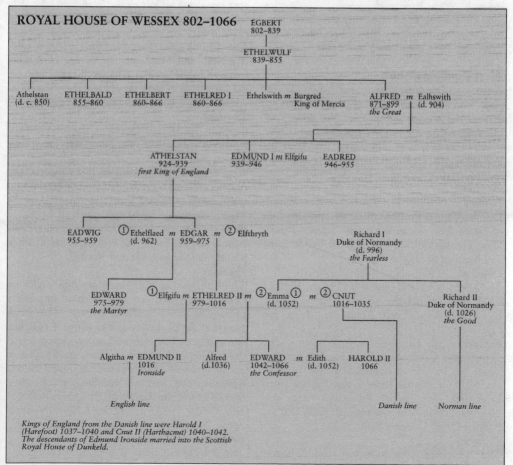

**ROYAL HOUSE OF WESSEX 802–1066**

Kings of England from the Danish line were Harold I (Harefoot) 1037–1040 and Cnut II (Harthacnut) 1040–1042. The descendants of Edmund Ironside married into the Scottish Royal House of Dunkeld.

of campaigning against nuclear weapons development at Greenham, Burghfield, and Aldermaston since 1981.

### Economy

Besides agriculture (dairy cattle, pig farming, including the local Berkshire pig), part of the local economy depends on horseracing, with training stables at Lambourn, East Ilsley, and West Ilsley. There is also a growing high-technology industry and commerce.

## West Bromwich

Industrial town in West Midlands, central England, 9 km/6 mi northwest of Birmingham, on the edge of the Black Country; population (1991) 144,700.

West Bromwich developed from the amalgamation of a collection of hamlets on the Tame, as small ironworks appeared; the discovery of coal in the vicinity led to the town's rapid development. With the completion in 1769 of a canal passing through West Bromwich, ancillary industries soon developed, and forges, furnaces, and foundries were established. In 1819 the population was 9,000; by 1854 it had risen to 36,500.

## West Dunbartonshire

Unitary authority in west central Scotland, created in 1996 from parts of two districts of Strathclyde region and part of the county of Dunbartonshire prior to 1975; population (1996) 97,800; area 177 sq km/68 sq mi. It is an industrial area. The main towns are ◊Dumbarton (administrative headquarters), Clydebank, and Alexandria.

### History

Dumbarton was the heart of the ancient kingdom of Strathclyde. As an important industrial area, West Dunbartonshire was targeted by Germans and bombed in World War II.

### Physical

The Leven valley and coastal land of the Firth of Clyde rise toward the upland plateau of the Kilpatrick Hills. Loch ◊Lomond is in the northwest.

### Features

Dumbarton Castle dates from the 6th century. There are 14 Sites of Special Scientific Interest, one National Nature Reserve, one Ramsar (wetland site), one Special Protection Area, one National Scenic Area, one regional park, and the Balloch Castle Country Park.

### Economy

The authority comes within the Glasgow economy. The area is undergoing transition as it seeks to redevelop following the loss of its industrial base; light manufacturing and service industries are emerging.

## Western Isles, also known as the Outer Hebrides

Island administrative unitary authority area in Scotland; population (1996) 27,800; area 3,057 sq km/1,180 sq mi. It includes the major islands of ◊Lewis (or Harris-with-Lewis), North and South Uist, Benbecula, and Barra. Harris and Lewis are often assumed to be two islands, but they are linked by a narrow neck of land. The chief towns are Stornoway on Lewis (administrative headquarters), Castlebay, Lochboisdale, Lochmaddy, and Tarbert. The Gaelic language and culture are thriving on the islands.

### History

A long history of settlement has left Stone, Bronze, and Iron Age remains, including those at ◊Callanish. From the 8th to 13th centuries the area remained subject to the Scandinavians; sites with remains are rare but language, customs, and place names are strongly related to this period. Associations with strong clans such as Macdonald, MacNeil, and MacLeod, the escape of Bonnie Prince Charlie (Prince Charles Edward Stuart), the formation of large estates and the 'clearances' are all integral parts of the history of this area.

### Physical

Open to the Atlantic Ocean on the west and the stormy Minch to the east, the islands are almost treeless and have extensive peat bogs. There are areas of hills and mountains on all the islands. The only fertile land is the sandy Machair on the west coast. Lewis is divided from the mainland by the Minch channel. The islands south of Lewis are divided from the Inner Hebrides by the Little Minch and the Sea of the Hebrides; uninhabited islands include St Kilda and Rockall.

### Features

The Callanish monolithic Stone Age circles on Lewis are regarded as one of the most impressive prehistoric monuments in Britain. The Black House at Arnol, Lewis, is a traditional thatched island house. The Butt of Lewis lighthouse is at the northern tip of Lewis. There are 53 Sites of Special Scientific Interest, four National Nature Reserves, two Ramsars (wetland sites), seven Special Protection Areas, two Biosphere Reserves, one World Heritage Site, and three National Scenic Areas.

### Economy

The main occupations of farming, weaving, and fishing are related to the crofting form of land holding and settlement. The larger settlements are all ports on the indented east side of all the main islands. Apart from the Harris ◊ tweed mills, there is little industry. Tourism is increasingly important. There are good air and sea connections from the larger islands.

## West Lothian

Unitary authority in central Scotland, south of the Firth of Forth and bordering the unitary authority of Edinburgh to the east; population (1996) 147,900; area 428 sq km/165 sq mi. It was previously a district within Lothian region (1975–96) and a county until 1974. The chief towns are Bathgate, Linlithgow, and Livingston (administrative headquarters).

### Physical

The area is low-lying and undulating area, with the River Almond flowing through it.

### Features

There is a prehistoric ritual site at Cairnpapple Hill, near Torpichen. The ruined Linlithgow Palace was once a royal residence and was the birthplace of Mary Queen of Scots. There are 17 Sites of Special Scientific Interest, one National Nature Reserve, one regional park, and three country parks.

### Economy

The area has a buoyant economy with the expansion of the development of the electronics industry.

## West Midlands

Metropolitan county of central England, created in 1974; population (1996) 2,642,500; area 900 sq km/347 sq mi. In 1986 most of the functions of the former county council were transferred to the metropolitan borough councils. The principal towns and cities are ◊ Birmingham, ◊ Coventry, ◊ Dudley, ◊ Solihull, ◊ Walsall, ◊ Wolverhampton (all administrative centres for districts of the same name), and Oldbury (administrative centre for Sandwell).

### History

Towards the end of the Middle Ages, Coventry became an important centre of the cloth trade. Metalworking began at Birmingham in the 16th century, but the town remained very small until the Industrial Revolution, when the presence of coal and iron ore transformed it into an industrial boom town. The Birmingham area and the nearby ◊ Black Country became highly industrialized, notoriously grimy, and densely populated. An enormous range of metal goods was manufactured. The area was substantially redeveloped in the 20th century.

### Physical

The county is almost entirely one urban conurbation.

### Features

High-rise buildings and new shopping centres are part of the 20th-century redevelopment of the area.

### Economy

The modern economy is dependent on a range of manufacturing, including aircraft and motor components, motor vehicles (Land Rover at Solihull), chemicals, electrical equipment, glass, and machine tools. Coal mining continues.

## Westminster, City of

Inner borough of central Greater London, on the north bank of the River Thames between Kensington and the City of London. It encompasses Bayswater, Belgravia, Mayfair, Paddington, Pimlico, Soho, St John's Wood, and Westminster; population (1991) 174,800.

### Features:

**Bayswater** a residential and hotel area north of Kensington Gardens; ◊ Tyburn, near ◊ Marble Arch, site of public executions until 1783.

**Belgravia** bounded to the north by Knightsbridge, has squares laid out 1825–30 by Thomas Cubitt; Grosvenor estate.

**Mayfair** between Oxford Street and Piccadilly, includes Park Lane and Grosvenor Square (with the US embassy).

**Paddington** includes Little Venice on the Grand Union Canal.

**Pimlico** has the ◊ Tate Gallery (Turner collection, British, and modern art); developed by Thomas Cubitt in 1830s.

**Soho** has many restaurants and a Chinese community around Gerrard Street. It was formerly known for strip clubs and sex shops.

**St John's Wood** has ◊ Lord's cricket ground and the studios at 3 Abbey Road where the Beatles recorded their music; famous residents included Edwin Landseer, Thomas Henry Huxley, George Frampton.

**Westminster** encompasses ◊ Buckingham Palace (royal residence), Green Park, St James's Park and ◊ St James's Palace (16th century), Marlborough House, ◊ Westminster Abbey, Westminster Hall (1097–1401), the only surviving part of the Palace of Westminster built by William II, the Houses of ◊ Parliament with Big Ben, ◊ Whitehall (government offices), ◊ Downing Street (homes of the prime minister at number 10 and the chancellor of the Exchequer at number 11), ◊ Hyde Park with the ◊ Albert Memorial (1876) opposite the ◊ Royal

Albert Hall (1871), ◊Trafalgar Square with the ◊National Gallery, the ◊National Portrait Gallery, and the church of St Martin in the Fields (designed by James Gibb 1722–24). The Palace of Westminster, Westminster Abbey, and St Margaret's Church are a World Heritage site.

## Westminster Abbey

Gothic church in central London, officially the Collegiate Church of St Peter. It was built 1050–1745 and consecrated under Edward the Confessor in 1065. Since William I nearly all English monarchs have been crowned in the abbey, and several are buried here, including Edward the Confessor, Henry III, Edward I, Henry VII, Elizabeth I, Mary Queen of Scots, Charles II, William III, Anne, and George II. Some 30 scientists, among them Isaac Newton and James Prescott, are also interred or commemorated here. Poets' Corner was established with the burial of Edmund Spenser in 1599. In the centre of the nave is the tomb of an 'Unknown Warrior' of World War I.

Fragments of Edward the Confessor's immense Romanesque church are embodied in the present building which was begun in 1245 by Henry III. Structurally, it is a French church, but much of the detail is English. The chapter-house was built

from 1245 to 1250 and is one of the largest in England. From the reign of Edward I until 1547 Parliament generally met here. It was completely restored by Gilbert Scott in 1865. The king's treasure chamber was once the crypt under the chapter-house. The west towers are by Nicholas ◊Hawksmoor, completed after his death in 1745.

Until recently the Coronation Chair included the Stone of ◊Scone on which Scottish kings were crowned, and which was brought here by Edward I in 1296. On the back of the tomb of Philippa of Hainault is the Westminster Retable, a 13th-century oak altarpiece with what is considered to be probably the finest early medieval painting in Europe.

Westminster School, a public school with ancient and modern buildings nearby, was once the abbey school. The Norman undercroft of the dormitory is now the abbey museum.

## Westminster Bridge

Bridge spanning the River Thames in central London, overlooking the House of Commons. Designed by Thomas Page between 1854 and 1862, it is a steel bridge 247 m/810 ft long. At its western end is a large statue of ◊Boudicca, Queen of the Iceni, (1902) by Thomas Thorneycroft.

The original Westminster Bridge was built between 1739 and 1750 by the Swiss architect Charles Labelye. Before that, the only bridge across the Thames in London was London Bridge.

The original bridge inspired the sonnet by William Wordsworth 'Upon Westminster Bridge' (1802).

## Westminster Cathedral

Roman Catholic Metropolitan church in London. The site, part of what was once known as Tothill Fields, was acquired by Cardinal Manning. His successor, Cardinal Vaughan, supervised the building of the cathedral, from 1895 to 1903. The architect, John Francis Bentley, designed a remarkable building in Early Byzantine style. The Stations of the Cross on the piers were carved by Eric Gill.

## Weston-super-Mare

Seaside resort and administrative headquarters (from 1996) of North Somerset unitary authority, southwest England, 32 km/20 mi from Bristol, on

**Westminster Abbey** Situated near the Houses of Parliament in London, Westminster Abbey is the burial place of many eminent Britons, including monarchs, scientists, and artists. In September 1997 the funeral service for Diana, Princess of Wales, was held here. Corel

the Bristol Channel; population (1991) 68,800. Industries include plastics and engineering.

Weston-super-Mare was a small fishing hamlet until it expanded rapidly as a resort in the late 19th century; by Edwardian times it had become one of the most popular resorts in the southwest of England. Amenities include sandy beaches, the Grand Pier (completed in 1904), public parks and gardens, and sports facilities.

## West Sussex

County of southern England created in 1974, formerly part of Sussex; population (1996) 737,300; area 1,990 sq km/768 sq mi. It has a southern coastline on the English Channel and part of the rolling South Downs, with open views and a number of coastal resorts. Inland the county has attractive wooded areas and picturesque villages. The main towns and cities are ◊Chichester (administrative headquarters), ◊Crawley, Horsham, Haywards Heath, and Shoreham (port); ◊Bognor Regis, Littlehampton, and ◊Worthing are resorts.

*Physical*

The county contains part of the ◊Weald and part of the ◊Downs, which are more wooded than in East Sussex, with beeches predominating in the Goodwood-Charlton area. Parts of the county are marshy, and there is a wide and fertile coastal plain stretching westwards from Worthing. The main rivers are the Adur, Arun, and West Rother. Along the coast there are beaches, as at Littlehampton and Bognor Regis, and shallow inlets, such as those at Pagham Harbour and Chichester Harbour, the latter with intricate channels.

*Features*

◊Fishbourne Palace is a key Roman site near Chichester. The fishing village of Selsey, south of Chichester, is the reputed landing place of the South Saxons in 447. Chichester, originally a Roman town, has a Norman cathedral and a fine harbour. Other fine historic buildings include the Norman castle at ◊Arundel; Bramber Castle; the 17th-century ◊Petworth House with paintings by J M W Turner and a room carved by Grinling Gibbons; ◊Uppark House (1685–90); ◊Goodwood House and racecourse; and Wakehurst Place, where the Royal Botanic Gardens, Kew, have additional grounds. The Weald and Downland Open Air Museum is at Singleton. The South Downs Way crosses the county.

*Economy*

◊Gatwick Airport, London's second airport, is a centre of employment. The county has agriculture and forestry. Industries include electronics and light engineering and industry; the holiday trade is important.

## Westward Ho!

Resort on the north coast of Devon, southwest England, 3 km/2 mi northwest of Bideford; population (1991) 1,400. Westward Ho! was named after a novel by Charles ◊Kingsley published in 1855.

The writer Rudyard ◊Kipling was educated at the United Services College (now a terrace of houses), which provided the background to his book of schoolboy stories *Stalky and Co* (1899). Pebble Ridge, jutting out into the Taw-Torridge estuary, is 3 km/2 mi long.

## West Yorkshire

Metropolitan county of northeast England, created in 1974; population (1996) 2,109,300; area 2,040 sq km/787 sq mi. West Yorkshire was formerly an important coal mining area and the towns were manufacturing centres for textiles in the 18th and 19th centuries; many of the textile mills have now been demolished but some have been converted for other uses. In the west there are unspoilt heather-clad moorlands, such as ◊Ilkley Moor and ◊Haworth Moor (home of the Brontë sisters), and in the east arable and pastoral land is interspersed with former coal-mining villages. In 1986 most of the functions of the former county council were transferred to the metropolitan borough councils. The main towns and cities are ◊Bradford, ◊Leeds, ◊Wakefield (administrative centres for districts of the same name), ◊Halifax (administrative centre of Calderdale district), and ◊Huddersfield (administrative centre of Kirklees district).

*Physical*

There are high Pennine moorlands in the west, also the well-known Ilkley Moor and Haworth Moor. The Vale of York is to the east. The main rivers are the Aire, Calder, Colne, and Wharfe.

*Features*

Part of the ◊Peak District National Park lies within the county. Haworth Parsonage, the family home of the Brontës, is a museum. The Piece Hall in Halifax (1779) is the only surviving cloth hall in the country. Part of the British Library is at Boston Spa (scientific, technical, and business documents). Eureka!, in Halifax, is an innovative hands-on museum of technology specifically designed for children. The National Coalmining Museum is in Wakefield. The Yorkshire Sculpture Park, also at Wakefield, contains works by Henry Moore, Barbara Hepworth, Elizabeth Frink, and others, displayed in 120 hectares/300 acres of parkland.

*Economy*
Coal mining and textile production have given way to mechanical and engineering trades; there are also financial services, for example the head-quarters of Halifax plc (formerly the Halifax Building Society) are in Halifax.

## wetland
Naturally flooding area that is managed for agriculture or wildlife. Wetlands include areas of marsh, fen, bog, flood plain, and shallow coastal areas. Wetlands are extremely fertile areas, and provide warm, sheltered waters for fisheries, lush vegetation for grazing livestock, and an abundance of wildlife. The ◊Royal Society for the Protection of Birds (RSPB) manages 2,800 hectares/7,000 acres of wetland, using sluice gates and flood-control devices to produce sanctuaries for wading birds and wild flowers. Some of these wetland sites are of international importance, and have been designated for protection under the EU Birds Directive known as the 'Ramsar Convention'. There are currently over 100 Ramsar sites in Britain.

## Weymouth
Seaport and resort in Dorset, on the south coast of England, at the mouth of the River Wey; population (1991) 45,900. It is linked by ferry to France and the Channel Islands. Industries include the quarrying of Portland stone, sailmaking, brewing, fishing, electronics, and engineering. Weymouth, dating from the 10th century, was the first place in England to suffer from the ◊Black Death in 1348. It was popularized as a bathing resort by George III.

Weymouth stands on both banks of the Wey, incorporating the area formerly known as Melcombe Regis. George III stayed at the Gloucester Hotel during his summer visits in Weymouth. To the south of Weymouth Bay is the limestone peninsula the Isle of ◊Portland.

## Wharfedale
Valley in West and North Yorkshire, England, in the Yorkshire ◊Dales National Park, extending from Wetherby to the source of the River Wharfe on Cam Fell. Lower Wharfedale is a rich agricultural district.

The area includes Harewood, where there is a ruined medieval castle, and ◊Ilkley, the largest town in the dale. Upper Wharfedale, above the ruins of Bolton Abbey, a priory founded in 1151, includes the village of Grassington. The village of Hubberholme lies at the northern end of the dale at the entrance to Langstrothdale.

## Whig Party
Predecessor of the Liberal Party. The name was first used of rebel Covenanters (Presbyterians) and then of those who wished to exclude James II from the English succession (as a Roman Catholic). They were in power continuously 1714–60 and pressed for industrial and commercial development, a vigorous foreign policy, and religious toleration. During the French Revolution, the Whigs demanded parliamentary reform in Britain, and from the passing of the Reform Bill 1832 became known as Liberals.

## whip (the whipper-in of hounds at a foxhunt)
The member of Parliament who ensures the presence of colleagues in the party when there is to be a vote in Parliament at the end of a debate. The written appeal sent by the whips to MPs is also called a whip; this letter is underlined once, twice, or three times to indicate its importance. A **three-line whip** is the most urgent, and every MP is expected to attend and vote with their party. An MP who fails to attend may be temporarily suspended from the party, a penalty known as 'having the whip withdrawn'.

## Whipsnade
Wild animal park in Bedfordshire, England, 5 km/3 mi south of Dunstable, on the edge of Dunstable Downs. Wild animals and birds are exhibited in spacious open-air enclosures intended to provide conditions resembling their natural state. The 240-ha/600-acre park, opened in 1931, runs conservation and breeding programmes for endangered species.

## whisky, or whiskey (Gaelic *uisge beatha*, water of life)
Distilled spirit made from cereals: Scotch whisky from malted barley, Irish whiskey usually from barley. Scotch is usually blended; pure malt whisky is more expensive. Whisky is generally aged in wooden casks for 4–12 years.

The spelling 'whisky' usually refers to Scotch or Canadian drink and 'whiskey' to Irish or American. The earliest written record of whisky comes from Scotland in 1494 but the art of distillation is thought to have been known before this time.

## Types of whisky:

**Scotch whisky** is made primarily from barley, malted, then heated over a peat fire. The flavoured malt is combined with water to make a mash, fermented to beer, then distilled twice to make whisky at 70% alcohol; this is reduced with water to 43% of volume.

**Irish whiskey** is made as Scotch, except that the malt is not exposed to the peat fire and thus does not have a smoky quality, and it is distilled three times. Irish whiskey is usually blended.

**Straight whisky** is unmixed or mixed with whisky from the same distillery or period; **blended whisky** is a mixture of neutral products with straight whiskies or may contain small quantities of sherry, fruit juice, and other flavours.

## Whitbread Literary Award

Annual prize of £23,000 open to writers in the UK and Ireland. Nominations are in four categories: novel, first novel, autobiography/biography, and poetry, each receiving £2,000. The overall winner receives a further £21,000. The award, which is administered by the Booksellers Association, was founded in 1971 by Whitbread, the UK brewing, food, and leisure company. The Whitbread Children's Book of the Year is a separate award worth £10,000.

## Whitby

Port and resort in North Yorkshire, northern England, on the North Sea coast, at the mouth of the River Esk, 32 km/20 mi northwest of Scarborough; population (1991) 13,800. Industries include tourism, boat building, fishing (particularly herring), and plastics. There are remains of a 13th-century abbey. Captain James ⬦Cook served his apprenticeship in Whitby and he sailed from here on his voyage to the Pacific Ocean in 1768. Bram Stoker's *Dracula* (1897) was set here.

Whitby was an important whaling centre and shipbuilding town in the 18th and 19th centuries. Mineral resources include jet, and Whitby also has potash reserves which run under the sea.

In 664 the Synod of Whitby, which affected the course of Christianity in England, was held here. The abbey was built on the site of a Saxon foundation established in 657 by St Hilda and destroyed by the Danes in 867. A Benedictine abbey was established in 1078, and the present ruins, reached from the town by 199 steps, date from 1220. Caedmon, the earliest-known English Christian poet, worked in the abbey in the 7th century. Near the abbey ruins stands the partly Norman parish church of St Mary. Captain

### Whitbread Literary Award Book of the Year

Winners are announced in November each year, and the overall winner (The Book of the Year) is awarded the £21,000 prize the following January.

| Year | Winner | Awarded for |
|------|--------|-------------|
| 1987 | Christopher Nolan | Under the Eye of the Clock |
| 1988 | Paul Sayer | The Comforts of Madness |
| 1989 | Richard Holmes | Coleridge: Early Visions |
| 1990 | Nicholas Mosley | Hopeful Monsters |
| 1991 | John Richardson | A Life of Picasso |
| 1992 | Jeff Torrington | Swing Hammer Swing! |
| 1993 | Joan Brady | Theory of War |
| 1994 | William Trevor | Felicia's Journey |
| 1995 | Kate Atkinson | Behind the Scenes at the Museum |
| 1996 | Seamus Heaney | The Spirit Level |
| 1997 | Ted Hughes | Tales from Ovid |
| 1998 | Ted Hughes | Birthday Letters |
| 1999 | Seamus Heaney | Beowulf |

Cook's ship *Resolution* was built in Whitby, and the Captain Cook Memorial Museum commemorates the life of the explorer.

## Whitehall

Street in Westminster, central London, between Trafalgar Square and the Houses of Parliament; it includes many of Britain's principal government offices and the Cenotaph war memorial.

The street derives its name from Whitehall Palace which was largely destroyed by fire in 1698. Of the palace only the Palladian Banqueting House (1622) survives, designed by Inigo Jones for James I. Whitehall is also the site of the headquarters (1753) of ⬦Horse Guards, the Household Cavalry. Among the many government offices in Whitehall are the Admiralty, Home Office, and Ministry of Defence.

### Whitehall Palace

A mansion was built here in the early 13th century by the justiciary, Hubert de Burgh. It was the residence of the archbishops of York from about 1250 until it was taken from Cardinal Wolsey by Henry VIII, who enlarged it and renamed it Whitehall; it remained the chief royal residence in London for about 150 years. The fine Banqueting

House includes a ceiling painted by Rubens. From a window in the hall Charles I stepped onto the scaffold for his execution in the street below.

---

*You must not miss Whitehall. At one end you will find a statue of one of our kings who was beheaded; at the other a monument to the man who did it. This is just an example of our attempts to be fair to everybody.*
**Edward Appleton** British physicist.
Referring to Charles I and Oliver Cromwell; speech, Stockholm, January 1948

---

## White Horse
Any of 17 ⟡hill figures in England, found particularly in the southern chalk downlands. The Uffington White Horse below Uffington Castle, a hillfort on the Berkshire Downs, is 110 m/360 ft long and probably a tribal totem of the late Bronze Age. The Westbury Horse on Bratton Hill, Wiltshire, was made in 1778 on the site of an older horse, said to commemorate Alfred the Great's victory over the Danes at Ethandun in AD 878.

### Uffington White Horse
The Uffington Horse has inspired many imitations, many of which date from the 18th and early 19th centuries. It has been known historically since at least AD 1084, when it was noted as a landmark in a charter of the Abbey of Abingdon, and by the 14th century it had given its name to the Vale of the White Horse. Theories regarding its origins have suggested that it was cut by Alfred the Great to celebrate his victory over the Danes at Ashdown in AD 871; that it was a memorial of the conversion of the Saxons to Christianity; and that it was made for some unknown purpose by the Druids or the Romans.

There is a stylistic similarity between the Uffington Horse and the horse represented on the gold and silver coins current in southeast England at the end of the early Iron Age. Similar horses appear on two artefacts of the same period, the Aylesford and Marlborough buckets. The nearby hillfort of Uffington Castle is also from the early Iron Age. According to recent excavation, the site has been used extensively since the Bronze Age, although the White Horse may not be contemporaneous with this, but a later modification to the landscape. Current opinion is that the Uffington Horse was a totem or cult object of the Belgae, a people who occupied much of southeast England between 50 BC and AD 50.

## Whithorn
Town and former royal burgh in Dumfries and Galloway unitary authority, Scotland, 18 km/11 mi south of Wigtown; population (1991) 1,000. Whithorn and Isle of Whithorn, a small port on Wigtown Bay lying 7 km/4 mi to the southeast, are associated with St Ninian, Scotland's earliest Christian missionary and bishop, who landed nearby around 397.

Candida Casa, his monastery and burial place, became a place of pilgrimage for many hundreds of years. Whithorn Priory, now in ruins, was built in the 12th century, and St Ninian's Chapel, founded in the 13th century, still stands at Isle of Whithorn. St Ninian's Cave lies on Port Castle Bay 4 km/2.5 mi to the southwest.

## Whitstable
Resort in Kent, southeast England, at the mouth of the River Swale, noted for its oysters; population (1991) 28,500. It is a yachting centre. In the Middle Ages it was a stopping place for pilgrims travelling to Canterbury, 11 km/7 mi to the southeast.

## Whittington, Dick (c. 1358–1423)
English cloth merchant who was mayor of London 1397–98, 1406–07, and 1419–20. According to legend, he came to London as a poor boy with his cat when he heard that the streets were paved with gold and silver. His cat first appears in a play from 1605.

## Whittle, Frank (1907–1996)
British engineer. He patented the basic design for the turbojet engine in 1930. In the Royal Air Force he worked on jet propulsion 1937–46. In May 1941 the Gloster E 28/39 aircraft first flew with the Whittle jet engine. Both the German (first operational jet planes) and the US jet aircraft were built using his principles.

## Widnes
Industrial town in Cheshire, England; population (1991) 56,000. It is linked with ⟡Runcorn on the other side of the River Mersey by road and rail bridges. Chemicals and metals are two of the main industries in Widnes.

## Wigan
Industrial town in Greater Manchester, northwest England, between Liverpool and Manchester, on the River Douglas; population (1991) 84,700.

Industries include tourism and leisure. The traditional coal and cotton industries have declined.

**Wigan Pier** was made famous by the writer George Orwell in *The Road to Wigan Pier* (1937). The pier was redeveloped to include a heritage centre, and was extended in 1996 with the addition of an art gallery.

### History

Wigan was the site of Roman and Saxon settlements. The town was granted borough status by charter of Henry III in 1246. It became an important trading centre in medieval times, on the road north through Lancashire between Warrington and Preston. Coalmining began in the area in the 15th century and Wigan prospered in the 19th century from the development of the cotton and engineering industries. Coal was distributed from here via the Liverpool–Leeds Canal to the Lancashire cotton mills. The Wigan School of Mines was founded in 1857. Thomas Linacre, one of the finest scholars of the 16th century and the first president of the Royal College of Physicians, was rector of Wigan 1519–24.

### Features

Wigan Pier; the area of the Leeds–Liverpool Canal basin, including Tencherfield Mill, the world's largest working mill steam-engine; Town Hall (1867); Market Hall (1877); Royal Albert Edward Infirmary (1873); Wigan Alps recreation area with ski slopes and water sports; sports and leisure complex at Robin Park.

## Wight, Isle of

Island and unitary authority of southern England; population (1996) 130,000; area 380 sq km/147 sq mi. It is opposite Southampton, Hampshire, separated from the mainland by the Solent and Spithead, and is a popular destination for holidays, especially as it a good area for sailing. The chief town is ◊Newport (administrative headquarters); Ryde, Sandown, Shanklin, and Ventnor are the main resorts. Cowes Week is an important annual sailing and social event.

### History

The Isle of Wight was called Vectis ('separate division') by the Romans, who conquered it in AD 43. Charles I was imprisoned 1647–48 in Carisbrooke Castle. Queen Victoria retired to Osborne House after the death of Prince Albert; it was her preferred residence, and she died there.

### Physical

The diamond-shaped island is low in the north and more hilly in the south. It has chalk cliffs and a ridge of downland running across the centre;

characteristic deep ravines are known locally as 'chines'. The highest point is St Boniface Down (240 m/787 ft). The Needles are a series of pointed chalk rocks up to 30 m/100 ft high in the sea at the western extreme of the island. Alum Bay has multicoloured cliff strata.

### Features

There are Roman villas at Newport and Brading. Quarr Abbey is the site of a Benedictine monastery. ◊Carisbrooke Castle, now ruined, is a Norman castle. ◊Osborne House is an Italianate palace overlooking the Solent, built in 1845. Parkhurst Prison is just outside Newport. ◊Cowes is the venue of Regatta Week and headquarters of the Royal Yacht Squadron.

### Economy

Tourism is important to the island. The mild climate enables cultivation of fine fruit and vegetables in the south. There is also boatbuilding, marine engineering, and high-technology industry. There are a range of services to the mainland, by water and air.

## Wightwick Manor

19th-century half-timbered house in the West Midlands, England, 5 km/3 mi west of Wolverhampton. It contains fabrics and wallpaper designed by William Morris, Pre-Raphaelite paintings, de Morgan ware, and Kempe glass. Geoffrey Mander gave the house and 7 ha/17 acres to the National Trust in 1937.

## Wilberforce, William (1759–1833)

English reformer. He was instrumental in abolishing slavery in the British Empire. He entered Parliament in 1780; in 1807 his bill banning the trade in slaves from the West Indies was passed, and in 1833, largely through his efforts, slavery was eradicated throughout the empire. He died shortly before the Slavery Abolition Act was passed.

---

*They charge me with fanaticism. If to be feelingly alive to the sufferings of my fellow-creatures is to be a fanatic, I am one of the most incurable fanatics ever permitted to be at large.*

**William Wilberforce** English reformer. Speech, 1816

---

Wilberforce was a member of a humanitarian group called the Clapham Sect, which exercised considerable influence on public policy, being closely identified with Sunday schools, and the

British and Foreign Bible Society, as well as the issue of slavery.

## Wilde, Oscar (1854–1900)

Irish writer. With his flamboyant style and quotable conversation, he dazzled London society and, on his lecture tour in 1882, the USA. He published his only novel, *The Picture of Dorian Gray*, in 1891, followed by a series of sharp comedies, including *A Woman of No Importance* (1893) and *The Importance of Being Earnest* (1895). In 1895 he was imprisoned for two years for homosexual offences; he died in exile.

Wilde studied at Dublin and Oxford, where he became known as a supporter of the ◊Aesthetic movement ('art for art's sake'). He published *Poems* (1881), and also wrote fairy tales and other stories, criticism, and a long, anarchic political essay, 'The Soul of Man Under Socialism' (1891). His elegant social comedies include *Lady Windermere's Fan* (1892) and *An Ideal Husband* (1895). The drama *Salome* (1893), based on the biblical character, was written in French; considered scandalous by the British censor, it was first performed in Paris in 1896 with the actress Sarah Bernhardt in the title role.

Among his lovers was Lord Alfred Douglas, whose father provoked Wilde into a lawsuit that led to his social and financial ruin and imprisonment. The long poem *Ballad of Reading Gaol* (1898) and a letter published as *De Profundis* (1905) were written in jail to explain his side of the relationship. After his release from prison in 1897,

he lived in France. He is buried in the Père Lachaise cemetery, Paris.

## William

Four kings of England:

### William (I) the Conqueror (c. 1027–1087)

King of England from 1066. He was the illegitimate son of Duke Robert the Devil and succeeded his father as Duke of Normandy in 1035. Claiming that his relative King Edward the Confessor had bequeathed him the English throne, William invaded the country in 1066, defeating ◊Harold II at Hastings, Sussex, and was crowned king of England.

William's coronation took place in Westminster Abbey on Christmas Day 1066. He completed the establishment of feudalism in England, compiling detailed records of land and property in the ◊Domesday Book, and kept the barons firmly under control. He died in Rouen after a fall from his horse and is buried in Caen, France. He was succeeded by his son William II.

---

*By the splendour of God I have taken possession of my realm; the earth of England is in my two hands.*
**William the Conqueror** King of England from 1066.
Said when he fell as he landed in England.
Attributed

---

### William (II) Rufus, 'the Red' (c. 1056–1100)

King of England from 1087, the third son of William the Conqueror. He spent most of his reign attempting to capture Normandy from his brother Robert II, Duke of Normandy. His extortion of money led his barons to revolt and caused confrontation with Bishop Anselm. He was killed while hunting in the New Forest, Hampshire, and was succeeded by his brother Henry I.

### William (III) of Orange (1650–1702)

King of Great Britain and Ireland from 1688, the son of William II of Orange and Mary, daughter of Charles I. He was offered the English crown by

**William (I) the Conqueror** The Great Seal of William I, the Norman king who mounted the last successful conquest of England. He subdued the country and imposed a new system of government dominated by an aristocratic Norman elite. Philip Sauvain Picture Collection

the parliamentary opposition to James II. He invaded England in 1688 and in 1689 became joint sovereign with his wife, ◊Mary II. He spent much of his reign campaigning, first in Ireland, where he defeated James II at the Battle of the ◊Boyne in 1690, and later against the French in Flanders. He was succeeded by Mary's sister, Anne.

Born in the Netherlands, William was made *stadtholder* (chief magistrate) in 1672 to resist the French invasion. He forced Louis XIV to make peace in 1678 and then concentrated on building up a European alliance against France. In 1677 he married his cousin Mary, daughter of the future James II. When invited by both Whig and Tory leaders to take the crown from James, he landed with a large force at Torbay, Devon. James fled to France, and his Scottish and Irish supporters were defeated at the battles of Dunkeld in 1689 and the Boyne in 1690.

## William IV (1765–1837)
King of Great Britain and Ireland from 1830, when he succeeded his brother George IV. Third son of George III, he was created Duke of Clarence in 1789, and married Adelaide of Saxe-Meiningen (1792–1849) in 1818. During the Reform Bill crisis he secured its passage by agreeing to create new peers to overcome the hostile majority in the House of Lords. He was succeeded by his niece Victoria.

## Williams
British racing-car manufacturing company started by Frank Williams in 1969 when he modified a Brabham BT26A. The first Williams Grand Prix car was designed by Patrick Head in 1978 and since then the team has been one of the most successful in Grand Prix racing, winning the Formula One Constructors' title a record-equalling nine times 1980–97.

## Wilmington
Village in East Sussex, southeast England, 8 km/5 mi northwest of Eastbourne. A ruined Benedictine monastery is now an agricultural museum. Nearby on the South ◊Downs is a ◊hill figure cut into the chalk of Windover Hill, the **Long Man of Wilmington**.

## Wilson, Angus (1913–1991)
English novelist, short-story writer, and biographer. His acidly humorous books include *Anglo-Saxon Attitudes* (1956) and *The Old Men at the Zoo* (1961). In his detailed portrayal of English

society, he extracted high comedy from its social and moral grotesqueries.

Wilson was deputy superintendent of the British Museum Reading Room from 1949–55, then worked as a full-time writer. He was professor of English literature at the University of East Anglia from 1966–78.

His first published works were the short-story collections *The Wrong Set* (1949) and *Such Darling Dodos* (1950). His other major novels include *Late Call* (1964), *No Laughing Matter* (1967), and *Setting the World on Fire* (1980). Knighted 1980.

## Wilson, Harold, Baron Wilson of Rievaulx (1916–1995)
British Labour politician, party leader from 1963, prime minister 1964–70 and 1974–76. His premiership was dominated by the issue of UK admission to membership of the European Community (now the European Union), the social contract (unofficial agreement with the trade unions), and economic difficulties.

---

*A week is a long time in politics.*
**Harold Wilson** British Labour prime minister.
Attributed remark

---

## Wilson, Richard (1714–1782)
Welsh painter. His landscapes, infused with an Italianate atmosphere, are painted in a Classical manner. His work influenced the development of English landscape painting, and Turner in particular.

## Wilton
Market town in Wiltshire, southwest England, 5 km/3 mi west of Salisbury; population (1991) 3,600. It manufactured carpets from the 16th century until 1995, when the Wilton Royal Carpet Factory closed. **Wilton House**, the seat of the earls of Pembroke, was built from designs by Hans Holbein and Inigo Jones.

Wilton was the seat of a bishopric until 1075, and was the capital of Wessex and the county town of Wiltshire in medieval times. The name of the county of Wiltshire is derived from 'Wiltonshire'.

Wilton House is associated with Shakespeare and with the Elizabethan courtier and poet Sir Philip Sidney. It is thought that the first performance of Shakespeare's play *As You Like It* took place at Wilton House in 1603 in front of James I. Sidney wrote part of his prose romance *Arcadia*

(1590) in Wilton House. Scenes from the book are illustrated in the dado round the Single Cube Room.

## Wiltshire

County of southwest England; population (1996) 593,300; area 3,480 sq km/1,343 sq mi. It is particularly known for its wealth of ancient monuments, of which Stonehenge is the most famous. The principal towns and cities are ◊Trowbridge (administrative headquarters), ◊Salisbury, ◊Wilton, Devizes, Chippenham, and Warminster. Since April 1997 ◊Swindon, formerly in Wiltshire, has been a separate unitary authority.

*Physical*

The Marlborough Downs pass through the county. ◊Savernake Forest, to the southeast of Marlborough, is largely a beech forest, covering some 1,620 ha/4,000 acres. In the county's centre is ◊Salisbury Plain (32 km/20 mi by 25 km/16 mi, lying at about 120 m/394 ft above sea-level), used as a military training area since Napoleonic times. The county's main rivers are the Kennet, Wylye, and Avons (Salisbury and Bristol).

*Features*

Wiltshire contains an exceptional number of important ancient monuments, the highlights being the Neolithic stone circle of ◊Stonehenge; Europe's largest stone circle at ◊Avebury; the artificial Neolithic mound of ◊Silbury Hill; and West Kennet Long Barrow (dating from the 3rd millennium BC). Salisbury Cathedral has the tallest spire in Britain (123 m/404 ft). Fine country houses include ◊Longleat House, home of the Marquess of Bath and site of the first safari park in England; Wilton House, home of the Earl of Pembroke, associated with Shakespeare; and Stourhead, with outstanding 18th-century landscaped gardens.

*Economy*

Agriculture remains important to Wiltshire's economy, supplemented by a range of industries including computing, electronics, pharmaceuticals, and plastics. Financial services, telecommunications, and research are growing areas. Portland stone is quarried. Tourism also contributes to the local economy.

## Wimbledon

English lawn-tennis centre used for international championship matches, situated in south London.

The first centre was at Worple Road when it was the home of the All England Croquet Club.

Tennis was first played there in 1875, and in 1877 the club was renamed the All England Lawn Tennis and Croquet Club. The first all England championship was held in the same year. The club and championship moved to their present site in Church Road in 1922. The Wimbledon championship, held in the last week of June and the first week of July, is one of the sport's four Grand Slam events; the others are the US Open, first held in 1881 as the US Championships, becoming the US Open in 1968; the French Championships, and the Australian Championships.

## Winchelsea

Town in East Sussex, southeast England, about 3 km/2 mi from Rye; population (1991) 2,300. The town was formerly one of the ◊Cinque Ports. During the 16th century the inlet to the sea became silted up, and Winchelsea is now more than 1 km/0.6 mi from the sea.

New Winchelsea was laid out in about 1290 by Edward I to replace Old Winchelsea, which was submerged by the sea in 1287. The plans were never the completed because the harbour silted up, and the church of St Thomas was also never finished, although the 14th-century chancel can still be seen.

## Winchester

Cathedral city and administrative headquarters of ◊Hampshire, England, on the River Itchen, 19 km/12 mi northeast of Southampton; population (1991) 36,100. Tourism is important, and there is also light industry. Originally a Roman town, Winchester was capital of the Anglo-Saxon kingdom of ◊Wessex, and later of England. Winchester Cathedral (1079–93) is the longest medieval church in Europe and was remodelled from Norman-Romanesque to ◊Perpendicular Gothic under the patronage of William of Wykeham (founder of Winchester College in 1382), who is buried there, as are Saxon kings, St Swithun, and the writers Izaac Walton and Jane Austen.

Winchester was a tribal centre of the Britons under the name Caer Gwent. On St Catherine's Hill can be seen the rampart and ditch made for defence by an Iron Age settlement in the 3rd century BC. Winchester was later one of the largest Roman settlements in Britain. It became capital of Wessex in 519 and under Alfred the Great and Canute was the seat of government. In 827 Egbert was crowned first king of all England here. Under William the Conqueror, Winchester was declared dual capital of England with London. A medieval 'reconstruction' of Arthur's Round Table is preserved in the 13th-century hall (all that survives) of the castle.

### Roman Winchester

During the Roman occupation of Britain, Winchester, called **Venta Belgarum**, was a route-centre and the commercial and administrative capital of a district. Many Roman finds from the city are in the city museum, and remains of Roman buildings were discovered during excavations from 1953 to 1963. The forum was excavated north of the cathedral in 1961 and 1963.

### The cathedral

The Saxon kings of Wessex are said to have been crowned in the old cathedral, which has now been fully excavated. Among kings of England crowned or recrowned at Winchester were William the Conqueror, and Richard I after his return from captivity. Here also Queen Mary was married to Philip of Spain. Not far from the cathedral lie the 12th-century ruins of the episcopal castle of Wolvesey, and adjoining them is the present official residence of the bishop, a building of the late-17th century. During the Saxon period the Winchester illuminators became famous. The most notable work produced was the Benedictional of St Aethelwold (created probably 975–80), formerly at Chatsworth and since 1957 in the British Museum. Another outstanding book is the 12th-century Winchester Bible, still in the cathedral library.

## Windermere

Largest lake in England, in the ◊Lake District, Cumbria, northwest England; length 17 km/10.5 mi; width 1.6 km/1 mi. Windermere is the principal centre of tourism in the Lake District. The town of the same name extends towards Bowness on the eastern shore of the lake.

The lake's shores are well-wooded, and the lake drains southwards into Morecambe Bay via the River Leven. The town of Windermere (population (1991) 7,700) developed around the railway station which was built in 1847. There is a car ferry service from Bowness across the lake to Sawrey.

## Windsor

Town in southern England, on the River Thames, 35 km/22 mi west of London; population (1991, with Eton) 30,600. Formerly in Berkshire, it joined with Maidenhead to become ◊Windsor and Maidenhead unitary authority in April 1998. Industries include tourism, computer services,

and financial services. It is the site of ◊Windsor Castle, a royal residence, and a 17th-century guildhall designed by Christopher Wren. Nearby is the prestigious private school ◊Eton College (founded in 1440).

### Features

The church of St John the Baptist (rebuilt in 1822) includes fine examples of woodcarvings by the Dutch woodcarver Grinling Gibbons, and a Jubilee statue of Queen Victoria. The parish church of Clewer St Andrew is a fine example of Norman architecture.

## Windsor and Maidenhead

Unitary authority in southern England, created in 1998 from part of the former county of Berkshire; population (1995) 140,200; area 198 sq km/76 sq mi. The principal towns are ◊Maidenhead (administrative headquarters) and ◊Windsor.

### Physical

The River Thames flows through the authority.

### Features

◊Windsor Castle is a royal residence, originally built by William (I) the Conqueror. Windsor Great Park is a remnant of a royal hunting ground. Legoland Windsor opened in 1996 on the site of the former Windsor Safari Park. ◊Eton College was founded by Henry VI in 1440. The Household Cavalry Museum is at Windsor. The Stanley Spencer Gallery contains works by the artist at ◊Cookham-on-Thames. The Royal Ascot race meeting is held annually at ◊Ascot in June.

### Economy

Tourism and service industries are important. Other activities include publishing, light engineering, electronics, and telecommunications.

## Windsor Castle

British royal residence in Windsor, Windsor and Maidenhead unitary authority, founded by William (I) the Conqueror on the site of an earlier fortress. It includes the ◊Perpendicular Gothic St George's Chapel and the Albert Memorial Chapel, beneath which George III, George IV, and William IV are buried. In the Home Park adjoining the castle is the Royal Mausoleum, ◊Frogmore, where Queen Victoria and Prince Albert are buried.

Beyond the Round Tower or Keep are the state apartments and the sovereign's private apartments. **Windsor Great Park** lies to the south. In 1990 the royal residence ◊Frogmore House, near Windsor Castle, as well as the Royal Mausoleum, were opened to the public.

On 20 November 1992 the castle was heavily damaged by a fire in its 14th-century St George's

Hall. In April 1993 the Queen decided to open Buckingham Palace to the public to raise money for the necessary repair work. St George's Hall was reopened in 1998.

## Windsor, House of

Official name of the British royal family since 1917, adopted in place of Saxe-Coburg-Gotha. Since 1960 those descendants of Elizabeth II not entitled to the prefix HRH (His/Her Royal Highness) have all borne the surname of Mountbatten-Windsor. See genealogy below.

## Woburn Abbey

House in Bedfordshire, England, 12 km/7 mi southeast of Milton Keynes. The present building contains an altered 17th-century wing but is otherwise of the 18th century, its main west range (1747–61) by Henry Flitcroft, who also built the stables, and its south range (1787–90) built by William Chambers or Henry Holland. Woburn attracts a large number of visitors, not only to the house, but also to the safari park in the grounds, and other entertainments.

The house contains many treasures, including 24 paintings by Canaletto, and works by Poussin, Claude, Reynolds, and Gainsborough. Woburn has been the seat of the earls and dukes of Bedford since 1547.

## Wodehouse, P(elham) G(renville) (1881–1975)

English novelist. He became a US citizen in 1955. His humorous novels and stories portray the accident-prone world of such characters as the socialite Bertie Wooster and his invaluable and impeccable manservant Jeeves, and Lord Emsworth of Blandings Castle with his prize pig, the Empress of Blandings.

---

*It is never difficult to distinguish between a Scotsman with a grievance and a ray of sunshine.*

**P G Wodehouse** English novelist.
Quoted in *Wodehouse at Work to the End*, by
Richard Usborne

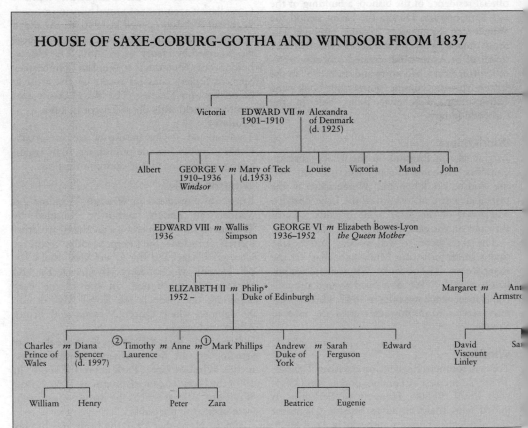

## HOUSE OF SAXE-COBURG-GOTHA AND WINDSOR FROM 1837

From 1906 Wodehouse also collaborated on the lyrics of Broadway musicals by Jerome Kern, Gershwin, and others. Staying in France in 1941 during World War II, he was interned by the Germans; he made some humorous broadcasts from Berlin, which were taken amiss in Britain at the time, but he was exonerated later and was knighted in 1975. His work is admired for its style, erudition, and geniality, and includes *Indiscretions of Archie* (1921), *The Clicking of Cuthbert* (1922), *The Inimitable Jeeves* (1932), and *Uncle Fred in the Springtime* (1939).

## Woking

Town in Surrey, southeast England, 37 km/23 mi southwest of London; population (1991) 82,300. It is largely residential and owes its growth to railway development after 1838, when a station opened 3 km/2 mi from Old Woking.

Britain's first custom-built mosque (1889) is here, and many commons and parks. The church of St Peter in Old Woking has Norman origins.

## Wokingham

Unitary authority in southeast England, created in 1998 from part of the former county of Berkshire; population (1995) 142,000; area 179 sq km/69 sq mi. The principal towns are Wokingham (administrative headquarters) and Twyford.

### Physical

The River Thames forms the northern border of authority. There are large areas of mixed woodland, including remnants of the old Royal Chase of Windsor Forest. Finchampstead Ridge lies to the south.

### Features

All Saints' Church, Wokingham, has a carved ◊Perpendicular Gothic font. Almshouses in the town date from 1451. The Royal Electrical and Mechanical Engineering Corps Museum is at Arborfield. Swallowfield Park was built for the 2nd Earl of Clarendon in 1690. The National Dairy Museum is here. Henley Regatta takes place annually at ◊Henley-on-Thames.

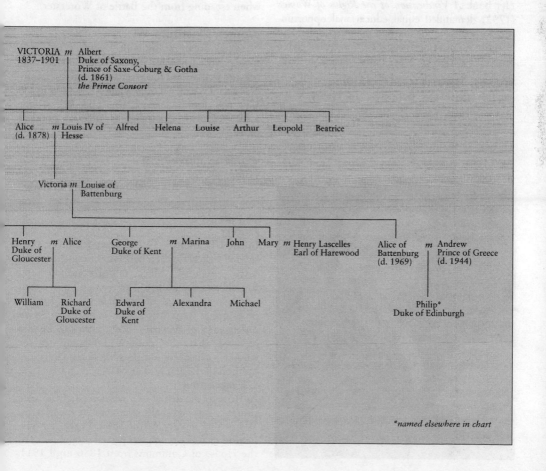

*named elsewhere in chart

*Economy*
Wokingham has been a market centre for over 500 years. Industries are mainly high tech (information technology, electronics, telecommunications, computer components and software); others include light engineering and plastics manufactures.

## wold (Old English *wald* 'forest')
Open, hilly country. The term refers specifically to certain areas in England, notably the Yorkshire and Lincolnshire Wolds and the ◊Cotswold Hills.

---

*I do not wish them [women] to have power over men; but over themselves.*

**Mary Wollstonecraft** English feminist and writer.
*Vindication of the Rights of Woman* ch 4

---

## Wollstonecraft, Mary (1759–1797)
British feminist. She was a member of a group of radical intellectuals called the English Jacobins. Her book *A Vindication of the Rights of Women* (1792) demanded equal educational opportunities for women. She married the philosopher and novelist William Godwin in 1797 and died giving birth to a daughter, Mary (later Mary ◊Shelley).

## Wolsey, Thomas (*c.* 1475–1530)
English cleric and politician. In Henry VIII's service from 1509, he became archbishop of York

**Mary Wollstonecraft** English author and early feminist Mary Wollstonecraft. Her best-known work is *A Vindication of the Rights of Woman*, written in 1792. She was also the mother of Mary Shelley. Corbis

in 1514, cardinal and lord chancellor in 1515, and began the ◊Dissolution of the Monasteries.

His reluctance to further Henry's divorce from Catherine of Aragón led to his downfall in 1529. He was charged with high treason in 1530 but died before being tried.

## Wolverhampton
Industrial town in West Midlands, central England, 20 km/12 mi northwest of Birmingham; population (1994) 256,100. Wolverhampton was a wool town in the Middle Ages and, situated at the heart of the industrial ◊Black Country, a centre of the iron industry from the 18th century.
*Features*
St Peter's Church was founded in 994 and some of its present structure dates from the 13th century. ◊Wightwick Manor nearby to the west was begun in 1887, and houses embroideries, carpets, and wallpaper designed by William Morris. Moseley Old Hall to the north is an Elizabethan timber-framed house, where Charles II stayed in 1651 when escaping from the Battle of Worcester.

## Women's Institute, WI
National organization with branches in many towns and villages for the 'development of community welfare and the practice of rural crafts'; the National Federation of Women's Institutes in the UK was founded in 1915. The WI is not associated with any religious faith or political party.

## women's movement
Campaign for the rights of women, including social, political, and economic equality with men (see also ◊suffragette and chronology of key dates on page 509).
*History*
In the UK, pioneer 19th-century feminists, considered radical for their belief in the equality of the sexes, included Mary ◊Wollstonecraft and Emmeline ◊Pankhurst. The women's movement was also supported in principle by the English philosopher John Stuart Mill, in his essay *On the Subjugation of Women* (1869), although he also believed that the political advocacy of the women's cause was not possible in the climate of opinion prevailing at that time.
*UK legislation*
In Britain, the denial of a woman's right to own property was eventually overcome by the Married Women's Property Act of 1882. Legislation giving the vote to women was passed several times by the House of Commons from 1886 until 1911,

## Women's Movement in Britain: Some key dates

**1775** King George III orders women and young children out of coal and salt mines.

**1792** The English writer and feminist Mary Wollstonecraft publishes her *Vindication of the Rights of Woman*.

**1845** Aged 18, Frances Buss sets up a girls' school in London; she later founds Camden School for Girls. Her work helps raise the status of women teachers as well as academic standards.

**11 June 1847** Millicent Garrett Fawcett (–1929), English suffragette leader for over 50 years, is born in Aldeburgh, Suffolk.

**1857** The Matrimonial Causes Act sets up divorce courts, allowing divorcees to remarry without recourse to a private act of Parliament, and outlines terms for divorce: men must prove adultery and women adultery and cruelty or desertion.

**14 July 1858** Emmeline Pankhurst (–1928), militant English suffragette, is born in Manchester.

**9 August 1870** The Married Women's Property Act is passed recognizing a woman's right to keep any money she earns and some of her own possessions.

**1871** The English educationalist Anne Clough provides a house of residence for the first women students at the University of Cambridge, which becomes Newnham College in 1875.

**1873** Legislation extends women's rights to claim custody of their children in divorce proceedings.

**1875** The London Medical School for Women is founded (women having previously been excluded from studying medicine).

**1882** The Married Women's Property Act gives married women the right of separate ownership of property of all kinds.

**23 October 1906** Women suffragettes demonstrate in the outer lobby of the House of Commons. Ten of the demonstrators are charged the following day, and sent to prison.

**1909** The suffragette Marion Wallace Dunlop becomes the first hunger striker in Britain: she is released after 91 hours.

**4 June 1913** The suffragette Emily Davison is killed when she runs under the king's horse at the Derby.

**28 November 1919** Lady Nancy Astor is elected in a by-election and becomes the first woman member of Parliament to take her seat.

**2 July 1928** Women's voting rights are extended to become equal with those of men.

**30 May 1929** In a general election, the first held under universal adult suffrage, the Labour Party wins 287 seats, Conservatives 260, Liberals, 59, others, 9.

**1930** Gertrude Denman, who introduced the Inter-uterine device (IUD) for birth control and published the best-selling *The Sex Factor in Marriage* earlier this year, becomes chair of the National Birth Control Council.

**23 May 1937** The Matrimonial Causes Act, introduced by the author, lawyer, and politician A P Herbert, gives women equality with men in divorce proceedings in England and Wales.

**1939** Dorothy Garrod becomes the first woman to receive a professorship at Cambridge University. She serves as professor of archaeology until 1952.

**6 November 1946** A royal commission favours equal pay for women.

**6 December 1947** Cambridge University votes to admit women to membership and degree courses.

**27 October 1967** Laws governing abortion are relaxed.

**23 April 1969** The government concedes universal adult suffrage In local elections in Northern Ireland, in response to Catholic civil-rights activists' demands.

**1973** The women's publishing house Virago is founded.

**October 1974** Five male colleges at Oxford University – Brasenose, Jesus, Wadham, Hertford, and St Catherine's – admit women for the first time.

**29 December 1975** The Sex Discrimination Act establishes the Equal Opportunities Commission.

**1979** The House of Commons has 19 women out of 635 members and the House of Lords has 51 women out of 1,107 members.

**4 May 1979** Conservative leader Margaret Thatcher becomes Britain's first woman prime minister.

**3 January 1980** A report shows that half of married British women go out to work, the largest proportion anywhere in the European Community.

**March 1984** Brenda Dean is the first woman to lead a major British union, when she is elected leader of print union SOGAT '82.

**1985** The General Synod of the Church of England approves by a large majority the ordination of women as deacons.

**1990** Britain introduces separate taxation for married women.

**27 April 1992** The Labour politician Betty Boothroyd becomes the first woman Speaker of the House of Commons.

**5 November 1993** Legislation to allow the Church of England to ordain women priests gains the royal assent.

**27 February 1998** The Home Office announces that Queen Elizabeth II supports plans to remove the gender bias from British succession rules that currently state that succession goes to the first-born son.

but was always vetoed by the House of Lords. The organized protests of women in the suffragette movement were abruptly terminated by the beginning of World War I in 1914, but opinion later turned in their favour owing to the work women did during the war. In 1918 a bill granting limited franchise was passed, and in 1928 full equality in voting was attained. In the UK since

1975 discrimination against women in employment, education, housing, and provision of goods, facilities, and services to the public has been illegal under the Sex Discrimination and Equal Pay Acts.

## woodland

Area in which trees grow more or less thickly; generally smaller than a forest. Woodland covers about 2.4 million hectares/6 million acres in the UK: about 8% of England, 15% of Scotland, 12% of Wales, and 6% of Northern Ireland. This is over 10% of the total land area – well below the 25% average in the rest of Europe. An estimated 33% of ancient woodland has been destroyed in Britain since 1945. The ◊Forestry Commission aims to double the area of woodlands in England by the middle of the 21st century.

### Woolf, Virginia born Stephen (1882–1941)

English novelist and critic. In novels such as *Mrs Dalloway* (1925), *To the Lighthouse* (1927), and *The Waves* (1931), she used a 'stream of consciousness' technique to render inner experience. In *A Room of One's Own* (1929, nonfiction), *Orlando* (1928), and *The Years* (1937), she examines the importance of economic independence for women and other feminist principles.

Her first novel, *The Voyage Out* (1915), explored the tensions experienced by women who want marriage and a career. *Night and Day* was published in 1919, but her first really characteristic work was *Jacob's Room* (1922). After the death of her father, Leslie Stephen, she and her siblings moved to Bloomsbury, forming the nucleus of the ◊Bloomsbury Group. She produced a succession of novels, short stories, and critical essays, included in *The Common Reader* (1925 and 1932). She was plagued by bouts of depression and committed suicide in 1941.

In 1912 Woolf married the writer **Leonard Woolf** (1880–1969), with whom she founded the Hogarth Press in 1917.

## woolsack

The seat of the lord chancellor in the House of Lords. The woolsack is a large square bag of wool, with a backrest but no arms, covered with red cloth. It is traditionally held to have been placed in the House during the reign of Edward III as a mark of the importance of the wool trade.

## Woolwich

District in east London, cut through by the River Thames, the northern part being in the borough of ◊Newham and the southern part in the borough of ◊Greenwich. The Thames barrier (a flood barrier, constructed in 1982) is here.

The Woolwich Royal Arsenal, an ordnance depot from 1518 and centre for the manufacture and testing of arms, is still partly in use. The Royal Military Academy and the Royal Artillery Institution Museum are located here.

Woolwich in the Middle Ages was a fishing village but it expanded in the 15th century when it became the site of a royal dockyard and the Royal Arsenal (developed from the Royal Laboratory, Carriage Department, and a Powder House, probably established about the same time as the dockyard). The main government foundry was moved here from Moorfields in 1716–17. The Royal Military Academy, established originally inside the Arsenal in 1741, was the first military school in Britain; it was amalgamated with the Royal Military College at Sandhurst in 1946. The population of Woolwich increased greatly after many factories were established here as a result of the Crimean War and World War I.

## Worcester

Cathedral city in west central England on the River Severn, and administrative headquarters of the county of Worcestershire, on the River Severn, 35 km/22 mi southwest of Birmingham; population (1991) 82,700. Industries include the manufacture of shoes, Worcestershire sauce, and Royal Worcester porcelain. The cathedral dates from the 13th and 14th centuries.

### *History*

Worcester was important as early as the 7th century due to its siting on a ford in the Severn. It has been an episcopal see since 680. In 964 St Oswald founded a new church here for Benedictine monks, and Bishop Wulfstan began rebuilding on a large scale in 1084. King John is buried between the shrines of Oswald and Wulfstan.

During the Civil War, the city supported the royalists. In 1651 Charles II lodged in the city, and from the cathedral tower watched his forces being routed by Cromwell's troops. Many royalist soldiers were imprisoned in the cathedral after the battle.

### *The cathedral*

The Cathedral of Christ and St Mary the Virgin includes a Norman crypt, an impressive geometrical west window, and a Perpendicular cloister. The circular Norman chapter house and the original refectory, now used by the King's School, remain. The building of the Early English choir and Lady chapel began in 1224. The last important addition to the cathedral was Prince Arthur's Chantry, with a magnificent Perpendicular screen, erected by Henry VII in memory of his eldest son. The exterior of the cathedral was extensively restored between 1857 and 1874.

## Other features

St Helen's is the oldest church in Worcester, dating back to 680, but rebuilt in the 13th and 15th centuries. St Andrew's and St Albans are other medieval ecclesiastical structures, but these three churches are not now used as places of worship.

The Commandery, formerly called the Hospital of St Wulfstan, was founded by Wulfstan (1085) for a master, priests, and brethren, under the rule of St Augustine; the present structure is 15th century. Medieval buildings still remain in New Street and Friar Street. From 'Queen Elizabeth's House', Queen Elizabeth I, according to tradition, addressed the people when she visited Worcester in 1574. Worcester is rich in Georgian buildings. The Guildhall (1721–23) is the work of Thomas White, a native of Worcester. The Royal Grammar School dates back to the 13th century. The Worcester Cathedral King's School was established and endowed out of the monastic funds by Henry VIII in 1541, and reorganized in 1884. More modern buildings include the Shire Hall, the Worcester Royal Infirmary, and the Victoria Institute. The birthplace of the composer Edward Elgar at nearby Broadheath is a museum.

## Industries past and present

From medieval times Worcester was the centre of a prosperous glove trade, and some firms still carry on this tradition today. The Royal Worcester Porcelain Factory was founded in 1751 by 'John Wall, doctor of Physic, and William Davis, Apothecary'; Wall was also connected with Worcester Royal Infirmary, which opened in a house in Silver Street in 1745.

Berrow's *Worcester Journal* traces its history to 1690, and is therefore one of the oldest newspapers in England.

# Worcestershire

County of west central England; population (1996) 535,700; area 1,640 sq km/1,020 sq mi. It was joined with Herefordshire 1974–98 to form the county of Hereford and Worcester, but in 1998 Herefordshire and Worcestershire regained their pre-1974 boundaries. The principal cities and towns are ◊Worcester (administrative headquarters), Bewdley, ◊Bromsgrove, Evesham, ◊Kidderminster, Pershore, Stourport, and Tenbury Wells.

## Physical

The south and southwest is hilly, with the highest point at Worcester Beacon (425 m/1,394 ft) in the Malvern Hills. Through the centre run the river valleys of the Severn, with its tributaries the Stour, Teme, and Avon, which runs through the fertile Vale of Evesham. The Lickey Hills and the Clent Hills rise in the north. The North Cotswold Hills and Bredon Hill lie along the southeast border of the county. Worcestershire is well wooded and contains the two ancient forests of Wyre and Malvern Chase. Canals connect the Severn with the Midland canal system.

## Features

The greater part of the county was at one time in the hands of the church, and there were no fewer than 13 great monastic foundations here. Of these there are ruins at Pershore and Evesham, both dating from the 8th century; Worcester Cathedral, and the priory church at Malvern, also of the same date; and ruins at Bordesley and Astley dating from the 13th century. The county is also rich in domestic architecture of the Tudor and Georgian periods, and possesses a number of notable country houses. Droitwich, once a Victorian spa, reopened its baths in 1985 (the town lies over a subterranean brine reservoir). The Three Choirs Festival is an annual event that takes place in rotation at Worcester, Hereford, and Gloucester.

## Economy

Much of the county is under cultivation, a large part being devoted to permanent pasture, notably for Hereford cattle. The county is otherwise known for producing carpets (Kidderminster) and porcelain (Worcester).

# Wordsworth, William (1770–1850)

English Romantic poet. In 1797 he moved with his sister Dorothy Wordsworth (1771–1855) to Somerset, where he lived near Samuel Taylor ◊Coleridge and collaborated with him on *Lyrical Ballads* (1798), which included 'Tintern Abbey', a meditation on his response to nature. His most notable individual poems were published in *Poems* (1807), including 'Intimations of Immortality'. At intervals between then and 1839 he revised *The Prelude* (posthumously published in 1850), the first part of his uncompleted philosophical, creative, and spiritual autobiography in verse. He was appointed poet laureate in 1843.

Wordsworth's first published works appeared in 1793, *The Evening Walk* and *Descriptive Sketches of a Pedestrian Tour in the Alps*. With his sister Dorothy he settled in Racedown, Dorset, then in Alfoxden in Somerset, near Nether Stowey where Coleridge was living. With the profits he made from the publication of *Lyrical Ballads* he went with Dorothy and Coleridge to Germany where he wrote some of his best short poems, including 'Strange fits...' and 'A slumber did my spirit seal'. In 1799 he and Dorothy moved to ◊ Dove Cottage in Grasmere, in the Lake District, and in 1802 he married his cousin Mary Hutchinson (1770–1859). In 1813 the Wordsworths moved to Rydal Mount. His later years were marred by his sister's ill health and the death of his daughter Dora in 1847.

A leader of the ◊ Romantic movement, Wordsworth is best known as the poet who reawakened his readers to the beauty of nature, describing the emotions and perceptive insights which natural beauty arouses in the sensitive observer. He advocated a poetry of simple feeling and the use of the language of ordinary speech, demonstrated in the unadorned simplicity of lyrics such as 'To the cuckoo' and 'I wandered lonely as a cloud'. At a deeper level, he saw himself as a philosophical poet and his nature mysticism had a strong, though diffuse, effect on his successors.

## World Heritage sites

There are 17 UK World Heritage sites, a term determined in 1972 by UNESCO for 'places or buildings of outstanding universal value'. Their formal titles are, in order of designation:

1986 The Giant's Causeway and Causeway coast

1986 Durham Castle and Cathedral

1986 Ironbridge Gorge

1986 Studley Royal Park, including the ruins of Fountains Abbey

1986 Stonehenge, Avebury, and associated sites

1986 The castles and town walls of King Edward in Gwynedd

1986 St Kilda

1987 Blenheim Palace

1987 City of Bath

1987 Hadrian's Wall

1987 Palace of Westminster, Abbey of Westminster, and St Margaret's church

1988 Henderson Island (in the South Pacific)

1988 The Tower of London

1988 Canterbury Cathedral, St Augustine's abbey, and St Martin's church

1995 Old and New Towns of Edinburgh

1995 Gough Island Wildlife Reserve (in the Atlantic)

1997 Maritime Greenwich

## World War I, 1914–1918

War between the Central Powers (Germany, Austria-Hungary, and allies) on one side, and the Triple Entente (Britain and the British Empire, France, and Russia) and their allies on the other. An estimated 10 million lives were lost and twice that number were wounded; the UK allies lost 600,000 men in just five months in 1916 in the Battle of the Somme. The war was fought on the eastern and western fronts, in the Middle East, in Africa, and at sea. Russia withdrew in 1917 because of the Russian Revolution; in the same year the USA entered the war on the side of Britain and France. The peace treaty of Versailles in 1919 was the formal end to the war. See also feature opposite.

---

*Fifty years were spent in the process of making Europe explosive. Five days were enough to detonate it.*

**Basil Liddell Hart** British military strategist. *The Real War, 1914–1918*

---

### The start of the war

The war was set in motion by the assassination in Sarajevo of the heir to the Austrian throne, Archduke Franz Ferdinand, by a Serbian nationalist in June 1914. Tension had already been mounting over many years between the major European powers who were divided, by a series of alliances, into two rival camps: one led by Germany and Austria-Hungary, and the other containing France, Britain, and Russia. Germany and Britain had both recently modernized their navies, and imperialist rivalries had led to a series of international crises: Russia against Austria over Bosnia 1908–09, and Germany against France and Britain over Agadir in 1911. When Austria declared war on Serbia on 28 July 1914, Russia mobilized along the German and Austrian frontier. Germany then declared war on Russia and France, taking a short cut in the west by invading neutral Belgium; on 4 August Britain declared war on Germany.

### The Western Front

The war against Germany was concentrated on the Western Front; the German advance was initially halted by the British Expeditionary Force under Sir John French at Mons and, following an allied counterattack at the Marne, the Germans were driven back to the Aisne River. The opposing lines then settled into trench warfare with neither side advancing more than a few miles over the next three years. Poison gas was first employed by the Germans at the second Battle of Ypres in 1915, and the British introduced tanks at the Battle of the Somme in 1916.

## ◆ THE EMBATTLED ISLAND: BRITAIN IN THE WORLD WARS ◆

War is often cited as a catalyst for change, and Britain's experience during the World Wars seems to prove the maxim. If World War I saw the birth of modern British society, World War II, to continue the analogy, saw its maturation.

### 'The War to End all Wars'

The events of July 1914 caught most of Britain by surprise. Despite Sir Edward Grey's apocalyptic remark 'the lamps are going out all over Europe; we shall not see them lit again in our lifetime', the majority of British people adhered to the popular belief that the European war would be over by Christmas. This belief goes some way to explain why the military encounter which consumed the next four years was so difficult for Britain; it proved to be a war of stalemate which established military thinking was powerless to break.

Reactions to the new reality of war were slow; neither British military nor political leaders were equipped for a major challenge to their accepted ideas. The prime minister, Asquith, was at first unwilling to treat the war as 'total', and then unable to implement the necessary control measures. The creation of Lloyd George's coalition in 1916 saw the first real political incursion into civilian life, ending the 'business as usual' attitude which had hampered the war effort until then.

The length of the conflict meant that resources were paramount, especially as Britain had traditionally been an importer of raw materials. Great efforts were made from 1916 to co-ordinate the country's requirements with industry's capabilities, and the rapid technical development which accompanied the war was effectively harnessed. The success of British agriculture is best shown in the delay of rationing until 1918.

Britain's most valuable resource in a war of attrition was its population. Kitchener's volunteer army had raised half a million by September 1914, but it was necessary to introduce conscription in 1916 for all males aged between 18 and 41. The labour market was filled by the allocation of women to the agricultural and industrial sectors, and their achievements gave weight to the call for emancipation, finally met in 1918.

World War I is remembered for its horrific casualties. It is estimated that of those who served 40% were either killed or suffered serious injuries. Both the reality and the image of these casualties haunted British society for decades afterwards. The late 20th century saw a revived interest in the war and its veterans.

### The interwar years

'What is our task? To make Britain a fit country for heroes to live in.' Lloyd George's slogan of 1918 reflected an admirable sentiment, but it proved unobtainable in the postwar world. By 1917, the war was costing Britain £7 million per day, the money coming largely from American loans. By 1918, the country was economically exhausted, and the impact of the war upon the international economy meant that Britain's usual revenue from exports was severely curtailed. The worldwide interwar depression further diminished Britain's economic standing, leaving the country facing the threat of Hitler in 1939 with limited resources, but at least with the experience of total war gleaned from the earlier conflict.

### The Finest Hour

During the 1930s, despite the policy of appeasement, Britain had been preparing for war; this is clearly demonstrated by the issue of gas masks as early as 1937. In May 1940, a coalition government was formed, with a War Cabinet of five. Led by Winston Churchill, this administration proved to be the most competent since the turn of the century. Conscription was introduced as soon as war broke out. In 1940 the Emergency Powers Act was enacted, effectively giving the government unlimited powers.

Although UK military casualties in World War II were about one-third of those suffered in World War I, the home population also faced direct attack. Fear of invasion and the horrors of the Blitz greatly increased civilian hardship caused by strict rationing, but tight government control of information ensured that no social breakdown occurred. Churchill's carefully contrived morale-boosting broadcasts also helped to maintain a spirit of national unity which transcended social divisions. As in World War I, effective management of resources was essential, and in Ernest Bevin Britain had an ideal minister of labour, directing workers nationally.

The financial consequence of a lengthy war was nevertheless a bankrupt Britain, and the war had highlighted huge social problems. Economist William Beveridge, working from the premise that 'warfare necessitates welfare', produced a report in 1942 which formed the blueprint for the Welfare State. Central to this plan was the creation of a system of universal secondary education, achieved by the 1944 Education Act, but many other welfare provisions were also floated. Thus on VE Day the British people really believed that they were entering a period of prosperity.

by Peter Martland

### The Eastern Front

On the Eastern Front the major Allied offensive was the Gallipoli campaign in 1915 which attempted to break through the Dardanelles and open up a route to assist Russia in its fight against the Turks. The failure of the campaign, and the great loss of mainly Australian and New Zealand troops, led to Winston Churchill's resignation as First Lord of the Admiralty. The Turks were also under attack in Mesopotamia, with Baghdad finally falling in 1917, and in Palestine where General Allenby, assisted by the Arab Revolt, won a series of victories that resulted in the Turkish armistice in October 1918.

### The war at sea

The war at sea involved, almost exclusively, the British and German navies, but the major sea battle at Jutland in 1916 was indecisive. The main impact at sea was by German U-boats (submarines) which, from January 1917, attempted to destroy Britain's merchant fleet and succeeded in bringing the country close to starvation. They were countered by the introduction, by British prime minister Lloyd George, of the convoy system, in which groups of vessels were protected by warships. As a result of the submarine threat the USA entered the war in April 1917.

### The final stages

In the spring of 1918 Germany launched a major offensive on the Western Front, which was halted at the second Battle of the Marne in August 1918, while in Italy the Austro-Hungarian army was defeated at Vittorio-Veneto. German capitulation began with naval mutinies at Kiel in October 1918, followed by uprisings in the major cities. Kaiser Wilhelm II abdicated, and on 11 November the armistice was signed. The peace conference at Versailles began in January 1919, and the treaty was signed by Germany in June 1919.

The terms of peace were negotiated separately with each of the Central Powers in the course of the next few years.

## World War II, 1939–45

War between Germany, Italy, and Japan (the Axis powers) on one side, and Britain, the Commonwealth, France, the USA, the USSR, and China (the Allied powers) on the other. The main theatres of war were Europe, the USSR, North Africa, and the Pacific and Atlantic seaboards. An estimated 55 million lives were lost, including 20 million citizens of the USSR and 6 million Jews killed in the holocaust. Germany surrendered in May 1945, but Japan fought on until the USA dropped atomic bombs on Hiroshima and Nagasaki in August.

---

*The British people have taken for themselves this motto – 'Business carried on as usual during alterations on the map of Europe'.*
**Winston Churchill** British Conservative prime minister.
Speech at the Guildhall 9 November 1914

---

### The start of the war

The war's origins lay in Germany's reluctance to accept the frontiers laid down at the peace of Versailles in 1920, and in the highly aggressive foreign policy of Adolf Hitler (German Chancellor from 1933). Britain and France declared war on Germany on 3 September 1939, two days after German forces had invaded Poland. In the following months (the 'phoney' war) little fighting took place, until April 1940 when the Germans invaded Denmark and Norway. The failure of Allied resistance led to the replacement of British prime minister Neville Chamberlain by Winston Churchill. By the end of May, Germany had invaded Holland, Belgium, and France, and 337,131 Allied troops had to be evacuated from the beaches of Dunkirk to England. Following the 1940 aerial bombardment of British cities, known as the ◊Blitz, German air attacks on British air bases were successfully resisted by the RAF in the ◊Battle of Britain, and the planned invasion of Britain was abandoned.

### The war in Russia

The Germans then moved east, invading Yugoslavia and Greece in April 1941, and launching an attack on the Russian front in June; by the end of the year they had come within 40 km/25 mi of Moscow and had begun to besiege Leningrad (now St Petersburg). After their initial success in the USSR, the Germans were gradually repulsed; Leningrad lost about a third of its population while resisting the German siege for nearly two years. The Germans were finally expelled from the USSR in August 1944.

### The US joins the Allies

The USA entered the war in December 1941 following the Japanese bombing of the US naval base at Pearl Harbour, Hawaii. The Japanese then took control of southeast Asia and Burma, capturing some 90,000 British and Commonwealth prisoners. They were only checked in June 1942 with a series of US naval victories culminating in the defeat of the Japanese fleet at Leyte Gulf in

# ◆ BREAKING WITH THE PAST: POST-WAR BRITAIN FROM ATTLEE TO THATCHER ◆

Britain emerged victorious from World War II, with its Empire intact. 'Now Win the Peace', said the election posters. The new Labour government promised planned economic growth, Keynesian remedies for unemployment, modernization of industry by national-ization, and welfare 'From the Cradle to the Grave'. It was little short of a social revolution, but high hopes were soon tempered by reality.

## The end of Empire
Internationally, the 'Big Three' were at best the 'Two-and-a-half'. The USA and USSR had contributed most to victory. When their rivalry turned into Cold War, Britain could not hope to compete in the arms race for long. At home, the staple British export industries (coal, steel, textiles, and ship-building) were in long-term decline. Markets lost during the war would never be fully recovered, and economic problems seemed endemic. These issues were linked: how could a nation with chronic balance of payments difficulties afford to remain a global power?

Despite austerity policies, by 1949 Britain had been forced to devalue the pound and reduce its overseas commitments by withdrawing from India and Palestine. Departure from these trouble-spots did not mean wholesale retreat. The government hoped to transform the British Empire into a freely co-operating Common-wealth of Nations with real political and economic significance. The aim was to satisfy colonial nationalism, while preserving a network of military bases and a trading bloc making international payments in sterling.

The weakness of this strategy was revealed by the Suez Crisis. When Britain attempted to exercise neo-imperial dominance in the Middle East by force, it failed and unleashed a wave of anti-British feeling. Harold Macmillan accelerated decolonization and accepted that the Commonwealth was going to be a very loose association. By 1964 most of the Empire had become independent. The 'special relationship' with the USA suffered as a result: Britain minus the colonies was simply not so valuable an ally. Fearing isolation, Britain turned to the European Community, only to find its application for membership vetoed by France. 'Great Britain has lost an Empire and has not yet found a role', observed Dean Acheson in 1962.

## 'East of Suez'
Britain meanwhile shared in the remarkable post-war economic recovery of the western world. 'Most of our people have never had it so good', said Macmillan in 1957. Both Conservatives and Labour were broadly committed to maintaining the mixed economy, the welfare state, and full employment. While living stan-dards rose, governments shrank from tackling the underlying problems of an uncompetitive economy with high wage demands and low investment. The Treasury merely operated short-term 'stop-go' policies as each spurt of growth ended in balance of payments deficits. These necessitated a second devaluation in 1967 and drastic cuts in overseas defence spending. All significant commitments 'East of Suez' were to be abandoned by 1971. Thus Britain broke through the status barrier: it was a world power no longer. Late-1960s society may have been affluent and per-missive, but the nation seemed in decline.

Edward Heath swung foreign policy decisively toward Europe. Britain entered the EC in 1973 but found it difficult to adjust to its institutions and policies. EC membership did not bring the dramatic material ben-efits expected. Nor did the discovery of North Sea oil. Rising unemployment, record levels of inflation, an energy crisis, industrial disputes, and violence in North-ern Ireland all added to the demoralization.

## The Thatcher years
The post-war consensus crumbled as politicians in both parties tried to find new policies. This plunged Labour into a decade of internal strife and permanent oppo-sition from 1979. The Conservatives, led by Margaret Thatcher, adopted a radical 'monetarist' programme intended to revitalize the economy through rapid deflation, deregulation, privatization, and the reduction of trade union power. But this economic shock treat-ment coincided with a global recession. British unem-ployment topped 3 million, amid signs of a growing divide between the depressed north and relatively prosperous south. Productivity improved and enterprise was encouraged in an economy increasingly based on services, but the 'economic miracle' of the mid-1980s proved short-lived, and unemployment remained high.

Thatcher sought to re-assert British influence in international affairs, but the prestige derived from the Falklands War and a revival of the 'special relationship' was not sustainable. When the end of the Cold War prompted further European integration British doubts about the EC resurfaced in the politics of the 1990s.

Britain has been transformed since 1945. The British Empire, built up over four centuries, came to an end in the 1960s. Traditional industries, chief sources of national wealth since the Industrial Revolution, with-ered away and all but died in the 1980s. The nation faced these changes with reluctance, but the era of empire and industry was over. A new era had begun.

by Jason Tomes

October 1944. The major turning point for the Allies occurred in North Africa, where German successes under Rommel were reversed when the British Eighth Army under ◊Montgomery won the decisive Battle of El Alamein in October–November 1942; by May 1943 the German army in Africa had surrendered. This left the Allies free to invade Sicily and, after the fall of the Italian dictator Mussolini in July 1943, mainland Italy. Rome fell in June 1944, and the Germans in Italy finally surrendered after the fall of Trieste in May 1945.

### The D-Day invasion

The Allies launched the successful ◊D-Day invasion of Normandy on 6 June 1944 under the command of Eisenhower; Paris was liberated by August and, in spite of the setback at Arnhem, the Allies pressed forward across the pre-war German frontier to link up in April 1945 with the Soviet army on the Elbe. The Germans surrendered at Rheims on 7 May. The Japanese continued to fight, despite the loss of Burma and the Philippines in 1945, and only surrendered after US atom bombs were dropped on the cities of Hiroshima and Nagasaki.

### Post-war

See feature on previous page.

## Worthing

Seaside resort in West Sussex, southeast England, 23 km/14 mi west of Brighton, at the foot of the South Downs; population (1991) 94,000. Industries include horticulture, retail, tourism, and leisure. There are traces of prehistoric and Roman occupation in the vicinity.

Worthing developed from a small fishing hamlet into a popular resort in the late 18th century. Regency terraces and crescents were built, including Park Crescent. Features include the Connaught Theatre, and a museum which contains Roman relics discovered in the area. Worthing includes the former separate villages of Broadwater, Durrington, and West Tarring.

## Wren, Christopher (1632–1723)

English architect. His ingenious use of a refined and sober Baroque style can be seen in his best-known work, ◊St Paul's Cathedral, London (1675–1711), and in the many churches he built in London including St Mary-le-Bow, Cheapside (1670–77), and St Bride's, Fleet Street (1671–78). His other works include the Sheldonian Theatre, Oxford (1664–69), Greenwich Hospital, London (begun 1694), and Marlborough House, London (1709–10; now much altered).

After studying science and mathematics at Oxford, he became Professor of Astronomy at Gresham College, London, in 1657 and Savilian Professor of Astronomy, Oxford, in 1661. He turned to architecture in about 1662, when he designed the chapel of Pembroke College, Cambridge. After the Great Fire of London in 1666, he prepared a plan for rebuilding the city on Classical lines, incorporating piazzas and broad avenues, but it was not adopted. Instead, he was commissioned to rebuild St Paul's and 51 City churches. He showed great skill both in fitting his buildings into the irregular sites of the destroyed churches, and in varying the designs, giving them a series of towers which characterized the London skyline until World War II.

In 1669 Wren became surveyor-general of the King's Works, his commissions including building and renovations at Hampton Court, Kensington, St James's, Westminster, Whitehall, Winchester, Windsor Castle, and Chelsea Hospital (1682–85).

## Wrexham

Unitary authority in northwest Wales, created in 1996 from part of the former county of Clywd; population (1996) 123,500; area 500 sq km/193 sq mi. The principal towns are Wrexham (administrative headquarters), Holt and Ruabon.

### Physical

The eastern side is mountainous, including Ruabon Mountain (511 m/1,677 ft). The River Dee flows through the area.

### Features

Clywedog Valley has notable countryside and industrial archaeology

### Economy

Activities include food processing, high tech industries, and the manufacture of plastics and pharmaceuticals.

## Wright, Joseph (1734–1797)

English painter. He was known as **Wright of Derby**, from his birthplace. He painted portraits, landscapes, and groups performing scientific experiments. His work is often dramatically lit – by fire, candlelight, or even volcanic explosion.

Several of his subjects are highly original, for example *The Experiment on a Bird in the Air Pump* (1768; National Gallery, London). His portraits include the reclining figure of *Sir Brooke Boothby* (1781; Tate Gallery, London).

## Wycherley, William (1640–c. 1716)

English Restoration dramatist. His first comedy, *Love in a Wood*, won him court favour in 1671, and later bawdy works include *The Country Wife* (1675) and *The Plain Dealer* (1676).

## Wycliffe, John (*c.* 1320–1384)

English religious reformer. Allying himself with the party of ◊John of Gaunt, which was opposed to ecclesiastical influence at court, he attacked abuses in the church, maintaining that the Bible rather than the church was the supreme authority. He criticized such fundamental doctrines as priestly absolution, confession, and indulgences, and set disciples to work on the first translation of the Bible into English. He wrote many popular tracts in English (rather than Latin). His followers were known as ◊Lollards.

## Wye, Welsh Gwy

River in Wales and England; length 208 km/130 mi. It rises on Plynlimon in northeast Ceredigion, flows southeast and east through Powys and Hereford and Worcester, and follows the Gwent–Gloucestershire border before joining the River Severn 4 km/2.5 mi south of Chepstow. It has salmon fisheries and is noted for its scenery.

## Wyndham, John (1903–1969)

English science-fiction writer. He wrote *The Day of the Triffids* (1951), describing the invasion of Earth by a strange plant mutation; *The Chrysalids* (1955); and *The Midwich Cuckoos* (1957). A recurrent theme in his work is people's response to disaster, whether caused by nature, aliens, or human error.

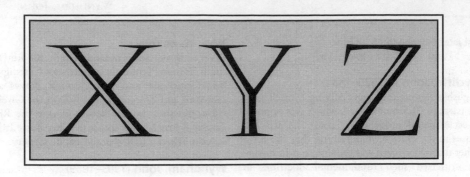

## yeoman

In England, a small landowner who farmed his own fields – a system that formed a bridge between the break-up of feudalism and the agricultural revolution of the 18th–19th centuries.

## Yeomen of the Guard

English military corps, popularly known as Beef-eaters, the sovereign's bodyguard since the corps was founded by Henry VII in 1485. Its duties are now purely ceremonial.

There are Yeomen warders at the Tower of London, and the uniform and weapons are much as they were in Tudor times. The nickname 'Beefeaters' is supposed to have originated in 1669 when the Grand Duke of Tuscany ascribed their fine appearance to beef.

## YMCA, Young Men's Christian Association

International organization founded in 1844 by George Williams (1821–1905) in London. It aims at self-improvement – spiritual, intellectual, and physical. YMCAs provide dormitories and rooms for both transients and residents; educational, sports, and civic programmes; and recreation facilities for members and for military troops in wartime.

From 1971 women were accepted as members.

## York

Cathedral and industrial city in northern England, on the River Ouse; population (1991) 127,700. Formerly part of the county of North Yorkshire, since 1996 it has been a unitary authority with an area of 271 sq km/105 sq mi. Industries include tourism (with some three million visitors a year), and the manufacture of scientific instruments, sugar, chocolate, and glass. The Gothic York Minster is England's largest medieval cathedral, and the town retains many of its medieval streets and buildings and much of its 14th-century city wall. The York Cycle of Mystery Plays, originally played on wagons in the street in the 14th and 15th centuries, are performed every four years; in 2000 they will be performed in the Minster for the first time.

### History

The town was founded in AD 71 as the Roman provincial capital **Eboracum**, and served as the base for the northern campaigns of Hadrian. The emperor Septimus Severus died in the city, and following the death here of the emperor Constantine Chlorus in 306, the troops proclaimed his son Constantine the Great emperor of the Western Roman Empire.

Under the Saxons York was known as **Eoforwic** and it became a Christian stronghold. The Roman missionary Paulinus became the first archbishop of York in 633. The Danes captured the city in 867, and it became the Viking trading centre of **Jorvik**. At the Battle of Stamford Bridge (1066), near York, Harold II defeated the army of King Harold of Norway.

At the time of the Norman Conquest the population was estimated to be 8,000, second in size only to that of London. An important commercial city in medieval times, it became a centre of the wool trade, and the small ships of its Merchant Adventurers sailed from York to the Hanseatic towns (a confederation of north European trading centres from the 12th to the 17th centuries). As the size of ships increased the city's European trade declined, and York lost its commercial importance, while retaining its ecclesiastical and much of its political importance. In the 15th century Richard, Duke of York (1411–1460), founded the dynasty of York which ruled England from 1461 to 1485.

The city was a Royalist stronghold during the

Civil War; in 1644 it was besieged by Parliamentary forces and surrendered after the Battle of Marston Moor. In the 18th century York became a fashionable resort, and in the 19th century its prosperity was again established when it became a railway centre.

## York Minster

It is thought that a wooden chapel was erected on the site of the present Minster in 627 for the baptism of King Edwin of Northumbria. A Norman structure was begun in about 1080, but the oldest surviving part of the present building dates from about 1220, and the central tower was completed in about 1480. The cathedral has fine stained-glass windows, and the Great East Window, dating from 1405, is thought to be the world's largest medieval stained-glass window.

## Churches

All Saints' Church (North Street) has 14th-and 15th-century glass and a graceful spire; All Saints' (in Pavement) is the only church in York to have a lantern tower. The last church to be built before the Reformation, St Michael-le-Belfry (1535) has in its register an entry recording the baptism in 1570 of Guy Fawkes, the conspirator in the Gunpowder Plot. St Olave's Church was established in the 11th century and contains 15th-century stained glass.

## Other features

The restored medieval Guildhall was originally built in 1448. There are three other guildhalls: the Merchant Adventurers Hall, built by York's most powerful guild which in the 15th–17th centuries controlled the export of cloth from the north of England; the Merchant Tailors' Hall which has a 17th–18th-century exterior; and the 15th-century St Anthony's Hall.

The city walls, built on earlier foundations, date mainly from the 14th century, although the gates include Norman work. The four main gateways or 'bars' are Walmgate Bar, Bootham Bar, Monk Bar, and Mickelgate Bar; Micklegate was the chief of these (and upon which the head of Richard of York was impaled in 1460).

Clifford's Tower (1245–1262) is all that remains of York Castle. It was built to replace the wooden tower built by William the Conqueror which was destroyed in 1190 when, during anti-Jewish riots in the city, 150 members of the Jewish population were put in the tower and took their own lives by setting fire to it, rather than fall into the hands of the mob.

The network of narrow medieval streets in the centre of York includes Stonegate, and the Shambles, the street of the butchers.

St Peter's School is one of the oldest private schools in England, claiming links with the school

**York Minster** The historic city of York is dominated by York Minster, seen here from the River Ouse. The vast cathedral is particularly noted for its stained glass. When fire, caused by a lightning strike, swept the south transept of the building in 1984, the famous Rose Window there was severely damaged, but has since been restored. Roger Scruton/Collections

of St Peter founded in 627. There are two Society of Friends' (Quaker) schools: the Mount School for girls (1785), and Bootham School (1823). York University was established in 1963.

York was the birthplace of the conspirator Guy Fawkes and the poet W H Auden. Dick Turpin, the highwayman, was hanged here in 1739.

*Museums and galleries*

The Yorkshire Museum contains fine archaeological, natural history, and geological collections. The Jorvik Viking Centre depicts life in York in the time of the Vikings and displays the archaeological remains discovered during excavations. The City Art Gallery has a large collection of European paintings. The Castle Museum is a folk museum which includes reconstructed 19th-century streets. The National Railway Museum houses a large collection of locomotives, as well as royal carriages and a replica of a section of the Channel Tunnel.

## York, House of

English dynasty founded by Richard, Duke of York (1411–1460). He claimed the throne through his descent from Lionel, Duke of Clarence (1338–1368), third son of Edward III, whereas the reigning monarch, Henry VI of the

rival house of Lancaster, was descended from the fourth son, John of Gaunt. The argument was fought out in the Wars of the ◊Roses. York was killed at the Battle of Wakefield in 1460, but the following year his son became King Edward IV. Edward was succeeded by his son Edward V and then by his brother Richard III, with whose death at Bosworth the line ended. The Lancastrian victor in that battle was crowned Henry VII, and consolidated his claim by marrying Edward IV's eldest daughter, Elizabeth, thus founding the House of Tudor.

See genealogy below.

## York, archbishop of

Metropolitan (archbishop with authority over bishops) of the northern province of the Anglican Church in England, hence primate of England.

The first archbishop of York was Egbert (732–66). The first Norman archbishop was Thomas of Bayeux (1070–1100). Pope Innocent VI (1352–62) decided that the archbishop of Canterbury should have precedence over the archbishop of York, with the title 'Primate of All England' as distinct from 'Primate of England' for York.

Recent noted archbishops of York have included Cosmo Gordon Lang (1908–28),

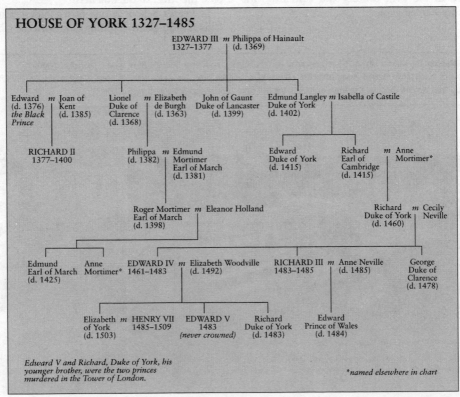

William Temple (1929–42), and Arthur Michael Ramsey (1956–61), all of whom went on to become archbishop of Canterbury. The current archbishop of York is David M Hope (appointed in 1995).

## Youth Hostels Association, YHA

Registered charity founded in Britain in 1930 to promote knowledge and care of the countryside by providing cheap overnight accommodation for young people on active holidays (such as walking or cycling). Types of accommodation range from castles to log cabins.

YHA membership is open to individuals of 14 or over (or 5 if accompanied by an adult). There are 260 hostels in England and Wales. In addition to basic accommodation, YHA provides sporting activities including climbing, windsurfing, hanggliding, and horse riding.

# APPENDICES

# Chronology of British history 1707–2000

| *Events involving Britain and Ireland* | *Other events* |
|---|---|
| **1707** Union of Scotland and England. | |
| | **1709** Battle of Poltava: Russians inflicted major defeat on Swedish invaders. |
| **1715** Jacobite Rebellion.<br>**1716** Septennial Act: maximum length of English parliament extended to seven years. | |
| **1720** South Sea Bubble.<br>**1721–42** Second ministry of Sir Robert Walpole. | |
| | **1740** War of Austrian Succession: Prussia conquered Silesia. |
| **1745** Jacobite Rebellion. | |
| **1756–63** Seven Years' War, ending with the Treaty of Paris. | |
| | **1772** First Partition of Poland. |
| **1776** American Declaration of Independence from Britain. | |
| **1781** Americans force British army to surrender at Yorktown. | |
| | **1789** Outbreak of French Revolution. |
| | **1792–97** War of the First Coalition.<br>**1793, 1795** Second and Third Partitions of Poland. |
| **1793** Revolutionary government in France declared war on Britain.<br>**1798** Battle of the Nile: Royal Navy defeated French navy in Egypt. | **1798–1801** War of the Second Coalition. |
| | **1799** In France, Napoleon overthrew the Directory. |
| **1801** Union of Britain and Ireland.<br>**1802** Britain made peace with France. | |
| **1805** Battle of Trafalgar: Royal Navy defeated French and Spanish fleets. | **1805–7** War of the Third Coalition. |
| | **1813–14** War of the Fourth Coalition, ending with the abdication of Napoleon. |
| **1815** Battle of Waterloo: Britain and allies defeated French. | **1815** Napoleon's 'Hundred Days' as restored emperor of France; Treaty of Vienna. |

## Society, economy, and science

**1709** Abraham Darby used coke to smelt iron.

**1712** Last execution for witchcraft in England.

**1721** Lady Mary Wortley Montague introduced inoculation for smallpox into England.

**1733** James Kay patented the 'flying shuttle', for use in weaving.
**1738** John Wesley received call to evangelism.

**1750** Foundation of the English Jockey Club and of the Hambledon Cricket Club.
**1754** Foundation of the Royal and Ancient Golf Club, St Andrew's.

**1768–71** James Cook's first voyage of discovery.

**1773–79** Construction of the cast-iron bridge at Ironbridge, Shropshire.
**1774** Joseph Priestley discovered oxygen.
**1776** Adam Smith, *An Inquiry into the Nature and Causes of the Wealth of Nations.*

**1787** Marylebone Cricket Club (MCC) founded.
**1789** Jeremy Bentham, *Introduction to the Principles of Morals and Legislation.*
**1790** Edmund Burke, *Reflections on the Revolution in France.*

**1798** Thomas Malthus, *Essay on the Principle of Population.*

**1802** John Dalton proposed atomic theory and compiled tables of atomic weights; William Paley, *Natural Theology.*

**1811** Luddite attacks on textile machinery in Nottingham and Yorkshire.

## Cultural history

**1710** George Berkeley, *A Treatise Concerning the Principles of Human Knowledge.*
**1712** Alexander Pope, *The Rape of the Lock.*

**1719** Daniel Defoe, *Robinson Crusoe.*

**1724** Foundation of Three Choirs Festival (for choirs in Gloucester, Hereford, and Worcester).
**1726** Jonathan Swift, *Gulliver's Travels.*
**1728** John Gay, *Beggar's Opera.*

**1739** David Hume, *Treatise on Human Nature.*

**1741** George Frideric Handel, *Messiah.*

**1749** Henry Fielding, *The History of Tom Jones, A Foundling.*

**1759** Opening of British Museum.

**1776** Edward Gibbon, *Decline and Fall of the Roman Empire* (–1788).

**1791** James Boswell, *Life of Johnson.*

**1813** Jane Austen, *Pride and Prejudice.*

**1817** Foundation of *The Scotsman.*

**1818** Lord Byron, *Don Juan* (–1823); Mary Shelley, *Frankenstein.*

| Events involving Britain and Ireland | Other events |
|---|---|
| **1829** Catholic Emancipation. | **1829** Greek kingdom established. |
| | **1830** July Revolution in France: Louis Philippe replaced Charles X. |
| **1832** Great Reform Act. | |
| **1845–46** Great Famine in Ireland. | |
| **1846** Abolition of Corn Laws; Conservative Party split. | |
| | **1848** Revolutions in Europe; republic established in France. |
| **1854–56** Crimean War: Britain and France fight Russia. | |
| | **1861–65** American Civil War. |
| | **1861** Kingdom of Italy proclaimed. |
| **1867** Second Reform Act. | |
| | **1870–71** Franco–Prussian War. |
| | **1871** German Empire proclaimed; Third Republic established in France. |
| **1884** Third Reform Act. | |
| **1885** Redistribution Act creates single-member constituencies. | |
| **1886** Gladstone's first Home Rule Bill for Ireland defeated; Liberal Party split. | |
| | **1894** Franco–Russian Alliance formed. |
| **1899–1902** Boer War. | |
| **1902** Anglo–Japanese Alliance formed. | |
| **1904** Anglo–French entente. | |
| | **1905** Attempted Revolution in Russia. |
| **1907** Anglo–Russian entente. | |
| | **1908** Austria-Hungary annexed Bosnia-Herzegovina. |
| **1909** Rejection of David Lloyd George's 'People's Budget' by Lords started constitutional crisis. | |
| **1911** Parliament Act reduced power of Lords. | |
| **1914** Irish Home Rule Act on statute book, but was suspended. | |
| **1914** Start of World War I: British forces involved in campaigns in NE France. | **1914** Assassination of Austrian Archduke Franz-Ferdinand in Sarajevo led to outbreak of World War I. |

## Society, economy, and science

**1825** Opening of the Stockton and Darlington Railway.
**1829** Foundation of the Metropolitan Police force (London).

**1833** John Keble begins the Oxford Movement in the Church of England.
**1834** Poor Law Amendment Act.

**1838** Working Men's Association draws up the People's Charter.
**1840** Introduction of Penny Postage.

**1843** Great Disruption in Scottish Church.
**1844** Foundation of the Co-operative Society.

**1851** Great Exhibition held in Hyde Park, London, in Joseph Paxton's Crystal Palace.

**1857** Matrimonial Causes Act established divorce courts in England and Wales.
**1859** Charles Darwin, *The Origin of Species*; J S Mill, *On Liberty*.

**1865** Debut of W G Grace, cricketer.
**1867** Karl Marx, *Das Kapital*, Vol. 1 (Vol. 2, 1885; Vol. 3, 1895).

**1871** Bank Holidays introduced in England and Wales.

**1882** Married Women's Property Act.

**1901** Guglielmo Marconi transmitted wireless message from Poldhu, Cornwall, to Newfoundland.
**1902** Balfour Education Act provided state secondary education and integrated state and church schools.

**1905** Foundation of the Automobile Association.

**1907** Formation of Boy Scouts (Girl Guides formed 1909).

**1911** Ernest Rutherford identified nuclear atom.

**1914** British government granted emergency powers.

## Cultural history

**1821** John Constable, *The Hay Wain*.
**1824** Foundation of the National Gallery, London.

**1836** Charles Dickens, *Sketches by Boz* and start of *Pickwick Papers*.

**1841** Publication of *Punch*.

**1847** W M Thackeray, *Vanity Fair* (–1848).

**1857** Anthony Trollope, *Barchester Towers*.

**1865** Lewis Carroll, *Alice's Adventures in Wonderland*.

**1871** George Eliot, *Middlemarch* (–1872).

**1872** Thomas Hardy, *Under The Greenwood Tree*.

**1889** J K Jerome, *Three Men in a Boat*.
**1892** A Conan Doyle, *The Adventures of Sherlock Holmes*.

**1895** Oscar Wilde, *The Importance of Being Earnest*; first series of Promenade Concerts at Queen's Hall, London, conducted by Henry Wood.
**1899** Edward Elgar, *Enigma Variations*.

**1902** Publication of the *Times Literary Supplement*.

**1903** G E Moore, *Principia Ethica*.

**1906** John Galsworthy, *The Man of Property* (Vol. I of The Forsyte Saga).

**1908** Kenneth Grahame, *The Wind in the Willows*.

**1911** Max Beerbohm, *Zuleika Dobson*.

## Events involving Britain and Ireland

**1915** Dardanelles campaign.
**1916** Easter Rising in Dublin; Battle of Jutland; Battle of the Somme.
**1917** Third Battle of Ypres (Passchendaele).

**1918** Counter-offensive against the Central Powers.

**1921** Partition of Ireland with separate governments in the north and the Irish Free State.

**1924** First Labour government, with Ramsay MacDonald as prime minister.

**1926** General Strike.

**1929** Second Labour government, with Ramsay MacDonald as prime minister.

**1931** Formation of coalition National Government, with Ramsay MacDonald as prime minister.

**1936** Abdication crisis: Edward VIII abdicates.

**1938** Munich crisis: Prime Minister Neville Chamberlain agreed to Hitler's demands on Czechoslovakia.
**1939** Following German invasion of Poland, Britain declared war on Germany.
**1940** Churchill appointed prime minister of coalition government; British withdrawal from Dunkirk; Battle of Britain.

**1942** Battle of El Alamein: British army defeated Germans under Erwin Rommel.

**1943** Anglo-American invasion of Italy.

**1944** D-Day invasion of France.

**1945** End of World War II.

**1947** Britain granted independence to India, Pakistan, and Burma.
**1949** Formation of NATO with Britain as member; southern Ireland became fully independent.
**1951** Festival of Britain.

## Other events

**1915** Italy joined War on Allied side.
**1916** Battle of Verdun on Western Front; Brusilov Offensive on Eastern Front.
**1917** 'February Revolution' in Russia (March), followed by the Bolshevik (Communist) 'October Revolution' (November) and civil war; USA enters War.
**1918** Treaty of Brest-Litovsk between Russia and Germany; end of War with Armistice of 11 November.
**1919** Treaty of Versailles, including creation of the League of Nations.
**1920** Russian Civil War ended with Bolshevik victory.

**1922** Benito Mussolini appointed prime minister of Italy.

**1925** Locarno Pact: Rhineland made a demilitarized zone.

**1929** Wall Street Crash and start of the Great Depression.

**1933** Adolf Hitler appointed chancellor of Germany.
**1934** Stalin started purge of political enemies and others in USSR.

**1936–9** Spanish Civil War.

**1937** Japanese invasion of China.

**1939** Soviet–German Pact; outbreak of World War II.

**1940** German invasion of Low Countries and France.

**1941** German invasion of USSR; Japan bombed Pearl Harbor and occupied SE Asia.
**1942** US Navy defeated Japan in Battle of Midway.

**1943** German army surrendered to Russians at Stalingrad.

**1945** Foundation of United Nations; end of World War II in Europe; atomic bombs halted war in Asia.
**1946–8** Communist governments established in E European countries.

| Society, economy, and science | Cultural history |
|---|---|
| **1916** Marie Stopes, *Married Love*. | |
| **1918** School leaving age increased to 14. | **1918** Lytton Strachey, *Eminent Victorians*. |
| **1919** John Maynard Keynes, *The Economic Consequences of the Peace*. | **1919** Edward Elgar, *Cello Concerto*. |
| **1922** Foundation of the British Broadcasting Company (Corporation from 1927). | **1922** T S Eliot, *The Waste Land*; James Joyce, *Ulysses*. |
| | **1923** William Walton, *Façade*. |
| **1925** UK divorce laws made inoperative in Irish Free State. | |
| **1926** John Logie Baird demonstrated television. | **1926** A A Milne, *Winnie the Pooh*. |
| | **1928** Virginia Woolf, *Orlando*. |
| **1929** Most Scottish Presbyterian churches united as Church of Scotland. | **1929** Noel Coward, *Bitter Sweet*; Robert Graves, *Goodbye to All That*. |
| **1930** First British Empire Games held (in Canada). | **1930** W H Auden, *Poems*. |
| **1932** James Chadwick discovered the neutron. | **1932** Aldous Huxley, *Brave New World*. |
| **1933** Controversial 'bodyline' MCC cricket tour of Australia. | |
| **1935** First successful experiments with radar. | |
| **1936** Billy Butlin opened first holiday camp, near Skegness; BBC started television broadcasting. | **1936** A J Ayer, *Language, Truth and Logic*. |
| | **1938** Graham Greene, *Brighton Rock*. |
| **1940** Howard Florey developed penicillin for medical use. | |
| **1942** William Beveridge, Social Security and Allied Services (the Beveridge Report); William Temple, *Christianity and the Social Order*. | |
| | **1943** T S Eliot, *Four Quartets*. |
| **1944** 'Butler' Education Act, creating three-school system of secondary education. | |
| | **1945** Benjamin Britten, *Peter Grimes*. |
| **1946** London Airport opened at Heathrow. | |
| | **1947** First Edinburgh Festival of the Arts. |
| **1949** Maiden flight of the Comet, the first jet airliner. | **1949** George Orwell, *Nineteen Eighty-four*. |
| **1953** Francis Crick and James Watson announced double-helix structure of DNA. | |
| **1954** Roger Bannister's four-minute mile. | **1954** Kingsley Amis, *Lucky Jim*; William Golding, *Lord of the Flies*. |

| Events involving Britain and Ireland | Other events |
|---|---|
| | **1955** Warsaw Pact signed. |
| **1956** Suez crisis. | |
| | **1957** Creation of the European Economic Community. |
| **1962** 'Night of Long Knives': Prime Minister Macmillan dismissed 7 of 21 cabinet ministers. | **1962** Cuban missile crisis. |
| **1963** British application to join European Common Market vetoed by France; Profumo Scandal. | **1963** In USA, assassination of President John F Kennedy. |
| **1964** Creation of the Welsh Office. | **1964** Growth of US involvement in Vietnam War. |
| **1965** Rhodesia made Unilateral Declaration of Independence from Britain. | **1965** Cultural Revolution in China. |
| **1967** Sterling devalued. | **1967** Six-Day War between Israel and Arab countries. |
| **1968** Enoch Powell's 'rivers of blood' speech advocating repatriation of immigrants. | **1968** Student unrest in France. |
| **1969** Outbreak of 'the troubles' in Northern Ireland. | |
| **1973** Britain joined the European Economic Community. | **1973** USA withdrew from Vietnam War. |
| **1974** Britain established direct rule of Northern Ireland. | |
| | **1975** In Spain, death of General Franco; succeeded by King Juan Carlos. |
| **1979** 'Winter of discontent': widespread strikes by public workers discredited Labour government; Margaret Thatcher elected first woman prime minister. | **1979** Peace Treaty between Egypt and Israel; USSR invaded Afghanistan. |
| | **1980** Death of President Tito of Yugoslavia; Ronald Reagan elected president of the USA. |
| **1981** Riots in Brixton (London) and Toxteth (Liverpool). | **1982** Martial Law declared in Poland and Solidarity Union suppressed. |
| **1982** Falklands War. | **1984** Prime Minister Indira Gandhi of India assassinated. |
| **1984–5** Miners' strike. | **1985** Mikhail Gorbachev appointed secretary general of Soviet Communist Party. |
| **1985** Anglo–Irish Agreement. | |
| | **1989** Tienanmen Square massacre in Beijing, China. |
| | **1989–90** Collapse of Communism in E Europe. |
| **1990** Resignation of Mrs Thatcher; succeeded by John Major. | **1990–91** Gulf War. |
| | **1991** Collapse of Soviet Union; formation of the Confederation of Independent States; Maastricht Treaty agreed. |
| **1992** Conservative Party's fourth consecutive victory in general election. | |
| **1994** Paramilitary organizations declared cease-fire in Northern Ireland. | **1994** Non-racial general election held in South Africa. |
| **1996** Northern Ireland ceasefire collapsed. | |

## Society, economy, and science

1956 Nuclear power station at Calder Hall opened.

1958 Munich air crash killed eight Manchester United players.
1959 Mini Minor on sale.
1960 Trial ruled that *Lady Chatterley's Lover* by D H Lawrence is not obscene.
1961 First betting shop opened; Michael Ramsey became 100th archbishop of Canterbury.

1963 Beeching Report proposed closure of quarter of railway network.

1966 England won World Cup.
1967 Completion of Cathedral of Christ the King, Liverpool; colour television introduced.

1969 Maiden flights of Concorde supersonic airliner; Open University founded.
1970 Age of majority reduced from 21 to 18.

1973 Introduction of commercial radio.

1975 Equal pay for both sexes compulsory.

1978 First test-tube baby born.

1982 First papal visit to Britain.

1986 GCSE examinations replaced O level and CSE.
1989 Ayatollah Khomeini of Iran issued fatwa sentencing British writer Salman Rushdie to death for blasphemy in his novel *The Satanic Verses*.

1991 Polytechnics permitted to become universities.

1992 Church of England voted to allow ordination of women to the priesthood.
1993 Queen Elizabeth II and Prince of Wales volunteered to pay income tax; Buckingham Palace was opened to the public.
1994 Privatization of British coal mines.
1994 Channel Tunnel opened.
1995 Baring's, Britain's oldest merchant bank, collapsed.
1996 Geneticists at the Roslin Institute in Edinburgh, Scotland, cloned an adult sheep, named Dolly.

## Cultural history

1955 Samuel Beckett, *Waiting for Godot*; Philip Larkin, *The Less Deceived*.
1956 John Osborne, *Look Back in Anger*.
1957 Richard Hoggart, *The Uses of Literacy*.
1958 John Betjeman, *Collected Poems*.

1961 Debut of The Beatles.

1962 Anthony Burgess, *A Clockwork Orange*; BBC broadcast *That Was The Week That Was*.
1963 John le Carré, *The Spy Who Came in from the Cold*.

1969 *Civilisation*, television series presented by Kenneth Clark; Rupert Murdoch purchased *The Sun*.
1970 Ted Hughes, *Crow*.
1972 Frederick Forsyth, *The Day of the Jackal*.

1978 *Evita*, musical by Tim Rice and Andrew Lloyd Webber.

1982 *Gandhi*, film directed by Richard Attenborough.

1984 First payments to authors on library loans under Public Lending Right.
1985 *Triumph of the West*, television series on world history presented by J M Roberts.

1989 John Tavener, *The Protecting Veil* for cello and string orchestra.

1990 Glasgow is 'Cultural Capital of Europe' for 1990.

1991 Closure of the *Listener* magazine (founded 1929).

1993 Rachel Whiteread awarded Turner Prize for *House* (plaster cast of inside of London house).

1995 Irish poet Seamus Heaney won Nobel Prize for Literature.

## Events involving Britain and Ireland

**1997** Victory of Labour Party in general election; Tony Blair became prime minister.

**1997** Paramilitary ceasefire resumed; multi-party talks on Northern Ireland began.

**1997** Following referendums in Wales and Scotland, the government announced plans for a Welsh Assembly and a Scottish Parliament.

**1998** Home Office announced that Queen Elizabeth II supports plans to remove the gender bias from British succession rules.

**1998** Ireland, Britain, and political parties in Northern Ireland reached peace agreement over Northern Ireland involving the devolution of a wide range of powers to a Northern Ireland Assembly. Surrender of arms by the IRA, however, was a stumbling block.

**1999** Scottish Parliament and National Assembly for Wales both opened officially. Northern Ireland Assembly became fully operational with the first meeting of the power-sharing executive on 2 December.

**2000** British government suspended the Northern Ireland Assembly owing to the stalemate over the decommissioning of weapons.

## Other events

**1998** Pakistan exploded five nuclear devices.

**1999** European parliament votes to place the European Commission on probation and instil wide-ranging reforms in an effort to stem corruption and fraud.

**1999** As Serb troops withdrew from Kosovo, NATO General Secretary Javier Solana officially declared an end to the alliance's 78 days of bombing in Yugoslavia.

**1999** Australian voters reject a referendum, by 55% to 45%, that would make the country a republic with a president elected by the federal parliament. Queen Elizabeth II remains head of state.

**2000** The new millennium is celebrated across the world, with fireworks, street parties, ceremonies and speeches.

## Society, economy, and science

**1997**  Death in a car accident in Paris of Diana, Princess of Wales.

**1999**  A new edition of the *Highway Code* is published. Amendments include warnings against using mobile phones, as well as other electronic equipment which can distract the driver.
**1999**  European Union legislation implemented in the UK requiring foods containing genetically modified (GM) protein or DNA to be labelled in restaurants and food shops.

## Cultural history

**1997**  Elton John's single 'Candle in the Wind' 97, a tribute to Diana, Princess of Wales, became the best-selling single of all time.
**1997**  *The Full Monty*, by Peter Cattaneo, became the biggest-grossing British film in the UK.

**1998**  David Trimble and John Hume jointly awarded Nobel peace prize for their part in the Northern Ireland peace process.

**1999**  Seamus Heaney's translation of *Beowulf* won the Whitbread Literary Award for Book of the Year.

**1999**  The Millennium Dome, Greenwich, London opened by Queen Elizabeth II, 31 December.

# Useful Web sites

**About the National Trust**
http://www.nationaltrust.org.uk/aboutnt.htm
Information about the charity, supported by 2.4 million members, entrusted with the care of large parts of the British countryside and many historic buildings. There is a brief history of the organization, outline of its work, and appeal for assistance.

**Art Guide – The Art Lover's Guide to Britain and Ireland**
http://www.artguide.org/
Regularly updated guide to the art world in Britain and Ireland. There is a searchable database of exhibitions, a clickable region-by-region directory, a listing of gallery Web sites, information about 1,900 artists, and a special section for children.

**BAFTA Awards**
http://www.bafta.org/
Home page of the British Academy of Film and Television Arts. As well as details of the annual awards, this site also includes a history of the organization, recent press releases, and details of various BAFTA events.

**BBC News**
http://news.bbc.co.uk/
Online news service from the BBC. Constantly updated, this is one of the best sources of news on the Internet. The long traditions of BBC news gathering are maintained at this site.

**Beaulieu**
http://www.beaulieu.co.uk/
Explore the buildings and history of Beaulieu Abbey and Palace House, the ancestral home of Lord Montagu and his family for over 400 years. The site comprises a detailed history of the estate and its buildings, a large collection of photographs, and history of the family, as well as information and pictures of the National Motor Museum which is based on the estate.

**Birmingham**
http://birmingham.gov.uk/
Full details on the city of Birmingham, England, for both visitors and residents. This official, illustrated site contains sections such as 'Tourism and leisure', 'Education and employment', 'Business' and 'Birmingham press cuttings'.

**Brief History of Wales**
http://www.britannia.com/wales/whist.html
From the Britannia Internet Magazine, a history of Wales in 21 chapters, written by Welsh historian Peter N Williams.

**British Army**
http://www.army.mod.uk/
Home page of the British Army. There is extensive information on the structure of the army, weapons systems, current deployments, and career opportunities. An 'Army World Challenge' game asks what you would do if faced with five challenging scenarios developed from actual current operational missions.

**British Library**
http://www.bl.uk/
Home page of the British Library. There is extensive information for users of the library's many services. The information provided is comprehensive and includes the capability to search through all the 9.5 million books catalogued since 1977.

**British Monarchy**
http://www.royal.gov.uk/
The official site of the British monarchy includes reviews of its history, its present role and character, and details on the formal order of accession, coronation, and succession that applies to each monarch. There are sections on the royal palaces and parks, the life of Lady Diana, and a guest book for visitors to sign.

**British Museum**
http://www.british-museum.ac.uk/
Comprehensive guide to the British Museum. The site has regularly updated information about current exhibitions. Maps of each floor of the museum allow a visit to be planned in advance.

**BT PhoneNet UK**
http://bt.com/phonenetuk/
At this site you can find the entire contents of this fully searchable version of the UK telephone directory.

**Buckingham Palace**
http://www.royal.gov.uk/palaces/bp.htm
Official guide to the London residence of the British queen. In addition to a history of the palace, there are sections on the Royal Mews, the State Coach, the State Room, the Queen's Gallery, and current art exhibitions. Information is provided on entry to those parts of the palace open to the public.

**Cabinet Office Home Page**
http://www.cabinet-office.gov.uk/
Site of the UK cabinet which includes the latest news from Whitehall, access to reports and papers from different departments, and statistics and information about government policy. There is also a full explanation of the 'Government Machine', with links to related sites.

**Canterbury Tour**
http://www.hillside.co.uk/tour/tour.html
Interactive tour of Canterbury, Kent. The tour features paired photographs of monuments and features, so you can see the view behind you as well as in front, and this site also features a history of the city.

**Cardiff, Capital City of Wales**
http://www.cardiff.co.uk/
Official guide to the Welsh capital. Local government functions are fully explained and investment opportunities outlined. There are many photos of the city and a listing of local amenities and historic sites.

**Conservative Party**
http://www.conservative-party.org.uk/
Official UK Conservative Party Web site, including an archive of press releases written by major party figures. There are also links to all the local constituency associations and a list of Conservative MPs sorted by various criteria.

**Countryside Agency**
http://www.countryside.gov.uk/
Guide to the work of the Commission and to the attractions of the British countryside. There is information on all of the UK's national parks and officially-designated areas of outstanding beauty. The Commission's work to preserve the countryside is fully explained and there are details of the latest scientific research.

*Economist*
http://www.economist.com
Includes the complete text of *The Economist* every week, as well as a searchable archive of back issues since 1995. Software downloads are also included, as is an online shop where Economist products can be bought.

**Edinburgh**
http://www.city.net/countries/united_kingdom/scotland/edinburgh/
Comprehensive guide to the Scottish capital, updated daily and including information on accommodation, food and drink, parks and gardens, and shopping.

*Electronic Telegraph*
http://www.telegraph.co.uk/
Online edition of *The Daily Telegraph*.

**English National Ballet**
http://www.ballet.org.uk/ballet/cgi-bin/index.cgi
The National Ballet's Web site includes a 'Tour schedule' and 'Company news', as well as the opportunity to contribute to the 'Online think tank' and 'Performance reviews'. There is also a 'Ballet school' for aspiring dancers.

**English National Opera**
http://www.eno.org/
Details of the company, its current productions, and the low-price ticket scheme 'Enjoy opera for schools'.

**Guide to the New Forest**
http://www.aard-vark.com/forest/
Automated guide to the flora, fauna, rivers, and walks of the New Forest in Hampshire. In a neat feature, the text and numerous photographs change automatically as you read.

**Hansard – House of Commons Debates**
http://www.parliament.the-stationery-office.co.uk/pa/cm/cmhansrd.htm
The complete proceedings of the House of Commons, posted each day at 12.30 p.m. You can also search archived proceedings going back to 1996.

### Her Majesty Queen Elizabeth the Queen Mother
http://www.royal.gov.uk/family/mother.htm
Official biography of the Queen Mother, presented by the British monarchy Web site. The Queen Mother's long life is comprehensively chronicled.

### Her Majesty the Queen
http://www.royal.gov.uk/family/hmqueen.htm
Official biography of the British queen, presented by the British monarchy Web site. There are full details of the queen's life and interests and links to other members of her family.

### Houses of Parliament Home Page
http://www.parliament.uk/
Site of the UK's House of Commons and House of Lords. There is a guide to visiting, and access to the many government publications and committees.

### Independent, The
http://www.independent.co.uk/
Online edition of *The Independent*, including full UCAS listings of UK university places.

### Labour Party
http://www.labour.org.uk
Home page of the British Labour Party. A brief glimpse of Tony Blair is followed by a menu offering a range of options. Search engines make it easy to identify and communicate with Labour parliamentarians and party representatives, and to find potted biographies. It is easy to access party policy by inputting key words.

### Lake District National Park Authority
http://www.lake-district.gov.uk/index.htm
Official guide to the attractions of Britain's largest national park. There are sections on geology, history, conservation activities, and exhibitions in the Park's visitor's centre. There is a daily weather report for keen walkers. There are also some fabulous photographs of Lakeland beauty spots.

### Liberal Democrats
http://www.libdems.org.uk
Home page of the Liberal Democrat Party in Britain. Their policy and principles are clearly set out. A search engine makes it easy to locate local and national party representatives and policy statements. There is also brief history of the party.

### LondonNet – The Net Magazine Guide to London
http://www.londonnet.co.uk/
Informative guide to London, suitable for both tourists and residents alike. There are notes on accommodation in London, covering hotels, apartments, and even places for the 'cost conscious'. Other areas covered here include the museums to visit, the best ways to travel, and the pick of the London nightlife. In addition, there are also notes on the places to shop and eat.

### Mary Rose
http://www.cix.co.uk/~mary-rose/
Wealth of information on the *Mary Rose* including a full virtual tour of the Mary Rose Museum. This provides information about historical context as well as detailed pictures of the ship itself. It also includes links to British and global maritime sites.

### Met Police
http://www.met.police.uk/
New Scotland Yard online that includes a complete history of the police in the UK, latest news, recruitment, and information about crime prevention. There is also a 'Youth page' section that includes several 'Streetwise' guides to safety.

### Millennium Commission
http://www.millennium.gov.uk/
Established to assist communities in the UK mark the millennium, the Millennium Commission's Web site includes details of how you can apply for a grant, and looks back over many of the events that took place in the UK to commemorate the millennium.

### Museum of Science
http://www.mos.org/
In Boston, Massachusetts, USA. This is a well-designed site with a range of programmes available to the public, including online tours and exhibitions.

### National Assembly for Wales
http://www.assembly.wales.gov.uk/index_e.html
Describes the structure and business of the Welsh Assembly, with 'Press notices', 'Who's who in the Assembly', and a 'Record of proceedings'.

### National Curriculum
http://www.nc.uk.net/
Well-designed official site of the UK National Curriculum, with information about what attainment levels are required in each of the subject areas.

### National Gallery, London
http://www.nationalgallery.org.uk/
Comprehensive guide to the National Gallery in London. This site includes full details about the gallery, as well as containing information about current and future exhibitions. There is also a 'Puzzling pictures' section which looks at works with an unusual history.

### National Maritime Museum
http://www.nmm.ac.uk/Index.htm
Extensive information about the museum's collections. The site contains resources for education, including a wide selection of useful fact sheets, and information about the Royal Observatory at Greenwich, London.

### National Portrait Gallery
http://www.npg.org.uk/index.htm
Information on this UK gallery, comprising floor plans, details of all the paintings on display in the various collections, information on current and future exhibitions and events, plus general information on such topics as opening hours and facilities. There is also a sound guide which takes you on an oral tour of the gallery.

### Natural History Museum
http://www.nhm.ac.uk/
Written features about all the museum's major areas, with many pictures. The site also includes practical information about the museum's opening times. One further section is dedicated to developing and displaying 3-D virtual reality models of exhibits.

### News Unlimited
http://www.newsunlimited.co.uk/
Online news service from *The Guardian* which is regularly updated throughout the day and contains a documentaries section, as well as web links related to the top stories. Although this site is free to use, you do have to register before you have full access.

### Northern Ireland Assembly
http://www.ni-assembly.gov.uk/index.htm
Information about the Assembly, its publications and committees, and a 'Register of members' interests'.

### Northern Ireland Tourist Board
http://www.ni-tourism.com/index.asp
This site covers the needs of anyone planning to visit Northern Ireland, from accommodation to events and attractions. It also features a virtual tour covering history, activities, food and drink, and places to stay.

### Ordnance Survey
http://www.ordsvy.gov.uk/home/index.html
Impressive site from the official body responsible for the mapping of Britain. Here you can download a selection of UK maps in a variety of formats. Other features include the 'Education' section which has a selection of teaching resources linked to maps and geography.

### Prince of Wales
http://www.royal.gov.uk/family/wales.htm
Official biography of the heir to the British throne, presented by the British monarchy Web site. There are full details of the Prince's education, military career, interests and overseas' visits. There are images of Charles and his family (but none of his late wife, Diana, Princess of Wales).

### Radio 1
http://www.bbc.co.uk/radio1/reception/reception.html
Radio 1's official Web site, which contains news, reviews, programmes, and coming attractions on air and around the UK. You can also listen to the current show and read biographies of the DJs.

### Railtrack – The Heart of the Railway
http://www.railtrack.co.uk/home.html
User-friendly Railtrack site which aims to simplify the planning of a railway journey in Britain. Input your destination and time of departure and a schedule rapidly appears. The site also includes corporate information. There are plans to include frequent updates of operational difficulties and advice to travellers.

### Royal Air Force
http://www.raf.mod.uk/
Well-organized and informative site of the UK's air force. In addition to information for would-be recruits, there is extensive information on the role of the RAF and profiles of all RAF aircraft, weapons systems, and bases. The PR-savvy RAF also puts its case for the need for continued low-flying operations.

**Royal Mail**
http://www.royalmail.co.uk
Official and comprehensive coverage of postal services in the UK, including a 'Postal rates calculator' and 'Postal services guide'. You can also find the post code for any part of the UK if you know the rest of the address.

**Royal Opera House**
http://www.royalopera.org/
Web site of Britain's leading opera house. There are sections providing practical information on current performances and bookings and a history of the Royal Opera. In addition, an education section has a host of practical activities designed to interest young people in opera and ballet.

**Royal Parks of London**
http://www.open.gov.uk/rp/rphome.htm
Locations and descriptions of London's nine royal parks. The history of each park is briefly described on this Web site, and a list of the amenities available in each park is also provided. There is even an 'active' map showing the locations of the parks: clicking on a name calls up details of that park.

**Royal Shakespeare Company**
http://www.stratford.co.uk/rsc/
Site of the prestigious British theatre company. In addition to full details of the RSC's current repertoire in London and Stratford, there is access to information about William Shakespeare.

**Scoot, the UK Business Directory**
http://www.scoot.co.uk/
Useful information service for the UK. Scoot allows you to specify the service you need, and the city or town in which you need it, and then provides you with a full list of business information matching that description, along with their distance in miles from the specified location, and provides a street map of the area in most cases as well. The site also includes a hotel booking service, and a cinema listing directory.

**Scottish Parliament**
http://www.scottish.parliament.uk/
Information about the Scottish Parliament and its activities, including 'The Parliament buildings', 'What's happening', 'Agenda and decisions', and information about the members of the Scottish Parliament.

**Shakespeare's Stratford**
http://www.stratford.co.uk/
Information about both this English town and one of its more famous inhabitants, William Shakespeare. There are details of local attractions and theatres, as well as a guide to eating out and accommodation in the town. The section of Shakespeare covers his life and times and also notes on 'performing Shakespeare', focusing on the work of the Royal Shakespeare Company and the Shakespeare Institute.

**Strolling.com**
http://www.strolling.com/
Very impressive site that allows you to visit London virtually. You can observe the tourist areas of the UK capital through 360° camera angles, and plan your real route through the city.

**Tate, the**
http://www.tate.org.uk/home/
Home of the leading gallery of British art. There is complete news of displays, exhibitions, and events at the two London galleries: Tate Britain and Tate Modern, and those in Liverpool and St Ives.

**10 Downing Street**
http://www.number-10.gov.uk/index.html
Official Web site of the British prime minister's residence includes a virtual tour, biographies of recent prime ministers, press releases, and copies of speeches and interviews.

**This Is Britain**
http://www.thisisbritain.co.uk/
Excellent news site which groups UK news headlines from regional sites, so you can easily find your local news. There is also a comprehensive directory of local news and sports sites.

**Times, The**
http://www.the-times.co.uk/
Online edition of *The Times*.

**UCAS Home Page**
http://www.ucas.ac.uk/
Official site for the organization that handles admissions to universities and colleges in the UK. This site is divided into four sections: a comprehensive search facility for all 'universites, colleges, and courses'; an 'advice centre' with information for both prospective students and parents, as well as details of how to apply for university electronically; information for 'for higher education staff'; and 'studentUK' which includes news, views, and advice for students.

**UK Maps**
http://www.multimap.com/uk/
This site allows you to search for maps of towns and cities in the UK. You can view the area in a variety of scales, from 1:50,000 to 1:200,000, and also see 'pages' next to your selected street; you can choose between colour or greyscale maps.

**UK National Lottery**
http://lottery.merseyworld.com/
History of the UK National Lottery, with links to the four shareholders who make up Camelot, the consortium licensed to run the lottery. Information is given on how to enter the lottery, and a breakdown is provided of how each pound is spent.

**UK Passport Agency**
http://www.open.gov.uk/ukpass/ukpass.htm
Information about the operations of the agency which issues British passports. There is comprehensive information on who is eligible to get one, how to obtain or renew a passport, and a regularly updated indication of how long you might have to wait for them to issue one.

**UK Theatre Web**
http://www.uktw.co.uk/
Regularly updated site on all things dramatic in the UK. It includes information on current amateur theatre, dance, opera, and gossip, as well as a fully searchable database of what's on at the theatre across the UK.

**UK Travel Guide**
http://www.uktravel.com/index.html
Essential resource for anyone planning to travel in the UK. It includes an A–Z of practical information from accommodation to the weather. The site also includes a 'clickable' map with features on towns and cities as well as several images.

**United Kingdom**
http://www.umsl.edu/services/govdocs/wofact96/258.htm
CIA's world fact book page on the UK. This page links to details held by the US intelligence agency on the UK. The site gives a lot more information than a standard atlas might, including details of international disputes, political inclinations, and economic performance amongst many others. For example, did you know Britain spent $35.1 billion on defence in 1995?

**UpMyStreet.com**
http://www.upmystreet.com/
Compare the property value, council tax, crime rates, and education levels of your postal area with either the national average or another post code. This site also provides a wealth of information about your local area, and a range of detailed maps of the UK.

**Victoria and Albert Museum**
http://www.vam.ac.uk/
Guide to the world's largest museum of the decorative arts. There is information on permanent displays, exhibitions, public events, publications, and talks. Other museums operated by the V&A are described and there are good summaries of the museum's main collections.

**Virtual Manchester**
http://www.manchester.com/home.html
Lively and comprehensive guide to the city of Manchester, with information on nightlife, education, events, enterprise, accommodation, maps, organizations, property, shopping, sport, and travel.

**Virtual River Thames**
http://www.riverthames.org/
Well-designed site that allows you to explore the River Thames. There is a description of virtually every part of the river from Cricklade, Wiltshire, all the way to London, and all the text is accompanied by photographs. The site also includes a 'River Thames calculator', which allows you to find out the distance between any two locks on the river.

**Visit Britain – British Tourist Authority**
http://www.visitbritain.com/frameset.htm
Comprehensive information on tourism in the British Isles, provided by the official tourist promotion agency. An interactive map and a good search engine make this a first-stop site for anyone contemplating a visit to Britain.

**Welcome to York**
http://www.britain.co.uk/tourism/wel2york.html
Complete guide to the English city of York. There is a guide to the many hotels of the city, featuring contact details as well as photographs of the places themselves. There are also notes on the many tourist attractions and places to eat out. A number of detailed maps complete this informative guide.

# The HUTCHINSON

# GUIDE TO
# BRITAIN